Student Edition

enVision® Integrated

MATHEMATICS III

Boston, Massachusetts Chandler, Arizona
Glenview, Illinois New York, New York

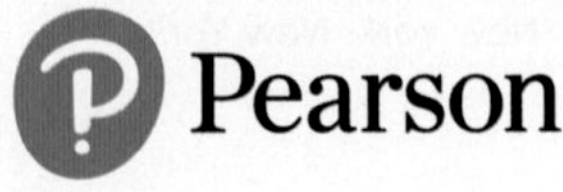

ISBN-13: 978-1418-28378-0
ISBN-10: 1418-28378-9

6 19

Contents in Brief

enVision Integrated MATHEMATICS III

Reviewers & Consultants

Mathematicians

David Bressoud, Ph.D.
Professor Emeritus of Mathematics
Macalester College
St. Paul, MN

Karen Edwards, Ph.D.
Mathematics Lecturer
Harvard University
Cambridge, MA

Teacher Reviewers

Jennifer Barkey
K-12 Math Supervisor
Gateway School District
Monroeville, PA

Miesha Beck
Math Teacher/Department Chair
Blackfoot School District
Blackfoot, ID

Joseph Brandell, Ph.D.
West Bloomfield High School
West Bloomfield Public Schools
West Bloomfield, MI

Andrea Coles
Mathematics Teacher
Mountain View Middle School
Blackfoot, ID

Julie Johnson
Mathematics/CS teacher (9 - 12)
Williamsville Central Schools
Williamsville, NY

Tamar McPherson
Plum Sr HS/Math Teacher
Plum School District
Pittsburgh, PA

Melisa Rice
Math Department Chairperson
Shawnee Public Schools
Shawnee, OK

Ben Wilson
Camille Casteel HS Teacher
Chandler Unified School District
Chandler, AZ

Erin Zitka
6-12 Math Coordinator
Forsyth County
Cumming, GA

Jeff Ziegler
Teacher
Pittsburgh City Schools
Pittsburgh, PA

Authors

Dan Kennedy, Ph.D

- Classroom teacher and the Lupton Distinguished Professor of Mathematics at the Baylor School in Chattanooga, TN
- Co-author of textbooks Precalculus: Graphical, Numerical, Algebraic and Calculus: Graphical, Numerical, Algebraic, AP Edition
- Past chair of the College Board's AP Calculus Development Committee.
- Previous Tandy Technology Scholar and Presidential Award winner

Eric Milou, Ed.D

- Professor of Mathematics, Rowan University, Glassboro, NJ
- Member of the author team for Pearson's **enVision**math**2.0** 6-8
- Member of National Council of Teachers of Mathematics (NCTM) feedback/advisory team for the Common Core State Standards
- Author of *Teaching Mathematics to Middle School Students*

Christine D. Thomas, Ph.D

- Professor of Mathematics Education at Georgia State University, Atlanta, GA
- Past-President of the Association of Mathematics Teacher Educators (AMTE)
- Past NCTM Board of Directors Member
- Past member of the editorial panel of the NCTM journal *Mathematics Teacher*
- Past co-chair of the steering committee of the North American chapter of the International Group of the Psychology of Mathematics Education

Rose Mary Zbiek, Ph.D

- Professor of Mathematics Education, Pennsylvania State University, College Park, PA
- Series editor for the NCTM *Essential Understanding* project

Contributing Author

Al Cuoco, Ph.D

- Lead author of CME Project, a National Science Foundation (NSF)-funded high school curriculum
- Team member to revise the Conference Board of the Mathematical Sciences (CBMS) recommendations for teacher preparation and professional development
- Co-author of several books published by the Mathematical Association of America and the American Mathematical Society
- Consultant to the writers of the Common Core State Standards for Mathematics and the PARCC Content Frameworks for high school mathematics

enVision® Integrated Mathematics III offers a carefully constructed lesson design to help you succeed in math.

Step 1 At the start of each lesson, you and your classmates will work together to come up with a solution strategy for the problem or task posed. After a class discussion, you'll be asked to reflect back on the processes and strategies you used in solving the problem.

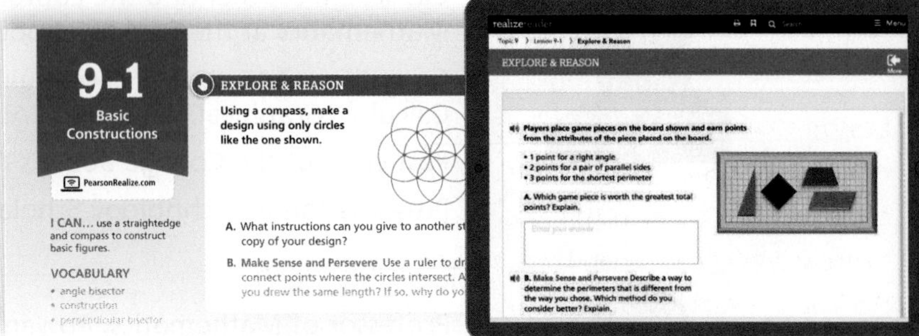

Step 2 Next, your teacher will guide you through new concepts and skills for the lesson.

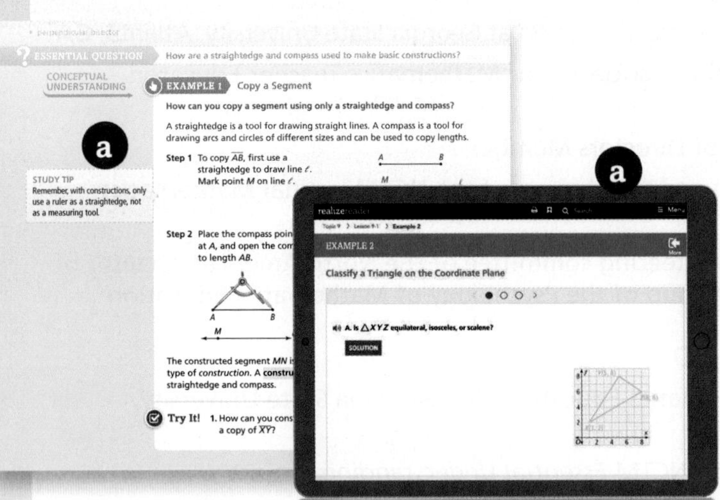

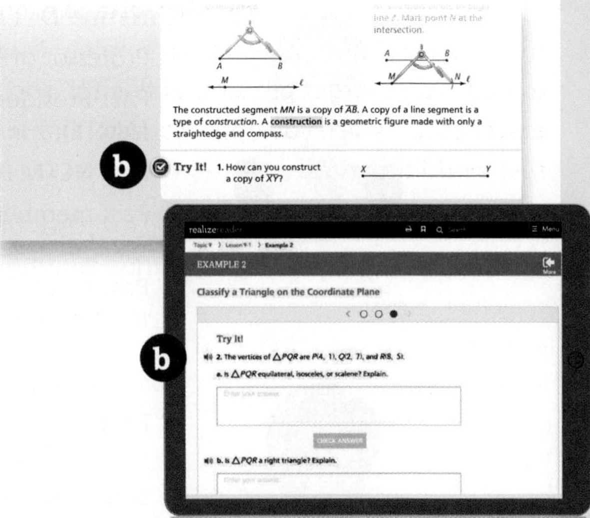

After each example **a**, you work out a problem called the **Try It!** **b** to solidify your understanding of these concepts.

In addition, you will periodically answer **Habits of Mind** **c** questions to refine your thinking and problem-solving skills.

Step 2 cont. This part of the lesson concludes with a Lesson Check that helps you to know how well you are understanding the new content presented in the lesson. With the exercises in the **Do You Understand?** and **Do You Know How?**, you can gauge your understanding of the lesson concepts.

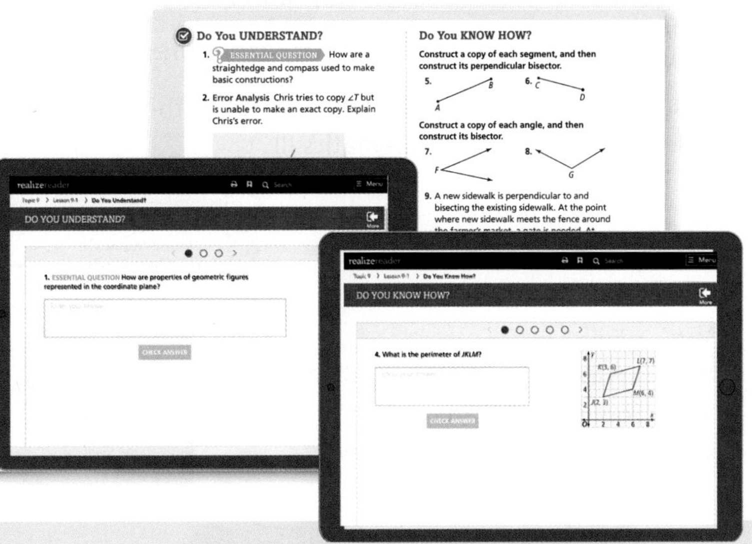

Step 3 In Step 3, you will find a balanced exercise set with **Understand** exercises that focus on conceptual understanding, **Practice** exercises that target procedural fluency, and **Apply** exercises for which you apply concept and skills to real-world situations **d**.

The **Assessment and Practice** **e** exercises offer practice for high stakes assessments. Your teacher may have you complete the assignment in your Student Edition, Student Companion, or online at PearsonRealize.com.

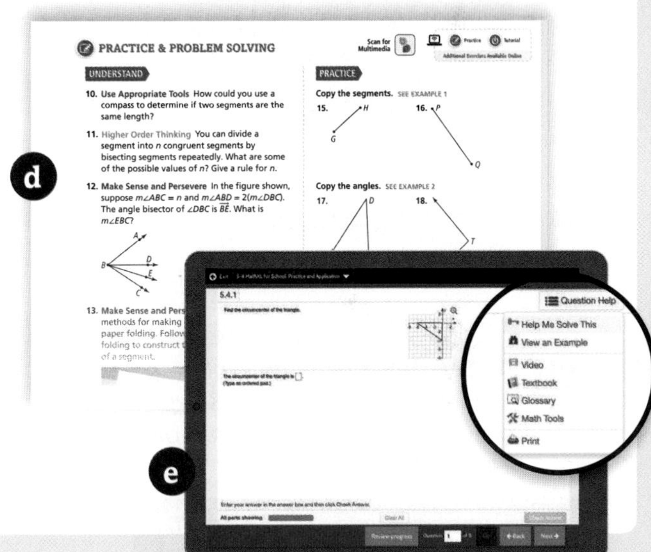

Step 4 Your teacher may have you take the Lesson Quiz after each lesson. You can take the quiz online or in print. To do your best on the quiz, review the lesson problems in that lesson.

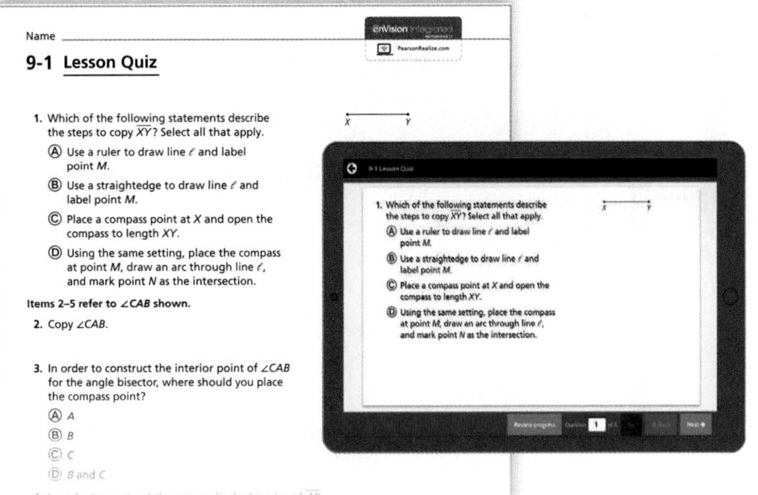

Digital Resources

Everything you need for math, anytime, anywhere.

PearsonRealize.com is your gateway to all of the digital resources for **enVision**® Integrated Mathematics III.

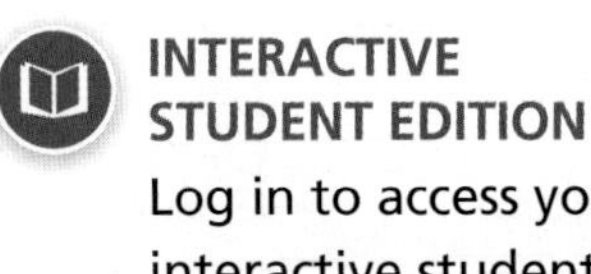

INTERACTIVE STUDENT EDITION
Log in to access your interactive student edition, called Realize Reader.

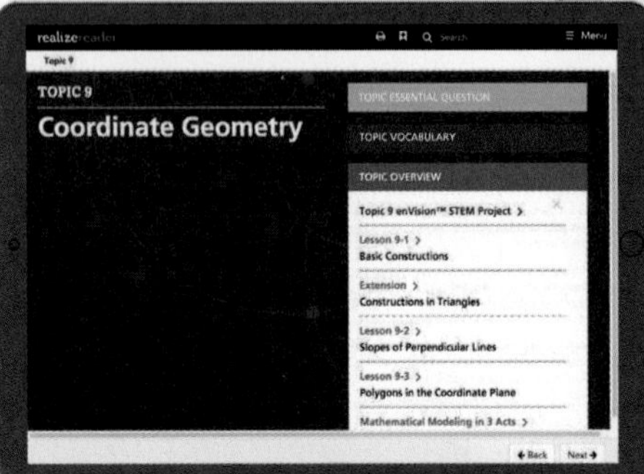

ACTIVITIES Complete *Explore & Reason, Model & Discuss, Critique & Explain* activities. Interact with *Examples* and *Try Its.*

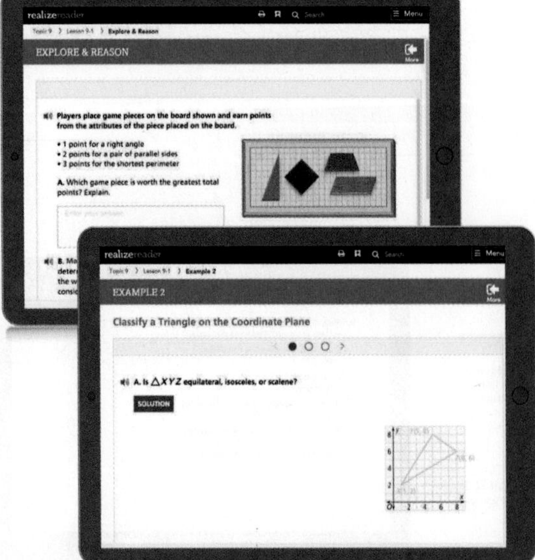

ANIMATION View and interact with real-world applications.

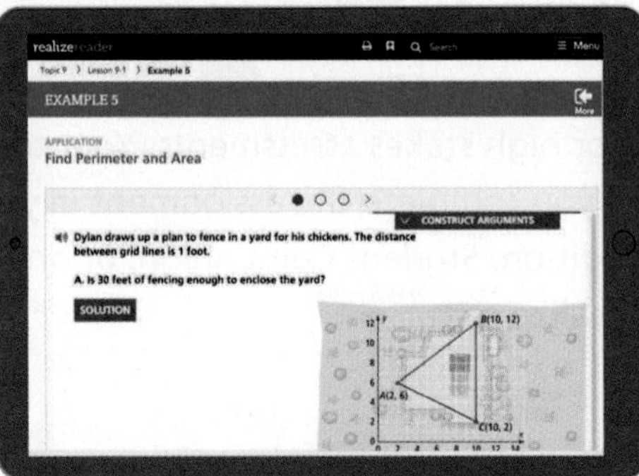

PRACTICE
Practice what you've learned.

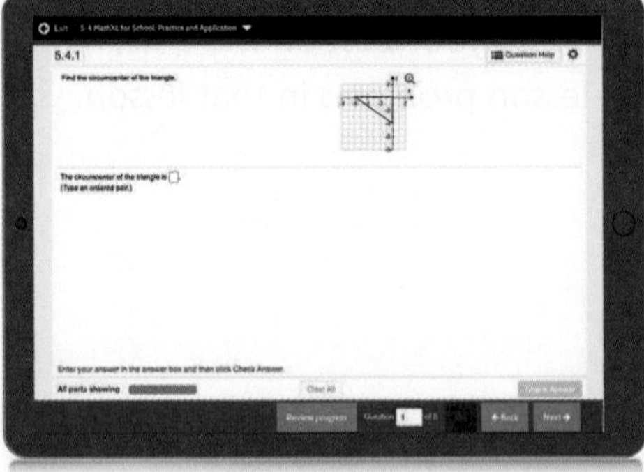

VIDEOS Watch clips to support Mathematical Modeling in 3 Acts Lessons and **enVision**® STEM Projects.

ASSESSMENT Show what you've learned.

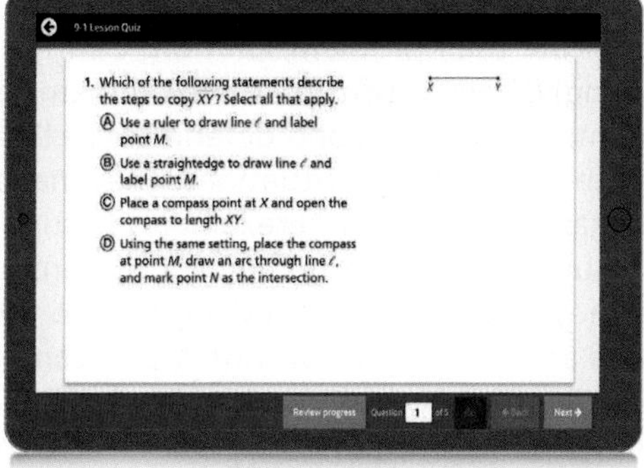

TUTORIALS Get help from Virtual Nerd, right when you need it.

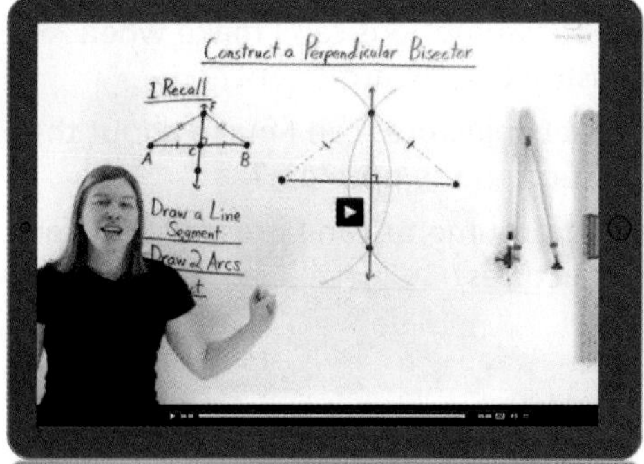

CONCEPT SUMMARY Review key lesson content through multiple representations.

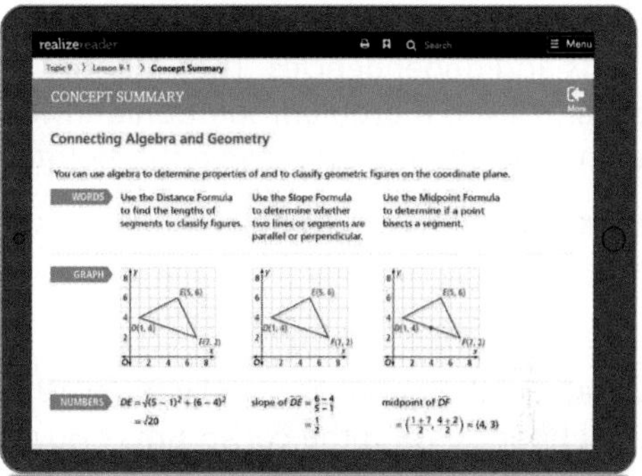

GLOSSARY Read and listen to English and Spanish definitions.

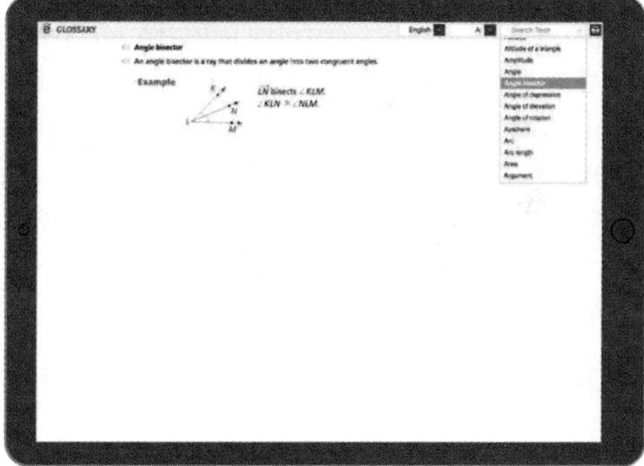

MATH TOOLS Explore math with digital tools and manipulatives.

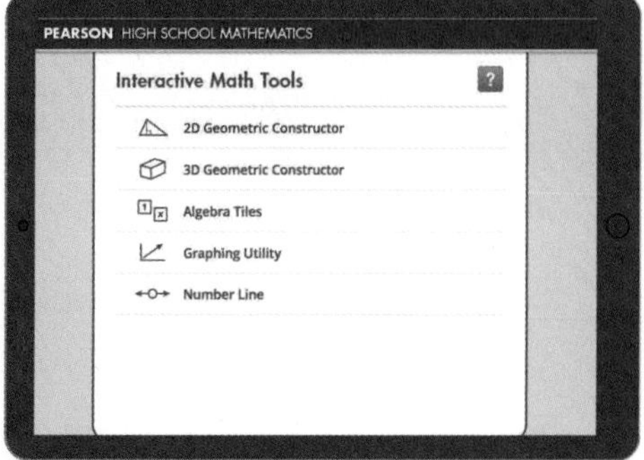

Mathematical Practices and Processes

Problem Solving

Make sense of problems and persevere in solving them.

Proficient math thinkers are able to read through a problem situation and can put together a workable solution path to solve the problem posed. They analyze the information provided and identify constraints and dependencies. They identify multiple entries to a problem solution and will choose an efficient and effective entry point.

Consider these questions to help you make sense of problems.

- What am I asked to find?
- What are the quantities and variables? The dependencies and the constraints? How do they relate?
- What are some possible strategies to solve the problem?

Attend to precision.

Proficient math thinkers communicate clearly and precisely the approach they are using. They identify the meaning of symbols that they use and always remember to specify units of measure and to label accurately graphical models. They use mathematical terms precisely and express their answers with the appropriate degree of accuracy.

Consider these questions to help you attend to precision.

- Have I stated the meaning of the variables and symbols I am using?
- Have I specified the units of measure I am using?
- Have I calculate accurately?

Reasoning and Communicating

Reason abstractly and quantitatively.

Proficient math thinkers make sense of quantities in problem situations. They represent a problem situation using symbols or equations and explain what the symbols or equation represent in relationship to a problem situation. As they model a situation symbolically or mathematically, they explain the meaning of the quantities.

Consider these questions to help you reason abstractly and quantitatively.

- How can I represent the problem using equations or formulas?
- What do the numbers, variables, and symbols in the equation or formula represent?

Construct viable arguments and critique the reasoning of others.

Proficient math thinkers and problem solvers communicate their problem solutions clearly and convincingly. They construct sound mathematical arguments and develop and defend conjectures to explain mathematical situations. They make use of examples and counterexamples to support their arguments and justify their conclusions. When asked, they respond clearly and logically to the positions and conclusions of others, and compare two arguments, identifying any flaws in logic or reasoning that the arguments may contain. They ask questions to clarify or improve the position of a classmate.

Consider these questions to help you construct mathematical arguments.

- What assumptions can I make when constructing an argument?
- What conjectures can I make about the solution to the problem?
- What arguments can I present to defend my conjectures?

Representing and Connecting

Model with mathematics.

Proficient math thinkers use mathematics to represent a problem situation and make connections between a real-world problem situation and mathematics. They see the applicability of mathematics to solve every-day problems and explain how geometry can be used to solve a carpentry problem or algebra to solve a proportional relationship problem. They define and map relationships among quantities in a problem, using appropriate tools. They analyze the relationships and draw conclusions about the solutions.

Consider these questions to help you model with mathematics.

- What representations can I use to show the relationship among quantities or variables?
- What assumptions can I make about the problem situation to simplify the problem?

Use appropriate tools strategically.

Proficient math thinkers strategize about which tools are more helpful to solve a problem situation. They consider all tools, from paper and pencil to protractors and rulers, to calculators and software applications. They articulate the appropriateness of different tools and recognize which would best serve the needs for a given problem. They are especially insightful about technological tools and use them in ways that deepen or extend their understanding of concepts. They also make use of mental tools, such as estimation, to determine the appropriateness of a solution.

Consider these questions to help you use appropriate tools.

- What tool can I use to help me solve the problem?
- How can technology help me solve the problem?

Seeing Patterns and Generalizing

Look for and make use of patterns.

Proficient math thinkers see mathematical patterns in the problems they are solving and generalize mathematics principles from these patterns. They see complicated expressions or equations as single objects composed of many parts.

Consider these questions to help you see structure.

- Can I see a pattern in the problem or solution strategy?
- How can I use the pattern I see to help me solve the problem?

Look for generalizations.

Proficient math thinkers notice when calculations are repeated and can uncover both general methods and shortcuts for solving similar problems.

Consider these questions to help you look for regularity in repeated reasoning.

- Do I notice any repeated calculations or steps?
- Are there general methods that I can use to solve the problem?
- What can I generalize from one problem to another?
- How reasonable are the results that I am getting?

Key Concepts in Integrated Mathematics III

Proficiency with key concepts and skills of **enVision®** Integrated Mathematics III is often cited as a requisite for college- and career readiness.

These foundational concepts of algebraic and geometric thinking provide the gateway to advanced mathematics.

Listed below are the key concepts that you will be studying in **enVision®** Integrated Mathematics III.

Number and Quantities

- Polynomials can be added, subtracted, and multiplied. Polynomials form a system that is closed under these operations. This system is analogous to the integers.
- Polynomials can be factored to reveal zeros. The zeros can be used to construct a rough graph of the function defined by the polynomial.
- Polynomial identities can be used to describe numerical relationships.
- Properties of rational and irrational numbers determine whether their sums and products are rational or irrational.
- The complex number i is equal to the square root of -1. Every complex number has the form $a + bi$ with a and b real numbers.
- The relation, $i^2 = -1$, and the properties of equality can be applied to add, subtract, and multiply complex numbers.
- The conjugate of $a + bi$ is $a - bi$. The conjugate can be used to find simplified forms of quotients of complex numbers.
- Polynomial identities can be extended to complex numbers.
- The Fundamental Theorem of Algebra states that every polynomial with complex coefficients has at least one complex root.
- The Remainder Theorem states that for a polynomial $p(x)$ and a number a, the remainder on division by $x - a$ is $p(a)$, so $p(a) = 0$ if and only if $x - a$ is a factor of $p(x)$.
- The Binomial Theorem describes the expansion of $(x + y)^n$ in terms of products of powers of x and y for a positive integer n with coefficients from Pascal's Triangle.
- Rational expressions can be rewritten in different forms to reveal different information about the relationships among the variables.
- Rational expressions form a system that is closed under the operations of addition, subtraction, multiplication, and division by a nonzero rational expression. This system is analogous to the rational numbers.

Exponential and Logarithmic Functions

- An exponential function increases or decreases by equal factors over equal intervals.
- An exponential function represents a situation in which a quantity grows or decays by a constant rate per unit interval relative to another.
- A geometric sequence is a type of exponential function. It can be defined recursively or explicitly.
- The properties of exponents can be used to interpret and transform expressions for exponential functions.

Trigonometric Functions, Equations, and Identities

- Simple trigonometric equations can be solved using inverse trigonometric functions.
- Radian measure of an angle is the length of the arc on the unit circle subtended by the angle.
- Trigonometric functions can be extended to all real numbers, interpreted as radian measures of angles traversed counterclockwise around the unit circle.
- The values of sine, cosine, tangent for $\frac{\pi}{3}$, $\frac{\pi}{4}$ and $\frac{\pi}{6}$, can be determined geometrically using special triangles.
- The unit circle can be used to explain symmetry (odd and even) and periodicity of trigonometric functions.
- Trigonometric functions can model periodic phenomena with specified amplitude, frequency, and midline.

Statistics

- Inferences can be made about population parameters based on a random sample from that population.
- Standard deviation of a data set is a measure of variance of a data set from the mean.
- Data from paired quantitative variables can be represented on a scatter plot.
- Randomization in data collections allows for more reliable inferences and conclusions about the sample or population.
- The margin of error represents a level of confidence that a sample statistic is close to a population parameter.
- Simulations can be carried out to decide whether differences between statistics are significant.

Key Concepts in Integrated Mathematics III

Circles

- All circles are similar.
- The length of the arc of a circle intercepted by an angle is proportional to the radius of the circle.
- The radian measure of an angle is the ratio of the arc length of a circle and the radius of the circle. It is a constant of proportionality between arc length and radius.
- The equation of a circle of given center and radius can be derived using the Pythagorean Theorem.
- Tangent lines only intersect the circle at one point. They are perpendicular to the radius that intersects the circle at that point.
- When two segments are tangent to a circle and have a common endpoint outside of the circle, the segments are congruent.
- When a quadrilateral is inscribed in a circle, opposite angles are supplementary.
- When a tangent intersects the endpoint of a chord, the measure of the angle formed is half the measure of its intercepted arc.
- The measure of an angle inscribed in a circle is half the measure of the arc it intercepts.
- An angle inscribed on the diameter is a right angle.
- Two inscribed angles that intercept the same arc are congruent.
- If the chords in a circle are congruent, their central angles are congruent.
- If chords are the same distance from the center of a circle, they are congruent.
- If the diameter intersects the chord at 90°, then it bisects the chord.
- If arcs of a circle are congruent, their chords are also congruent.

Geometric Figures and Measurements

- Volume formulas for cylinders, pyramids, cones, and spheres can help solve real-world and mathematical problems.
- The cross-sections of three-dimensional objects are two-dimensional figures.
- The properties and measures of geometric figures can be used to describe real-world objects.
- Concepts of density based on area and volume can be used to model real-world situations.
- Geometric methods can help solve design problems.

TOPIC 1

Linear Functions and Systems

TOPIC 2

Polynomial Functions

TOPIC 3

Rational Functions

TOPIC 4

Rational Exponents and Radical Functions

TOPIC 5

Exponential and Logarithmic Functions

TOPIC 6

Trigonometric Functions

TOPIC 7

Trigonometric Equations and Identities

TOPIC 8

Data Analysis and Statistics

TOPIC 9

Coordinate Geometry

TOPIC 10

Circles

TOPIC 11

Two- and Three-Dimensional Models

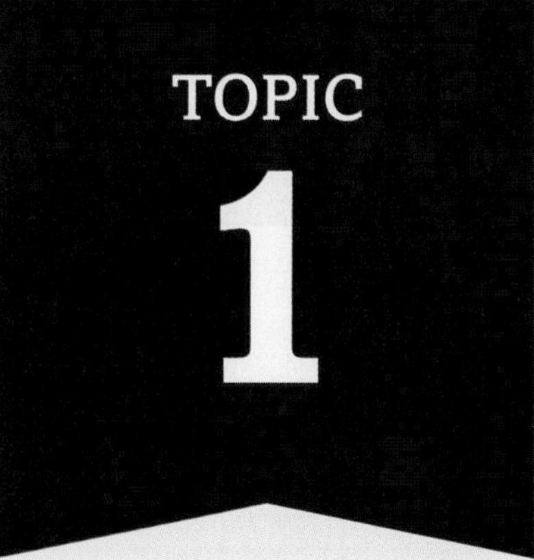

Linear Functions and Systems

What are the ways in which functions can be used to represent and solve problems involving quantities?

Topic Overview

Topic Vocabulary

- arithmetic sequence
- arithmetic series
- average rate of change
- common difference
- compression
- explicit definition
- inconsistent system
- interval notation
- maximum
- minimum
- piecewise-defined function
- recursive definition
- reflection
- sequence
- series
- set-builder notation
- sigma notation
- solution of a system of linear equations
- step function
- stretch
- system of linear equations
- system of linear inequalities
- transformation
- translation
- zero of a function

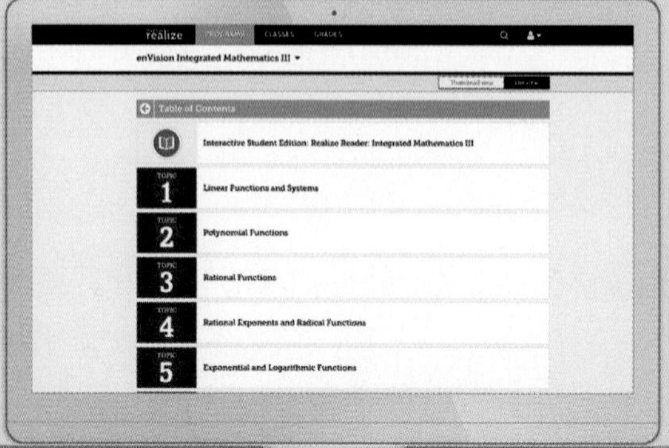

Go online | **PearsonRealize.com**

Digital Experience

INTERACTIVE STUDENT EDITION Access online or offline.

ACTIVITIES Complete ***Explore & Reason, Model & Discuss***, and ***Critique & Explain*** activities. Interact with Examples and Try Its.

ANIMATION View and interact with real-world applications.

PRACTICE Practice what you've learned.

Current Events

You might say that someone who loses their temper has "blown a fuse." However, it's rare to hear about electrical fuses blowing these days. That's because most fuses have been replaced by circuit breakers. A fuse must be replaced once it's blown, but a circuit breaker can be reset.

Ask for permission to look at the electrical panel in your home. If there is a series of switches inside, each of those is a circuit breaker, designed to interrupt the circuit when the electrical current inside is too dangerous. How much electricity does it take to trip a circuit breaker? Think about this question during the Mathematical Modeling in 3-Acts lesson.

TOPIC 1

VIDEOS Watch clips to support ***Mathematical Modeling in 3 Acts Lessons*** and **enVision® *STEM Projects.***

CONCEPT SUMMARY Review key lesson content through multiple representations.

ASSESSMENT Show what you've learned.

GLOSSARY Read and listen to English and Spanish definitions.

TUTORIALS Get help from ***Virtual Nerd***, right when you need it.

MATH TOOLS Explore math with digital tools and manipulatives.

Did You Know?

Carbon dioxide (CO_2) is composed of 1 atom of carbon and 2 atoms of oxygen. A gas that occurs naturally on Earth, CO_2 also produced by burning fossil fuels. In its solid form, CO_2 is commonly called "dry ice."

This hybrid hatchback averages 59 mpg in the city.

This large SUV averages **10 mpg** in the city.

In the United States, each state determines the **tax rate** on gasoline, so the state in which you buy your gas determines how much it costs to fill your tank.

How much **crude oil** do you use when filling up your car?

2 full tanks

10-gal. 10-gal.

19 gallons of gasoline

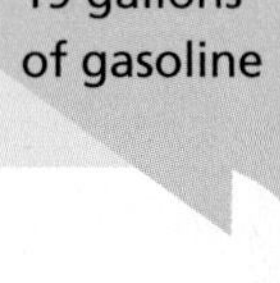

1 barrel = 42 gallons unrefined crude oil

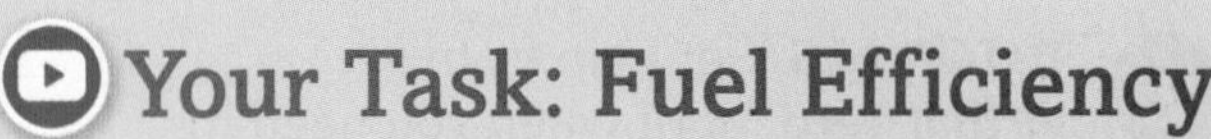

Your Task: Fuel Efficiency

You and your classmates will analyze cars' fuel efficiency. If you were designing a car to come out in 2024, what gas mileage would you target?

Activity Assess

1-1 Key Features of Functions

PearsonRealize.com

I CAN... interpret key features of linear, quadratic, and absolute value functions given an equation or a graph.

VOCABULARY

- average rate of change
- interval notation
- maximum
- minimum
- set-builder notation
- zero of a function

EXPLORE & REASON

A diver is going through ocean search-and-rescue training. The graph shows the relationship between her depth and the time in seconds since starting her dive.

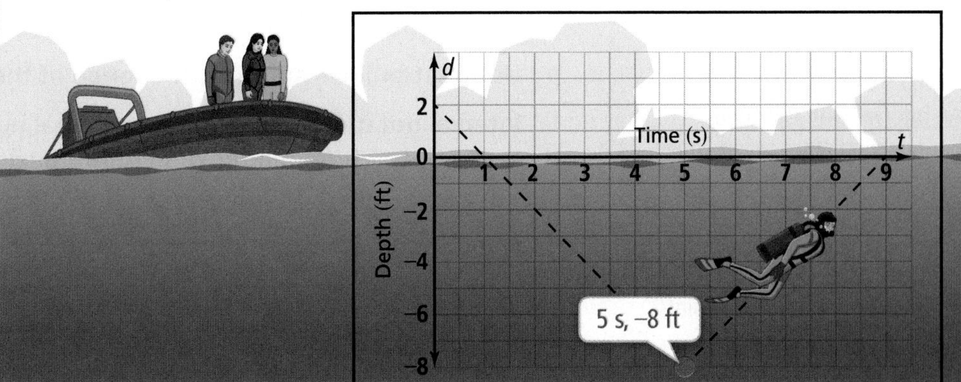

A. What details can you determine about the dive from the coordinates of the point (5, –8)?

B. What is the average speed of the diver in the water? How can you tell from the graph?

C. Which point on the graph shows the starting location of the diver? Explain.

D. **Communicate Precisely** What does the V-shape of the graph tell you about the dive? What information does it not tell you about the dive?

ESSENTIAL QUESTION

How do graphs and equations reveal information about a relationship between two quantities?

EXAMPLE 1 Understand Domain and Range

A. What are the domain and range of the function defined by $y = x^2 - 3$?

The set of all possible inputs for a relation is called the *domain*.

You can square any real number, so any number can be input for x.

The square of a real number is greater than or equal to 0. So the minimum value of $y = x^2 - 3$ is $0 - 3$, or -3.

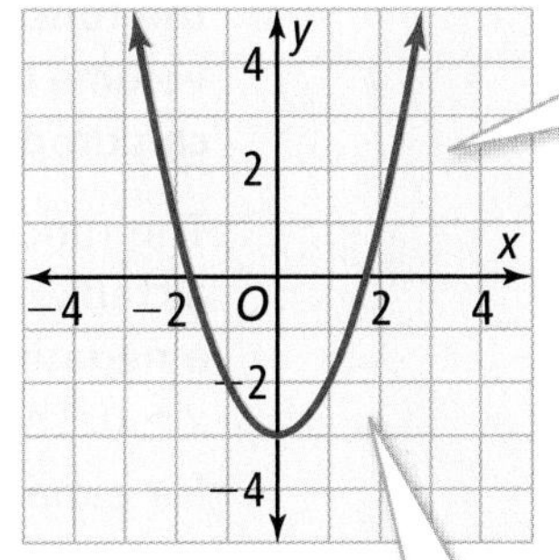

This graph represents a *function* because each input has exactly one output.

The set of all possible outputs for a relation is called the *range*.

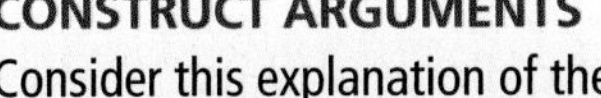

CONSTRUCT ARGUMENTS Consider this explanation of the function's minimum value. How do you know that the function has no maximum value?

There are two notations used to represent intervals of numbers like domain and range.

Set-Builder Notation uses a verbal description or an inequality to describe the numbers.

CONTINUED ON THE NEXT PAGE

EXAMPLE 1 CONTINUED

Using set-builder notation, the domain of this function is $\{x \mid x \text{ is a real number}\}$.

This is read *"The set of all x such that x is a real number."*

This is read *"The set of all y such that y is greater than or equal to −3."*

Using set-builder notation, the range of the function is $\{y \mid y \geq -3\}$.

STUDY TIP
An interval with excluded boundary points is called "open" and is represented by open circle end points on the graph. An interval with included boundary points is called "closed" and is represented by solid end points.

Interval notation represents a set of real numbers by the pair of values that are its left (minimum) and right (maximum) boundaries. Using interval notation, the domain of the function is $(-\infty, \infty)$.

Using interval notation, the range is $[-3, \infty)$.

To summarize the ways in which we can indicate intervals of numbers, refer to the table below.

Interval Notation	Words	Set Notation
$[3, 4]$	All real numbers that are greater or equal to 3 and less than or equal to 4	$\{x \mid 3 \leq x \leq 4\}$
$(3, 4]$	All real numbers that are greater than 3 and less than or equal to 4	$\{x \mid 3 < x \leq 4\}$
$[3, 4)$	All real numbers that are greater than or equal to 3 and less than 4	$\{x \mid 3 \leq x < 4\}$
$(3, 4)$	All real numbers that are greater than 3 and less than 4	$\{x \mid 3 < x < 4\}$
$[3, \infty)$	All real numbers greater than or equal to 3	$\{x \mid 3 \leq x < \infty\}$
$(-\infty, 3]$	All real numbers less than or equal to 3	$\{x \mid -\infty < x \leq 3\}$
$(-\infty, \infty)$	All real numbers	$\{x \mid -\infty < x < \infty\}$

B. An airtanker flies over forest fires and drops water at a constant rate until its tank is empty. What are the domain and range of the function that represents the volume of water the airtanker can drop in *x* seconds?

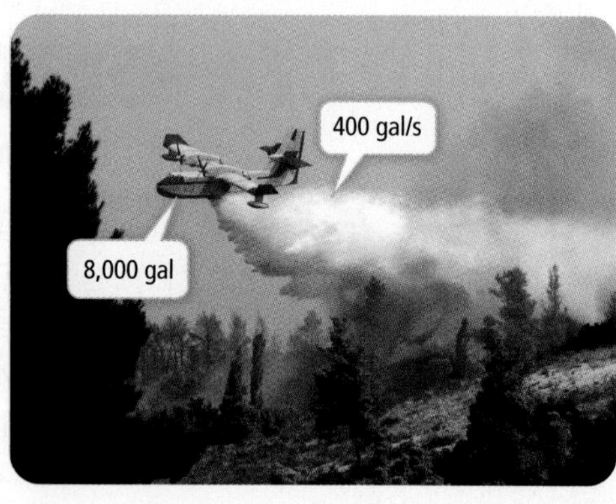

The function is $f(x) = 400x$. The airtanker cannot drop water for a negative number of seconds, so $x \geq 0$. The tanker can drop water for a maximum of $\frac{8{,}000}{400} = 20$ s before running out of water, so $x \leq 20$.

The domain is $\{x \mid 0 \leq x \leq 20\}$, or $[0, 20]$.

The airtanker cannot drop a negative number of gallons, and its maximum capacity is 8,000 gal.

The range is $\{y \mid 0 \leq y \leq 8{,}000\}$, or $[0, 8{,}000]$.

Try It! 1. What are the domain and range of each function? Write the domain and range in set-builder notation and interval notation.

a. $y = |x - 4|$

b. $y = 6x - 2x^2$

Activity

Assess

APPLICATION

EXAMPLE 2 Find x- and y-intercepts

A. A car starts a journey with a full tank of gas. The equation $y = 16 - 0.05x$ relates the number of gallons of gas, y, left in the tank to the number of miles the car has traveled, x. What are the x- and y-intercepts of the graph of this equation, and what do they represent about the situation?

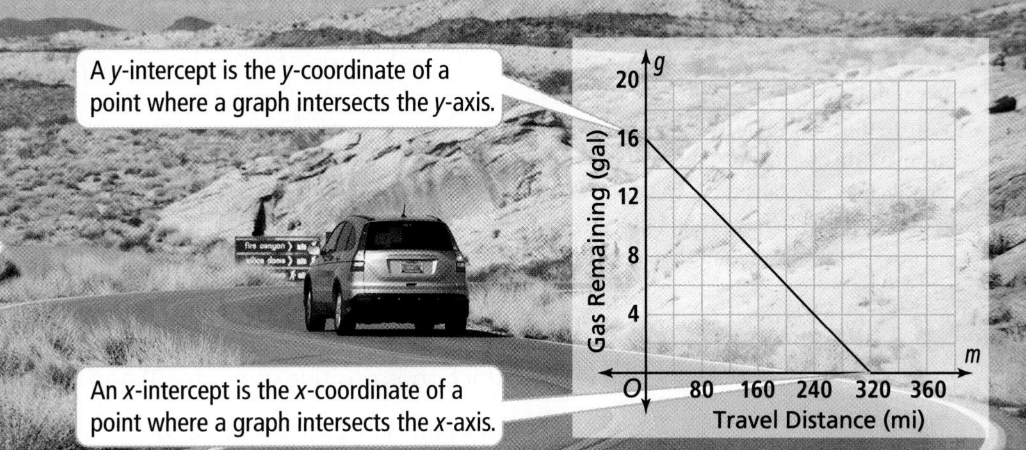

STUDY TIP

Depending on the situation modeled by a function, the intercept(s) may not be in the domain of the function, and may not represent anything important in the situation.

The graph above intersects the x-axis at (320, 0), so the x-intercept is 320. This means that the car can travel 320 mi before it runs out of gas.

The graph intersects the y-axis at (0, 16), so the y-intercept is 16. This means the car has 16 gal of gas when it starts its trip.

B. What are the x- and y-intercepts of the graph of $y = |x| - 3$?

Find the x-intercept(s) algebraically:

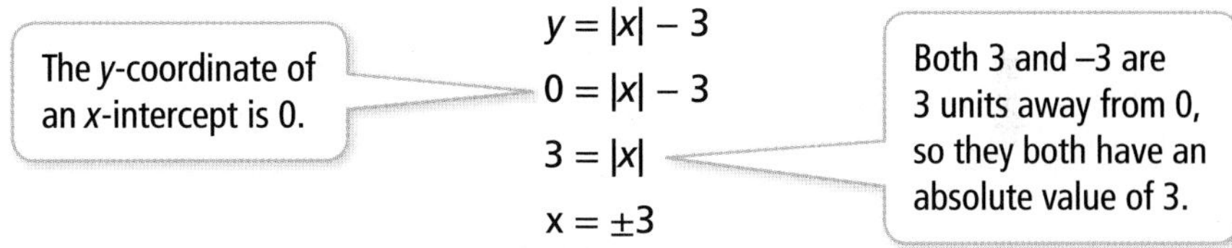

$$y = |x| - 3$$
$$0 = |x| - 3$$
$$3 = |x|$$
$$x = \pm 3$$

The x-intercepts of the graph of $y = |x| - 3$ are -3 and 3. The x-intercepts are also the **zeros of the function** because they are the input values that result in a function output value of 0.

Find the y-intercept algebraically:

$$\mathbf{y = |x| - 3}$$
$$y = |0| - 3$$
$$y = 0 - 3$$
$$y = -3$$

The x-coordinate at the y-intercept is 0.

The y-intercept of the graph of $y = |x| - 3$ is -3.

Try It! 2. What are the x- and y-intercepts of $g(x) = 4 - x^2$?

EXAMPLE 3 Identify Positive or Negative Intervals

For what intervals is $f(x) = x^2 - 9$ positive? For what intervals is the function negative?

Use technology to graph the function:

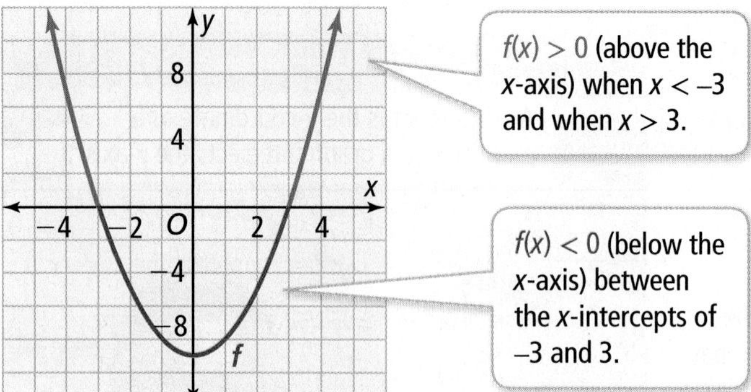

COMMON ERROR
Be careful not to confuse a positive function value and a positive rate of change. A positive rate of change means the y-values of the function are increasing but are not necessarily greater than 0.

The function is positive at $(-\infty, -3)$ and $(3, \infty)$.

Parentheses indicate that a boundary point is not included.

The function is negative at $(-3, 3)$.

The function is neither positive nor negative at the x-intercepts of -3 and 3.

 **Try It!** **3. a.** For what interval(s) is $h(x) = 2x + 10$ positive?

b. For what interval(s) is the function negative?

EXAMPLE 4 Identify Where a Function Increases or Decreases

For what values of x is $g(x) = 2 - |x|$ increasing? For what values is it decreasing?

Construct a table and sketch a graph to represent the function.

x	$g(x)$
−3	−1
−2	0
−1	1
0	2
1	1
2	0
3	−1

$g(x)$ is increasing from $-\infty$ to 0.

$g(x)$ is decreasing from 0 to ∞.

The greatest value a function attains is the ***maximum*** of the function. The least value a function attains is the ***minimum***.

The values of $g(x)$ are increasing on the interval $(-\infty, 0)$.

The values of $g(x)$ are decreasing on the interval $(0, \infty)$.

 **Try It!** **4.** For what values of x is each function increasing? For what values of x is it decreasing?

a. $f(x) = x^2 - 4x$

b. $f(x) = -2x - 3$

CONCEPTUAL UNDERSTANDING

EXAMPLE 5 Understand Average Rate of Change Over an Interval

A. What is the average rate of change of a function $y = f(x)$ over the interval $[a, b]$?

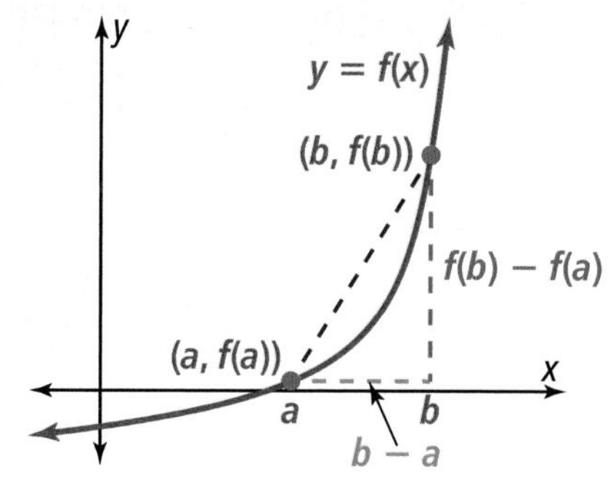

The interval starts at a value of $f(a)$ when $x = a$ and ends at a value of $f(b)$ when $x = b$.

The total change in the function values is $f(b) - f(a)$.

The length of the interval is $b - a$.

The **average rate of change** is the ratio $\frac{f(b) - f(a)}{b - a}$. This is the same as the slope of the line segment between the points $(a, f(a))$ and $(b, f(b))$.

B. What do the average rates of change over the intervals [−2, 0], [0, 3], and [−2, 3] indicate about the given functions?

LOOK FOR RELATIONSHIPS
If (x_1, y_1) and (x_2, y_2) are points on the graph of the linear function $y = mx + b$, then the average rate of change in the interval $[x_1, x_2]$ is $m = \frac{y_2 - y_1}{x_2 - x_1}$.

	$f(x) = 1$	$g(x) = \frac{1}{2}x - 1$	$h(x) = x^2$
	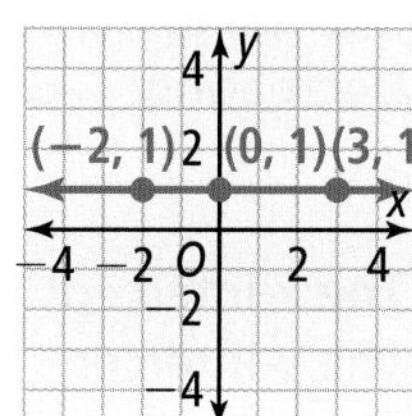	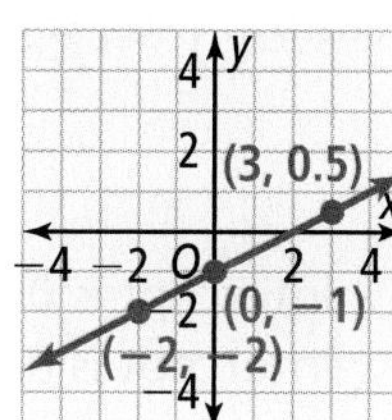	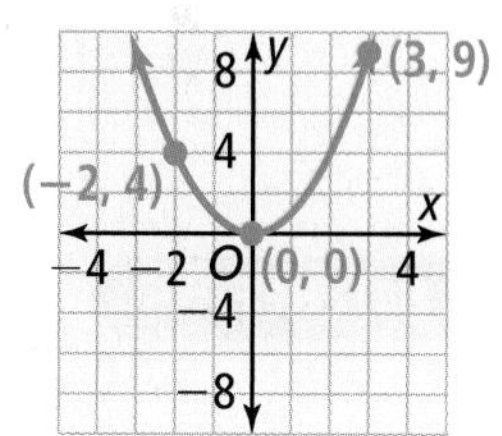
[−2, 0]	$\frac{1-1}{0-(-2)} = 0$	$\frac{-1-(-2)}{0-(-2)} = \frac{1}{2}$	$\frac{0-4}{0-(-2)} = -2$
[0, 3]	$\frac{1-1}{3-0} = 0$	$\frac{0.5-(-1)}{3-0} = \frac{1}{2}$	$\frac{9-0}{3-0} = 3$
[−2, 3]	$\frac{1-1}{3-(-2)} = 0$	$\frac{0.5-(-2)}{3-(-2)} = \frac{1}{2}$	$\frac{9-4}{3-(-2)} = 1$
	$f(x) = 1$ has the same rate of change, 0, over every interval $[a, b]$. This means it is a constant function.	$g(x) = \frac{1}{2}x - 1$ has a constant rate of change, $\frac{1}{2}$, over every interval $[a, b]$. This means it is a linear function.	$h(x) = x^2$ does not have a constant rate of change over every interval $[a, b]$. This means it is a nonlinear function.

 **Try It!** 5. What do the average rates of change of the function $y = |x| + 2$ over the intervals [−2, 0], [0, 3], and [−2, 3] indicate about the function?

  Concept Summary  Assess

CONCEPT SUMMARY Some Functions With Key Features

FUNCTION	Linear $y = x$	Quadratic $y = x^2$	Absolute Value $y = \|x\|$	Constant $y = 1$
GRAPH	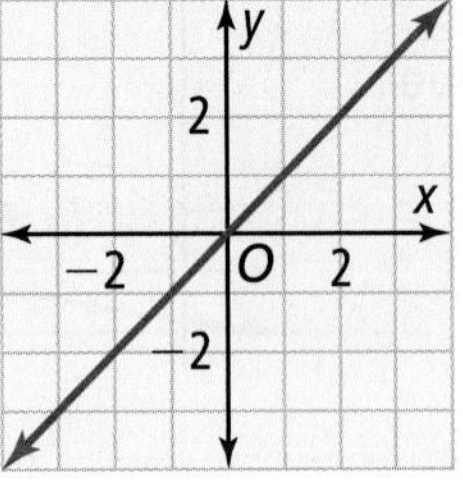	vertex; axis of symmetry = y-axis	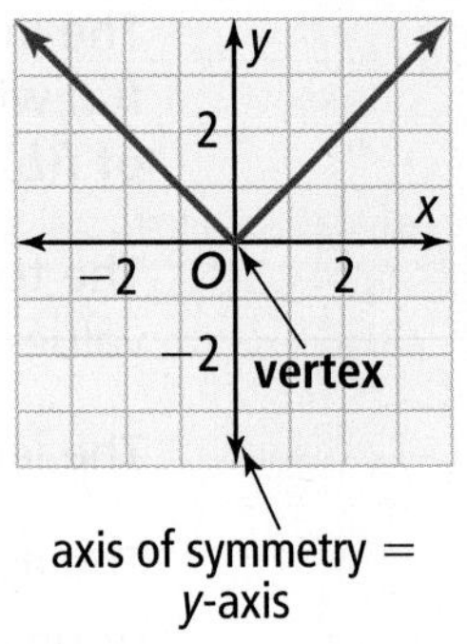 vertex; axis of symmetry = y-axis	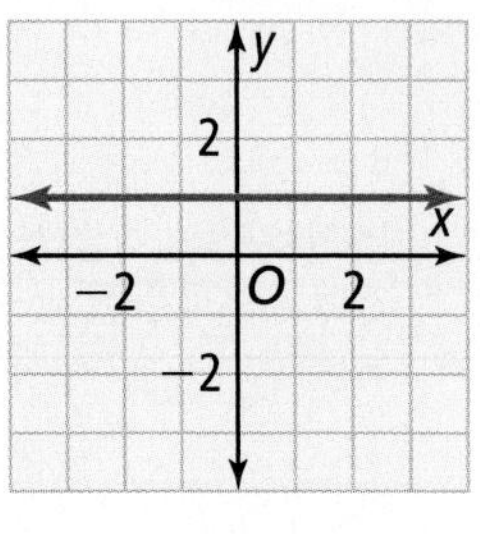
KEY FEATURES	Domain: $(-\infty, \infty)$ Range: $(-\infty, \infty)$ Increasing: $(-\infty, \infty)$	Domain: $(-\infty, \infty)$ Range: $[0, \infty)$ Increasing: $(0, \infty)$ Decreasing: $(-\infty, 0)$	Domain: $(-\infty, \infty)$ Range: $[0, \infty)$ Increasing: $(0, \infty)$ Decreasing: $(-\infty, 0)$	Domain: $(-\infty, \infty)$ Range: $\{y \mid y = 1\}$
INTERCEPTS	The x-intercept is 0. The y-intercept is 0.	The x-intercept is 0. The y-intercept is 0.	The x-intercept is 0. The y-intercept is 0.	There is no x-intercept. The y-intercept is 1.

 Do You UNDERSTAND?

1. ESSENTIAL QUESTION How do graphs and equations reveal information about a relationship between two quantities?

2. **Vocabulary** Define the term *zero of a function* in your own words.

3. **Error Analysis** Lonzell said the function shown in the graph is positive on the interval $(-1, 5)$ and negative on the interval $(-5, -1)$. Identify and correct Lonzell's error.

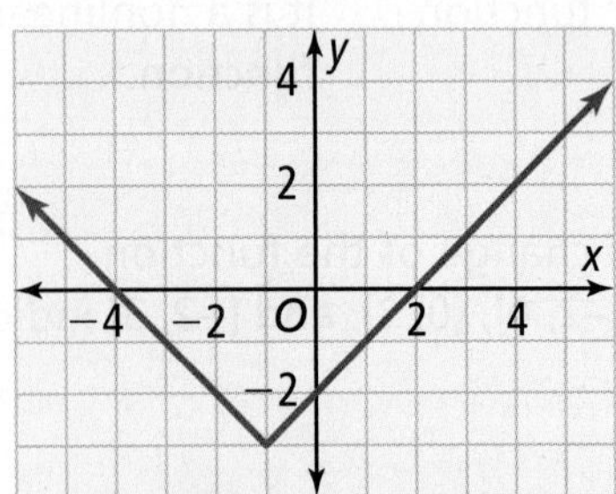

Do You KNOW HOW?

Find each key feature.

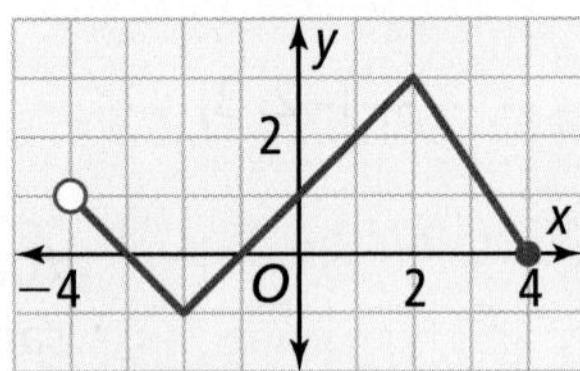

4. domain

5. range

6. x-intercept(s)

7. y-intercept(s)

8. interval(s) where the graph is positive

9. interval(s) where the graph is decreasing

10. interval(s) where the graph is increasing

11. rate of change on $[-1, 4]$

PRACTICE & PROBLEM SOLVING

Scan for Multimedia

Practice Tutorial

Additional Exercises Available Online

UNDERSTAND

12. **Reason** The graph of $y = -\frac{1}{2}x + 2$ is negative over the interval $(4, \infty)$ and positive over the interval $(-\infty, 4)$. What happens on the graph when $x = 4$? Explain.

13. **Error Analysis** Describe and correct the error a student made in finding the interval(s) over which the function is positive and negative.

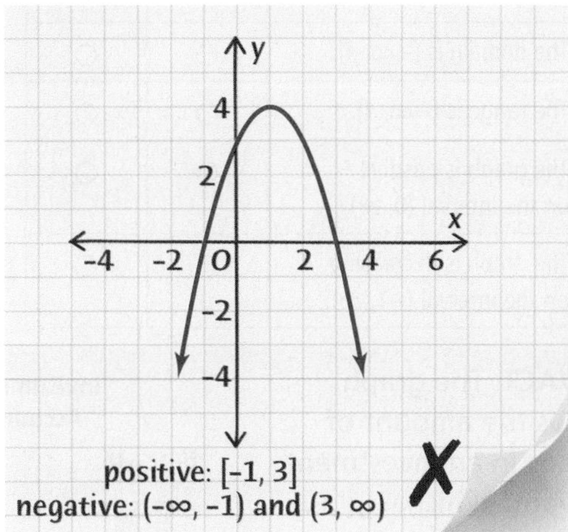

14. **Use Structure** Sketch a graph given the following key features.

domain: $(-4, 4)$	range: $(-4, 6]$
increasing: $(-4, 1)$	decreasing: $(1, 4)$
x-intercepts: $(-2, 0)$, $(3, 0)$	y-intercept: $(0, 4)$
negative: $(-4, -2)$ and $(3, 4)$	positive: $(-2, 3)$

15. **Construct Arguments** A student says that all linear functions are either increasing or decreasing. Do you agree? Explain.

16. **Higher Order Thinking** A relative maximum of a function occurs at the highest point on a graph over a certain interval. A relative minimum of a function occurs at the lowest point on a graph over a certain interval. Explain how to identify a relative maximum and a relative minimum of a function using key features.

17. **Model With Mathematics** For a graph of speed in miles per hour as a function of time in hours, what does it mean when the function is increasing? Decreasing?

PRACTICE

Use the graph of the function for Exercises 18–22.

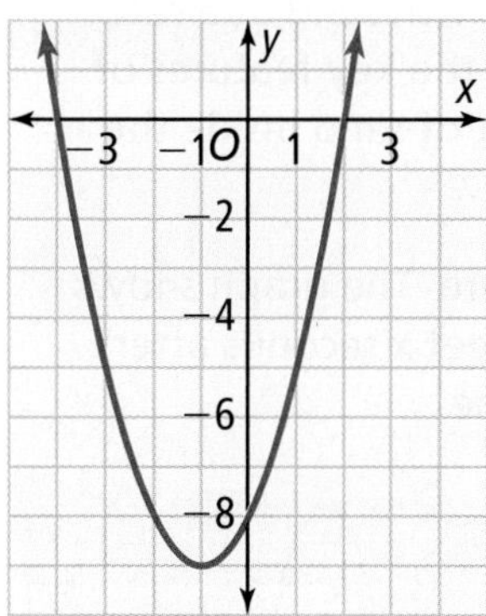

18. Identify the domain and range of the function. SEE EXAMPLE 1

19. Identify the x- and y-intercepts of the function. SEE EXAMPLE 2

20. On what intervals is the function positive? On what intervals is it negative? SEE EXAMPLE 3

21. On what intervals is the function increasing? On what intervals is it decreasing? SEE EXAMPLE 4

22. What is the average rate of change over the interval $(-3, 2)$? SEE EXAMPLE 5

Use the graph of the function for Exercises 23–27.

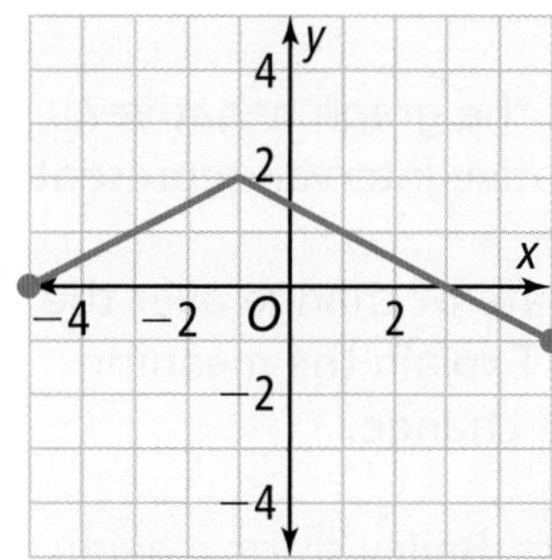

23. Identify the domain and range of the function. SEE EXAMPLE 1

24. Identify the x- and y-intercepts of the function. SEE EXAMPLE 2

25. Determine over what interval the function is positive or negative. SEE EXAMPLE 3

26. Determine over what interval the function is increasing or decreasing. SEE EXAMPLE 4

27. What is the average rate of change over the interval $(-1, 5)$? SEE EXAMPLE 5

PRACTICE & PROBLEM SOLVING

Mixed Review Available Online

APPLY

28. Communicate Precisely Kathryn is filling an empty 100 ft^3 container with sand at a rate of 1.25 ft^3/min. Describe the key features of the graph of the amount of sand inside the container.

29. Make Sense and Persevere The graph shows a jumper's height, y, in feet x seconds after getting onto a trampoline.

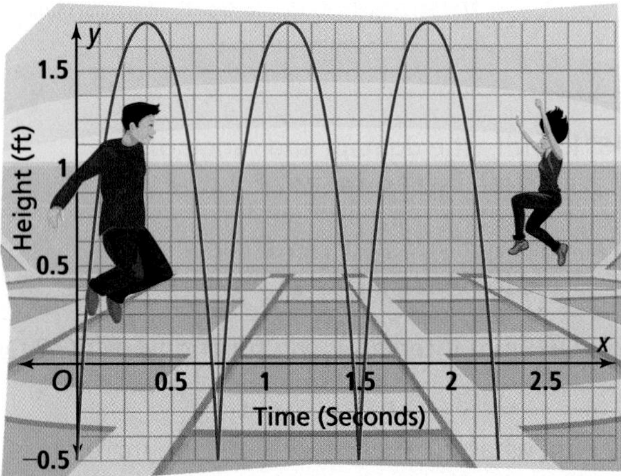

a. What are the x- and y-intercepts? Explain what the x- and y-intercepts represent.

b. Over what intervals is the graph positive? Explain what the positive intervals represent.

c. Over what intervals is the graph negative? Explain what the negative intervals represent.

d. What is the average rate of change over the interval [0.75, 1.125]? Explain the meaning of the average rate of change.

30. Model With Mathematics Bailey starts playing a game on her cell phone with the battery fully charged, and plays until the phone battery dies. While playing the game, the charge in Bailey's battery decreases by half a percent per minute.

a. Write a function for the percent charge in the battery while Bailey is playing the game.

b. What is the domain and range of the function?

c. How long can Bailey play the game?

ASSESSMENT PRACTICE

31. Given the graph, select yes or no for each statement.

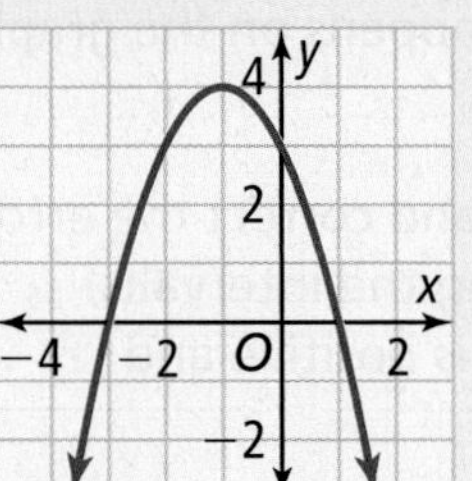

	Yes	No
a. The domain is $(-\infty, 4]$.	○	○
b. The range is $(-\infty, 4]$.	○	○
c. The graph is positive on the interval $(0, \infty)$.	○	○
d. The graph is decreasing on the interval $(-1, \infty)$.	○	○

32. SAT/ACT The graph shows the amount of money in an investment account. Which statement is true?

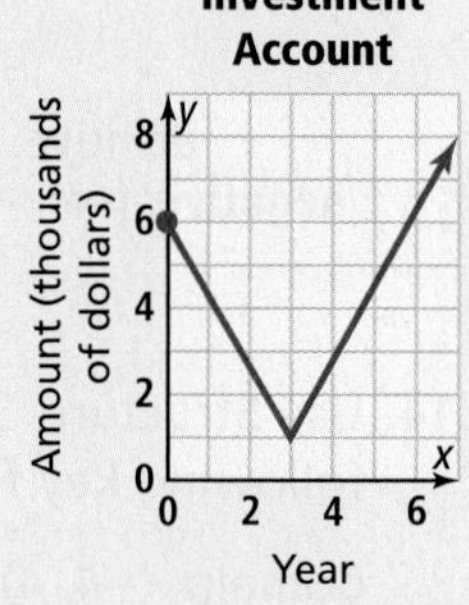

Ⓐ $6,000 was initially invested in the account.

Ⓑ $1,000 was initially invested in the account.

Ⓒ At Year 3, there was $0 in the account.

Ⓓ At Year 7, there was $0 in the account.

33. Performance Task The graph shows the amount of water in a water tank over several hours.

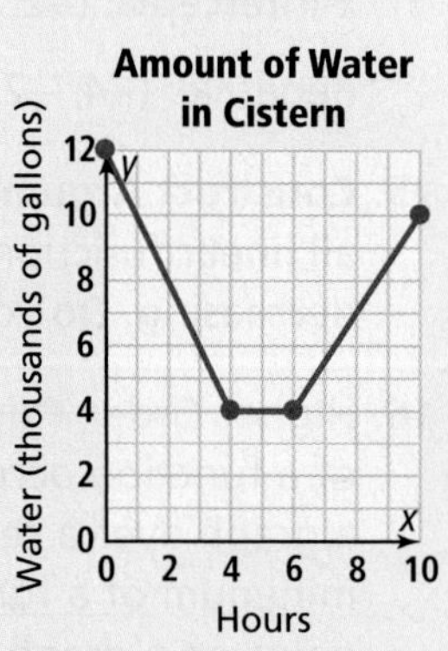

Part A What is the average rate of change on the interval [0, 4] and on the interval [6, 10]? What is a possible explanation for what each rate of change indicates?

Part B What is a possible explanation for what occurred between 4 and 6 h?

Part C What is the average rate of change on the interval [0, 10]? What does the rate of change mean? Does this rate of change give a good indication as to what is happening with the water in the cistern from 0 h to 10 h? Explain.

1-2

Transformations of Functions

  Activity  Assess

I CAN… apply transformations to graph functions and write equations.

VOCABULARY

- compression
- reflection
- stretch
- transformation
- translation

EXPLORE & REASON

The graph of the function $f(x) = |x|$ is shown.

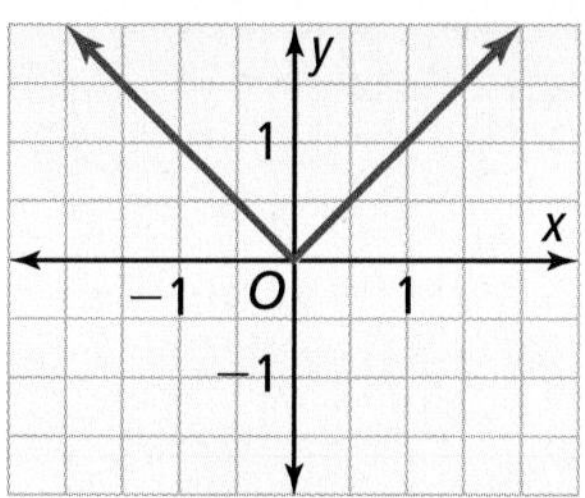

A. Graph the function $g(x) = |x + c|$ several times with different values for c (any value from −5 to 5).

B. Look for Relationships Predict what will happen to the graph if c is a number greater than 100. What if c is a number between 0 and $\frac{1}{2}$?

ESSENTIAL QUESTION

What do the differences between the equation of a function and the equation of its parent function tell you about the differences in the graphs of the two functions?

EXAMPLE 1 Translate a Function

A. Graph the function $f(x) = x^2$ for the domain [−2, 2]. The graph of g is the graph of f after a translation of 3 units down. How are the equations, domains, and ranges of f and g related?

Every point on the graph of g is 3 units below a corresponding point on the graph of f.

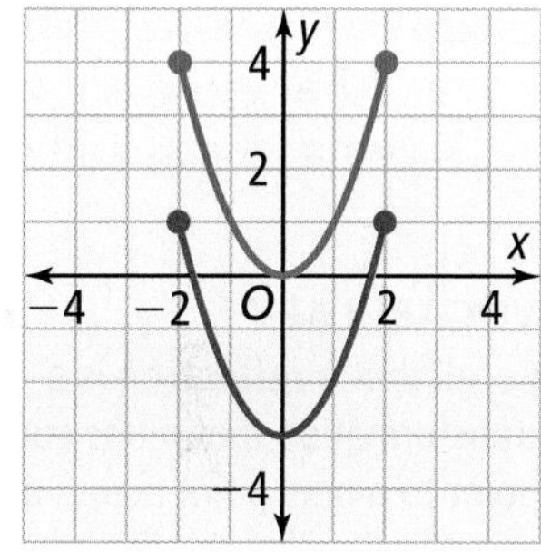

$$(x, f(x)) \rightarrow (x, f(x) - 3) = (x, g(x))$$

$$g(x) = f(x) - 3$$

The domains of f and g are the same: [−2, 2]. The range values of g are 3 units less than the range values of f. The range of f is [0, 4] and the range of g is [−3, 1].

LOOK FOR RELATIONSHIPS
This type of transformation slides the graph up or down. You could perform a transformation like this to a non-vertical line and produce a parallel line.

A **translation** like this one is a particular kind of transformation of a function, one that shifts each point on a graph the same distance and direction.

Other kinds of **transformations** of a function may reflect its graph across an axis, or stretch or compress its graph.

In general, if $g(x) = f(x) + k$, then the graph of g is a vertical translation of the graph of f by k units.

CONTINUED ON THE NEXT PAGE

EXAMPLE 1 CONTINUED

B. Graph the function $f(x) = x^2$ for the domain [−2, 2]. The graph of the function g is the graph of f after a translation 3 units to the right. How are the equations, domains, and ranges of f and g related?

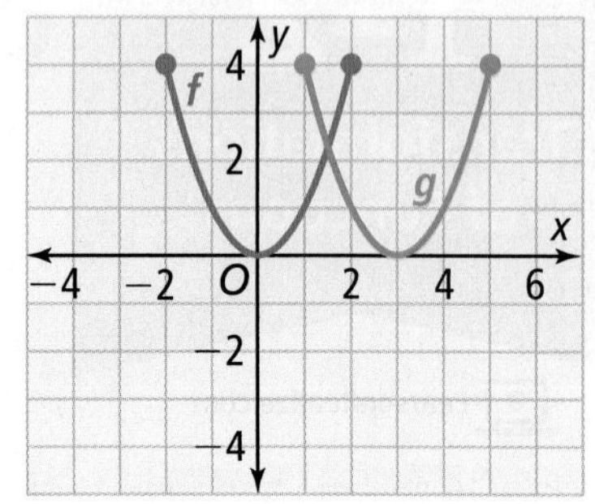

Every point on the graph of g is 3 units to the right of the corresponding point on the graph of f.

$(x, f(x)) \rightarrow (x, g(x + 3))$

The translation of the graph of f to the graph of g can be described as $g(x + 3) = f(x)$, or $g(x) = f(x - 3)$.

The range values of f and g are the same: [0, 4]. The domain values of g are 3 units more than the domain values of f. The domain of f is [−2, 2] and the domain of g is [1, 5].

In general, if $g(x) = f(x - h)$, then the graph of g is a horizontal translation of the graph of f by h units.

Try It! **1. a.** How did the transformation of f to g in part (a) affect the intercepts?

b. How did the transformation of f to g in part (b) affect the intercepts?

EXAMPLE 2 Reflect a Function Across the x- or y-Axis

VOCABULARY
Recall that a **reflection** is a transformation that maps each point to a new point across a given line, called the *line of reflection*. The line of reflection is the perpendicular bisector of the segment between the point and its image.

A. Graph $f(x) = 2x - 6$ and the function g, whose graph is the reflection of the graph of f across the x-axis. How are their equations related?

Graph f. Then graph g by reflecting each point of the graph of f across the x-axis. For each point (x, y) on the graph of f, plot the point (x, −y) to get the graph of g.

Since the y-values of the new function have the opposite sign, $g(x) = -f(x)$.

From the graph, you can see that $g(x) = -2x + 6$.

You can check that $g(x) = -f(x)$ by substituting for $f(x)$.

$$g(x) = -f(x)$$
$$= -(2x - 6)$$
$$g(x) = -2x + 6$$

The expression that defines g is the opposite of the expression that defines f.

The y-intercept of g, 6, is the opposite of the y-intercept of f, −6.

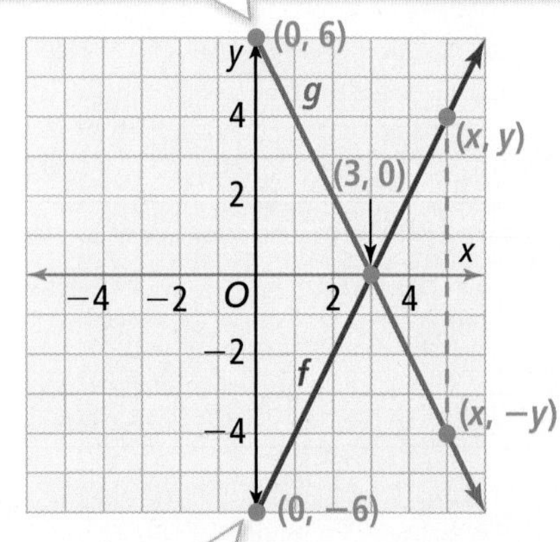

The slope of the graph of f is 2, while the slope of the graph of g is −2.

CONTINUED ON THE NEXT PAGE

EXAMPLE 2 CONTINUED

B. Graph $f(x) = 2x - 6$ and the function h, whose graph is the reflection of the graph of f across the y-axis. How are their equations related?

Graph f. Then reflect every point on the graph of f over the y-axis to produce the graph of h.

From the graph, you can see that $h(x) = -2x - 6$.

You can check that $h(x) = f(-x)$ by substituting for $f(-x)$.

$$h(x) = f(-x)$$
$$= 2(-x) - 6$$
$$h(x) = -2x - 6$$

The slope of the graph of f is 2, and the slope of the graph of h is -2.

For any point (x, y) on the graph of f, there is a reflected point $(-x, y)$ on the graph of h, so $h(x) = f(-x)$. The x-intercept of h, -3, is the opposite of the x-intercept of f, 3.

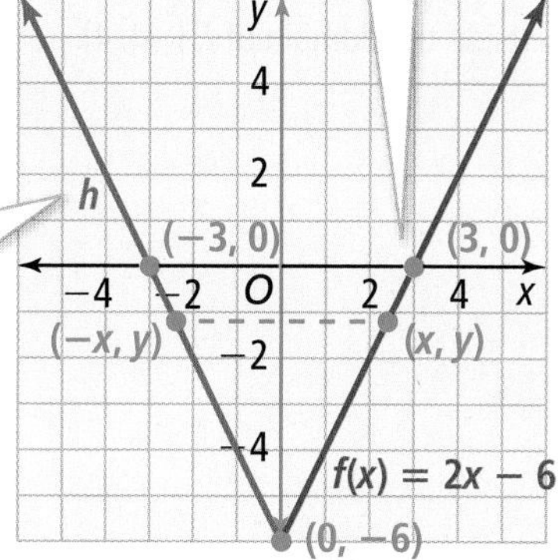

The function h has a slope that is the opposite of the slope of f but with the same y-intercept.

USE STRUCTURE
Why does $g(x) = -f(x)$ affect the y-coordinate of each point and $g(x) = f(-x)$ affect the x-coordinate of each point?

Try It! 2. What is an equation for the reflected graph? Check by graphing.

a. the graph of $f(x) = x^2 - 2$ reflected across the x-axis

b. the graph of $f(x) = x^2 - 2$ reflected across the y-axis

CONCEPTUAL UNDERSTANDING

EXAMPLE 3 Understand Stretches and Compressions

A. Graph $f(x) = |x|$ with domain $[-4, 4]$ and $g(x) = 2 \cdot f(x)$. How are the domains and ranges related?

Use a table to find points on the graph of g.

x	$f(x)$	$g(x) = 2 \cdot f(x)$	$(x, g(x))$
−4	4	$2 \cdot f(-4) = 2(4) = 8$	(−4, 8)
−2	2	$2 \cdot f(-2) = 2(2) = 4$	(−2, 4)
0	0	$2 \cdot f(0) = 2(0) = 0$	(0, 0)
2	2	$2 \cdot f(2) = 2(2) = 4$	(2, 4)
4	4	$2 \cdot f(4) = 2(4) = 8$	(4, 8)

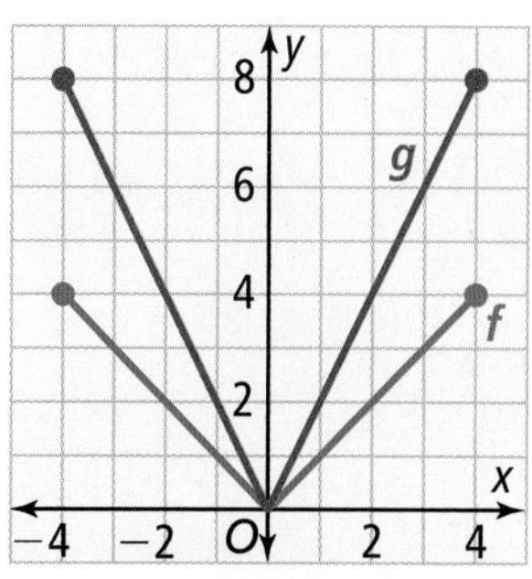

The domains of f and g are the same. Each y-value is multiplied by 2, so for the function with the given domain, the range of f, [0, 4], is doubled for g to [0, 8].

A transformation that increases the distance between the points of a graph and a given line by the same factor is called a **stretch.** The graph of g is a vertical stretch of the graph of f by a factor of 2.

CONTINUED ON THE NEXT PAGE

EXAMPLE 3 CONTINUED

B. Graph $f(x) = |x|$ with domain $[-4, 4]$ and $h(x) = f(2x)$. How are the domains and ranges related?

Use a table to find points on the graph of h.

x	$f(x)$	$h = f(2x)$	$(x, h(x))$
−2	2	$f(2(-2)) = f(-4) = 4$	(−2, 4)
−1	1	$f(2(-1)) = f(-2) = 2$	(−1, 2)
0	0	$f(2(0)) = f(0) = 0$	(0, 0)
1	1	$f(2(1)) = f(2) = 2$	(1, 2)
2	2	$f(2(2)) = f(4) = 4$	(2, 4)

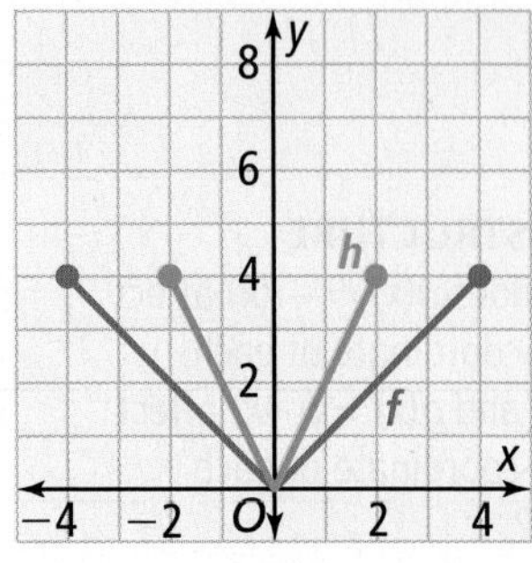

COMMON ERROR
Be careful not to assume that the domain of a transformed function is the same as the domain of the original function. Notice that $h(-4)$ would equal $f(-8)$, which is outside the domain of f, $[-4, 4]$.

For each corresponding output, the value of the input for h is half the value of the input for f. The two functions have the same range, but the values in the domain of h, $[-2, 2]$, are half as large as the values in the domain of f, $[-4, 4]$.

A transformation that decreases the distance between the points of a graph and a given line by the same factor is called a **compression**. The graph of h is a horizontal compression of the graph of f by a factor of 2.

 **Try It!** 3. Show that $j(x) = f\left(\frac{1}{2}x\right)$ is a horizontal stretch of the graph of f.

CONCEPT Stretches and Compressions

Vertical Stretches and Compressions:

If $a > 1$, then $g(x) = a \cdot f(x)$ is a vertical stretch of f by the factor a.

If $0 < a < 1$, then $g(x) = a \cdot f(x)$ is a vertical compression of f by the factor $\frac{1}{a}$.

Horizontal Stretches and Compressions:

If $a > 1$, then $g(x) = f(ax)$ is a horizontal compression of f by the factor a.

If $0 < a < 1$, then $g(x) = f(ax)$ is a horizontal stretch of f by the factor $\frac{1}{a}$.

EXAMPLE 4 Graph a Combination of Transformations

The graph represents $y = f(x)$. Using $y = f(x)$, how can you graph a combination of transformations?

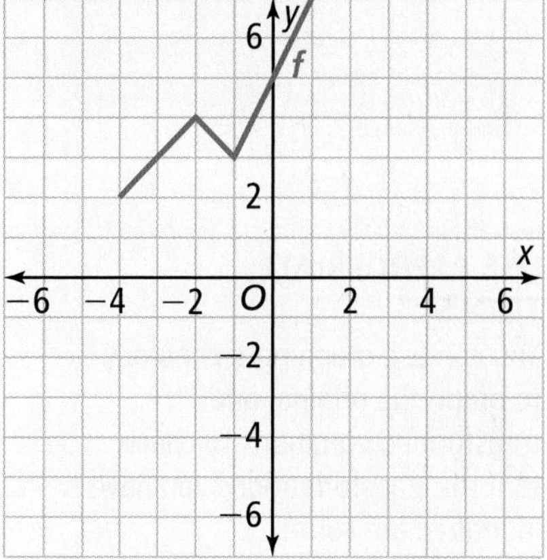

A. Graph $y = -f(x + 2)$.

Graph $g(x) = f(x + 2)$, which is a translation of f left 2 units.

Graph $h(x) = -f(x + 2)$, which is a reflection of g across the x-axis.

The graph of h is a translation of f left 2 units followed by a reflection across the x-axis.

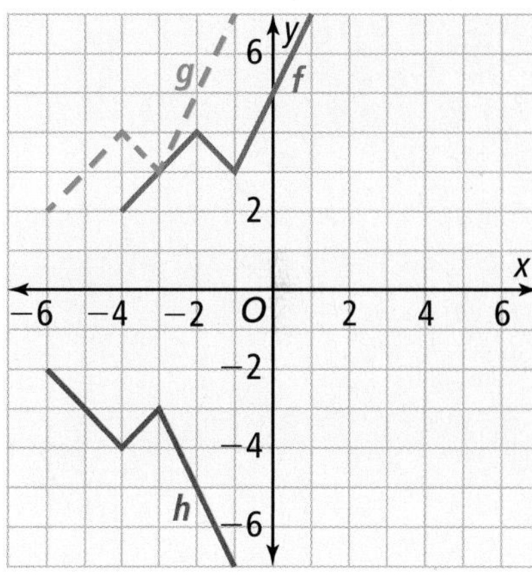

STUDY TIP
It is easier to perform one transformation at a time. Trying to perform both transformations at the same time will often result in an incorrect graph.

B. Graph $y = \frac{1}{2} f(x) + 3$.

Graph $g(x) = \frac{1}{2} f(x)$, which is a vertical compression of f by a factor of 2.

Graph $h(x) = \frac{1}{2} f(x) + 3$, which is a translation of g up 3 units.

The graph of h is a vertical compression of f by a factor of 2 followed by a translation 3 units up.

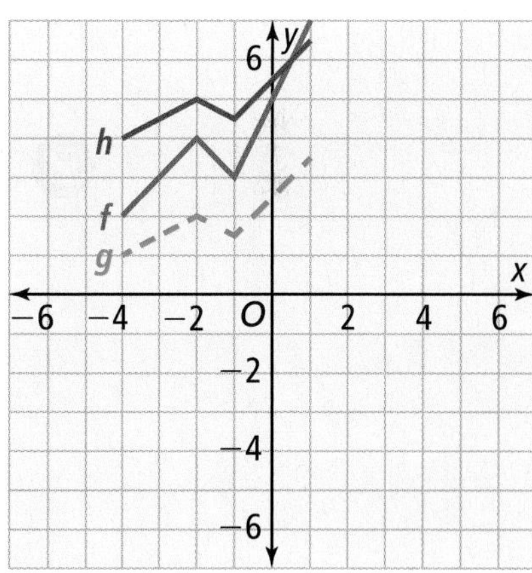

Try It! 4. Using the graph of f above, graph each equation.

a. $y = f(2x) - 4$ **b.** $y = f(2x - 3) - 2$

EXAMPLE 5 Identify Transformations From an Equation

What transformations of $f(x) = x^2$ result in the graph of the function g?

A. $g(x) = -\left(\frac{1}{3}x\right)^2$

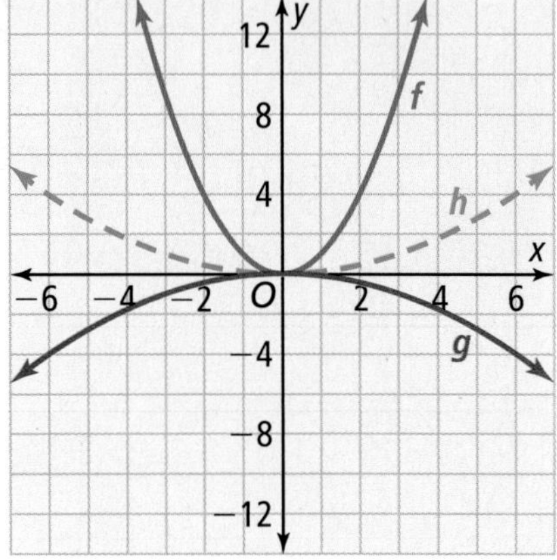

$h(x) = f\left(\frac{1}{3}x\right) = \left(\frac{1}{3}x\right)^2$ represents a horizontal stretch of the graph of f by a factor of 3.

$g(x) = -h(x) = -f\left(\frac{1}{3}x\right) = -\left(\frac{1}{3}x\right)^2$ represents a reflection across the x-axis of $f\left(\frac{1}{3}x\right)$.

The graph of g is a horizontal stretch by a factor of 3 and a reflection across the x-axis of the graph of f.

USE APPROPRIATE TOOLS
You can use graphing technology to graph the original and transformed equations to check that the transformations you have identified are correct.

B. $g(x) = (x - 4)^2 + 5$

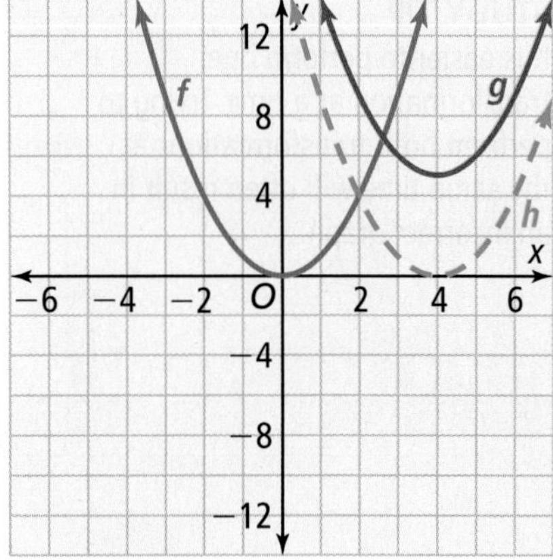

$h(x) = f(x - 4) = (x - 4)^2$ represents a translation 4 units to the right of the graph of f.

$g(x) = h(x) + 5 = f(x - 4) + 5 = (x - 4)^2 + 5$ represents a translation 5 units up of the graph of $f(x - 4)$.

The graph of g is a translation 4 units right and 5 units up of the graph of f.

Try It! **5.** What transformations of the graph of $f(x) = |x|$ are applied to graph the function g?

a. $g(x) = \frac{1}{2}|x + 3|$ **b.** $g(x) = -|x| + 2$

APPLICATION

EXAMPLE 6 Write an Equation From a Graph

A scenic train ride makes trips on an old mining line. The graph shows the distance y in kilometers of the train from the station x minutes after the ride begins. What equation represents the distance from the station as a function of time? What is its domain?

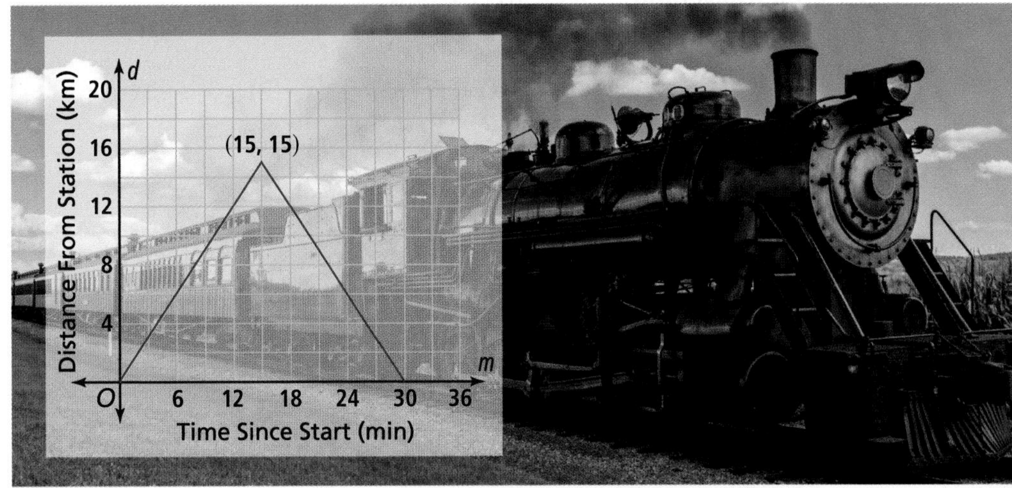

The graph shows a reflection of an absolute value graph across the x-axis and a translation upward and to the right. The general form of this absolute value function is $y = -a|x - h| + k$, where the point (h, k) represents the vertex and $-a$ indicates that the graph opens downward.

Substituting the point of the vertex (15, 15) for (h, k) gives the equation $y = -a|x - 15| + 15$.

To solve for a, you can use any point on the graph. Using the point (0, 0) to substitute for (x, y) in the equation simplifies the computation:

$$y = -a|x - 15| + 15$$

$$0 = -a|0 - 15| + 15$$

$$0 = -15a + 15$$

$$-15 = -15a$$

$$a = 1$$

STUDY TIP
Solving algebraically is only one method for determining a stretch or compression factor.

Now you can write the equation for distance as a function of time:

$$y = -|x - 15| + 15.$$

According to the graph, the train returns to its station after 30 minutes, so the function's domain is [0, 30].

Try It! **6.** How would the graph and equation be affected if the train traveled twice as far in the same amount of time?

CONCEPT SUMMARY Transformations of Functions

For a function $f(x)$, the graph of $f(x) = a \cdot f[b(x - h)] + k$ represents a transformation of the graph of that function by translation, reflection, or stretching.

WORDS	EQUATIONS	GRAPHS
Horizontal translation of *f* right 2 units (altering *h*)	$f(x)$ becomes $g(x) = f(x - 2)$ $f(x) = x^2 + x$ $g(x) = (x - 2)^2 + (x - 2) = x^2 - 3x + 2$	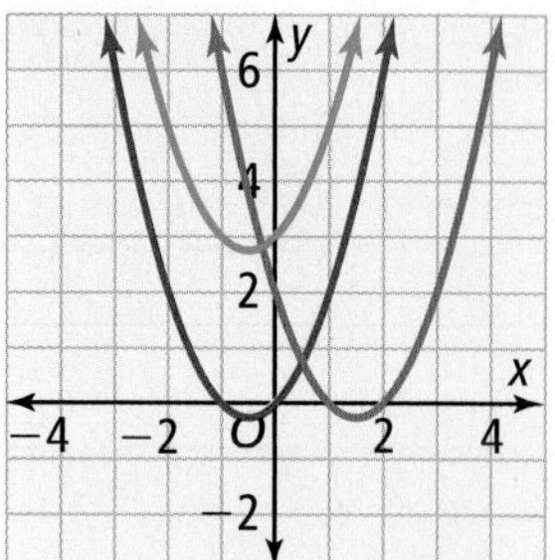
Vertical translation of *f* up 3 units (altering *k*)	$f(x)$ becomes $h(x) = f(x) + 3$ $f(x) = x^2 + x$ $h(x) = x^2 + x + 3$	
Reflection of *f* across the *x*-axis (altering *a*)	$f(x)$ becomes $-f(x)$ $f(x) = x^2 + x$ $-f(x) = -(x^2 + x) = -x^2 - x$	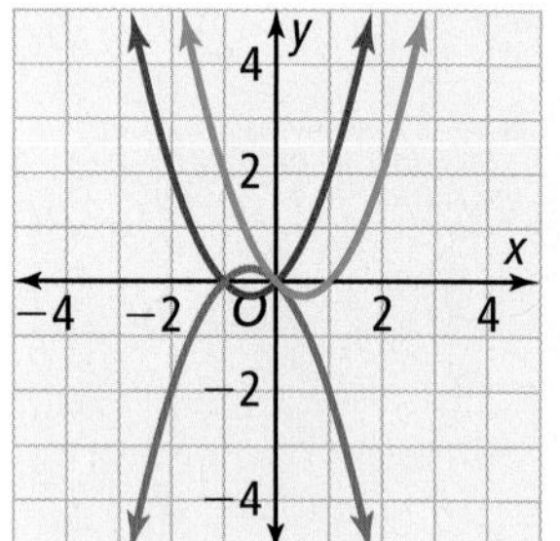
Reflection of *f* across the *y*-axis (altering *b*)	$f(x)$ becomes $f(-x)$ $f(x) = x^2 + x$ $f(-x) = (-x)^2 + (-x) = x^2 - x$	
Horizontal stretch of *f* by a factor of 2 (altering *b*)	$f(x)$ becomes $f\left(\frac{1}{2}x\right)$ $f(x) = x^2 + x$ $f\left(\frac{1}{2}x\right) = \left(\frac{1}{2}x\right)^2 + \frac{1}{2}x = \frac{1}{4}x^2 + \frac{1}{2}x$	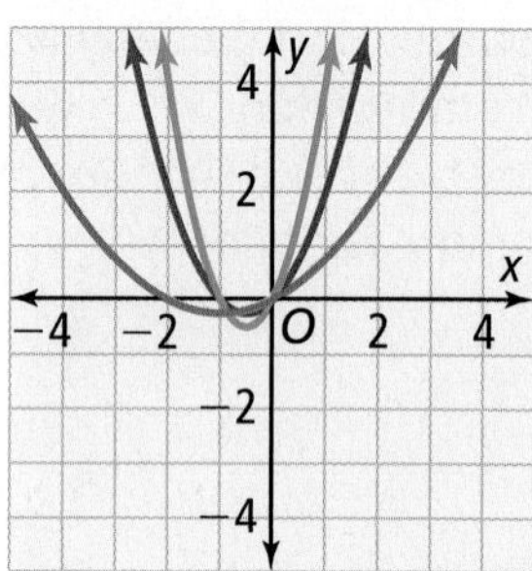
Vertical stretch of *f* by a factor of 2 (altering *a*)	$f(x)$ becomes $2f(x)$ $f(x) = x^2 + x$ $2f(x) = 2(x^2 + x) = 2x^2 + 2x$	

Do You UNDERSTAND?

1. **ESSENTIAL QUESTION** What do the differences between the equation of a function and the equation of its parent function tell you about the differences in the graphs of the two functions?

2. **Reason** Do k and h affect the input or output for $g(x) = f(x) + k$ and $g(x) = f(x - h)$? Explain.

3. **Error Analysis** Margo is comparing the functions $f(x) = |x|$ and $g(x) = |x + 1| - 5$. She said the graph of g is a vertical translation of the graph of f 5 units down and a horizontal translation of the graph of f 1 unit right. What is Margo's error?

Do You KNOW HOW?

Graph each function and its parent function.

4. $g(x) = |x| - 1$
5. $g(x) = (x - 3)^2$
6. $g(x) = -|x|$
7. $g(x) = -x$
8. $g(x) = x^2 - 2$
9. $g(x) = \frac{1}{2}|x|$
10. $g(x) = 4x$
11. $g(x) = |5x|$
12. Which types of transformations in Exercises 4–11 do not change the shape of a graph? Which types of transformations change the shape of a graph? Explain.

PRACTICE & PROBLEM SOLVING

UNDERSTAND

13. **Use Structure** Write a function g with the parent function $f(x) = x^2$ that has a vertex at (3, –6).

14. **Error Analysis** Describe and correct the error a student made in graphing $g(x) = f(-x)$ as a reflection across the y-axis of the graph of $f(x) = |x + 2| + 1$.

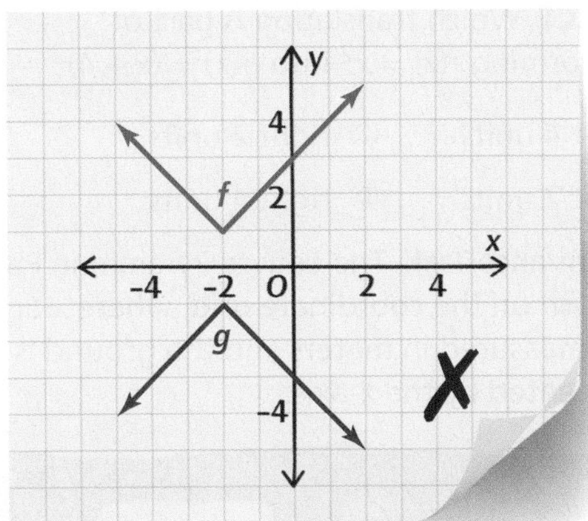

15. **Higher Order Thinking** Describe the transformation g of $f(x) = |x|$ as a stretch and as a compression. Then write two equations to represent the function. What can you conclude? Explain.

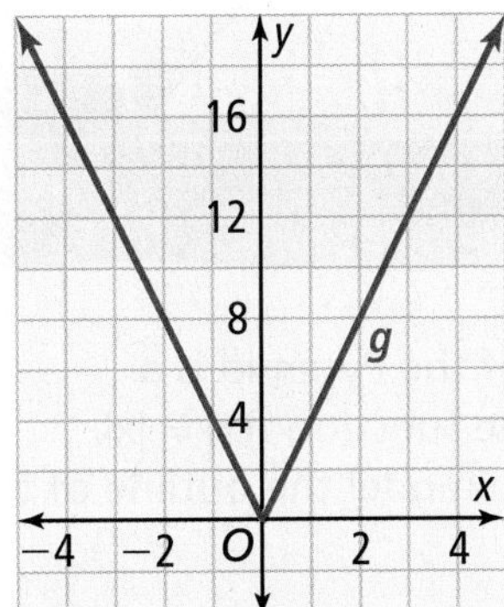

16. **Use Structure** The graph of the parent function $f(x) = x^2$ is reflected across the y-axis. Write an equation for the function g after the reflection. Show your work. Based on your equation, what happens to the graph? Explain.

17. **Error Analysis** Monisha is comparing $f(x) = |x|$ and $g(x) = |2x - 4|$. She said the graph of g is a horizontal translation of the graph of f 4 units to the right and a horizontal compression of the graph of f by a factor of 2. What is Monisha's error?

PRACTICE

Graph each function as a translation of its parent function, *f*. How did the transformation affect the domain and range? SEE EXAMPLE 1

18. $g(x) = |x| - 5$
19. $g(x) = (x + 1)^2$
20. $g(x) = |x - 3|$
21. $g(x) = x^2 + 2$

What is the equation for the image graph? Check by graphing. SEE EXAMPLE 2

22. Reflect $f(x) = x^2 + 1$ across the x-axis.

23. Reflect $f(x) = x^2 + 1$ across the y-axis.

Graph each function as a vertical stretch or compression of its parent function.
SEE EXAMPLE 3

24. $g(x) = 0.25|x|$
25. $g(x) = 3x^2$
26. $g(x) = 1.5|x|$
27. $g(x) = 0.75x^2$

28. Use the graph of $f(x)$ to graph $y = f(x + 1) + 2$. SEE EXAMPLE 4

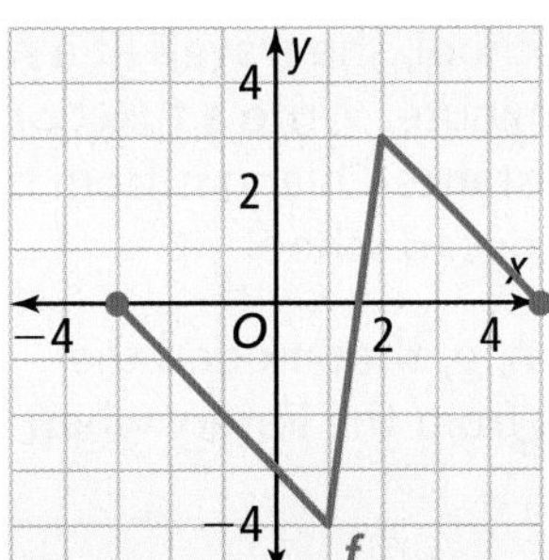

What transformations of $f(x) = x^2$ are applied to the function *g*? SEE EXAMPLE 5

29. $g(x) = 2(x + 1)^2$
30. $g(x) = (x - 3)^2 + 5$
31. $g(x) = -x^2 - 6$
32. $g(x) = 4(x - 7)^2 - 9$

33. The graph shows the height y in feet of a flying insect x seconds after taking off from the ground. Write an equation that represents the height of the insect as a function of time.
SEE EXAMPLE 6

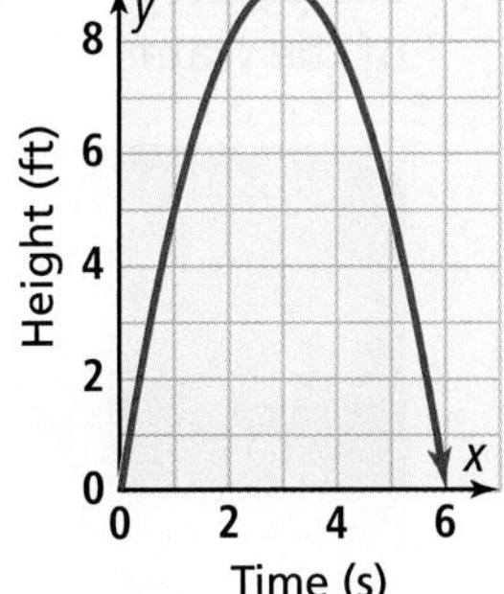

PRACTICE & PROBLEM SOLVING

APPLY

34. Model With Mathematics Chiang walks to school each day. She passes the library halfway on her walk to school. She walks at a rate of 1 block per minute. The graph shows the distance Chiang is from the library as she walks to school.

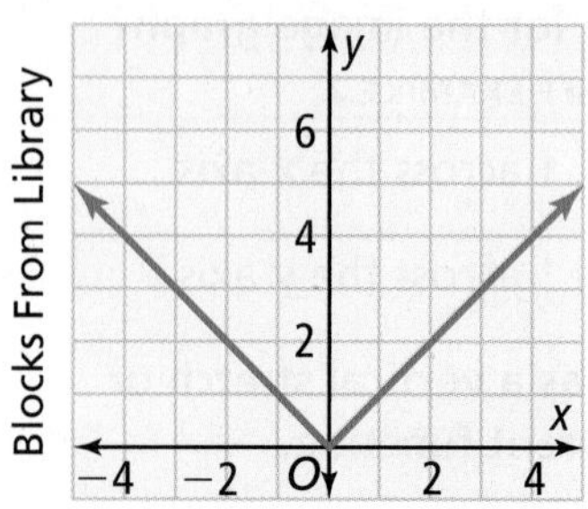

a. Write a function, f, to model the distance Chiang is from the library when she walks to school.

b. If Chiang jogs to school, she travels at a rate of 2.5 blocks per minute. Write a function, g, to model the distance Chiang is from the library when she jogs to school.

c. Graph the function, g, that models the distance Chiang is from the library when she jogs to school.

35. Model With Mathematics The archer fish spits water at flying insects to knock them into the water. The path of the water is shown with x and y distances in feet. Write an equation to represent the path of the water in relation to the coordinate grid. Then determine the coordinates of the point of maximum height of the water.

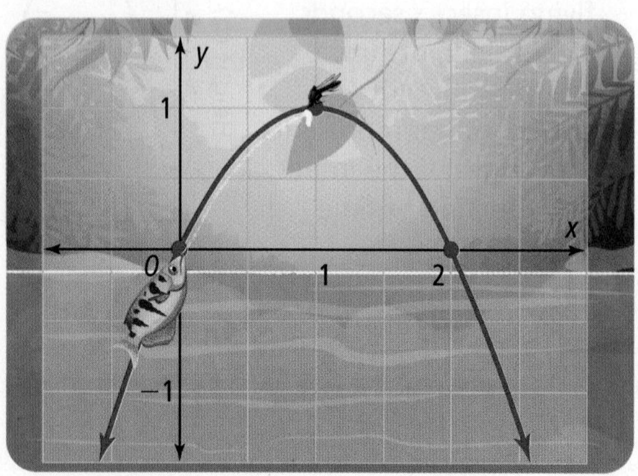

ASSESSMENT PRACTICE

36. Match each equation on the left to an equation on the right that has the same translation of $y = |x|$.

A. $y = |x| - 1$
B. $y = -|x + 1|$
C. $y = -|x + 1| - 1$
D. $y = |x + 1| - 1$
E. $y = 2|x| - 1$
F. $y = |x + 1|$

37. SAT/ACT Which translation is part of transforming $f(x) = x^2$ into $h(x) = (x + 4)^2 - 2$?

Ⓐ left 4 units
Ⓑ left 2 units
Ⓒ right 2 units
Ⓓ right 4 units

38. Performance Task The Louvre Pyramid in Paris is shown on the coordinate grid, where x and y are measured in meters and the ground is represented by the x-axis.

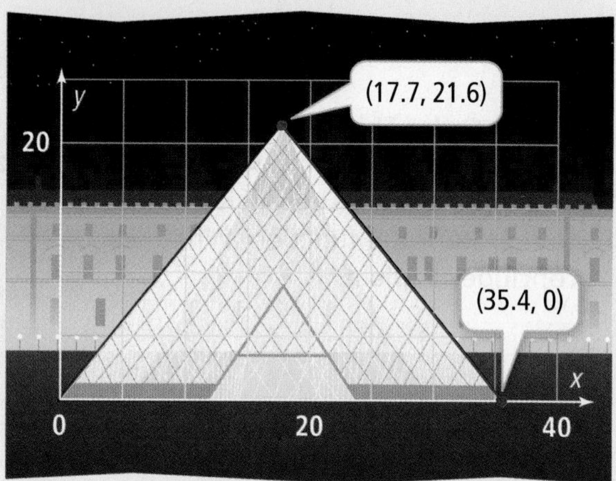

Part A The outline of the Pyramid is a transformation of the function $f(x) = |x|$. Write a function g to model the outline of the Pyramid.

Part B What is the domain and range of the function that models the outline of the Pyramid? What do the domain and range represent?

1-3 Piecewise-Defined Functions

 PearsonRealize.com

Activity Assess

I CAN… graph and interpret piecewise-defined functions.

VOCABULARY

- piecewise-defined function
- step function

MODEL & DISCUSS

A music teacher needs to buy guitar strings for her class. At store A, the guitar strings cost \$6 each. At store B, the guitar strings are \$20 for a pack of 4.

A. Make graphs that show the income each store receives if the teacher needs 1–20 guitar strings

B. Describe the shape of the graph for store A. Describe the shape of the graph for store B. Why are the graphs different?

C. Communicate Precisely Compare the graphs for stores A and B. For what numbers of guitar strings is it cheaper to buy from store B? Explain how you know.

? ESSENTIAL QUESTION

How do you model a situation in which a function behaves differently over different parts of its domain?

CONCEPTUAL UNDERSTANDING

EXAMPLE 1 Model With a Piecewise-Defined Function

Alani has a summer job as a lifeguard. She makes \$8/h for up to 40 h each week. If she works more than 40 h, she makes 1.5 times her hourly pay, or \$12/h, for each hour over 40 h. How could you make a graph and write a function that shows Alani's weekly earnings based on the number of hours she worked?

Step 1 Make a table of values and a graph.

STUDY TIP
Remember that Alani makes \$8/h for the first 40 h and \$12/h for any additional hours after that.

Hours Worked	Pay
20	160
25	200
30	240
35	280
40	320
45	380
50	440
55	500

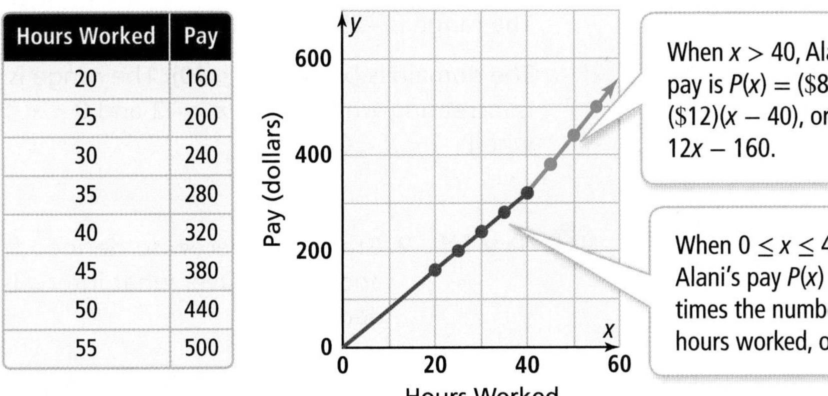

When $x > 40$, Alani's pay is $P(x) = (\$8)(40) + (\$12)(x - 40)$, or $P(x) = 12x - 160$.

When $0 \leq x \leq 40$, Alani's pay $P(x)$ is \$8/h times the number of hours worked, or $8x$.

Step 2 Notice that the plot contains two linear segments with a slope that changes slightly at $x = 40$. A function that has different rules for different parts of its domain is called a **piecewise-defined function.**

Step 3 Write an equation for each piece of the graph.

USE STRUCTURE
This notation is used for piecewise-defined functions to indicate the different functions at different parts of the domain.

$$P(x) = \begin{cases} 8x, & 0 \leq x \leq 40 \\ 12x - 160, & x > 40 \end{cases}$$

CONTINUED ON THE NEXT PAGE

Activity

Assess

EXAMPLE 1 CONTINUED

Try It! 1. How much will Alani earn if she works:

a. 37 hours?

b. 43 hours?

EXAMPLE 2 Graph a Piecewise-Defined Function

How do you graph a piecewise defined function?

$$f(x) = \begin{cases} 4x + 11, & -10 \leq x < -2 \\ x^2 - 1, & -2 \leq x \leq 2 \\ x + 1, & 2 < x \leq 10 \end{cases}$$

What are the domain and range? Over what intervals is the function increasing or decreasing?

COMMON ERROR

The values of −2 and 2 are only included in one piece of the graph. If they were included in more than one piece and had different values for different pieces, this would not be a function.

Sketch the graph of $y = 4x + 11$ for values of x between −10 and −2.

Sketch the graph of $y = x^2 - 1$ for values of x between −2 and 2.

Sketch the graph of $y = x + 1$ for values between 2 and 10.

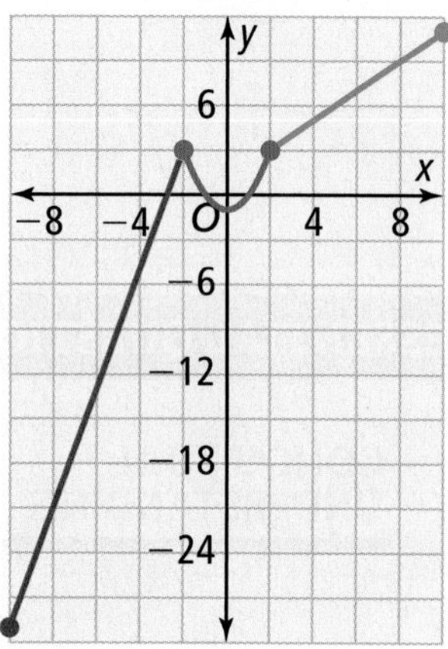

To determine the range, calculate the y-values that correspond to the minimum and maximum x-values on the graph. For this graph, these values occur at the endpoints of the domain of the piecewise function, $-10 \leq x \leq 10$.

Evaluate $y = 4x + 11$ for $x = -10$

$y = 4(-10) + 11$

$y = -29$

Evaluate $y = x + 1$ for $x = 10$

$y = 10 + 1$

$y = 11$

The range is $-29 \leq y \leq 11$.

The domain is $\{x | -10 \leq x \leq 10\}$. The range is $\{y \mid -29 \leq y \leq 11\}$. The function is increasing when $-10 \leq x < -2$ and $0 < x \leq 10$. The function is decreasing when $-2 < x < 0$.

Try It! 2. Graph the piecewise-defined function. What are the domain and range? Over what intervals is the function increasing or decreasing?

a. $f(x) = \begin{cases} 2x + 5, & -6 \leq x \leq -2 \\ 2x^2 - 7, & -2 < x < 1 \\ -4 - x, & 1 \leq x \leq 3 \end{cases}$

b. $f(x) = \begin{cases} 3, & -4 < x \leq 0 \\ -x, & 0 \leq x \leq 2 \\ 3 - x, & 2 < x < 4 \end{cases}$

EXAMPLE 3 Write a Piecewise-Defined Rule From a Graph

STUDY TIP
A closed circle on the graph means the coordinates of the point are included in the domain and range of the function. An open circle indicates they are not included.

What is the rule that describes the piecewise-defined function shown in the graph?

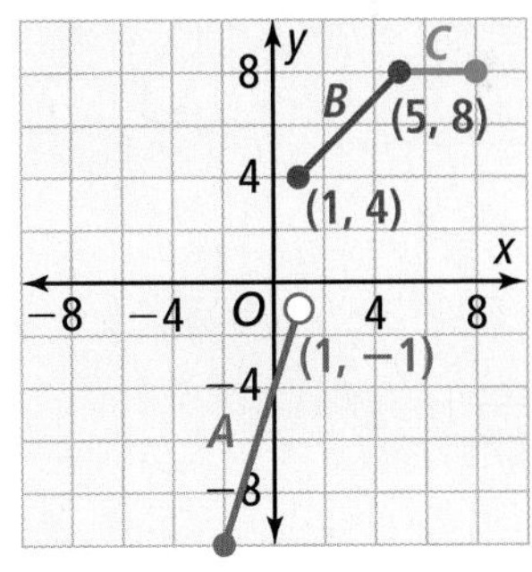

Step 1 Notice three separate linear pieces that make up the function.

Step 2 Determine the domain of each segment.

Step 3 For each segment, use the graph to locate points on the line and to find the slope.

Step 4 You can use the slope-intercept form of a linear function, $f(x) = mx + b$, to define the function for each segment.

Segment A	Segment B	Segment C
Domain: $-2 \le x < 1$	**Domain: $1 \le x \le 5$**	**Domain: $5 < x \le 8$**
(1, −1), slope = 3	(1, 4), slope = 1	(5, 8), slope = 0
$y = mx + b$ $-1 = (3)(1) + b$ $b = -4$	$y = mx + b$ $4 = (1)(1) + b$ $b = 3$	$y = mx + b$ $8 = (0)(5) + b$ $b = 8$
$f(x) = 3x - 4$	$f(x) = x + 3$	$f(x) = 8$

The rule for this function is:

$$f(x) = \begin{cases} 3x - 4, & -2 \le x < 1 \\ x + 3, & 1 \le x \le 5 \\ 8, & 5 < x \le 8 \end{cases}$$

Try It! 3. What rule defines the function in each of the following graphs?

a.

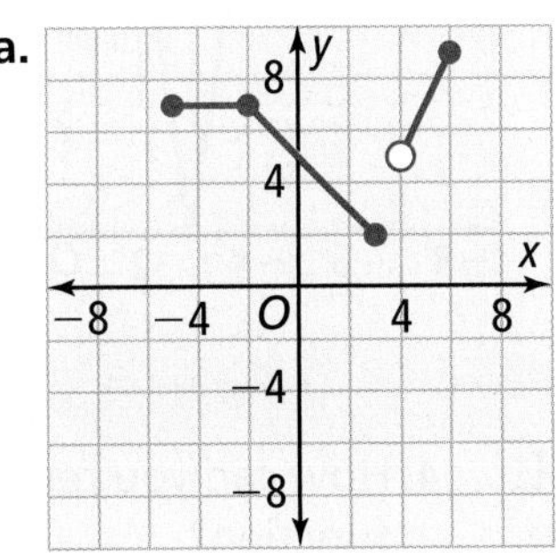

b.

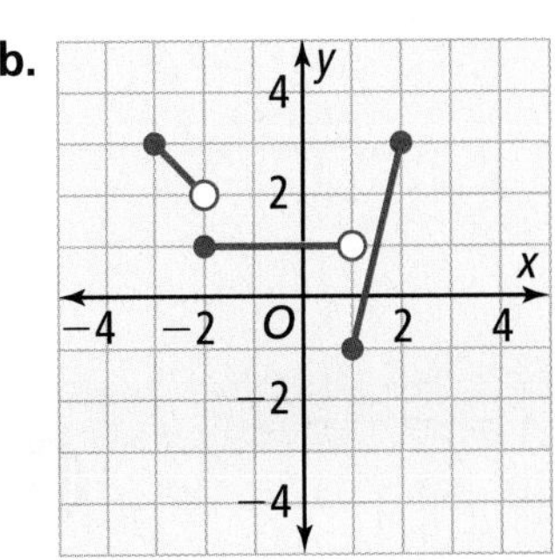

EXAMPLE 4 Write a Rule for an Absolute Value Function

How can you rewrite the function $f(x) = |6x + 18|$ as a piecewise-defined fuction?

Step 1 Write the function in the form $f(x) = a|x - h| + k$ to find the vertex of the function.

$$f(x) = |6x + 18|$$
$$= |6(x + 3)|$$
$$= 6|x - (-3)| + 0$$

$k = 0$

$h = -3$

The vertex is $(h, k) = (-3, 0)$. The graph has two linear pieces, one to the left of $x = -3$, and one to the right of $x = -3$.

Step 2 Determine the slope and equation of each piece of the function by testing x-values on either side of -3.

	Choose a point so that $x < -3$: let $x = -4$	Choose a point so that $x > -3$: let $x = 0$
Point	$(-4, 6)$	$(0, 18)$
Slope to $(-3, 0)$	-6	6
Equation	$y = -6x - 18$	$y = 6x + 18$

GENERALIZE
The parent absolute value function $f(x) = |x|$ is a piecewise-defined function:

$$f(x) = \begin{cases} x, & x \geq 0 \\ -x, & x < 0 \end{cases}$$

Step 3 Write the piecewise-defined function.

The absolute value function $f(x) = |6x + 18|$ can be written as the piecewise-defined function:

$$f(x) = \begin{cases} -6x - 18, & x < -3 \\ 6x + 18, & x \geq -3 \end{cases}$$

Step 4 Confirm by graphing.

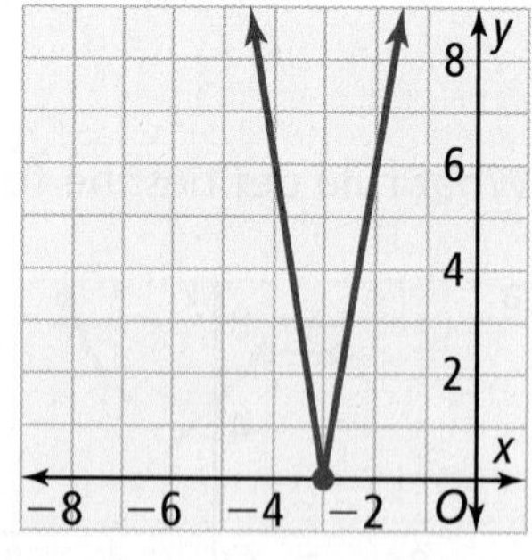

The vertex is $(-3, 0)$.

Try It! 4. How can you rewrite each function as a piecewise-defined function?

a. $f(x) = |-5x - 10|$

b. $f(x) = -|x| + 3$

APPLICATION

EXAMPLE 5 Graph a Step Function

The shipping cost of items purchased from an online store is dependent on the weight of the items. The table represents shipping costs y based on the weight x. Graph the function. What are the domain and range of the function? What are the maximum and minimum values?

Weight of Items	$0 < x \leq 2$ lb	$2 < x \leq 4$ lb	$4 < x \leq 6$ lb	$6 < x \leq 8$ lb
Shipping Cost	$5	$8	$11	$14

The graph of the function looks like the steps of a staircase. This is called a **step function** since it pairs every input in an interval with the same output value.

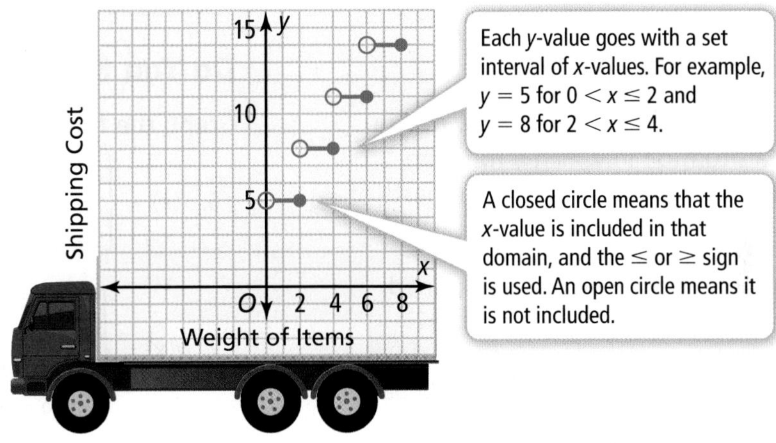

COMMON ERROR
You might think that the range of this function would be the interval [5, 14], but only the values 5, 8, 11, and 14 are possible outputs.

Domain: $\{x \mid 0 < x \leq 8\}$

Range: $\{5, 8, 11, 14\}$

This function has a minimum of 5 and a maximum of 14.

Try It! 5. The table below represents fees for a parking lot. Graph the function. What are the domain and range of the function? What are the maximum and minimum values?

Time	$0 < t \leq 3$h	$3 < t \leq 6$h	$6 < t \leq 9$h	$9 < t \leq 12$h
Cost	$10	$15	$20	$25

Concept Summary Assess

CONCEPT SUMMARY Piecewise-Defined Functions

WORDS

A piecewise function has different rules for different parts of its domain.

ALGEBRA

$$f(x) = \begin{cases} 7, & -5 \le x \le -2 \\ 5 - x, & -2 < x \le 3 \\ 2x - 3, & 4 < x \le 6 \end{cases}$$

GRAPH

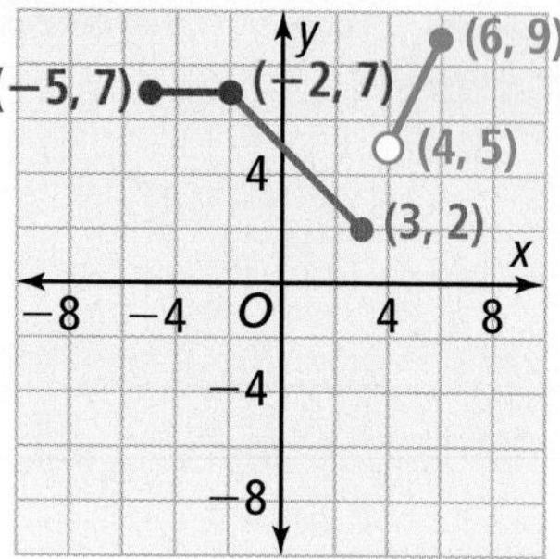

Do You UNDERSTAND?

1. ESSENTIAL QUESTION How do you model a situation in which a function behaves differently over different parts of its domain?

2. **Vocabulary** How do piecewise-defined functions differ from step functions?

3. **Error Analysis** Given the function
$$f(x) = \begin{cases} 2x + 5, & -2 < x \le 4 \\ -4x - 7, & 4 < x \le 9 \end{cases}$$
Rebecca says there is an open circle at $x = 4$ for both pieces of the function. Explain her error.

4. **Communicate Precisely** What steps do you follow when graphing a piecewise-defined function?

5. **Make Sense and Persevere** Is the relation defined by the following piecewise rule a function? Explain.
$$y = \begin{cases} 7x - 4, & x < 2 \\ -x + 5, & x \ge -2 \end{cases}$$

Do You KNOW HOW?

Graph the function.

6. $$f(x) = \begin{cases} -x + 1, & -10 \le x < -3 \\ x^2 - 9, & -3 \le x \le 3 \\ 2x + 1, & 3 < x < 5 \end{cases}$$

7. $$g(x) = \begin{cases} 1, & 0 \le x < 2 \\ 3, & 2 \le x < 4 \\ 5, & 4 \le x < 6 \\ 7, & 6 \le x < 8 \end{cases}$$

8. Given the function
$$f(x) = \begin{cases} -2x + 4, & 0 \le x < 8 \\ -5x + 11, & x \ge 8 \end{cases}$$
is the function increasing or decreasing over the interval [2, 7]? Find the rate of change over this interval.

9. What is the rule that defines the function shown in the graph?

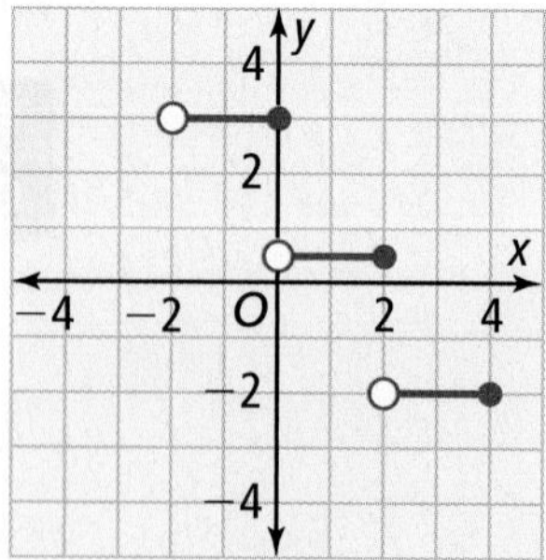

PRACTICE & PROBLEM SOLVING

UNDERSTAND

10. Communicate Precisely What do closed circles and open circles on the graph of a step function indicate?

11. Error Analysis What error did Damian make when defining the domain of the graph? Explain.

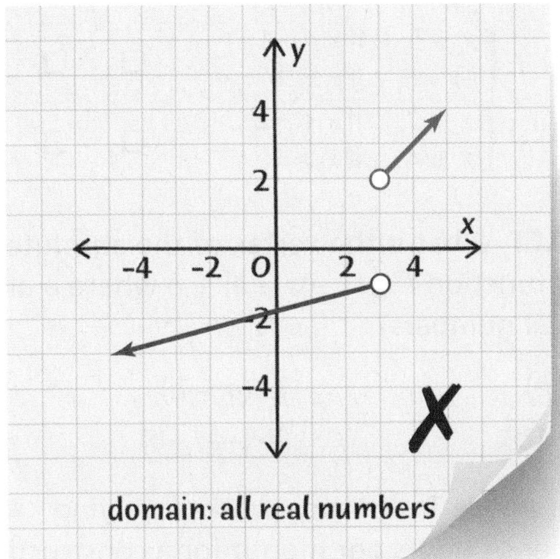

12. Communicate Precisely For what values of x is the function $f(x) = \begin{cases} -3x + 4, & -2 < x \leq 3 \\ 2x + 1, & 4 \leq x < 9 \end{cases}$ defined?

13. Mathematical Connections For the piecewise-defined function $f(x) = \begin{cases} 7, & x > 3 \\ 5x - 3, & x \leq 3 \end{cases}$ find two x-values that have the same y-value and the sum of the x-values is 10.

14. Higher Order Thinking The function $f(x) = \lfloor x \rfloor$ is called the greatest integer function because the output returned is the greatest integer less than or equal to x. For example, $f(3.2) = \lfloor 3.2 \rfloor = 3$ and $f(0.975) = \lfloor 0.975 \rfloor = 0$. Graph the function $f(x) = \lfloor x \rfloor$. What type of graph does this look like?

PRACTICE

15. A phone company offers a monthly cellular phone plan for \$25. The plan includes 250 anytime minutes, and charges \$0.20 per minute above 250 min. Write a piecewise-defined function for $C(x)$, the cost for using x minutes in a month. SEE EXAMPLE 1

16. Graph the piecewise-defined function. State the domain and range. Identify whether the function is increasing, constant, or decreasing on each interval of the domain. SEE EXAMPLE 2

$$f(x) = \begin{cases} \frac{1}{4}x + 3, & -2 < x \leq 0 \\ 2, & 0 < x \leq 4 \\ 3 - x, & 4 < x \leq 7 \end{cases}$$

17. Write the rule that defines the function in the following graph. SEE EXAMPLE 3

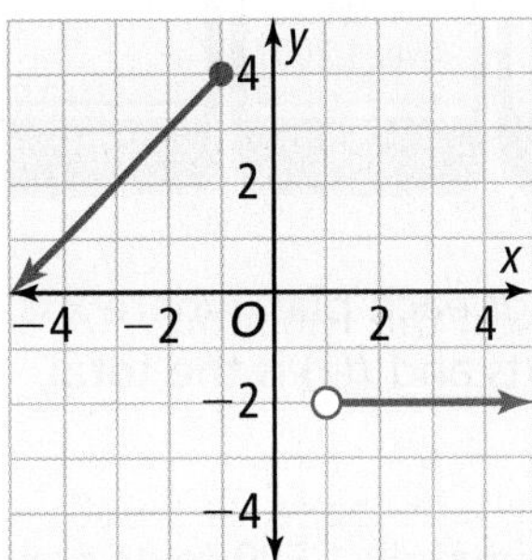

Write each absolute value function as a piecewise-defined function. SEE EXAMPLE 4

18. $f(x) = |3x + 1|$

19. $g(x) = |-2x - 6|$

Graph the step function. SEE EXAMPLE 5

20. $f(x) = \begin{cases} 2, & -3 \leq x < 1 \\ 5, & 1 \leq x < 4 \\ 8, & 4 \leq x < 6 \\ 9, & 6 \leq x < 10 \end{cases}$

21. The parking rates for a parking garage are shown. Graph the function for the cost of parking rates at the garage. SEE EXAMPLE 5

PRACTICE & PROBLEM SOLVING

APPLY

22. Model With Mathematics If Kyle works more than 40 h per week, his hourly wage for the extra hour(s) is 1.5 times the normal hourly wage of \$10 per hour. Write a piecewise-defined function that gives Kyle's weekly pay P in terms of the number h of hours he works. Determine how much Kyle will get paid if he works 45 h.

23. Model With Mathematics Text message plans offered at a phone company, along with overage charges, are shown.

a. Write a function for each plan where x is the number of texts and $f(x)$ is the total monthly cost.

b. Sarah uses approximately 1,500 texts per month. What is the monthly cost under each text message plan?

c. Write an interval for the number of text messages that would make each plan the best one to purchase.

24. Reason The cost C (in dollars) of sending next-day mail depends on the weight x (in ounces) of a package. The cost of packages, up to 5 lb, is given by the function below. What are the domain and range of the function?

$$f(x) = \begin{cases} 12.25, & 0 < x \leq 8 \\ 16.75, & 8 < x \leq 32 \\ 19.50, & 32 < x \leq 48 \\ 23.50, & 48 < x \leq 64 \\ 25.25, & 64 < x \leq 80 \end{cases}$$

ASSESSMENT PRACTICE

25. Does the function have a range of $(-\infty, 4)$? Write **yes** or **no.**

	Yes	No
a. $f(x) = \begin{cases} x-3, & \text{if } x < -2 \\ 5-x, & \text{if } x > 1 \end{cases}$	❑	❑
b. $h(x) = \begin{cases} x-1, & \text{if } x < -1 \\ 3-x, & \text{if } x > 2 \end{cases}$	❑	❑
c. $g(x) = \begin{cases} x+5, & \text{if } x < -1 \\ -x-5, & \text{if } x > 1 \end{cases}$	❑	❑
d. $k(x) = \begin{cases} x+2, & \text{if } x < -2 \\ x+4, & \text{if } x > 1 \end{cases}$	❑	❑

26. SAT/ACT What is the vertex of the absolute value function $f(x) = -|x - a| + b$ where a and b are real numbers?

Ⓐ (a, b)
Ⓑ $(-a, b)$
Ⓒ $(a, -b)$
Ⓓ $(-a, -b)$

27. Performance Task Yama works a varying number of hours per month for a construction company. The following scatter plot shows how much money he earns for each number of hours he works. Write the piecewise-defined function that represents Yama's earnings as a function of his hours worked.

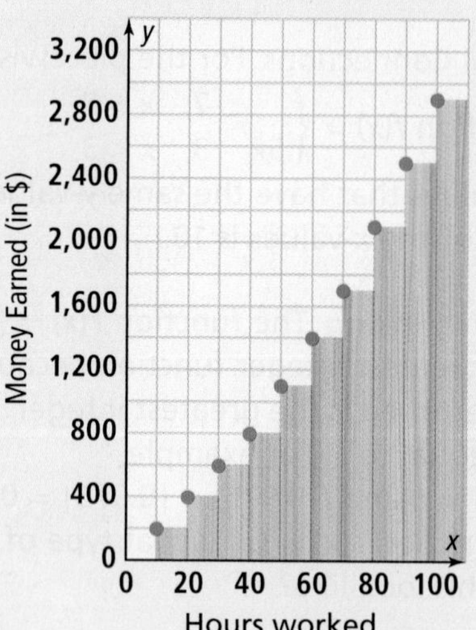

  Activity  Assess

1-4 Arithmetic Sequences and Series

 PearsonRealize.com

I CAN… interpret arithmetic sequences and series.

VOCABULARY

- arithmetic sequence
- arithmetic series
- common difference
- explicit definition
- recursive definition
- sequence
- series
- sigma notation

CRITIQUE & EXPLAIN

Yumiko and Hugo are looking at the table of data.

Input	Output
0	1
1	5
2	9
3	13
4	17

Yumiko writes $f(1) = 1 + 4 = 5$,

$f(2) = f(1) + 4 = 5 + 4 = 9$,

$f(3) = f(2) + 4 = 9 + 4 = 13$,

$f(4) = f(3) + 4 = 13 + 4 = 17$.

Hugo writes $g(x) = 1 + 4x$.

A. Describe the pattern Yumiko found for finding an output value.

B. Describe the pattern Hugo found for finding an output value.

C. **Use Structure** Compare the two methods. Which method would be more useful in finding the 100th number in the list? Why?

ESSENTIAL QUESTION

What is an arithmetic sequence, and how do you represent and find its terms and their sums?

CONCEPTUAL UNDERSTANDING

EXAMPLE 1 Understand Arithmetic Sequences

A. Is the sequence arithmetic? If so, what is the common difference? What is the next term in the sequence?

3, 8, 13, 18, 23, …

This is a **sequence**, a function whose domain is the Natural numbers.

Create a table that shows the term number, or domain, and the term, or range.

Term Number	Term
1	3
2	8
3	13
4	18
5	23
6	?

+5, +5, +5, +5, +5

The difference between consecutive numbers in the range is 5.

An **arithmetic sequence** is a sequence with a constant difference between consecutive terms. This difference is known as the **common difference**, or d.

This sequence is an arithmetic sequence with the common difference, $d = 5$. The next term in the sequence is 23 + 5, or 28.

COMMON ERROR
The common difference is always calculated by subtracting a term from the next term; $d = a_n - a_{n-1}$.

CONTINUED ON THE NEXT PAGE

EXAMPLE 1 CONTINUED

B. How could you write a formula for finding the next term in the sequence?

Each term can be represented by $f(n)$ where n represents the number of the term.

So, for $n = 1$, $f(1) = 3$.

If $n > 1$, each term is the sum of the previous term and 5.

$$f(2) = f(1) + 5$$

$$f(3) = f(2) + 5$$

$$f(n) = f(n - 1) + 5$$

Write the general rule for an arithmetic sequence as a piecewise-defined function:

$$f(n) = \begin{cases} f(1), & n = 1 \\ f(n-1) + d, & n > 1 \end{cases}$$

This is the **recursive definition** for an arithmetic sequence. Each term is defined by operations on the previous term.

Another way to write a recursive definition is to use subscript notation.

$$a_n = \begin{cases} a_1, & n = 1 \\ a_{n-1} + d, & n > 1 \end{cases}$$

With the notation, the subscript shows the number of the term.

C. Is the sequence 4, 7, 10, 13, 16, ... arithmetic? If so, write the recursive definition for the sequence.

$a_1 = 4$ — 4, 7, 10, 13, 16 — The common difference, d, is 3, so this is an arithmetic sequence.

The recursive definition for this sequence is

$$a_n = \begin{cases} 4, & n = 1 \\ a_{n-1} + 3, & n > 1. \end{cases}$$

STUDY TIP

An arithmetic sequence is a function, so you can write the terms using function notation.

Try It! 1. Are the following sequences arithmetic? If so, what is the recursive definition, and what is the next term in the sequence?

a. 25, 20, 15, 10, ...

b. 2, 4, 7, 12, 13, ...

  Activity  Assess

EXAMPLE 2 Translate Between Recursive and Explicit Forms

A. Given the recursive definition $a_n = \begin{cases} 3, n = 1 \\ a_{n-1} + 0.5, n > 1 \end{cases}$ **what is an explicit definition for the sequence?**

An **explicit definition**, also written as $a_n = a_1 + d(n - 1)$, allows you to find any term in the sequence without knowing the previous term.

Use the recursive definition to find a pattern:

USE STRUCTURE
Since $a_2 = a_1 + 0.5$, use substitution to simplify the expression.

$a_1 = 3$

$a_2 = 3 + 0.5$

$a_3 = a_2 + 0.5 = [3 + 0.5] + 0.5 = 3 + 2(0.5)$

$a_4 = a_3 + 0.5 = [3 + 2(0.5)] + 0.5 = 3 + 3(0.5)$

The first term has 0 common differences added. The second term has 1 common difference added to the first term. The third term has 2 common differences added, and so on.

So the explicit definition is $a_n = 3 + (n - 1)(0.5)$.

In general, the explicit definition of an arithmetic sequence is $a_n = a_1 + d(n - 1)$.

B. Given the explicit definition $a_n = 16 - 3(n - 1)$**, what is the recursive definition for the arithmetic sequence?**

The common difference d is -3 and $a_1 = 16$.

The recursive definition is $a_n = \begin{cases} 16, n = 1 \\ a_{n-1} - 3, n > 1. \end{cases}$

 **Try It!** **2. a.** For the recursive definition $a_n = \begin{cases} 45, n = 1 \\ a_{n-1} - 2, n > 1, \end{cases}$ what is the explicit definition?

b. For the explicit definition $a_n = 1 + 7(n - 1)$, what is the recursive definition?

APPLICATION

EXAMPLE 3 Solve Problems With Arithmetic Sequences

A high school auditorium has 18 seats in the first row and 26 seats in the fifth row. The number of seats in each row forms an arithmetic sequence.

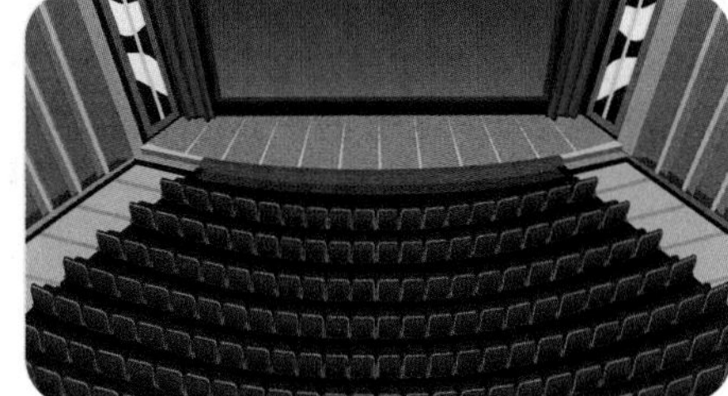

A. What is the explicit definition for the sequence?

The problem states that $a_1 = 18$, $n = 5$, and $a_5 = 26$.

$a_n = a_1 + d(n - 1)$	Write the general explicit formula.
$26 = 18 + d(5 - 1)$	Substitute.
$26 = 18 + 4d$	Simplify.
$8 = 4d$	Simplify.
$2 = d$	Solve.

Each row has two more seats than the previous row.

The explicit definition is $a_n = 18 + 2(n - 1)$.

CONTINUED ON THE NEXT PAGE

EXAMPLE 3 CONTINUED

B. How many seats are in the twelfth row?

$a_n = 18 + 2(n - 1)$ ········ Write the explicit formula.

$a_{12} = 18 + 2(12 - 1)$ ········ Substitute 12 for n.

$a_{12} = 40$ ········ Simplify.

The twelfth row has 40 seats.

Try It! 3. Samantha is training for a race. The distances of her training runs form an arithmetic sequence. She runs 1 mi the first day and 2 mi the seventh day.

a. What is the explicit definition for this sequence?

b. How far does she run on day 19?

EXAMPLE 4 Find the Sum of an Arithmetic Series

A. What is the sum of the terms in the arithmetic sequence 1, 4, 7, 10, 13? What is a general formula for an arithmetic series?

A finite **series** is the sum of the terms in a finite sequence. A finite **arithmetic series** is the sum of the terms in an arithmetic sequence. For the sum of n numbers in a sequence, you can use a recursive formula, or simply add the terms.

$$S_n = a_1 + a_2 + a_3 + a_4 + \cdots + a_n$$

This represents a partial sum of a series because it is the sum of a finite number of terms, n, in the series.

$$\mathbf{1 + 4 + 7 + 10 + 13 = 35}$$

To find the sum of a series with many terms, you can use an explicit definition.

STUDY TIP
The finite series represents an equation which can be added to a second related equation to help you.

Step 1 To find the explicit definition for the sum, use the Commutative Property of Addition and reverse the order of the terms in the recursive series.

$$S_5 = 13 + 10 + 7 + 4 + 1$$

Substitute the values from the series.

Step 2 Add the two expressions for the series, so you are adding the first term to the last term and the second term to the second-to-last term, and so on.

$$\begin{aligned} S_5 &= 1 + 4 + 7 + 10 + 13 \\ + S_5 &= 13 + 10 + 7 + 4 + 1 \\ \hline 2S_5 &= 14 + 14 + 14 + 14 + 14 \end{aligned}$$

Step 3 Simplify.

$$2 \cdot S_5 = 5(14)$$

$$S_5 = \frac{5(1 + 13)}{2}$$

Notice that 14 is the sum of the first and last terms, or $a_1 + a_5$.

Step 4 Write the general formula.

$$S_n = \frac{n(a_1 + a_n)}{2}$$

CONTINUED ON THE NEXT PAGE

EXAMPLE 4 CONTINUED

B. What is the sum of the following arithmetic sequence?
2, 6, 10, 14, 18, 22

$n = 6 \qquad a_1 = 2 \qquad a_n = 22$

Use the general formula to find the sum.

$$S_n = \frac{n(a_1 + a_n)}{2} \qquad S_n = \frac{6(2 + 22)}{2} = \frac{144}{2} = 72$$

The sum of the terms in the sequence is 72.

Try It! **4.** Find the sum of each arithmetic series.

a. series with 12 terms, $a_1 = 3$ and $a_{12} = 25$

b. $5 + 11 + 17 + 23 + 29 + 35 + 41$

CONCEPT Sigma Notation

The sum of n terms of a sequence can be written using **sigma notation:**

$$\sum_{i=1}^{n} a_i$$

The index i counts through the terms in the partial sum. Here it takes the values from 1 up to n, the last term in the partial series. The value of the ith term is a_i. You can use the explicit formula for the sequence in place of a_i.

EXAMPLE 5 Use Sigma Notation

A. What is $\sum_{i=1}^{9} 2i - 6$?

Find the sum by writing out all of the terms in the series.

$a_1 = 2(1) - 6 = -4 \qquad a_4 = 2(4) - 6 = 2 \qquad a_7 = 2(7) - 6 = 8$

$a_2 = 2(2) - 6 = -2 \qquad a_5 = 2(5) - 6 = 4 \qquad a_8 = 2(8) - 6 = 10$

$a_3 = 2(3) - 6 = 0 \qquad a_6 = 2(6) - 6 = 6 \qquad a_9 = 2(9) - 6 = 12$

$$\sum_{i=1}^{9} 2i - 6 = S_9 = -4 - 2 + 0 + 2 + 4 + 6 + 8 + 10 + 12 = 36$$

LOOK FOR RELATIONSHIPS
You can quickly see that the common difference in this series is 2.

B. How can you write the series $2 + 9 + 16 + \cdots + 79$ using sigma notation? What is the sum?

Step 1 Solve for n to find the number of terms in the series: $a_1 = 2$, $d = 7$, and $a_n = 79$.

$a_n = a_1 + d(n - 1)$ .... Write the explicit formula.

$79 = 2 + (7)(n - 1)$ .... Substitute a_n, a_1, and d.

$77 = (7)(n - 1)$ .... Simplify.

$11 = n - 1$ .... Simplify.

$n = 12$ .... Solve.

There are 12 terms in the series.

CONTINUED ON THE NEXT PAGE

EXAMPLE 5 CONTINUED

Step 2 Write the explicit formula for the series.

$$a_n = 2 + 7(n - 1) = 7n - 5$$

Step 3 Write using sigma notation.

The index i will count from 1 to $n = 12$.

The explicit definition gives $a_i = 7i - 5$.

$$\sum_{i=1}^{12} 7i - 5$$

Step 4 Find the sum of the series.

$$S_n = \frac{n(a_1 + a_n)}{2}$$

$$S_{12} = \frac{12(2 + 79)}{2} = 486$$

So the series can be written $\sum_{i=1}^{12} 7i - 5$ in sigma notation. The sum of the series is 486.

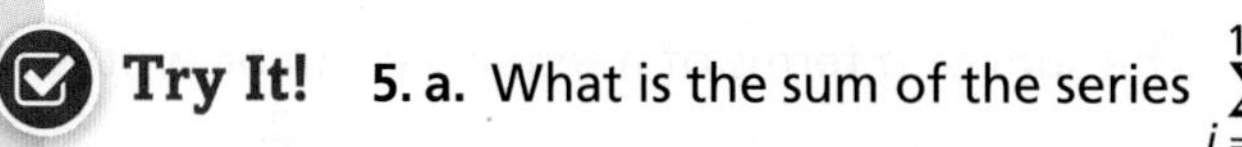

Try It! **5. a.** What is the sum of the series $\sum_{i=1}^{13} 3i + 2$?

b. How can you write the series $8 + 13 + 18 + \ldots + 43$ using sigma notation? What is the sum?

APPLICATION

EXAMPLE 6 Use a Finite Arithmetic Series

A pyramid of cans is on display in a supermarket. The top row has 1 can, the second row has 2 cans, and the third row has 3 cans. If there are 10 rows of cans, how many total cans were used to make the pyramid?

This is an arithmetic series where the common difference is 1.

Step 1 Find a_1 and a_{10}.

$$a_1 = 1$$

$$a_{10} = a_1 + d(n - 1)$$
$$= 1 + 1(10 - 1)$$
$$= 10$$

STUDY TIP
Since you know n, a_1, and a_{10}, you can use the explicit formula to find the sum of the series efficiently.

Step 2 Use the explicit formula for finding the sum of a series.

$$S_n = \frac{n(a_1 + a_n)}{2}$$

$$S_n = \frac{10(1 + 10)}{2} = 55$$

There are 55 cans in the display.

Try It! **6.** A flight of stairs gets wider as it descends. The top stair is 15 bricks across, the second stair is 17 bricks across, and the third stair is 19 bricks across. What is the total number of bricks used in all 16 stairs?

CONCEPT SUMMARY Arithmetic Sequences and Series

In an arithmetic sequence, each term is equal to the previous term plus a constant d, the common difference.

	Recursive Formula	Explicit Formula	Arithmetic Series
ALGEBRA	$a_n = \begin{cases} a_1, n = 1 \\ a_{n-1} + d, n > 1 \end{cases}$	$a_n = a_1 + d(n - 1)$	$S_n = \frac{n(a_1 + a_n)}{2}$
NUMBERS	For $a_1 = 1$ and $d = 7$, $a_2 = 1 + 7 = 8$ $a_3 = 8 + 7 = 15$ $a_4 = 15 + 7 = 22$ ....and so on	For $a_1 = 90$ and $d = -4$, $a_2 = 90 + 1(-4) = 86$ $a_3 = 90 + 2(-4) = 82$ $a_4 = 90 + 3(-4) = 78$ ....and so on	$\sum_{i=1}^{8} 5i - 2$ $3 + 8 + 13 + 18 + 23 + 28 + 33 + 38 = 164$ or $S_8 = \frac{8(3 + 38)}{2} = 164$

Do You UNDERSTAND?

1. ESSENTIAL QUESTION What is an arithmetic sequence, and how do you represent and find its terms and their sums?

2. **Vocabulary** How do arithmetic sequences differ from arithmetic series?

3. **Error Analysis** A student claims the sequence 0,1,3, 6, ... is an arithmetic sequence, and the next number is 10. What error did the student make?

4. **Communicate Precisely** How would you tell someone how to calculate $\sum_{n=1}^{5} (2n + 1)$?

Do You KNOW HOW?

Find the common difference and the next three terms of each arithmetic sequence.

5. $\frac{1}{4}, \frac{1}{2}, \frac{3}{4}, 1, \frac{5}{4}, \ldots$

6. 6, 1, −4, −9, −14, . . .

7. 215, 227, 239, 251, . . .

8. −4, −5, −6, −7, . . .

9. 4.1, 6.3, 8.5, 10.7, . . .

10. −17, −9, −1, 7, 15, . . .

11. In June, you start a holiday savings account with a deposit of $30. You increase each monthly deposit by $4 until the end of the year. How much money will you have saved by the end of December?

PRACTICE & PROBLEM SOLVING

Scan for Multimedia

Practice Tutorial

Additional Exercises Available Online

UNDERSTAND

12. **Use Structure** Write an arithmetic sequence with at least four terms, and describe it using both an explicit and recursive definition.

13. **Error Analysis** Alex says the common difference for an arithmetic sequence is always negative because of the definition of *difference*. Why is he wrong? Write an arithmetic sequence to show he is wrong.

14. **Use Structure** A company will pay Becky \$120 for her first sale. For each sale after that, they will pay an extra \$31.50 per sale. So, she will make \$151.50 for the second sale, \$183 for the third sale, and so on. How many sales will Becky have to make to earn at least \$2,000?

15. **Higher Order Thinking** Felipe and Gregory are given the arithmetic sequence −1, 6, 13, ... Gregory wrote the explicit definition $a_n = -1 + 7(n - 1)$ for the sequence. Felipe wrote the definition as $a_n = 7n - 8$. Which one of them is correct? Explain.

16. **Model With Mathematics** Suppose you are building 10 steps with 8 concrete blocks in the top step and 80 blocks in the bottom step. If the number of blocks in each step forms an arithmetic sequence, find the total number of concrete blocks needed to build the steps.

17. **Model With Mathematics** With her half-marathon quickly approaching, Talisa decides to train every day up to the day of the race. She plans to run 2 mi the first day and 3.2 mi the fifth day.

    a. What is the explicit definition for this sequence?

    b. Which day of training will she run the distance of a half-marathon (13.1 mi)?

PRACTICE

Are the following sequences arithmetic? If so, what is the common difference? What is the next term in the sequence? SEE EXAMPLE 1

18. 10, 20, 30, 40, . . .

19. 97, 86, 75, 64, . . .

20. 1, 4, 9, 16, . . .

21. 3, 7, 11, 15, . . .

Translate between the recursive and explicit definitions for each sequence. SEE EXAMPLE 2

22. $a_n = \begin{cases} 2, n = 1 \\ a_{n-1} + 2, n > 1 \end{cases}$

23. $a_n = -2 + 7(n - 1)$

24. $a_n = \frac{1}{8}(n - 1)$

25. $a_n = \begin{cases} -4, n = 1 \\ a_{n-1} - 4, n > 1 \end{cases}$

26. The members of a school's color guard begin their performance in a pyramid formation. The first row has 1 member, and the third row has 5 members. SEE EXAMPLE 3

    a. What is the explicit definition for this sequence?

    b. How many members are in the eighth row?

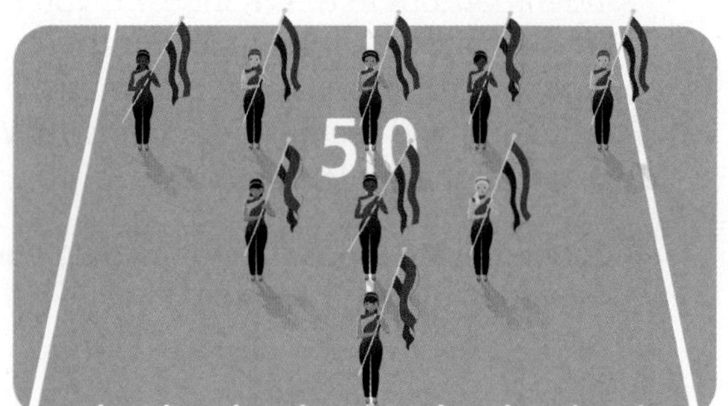

Find the sum of an arithmetic series with the given number of terms, a_1, and a_n. SEE EXAMPLE 4

27. 10 terms, $a_1 = 4$, $a_{10} = 31$

28. 15 terms, $a_1 = 17$, $a_{15} = 129$

What is the sum of each of the following series? SEE EXAMPLE 5

29. $\sum_{n=1}^{11} (3 + 2n)$

30. $\sum_{n=1}^{12} \left(\frac{n}{2} - 9\right)$

31. The number of seats in each row of an auditorium increases as you go back from the stage. The front row has 24 seats, the second row has 29 seats, and the third row has 34 seats. If there are 35 rows, how many seats are in the auditorium? SEE EXAMPLE 6

PRACTICE & PROBLEM SOLVING

Practice Tutorial
Mixed Review Available Online

APPLY

32. Make Sense and Persevere A piece of tile artwork is in the shape of a triangle. The top row has 1 tile, the second row has 2 tiles, and the third row has 3 tiles. If there are 14 rows of tiles, how many tiles were used to make the artwork?

33. Model With Mathematics A race car driver travels 34 ft in the first second of a race. If the driver travels 3.5 additional feet each subsequent second, how many feet did the driver travel in 52 s?

34. Construct Arguments A school board committee has decided to spend its annual technology budget this year on 90 student laptops and plans to buy 40 new laptops each year from now on.

a. The school board decided that each student in the school should have access to a laptop in the next ten years. If there are 500 students, will the technology coordinator meet this goal? Explain.

b. What are some pros and cons of buying student laptops in this manner? If you could change the plan, would you? If so, how would you change it?

35. Make Sense and Persevere On October 1, Nadia starts a push-up challenge by doing 18 push-ups. On October 2, she does 21 push-ups. On October 3, she does 24 push-ups. She continues until October 16, when she does the final push-ups in the challenge.

a. Write an explicit definition to model the number of push-ups Nadia does each day.

b. Write a recursive definition to model the number of push-ups Nadia does each day.

c. How many push-ups will Nadia do on October 16?

d. What is the total number of push-ups Nadia does from October 1 to October 16?

ASSESSMENT PRACTICE

36. Which of the following are also numbers in the arithmetic sequence 4, 11, 18, 25, 32, . . . ? Write the numbers in the correct box.

60 68 75 39 81

In the sequence	Not in the sequence

37. SAT/ACT Tamika is selling magazines door to door. On her first day, she sells 12 magazines, and she intends to sell 5 more magazines per day than on the previous day. If she meets her goal and sells magazines for a total of 10 days, how many magazines would she sell?

Ⓐ 314 Ⓑ 345 Ⓒ 415 Ⓓ 474 Ⓔ 505

38. Performance Task The chart shows the population of Edgar's beehive over the first four weeks. Assume the population will continue to grow at the same rate.

Part A Write an explicit definition for the sequence.

Part B If Edgar's bees have a mass of 1.5 g each, what will the total mass of all his bees be in 12 wk?

Part C When the colony reaches 1,015 bees, Edgar's beehive will not be big enough for all of them. In how many weeks will the bee population be too large?

1-5

Solving Equations and Inequalities by Graphing

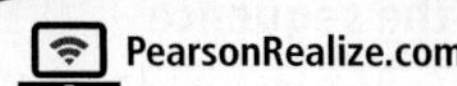

PearsonRealize.com

I CAN... use graphs and tables to approximate solutions to algebraic equations and inequalities.

MODEL & DISCUSS

A homeowner has 32 feet of fencing to build three sides of a rectangular chicken run.

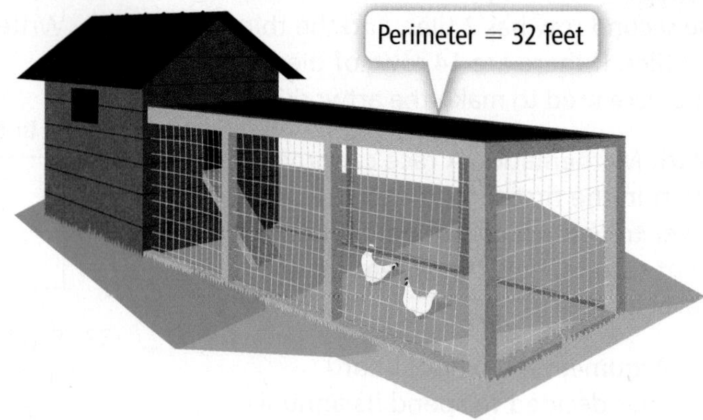

A. Make a table of values for the length, width, and area of different rectangular chicken runs that will utilize 32 feet of fencing. Then write a function for the area, in terms of width, of a rectangular run using this much fencing.

B. Graph your function.

C. Reason Explain what happens where the graph intersects the x-axis.

ESSENTIAL QUESTION

How can you solve an equation or inequality by graphing?

CONCEPTUAL UNDERSTANDING

EXAMPLE 1 Use a Graph to Solve an Equation

How can you use a graph to solve an equation?

A. Solve $-3x + 20 = 5$ by graphing.

An equation is a statement that two expressions are equal. The values of x that make the equation true are the solutions.

To solve an equation by graphing, write two new equations by setting y equal to each in the original equation.

$$-3x + 20 = 5$$

$$y = -3x + 20 \qquad y = 5$$

Graph the two equations and identify the points of intersection. These points will have x-values that produce the same y-values for both expressions. Each of the x-values is a solution to the original equation.

Graph $y = -3x + 20$ and $y = 5$.

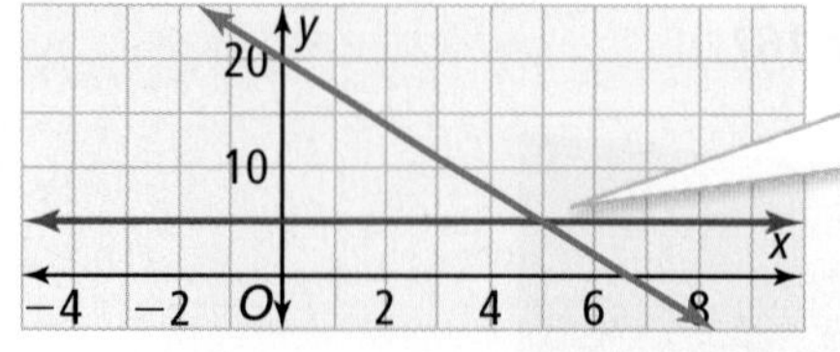

LOOK FOR RELATIONSHIPS
This method is similar to solving an equation by finding the x-intercept, where the solution is the intersection of the line and the line $y = 0$.

So $-3x + 20 = 5$ when $x = 5$. This is the only point on the graph where the value of the functions $y = -3x + 20$ and $y = 5$ are equal.

CONTINUED ON THE NEXT PAGE

EXAMPLE 1 CONTINUED

B. Solve $|x - 4| = \frac{1}{2}x + 1$ by graphing.

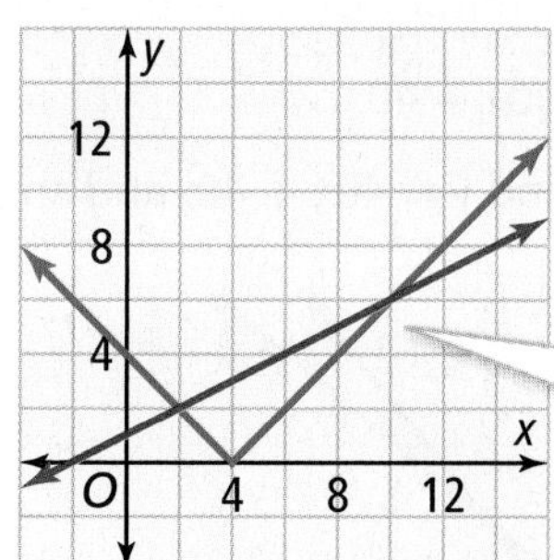

To solve $|x - 4| = \frac{1}{2}x + 1$, write two equations $y = |x - 4|$ and $y = \frac{1}{2}x + 1$, and graph.

It appears that $y = |x - 4|$ and $y = \frac{1}{2}x + 1$ intersect at $x = 2$ and $x = 10$.

The solutions to the equation $|x - 4| = \frac{1}{2}x + 1$ are $x = 2$ and $x = 10$. You can verify these values by substituting them back into the original equation.

Try It! **1. Use a graph to solve the equation.**

a. $5x - 12 = 3$

b. $-|x - 2| = -\frac{1}{2}x - 2$

APPLICATION

EXAMPLE 2 Solve a One-Variable Inequality by Graphing

How can you use a graph to solve an inequality?

A. Solve $x^2 - 4 > 0$.

To solve the inequality, identify the values of x that make the value of the expression $x^2 - 4$ greater than 0. Graph the equation $y = x^2 - 4$ by translating the parent function $y = x^2$ down 4 units.

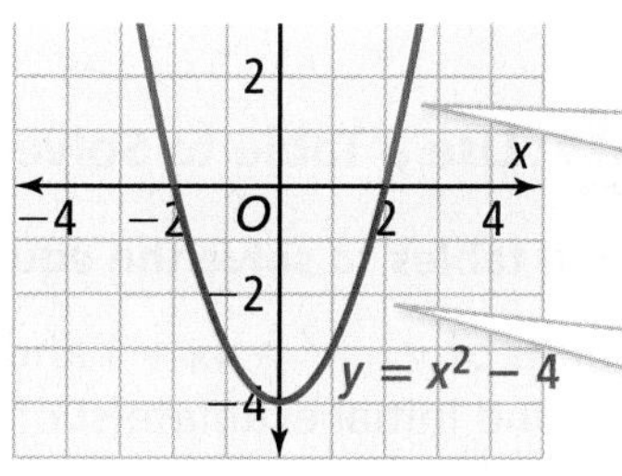

Look for the points on the graph where the value of the function is positive.

The intercepts appear to be $x = 2$ and $x = -2$.

COMMON ERROR

You may think that you need to find interval(s) where $x > 0$. However, you need to find where $x^2 - 4 > 0$, so you are looking for interval(s) where $y > 0$.

The graph of the function is positive over the intervals $(-\infty, -2)$ and $(2, \infty)$. So $x^2 - 4 > 0$ when $x < -2$ or $x > 2$.

B. A motorcycle is 40 mi ahead of a car. The motorcycle travels at an average rate of 40 mph. The car travels at a rate of 60 mph. When will the car be ahead of the motorcycle?

Let x represent the number of hours since the car started traveling. The expression $60x$ represents the distance the car travels in x hours. The expression $40x$ represents the distance the motorcycle travels in x hours.

CONTINUED ON THE NEXT PAGE

EXAMPLE 2 CONTINUED

To solve, we need to determine when the number of miles the car travels exceeds the number of miles the motorcycle travels.

Solve $60x > 40x + 40$.

Set $y = 60x$ and $y = 40x + 40$, and then graph both equations.

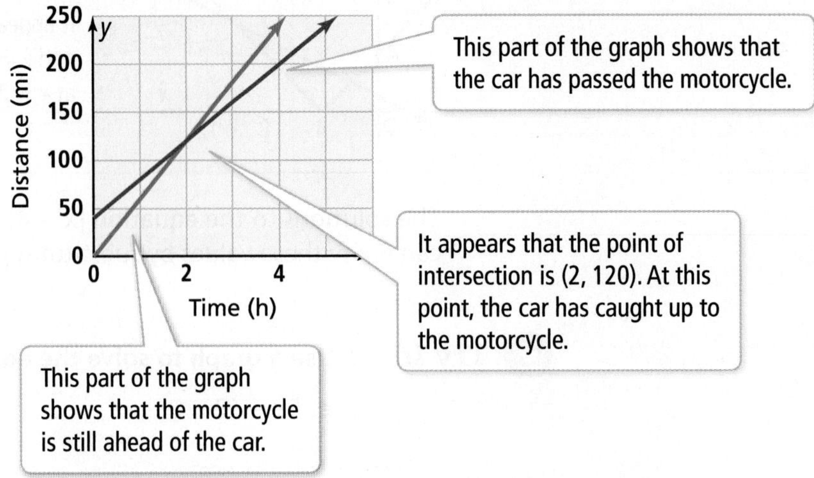

This part of the graph shows that the motorcycle is still ahead of the car.

The car will be ahead of the motorcycle any time after 2 h. You can verify the solution by selecting any number greater than 2 and substituting it into the original inequality.

Try It! **2.** Use a graph to solve each inequality.

a. $x^2 + 6x + 5 \geq 0$

b. $x + 3 > 7 - 3x$

EXAMPLE 3 Use a Table to Solve an Equation

Use a graph and tables to solve the equation $x^2 - 4x + 1 = x - 2$.

Sketch the graphs of $y = x^2 - 4x + 1$ and $y = x - 2$. Identify the points of intersection to find initial estimate(s) of the solution value(s).

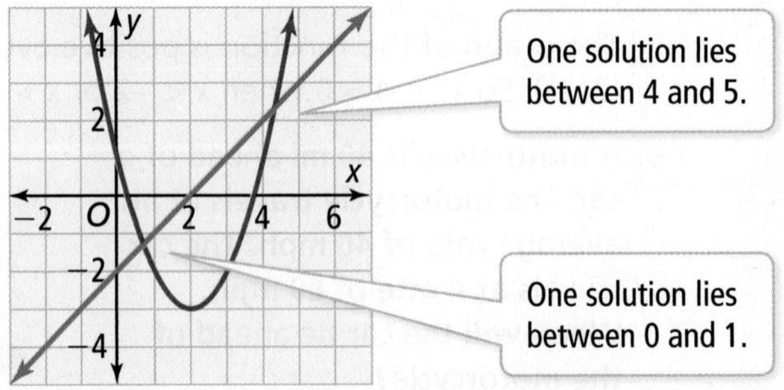

Neither solution appears to correspond to a grid point. You can use a table to get more accurate estimates for the solutions.

CONTINUED ON THE NEXT PAGE

EXAMPLE 3 CONTINUED

x	$x - 2$	$x^2 - 4x + 1$
0.5	−1.5	−0.75
0.6	−1.4	−1.04
0.7	−1.3	−1.31
0.8	−1.2	−1.56
0.9	−1.1	−1.79
1	−1	−2

If $x \leq 0.6$, then $x^2 - 4x + 1 > x - 2$. If $x \geq 0.7$, then $x^2 - 4x + 1 < x - 2$.

x	$x - 2$	$x^2 - 4x + 1$
0.65	−1.35	−1.1775
0.66	−1.34	−1.2044
0.67	−1.33	−1.2311
0.68	−1.32	−1.2576
0.69	−1.31	−1.2839
0.7	−1.3	−1.31

Look for values where graphs will cross. Use these values to "zoom in," finding better and better approximations.

x	$x - 2$	$x^2 - 4x + 1$
0.69	−1.31	−1.2839
0.691	−1.309	−1.28652
0.692	−1.308	−1.28914
0.693	−1.307	−1.29175
0.694	−1.306	−1.29436
0.695	−1.305	−1.29698
0.696	−1.304	−1.29958
0.697	−1.303	−1.30219
0.698	−1.302	−1.30480

Choose the x-value with the smallest difference in the function values.

USE APPROPRIATE TOOLS
Create tables using a calculator or spreadsheet. When you let technology perform the calculations, you can concentrate on what the numbers mean.

One solution is approximately $x = 0.697$.

You can use a similar method to approximate the second solution.

Try It! 3. The equation $x^2 - 4x + 1 = x - 2$ has a second solution in the interval $4 < x < 5$. Use a spreadsheet to approximate this solution to the nearest thousandth.

EXAMPLE 4 Use Graphing Technology to Solve Equations

Use graphing technology to approximate the solutions of the equation $-x^2 + 8x - 13 = |x - 4|$ to the nearest tenth.

Graph $y = -x^2 + 8x - 13$ and $y = |x - 4|$.

Use the INTERSECT feature to find the approximate solutions.

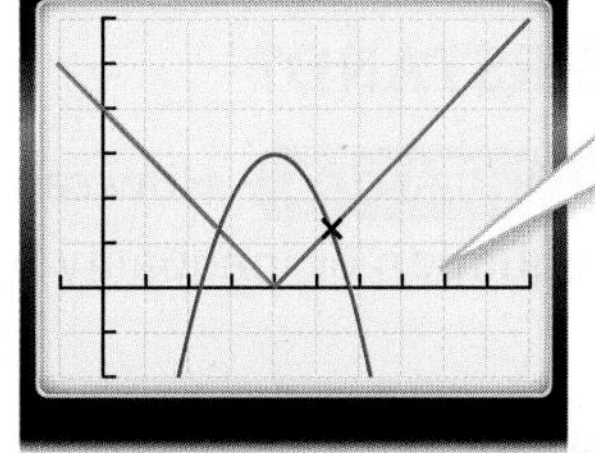

$x = 2.6972244$ $y = 1.3027756$ $x = 5.3027756$ $y = 1.3027756$

Remember that you are looking for the values of x where the graphs intersect.

STUDY TIP
Test your approximate solutions in the *original equation*. The value of the expression on the left side should be very close to the value of the expression on the right.

The INTERSECT feature shows that the equation has solutions $x \approx 2.7$ and $x \approx 5.3$.

Try It! 4. Use graphing technology to approximate the solutions of the equation $x^2 + 2x - 1 = |x + 2| + 2$ to the nearest tenth.

CONCEPT SUMMARY Solving Equations and Inequalities by Graphing

Solve $|3x + 5| = \frac{1}{3}x + 5$.

Let $f(x) = |3x + 5|$ and $g(x) = \frac{1}{3}x + 5$

GRAPHS Graph each function, and identify the x-coordinates of the points of intersection.

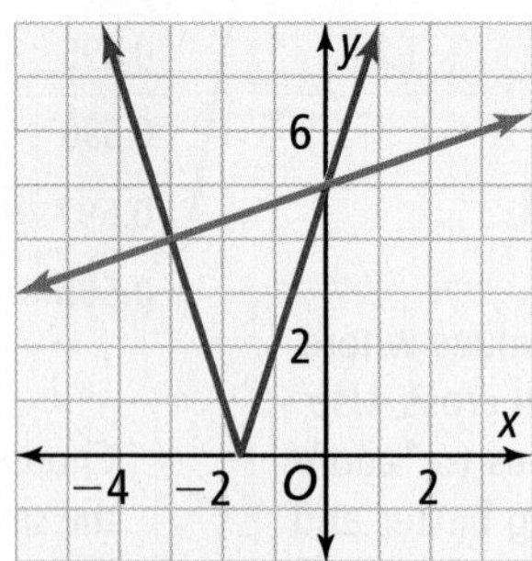

One solution appears to be 0. The second solution appears to be –3.

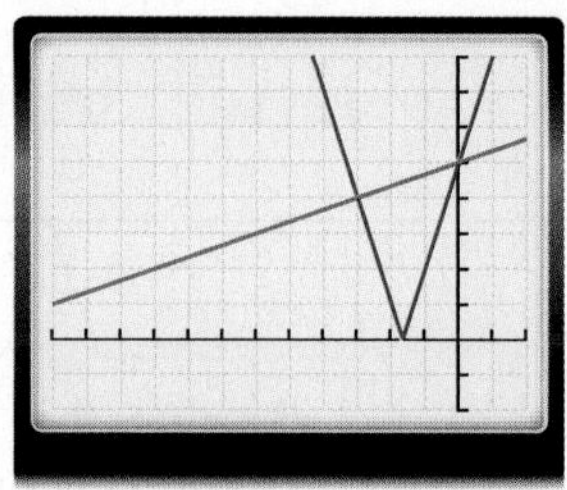

x = 0   y = 5

When graphing with technology, use the INTERSECT feature to find the exact solution(s).

TABLE Graphs may not always yield integer results. Tables may be used to find solutions.

x	$f(x)$	$g(x)$
–3.3	4.9	3.9
–3.2	4.6	3.9333
–3.1	4.3	3.9667
–3.0	4	4
–2.9	3.7	4.0333

Do You UNDERSTAND?

1. ESSENTIAL QUESTION How can you solve an equation or inequality by graphing?

2. **Communicate Precisely** What is an advantage of solving an equation graphically by finding the points of intersection?

3. **Error Analysis** Ben said the graph of the inequality $-x^2 + 9 > 0$ shows the solution is $x < -3$ or $x > 3$. Is Ben correct? Explain.

Do You KNOW HOW?

4. Using the graph below, what is the solution to $-2x + 4 = -2$? How can you tell?

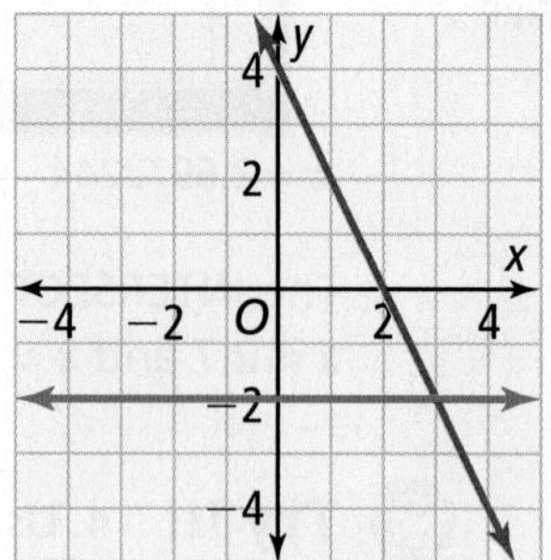

PRACTICE & PROBLEM SOLVING

Scan for Multimedia

Practice Tutorial

Additional Exercises Available Online

UNDERSTAND

5. **Construct Arguments** Use a graph to solve the equation $3x - 5 = 2 + 3x$. How can you use algebra to confirm that your graph shows the correct solution?

6. **Error Analysis** Victor graphed the equation $x^2 + 2x - 5 = -0.6x + 1$. He used the INTERSECT feature on his graphing calculator to find the solution. Victor said one of the solutions is $x \approx 0.116$. Describe and correct the error Victor made.

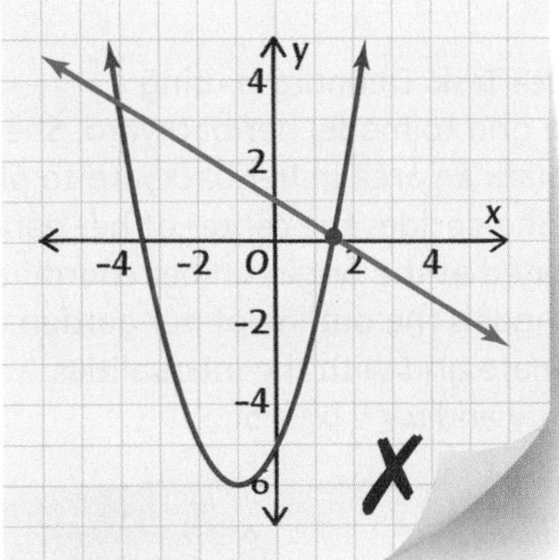

7. **Higher Order Thinking** Sadie used a graph to solve an equation. What equation did Sadie solve? Explain how to verify your equation is correct.

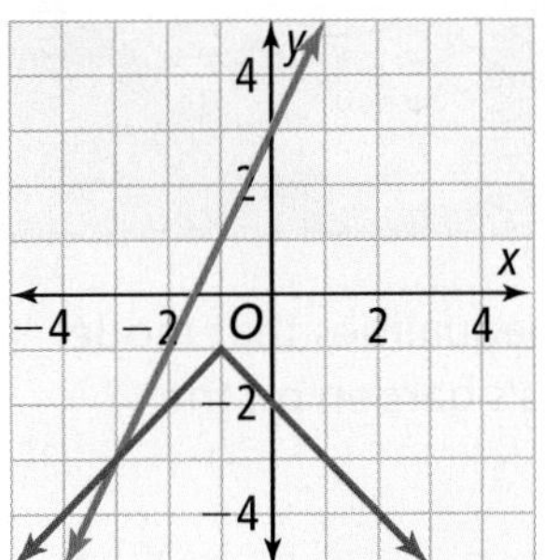

8. **Communicate Precisely** Explain how to use the table to find the approximate solution to the equation $f(x) = g(x)$.

x	$f(x)$	$g(x)$
1.1426	1.8556	1.857175
1.1427	1.8562	1.8571625
1.1428	1.8568	1.85715
1.1429	1.8574	1.8571375
1.1430	1.858	1.857125

PRACTICE

Use a graph to solve each equation. SEE EXAMPLE 1

9. $-x + 4 = 2$

10. $|x - 4| - 4 = \frac{1}{2}x$

11. $3x + 2 = x + 4$

12. $-\frac{1}{4}x + 6 = \frac{1}{2}x + 3$

13. $\frac{3}{4}x = 2x - 10$

14. $|x + 8| = |x - 2|$

Use a graph to solve each inequality. SEE EXAMPLE 2

15. $x^2 - 7x - 8 > 0$

16. $x - 5 > -2x + 4$

17. $x^2 + x - 6 < 0$

18. $x^2 + 2x - 8 \leq 0$

19. $-x^2 - 2x + 15 \leq 0$

20. $-x + 5 < \frac{1}{2}x - 1$

21. Cindy is longboarding 6 mi ahead of Tamira. Cindy is traveling at an average rate of 2 mph. Tamira is traveling at a rate of 4 mph. Let x represent the number of hours since Tamira started longboarding. When will Tamira be ahead of Cindy? Write an inequality to represent this situation.

Use a graph and tables to solve the equation. SEE EXAMPLE 3

22. $x^2 - 8x + 5 = x + 3$

23. $\frac{1}{4}x + 3 = x^2 - x + 2$

24. $2x^2 - 5 = -x^2 + 2x - 1$

25. $3x - 4 = \frac{1}{2}|x - 5|$

Use graphing technology to approximate the solutions of the equation to the nearest tenth. SEE EXAMPLE 4

26. $x^2 + 6x - 8 = |x - 1| + 3$

27. $|x + 2| - 6 = x^2 - 7x - 2$

28. $\frac{1}{5}|x + 2| - 3 = -|x - 1| + 5$

29. $x^2 + 3x - 7 = -2x^2 - 6x + 9$

PRACTICE & PROBLEM SOLVING

Practice Tutorial

Mixed Review Available Online

APPLY

30. **Reason** Jack is running 2.45 mi ahead of Zhang. Jack is running at an average rate of 5.5 mph. Zhang is running at a rate of 7.75 mph. Let x represent the number of hours since Zhang started jogging.

    a. Write an inequality to represent this situation.

    b. Use graphing technology to find when Zhang will be ahead of Jack. Round to the nearest hundredth.

31. **Use Structure** In a kickball game, a ball is kicked and travels along a parabolic path. The height h, in feet, of the kickball t seconds after the kick can be modeled by the equation $h(t) = -16t^2 + 24t$.

    a. A fielder runs a route that will allow him to catch the kickball at about 3 ft above the ground. Write an equation that can be used to find when the fielder will catch the ball.

    b. Use graphing technology to find out how long the kickball has been in the air when the fielder catches it on its descent. Round to the nearest hundredth.

32. **Make Sense and Persevere** The amount, in millions of dollars, that a company earns in revenue for selling x items, in thousands, is $R = -2x^2 + 18x - 2$. The expenses, in millions of dollars, for selling x items, in thousands, is $E = -0.25x + 6$.

    a. The profit P, in millions of dollars, for selling x items, in thousands, is the difference between the revenues and the expenses. Write an inequality that models the company earning a profit.

    b. Use graphing technology to find how many items the company must sell to earn a profit. Round to the nearest item.

ASSESSMENT PRACTICE

33. Graph the equation $x^2 - 3 = x + 3$. What are the solutions to the equation?

34. **SAT/ACT** A graph shows the solution to the equation $-\frac{1}{2}x + \frac{7}{2} = -x + a$ is $x = -1$. What is the value of a?

    Ⓐ −3
    Ⓑ −2
    Ⓒ 1
    Ⓓ 2
    Ⓔ 3

35. **Performance Task** Deondra is using a coordinate grid to model her backyard. She wants to mark an area in her backyard to plant a garden. She decides the center of her garden will be located at the origin on her coordinate grid. She models the outline of her garden on the coordinate grid with the inequalities $-\frac{1}{2}|x| + 5 \geq y$ and $y \leq \frac{1}{2}|x| - 5$.

Part A Graph the inequalities that model the area of Deondra's garden on the coordinate grid.

Part B What shape is Deondra's garden?

Part C Deondra wants to cover her garden with garden soil. She wants the soil to be $\frac{1}{2}$ ft deep. If each unit on the coordinate grid represents 1 ft^2, how much garden soil will Deondra need?

1-6 Linear Systems

I CAN… use a variety of tools to solve systems of linear equations and inequalities.

VOCABULARY

- inconsistent system
- solution of a system of linear equations
- system of linear equations
- system of linear inequalities

Activity Assess

EXPLORE & REASON

The graph shows two lines that intersect at one point.

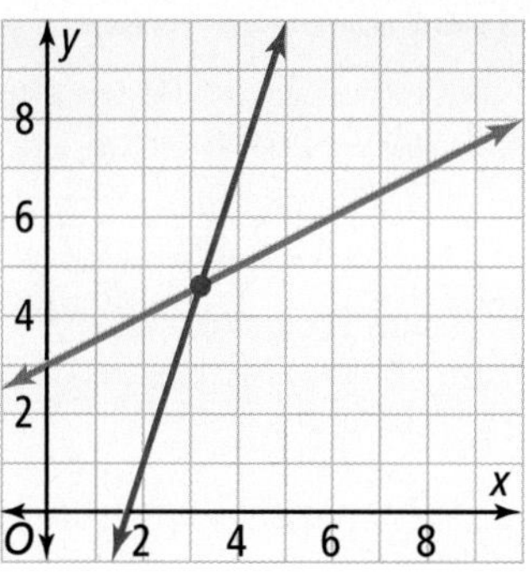

A. What are the approximate coordinates of the point of intersection?

B. How could you verify whether the coordinates you estimated are, in fact, the solution? Is the point the solution to the equations of both lines?

C. Make Sense and Persevere Use your result to refine your approximation, and try again. Can you find the point of intersection this way? Is there a more efficient way?

ESSENTIAL QUESTION

How can you find and represent solutions of systems of linear equations and inequalities?

CONCEPTUAL UNDERSTANDING

EXAMPLE 1 Solve a System of Linear Equations

What is the solution of the system of linear equations $\begin{cases} x + 2y = 3 \\ x - 2y = 4 \end{cases}$**?**

A **system of linear equations** is a set of two or more equations using the same variables. The **solution of a system of linear equations** is the set of all ordered coordinates that simultaneously make all equations in the system true.

Sketch the graph of each equation to estimate the solutions. Then solve algebraically.

GENERALIZE
Recall that there are three possible outcomes when solving a system of two linear equations: no solution, one solution, or an infinite number of solutions.

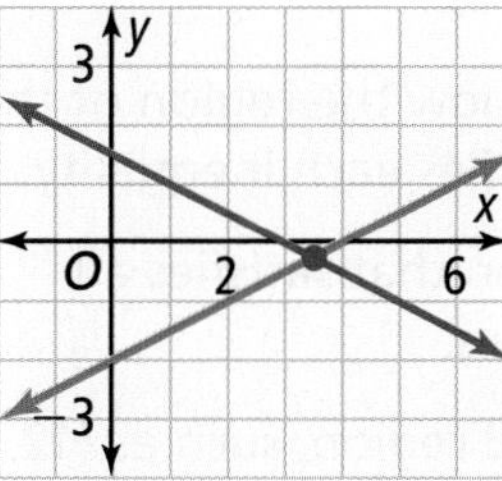

The x-coordinate of the solution is between 3 and 4, and the y-coordinate of the solution is between −1 and 0.

$$x + 2y = 3 \Rightarrow x = 3 - 2y$$
$$x - 2y = 4 \Rightarrow x = 4 + 2y$$
$$\Downarrow$$

Substitute for x in both equations and solve.

$$3 - 2y = 4 + 2y$$
$$-1 = 4y$$
$$-\frac{1}{4} = y$$

Substitute the value for y into either original equation to find the value of x.

$$x = 3 - 2\left(-\frac{1}{4}\right)$$
$$x = \frac{7}{2}$$

The solution is $\left(\frac{7}{2}, -\frac{1}{4}\right)$. These values are close to the estimate made from the graph. You can check to confirm that these values satisfy both equations.

Try It! **1.** Solve each system of equations.

a. $\begin{cases} 2x + y = -1 \\ 5y - 6x = 7 \end{cases}$

b. $\begin{cases} 3x + 2y = 5 \\ 6x + 4y = 3 \end{cases}$

APPLICATION

EXAMPLE 2 Solve a System of Linear Inequalities

Malcolm earns \$20 per hour mowing lawns and \$10 per hour walking dogs. His goal is to earn at least \$200 each week, but he can work a maximum of 20 h per week. Malcolm must spend at least 5 h per week walking his neighbors' dogs. For how many hours should Malcolm work at each job in order to meet his goals?

A **system of linear inequalities** is a set of two or more inequalities using the same variables.

Step 1 Define the variables.

x = number of hours spent mowing lawns

y = number of hours spent walking dogs

Step 2 Write inequalities to model the constraints.

Malcolm wants to earn at least \$200 each week at \$20 per hour mowing lawns and \$10 per hour walking dogs: $20x + 10y \geq 200$.

Malcolm cannot work more than 20 h each week: $x + y \leq 20$.

Malcolm must spend at least 5 h walking dogs each week: $y \geq 5$.

Step 3 Solve each inequality for y, then graph the inequalities on the same coordinate plane.

$y \geq 20 - 2x$

$y \leq 20 - x$

$y \geq 5$

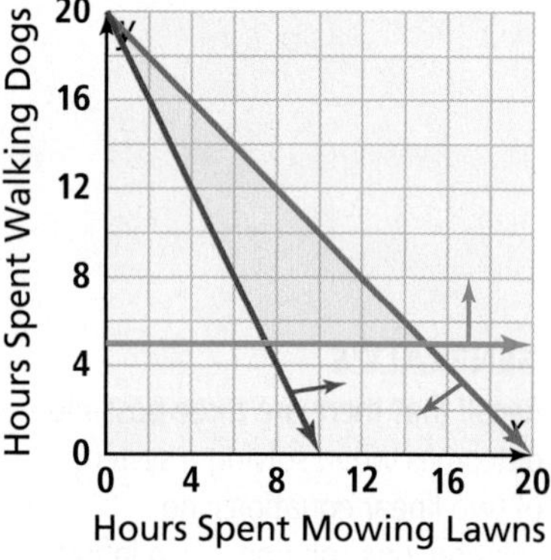

Use arrows to show the region of the graph that satisfies each inequality.

Shade the region that satisfies all three inequalities.

STUDY TIP
Using color to sketch graphs of equations or inequalities can make the graph easier to analyze.

Any point in the shaded region, such as (12, 7), is a solution to the system of inequalities. So if Malcolm spends 12 h mowing lawns and 7 h walking dogs, he will have met his goals.

Try It! 2. Sketch the graph of the set of all points that solve this system of linear inequalities.

$$\begin{cases} 2x + y \leq 14 \\ x + 2y \leq 10 \\ x \geq 0 \\ y \geq 0 \end{cases}$$

EXAMPLE 3 Solve a System of Equations in Three Variables

How can you solve a system of equations in three variables?

A. What is the solution of this system? $\begin{cases} 2x + y - z = -10 \\ -x + 2y + z = 3 \\ x + 2y + 3z = 13 \end{cases}$

$$\begin{aligned} 2x + y - z &= -10 \quad \text{(A)} \\ -x + 2y + z &= 3 \quad \text{(B)} \\ x + 2y + 3z &= 13 \quad \text{(C)} \end{aligned}$$

$$\boxed{\begin{aligned} x + 3y &= -7 \quad \text{(D)} \\ 3x - 6y - 3z &= -9 \quad \text{(E)} \\ x + 2y + 3z &= 13 \quad \text{(F)} \end{aligned}}$$

(D) = (A) + (B)
(E) = −3 × (B)
(F) = (C)

$$\boxed{\begin{aligned} x + 3y &= -7 \quad \text{(G)} \\ 4x - 4y &= 4 \quad \text{(H)} \\ x + 2y + 3z &= 13 \quad \text{(J)} \end{aligned}}$$

(G) = (D)
(H) = (E) + (F)
(J) = (F)

$$\boxed{\begin{aligned} x + 3y &= -7 \quad \text{(K)} \\ -x + y &= -1 \quad \text{(L)} \\ x + 2y + 3z &= 13 \quad \text{(M)} \end{aligned}}$$

(K) = (G)
(L) = (H) ÷ (−4)
(M) = (J)

$$\boxed{\begin{aligned} 4y &= -8 \quad \text{(N)} \\ -x + y &= -1 \quad \text{(P)} \\ x + 2y + 3z &= 13 \quad \text{(Q)} \end{aligned}}$$

(N) = (K) + (L)
(P) = (L)
(Q) = (M)

From equation (N):
$y = -2$

Substituting into (P):
$-x + (-2) = -1$
$x = -1$

Substituting into (A):
$2(-1) + (-2) - z = -10$
$z = 6$

The solution is (−1, −2, 6).

B. What is the solution of this system of equations? $\begin{cases} 2x - y + z = 3 \\ x + y + z = 5 \\ -4x + 2y - 2z = 0 \end{cases}$

$$\begin{aligned} 2x - y + z &= 3 \quad \text{(A)} \\ x + y + z &= 5 \quad \text{(B)} \\ -4x + 2y - 2z &= 0 \quad \text{(C)} \end{aligned}$$

$$\boxed{\begin{aligned} 3x + 2z &= 8 \quad \text{(D)} \\ x + y + z &= 5 \quad \text{(E)} \\ -6x - 4z &= -10 \quad \text{(F)} \end{aligned}}$$

(D) = (A) + (B)
(E) = (B)
(F) = −2(B) + (C)

$$\boxed{\begin{aligned} 3x + 2z &= 8 \quad \text{(G)} \\ x + y + z &= 5 \quad \text{(H)} \\ 0 &= 6 \quad \text{(J)} \end{aligned}}$$

(G) = (D)
(H) = (E)
(J) = 2(D) + (F)

Equation (J) is not true. There is no solution for this system of equations; it is an **inconsistent system.**

CONTINUED ON THE NEXT PAGE

LOOK FOR RELATIONSHIPS
The following actions do not change the solutions of a system of equations:

- rearranging the order of the list
- multiplying an equation by a nonzero number
- adding one equation to another and replacing one of these equations with the sum

EXAMPLE 3 CONTINUED

 **Try It!** 3. Solve the following systems of equations.

a. $\begin{cases} x + y + z = 3 \\ x - y + z = 1 \\ x + y - z = 2 \end{cases}$ b. $\begin{cases} 2x + y - 2z = 3 \\ x - 2y + 7z = 12 \\ 3x - y + 5z = 10 \end{cases}$

 **CONCEPT SUMMARY Linear Systems**

	System of linear equations	System of linear inequalities
WORDS	a set of two or more equations using the same variables	a set of two or more inequalities using the same variables
ALGEBRA	$\begin{cases} 4x - 3y = 4 \\ -x + 2y = 5 \end{cases}$	$\begin{cases} y \geq 16 - 2x \\ y \leq 16 - x \\ y \geq 6 \end{cases}$
GRAPHS	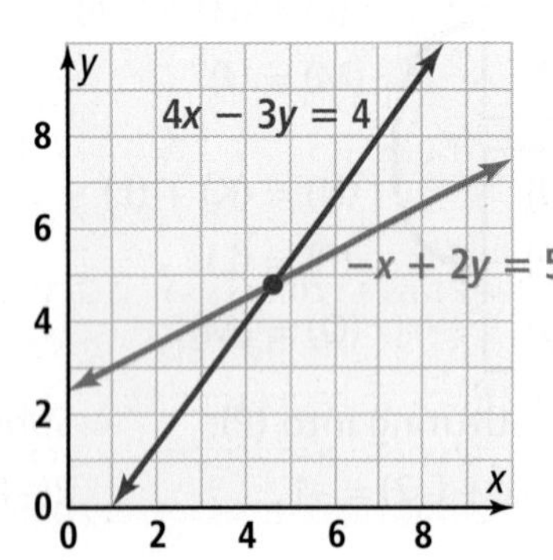	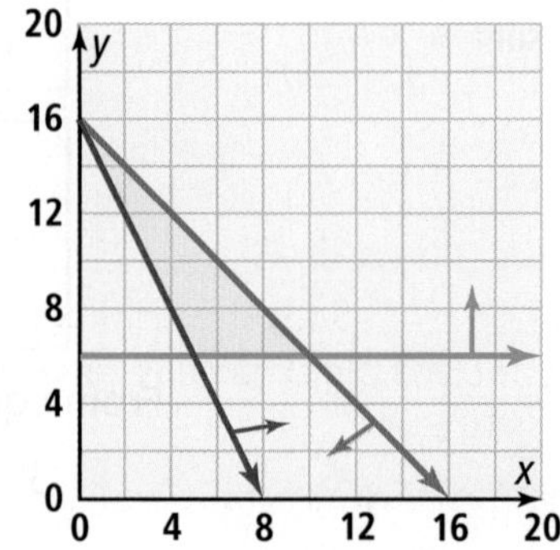

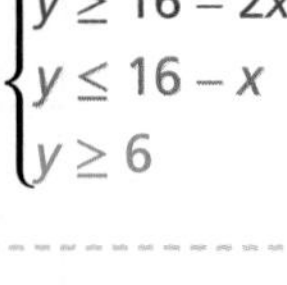

Do You UNDERSTAND?

1. ESSENTIAL QUESTION How can you find and represent solutions of systems of linear equations and inequalities?

2. **Error Analysis** Shandra said the solution of the system of equations $\begin{cases} 2x + y = 3 \\ -x + 4y = -6 \end{cases}$ is (–1, 2). Is she correct? Explain.

3. **Communicate Precisely** Why is a system of linear inequalities often solved graphically?

4. **Make Sense and Persevere** How does knowing how to solve a system of two equations in two variables help you to solve a system of three equations in three variables?

5. **Vocabulary** What is the difference between a system of linear equations and a system of linear inequalities?

Do You KNOW HOW?

6. Solve the following system of equations.
$\begin{cases} 2x + 2y = 10 \\ x + 5y = 13 \end{cases}$

7. Graph the following system of inequalities.
$\begin{cases} -x + 2y < 1 \\ x \geq 0 \\ y \geq 0 \end{cases}$

8. Solve the following system of equations.
$2x - y + z = 3$
$3x + y + 3z = 10$
$x - 2y - 2z = 3$

9. Equations with two variables that are raised only to the first power represent lines. There are three possible outcomes for the intersections of two lines. Describe the outcomes.

UNDERSTAND

10. Communicate Precisely Consider a point that lies on the border of the shaded region of the graph of a system of linear inequalities. Under what conditions is that point a solution to the system?

11. Error Analysis Describe and correct the error a student made in solving the system of equations.

$$\begin{aligned} 2x + 4y &= 0 &\Rightarrow\quad 2x + 4y &= 0 \\ 3x - 2y &= -24 &\Rightarrow\quad 6x - 4y &= -24 \end{aligned}$$

$$\Downarrow$$

$$8x = -24$$
$$x = -3$$

$$\Downarrow$$

$$2(-3) + 4y = 0$$
$$-6 + 4y = 0$$
$$4y = 6$$
$$y = \frac{3}{2} \quad ✗$$

12. Higher Order Thinking Suppose that solving a system of equations algebraically gives the following result: $0 = 0$

What does this mean graphically?

13. Use Structure Write a system of equations in three variables with integer solutions. Give the solution. Explain your process.

14. Make Sense and Persevere Write a system of inequalities for the shaded region.

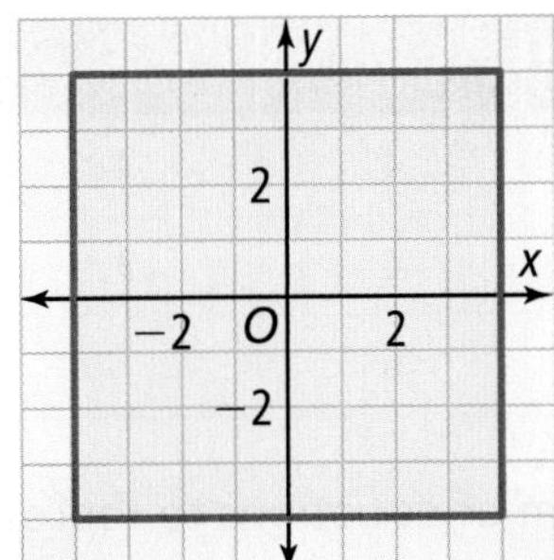

15. Mathematical Connections Consider the following system of equations.

$$\begin{cases} x = 5 - 3y \\ y = -2x \end{cases}$$

Write a system of inequalities whose solution includes the solution to the system of equations above.

PRACTICE

Solve the following systems of equations.
SEE EXAMPLE 1

16. $\begin{cases} x = 2y - 5 \\ 3x - y = 5 \end{cases}$

17. $\begin{cases} y = 2x + 3 \\ 2y - x = 12 \end{cases}$

18. $\begin{cases} x - 3y = 1 \\ 2x - y = 7 \end{cases}$

19. $\begin{cases} x + 2y = -4 \\ 3x - y = -5 \end{cases}$

Write a system of linear equations that has the solution shown.

20. $(-3, 5)$

21. $(10, -1)$

Sketch the graph of the set of all points that solve each system of linear inequalities. SEE EXAMPLE 2

22. $\begin{cases} 0 < x \leq 125 \\ x \geq 2y > 0 \\ 2x + 2y \leq 300 \end{cases}$

23. $\begin{cases} y + 2x < 10 \\ x - 2y < 8 \\ x > 0 \\ y > 0 \end{cases}$

24. $\begin{cases} y \leq -2x + 19 \\ y \geq \frac{3}{7}x + 2 \\ x \leq 7 \end{cases}$

25. $\begin{cases} y < \frac{3}{2}x \\ 3x + 2y < 36 \\ 3 < y < 6 \end{cases}$

26. Charles has a collection of dimes and quarters worth \$1.25. He has 8 coins. Write a system of equations to represent this situation. Then solve the system to determine how many dimes and how many quarters Charles has. SEE EXAMPLE 2

27. A set of triangular and square tiles contains 50 pieces and 170 sides. Write a system of equations to represent this situation. Then solve the system to determine how many triangular and how many square tiles there are. SEE EXAMPLE 2

Solve the following systems of equations.
SEE EXAMPLE 3

28. $\begin{cases} 2x - y - 3z = 20 \\ 3x + y + 6z = 4 \\ x + 2y + 9z = -16 \end{cases}$

29. $\begin{cases} 2x + 5y - 3z = 14 \\ x - 2y + 4z = -12 \\ -x + 3y - 2z = 13 \end{cases}$

30. $\begin{cases} 8x - y + 2z = 1 \\ -2x + 3y + 7z = 8 \\ 4x - 2y + z = -4 \end{cases}$

31. $\begin{cases} 7x - y - 5z = -27 \\ 2x + y + 3z = -19 \\ x + 3y + z = 5 \end{cases}$

PRACTICE & PROBLEM SOLVING

Practice | Tutorial
Mixed Review Available Online

APPLY

32. **Model With Mathematics** In basketball, a successful free throw is worth 1 point, a basket made from inside the 3-point arc is worth 2 points, and a basket made from outside the 3-point arc basket is worth 3 points. How many of each type of basket did Pilar make?

33. **Reason** Raul is paid $75 per week plus $5 for each new gym membership he sells. He may switch to a gym that pays $50 per week and $7.50 for each new membership. How many memberships per week does Raul have to sell for the new gym to be a better deal for him?

34. **Reason** Keisha is designing a rectangular giraffe enclosure with a length of at most 125 m. The animal sanctuary can afford at most 300 m of fencing, and the length of the enclosure must be at least double the width.

a. Write inequalities to represent each constraint where x = width and y = length.

b. Graph and solve the linear system of inequalities.

c. What does the solution mean?

35. **Make Sense and Persevere** Ramona needs 10 mL of a 30% saline solution. She has a 50% saline solution and a 25% saline solution. How many milliliters of each solution does she need to create the 30% solution?

ASSESSMENT PRACTICE

36. One equation in a system of equations with one solution is $4x + 2y = 14$. Select all equations that could be the second equation in the system.

☐ **A.** $2x + y = 7$
☐ **B.** $3x - 6y = -12$
☐ **C.** $2x + 6y = 32$
☐ **D.** $-3x + 10y = 1$
☐ **E.** $2x + y = 5$

37. **SAT/ACT** What value of a gives $(-1, 1)$ as the solution of the system $\begin{cases} 3x + 5y = 2 \\ ax + 8y = 14 \end{cases}$?

Ⓐ −22 Ⓑ −6 Ⓒ 0 Ⓓ 6 Ⓔ 22

38. **Performance Task** Each Sophomore, Junior, and Senior at a high school collected aluminum cans and plastic bottles. The table shows the average number of cans and bottles collected per student, by grade level during a 3 week recyling drive.

	Sophomores	Juniors	Seniors
Week 1	3	4	4
Week 2	4	4	3
Week 3	5	6	7

Part A Write a system of equations to represent the situation.

Part B Find the solution of the system of equations you found in Part A.

Part C What does your solution to part B represent in terms of this scenario?

MATHEMATICAL MODELING IN 3 ACTS

PearsonRealize.com

Current Events

You might say that someone who loses their temper has "blown a fuse." However, it's rare to hear about electrical fuses blowing these days. That's because most fuses have been replaced by circuit breakers. A fuse must be replaced once it's blown, but a circuit breaker can be reset.

Ask for permission to look at the electrical panel in your home. If there is a series of switches inside, each of those is a circuit breaker, designed to interrupt the circuit when the electrical current inside is too dangerous. How much electricity does it take to trip a circuit breaker? Think about this question during the Mathematical Modeling in 3-Acts lesson.

ACT 1 Identify the Problem

1. What is the first question that comes to mind after watching the video?
2. Write down the main question you will answer about what you saw in the video.
3. Make an initial conjecture that answers this main question.
4. Explain how you arrived at your conjecture.
5. What information will be useful to know to answer the main question? How can you get it? How will you use that information?

ACT 2 Develop a Model

6. Use the math that you have learned in this Topic to refine your conjecture.

ACT 3 Interpret the Results

7. Did your refined conjecture match the actual answer exactly? If not, what might explain the difference?

TOPIC 1

Topic Review

TOPIC ESSENTIAL QUESTION

1. What are different ways in which functions can be used to represent and solve problems involving quantities?

Vocabulary Review

Choose the correct term to complete each sentence.

2. The __________ pairs every input in an interval with the same output value.
3. The point at which a function changes from increasing to decreasing is the __________ of the function.
4. A __________ of a function $y = af(x - h) + k$ is a change made to at least one of the values a, h, and k.
5. A __________ is the value of x when $y = 0$.
6. A __________ is defined by two or more functions, each over a different interval.

- step function
- piecewise-defined function
- minimum
- maximum
- system of linear equations
- transformation
- zero of the function

Concepts & Skills Review

LESSON 1-1 Key Features of Functions

Quick Review

The domain of a function is the set of input values, or x-values. The range of a function is the set of output values, or y-values. These sets can be described using **interval notation** or **set-builder notation.**

A y-intercept is a point on the graph of a function where $x = 0$. An x-intercept is a point on the graph where $y = 0$. An x-intercept may also be a **zero of a function.**

Example

Find the zeros of the function. Then determine over what domain the function is positive or negative.

The point where the line crosses the x-axis is (1, 0), so $x = 1$ is a zero of the function. The function is positive on the interval $(-\infty, 1)$ and negative on the interval $(1, \infty)$.

Practice & Problem Solving

Identify the domain and range of the function in interval notation. Find the zeros of the function. Then determine for which values of x the function is positive and for which it is negative.

7.

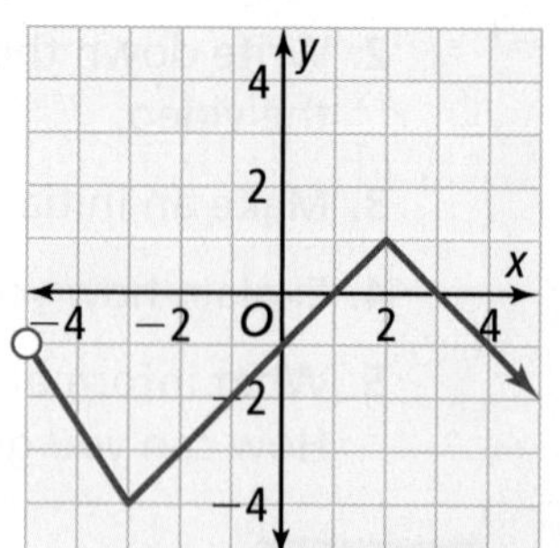

8.

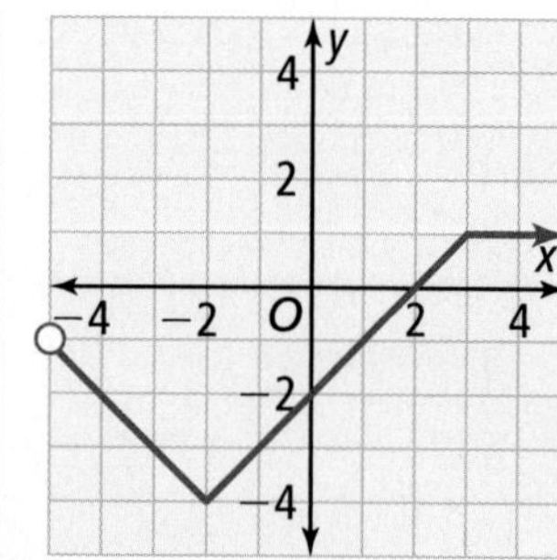

9. **Use Structure** Sketch a graph given the following key features.
domain: $(-5, 5)$; decreasing: $(-3, 1)$; x-intercepts: -4, -2; positive: $(-4, -2)$

10. **Communicate Precisely** Jeffrey is emptying a 50 ft^3 container filled with water at a rate of 0.5 ft^3/min. Find and interpret the key features for this situation.

LESSON 1-2 Transformations of Functions

Quick Review

There are different types of **transformations** that change the graph of the parent function. A **translation** shifts each point on a graph the same distance and direction. A **reflection** maps each point to a new point across a given line. A **stretch** or a **compression** increases or decreases the distance between the points of a graph and a given line by the same factor.

Example

Graph the parent function $f(x) = |x|$ and $g(x) = -|x + 2| - 1$. Describe the transformation.

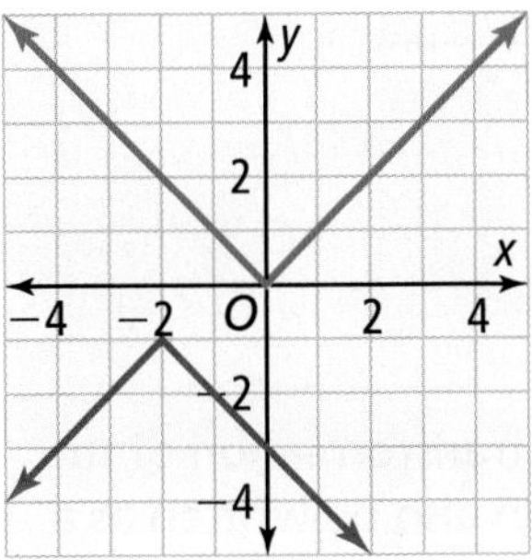

Multiplying the absolute value expression by −1 indicates a reflection over the *x*-axis.

Adding 2 to *x* indicates a translation 2 units to the left and subtracting 1 from the absolute value expression indicates a translation 1 unit down.

So the graph of *g* is a reflection of the graph of the parent function *f* over the *x*-axis, and then a translation 2 units left and 1 unit down.

Practice & Problem Solving

Graph each function as a translation of its parent function, *f*.

11. $g(x) = |x| - 7$

12. $g(x) = x^2 + 5$

Graph the function, *g*, as a reflection of the graph of *f* across the given axis.

13. across the *x*-axis

14. across the *y*-axis

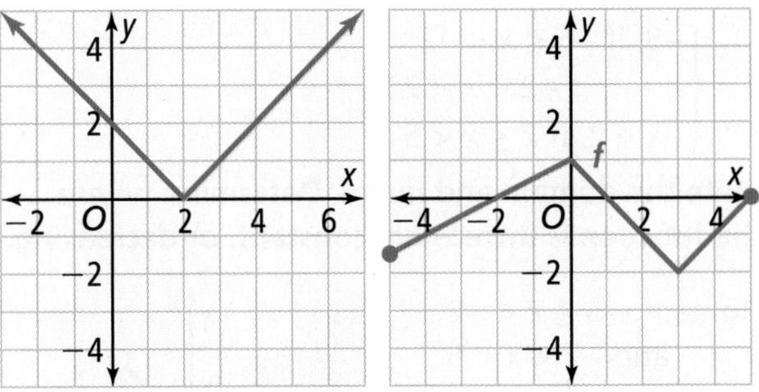

15. **Look for Relationships** Describe the effect of a vertical stretch by a factor greater than 1 on the graph of the absolute value function. How is that different from the effect of a horizontal stretch by the same factor?

16. **Use Structure** Graph the function that is a vertical stretch by a factor of 3.5 of the parent function $f(x) = |x|$.

17. **Use Structure** Graph the function that is a horizontal translation 1 unit to the right of the parent function $f(x) = x^2$.

LESSON 1-3 Piecewise-Defined Functions

Quick Review

A **piecewise-defined function** is a function defined by two or more function rules over different intervals. A **step function** pairs every number in an interval with a single value.

Example

Graph the function.

$$y = \begin{cases} -3, \text{ if } -5 \leq x < -2 \\ x + 1, \text{ if } -2 < x < 2 \\ -x + 2, \text{ if } 2 \leq x < 5 \end{cases}$$

State the domain and range. Determine where the function is increasing, constant, or decreasing.

Domain: $-5 \leq x < -2$ and $-2 < x < 5$

Range: $-3 \leq y < 3$

Increasing: $-2 < x < 3$

Constant: $-5 < x < -2$

Decreasing: $2 < x < 5$

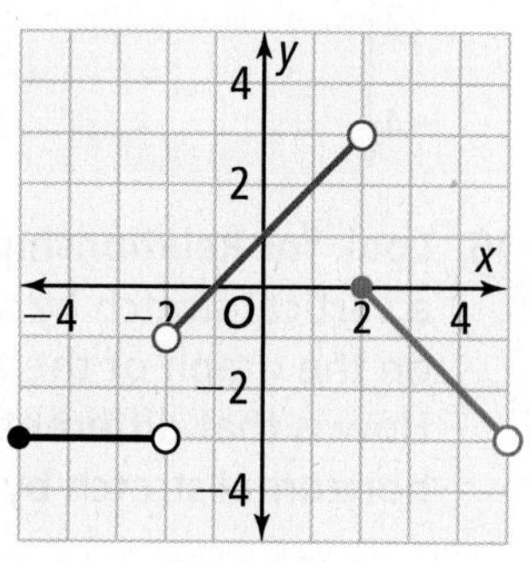

Practice & Problem Solving

18. Graph the function.

$$y = \begin{cases} -3, \text{ if } -4 \leq x < -2 \\ -1, \text{ if } -2 \leq x < 0 \\ 1, \text{ if } 0 \leq x < 2 \\ 3, \text{ if } 2 \leq x < 4 \end{cases}$$

19. What rule defines the function in the following graph?

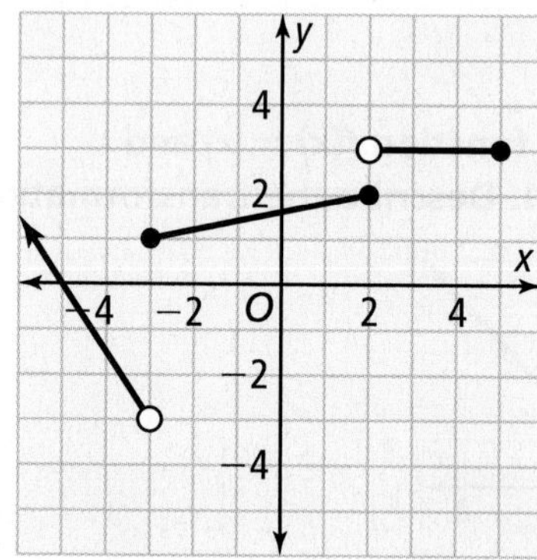

20. Generalize Can every transformation of the absolute value function also be written as a piecewise-defined function? Explain.

LESSON 1-4 Arithmetic Sequences and Series

Quick Review

An **arithmetic sequence** is a sequence with a constant difference between consecutive terms.

recursive definition: $a_n = \begin{cases} a_1, \text{ if } n = 1 \\ a_{n-1} + d, \text{ if } n > 1 \end{cases}$

explicit definition: $a_n = a_1 + (n - 1)d$

Example

Given the sequence 22, 17, 12, 7, ..., write the explicit formula. Then find the 6th term.

$d = -5$ .... Find the common difference.

$a_n = 22 + (n - 1)(-5)$ .... Substitute 22 for a_1 and -5 for d.

$a_n = 22 - 5(n - 1)$ .... Simplify.

$a_6 = 22 - 5(6 - 1)$ .... Substitute 6 for n.

$a_6 = -3$ .... Solve for the 6th term.

Practice & Problem Solving

What are the common difference, the next term, and the recursive and explicit functions for each arithmetic sequence?

21. 3, 15, 27, 39, ...

22. 19, 13, 7, 1, ...

Find the sum of an arithmetic sequence with the given number of terms and values of a_1 and a_n.

23. 8 terms, $a_1 = 2$, $a_8 = 74$

24. 12 terms, $a_1 = 87$, $a_{12} = 10$

What is the value of each of the following series?

25. $\sum_{n=1}^{9} (1 + 3n)$

26. $\sum_{n=1}^{6} (5n - 2)$

27. Make Sense and Persevere Cubes are stacked in the shape of a pyramid. The top row has 1 cube, the second row has 3, and the third row has 5. If there are 9 rows of cubes, how many cubes were used to make the front of the pyramid?

LESSON 1-5 Solving Equations and Inequalities by Graphing

Quick Review

To solve an equation by graphing, write two new equations by setting y equal to each expression in the original equation. Approximate coordinates of any points of intersection. The x-values of these points are the solutions to the equation. You can also solve equations using tables or graphing technology.

Example

Solve $|x + 3| - 5 = \frac{1}{2}x - 2$ by graphing.

Graph $y = |x + 3| - 5$ and $y = \frac{1}{2}x - 2$.

It appears that $x = -4$ and $x = 0$ are solutions.

Confirm the solutions by substituting into the original equation.

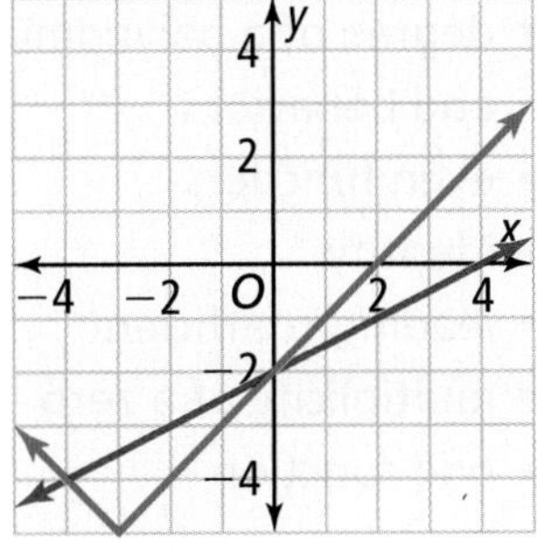

Practice & Problem Solving

Use a graph to solve each equation.

28. $-x + 2 = x^2$

29. $\frac{1}{4}|x + 3| = 2$

Use a graph to solve each inequality.

30. $x^2 + 2x - 3 > 0$

31. $x^2 - 7x - 8 < 0$

32. Construct Arguments Is graphing always the most convenient method for solving an equation? Why or why not?

33. Model With Mathematics A truck is traveling 30 mi ahead of a car at an average rate of 55 mph. The car is traveling at a rate of 63 mph. Let x represent the number of hours that the car and truck travel. Write an inequality to determine at what times the car will be ahead of the truck and graph the inequality to solve.

LESSON 1-6 Linear Systems

Quick Review

A **system of linear equations** is a set of two or more equations using the same variables. The **solution of a system of linear equations** is the set of all ordered coordinates that simultaneously make all equations in the system true. A **system of linear inequalities** is a set of two or more inequalities using the same variables.

Example

Solve the system. $\begin{cases} -4x + 4y = 16 \\ -x + 2y = 10 \end{cases}$

$x = 2y - 10$ .... Solve the second equation for x.

$-4(2y - 10) + 4y = 16$
$y = 6$ .... Substitute $2y - 10$ for x. Solve for y.

$x = 2(6) - 10$
$x = 2$ .... Substitute 6 for y in the equation $x = 2y - 10$.

Practice & Problem Solving

Solve each system of equations.

34. $\begin{cases} y = 2x + 5 \\ 2x + 4y = 10 \end{cases}$

35. $\begin{cases} y = 2x - 6 \\ 6x + y = 10 \end{cases}$

36. Use Structure Write a linear system in two variables that has infinitely many solutions.

37. Model With Mathematics It takes Leo 12 h to make a table and 20 h to make a chair. In 8 wk, Leo wants to make at least 5 tables and 8 chairs to display in his new shop. Leo works 40 h a week. Write a system of linear inequalities relating the number of tables x and the number of chairs y Leo will be able to make. List two different combinations of tables and chairs Leo could have to display at the opening of his new shop.

TOPIC 2

Polynomial Functions

TOPIC ESSENTIAL QUESTION

What can the rule for a polynomial function reveal about its graph, and what can the graphs of polynomial functions reveal about the solutions of polynomial equations?

Topic Overview

Topic Vocabulary

- Binomial Theorem
- degree of a polynomial
- end behavior
- even function
- identity
- leading coefficient
- multiplicity of a zero
- odd function
- Pascal's triangle
- polynomial function
- relative maximum
- relative minimum
- Rational Root Theorem
- Remainder Theorem
- standard form of a polynomial
- synthetic division
- turning point

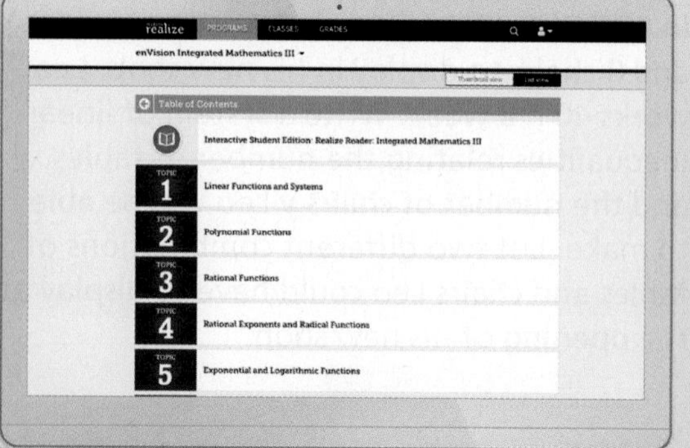

Go online | **PearsonRealize.com**

Digital Experience

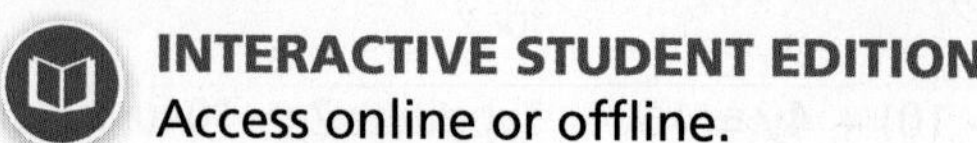

INTERACTIVE STUDENT EDITION Access online or offline.

ACTIVITIES Complete ***Explore & Reason, Model & Discuss,*** and ***Critique & Explain*** activities. Interact with Examples and Try Its.

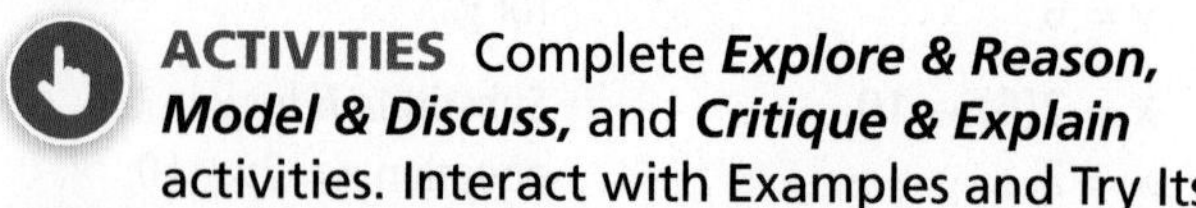

ANIMATION View and interact with real-world applications.

PRACTICE Practice what you've learned.

What Are the Rules?

All games have rules about how to play the game. The rules outline such things as when a ball is in or out, how a player scores points, and how many points a player gets for each winning shot.

If you didn't alreay know how to play tennis, or some other game, could you figure out what the rules were just by watching? What clues would help you understand the game? Think about this during the Mathematical Modeling in 3 Acts lesson.

TOPIC 2

VIDEOS Watch clips to support **Mathematical Modeling in 3 Acts Lessons** and **enVision® STEM Projects.**

CONCEPT SUMMARY Review key lesson content through multiple representations.

ASSESSMENT Show what you've learned.

GLOSSARY Read and listen to English and Spanish definitions.

TUTORIALS Get help from *Virtual Nerd*, right when you need it.

MATH TOOLS Explore math with digital tools and manipulatives.

Video

Did You Know?

In a 2013–2015 overhaul, Texas A&M's football stadium increased its seating from 80,600 to 102,512. The renovation cost $450 million and included lowering the field and adding overhangs to two sides.

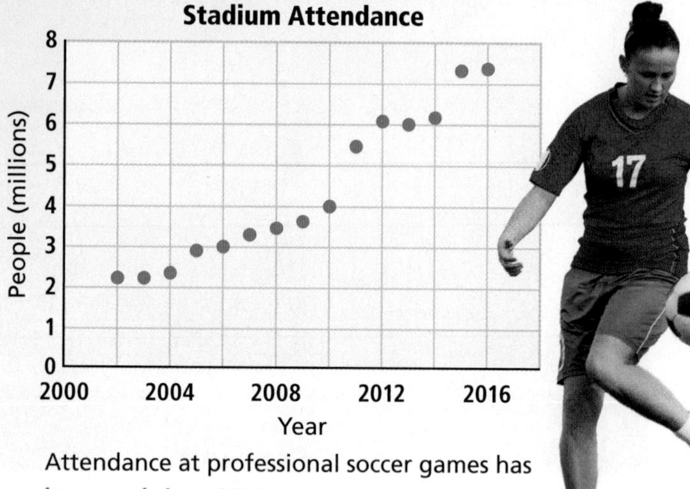

Attendance at professional soccer games has increased since 2002.

The new home of the Minnesota Vikings, opened in Minneapolis in July 2016, includes approximately 1.6 million square feet of space. The stadium seats 66,200 spectators for most events but can expand to seat 73,000. The first row of seats is 41 feet from the sideline.

Your Task: Design a Stadium

You and your classmates will plan the seating at a new stadium. You will explore attendance at the current stadium and use fitted curves to support your predictions of future attendance.

2-1 Graphing Polynomial Functions

PearsonRealize.com

I CAN… predict the behavior of polynomial functions.

VOCABULARY

- degree of a polynomial
- leading coefficient
- polynomial function
- relative maximum
- relative minimum
- standard form of a polynomial
- turning point

EXPLORE & REASON

Consider functions of the form $f(x) = x^n$, where n is a positive integer.

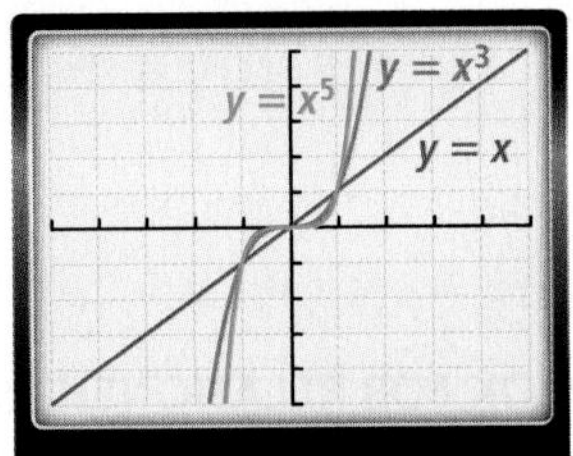

A. Graph $f(x) = x^n$ for $n = 1$, 3, and 5. Look at the graphs in Quadrant I. As the exponent increases, what is happening to the graphs? Which quadrants do the graphs pass through?

B. Look for Relationships Now graph $f(x) = x^n$ for $n = 2$, 4, and 6. What happens to these graphs in Quadrant I as the exponent increases? Which quadrants do the graphs pass through?

C. Write two equations in the form $f(x) = x^n$ with graphs that you predict are in Quadrants I and II. Write two equations with graphs that you predict are in Quadrants I and III. Use graphing technology to test your predictions.

ESSENTIAL QUESTION

How do the key features of a polynomial function help you sketch its graph?

EXAMPLE 1 Classify Polynomials

How can you write a polynomial in standard form and use it to identify the leading coefficient, the degree, and the number of terms?

$$-4x + 9 + 2x^3$$

Recall that a polynomial is a monomial or the sum of one or more monomials, called terms. The degree of a term with one variable is the exponent of that variable.

Degree of $-4x$: 1   Degree of 9: 0   Degree of $2x^3$: 3

Standard form of a polynomial shows any like terms combined and the terms by degree in descending numerical order.

Standard form of this polynomial is:

$$2x^3 - 4x + 9$$

The polynomial has three terms, so it is called a *trinomial*.

The **leading coefficient** refers to the non-zero factor that is multiplied by the greatest power of x. The leading coefficient of this polynomial is 2.

The **degree of a polynomial** is the greatest degree of any of the terms. This is a polynomial of degree 3, also known as a *cubic polynomial*.

USE STRUCTURE
Note that there is no x^2-term in the polynomial $2x^3 - 4x + 9$. In some cases, it may be useful to write the polynomial as $2x^3 + 0x^2 - 4x + 9$.

Try It! **1.** What is each polynomial in standard form and what are the leading coefficient, the degree, and the number of terms of each?

a. $2x - 3x^4 + 6 - 5x^3$

b. $x^5 + 2x^6 - 3x^4 - 8x + 4x^3$

CONCEPTUAL UNDERSTANDING

Understand End Behavior of Polynomial Functions

How do the sign of the leading coefficient and the degree of a polynomial affect the end behavior of the graph of a polynomial function?

A **polynomial function** is a function whose rule is a polynomial. The **end behavior** of a graph describes what happens to the function values as x approaches positive and negative infinity.

LOOK FOR RELATIONSHIPS
Though a polynomial function may have many terms, the leading term determines the end behavior because it has the greatest exponent and therefore the greatest impact on function values when x is very large or very small.

Odd Degree Positive Leading Coefficient	Even Degree Positive Leading Coefficient
$f(x) = x$; degree 1 $g(x) = 0.5x^3 - x^2 + 3$; degree 3 $h(x) = 2x^5 - x^2 - x - 2$; degree 5	$f(x) = x^2$; degree 2 $g(x) = 0.9x^4 - 2x^3 + x^2 - 2x$; degree 4 $h(x) = 2x^6 + x^2 - 2$; degree 6
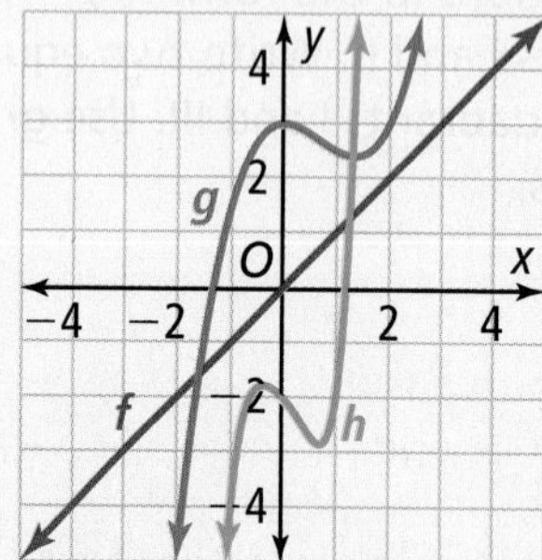	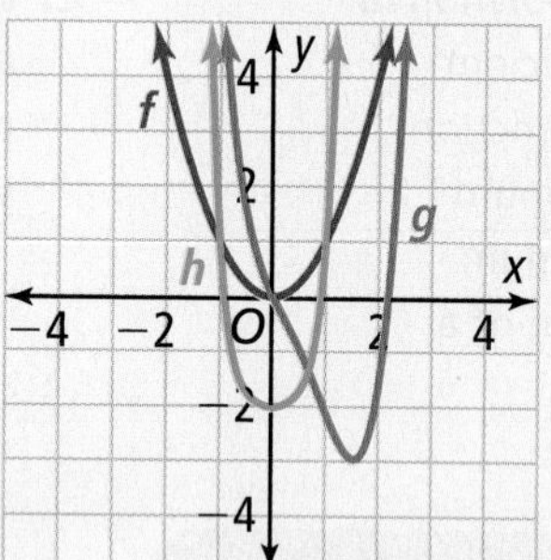
End behavior is similar to the linear parent function $f(x) = x$.	End is behavior similar to the quadratic parent function $f(x) = x^2$.

Recall that a reflection of a function across the x-axis occurs when the function is negated: $f(x)$ becomes $-f(x)$. The end behavior of a function is similarly affected when the leading coefficient is negative.

Odd Degree Negative Leading Coefficient	Even Degree Negative Leading Coefficient
$f(x) = -x$; degree 1 $g(x) = -0.5x^3 - x^2 - 3$; degree 3 $h(x) = -2x^5 + x^2 + x + 2$; degree 5	$f(x) = -x^2$; degree 2 $g(x) = -0.9x^4 + 2x^3 - x^2 + 2x$; degree 4 $h(x) = -2x^6 - x^2 + 2$; degree 6
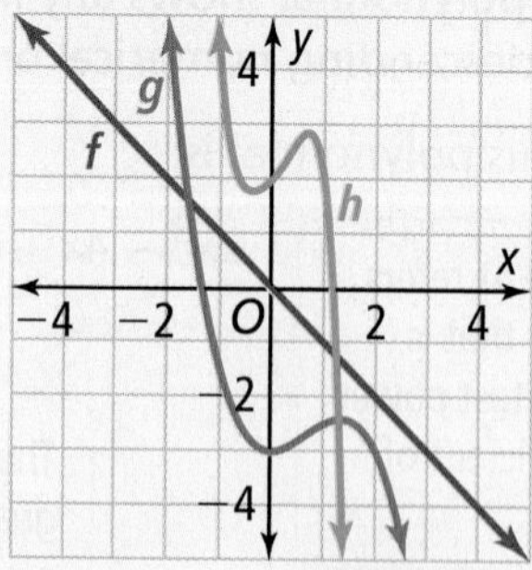	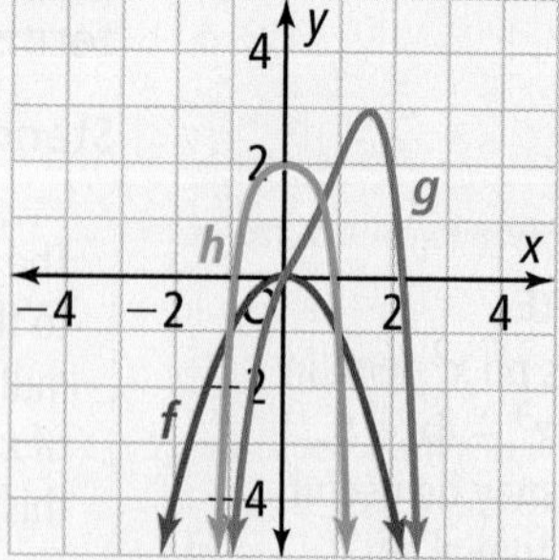
End behavior is similar to $f(x) = -x$.	End behavior is similar to $f(x) = -x^2$.

Try It! **2.** Use the leading coefficient and degree of the polynomial function to determine the end behavior of each graph.

a. $f(x) = 2x^6 - 5x^5 + 6x^4 - x^3 + 4x^2 - x + 1$

b. $g(x) = -5x^3 + 8x + 4$

EXAMPLE 3 Graph a Polynomial Function

Consider the polynomial function $f(x) = -0.5x^4 + 3x^2 + 2$.

A. How can you use a table of values to identify key features and sketch a graph of the function?

Make a table of values and identify intervals where the function is increasing and decreasing.

x	$f(x)$
−3	−11.5
−2	6
−1	4.5
0	2
1	4.5
2	6
3	−11.5

increasing (−3 to −2)

decreasing (−2 to 0)

increasing (0 to 2)

decreasing (2 to 3)

Points where the function values change from increasing to decreasing, or vice-versa, are **turning points**. This function has approximate turning points when the value of x is between −2 and −1, −1 and 0, and 1 and 2.

USE APPROPRIATE TOOLS
It can be very difficult to locate the precise turning points and zeros of polynomial functions. Graphing technology can help identify these points.

This is a polynomial function with an even degree and a negative leading coefficient, so both ends of the graph will trend toward $-\infty$.

Plot the points and sketch the graph with a smooth curve.

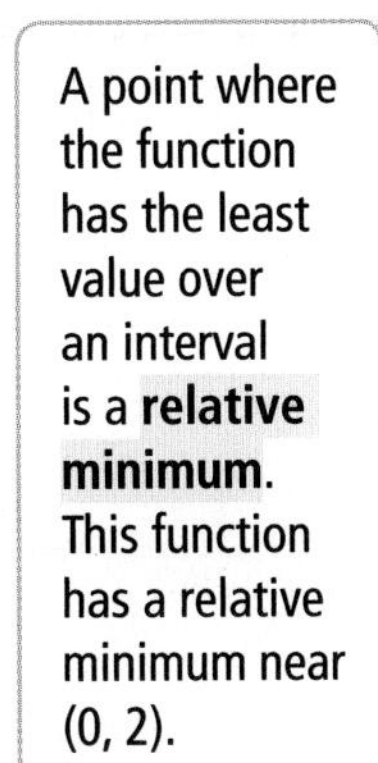

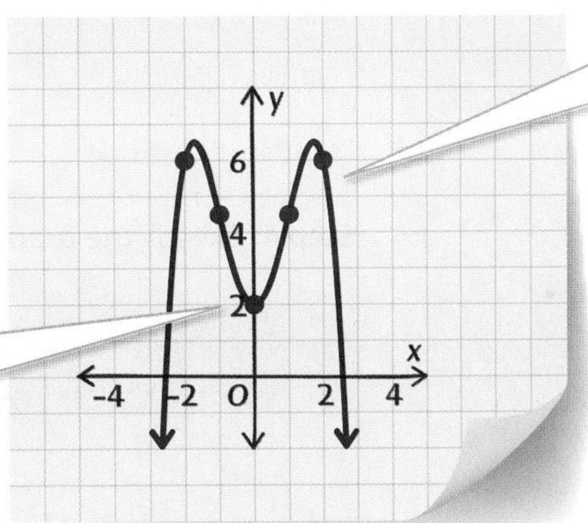

A point where the function has the greatest value over an interval is a **relative maximum**. This function has two relative maximums near (−2, 6) and (2, 6).

B. How can you use the graph to estimate the average rate of change over the interval [−2, 0]?

Recall that the average rate of change is $\frac{f(b) - f(a)}{b - a}$ for two points on a graph $(a, f(a))$ and $(b, f(b))$.

$$\text{Average rate of change} = \frac{f(b) - f(a)}{b - a}$$
$$= \frac{2 - 6}{0 - (-2)}$$
$$= -2$$

Substitute (−2, 6) and (0, 2).

The average rate of change over the interval [−2, 0] is −2.

Try It! **3.** Consider the polynomial function $f(x) = x^5 + 18x^2 + 10x + 1$.

a. Make a table of values to identify key features and sketch a graph of the function.

b. Find the average rate of change over the interval [0, 2].

 Activity 

EXAMPLE 4 Sketch the Graph from a Verbal Description

How can you sketch a graph of the polynomial function *f* from a verbal description?

- ***f*(*x*) is positive on the intervals $(-\infty, -4)$ and $(-1, 4)$.**
- ***f*(*x*) is negative on the intervals $(-4, -1)$ and $(4, \infty)$.**
- ***f*(*x*) is decreasing on the intervals $(-\infty, -2.67)$ and $(2, \infty)$.**
- ***f*(*x*) is increasing on the interval $(-2.67, 2)$.**

COMMON ERROR
Positive/negative behavior only tells where the function's graph lies above or below the *x*-axis. It does not indicate whether the function is increasing or decreasing.

Step 1: Identify or estimate *x*-intercepts. The function values change signs at $x = -4$, $x = -1$, and $x = 4$.

Step 2: Identify or estimate turning points. The function changes direction at $x = -2.67$ and $x = 2$.

- There is a relative minimum at $x = -2.67$.
- There is a relative maximum at $x = 2$.

Step 3: Evaluate end behavior.

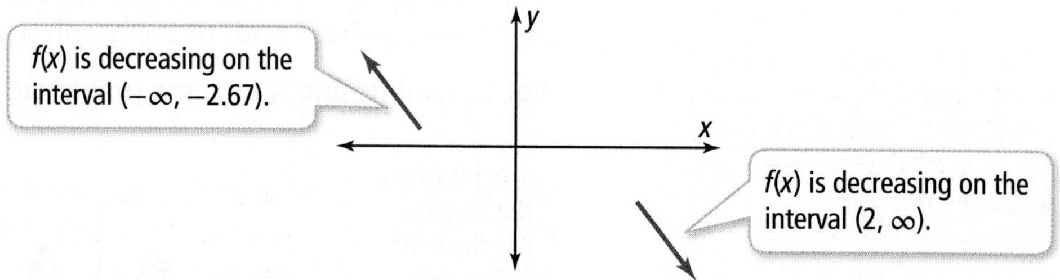

Step 4: Sketch the graph.

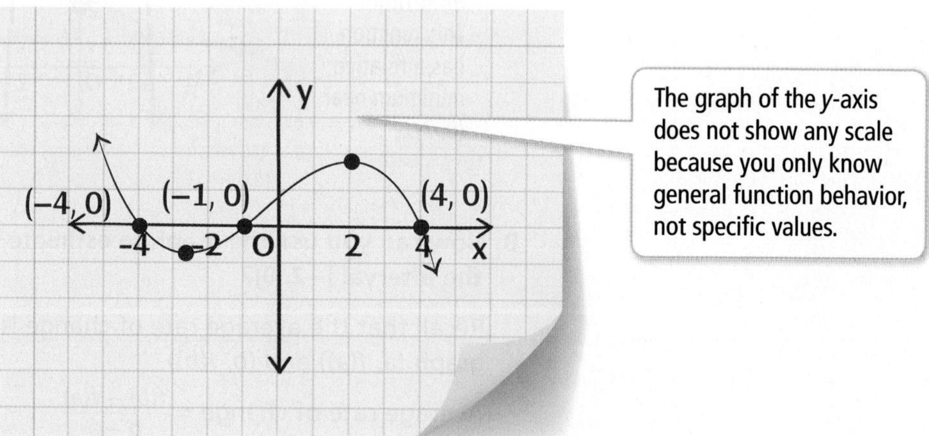

 **Try It!** 4. Use the information below to sketch a graph of the polynomial function $y = f(x)$.

- $f(x)$ is positive on the intervals $(-2, -1)$ and $(1, 2)$.
- $f(x)$ is negative on the intervals $(-\infty, -2)$, $(-1, 1)$, and $(2, \infty)$.
- $f(x)$ is increasing on the interval $(-\infty, -1.5)$ and $(0, 1.5)$.
- $f(x)$ is decreasing on the intervals $(-1.5, 0)$ and $(1.5, \infty)$.

Activity Assess

APPLICATION

EXAMPLE 5 Interpret a Polynomial Model

In science class, Abby mixes a fixed amount of baking soda with different amounts of vinegar in a bottle capped by a balloon. She records the amount of time it takes the gases produced by the reaction to inflate the balloon.

From her data, Abby created a function to model the situation. For x quarter-cups of vinegar, it takes $t(x) = -0.12x^3 + x^2 - 3.38x + 13.16$ seconds to inflate the balloon.

A. How long would it take to inflate the balloon with 5 quarter-cups of vinegar?

Use technology to sketch the graph.

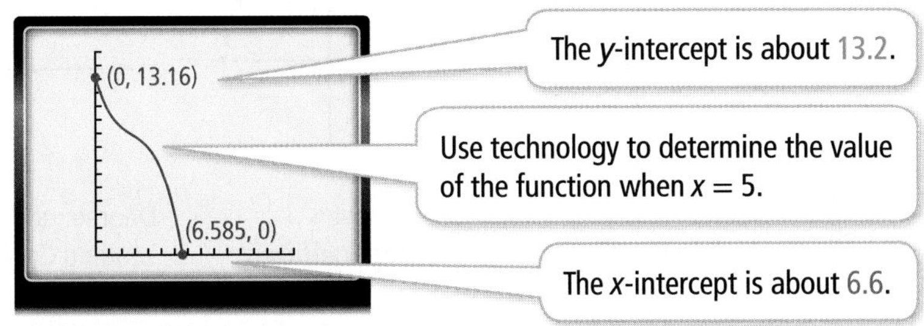

When $x = 5$, the value of the function is about 6.3. This means that if Abby uses 5 quarter-cups of vinegar, the balloon will inflate in approximately 6.3 seconds.

B. What do the x- and y-intercepts of the graph mean in this context? Do those values make sense?

The x-intercept is approximately 6.6 which means that if 6.6 cups of vinegar are used, the balloon would inflate in 0 seconds.

The y-intercept is approximately 13.2, which means that if no vinegar is used, the balloon will inflate in 13.2 seconds.

Neither the x- nor the y-intercept make sense in this context. Therefore, we must limit the domain and range when considering this model.

STUDY TIP

Recall that when you are using a graph in a real-world context, you need to consider the context when thinking about domain and range. Does it make sense for x to be negative? Does it make sense for y to be negative?

Try It! 5. Danielle is engineering a new brand of shoes. For x shoes sold, in thousands, a profit of $p(x) = -3x^4 + 4x^3 - 2x^2 + 5x + 10$ dollars, in ten thousands, will be earned.

a. How much will be earned in profit for selling 1,000 shoes?

b. What do the x- and y-intercepts of the graph mean in this context? Do those values make sense?

Concept Summary Assess

CONCEPT SUMMARY Graphing Polynomial Functions

WORDS A **polynomial function** is a function whose rule is either a monomial or a sum of monomials.

KEY FEATURES **Turning points** – function values change from increasing to decreasing, or vice-versa

Relative minimum – changes from decreasing to increasing

Relative maximum – changes from increasing to decreasing

GRAPHS End behavior depends on the degree of the polynomial and the sign of its leading coefficient.

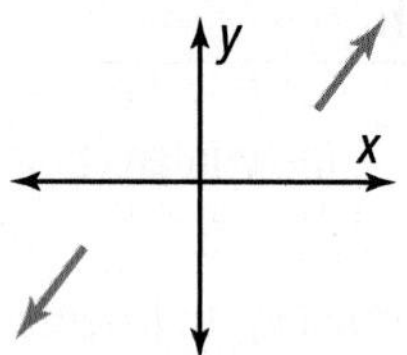

Degree: odd
Leading Coefficient: +

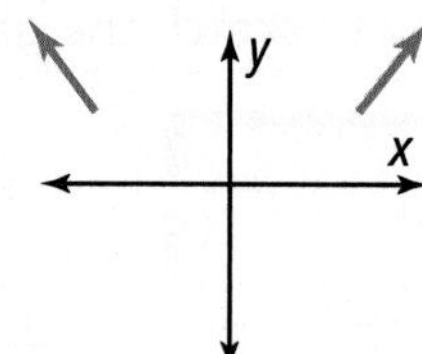

Degree: even
Leading Coefficient: +

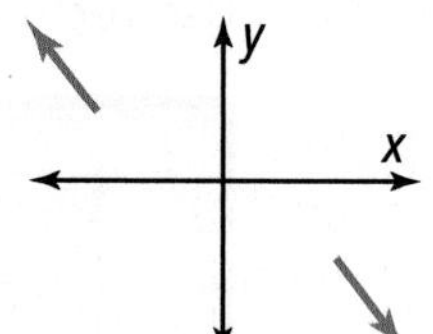

Degree: odd
Leading Coefficient: −

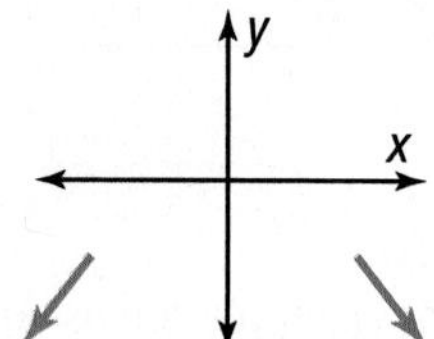

Degree: even
Leading Coefficient: −

Do You UNDERSTAND?

1. ESSENTIAL QUESTION How do the key features of a polynomial function help you sketch its graph?

2. **Error Analysis** Allie said the degree of the polynomial function $f(x) = x^5 + 2x^4 + 3x^3 - 2x^6 - 9x^2 - 6x + 4$ is 5. Explain and correct Allie's error.

3. **Vocabulary** Explain how to determine the leading coefficient of a polynomial function.

4. **Look for Relationships** What is the relationship between the degree and leading coefficient of a polynomial function and the end behavior of the polynomial?

Do You KNOW HOW?

The graph shows the function $f(x) = x^4 + 2x^3 - 13x^2 - 14x + 24$. Find the following.

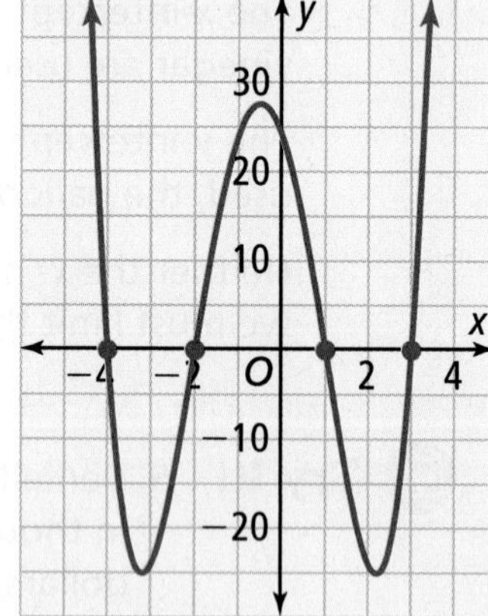

5. number of terms
6. degree
7. leading coefficient
8. end behavior
9. turning point(s)
10. x-intercept(s)
11. relative minimum(s)
12. relative maximum(s)

PRACTICE & PROBLEM SOLVING

Scan for Multimedia   

Practice Tutorial

Additional Exercises Available Online

UNDERSTAND

13. **Make Sense and Persevere** The table shows some values of a polynomial function. Deshawn says there are turning points between the x-values -3 and -2 and between 0 and 1. He also says there is a relative minimum between the x-values -3 and -2, and a relative maximum between 0 and 1. Sketch a graph that shows how Deshawn could be correct and another graph that shows how Deshawn could be incorrect.

x	-5	-4	-3	-2	-1	0	1	2
$f(x)$	-1004	129	220	85	12	1	4	165

14. **Higher Order Thinking** Use the information below about a polynomial function in standard form to write a possible polynomial function. Explain how you determined your function and graph it to verify that it satisfies the criteria.
    - 6 terms
    - y-intercept at 1
    - end behavior: As $x \to -\infty$, $y \to +\infty$.
      As $x \to +\infty$, $y \to -\infty$.

15. **Reason** An analyst for a new company used the first three years of revenue data to project future revenue for the company. The analyst predicts the function $f(x) = -2x^5 + 6x^4 - x^3 + 5x^2 + 6x + 50$ will give the revenue after x years. Should the CEO expect the company to be successful? Explain.

16. **Look for Relationships** Sketch a graph of each of the functions described below.
    - a cubic function with one x-intercept
    - a cubic function with 2 x-intercepts
    - a cubic function with 3 x-intercepts

17. **Make Sense and Persevere** Compare the rate of change for the function $f(x) = x^3 - 2x^2 + x + 1$ over the intervals [0, 2] and [2, 4].

PRACTICE

Write each polynomial function in standard form. For each function, find the degree, number of terms, and leading coefficient.
SEE EXAMPLE 1

18. $f(x) = -3x^3 + 2x^5 + x + 8x^3 - 6 + x^4 - 3x^2$

19. $f(x) = 8x^2 + 10x^7 - 7x^3 - x^4$

20. $f(x) = -x^3 + 9x + 12 - x^4 + 5x^2$

Use the leading coefficient and degree of the polynomial function to determine the end behavior of the graph. SEE EXAMPLE 2

21. $f(x) = -x^5 + 2x^4 + 3x^3 + 2x^2 - 8x + 9$

22. $f(x) = 7x^4 - 4x^3 + 7x^2 + 10x - 15$

23. $f(x) = -x^6 + 7x^5 - x^4 + 2x^3 + 9x^2 - 8x - 2$

Use a table of values to estimate the intercepts and turning points of the function. Then graph the function. SEE EXAMPLE 3

24. $f(x) = x^3 + 2x^2 - 5x - 6$

25. $f(x) = x^4 - x^3 - 21x^2 + x + 20$

26. Use the information below to sketch a graph of the polynomial function $y = f(x)$. SEE EXAMPLE 4
    - $f(x)$ is positive on the intervals $(-\infty, -3)$, $(-2, 0)$, and $(2, 3)$.
    - $f(x)$ is negative on the intervals $(-3, -2)$, $(0, 2)$, and $(3, \infty)$.
    - $f(x)$ is increasing on the interval $(-2.67, -1)$ and $(1, 2.5)$.
    - $f(x)$ is decreasing on the intervals $(-\infty, -2.67)$, $(-1, 1)$, and $(2.5, \infty)$.

27. The equation shown models the average depth y, in feet, of a lake, x years after 2016, where $0 < x < 6$. Use technology to graph the function. In what year does this model predict a relative minimum value for the depth? SEE EXAMPLE 5

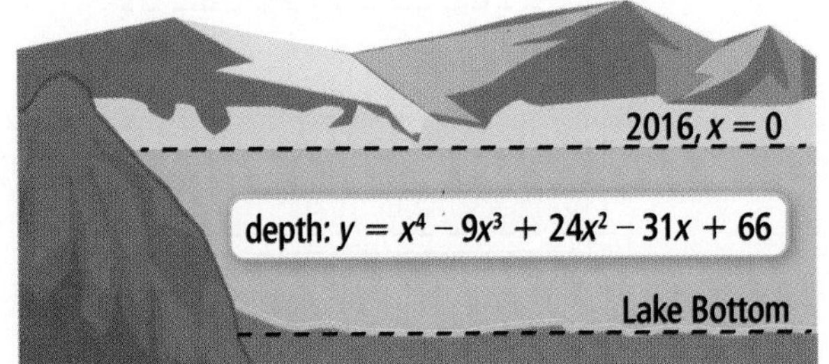

Practice Tutorial

Mixed Review Available Online

PRACTICE & PROBLEM SOLVING

APPLY

28. Reason Allie has a piece of construction paper that she wants to use to make an open rectangular prism. She will cut a square with side length x from each corner of the paper, so the length and width is decreased by $2x$ as shown in the diagram.

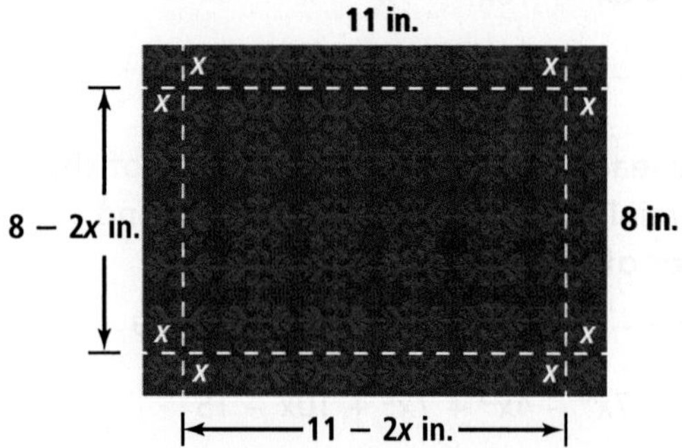

a. Write a function that models the volume of the rectangular prism.

b. Graph the function and identify a reasonable domain.

c. What do the x-intercepts of the graph mean in this context?

d. If Allie wants to maximize the volume of the box, what is the side length of the squares that should be cut from each corner of the piece of construction paper? Explain.

29. Make Sense and Persevere Alberto is designing a container in the shape of a rectangular prism to ship electronic devices. The length of the container is 10 inches longer than the height. The sum of the length, width, and height is 25 inches. The volume of the container, in terms of height x, is shown. Use a graphing calculator to graph the function. What do the x-intercepts of the graph mean in this context? What dimensions of the container will maximize the volume?

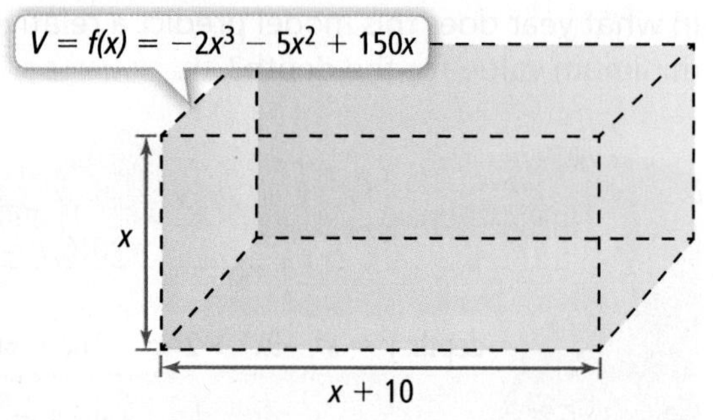

ASSESSMENT PRACTICE

30. Copy and complete the table to give the leading coefficient of each polynomial function.

Polynomial Function	Leading coefficient
$f(x) = 3x^3 + 2x^2 + 9x - 6$	
$f(x) = -3x^4 + 8x^2 - 2x + 7x^5$	
$f(x) = -3x^5 + 7x^3 + 6x^2 - 2$	
$f(x) = 3x^2 - 12x^4 - 3x^6 - 3x^3$	
$f(x) = 6x^3 + 9x^2 - 5x - 3$	

31. SAT/ACT What is the maximum number of terms a fourth-degree polynomial function in standard form can have?

Ⓐ 1 Ⓑ 2 Ⓒ 3 Ⓓ 4 Ⓔ 5

32. Performance Task In the year 2000, a demographer predicted the estimated population of a city, which can be modeled by the function $f(x) = 5x^4 - 4x^3 + 25x + 8{,}000$. Several years later, a statistician, using data from the U.S. Census Bureau, modeled the actual population with the function $P(x) = 7x^4 - 6x^3 + 5x + 8{,}000$. The graphs of the functions are shown.

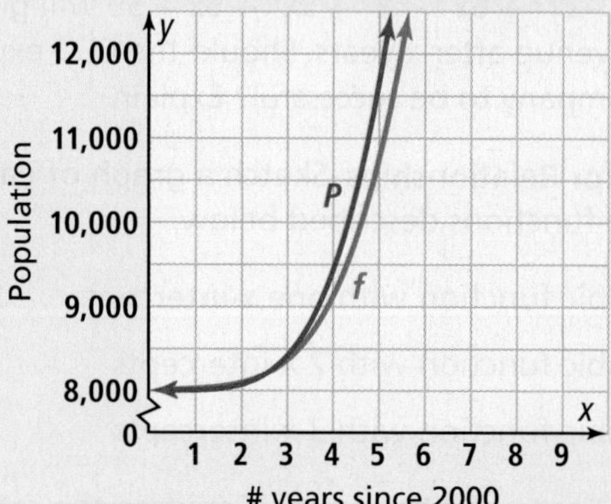

Part A What is the y-intercept of each function, and what does it represent?

Part B Identify the end behaviors of f and P.

Part C Compare the average rates of change of f and P from 2003 to 2005.

 Activity  Assess

2-2 Adding, Subtracting, and Multiplying Polynomials

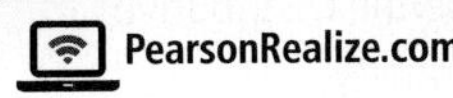

PearsonRealize.com

I CAN… add, subtract, and multiply polynomials.

EXPLORE & REASON

Let S be the set of expressions that can be written as $ax + b$ where a and b are real numbers.

A. Describe the Associative Property, Commutative Property, and the Distributive Property. Then, explain the role of each in simplifying the sum $(3x + 2) + (7x - 4)$. Identify the leading coefficient and the constant term in the result.

B. Is the sum you found in part A a member of S? Explain.

C. **Construct Arguments** Is the product of two expressions in S also a member of S? Explain why or produce a counterexample.

ESSENTIAL QUESTION

How do you add, subtract, and multiply polynomials?

EXAMPLE 1 Add and Subtract Polynomials

How do you add or subtract the polynomials?

To add and subtract polynomials, use the Commutative and Associative Properties to group like terms. Then combine like terms.

A. $(6x^3 + 4x + x^2 - 7) + (2x^3 - 8x^2 + 3)$

$= (6x^3 + 2x^3) + 4x + (x^2 - 8x^2) + (-7 + 3)$ Apply the Commutative and Associative Properties.

$= 8x^3 + 4x - 7x^2 - 4$ Combine like terms.

$= 8x^3 - 7x^2 + 4x - 4$ Write in standard form.

USE STRUCTURE
In order for terms to be *like terms*, the variables and their corresponding exponents must be identical.

B. $(3x^2y^2 + 2xy^2 + 6x^2) - (2x^2y^2 + 3xy^2 - 2x^2)$

$= 3x^2y^2 + 2xy^2 + 6x^2 - 2x^2y^2 - 3xy^2 + 2x^2$ Distribute the factor of −1.

$= (3x^2y^2 - 2x^2y^2) + (2xy^2 - 3xy^2) + (6x^2 + 2x^2)$

$= x^2y^2 - xy^2 + 8x^2$

The degree of a multi-variable polynomial is the greatest sum of powers in any term.

Try It! 1. Add or subtract the polynomials.

a. $(4a^4 - 6a^3 - 3a^2 + a + 1) + (5a^3 + 7a^2 + 2a - 2)$

b. $(2a^2b^2 + 3ab^2 - 5a^2b) - (3a^2b^2 - 9a^2b + 7ab^2)$

EXAMPLE 2 Multiply Polynomials

How do you multiply the polynomials?

To multiply polynomials, use the Distributive Property, then group like terms and combine.

A. $(2m + 5)(3m^2 - 4m + 2)$

$= 2m(3m^2 - 4m + 2) + 5(3m^2 - 4m + 2)$ .... Use the Distributive Property.

$= 6m^3 - 8m^2 + 4m + 15m^2 - 20m + 10$ .... Use the Distributive Property.

$= 6m^3 + (-8m^2 + 15m^2) + (4m - 20m) + 10$ .... Group like terms.

$= 6m^3 + 7m^2 - 16m + 10$ .... Combine like terms.

B. $(mn + 1)(mn - 2)(mn + 4)$

$= [(mn + 1)(mn - 2)](mn + 4)$ .... Multiply two binomials first.

$= (m^2n^2 - 2mn + mn - 2)(mn + 4)$ .... Use the Distributive Property.

$= (m^2n^2 - mn - 2)(mn + 4)$ .... Combine like terms.

$= m^2n^2(mn + 4) + (-mn)(mn + 4) + (-2)(mn + 4)$ .... Use the Distributive Property.

$= m^3n^3 + 4m^2n^2 - m^2n^2 - 4mn - 2mn - 8$ .... Use the Distributive Property.

$= m^3n^3 + (4m^2n^2 - m^2n^2) + (-4mn - 2mn) - 8$ .... Group like terms.

$= m^3n^3 + 3m^2n^2 - 6mn - 8$ .... Combine like terms.

Try It! 2. Multiply the polynomials.

a. $(6n^2 - 7)(n^2 + n + 3)$

b. $(mn + 1)(m^2n - 1)(mn^2 + 2)$

CONCEPTUAL UNDERSTANDING

EXAMPLE 3 Understand Closure

Is the set of polynomials closed under addition and subtraction? Explain.

COMMUNICATE PRECISELY
Can you think of two real numbers such that when you add them, the result is NOT a real number?

The set of real numbers is closed under addition: if a and b are real and $a + b = c$, then c is also real.

Add two polynomials:

$$\begin{array}{l} (a_nx^n + a_{n-1}x^{n-1} + \ldots + a_2x^2 + a_1x + a_0) \\ +\,(b_nx^n + b_{n-1}x^{n-1} + \ldots + b_2x^2 + b_1x + b_0) \\ \hline (a_n + b_n)x^n + (a_{n-1} + b_{n-1})x^{n-1} + \ldots + (a_2 + b_2)x^2 + (a_1 + b_1)x + (a_0 + b_0) \end{array}$$

Adding like terms does not change the variable factor(s) of the terms, only the coefficient: $-3x^2y^2 + 9x^2y^2 = 6x^2y^2$.

Since a and b are real, $(a + b)$ is also real. The exponents are unchanged. The sum is still a polynomial, so the set of polynomials is closed under addition.

Using the same logic, you can determine that the set of polynomials is closed under subtraction.

Try It! 3. Is the set of monomials closed under multiplication? Explain.

Activity

Assess

APPLICATION

EXAMPLE 4 Write a Polynomial Function

Carolina makes wind chimes to sell at the local street market.

As Carolina produces a greater number of wind chimes, she can lower the price per unit. The function $v(x) = 48 - 2x$ relates the price v to the number produced x. The cost c of making x wind chimes can be represented with the function $c(x) = 12x + 64$.

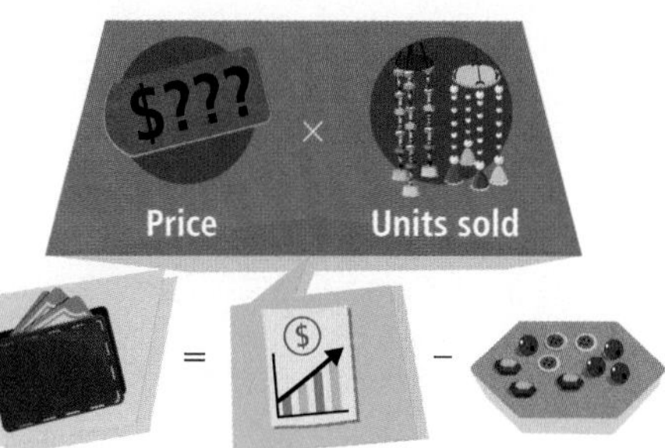

How many wind chimes should Carolina sell each week to maximize her profit P?

Formulate Write a function for revenue R by multiplying the price $v(x) = 48 - 2x$ of each item by the number sold x.

$$R(x) = (48 - 2x)x$$

Then write the function for profit P.

$$P(x) = R(x) - c(x) \quad \text{Profit = Revenue − Cost}$$

$$= (48 - 2x)x - (12x + 64). \quad \text{Substitute for } R(x) \text{ and } c(x).$$

Compute Simplify the function.

$$P(x) = (48 - 2x)x - (12x + 64) \quad \text{Write the profit function.}$$

$$= (48x - 2x^2) - (12x + 64) \quad \text{Use the Distributive Property.}$$

$$= 48x - 2x^2 - 12x - 64 \quad \text{Distribute the factor of } -1.$$

$$= -2x^2 + 36x - 64 \quad \text{Combine like terms.}$$

Carolina's profit function is $P(x) = -2x^2 + 36x - 64$.

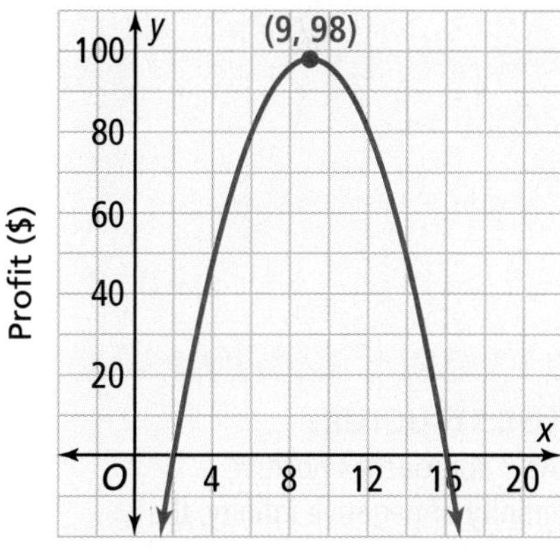

Interpret Carolina's profit is modeled by a quadratic function. The domain of the function is the set of whole numbers. Her maximum profit corresponds to the vertex of the graph.

Carolina's best business plan is to produce and sell 9 wind chimes per week, for a weekly profit of $98.

Try It! 4. The cost of Carolina's materials changes so that her new cost function is $c(x) = 4x + 42$.

Find the new profit function. Then find the quantity that maximizes profit and calculate the profit.

APPLICATION

EXAMPLE 5 Compare Two Polynomial Functions

Carolina's profit function, $y = P(x)$ is represented by the graph. Kiyo's profit from selling x flowerpots can be modeled by the function shown.

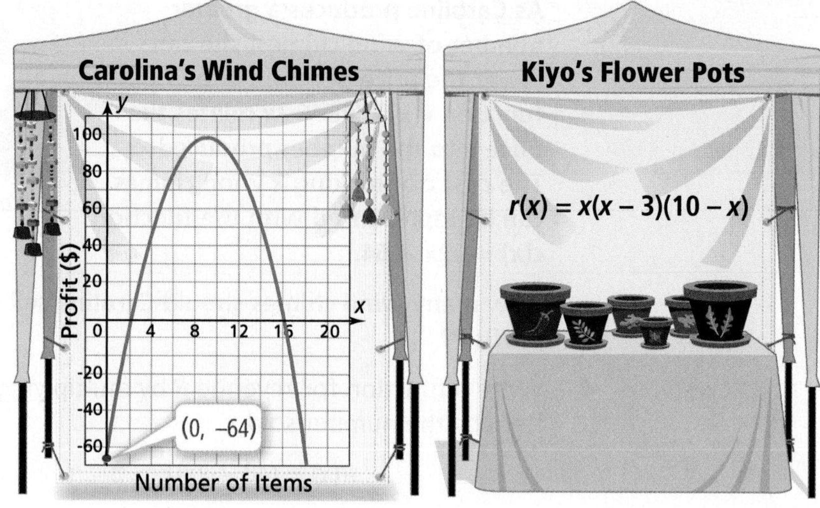

A. Find the y-intercept of each function. Who would lose more money if neither person sold any items?

The y-intercept of $P(x)$ is -64. If Carolina does not sell any wind chimes this week, she will lose \$64.

Carolina has startup costs, which she pays whether she sells any items or not.

Substitute 0 for x in r to find the y-intercept.

$r(0) = 0(0 - 3)(10 - 0)$ Substitute 0 for x.

$= 0$ Simplify.

Kiyo has no startup costs.

The y-intercept of r is 0. If Kiyo does not sell any flowerpots, he will not lose any money. So, Carolina loses more money by not making any sales.

B. Interpret the end behavior of the functions.

The domain of each function includes only non-negative values.

The graph of $P(x)$ shows that the end behavior, as $x \to \infty$, is $y \to -\infty$.

Rewrite the function r in standard form to identify end behavior.

$r(x) = x(x - 3)(10 - x)$

$= (x^2 - 3x)(10 - x)$ Use the Distributive Property.

$= -x^3 + 13x^2 - 30x$ Combine like terms.

Because the leading coefficient is negative, we know that as $x \to \infty$, $y \to -\infty$.

USE STRUCTURE
As x approaches positive infinity or negative infinity, the leading term of the polynomial determines the end behavior of the graph of the function.

Kiyo and Carolina each have a finite number of items they should sell to maximize profits.

Try It! 5. Compare the profit functions of two additional market sellers modeled by the graph of f and the equation $g(x) = (x + 1)(5 - x)$. Compare and interpret the y-intercepts of these functions and their end behavior.

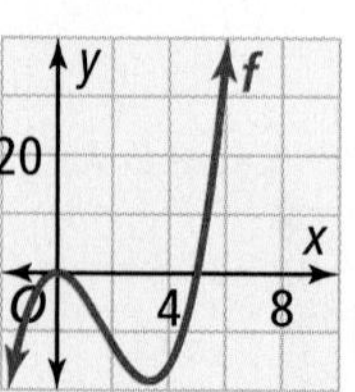

CONCEPT SUMMARY Adding, Subtracting, and Multiplying Polynomials

ADD To add polynomials, use the Associative and Commutative Properties to group like terms. Then use the Distributive Property to combine like terms.

$$(2x^2 + 5x - 7) + (3x^2 - 9x + 12)$$
$$= (2x^2 + 3x^2) + (5x - 9x) + (-7 + 12)$$
$$= 5x^2 - 4x + 5$$

SUBTRACT To subtract polynomials, distribute the factor of −1. Then, group and combine like terms.

$$(6x^3 + 2x^2 + 14) - (4x^3 + 4x^2 - 8)$$
$$= 6x^3 + 2x^2 + 14 - 4x^3 - 4x^2 + 8$$

Distribute the factor of −1 to each term.

$$= (6x^3 - 4x^3) + (2x^2 - 4x^2) + (14 + 8)$$
$$= 2x^3 - 2x^2 + 22$$

MULTIPLY To multiply polynomials, use the Distributive Property. Then, group and combine like terms.

$$(x + 5)(3x^2 - 2x + 4)$$
$$= x(3x^2 - 2x + 4) + 5(3x^2 - 2x + 4)$$
$$= 3x^3 - 2x^2 + 4x + 15x^2 - 10x + 20$$
$$= 3x^3 + (-2x^2 + 15x^2) + (4x - 10x) + 20$$
$$= 3x^3 + 13x^2 - 6x + 20$$

Do You UNDERSTAND?

1. **ESSENTIAL QUESTION** How do you add, subtract, and multiply polynomials?

2. **Error Analysis** Chen subtracted two polynomials as shown. Explain Chen's error.

$p^2 + 7mp + 4 - (-2p^2 - mp + 1)$

$p^2 + 2p^2 + 7mp - mp + 4 + 1$

$3p^2 + 6mp + 5$ ✗

3. **Communicate Precisely** Why do we often write the results of polynomial calculations in standard form?

4. **Construct Arguments** Is the set of whole numbers closed under subtraction? Explain why you think so, or provide a counterexample.

Do You KNOW HOW?

Add or subtract the polynomials.

5. $(-3a^3 + 2a^2 - 4) + (a^3 - 3a^2 - 5a + 7)$

6. $(7x^2y^2 - 6x^3 + xy) - (5x^2y^2 - x^3 + xy + x)$

Multiply the polynomials.

7. $(7a + 2)(2a^2 - 5a + 3)$

8. $(xy - 1)(xy + 6)(xy - 8)$

9. The length of a rectangular speaker is three times its width, and the height is four more than the width. Write an expression for the volume V of the rectangular prism in terms of its width w.

PRACTICE & PROBLEM SOLVING

Scan for Multimedia

 Practice  Tutorial

Additional Exercises Available Online

UNDERSTAND

10. **Generalize** Explain two methods by which $(2m^3 + 4n^2)^2$ can be simplified. Which method do you prefer and why?

11. **Use Structure** Polynomial function P is the sum of two polynomial functions, one with degree 2 and a positive leading coefficient and one with degree 3 and a negative leading coefficient. Describe the end behavior of P. Write an example of two polynomial functions and their sum, P, to justify your description.

12. **Generalize** Multiply the polynomials $(a + b)(a + b)(a + b)$ to develop a general formula for cubing a binomial, $(a + b)^3$.

13. **Reason** Polynomial function R is the difference of two degree-two polynomial functions. What are the possible degrees for R? Explain.

14. **Error Analysis** Describe and correct the error a student made in multiplying the polynomials.

$(y - 2)(3y^2 - y - 7)$
$= y(3y^2 - y - 7) - 2(3y^2 - y - 7)$
$= 3y^3 - y^2 - 7y + (-6y^2) + (-2y) - 14$
$= 3y^3 - 7y^2 - 9y - 14$ ✗

15. **Higher Order Thinking** Do you think polynomials are closed under division? Explain why you think so, or provide a counterexample.

16. **Construct Arguments** Explain why the expression $9x^3 + \frac{1}{2}x^2 + 3x^{-1}$ is not a polynomial.

17. **Communicate Precisely** Explain the difference between the graphs of polynomial functions with a degree of 3 that have a positive leading coefficient and the graphs of those with a negative leading coefficient.

PRACTICE

Add or subtract the polynomials. SEE EXAMPLE 1

18. $(2x^3 + 3x^2 + 4) + (6x^3 - x^2 - 5x)$

19. $(5y^4 + 3y^3 - 6y^2 + 14) - (-y^4 + y^2 - 7y - 1)$

20. $(4p^2q^2 + 2p^2q - 7pq) - (9p^2q^2 + 5pq^2 - 11pq)$

Multiply the polynomials. SEE EXAMPLE 2

21. $-4xy(5x^2 - 9xy - y^2)$

22. $(3c - 4)(2c^2 - 5c + 7)$

23. $(z + 5)(z - 9)(1 - z)$

24. Is the set of monomials closed under addition? Explain why you think so, or provide a counterexample. SEE EXAMPLE 3

25. An online shopping club has 13,500 members when it charges \$8 per month for membership. For each \$1 monthly increase in membership fee, the club loses approximately 500 of its existing members.

Write and simplify a function R to represent the monthly revenue received by the club when x represents the price increase.

Hint Monthly revenue = # members • monthly fee SEE EXAMPLE 4

26. The graph shows a polynomial function f. Polynomial function g is defined by $g(x) = x^2(6 - x)$. Compare the maximum values and the end behavior of the functions f and g when $x > 0$.
SEE EXAMPLE 5

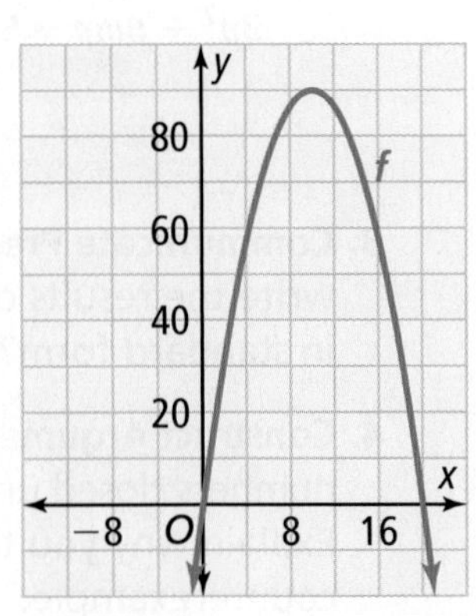

PRACTICE & PROBLEM SOLVING

Practice Tutorial

Mixed Review Available Online

APPLY

Use this information for 27 and 28. A foundry manufactures aluminum trays from pieces of sheet metal as shown.

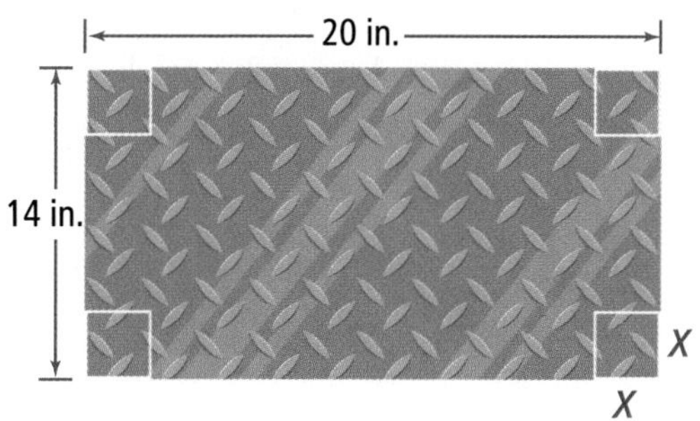

27. **Model With Mathematics** Let x represent the side length of each square.

    a. Write expressions for the length, width, and height of the metal tray.

    b. Write and simplify a polynomial function V to represent the volume of the tray.

    c. Using the graph of the function V, explain what the marked relative maximum represents.

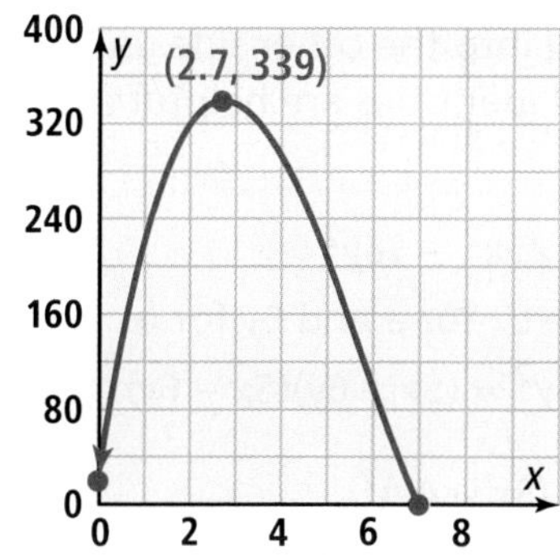

28. **Reason** Suppose the foundry manufacturer has a new design where the squares cut from the corners have sides that are half the length of the squares in the previous design.

    a. Write expressions for the length, width, and height of this tray.

    b. Write and simplify the polynomial function $v(x)$, to represent the volume of the new tray.

    c. Write the function $D(x)$ that represents the difference, $V(x) - v(x)$.

29. **Make Sense and Persevere** Jacy has $1,000 to invest in a fund that pays approximately 4.6% per year or in a savings account with an annual interest rate of 1.8%. Write a polynomial function $S(x)$ to represent the interest Jacy will earn in 1 year by investing x dollars in the fund and the remainder in the savings account.

ASSESSMENT PRACTICE

30. Are polynomials open or closed under each operation? Classify each operation as *open* or *closed*.

    a. addition

    b. subtraction

    c. multiplication

    d. division

31. **SAT/ACT** Which of the following functions is NOT a polynomial function?

    Ⓐ $2y^2 + 9y - 8$

    Ⓑ $-\frac{1}{2}x^3 + 8$

    Ⓒ $(x - 1)(5 - x)(x + 4)$

    Ⓓ $9z^4 + 2z + \frac{1}{z}$

32. **Performance Task** Consider the polynomial functions $P(x) = x^2 - 4$ and $R(x) = -x^2 - 2x$.

    Part A Write and simplify a polynomial function $T(x)$ that is the product of P and R.

    Part B Copy and complete the table of values for all three functions.

x	$P(x)$	$R(x)$	$T(x)$
–3			
–2			
–1			
0			
1			
2			
3			

Part C Graph the functions on the same coordinate grid.

Part D How do the zeros of T relate to the zeros of P and R?

Part E Explain how you can identify the intervals in which T is positive by analyzing the R and P.

Activity Assess

2-3 Polynomial Identities

I CAN... prove and use polynomial identities.

VOCABULARY

- Binomial Theorem
- identity
- Pascal's Triangle

EXPLORE & REASON

Look at the following triangle.

Each number is the sum of the two numbers diagonally above. If there is not a second number, think of it as 0.

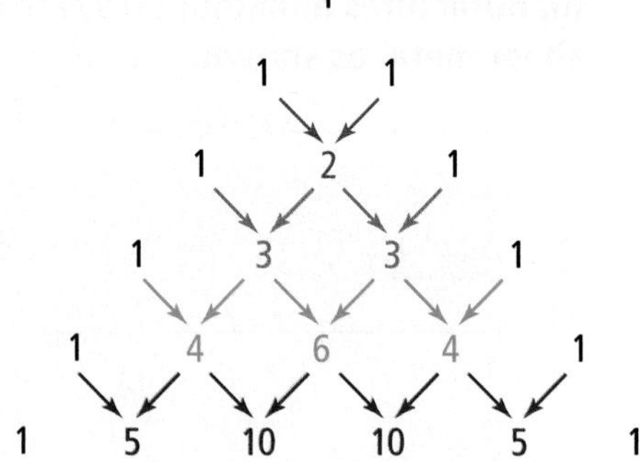

A. Write the numbers in the next three rows.

B. Look for Relationships What other patterns do you see?

C. Find the sum of the numbers in each row of the triangle. Write a formula for the sum of the numbers in the nth row.

ESSENTIAL QUESTION

How can you use polynomial identities to rewrite expressions efficiently?

CONCEPT Polynomial Identities

A mathematical statement that equates two polynomial expressions is an **identity** if one side can be transformed into the other side using mathematical operations. These polynomial identities are helpful tools used to multiply and factor polynomials.

Difference of Squares

$a^2 - b^2 = (a + b)(a - b)$

Example: $25x^2 - 36y^2$

Substitute $5x$ for a and $6y$ for b.

$25x^2 - 36y^2 = (5x + 6y)(5x - 6y)$

Square of a Sum

$(a + b)^2 = a^2 + 2ab + b^2$

Example: $(3x + 4y)^2$

Substitute $3x$ for a and $4y$ for b.

$(3x + 4y)^2 = (3x)^2 + 2(3x)(4y) + (4y)^2$

$= 9x^2 + 24xy + 16y^2$

Difference of Cubes

$a^3 - b^3 = (a - b)(a^2 + ab + b^2)$

Example: $8m^3 - 27$

Substitute $2m$ for a and 3 for b.

$8m^3 - 27 = (2m - 3)[(2m)^2 + (2m)(3) + 3^2]$

$= (2m - 3)(4m^2 + 6m + 9)$

Sum of Cubes

$a^3 + b^3 = (a + b)(a^2 - ab + b^2)$

Example: $g^3 + 64h^3$

Substitute g for a and $4h$ for b.

$g^3 + 64h^3 = (g + 4h)[g^2 - (g)(4h) + (4h)^2]$

$= (g + 4h)(g^2 - 4gh + 16h^2)$

EXAMPLE 1 Prove a Polynomial Identity

How can you prove the Sum of Cubes Identity, $a^3 + b^3 = (a + b)(a^2 - ab + b^2)$?

To prove an identity, start with the expression on one side of the equation and use properties of operations on polynomials to transform it into the expression on the other side.

USE STRUCTURE
Another way to establish the identity is to multiply each term of the second factor by $(a + b)$, and then combine like terms.

$(a + b)(a^2 - ab + b^2)$

$= a(a^2 - ab + b^2) + b(a^2 - ab + b^2)$ ······ Use the Distributive Property.

$= a^3 - a^2b + ab^2 + a^2b - ab^2 + b^3$ ······ Use the Distributive Property.

$= a^3 + (-a^2b + a^2b) + (ab^2 - ab^2) + b^3$ ······ Group like terms.

$= a^3 + b^3$ ······ Combine like terms.

So, $a^3 + b^3 = (a + b)(a^2 - ab + b^2)$.

Try It! **1.** Prove the Difference of Cubes Identity.

EXAMPLE 2 Use Polynomial Identities to Multiply

How can you use polynomial identities to multiply expressions?

A. $(2x^2 + y^3)^2$

The sum is a binomial, and the entire sum is being raised to the second power.

COMMON ERROR
When finding $(a + b)^2$, recall that it is not sufficient to square the first term and square the second term. You must distribute the two binomials.

Use the Square of a Sum Identity to find the product:

$(a + b)^2 = a^2 + 2ab + b^2$

$(2x^2 + y^3)^2 = (2x^2)^2 + 2(2x^2)(y^3) + (y^3)^2$ ······ Substitute $2x^2$ for a and y^3 for b.

$= 4x^4 + 4x^2y^3 + y^6$ ······ Simplify.

So, $(2x^2 + y^3)^2 = 4x^4 + 4x^2y^3 + y^6$.

B. $41 \bullet 39$

Rewrite the expression in terms of a and b.

$41 \bullet 39 = (a + b)(a - b)$

$= (40 + 1)(40 - 1)$

Use the Difference of Squares Identity:

$(40 + 1)(40 - 1) = 40^2 - 1^2$

$= 1{,}600 - 1$

$= 1{,}599$

So $41 \bullet 39 = 1{,}599$.

Try It! **2.** Use polynomial identities to multiply the expressions.

a. $(3x^2 + 5y^3)(3x^2 - 5y^3)$ **b.** $(12 + 15)^2$

EXAMPLE 3 Use Polynomial Identities to Factor and Simplify

How can you use polynomial identities to factor polynomials and simplify numerical expressions?

A. $9m^4 - 25n^6$

$9m^4$ and $25n^6$ are both perfect squares.

A square term includes an even exponent, not necessarily an exponent that is a perfect square.

$9m^4 = (3m^2)^2$

$25n^6 = (5n^3)^2$

Use the Difference of Squares Identity: $a^2 - b^2 = (a + b)(a - b)$.

$9m^4 - 25n^6 = (3m^2)^2 - (5n^3)^2$ Express each term as a square.

$= (3m^2 + 5n^3)(3m^2 - 5n^3)$ Write the factors.

So, $9m^4 - 25n^6 = (3m^2 + 5n^3)(3m^2 - 5n^3)$.

B. $x^3 - 216$

x^3 and 216 are both perfect cubes.

$x^3 = (x)^3$

$216 = 6^3$

Use the Difference of Cubes Identity: $a^3 - b^3 = (a - b)(a^2 + ab + b^2)$.

$x^3 - 216 = (x)^3 - (6)^3$ Express each term as a cube.

$= (x - 6)(x^2 + 6x + 36)$ Write the factors.

So, $x^3 - 216 = (x - 6)(x^2 + 6x + 36)$.

COMMON ERROR
The second factor is *almost* a Square of a Sum. Remember that the middle term of the Difference of Cubes Identity is the product *ab*, not 2*ab*.

C. $11^3 + 5^3$

Use the Sum of Cubes Identity: $a^3 + b^3 = (a + b)(a^2 - ab + b^2)$.

$11^3 + 5^3 = (11 + 5)(11^2 - 11(5) + 5^2)$

$= (16)(121 - 55 + 25)$

$= 16(91)$

$= 1{,}456$

So, $11^3 + 5^3 = 1{,}456$.

 **Try It!** **3.** Use polynomial identities to factor each polynomial.

a. $m^8 - 9n^{10}$ **b.** $27x^9 - 343y^6$ **c.** $12^3 + 2^3$

Activity

Assess

CONCEPTUAL UNDERSTANDING

EXAMPLE 4 Expand a Power of a Binomial

How is $(x + y)^n$ obtained from $(x + y)^{n-1}$?

A. What are $(x + y)^3$ and $(x + y)^4$?

$$(x + y)^3 = (x + y)(x + y)^2$$
$$= (x + y)(x^2 + 2xy + y^2)$$

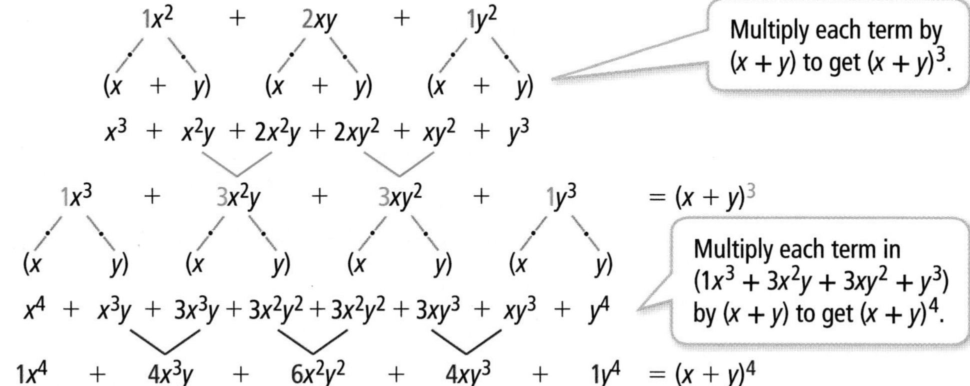

$1x^3 + 3x^2y + 3xy^2 + 1y^3 = (x + y)^3$

$(x \quad y) \quad (x \quad y) \quad (x \quad y) \quad (x \quad y)$

$x^4 + x^3y + 3x^3y + 3x^2y^2 + 3x^2y^2 + 3xy^3 + xy^3 + y^4$

Multiply each term in $(1x^3 + 3x^2y + 3xy^2 + y^3)$ by $(x + y)$ to get $(x + y)^4$.

$1x^4 + 4x^3y + 6x^2y^2 + 4xy^3 + 1y^4 = (x + y)^4$

The coefficients of $(x + y)^n$ are produced by adding the coefficients of $(x + y)^{n-1}$, producing an array known as Pascal's Triangle. **Pascal's Triangle** is the triangular pattern of numbers where each number is the sum of the two numbers diagonally above it. If there is not a second number diagonally above in the triangle, think of the missing number as 0.

Row	Coefficients	Expansion	Power
Row 0	1	1	$(x + y)^0$
Row 1	1 1	$1x + 1y$	$(x + y)^1$
Row 2	1 2 1	$1x^2 + 2xy + 1y^2$	$(x + y)^2$
Row 3	1 3 3 1	$1x^3 + 3x^2y + 3xy^2 + 1y^3$	$(x + y)^3$
Row 4	1 4 6 4 1	$1x^4 + 4x^3y + 6x^2y^2 + 4xy^3 + 1y^4$	$(x + y)^4$

STUDY TIP
Notice the patterns of the powers. The powers of x decrease from n to 0 and the powers of y increase from 0 to n when reading the terms from left to right.

You can obtain $(x + y)^n$ by adding adjacent pairs of coefficients from $(x + y)^{n-1}$.

B. Use Pascal's Triangle to expand $(x + y)^5$.

Add pairs of coefficients from Row 4 to complete Row 5.

Row 4   1   4   6   4   1

Row 5   1   5   10   10   5   1

Write the expansion. Use the coefficients from Row 5 with powers of x starting at 5 and decreasing to 0 and with powers of y starting at 0 and increasing to 5.

The sum of the exponents in each term is equal to the exponent on the original binomial.

$$(x + y)^5 = 1x^5 + 5x^4y + 10x^3y^2 + 10x^2y^3 + 5xy^4 + 1y^5$$

Try It! **4.** Use Pascal's Triangle to expand $(x + y)^6$.

CONCEPT Binomial Theorem

The **Binomial Theorem** states that, for every positive integer n,

$$(a + b)^n = C_0a^n + C_1a^{n-1}b + C_2a^{n-2}b^2 + \ldots + C_{n-1}ab^{n-1} + C_nb^n.$$

The coefficients $C_0, C_1, C_2, \ldots, C_{n-1}, C_n$ are the numbers in Row n of Pascal's Triangle.

Notice that the powers of a are decreasing while the powers of b are increasing, and that the sum of the powers of a and b in each term is always n.

EXAMPLE 5 Apply the Binomial Theorem

Use the Binomial Theorem to expand the expressions.

A. Find $(x - 3)^4$.

Step 1 Use the Binomial Theorem to write the expansion when $n = 4$.

$$C_0a^4 + C_1a^3b + C_2a^2b^2 + C_3ab^3 + C_4b^4$$

Step 2 Use Row 4 in Pascal's Triangle to write the coefficients.

$$a^4 + 4a^3b + 6a^2b^2 + 4ab^3 + b^4$$

Pascal's Triangle

1
1 1
1 2 1
1 3 3 1
1 4 6 4 1
1 5 10 10 5 1

Step 3 Identify a and b.

$$a = x \text{ and } b = -3$$

COMMON ERROR
Remember that the base of $(a + b)^n$ in the Binomial Theorem is $(a + b)$. If the terms are being subtracted, use the opposite of b in the expansion.

Step 4 Substitute x for a and -3 for b in the pattern. Then simplify.

$$x^4 + 4x^3(-3) + 6x^2(-3)^2 + 4x(-3)^3 + (-3)^4$$

$$x^4 - 12x^3 + 54x^2 - 108x + 81$$

So $(x - 3)^4 = x^4 - 12x^3 + 54x^2 - 108x + 81$.

B. Find $(s^2 + 3)^5$.

The expansion of $(a + b)^5$ is $a^5 + 5a^4b + 10a^3b^2 + 10a^2b^3 + 5ab^4 + b^5$.

Since $a = s^2$ and $b = 3$, the expansion is:

$$(s^2 + 3)^5 = (s^2)^5 + 5(s^2)^4(3) + 10(s^2)^3(3)^2 + 10(s^2)^2(3)^3 + 5(s^2)(3)^4 + (3)^5$$

$$= s^{10} + 15s^8 + 90s^6 + 270s^4 + 405s^2 + 243$$

So $(s^2 + 3)^5 = s^{10} + 15s^8 + 90s^6 + 270s^4 + 405s^2 + 243$.

Try It! 5. Use the Binomial Theorem to expand each expression.

a. $(x - 1)^7$

b. $(2c + d)^6$

CONCEPT SUMMARY Polynomial Identities

POLYNOMIAL IDENTITIES

Special polynomial identities can be used to multiply and factor polynomials.

Difference of Squares

$a^2 - b^2 = (a + b)(a - b)$

Square of a Sum

$(a + b)^2 = a^2 + 2ab + b^2$

Difference of Cubes

$a^3 - b^3 = (a - b)(a^2 + ab + b^2)$

Sum of Cubes

$a^3 + b^3 = (a + b)(a^2 - ab + b^2)$

BINOMIAL EXPANSION

The binomial expansion of $(a + b)^n$ has the following properties:

1) The expansion contains $n + 1$ terms.

2) The coefficients of each term are numbers from the nth row of Pascal's Triangle.

3) The exponent of a is n in the first term and decreases by 1 in each successive term.

4) The exponent of b is 0 in the first term and increases by 1 in each successive term.

5) The sum of the exponents in any term is n.

Row	Pascal's Triangle	Expansion	Binomial
Row 0	1	1	$(x + y)^0$
Row 1	1 1	$1x + 1y$	$(x + y)^1$
Row 2	1 2 1	$1x^2 + 2xy + 1y^2$	$(x + y)^2$
Row 3	1 3 3 1	$1x^3 + 3x^2y + 3xy^2 + 1y^3$	$(x + y)^3$
Row 4	1 4 6 4 1	$1x^4 + 4x^3y + 6x^2y^2 + 4xy^3 + 1y^4$	$(x + y)^4$

Do You UNDERSTAND?

1. ESSENTIAL QUESTION How can you use polynomial identities to rewrite expressions efficiently?

2. **Reason** Explain why the middle term of $(x + 5)^2$ is $10x$.

3. **Communicate Precisely** How are Pascal's Triangle and a binomial expansion, such as $(a + b)^5$, related?

4. **Use Structure** Explain how to use a polynomial identity to factor $8x^6 - 27y^3$.

5. **Make Sense and Persevere** What number does C_3 represent in the expansion $C_0a^5 + C_1a^4b + C_2a^3b^2 + C_3a^2b^3 + C_4ab^4 + C_5b^5$? Explain.

6. **Error Analysis** Dakota said the third term of the expansion of $(2g + 3h)^4$ is $36g^2h^2$. Explain Dakota's error. Then correct the error.

Do You KNOW HOW?

Use polynomial identities to multiply each expression.

7. $(2x + 8y)(2x - 8y)$

8. $(x + 3y^3)^2$

Use polynomial identities to factor each polynomial.

9. $36a^6 - 4b^2$

10. $8x^6 - y^3$

11. $m^9 + 27n^6$

Find the term of the binomial expansion.

12. fifth term of $(x + y)^5$

13. third term of $(a - 3)^6$

Use Pascal's Triangle to expand each expression.

14. $(x + 1)^5$

15. $(a - b)^6$

Use the Binomial Theorem to expand each expression.

16. $(d - 1)^4$

17. $(x + y)^7$

PRACTICE & PROBLEM SOLVING

Scan for Multimedia

 Practice  Tutorial

Additional Exercises Available Online

UNDERSTAND

18. Use Structure Expand $(3x + 4y)^3$ using Pascal's Triangle and the Binomial Theorem.

19. Error Analysis Emma factored $625g^{16} - 25h^4$. Describe and correct the error Emma made in factoring the polynomial.

$625g^{16} - 25h^4$
$= (25g^4)^2 - (5h^2)^2$
$= (25g^4 + 5h^2)(25g^4 - 5h^2)$
X

20. Higher Order Thinking Use Pascal's Triangle and the Binomial Theorem to expand $(x + i)^4$. Justify your work.

21. Use Structure Expand the expression $(2x - 1)^4$. What is the sum of the coefficients?

22. Error Analysis A student says that the expansion of the expression $(-4y + z)^7$ has seven terms. Describe and correct the error the student may have made.

23. Reason The sum of the coefficients in the expansion of the expression $(a + b)^n$ is 64. Use Pascal's Triangle to find the value of n.

24. Use Structure Factor $x^3 - 125y^6$ in the form $(x - A)(x^2 + Bx + C)$. What are the values of A, B, and C?

25. Generalize How many terms will there be in the expansion of the expression $(x + 3)^n$? Explain how you know.

26. Make Sense and Persevere How could you use polynomial identities to factor the expression $x^6 - y^6$?

PRACTICE

27. Prove the polynomial identity.
$x^4 - y^4 = (x - y)(x + y)(x^2 + y^2)$
SEE EXAMPLE 1

Use polynomial identities to multiply the expressions. SEE EXAMPLE 2

28. $(x + 9)(x - 9)$
29. $(x + 6)^2$
30. $(3x - 7)^2$
31. $(2x - 5)(2x + 5)$
32. $(4x^2 + 6y^2)(4x^2 - 6y^2)$
33. $(x^2 + y^6)^2$
34. $(8 - x^2)(8 + x^2)$
35. $(6 - y^3)^2$
36. $18 \bullet 22$
37. $103 \bullet 97$
38. $(7 + 9)^2$
39. $(10 + 5)^2$

Use polynomial identities to factor the polynomials or simplify the expressions. SEE EXAMPLE 3

40. $x^8 - 9$
41. $x^9 - 8$
42. $8x^3 + y^9$
43. $x^6 - 27y^3$
44. $4x^2 - y^6$
45. $216 + 27y^{12}$
46. $64x^3 - 125y^6$
47. $\frac{1}{16}x^6 - 25y^4$
48. $9^3 + 6^3$
49. $10^3 + 5^3$
50. $10^3 - 3^3$
51. $8^3 - 2^3$

Use the Binomial Theorem to expand the expressions. SEE EXAMPLES 4 and 5

52. $(x + 3)^3$
53. $(2a - b)^5$
54. $\left(b - \frac{1}{2}\right)^4$
55. $(x^2 + 1)^4$
56. $\left(2x + \frac{1}{3}\right)^3$
57. $(x^3 + y^2)^6$
58. $(d - 3)^4$
59. $(2m + 2n)^6$
60. $(n + 5)^5$
61. $(3x - 0.2)^3$
62. $(4g + 2h)^4$
63. $\left(m^2 + \frac{1}{2}n\right)^3$

PRACTICE & PROBLEM SOLVING

APPLY

64. Reason A medium-sized shipping box with side length s units has a volume of s^3 cubic units.

a. A large shipping box has side lengths that are 3 units longer than the medium shipping box. Write a binomial expression for the volume of the large shipping box.

b. Expand the polynomial in part a to simplify the volume of the large shipping box.

c. A small shipping box has side lengths that are 2 units shorter than the medium shipping box. Write a binomial expression for the volume of the small shipping box.

d. Expand the polynomial in part c to simplify the volume of the small shipping box.

65. Use Structure The dimensions of a rectangle are shown. Write the area of the rectangle as a sum of cubes.

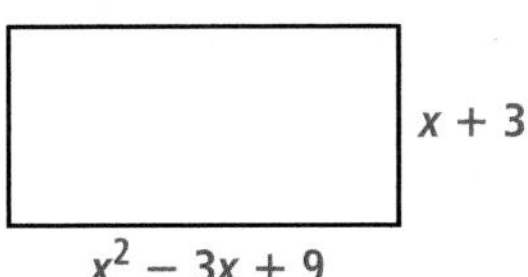

66. A Pythagorean triple is a set of three positive integers a, b, and c that satisfy $a^2 + b^2 = c^2$. The identity $(x^2 - y^2)^2 + (2xy)^2 = (x^2 + y^2)^2$ can be used to generate Pythagorean triples. Use the identity to generate a Pythagorean triple when $x = 5$ and $y = 4$.

ASSESSMENT PRACTICE

67. Are the expressions below perfect square trinomials? Select *Yes* or *No*.

	Yes	No
$x^2 + 16x + 64$		
$4x^2 - 44x + 121$		
$9x^2 - 15x + 25$		

68. SAT/ACT How many terms are in the expansion of $(2x + 7y)^9$?

Ⓐ 2 Ⓑ 7 Ⓒ 8 Ⓓ 9 Ⓔ 10

69. Performance Task If an event has a probability of success p and a probability of failure q, then each term in the expansion of $(p + q)^n$ represents a probability. For example, if a basketball player makes 60% of his free throw attempts, $p = 0.6$ and $q = 0.4$. To find the probability the basketball player will make exactly h out of k free throws, find $C_{k-h}p^hq^{k-h}$, where C_{k-h} is a coefficient of row k of Pascal's Triangle, p is the probability of success, and q is the probability of failure.

Part A What is the probability the basketball player will make exactly 6 out of 10 free throws? Round to the nearest percent.

Part B Another basketball player makes 80% of her free throw attempts. Write an expression to find the probability of this basketball player making exactly 7 out of 10 free throws. Describe what each variable in the expression represents.

Part C Find the probability that the basketball player from Part B will make exactly 7 out of 10 free throws. Round to the nearest percent.

2-4 Dividing Polynomials

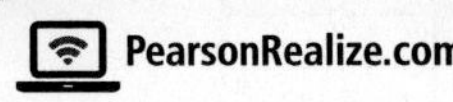

I CAN... divide polynomials.

VOCABULARY

- Factor Theorem
- Remainder Theorem
- synthetic division

EXPLORE & REASON

Benson recalls how to divide whole numbers by solving a problem with 6 as the divisor and 83 as the dividend. He determines that the quotient is 13 with remainder 5.

A. Explain the process of long division using Benson's example.

B. How can you express the remainder as a fraction?

C. Use Structure Use the results of the division problem to write two expressions for 83 that include the divisor, quotient, and remainder.

ESSENTIAL QUESTION

How can you divide polynomials?

EXAMPLE 1 Use Long Division to Divide Polynomials

How can you use long division to divide *P*(*x*) by *D*(*x*)? Write the polynomial *P*(*x*) in terms of the quotient and remainder.

LOOK FOR RELATIONSHIPS
Compare the long division of these two polynomials to this numerical long division problem.

$$\begin{array}{r} 120 \\ 13\overline{)1{,}569} \\ \underline{-13} \\ 26 \\ \underline{-26} \\ 09 \end{array}$$

A. Let $P(x) = x^3 + 5x^2 + 6x + 9$ and $D(x) = x + 3$.

Long division of polynomials is similar to long division of numbers.

$$\begin{array}{r} x^2 + 2x \\ x + 3\overline{)x^3 + 5x^2 + 6x + 9} \\ \underline{-(x^3 + 3x^2)} \\ 2x^2 + 6x + 9 \\ \underline{-(2x^2 + 6x)} \\ 9 \end{array}$$

- Divide the leading terms: $x^3 \div x = x^2$.
- Multiply: $x^2(x + 3) = x^3 + 3x$. Then subtract.
- Divide the leading terms again: $2x^2 \div x = 2x$.
- Multiply: $2x(x + 3) = 2x + 6x$.
- Subtract. The remainder is 9.

When you divide polynomials, you can express the relationship of the quotient and remainder to the dividend and divisor in two ways.

$$\frac{\text{dividend}}{\text{divisor}} = \text{quotient} + \frac{\text{remainder}}{\text{divisor}}$$

$$\text{dividend} = \text{quotient} \times \text{divisor} + \text{remainder}$$

$$\frac{x^3 + 5x^2 + 6x + 9}{x + 3} = x^2 + 2x + \frac{9}{x + 3}$$

$$x^3 + 5x^2 + 6x + 9 = (x^2 + 2x)(x + 3) + 9$$

CONTINUED ON THE NEXT PAGE

EXAMPLE 1 CONTINUED

B. Let $P(x) = 8x^3 + 27$ and $D(x) = 2x + 3$.

The dividend is a cubic polynomial with no first- or second-degree term.

$$\begin{array}{r} 4x^2 - 6x + 9 \\ 2x + 3 \overline{)8x^3 + 0x^2 + 0x + 27} \\ \underline{-(8x^3 + 12x^2)} \\ -12x^2 + 0x + 27 \\ \underline{-(-12x^2 - 18x)} \\ 18x + 27 \\ \underline{-(18x + 27)} \\ 0 \end{array}$$

Use 0 as the coefficient for the missing 1st- and 2nd-degree terms.

The remainder is 0. This means the divisor is a factor of the dividend.

GENERALIZE
When the remainder is 0, you can use the results of the long division to write $P(x)$ in factored form.

So, $\frac{8x^3 + 27}{2x + 3} = 4x^2 - 6x + 9$ and $8x^3 + 27 = (2x + 3)(4x^2 - 6x + 9)$.

Try It! 1. Use long division to divide the polynomials. Then write the dividend in terms of the quotient and remainder.

a. $x^3 - 6x^2 + 11x - 6$ divided by $x^2 - 4x + 3$

b. $16x^4 - 85$ divided by $4x^2 + 9$

EXAMPLE 2 Use Synthetic Division to Divide by $x - a$

What is $2x^3 - 7x^2 - 4$ divided by $x - 3$? Use synthetic division.

Synthetic division is a method used to divide a polynomial by a linear expression in the form $x - a$. Note that the leading coefficient of the divisor is 1, and that a is the zero of the divisor.

Step 1 To change from long division format to synthetic division format, write only the zero of the divisor and the coefficients of the dividend.

$$x - 3\overline{)2x^3 - 7x^2 + 0x - 4}$$

$$\begin{array}{c|cccc} \downarrow & \downarrow & \downarrow & \downarrow & \downarrow \\ 3 & 2 & -7 & 0 & -4 \end{array}$$

zero of the divisor, a

coefficients of the dividend

Separate a from the dividend.

Step 2 Bring down the first coefficient. Multiply the zero of the divisor by the first coefficient. Add the result to the second coefficient.

$$\begin{array}{c|cccc} 3 & 2 & -7 & 0 & -4 \\ & & 6 & & \\ \hline & 2 & -1 & & \end{array}$$

$3 \cdot 2 = 6$

$-7 + 6 = -1$

CONTINUED ON THE NEXT PAGE

EXAMPLE 2 CONTINUED

Step 3 Repeat the process until all the columns are complete.

COMMON ERROR
Remember to keep track of all positive and negative signs when multiplying.

$$\begin{array}{r|rrrr} 3 & 2 & -7 & 0 & -4 \\ & & 6 & -3 & \\ \hline & 2 & -1 & -3 & \end{array}$$

$3 \cdot -1 = -3$

$$\begin{array}{r|rrrr} 3 & 2 & -7 & 0 & -4 \\ & & 6 & -3 & -9 \\ \hline & 2 & -1 & -3 & -13 \end{array}$$

$3 \cdot -3 = -9$

Step 4 Use the numbers in the last row to write the quotient and remainder.

$$\begin{array}{r|rrrr} 3 & 2 & -7 & 0 & -4 \\ & & 6 & -3 & -9 \\ \hline & 2 & -1 & -3 & -13 \end{array}$$

remainder

coefficients of the quotient

$2x^2 - 1x - 3 - \frac{13}{x-3}$

USE STRUCTURE
You can use the result to write the dividend $2x^3 - 7x - 4$ in the form $(2x^2 - x - 3)(x - 3) - 13$.

Since the dividend is cubic and the divisor is linear, the quotient is quadratic.

So, $\frac{2x^3 - 7x^2 - 4}{(x-3)} = 2x^2 - x - 3 - \frac{13}{x-3}$.

 **Try It!** **2.** Use synthetic division to divide $3x^3 - 5x + 10$ by $x - 1$.

CONCEPTUAL UNDERSTANDING

EXAMPLE 3 Relate $P(a)$ to the Remainder of $P(x) \div (x - a)$

How is the value of $P(a)$ related to the remainder of $P(x) \div (x - a)$?

To explore this question, let $P(x) = x^3 + 10x^2 + 29x + 24$. Use synthetic division to divide $P(x)$ by $x + 5$.

To identify the value of a, write the divisor $x + 5$ in the form $x - a$.

$x + 5 = x - (-5)$ $a = -5$

$$\begin{array}{r|rrrr} -5 & 1 & 10 & 29 & 24 \\ & & -5 & -25 & -20 \\ \hline & 1 & 5 & 4 & 4 \end{array}$$

The remainder is 4.

The quotient is $x^2 + 5x + 4$.

So, $P(x) = (x^2 + 5x + 4)(x + 5) + 4$. Use this form to evaluate $P(-5)$.

$$\begin{aligned} P(-5) &= [((-5)^2 + 5(-5) + 4)(-5 + 5)] + 4 \\ &= [(25 - 25 + 4)(0)] + 4 \\ &= 0 + 4 \\ &= 4 \end{aligned}$$

-5 is the zero of the divisor, so the product of the quotient and the divisor is 0.

So, $P(-5)$ is the remainder, 4, of $P(x)$ divided by $x - (-5)$.

CONTINUED ON THE NEXT PAGE

EXAMPLE 3 CONTINUED

In general, dividing $P(x)$ by $x - a$ results in a quotient $Q(x)$ and a remainder r.

$$\begin{aligned} P(x) &= Q(x)(x - a) + r \\ P(a) &= Q(x)(a - a) + r \\ &= Q(x)(0) + r \\ &= r \end{aligned}$$

Evaluating $P(x)$ at a, the zero of the divisor, shows that $P(a) = r$.

So, the for a polynomial $P(x)$ the value of $P(a)$ is equal to the remainder of the division $P(x) \div (x - a)$.

Try It! **3.** Use synthetic division to show that the remainder of $f(x) = x^3 + 8x^2 + 12x + 5$ divided by $x + 2$ is equal to $f(-2)$.

CONCEPT Remainder Theorem and Factor Theorem

The **Remainder Theorem** states that if a polynomial $P(x)$ is divided by $x - a$, the remainder is $P(a)$.

When $x - a$ is a factor of $P(x)$, we can show that $P(a) = 0$.

$$\begin{aligned} P(x) &= Q(x)(x - a) \\ P(a) &= Q(x)(a - a) \\ P(a) &= 0 \end{aligned}$$

Conversely, when $P(a) = 0$, we can show that $x - a$ is a factor.

$$\begin{aligned} P(x) &= Q(x)(x - a) + r \\ P(x) &= Q(x)(x - a) + P(a) \\ P(x) &= Q(x)(x - a) + 0 \\ P(x) &= Q(x)(x - a) \end{aligned}$$

Use the Remainder Theorem.

The Factor Theorem formalizes these two points.

The **Factor Theorem** states that the expression $x - a$ is a factor of a polynomial $P(x)$ if and only if $P(a) = 0$.

APPLICATION

EXAMPLE 4 Use the Remainder Theorem to Evaluate Polynomials

The population of tortoises on an island is modeled by the function $P(x) = -x^3 + 6x^2 + 12x + 325$ where x is the number of years since 2015. Use the Remainder Theorem to estimate the population in 2023.

Use synthetic division to find $P(a)$ when $a = 8$.

$$\begin{array}{r|rrrr} 8 & -1 & 6 & 12 & 325 \\ & & -8 & -16 & -32 \\ \hline & -1 & -2 & -4 & 293 \end{array}$$

The estimated population in 2023 is 293 tortoises.

Try It! **4.** A technology company uses the function $R(x) = -x^3 + 12x^2 + 6x + 80$ to model expected annual revenue, in thousands of dollars, for a new product, where x is the number of years after the product is released. Use the Remainder Theorem to estimate the revenue in year 5.

 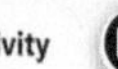 Activity Assess

EXAMPLE 5 Check Whether $x - a$ is a Factor of $P(x)$

How can you use the Remainder and Factor Theorems to determine whether the given binomial is a factor of $P(x)$? If it is a factor, write the polynomial in factored form.

A. $P(x) = x^4 - 8x^3 + 16x^2 - 23x - 6$; binomial: $x - 6$

The binomial $x - 6$ is a factor of $P(x)$ if 6 is a zero of $P(x)$.

Method 1 Use synthetic substitution.

6	1	−8	16	−23	−6
		6	−12	24	6
	1	−2	4	1	0

Method 2 Use direct substitution.

$P(6) = 6^4 - 8(6^3) + 16(6^2) - 23(6) - 6$

$= 1{,}296 - 1{,}728 + 576 - 138 - 6$

$= 0$

Because $P(6) = 0$, you can use the Factor Theorem to conclude that $x - 6$ is a factor of $P(x)$: $P(x) = (x^3 - 2x^2 + 4x + 1)(x - 6)$.

B. $P(x) = x^5 - 5x^3 + 9x^2 - x + 3$; binomial: $x + 3$

COMMON ERROR
When using synthetic division, remember to include 0 coefficients for any missing terms.

Method 1 Use synthetic substitution.

−3	1	0	−5	9	−1	3
		−3	9	−12	9	−24
	1	−3	4	−3	8	−21

Method 2 Use direct substitution.

$P(-3) = (-3)^5 - 5((-3)^3) + 9((-3)^2) - (-3) + 3$

$P(-3) = -243 + 135 + 81 + 3 + 3$

$P(-3) = -21$

Because −3 is a not a zero of $P(x)$, you can use the Factor Theorem to conclude that $x + 3$ is not a factor of $P(x)$.

 **Try It!** 5. Use the Remainder and Factor Theorems to determine whether the given binomial is a factor of $P(x)$.

a. $P(x) = x^3 - 10x^2 + 28x - 16$; binomial: $x - 4$

b. $P(x) = 2x^4 + 9x^3 - 2x^2 + 6x - 40$; binomial: $x + 5$

CONCEPT SUMMARY Dividing Polynomials

Example: Divide $x^3 - 8x^2 - 5x - 30$ by $x - 9$.

LONG DIVISION

Can be used for any polynomial division.

$$\begin{array}{r} x^2 + x + 4 \\ x - 9\overline{)x^3 - 8x^2 - 5x - 30} \\ \underline{-(x^3 - 9x^2)} \\ x^2 - 5x - 30 \\ \underline{-(x^2 - 9x)} \\ 4x - 30 \\ \underline{-(4x - 36)} \\ 6 \end{array}$$

SYNTHETIC DIVISION

Most readily used when the divisor is linear and its leading coefficient is 1.

$$\begin{array}{r|rrrr} 9 & 1 & -8 & -5 & -30 \\ & & 9 & 9 & 36 \\ \hline & 1 & 1 & 4 & 6 \end{array}$$

Either method shows that $x^3 - 8x^2 - 5x - 30 = (x^2 + x + 4)(x - 9) + 6$

REMAINDER THEOREM

If a polynomial $P(x)$ is divided by a linear divisor $x - a$, the remainder is $P(a)$.

$P(x) = x^3 - 2x + 1$ divided by $x - 2$ has remainder 5.

$$\begin{array}{r|rrrr} 2 & 1 & 0 & -2 & 1 \\ & & 2 & 4 & 4 \\ \hline & 1 & 2 & 2 & 5 \end{array}$$

$P(2) = 5$

FACTOR THEOREM

The binomial $x - a$ is a factor of $P(x)$ if and only if $P(a) = 0$.

$P(x) = 2x^4 - 5x^3 - 12x^2 + x - 4$ divided by $x - 4$ has remainder 0.

$$\begin{array}{r|rrrrr} 4 & 2 & -5 & -12 & 1 & -4 \\ & & 8 & 12 & 0 & 4 \\ \hline & 2 & 3 & 0 & 1 & 0 \end{array}$$

Do You UNDERSTAND?

1. ESSENTIAL QUESTION How can you divide polynomials?

2. **Error Analysis** Ella said the remainder of $x^3 + 2x^2 - 4x + 6$ divided by $x + 5$ is 149. Is Ella correct? Explain.

3. **Look for Relationships** You divide a polynomial $P(x)$ by a linear expression $D(x)$. You find a quotient $Q(x)$ and a remainder $R(x)$. How can you check your work?

Do You KNOW HOW?

4. Use long division to divide $x^4 - 4x^3 + 12x^2 - 3x + 6$ by $x^2 + 8$.

5. Use synthetic division to divide $x^3 - 8x^2 + 9x - 5$ by $x - 3$.

6. Use the Remainder Theorem to find the remainder of $2x^4 + x^2 - 10x - 1$ divided by $x + 2$.

7. Is $x + 9$ a factor of the polynomial $P(x) = x^3 + 11x^2 + 15x - 27$? If so, write the polynomial as a product of two factors. If not, explain how you know.

PRACTICE & PROBLEM SOLVING

Scan for Multimedia

Practice | Tutorial

Additional Exercises Available Online

UNDERSTAND

8. **Reason** Write a polynomial division problem with a quotient of $x^2 - 5x + 7$ and a remainder of 2. Explain your reasoning. How can you verify your answer?

9. **Communicate Precisely** Show that $x - 3$ and $x + 5$ are factors of $x^4 + 2x^3 - 16x^2 - 2x + 15$. Explain your reasoning.

10. **Error Analysis** Alicia divided the polynomial $2x^3 - 4x^2 + 6x + 10$ by $x^2 + x$. Describe and correct the error Alicia made in dividing the polynomials.

$$
\begin{array}{r}
2x - 6 + \dfrac{10}{x^2 + x} \\
x^2 + x \enclose{longdiv}{2x^3 - 4x^2 + 6x + 10} \\
\underline{-(2x^3 + 2x^2)} \\
-6x^2 + 6x \\
\underline{-(-6x^2 - 6x)} \\
10
\end{array}
$$

X

11. **Higher Order Thinking** When dividing polynomial $P(x)$ by polynomial $d(x)$, the remainder is $R(x)$. The remainder can also be written as $\frac{R(x)}{d(x)}$. How can you use the degrees of $R(x)$ and $d(x)$ to determine whether you are finished dividing?

12. **Look for Relationships** When dividing polynomial $P(x)$ by polynomial $x - n$, the remainder is 0. When graphing $P(x)$, what is an x-intercept of the graph?

13. **Reason** When dividing $x^3 + nx^2 + 4nx - 6$ by $x + 3$, the remainder is –48. What is the value of n?

14. **Mathematical Connections** Use polynomial long division to divide $8x^3 + 27$ by $2x + 3$. How can you use multiplication to check your answer? Show your work.

PRACTICE

Use long division to divide. SEE EXAMPLE 1

15. $x^3 + 5x^2 - x - 5$ divided by $x - 1$

16. $2x^3 + 9x^2 + 10x + 3$ divided by $2x + 1$

17. $3x^3 - 2x^2 + 7x + 9$ divided by $x^2 - 3x$

18. $2x^4 - 6x^2 + 3$ divided by $2x - 6$

Use synthetic division to divide. SEE EXAMPLE 2

19. $x^4 - 25x^2 + 144$ divided by $x - 4$

20. $x^3 + 6x^2 + 3x - 10$ divided by $x + 5$

21. $x^5 + 2x^4 - 3x^3 + x - 1$ divided by $x + 2$

22. $-x^4 + 7x^3 + x^2 - 2x - 12$ divided by $x - 3$

23. Use synthetic division to show that the remainder of $f(x) = x^4 - 6x^3 - 33x^2 + 46x + 75$ divided by $x - 9$ is $P(9)$. SEE EXAMPLE 3

Use the Remainder Theorem to evaluate each polynomial for the given value of x. SEE EXAMPLE 4

24. $f(x) = x^3 + 9x^2 + 3x - 7$; $x = -5$

25. $f(x) = 2x^3 - 3x^2 + 4x + 13$; $x = 3$

26. $f(x) = -x^4 + 2x^3 - x^2 + 4x + 8$; $x = -2$

27. $f(x) = x^5 - 3x^4 - 2x^3 + x^2 - 2x - 1$; $x = 4$

Is each given binomial a factor of the given polynomial? If so, write the polynomial as a product of two factors. SEE EXAMPLE 5

28. polynomial: $P(x) = 8x^3 - 10x^2 + 28x - 16$; binomial: $x - 3$

29. polynomial: $P(x) = 4x^4 - 9x^3 - 7x^2 - 2x + 25$; binomial: $x + 4$

30. polynomial: $P(x) = -x^5 + 12x^3 + 6x^2 - 23x + 1$; binomial: $x - 2$

31. polynomial: $P(x) = 2x^3 + 3x^2 - 8x - 12$; binomial: $2x + 3$

PRACTICE & PROBLEM SOLVING

 Practice  Tutorial

Mixed Review Available Online

APPLY

32. Model With Mathematics Darren is placing shipping boxes in a storage unit with a floor area of $x^4 + 5x^3 + x^2 - 20x - 14$ square units. Each box has a volume of $x^3 + 10x^2 + 29x + 20$ cubic units and can hold a stack of items with a height of $x + 5$ units.

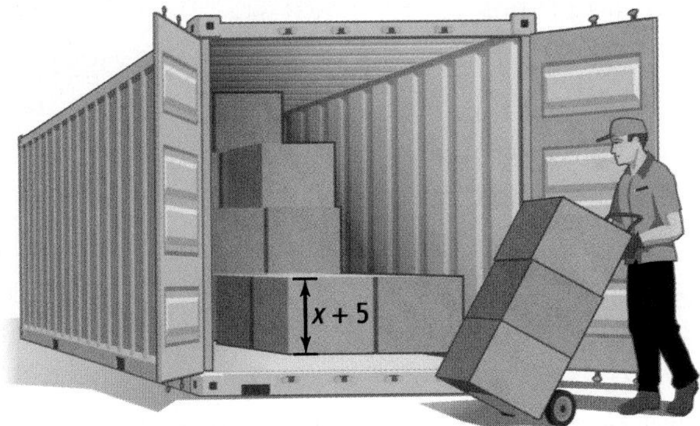

a. How much floor space will each box cover?

b. What is the maximum number of boxes Darren can place on the floor of the storage unit?

c. Assume Darren places the maximum number of boxes on the floor of the storage unit, with no overlap. How much of the floor space is not covered by a box?

33. Reason Lauren wants to determine the length and height of her DVD stand. The function $f(x) = x^3 + 14x^2 + 57x + 72$ represents the volume of the DVD stand, where the width is $x + 3$ units. What are possible dimensions for the length and height of the DVD stand? Explain.

34. Make Sense and Persevere A truck traveled $6x^3 + x^2 + 20x - 11$ miles in $2x - 1$ hours. At what rate did the semi-truck travel? (*Hint:* Use the formula $d = rt$, where d is the distance, r is the rate, and t is the time.)

ASSESSMENT PRACTICE

35. When polynomial $P(x)$ is divided by the linear factor $x - n$, the remainder is 0. What can you conclude? Select all that apply.

Ⓐ $P(x) = 0$
Ⓑ $P(n) = 0$
Ⓒ $P(-n) = 0$
Ⓓ $x - n$ is a factor of $P(x)$.
Ⓔ $x + n$ is a factor of $P(x)$.

36. SAT/ACT $x + 3$ is a factor of the polynomial $x^3 + 2x^2 - 5x + n$. What is the value of n?

Ⓐ −6
Ⓑ −3
Ⓒ −2
Ⓓ 3
Ⓔ 6

37. Performance Task The table shows some quotients of the polynomial $x^n - 1$ divided by the linear factor $x - 1$.

Dividend	Divisor	Quotient
$x^2 - 1$	$x - 1$	$x + 1$
$x^3 - 1$	$x - 1$	$x^2 + x + 1$
$x^4 - 1$	$x - 1$	
$x^5 - 1$	$x - 1$	
$x^6 - 1$	$x - 1$	

Part A Use long division or synthetic division to find the missing quotients to complete the table.

Part B Look for a pattern. Then describe the pattern when $x^n - 1$ is divided by $x - 1$.

Part C Use the pattern to find the quotient when $x^{10} - 1$ is divided by $x - 1$.

Activity Assess

2-5 Zeros of Polynomial Functions

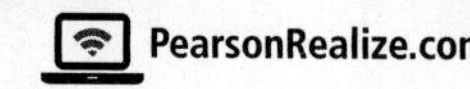

PearsonRealize.com

I CAN… model and solve problems using the zeros of a polynomial function.

VOCABULARY

- multiplicity of a zero

MODEL & DISCUSS

Charlie and Aisha built a small rocket and launched it from their backyard. The rocket fell to the ground 10 s after it launched.

The height h, in feet, of the rocket relative to the ground at time t seconds can be modeled by the function shown.

A. How are the launch and landing times related to the modeling function?

B. What additional information about the rocket launch could you use to construct an accurate model for the rocket's height relative to the ground?

C. Construct Arguments Charlie believes that the function $h(t) = -16t^2 + 160t$ models the height of the rocket with respect to time. Do you agree? Explain your reasoning and indicate the domain of this function.

ESSENTIAL QUESTION

How are the zeros of a polynomial function related to an equation and graph of the function?

CONCEPTUAL UNDERSTANDING

EXAMPLE 1 Use Zeros to Graph a Polynomial Function

What are the zeros of $f(x) = x(x - 4)(x + 3)$? Graph the function.

A *zero* of a polynomial function is a value for which the function is equal to 0. By the Zero-Product Property, the zeros of the function are –3, 0, and 4.

The zeros divide a number line into four intervals.

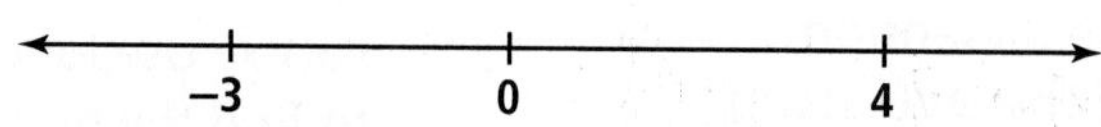

To see how the graph of the function behaves on each interval, look at the sign of each factor on each interval, and the sign of the product.

Interval	Sign			
	x	$x - 4$	$x + 3$	Product
$x < -3$	–	–	–	–
$-3 < x < 0$	–	–	+	+
$0 < x < 4$	+	–	+	–
$x > 4$	+	+	+	+

The last column shows the sign of the product of the three factors.

CONTINUED ON THE NEXT PAGE

STUDY TIP
Using the zeros to sketch a rough graph does not tell you how the function behaves within each interval other than whether it is positive or negative.

EXAMPLE 1 CONTINUED

Sketch the graph. Draw a continuous curve that passes through each zero on the x-axis, and is below the x-axis when the function is negative, and above the x-axis when the function is positive.

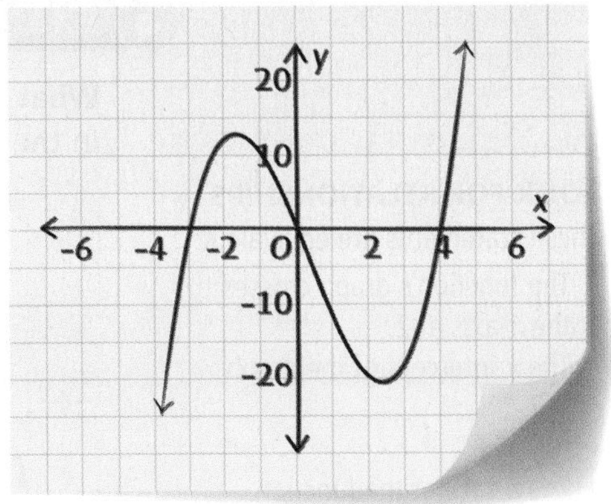

Try It! 1. Factor each function. Then use the zeros to sketch its graph.

a. $f(x) = 4x^3 + 4x^2 - 24x$

b. $g(x) = x^4 - 81$

EXAMPLE 2 Understand How a Multiple Zero Can Affect a Graph

How does a multiple zero affect the graph of a polynomial function?

The **multiplicity of a zero** of a polynomial function is the number of times its related factor appears in the factored form of the polynomial. Notice the behavior of each graph as it approaches the x-axis. What can you conclude about the multiplicity of a zero and its effect on the graph of the function?

STUDY TIP
Close to a zero, the graph looks like a polynomial function with degree equal to the multiplicity of the zero.

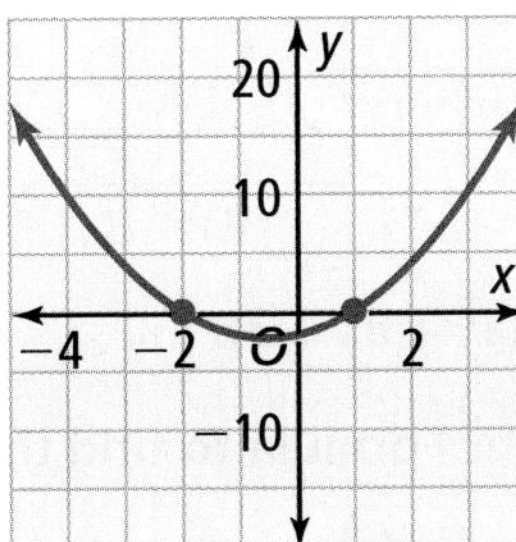

$f(x) = (x - 1)(x + 2)$

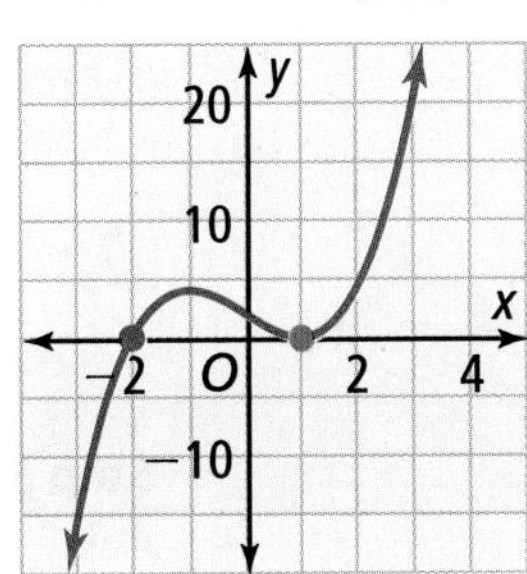

$f(x) = (x - 1)^2(x + 2)$

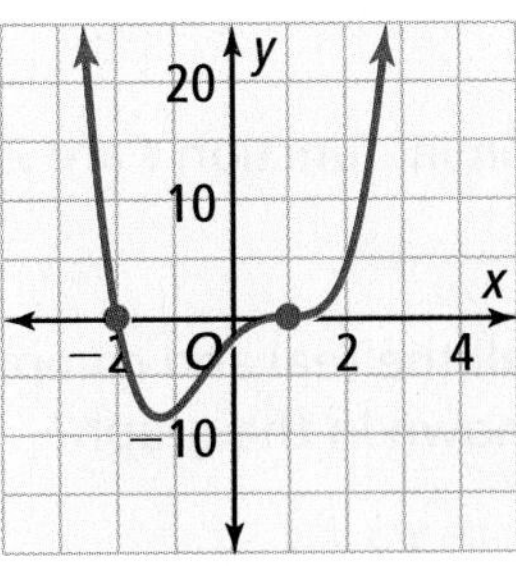

$f(x) = (x - 1)^3(x + 2)$

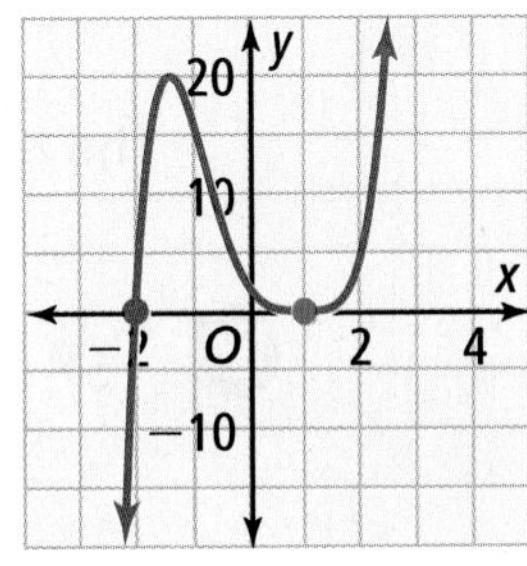

$f(x) = (x - 1)^4(x + 2)$

When the multiplicity of a zero is odd, the function crosses the x-axis. When the multiplicity of a zero is even, the graph has a turning point at the x-axis.

Try It! 2. Describe the behavior of the graph of the function at each of its zeros.

a. $f(x) = x(x + 4)(x - 1)^4$

b. $f(x) = (x^2 + 9)(x - 1)^5(x + 2)^2$

EXAMPLE 3 Find Real and Complex Zeros

What are all the real and complex zeros of the polynomial function shown in the graph?

LOOK FOR RELATIONSHIPS
These statements are equivalent:
- The function's graph crosses the x-axis at 2.
- The x-intercept of the graph is 2.
- $f(2) = 0$
- 2 is a zero of the function.
- $x - 2$ is a factor of the polynomial.

$f(x) = x^3 + x^2 - 3x - 6$

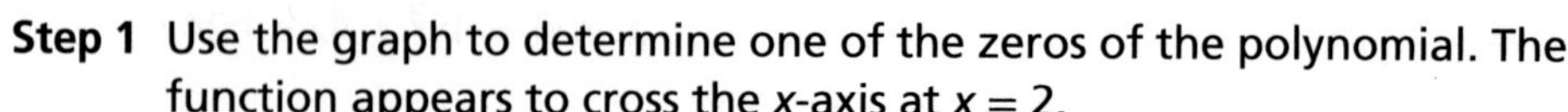

Step 1 Use the graph to determine one of the zeros of the polynomial. The function appears to cross the x-axis at $x = 2$.

Confirm that 2 is a zero of the function.

$$f(2) = (2)^3 + (2)^2 - 3(2) - 6$$
$$= 0$$

So 2 is a zero of the function. By the Factor Theorem, $x - 2$ is a factor of the related polynomial.

Step 2 Use synthetic division to factor the polynomial.

$$\begin{array}{r|rrrr} 2 & 1 & 1 & -3 & -6 \\ & & 2 & 6 & 6 \\ \hline & 1 & 3 & 3 & 0 \end{array}$$

So $f(x) = (x - 2)(x^2 + 3x + 3)$.

Step 3 Use the Quadratic Formula to find the remaining zeros.

$$x = \frac{-3 \pm \sqrt{3^2 - 4(1)(3)}}{2(1)}$$
$$= -\frac{3}{2} \pm \frac{\sqrt{3}}{2}i$$

The zeros of the polynomial function f are 2, $-\frac{3}{2} + \frac{\sqrt{3}}{2}i$, and $-\frac{3}{2} - \frac{\sqrt{3}}{2}i$.

Try It! 3. What are all the real and complex zeros of the polynomial function shown in the graph?

a.

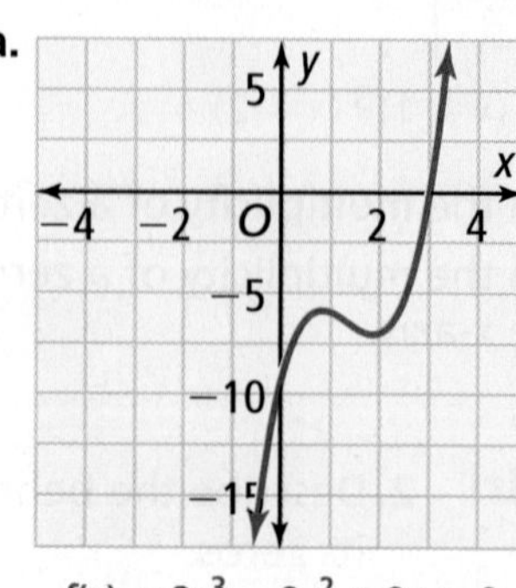

$f(x) = 2x^3 - 8x^2 + 9x - 9$

b.

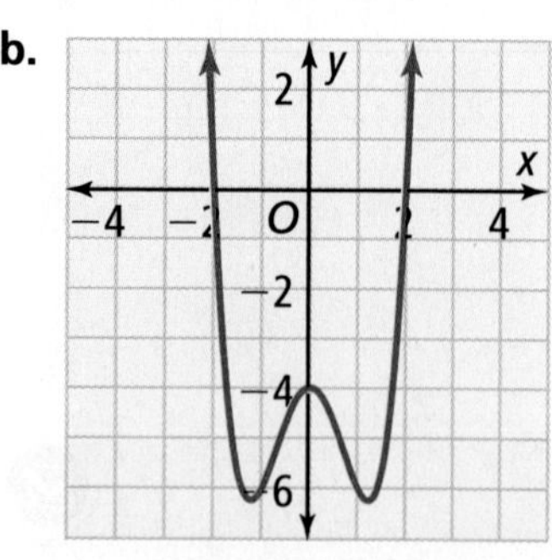

$f(x) = x^4 - 3x^2 - 4$

Go Online | PearsonRealize.com

APPLICATION

EXAMPLE 4 Interpret the Zeros of a Function

Acme Innovations makes and sells lamps. Their profit *P*, in hundreds of dollars earned, is a function of the number of lamps sold *x*, in thousands.

From historical data, they know that their company's profit is modeled by the function shown.

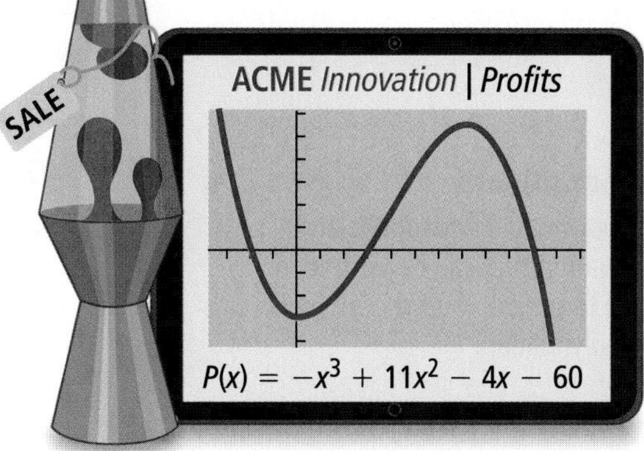

What do the zeros of the function tell you about the number of lamps that Acme Innovations should produce?

Formulate A profit for the company corresponds to the portions of the graph that lie above the *x*-axis. Find the zeros of the function to determine where the graph crosses the *x*-axis.

Based on the graph, the zeros of the function appear to be –2, 3, and 10. If these are the zeros of the function, then by the Factor Theorem you can determine the factors of the related polynomial.

Zero of *P*	Factor of *P*(*x*)
-2	$x + 2$
3	$x - 3$
10	$x - 10$

Compute Multiply these factors to verify that the product is equal to the polynomial given.

$$(x + 2)(x - 3)(x - 10) = (x + 2)(x^2 - 13x + 30)$$
$$= x^3 - 13x^2 + 30x + 2x^2 - 26x + 60$$
$$= x^3 - 11x^2 + 4x + 60$$

The result is equal to $-P(x)$, not $P(x)$. But both polynomials have the same factors since $P(x) = -(x + 2)(x - 3)(x - 10)$.

So the zeros of the function are –2, 3, and 10.

Interpret When $P(x)$ is positive, Acme Innovations earns a profit. The profit is positive when $x < -2$ or $3 < x < 10$. Acme Innovations cannot produce a negative number of lamps, so disregard the interval $x < -2$. Since *x* represents the number of lamps in hundreds, the company should make between 3,000 and 10,000 lamps.

Try It! 4. Due to a decrease in the cost of materials, the profit function for Acme Innovations has changed to $Q(x) = -x^3 + 10x^2 + 13x - 22$. How many lamps should they make in order to make a profit?

EXAMPLE 5 Solve Polynomial Equations

What are the solutions of $2x^3 + 5x^2 - 3x = 3x^3 + 8x^2 + 1$?

Rewrite the equation in the form $P(x) = 0$.

$$2x^3 + 5x^2 - 3x = 3x^3 + 8x^2 + 1$$
$$x^3 + 3x^2 + 3x + 1 = 0$$

Combine like terms on one side of the equation.

VOCABULARY
A *polynomial equation* is an equation that can be written in the form $P(x) = 0$, where $P(x)$ is a polynomial.

The roots are the zeros of the function $P(x) = x^3 + 3x^2 + 3x + 1$.

$(x + 1)^3 = 0$ ······ Cube of a binomial.

$x + 1 = 0$ ······ Zero-Product Property.

$x = -1$ ······ Subtract 1 from each side.

To check, write each side of the equation as a separate polynomial and graph. Use the INTERSECT feature to confirm that the graphs intersect at $x = -1$.

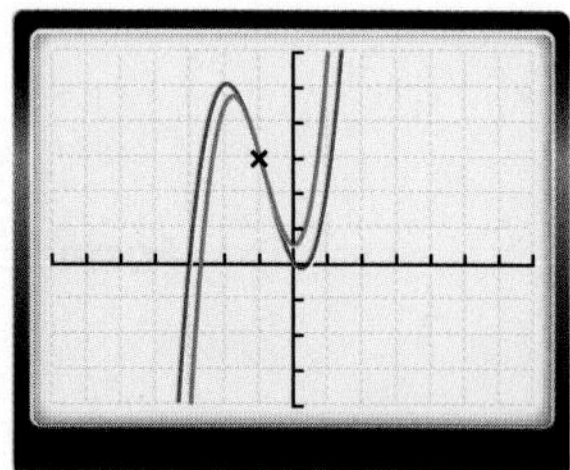

x scale: 1 *y scale: 2*

Try It!

5. What is the solution of the equation?

a. $x^3 - 7x + 6 = x^3 + 5x^2 - 2x - 24$ b. $x^4 + 2x^2 = -x^3 - 2x$

EXAMPLE 6 Solve a Polynomial Inequality by Graphing

What are the solutions of $x^3 - 16x < 0$?

The solutions are all values of x that make the inequality true. The polynomial $x^3 - 16x$ defines a polynomial function $P(x) = x^3 - 16x$.

Factor to find the zeros of the function.

$x^3 - 16x = 0$

$x(x^2 - 16) = 0$ ······ Factor out the greatest common factor.

$x(x - 4)(x + 4) = 0$ ······ Difference of squares.

By the Zero-Product Property, the zeros of P are –4, 0, and 4.

Sketch the function, and use the graph to determine where $P(x) < 0$.

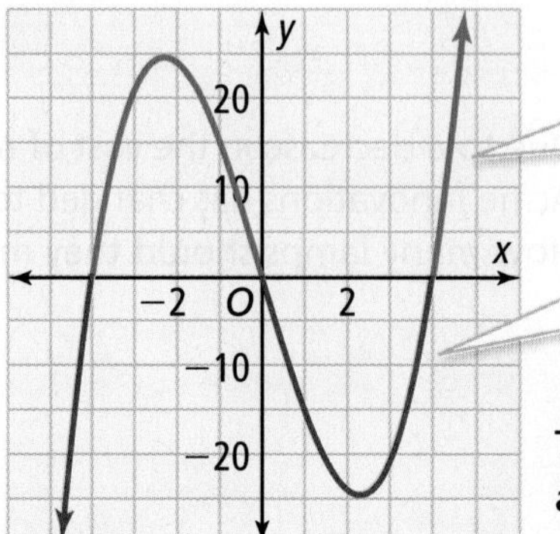

The blue portions show where $P(x) > 0$.

The red portions show where $P(x) < 0$.

The solutions of the inequality $x^3 - 16x < 0$ are all real numbers such that $x < -4$ or $0 < x < 4$.

CONTINUED ON THE NEXT PAGE

EXAMPLE 6 CONTINUED

Try It! 6. What are the solutions of the inequality?

a. $2x^3 + 12x^2 + 12x < 0$

b. $(x^2 - 1)(x^2 - x - 6) > 0$

CONCEPT SUMMARY Zeros of Polynomials

FUNCTION $f(x) = (x - a)^2(x - b)^3(x - c)$

GRAPH

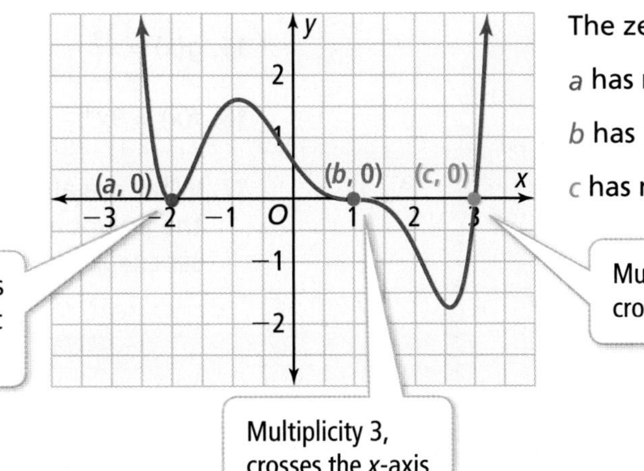

The zeros are a, b, and c.

a has multiplicity 2.

b has multiplicity 3.

c has multiplicity 1.

Do You UNDERSTAND?

1. ESSENTIAL QUESTION How are the zeros of a polynomial function related to the equation and graph of a function?

2. **Error Analysis** In order to identify the zeros of the function, a student factored the cubic function $f(x) = x^3 - 3x^2 - 10x$ as follows:

$$f(x) = x^3 - 3x^2 - 10x$$
$$= x(x^2 - 3x - 10)$$
$$= x(x - 5)(x + 2)$$
$$x = 0, x = -5, x = 2$$

Describe and correct the error the student made.

3. **Make Sense and Persevere** Explain how you can determine that the function $f(x) = x^3 + 3x^2 + 4x + 2$ has both real and complex zeros.

Do You KNOW HOW?

4. If the graph of the function f has a multiple zero at $x = 2$, what is a possible exponent of the factor $x - 2$? Justify your reasoning.

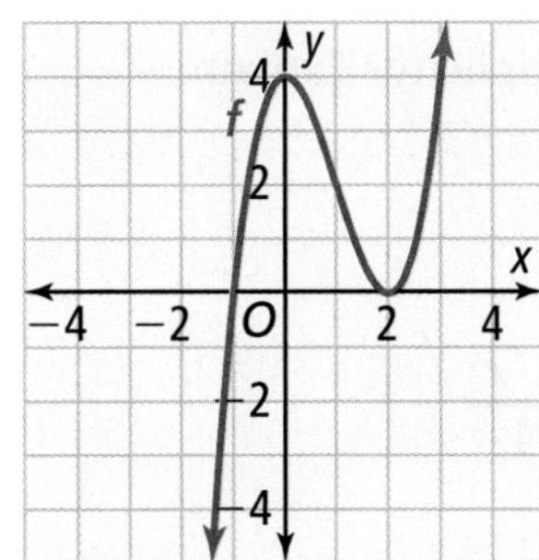

5. Energy Solutions manufactures LED light bulbs. The profit p, in thousands of dollars earned, is a function of the number of bulbs sold, x, in ten thousands. Profit is modeled by the function $-x^3 + 9x^2 - 11x - 21$.

For what number of bulbs manufactured does the company make a profit?

PRACTICE & PROBLEM SOLVING

UNDERSTAND

6. **Reason** If you use zeros to sketch the graph of a polynomial function, how can you verify that your graph is correct?

7. **Error Analysis** Describe and resolve two errors that Tonya may have made in finding all the roots of the polynomial function, $f(x) = x^3 + 3x^2 + 7x + 5$.

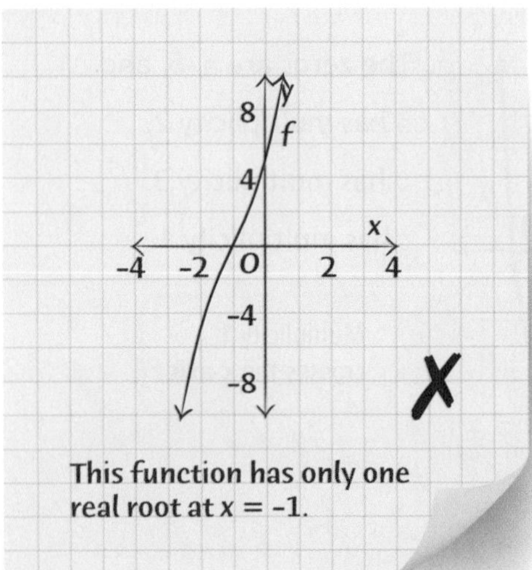

8. **Higher Order Thinking** How could you use your graphing calculator to determine that $f(x) = (x + 2)(x + 6)(x - 1)$ is not the correct factorization of $f(x) = x^3 + 7x^2 + 16x + 12$? Explain.

9. **Generalize** How can you determine that the polynomial function shown does not have any zeros with even multiplicity? Explain.

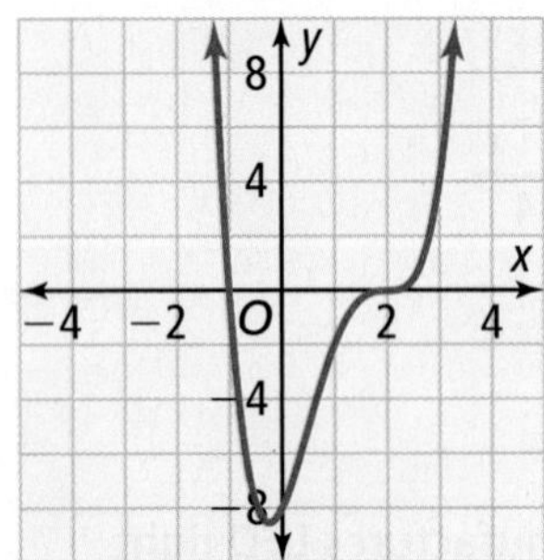

10. **Use Structure** Factor the polynomial $x^4 - 16$. How many real zeros does the function $g(x) = x^4 - 16$ have?

11. At what points do the graphs of $f(x) = x^3 - 2x^2 - 16x + 20$ and $g(x) = -12$ intersect?

PRACTICE

Sketch the graph of the function by finding the zeros. SEE EXAMPLE 1

12. $f(x) = 3x^3 - 9x^2 - 12x$

13. $g(x) = (x + 3)(x - 1)(x - 4)$

Find the zeros of the function, and describe the behavior of the graph at each zero. SEE EXAMPLE 2

14. $f(x) = x^3 - 8x^2 + 16x$

15. $g(x) = x^3 - x^2 - 25x + 25$

16. $f(x) = 9x^4 - 40x^2 + 16$

17. What are all the real and complex zeros of the polynomial function shown in the graph? SEE EXAMPLE 3

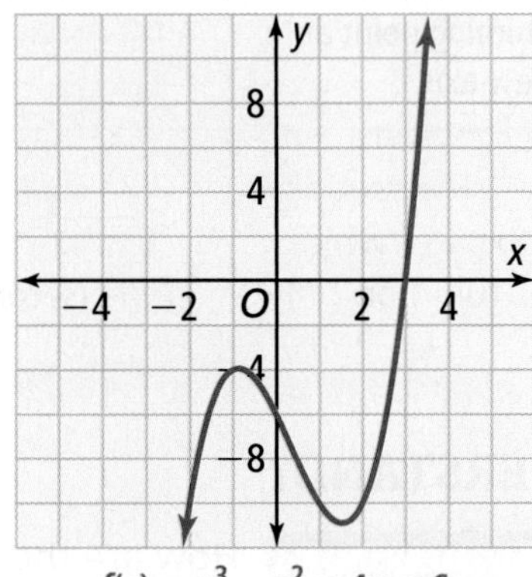

$f(x) = x^3 - x^2 - 4x - 6$

18. Waterworks is a company that manufactures and sells paddleboards. Their profit P, in hundreds of dollars earned, is a function of the number of paddleboards sold x, measured in thousands. Profit is modeled by the function $P(x) = -3x^3 + 48x^2 - 144x$. What do the zeros of the function tell you about the number of paddleboards that Waterworks should produce? SEE EXAMPLE 4

What are the solution(s) of the equation? SEE EXAMPLE 5

19. $-3x^3 - x^2 + 54x - 40 = 2x^2 + 6x + 20$

20. $2x^3 + 3x^2 - 36 = x^3 - x^2 + 9x$

21. $-5x^4 + 4x^2 - 12x = -6x^4 + 3x^3$

What are the solutions of the inequality? SEE EXAMPLE 6

22. $x^3 - 9x > 0$

23. $0 > 4x^3 + 8x^2 - x - 2$

24. $64x^2 > -4x^3 - x - 16$

PRACTICE & PROBLEM SOLVING

Mixed Review Available Online

APPLY

25. Make Sense and Persevere A firework is launched vertically into the air. Its height in meters is given by the function shown, where t is measured in seconds.

a. What is a reasonable domain of the function?

b. What are the zeros of the function? Explain what they represent in this situation.

c. Use technology to find the vertex. What does it represent in this situation?

26. The height of a baseball thrown in the air can be modeled by the function $h(t) = -16t^2 + 32t + 6.5$, where $h(t)$ represents the height in feet of the baseball after t seconds. Explain why the graph of this function only shows one zero.

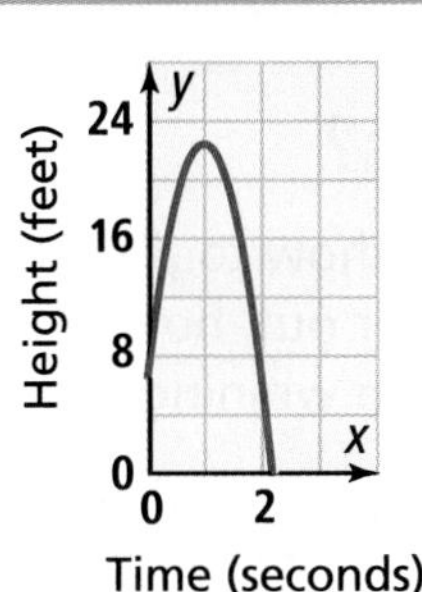

27. Model With Mathematics The height of a rectangular storage box is less than both its length and width. The function $f(x) = x^3 + 2x^2 - 3x$ represents the volume of the rectangular box, where x represents the width of the box, in feet.

a. Find the factored form of $f(x)$.

b. Find the zeros of the function.

c. You know x represents the width of the box. What do the other two factors represent?

d. Find the dimensions of the box when the volume is 10 ft^3.

ASSESSMENT PRACTICE

28. Complete each statement so it means the same as 4 is *a zero of the function*.

The graph of the function crosses the __________ at 4. ______________ is a factor of the polynomial.

29. SAT/ACT Without the use of a graphing calculator, determine which of the following functions is the graph of $f(x) = x^3 + x^2 - 4x$.

Ⓐ 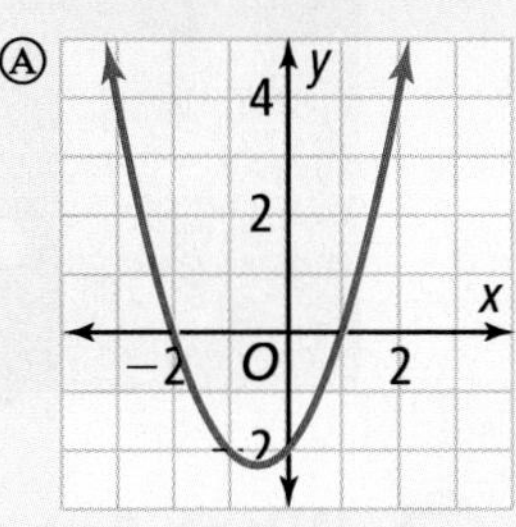

Ⓑ 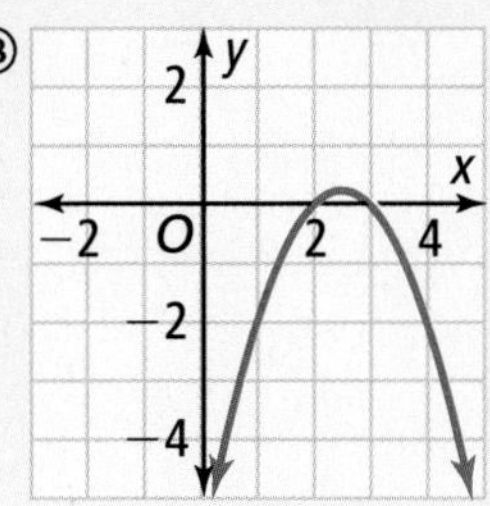

Ⓒ 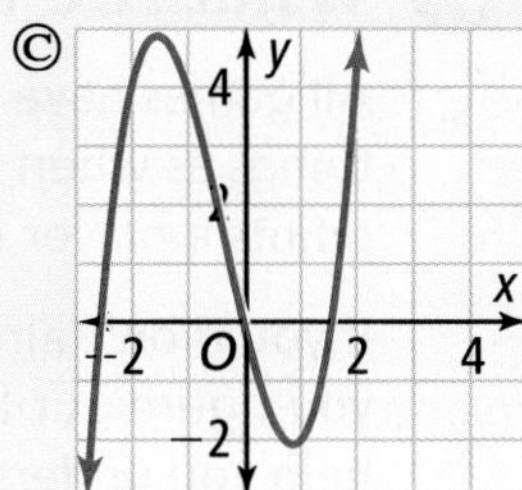

Ⓓ 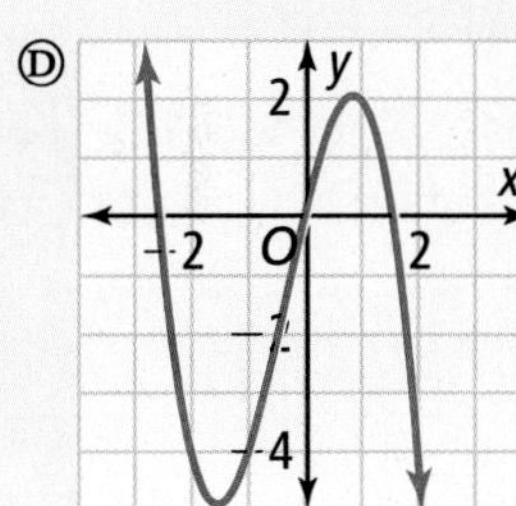

30. Performance Task Venetta opened several deli sandwich franchises in 2000. The profit P (in hundreds of dollars) of the franchises in t years (since the franchises opened) can be modeled by the function $P(t) = t^3 + t^2 - 6t$.

Part A Sketch a graph of the function.

Part B Based on the model, during what years did Venetta not make a profit?

Part C If the model is appropriate, predict the amount of profit Venetta will receive from her franchises in 2020.

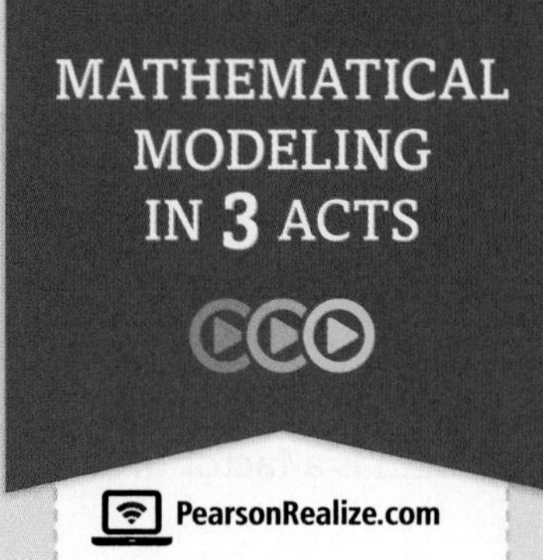

PearsonRealize.com

What Are the Rules?

All games have rules about how to play the game. The rules outline such things as when a ball is in or out, how a player scores points, and how many points a player gets for each winning shot.

If you didn't already know how to play tennis, or some other game, could you figure out what the rules were just by watching? What clues would help you understand the game? Think about this during the Mathematical Modeling in 3-Acts lesson.

ACT 1 Identify the Problem

1. What is the first question that comes to mind after watching the video?
2. Write down the main question you will answer about what you saw in the video.
3. Make an initial conjecture that answers this main question.
4. Explain how you arrived at your conjecture.
5. What information will be useful to know to answer the main question? How can you get it? How will you use that information?

ACT 2 Develop a Model

6. Use the math that you have learned in this Topic to refine your conjecture.

ACT 3 Interpret the Results

7. Did your refined conjecture match the actual answer exactly? If not, what might explain the difference?

2-6 Theorems About Roots of Polynomial Equations

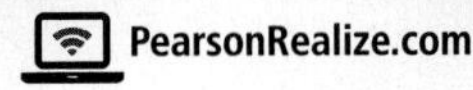

I CAN… use roots of a polynomial equation to find other roots.

CRITIQUE & EXPLAIN

Look at the polynomial functions shown.

$$g(x) = x^2 - 7x - 18$$

$$h(x) = 5x^2 + 24x + 16$$

A. Avery has a conjecture that the zeros of a polynomial function have to be positive or negative factors of its constant term. Factor $g(x)$ completely. Are the zeros of g factors of -18?

B. Look for Relationships Now test Avery's conjecture by factoring $h(x)$. Does Avery's conjecture hold? If so, explain why. If not, make a new conjecture.

ESSENTIAL QUESTION

How are the roots of a polynomial equation related to the coefficients and degree of the polynomial?

CONCEPT The Rational Root Theorem

Let $P(x) = a_nx^n + a_{n-1}x^n + \ldots + a_1x + a_0$ be a polynomial with integer coefficients.

If the polynomial equation $P(x) = 0$ has any rational roots, then each rational root is of the form $\frac{p}{q}$, where p is a factor of the constant term, a_0, and q is a factor of the leading coefficient, a_n.

EXAMPLE 1 Identify Possible Rational Solutions

From the graph it appears that 4 is a zero of the function $P(x) = 8x^5 - 32x^4 + x^2 - 4$. Without substituting, how can you determine if 4 is a possible solution to $P(x) = 0$?

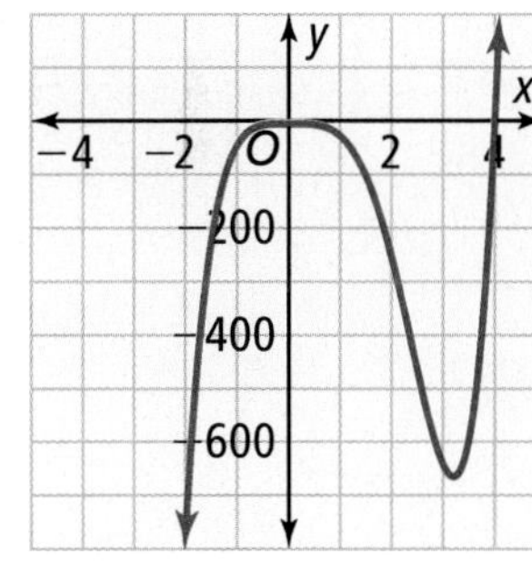

List all the factors of the leading coefficient and the constant term of $P(x)$.

constant term = −4 factors: ±1, ±2, ±4

leading coefficient = 8 factors: ±1, ±2, ±4, ±8

The Rational Root Theorem states that the possible rational roots of $P(x) = 0$ are

$\pm\frac{1}{1}, \pm\frac{1}{2}, \pm\frac{1}{4}, \pm\frac{1}{8}, \pm\frac{2}{1}, \pm\frac{2}{2}, \pm\frac{2}{4}, \pm\frac{2}{8}, \pm\frac{4}{1}, \pm\frac{4}{2}, \pm\frac{4}{4}, \pm\frac{4}{8}$

Values in the numerator are factors of the constant term.

Values in the denominator are factors of the leading coefficient.

$\frac{4}{1}$ is equal to 4, so it is a possible solution to $8x^5 - 32x^4 + x^2 - 4 = 0$ according to the Rational Roots Theorem.

COMMON ERROR
These are *possible* roots of the equation. You still need to test them to determine whether they are *actual* roots.

 **Try It!** 1. List all the possible rational solutions for each equation.

a. $4x^4 + 13x^3 - 124x^2 + 212x - 8 = 0$

b. $7x^4 + 13x^3 - 124x^2 + 212x - 45 = 0$

  Activity  Assess

APPLICATION

EXAMPLE 2 Use the Rational Root Theorem

A storage company is designing a new storage unit. Based on the dimensions shown, the volume of a container is modeled by the polynomial $v(x) = 2x^3 - 7x^2 + 6x$, where x is the width in feet. What are the dimensions of the container in feet if the volume of the unit is 154 ft^3?

Formulate The volume is 154 ft^3, so find solutions to the equation $2x^3 - 7x^2 + 6x = 154$.

The zeros of the polynomial will be rational roots of the equation in standard form: $2x^3 - 7x^2 + 6x - 154 = 0$.

Compute List the factors of the constant term and the leading coefficient.

constant term = −154

factors: ±1, ±2, ±7, ±11, ±14, ±22, ±77, ±154

leading coefficient = 2

factors: ±1, ±2

List all possible rational roots, eliminating repeated values.

Use a spreadsheet or a programmable calculator to test the possible roots.

$$\pm\frac{1}{1}, \pm\frac{2}{1}, \pm\frac{7}{1}, \pm\frac{11}{1}, \pm\frac{14}{1}, \pm\frac{22}{1}, \pm\frac{77}{1}, \pm\frac{154}{1}, \pm\frac{1}{2}, \pm\frac{7}{2}, \pm\frac{11}{2}, \pm\frac{77}{2}$$

Look for an x-value where $2x^3 - 7x^2 + 6x - 154 = 0$.

Testing shows that $\frac{11}{2}$ is a solution to the equation. Once you find one root, you can use synthetic division to find the other factor.

$$\begin{array}{c|rrrr} \frac{11}{2} & 2 & -7 & 6 & -154 \\ & & 11 & 22 & 154 \\ \hline & 2 & 4 & 28 & 0 \end{array}$$

The factored form of the equation is $\left(x - \frac{11}{2}\right)(2x^2 + 4x + 28) = 0$.

The discriminant of the quadratic factor is –208, so there are no real zeros for this factor. Therefore $\frac{11}{2}$ is the only real solution to the original equation.

Interpret The width of the container is $\frac{11}{2}$, or 5.5 ft; its length is $\frac{11}{2} - 2$, or 3.5 ft; and its height is $2\left(\frac{11}{2}\right) - 3$, or 8 ft.

Try It! 2. A jewelry box measures $2x + 1$ in. long, $2x - 6$ in. wide, and x in. tall. The volume of the box is given by the function $v(x) = 4x^3 - 10x^2 - 6x$. What is the height of the box, in inches, if its volume is 28 in.^{3}?

CONCEPT Fundamental Theorem of Algebra

If $P(x)$ is a polynomial of degree $n \geq 1$, then $P(x) = 0$ has exactly n solutions in the set of complex numbers.

If $P(x)$ has any factor of multiplicity m, count the solution associated with that factor m times. For example, the equation $(x - 3)^4 = 0$ has four solutions, each equal to 3.

EXAMPLE 3 Find All Complex Roots

What are all the complex roots of the polynomial equation?

$$3x^4 + 4x^3 + 2x^2 - x - 2 = 0$$

Step 1 List the factors of the constant term and leading coefficient

constant term = −2 factors: ±1, ±2

leading coefficient = 3 factors: ±1, ±3

Step 2 List the possible rational roots.

$\pm\frac{1}{3}, \pm\frac{2}{3}, \pm 1, \pm 2$

STUDY TIP
Remember that if you use synthetic division to test for factors, the result also tells you the quotient after division by the factor.

Step 3 Testing with synthetic division reveals that $\frac{2}{3}$ and −1 are roots.

Divide $3x^4 + 4x^3 + 2x^2 - x - 2$ by $x - \frac{2}{3}$.

$\frac{2}{3}$	3	4	2	−1	−2
		2	4	4	2
	3	6	6	3	0

So $3x^4 + 4x^3 + 2x^2 - x - 2 = \left(x - \frac{2}{3}\right)(3x^3 + 6x^2 + 6x + 3)$.

Now divide the cubic factor by $x - (-1)$.

−1	3	6	6	3
		−3	−3	−3
	3	3	3	0

After factoring out 3 from the final quotient, the polynomial equation can be written as $3(x - \frac{2}{3})(x + 1)(x^2 + x + 1) = 0$.

Step 4 Use the Quadratic Formula to find the last two roots.

If $x^2 + x + 1 = 0$, then $x = \frac{-1 \pm \sqrt{1^2 - 4(1)(1)}}{2(1)}$

$= \frac{-1 \pm i\sqrt{3}}{2}$

The complex numbers $\frac{2}{3}$, −1, $\frac{-1 - i\sqrt{3}}{2}$, and $\frac{-1 + i\sqrt{3}}{2}$ are all roots of the equation. Since the polynomial has degree 4, the Fundamental Theorem of Algebra states that these are the only four roots of the equation.

Try It! **3.** What are all the complex roots of the equation $x^3 - 2x^2 + 5x - 10 = 0$?

CONCEPTUAL UNDERSTANDING

EXAMPLE 4 Irrational Roots and the Coefficients of a Polynomial

How are the types of zeros of a polynomial function related to the coefficients of the polynomial?

A. Suppose a quadratic polynomial function *P* has one rational zero *c* and one irrational zero $a + \sqrt{b}$ where *a* and *b* are rational numbers. Are all the coefficients of *P* rational?

LOOK FOR RELATIONSHIPS
Remember that if *r* is a zero of a polynomial, then $x - r$ is a factor of the polynomial.

Write $P(x)$ in terms of its factors.

$$P(x) = (x - c)(x - (a + \sqrt{b}))$$
$$= x^2 - (a + \sqrt{b} + c)x + (a + \sqrt{b})c$$

Multiply and collect like terms.

No, the function *P* has two irrational coefficients.

B. Suppose a quadratic polynomial function *R* has two irrational zeros: a conjugate pair $a + \sqrt{b}$ and $a - \sqrt{b}$ (where *a* and *b* are rational numbers). Are all the coefficients of *R* rational?

$R(x) = (x - (a + \sqrt{b}))\,(x - (a - \sqrt{b}))$ ········ Write $R(x)$ in terms of its factors.

$= (x - a - \sqrt{b})(x - a + \sqrt{b})$ ········ Distribute.

$= ((x - a) - \sqrt{b})((x - a) + \sqrt{b})$ ········ Regroup the factors.

$= (x - a)^2 - (\sqrt{b})^2$ ········ Rewrite as the difference of squares.

$= x^2 - 2ax + (a^2 - b)$ ········ Expand.

rational numbers

Yes, *R* has only rational coefficients.

So a quadratic function with one rational zero and one irrational zero $a + \sqrt{b}$ (where *a* and *b* are rational) will have some irrational coefficients. But a quadratic with a conjugate pair of irrational zeros $a + \sqrt{b}$ and $a - \sqrt{b}$ (where *a* and *b* are rational) will have only rational coefficients.

Try It! **4.** Suppose a quadratic polynomial function *f* has two complex zeros which are a conjugate pair, $a - bi$ and $a + bi$ (where *a* and *b* are real numbers). Are all the coefficients of *f* real? Explain.

CONCEPT Conjugate Root Theorems

- Let *P* be a polynomial function with rational coefficients and let *a* and *b* be real numbers. Then if $a + \sqrt{b}$ is a root of $P(x) = 0$, then $a - \sqrt{b}$ is also a root of $P(x) = 0$.
- Let *P* be a polynomial function with real coefficients and let *a* and *b* be real numbers. Then if $a + bi$ is a root of $P(x) = 0$, then $a - bi$ is also a root of $P(x) = 0$.

 Activity  Assess

EXAMPLE 5 Write Polynomial Functions Using Conjugates

A. What is a quadratic function *P* with rational coefficients in standard form such that $P(x) = 0$ has $2 + 5i$ as a root?

By the Fundamental Theorem of Algebra, you know that a quadratic equation has two complex roots. Since $2 + 5i$ is one root, its complex conjugate, $2 - 5i$, must be the other.

Use the Factor Theorem to write the quadratic function using the two roots.

$P(x) = (x - (2 + 5i))(x - (2 - 5i))$ .... Write *P* in factored form.

$= (x - 2 - 5i)(x - 2 + 5i)$ .... Distribute.

$= ((x - 2) - 5i)((x - 2) + 5i))$ .... Associative Property.

$= (x - 2)^2 - (5i)^2$ .... Rewrite as the difference of squares.

$= x^2 - 4x + 4 - (-25)$ .... Simplify.

$= x^2 - 4x + 29$

So the equation $x^2 - 4x + 29$ is a quadratic equation with $2 + 5i$ as root.

STUDY TIP
Any equation of the form $cP(x) = 0$, where $c \neq 0$, is another equation with the same roots.

B. A polynomial function *Q* of degree 4 with rational coefficients has zeros $3 - \sqrt{7}$ and $4i$. What is a polynomial equation in standard form with these roots?

The zeros of *Q* are the same as the roots of $Q(x) = 0$. Since one root is irrational and the other is complex with a non-zero imaginary component, their conjugates are also roots.

Factors of $Q(x)$: $x - (3 - \sqrt{7})$ and $x - (3 + \sqrt{7})$

$x - 4i$ and $x - (-4i)$

Multiply the four factors of $Q(x)$.

$Q(x) = (x - (3 - \sqrt{7}))(x - (3 + \sqrt{7}))(x - 4i)(x - (-4i))$

$= ((x - 3) + \sqrt{7}))((x - 3) - \sqrt{7}))(x - 4i)(x + 4i)$ .... Distribute and regroup.

$= ((x - 3)^2 - (\sqrt{7})^2)(x^2 - (4i)^2)$ .... Rewrite as the difference of squares.

$= (x^2 - 6x + 2)(x^2 + 16)$ .... Simplify.

$= x^4 - 6x^3 + 18x^2 - 96x + 32$

The polynomial equation $x^4 - 6x^3 + 18x^2 - 96x + 32 = 0$ has roots $3 - \sqrt{7}$ and $4i$.

Try It! **5a.** What is a quadratic equation in standard form with rational coefficients that has a root of $5 + 4i$?

b. What is a polynomial function *Q* of degree 4 with rational coefficients such that $Q(x) = 0$ has roots $2 - \sqrt{3}$ and $5i$?

CONCEPT SUMMARY Theorems About Roots of Polynomial Equations

	Words	Example
RATIONAL ROOT THEOREM	For the polynomial equation $0 = a_nx^n + a_{n-1}x^{n-1} + ... + a_1x^1 + a_0$, there are a limited number of possible rational roots. Rational roots must have reduced form $\frac{p}{q}$ where p is an integer factor of a_0 and q is an integer factor of a_n. Use substitution or synthetic division to check roots.	$2x^3 + 3x^2 - 10x - 15 = 0$ $p = -15$; Factors of p: $\pm1, \pm3, \pm5, \pm15$ $q = 2$; Factors of q: $\pm1, \pm2$ Possible rational roots: $\pm1, \pm3, \pm5, \pm15, \pm\frac{1}{2}, \pm\frac{3}{2}, \pm\frac{5}{2}, \pm\frac{15}{2}$ $-\frac{3}{2}$ is a root of the equation.
FUNDAMENTAL THEOREM OF ALGEBRA	If $P(x)$ is a polynomial of degree $n \geq 1$, then $P(x) = 0$ has exactly n solutions in th set of complex numbers.	
CONJUGATE ROOT THEOREMS	**Irrational Conjugates**	**Complex Conjugates**
	Let P be a polynomial function with rational coefficients and let a and b be real numbers. Then if $a + \sqrt{b}$ is a root of $P(x) = 0$, then $a - \sqrt{b}$ is also a root of $P(x) = 0$.	Let P be a polynomial function with real coefficients and let a and b be re numbers. Then if $a + bi$ is a root of $P(x) = 0$, then $a - bi$ is also a root of $P(x) = 0$.

Do You UNDERSTAND?

1. ESSENTIAL QUESTION How are the roots of a polynomial equation related to the coefficients and degree of the polynomial?

2. **Error Analysis** Renaldo said that a polynomial equation with rational coefficients that has zeros $-1 + 2i$ and $3 + \sqrt{5}$ has a degree of 4. Is Renaldo correct? Explain.

3. **Use Structure** A fifth degree polynomial $P(x)$ with rational coefficients has zeros $2i$ and $\sqrt{7}$. What other zeros does $P(x)$ have? Explain.

4. **Construct Arguments** If one root of a polynomial equation with real coefficients is $4 + 2i$, is it certain that $4 - 2i$ is also a root of the equation? Explain.

Do You KNOW HOW?

List all the possible rational solutions for each equation according to the Rational Roots Theorem. Then find all of the rational roots.

5. $0 = x^3 + 4x^2 - 9x - 36$

6. $0 = x^4 - 2x^3 - 7x^2 + 8x + 12$

7. $0 = 4x^3 + 8x^2 - x - 2$

8. $0 = 9x^4 - 40x^2 + 16$

A polynomial equation with rational coefficients has the given roots. List two more roots of each equation.

9. $1 + \sqrt{11}$ and $-3 + \sqrt{17}$

10. $5 + 12i$ and $-9 - 7i$

11. $12 + 5i$ and $6 - \sqrt{13}$

12. $5 - 15i$ and $17 + \sqrt{23}$

PRACTICE & PROBLEM SOLVING

Scan for Multimedia

Additional Exercises Available Online

UNDERSTAND

13. **Construct Arguments** Consider the polynomial $P(x) = 5x^3 + ms^2 + nx + 6$, where m and n are rational coefficients. Is 3 *sometimes, always,* or *never* a root? Explain.

14. **Use Structure** Write a fourth-degree polynomial function Q with roots -1, 0, and $2i$.

15. **Error Analysis** A student says that a fifth-degree polynomial equation with rational coefficients has roots -5, -3, 1, 2, and $\sqrt{3}$. Describe possible errors the student may have made.

16. **Reason** Write a third-degree polynomial with rational coefficients that has the following possible roots. Explain your reasoning.

$$\pm\frac{1}{1}, \pm\frac{1}{2}, \pm\frac{2}{1}, \pm\frac{2}{2}, \pm\frac{5}{1}, \pm\frac{5}{2}, \pm\frac{10}{1}, \pm\frac{10}{2}$$

17. **Error Analysis** Describe and correct the error a student made in finding the roots of the polynomial equation $2x^3 - x^2 - 10x + 5 = 0$.

List all possible rational roots.

$\pm 1, \pm\frac{1}{2}, \pm 5, \pm\frac{5}{2}$

Testing reveals that $\frac{1}{2}$ is a root.

Dividing the polynomial by the binomial $x - \frac{1}{2}$ results in the factored form

$f(x) = (x - \frac{1}{2})(2x^2 - 10)$

The equation $2x^2 - 10 = 0$ has two irrational roots, $\sqrt{10}$ and $-\sqrt{10}$.

The complete set of roots is $\{\frac{1}{2}, \sqrt{10}, -\sqrt{10}\}$.

18. **Higher Order Thinking** What is the least number of terms a fifth-degree polynomial with root $3i$ can have? Give an example of such a polynomial equation. Explain.

19. **Use Structure** Show that the Fundamental Theorem of Algebra is true for all quadratic equations with real coefficients. (*Hint*: Use the Quadratic Formula and examine the possibilities for the value of the discriminant.)

PRACTICE

List all the possible rational solutions for each equation. SEE EXAMPLE 1

20. $0 = x^3 - 3x^2 + 4x - 12$

21. $0 = 2x^4 + 13x^3 - 47x^2 - 13x + 45$

22. $0 = 4x^3 + 64x^2 - x - 16$

23. $0 = 8x^3 + 11x^2 - 13x - 6$

24. A closet in the shape of a rectangular prism has the measurements shown. What is the height of the closet, in feet, if its volume is 220 ft^3? SEE EXAMPLE 2

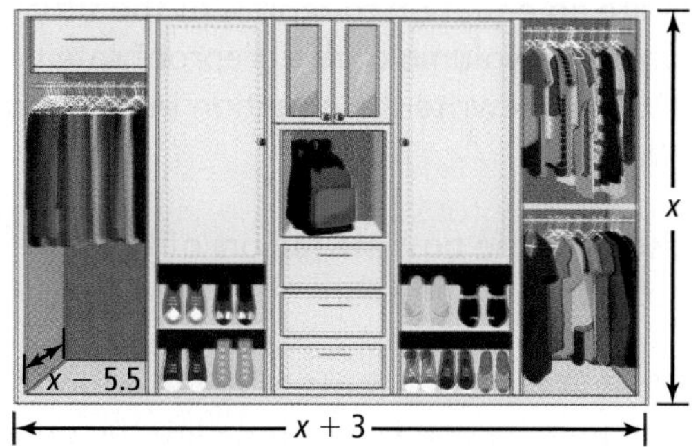

What are all real and complex roots of the following functions? SEE EXAMPLE 3

25. $0 = x^3 - 3x - 52$

26. $0 = x^3 + 9x^2 - 7x - 63$

27. $0 = x^4 + 34x^2 - 72$

28. $0 = x^6 + 4x^4 - 41x^2 + 36$

29. Suppose a cubic polynomial f has one rational zero c and two irrational zeros which are a conjugate pair $a + \sqrt{b}$ and $a - \sqrt{b}$, where a and b are rational numbers. Does f have rational coefficients? SEE EXAMPLE 4

Find a polynomial function $P(x)$ such that P has the degree and $P(x) = 0$ has the root(s) listed. SEE EXAMPLE 5

30. degree of $P = 2$;
zero: $1 + 6i$

31. degree of $P = 4$;
zeros: $3 - \sqrt{11}$ and $-9i$

32. degree of $P = 3$;
zeros: -5 and $4 - 8i$

Mixed Review Available Online

PRACTICE & PROBLEM SOLVING

APPLY

33. Make Sense and Persevere A fireproof safe has the measurements shown.

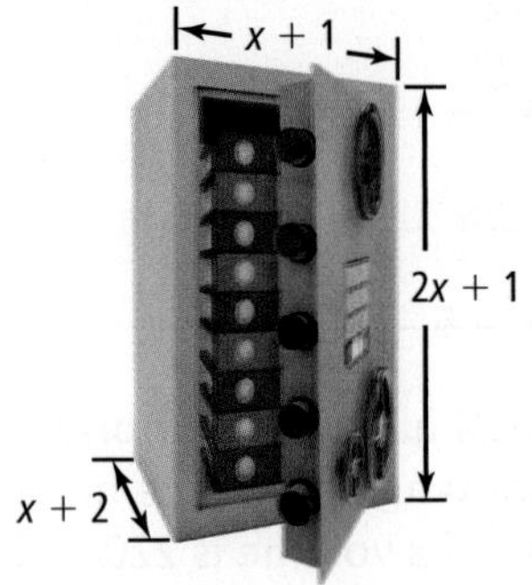

a. Write an equation to represent the situation when the volume of the fireproof safe is 270 in.^{3}. Rewrite the equation in the form $P(x) = 0$.

b. List all of the possible factors of the polynomial expression.

c. What are the real roots of the equation? Explain how you know these are the only real roots.

d. What are the length, width, and height of the fireproof safe?

34. Reason What are the dimensions of the fish tank, in feet, if its volume is 176 ft^3?

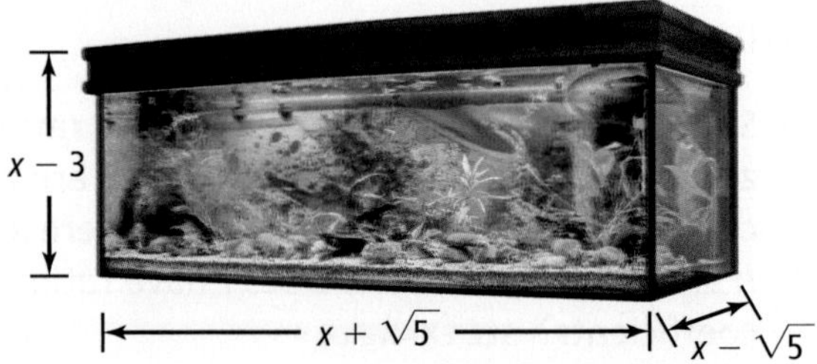

35. Reason The cost of producing x video game consoles is modeled by the function $C(x) = x^4 - 5x^3 - 12x^2 - 22x - 40$. If a company spent \$1,706 to produce video game consoles, how many consoles were made?

ASSESSMENT PRACTICE

36. A fifth-degree polynomial equation with rational coefficients has the roots 3, $8i$, and $7 - \sqrt{5}$. Which are also roots of the polynomial equation? Select all that apply.

Ⓐ -3
Ⓑ $-8i$
Ⓒ $1 - 8i$
Ⓓ $-7 - \sqrt{5}$
Ⓔ $7 + \sqrt{5}$

37. SAT/ACT Which is a third-degree polynomial equation with rational coefficients that has roots -2 and $6i$?

Ⓐ $x^3 + 2x^2 + 36x + 72$
Ⓑ $x^3 - 2x^2 + 36x - 72$
Ⓒ $x^3 + 2x^2 - 36x - 72$
Ⓓ $x^2 + (6i - 2)x - 12$
Ⓔ $x^2 - (6i - 2)x - 12$

38. Performance Task The table shows the number of possible real and imaginary roots for an nth degree polynomial equation with rational coefficients.

Degree	Real Roots	Imaginary Roots
3	3	0
3	1	2
5	5	0
5	3	2
5	1	4

Part A List all of the possible combinations of real and imaginary roots for a seventh-degree polynomial equation.

Part B What do you notice about the number of real roots of a polynomial equation with an odd degree?

2-7 Transformations of Polynomial Functions

I CAN... identify symmetry in and transform polynomial functions.

VOCABULARY

- even function
- odd function

EXPLORE & REASON

Look at the polynomial graphs below.

$f(x) = x^2$

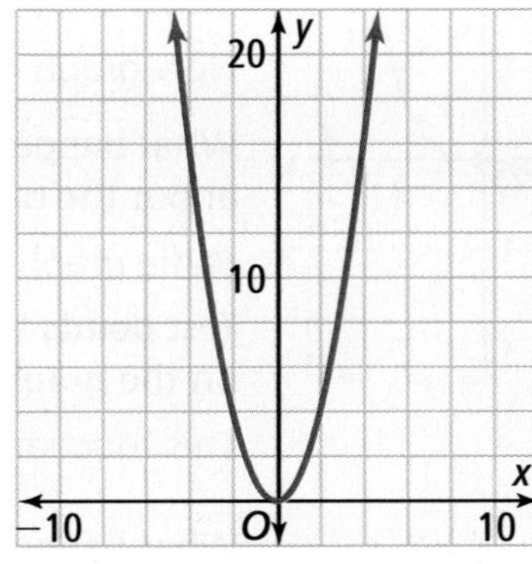

$g(x) = x^3$

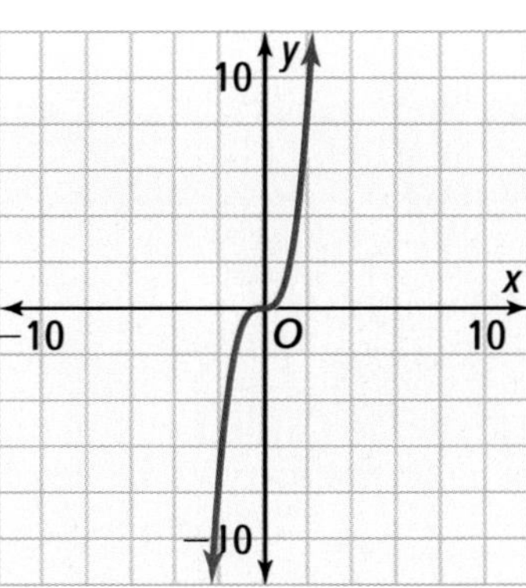

A. Is the graph of f or g symmetric about the y-axis? Is the graph of f or g symmetric about the origin? Explain.

B. Look for Relationships Graph more functions of the form $y = x^n$ where n is a natural number. Which of these functions are symmetric about the origin? Which are symmetric about the y-axis? What conjectures can you make?

ESSENTIAL QUESTION

How are symmetry and transformations represented in the graph and equation of a polynomial function?

CONCEPT Odd and Even Functions

A polynomial function $P(x) = a_nx^n + a_{n-1}x^{n-1} + \cdots + a_1x^1 + a_0$ is an **even function** if it is symmetric about the y-axis and an **odd function** if it is symmetric about the origin.

Other types of functions can also be classified as odd or even. For example, the function $y = |x|$ is an even function.

Even Function

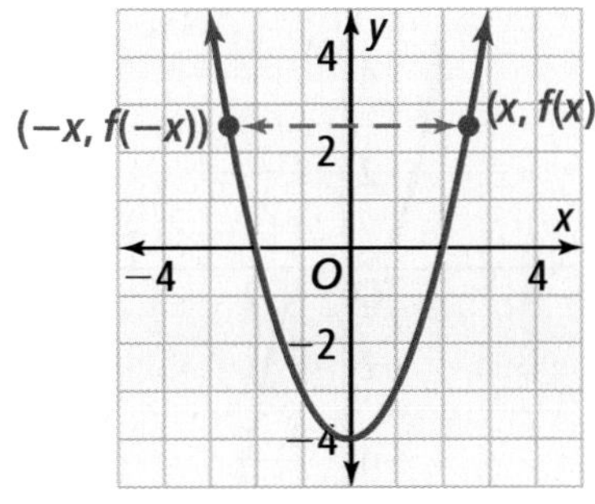

For all x in the domain,

$f(x) = f(-x)$.

Odd Function

Neither

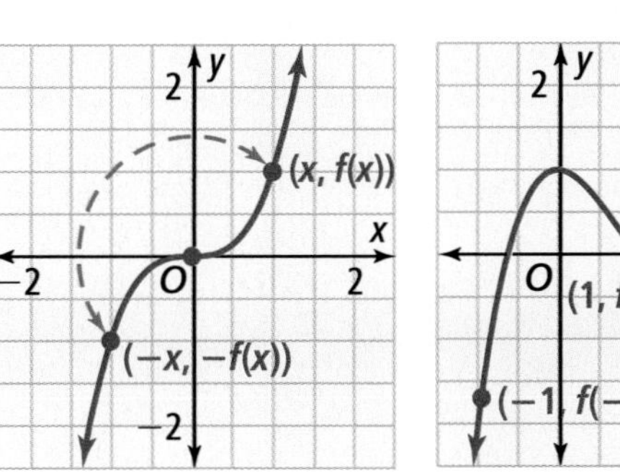

For all x in the domain,

$f(-x) = -f(x)$.

$f(1) \neq f(-1)$ (not even)

$f(-1) \neq -f(1)$ (not odd)

EXAMPLE 1 Identify Even and Odd Functions From Their Graphs

Use the graph to classify the polynomial function. Is it even, odd, or neither?

A.

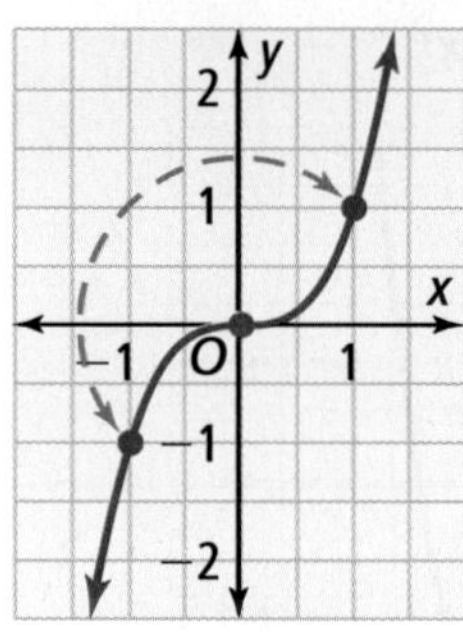

What happens when you reflect the graph across the *y*-axis?

New graph – not even.

What happens when you rotate the graph 180° about the origin?

Same graph – odd

Test points to confirm: (1, 1) and (−1, −1) are both on the graph.

This function is odd.

B.

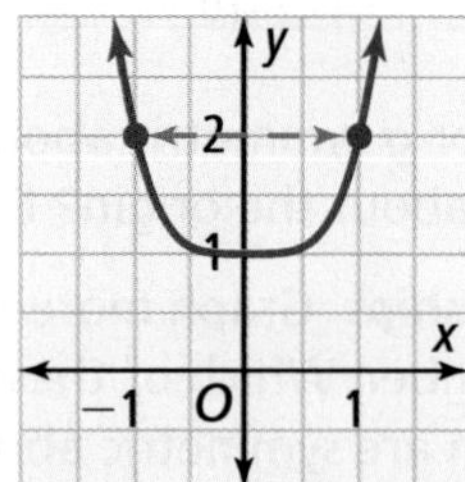

What happens when you reflect the graph across the *y*-axis?

Same graph – even

Test points to confirm: (1, 2) and (−1, 2) are both on the graph.

This function is even.

C.

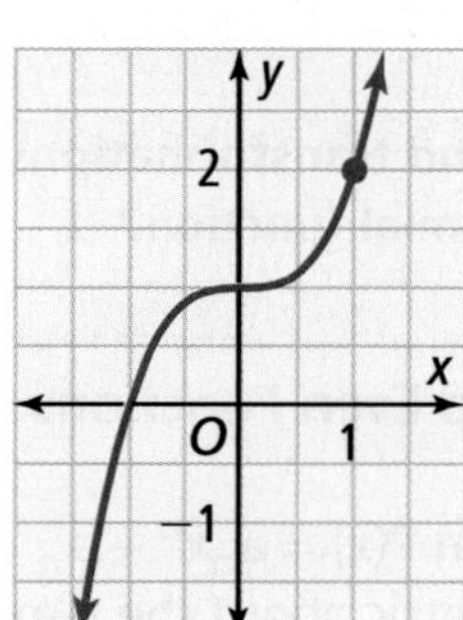

What happens when you reflect the graph across the *y*-axis?

New graph – not even

What happens when you rotate the graph 180° about the origin?

New graph – not odd

Test points to confirm: (1, 2) is on the graph, but (−1, 2) and (−1, −2) are not.

This function is neither even nor odd.

COMMON ERROR

An odd degree polynomial function may have rotational symmetry around a point other than (0, 0). It is only an odd function if the symmetry is around the origin.

Try It! 1. Classify the polynomial functions as even or odd based on the graphs.

a.

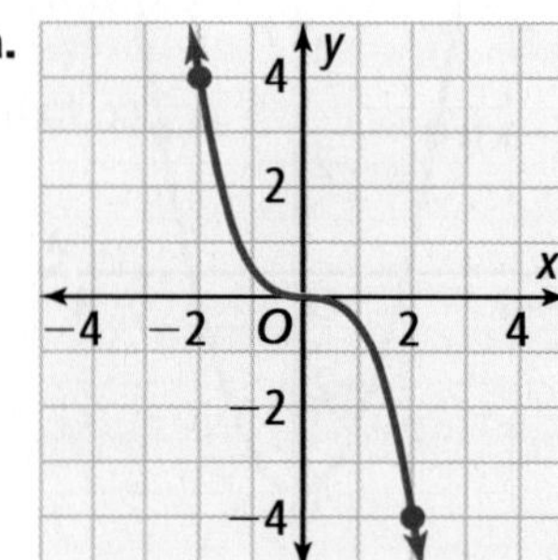

b.

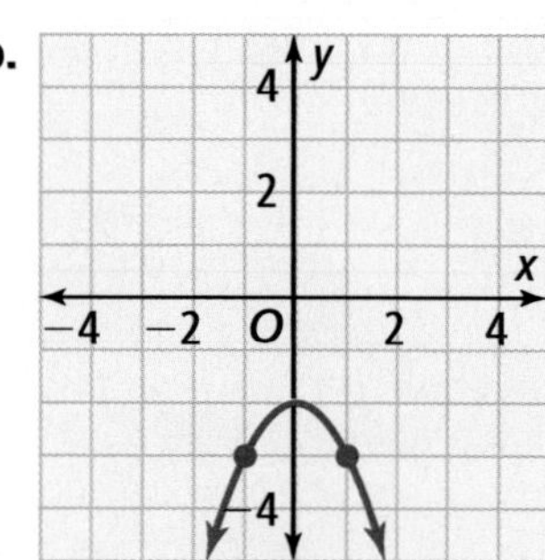

EXAMPLE 2 Identify Even and Odd Functions From Their Equations

Is the function odd, even, or neither?

A. $f(x) = 4x^4 + 5$

$f(-x) = 4(-x)^4 + 5$ .... Replace x with $-x$.

$f(-x) = 4x^4 + 5$ .... Simplify.

Since $f(x) = f(-x)$, $f(x) = 4x^4 + 5$ is an even function.

B. $g(x) = 2x^3 + 3x$

$g(-x) = 2(-x)^3 + 3(-x)$ .... Replace x with $-x$.

$g(-x) = -2x^3 - 3x = -(2x^3 + 3x)$ .... Simplify.

Since $g(-x) = -g(x)$, $g(x) = 2x^3 + 3x$ is an odd function.

CONSTRUCT ARGUMENTS
Why use a variable rather than a specific value? You must show that $f(x) = f(-x)$ or that $-f(x) = f(-x)$ for all x in the domain, not just one value.

Try It! 2. Is the function odd, even, or neither?

a. $f(x) = 7x^5 - 2x^2 + 4$

b. $f(x) = x^6 - 2$

EXAMPLE 3 Graph Transformations of Cubic and Quartic Parent Functions

How do transformed graphs compare to the graph of the parent function?

A. $g(x) = 3x^4 - 18$

Identify the transformations: $g(x) = 3x^4 - 18$.

Parent function: $f(x) = x^4$

Leading coefficient, 3, stretches the graph vertically, making it narrower than the graph of the parent function.

Subtracting 18 translates the graph down 18 units.

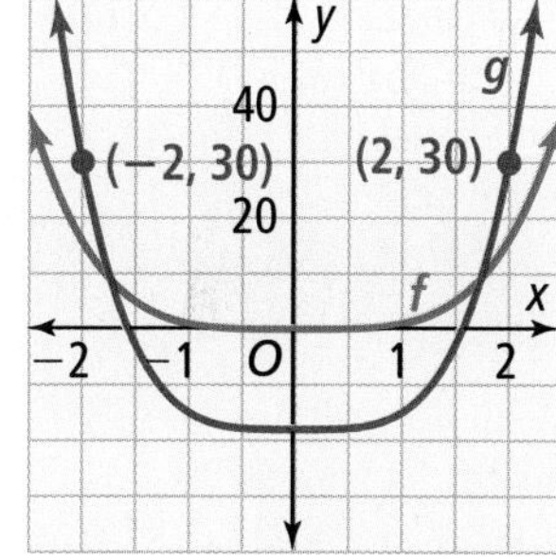

USE APPROPRIATE TOOLS
The graph of the parent function is a valuable tool, because it provides the foundation for sketching the graphs of related functions using transformations.

B. $h(x) = 5(x - 2)^3 + 4$

Identify the transformations: $h(x) = 5(x - 2)^3 + 4$.

Parent function: $f(x) = x^3$

Subtracting 2 (before calculating the cube) shifts the parent graph to the right 2 units.

Multiplying by 5 stretches the translated graph vertically, making it narrower than the graph of the parent function.

Adding 4 translates the stretched graph up 4 units.

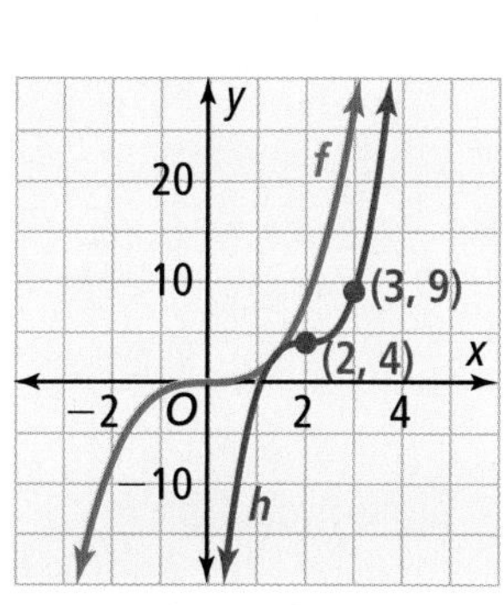

Try It! 3. How does the graph of the function $g(x) = 2x^3 - 5$ differ from the graph of its parent function?

CONCEPTUAL UNDERSTANDING

EXAMPLE 4 Identify a Transformation

VOCABULARY
A cubic function is 3rd degree. A quartic function is 4th degree.

Each of the given graphs is a transformation of the parent cubic function or parent quartic function. How can you determine the equation of the graph?

A.

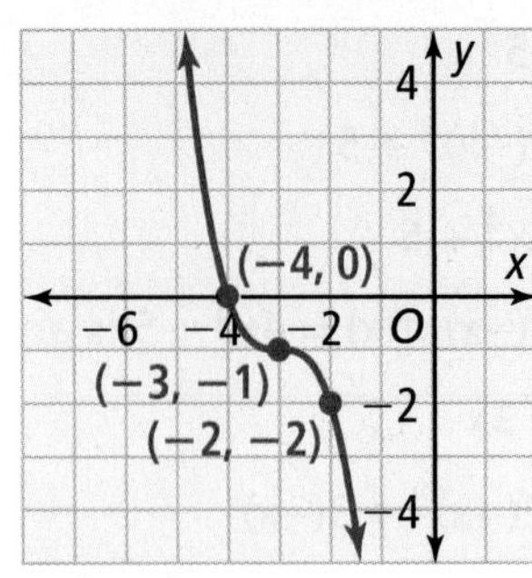

Since the ends extend in opposite directions, the end behavior shows that the parent function has odd degree: $y = x^3$.

The end behavior indicates a negative leading coefficient so this graph is a reflection across the x-axis, such as $y = -x^3$.

The point (0, 0) has shifted to (−3, −1), which shows that the graph has been translated:

Left 3 units

$$y = -(x + 3)^3$$

Down 1 unit

$$y = -(x + 3)^3 - 1$$

The function is $f(x) = -(x + 3)^3 - 1$.

B.

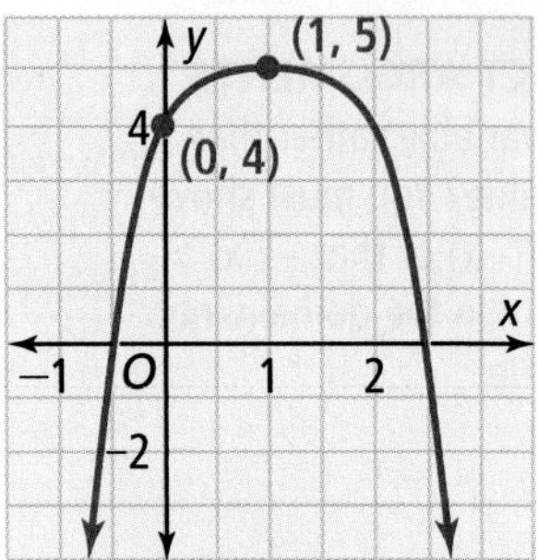

Since the ends extend in the same direction, the end behavior shows that the parent function has even degree: $y = x^4$.

The end behavior indicates a negative leading coefficient so this graph is a reflection across the x-axis, such as $y = -x^4$.

The point (0, 0) has shifted to (1, 5), which shows that the graph has been translated:

Right 1 unit

$$y = -(x - 1)^4$$

Up 5 units

$$y = -(x - 1)^4 + 5$$

The function is $f(x) = -(x - 1)^4 + 5$.

Try It! 4. Determine the equation of each graph as it relates to its parent cubic function or quartic function.

a.

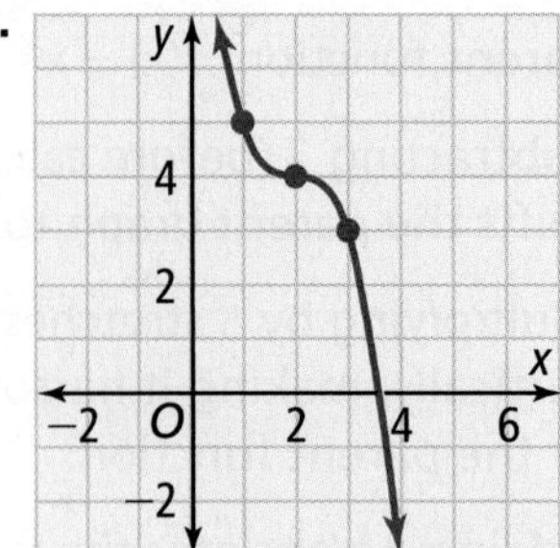

b.

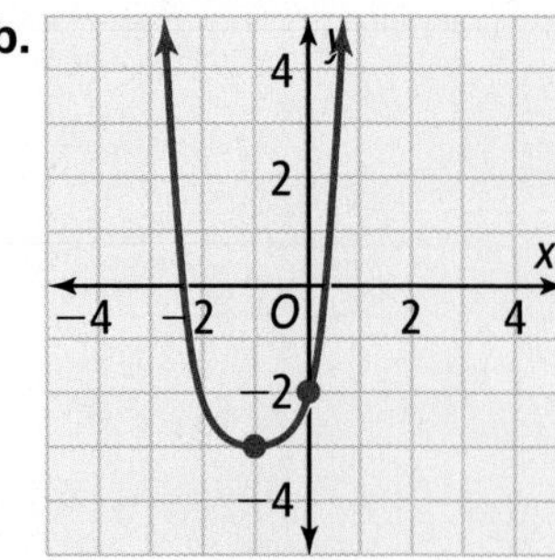

  Activity  Assess

APPLICATION

EXAMPLE 5 Apply a Transformation of a Cubic Function

A. The volume of a box, in cubic yards, is given by the function $V(x) = x^3$. The post office lists permissible shipping volumes in cubic feet. Write a function for the volume in cubic feet if x is the edge length in yards.

Replace x with $3x$ ······ Convert yards to feet.

$V(3x) = (3x)^3$ ······ Evaluate $V(x)$ for the value $3x$.

$V(x) = 27x^3$ ······ Simplify to write the function in units of cubic feet.

The function that represents the volume of the box, in cubic feet, is $V(x) = 27x^3$.

COMMON ERROR
Remember to apply exponents correctly: $(3x)^3 \neq 3x^3$.

B. A terrarium is in the shape of a rectangular prism. The volume of the tank is given by $V(x) = (x)(2x)(x + 5) = 2x^3 + 10x^2$, where x is measured in inches. The manufacturer wants to compare the volume of this tank with one that has a width 2 inches shorter but maintains the relationships between the width and the other dimensions. Write a new function for the volume of this smaller tank.

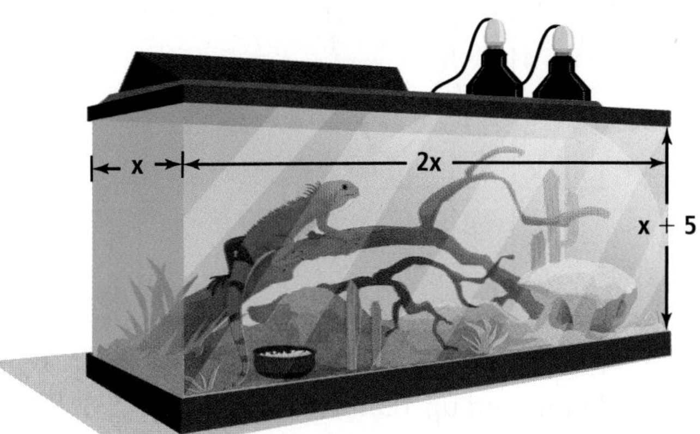

$$V(x - 2) = (x - 2)[2(x - 2)][(x - 2) + 5]$$ Replace x with $x - 2$.

$$= (x - 2)(2x - 4)(x + 3)$$

$$= (2x^2 - 8x + 8)(x + 3)$$

$$= 2x^3 - 2x^2 - 16x + 24$$

The function that represents the volume of the smaller tank is $V(x - 2) = 2x^3 - 2x^2 - 16x + 24$.

 **Try It!** 5a. The volume of a cube, in cubic feet, is given by the function $V(x) = x^3$. Write a function for the volume of the cube in cubic inches if x is the edge length in feet.

b. A storage unit is in the shape of a rectangular prism. The volume of the storage unit is given by $V(x) = (x)(x)(x - 1) = x^3 - x^2$, where x is measured in feet. A potential customer wants to compare the volume of this storage unit with that of another storage unit that is 1 foot longer in every dimension. Write a function for the volume of this larger unit.

CONCEPT SUMMARY Understand Polynomial Functions

	Even Function	Odd Function
DEFINITION	Line of symmetry: y-axis For all x, $f(x) = f(-x)$.	Point of symmetry: origin For all x, $f(-x) = -f(x)$.
PARENT FUNCTION	Has even degree: $y = x^2, y = x^4, y = x^6, \ldots$	Has odd degree: $y = x, y = x^3, y = x^5, \ldots$
END BEHAVIOR (positive leading coefficient) (negative leading coefficient)	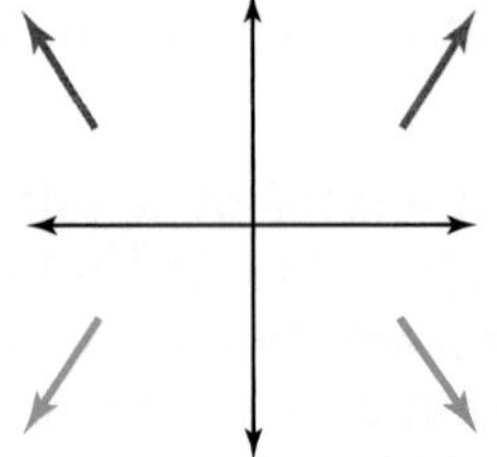	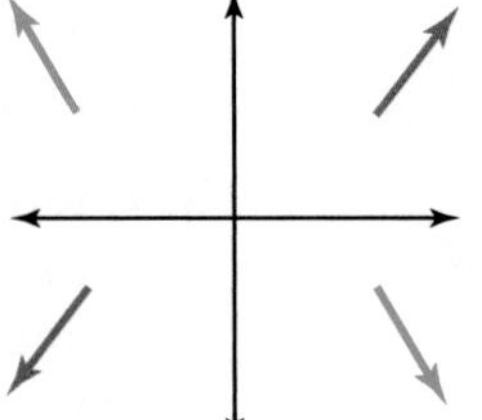
TRANSLATION	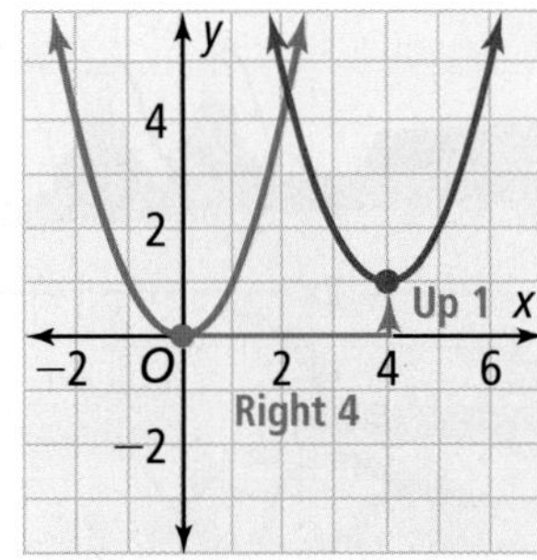 The vertex moves to the right 4 units and up 1 unit. $y = x^2 \rightarrow y = (x - 4)^2 + 1$	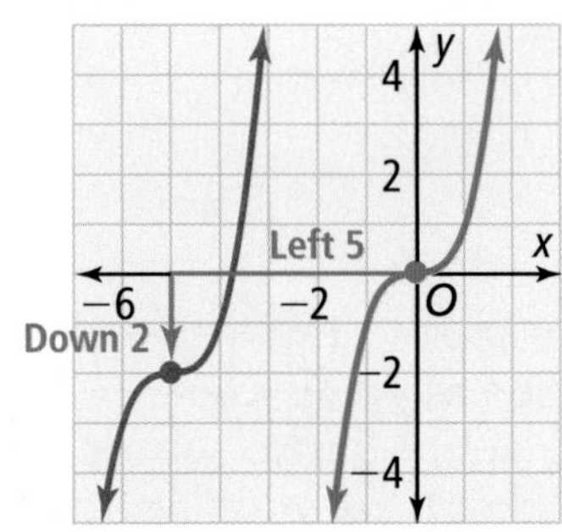 The graph of the function moves to the left 5 units and down 2 units. $y = x^3 \rightarrow y = (x + 5)^3 - 2$

Do You UNDERSTAND?

1. **ESSENTIAL QUESTION** How are symmetry and transformations represented in the graph and equation of a polynomial function?

2. **Vocabulary** What is the difference between the graph of an even function and the graph of an odd function?

3. **Error Analysis** A student identified the transformations of the polynomial function $f(x) = 3(x - 1)^3 - 6$ as follows:

   The function shifted to the left 1 unit, stretched vertically, and shifted downward 6 units.

   Describe and correct the error the student made.

Do You KNOW HOW?

4. Classify the function on the graph as odd, even, or neither.

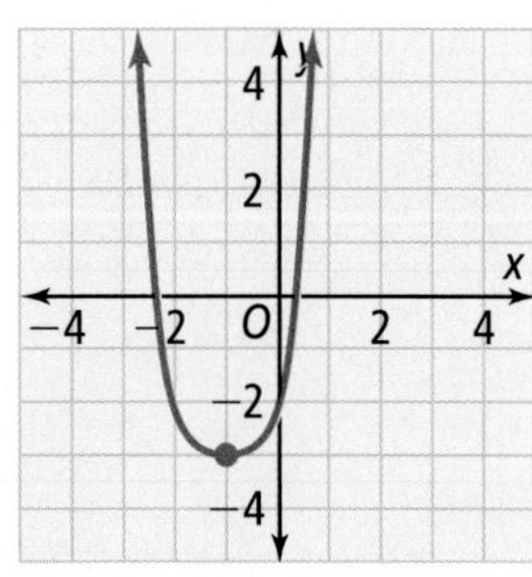

5. Use the equation to classify the function as odd, even, or neither.

   $$g(x) = 4x^3 - x$$

6. The volume of a cardboard box is given by the function $V(x) = x(x - 2)(x) = x^3 - 2x^2$. Write a new function for the volume of a cardboard box that is 2 units longer in every dimension.

PRACTICE & PROBLEM SOLVING

Scan for Multimedia

Practice Tutorial

Additional Exercises Available Online

UNDERSTAND

7. **Make Sense and Persevere** If you use a graph to determine the equation of a function, explain how to check that your equation is correct.

8. **Error Analysis** Describe the error Terrence made in graphing the transformation of the cubic function $g(x) = x^3$ to $f(x) = -\frac{1}{2}x^3 + 10$.

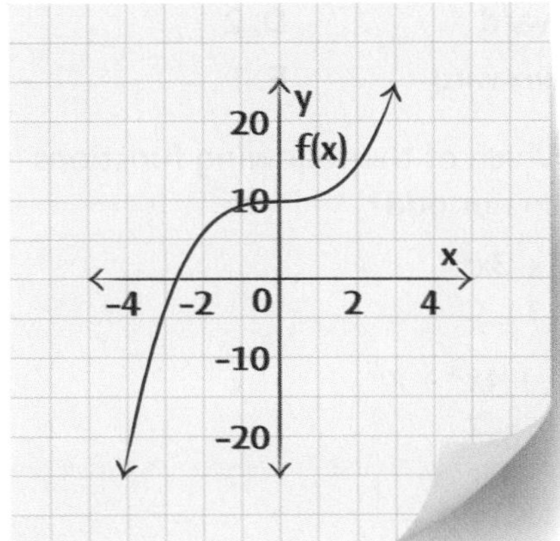

9. **Higher Order Thinking** Explain how to identify a transformation of the function $y = x^3$ by looking at a graph. What do you look for to determine a translation? A reflection? A stretch or compression?

10. **Use Structure** Describe the steps used to determine the equation of the graph of the transformed parent quartic function.

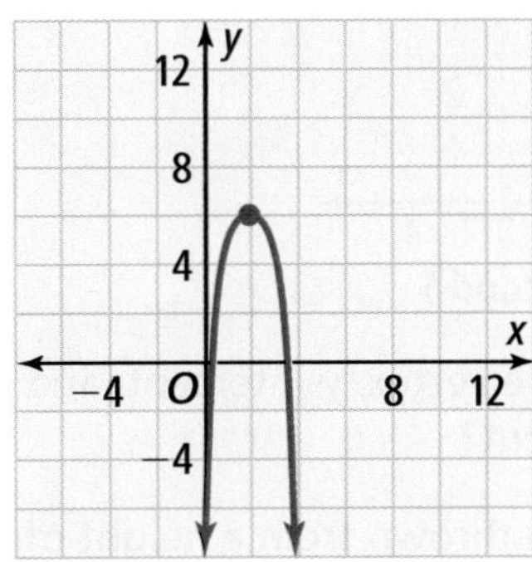

11. **Construct Arguments** Explain why the function $g(x) = 2x^5 + 3x^4 + 1$ is neither even nor odd.

12. **Construct Arguments** Provide an example that demonstrates the following statement is not true.

If the degree of a function is an even number, then the function is an even function.

PRACTICE

Use the graph to classify the polynomial function. Is it even, odd, or neither? SEE EXAMPLE 1

13.

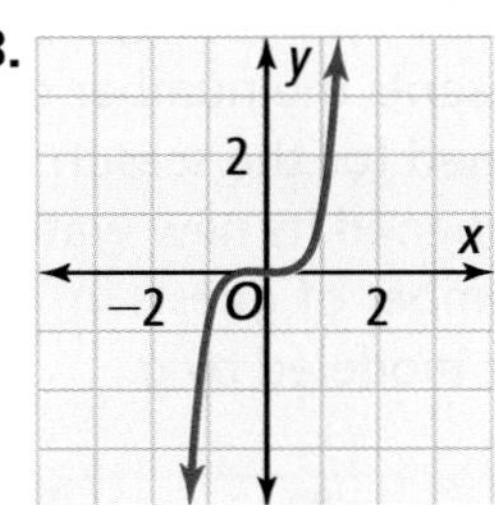

14.

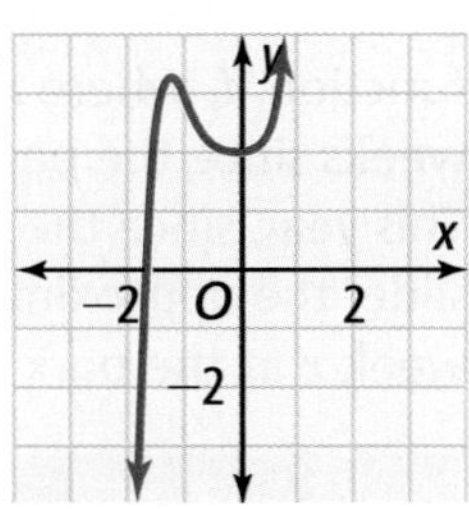

Use the equation to classify the polynomial function. Is it even, odd, or neither? SEE EXAMPLE 2

15. $f(x) = 2x^5 + 4x^2$

16. $g(x) = 6x^4 + 2x^2$

How do the graphs of transformations compare to the graph of the parent function? SEE EXAMPLE 3

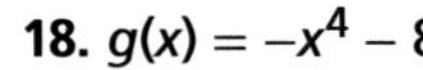

17. $f(x) = 3(x + 1)^3 - 2$

18. $g(x) = -x^4 - 8$

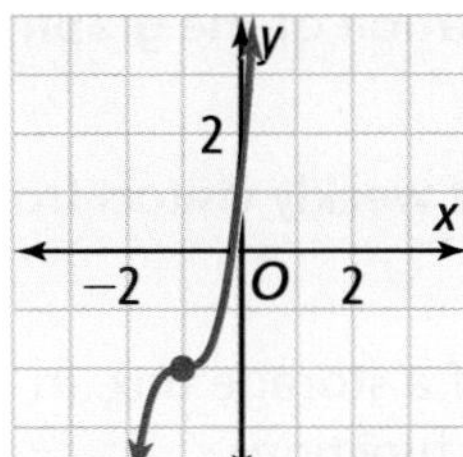

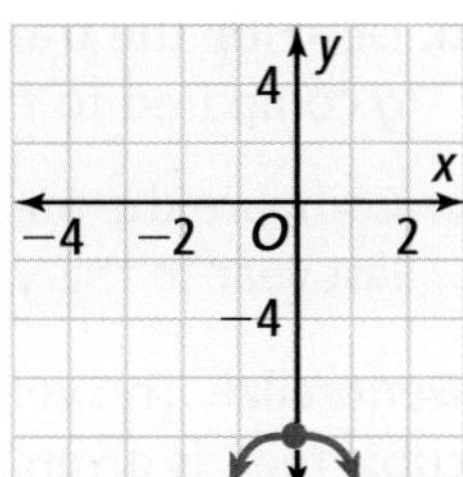

Each graph is a transformation of the parent cubic function or quartic function. Determine the equation of the graph. SEE EXAMPLE 4

19.

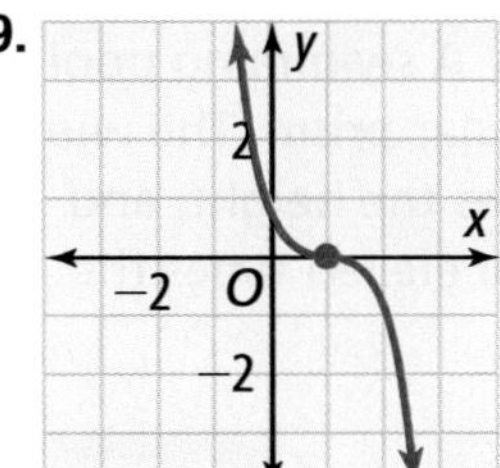

20.

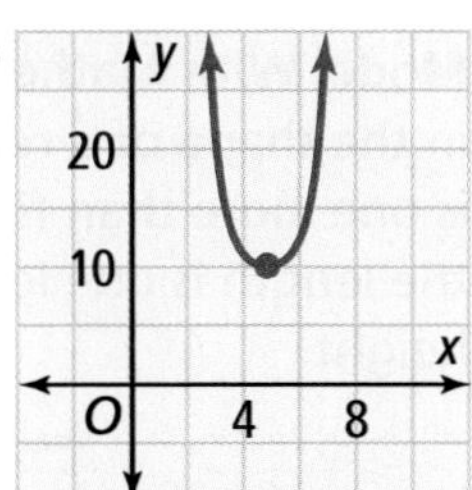

21. The volume of a rectangular room, in cubic yards, is given by the function shown. Write a function for the volume in cubic feet if x is in yards. SEE EXAMPLE 5

PRACTICE & PROBLEM SOLVING

APPLY

22. **Make Sense and Persevere** Last season the approximate number of guests in week x at an amusement park could be modeled by the function, f, where x represents the number of weeks since the park opened for the season. This year, since the park opened its new water slide, the approximate number of guests in week x at the park can be modeled by g.

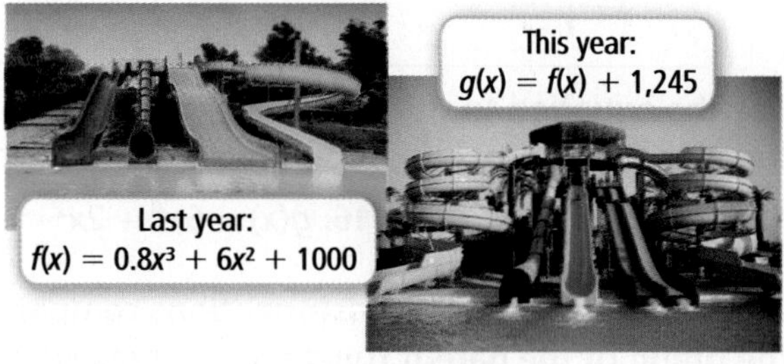

   a. Write the function g in terms of x.

   b. Describe the transformation of the graph of g compared to f.

   c. Compare the number of weekly visitors from last year to this year.

23. **Generalize** The volume of a storage box, in cubic feet, is given by the function $V(x) = (x)(x + 1)^2$. A freight company lists the shipping rates of items in cubic inches. Write a function for the volume of the box in cubic inches if x is its width in feet.

24. **Model With Mathematics** A swimming pool is in the shape of a rectangular prism. The width is one more than five times the height, and the length is one less than eleven times the height.

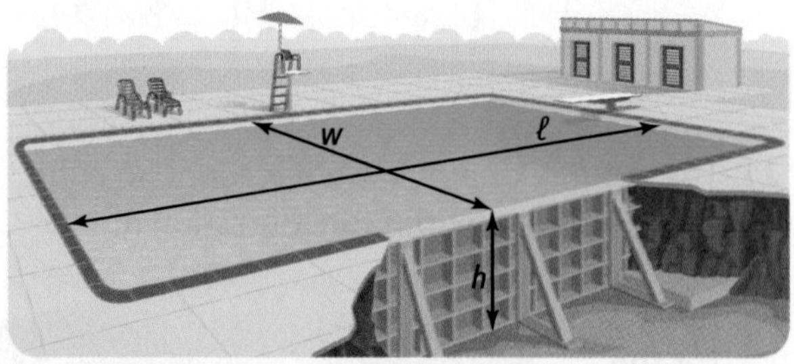

   a. Using x for the height, write a function $V(x)$ to represent the volume of the pool.

   b. Compare the volume of this pool with a larger one that is the same height, but twice the length and twice the width of this pool. Write a function $Z(x)$ for the volume of this larger pool.

ASSESSMENT PRACTICE

25. Match the number in each function with its effect on the parent function.

$f(x) = 2(x - 1)^4 + 5$

$g(x) = (x + 3)^6 - 7$

I vertical stretch	**A.** 7
II shift to the left	**B.** 5
III shift to the right	**C.** 3
IV shift upward	**D.** 2
V shift downward	**E.** 1

26. **SAT/ACT** Which of the following functions is neither even nor odd?

Ⓐ $f(x) = x^4 + 3x^2$

Ⓑ $g(x) = 5x^3 - x$

Ⓒ $h(x) = x^5 + 4x^3 + x^2$

Ⓓ $k(x) = 9 - 8x^2$

Ⓔ $p(x) = 5$

27. **Performance Task** The height of a ball thrown in the air can be modeled by the function $h(x) = -16t^2 + 32t + 6$, where $h(x)$ represents the height in feet of the ball after t seconds. The graph of this function is shown below.

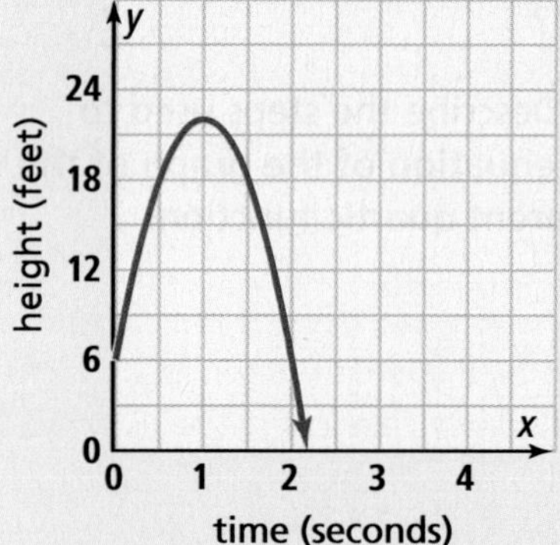

Part A What do the vertex, y-intercept, and x-intercept represent?

Part B If the ball is thrown from a height of 10 ft, how will this transform the graph?

Part C About how much longer will the ball be in the air when it is thrown from 10 ft compared to when it was thrown from 6 ft? (Hint: You may want to use your graphing calculator to compare the two graphs.)

TOPIC 2

Topic Review

TOPIC ESSENTIAL QUESTION

1. What can the rule for a polynomial function reveal about its graph, and what can the graphs of polynomial functions reveal about the solutions of polynomial equations?

Vocabulary Review

Choose the correct term to complete each sentence.

2. The ________ is the greatest power of the variable in a polynomial expression.
3. The ________ is the non-zero constant multiplied by the greatest power of the variable in a polynomial expression.
4. The ________ of a function describes what happens to its graph as x approaches positive and negative infinity.
5. ________ is the triangular pattern of numbers where each number is the sum of two numbers above it.
6. The ________ determines whether the graph of the function will cross the x-axis at the point or merely touch it.
7. The ________ is a formula that can be used to expand powers of binomial expressions.
8. ________ is a method to divide a polynomial by a linear factor whose leading coefficient is 1.

- Binomial Theorem
- degree of a polynomial
- end behavior
- even function
- Factor Theorem
- identity
- leading coefficient
- multiplicity of a zero
- Pascal's Triangle
- synthetic division

Concepts & Skills Review

LESSON 2-1 Graphing Polynomial Functions

Quick Review

A **polynomial** can be either a monomial or a sum of monomials. When a polynomial has more than one monomial, the monomials are also referred to as **terms**.

Example

Graph the function $f(x) = 2x^3 - x^2 - 13x - 6$.

There are zeros at $x = -2$, $x = -0.5$, and $x = 3$.

There are turning points between −2 and −0.5 and between −0.5 and 3.

As $x \to -\infty$, $y \to -\infty$.

As $x \to +\infty$, $y \to +\infty$.

Practice & Problem Solving

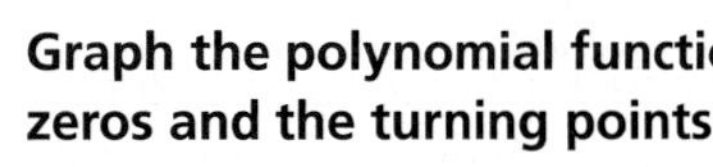

Graph the polynomial function. Estimate the zeros and the turning points of the graph.

9. $f(x) = x^5 + 2x^4 - 10x^3 - 20x^2 + 9x + 18$

10. $f(x) = x^4 + x^3 - 16x^2 - 4x + 48$

11. **Reason** A polynomial function has the following end behavior: As $x \to -\infty$, $y \to +\infty$. As $x \to +\infty$, $y \to -\infty$. Describe the degree and leading coefficient of the polynomial function.

12. **Make Sense and Persevere** After x hours of hiking, Sadie's elevation is $p(x) = -x^3 + 11x^2 - 34x + 24$, in meters. After how many hours will Sadie's elevation be 18 m below sea level? What do the x- and y-intercepts of the graph mean in this context?

LESSONS 2-2 & 2-3 Adding, Subtracting, and Multiplying Polynomials and Polynomial Identities

Quick Review

To add or subtract polynomials, add or subtract like terms. To multiply polynomials, use the Distributive Property.

Polynomial identities can be used to factor or multiply polynomials.

Example

Add $(-2x^3 + 5x^2 + 2x - 3) + (x^3 - 6x^2 + x + 12)$.

Use the Commutative and Associative Properties. Then combine like terms.

$(-2x^3 + 5x^2 + 2x - 3) + (x^3 - 6x^2 + x - 12)$

$= (-2x^3 + x^3) + (5x^2 - 6x^2) + (2x + x) + (-3 + 12)$

$= -x^3 - x^2 + 3x + 9$

Example

Use polynomial identities to factor $8x^3 + 27y^3$.

Use the Sum of Cubes Identity. Express each term as a square. Then write the factors.

$a^3 + b^3 = (a + b)(a^2 - ab + b^2)$

$8x^3 + 27y^3 = (2x)^3 + (3y)^3$

$= (2x + 3y)(4x^2 - 6xy + 9y^2)$

Practice & Problem Solving

Add or subtract the polynomials.

13. $(-8x^3 + 7x^2 + x - 9) + (5x^3 + 3x^2 - 2x - 1)$
14. $(9y^4 - y^3 + 4y^2 + y - 2) - (2y^4 - 3y^3 + 6y - 7)$

Multiply the polynomials.

15. $(9x - 1)(x + 5)(7x + 2)$

Use polynomial identities to multiply each polynomial.

16. $(5x + 8)^2$
17. $(7x - 4)(7x + 4)$

Factor the polynomial.

18. $x^6 - 64$
19. $27x^3 + y^6$

Use Pascal's Triangle or the Binomial Theorem to expand the expressions.

20. $(x - 2)^4$
21. $(x + 5y)^5$
22. **Communicate Precisely** Explain why the set of polynomials is closed under subtraction.
23. **Reason** The length of a rectangle is represented by $3x^3 - 2x^2 + 10x - 4$, and the width is represented by $-x^3 + 6x^2 - x + 8$. What is the perimeter of the rectangle?

LESSON 2-4 Dividing Polynomials

Quick Review

Polynomials can be divided using long division or synthetic division. **Synthetic division** is a method to divide a polynomial by a linear factor whose leading coefficient is 1.

Example

Use synthetic division to divide $x^4 - 5x^3 - 6x^2 + 2x - 8$ by $x + 3$.

−3	1	−5	−6	2	−8
		−3	24	−54	156
	1	−8	18	−52	148
	↓	↓	↓	↓	↓
	x^3	$-8x^2$	$+18x$	-52	$+\frac{148}{x+3}$

The quotient is $x^3 - 8x^2 + 18x - 52$, and the remainder is 148.

Practice & Problem Solving

Use long division to divide.

24. $x^4 + 2x^3 - 8x^2 - 3x + 1$ divided by $x + 2$

Use synthetic division to divide.

25. $x^4 + 5x^3 + 7x^2 - 2x + 17$ divided by $x - 3$
26. **Make Sense and Persevere** A student divided $f(x) = x^3 + 8x^2 - 9x - 3$ by $x - 2$ and got a remainder of 19. Explain how the student could verify the remainder is correct.
27. **Reason** The area of a rectangle is $4x^3 + 14x^2 - 18$ in.^{2}. The length of the rectangle is $x + 3$ in. What is the width of the rectangle?

LESSONS 2-5 & 2-6 Zeros of Polynomial Functions and Theorems About Roots of Polynomial Equations

Quick Review

You can factor and use synthetic division to find zeros of polynomial functions. Then you can use the zeros to sketch a graph of the function.

The **Rational Root Theorem** states that the possible rational roots, or zeros, of a polynomial equation with integer coefficients come from the list of numbers of the form: $\pm \frac{\textit{factor of } a_0}{\textit{factor of } a_n}$.

Example

List all the possible rational solutions for the equation $0 = 2x^3 + x^2 - 7x - 6$. Then find all of the rational roots.

$\pm 1, \pm 2, \pm 3, \pm 6$ Factors of the constant term

$\pm 1, \pm 2$ Factors of the leading coefficient

List the possible roots, eliminating duplicates.

$\pm\frac{1}{1}, \pm\frac{1}{2}, \pm\frac{2}{1}, \pm\frac{3}{1}, \pm\frac{3}{2}, \pm\frac{6}{1}$

Use synthetic division to find that the roots are $-\frac{3}{2}$, -1, and 2.

Practice & Problem Solving

Sketch the graph of the function.

28. $f(x) = 2x^4 - x^3 - 32x^2 + 31x + 60$

29. $g(x) = x^3 - x^2 - 20x$

30. What x-values are solutions to the equation $x^3 + 2x^2 - 4x + 8 = x^2 - x + 4$?

31. What values of x are solutions to the inequality $x^3 + 3x^2 - 4x - 12 > 0$?

32. What are all of the real and complex roots of the function $f(x) = x^4 - 4x^3 + 4x^2 - 36x - 45$?

33. A polynomial function Q of degree 4 with rational coefficients has zeros $1 + \sqrt{5}$ and $-7i$. What is an equation for Q?

34. Reason What does the graph of a function tell you about the multiplicity of a zero?

35. Make Sense and Persevere A storage unit in the shape of a rectangular prism measures $2x$ ft long, $x + 8$ ft wide, and $x + 9$ ft tall. What are the dimensions of the storage unit, in feet, if its volume is 792 ft^3?

LESSON 2-7 Transformations of Polynomial Functions

Quick Review

Polynomial functions can be translated, reflected, and stretched in similar ways to other functions you have studied.

Example

How does the graph of $f(x) = 2(x + 1)^3 - 3$ compare to the graph of the parent function?

Parent function: $y = x^3$

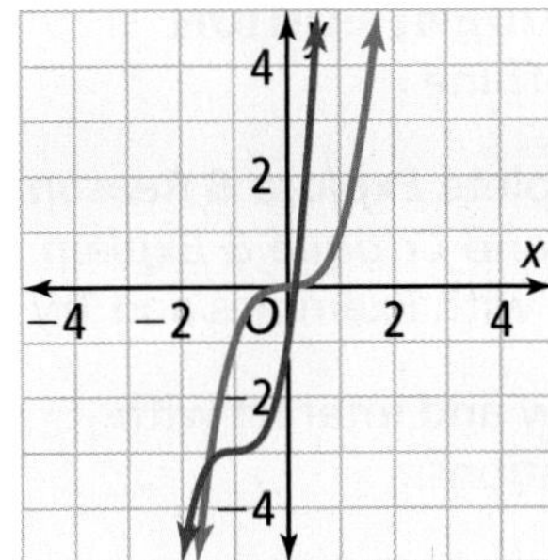

Adding 1 shifts the graph to the left 1 unit.

Multiplying by 2 stretches the graph vertically.

Subtracting 3 shifts the graph down 3 units.

Practice & Problem Solving

Classify each function as even, odd, or neither.

36.

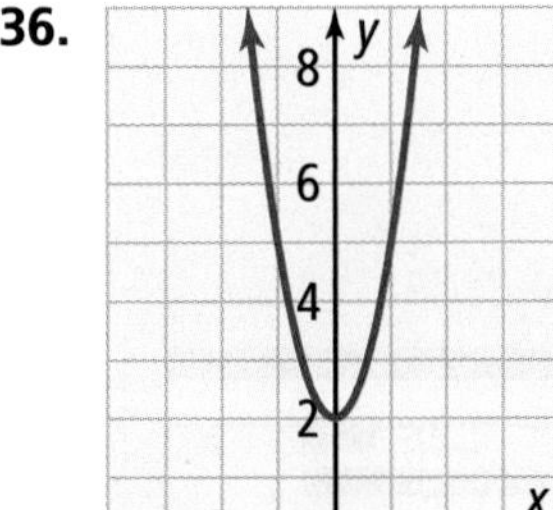

37.

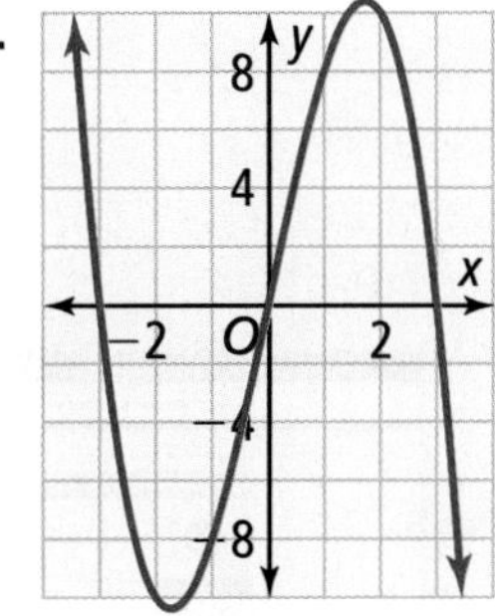

38. Error Analysis A student says the graph of $f(x) = 0.5x^4 + 1$ is a vertical stretch and a translation up 1 unit of the parent function. Explain the student's error.

39. Make Sense and Persevere The volume of a refrigerator, in cubic centimeters, is given by the function $V(x) = (x)(x + 1)(x - 2)$. Write a new function for the volume of the refrigerator in cubic millimeters if x is in centimeters.

TOPIC

3

Rational Functions

? TOPIC ESSENTIAL QUESTION

How do you calculate with functions defined as quotients of polynomials, and what are the key features of their graphs?

Topic Overview

Topic Vocabulary

- asymptote
- compound fraction
- constant of variation
- extraneous solution
- inverse variation
- rational equation
- rational expression
- rational function
- reciprocal function
- simplified form of a rational expression

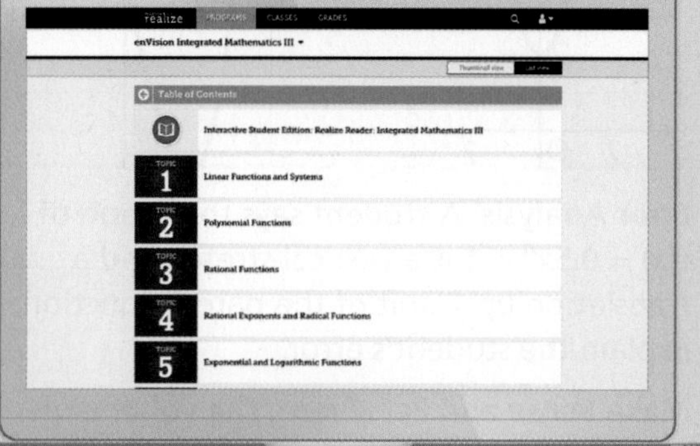

Go online | **PearsonRealize.com**

Digital Experience

INTERACTIVE STUDENT EDITION Access online or offline.

ACTIVITIES Complete ***Explore & Reason, Model & Discuss***, and ***Critique & Explain*** activities. Interact with Examples and Try Its.

ANIMATION View and interact with real-world applications.

PRACTICE Practice what you've learned.

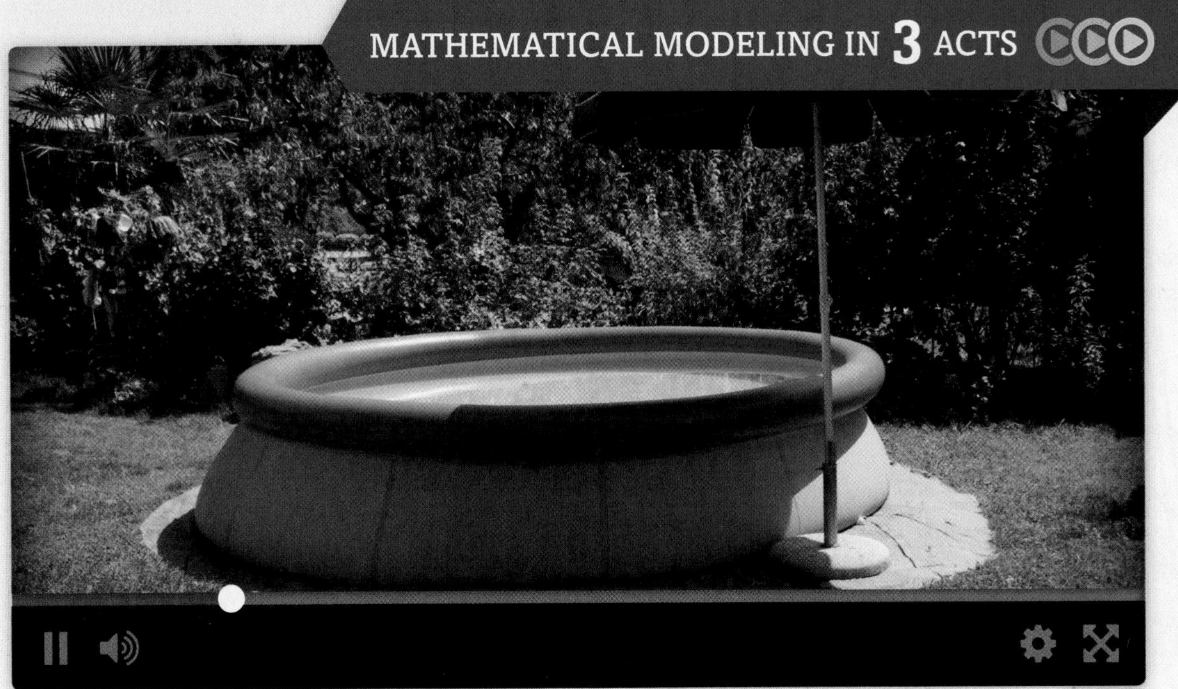

Real Cool Waters

Nothing feels better on a hot day than jumping into a pool! Many cities have swimming pools that people can go to for a small fee. Some people have swimming pools in their backyards that they can enjoy any time. If neither of these options are available, you can always create your own beach paradise! Get a kiddie pool, a lawn chair, and a beach umbrella. Think about your beach paradise during the Mathematical Modeling in 3 Acts lesson.

TOPIC 3

VIDEOS Watch clips to support ***Mathematical Modeling in 3 Acts Lessons*** and **enVision® *STEM Projects*.**

CONCEPT SUMMARY Review key lesson content through multiple representations.

ASSESSMENT Show what you've learned.

GLOSSARY Read and listen to English and Spanish definitions.

TUTORIALS Get help from ***Virtual Nerd***, right when you need it.

MATH TOOLS Explore math with digital tools and manipulatives.

Did You Know?

All business-related costs are either *fixed* or *variable*. **Fixed costs** for a business include rent and machinery to make items to be sold by the business. **Variable costs** include the materials needed to make the items.

In 2013, **Delta Airlines** began purchasing used aircraft instead of new aircraft, lowering its fixed costs (buying aircraft) and raising its variable costs (maintaining its aircraft).

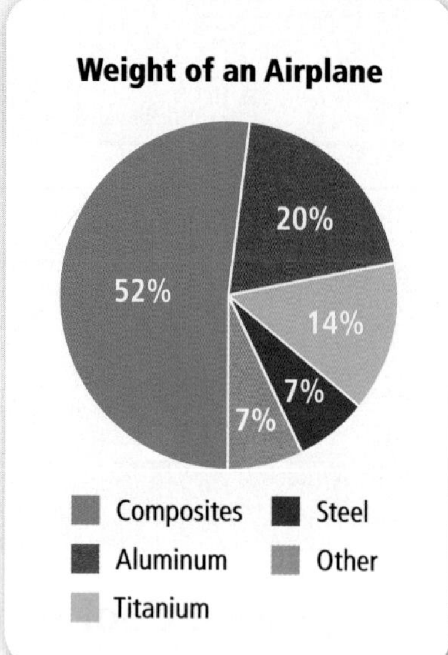

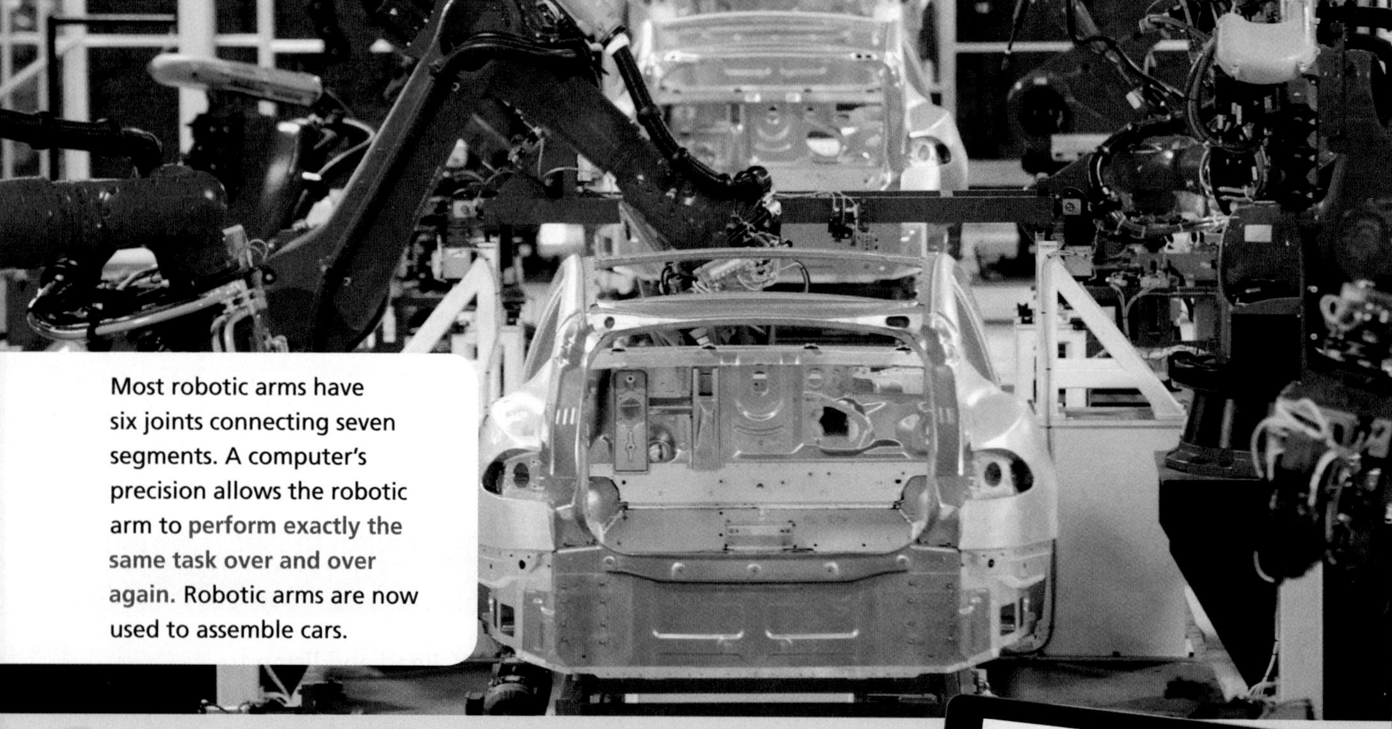

Most robotic arms have six joints connecting seven segments. A computer's precision allows the robotic arm to **perform exactly the same task over and over again.** Robotic arms are now used to assemble cars.

Your Task: Manufacturing Costs

You and your classmates will collect data about a potential business venture, and determine the number of items that must be built and sold in order for the business to be profitable. Based on this and other information, you will give advice about whether or not the business venture is viable and how to improve it.

3-1 Inverse Variation and the Reciprocal Function

I CAN... use inverse variation and graph translations of the reciprocal function.

VOCABULARY

- asymptote
- constant of variation
- inverse variation
- reciprocal function

Activity Assess

MODEL & DISCUSS

The two rectangles shown both have an area of 144 square units.

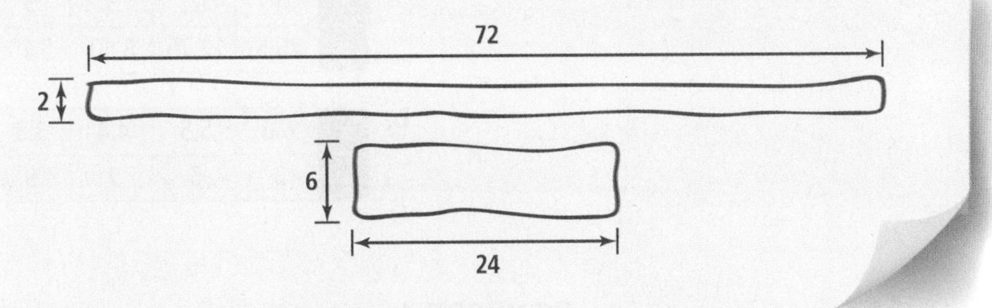

A. Sketch as many other rectangles as you can that have the same area. Organize and record your data for the lengths and widths of the rectangles.

B. Use Structure Considering rectangles with an area of 144 square units, what happens to the width of the rectangle as the length increases?

C. Examine at least five other pairs of rectangles, each pair sharing the same area. How would you describe the relationship between the lengths and widths?

ESSENTIAL QUESTION

How are inverse variations related to the reciprocal function?

EXAMPLE 1 Identify Inverse Variation

How do you determine if a relationship represents an inverse variation?

A. Does the table of values represent an inverse variation?

x	1	2	3	4	6	12
y	12	6	4	3	2	1

An **inverse variation** is a relation between two variables such that as one variable increases, the other decreases proportionally. For the table to represent an inverse variation, the product of x and y must be constant. Find the product, xy, for each column in the table.

x	1	2	3	4	6	12
y	12	6	4	3	2	1
xy	12	12	12	12	12	12

Since the product of the values is constant, *the table of values represents an inverse variation*.

STUDY TIP

Be sure to check the products for every pair of values before drawing a conclusion.

B. Does the table of values represent an inverse variation?

x	1	2	3	4	5	6
y	20	17	14	11	8	5

Find the products.

x	1	2	3	4	5	6
y	20	17	14	11	8	5
xy	20	34	42	44	40	30

Since the products are not constant, *the table does not represent an inverse variation*.

CONTINUED ON THE NEXT PAGE

Try It! 1. Determine if each table of values represents an inverse variation.

a.

x	1	2	3	5	6	15
y	25.5	12.75	8.50	5.10	4.25	1.70

b.

x	6.6	5.5	4.4	3.3	2.2	1.1
y	3	5	7	9	11	13

CONCEPT Inverse Variation

When a relation between x and y is an inverse variation, we say that x varies inversely as y. Inverse variation is modeled by the equation $y = \frac{k}{x}$, or with an equivalent form $x = \frac{k}{y}$ or $xy = k$, where $k \neq 0$. The variable k represents the **constant of variation**, the number that relates the two variables in an inverse variation.

In this table, the constant of variation is 24.

x	1	2	3	4	6	8	12	24
y	24	12	8	6	4	3	2	1

Notice how as x doubles in value from 1 to 2 to 4 to 8, . . .

. . . the value of y is halved from 24 to 12 to 6 to 3.

EXAMPLE 2 Use Inverse Variation

In an inverse variation, $x = 10$ when $y = 3$. Write an equation to represent the inverse variation. Then find the value of y when $x = -6$.

$y = \frac{k}{x}$ Write the equation for an inverse variation.

$3 = \frac{k}{10}$ Substitute 10 and 3 for x and y.

$30 = k$ Multiply both sides by 10 to solve for k.

After solving for k, write an equation for the inverse variation.

$y = \frac{30}{x}$ Write the equation to represent the inverse variation.

$y = \frac{30}{-6}$ Substitute −6 for x in the equation.

$y = -5$ Divide.

The equation that represents the inverse relation is $y = \frac{30}{x}$. When $x = -6$, $y = -5$.

COMMON ERROR
Remember to keep track of any negative signs when substituting into equations and performing calculations.

Try It! 2. In an inverse variation, $x = 6$ and $y = \frac{1}{2}$.

a. What is the equation that represents the inverse variation?

b. What is the value of y when $x = 15$?

APPLICATION

EXAMPLE 3 Use an Inverse Variation Model

On a guitar, the string length, *s*, varies inversely with the frequency, *f*, of its vibrations.

MAKE SENSE AND PERSEVERE
Use what you know about inverse variation to mentally compute an approximate value of your answer.

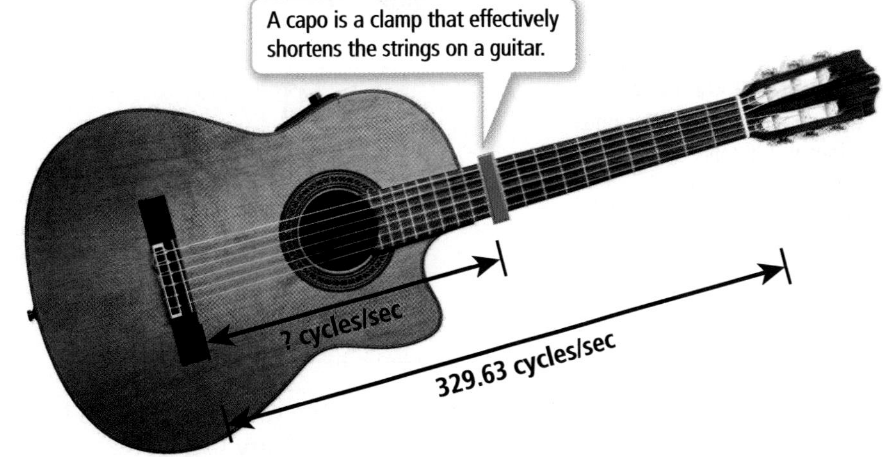

The frequency of a 26-inch E-string is 329.63 cycles per second. What is the frequency when the string length is 13 inches?

$s = \frac{k}{f}$ .... Write the equation for an inverse variation.

$26 = \frac{k}{329.63}$ .... Substitute 26 and 329.63 for *s* and *f*.

$8{,}570.38 = k$ .... Multiply by 329.63 to solve for *k*.

After solving for *k*, write an equation for the inverse variation.

$s = \frac{8{,}570.38}{f}$ .... Substitute 8,570.38 for *k* in the equation.

$13 = \frac{8{,}570.38}{f}$ .... Substitute 13 for *s* in the equation.

$f = 659.26$ .... Solve for *f*.

So the frequency of the 13-inch string is 659.26 cycles per second.

Try It! 3. The amount of time it takes for an ice cube to melt varies inversely to the air temperature, in degrees. At 20° Celsius, the ice will melt in 20 minutes. How long will it take the ice to melt if the temperature is 30° Celsius?

CONCEPTUAL UNDERSTANDING

EXAMPLE 4 Graph the Reciprocal Function

How do you graph the reciprocal function, $y = \frac{1}{x}$?

The **reciprocal function** maps every non-zero real number to its reciprocal.

Step 1: Consider the domain and range of the function.

Domain: $\{x \mid x \neq 0\}$

Range: $\{y \mid y \neq 0\}$

If $x = 0$ that will result in an undefined expression, so $x \neq 0$.

CONTINUED ON THE NEXT PAGE

Activity

EXAMPLE 4 CONTINUED

Step 2: Graph the function.

x	-3	-2	-1	$-\frac{1}{2}$	$-\frac{1}{3}$	0	$\frac{1}{3}$	$\frac{1}{2}$	1	2	3
$f(x)$	$-\frac{1}{3}$	$-\frac{1}{2}$	-1	-2	-3	Undefined	3	2	1	$\frac{1}{2}$	$\frac{1}{3}$

USE APPROPRIATE TOOLS
For an equation such as this one, that does not involve a lot of parameters, graphing by hand makes sense. As you encounter more complex equations, it may be appropriate to graph with technology.

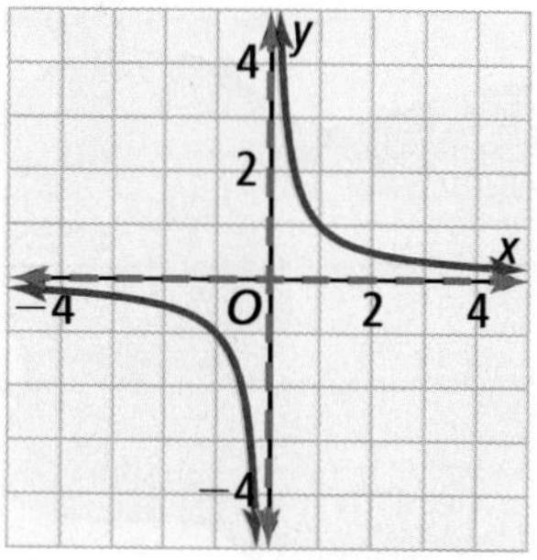

Use a table of values or technology to graph the function.

Step 3: Observe the graph of $y = \frac{1}{x}$ as it approaches positive infinity and negative infinity.

x	1	10	100	1,000	10,000
$f(x)$	1	$\frac{1}{10}$	$\frac{1}{100}$	$\frac{1}{1,000}$	$\frac{1}{10,000}$

As x gets larger, the denominator gets larger and the value of the function approaches zero.

An **asymptote** is a line that a graph approaches. Asymptotes guide the end behavior of a function.

As x approaches infinity, $f(x)$ approaches 0. The same is true as x-values approach negative infinity, so the line $y = 0$ is a *horizontal asymptote*.

Step 4: Observe the graph of $y = \frac{1}{x}$ as x approaches 0 for positive and negative x-values.

x	1	$\frac{1}{10}$	$\frac{1}{100}$	$\frac{1}{1,000}$	$\frac{1}{10,000}$
$f(x)$	1	10	100	1,000	10,000

As x gets closer to 0, the value of the function gets larger and larger.

For positive values of x, as x approaches 0, $f(x)$ approaches positive infinity.

x	-1	$-\frac{1}{10}$	$-\frac{1}{100}$	$-\frac{1}{1,000}$	$-\frac{1}{10,000}$
$f(x)$	-1	-10	-100	$-1,000$	$-10,000$

As x gets closer to 0, the value of the function approaches negative infinity.

For negative values of x, as x approaches 0, $f(x)$ approaches negative infinity. The domain of the function excludes 0, so the graph will never touch the line $x = 0$. The line $x = 0$ is a *vertical asymptote*.

Try It! 4. Graph the function $y = \frac{10}{x}$. What are the domain, range, and asymptotes of the function?

EXAMPLE 5 Graph Translations of the Reciprocal Function

Graph $g(x) = \frac{1}{x-3} + 2$. What are the equations of the asymptotes? What are the domain and range?

Start with the graph of the parent function, $f(x) = \frac{1}{x}$.

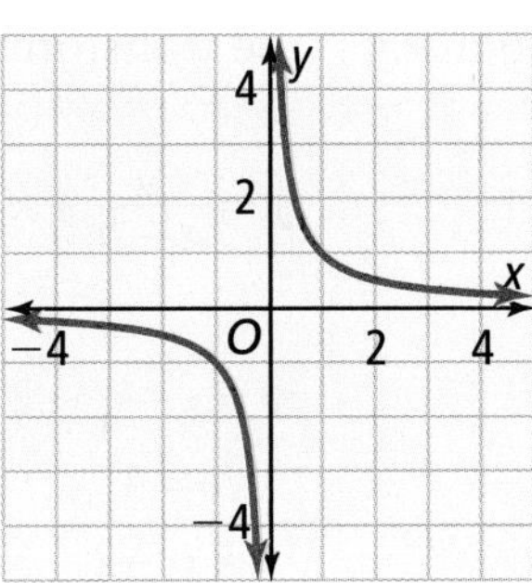

Recall that adding h to x in the definition of f translates the graph of f horizontally. Adding k to $f(x)$ translates the graph of f vertically.

The function $q(x) = \frac{1}{x-h} + k$ is a transformation of the parent function f that shifts the graph of f horizontally by h units and then shifts the graph of f vertically by k units.

The graph of $g(x) = \frac{1}{x-3} + 2$ is a translation of the graph of the parent function 3 units right and 2 units up.

MAKE SENSE AND PERSEVERE
Not only are the points of the graph translated, but the asymptotes are translated as well.

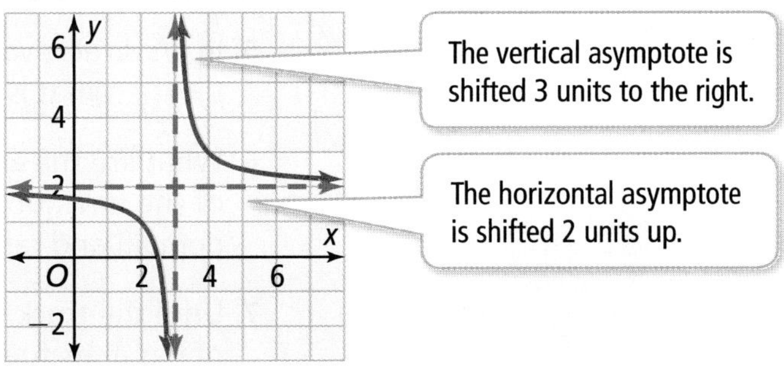

The line $x = 3$ is a vertical asymptote. The line $y = 2$ is a horizontal asymptote.

The domain is $\{x \mid x \neq 3\}$.

The range is $\{y \mid y \neq 2\}$.

Try It! 5. Graph $g(x) = \frac{1}{x+2} - 4$. What are the equations of the asymptotes? What are the domain and range?

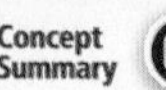

CONCEPT SUMMARY Inverse Variation and the Reciprocal Function

	Inverse Variation	Transformations of the Reciprocal Function
WORDS	An inverse variation is a relation between two variables such that as one variable increases, the other decreases proportionally.	The reciprocal function models the inverse variation, $y = \frac{1}{x}$. Like other functions, it can be transformed.
ALGEBRA	$y = \frac{k}{x}$, where $k \neq 0$	$y = \frac{a}{x-h} + k$
EXAMPLES	$y = \frac{1}{x}$ asymptotes: $x = 0$ $y = 0$ 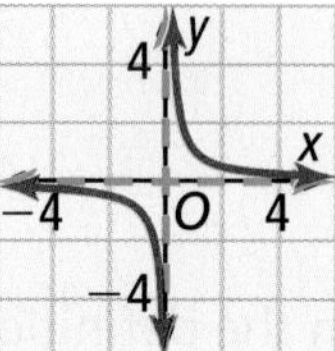	$y = \frac{1}{x-4} - 2$ $h = 4$ $k = -2$ Parent is transformed down 2 and right 4. asymptotes: $x = 4$ $y = -2$ 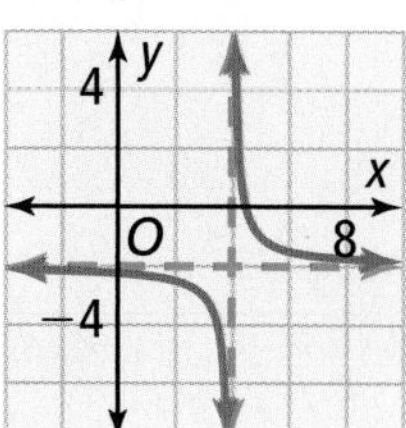

Do You UNDERSTAND?

1. ESSENTIAL QUESTION How are inverse variations related to the reciprocal function?

2. **Construct Arguments** Explain why the amount of propane in a grill's tank and the time spent grilling could represent an inverse variation.

3. **Vocabulary** Why is it impossible for the graph of the function $y = \frac{1}{x}$ to intersect the horizontal asymptote at the x-axis?

4. **Error Analysis** Carmen said the table of values shown represents an inverse variation. Explain why Carmen is mistaken.

x	1	2	3	4	8	16
y	24	12	8	6	3	2

Do You KNOW HOW?

5. In an inverse variation, $x = -8$ when $y = -\frac{1}{4}$. What is the value of y when $x = 4$?

6. What are the equations of the asymptotes of the function $f(x) = \frac{1}{x-5} + 3$? What are the domain and range?

7. Until the truck runs out of gas, the amount of gas in its fuel tank varies inversely with the number of miles traveled. Model a relationship between the amount of gas in a fuel tank of a truck and the number of miles traveled by the truck as an inverse variation.

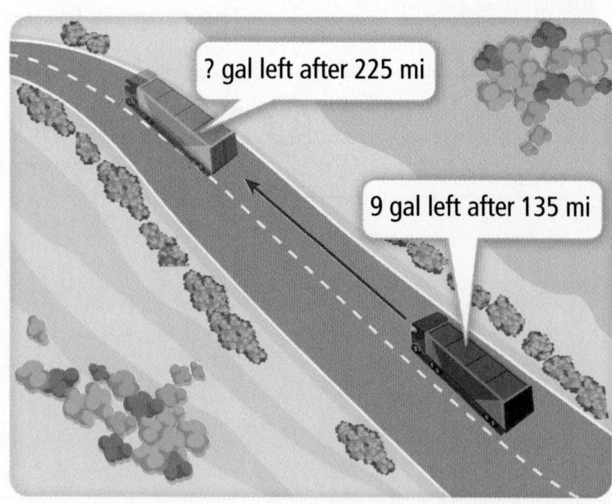

PRACTICE & PROBLEM SOLVING

Scan for Multimedia

Additional Exercises Available Online

UNDERSTAND

8. **Communicate Precisely** Explain the difference between the graphs of inverse variation functions when $k > 0$ and when $k < 0$.

9. **Generalize** Just from looking at the table of values, how can you determine that the data do *not* represent an inverse variation?

x	−2	2	4	6	8	10
y	−6	6	12	18	24	30

10. **Construct Arguments** Explain why zero cannot be in the domain of an inverse variation.

11. **Error Analysis** Describe and correct the error a student made in graphing the function $y = \frac{5}{x}$.

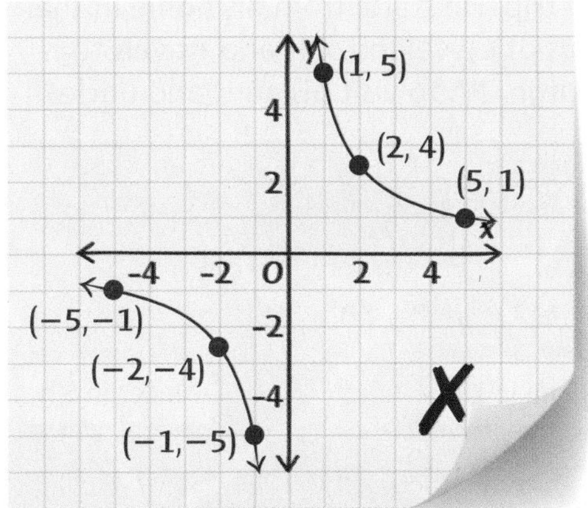

12. **Higher Order Thinking** The cost to rent a condominium at the beach is \$1,500 per week. If two people share the cost, they each have to pay \$750. Explain why the relationship between the cost per person varies inversely with the number of persons sharing the cost. Then write an inverse variation function that can be used to calculate the cost per person, c, of p persons sharing the rental fee.

13. **Generalize** For an inverse variation, write an equation that gives the value of k in terms of x and y.

PRACTICE

Do the tables of values represent inverse variations? Explain. SEE EXAMPLE 1

14.

x	$-\frac{1}{4}$	$-\frac{1}{2}$	$\frac{1}{3}$	2	5	11
y	$-\frac{9}{2}$	−9	6	36	90	198

15.

x	1	2	3	4	5	6
y	60	30	20	15	12	10

16. If x and y vary inversely and $x = 3$ when $y = \frac{2}{3}$, what is the value of y when $x = -1$? SEE EXAMPLE 2

17. The wavelength, w, of a radio wave varies inversely to its frequency, f, as shown in the graph.

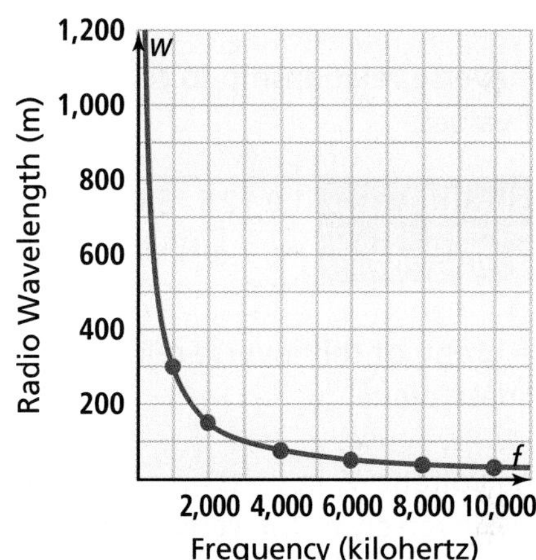

A radio wave with a frequency of 1,000 kilohertz has a length of 300 m. What is the frequency when the wave-length is 375 m? SEE EXAMPLE 3

18. Graph the function $y = \frac{-2}{x}$. What are the domain, range, and asymptotes of the function? SEE EXAMPLE 4

19. Graph $g(x) = \frac{1}{x-2} + 6$. What are the equations of the asymptotes? What are the domain and range? SEE EXAMPLE 5

PRACTICE & PROBLEM SOLVING

Practice Tutorial

Mixed Review Available Online

APPLY

20. **Model With Mathematics** The time t required to empty a water tank varies inversely as the rate of pumping p. A pump can empty a water tank in 40 min at the rate of 120 gal/min. Write the equation of the inverse variation. How long it will take the pump to empty the water tank at the rate of 200 gal/min?

21. **Use Structure** The number of downloaded games that can be stored on a video game system varies inversely with the average size of a video game. A certain video game system can store 160 games when the average size of a game is 2.0 gigabytes (GB).

    a. Write an inverse equation that relates the number of games n that will fit on the video game system as a function of the average game size s in GB.

    b. Use the inverse relationship to complete the table of values.

Game Size (GB), s	1.0	2.5	3.0	4.0
Number of Games, n	■	■	■	■

    c. Sketch a graph of this inverse relationship on a coordinate plane.

22. **Reason** The voltage V, in volts, in an electrical circuit varies inversely as the resistance R in ohms. The voltage in the circuit is 15 volts when the resistance is 192 ohms.

    a. Write the equation of the inverse variation.

    b. Find the voltage in the circuit when the resistance is 144 ohms.

23. Boyle's Law states that the pressure exerted by fixed quantity of a gas, P, varies inversely with the volume the gas occupies, V, assuming constant temperature.

    The volume and air pressure of a volleyball are 300 in.^{3} and 4.5 psi. The volume and air pressure of a basketball are 415 in.^{3} and 8 psi. How much smaller would the volleyball have to be to equal the air pressure of the basketball?

ASSESSMENT PRACTICE

24. Given that $\frac{A}{B} = k$, which of the following is true?

    Ⓐ k varies inversely with A.

    Ⓑ k varies inversely with B.

    Ⓒ A varies inversely with k.

    Ⓓ A varies inversely with B.

25. **SAT/ACT** Suppose y varies inversely as the square of x. If x is multiplied by 4, which of the following is true for the value of y?

    Ⓐ It is multiplied by 4.

    Ⓑ It is multiplied by 16.

    Ⓒ It is multiplied by $\frac{1}{4}$.

    Ⓓ It is multiplied by $\frac{1}{16}$.

26. **Performance Task** Suppose Cameron takes a road trip. He starts from his home in the suburbs of Cleveland, OH and travels to Pittsburgh, PA to visit his aunt and uncle.

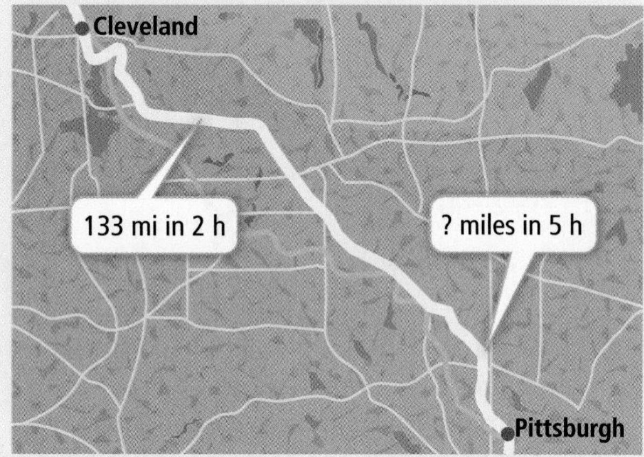

Part A The distance Cameron drives from Cleveland to Pittsburgh is 133 miles. The trip takes him 2 hours. The distance d in miles that Cameron drives varies directly with the amount of time t in hours, he spends driving. Write the equation of the direct variation. Use the given relationship and the equation to find the number of miles Cameron would travel if he continues on for 5 more hours.

Part B The amount of gas in Cameron's car is 9 gal after he drives for 2 h. The amount of gas g in gallons in his tank varies inversely with the amount of time t, in hours, he spends driving. Write the equation of the inverse variation. Use the given relationship and the equation to find the number of gallons in Cameron's tank after 5 more hours of driving.

3-2 Graphing Rational Functions

I CAN… graph rational functions.

VOCABULARY
- rational expression
- rational function

EXPLORE & REASON

Look at the three functions shown.

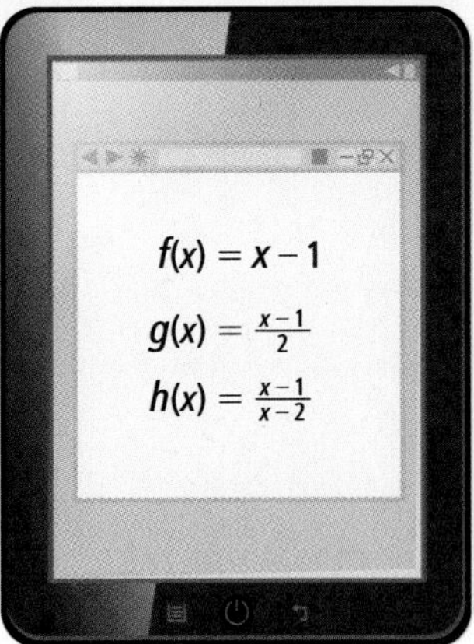

A. Look for Relationships Graph each function. Determine which of the functions are linear. Find the *y*-intercept of each function and the slope, if appropriate.

B. What is the effect on the graph of *f* when dividing $x - 1$ by 2?

C. What happens to the graph of *h* as *x* approaches 2?

D. Communicate Precisely What is the effect on the graph of $f(x)$ when dividing $x - 1$ by $x - 2$? (Hint: Compare it to what you found in part (B).)

ESSENTIAL QUESTION

How can you graph a rational function?

EXAMPLE 1 Rewrite a Rational Function to Identify Asymptotes

Rewrite $g(x) = \frac{4x}{x-3}$ using long division. How is the quotient related to the reciprocal function, $f(x) = \frac{1}{x}$? Sketch the graph.

$g(x) = \frac{4x}{x-3}$ — Write the equation.

$= x - 3\overline{)\,4x}$ with quotient 4 — Divide 4x by x.

$\ -(4x - 12)$, remainder 12 — Multiply $x - 3$ by 4 and subtract from 4x.

$g(x) = 4 + \frac{12}{x-3}$ — Write the remainder as a fraction in the quotient.

Rewrite *g* in the form $g(x) = \frac{a}{x-h} + k$ to identify the transformation of the parent function, $f(x) = \frac{1}{x}$.

$$g(x) = 4 + \frac{12}{x-3}$$

In the graph, the parent function *f* has been shifted up 4 units and then right 3 units. The resulting graph has been stretched vertically by a factor of 12.

There is a vertical asymptote at $x = 3$ and a horizontal asymptote at $y = 4$.

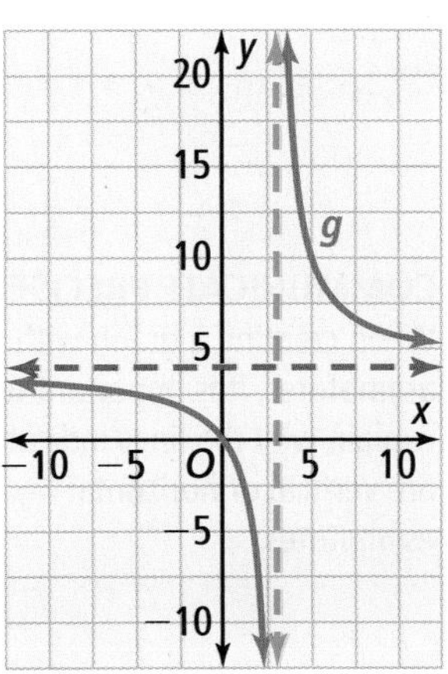

USE STRUCTURE Rewriting *g* in this way is similar to rewriting an improper fraction as a mixed number.

Try It! 1. Use long division to rewrite each rational function. Find the asymptotes of *f* and sketch the graph.

a. $f(x) = \frac{6x}{2x+1}$

b. $f(x) = \frac{x}{x-6}$

Activity Assess

CONCEPT BOX Rational Functions

Just as a rational number is a number that can be expressed the ratio of two integers, a **rational expression** is an expression that can be expressed as the ratio of two polynomials, such as $\frac{P(x)}{Q(x)}$, where the value of $Q(x) \neq 0$.

A **rational function** is any function defined by a rational expression, such as $R(x) = \frac{P(X)}{Q(X)}$. The domain of $R(x)$ is all values of x for which $Q(x) \neq 0$.

The function $g(x) = \frac{4x}{x-3}$ is a rational function.

CONCEPTUAL UNDERSTANDING

EXAMPLE 2 Find Asymptotes of a Rational Function

How do you find vertical and horizontal asymptotes of a rational function?

A. What are the vertical asymptotes for the graph of $f(x) = \frac{3x-2}{x^2+7x+12}$?

Vertical asymptotes can occur at the *x*-values where the function is undefined. Determine where the denominator of the rational function is equal to 0.

$x^2 + 7x + 12 = 0$ ········ Set the denominator equal to 0.

$(x+3)(x+4) = 0$ ········ Factor.

$x + 3 = 0$ or $x + 4 = 0$ ········ Use the Zero Product Property.

$x = -3$ or $x = -4$ ········ Solve using the Addition Property of Equality.

The possible vertical asymptotes are $x = -3$ and $x = -4$.

Graph the function to determine if there are asymptotes at $x = -3$ or $x = -4$.

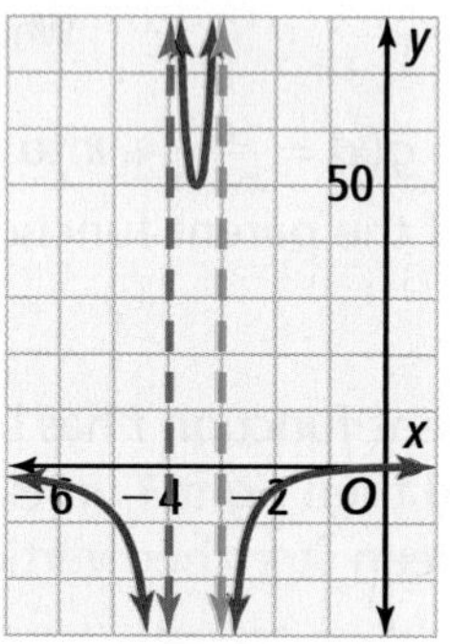

Use the TRACE feature on the graphing calculator to confirm that the graph is not defined at $x = -3$ or $x = -4$.

The graph is not defined at $x = -3$ or $x = -4$. These lines are vertical asymptotes.

COMMUNICATE PRECISELY
When creating a graph with asymptotes, it is important to explain why the lines indicated are vertical or horizontal asymptotes.

CONTINUED ON THE NEXT PAGE

Activity Assess

EXAMPLE 2 CONTINUED

B. What are the horizontal asymptotes for the graph $f(x) = \frac{3x-2}{x^2+7x+12}$?

To identify *horizontal asymptotes*, we have to consider three cases.

Case 1: The degree of the numerator is less than the degree of the denominator.

Consider $g(x) = \frac{x+4}{x^2+1}$

As the value of x increases, the value of the denominator gets very large in relation to the numerator. The value of the function gets closer and closer to 0.

When the degree of the numerator is less than the degree of the denominator, there exists a horizontal asymptote at $y = 0$.

Case 2: The degree of the numerator is greater than the degree of the denominator.

Consider $h(x) = \frac{x^2+1}{x+2}$

As the value of x increases, the value of the numerator gets very large in relation to the denominator. The value of the function continues to increase.

When the degree of the numerator is greater than the degree of the denominator, there are no horizontal asymptotes.

Case 3: The degree of the numerator and the denominator are the same.

Consider $k(x) = \frac{2x^2+x+1}{x^2-1}$

Using long division, we can rewrite this as $k(x) = 2 + \frac{x+3}{x^2-1}$.

As the value of x increases, the value of the rational part of the quotient approaches 0, so the value of the function approaches 2.

$k(x) = \frac{2x^2+x+1}{x^2-1}$ has a horizontal asymptote at $y = 2$.

When the degree of the numerator is equal to the degree of the denominator, the horizontal asymptote is the ratio of the leading coefficients.

For the function $k(x) = \frac{3x-2}{x^2+7x+12}$, the degree of the numerator is less than the degree of the denominator.

It has a horizontal asymptote at $y = 0$.

STUDY TIP

The vertical asymptote(s) are found by factoring the denominator of the function.

The horizontal asymptote(s) are found using the relationship between the degree of the numerator and the degree of the denominator.

MAKE SENSE AND PERSEVERE

To show that the horizontal asymptote is accurate, try substituting different values for x and see if the values for y approach the asymptote(s).

Try It! 2. What are the vertical and horizontal asymptotes of the graph of each function?

a. $g(x) = \frac{2x^2+x-9}{x^2-2x-8}$

b. $\frac{x^2+5x+4}{3x^2-12}$

Activity Assess

EXAMPLE 3 Graph a Function of the Form $\frac{ax+b}{cx+d}$

What is the graph of the function $f(x) = \frac{2x+1}{3x-4}$?

Step 1: Determine if there is a vertical asymptote.

$3x - 4 = 0$ ······ Set the denominator equal to 0.

$3x = 4$ ······ Solve.

$x = \frac{4}{3}$ ······ Divide to isolate the variable.

At $x = \frac{4}{3}$, the value of the denominator is 0. There is a vertical asymptote at $x = \frac{4}{3}$.

COMMON ERROR
The ratio of the leading terms cannot be used as an approximation unless x is approaching positive or negative infinity.

Step 2: Determine if there is a horizontal asymptote.

$y \approx \frac{2x}{3x}$ ······ Approximate f with ratio of leading terms.

$y \approx \frac{2}{3}$ ······ Simplify.

As $x \to \pm\infty$, $y \to \frac{2}{3}$.

There is a horizontal asymptote at $y = \frac{2}{3}$.

Step 3: Graph the function.

- Indicate the asymptotes.
- Choose x-values on either side of the vertical asymptote, and evaluate the function for those x-values to create coordinate points.
- Plot the points.

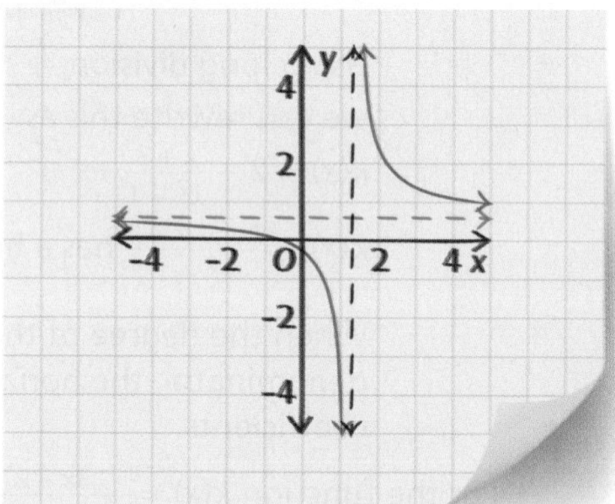

Try It! 3. Graph each function.

a. $f(x) = \frac{4x-3}{x+8}$

b. $g(x) = \frac{3x+2}{x-1}$

APPLICATION

EXAMPLE 4 Use a Rational Function Model

The cost of removing a pollutant is modeled by the given function where *f*(*p*) is the cost, in millions of dollars, of removing *p* percent of the pollutant. What percent of the pollutant can be removed for $78.3 million?

Formulate Since p is a percent, you know that $0 \leq p \leq 100$.

Compute Find the vertical asymptote by solving $100 - p = 0$:

$p = 100$.

Refine the domain: $0 \leq p < 100$.

Graph $y = 78.3$ and $y = \dfrac{8.7p}{100 - p}$.

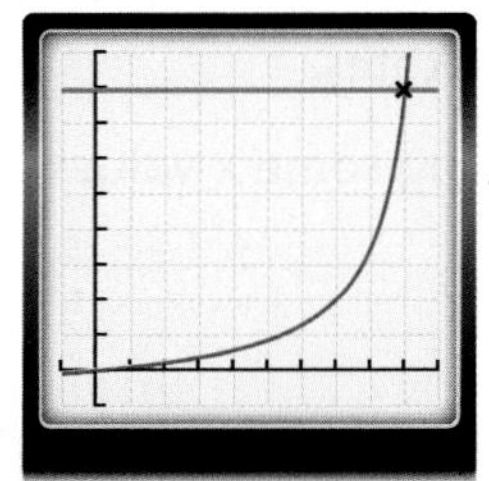

Use graphing technology to find the point of intersection.

The point (90, 78.3) lies on both graphs.

Interpret 90% of the pollutant can be removed for $78.3 million.

 **Try It!** **4.** New techniques have changed the cost function. For the new function $g(p) = \dfrac{3.2p + 1}{100 - p}$, what percent of the pollutant can be removed for $50 million?

Activity Assess

EXAMPLE 5 Graph a Rational Function

What is the graph of $f(x) = \dfrac{4x^2 - 9}{x^2 + 2x - 15}$?

Step 1 Determine if there are any vertical asymptotes.

$x^2 + 2x - 15 = 0$ .... Set the denominator equal to 0.

$(x + 5)(x - 3) = 0$ .... Factor.

$x + 5 = 0$ or $x - 3 = 0$ .... Use the Zero Product Property.

$x = -5$ or $x = 3$

Neither of these values makes the numerator equal to 0, but they each make the denominator equal to 0.

Vertical asymptotes: $x = -5$ and $x = 3$

Step 2 Determine if there is a horizontal asymptote.

$y \approx \dfrac{4x^2}{x^2}$ .... Approximate f with ratio of leading terms.

≈ 4 .... Simplify.

As $x \to \pm\infty$, $y \to 4$.

There is a horizontal asymptote at $y = 4$.

COMMUNICATE PRECISELY
When graphing, it is important to indicate and clearly label both horizontal and vertical asymptotes.

Step 3 Sketch the graph.

Indicate the asymptotes.

Plot points, choosing some x-values from each area of the graph.

x	$f(x)$
−20	4.61
−15	4.95
−10	6.02
−4	−7.86
0	0.60
4	6.11
7	3.90
13	3.71
20	3.74

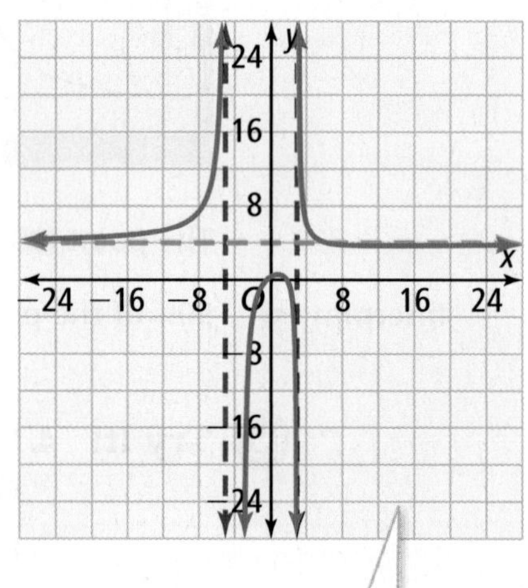

For $x > 3$ as the x values get larger, this graph drops below the horizontal asymptote and then approaches it from below.

Try It! 5. Identify the asymptotes and sketch the graph of $g(x) = \dfrac{x^2 - 5x + 6}{2x^2 - 10}$.

CONCEPT SUMMARY Graphing Rational Functions

RATIONAL FUNCTION A function that is expressible as a fraction with polynomials in the numerator and the denominator

ASYMPTOTES

Vertical

Vertical asymptotes are guides for the behavior of a graph as it approaches a vertical line.

- The line $x = a$ is a vertical asymptote of $\frac{P(x)}{Q(x)}$, if $Q(a) = 0$ and $P(a) \neq 0$.
- The up or down behavior of the function as it approaches the asymptote can be determined by substituting values close to a on either side of the asymptote.

Horizontal

Horizontal asymptotes are guides for the end behavior of a graph as it approaches a horizontal line.

If the degree of the numerator is

- less than the degree of the denominator, the horizontal asymptote is at $y = 0$.
- greater than the denominator, there is no horizontal asymptote.
- equal to the degree of the denominator, set y equal to the ratio of the leading coefficients. The graph of this line is the horizontal asymptote.

ALGEBRA

$f(x) = \frac{8x - 3}{4x + 1}$

Vertical Asymptote: Let $4x + 1 = 0$ and solve.

$x = -\frac{1}{4}$

Horizontal Asymptote: Find the ratio of the leading coefficients $\left(\frac{8}{4}\right)$.

$y = 2$

GRAPH

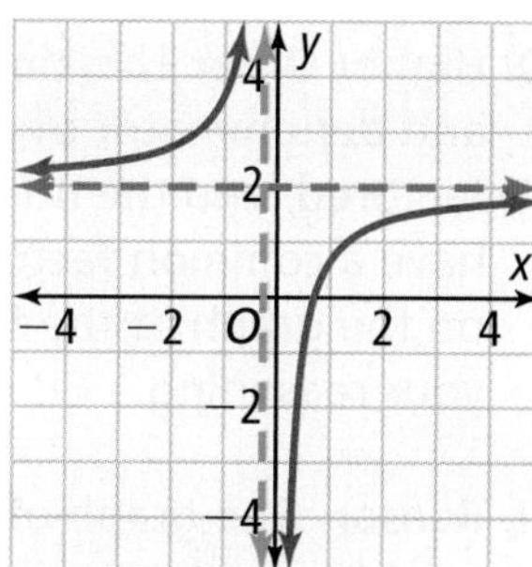

Do You UNDERSTAND?

1. **ESSENTIAL QUESTION** How can you graph a rational function?

2. **Vocabulary** Why does it make sense to call the expressions in this lesson *rational* functions?

3. **Error Analysis** Ashton said the graph of $f(x) = \frac{x + 2}{2x^2 + 4x - 6}$ has a horizontal asymptote at $y = \frac{1}{2}$. Describe and correct Ashton's error.

4. **Reason** When will the graph of a rational function have no vertical asymptotes? Give an example of such a function.

Do You KNOW HOW?

Find the vertical asymptote(s) and horizontal asymptote(s) of the rational function. Then graph the function.

5. $f(x) = \frac{x + 2}{x - 3}$

6. $f(x) = \frac{x - 1}{2x + 1}$

7. A trainer mixed water with an electrolyte solution. The concentration of electrolytes can be modeled by $f(x) = \frac{4}{x + 12}$. Graph the function.

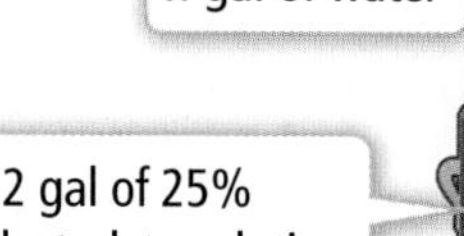

PRACTICE & PROBLEM SOLVING

Scan for Multimedia

Practice | Tutorial

Additional Exercises Available Online

UNDERSTAND

8. **Communicate Precisely** What is the horizontal asymptote of the rational function $f(x) = \frac{ax^2 + bx + c}{dx^2 + ex + f}$? Explain.

9. **Error Analysis** Juanita is trying to determine the vertical and horizontal asymptotes for the graph of the function $f(x) = \frac{x^2 + 3x - 4}{x^2 - x - 12}$. Describe and correct the error Juanita made in determining the vertical and horizontal asymptotes.

$$f(x) = \frac{x^2 + 3x - 4}{x^2 - x - 12}$$
$$= \frac{(x + 4)(x - 1)}{(x + 3)(x - 4)}$$

vertical asymptote: $x = -3, x = 4$
horizontal asymptote: $y = -4, y = 1$ ✗

10. **Higher Order Thinking** Suppose the numerator and denominator of a rational function are factored, and the numerator and denominator have a common factor of $x + a$. What happens on the graph of the function at $x = -a$? Explain your reasoning.

11. **Reason** The graph of a rational function has vertical asymptotes at $x = -3$ and $x = 1$ and a horizontal asymptote at $y = 3$.
    a. Write a function that has these attributes.
    b. Graph your function to verify it is correct.
    c. Is it possible to have a different graph with the same attributes? Explain.

12. **Communicate Precisely** Explain how to use the end behavior of the function $f(x) = \frac{x^2 + 6}{4x^2 - 3x - 1}$ to determine the horizontal asymptote of the graph. Then explain why using end behavior for finding the horizontal asymptote works the same as using the ratio of the leading terms.

PRACTICE

Use long division to rewrite each rational function. What are the asymptotes of *f*? Sketch the graph.
SEE EXAMPLE 1

13. $f(x) = \frac{2x}{x + 4}$

14. $f(x) = \frac{5x}{x - 2}$

15. $f(x) = \frac{6x^2}{3x^2 + 1}$

16. $f(x) = \frac{x^2}{2x^2 - 2}$

Identify the vertical and horizontal asymptotes of each rational function. SEE EXAMPLE 2

17. $f(x) = \frac{3x^2}{4x^2 - 1}$

18. $f(x) = \frac{5x + 6}{x^2 - 9x + 18}$

19. $f(x) = \frac{4x + 3}{x^2 - 4}$

20. $f(x) = \frac{5x^2 - 19x - 4}{2x^2 - 2}$

Graph each function. SEE EXAMPLE 3

21. $f(x) = \frac{-1}{x + 3}$

22. $f(x) = \frac{3x}{x - 1}$

23. $f(x) = \frac{x + 2}{-x + 1}$

24. $f(x) = \frac{2x - 3}{3x + 4}$

25. An owner tracks her sales each day since opening her marketing company. The daily sales, in dollars, after day x is given by the function $f(x) = \frac{200{,}000x}{x^2 + 150}$. On approximately which day(s) will the daily sales be $3,000?
SEE EXAMPLE 4

AC ADVERTISING COMPANY

DAILY SALES TRACKER

DAYS	SALES
1	$1,324.50
2	$2,597.40
3	$3,773.58
4	$4,819.28

Graph each function, labeling all horizontal or vertical asymptotes of the form $x = a$ or $y = b$.
SEE EXAMPLE 5

26. $f(x) = \frac{x + 4}{2x^2 - 13x - 7}$

27. $f(x) = \frac{2x - 1}{x^2 - 3x - 10}$

28. $f(x) = \frac{x^2 + x - 2}{2x^2 - 9x - 18}$

29. $f(x) = \frac{6x^2 - 12x}{x^2 + 5x - 24}$

PRACTICE & PROBLEM SOLVING

 Practice  Tutorial

Mixed Review Available Online

APPLY

30. Make Sense and Persevere Amaya made 10 three-point shots out of 25 attempts. If she then goes on to make x consecutive three-point shots, her success would be given by the function $f(x) = \frac{x + 10}{x + 25}$.

a. Identify the vertical asymptote(s) and horizontal asymptote(s).

b. Graph the function.

31. Model With Mathematics A software CD can be manufactured for \$0.10 each. The development cost to produce the software is \$500,000. The first 200 CDs were used by testers to test the functionality of the software and were not sold.

a. Write a function f for the average cost, in dollars, of a salable software CD where x is the number of salable software CDs.

b. What are the vertical asymptotes of the graph?

c. What are the horizontal asymptotes of the graph?

d. Graph the function.

e. What do the asymptotes mean?

32. Reason After diluting salt water, the concentration of salt in the water is given by the function $f(x) = \frac{0.5x}{x^2 - 1}$, where x is the time in hours since the dilution.

a. What is the concentration of salt in the water after 4 hours?

b. After how many hours will the concentration of salt in the water be 0.2? Round to the nearest hundredth.

ASSESSMENT PRACTICE

33. Which function has a graph with a vertical asymptote at $x = 3$? Select all that apply.

Ⓐ $f(x) = \frac{x - 2}{x^2 + 2x - 15}$

Ⓑ $f(x) = \frac{x - 3}{x^2 + 7x + 12}$

Ⓒ $f(x) = \frac{x^2 - 9}{x + 9}$

Ⓓ $f(x) = \frac{x^2 + 6x + 5}{x^2 - 9}$

34. SAT/ACT Which function has a graph with a horizontal asymptote at $y = -1$?

Ⓐ $f(x) = \frac{x + 5}{x - 3}$

Ⓑ $f(x) = \frac{-x + 9}{x - 8}$

Ⓒ $f(x) = \frac{x^2 + 4}{x^2 - 1}$

Ⓓ $f(x) = \frac{2x^2}{x^2 - x - 2}$

35. Performance Task There is a relationship between the degree of the numerator and denominator of a rational function and the function's horizontal asymptote.

Function	Horizontal Asymptote
$f(x) = \frac{2x}{x^2}$	
$f(x) = \frac{5x^2}{2x^3}$	
$f(x) = \frac{9x^6}{7x}$	
$f(x) = \frac{-3x^7}{4x^4}$	

Part A Complete the right column of the table.

Part B What is the relationship between the degree of the numerator and denominator when the horizontal asymptote is $y = 0$?

Part C What is the relationship between the degree of the numerator and denominator when there is no a horizontal asymptote?

3-3 Multiplying and Dividing Rational Expressions

I CAN… find the product and the quotient of rational expressions.

VOCABULARY

- simplified form of a rational expression

EXPLORE & REASON

Consider the following graph of the function $y = x + 2$.

A. What is the domain of this function?

B. Sketch a function that resembles the graph, but restrict its domain to exclude 2.

C. Use Structure Consider the function you have sketched. What kind of function might have a graph like this? Explain.

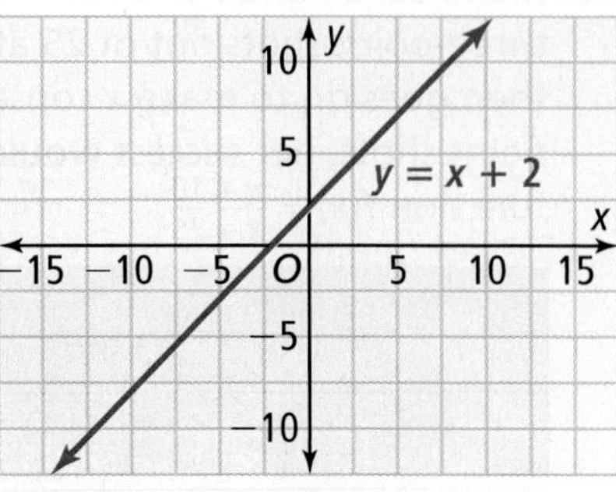

ESSENTIAL QUESTION

How does understanding operations with fractions help you multiply and divide rational expressions?

CONCEPT Rational Expression

A *rational expression* is the quotient of two polynomials. The domain is all real numbers except those for which the denominator is equal to 0.

$\frac{x^2}{x^2 - 9}$ is an example of a rational expression.

Since the denominator cannot equal 0, $x^2 - 9 \neq 0$.

$x^2 \neq 9 \rightarrow x \neq 3$ or -3.

So the domain of $\frac{x^2}{x^2 - 9}$ is all real numbers except 3 and –3.

CONCEPTUAL UNDERSTANDING

EXAMPLE 1 Write Equivalent Rational Expressions

When are two rational expressions equivalent?

Rational expressions can be simplified in a process that is similar to the process for simplifying rational numbers.

$$\frac{12}{16} = \frac{3 \cdot 2 \cdot 2}{2 \cdot 2 \cdot 2 \cdot 2} = \frac{3}{2 \cdot 2} \cdot \frac{2}{2} \cdot \frac{2}{2} = \frac{3}{2 \cdot 2} \cdot 1 \cdot 1 = \frac{3}{4}$$

By replacing quotients of common factors between the numerator and denominator with 1, you learn that $\frac{12}{16}$ is equivalent to $\frac{3}{4}$.

Write an expression that is equivalent to $\frac{x^3 - 5x^2 - 24x}{x^3 + x^2 - 72x}$.

Step 1 Factor the numerator and the denominator.

$$\frac{x^3 - 5x^2 - 24x}{x^3 + x^2 - 72x} = \frac{x(x^2 - 5x - 24)}{x(x^2 + x - 72)} = \frac{x(x - 8)(x + 3)}{x(x - 8)(x + 9)}$$

Step 2 Find the domain of the rational expression.

The domain is all real numbers except 0, 8, and –9.

Both $\frac{x^3 - 5x^2 - 24x}{x^3 + x^2 - 72x}$ and $\frac{x(x - 8)(x + 3)}{x(x - 8)(x + 9)}$ have the same domain.

CONTINUED ON THE NEXT PAGE

  Activity Assess

EXAMPLE 1 CONTINUED

COMMUNICATE PRECISELY
A statement of equivalence between two expressions is an identity. The identity is only valid where both expressions are defined.

Step 3 Recognize that the ratio of the common factors in the numerator and denominator are equal to 1.

$$\frac{x(x-8)(x+3)}{x(x-8)(x+9)} = \frac{x}{x} \cdot \frac{(x-8)}{(x-8)} \cdot \frac{(x+3)}{(x+9)} = 1 \cdot 1 \cdot \frac{(x+3)}{(x+9)} = \frac{x+3}{x+9}$$

So $\frac{x^3-5x^2-24x}{x^3+x^2-72x}$ is equivalent to $\frac{x+3}{x+9}$ for all x except –9, 0, and 8.

Like the original expression, the domain of $\frac{x+3}{x+9}$ excludes –9. But the domain of the original expression also excludes 0 and 8.

 **Try It!** 1. Write an expression equivalent to $\frac{3x^5-18x^4-21x^3}{2x^6-98x^4}$. Remember to give the domain for your expression.

EXAMPLE 2 Simplify a Rational Expression

What is the simplified form of the rational expression? What is the domain for which the identity between the two expressions is valid?

$$\frac{4-x^2}{x^2+3x-10}$$

The **simplified form of a rational expression** has no common factors, other than 1, in the numerator and the denominator.

$$\frac{4-x^2}{x^2+3x-10} = \frac{(2-x)(2+x)}{(x-2)(x+5)}$$ Factor the polynomials.

The domain is all real numbers except 2 and –5. Identify the domain from the original expression.

$$= \frac{-(x-2)(x+2)}{(x-2)(x+5)}$$ Divide out common factors.

The simplified form of $\frac{4-x^2}{x^2+3x-10}$ is $-\frac{x+2}{x+5}$ for all real numbers except 2 and –5.

COMMON ERROR
Be sure to factor out –1 from $2-x$ before dividing out common factors: $2-x=-(x-2)$

 **Try It!** 2. Simplify each expression and state the domain.

a. $\frac{x^2+2x+1}{x^3-2x^2-3x}$

b. $\frac{x^3+4x^2-x-4}{x^2+3x-4}$

EXAMPLE 3 Multiply Rational Expressions

A. What is the product of $\frac{2xy}{z}$ and $\frac{3x^2}{4yz}$?

To multiply rational expressions, follow a similar method to that for multiplying two numerical fractions.

The domain is $z \neq 0$ and $y \neq 0$.

$$\frac{2xy}{z} \cdot \frac{3x^2}{4yz} = \frac{(2xy)(3x^2)}{z(4yz)}$$ Multiply the expressions.

$$= \frac{2 \cdot 3 \cdot x^3 \cdot y}{2 \cdot 2 \cdot y \cdot z^2}$$ Divide out common factors.

$$= \frac{3x^3}{2z^2}$$

The product of $\frac{2xy}{z}$ and $\frac{3x^2}{4yz}$ is $\frac{3x^3}{2z^2}$ for $y \neq 0$ and $z \neq 0$.

USE STRUCTURE
Recall that when multiplying $\frac{a}{b} \times \frac{c}{d}$ you can often simplify by dividing both a and d (or both b and c) by the greatest common factor.

CONTINUED ON THE NEXT PAGE

 Activity  Assess

EXAMPLE 3 CONTINUED

STUDY TIP
It is easier to find the domain after factoring the denominator. Use the Zero Product Property to find values that will make the expression undefined. In this example, x cannot be −3, −1, or 2.

B. What is the simplified form of $\frac{5x}{x+3} \cdot \frac{x^2+x-6}{x^2+2x+1} \cdot \frac{x^2+x}{5x-10}$?

$$\frac{5x}{x+3} \cdot \frac{x^2+x-6}{x^2+2x+1} \cdot \frac{x^2+x}{5x-10} = \frac{5x(x+3)(x-2)x(x+1)}{(x+3)(x+1)^2 5(x-2)}$$ Multiply and factor the expressions.

$$= \frac{5x(x+3)(x-2)x(x+1)}{(x+3)(x+1)(x+1)5(x-2)}$$ Divide out common factors.

$$= \frac{x^2}{x+1}$$ Simplify.

So $\frac{5x}{x+3} \cdot \frac{x^2+x-6}{x^2+2x+1} \cdot \frac{x^2+x}{5x-10} = \frac{x^2}{x+1}$ for $x \neq -3, -1$, or 2.

Try It! 3. Find the simplified form of each product, and give the domain.

a. $\frac{x^2-16}{9-x} \cdot \frac{x^2+x-90}{x^2+14x+40}$

b. $\frac{x+3}{4x} \cdot \frac{3x-18}{6x+18} \cdot \frac{x^2}{4x+12}$

EXAMPLE 4 Multiply a Rational Expression by a Polynomial

STUDY TIP
This process is similar to writing a whole number with a denominator of 1 when multiplying a fraction and a whole number.

What is the product of $\frac{x+2}{x^4-16}$ and x^3+4x^2-12x?

$$\frac{x+2}{x^4-16} \cdot (x^3+4x^2-12x) = \frac{x+2}{x^4-16} \cdot \frac{x^3+4x^2-12x}{1}$$

$$= \frac{(x+2)x(x^2+4x-12)}{1(x^2+4)(x^2-4)}$$

$$= \frac{(x+2)x(x+6)(x-2)}{1(x^2+4)(x+2)(x-2)}$$

The domain is $x \neq -2$ or 2.

So $\frac{x+2}{x^4-16} \cdot (x^3+4x^2-12x) = \frac{x(x+6)}{x^2+4}$ for $x \neq -2$ or 2.

Try It! 4. Find the simplified form of each product and the domain.

a. $\frac{x^3-4x}{6x^2-13x-5} \cdot (2x^3-3x^2-5x)$

b. $\frac{3x^2+6x}{x^2-49} \cdot (x^2+9x+14)$

EXAMPLE 5 Divide Rational Expressions

What is the quotient of $\frac{x^3+3x^2+3x+1}{1-x^2}$ and $\frac{x^2+5x+4}{x^2+3x-4}$?

$$\frac{x^3+3x^2+3x+1}{1-x^2} \div \frac{x^2+5x+4}{x^2+3x-4} = \frac{x^3+3x^2+3x+1}{1-x^2} \cdot \frac{x^2+3x-4}{x^2+5x+4}$$

Multiply by the reciprocal of the divisor.

$$= \frac{(x+1)(x+1)(x+1)(x+4)(x-1)}{-(x-1)(x+1)(x+1)(x+4)}$$

The domain is $x \neq -4, -1$, or 1.

COMMON ERROR
Remember to include the factor of −1!

$$= \frac{(x+1)}{-1} \cdot \frac{(x+1)}{(x+1)} \cdot \frac{(x+1)}{(x+1)} \cdot \frac{(x-1)}{(x-1)} \cdot \frac{(x+4)}{(x+4)}$$

$$= -(x+1)$$

The quotient is $-(x+1)$, $x \neq -4, -1$, or 1.

CONTINUED ON THE NEXT PAGE

EXAMPLE 5 CONTINUED

Try It! 5. Find the simplified quotient and the domain of each expression.

a. $\frac{1}{x^2 + 9x} \div \left(\frac{6 - x}{3x^2 - 18x}\right)$

b. $\frac{2x^2 - 12x}{x + 5} \div \left(\frac{x - 6}{x + 5}\right)$

APPLICATION

EXAMPLE 6 Use Division of Rational Expressions

A company is evaluating two packaging options for its product line. The more efficient design will have the lesser ratio of surface area to volume. Should the company use packages that are cylinders or rectangular prisms?

Option 1: A rectangular prism with a square base

Option 2: A cylinder with the same height as the prism, and diameter equal to the side length of the prism's base

STUDY TIP
Recall that surface area tells how much packaging material is needed and volume tells how much product the package can hold.

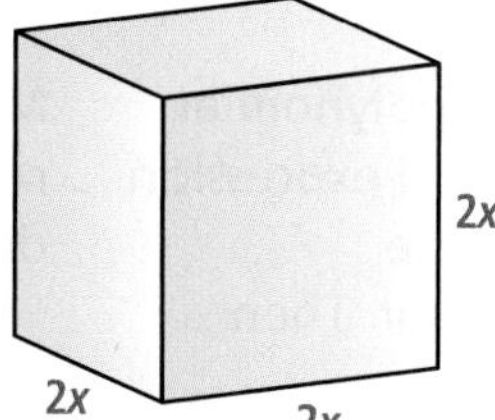

Surface Area: $2(2x)^2 + 4(2x)^2$
Volume: $(2x)^3$

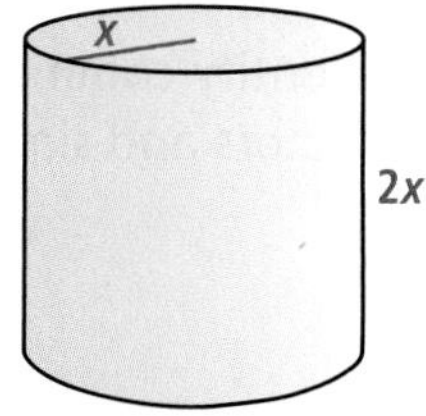

Surface Area: $2\pi x^2 + 2\pi x(2x)$
Volume: $\pi x^2(2x)$

The efficiency ratio is $\frac{SA}{V}$, where SA represents surface area and V represents volume.

Option 1:

$$\frac{SA}{V} = \frac{2(4x^2) + 4(4x^2)}{8x^3}$$
$$= \frac{24x^2}{8x^3}$$
$$= \frac{3}{x}$$

Option 2:

$$\frac{SA}{V} = \frac{2\pi x^2 + 4\pi x^2}{2\pi x^3}$$
$$= \frac{6\pi x^2}{2\pi x^3}$$
$$= \frac{3}{x}$$

The company can now compare the efficiency ratio of the package designs.

Prism: $\frac{3}{x}$ Cylinder: $\frac{3}{x}$

In this example, the efficiency ratio of the cylinder is equal to that of the prism. So the company should choose their package design based on other criteria.

Regardless of what positive value is selected for x, the efficiency ratios for these two package designs will be the same.

CONTINUED ON THE NEXT PAGE

EXAMPLE 6 CONTINUED

Try It! 6. The company compares the ratios of surface area to volume for two more containers. One is a rectangular prism with a square base. The other is a rectangular prism with a rectangular base. One side of the base is equal to the side-length of the first container, and the other side is twice as long. The surface area of this second container is $4x^2 + 6xh$. The heights of the two containers are equal. Which has the smaller surface area-to-volume ratio?

CONCEPT SUMMARY Products and Quotients of Rational Expressions

	Multiply	Multiply an Integer or a Polynomial	Divide
RATIONAL EXPRESSIONS	$\frac{3x}{x+1} \bullet \frac{x^2+x}{3x-6}$ The domain is $x \neq -1$ or 2.	$\frac{x+2}{x^2-4} \bullet (x^2-2x)$ $= \frac{x+2}{x^2-4} \bullet \frac{x^2-2x}{1}$ The domain is $x \neq -2$ or 2.	$\frac{1-x^2}{x^2+3x-4} \div \frac{x+1}{x+4}$ $= \frac{1-x^2}{x^2+3x-4} \bullet \frac{x+4}{x+1}$ The domain is $x \neq -4$, -1, or 1.
WORDS	Identify common factors and simplify.	Write the polynomial as a rational expression with 1 in the denominator. Then multiply.	Multiply by the reciprocal of the divisor.

Do You UNDERSTAND?

1. ESSENTIAL QUESTION How does understanding operations with fractions help you multiply and divide rational expressions?

2. **Vocabulary** In your own words, define *rational expression* and provide an example of a rational expression.

3. **Error Analysis** A student divided the rational expressions as follows:

$$\frac{4x}{5y} \div \frac{20x^2}{25y^2} = \frac{4x}{\cancel{5}y} \div \frac{\overset{4}{\cancel{20}}x^2}{25y^2} = \frac{16x^3}{25y^3}.$$

Describe and correct the errors the student made.

4. **Communicate Precisely** Why do you have to state the domain when simplifying rational expressions?

Do You KNOW HOW?

5. What is the simplified form of the rational expression $\frac{x^2-36}{x^2+3x-18}$? What is the domain?

6. Find the product and give the domain of $\frac{y+3}{y+2} \bullet \frac{y^2+4y+4}{y^2-9}$.

7. Find and simplify the ratio of the volume of Figure A to the volume of Figure B.

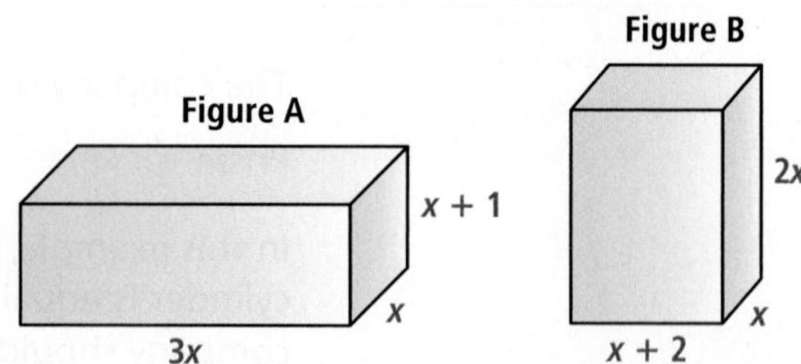

PRACTICE & PROBLEM SOLVING

Scan for Multimedia

Practice Tutorial

Additional Exercises Available Online

UNDERSTAND

8. **Reason** Explain why $\frac{4x^2-7}{4x^2-7} = 1$ is a valid identity under the domain of all real numbers except $\pm\frac{\sqrt{7}}{2}$.

9. **Error Analysis** Describe the error a student made in multiplying and simplifying $\frac{x+2}{x-2} \bullet \frac{x^2-4}{x^2+x-2}$.

$$\frac{x+2}{x-2} \cdot \frac{x^2-4}{x^2+x-2}$$
$$= \frac{x+2}{x-2} \cdot \frac{(x+2)(x-2)}{(x+2)(x-1)}$$
$$= \frac{2}{-1}$$

✗

10. Higher Order Thinking Explain why the process of dividing by a rational number is the same as multiplying by its reciprocal.

11. **Use Appropriate Tools** Explain how you can use your graphing calculator to show that the rational expressions $\frac{-6x^2+21x}{3x}$ and $-2x+7$ are equivalent under a given domain. What is true about the graph at $x = 0$ and why?

12. **Generalize** Explain the similarities between rational numbers and rational expressions.

13. **Use Structure** Determine whether $\frac{5x+11}{6x+11} = \frac{5}{6}$ is *sometimes, always,* or *never* true. Justify your reasoning.

14. **Construct Arguments** Explain how you can tell whether a rational expression is in simplest form.

15. **Communicate Precisely** When multiplying $\frac{15}{x} \bullet \frac{x}{3} = 5$, is it necessary to make the restriction $x \neq 0$? Why or why not?

16. **Reason** If the denominator of a rational expression is $x^3 + 3x^2 - 10x$, what value(s) must be restricted from the domain for x?

PRACTICE

Write an equivalent expression. State the domain. SEE EXAMPLE 1

17. $\frac{x^3+4x^2-12x}{x^2+x-30}$

18. $\frac{3x^2+15x}{x^2+3x-10}$

What is the simplified form of each rational expression? What is the domain? SEE EXAMPLE 2

19. $\frac{y^2-5y-24}{y^2+3y}$

20. $\frac{ab^3-9ab}{12ab^2+12ab-144a}$

21. $\frac{x^2+8x+15}{x^2-x-12}$

22. $\frac{x^3+9x^2-10x}{x^3-9x^2-10x}$

Find the product and the domain. SEE EXAMPLE 3

23. $\frac{x^2+6x+8}{x^2+4x+3} \bullet \frac{x+3}{x+2}$

24. $\frac{(x-y)^2}{x+y} \bullet \frac{3x+3y}{x^2-y^2}$

Find the product and the domain. SEE EXAMPLE 4

25. $\frac{(x+5)}{(x^3-25x)} \bullet (2x^3-11x^2+5x)$

26. $\frac{(2x^2-10x)}{(x-5)(x^2-1)} \bullet (3x^2+4x+1)$

Find the quotient and the domain. SEE EXAMPLE 5

27. $\frac{y^2-16}{y^2-10y+25} \div \frac{3y-12}{y^2-3y-10}$

28. $\frac{(x-y)^2}{x+y} \div \frac{3x+3y}{x^2-y^2}$

29. $\frac{25x^2-4}{x^2-9} \div \frac{5x-2}{x+3}$

30. $\frac{x^4+x^3-30x^2}{x^2-3x-18} \div \frac{x^3+x^2-30x}{x^2-36}$

31. A rectangular prism with a volume of $3x^3 + 7x^2 + 2x$ cubic units has a base area of $x^2 + 2x$ square units. Find the height of the rectangular prism. SEE EXAMPLE 6

Practice | Tutorial

Mixed Review Available Online

PRACTICE & PROBLEM SOLVING

APPLY

32. Make Sense and Persevere An engineering firm wants to construct a cylindrical structure that will maximize the volume for a given surface area. Compare the ratios of the volume to surface area of each of the cylindrical structures shown, using the following formulas for volume and surface area of cylinders.

Volume $(V) = \pi r^2 h$

Surface Area $(SA) = 2\pi rh + 2\pi r^2$

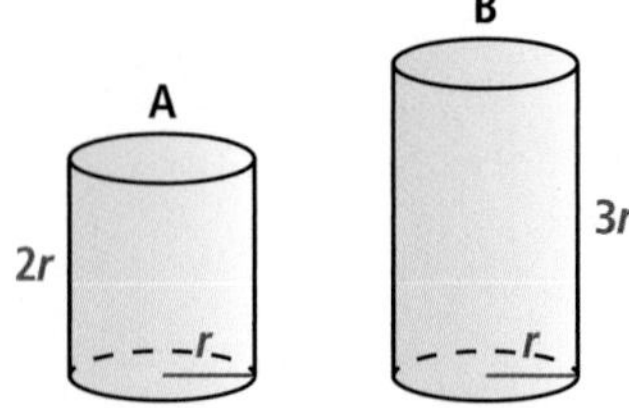

a. Calculate the ratio of volume to surface area for cylinder A.

b. Calculate the ratio of volume to surface area for cylinder B.

c. Which of these cylinders has a greater ratio of volume to surface area?

33. Look for Relationships A parallelogram with an area of $\frac{3x + 12}{10x + 25}$ square units has a height shown. Find the length of the base of the parallelogram.

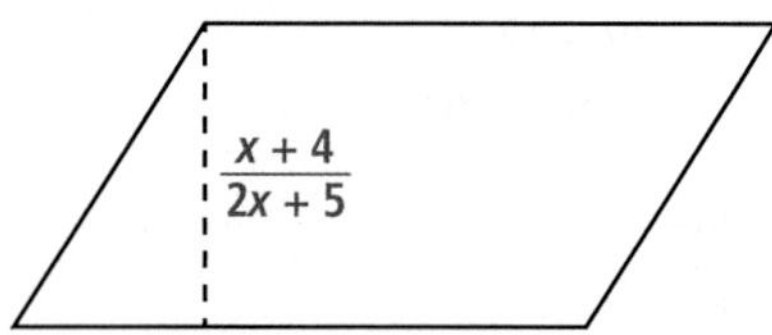

34. Model With Mathematics Brie designed a carnival game that involves tossing a beanbag into the box shown. In order to win a prize, the beanbag must fall inside the black rectangle. The probability of winning is equal to the ratio of the area of the black rectangle to the total area of the face of the box shown. Find this probability in simplified form.

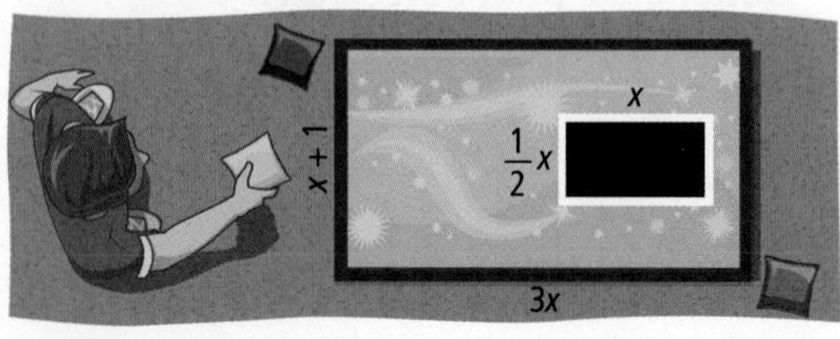

ASSESSMENT PRACTICE

35. Which of the following rational expressions simplify to $\frac{y}{y+3}$? Select all that apply.

Ⓐ $\frac{(2y^2 + y)(y + 3)}{(4y + 2)(y + 3)^2}$

Ⓑ $\frac{3y^2 + y}{3y^2 + 10y + 3}$

Ⓒ $\frac{2y^3 + 3y^2 + y}{(2y + 1)(y^2 + 4y + 3)}$

Ⓓ $\frac{y^2 + 2y}{y^2 + 4y + 3}$

Ⓔ $\frac{\frac{1}{y}}{y + 3}$

36. SAT/ACT For what value of x is $\frac{2x^2 + 8x}{(x + 4)(x^2 - 9)}$ undefined?

Ⓐ −8

Ⓑ −3

Ⓒ 0

Ⓓ 4

Ⓔ 9

37. Performance Task The approximate annual interest rate r of a monthly installment loan is given by the formula:

$$r = \frac{\left[\frac{24(nm - p)}{n}\right]}{\left(p + \frac{nm}{12}\right)},$$

where n is the total number of payments, m is the monthly payment, and p is the amount financed.

Part A Find the approximate annual interest rate (to the nearest percent) for a four-year signature loan of \$20,000 that has monthly payments of \$500.

Part B Find the approximate annual interest rate (to the nearest tenth percent) for a five-year auto loan of \$40,000 that has monthly payments of \$750.

3-4 Adding and Subtracting Rational Expressions

I CAN... find the sum or difference of rational expressions.

VOCABULARY

- compound fraction

CRITIQUE & EXPLAIN

Teo and Shannon find the following exercise in their homework:

$$\frac{1}{2}+\frac{1}{3}+\frac{1}{9}$$

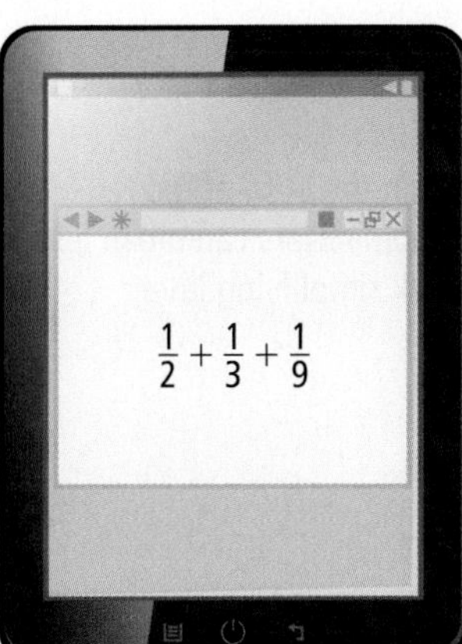

A. Teo claims that a common denominator of the sum is $2 + 3 + 9 = 14$. Shannon claims that it is $2 \cdot 3 \cdot 9 = 54$. Is either student correct? Explain why or why not.

B. Find the sum, explaining the method you use.

C. Construct Arguments Timothy states that the quickest way to find the sum of any two fractions with unlike denominators is to multiply their denominators to find a common denominator, and then rewrite each fraction with that denominator. Do you agree?

ESSENTIAL QUESTION

How do you rewrite rational expressions to find sums and differences?

EXAMPLE 1 Add Rational Expressions With Like Denominators

USE STRUCTURE
Compare addition of numerical and algebraic fractions:

$\frac{1}{5}+\frac{3}{5}=\frac{1+3}{5}=\frac{4}{5}$

In the same way,

$\frac{x}{x+4}+\frac{5}{x+4}=\frac{x+5}{x+4}$.

What is the sum?

A. $\frac{x}{x+4}+\frac{5}{x+4}$

$=\frac{x+5}{x+4}$ ······ When denominators are the same, add the numerators.

So $\frac{x}{x+4}+\frac{5}{x+4}=\frac{x+5}{x+4}$

B. $\frac{2x+1}{x^2+3x}+\frac{3x-8}{x(x+3)}$

$=\frac{(2x+1)+(3x-8)}{x^2+3x}$ ······ Add the numerators.

$=\frac{(2x+3x)+(1-8)}{x^2+3x}$ ······ Use the Commutative and Associative Properties.

$=\frac{5x-7}{x^2+3x}$ ······ Combine like terms.

So $\frac{2x+1}{x^2+3x}+\frac{3x-8}{x(x+3)}=\frac{5x-7}{x^2+3x}$

Try It! 1. Find the sum.

a. $\frac{10x-5}{2x+3}+\frac{8-4x}{2x+3}$

b. $\frac{x-5}{x+5}+\frac{3x-21}{x+5}$

CONCEPTUAL UNDERSTANDING

EXAMPLE 2 Identify the Least Common Multiple of Polynomials

How can you find the least common multiple (LCM) of polynomials?

STUDY TIP
Using the LCM of the denominators can mean less work simplifying later.

A. $(x + 2)^2$, $x^2 + 5x + 6$

Factor each polynomial.

$(x + 2)^2 = (x + 2)(x + 2)$

$x^2 + 5x + 6 = (x + 2)(x + 3)$

The LCM is the product of the factors. Duplicate factors are raised to the greatest power represented.

LCM: $(x + 2)(x + 2)(x + 3)$ or $(x + 2)^2(x + 3)$

B. $x^3 - 9x$, $x^2 - 2x - 15$, $x^2 - 5x$

Factor each polynomial.

$x^3 - 9x = x(x^2 - 9) = x(x + 3)(x - 3)$

$x^2 - 2x - 15 = (x + 3)(x - 5)$

$x^2 - 5x = x(x - 5)$

LCM: $x(x + 3)(x - 3)(x - 5)$

Each original polynomial is a factor of the LCM.

Try It! 2. Find the LCM for each set of expressions.

a. $x^3 + 9x^2 + 27x + 27$, $x^2 - 4x - 21$

b. $10x^2 - 10y^2$, $15x^2 - 30xy + 15y^2$, $x^2 + 3xy + 2y^2$

EXAMPLE 3 Add Rational Expressions With Unlike Denominators

What is the sum of $\frac{x + 3}{x^2 - 1}$ and $\frac{2}{x^2 - 3x + 2}$?

Follow a similar procedure to the one you use to add numerical fractions with unlike denominators.

USE STRUCTURE
The LCM of 6 and 15 is 30, not 90.
$\frac{1}{6} + \frac{1}{15} = \frac{1}{2 \cdot 3} + \frac{1}{3 \cdot 5} = \frac{1 \cdot 5 + 1 \cdot 2}{2 \cdot 3 \cdot 5}$
The LCM does not contain the common factor 3 twice. In the example problem, the common factor $(x - 1)$ is not used twice.

$\frac{x + 3}{x^2 - 1} + \frac{2}{x^2 - 3x + 2} = \frac{x + 3}{(x + 1)(x - 1)} + \frac{2}{(x - 1)(x - 2)}$ — Factor each denominator.

$= \frac{(x + 3)(x - 2)}{(x + 1)(x - 1)(x - 2)} + \frac{2(x + 1)}{(x + 1)(x - 1)(x - 2)}$ — Use the LCM as the least common denominator (LCD).

$= \frac{(x + 3)(x - 2) + 2(x + 1)}{(x + 1)(x - 1)(x - 2)}$ — Add the numerators.

$= \frac{(x^2 + x - 6) + (2x + 2)}{(x + 1)(x - 1)(x - 2)}$ — Distribute.

$= \frac{x^2 + 3x - 4}{(x + 1)(x - 1)(x - 2)}$ — Combine like terms.

$= \frac{(x + 4)(x - 1)}{(x + 1)(x - 1)(x - 2)}$ — Factor.

$= \frac{(x + 4)}{(x + 1)(x - 2)} \cdot \frac{(x - 1)}{(x - 1)}$ — Rewrite to identify unit factors.

$= \frac{x + 4}{(x + 1)(x - 2)}$ for $x \neq -1, 1$, and 2 — Simplify and state the domain.

The sum of $\frac{x + 3}{x^2 - 1}$ and $\frac{2}{x^2 - 3x + 2}$ is $\frac{x + 4}{(x + 1)(x - 2)}$ for $x \neq -1, 1$, and 2.

Try It! 3. Find the sum.

a. $\frac{x + 6}{x^2 - 4} + \frac{2}{x^2 - 5x + 6}$

b. $\frac{2x}{3x + 4} + \frac{4x^2 - 11x - 12}{6x^2 + 5x - 4}$

EXAMPLE 4 Subtract Rational Expressions

What is the difference between $\frac{x+1}{x^2-6x-16}$ and $\frac{x+1}{x^2+6x+8}$?

$$\frac{x+1}{x^2-6x-16}-\frac{x+1}{x^2+6x+8}=\frac{x+1}{(x-8)(x+2)}-\frac{x+1}{(x+2)(x+4)}$$

The LCD is $(x-8)(x+2)(x+4)$.

$$=\frac{(x+1)(x+4)}{(x-8)(x+2)(x+4)}-\frac{(x-8)(x+1)}{(x-8)(x+2)(x+4)}$$

$$=\frac{(x^2+5x+4)-(x^2-7x-8)}{(x-8)(x+2)(x+4)}$$

$$=\frac{x^2+5x+4-x^2+7x+8}{(x-8)(x+2)(x+4)}$$

$$=\frac{12x+12}{(x-8)(x+2)(x+4)}$$

$$=\frac{12(x+1)}{(x-8)(x+2)(x+4)}$$

Check for common factors in the numerator and denominator and simplify, if possible.

COMMON ERROR
When subtracting polynomials, remember to distribute -1 when removing the parentheses.

The difference between $\frac{x+1}{x^2-6x-16}$ and $\frac{x+1}{x^2+6x+8}$ is $\frac{12(x+1)}{(x-8)(x+2)(x+4)}$ for $x \neq -4, -2$, and 8.

Try It! 4. Simplify.

a. $\frac{1}{3x}+\frac{1}{6x}-\frac{1}{x^2}$

b. $\frac{3x-5}{x^2-25}-\frac{2}{x+5}$

APPLICATION

EXAMPLE 5 Find a Rate

Leah drives her car to the mechanic, then she takes the commuter rail train back to her neighborhood. The average speed for the 10-mile trip is 15 miles per hour faster on the train. Find an expression for Leah's total travel time. If she drove 30 mph, how long did this take?

USE APPROPRIATE TOOLS
Use a table to organize information and help create an accurate model of the situation.

	Distance	Rate	Time
Car	10	r	$\frac{10}{r}$
Commuter Rail	10	$r+15$	$\frac{10}{r+15}$

Remember: distance = rate • time, so time = $\frac{\text{distance}}{\text{rate}}$.

Total time for the trip:

$$\frac{10}{r}+\frac{10}{r+15}=\frac{10(r+15)}{r(r+15)}+\frac{10r}{r(r+15)}$$

Add the times for each part of the trip.

$$=\frac{10r+150+10r}{r(r+15)}$$

$$=\frac{20r+150}{r(r+15)}$$

CONTINUED ON THE NEXT PAGE

EXAMPLE 5 CONTINUED

At a driving rate of 30 mph, you can find the total time.

$$\frac{20r + 150}{r(r+15)} = \frac{20(30) + 150}{30(30+15)}$$

$$= \frac{750}{1{,}350}$$

$$= \frac{5}{9}$$

Substitute 30 mph for the rate, and simplify.

The expression for Leah's total travel time is $\frac{20r + 150}{r(r+15)}$. The total time is $\frac{5}{9}$ h, or about 33 min.

Try It! 5. On the way to work Juan carpools with a fellow co-worker, then takes the city bus back home in the evening. The average speed of the 20-mile trip is 5 miles per hour faster in the carpool. Write an expression that represents Juan's total travel time.

EXAMPLE 6 Simplify a Compound Fraction

A compound fraction is in the form of a fraction and has one or more fractions in the numerator and/or the denominator. How can you write a simpler form of a compound fraction?

$$\frac{\frac{1}{x} + \frac{2}{x+1}}{\frac{1}{y}}$$

Method 1 Find the Least Common Multiple (LCM) of the fractions in the numerator and denominator. Multiply the numerator and the denominator by the LCM.

$$\frac{\frac{1}{x} + \frac{2}{x+1}}{\frac{1}{y}} = \frac{\left[\frac{1}{x} + \frac{2}{x+1}\right] \cdot [x(x+1)y]}{\frac{1}{y} \cdot [x(x+1)y]}$$ Multiply the numerator and the denominator by the LCD.

$$= \frac{(x+1)y + 2xy}{x(x+1)}$$ Use the Distributive Property to eliminate the fractions.

$$= \frac{xy + y + 2xy}{x(x+1)}$$ Simplify.

$$= \frac{(3x+1)y}{x(x+1)}$$ Factor.

Method 2 Express the numerator and denominator as single fractions. Then multiply the numerator by the reciprocal of the denominator.

$$\frac{\frac{1}{x} + \frac{2}{x+1}}{\frac{1}{y}} = \frac{\frac{1}{x} \cdot \frac{x+1}{x+1} + \frac{2}{x+1} \cdot \frac{x}{x}}{\frac{1}{y}}$$ Multiply the numerator by the LCD.

$$= \frac{\frac{(x+1) + 2x}{x(x+1)}}{\frac{1}{y}}$$ Simplify.

$$= \frac{3x+1}{x(x+1)} \cdot \frac{y}{1}$$ Multiply the numerator by the reciprocal of the denominator.

$$= \frac{(3x+1)y}{x(x+1)}$$ Simplify.

Using either method, $\frac{\frac{1}{x} + \frac{2}{x+1}}{\frac{1}{y}}$ is equal to $\frac{(3x+1)y}{x(x+1)}$ when $x \neq -1, 0$ and $y \neq 0$.

USE STRUCTURE
Remember that the fraction bar separating the numerator and denominator represents division.

Try It! 6. Simplify each compound fraction.

a. $\dfrac{\frac{1}{x-1}}{\frac{x+1}{3} + \frac{4}{x-1}}$

b. $\dfrac{2 - \frac{1}{x}}{x + \frac{2}{x}}$

CONCEPT SUMMARY Find Sums and Differences of Rational Expressions

WORDS	To add or subtract rational expressions with common denominators, add the numerators and keep the denominator the same.	To add or subtract rational expressions with different denominators, rewrite each expression so that its denominator is the LCD, then add or subtract the numerators.
NUMBERS	$\frac{1}{5}+\frac{3}{5}=\frac{1+3}{5}=\frac{4}{5}$	$\frac{1}{6}+\frac{1}{15}=\frac{1}{2\cdot 3}+\frac{1}{3\cdot 5}$ $=\frac{1\cdot 5+1\cdot 2}{2\cdot 3\cdot 5}$
ALGEBRA	$\frac{x}{x+4}+\frac{5}{x+4}=\frac{x+5}{x+4}$	$\frac{x+3}{x^2-1}+\frac{2}{x^2-3x+2}$ $=\frac{x+3}{(x+1)(x-1)}+\frac{2}{(x-1)(x-2)}$ Rewrite the rational expressions using the LCD. $=\frac{(x+3)(x-2)}{(x+1)(x-1)(x-2)}+\frac{2(x+1)}{(x+1)(x-1)(x-2)}$

Do You UNDERSTAND?

1. **ESSENTIAL QUESTION** How do you rewrite rational expressions to find sums and differences?

2. **Vocabulary** In your own words, define **compound fraction** and provide an example of one.

3. **Error Analysis** A student added the rational expressions as follows:
$$\frac{5x}{x+7}+\frac{7}{x}=\frac{5x}{x+7}+\frac{7(7)}{x+7}=\frac{5x+49}{x+7}$$
Describe and correct the error the student made.

4. **Construct Arguments** Explain why, when stating the domain of a sum or difference of rational expressions, not only should the simplified sum or difference be considered but the original expression should also be considered.

5. **Make Sense and Persevere** In adding or subtracting rational expressions, why is the L in LCD significant?

Do You KNOW HOW?

6. Find the sum of $\frac{3}{x+1}+\frac{11}{x+1}$.

Find the LCM of the polynomials.

7. x^2-y^2 and $x^2-2xy+y^2$

8. $5x^3y$ and $15x^2y^2$

Find the sum or difference.

9. $\frac{3x}{4y^2}-\frac{y}{10x}$

10. $\frac{9y+2}{3y^2-2y-8}+\frac{7}{3y^2+y-4}$

11. Find the perimeter of the quadrilateral in simplest form.

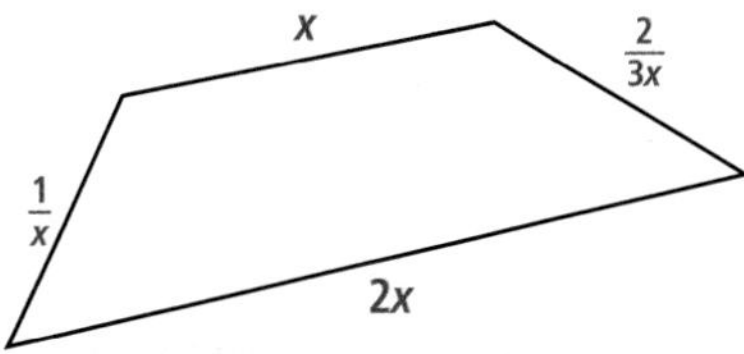

PRACTICE & PROBLEM SOLVING

Scan for Multimedia

Practice Tutorial

Additional Exercises Available Online

UNDERSTAND

12. Generalize Explain how addition and subtraction of rational expressions is similar to and different from addition and subtraction of rational numbers.

13. Error Analysis Describe and correct the error a student made in adding the rational expressions.

$$\frac{1}{x^2+3x+2}+\frac{x^2+4x}{4x+8}=\frac{1}{(x+1)(x+2)}+\frac{x(x+4)}{4(x+2)}$$
$$=\frac{4}{4(x+1)(x+2)}+\frac{x(x+4)}{4(x+1)(x+2)}$$
$$=\frac{4+x^2+4x}{4(x+1)(x+2)}$$
$$=\frac{x^2+4x+4}{4(x+1)(x+2)}$$
$$=\frac{(x+2)(x+2)}{4(x+1)(x+2)}$$
$$=\frac{x+2}{4(x+1)}\cdot\frac{(x+2)}{(x+2)}$$
$$=\frac{x+2}{4(x+1)}\quad ✗$$

14. Higher Order Thinking Find the slope of the line that passes through the points shown. Express in simplest form.

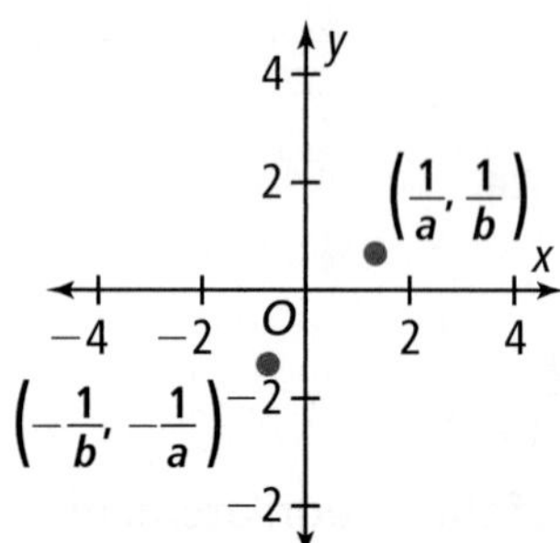

15. Reason For what values of x is the sum of $\frac{x-5y}{x+y}$ and $\frac{x+7y}{x+y}$ undefined? Explain.

16. Error Analysis A student says that the LCM of $3x^2+7x+2$ and $9x+3$ is $(3x^2+7x+2)(9x+3)$. Describe and correct the error the student made.

PRACTICE

Find the sum. SEE EXAMPLE 1

17. $\frac{4x}{x+7}+\frac{9}{x+7}$

18. $\frac{3y-1}{y^2+4y}+\frac{9y+6}{y(y+4)}$

Find the LCM for each group of expressions. SEE EXAMPLE 2

19. $x^2-7x+6,\ x^2-5x-6$

20. $y^2+2y-24,\ y^2-16,\ 2y$

Find the sum. SEE EXAMPLE 3

21. $\frac{6x}{x^2-8x}+\frac{4}{2x-16}$

22. $\frac{3y}{2y^2-y}+\frac{2}{2y}$

Find the difference. SEE EXAMPLE 4

23. $\frac{4x}{x^2-1}-\frac{4}{x-1}$

24. $\frac{y-1}{3y+15}-\frac{y+3}{5y+25}$

25 On Saturday morning, Ahmed decided to take a bike ride from one end of the 15-mile bike trail to the other end of the bike trail and back. His average speed the first half of the ride was 2 mph faster than his speed on the second half. Find an expression for Ahmed's total travel time. If his average speed for the first half of the ride was 12 mph, how long was Ahmed's bike ride? SEE EXAMPLE 5

Rewrite as a rational expression. SEE EXAMPLE 6

26. $\dfrac{1+\frac{1}{x}}{x-\frac{1}{x}}$

27. $\dfrac{\frac{3}{y}+\frac{7}{x}}{\frac{1}{y}-\frac{2}{x}}$

28. $\dfrac{\frac{1}{a}+\frac{1}{b}}{\frac{a^2-b^2}{ab}}$

29. $\dfrac{\frac{z^2-z-12}{z^2-2z-15}}{\frac{z^2+8z+12}{z^2-5z-14}}$

PRACTICE & PROBLEM SOLVING

Practice Tutorial

Mixed Review Available Online

APPLY

30. Use Structure Aisha paddles a kayak 5 miles downstream at a rate 3 mph faster than the river's current. She then travels 4 miles back upstream at a rate 1 mph slower than the river's current. Hint: Let x represent the rate of the river current.

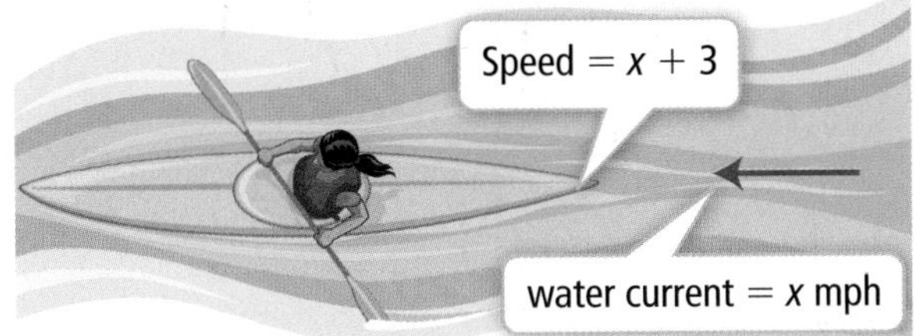

a. Write and simplify an expression to represent the total time it takes Aisha to paddle the kayak 5 miles downstream and 4 miles upstream.

b. If the rate of the river current, x, is 2 mph, how long was Aisha's entire kayak trip?

31. Model With Mathematics Rectangles A and B are similar. An expression that represents the width of each rectangle is shown. Find the scale factor of rectangle A to rectangle B in simplest form.

A: $\frac{x^2 - 25}{x - 4}$ B: $\frac{x + 5}{x^2 - 16}$

32. Reason The Taylor family drives 180 miles (round trip) to a professional basketball game. On the way to the game, their average speed is approximately 8 mph faster than their speed on the return trip home.

a. Let x represent their average speed on the way home. Write and simplify an expression to represent the total time it took them to drive to and from the game.

b. If their average speed going to the game was 72 mph, how long did it take them to drive to the game and back?

ASSESSMENT PRACTICE

33. Which of the following compound fractions simplifies to $\frac{x+1}{x-3}$? Select all that apply.

Ⓐ $\dfrac{\frac{x^2 + 5x + 4}{x^2 + 2x - 8}}{\frac{x^2 - 4x + 3}{x^2 - 3x + 2}}$ Ⓑ $\dfrac{\frac{x^2 - 1}{x^2 - 4}}{\frac{x^2 + x - 7}{x^2 + 5x + 6}}$

Ⓒ $\dfrac{\frac{x^2 + 3x - 10}{x^2 - 16}}{\frac{x^2 - 4x - 5}{x^2 - 1}}$ Ⓓ $\dfrac{\frac{x^2 + 3x - 10}{x^2 - 5x + 6}}{\frac{x^2 - 25}{x^2 - 4x - 5}}$

34. SAT/ACT What is the difference between $\frac{x}{9}$ and $\frac{x-y}{6}$?

Ⓐ $\frac{5x - y}{18}$ Ⓑ $\frac{5x + y}{18}$

Ⓒ $\frac{-x + 3y}{18}$ Ⓓ $\frac{-x - 3y}{18}$

35. Performance Task The lens equation $\frac{1}{f} = \frac{1}{d_i} + \frac{1}{d_o}$ represents the relationship between f, the focal length of a camera lens, d_i, the distance from the lens to the film, and d_o, the distance from the lens to the object.

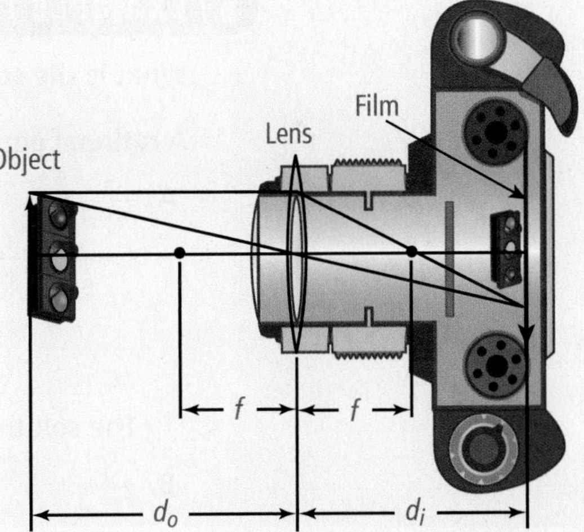

Part A Find the focal length of a camera lens if an object that is 12 cm from a camera lens is in focus on the film when the lens is 6 cm from the film.

Part B Suppose the focal length of another camera lens is 3 inches, and the object to be photographed is 5 feet away. What distance (to the nearest tenth inch) should the lens be from the film?

Activity Assess

3-5 Solving Rational Equations

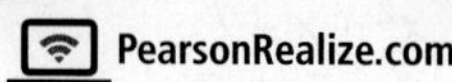
PearsonRealize.com

I CAN… solve rational equations and identify extraneous solutions.

VOCABULARY
- rational equation
- extraneous solution

CRITIQUE & EXPLAIN

Nicky and Tavon used different methods to solve the equation $\frac{1}{2}x + \frac{2}{5} = \frac{9}{10}$.

Nicky	Tavon
$\frac{1}{2}x + \frac{2}{5} = \frac{9}{10}$	$\frac{1}{2}x + \frac{2}{5} = \frac{9}{10}$
$\frac{1}{2}x = \frac{9}{10} - \frac{2}{5}$	$10\left(\frac{1}{2}x + \frac{2}{5} = \frac{9}{10}\right)$
$\frac{1}{2}x = \frac{5}{10}$	$5x + 4 = 9$
$x = 1$	$5x = 5$
	$x = 1$
The solution is 1.	The solution is 1.

A. Explain the different strategies that Nicky and Tavon used and the advantages or disadvantages of each.

B. Did Nicky use a correct method to solve the equation? Did Tavon?

C. **Use Structure** Why might Tavon have chosen to multiply both sides of the equation by 10? Could he have used another number? Explain.

? ESSENTIAL QUESTION **How can you solve rational equations and identify extraneous solutions?**

EXAMPLE 1 Solve a Rational Equation

What is the solution to each rational equation?

A **rational equation** is an equation that contains a rational expression.

A. $\frac{1}{x+4} = 2$

$$(x+4)\left(\frac{1}{x+4}\right) = 2(x+4)$$
$$1 = 2x + 8$$
$$x = -\frac{7}{2}$$

Multiply both sides of the equation by the common denominator to eliminate the fractions. Then solve. Confirm that the solution is valid in the original equation.

The solution is $x = -\frac{7}{2}$.

B. $\frac{1}{x-3} = 5$

$$(x-3)\left(\frac{1}{x-3}\right) = 5(x-3)$$
$$1 = 5x - 15$$
$$x = \frac{16}{5}$$

The solution is $x = \frac{16}{5}$.

STUDY TIP
A fraction with a denominator equal to zero is undefined.

Try It! 1. What is the solution to each equation?

a. $\frac{2}{x+5} = 4$ **b.** $\frac{1}{x-7} = 2$

APPLICATION

EXAMPLE 2 Solve a Work-Rate Problem

Arthur and Cheyenne can paint a wall in 6 hours when working together. Cheyenne works twice as fast as Arthur. How long would it take Cheyenne to paint the wall if she were working alone?

Step 1 Determine the work-rates of Arthur and Cheyenne.

Let x represent the number of hours Arthur needs to paint the wall himself.

The fraction of a job completed *per hour* is the work-rate.

Arthur can paint 1 wall in x hours, or $\frac{1}{x}$ of a wall in 1 hour.

Cheyenne is twice as fast, so Cheyenne paints $\frac{2}{x}$ of a wall in 1 hour.

Together they paint 1 wall in 6 hours, or $\frac{1}{6}$ of a wall in 1 hour.

COMMON ERROR
You might have multiplied x by 2 because Cheyenne works twice as fast. However, it takes Cheyenne *half* the time to paint the wall.

Step 2 Write the equation for their rates working together.

$$\frac{1}{x} + \frac{2}{x} = \frac{1}{6}$$

$$6x\left(\frac{1}{x} + \frac{2}{x}\right) = 6x\left(\frac{1}{6}\right)$$

$$6 + 12 = x$$

$$18 = x$$

Write the equation for their rates working together. Then solve.

It takes Arthur 18 hours to paint the wall alone. Since Cheyenne works twice as fast as Arthur, it would take her 9 hours to paint the wall alone.

 **Try It!** 2. It takes 12 hours to fill a pool with two pipes, where the water in one pipe flows three times as fast as the other pipe. How long will it take the slower pipe to fill the pool by itself?

Activity

Assess

CONCEPTUAL UNDERSTANDING

EXAMPLE 3 Identify an Extraneous Solution

What is the solution of the equation $\frac{1}{x-5} + \frac{x}{x-3} = \frac{2}{x^2 - 8x + 15}$?

Step 1 Multiply each side of the equation by the common denominator, $(x - 5)(x - 3)$.

$$(x-5)(x-3)\left(\frac{1}{x-5} + \frac{x}{x-3}\right) = \frac{2(x-5)(x-3)}{x^2 - 8x + 15}$$

Step 2 Continue to simplify.

$$\frac{(x-5)(x-3)}{x-5} + \frac{x(x-5)(x-3)}{x-3} = \frac{2(x-5)(x-3)}{x^2 - 8x + 15}$$

Step 3 Divide out common factors in the numerator and the denominator.

$$\frac{\cancel{(x-5)}(x-3)}{\cancel{x-5}} + \frac{x(x-5)\cancel{(x-3)}}{\cancel{x-3}} = \frac{2\cancel{(x-5)}\cancel{(x-3)}}{\cancel{x^2 - 8x + 15}}$$

You can divide out common factors under the assumption that $\frac{(x-5)}{(x-5)} = 1$ and $\frac{(x-3)}{(x-3)} = 1$. This is only true if $x \neq 5$ or 3.

Step 4 Solve the equation.

$$(x-3) + x(x-5) = 2$$
$$x - 3 + x^2 - 5x = 2$$
$$x^2 - 4x - 3 = 2$$
$$x^2 - 4x - 5 = 0$$
$$(x-5)(x+1) = 0$$
$$x = 5 \text{ and } x = -1$$

Consider both solutions. If either solution makes the value of the denominator 0, it is not valid.

The solution $x = 5$ is an **extraneous solution** because it makes the value of a denominator in the original equation equal to 0.

The solution of the equation $\frac{1}{x-5} + \frac{x}{x-3} = \frac{2}{x^2 - 8x + 15}$ is −1.

Confirm with a graph.

Consider the graphs of $\frac{1}{x-5} + \frac{x}{x-3}$ and $\frac{2}{x^2 - 8x + 15}$.

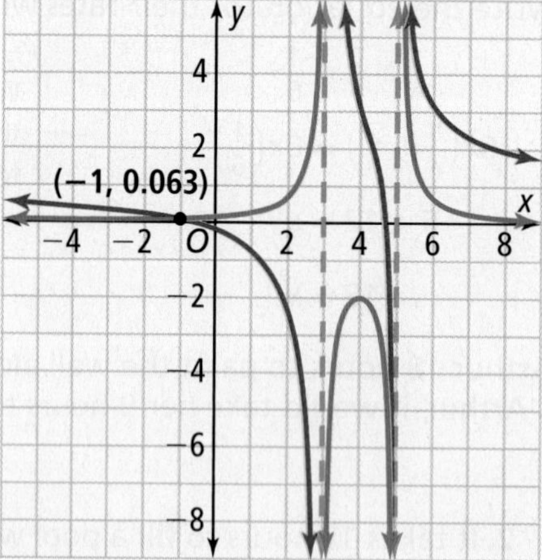

LOOK FOR RELATIONSHIPS
How are an extraneous solution and an asymptote related? Is this always true?

Note that each graph has a vertical asymptote at $x = 3$ and $x = 5$. Therefore, neither graph has a value at $x = 5$. The graphs only intersect in one point, at $x = -1$.

Try It! 3. What is the solution to the equation $\frac{1}{x+2} + \frac{1}{x-2} = \frac{4}{(x+2)(x-2)}$?

EXAMPLE 4 Solve Problems With Extraneous Solutions

What are the solutions to the following equations?

A. $\frac{5x}{x-2} = 7 + \frac{10}{x-2}$

STUDY TIP
Remember to multiply all terms on both sides of the equation by the least common denominator.

$\frac{5x}{x-2} = 7 + \frac{10}{x-2}$ .... Write the original equation.

$(x-2)\left(\frac{5x}{x-2}\right) = \left(7 + \frac{10}{x-2}\right)(x-2)$ .... Multiply by the LCD.

$5x = 7(x-2) + 10$ .... Distributive Property

$5x = 7x - 14 + 10$ .... Distributive Property

$-2x = -4$ .... Collect terms and simplify.

$x = 2$ .... Solve for x.

Check the solution in the original equation. The value 2 is an extraneous solution because it would cause the denominator in the original equation to be equal to 0. This equation has no solution.

B. $\frac{3}{x-3} = \frac{x}{x-3} - \frac{x}{4}$

$\frac{3}{x-3} = \frac{x}{x-3} - \frac{x}{4}$ .... Write original equation.

$(4)(x-3)\left(\frac{3}{x-3}\right) = \left(\frac{x}{x-3} - \frac{x}{4}\right)(4)(x-3)$ .... Multiply by LCD.

$4(3) = 4(x) - x(x-3)$ .... Distributive Property

$12 = 4x - x^2 + 3x$ .... Simplify.

$x^2 - 7x + 12 = 0$ .... Write in standard form

$(x-3)(x-4) = 0$ .... Factor.

$x - 3 = 0$ or $x - 4 = 0$ .... Solve using the Zero Product Property.

$x = 3$ or $x = 4$ .... Solve for x.

Check the solutions in the original equation. The value 3 is an extraneous solution because it would cause the denominator of the original equation to be equal to zero. The only solution to the equation is $x = 4$.

 **Try It!** **4.** What are the solutions to the following equations?

a. $x + \frac{6}{x-3} = \frac{2x}{x-3}$

b. $\frac{x^2}{x+5} = \frac{25}{x+5}$

APPLICATION

EXAMPLE 5 Solve a Rate Problem

Paddling with the current in a river, Jake traveled 16 miles. Even though he paddled upstream for an hour longer than the amount of time he paddled downstream, Jake could only travel 6 miles against the current. In still water, Jake paddles at a rate of 5 mph. What is the speed of the current in the river?

Formulate Let c be the rate of the river's current.

Recall that distance = rate • time so time = $\frac{\text{distance}}{\text{rate}}$.

$$\frac{16}{5+c} + 1 = \frac{6}{5-c}$$

Jake's paddle rate in still water + the rate of the current

Jake paddles 1 h longer upstream than downstream.

Jake's paddle rate in still water − the rate of the current

Compute Solve the equation for c.

$$\frac{16}{5+c} + 1 = \frac{6}{5-c}$$

$(5+c)(5-c)\left(\frac{16}{5+c} + 1\right) = \left(\frac{6}{5-c}\right)(5+c)(5-c)$ .... Multiply both sides by a common denominator.

$80 - 16c + 25 - c^2 = 30 + 6c$ .... Combine like terms.

$0 = c^2 + 22c - 75$ .... Write in standard form.

$0 = (c + 25)(c - 3)$ .... Factor.

$0 = c + 25 \quad 0 = c - 3$ .... Use the Zero Product Property.

$c = -25 \quad c = 3$ .... Solve.

Interpret The solution $c = -25$ is extraneous because the speed of the current cannot be negative.

The speed of the current is 3 mph.

Try It! 5. Three people are planting tomatoes in a community garden. Marta takes 50 minutes to plant the garden alone, Benito takes x minutes and Tyler takes $x + 15$ minutes. If the three of them take 20 minutes to finish the garden, how long would it have taken Tyler alone?

CONCEPT SUMMARY Solving Rational Equations

WORDS A rational equation is an equation that contains a rational expression. To solve, identify the domain for the variable. Then multiply both sides of the equation by a common denominator and solve. An extraneous solution is a solution that is not valid because that value is excluded from the domain of the original equation.

ALGEBRA

$$\frac{1}{x} + \frac{2}{x} = \frac{1}{6}$$ Domain: $x \neq 0$

$$6x\left(\frac{1}{x} + \frac{2}{x}\right) = 6x\left(\frac{1}{6}\right)$$

$$6 + 12 = x$$

$$18 = x$$

The domain includes $x = 18$, so the solution to the equation is 18.

$$\frac{x^2 + 4}{x - 1} = \frac{5}{x - 1}$$ Domain: $x \neq 1$

$$(x - 1)\left(\frac{x^2 + 4}{x - 1}\right) = (x - 1)\left(\frac{5}{x - 1}\right)$$

$$x^2 + 4 = 5$$

$$x^2 = 1$$

$$x = \pm 1$$

The domain does not include $x = 1$, so 1 is an extraneous solution. It does include $x = -1$, so the solution to the equation is -1.

Do You UNDERSTAND?

1. **ESSENTIAL QUESTION** How can you solve rational equations and identify extraneous solutions?

2. **Vocabulary** Write your own example of a rational equation that, when solved, has at least one **extraneous solution**.

3. **Error Analysis** A student solved the rational equation as follows:

$$\frac{1}{2x} - \frac{2}{5x} = \frac{1}{10x} - 3; x = 0$$

Describe and correct the error the student made.

4. **Construct Arguments** Yuki says, "*You can check the solution(s) of rational equations in any of the steps of the solution process.*" Explain why her reasoning is incorrect.

Do You KNOW HOW?

Solve.

5. $\frac{4}{x + 6} = 2$

6. $\frac{x^2}{x + 3} = \frac{9}{x + 3}$

7. Organizing given information into a table can be helpful when solving rate problems. Use this table to solve the following problem.

	Distance	Rate	Time
Upstream			
Downstream			

The speed of a stream is 4 km/h. A boat can travel 6 km upstream in the same time it takes to travel 12 km downstream. Find the speed of the boat in still water.

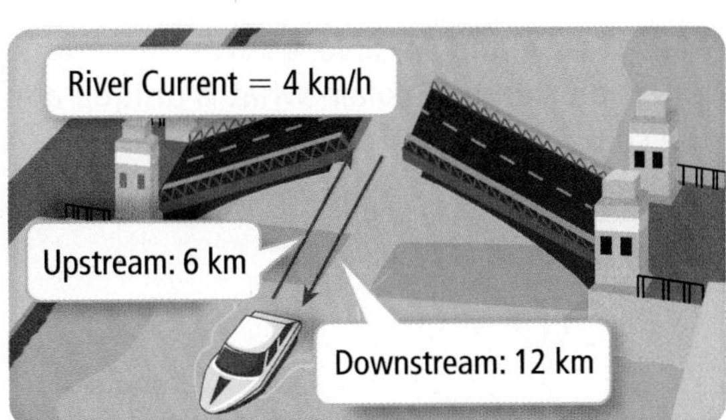

PRACTICE & PROBLEM SOLVING

UNDERSTAND

8. **Reason** If you solve a work-rate problem and your solution, which represents the amount of time it would take *working together,* exceeds the individual *working alone* times that are given, then how do you know your solution is unreasonable? Explain.

9. **Construct Arguments** Explain why a negative solution must be eliminated as an extraneous solution when solving a rational equation for an unknown rate.

10. **Error Analysis** Describe and correct the error Miranda made in solving the rational equation.

$$\frac{1}{x-2} + \frac{x-2}{x+2} = \frac{x-4}{x-2}$$

$$(x+2)(x-2)\left(\frac{1}{x-2} + \frac{x-2}{x+2}\right) = \left(\frac{x-4}{x-2}\right)(x+2)(x-2)$$

$$(x+2)(1) + (x-2)(x-2) = (x+4)(x+2)$$

$$x + 2 + \cancel{x^2} - 4x + 4 = \cancel{x^2} + 6x + 8$$

$$-3x + 6 = 6x + 8$$

$$-2 = 9x; \text{ or } x = -\frac{2}{9}$$ ✗

11. **Generalize** In addition to identifying extraneous solutions, why else is it important to substitute your solution into the original equation?

12. **Mathematical Connections** Explain how solving rational equations is related to solving linear and quadratic equations.

13. **Higher Order Thinking** Write a rational equation that cannot have 2 or −6 as solutions.

14. **Make Sense and Persevere** Solve the rational equation shown. Explain what is unique about the solution.

$$\frac{x^2 - 7x - 18}{x+2} = x - 9$$

PRACTICE

Solve the equation. SEE EXAMPLE 1

15. $\frac{1}{x-3} = 10$

16. $\frac{15}{x+3} = 3$

17. $\frac{12}{x-4} = 9$

18. $\frac{5}{3-x} = 1$

Solve the problem. SEE EXAMPLE 2

19. Paige can complete a landscaping job in 6 hours. Malia can complete the same job in 4 hours. Working together, how long would it take them to complete the job?

20. Russel and Aaron can build a shed in 8 hours when working together. Aaron works three times as fast as Russel. How long would it take Russel to build the shed if he were to work alone?

Solve the equation. SEE EXAMPLE 3

21. $\frac{x}{x-3} - 4 = \frac{3}{x-3}$

22. $\frac{x^2}{x-10} = \frac{100}{x-10} - 10$

Solve the equation. SEE EXAMPLE 4

23. $\frac{4}{3(x+1)} = \frac{12}{x^2-1}$

24. $\frac{x}{x-3} + \frac{2x}{x+3} = \frac{18}{(x+3)(x-3)}$

Solve the problem. SEE EXAMPLE 5

25. A boat travels 8 miles upstream in the same amount of time it can travel 12 miles downstream. In still water the speed of the boat is 5 mi/h. What is the speed of the current?

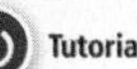

Practice Tutorial

Mixed Review Available Online

PRACTICE & PROBLEM SOLVING

APPLY

26. **Make Sense and Persevere** Kenji can finish a puzzle in 2 hours working alone. Oscar can finish the same puzzle in 3 hours working alone. How long would it take Oscar and Kenji to finish the puzzle if they worked on it together?

27. **Use Structure** A commercial jet flies 1,500 miles with the wind. In the same amount of time it can fly 1,000 miles against the wind. The speed of the jet in still air is 550 mph. Find the speed of the wind.

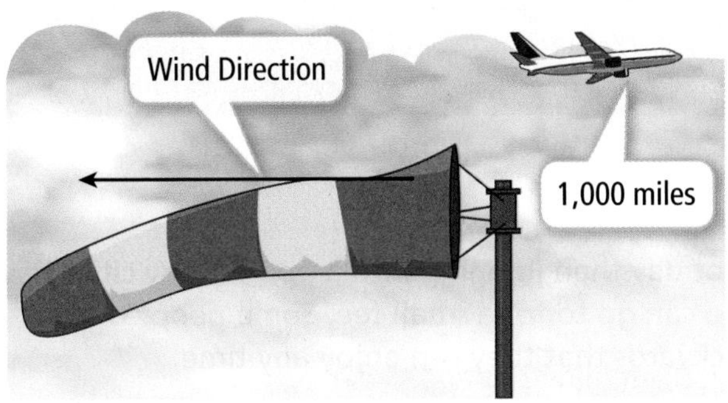

a. Organize the given information and what you need to find in a table.

b. Write and solve a rational equation to find the wind speed.

28. **Reason** During their day at the beach, Jae and his friends rent a Jet Ski. They split the \$120 rental fee evenly among themselves. Then Jae, with only his friend Morgan, share the cost of a \$16 pizza. If Jae spends a total of \$48 for both, then find the number of friends, *n*, with whom he shared the cost of the Jet Ski rental.

29. **Make Sense and Persevere** When driving to their family reunion, River's mom drove 10 miles at a rate of x mph and then 25 miles at a rate of $x + 10$ mph. The total driving time was 45 minutes. What were the two driving speeds at which River's mom drove?

30. **Generalize** So far this baseball season, Philip has gotten a hit 8 times out of 40 at-bats. He wants to increase his batting average to 0.333. Calculate the number of consecutive hits, *h*, he would need in order to achieve this goal. Round your answer to the nearest whole number.

ASSESSMENT PRACTICE

31. Which of the following rational equations have at least one extraneous solution? Select all that apply.

Ⓐ $\frac{2}{x} = \frac{3}{x-4}$

Ⓑ $\frac{x^2}{x-3} = \frac{9}{x-3}$

Ⓒ $\frac{x-1}{x-5} = \frac{9}{x-5}$

Ⓓ $x + \frac{3}{x} = 4$

Ⓔ $\frac{x}{x-3} - \frac{3}{2} = \frac{3}{x-3}$

32. **SAT/ACT** Which of the following is the solution of $\frac{3}{x+1} = \frac{2}{x-3}$?

Ⓐ $x = -11$

Ⓑ $x = -\frac{7}{5}$

Ⓒ $x = \frac{7}{5}$

Ⓓ $x = 11$

33. **Performance Task** A chemist needs alcohol solution in the correct concentration for her experiment. She adds a 6% alcohol solution to 50 gallons of solution that is 2% alcohol. The function that represents the percent of alcohol in the resulting solution is $f(x) = \frac{50(0.02) + x(0.06)}{50 + x}$, where x is the amount of 6% solution added.

Part A How much 6% solution should be added to create a solution that is 5% alcohol?

Part B Use Appropriate Tools Explain the steps you could take to use your graphing calculator to verify the correctness of your answer to part (A).

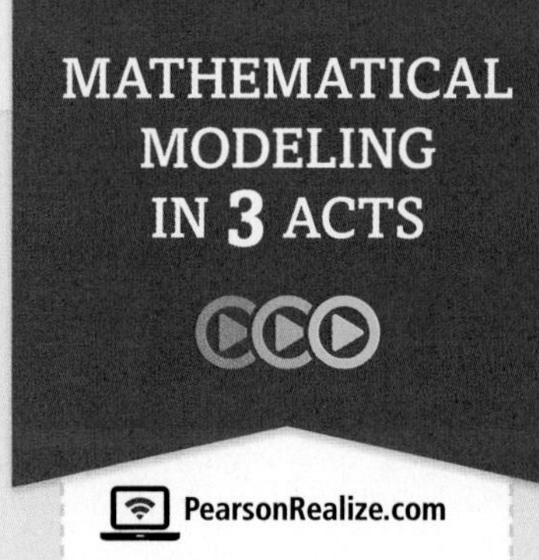

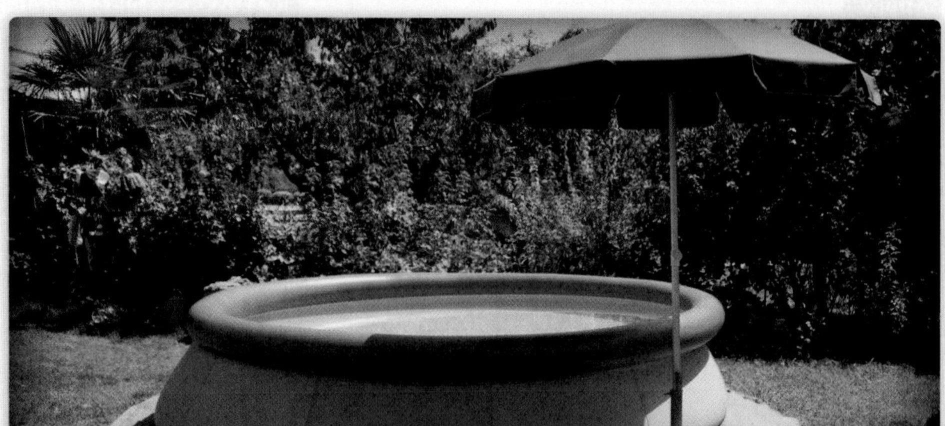

Real Cool Waters

Nothing feels better on a hot day than jumping into a pool! Many cities have swimming pools that people can go to for a small fee. Some people have swimming pools in their backyards that they can enjoy any time.

If neither of these options are available, you can always create your own beach paradise! Get a kiddie pool, a lawn chair, and a beach umbrella. Think about your beach paradise during the Mathematical Modeling in 3 Acts lesson.

ACT 1 Identify the Problem

1. What is the first question that comes to mind after watching the video?
2. Write down the main question you will answer about what you saw in the video.
3. Make an initial conjecture that answers this main question.
4. Explain how you arrived at your conjecture.
5. Write a number that you know is too small.
6. Write a number that you know is too large.
7. What information will be useful to know to answer the main question? How can you get it? How will you use that information?

ACT 2 Develop a Model

8. Use the math that you have learned in this Topic to refine your conjecture.

ACT 3 Interpret the Results

9. Is your refined conjecture between the highs and lows you set up earlier?
10. Did your refined conjecture match the actual answer exactly? If not, what might explain the difference?

TOPIC 3

Topic Review

TOPIC ESSENTIAL QUESTION

1. How do you calculate with functions defined as quotients of polynomials, and what are the key features of their graphs?

Vocabulary Review

Choose the correct term to complete each sentence.

2. The __________ can be represented by the equation $y = \frac{1}{x}$.
3. A(n) __________ is any function $R(x) = \frac{P(x)}{Q(x)}$ where $P(x)$ and $Q(x)$ are polynomials and $Q(x) \neq 0$.
4. __________ can be modeled by the equation $y = \frac{k}{x}$.
5. A(n) __________ is the quotient of two polynomials.
6. A(n) __________ is a line that a graph approaches but may not touch.
7. A(n) __________ is a fraction that has one or more fractions in the numerator and/or the denominator.
8. A(n) __________ is a value that is a solution to an equation that is derived from an original equation but does not satisfy the original equation.

- inverse variation
- constant of variation
- reciprocal function
- asymptote
- rational function
- extraneous solution
- rational expression
- compound fraction

Concepts & Skills Review

LESSON 3-1 Inverse Variation and the Reciprocal Function

Quick Review

The equation $y = \frac{k}{x}$, or $xy = k$, $k \neq 0$, represents an **inverse variation**, where k is the **constant of variation**. The parent **reciprocal function** is $y = \frac{1}{x}$.

Example

In an inverse variation, $x = 9$ when $y = 2$. What is the value of y when $x = 3$?

$2 = \frac{k}{9}$ .... Substitute 9 and 2 for x and y.

$18 = k$ .... Solve for k.

$y = \frac{18}{3}$ .... Substitute 18 and 3 for k and x, respectively.

$y = 6$ .... Divide.

Practice & Problem Solving

9. In an inverse variation, $x = 2$ when $y = -4$. What is the value of y when $x = 16$?
10. In an inverse variation, $x = 6$ when $y = \frac{1}{12}$. What is the value of x when $y = 2$?
11. Graph the function $y = \frac{5}{x}$. What are the domain, range, and asymptotes of the function?
12. **Look for Relationships** How is the parent reciprocal function related to an inverse variation?
13. **Make Sense and Persevere** The volume, V, of a gas varies inversely with pressure, P. If the volume of a gas is 6 cm^3 with pressure 25 kg/cm^2, what is the volume of a gas with pressure 15 kg/cm^2?

LESSON 3-2 Graphing Rational Functions

Quick Review

Vertical asymptotes may occur when the denominator of a rational function is equal to 0.

Horizontal asymptotes guide the end behavior of a graph and depend on the degrees of the numerator and denominator.

Example

What is the graph of $f(x) = \frac{9x^2 - 25}{x^2 - 5x - 6}$?

Find vertical asymptotes.

$x^2 - 5x - 6 = 0$ ········ Set denominator equal to 0.

$(x + 1)(x - 6) = 0$ ········ Factor.

$x = -1 \quad x = 6$ ········ Solve.

Find horizontal asymptotes.

Find the ratio of leading terms.

$f(x) = \frac{9x^2}{x^2} = 9$

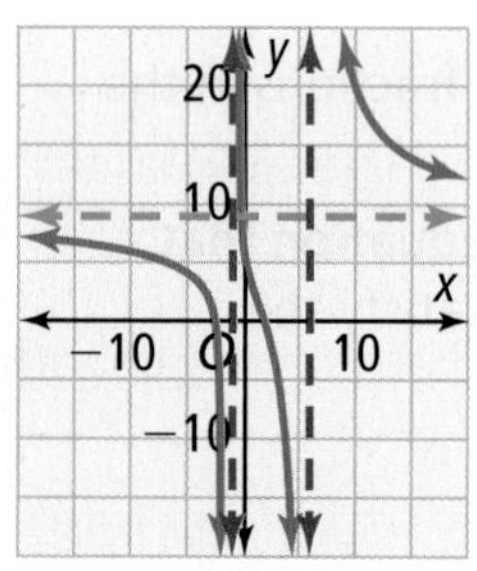

Practice & Problem Solving

Identify the vertical and horizontal asymptotes of each rational function.

14. $f(x) = \frac{x - 8}{x^2 + 9x + 14}$

15. $f(x) = \frac{2x + 1}{x^2 + 5x - 6}$

16. $f(x) = \frac{x^2 - 9}{2x^2 + 25}$

17. $f(x) = \frac{16x^2 - 1}{x^2 - 6x - 16}$

Graph each function and identify the horizontal and vertical asymptotes.

18. $f(x) = \frac{x}{x^2 - 1}$

19. $f(x) = \frac{3}{x - 2}$

20. $f(x) = \frac{2x^2 + 7}{x^2 + 2x + 1}$

21. $f(x) = \frac{3x^2 - 11x - 4}{4x^2 - 25}$

22. **Reason** The daily attendance at an amusement park after day x is given by the function $f(x) = \frac{3{,}000x}{x^2 - 1}$. On approximately which day will the attendance be 1,125 people?

LESSON 3-3 Multiplying and Dividing Rational Expressions

Quick Review

To multiply **rational expressions**, divide out common factors and simplify. To divide rational expressions, multiply by the reciprocal of the divisor.

Example

What is the quotient of $\frac{x^2 + x - 2}{x + 3}$ and $\frac{x^2 + 3x - 4}{2x + 6}$?

$= \frac{x^2 + x - 2}{x + 3} \cdot \frac{2x + 6}{x^2 + 3x - 4}$ ········ Multiply by reciprocal.

$= \frac{(x + 2)\cancel{(x - 1)}}{\cancel{x + 3}} \cdot \frac{2\cancel{(x + 3)}}{(x + 4)\cancel{(x - 1)}}$ ········ Divide out common factors.

$= \frac{2(x + 2)}{x + 4}$ ········ Simplify.

Practice & Problem Solving

Find the simplified product, and state the domain.

23. $\frac{x^2 + x - 12}{x^2 - x - 6} \cdot \frac{x + 2}{x + 4}$

24. $\frac{x^2 + 8x}{x^3 + 5x^2 - 24x} \cdot (x^3 + 2x^2 - 15x)$

Find the simplified quotient, and state the domain.

25. $\frac{x^2 - 36}{x^2 - 3x - 18} \div \frac{x^2 + 2x - 24}{x^2 + 7x + 12}$

26. $\frac{2x^2 + 5x - 3}{x^2 - 4x - 21} \div \frac{2x^2 + 5x - 3}{3x + 9}$

27. **Reason** The volume, in cubic units, of a rectangular prism with a square base can be represented by $25x^3 + 200x^2$. The height, in units, can be represented by $x + 8$. What is the side length of the base of the rectangular prism, in units?

LESSON 3-4 Adding and Subtracting Rational Expressions

Quick Review

To add or subtract rational expressions, multiply each expression in both the numerator and denominator by a common denominator. Add or subtract the numerators. Then simplify.

Example

What is the sum of $\frac{x-2}{x^2-25}$ and $\frac{3}{x+5}$?

$\frac{x-2}{(x+5)(x-5)} + \frac{3}{x+5}$ .... Factor denominators.

$= \frac{x-2}{(x+5)(x-5)} + \frac{3(x-5)}{(x+5)(x-5)}$ .... Find common denominator.

$= \frac{x-2+3(x-5)}{(x+5)(x-5)}$ .... Add numerators.

$= \frac{x-2+3x-15}{(x+5)(x-5)}$ .... Multiply.

$= \frac{4x-17}{(x+5)(x-5)}$ .... Simplify.

Practice & Problem Solving

Find the sum or difference.

28. $\frac{2x}{x+6} + \frac{3}{x-1}$

29. $\frac{x}{x^2-4} - \frac{5}{x-2}$

Simplify.

30. $\frac{2+\frac{2}{x}}{2-\frac{2}{x}}$

31. $\frac{\frac{-1}{x}+\frac{3}{y}}{\frac{4}{x}-\frac{5}{y}}$

32. Communicate Precisely Why is it necessary to consider the domain when adding and subtracting rational expressions?

33. Make Sense and Persevere Mia paddles a kayak 6 miles downstream at a rate 4 mph faster than the river's current. She then travels 6 miles back upstream at a rate 2 mph faster than the river's current. Write and simplify an expression for the time it takes her to make the round trip in terms of the river's current c.

LESSON 3-5 Solving Rational Equations

Quick Review

A **rational equation** is an equation relating rational expressions. An **extraneous solution** is a value that is a solution to an equation that is derived from an original equation but does not satisfy the original equation.

Example

What are the solutions to the equation $\frac{2}{x-2} = \frac{x}{x-2} - \frac{x}{4}$?

$(4)(x-2)\left(\frac{2}{x-2}\right)$

$= \left(\frac{x}{x-2} - \frac{x}{4}\right)(4)(x-2)$ .... Multiply by the LCD.

$8 = 4x - x^2 + 2x$ .... Multiply.

$x^2 - 6x + 8 = 0$ .... Write in standard form.

$(x-2)(x-4) = 0$ .... Factor.

$x-2=0$ or $x-4=0$ .... Zero Product Property

$x=2$ or $x=4$ .... Solve to identify possible solutions.

The solution $x = 2$ is extraneous. The only solution to the equation is $x = 4$.

Practice & Problem Solving

Solve the equation.

34. $\frac{18}{x+4} = 6$

35. $\frac{9}{x-1} = 3$

36. $-\frac{4}{3} + \frac{2}{x} = 8$

37. $\frac{2x}{x+3} = 5 + \frac{6x}{x+3}$

38. $-8 + \frac{64}{x-8} = \frac{x^2}{x-8}$

39. $\frac{9}{x^2-9} = \frac{3}{6(x-3)}$

40. Communicate Precisely Explain how to check if a solution to a rational equation is an extraneous solution.

41. Reason Diego and Stacy can paint a doghouse in 5 hours when working together. Diego works twice as fast as Stacy. Let x be the number of hours it would take Diego to paint the doghouse and y be the number of hours it would take Stacy to paint the doghouse. How long would it take Stacy to paint the doghouse if she was working alone? How long would it take Diego to paint the doghouse if he was working alone?

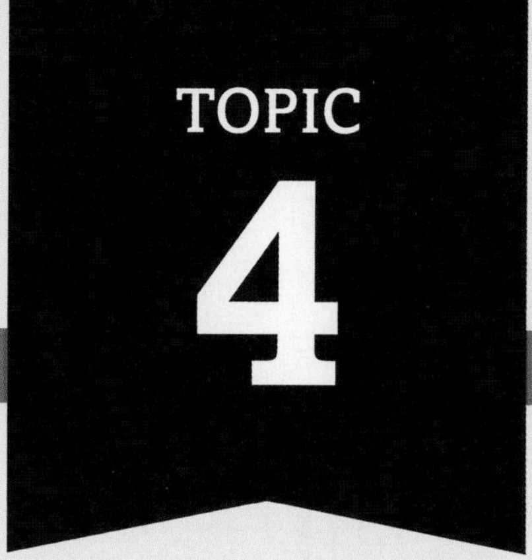

Rational Exponents and Radical Functions

How are rational exponents and radical equations used to solve real-world problems?

Topic Overview

enVision® STEM Project:
Tune a Piano

4-1 *n*th Roots, Radicals, and Rational Exponents

4-2 Properties of Exponents and Radicals

4-3 Graphing Radical Functions

4-4 Solving Radical Equations

Mathematical Modeling in 3 Acts:
The Snack Shack

4-5 Function Operations

4-6 Inverse Relations and Functions

Topic Vocabulary

- composite function
- composition of functions
- extraneous solution
- index
- inverse function
- inverse relation
- like radicals
- *n*th root
- radical function
- radical symbol
- radicand
- reduced radical form

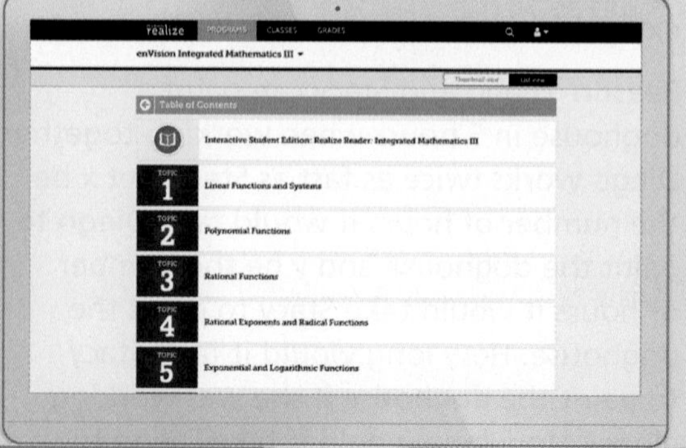

Go online | **PearsonRealize.com**

Digital Experience

INTERACTIVE STUDENT EDITION Access online or offline.

ACTIVITIES Complete ***Explore & Reason, Model & Discuss***, and ***Critique & Explain*** activities. Interact with Examples and Try Its.

ANIMATION View and interact with real-world applications.

PRACTICE Practice what you've learned.

MATHEMATICAL MODELING IN 3 ACTS

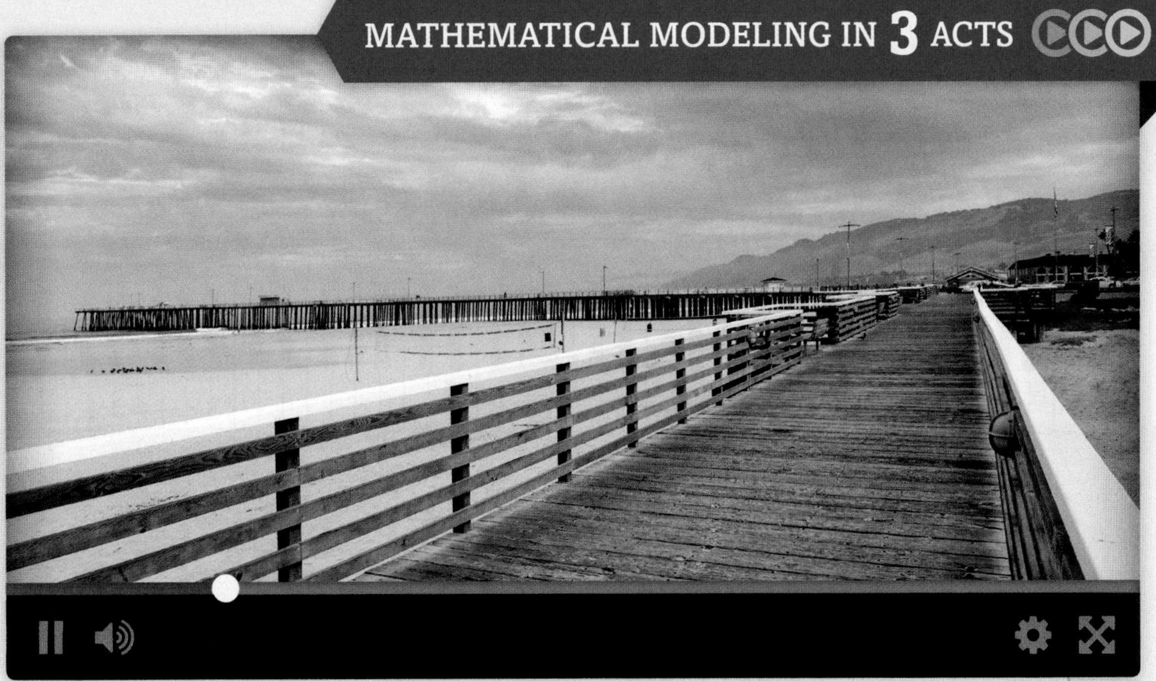

The Snack Shack

Many Americans love the beach! When visiting the beach, some people bring coolers packed with food and drinks. Others prefer to take advantage of snack bars and shops set up along the beach.

Some beachside communities have built long wooden walkways, or boardwalks, to make it easier for beachgoers to walk to the snack bars and stores. How easy do you find walking in the sand? Think about this during the Mathematical Modeling in 3 Acts lesson.

TOPIC 4

VIDEOS Watch clips to support ***Mathematical Modeling in 3 Acts Lessons*** and **enVision®** ***STEM Projects.***

CONCEPT SUMMARY Review key lesson content through multiple representations.

ASSESSMENT Show what you've learned.

GLOSSARY Read and listen to English and Spanish definitions.

TUTORIALS Get help from ***Virtual Nerd,*** right when you need it.

MATH TOOLS Explore math with digital tools and manipulatives.

Did You Know?

The size of an instrument can affect the range of pitches it can produce.

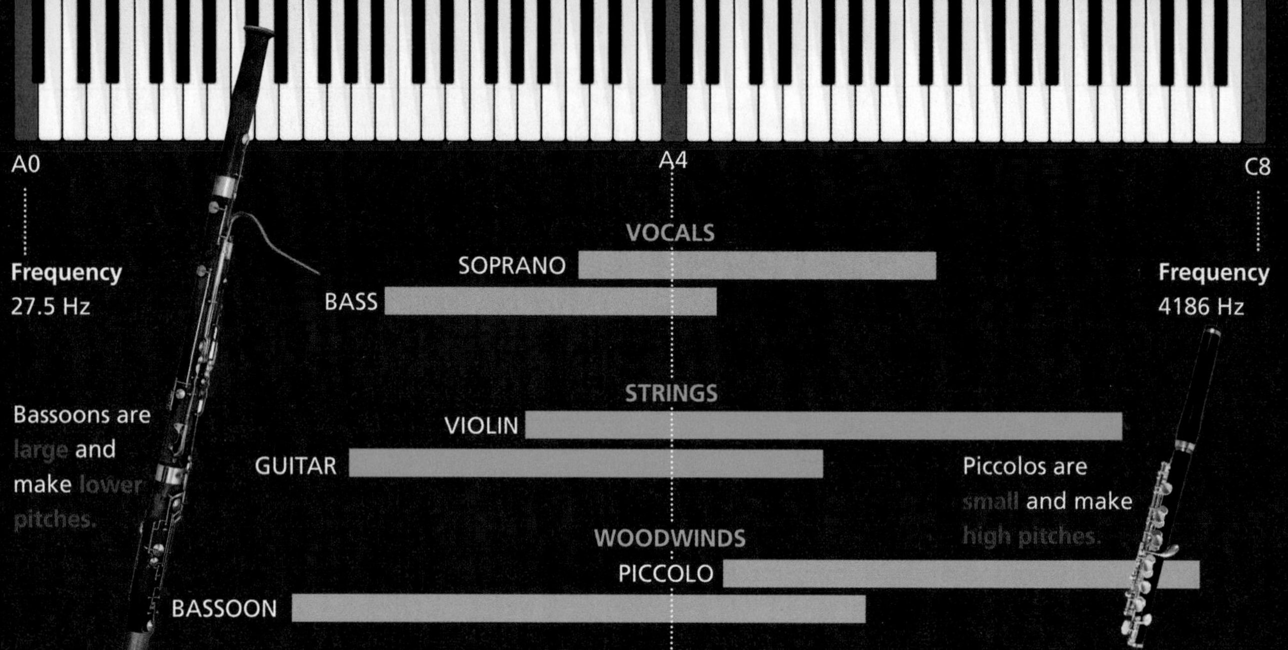

Digital music programs allow musicians, audio technicians, and music producers to **alter a tone or pitch**, edit music, and visualize sounds.

Where you press down on a guitar string affects the pitch of the string when plucked. Pressing halfway down the string **produces a pitch an octave higher** than pressing the top of the string.

Your Task: Tune a Piano

You and your classmates will investigate different ways to tune a piano. You will select a musical piece and then decide what tuning sounds best for it.

4-1

*n*th Roots, Radicals, and Rational Exponents

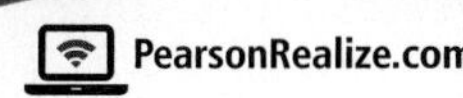
PearsonRealize.com

I CAN… relate roots and rational exponents and use them to simplify expressions and solve equations.

VOCABULARY

- index
- *n*th root
- radical symbol
- radicand

Activity Assess

EXPLORE & REASON

The graph shows $y = x^2$.

A. Find *all* possible values of *x* or *y* so that the point is on the graph.

(a) (2, ___) (b) (3, ___)

(c) (−3, ___) (d) (5, ___)

(e) (___, 4) (f) (___, −16)

(g) (___, 7) (h) (___, 5)

B. Communicate Precisely Write a precise set of instructions that show how to find an approximate value of $\sqrt{13}$ using the graph.

C. Draw a graph of $y = x^3$. Use the graph to approximate each value.

(a) $\sqrt[3]{5}$ (b) $\sqrt[3]{-5}$

(c) $\sqrt[3]{8}$ (d) A solution to $x^3 = 5$

(e) A solution to $x^3 = -5$ (f) A solution to $x^3 = 8$

ESSENTIAL QUESTION **How are exponents and radicals used to represent roots of real numbers?**

EXAMPLE 1 Find All Real *n*th Roots

A. What are all the real cube roots of 125?

An ***n*th root** of a number *c* is *x*, such that $x^n = c$. An *n*th root can be denoted by a **radical symbol** with an **index** of *n*: $\sqrt[n]{c}$; *c* is called the **radicand.**

To represent the real cube root of 125, write $x = \sqrt[3]{125}$.

Find the value of *x* such that $x^3 = 125$.

To solve $x^3 = 125$, note that $5^3 = 125$, so 5 is a root.

> Recall that complex solutions to polynomial equations come in pairs. The number of real roots depends on the degree of the equation.
> - odd degree → odd number of real roots
> - even degree → even number of real roots

Consider if there are others.
To determine this, set the expression equal to 0 and factor.

$x^3 - 125 = 0$

$(x - 5)(x^2 + 5x + 25)$

$x - 5 = 0$ gives the root 5

$x^2 + 5x + 25 = 0$

> **MAKE SENSE AND PERSEVERE**
> Recall that third degree equations have three solutions; here, one solution is real and two are complex.

The discriminant of the expression is $5^2 - 4(1)(25)$, or −75.
The roots are not real.

Therefore, 5 is the only real cube root of 125.

CONTINUED ON THE NEXT PAGE

EXAMPLE 1 CONTINUED

B. What are all the real fourth roots of 16?

The index is 4 and the radicand is 16. Write $x = \sqrt[4]{16}$.

Find the value of x such that $x^4 = 16$.

Set the expression equal to 0 and factor.

$$x^4 - 16 = 0$$

$$(x^2 - 4)(x^2 + 4) = 0$$

$$(x + 2)(x - 2)(x^2 + 4) = 0$$

$$x = 2, -2$$

$x^2 + 4 = 0$ leads to imaginary roots.

The real roots of $x^4 = 16$ are 2 and -2.

The radical symbol represents the positive (principal) root.

Try It! 1. Find the specified roots of each number.

a. real fourth roots of 81 b. real cube roots of 64

CONCEPTUAL UNDERSTANDING

 **EXAMPLE 2 Understand Rational Exponents**

A. What is the meaning of the exponent in the expression $16^{\frac{1}{4}}$?

To interpret a rational exponent, look at what happens if you extend the properties of *integer* exponents to *rational* exponents.

Assume the Power of a Power Property applies to exponents in the form $\frac{1}{n}$.

STUDY TIP
It is important to recognize multiple representations of the same value so you can select the form that is most efficient for a given situation.

$$\left(16^{\frac{1}{4}}\right) = (2^4)^{\frac{1}{4}} = 2 = \sqrt[4]{16}$$

$16^{\frac{1}{4}}$ is a number you raise to the 4th power to get 16.

This means you can define $16^{\frac{1}{4}}$ to be $\sqrt[4]{16}$, or 2.

In general, for positive integer n, $x^{\frac{1}{n}}$ is defined to be $\sqrt[n]{x}$.

$$x^{\frac{1}{n}} = \sqrt[n]{x}$$

Both the exponent $\frac{1}{n}$ and the radical symbol $\sqrt[n]{x}$ indicate the principal nth root.

B. What is the meaning of the exponent in the expression $27^{\frac{2}{3}}$?

$27^{\frac{2}{3}} = \left(27^{\frac{1}{3}}\right)^2$ .... Rewrite using the Power of a Power Property.

$= (\sqrt[3]{27})^2$ .... Use the definition of the exponent $\frac{1}{n}$, $x = \sqrt[n]{x}$.

$= 3^2$

$= 9$

This means that you can define $27^{\frac{2}{3}}$ to be the $(\sqrt[3]{27})^2$, or 9.

 **Try It!** 2. Explain what each fractional exponent means, then evaluate.

a. $25^{\frac{1}{2}}$ b. $32^{\frac{2}{5}}$

 Activity  Assess

CONCEPT Interpreting Fractional Exponents

The index of a radical is equivalent to the denominator of a fractional exponent.

In general, if the *n*th root of *c* is a real number, $\sqrt[n]{c} = c^{\frac{1}{n}}$.

Furthermore, if *m* is an integer and $\frac{m}{n}$ is in lowest terms, then $c^{\frac{m}{n}} = (c^{\frac{1}{n}})^m = (\sqrt[n]{c})^m$ and $\sqrt[n]{c^m} = (c^m)^{\frac{1}{n}} = c^{\frac{m}{n}}$.

APPLICATION

USE APPROPRIATE TOOLS
Many expressions with integer roots can be evaluated using mental math. However, when the root is not an integer, it can be efficient to use the power function of a calculator to compute rational roots.

EXAMPLE 3 Evaluate Expressions With Rational Exponents

A. Evaluate the expressions $32^{\frac{3}{5}}$, $27^{-\frac{2}{3}}$, $50^{\frac{3}{4}}$.

$$32^{\frac{3}{5}} = \left(32^{\frac{1}{5}}\right)^3 = 2^3 = 8$$

$$27^{-\frac{2}{3}} = \left(27^{\frac{1}{3}}\right)^{-2} = (3)^{-2} = \frac{1}{9}$$

Since 50 does not have a perfect 4th root, use a calculator to approximate: $50^{\frac{3}{4}} \approx 18.80$

B. The Fujita scale rating, *F*, of a tornado is represented by $F = \sqrt[3]{\left(\frac{W}{14.1}\right)^2} - 2$, where *W* is the estimated wind speed of the tornado in miles per hour. What is the Fujita scale rating of a tornado with estimated wind speeds of 100 mph?

$F = \sqrt[3]{\left(\frac{100}{14.1}\right)^2} - 2$ ········ Substitute 100 for *W* in the formula.

$= \left(\frac{100}{14.1}\right)^{\frac{2}{3}} - 2$ ········ Rewrite the radical using an exponent.

$\approx (7.09)^{\frac{2}{3}} - 2$ ········ Divide 100 by 14.1.

$\approx 3.69 - 2$ ········ Evaluate the exponent.

≈ 1.69 ········ Subtract.

A tornado with estimated wind speeds of 100 mph is classified as F1 according to the Fujita scale.

 **Try It!** **3.** What is the value of each expression? Round to the nearest hundredth if necessary.

a. $-\left(16^{\frac{3}{4}}\right)$ **b.** $\sqrt[5]{3.5^4}$

EXAMPLE 4 Simplify *n*th Roots

Simplify each expression.

A. $\sqrt[5]{32m^{15}}$

$\sqrt[5]{2^5m^{15}} = \sqrt[5]{(2m^3)^5}$ — Write the radicand as an expression to the 5th power.

$= 2m^3$

So, $\sqrt[5]{32m^{15}} = 2m^3$.

COMMON ERROR
You may think that because 20 and 8 do not have perfect fourth roots this expression cannot be simplified. However, each exponent is a multiple of 4, and: $(n^4)^m = n^{4m}$.

B. $\sqrt[4]{x^{20}y^8}$

$\sqrt[4]{x^{20}y^8} = \sqrt[4]{(x^5y^2)^4}$ — Write the radicand as an expression to the 4th power.

$= |x^5y^2|$

$= |x^5|y^2$ — Recall that the y^2 will always be positive and does not require absolute value.

So, $\sqrt[4]{x^{20}y^8} = |x^5|y^2$.

Try It! **4.** Simplify each expression.

a. $\sqrt[3]{-8a^3b^9}$ **b.** $\sqrt[4]{256x^{12}y^{24}}$

EXAMPLE 5 Use *n*th Roots to Solve Equations

Solve the equation $2x^5 = 64$.

GENERALIZE
Raise both sides of the equation to a power so that the exponent of the variable becomes 1. Using the Power of a Power Property, $(x^n)^{\frac{1}{n}} = x^1$.

$2x^5 = 64$

$x^5 = 32$

$(x^5)^{\frac{1}{5}} = 32^{\frac{1}{5}}$ — Raise each side of the equation to the $\frac{1}{5}$ power.

$x = 2$ — Use Power of a Power Property on the left, and simplify the rational exponent on the right.

The solution to the equation is $x = 2$.

Try It! **5. a.** Solve the equation $5x^3 = 320$.

b. Solve the equation $2p^4 = 162$.

 Activity Assess

CONCEPT Solving an Equation in the Form $x^n = c$

To solve an equation in the form $x^n = c$, find the nth root of both sides by raising each expression to the $\frac{1}{n}$ power.

$$(x^n)^{\frac{1}{n}} = (c)^{\frac{1}{n}}$$

APPLICATION

EXAMPLE 6 Use nth Roots to Solve Problems

One cube-shaped container has an edge length 2 cm longer than the edge length of a second cube. The volume of the larger cube is 729 cm^3. When the larger cube empties into the smaller cube, how much water will spill?

MODEL WITH MATHEMATICS
Use the information in the problem to write an equation that models the situation.

$$(x + 2)^3 = 729$$
$$[(x + 2)^3]^{\frac{1}{3}} = (729)^{\frac{1}{3}}$$
$$x + 2 = 9$$
$$x = 7$$

Raise both sides to the $\frac{1}{3}$ power and solve.

The volume of the smaller cube is 7^3, or 343 cm^3.

The volume of the larger cube is 729 cm^3.

The amount of water that spills is $729 - 343 = 386$.

When the larger cube empties into the smaller cube, 386 cm^3 of water will spill out.

 **Try It!** 6. One cube has an edge length 3 cm shorter than the edge length of a second cube. The volume of the smaller cube is 200 cm^3. What is the volume of the larger cube?

CONCEPT SUMMARY *n*th Roots, Radicals, and Rational Exponents

	Relating Radical and Exponential Forms	Solving an Equation in the Form $x^n = c$
WORDS	The index of a radical is equivalent to the denominator of a fractional exponent. The exponent of the radicand is equivalent to the numerator of a fractional exponent.	To solve an equation in the form $x^n = c$, find the *n*th root of both sides of the equation by raising each expression to the $\frac{1}{n}$ power.
NUMBERS	**Radical Form** $\sqrt[5]{32^4} = (32^4)^{\frac{1}{5}} = 32^{\frac{4}{5}}$ **Exponential Form** $729^{\frac{5}{6}} = \left(729^{\frac{1}{6}}\right)^5 = (\sqrt[6]{729})^5$	$x^3 = 1{,}728$ $(x^3)^{\frac{1}{3}} = (1{,}728)^{\frac{1}{3}}$ $x = 12$
ALGEBRA	**Radical Form** $\sqrt[n]{c^m} = (c^m)^{\frac{1}{n}} = c^{\frac{m}{n}}$ **Exponential Form** $c^{\frac{m}{n}} = \left(c^{\frac{1}{n}}\right)^m = \sqrt[n]{c^m}$	$x^n = c$ $(x^n)^{\frac{1}{n}} = (c)^{\frac{1}{n}}$ $x = c^{\frac{1}{n}}$

Do You UNDERSTAND?

1. **ESSENTIAL QUESTION** How are exponents and radicals used to represent roots of real numbers?

2. **Error Analysis** Kaitlyn said $\sqrt[3]{10} = 10^3$. Explain Kaitlyn's error.

3. **Vocabulary** In the radical expression $\sqrt[5]{125}$, what is the index? What is the radicand?

4. **Use Structure** Why is $75^{\frac{3}{5}}$ equal to $\left(75^{\frac{1}{5}}\right)^3$?

5. **Construct Arguments** Anastasia said that $(x^8)^{\frac{1}{4}} = \frac{x^8}{x^4} = x^4$. Is Anastasia correct? Explain.

6. **Make Sense and Persevere** Is it possible for a rational exponent to be an improper fraction? Explain how $27^{\frac{4}{3}}$ is evaluated or why it cannot be evaluated.

Do You KNOW HOW?

Write each expression in radical form.

7. $a^{\frac{1}{5}}$

8. $7^{\frac{2}{3}}$

Write each expression in exponential form.

9. $\sqrt[3]{b}$

10. $\sqrt[4]{p^7}$

11. How many real third roots does 1,728 have?

12. How many real sixth roots does 15,625 have?

13. Solve the equation $4x^3 = 324$.

14. Solve the equation $2x^4 = 2{,}500$.

Simplify each expression.

15. $\sqrt[3]{27x^{12}y^6}$

16. $\sqrt[5]{-32x^5y^{30}}$

17. A snow globe is packaged in a cubic container that has volume 64 in.^{3} A large shipping container is also a cube, and its edge length is 8 inches longer than the edge length of the snow globe container. How many snow globes can fit into the larger shipping container?

PRACTICE & PROBLEM SOLVING

Scan for Multimedia

Practice Tutorial

Additional Exercises Available Online

UNDERSTAND

18. **Construct Arguments** Justice found that the fifth root of $243x^{15}y^5$ is $3x^3y$. Is Justice correct? Explain your reasoning.

19. **Make Sense and Persevere** For a show, each sphere was inflated to have a volume of $4{,}186\frac{2}{3}$ in.^{3} Explain how to find the radius r of one of the inflated spheres. Use technology to compute your answer.

20. **Error Analysis** Describe and correct the error a student made in writing this exponential expression in radical form.

$$x^{\frac{4}{3}} = (x^4)^{\frac{1}{3}}$$
$$(x^4)^{\frac{1}{3}} = \sqrt[4]{x^3} \quad ✗$$

21. **Construct Arguments** Determine whether $\sqrt[3]{x^2}$ is equal to $(\sqrt[3]{x})^2$. Explain your reasoning.

22. **Use Structure** How many third roots does −512 have? Explain your reasoning.

23. **Higher Order Thinking** The annual interest formula below calculates the final balance of an account, F, given a starting balance, S, and an interest rate, r, after 10 years.

$$F = S(1 + r)^{10}$$

When solving for r, why can the negative root be ignored?

24. **Mathematical Connections** The lengths of the two legs of a right triangle are 4 and 8. What is the length of the hypotenuse, in simplest radical form?

PRACTICE

Find the specified roots of each number. SEE EXAMPLE 1

25. the real fourth roots of 81

26. the real third roots of 343

27. the real fifth roots of 1,024

28. the real square roots of 25

Rewrite each expression using a fractional exponent. SEE EXAMPLE 2

29. $\sqrt[4]{16^2}$

30. $\sqrt[6]{729}$

31. $\sqrt[7]{x^2}$

32. $\sqrt[4]{ab}$

What is the value of each expression? Round to the nearest hundredth if necessary. SEE EXAMPLE 3

33. $\sqrt[4]{25^2}$

34. $-\sqrt[3]{125^5}$

Simplify each expression. SEE EXAMPLE 4

35. $\sqrt[3]{8y^9}$

36. $\sqrt[4]{q^{12}z^4}$

37. $\sqrt[6]{729a^{24}b^{18}}$

38. $\sqrt[8]{v^8g^{40}}$

Solve each equation. SEE EXAMPLE 5

39. $1{,}125 = 9x^3$

40. $6{,}480 = 5w^4$

41. $270 = 10q^3$

42. $256 = 4h^6$

43. A small cube has the volume shown. Its side length is 1.5 in. less than a second, larger cube. What is the volume of the larger cube?
SEE EXAMPLE 6

PRACTICE & PROBLEM SOLVING

Practice Tutorial

Mixed Review Available Online

APPLY

44. **Model With Mathematics** A water-walking ball has a volume of approximately 4.19 m^3. What is the radius, r, of the ball?

45. **Make Sense and Persevere** Ahmed received a box of gifts. The box is a rectangular prism with the same height and width, and the length is twice the width. The volume of the box is 3,456 $in.^3$ What is the height of the box?

46. **Make Sense and Persevere** Amelia's bank account earns interest annually. The equation shows her starting balance of \$200 and her balance at the end of four years, \$220.82. At what rate, r, did Amelia earn interest?

$$220.82 = 200(1 + r)^4$$

47. **Model With Mathematics** One measure of a patient's body surface area is found using the expression $\sqrt{\frac{H \cdot W}{3{,}600}}$. Write this with a fractional exponent.

ASSESSMENT PRACTICE

48. Determine if each expression is another way to write $b^{\frac{3}{4}}$. Select *Yes* or *No*.

	Yes	No
a. $\sqrt[4]{b^3}$	❑	❑
b. $(b^3)^{\frac{1}{4}}$	❑	❑
c. $b^{\frac{4}{3}}$	❑	❑
d. $\sqrt[3]{b^4}$	❑	❑
e. $\frac{b^3}{b^4}$	❑	❑

49. **SAT/ACT** Which of the following is equivalent to $\sqrt[6]{4{,}096x^{18}y^{30}}$?

Ⓐ $682.7x^{15}y^{24}$

Ⓑ $4x^{1.6}y^{1.8}$

Ⓒ $4{,}096x^3y^5$

Ⓓ $4x^3y^5$

Ⓔ $682.7x^3y^5$

50. **Performance Task** A milk processing company uses cylindrical-shaped containers. The height of the container is equal to the diameter of the base.

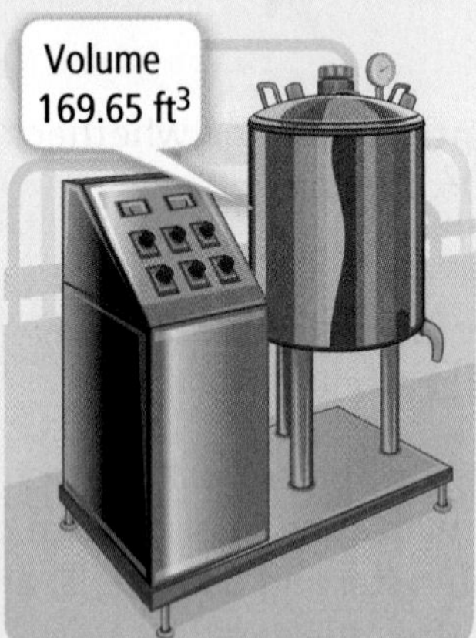

Part A The volume of one container is about 169.65 ft^3. How much material is needed to make the lateral surface of the shipping container?

Part B The cargo hold of a ship is 20 ft high. What is the largest number of these shipping containers that could be stacked on top of each other inside the cargo hold?

 Activity  Assess

4-2 Properties of Exponents and Radicals

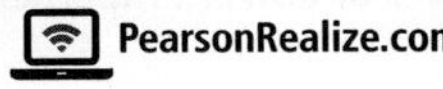

I CAN… use properties of exponents and radicals to simplify radical expressions.

VOCABULARY

- like radicals
- reduced radical form

CRITIQUE & EXPLAIN

Olivia was practicing evaluating and simplifying expressions. Her work for three expressions is shown.

1. $24^2 = 400 + 16 = 416$
2. $3^6 = 9(27) = 270 - 27 = 243$
3. $\sqrt{625} = \sqrt{400} + \sqrt{225} = 20 + 15 = 35$

A. Is Olivia's work in the first example correct? Explain your thinking.

B. Is Olivia's work in the second example correct? Explain your thinking.

C. Is Olivia's work in the third example correct? Explain your thinking.

D. **Make Sense and Persevere** What advice would you give Olivia on simplifying expressions?

ESSENTIAL QUESTION

How can properties of exponents and radicals be used to rewrite radical expressions?

CONCEPT Properties of Rational Exponents

The properties of exponents apply not only to integer exponents, but to *rational* exponents as well. Now let m and n represent *rational* numbers, with a, b nonnegative real numbers.

	Property	Example
Product of Powers	$a^m \cdot a^n = a^{m+n}$	$4^{\frac{2}{3}} \cdot 4^{-\frac{1}{3}} = 4^{\frac{1}{3}}$
Quotient of Powers	$\frac{a^m}{a^n} = a^{m-n}$	$\frac{3^4}{3^2} = 3^{4-2} = 3^2 = 9$
Power of Power	$(a^m)^n = a^{mn}$	$(7^3)^{\frac{2}{3}} = 7^2$
Power of Product	$(ab)^m = a^m b^m$	$(16x)^{\frac{1}{2}} = (16^{\frac{1}{2}}x^{\frac{1}{2}}) = 4x^{\frac{1}{2}}$
Negative Exponent	$a^{-m} = \frac{1}{a^m}$	$5^{-\frac{1}{2}} = \frac{1}{5^{\frac{1}{2}}}$

EXAMPLE 1 Use Properties of Exponents

How can you rewrite each expression using the properties of exponents?

USE STRUCTURE When multiplying numbers with the same base, adding a negative exponent gives the same result as subtracting its opposite.

A. $81^{\frac{5}{6}} \cdot 81^{-\frac{1}{3}}$

$81^{\frac{5}{6}} \cdot 81^{-\frac{1}{3}} = 81^{\frac{5}{6} - \frac{1}{3}}$ .... Use the Product of Powers Property.

$= 81^{\frac{1}{2}}$ .... Simplify the exponent.

$= 9$ .... Evaluate.

You can rewrite $81^{\frac{5}{6}} \cdot 81^{-\frac{1}{3}}$ as 9.

CONTINUED ON THE NEXT PAGE

EXAMPLE 1 CONTINUED

B. $\left(\dfrac{xy^3}{x^{\frac{1}{2}}}\right)^{\frac{2}{3}}$

$$\left(\frac{xy^3}{x^{\frac{1}{2}}}\right)^{\frac{2}{3}} = \left(x^{1-\frac{1}{2}}y^3\right)^{\frac{2}{3}} \quad \text{Use the Quotient of Powers Property.}$$

$$= \left(x^{\frac{1}{2}}y^3\right)^{\frac{2}{3}} \quad \text{Simplify.}$$

$$= x^{\frac{1}{3}}y^2 \quad \text{Use the Power of Product and Power of Power Properties.}$$

$$= y^2\sqrt[3]{x} \quad \text{Write in radical form.}$$

You can rewrite $\left(\dfrac{xy^3}{x^{\frac{1}{2}}}\right)^{\frac{2}{3}}$ as $y^2\sqrt[3]{x}$.

COMMON ERROR
Remember to subtract the exponents, not divide them. Be careful not to write x^2.

Try It! 1. How can you rewrite each expression using the properties of exponents?

a. $\left(\dfrac{3}{32^{\frac{2}{5}}}\right)^{\frac{1}{2}}$

b. $2a^{\frac{1}{3}}\left(ab^{\frac{1}{2}}\right)^{\frac{2}{3}}$

CONCEPTUAL UNDERSTANDING

EXAMPLE 2 Use Properties of Exponents to Rewrite Radicals

How can you extend the properties of exponents to derive the properties of radicals?

A. How can you rewrite $\sqrt[n]{ab}$ using the properties of exponents?

$$\sqrt[n]{ab} = (ab)^{\frac{1}{n}} \quad \text{Rewrite the radical as a rational exponent.}$$

$$= a^{\frac{1}{n}}b^{\frac{1}{n}} \quad \text{Rewrite using the Power of a Product Property.}$$

$$= \sqrt[n]{a}\,\sqrt[n]{b} \quad \text{Rewrite the rational exponents as radicals.}$$

So, $\sqrt[n]{ab} = \sqrt[n]{a}\,\sqrt[n]{b}$.

You can use a similar method to show that $\sqrt[n]{\dfrac{a}{b}} = \dfrac{\sqrt[n]{a}}{\sqrt[n]{b}}$.

B. How can you rewrite $\sqrt[3]{16x^5}$ using the properties of exponents?

$$\sqrt[3]{16x^5} = \sqrt[3]{8x^3 \cdot 2x^2}$$

$$= \sqrt[3]{8x^3} \cdot \sqrt[3]{2x^2}$$

$$= 2x\sqrt[3]{2x^2}$$

Factors of 16 and x^5 that are perfect cubes

Remaining factors of 16 and x^5 that are not perfect cubes

So, $\sqrt[3]{16x^5} = 2x\sqrt[3]{2x^2}$.

Writing the expression as $2x\sqrt[3]{2x^2}$ may be referred to as the **reduced radical form** of the expression because all *n*th roots of perfect *n*th powers in the radicand have been simplified, and no radicals remain in the denominator.

Try It! 2. How can you rewrite each expression?

a. $\sqrt[4]{81a^8b^5}$

b. $\sqrt[3]{\dfrac{x^4y^2}{125x}}$

CONCEPT Properties of Radicals

LOOK FOR RELATIONSHIPS
The Product of Powers and Quotient of Powers Properties lead to the Product and Quotient Properties for Radicals.

Product Property of Radicals
The nth root of a product of nonnegative real numbers is equal to the product of the nth roots of those numbers.

$\sqrt[n]{ab} = \sqrt[n]{a}\sqrt[n]{b}$ $\qquad (ab)^{\frac{1}{n}} = a^{\frac{1}{n}}b^{\frac{1}{n}}$

Quotient Property of Radicals
The nth root of a quotient of nonnegative real numbers is equal to the quotient of the nth roots of those numbers.

$\sqrt[n]{\frac{a}{b}} = \frac{\sqrt[n]{a}}{\sqrt[n]{b}}$ $\qquad \left(\frac{a}{b}\right)^{\frac{1}{n}} = \frac{a^{\frac{1}{n}}}{b^{\frac{1}{n}}}$

EXAMPLE 3 Rewrite the Product or Quotient of a Radical

A. What is $\sqrt[5]{16} \cdot \sqrt[5]{8}$ in reduced radical form?

$\sqrt[5]{16} \cdot \sqrt[5]{8} = \sqrt[5]{16 \cdot 8}$ .... Use the Product Property of Radicals.

$= \sqrt[5]{128}$ .... Multiply radicands.

$= \sqrt[5]{32} \cdot \sqrt[5]{4}$ .... Use the Product Property of Radicals.

$= 2\sqrt[5]{4}$ .... Simplify.

In reduced radical form $\sqrt[5]{16} \cdot \sqrt[5]{8}$ is $2\sqrt[5]{4}$.

B. What is $\sqrt[6]{8x} \cdot \sqrt[3]{2x}$ in reduced radical form?

Use rational exponents.

$\sqrt[6]{8x} \cdot \sqrt[3]{2x} = (8x)^{\frac{1}{6}} \cdot (2x)^{\frac{1}{3}}$ .... Rewrite using rational exponents.

$= (8x)^{\frac{1}{6}} \cdot (2x)^{\frac{2}{6}}$ .... Write with common index (denominator).

$= \left(8x \cdot (2x)^2\right)^{\frac{1}{6}}$ .... Use the Product Property of Radicals.

$= \sqrt[6]{32x^3}$ .... Simplify.

In reduced radical form $\sqrt[6]{8x} \cdot \sqrt[3]{2x}$ is $\sqrt[6]{32x^3}$.

C. What is $\sqrt[3]{\frac{2n}{9m}}$ in reduced radical form?

To rationalize the denominator of an expression, rewrite it so there are no radicals in any denominator and no denominators in any radical.

REASON
Think about the simplest factor by which you can multiply the denominator to eliminate the radical. There are many options, but it is more efficient to choose the simplest factor.

$\sqrt[3]{\frac{2n}{9m}} = \frac{\sqrt[3]{2n}}{\sqrt[3]{9m}}$

To rationalize the denominator, find a factor so that a cube root of a perfect cube is created.

$= \frac{\sqrt[3]{2n}}{\sqrt[3]{9m}} \cdot \frac{\sqrt[3]{3m^2}}{\sqrt[3]{3m^2}}$

9 is a factor of the perfect cube 27, and m^1 is a factor of m^3. Multiply the denominator and numerator by $\sqrt[3]{3m^2}$ to create a perfect cube.

$= \frac{\sqrt[3]{6nm^2}}{\sqrt[3]{27m^3}}$

$= \frac{\sqrt[3]{6nm^2}}{3m}$

In reduced radical form $\sqrt[3]{\frac{2n}{9m}}$ is $\frac{\sqrt[3]{6nm^2}}{3m}$.

Try It! 3. What is the reduced radical form of each expression?

a. $\sqrt[5]{\frac{7}{16x^3}}$

b. $\sqrt[4]{27x^2} \cdot \sqrt{3x}$

EXAMPLE 4 Add and Subtract Radical Expressions

A. What is the sum of $\sqrt{20} - \sqrt[3]{16} + \sqrt[3]{250} - \sqrt{5}$?

Like radicals have the same index and the same radicand. Only like radicals can be combined with addition and subtraction.

$\sqrt{20} - \sqrt[3]{16} + \sqrt[3]{250} - \sqrt{5}$

$\sqrt{20} - \sqrt{5} - \sqrt[3]{16} + \sqrt[3]{250}$ ······ Group radical terms with like indices.

$2\sqrt{5} - \sqrt{5} - 2\sqrt[3]{2} + 5\sqrt[3]{2}$ ······ Simplify each radical term.

$(2 - 1)\sqrt{5} + (-2 + 5)\sqrt[3]{2}$ ······ Factor out the radicals with the inverse of the Distributive Property.

$\sqrt{5} + 3\sqrt[3]{2}$ ······ Combine like radical terms.

The expression $\sqrt{20} - \sqrt[3]{16} + \sqrt[3]{250} - \sqrt{5}$ is equivalent to $\sqrt{5} + 3\sqrt[3]{2}$.

STUDY TIP
Use the inverse of the Distributive Property to combine like radicals in the same way that you would combine like terms.

APPLICATION

B. The design shows the boards needed for bracing the back of some set scenery. Will 75 ft of wood be enough for all of the bracing?

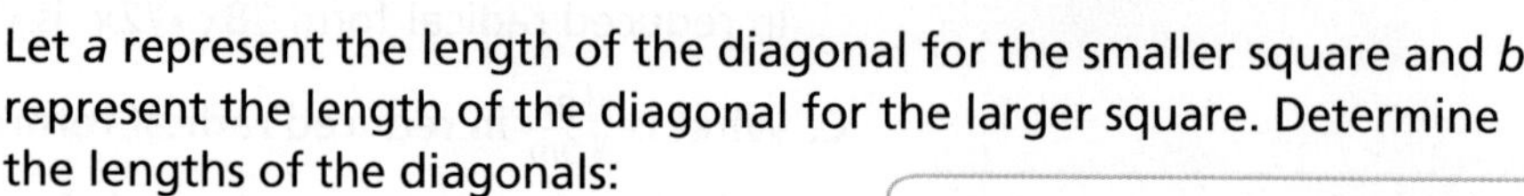

Let a represent the length of the diagonal for the smaller square and b represent the length of the diagonal for the larger square. Determine the lengths of the diagonals:

$$4^2 + 4^2 = a^2 \qquad 7^2 + 7^2 = b^2$$

$$32 = a^2 \qquad 98 = b^2$$

$$4\sqrt{2} = a \qquad 7\sqrt{2} = b$$

Take the square root of both sides of the equation and simplify the radical. Since the context is length, the negative solution may be disregarded.

There are 3 edges that are 4 ft, 4 edges that are 7 ft, and 2 diagonals each of $4\sqrt{2}$ ft and $7\sqrt{2}$ ft in length. Determine the total length of the boards:

$$3(4) + 4(7) + 2(4\sqrt{2}) + 2(7\sqrt{2}) = 40 + 22\sqrt{2}$$

Evaluating the expression, $40 + 22\sqrt{2} \approx 71.1$.
So 75 ft of wood is enough to make the bracing for the set scenery.

 **Try It!** 4. How can you rewrite each expression in a simpler form?

a. $\sqrt[3]{2{,}000} + \sqrt{2} - \sqrt[3]{128}$

b. $\sqrt{20} - \sqrt{600} - \sqrt{125}$

EXAMPLE 5 Multiply Binomial Radical Expressions

What is the reduced radical form of each product?

A. $\sqrt[3]{7}(2 - \sqrt[3]{49})$

$\sqrt[3]{7}(2) - \sqrt[3]{7}\sqrt[3]{49}$	Use the Distributive Property.
$\sqrt[3]{7}(2) - \sqrt[3]{343}$	Multiply radicands with like indices.
$2\sqrt[3]{7} - 7$	Simplify each radical term.

The product is $2\sqrt[3]{7} - 7$.

B. $(2x - \sqrt{3})(2x - \sqrt{3})$

$4x^2 - 2x\sqrt{3} - 2x\sqrt{3} + \sqrt{9}$	Expand the product.
$4x^2 - 4x\sqrt{3} + 3$	Combine like terms.

The product is $4x^2 - 4x\sqrt{3} + 3$.

STUDY TIP
Recall that there are different methods for expanding the product of binomial factors.

Try It! 5. Multiply.

a. $(x - \sqrt{10})(x + \sqrt{10})$

b. $\sqrt{6}(5 + \sqrt{3})$

EXAMPLE 6 Rationalize a Binomial Denominator

How can you rewrite $\frac{1}{2 + \sqrt{5}}$ without a radical in the denominator?

To rationalize a denominator that has a binomial denominator, multiply by the conjugate of the denominator.

STUDY TIP
The product of conjugates is $a^2 - b^2$, which eliminates radicals from the denominator.

$\frac{1}{2 + \sqrt{5}} \cdot \frac{2 - \sqrt{5}}{2 - \sqrt{5}}$	Multiply the numerator and denominator by the conjugate of the denominator.
$\frac{2 - \sqrt{5}}{4 - 5}$	Multiply the numerators and the denominators.
$\frac{2 - \sqrt{5}}{-1}$	Subtract the terms in the denominators.
$\sqrt{5} - 2$	Simplify.

$\frac{1}{2 + \sqrt{5}}$ can be rewritten as $\sqrt{5} - 2$.

Try It! 6. What is the reduced radical form of each expression?

a. $\frac{5 - \sqrt{2}}{2 - \sqrt{3}}$

b. $\frac{-4x}{1 - \sqrt{x}}$

  Concept Summary   Assess

CONCEPT SUMMARY Properties of Radicals

	Product Property of Radicals	Quotient Property of Radicals	Rationalize the Denominator
WORDS	The *n*th root of a product is equal to the product of the *n*th roots of the factors.	The *n*th root of a quotient is equal to the quotient of the *n*th roots of the factors.	To rationalize the denominator of an expression, multiply by the conjugate of the denominator.
ALGEBRA	$\sqrt[n]{ab} = \sqrt[n]{a} \cdot \sqrt[n]{b}$	$\sqrt[n]{\frac{a}{b}} = \frac{\sqrt[n]{a}}{\sqrt[n]{b}}$	$\frac{3}{\sqrt{x}} \cdot \frac{\sqrt{x}}{\sqrt{x}} = \frac{3\sqrt{x}}{x}$
NUMBERS	$\sqrt[3]{2} \cdot \sqrt[3]{20} = \sqrt[3]{40}$ $\sqrt[3]{40} = \sqrt[3]{8} \cdot \sqrt[3]{5} = 2\sqrt[3]{5}$	$\sqrt{\frac{8}{9}} = \frac{\sqrt{8}}{\sqrt{9}} = \frac{2\sqrt{2}}{3}$	$\frac{2}{\sqrt{5}} \cdot \frac{\sqrt{5}}{\sqrt{5}} = \frac{2\sqrt{5}}{5}$

Using Properties of Radicals

SIMPLIFY

$$\sqrt[4]{32x^9} = \sqrt[4]{16x^8} \cdot \sqrt[4]{2x}$$
$$= 2x^2\sqrt[4]{2x}$$

Find factors that have a perfect 4th root.

$$\frac{5}{x-\sqrt{8}} \cdot \frac{x+\sqrt{8}}{x+\sqrt{8}} = \frac{5(x+\sqrt{8})}{x^2 + x\sqrt{8} - x\sqrt{8} - 8} = \frac{5x+5\sqrt{8}}{x^2-8}$$

Since the denominator is a binomial, multiply the numerator and the denominator by the conjugate of the denominator.

Do You UNDERSTAND?

1. ESSENTIAL QUESTION How can properties of exponents and radicals be used to rewrite radical expressions?

2. **Vocabulary** How can you determine if a radical expression is in reduced form?

3. **Use Structure** Explain why $(-64)^{\frac{1}{3}}$ equals $-64^{\frac{1}{3}}$ but $(-64)^{\frac{1}{2}}$ does not equal $-64^{\frac{1}{2}}$.

4. **Error Analysis** Explain the error in Julie's work in rewriting the radical expression.
$\sqrt{-3} \cdot \sqrt{-12} = \sqrt{-3\,(-12)} = \sqrt{36} = 6$

Do You KNOW HOW?

What is the reduced radical form of each expression?

5. $49^{\frac{3}{4}} \cdot 49^{\frac{-1}{4}}$

6. $\left(\frac{a^2b^8}{a^{\frac{1}{3}}}\right)^{\frac{3}{4}}$

7. $\sqrt[4]{1{,}024x^9y^{12}}$

8. $\sqrt[3]{\frac{4}{9m^2}}$

9. $\sqrt{63} - \sqrt{700} - \sqrt{112}$

10. $\sqrt{5}(6 + \sqrt{2})$

11. $\frac{3}{\sqrt{6}}$

12. $\frac{\sqrt{7}}{\sqrt{5} + 3}$

PRACTICE & PROBLEM SOLVING

Scan for Multimedia

Practice Tutorial

Additional Exercises Available Online

UNDERSTAND

13. **Model With Mathematics** In the expression $PV^{\frac{4}{3}}$, P represents the pressure and V represents the volume of a sample of a gas. Evaluate the expression for $P = 7$ and $V = 8$.

14. **Reason** Describe the possible values of k such that $\sqrt{32} + \sqrt{k}$ can be rewritten as a single term.

15. **Error Analysis** Explain why the following work is incorrect. Find the correct answer.

$$5\left(4 - 5^{\frac{1}{2}}\right) = 5(4) - 5\left(5^{\frac{1}{2}}\right)$$
$$= 20 - 25^{\frac{1}{2}}$$
$$= 15 \quad ✗$$

16. **Communicate Precisely** Discuss the advantages and disadvantages of first rewriting $\sqrt{27} + \sqrt{48} + \sqrt{147}$ in order to estimate its decimal value.

17. **Higher Order Thinking** Write $\sqrt{\frac{4}{5}}$ in two different ways, one where the numerator is simplified and another where the denominator is rationalized.

18. **Construct Arguments** Justify each step used in simplifying the expression below.

$$\left(\frac{a^2}{a^{\frac{3}{4}}}\right)^{\frac{1}{5}} = \left(a^{2-\frac{3}{4}}\right)^{\frac{1}{5}}$$
$$= \left(a^{\frac{5}{4}}\right)^{\frac{1}{5}}$$
$$= a^{\frac{1}{4}}$$
$$= \sqrt[4]{a}$$

PRACTICE

What is the reduced radical form of each expression? SEE EXAMPLE 1

19. $\left(3x^{\frac{1}{2}}\right)\left(4x^{\frac{2}{3}}\right)$

20. $2b^{\frac{1}{2}}\left(3b^{\frac{1}{2}}c^{\frac{1}{3}}\right)^2$

21. $\left(x^{\frac{1}{2}} \cdot x^{\frac{5}{12}}\right)^4 \div x^{\frac{2}{3}}$

22. $\left(\frac{16c^{14}}{81d^{18}}\right)^{\frac{1}{2}}$

What is the reduced radical form of each expression? SEE EXAMPLE 2

23. $\sqrt[3]{250y^2z^4}$

24. $\sqrt[4]{256v^7w^{12}}$

25. $\sqrt{\frac{48x^3}{3xy^2}}$

26. $\sqrt{\frac{56x^5y^5}{7xy}}$

27. $\sqrt[3]{216m}$

28. $\sqrt[3]{\frac{250f^7g^3}{2f^2g}}$

What is the reduced radical form of each expression? SEE EXAMPLE 3

29. $\sqrt{x^5y^5} \cdot 3\sqrt{2x^7y^6}$

30. $\sqrt[3]{\frac{18n^2}{24n}}$

31. $\sqrt[3]{3x^2} \cdot \sqrt[3]{x^2} \cdot \sqrt[3]{9x^3}$

32. $\sqrt{\frac{162a}{6a^3}}$

33. $\sqrt[5]{2pq^6} \cdot 2\sqrt{2p^3q}$

34. $\sqrt[3]{\frac{x^2}{9y}}$

35. $\sqrt[3]{6} \cdot \sqrt[3]{16}$

36. $\sqrt[4]{\frac{2}{5x}}$

What is the reduced radical form of each expression? SEE EXAMPLE 4

37. $4\sqrt[3]{81} - 2\sqrt[3]{72} - \sqrt[3]{24}$

38. $6\sqrt{45y^2} - 4\sqrt{20y^2}$

39. $3\sqrt{12} - \sqrt{54} + 7\sqrt{75}$

40. $\sqrt{32h} + 4\sqrt{98h} - 3\sqrt{50h}$

Multiply. SEE EXAMPLE 5

41. $(3\sqrt{p} - \sqrt{5})(\sqrt{p} + 5\sqrt{5})$

42. $(4m - \sqrt{3})(4m - \sqrt{3})$

43. $(3\sqrt{2} + 8)(3\sqrt{2} - 8)$

44. $\sqrt[3]{3}(5\sqrt[3]{9} - 4)$

What is the reduced radical form of each expression? SEE EXAMPLE 6

45. $\frac{4}{1 - \sqrt{3}}$

46. $\frac{20}{3 + \sqrt{2}}$

47. $\frac{3 + \sqrt{8}}{2 - 2\sqrt{8}}$

48. $\frac{-2x}{3 + \sqrt{x}}$

PRACTICE & PROBLEM SOLVING

Practice | Tutorial

Mixed Review Available Online

APPLY

49. **Model With Mathematics** A triangular swimming area is marked off by a rope.

    a. If a woman swims around the perimeter of the swimming area, how far will she swim?

    b. What is the area of the roped off section?

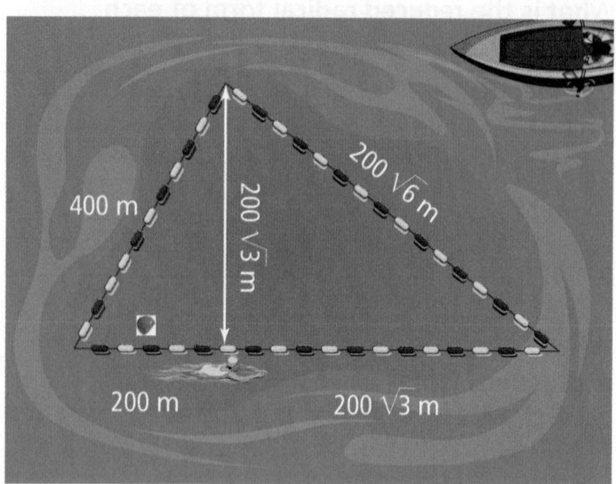

50. **Use Structure** The interest rate r required to increase your investment p to the amount a in m months is found by $r = \left(\frac{a}{p}\right)^{\frac{1}{m}} - 1$. What interest rate would be required to increase your investment of \$3,600 to \$6,400 over 7 months? Round your answer to the nearest tenth of a percent.

51. **Use Structure** The length of a rectangle is $(2 + \sqrt{5})y$. The width is $(4 + 3\sqrt{5})z$. What is the area of the rectangle?

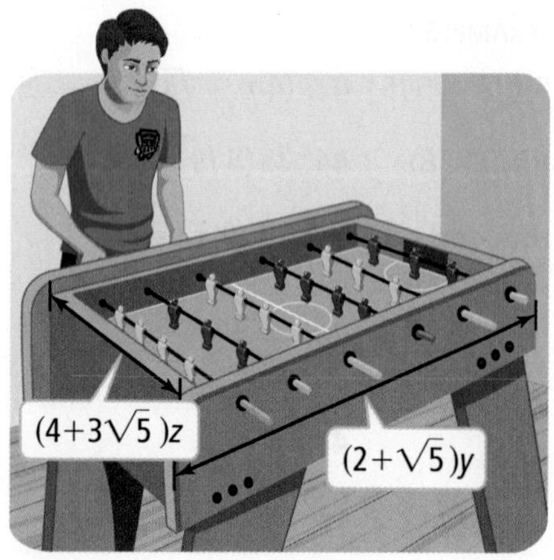

52. **Model With Mathematics** A rectangular boardroom table is $\sqrt{440}$ ft by $\sqrt{20}$ ft. Find its area.

ASSESSMENT PRACTICE

53. Aaron is rewriting $\frac{1+\sqrt{3}}{5-\sqrt{3}}$ into reduced radical form. Determine if Aaron would have written the steps below to show his work. Select *Yes* or *No*.

	Yes	No
$\frac{6+4\sqrt{3}-3}{25+9}$	❑	❑
$\frac{5+\sqrt{3}+5\sqrt{3}+\sqrt{9}}{25+5\sqrt{3}-5\sqrt{3}-\sqrt{9}}$	❑	❑
$\frac{4+3\sqrt{3}}{11}$	❑	❑
$\frac{8+6\sqrt{3}}{28}$	❑	❑
$\frac{5+6\sqrt{3}+3}{25-3}$	❑	❑

54. **SAT/ACT** Which expression cannot be rewritten as -10?

    Ⓐ $\sqrt{25} \cdot \sqrt[3]{-8}$

    Ⓑ $\sqrt[3]{-125} \cdot \sqrt[4]{16}$

    Ⓒ $-\sqrt[3]{1,000}$

    Ⓓ $-\sqrt{25} \cdot \sqrt[5]{-32}$

    Ⓔ $\sqrt{4} \cdot -\sqrt[3]{125}$

55. **Performance Task** The volume of a sphere of radius r is $V = \frac{4}{3}\pi r^3$.

    Part A Use the formula to find r in terms of V. Rationalize the denominator.

    Part B A snowman is made using three spherical snowballs. The top snowball for the head has a volume of 500 in.^{3}. What is the diameter of the top snowball?

Part C The volumes of the other two snowballs are 750 in.^{3} and 1,000 in.^{3}. How tall is the snowman?

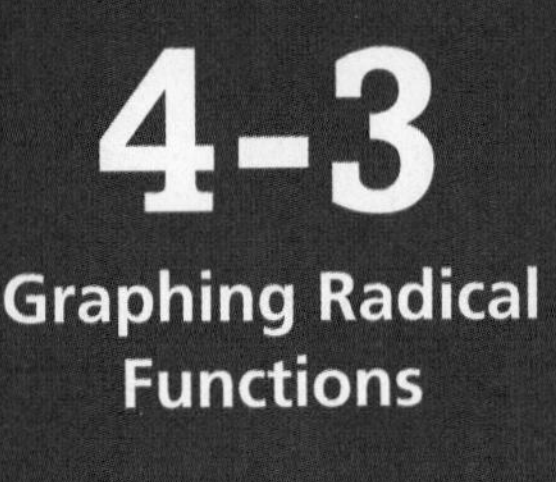

4-3 Graphing Radical Functions

PearsonRealize.com

I CAN… graph and transform radical functions.

VOCABULARY

- radical function

EXPLORE & REASON

Consider the formula for the area of a square: $A = s^2$

A. Graph the function that represents area as a function of side length.

B. On the same set of axes, graph the function that represents side length as a function of area.

C. Look for Relationships How are the two graphs related?

ESSENTIAL QUESTION

How can you use what you know about transformations of functions to graph radical functions?

EXAMPLE 1 Graph Square Root and Cube Root Functions

Graph the following functions. What are the domain and range of each function? Is the function increasing or decreasing?

A. $f(x) = \sqrt{3x}$

Make a table of values and graph.

x	0	3	12	27
y	0	3	6	9

For ease, choose x-values that make the radicand a perfect square.

For a square root function, the radicand cannot be negative, so the domain of the function is $\{x \mid x \geq 0\}$.

Radical functions do not have a horizontal asymptote; they grow without limit.

LOOK FOR RELATIONSHIPS
How does the graph of the function shown compare to the graph of its parent function?

The solution to a square root function always returns a positive value or 0, so the range is $\{y \mid y \geq 0\}$. As x increases, y increases, so the function is increasing.

B. $g(x) = \sqrt[3]{2x}$

Make a table of values, and graph.

x	−13.5	−4	0	4	13.5
y	−3	−2	0	2	3

The radicand in a cube root function can be positive or negative.

CONTINUED ON THE NEXT PAGE

EXAMPLE 1 CONTINUED

There are no restrictions on the radicand of a cube root function, so the domain and range of the function is all real numbers.

The function is increasing over the entire domain.

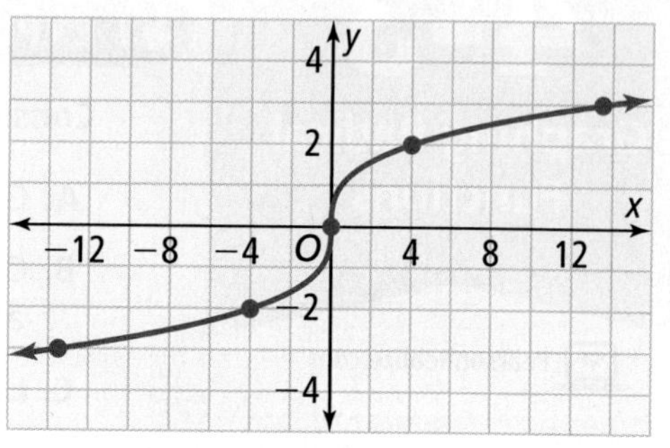

LOOK FOR RELATIONSHIPS
Odd functions are symmetric about the origin. The cube root parent is an odd function. *Even functions* are symmetric about the *y*-axis.

Try It! 1. Graph the following functions. What are the domain and range of each function? Is the function increasing or decreasing?

a. $f(x) = \sqrt{x - 5}$ b. $g(x) = \sqrt[3]{x + 1}$

CONCEPT Radical Function

A **radical function** is a function of the form $f(x) = a\sqrt[n]{x - h} + k$, where

- *a* determines a vertical stretch or compression.
- *h* determines a horizontal translation.
- *k* determines a vertical translation.

EXAMPLE 2 Graph a Transformation of a Radical Function

Graph $g(x) = 2\sqrt{(x + 3)} + 5$. What transformations map the graph of $f(x) = \sqrt{x}$ to the graph of *g*? How do the domain and range of *g* differ from those of *f*?

STUDY TIP
The radicand $x + 3$ can be written as $x - (-3)$, which relates more directly to the general form of a radical function. The horizontal translation, *h*, is −3, so the graph of the function will shift (or translate) *left* 3 units.

Step 1 Identify the parameters in $g(x) = 2\sqrt{(x + 3)} + 5$.

$$g(x) = 2\sqrt{x - (-3)} + 5$$

- $a = 2$, so the function is stretched vertically by a factor of 2.
- $h = -3$, so the graph is translated left 3 units.
- $k = 5$, so the graph is translated up 5 units.

Step 2 Graph the parent function *f*, and use it as a guide to graph *g*.

x	0	1	4	9	16
f(x)	0	1	2	3	4

This stretched graph is then translated 3 units left and 5 units up to show the graph of *g*.

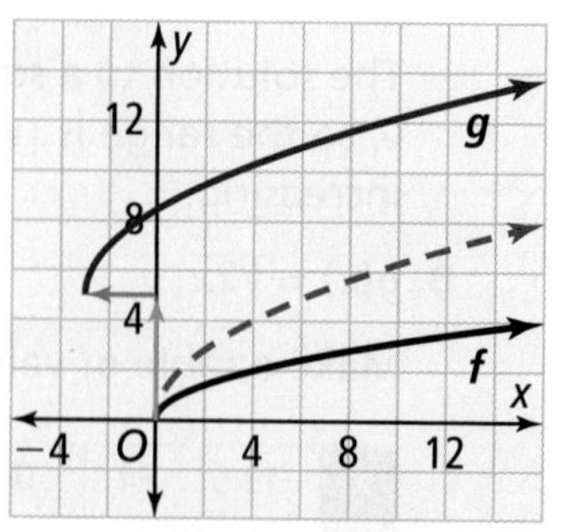

The graph of *f* is stretched vertically by a factor of 2, so each *y*-value is twice as far from the *x*-axis.

The domain of *f* is $\{x \mid x \geq 0\}$, while the domain of *g* is $\{x \mid x \geq -3\}$.
The range of *f* is $\{y \mid y \geq 0\}$, while the range of *g* is $\{y \mid y \geq 5\}$.

CONTINUED ON THE NEXT PAGE

Try It! 2. Graph $g(x) = \frac{1}{2}\sqrt{x-1} - 3$. What transformations of the graph of $f(x) = \sqrt{x}$ produce the graph of g? What is the effect of the transformations on the domain and range of g?

CONCEPTUAL UNDERSTANDING

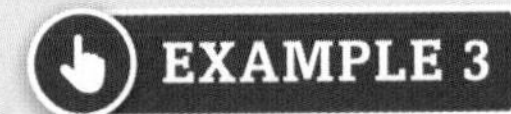

EXAMPLE 3 Rewrite Radical Functions to Identify Transformations

STUDY TIP

You may recall that the parameter k in $f(kx)$ determines horizontal stretch or compression. In this example, $g(x)$ can be described as either a horizontal compression or a vertical stretch. Both transformations of the parent function result in the same graph.

How can you rewrite the following radical functions to identify their transformations from the parent graph of $f(x) = \sqrt{x}$?

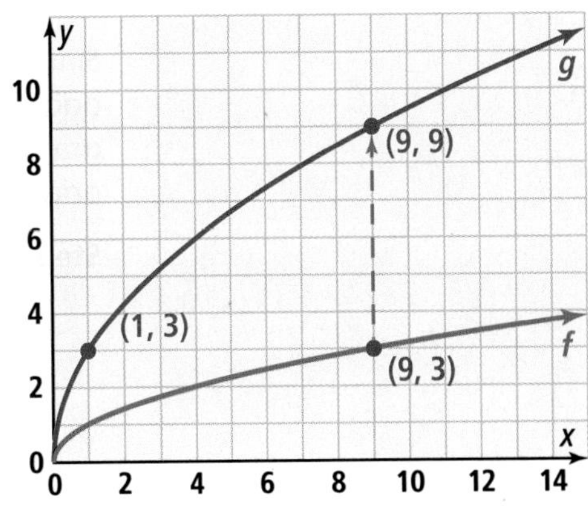

A. $g(x) = \sqrt{9x}$

Use the properties of radicals to rewrite the function and identify a vertical change.

$g(x) = \sqrt{9x}$ .... Write the original equation.

$= \sqrt{9} \bullet \sqrt{x}$ .... Use the Product Property of Radicals.

$= 3\sqrt{x}$ .... Simplify.

$a = 3$, so the graph of g is stretched vertically by a factor of 3 from the parent graph. Both h and k are 0, so there is no translation of the graph.

B. $h(x) = \sqrt{4x + 16} + 7$

Rewrite the function in the form $h(x) = a\sqrt{x - h} + k$.

$h(x) = \sqrt{4x + 16} + 7$ .... Write the original equation.

$= \sqrt{4(x + 4)} + 7$ .... Factor the radicand.

$= \sqrt{4} \bullet \sqrt{x + 4} + 7$ .... Use the Product Property of Radicals.

$= 2\sqrt{x + 4} + 7$ .... Simplify.

The graph of $h(x)$ is a vertical stretch of the parent function by a factor of 2, followed by a translation of 4 units to the left, and a translation of 7 units up.

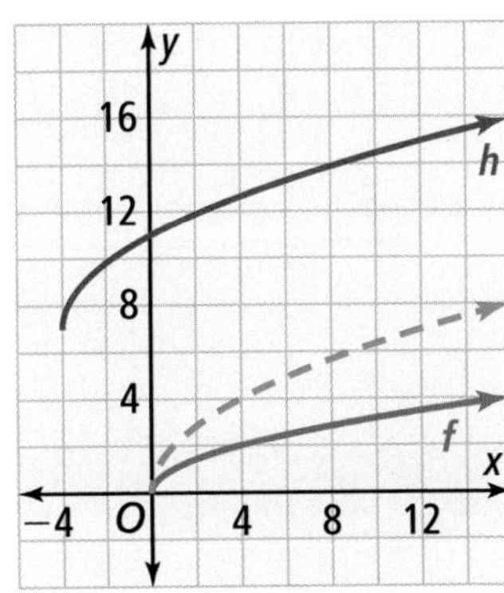

Try It! 3. What transformations of the parent graph of $f(x) = \sqrt{x}$ produce the graphs of the following functions?

a. $m(x) = \sqrt{7x - 3.5} - 10$ b. $j(x) = -2\sqrt{12x} + 4$

Activity Assess

EXAMPLE 4 Write an Equation of a Transformation

What radical function is represented in the graph?

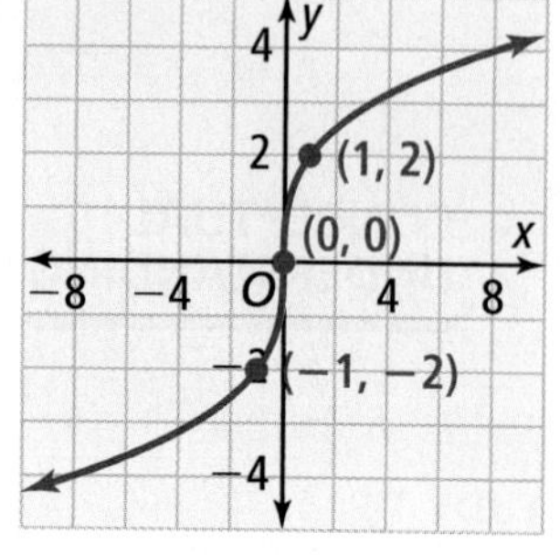

Compare the graph to the parent graph of $f(x) = \sqrt[3]{x}$.

Step 1 Check to see if any vertical or horizontal translations have been performed.

Since $f(-x) = -f(x)$, you know that the function is odd. Like the graph of the parent function, the graph of this function is symmetric about the origin, so no translation has been performed.

Step 2 Check for a vertical and horizontal stretch.

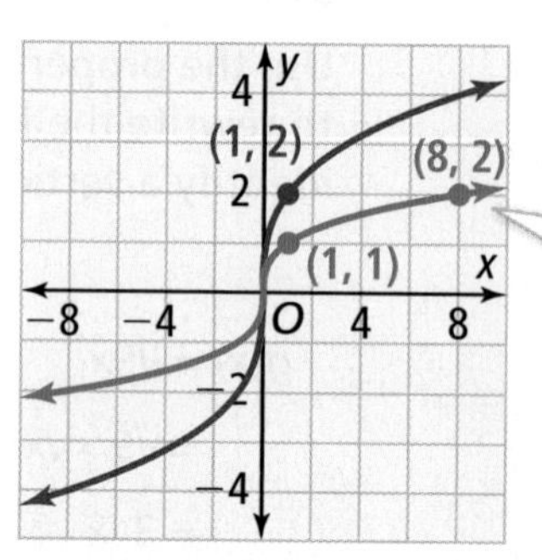

The function has either been vertically stretched by a factor of 2 or horizontally compressed by a factor of 8.

STUDY TIP

Vertical stretch is written as $f(x) = k\sqrt{x}$, and horizontal compression is written as $f(x) = \sqrt{kx}$.

Either transformation maps the initial graph to the same resulting graph.

Step 3 Identify the transformation.

The function g can be written as $g(x) = 2\sqrt[3]{x}$ or $g(x) = \sqrt[3]{8x}$.

Try It! 4. What radical function is represented in each graph below?

a.

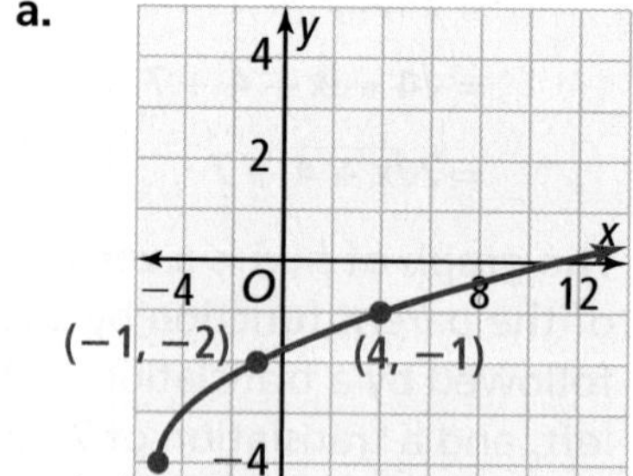

b.

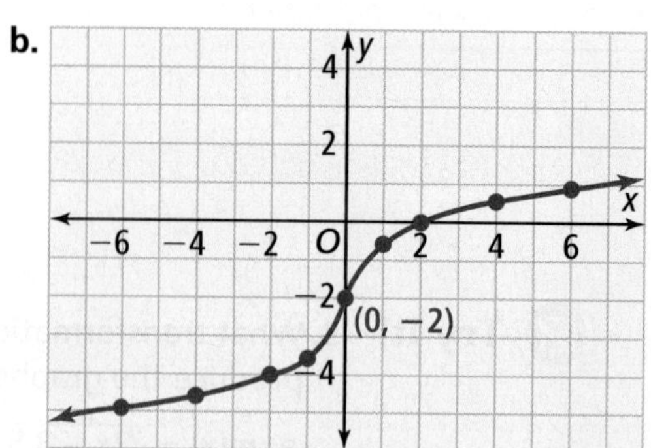

APPLICATION

EXAMPLE 5 Interpret a Radical Function Model

Looking out to the sea, the visibility in miles from a certain spot on a cliff can be calculated using the function $d(x) = \sqrt{1.5x}$, where x is the height in feet above sea level. Sasha walks through elevations ranging from 5 ft to 40 ft above sea level. What are the minimum and maximum distances that she can see?

USE STRUCTURE
Think about the shape of the radical function's graph. It is always increasing or decreasing, so the maximum and minimum points will always be the endpoints of the context's domain.

Step 1 Graph the function over the given domain.

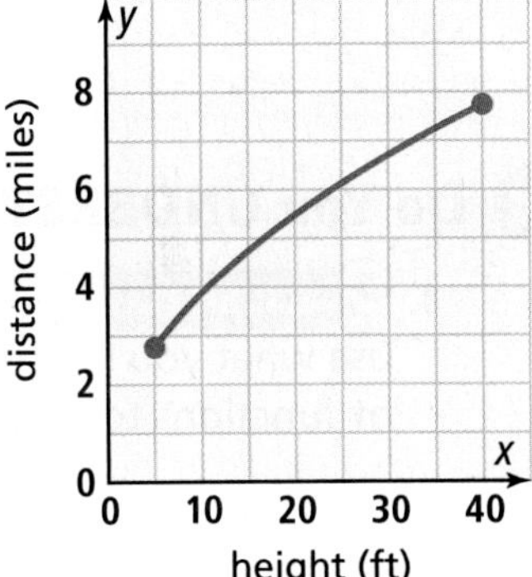

Step 2 Look for the minimum and maximum points on the graph. Notice they are the endpoints of the graph of the function along the given domain.

Step 3 Find the value of the function at the minimum and maximum value of the domain to determine the minimum and maximum distances that Sasha can see.

$$d(5) = \sqrt{(1.5)(5)} \approx 2.74$$

$$d(40) = \sqrt{(1.5)(40)} \approx 7.75$$

The minimum and maximum distances that Sasha can see are approximately 2.74 mi and 7.75 mi.

Try It! **5.** Use the same function as in Example 5. Suppose Sasha's brother walks through elevations ranging from 8 ft to 48 ft. What are the minimum and maximum distances that he can see?

  Concept Summary  Assess

CONCEPT SUMMARY Use Transformations to Graph Radical Functions

ALGEBRA Understand how the values of a radical function transform the graph of the parent function.

$$f(x) = a\sqrt[n]{x - h} + k$$

a determines a vertical stretch or compression.

h determines a horizontal translation.

k determines a vertical translation.

GRAPHS Understand the relationship between the graph of the parent function and the graph of the radical function.

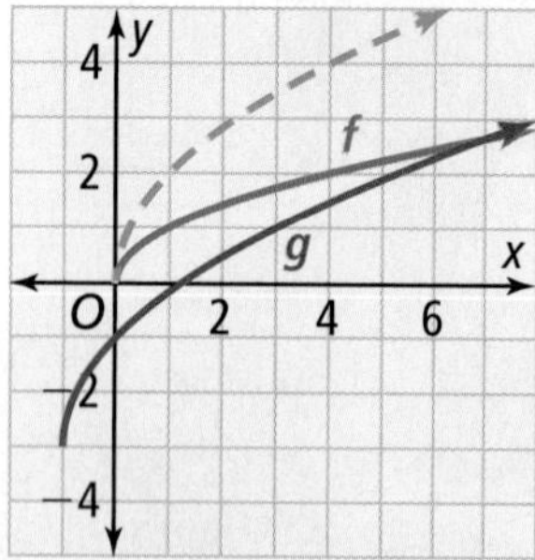

$f(x) = \sqrt{x}$ is the parent square root function.

$g(x) = 2\sqrt{x + 1} - 3$ is the result of a vertical stretch by a factor of 2, a translation 1 unit left, and a translation 3 units down from the parent function.

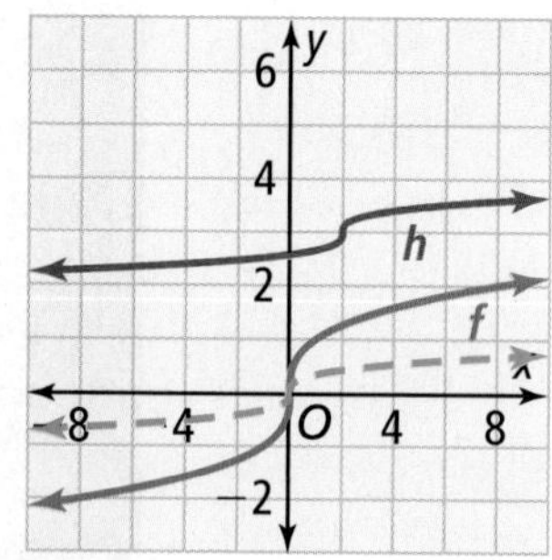

$f(x) = \sqrt[3]{x}$ is the parent cube root function.

$h(x) = \frac{1}{3}\sqrt[3]{x - 2} + 3$ is the result of a vertical compression by a factor of 3, a translation 2 units right, and a translation 3 units up from the parent function.

Do You UNDERSTAND?

1. **ESSENTIAL QUESTION** How can you use what you know about transformations of functions to graph radical functions?

2. **Error Analysis** Parker said the graph of the radical function $g(x) = -\sqrt{x + 2} - 1$ is a translation 2 units left and 1 unit down from the parent function $f(x) = \sqrt{x}$. Describe and correct the error.

3. **Reason** What effect does a have on the graph of $f(x) = a\sqrt{x}$?

Do You KNOW HOW?

Graph each function. Then identify its domain and range.

4. $f(x) = \sqrt{x - 2}$

5. $f(x) = \sqrt[3]{x + 2}$

6. $f(x) = \sqrt{x + 1} - 2$

7. $f(x) = \sqrt[3]{x - 3} + 2$

8. $f(x) = 3\sqrt{x - 5}$

9. $f(x) = \frac{1}{2}\sqrt[3]{x} + 1$

10. The volume of a cube is a function of the cube's side length. The function can be written as $V(s) = s^3$, where s is the length of the cube's edge and V is the volume.

    a. Express a cube's edge length as a function of its volume, $s(V)$.

    b. Graph $V(s)$ and $s(V)$. What are the domain and range of the functions? Explain.

PRACTICE & PROBLEM SOLVING

Scan for Multimedia

Practice | Tutorial

Additional Exercises Available Online

UNDERSTAND

11. **Communicate Precisely** What is the domain and range of the radical function $h(x) = \sqrt{x + a} + b$? Is the function increasing or decreasing? Explain.

12. **Model with Mathematics** The graph of a cube root function has a horizontal translation that is three times the vertical translation. The vertical translation is negative.

    a. Write a function, g, that has these attributes.

    b. Graph your function and the parent function, f, to verify it is correct.

13. **Error Analysis** Helena is trying to write a radical function that is represented by the graph below. Describe and correct the error Helena made in writing the radical function.

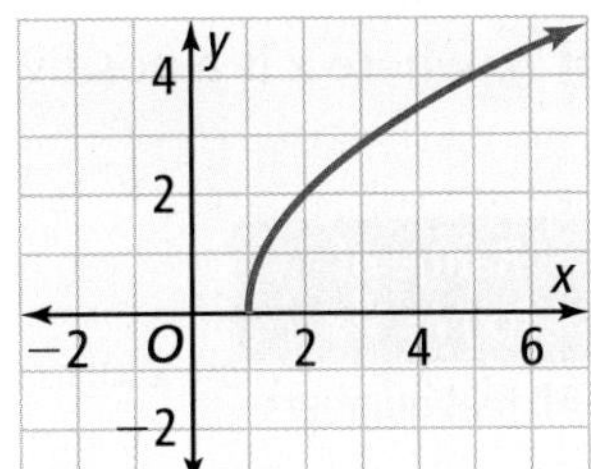

$f(x) = \sqrt{x - 1}$ ✗

14. **Higher Order Thinking** Rewrite the radical function $g(x) = \sqrt[3]{8x + 64} - 3$ to identify the transformations from the parent graph of $f(x) = \sqrt[3]{x}$. Explain how you rewrote the radical function.

15. **Reason** The parent function $f(x) = \sqrt{x}$ and a transformation of the parent function, $g(x)$, are reflections of each other over the x-axis. Write the function $g(x)$.

16. **Mathematical Connections** How do the transformations of a radical function compare to the transformations of an absolute value function?

PRACTICE

Graph the following functions. State the domain and range. Is the function increasing or decreasing? SEE EXAMPLE 1

17. $f(x) = \sqrt{x} + 2$

18. $f(x) = \sqrt[3]{x} - 4$

19. $f(x) = \sqrt[3]{x - 8}$

20. $f(x) = \sqrt{x + 6}$

21. Graph $f(x) = \sqrt[3]{x}$ and $g(x) = 3\sqrt[3]{x + 9} - 8$. What transformations of the graph of f produce the graph of g? What effect do the transformations have on the domain and range of g? SEE EXAMPLE 2

Rewrite the following radical functions to identify their transformations from the parent graph $f(x) = \sqrt{x}$. SEE EXAMPLE 3

22. $f(x) = \sqrt{16x}$

23. $f(x) = \sqrt{25x + 75}$

24. $f(x) = \sqrt{9x - 45}$

25. $f(x) = \sqrt{4x - 24} - 6$

What radical function is represented in each graph? SEE EXAMPLE 4

26.

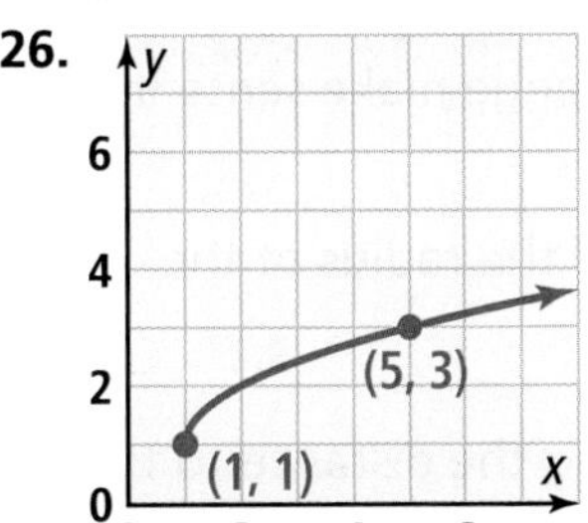

27.

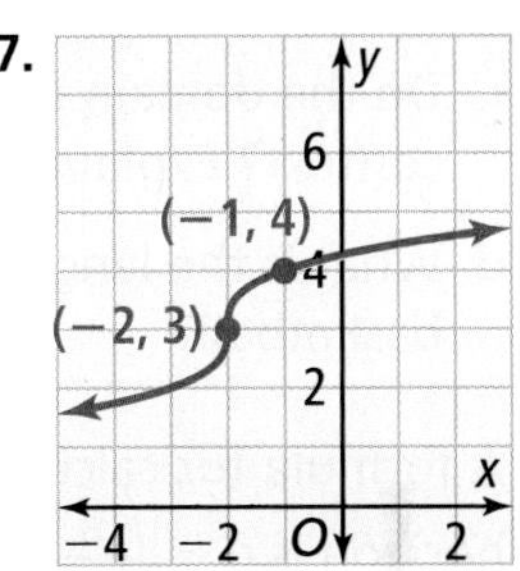

28. The hull speed, y, measured in knots, of a sailboat can be estimated by the function $y = 1.34\sqrt{x}$, where x is the waterline length of the sailboat, in feet. Luis works at a sailboat rental business with boats that have a waterline length between 25 ft and 64 ft. SEE EXAMPLE 5

    a. Graph the relationship between the hull speed of a sailboat and its waterline length.

    b. What are the minimum and maximum hull speeds of the sailboats at the rental business?

PRACTICE & PROBLEM SOLVING

Practice Tutorial

Mixed Review Available Online

APPLY

29. Make Sense and Persevere The radius of a sphere can be found using the function $r = \sqrt[3]{\frac{3V}{4\pi}}$, where V is the volume of the sphere. Heather filled a basketball with 448.92 in.^{3} of air.

a. Graph the function.

b. Identify the domain and range of the graph.

c. Do the domain and range make sense in this context? Explain.

d. What is the length of the radius of the basketball?

30. A formula for calculating the distance to the horizon is $d = \sqrt{\frac{h}{0.57}}$, where d is the distance to the horizon, in miles, and h is the height above the surface, in feet.

a. Graph the function.

b. Reason What is your height above the surface if you can see a distance of 5 mi to the horizon?

ASSESSMENT PRACTICE

31. Choose yes or no to tell whether the function is an odd function.

a. $f(x) = 5\sqrt{x - 10} - 12$	○ Yes	○ No
b. $f(x) = \frac{1}{4}\sqrt[3]{x}$	○ Yes	○ No
c. $f(x) = \frac{1}{2}\sqrt{x + 8} - 1$	○ Yes	○ No
d. $f(x) = 6\sqrt[3]{x}$	○ Yes	○ No
e. $f(x) = 9\sqrt[3]{x - 7} + 8$	○ Yes	○ No

32. SAT/ACT Which function has a graph with domain $x \geq -1$ and range $y \geq -2$?

Ⓐ $f(x) = \sqrt{x - 1} + 2$

Ⓑ $f(x) = \sqrt[3]{x + 1} - 2$

Ⓒ $f(x) = \sqrt[3]{x - 1} + 2$

Ⓓ $f(x) = \sqrt{x + 1} - 2$

33. Performance Task The table shows the domain and range of the function $f(x) = \sqrt[n]{x}$ for different values of n, where x is a positive real number.

n	Domain of $f(x) = \sqrt[n]{x}$	Range of $f(x) = \sqrt[n]{x}$
1	All real numbers	All real numbers
2	$x \geq 0$	$y \geq 0$
3	All real numbers	All real numbers
4		
5		
6		
7		
8		

Part A Identify the domain and range of the function $f(x) = \sqrt[n]{x}$ when $n = 4, 5, 6, 7$, and 8.

Part B Make a conjecture about the values of n that gives a domain and range of all real numbers.

Part C Make a conjecture about the values of n that gives a domain of $x \geq 0$ and a range of $y \geq 0$.

4-4 Solving Radical Equations

PearsonRealize.com

EXPLORE & REASON

A. Solve $3(a + 1)^2 + 2 = 11$. Use at least two different methods.

B. Try each of the methods you used in part (a) to solve $3\sqrt{(a + 1)} + 2 = 11$.

C. Generalize Which of the methods is better suited for solving an equation with a radical? What problems arise when using the other method?

I CAN...solve radical equations and inequalities.

VOCABULARY

- extraneous solution

ESSENTIAL QUESTION

How can you solve equations that include radicals or rational exponents?

EXAMPLE 1 Solve an Equation With One Radical

A. Solve the radical equation $\sqrt{x + 5} - 1 = 3$.

To solve this equation, you can isolate the radical. Then you can square both sides of the equation to eliminate the radical and solve for x.

$\sqrt{x + 5} - 1 = 3$	Write the original equation.
$\sqrt{x + 5} = 4$	Add 1 to each side.
$\left(\sqrt{x + 5}\right)^2 = 4^2$	Square both sides to eliminate the radical.
$x + 5 = 16$	Simplify.
$x = 11$	Subtract 5 from each side.

LOOK FOR RELATIONSHIPS
When you square both sides of an equation, you are multiplying each side by the same quantity. The expression for the quantity differs, but $\sqrt{x + 5}$ and 4 are equal.

So the solution to the radical equation is $x = 11$.

Check your answer by substituting 11 for x in the original equation:
$\sqrt{11 + 5} - 1 = \sqrt{16} - 1 = 4 - 1 = 3$ ✓
You can also check by graphing $y = \sqrt{x + 5} - 1$ and $y = 3$ on the same coordinate axes. The graphs of the equations intersect at (11, 3).

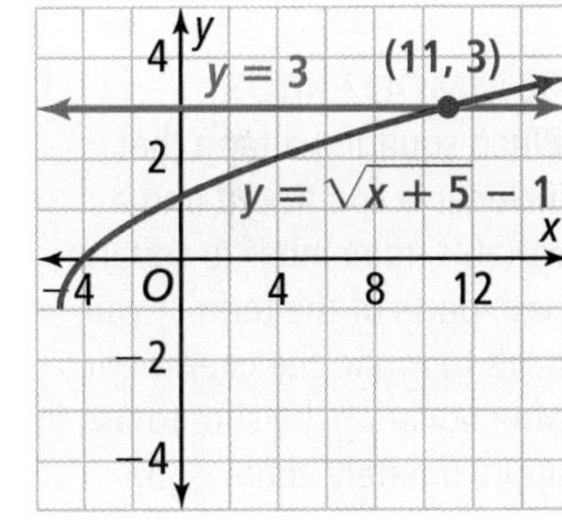

B. Solve the radical equation $\sqrt[3]{x} + 2 = 4$.

$\sqrt[3]{x} + 2 = 4$	Write the original equation.
$\sqrt[3]{x} = 2$	Subtract 2 from each side to isolate the radical.
$(\sqrt[3]{x})^3 = 2^3$	Cube both sides to eliminate the cube root.
$x = 8$	Simplify.

So the solution to the radical equation is $x = 8$.

Check your answer by substituting 8 for x in the original equation:
$\sqrt[3]{8} + 2 = 2 + 2 = 4$ ✓

 **Try It!** 1. Solve each radical equation.

a. $\sqrt{x - 2} + 3 = 5$

b. $\sqrt[3]{x - 1} = 2$

APPLICATION

EXAMPLE 2 Rewrite a Formula

The suspension cables from the Golden Gate Bridge's towers are farther above the roadway near the towers and closer to the roadway near the middle of the bridge. You can figure out your distance from the middle of the bridge, x, in feet, and the height of the suspension cable, y, in feet, at your position by using the equation $x = \frac{\sqrt{y-220}}{0.010583}$. About how far is the cable from the roadway when you are 200 ft from the middle of the bridge?

Rewrite the equation to isolate y so you can express the vertical distance between the roadway of the bridge and the suspension cable in terms of x.

$x = \frac{\sqrt{y-220}}{0.010583}$ .... Write the original function.

$0.010583x = \sqrt{y-220}$ .... Multiply both sides by 0.010583.

$(0.010583x)^2 = (\sqrt{y-220})^2$ .... Square both sides.

$0.000112x^2 \approx y - 220$ .... Simplify.

$0.000112x^2 + 220 \approx y$ .... Add 220 to both sides.

$0.000112(200)^2 + 220 \approx y$ .... Substitute 200 for x.

$224.48 \approx y$ .... Simplify.

COMMON ERROR

When squaring a term that includes a coefficient and a variable, remember to square both parts of the term. If you have to round the coefficient after squaring, be sure to use the approximately equal sign.

The equation $0.000112x^2 + 220 \approx y$ gives the vertical distance between the deck and the suspension cable for different values of x.

The cable is about 224 ft above the bridge's roadway when you are 200 ft from the middle of the bridge.

Try It! 2. The speed, v, of a vehicle in relation to its stopping distance, d, is represented by the equation $v = 3.57\sqrt{d}$. What is the equation for the stopping distance in terms of the vehicle's speed?

CONCEPTUAL UNDERSTANDING

EXAMPLE 3 Identify an Extraneous Solution

A. Solve the radical equation $\sqrt{3x-2} = x - 4$.

$\sqrt{3x-2} = x - 4$	Write the original equation.
$(\sqrt{3x-2})^2 = (x-4)^2$	Square both sides.
$3x - 2 = x^2 - 8x + 16$	Simplify the left side; expand the right side using the Distributive Property.
$0 = x^2 - 11x + 18$	Write in standard form.
$0 = (x-9)(x-2)$	Factor.
$x = 9$ or $x = 2$	Use the Zero-Product Property to solve.

Check the potential solutions by substituting the solutions for x in the original equation:

$\sqrt{3x-2} = x - 4$	$\sqrt{3x-2} = x - 4$
$\sqrt{3(9)-2} = 9 - 4$	$\sqrt{3(2)-2} = 2 - 4$
$\sqrt{25} = 5$ ✓	$\sqrt{4} \neq -2$ ✗

So 9 is the only solution to the equation and 2 is an extraneous solution.

VOCABULARY
An **extraneous solution** is a solution of an equation *derived* from an original equation, but it is *not* a solution of the original equation.

B. Why does this extraneous solution arise?

Your first step in solving the equation in part (a) was to square both sides. You now have two equations. Are they equivalent equations?

Use graphs to represent both the original equation from part (a) and the equation you got after squaring both sides of the original equation:

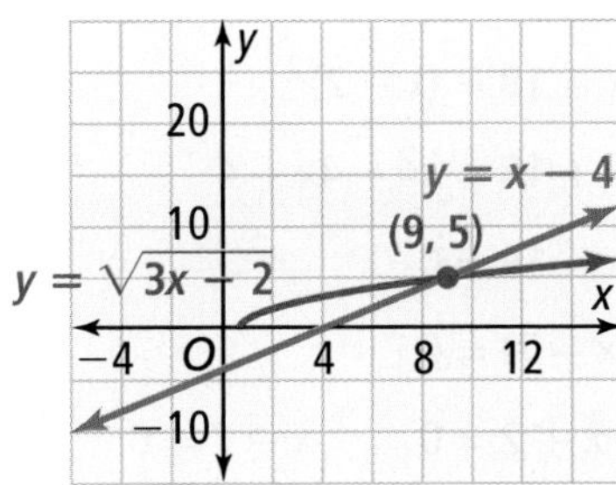

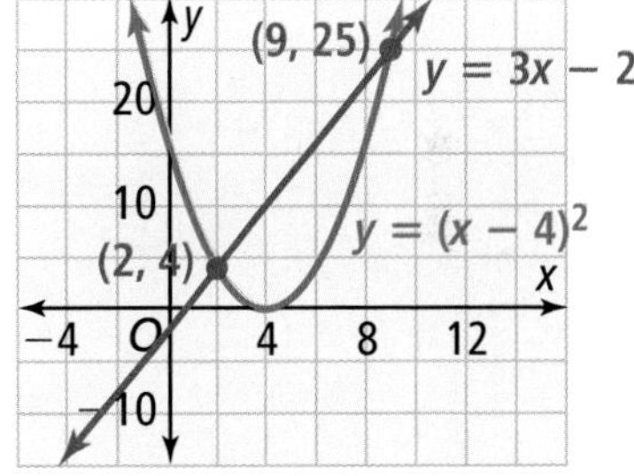

The graphs of $y = \sqrt{3x-2}$ and $y = x - 4$ intersect at (9, 5), so the solution to $\sqrt{3x-2} = x - 4$ is $x = 9$.

The graphs of $3x - 2$ and $(x-4)^2$ intersect at (2, 4) and (9, 25), so the solution to $(\sqrt{3x-2})^2 = (x-4)^2$ is $x = 2$ and $x = 9$.

This means that the equations $\sqrt{3x-2} = x - 4$ and $(\sqrt{3x-2})^2 = (x-4)^2$ are not equivalent. Both graphs have an intersection point at $x = 9$, but the second graph also has an intersection point at $x = 2$. Squaring both sides of the original equation created an extraneous solution.

Try It! 3. Solve each radical equation. Identify any extraneous solutions.

a. $x = \sqrt{7x+8}$

b. $x + 2 = \sqrt{x+2}$

EXAMPLE 4 Solve Equations With Rational Exponents

A. What are the solutions to the equation $(x^2 + 5x + 5)^{\frac{5}{2}} = 1$?

$$(x^2 + 5x + 5)^{\frac{5}{2}} = 1$$

$$\left((x^2 + 5x + 5)^{\frac{5}{2}}\right)^{\frac{2}{5}} = (1)^{\frac{2}{5}}$$

Raise both sides to the reciprocal power.

$$x^2 + 5x + 5 = 1$$

$$x^2 + 5x + 4 = 0$$

$$(x + 4)(x + 1) = 0$$

$$x + 4 = 0 \text{ or } x + 1 = 0$$

Use the Zero-Product Property.

$$x = -4 \text{ or } x = -1$$

STUDY TIP

An equation can have one solution, multiple solutions, or no solutions, so it's important to check all potential solutions.

Check for extraneous solutions.

$$((-4)^2 + 5(-4) + 5)^{\frac{5}{2}} \stackrel{?}{=} 1 \qquad ((-1)^2 + 5(-1) + 5)^{\frac{5}{2}} \stackrel{?}{=} 1$$

$$(16 - 20 + 5)^{\frac{5}{2}} \stackrel{?}{=} 1 \qquad (1 - 5 + 5)^{\frac{5}{2}} \stackrel{?}{=} 1$$

$$(1)^{\frac{5}{2}} \stackrel{?}{=} 1 \qquad (1)^{\frac{5}{2}} \stackrel{?}{=} 1$$

$$1 = 1 \checkmark \qquad 1 = 1 \checkmark$$

This equation has two solutions, $x = -4$ and $x = -1$. There are no extraneous solutions.

B. What is the solution to $(x + 18)^{\frac{3}{2}} = (x - 2)^3$?

$$(x + 18)^{\frac{3}{2}} = (x - 2)^3$$

$$\left((x + 18)^{\frac{3}{2}}\right)^{\frac{2}{3}} = \left((x - 2)^3\right)^{\frac{2}{3}}$$

Raise both sides to the reciprocal power.

$$x + 18 = (x - 2)^2$$

$$x + 18 = x^2 - 4x + 4$$

$$x^2 - 5x - 14 = 0$$

$$(x + 2)(x - 7) = 0$$

$$x + 2 = 0 \qquad x - 7 = 0$$

Use the Zero-Product Property.

$$x = -2 \qquad x = 7$$

Check for extraneous solutions.

$$(-2 + 18)^{\frac{3}{2}} \stackrel{?}{=} (-2 - 2)^3 \qquad (7 + 18)^{\frac{3}{2}} \stackrel{?}{=} (7 - 2)^3$$

$$16^{\frac{3}{2}} \stackrel{?}{=} (-4)^3 \qquad 25^{\frac{3}{2}} \stackrel{?}{=} 5^3$$

$$64 \neq -64 \ \text{✗} \qquad 125 = 125 \checkmark$$

So 7 is the only solution to the equation, and −2 is an extraneous solution.

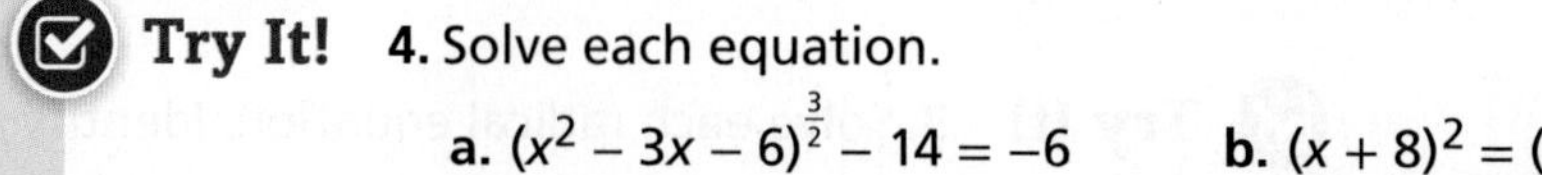

Try It! **4.** Solve each equation.

a. $(x^2 - 3x - 6)^{\frac{3}{2}} - 14 = -6$ **b.** $(x + 8)^2 = (x - 10)^{\frac{5}{2}}$

EXAMPLE 5 Solve an Equation With Two Radicals

Solve the radical equation $\sqrt{x+9} - \sqrt{2x} = 3$.

When an equation has two radicals, start the solution process by isolating one radical.

COMMON ERROR
A common mistake when squaring an expression like $\sqrt{2x} + 3$ is to only square the radical portion. Square this expression as you would any binomial, by using the Distributive Property.

$\sqrt{x+9} - \sqrt{2x} = 3$	Write the original equation.
$\sqrt{x+9} = \sqrt{2x} + 3$	Add $\sqrt{2x}$ to both sides to isolate $\sqrt{x+9}$.
$(\sqrt{x+9})^2 = (\sqrt{2x} + 3)^2$	Square both sides.
$x + 9 = 2x + 6\sqrt{2x} + 9$	Simplify the left side; expand the right side using the Distributive Property.
$0 = x + 6\sqrt{2x}$	Simplify.
$-x = 6\sqrt{2x}$	Isolate the radical expression.
$(-x)^2 = (6\sqrt{2x})^2$	Square both sides again.
$x^2 - 72x = 0$	Simplify and write in standard form.
$x(x - 72) = 0$	Factor completely.
$x = 0$ or $x = 72$	Use the Zero-Product Property.

Check the potential solutions by substituting 0 and 72 for x in the original equation:

$\sqrt{x+9} - \sqrt{2x} \stackrel{?}{=} 3$	$\sqrt{x+9} - \sqrt{2x} \stackrel{?}{=} 3$
$\sqrt{(0)+9} - \sqrt{2(0)} \stackrel{?}{=} 3$	$\sqrt{(72)+9} - \sqrt{2(72)} \stackrel{?}{=} 3$
$\sqrt{9} - \sqrt{0} \stackrel{?}{=} 3$	$\sqrt{81} - \sqrt{144} \stackrel{?}{=} 3$
$3 - 0 \stackrel{?}{=} 3$	$9 - 12 \stackrel{?}{=} 3$
$3 = 3$ ✓	$-3 \neq 3$ ✗

The only solution is 0. The value 72 does not make the original equation true, so it is an extraneous solution.

You can also see this by graphing $y = \sqrt{x+9} - \sqrt{2x}$ and $y = 3$ together. They intersect only at $x = 0$.

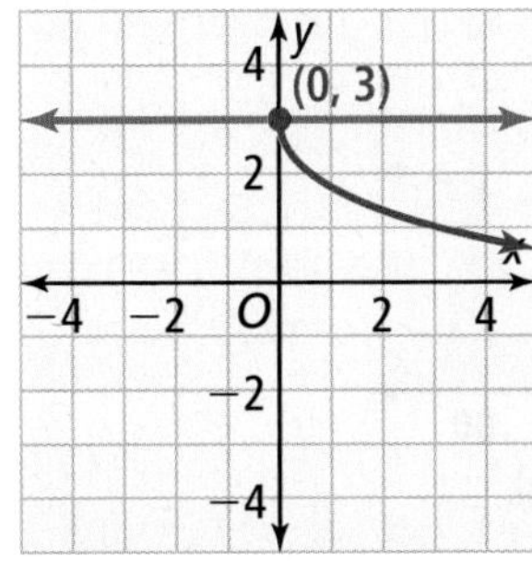

Try It! 5. Solve each radical equation. Check for extraneous solutions.

a. $\sqrt{x+4} - \sqrt{3x} = -2$

b. $\sqrt{15-x} - \sqrt{6x} = -3$

APPLICATION

EXAMPLE 6 Solve a Radical Inequality

The body surface area (BSA) of a human being is used to determine doses of medication. The formula for finding BSA is $BSA = \sqrt{\frac{H \cdot M}{3{,}600}}$, where H is the height in centimeters and M is the mass in kilograms.

A doctor calculates a particular dose of medicine for a patient whose BSA is less than 1.9. If the patient is 160 cm tall, what must the mass of the person be for the dose to be appropriate?

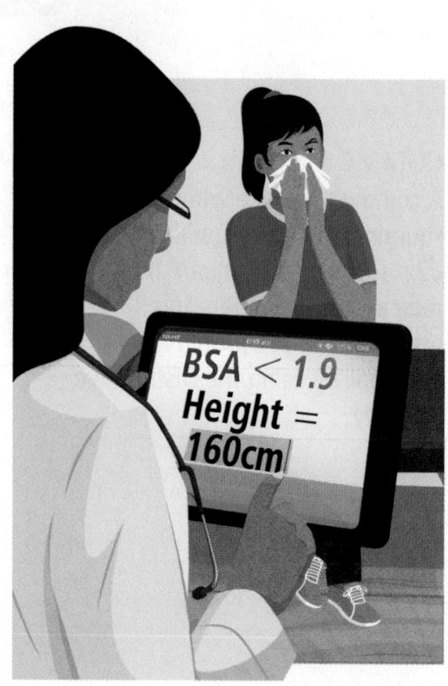

LOOK FOR RELATIONSHIPS
Recall that you solve an inequality just as you do an equation, using an inequality sign instead of an equal sign.

$BSA = \sqrt{\frac{H \cdot M}{3{,}600}}$ Write the BSA model.

$\sqrt{\frac{160 \cdot M}{3{,}600}} < 1.9$ Write an inequality to represent the situation. Substitute 160 for H.

$\left(\sqrt{\frac{160 \cdot M}{3{,}600}}\right)^2 < (1.9)^2$ Square both sides to remove the radical sign.

$\frac{160 \cdot M}{3{,}600} < 3.61$ Simplify.

$160 \cdot M < 12{,}996$ Multiply both sides by 3,600.

$M < 81.225$ Divide both sides by 160.

The mass of the individual must be less than 81.225 kg for the dose to be appropriate.

The graph of the inequality $y < \sqrt{\frac{160 \cdot M}{3{,}600}}$ shows that when the BSA is 1.9, the mass of the individual must be less than approximately 81 kg.

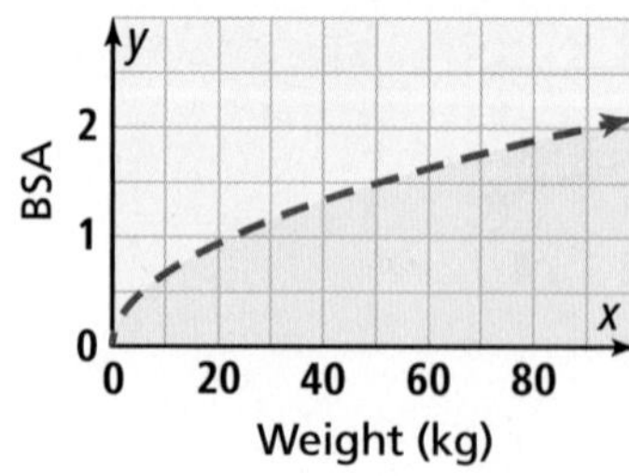

Try It! 6. A doctor calculates that a particular dose of medicine is appropriate for an individual whose BSA is less than 1.8. If the mass of the individual is 75 kg, how many cm tall can he or she be for the dose to be appropriate?

CONCEPT SUMMARY Solving Radical Equations

	WORDS	ALGEBRA	GRAPH
Step 1	Isolate the radical term.	$2\sqrt{x+3} - x = 0$ $2\sqrt{x+3} = x$	
Step 2	Square both sides to remove the radical.	$\left(2\sqrt{x+3}\right)^2 = (x)^2$	
Step 3	Solve the equation.	$4(x+3) = x^2$ $x^2 - 4x - 12 = 0$ $(x-6)(x+2) = 0$ $x = 6$ or $x = -2$	$y = x$, $y = 2\sqrt{x+3}$, (6, 6)
Step 4	Eliminate extraneous solutions.	$2\sqrt{6+3} - 6 \stackrel{?}{=} 0$ $2\sqrt{-2+3} - (-2) \stackrel{?}{=} 0$ $2\sqrt{9} \stackrel{?}{=} 6$ $2\sqrt{1} \stackrel{?}{=} -2$ $6 \stackrel{?}{=} 6$ $2 \stackrel{?}{=} -2$ $6 = 6$ ✓ $2 \neq -2$ ✗	

Do You UNDERSTAND?

1. **ESSENTIAL QUESTION** How can you solve equations that include radicals or rational exponents?

2. **Construct Arguments** How can you use a graph to show that the solution to $\sqrt[3]{84x+8} = 8$ is 6?

3. **Vocabulary** Why does solving a radical equation sometimes result in an extraneous solution?

4. **Error Analysis** Neil said that −3 and 6 are the solutions to $\sqrt{3x+18} = x$. What error did Neil make?

5. **Communicate Precisely** Describe how you would solve the equation $x^{\frac{2}{3}} = n$. How is this solution method to be interpreted if the equation had been written in radical form instead?

Do You KNOW HOW?

Solve for x.

6. $3\sqrt{x+22} = 21$

7. $\sqrt[3]{5x} = 25$

In 8 and 9, find the extraneous solution.

8. $\sqrt{8x+9} = x$

9. $x = \sqrt{24-2x}$

10. Rewrite the equation $y = \sqrt{\frac{x-48}{6}}$ to isolate x.

11. Use a graph to find the solution to the equation $9 = \sqrt{3x+11}$.

Solve each equation.

12. $(3x+2)^{\frac{2}{5}} = 4$

13. $\sqrt{2x-5} - \sqrt{x-3} = 1$

14. $\sqrt{x+2} + \sqrt{3x+4} = 2$

PRACTICE & PROBLEM SOLVING

Scan for Multimedia

Practice | Tutorial

Additional Exercises Available Online

UNDERSTAND

15. **Generalize** Explain how to identify an extraneous solution for an equation containing a radical expression.

16. **Look for Relationships** Write a radical equation that relates a square's perimeter to its area. Explain your reasoning. Use s to represent the side length of the square.

17. **Error Analysis** Describe and correct the error a student made in rewriting the equation to isolate y.

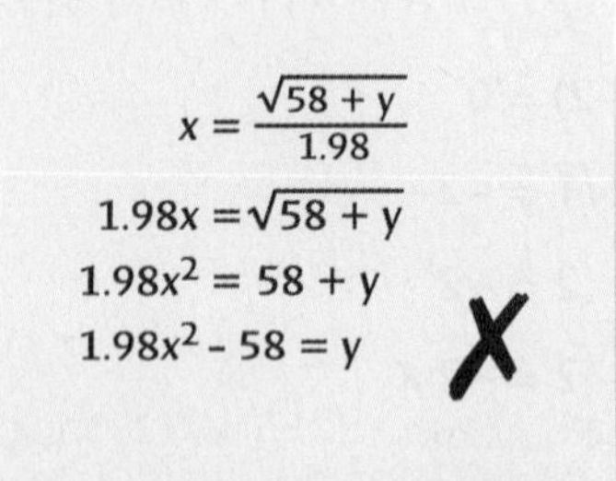

$$x = \frac{\sqrt{58 + y}}{1.98}$$
$$1.98x = \sqrt{58 + y}$$
$$1.98x^2 = 58 + y$$
$$1.98x^2 - 58 = y$$

18. **Use Appropriate Tools** Use the equations represented in the graph below to find the point of intersection.

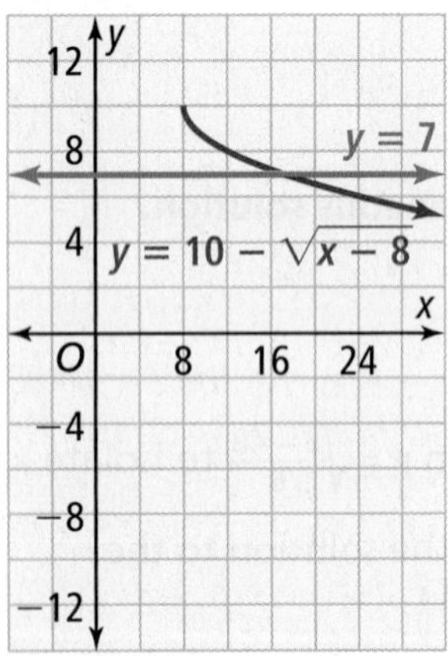

19. **Higher Order Thinking** Some, but not all, equations with rational exponents have extraneous solutions. What is the relationship between the exponents and the possibility of having extraneous solutions for equations with rational exponents? Explain your reasoning.

20. **Communicate Precisely** Describe the process used to solve an equation with two radical expressions. How is this process different from solving an equation with only one radical expression?

PRACTICE

Solve each radical equation. SEE EXAMPLE 1

21. $\sqrt[3]{x} + 8 = 13$

22. $\sqrt{4x} = 11$

23. $\sqrt{75 + x} - 6 = 14$

24. $25 - \sqrt[4]{x} = 22$

Solve for y. SEE EXAMPLE 2

25. $x = 3(\sqrt[3]{15 + y})$

26. $x = \frac{\sqrt{2y}}{26}$

27. $x = \frac{\sqrt{y - 14.2}}{0.05}$

28. $x = \frac{1}{3}(\sqrt[4]{y})$

Solve each radical equation. Check for extraneous solutions. SEE EXAMPLE 3

29. $x = \sqrt{x + 6}$

30. $2x = \sqrt{17x - 15}$

31. $4x = \sqrt{6x + 10}$

32. $x = \sqrt{56 - x}$

Solve. SEE EXAMPLE 4

33. $0.5(x^2 + 5x + 136)^{\frac{2}{3}} = 50$

34. $2(x^2 - 12x - 4)^{\frac{1}{2}} - 3 = 15$

35. $(x^2 + 4x + 5)^{\frac{3}{2}} + 1 = 0$

Solve each radical equation. Check for extraneous solutions. SEE EXAMPLE 5

36. $\sqrt{6 + x} - \sqrt{x - 5} = 2$

37. $\sqrt{4x + 5} - \sqrt{x + 1} = 1$

38. $\sqrt{x + 1} + 1 = \sqrt{x + 3}$

Solve using the formula $BSA = \sqrt{\frac{H \cdot M}{3{,}600}}$. SEE EXAMPLE 6

39. A sports medicine specialist determines that a hot-weather training strategy is appropriate for a 165 cm tall individual whose BSA is less than 2.0. To the nearest hundredth, what can the mass of the individual be for the training strategy to be appropriate?

PRACTICE & PROBLEM SOLVING

Practice Tutorial

Mixed Review Available Online

APPLY

40. Use Structure Specialists can determine the speed a vehicle was traveling from the length of its skid marks, d, and the coefficient of friction, f. The formula for calculating the speed, s, is $s = 15.9\sqrt{df}$. Rewrite the formula to solve for the length of the skid marks.

41. Make Sense and Persevere The half-life of a certain type of soft drink is 5 h. If you drink 50 mL of this drink, the formula $y = 50(0.5)^{\frac{t}{5}}$ tells the amount of the drink left in your system after t hours. How much of the soft drink will be left in your system after 16 hours?

42. Model With Mathematics Big Ben's pendulum takes 4 s to swing back and forth. The formula $t = 2\pi\sqrt{\frac{L}{32}}$ gives the swing time, t, in seconds, based on the length of the pendulum, L, in feet. What is the minimum length necessary to build a clock with a pendulum that takes longer than Big Ben's pendulum to swing back and forth?

43. Make Sense and Persevere Derek is hang gliding on a clear day at an altitude of a feet. His visibility, v, is 67.1 mi. Use the formula $v = 1.225\sqrt{a}$ to find the altitude at which Derek is hang gliding.

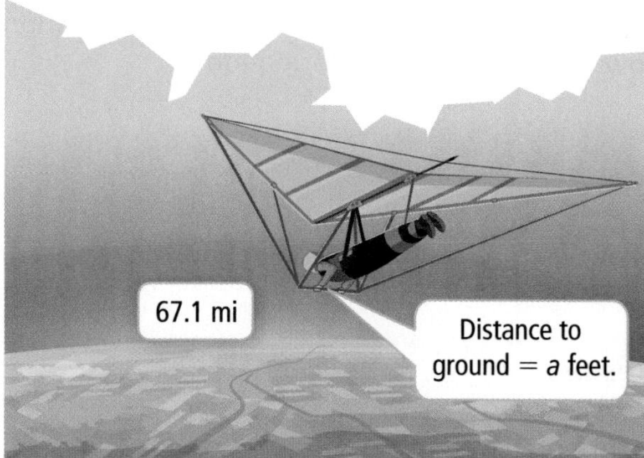

ASSESSMENT PRACTICE

44. Complete the table to solve for the unknown value in the equation $y = \sqrt[3]{2x + z} - 12$, using the given values in each row.

y	x	z
0	462	
−3		439
−10	1.25	
3		16

45. SAT/ACT What is the solution to the equation $(x^2 + 5x + 25)^{\frac{3}{2}} = 343$?

Ⓐ −8 only

Ⓑ 3 only

Ⓒ 77 only

Ⓓ −8 and 3

Ⓔ There are no solutions.

46. Performance Task Escape velocity is the velocity at which an object must be traveling to leave a star or planet without falling back to its surface or into orbit. Escape velocity, v, depends on the gravitational constant, G, the mass, M, and radius, r, of the star or planet.

$$v = \sqrt{\frac{2GM}{r}}$$

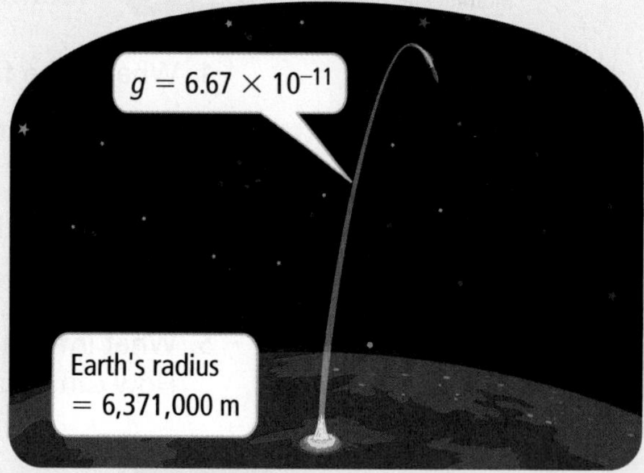

Part A Rewrite the equation to solve for mass.

Part B The escape velocity of Earth is 11,200 m/s and its radius is 6,371,000 m. The gravitational constant is 6.67×10^{-11}. What is Earth's mass in kilograms?

The Snack Shack

Americans seem to love the beach! When the weather is warm, people flock to the beach. Some people bring coolers packed with food and drinks. Others prefer to take advantage of snack bars and shops set up along the beach.

Some beachside communities have built long wooden walkways, or boardwalks, to make it easier for beachgoers to walk to the snack bars and stores. How easy do you find walking in the sand? Think about this during the Mathematical Modeling in 3 Acts lesson.

Scan for Multimedia

ACT 1 Identify the Problem

1. What is the first question that comes to mind after watching the video?
2. Write down the main question you will answer about what you saw in the video.
3. Make an initial conjecture that answers this main question.
4. Explain how you arrived at your conjecture.
5. What information will be useful to know to answer the main question? How can you get it? How will you use that information?

ACT 2 Develop a Model

6. Use the math that you have learned in this Topic to refine your conjecture.

ACT 3 Interpret the Results

7. Did your refined conjecture match the actual answer exactly? If not, what might explain the difference?

4-5 Function Operations

PearsonRealize.com

I CAN... perform operations on functions to answer real-world questions.

VOCABULARY

- composite function
- composition of functions

MODEL & DISCUSS

In business, the term *profit* is used to describe the difference between the money the business earns (revenue) and the money the business spends (cost).

A. Grooming USA charges $25 for every pet that is groomed. Let x represent the number of pets groomed in a month. Define a revenue function for the business.

B. Materials and labor for each pet groomed cost $15. The business also has fixed costs of $1,000 each month. Define a cost function for this business.

C. Last month, Grooming USA groomed 95 pets. Did they earn a profit? What would the profit be if the business groomed 110 pets in a month?

D. **Generalize** Explain your procedure for calculating the profit for Grooming USA. Suppose you wanted to calculate the profit for several different scenarios. How could you simplify your process?

ESSENTIAL QUESTION

How do you combine, multiply, divide, and compose functions, and how do you find the domain of the resulting function?

EXAMPLE 1 Add and Subtract Functions

How do you define the sum, $f + g$, and the difference, $f - g$, of the functions $f(x) = 3x + 4$ and $g(x) = x^2 - 5x + 2$?

A. What is the sum of $f(x) = 3x + 4$ and $g(x) = x^2 - 5x + 2$?

To define the sum of two functions with known rules, add their rules.

$(f + g)(x) = f(x) + g(x)$

$= (3x + 4) + (x^2 - 5x + 2)$ .... Substitute the rule of each function.

$= x^2 + (3x - 5x) + (4 + 2)$ .... Group like terms.

$= x^2 - 2x + 6$ .... Combine like terms.

The domain of f is $\{x \mid x \text{ is a real number}\}$.

The domain of g is $\{x \mid x \text{ is a real number}\}$.

So the domain of $f + g$ is $\{x \mid x \text{ is a real number}\}$.

The sum of the two functions is $x^2 - 2x + 6$.

COMMUNICATE PRECISELY
Defining a function includes describing its domain. The domain of $f \pm g$ is the intersection of the domains of f and g.

CONTINUED ON THE NEXT PAGE

EXAMPLE 1 CONTINUED

B. What is the difference of $f(x) = 3x + 4$ and $g(x) = x^2 - 5x + 2$?

To define the difference of two functions with known rules, subtract their rules.

$(f - g)(x) = f(x) - g(x)$

$= (3x + 4) - (x^2 - 5x + 2)$ ········ Substitute the rule of each function.

$= 3x + 4 - x^2 + 5x - 2$ ········ Use the Distributive Property.

$= -x^2 + 8x + 2$ ········ Combine like terms.

The domain of f is $\{x \mid x$ is a real number$\}$. The domain of g is $\{x \mid x$ is a real number$\}$. So the domain of $f - g$ is $\{x \mid x$ is a real number$\}$.

The difference of the two functions is $-x^2 + 8x + 2$.

Try It! 1. Let $f(x) = 2x^2 + 7x - 1$ and $g(x) = 3 - 2x$. Identify rules for the following functions.

a. $f + g$ **b.** $f - g$

APPLICATION

EXAMPLE 2 Multiply Functions

The demand d, in units sold, for a company's new brand of cell phone at price x, in dollars, is $d(x) = 5{,}000 - 10x$. What is the company's expected revenue from cell phone sales in terms of the price, x?

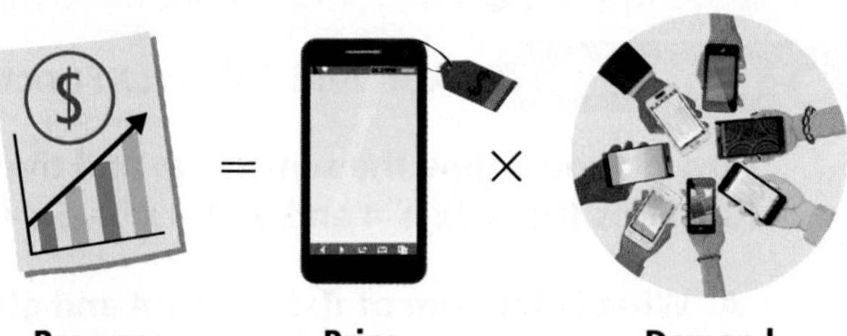

The company's revenue will equal the price of its cell phones multiplied by the demand for its cell phones.

Revenue = price × demand

The demand is the function $d(x)$. The price is the function $p(x)$.

The product of two functions is the product of their rules: $(p \cdot d) = p(x) \cdot d(x)$.

> **USE STRUCTURE**
> You can use the Associative and Commutative Properties to add and multiply functions, since these operations are based on addition and multiplication of real numbers.

		Domains
Price:	$p(x) = x$	$p(x)$: $0 \le x$
Demand:	$d(x) = 5{,}000 - 10x$	$d(x)$: $x \le 500$
Revenue:	$R(x) = p(x) \cdot d(x)$	$R(x)$: $0 \le x \le 500$
	$= x(5{,}000 - 10x)$	
	$= 5{,}000x - 10x^2$	

Price cannot be negative.

Demand cannot be negative: $0 \le 5{,}000 - 10x$

Domain is the intersection of the domains of p and d.

CONTINUED ON THE NEXT PAGE

  Activity  Assess

EXAMPLE 2 CONTINUED

The revenue the company will earn in terms of the cell phone price x is represented by $R(x) = 5{,}000x - 10x^2$.

Try It! 2. Suppose demand, d, for a company's product at cost, x, is predicted by the function $d(x) = -0.25x^2 + 1{,}000$, and the price, p, that the company can charge for the product is given by $p(x) = x + 16$. Find the company's revenue function.

EXAMPLE 3 Divide Functions

How do you define the quotient $\frac{f}{g}$ of the functions $f(x) = x - 7$ and $g(x) = 2x^2 - 13x - 7$?

To define the quotient of two functions, take the quotient of their rules: $\left(\frac{f}{g}\right)(x) = \frac{f(x)}{g(x)}$

$$\left(\frac{f}{g}\right)(x) = \frac{f(x)}{g(x)} = \frac{x-7}{2x^2 - 13x - 7} \quad \text{Substitute the rule of each function.}$$

$$= \frac{x-7}{(2x+1)(x-7)} \quad \text{Factor the denominator.}$$

$$= \frac{1}{2x+1} \quad \text{Simplify.}$$

The quotient of $\frac{f}{g}$ is $\frac{1}{2x+1}$. The domain of $\frac{f}{g}$ is the set of all values for which f, g, and $\frac{f}{g}$ are defined, so g cannot be 0. This is the set of all real numbers x such that $x \neq 7$ and $x \neq -\frac{1}{2}$.

COMMON ERROR
You may think that the domain of $\frac{f}{g}$ is the set of real numbers. However, $x \neq -\frac{1}{2}$. Remember to identify the domain ***before*** simplifying the rational function.

Try It! 3. Identify the rule and domain for $\frac{f}{g}$ for each pair of functions.

a. $f(x) = x^2 - 3x - 18$, $g(x) = x + 3$

b. $f(x) = x - 3$, $g(x) = x^2 - x - 6$

CONCEPTUAL UNDERSTANDING

EXAMPLE 4 Compose Functions

Let $f(x) = x^2$ and let $g(x) = x + 1$. Investigate what happens when you apply the rule for g and then the rule for f to a number or variable.

A. Find the value of $f(g(3))$.

$$g(3) = 3 + 1 = 4 \quad \text{Apply the rule for } g.$$

$$f(g(3)) = f(4) \quad \text{Apply the rule for } f \text{ to the result.}$$

$$= 4^2 \quad \text{Use the rule for } f.$$

$$= 16 \quad \text{Simplify.}$$

$$f(g(3)) = 16$$

LOOK FOR RELATIONSHIPS
When finding the rule for $f(g(x))$, work from the inside out. Notice that $g(x)$ takes the place of the variable x in the function $f(x)$.

CONTINUED ON THE NEXT PAGE

EXAMPLE 4 CONTINUED

B. Find the rule for $f(g(x))$.

$g(x) = x + 1$ .... Apply the rule for g.

$f(g(x)) = f(x + 1)$ .... Apply the rule for f to the result.

$= (x + 1)^2$ .... Use the rule for f.

$= x^2 + 2x + 1$ .... Square the binomial.

$f(g(x)) = x^2 + 2x + 1$

When you apply the rule for one function to the rule of another function, you create an entirely new function.

 **Try It!** **4.** Let $f(x) = 2x - 1$ and $g(x) = 3x$. Identify the rule for the following functions.

a. $f(g(2))$

b. $f(g(x))$

CONCEPT Composite Function

A **composite function** is the result of applying the rule for one function, f, to the rule of another function, g. The new rule is denoted as $f \circ g$.

$$(f \circ g)(x) = f(g(x))$$

The operation $\circ$ that forms a composite functions is called **composition of functions**.

The domain of $f \circ g$ is the set of all real numbers x in the domain of g such that $g(x)$ is in the domain of f.

So the domain of the composition is the intersection of the domains of g and $f \circ g$, but not f.

EXAMPLE 5 Write a Rule for a Composite Function

What is the rule for the composition $(f \circ g)(x)$?

MAKE SENSE AND PERSEVERE
When finding the rule for the composition of functions, $f \circ g$, the rule for g is substituted into the rule for f just like substituting a value in for a variable. How might you find the rule for $g \circ f$?

A. $f(x) = \sqrt{x + 7}$ and $g(x) = 2x - 5$

$(f \circ g)(x) = f(g(x))$

$= f(2x - 5)$ .... Apply the rule for g.

$= \sqrt{(2x - 5) + 7}$ .... Apply the rule for f.

$= \sqrt{2x + 2}$ .... Simplify.

The rule for the composition $(f \circ g)(x)$ is $\sqrt{2x + 2}$, and the domain is $x > -1$.

CONTINUED ON THE NEXT PAGE

EXAMPLE 5 CONTINUED

B. $f(x) = x^2 + x + 2$ and $g(x) = 4 - x$

$$(f \circ g)(x) = f(g(x))$$

$= f(4 - x)$ ······ Apply the rule for g.

$= (4 - x)^2 + (4 - x) + 2$ ······ Apply the rule for f.

$= 16 - 8x + x^2 + 4 - x + 2$ ······ Expand the binomial.

$= x^2 - 9x + 22$ ······ Combine like terms.

The rule for the composition $(f \circ g)(x)$ is $x^2 - 9x + 22$, and the domain is all real numbers.

Try It! **5.** Identify the rules for $f \circ g$ and $g \circ f$.

a. $f(x) = x^3$, $g(x) = x + 1$

b. $f(x) = x^2 + 1$, $g(x) = x - 5$

APPLICATION

EXAMPLE 6 Use a Composite Function Model

Clothes U Wear posts discounts on social media. The store allows customers to use multiple discounts. They simply need to tell the cashier in which order they would like the discounts to be applied.

On your next trip to Clothes U Wear, in which order should you ask for the discounts?

Write functions to model the discounts, letting x represent the price of the purchase.

$f(x) = x - 5$

$g(x) = x - 0.1x$ ← price − 10% of price

$= 0.9x$

STUDY TIP

Using a model can help solve a problem. By writing functions to model the discounts, determine which sequence of functions provides a better deal for the customer.

10% off, then \$5 off ⇒ Identify the rule for $f \circ g$.

$(f \circ g)(x) = f(g(x))$

$= f(0.9x)$

$= 0.9x - 5$ ← This is the better deal.

\$5 off, then 10% off ⇒ Identify the rule for $g \circ f$.

$(f \circ g)(x) = g(f(x))$

$= g(x - 5)$

$= 0.9(x - 5)$

$= 0.9x - 4.5$

Suppose a shirt costs \$30.00 before the discounts. Applying the discounts as $(f \circ g)(x)$ means the new cost is $(0.9)(30) - 5 = 22$, or \$22.00. Applying the discounts as $(f \circ g)(x)$ means the new cost is $(0.9)(30) - 4.5 = 22.5$, or \$22.50.

The first method yields the better deal.

Try It! **6.** As a member of the Games Shop rewards program, you get a 20% discount on purchases. All sales are subject to a 6% sales tax. Write functions to model the discount and the sales tax, then identify the rule for the composition function that calculates the final price you would pay at Games Shop.

CONCEPT SUMMARY Function Operations

	Add or Subtract Functions	Multiply or Divide Functions	Compose Functions
ALGEBRA	$(f+g)(x) = f(x) + g(x)$ $(f-g)(x) = f(x) - g(x)$	$(f \cdot g)(x) = f(x) \cdot g(x)$ $\left(\frac{f}{g}\right)(x) = \frac{f(x)}{g(x)}$	$(f \circ g)(x) = f(g(x))$ $(g \circ f)(x) = g(f(x))$
WORDS	The domain of the sum or difference of f and g is the intersection of the domain of f and the domain of g.	The domain is the set of all real numbers for which f and g and the new function are defined.	The **domain** of $f \circ g$ is the set of all real numbers x, in the domain of g, such that $g(x)$ is in the domain of f.
NUMBERS	For $f(x) = 3x + 5$ and $g(x) = x - 3$, $f + g = (3x + 5) + (x - 3) = 4x + 2$ and $f - g = (3x + 5) - (x - 3) = 2x + 8$	For $f(x) = 3x + 5$ and $g(x) = x - 3$, $f \cdot g = (3x + 5)(x - 3) = 3x^2 - 4x - 15$ and $\frac{f}{g} = \frac{3x+5}{x-3}$ for $x \neq 3$	For $f(x) = 3x + 5$ and $g(x) = x - 3$, $f \circ g = 3(x - 3) + 5 = 3x - 4$ and $g \circ f = (3x + 5) - 3 = 3x + 2$

Do You UNDERSTAND?

1. ESSENTIAL QUESTION How do you combine, multiply, divide, and compose functions, and how do you find the domain of the resulting function?

2. **Vocabulary** In your own words, define and provide an example of a composite function.

3. **Error Analysis** Reagan said the domain of $\frac{f}{g}$ when $f(x) = 5x^2$ and $g(x) = x + 3$ is the set of real numbers. Explain why Reagan is incorrect.

4. **Use Structure** Explain why changing the order in which two functions occur affects the result when subtracting and dividing the functions.

Do You KNOW HOW?

Let $f(x) = 3x^2 + 5x + 1$ and $g(x) = 2x - 1$.

5. Identify the rule for $f + g$.

6. Identify the rule for $f - g$.

7. Identify the rule for $g - f$.

Let $f(x) = x^2 + 2x + 1$ and $g(x) = x - 4$.

8. Identify the rule for $f \cdot g$.

9. Identify the rule for $\frac{f}{g}$, and state the domain.

10. Identify the rule for $\frac{g}{f}$, and state the domain.

11. If $f(x) = 2x^2 + 5$ and $g(x) = -3x$, what is $f(g(x))$?

PRACTICE & PROBLEM SOLVING

Scan for Multimedia

Additional Exercises Available Online

UNDERSTAND

12. **Generalize** Does $f \circ g$ always equal $g \circ f$? Justify your response.

13. **Construct Arguments** Explain why the domain for the quotient of functions might not be the set of all real numbers.

14. **Error Analysis** Describe and correct the error a student made in finding the rule for the composition $f \circ g$ of the functions $f(x) = 3x^2 - x + 2$ and $g(x) = 2x + 1$.

$$\begin{aligned} f \cdot g &= f(g(x)) \\ &= 3(2x + 1)^2 - 2x + 1 + 2 \\ &= 3(4x^2 + 4x + 1) - 2x + 1 + 2 \\ &= 12x^2 + 12x + 3 - 2x + 1 + 2 \\ &= 12x^2 + 10x + 6 \end{aligned}$$

X

15. **Make Sense and Persevere** Identify the rules for two functions, $f(x)$ and $g(x)$, for which $f \circ g = g \circ f$.

16. **Higher Order Thinking** Suppose two functions, $f(x)$ and $g(x)$ are only defined by the ordered pairs listed below.

$f = (6, 7), (5, 2), (4, 1), (10, 8)$
$g = (5, 4), (3, 6), (1, 5), (2, 10)$
Find the ordered pairs that comprise $(f \circ g)(x)$.

17. **Mathematical Connections** How is the process of finding the rule for the composition of functions related to the order of operations in arithmetic?

18. **Make Sense and Persevere** Recalling that the identity function is $f(x) = x$, identify the rules for two functions $f(x)$ and $g(x)$, for which $f(g(x)) = x$.

19. **Construct Arguments** Is it possible that the result of subtracting two linear functions is a horizontal line? If so, give an example. What must be true about the two linear functions? If not, explain why it is not possible.

PRACTICE

Let $f(x) = 2x^2 + 5x - 1$ and $g(x) = 3x + 2$. Identify the rules for the following functions. SEE EXAMPLE 1

20. $f + g$

21. $f - g$

22. Suppose the demand d, in units sold, for a company's jeans at price x, in dollars, is $d(x) = 600 - 4x$.

a. If revenue = price × demand, write the rule for the function $r(x)$, which represent the company's expected revenue in jean sales. Then state the domain of this function.

b. If the price is \$40, how much revenue will the company earn? SEE EXAMPLE 2

23. Identify the rule and domain for $\frac{f}{g}$ when $f(x) = x^2 + 3x - 28$ and $g(x) = x + 7$. SEE EXAMPLE 3

Let $f(x) = 4x - 5$ and $g(x) = -7x$. Evaluate each expression. SEE EXAMPLE 4

24. $f(g(3))$

25. $f(g(x))$

26. $g(f(2))$

27. $g(f(x))$

Let $f(x) = x^2 + x$ and $g(x) = 9 - 2x$. Identify the rules for the following functions. SEE EXAMPLE 5

28. $f \circ g$

29. $g \circ f$

30. A sporting goods store is running a summer sale on its snowboards. Kayden is interested in a snowboard that normally costs \$400. The store is offering a \$50 instant rebate, as well as a 10% discount.

In which order should these special offers be applied to the cost of the snowboard in order to benefit Kayden? Explain. SEE EXAMPLE 6

PRACTICE & PROBLEM SOLVING

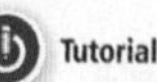

Mixed Review Available Online

APPLY

31. Model With Mathematics The cost (in dollars) to produce x shovels in a factory is given by the function $C(x) = 20x + 500$. The number of shovels that can be produced in h hours is given by the function $x(h) = 30h$.

a. Find the rule for $C(x(h))$.

b. Find the cost when $h = 8$ hours.

c. Explain what the answer to part (b) represents.

32. Use Structure A music store is running the following promotions.

a. Use composition of functions to find the sale price of a \$90 purchase when the \$5 off discount is applied prior to the 15% off discount.

b. Use composition of functions to find the sale price of a \$90 purchase when the 15% off discount is applied prior to the \$5 off discount.

c. In which order is the deal better for the consumer? Explain.

33. Reason From 2000 to 2015, the number of births, b, (in the hundreds) in Fairfield County can be modeled by the function $b(x) = 300 - 5x$. The number of deaths, d, (in the hundreds) can be modeled by the function $d(x) = 10x + 5$. The variable x represents the number of years since 2000.

a. Which function operation can be used to represent the net increase in the population?

b. Write and simplify a function which represents the net increase in the population, p, against x, the number of years since 2000. State the domain of this function.

ASSESSMENT PRACTICE

34. Given that $f(x) = x^2 + 8x + 3$ and $g(x) = -x - 7$, which of the following are true? Select all that apply.

Ⓐ $f + g = x^2 + 7x - 4$

Ⓑ $f(g(x)) = x^2 + 6x - 4$

Ⓒ The domain of $\frac{f}{g}$ is the set of all real numbers.

Ⓓ $f(x) \cdot g(x) = -x^3 - 15x^2 + 53x + 21$

Ⓔ In the composition $g \circ f$, the output $f(x)$ is used as the input for g.

35. SAT/ACT Find the value of $f(g(5))$ if $f(x) = 4x + 1$ and $g(x) = x^2 + 6$.

Ⓐ 101 Ⓑ 124 Ⓒ 125 Ⓓ 676 Ⓔ 682

36. Performance Task The temperature in degrees Celsius is 32 less than the Fahrenheit temperature, multiplied by five ninths. The temperature in degrees Kelvin is the number of degrees Celsius plus 273.

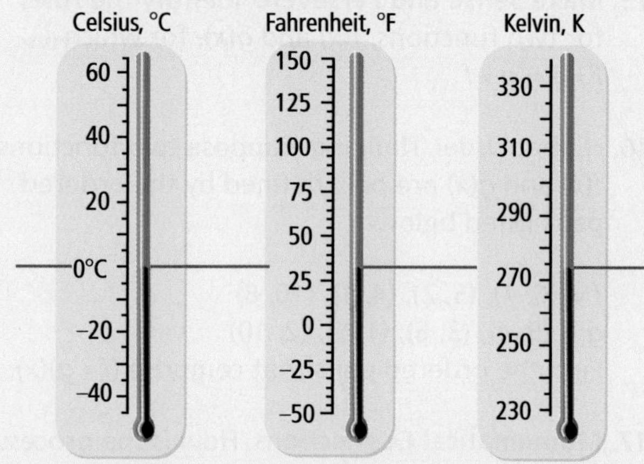

Part A Derive a conversion formula for finding the number of degrees Kelvin, given the temperature in Fahrenheit.

Part B Using your conversion formula from part (a), find the temperature in degrees Kelvin when the temperature is 27°F. Round to the nearest whole number if necessary.

Activity Assess

4-6 Inverse Relations and Functions

I CAN… represent the inverse of a relation using tables, graphs, and equations.

VOCABULARY
- inverse function
- inverse relation

EXPLORE & REASON

Each number path will lead you from a number in the domain, the set of all real numbers, to a number in the range.

Number Path f: $x \to f(x)$
- Start with x.
- Subtract 3.
- Multiply by −2.
- Add 5.

Number Path g: $x \to g(x)$
- Start with x.
- Add 1.
- Square the value.
- Subtract 2.

A. Follow the number paths to find $f(1)$ and $g(1)$.

B. Identify all possible values of x that lead to $f(x) = 7$ and all values that lead to $g(x) = 7$.

C. Communicate Precisely Based on the two Number Paths, under what conditions can you follow a path back to a unique value in the domain?

ESSENTIAL QUESTION

How can you find the inverse of a function and verify the two functions are inverses?

CONCEPTUAL UNDERSTANDING

EXAMPLE 1 Represent the Inverse of a Relation

What is the inverse of the relation represented in the table?

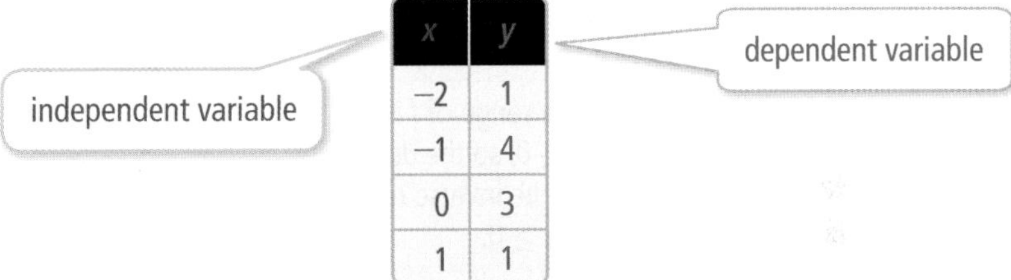

x	y
−2	1
−1	4
0	3
1	1

Recall that a relation is any set of ordered pairs (x, y), where x is the independent variable and y is the dependent variable. An **inverse relation** is formed when the roles of the independent and dependent variables are reversed.

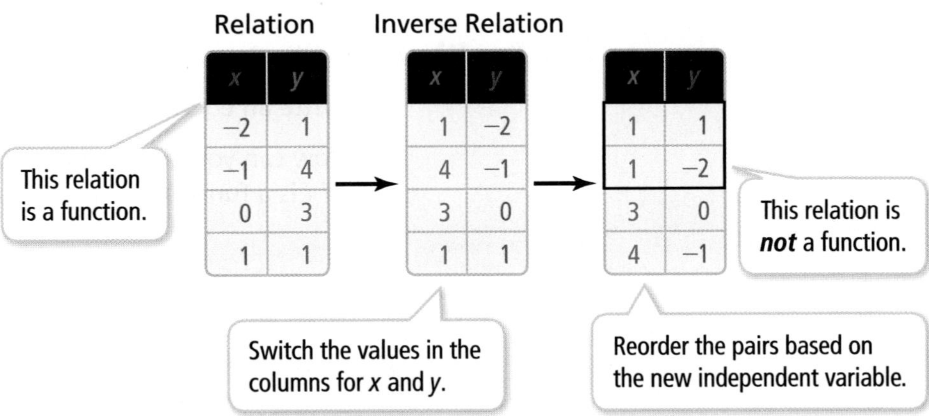

Relation:

x	y
−2	1
−1	4
0	3
1	1

Inverse Relation:

x	y
1	−2
4	−1
3	0
1	1

x	y
1	1
1	−2
3	0
4	−1

LOOK FOR RELATIONSHIPS
If two distinct values in the domain of f have the same image, then the inverse of f is not a function.

If an inverse relation of a function, f, is itself a function, it is called the **inverse function** of f, which is written $f^{-1}(x)$.

CONTINUED ON THE NEXT PAGE

EXAMPLE 1 CONTINUED

Try It! 1. Identify the inverse relation. Is it a function?

x	−1	0	1	2	3	4
y	9	7	5	3	1	−1

EXAMPLE 2 Find an Equation of an Inverse Relation

Let $f(x) = x^2$.

A. How can you represent the inverse relation of f algebraically?

$f(x) = x^2 \rightarrow y = x^2$

$x = y^2$ .... Switch the roles of x and y.

$y = \pm\sqrt{x}$ .... Solve for y.

The inverse of f can be represented algebraically by the equation $y = \pm\sqrt{x}$.

B. How are the graphs of $y = x^2$ and $y = \pm\sqrt{x}$ related?

LOOK FOR RELATIONSHIPS
The domain of a relation becomes the range of its inverse, and the range of a relation becomes the domain of its inverse.

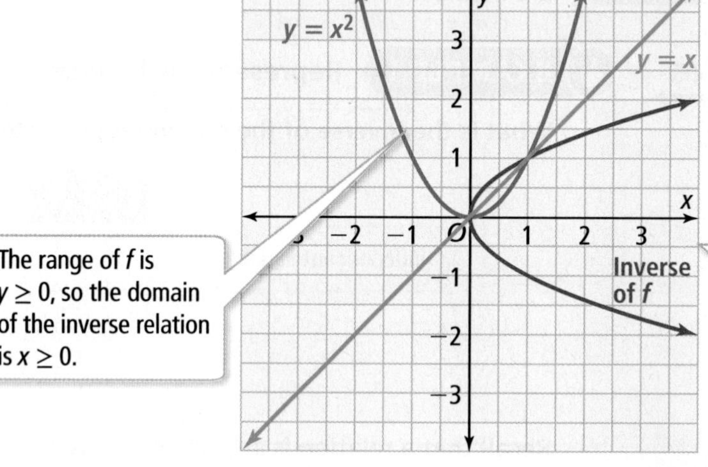

The graph of the inverse of f is the reflection of the graph of $y = x^2$ across the line $y = x$.

Try It! 2. Let $f(x) = 2x + 1$.

a. Write an equation to represent the inverse of f.

b. How can you use the graph of f to determine if the inverse of f is a function? Explain your answer.

EXAMPLE 3 Restrict a Domain to Produce an Inverse Function

Consider again the function $f(x) = x^2$. Under what domain will the inverse relation be a function?

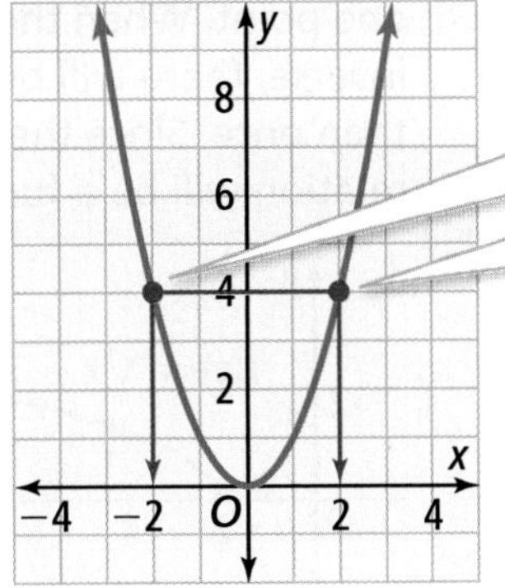

The inverse relation is not a function since it would contain the inverse of these two points, (4, −2) and (4, 2).

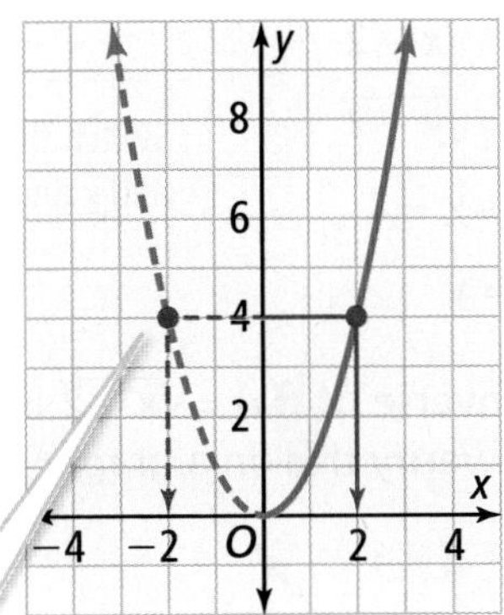

For the inverse to be a function, all of the duplicate *y*-values would have to be eliminated from the original function.

Restrict the domain of *f* to be $x \geq 0$.

If a function has two *x*-values for the same *y*-value, its inverse will not be a function. You can restrict the domain in many different ways to create a function that will have an inverse that is a function.

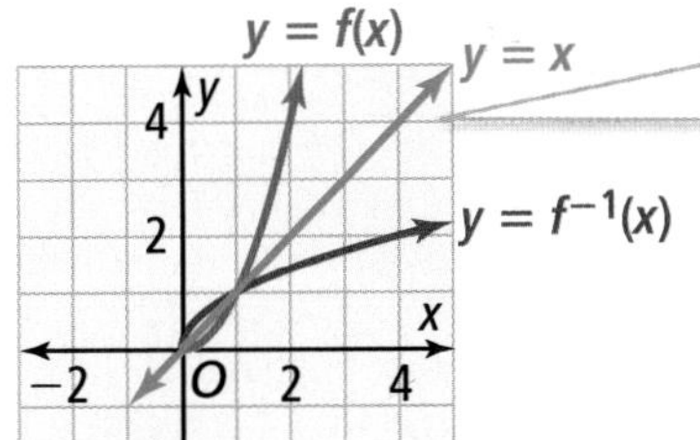

The graph of the inverse function of *f* is the reflection of the graph of $f(x)$ across the line $y = x$.

STUDY TIP
There is more than one way to restrict the domain of a function. The context of a situation often influences the choice of domain.

The inverse relation of $f(x) = x^2$ is $y = \pm\sqrt{x}$. If the domain of $f(x) = x^2$ is restricted to $x \geq 0$, then the inverse is the function defined as $f^{-1}(x) = \sqrt{x}$.

Try It! 3. Find the inverse of each function by identifying an appropriate restriction of its domain.

a. $f(x) = x^2 + 8x + 16$

b. $f(x) = x^2 - 9$

 Activity  Assess

EXAMPLE 4 Find an Equation of an Inverse Function

A. Find an equation of the inverse function of $f(x) = \sqrt{x-2}$.

The graph shows that no horizontal line intersects the graph in more than one point. When the graph is reflected over the line $y = x$ to produce an inverse, there will be no vertical line that will intersect the graph more than once. Since the inverse will pass the vertical line test, the inverse relation will be a function.

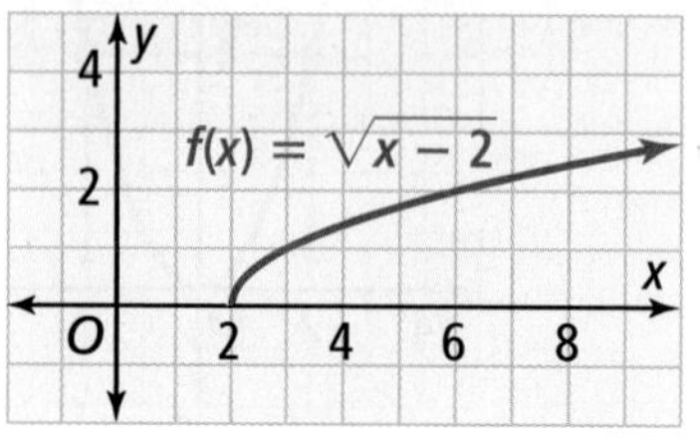

Use the graph to identify the domain and range of f and f^{-1}.

	domain	range
f	$x \geq 2$	$y \geq 0$
f^{-1}	$x \geq 0$	$y \geq 2$

COMMON ERROR
Don't apply f^{-1} notation too quickly. This notation is only used when the inverse of f is a function.

$$y = \sqrt{x-2}$$
$$x = \sqrt{y-2}$$
$$x^2 = y - 2$$
$$x^2 + 2 = y$$

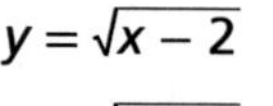

Switch the roles of x and y and solve for y.

So the inverse of $f(x) = \sqrt{x-2}$ is a function, $f^{-1}(x) = x^2 + 2,\ x \geq 0$. You can verify this on a graph.

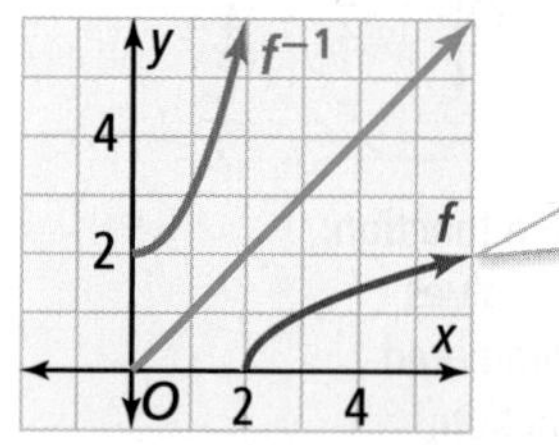

The graphs of f and f^{-1} are both functions and are reflections over the line $y = x$.

B. Find an equation of the inverse function of $f(x) = -\sqrt[3]{4x}$.

The graph shows that no horizontal line intersects the graph in more than one point, so the inverse relation will be a function.

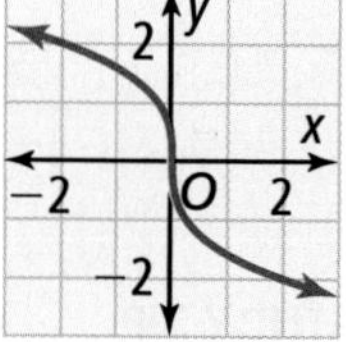

$$y = -\sqrt[3]{4x}$$
$$x = -\sqrt[3]{4y}$$
$$x^3 = -4y$$
$$\frac{-x^3}{4} = y$$

Since the inverse is a function, $f^{-1}(x) = \frac{-x^3}{4}$ for all real x. You can verify this on a graph.

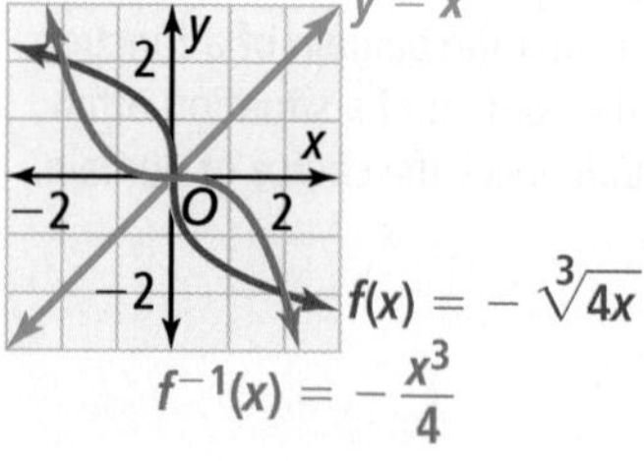

Try It! 4. Let $f(x) = 2 - \sqrt[3]{x+1}$.

a. Sketch the graph of f.

b. Verify that the inverse will be a function and write an equation for $f^{-1}(x)$.

 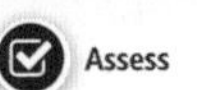

Activity Assess

EXAMPLE 5 Use Composition to Verify Inverse Functions

A. What is the inverse of $f(x) = 2x + 5$, and how can you verify this?

$y = 2x + 5 \rightarrow x = 2y + 5$ .... Switch x and y.

$2y = x - 5$ .... Isolate y-term.

$y = \frac{1}{2}x - \frac{5}{2}$ .... Divide by 2.

So the inverse of f is $g(x) = \frac{1}{2}x - \frac{5}{2}$. You can verify this with function composition: To be inverse functions, $(f \circ g)(x) = x$ and $(g \circ f)(x) = x$.

$$\begin{aligned}(f \circ g)(x) &= f(g(x)) \\ &= 2(g(x)) + 5 \\ &= 2\left(\tfrac{1}{2}x - \tfrac{5}{2}\right) + 5 \\ &= x - 5 + 5 \\ &= x\end{aligned}$$

$$\begin{aligned}(g \circ f)(x) &= g(f(x)) \\ &= \tfrac{1}{2}(f(x)) - \tfrac{5}{2} \\ &= \tfrac{1}{2}(2x + 5) - \tfrac{5}{2} \\ &= x + \tfrac{5}{2} - \tfrac{5}{2} \\ &= x\end{aligned}$$

LOOK FOR RELATIONSHIPS
Because a function's inverse reverses the action of the original function, the composition of the two (in either order) simplifies to the identity function.

Since $(f \circ g)(x) = x$ and $(g \circ f)(x) = x$, the functions $f(x) = 2x + 5$ and $g(x) = \frac{1}{2}x - \frac{5}{2}$ are inverses.

You can also verify $g(x)$ is the inverse of $f(x)$ by graphing.

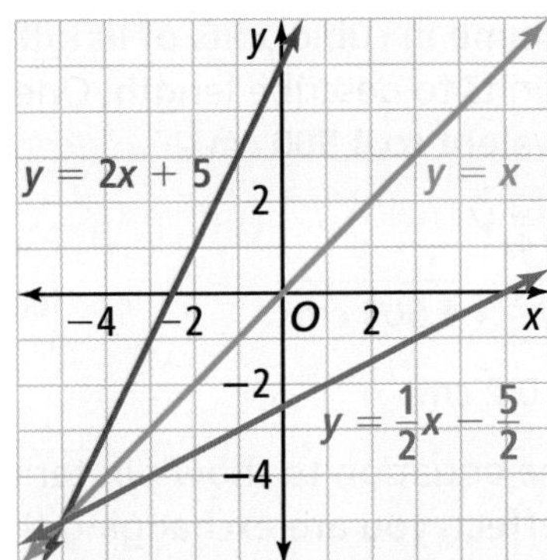

The graph of $y = \frac{1}{2}x - \frac{5}{2}$ is a reflection of the graph of $y = 2x + 5$ across the line $y = x$.

B. Are the two functions $f(x) = x^2 + 5$ and $g(x) = \sqrt{x} - 5$ inverses of each other?

To be inverse functions, $(f \circ g)(x) = x$ and $(g \circ f)(x) = x$.

$$\begin{aligned}(f \circ g)(x) &= f(g(x)) \\ &= (g(x))^2 + 5 \\ &= (\sqrt{x} - 5)^2 + 5 \\ &= x - 10\sqrt{x} + 25 + 5 \\ &= x - 10\sqrt{x} + 30\end{aligned}$$

$$\begin{aligned}(g \circ f)(x) &= g(f(x)) \\ &= \sqrt{f(x)} - 5 \\ &= \sqrt{x^2 + 5} - 5\end{aligned}$$

Since neither $(f \circ g)(x)$ nor $(g \circ f)(x)$ simplify to the identity function, the functions are not inverses.

Try It! 5. Use composition to determine whether f and g are inverse functions.

a. $f(x) = \frac{1}{4}x + 7$, $g(x) = 4x - 7$

b. $f(x) = \sqrt[3]{x - 1}$, $g(x) = x^3 + 1$

APPLICATION

EXAMPLE 6 Rewrite a Formula

A sculpture artist is making an ice sculpture of Earth for a display. He created a mold that can hold 4.5 L of ice. What will the radius of the ice sculpture be if he fills the mold all of the way?

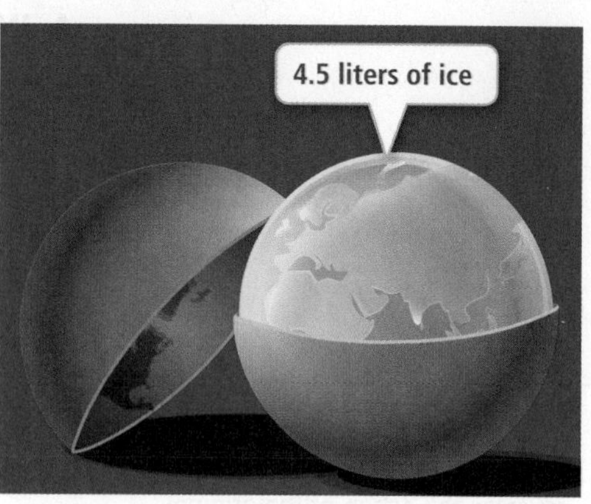

The volume of a sphere is calculated using the formula $V = \frac{4}{3}\pi r^3$.

Rewrite the formula to find the length of the radius.

$$\frac{4}{3}\pi r^3 = V$$

$$\pi r^3 = \frac{3}{4}V$$

$$r^3 = \frac{3}{4\pi}V$$

$$r = \sqrt[3]{\frac{3}{4\pi}V}$$

Since a liter is a measure of capacity, or volume, it can be expressed using cubic units of length. When you take the cube root of an expression involving volume in cubic units of length, the units of the result will be in the correct units to describe length. One liter is equivalent to 1,000 cm^3, so 4.5 L is equivalent to 4,500 cm^3.

MAKE SENSE AND PERSEVERE
If this seems smaller than expected, remember that this is the radius—the diameter of the ice sculpture mold is about 20.4 cm.

$$r = \sqrt[3]{\frac{3}{4\pi}V}$$

$$= \sqrt[3]{\frac{3}{4\pi} \cdot 4{,}500 \text{ cm}^3}$$

Substitute 4,500 cm^3 for V.

$$\approx 10.2 \text{ cm}$$

Rewriting the equation to show r in terms of V is similar to finding the inverse. In effect, you are exchanging the roles of the dependent and independent variables.

$$V = \frac{4}{3}\pi r^3 \qquad r = \sqrt[3]{\frac{3V}{4\pi}}$$

In the original equation, you can see how the value of V *depends* on the value of r.

In this form of the equation, you can see how the value of r can be determined by, and depends on, a given value of V.

The ice sculpture mold will have a radius of about 10 cm.

Try It! 6. The manufacturer of a gift box designs a box with length and width each twice as long as its height. Find a formula that gives the height h of the box in terms of its volume V. Then give the length of the box if the volume is 640 cm^3.

CONCEPT SUMMARY Inverse Functions

To find the **inverse** of a function, exchange the roles of the independent and dependent variables.

TABLES Switch the columns.

f	
x	y
0	2
1	4
2	6
3	8
4	10

f^{-1}	
x	y
2	0
4	1
6	2
8	3
10	4

ALGEBRA

Exchange the roles of the independent and dependent variables. Solve for the new dependent variable.

$$y = x + 9$$
$$x = y + 9$$
$$x - 9 = y$$
$$y = x - 9$$

GRAPHS

Reflect the graph across the line $y = x$.

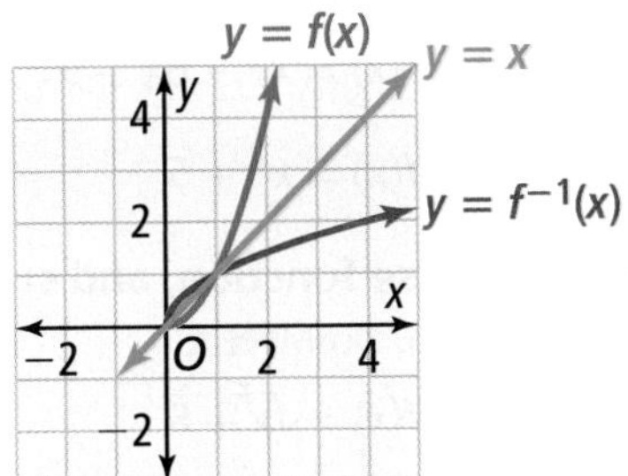

If needed, **restrict the domain** of the original function to find an appropriate inverse for the function.

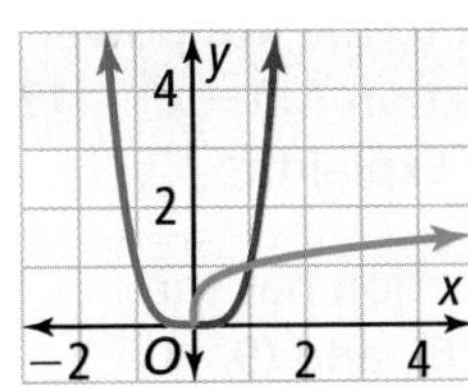

Restrict the domain of $y = x^4$ to $x \geq 0$.

Composition verifies inverses: $f(f^{-1}(x)) = x$ and $f^{-1}(f(x)) = x$.

Do You UNDERSTAND?

1. **ESSENTIAL QUESTION** How can you find the inverse of a function and verify the two functions are inverses?

2. **Error Analysis** Abi said the inverse of $f(x) = 3x + 1$ is $f^{-1}(x) = \frac{1}{3}x - 1$. Is she correct? Explain.

3. **Construct Arguments** Is the inverse of a function always a function? Explain.

Do You KNOW HOW?

Consider the function $f(x) = -\frac{1}{2}x + 5$.

4. Write an equation for the inverse of f.

5. Use composition to show that f and the equation you wrote are inverses.

6. Sketch a graph of f and its inverse.

7. How can you verify by the graph of f and its inverse that they are indeed inverses?

8. Is the inverse of f a function? Explain.

PRACTICE & PROBLEM SOLVING

Scan for Multimedia

Practice Tutorial

Additional Exercises Available Online

UNDERSTAND

9. **Reason** Explain how to find the range of the inverse of $f(x) = \sqrt{2x - 3}$ without finding $f^{-1}(x)$.

10. **Error Analysis** Describe and correct the error a student made in finding the inverse of the function $f(x) = x^2 - 4$.

$$f(x) = x^2 - 4$$
$$x = y^2 - 4$$
$$\sqrt{x} = \sqrt{y^2 - 4}$$
$$\sqrt{x} = y - 2$$
$$\sqrt{x} + 2 = y$$
$$f^{-1}(x) = \sqrt{x} + 2$$

✗

11. **Higher Order Thinking** What is the inverse operation of raising a number to the 4th power? How can you use the inverse operation of a number raised to the 4th power to find the inverse of the function $f(x) = x^4 - 1$? Is the inverse of f a function? Explain.

12. **Communicate Precisely** A function has the ordered pairs (1, 3), (7, 4), (8, 6), and (9, y). What restrictions are there on the value of y so that the inverse of the function is also a function? Explain.

13. **Construct Arguments** What is the inverse of the function $a(b) = \frac{1}{4}b^2$? Show how to use composition of functions to prove you found the correct inverse.

14. **Construct Arguments** A relation has one element in its domain and two elements in its range. Is the relation a function? Is the inverse of the relation a function? Explain.

15. **Mathematical Connections** Find the x- and y-intercepts of the function $y = 2x + 1$. What are the intercepts of the inverse function? How are the intercepts related?

PRACTICE

Identify the inverse relation. Is it a function? SEE EXAMPLE 1

16.

x	−2	−1	0	1	2	3
y	9	3	−4	8	−6	3

17.

x	−2	1	0	1	2	3
y	−7	6	8	−1	3	7

Write an equation to represent the inverse of f. Sketch the graphs of f, $y = x$, and the inverse of f on the same coordinate axes. Is the inverse of f a function? SEE EXAMPLE 2

18. Let $f(x) = x + 3$.

19. Let $f(x) = 4x - 1$.

20. Let $f(x) = x^2 + 1$.

21. Let $f(x) = \sqrt{x + 5}$.

Find the inverse of the function by identifying an appropriate restriction of its domain. SEE EXAMPLE 3

22. $f(x) = x^2 + 4x + 4$

23. $f(x) = x^2 - 6x + 9$

24. $f(x) = x^2 - 2$

25. $f(x) = x^2 + 5$

Find an equation of the inverse function, and state the domain of the inverse. SEE EXAMPLE 4

26. $f(x) = 2x^2 - 5$

27. $f(x) = \sqrt{x + 6}$

28. $f(x) = 3x + 10$

29. $f(x) = \sqrt{x - 9}$

Use composition to determine whether f and g are inverse functions. SEE EXAMPLE 5

30. $f(x) = 2x - 9$, $g(x) = \frac{1}{2}x + 9$

31. $f(x) = \sqrt{\frac{x + 4}{3}}$, $g(x) = 3x^2 - 4$

32. A manager purchased cones for ice cream. Find a formula for the length of the radius, r, of a cone in terms of its volume, V. Then find the length of the radius of a cone if the volume is 290π cm^3 and the height is 15 cm. SEE EXAMPLE 6

PRACTICE & PROBLEM SOLVING

Practice Tutorial

Mixed Review Available Online

APPLY

33. Model With Mathematics The formula for converting Celsius to Fahrenheit is $F = \frac{5}{9}(C - 32)$. Find the inverse formula, and use it to find the Celsius temperature when the Fahrenheit temperature is 56° F.

34. Reason A DJ charges an hourly fee and an equipment setup fee.

a. Write a function for the cost, C, of hiring a DJ for n hours.

b. Find the inverse of the cost function. What does the function represent?

c. If the DJ charged \$550, for how many hours was she hired? Use the inverse function.

35. Reason A coffee can is in the shape of a cylinder.

a. Find the formula that gives the radius of the coffee can r in terms of the volume V and height h.

b. Describe any restrictions on the formula.

c. What is the radius of a coffee can given the volume is 67.5π in.^{3} and the height is 7.5 in.?

ASSESSMENT PRACTICE

36. Choose Yes or No to tell whether each function has an inverse that is a function.

	Yes	No
a. $f(x) = 2x - 9$	❑	❑
b. $f(x) = x^2 + 4$	❑	❑
c. $f(x) = x^3 - 6$	❑	❑
d. $f(x) = \sqrt{2x + 7}$	❑	❑
e. $f(x) = x^2 - 10x + 25$	❑	❑

37. SAT/ACT What is the range of the inverse of $f(x) = \sqrt{-ax + b} - c$, where a, b, and c are real numbers?

Ⓐ $y \geq \frac{a}{b}$

Ⓑ $y \leq \frac{b}{a}$

Ⓒ $y \geq -\frac{a}{b}$

Ⓓ $y \geq -\frac{b}{a}$

Ⓔ $y \geq c$

38. Performance Task The table shows several functions and some of the inverses of those functions. The table also shows whether some of the inverses are functions.

Function	Inverse	Is the inverse a function?
$f(x) = x$	$f^{-1}(x) = x$	yes
$g(x) = x^2$	$g^{-1}(x) = \pm\sqrt{x}$	no
$h(x) = x^3$	$h^{-1}(x) = \sqrt[3]{x}$	yes
$k(x) = x^4$		
$m(x) = x^5$		
$n(x) = x^6$		

Part A Determine the inverses of the remaining functions in the table.

Part B Determine if the inverses of the remaining functions in the table are functions.

Part C Make a conjecture about the power of a function if the inverse of that function is a function.

TOPIC 4

Topic Review

TOPIC ESSENTIAL QUESTION

1. How are rational exponents and radical equations used to solve real-world problems?

Vocabulary Review

Choose the correct term to complete each sentence.

2. In the expression $\sqrt[n]{c}$, n is the ________.
3. In the expression $\sqrt[n]{c}$, c is the ________.
4. Radicals with the same index and the same radicand are ________.
5. A(n) ________ is a function defined by a radical expression.
6. A(n) ________ of a number c is x, such that $x^n = c$.
7. A(n) ________ is a potential solution that must be rejected because it does not satisfy the original equation.
8. When all nth roots of perfect nth powers have been simplified and no radicals remain in the denominator, an expression is in ________.
9. A(n) ________ results from the application of one function to the output of another function.

- composite function
- extraneous solution
- index
- inverse function
- like radicals
- *n*th root
- radical function
- radicand
- reduced radical form

Concepts & Skills Review

LESSON 4-1 *n*th Roots, Radicals, and Rational Exponents

Quick Review

An ***n*****th root** of a number c is x, such that $x^n = c$. The nth root of c can be represented as $\sqrt[n]{c}$, where n is the **index** and c is the **radicand**.

Example

Solve the equation $2x^4 = 162$.

$2x^4 = 162$ Write the original equation.

$x^4 = 81$ Divide both sides by 2.

$(x^4)^{\frac{1}{4}} = (81)^{\frac{1}{4}}$ Raise both sides to the reciprocal of the exponent of x.

$x = 3$ Use the Power of a Power Property.

Practice & Problem Solving

What is the value of each expression? Round to the nearest hundredth, if necessary.

10. $\sqrt[4]{16^2}$

11. $-\sqrt[3]{25^6}$

Simplify each expression.

12. $\sqrt[3]{27x^{12}}$

13. $\sqrt[4]{16a^{24}b^8}$

Solve each equation.

14. $750 = 6y^3$

15. $1{,}280 = 5z^4$

16. **Communicate Precisely** Describe the relationship between a rational exponent and a root of a number x.

17. **Make Sense and Persevere** The function $d(t) = 9.8t^2$ represents how far an object falls, in meters, in t seconds. How long would it take a rock to fall from a height of 300 m? Round to the nearest hundredth of a second.

LESSON 4-2 Properties of Exponents and Radicals

Quick Review

To simplify radical expressions, look for factors that are perfect *n*th power factors.

The Product Property of Radicals and Quotient Property of Radicals can also be used to rewrite radical expressions.

Product Property of Radicals $\sqrt[n]{ab} = \sqrt[n]{a} \cdot \sqrt[n]{b}$

Quotient Property of Radicals $\sqrt[n]{\frac{a}{b}} = \frac{\sqrt[n]{a}}{\sqrt[n]{b}}$

Example

What is $\sqrt[4]{64} \cdot \sqrt[4]{2}$ in reduced radical form?

$\sqrt[4]{64} \cdot \sqrt[4]{2}$ .... Write the original expression.

$\sqrt[4]{64 \cdot 2}$ .... Use the Product Property of Radicals.

$\sqrt[4]{128}$ .... Multiply.

$\sqrt[4]{16} \cdot \sqrt[4]{8}$ .... Rewrite using the Product Property of Radicals.

$2\sqrt[4]{8}$ .... Simplify.

Practice & Problem Solving

What is the reduced radical form of each expression?

18. $\sqrt{x^6y^4} \cdot \sqrt{x^8y^6}$

19. $\sqrt[3]{\frac{243m^4}{3m}}$

20. $\sqrt[3]{5x^4} \cdot \sqrt[3]{x^2} \cdot \sqrt[3]{25x^3}$

21. $\sqrt{\frac{98a^{10}}{2a^4}}$

Multiply.

22. $(\sqrt{n} - \sqrt{7})(\sqrt{n} + 3\sqrt{7})$

23. $(9x + \sqrt{2})(9x + \sqrt{2})$

24. $(5\sqrt{3} + 6)(5\sqrt{3} - 6)$

25. $\sqrt[3]{4}(6\sqrt[3]{2} - 1)$

How can you rewrite each expression so there are no radicals in the denominator?

26. $\frac{6}{1 + \sqrt{2}}$

27. $\frac{5}{2 - \sqrt{5}}$

28. $\frac{4 + \sqrt{6}}{3 - 3\sqrt{6}}$

29. $\frac{-9x}{\sqrt{x}}$

30. **Error Analysis** Describe and correct the error made in rewriting the radical expression.
$5\sqrt{18} - \sqrt{27} = 7\sqrt{2}$

31. **Reason** A rectangular wall is $\sqrt{240}$ ft by $\sqrt{50}$ ft. You need to paint the wall twice to cover the area with two coats of paint. If each can of paint can cover 60 square feet, how many cans of paint will you need?

LESSON 4-3 Graphing Radical Functions

Quick Review

A **radical function** is a function defined by a radical expression. To determine transformations of a radical function, write the radical function in the form $h(x) = a\sqrt[n]{x - h} + k$ and compare it to the parent function.

Example

Graph $g(x) = 2\sqrt{x - 1} + 3$.

$g(x) = 2\sqrt{x - 1} + 3$ is a vertical stretch by a factor of 2, a horizontal shift 1 unit to the right, and a vertical shift 3 units up from the parent function $f(x) = \sqrt{x}$.

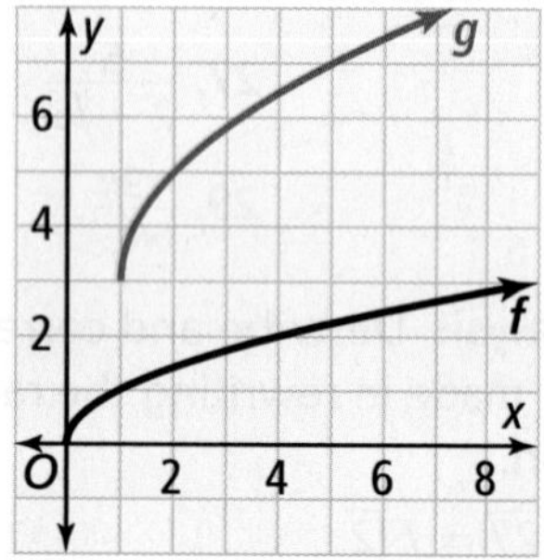

Practice & Problem Solving

Graph the following functions. What are the domain and range? Is the function increasing or decreasing?

32. $f(x) = \sqrt{x} - 1$

33. $f(x) = \sqrt[3]{x} + 2$

34. $f(x) = \frac{1}{2}\sqrt{x + 1}$

35. $f(x) = 2\sqrt[3]{x} - 1$

36. $f(x) = \sqrt[3]{x - 3}$

37. $f(x) = \sqrt{x + 4} - 2$

38. Communicate Precisely Explain how to rewrite the function $g(x) = \sqrt[3]{8x - 24} + 1$ to identify the transformations from the parent graph $f(x) = \sqrt[3]{x}$.

39. Reason The speed s, in miles per hour, of a car when it starts to skid can be estimated using the formula $s = \sqrt{30 \cdot 0.5d}$, where d is the length of the skid marks, in feet. Graph the function. If a car's skid marks measure 40 ft in a zone where the speed limit is 25 mph, was the car speeding? Explain.

LESSON 4-4 Solving Radical Equations

Quick Review

To solve a radical equation, isolate the radical. Raise both sides of the equation to the appropriate power to eliminate the radical and solve for x. Then check for **extraneous solutions**. If the equation includes more than one radical, eliminate one radical at a time using a similar process.

Example

Solve the radical equation $\sqrt{6 - x} = x$.

$\sqrt{6 - x} = x$	Write the original equation.
$(\sqrt{6 - x})^2 = (x)^2$	Square both sides.
$6 - x = x^2$	Simplify.
$0 = x^2 + x - 6$	Write in standard form.
$0 = (x + 3)(x - 2)$	Factor.
$x = -3$ or $x = 2$	Use the Zero-Product Property.

Check the solutions to see if they both make the original equation true.

Practice & Problem Solving

Solve each radical equation. Check for extraneous solutions.

40. $\sqrt[3]{x} - 2 = 7$

41. $\sqrt{2x} = 12$

42. $\sqrt{25 + x} + 5 = 9$

43. $13 - \sqrt[4]{x} = 10$

44. $\sqrt{5x + 1} + 1 = x$

45. $\sqrt{6x - 20} - x = -6$

46. Construct Arguments Give an example of a radical equation that has no real solutions. Explain your reasoning.

47. Make Sense and Persevere The formula $d = \frac{\sqrt{15w}}{3.14}$ gives the diameter d, in inches, of a rope needed to lift a weight of w, in tons. How much weight can be lifted with a rope that has a diameter of 4 in?

LESSON 4-5 Function Operations

Quick Review

You can add, subtract, multiply, or divide functions. When adding, subtracting, and multiplying functions, the domain is the intersection of the domains of the two functions. When dividing functions, the domain is the set of all real numbers for which both original functions and the new function are defined. You can also compose functions, by using one function as the input for another function. These are called **composite functions.**

Example

Let $f(x) = 5x$ and $g(x) = 3x - 1$. What is the rule for the composition $f \circ g$?

$f \circ g = f(g(x))$ ······ Apply the definition.

$= f(3x - 1)$ ······ Apply the rule for g.

$= 5(3x - 1)$ ······ Apply the rule for f.

$= 15x - 5$ ······ Distribute.

Practice & Problem Solving

Let $f(x) = -x + 6$ and $g(x) = 5x$. Identify the rule for the following functions.

48. $f + g$

49. $f - g$

50. $g(f(2))$

51. $f(g(-1))$

52. Reason For the functions f and g, what is the domain of $f \circ g$? $\frac{f}{g}$? $\frac{g}{f}$?

53. Make Sense and Persevere A test has a bonus problem. If you get the bonus problem correct, you will receive 2 bonus points and your test score will increase by 3% of your score. Let $f(x) = x + 2$ and $g(x) = 1.03x$, where x is the test score without the bonus problem. Find $g(f(78))$. What does $g(f(78))$ represent?

LESSON 4-6 Inverse Relations and Functions

Quick Review

An **inverse relation** is formed when the roles of the independent and dependent variables are reversed. If an inverse relation of a function, f, is itself a function, it is called the **inverse function** of f, which is written $f^{-1}(x)$.

Example

What is the inverse of the relation represented in the table?

x	y
−2	0
−1	6
0	5
1	3
3	−1

Switch the values of x and y. Then reorder the ordered pairs.

x	y
−1	3
0	−2
3	1
5	0
6	−1

Practice & Problem Solving

Find an equation of the inverse function.

54. $f(x) = -4x^2 + 3$

55. $f(x) = \sqrt{x - 4}$

56. $f(x) = 9x + 5$

57. $f(x) = \sqrt{x + 7} - 1$

58. Error Analysis Jamie said the inverse of $f(x) = \sqrt{x - 9}$ is $f^{-1}(x) = (x + 9)^2$. Is Jamie correct? Explain.

59. Make Sense and Persevere An electrician charges \$50 for a house visit plus \$40 per hour. Write a function for the cost C of an electrician charging for h hours. Find the inverse of the function. If the bill is \$150, how long did the electrician work?

TOPIC 4 REVIEW

TOPIC 5

Exponential and Logarithmic Functions

TOPIC ESSENTIAL QUESTION

How do you use exponential and logarithmic functions to model situations and solve problems?

Topic Overview

enVision® STEM Project:
Analyze Elections

5-1 Key Features of Exponential Functions

5-2 Exponential Models

Extension 5-2a: Analyzing Residuals

Mathematical Modeling in 3 Acts:
The Crazy Conditioning

5-3 Linear, Exponential, and Quadratic Models

5-4 Logarithms

5-5 Logarithmic Functions

5-6 Properties of Logarithms

5-7 Exponential and Logarithmic Equations

5-8 Geometric Sequences and Series

Topic Vocabulary

- Change of Base Formula
- common logarithm
- compound interest
- continuously compounded interest
- decay factor
- exponential equation
- exponential function
- exponential decay function
- exponential growth function
- growth factor
- logarithm
- logarithmic equation
- logarithmic function
- natural base *e*
- natural logarithm

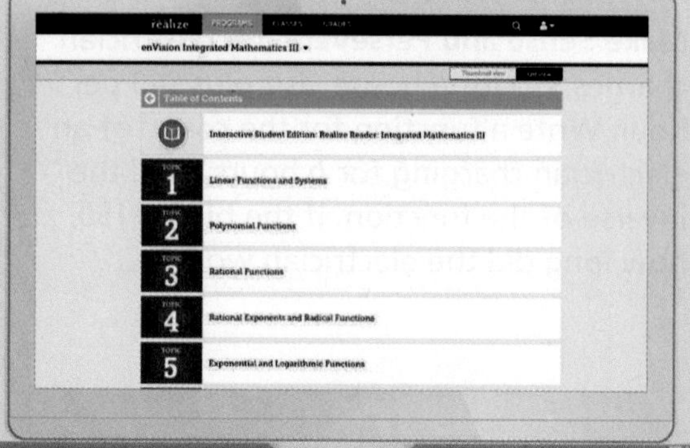

Go online | **PearsonRealize.com**

Digital Experience

INTERACTIVE STUDENT EDITION
Access online or offline.

ACTIVITIES Complete ***Explore & Reason, Model & Discuss***, and ***Critique & Explain*** activities. Interact with Examples and Try Its.

ANIMATION View and interact with real-world applications.

PRACTICE Practice what you've learned.

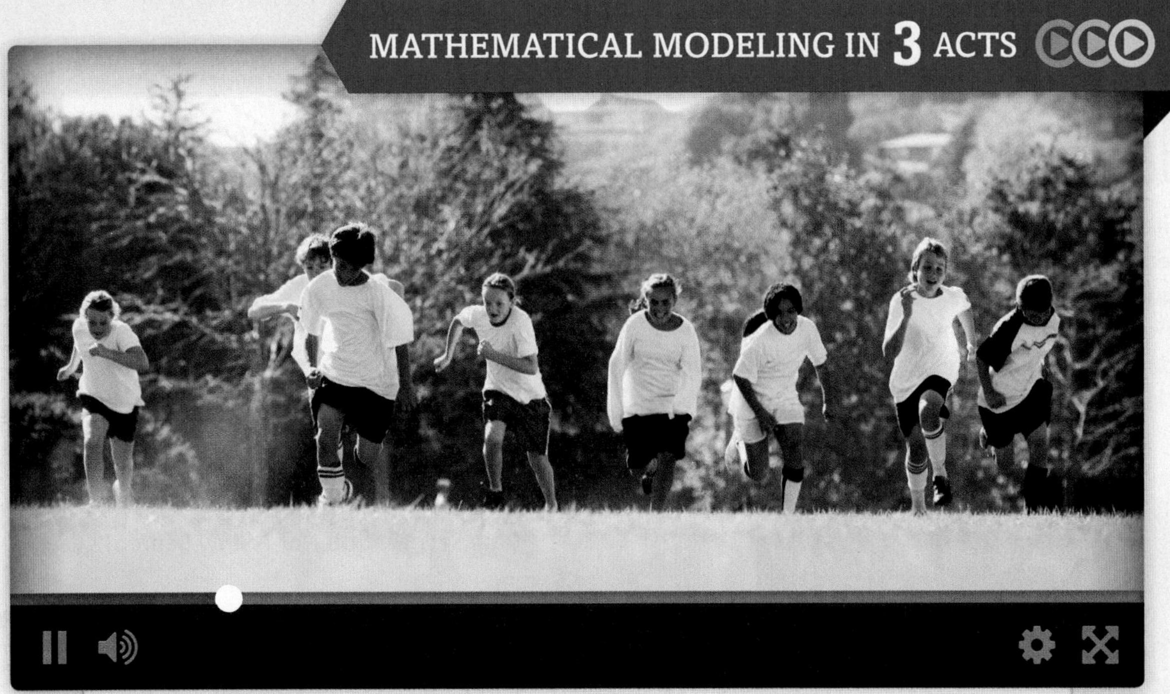

The Crazy Conditioning

Like all sports, soccer requires its players to be well trained. That is why players often have to run sprints in practice.

To make sprint drills more interesting, many coaches set up competitions. Coaches might split the players into teams and have them run relay races against each other. Or they might have the players sprint around cones and over barriers. What other ways would make doing sprints more fun? Think about this during the Mathematical Modeling in 3 Acts lesson.

TOPIC 5

VIDEOS Watch clips to support ***Mathematical Modeling in 3 Acts Lessons*** and **enVision® *STEM Projects.***

CONCEPT SUMMARY Review key lesson content through multiple representations.

ASSESSMENT Show what you've learned.

GLOSSARY Read and listen to English and Spanish definitions.

TUTORIALS Get help from ***Virtual Nerd***, right when you need it.

MATH TOOLS Explore math with digital tools and manipulatives.

Did You Know?

While you might expect the digits 1 through 9 to lead off the numbers in a data set with equal frequency, Benford's Law shows that they do not. Benford's Law states that, in real-world data, the leading digit is 1 more than 30% of the time, while the leading digit is 9 less than 5% of the time.

Data Sets That Follow Benford's Law

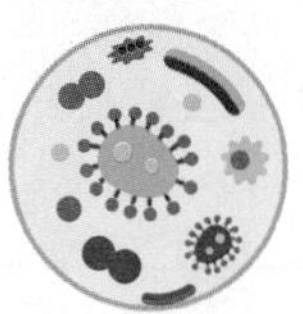

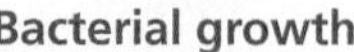

Bacterial growth | Expansion of 2^n | Price × Quantity

Data Sets That Do Not Follow Benford's Law

Price | Quantity | Zip Codes | Social Security numbers

Bacteria (plural of bacterium) exist in soil, water, plants, glaciers, hot springs, and the oceans. Bacteria grow by duplicating themselves, so a population grows by doubling. In a laboratory, a population can double at regular intervals. These intervals vary from about 12 minutes to as much as 24 hours.

Your Task: Analyze Elections

You and your classmates will use Benford's law to analyze election results and determine which, if any, may be fraudulent.

5-1 Key Features of Exponential Functions

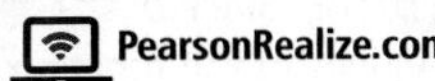
PearsonRealize.com

I CAN… recognize the key features of exponential functions.

VOCABULARY

- decay factor
- exponential decay function
- exponential function
- exponential growth function
- growth factor

EXPLORE & REASON

Margaret investigates three functions: $y = 3x$, $y = x^3$, and $y = 3^x$. She is interested in the differences and ratios between consecutive y-values. Here is the table she started for $y = 3x$.

Investigating y = 3x			
x	y	Difference between y-values	Ratio between y-values
1	3		
2	6	$6 - 3 = 3$	$\frac{6}{3} = 2$
3	9	$9 - 6 = 3$	$\frac{9}{6} = 1.5$
4	12	$12 - 9 = 3$	$\frac{12}{9} \approx 1.33$

A. Create tables like Margaret's for all three functions and fill in more rows.

B. Which functions have a constant difference between consecutive y-values? Constant ratio?

C. Use Structure Which of these three functions will have y-values that increase the fastest as x increases? Why?

ESSENTIAL QUESTION

How do graphs and equations reveal key features of exponential growth and decay functions?

EXAMPLE 1 Identify Key Features of Exponential Functions

What are the key features of each function? Include domain, range, intercepts, asymptotes, and end behavior.

An **exponential function** is any function of the form $y = a \cdot b^x$ where a and b are constants with $a \neq 0$, and $b > 0$, $b \neq 1$.

A. $f(x) = 2^x$

Graphing $y = a \cdot b^x$	
x	$f(x) = 2^x$
−2	0.25
−1	0.5
0	1
1	2
2	4

For f, $b = 2$. Since $b > 1$, the y-values of the function increase.

For $y = a \cdot b^x$, the value of a is the y-intercept.

STUDY TIP
Recall your investigation of the ratios of consecutive y-values in the Explore & Reason activity. That ratio, which was 3 for the function $y = 3^x$, is equal to the value of b in the equation $y = a \cdot b^x$.

Domain: all real numbers
Range: $\{y \mid y > 0\}$
y-intercept: 1;

Asymptote: x-axis
End Behavior:
As $x \to -\infty$, $y \to 0$. As $x \to \infty$, $y \to \infty$.

CONTINUED ON THE NEXT PAGE

EXAMPLE 1 CONTINUED

B. $g(x) = 5\left(\frac{1}{2}\right)^x$

Graphing $y = a \cdot b^x$	
x	$g(x) = 5\left(\frac{1}{2}\right)^x$
−2	20
−1	10
0	5
1	2.5
2	1.25

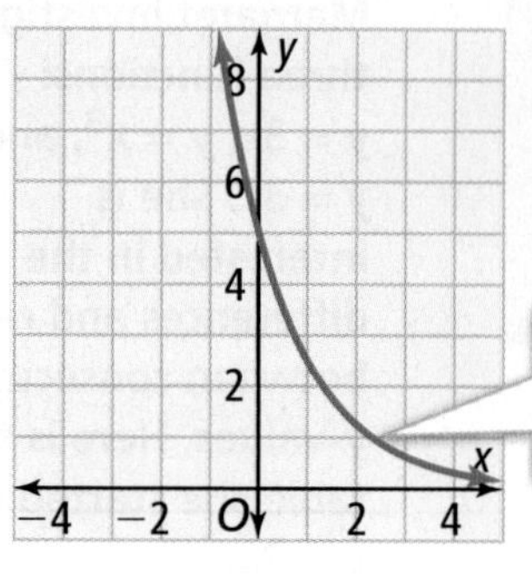

For g, $b = \frac{1}{2}$. Since $b < 1$, the y-values of the function decrease.

Domain: all real numbers
Range: $\{y \mid y > 0\}$
y-intercept: 5;
Asymptote: x-axis
End Behavior: As $x \to -\infty$, $y \to \infty$.
As $x \to \infty$, $y \to 0$.

 **Try It!** 1. Graph $f(x) = 4(0.5)^x$. What are the domain, range, intercepts, asymptote, and the end behavior for this function?

EXAMPLE 2 Graph Transformations of Exponential Functions

Graph each function. Describe the graph in terms of transformations of the parent function $f(x) = 3^x$. How do the asymptote and intercept of the given function compare to the asymptote and intercept of the parent function?

COMMON ERROR
You may confuse reflection across the axes. Recall that if the y-value is multiplied by −1 (as in this case, with $g(x) = -3^x$), the reflection is across the x-axis. Each y-value is replaced by its opposite.

A. $g(x) = -3^x$

When the sign of a changes, the function is reflected across the x-axis.

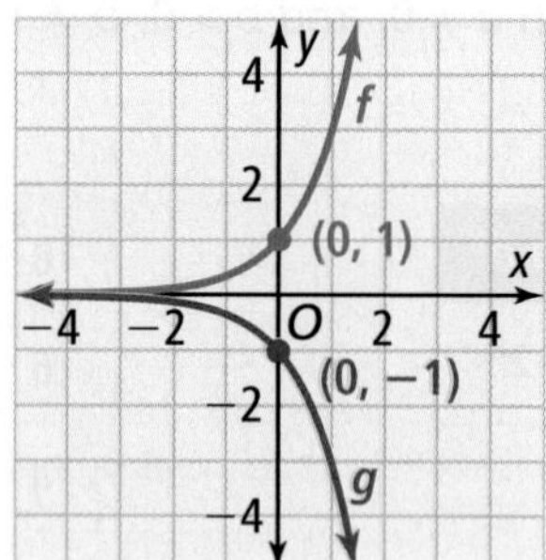

$g(x) = -3^x = -f(x)$

The intercept changes from a to $-a$.

The asymptote of the function does not change. It is still the x-axis.

B. $h(x) = 3^x - 4$

When adding a constant k, the function shifts vertically by k units.

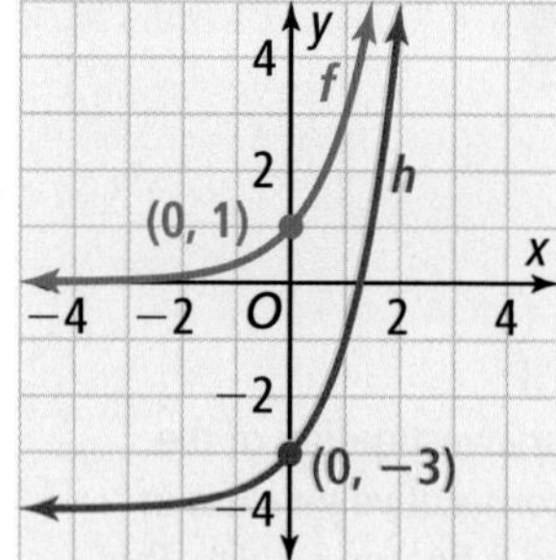

$h(x) = 3^x - 4 = f(x) - 4$

The intercept changes from 1 to $1 + K$.

The asymptote of the function also changes. It is $y = k$ or $y = -4$.

 **Try It!** 2. How do the asymptote and intercept of the given function compare to the asymptote and intercept of the function $f(x) = 5^x$?

a. $g(x) = 5^{x+3}$

b. $h(x) = 5^{-x}$

  Activity  Assess

CONCEPTUAL UNDERSTANDING

EXAMPLE 3 Model with Exponential Functions

The population of a large city was about 4.6 million in the year 2010 and grew at a rate of 1.3% for the next four years.

A. What exponential function models the population of the city over that 4-year period?

Compute the population for the first few years to look for a pattern.

USE STRUCTURE
Exponential functions of the form $y = a \cdot b^x$ involve repeated multiplication by the factor b. To understand how to model population with an exponential function, look for repeated multiplication in your computations.

The population can be modeled by the exponential function:

$$P = 4.6(1.013)^t$$

B. If the population continues to grow at the same rate, what will the population be in 2040?

To find the population in 2040, solve the equation for $t = 30$:

$P = 4.6(1.013)^{30} \approx 6.78.$

In 2040, the population will be about 6.78 million.

 **Try It!** 3. A factory purchased a 3D printer in 2010. The value of the printer is modeled by the function $f(x) = 30(0.93)^x$, where x is the number of years since 2010.

a. What is the value of the printer after 10 years?

b. Does the printer lose more of its value in the first 10 years or in the second 10 years after it was purchased?

Activity Assess

CONCEPT Exponential Growth and Decay Models

Exponential growth and **exponential decay** functions model quantities that increase or decrease by a fixed percent during each time period. Given an initial amount a and the rate of increase or decrease r, the amount $A(t)$ after t time periods is given by:

Exponential Growth Model	Exponential Decay Model
$A(t) = a(1 + r)^t$	$A(t) = a(1 - r)^t$
$a > 0, b > 1, b = 1 + r$	$a > 0, 0 < b < 1, b = 1 - r$

The **growth or decay factor** is equal to b, and is the ratio between two consecutive y-values.

EXAMPLE 4 Interpret an Exponential Function

A car was purchased for \$24,000. The function $y = 24 \cdot 0.8^x$ can be used to model the value of the car (in thousands of dollars) x years after it was purchased.

A. Does the function represent exponential growth or decay?

$$y = 24 \cdot 0.8^x$$

$b = 0.8$, so $b < 1$ and the function represents exponential decay.

B. What is the rate of decay for this function? What does it mean?

$$b = 1 - r$$
$$0.8 = 1 - r$$
$$r = 0.2$$

STUDY TIP
For a function of the form $y = a \cdot b^x$, if $b > 1$, the function is increasing. If $0 < b < 1$, the function is decreasing.

The rate of decay is 0.2, or 20%. This means that the value of the car decreases by 20% each year.

C. Graph the function on a reasonable domain. What do the y-intercept and asymptote represent? When will the value of the car be about \$5,000?

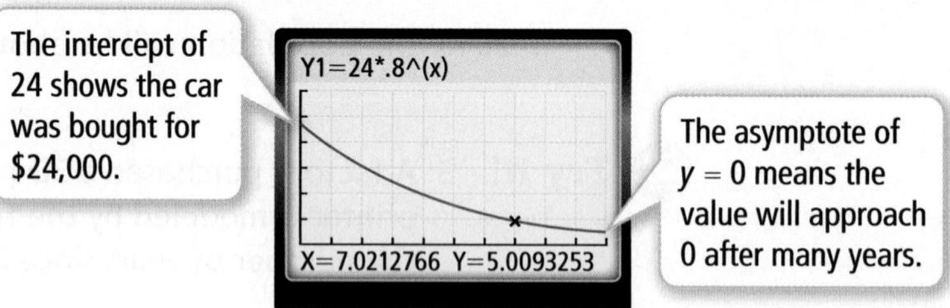

Find the value of x when $y = 5$.

The graph (approximately) passes through the point (7, 5). This means that the value of the car will be about \$5,000 after 7 years.

CONTINUED ON THE NEXT PAGE

Try It! 4. Two-hundred twenty hawks were released into a region on January 2, 2016. The function $f(x) = 220(1.05)^x$ can be used to model the number of hawks in the region x years after 2016.

a. Is the population increasing or decreasing? Explain.

b. In what year will the number of hawks reach 280?

APPLICATION

EXAMPLE 5 Compare Two Exponential Functions

A museum purchased a painting and a sculpture in the same year. Their changing values are modeled as shown. Find the average rate of change of the value of each art work over the 5-year period. Which art work's value is increasing more quickly?

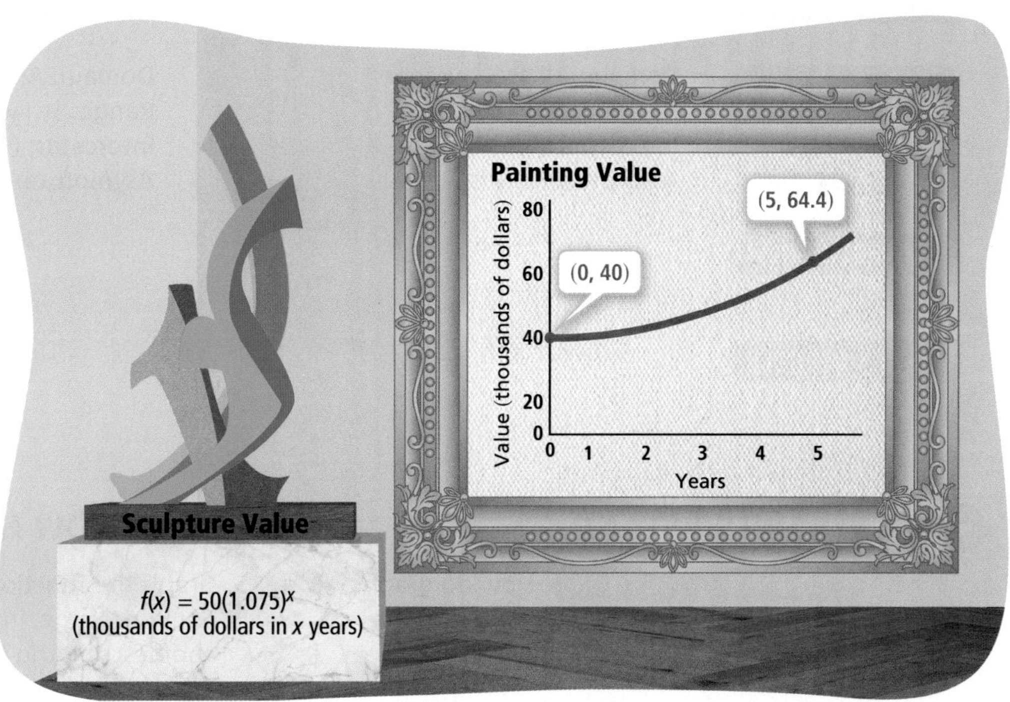

Sculpture

$$f(0) = 50(1.075)^0 = 50$$

$$f(5) = 50(1.075)^5 \approx 71.78$$

$$\frac{y_2 - y_1}{x_2 - x_1} = \frac{71.78 - 50}{5 - 0} = \frac{21.78}{5} = 4.356$$

The sculpture's value increased at an average of $4,356 per year.

Painting

$$\frac{y_2 - y_1}{x_2 - x_1} = \frac{64.4 - 40}{5 - 0} = \frac{24.4}{5} = 4.88$$

The painting's value increased at an average of $4,880 per year.

MODEL WITH MATHEMATICS
The average rate of change of $f(x)$ from x_1 to x_2 is the slope of the line containing the points $(x_1, f(x_1))$ and $(x_2, (f(x_2))$.

Over the 5-year period, the value of the painting increased at a greater average rate than the value of the sculpture.

Try It! 5. In Example 5, will the value of the painting ever surpass the value of the sculpture according to the models? Explain.

 CONCEPT SUMMARY Key Features of Exponential Functions

	Exponential Growth	Exponential Decay
GRAPHS	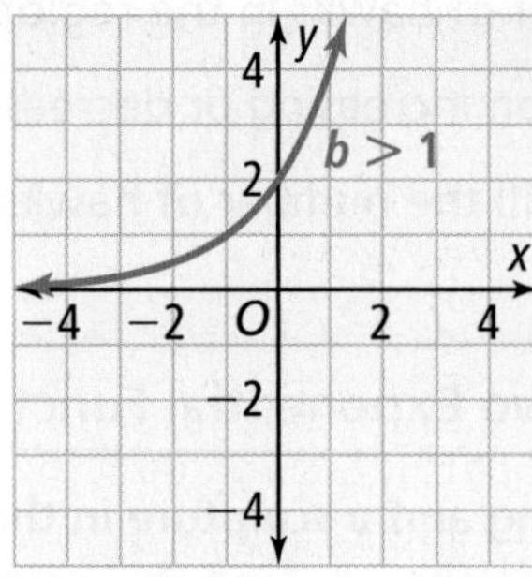 Growth factor: $1 + r$	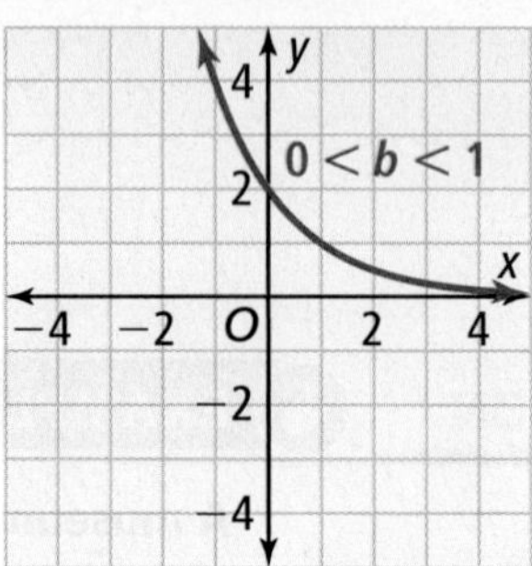 Decay factor: $1 - r$
EQUATIONS	$y = a \cdot b^x$, for $b > 1$	$y = a \cdot b^x$, for $0 < b < 1$
KEY FEATURES	Domain: All real numbers Range: $\{y \mid y \geq 0\}$ Intercepts: $(0, a)$ Asymptote: x-axis	Domain: All real numbers Range: $\{y \mid y \geq 0\}$ Intercepts: $(0, a)$ Asymptote: x-axis
END BEHAVIOR	As $x \to -\infty$, $y \to 0$ As $x \to \infty$, $y \to \infty$	As $x \to -\infty$, $y \to \infty$ As $x \to \infty$, $y \to 0$
MODELS	Growth: $A(t) = a(1 + r)^t$	Decay: $A(t) = a(1 - r)^t$

Do You UNDERSTAND?

1. ESSENTIAL QUESTION How do graphs and equations reveal key features of exponential growth and decay functions?

2. **Vocabulary** How do *exponential functions* differ from polynomial and rational functions?

3. **Error Analysis** Charles claimed the function $f(x) = \left(\frac{3}{2}\right)^x$ represents exponential decay. Explain the error Charles made.

4. **Communicate Precisely** How are exponential growth functions similar to exponential decay functions? How are they different?

Do You KNOW HOW?

5. Graph the function $f(x) = 4 \times 3^x$. Identify the domain, range, intercept, and asymptote, and describe the end behavior.

6. The exponential function $f(x) = 2500(0.4)^x$ models the amount of money in Zachary's savings account over the last 10 years. Is Zachary's account balance increasing or decreasing? Write the base in terms of the rate of growth or decay.

7. Describe how the graph of $g(x) = 4(0.5)^{x-3}$ compares to the graph of $f(x) = 4(0.5)^x$.

8. Two trucks were purchased by a landscaping company in 2016. Their values are modeled by the functions $f(x) = 35(0.85)^x$ and $g(x) = 46(0.75)^x$ where x is the number of years since 2016. Which function models the truck that is worth the most after 5 years? Explain.

PRACTICE & PROBLEM SOLVING

Scan for Multimedia

Additional Exercises Available Online

UNDERSTAND

9. Use Structure What value of a completes the equation $y = a \cdot 2^x$ for the exponential growth function shown below?

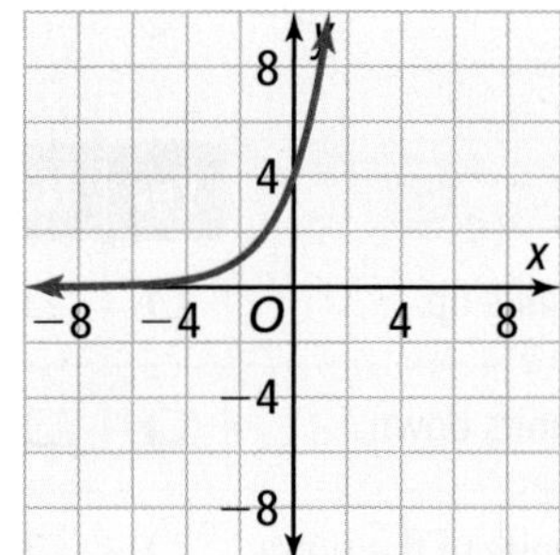

10. Make Sense and Persevere Cindy found a collection of baseball cards in her attic worth \$8,000. The collection is estimated to increase in value by 1.5% per year. Write an exponential growth function and find the value of the collection after 7 years.

11. Error Analysis Describe and correct the error a student made in identifying the growth or decay factor for the function $y = 2.55(0.7)^x$.

Step 1 The base of the function is 0.7, so it represents exponential decay.

Step 2 The function in the form $y = a(1 - r)^x$ is $y = 2.55(1 - 0.7)^x$.

Step 3 The decay factor is 0.3.

12. Reason In 2000, the population of St. Louis was 346,904, and it decreased to 319,257 in 2010. If this population decrease were modeled by an exponential decay function, what value would represent the y-intercept? Explain your reasoning.

13. Mathematical Connections Describe how the graph of $g(x) = 6 \cdot 2^{x+1} - 4$ compares to the graph of $f(x) = 6 \cdot 2^x$.

PRACTICE

Identify the domain, range, intercept, and asymptote of each exponential function. Then describe the end behavior. SEE EXAMPLE 1

14. $f(x) = 5 \cdot 3^x$

15. $f(x) = 0.75\left(\frac{2}{3}\right)^x$

16. $f(x) = 4\left(\frac{1}{2}\right)^x$

17. $f(x) = 7 \cdot 2^x$

Determine whether each function represents exponential growth or decay. Write the base in terms of the rate of growth or decay, identify *r*, and interpret the rate of growth or decay.
SEE EXAMPLES 3 AND 4

18. $y = 100 \cdot 2.5^x$

19. $f(x) = 10{,}200\left(\frac{3}{5}\right)^x$

20. $f(x) = 12{,}000\left(\frac{7}{10}\right)^x$

21. $y = 450 \cdot 2^x$

22. The function $f(x)$, shown in the graph, represents an exponential growth function. Compare the average rate of change of $f(x)$ to the average rate of change of the exponential growth function $g(x) = 25\,(1.4)^x$. Use the interval [0, 4]. SEE EXAMPLE 5

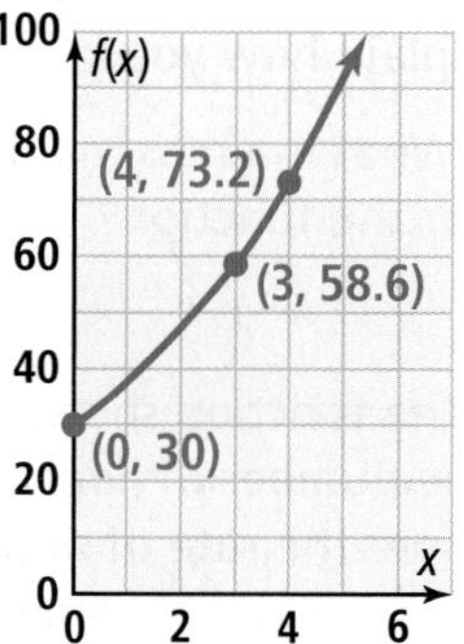

23. Write a function $g(x)$ that represents the exponential function $f(x) = 2^x$ after a vertical stretch of 6 and a reflection across the x-axis. Graph both functions. SEE EXAMPLE 2

24. The population of Medway, Ohio, was 4,007 in 2000. It is expected to decrease by about 0.36% per year. Write an exponential decay function and use it to approximate the population in 2020. SEE EXAMPLE 4

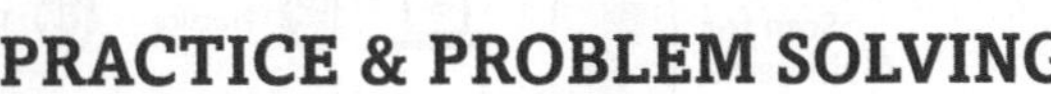

PRACTICE & PROBLEM SOLVING

Practice Tutorial

Mixed Review Available Online

APPLY

25. **Model With Mathematics** A colony of bacteria starts with 50 organisms and quadruples each day. Write an exponential function, $P(t)$, that represents the population of the bacteria after t days. Then find the number of bacteria that will be in the colony after 5 days.

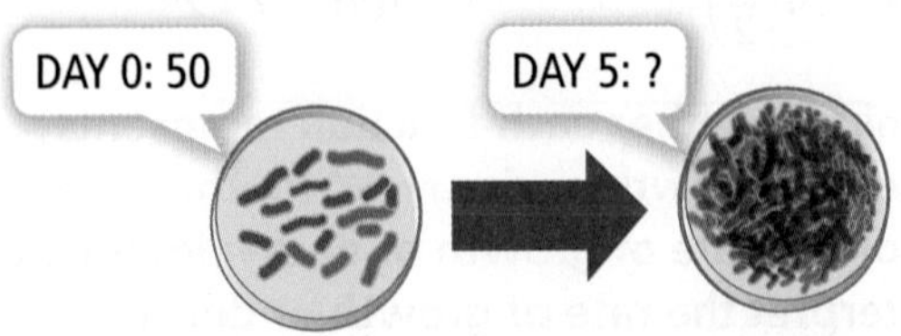

26. **Higher Order Thinking** The number of teams y remaining in a single elimination tournament can be found using the exponential function $y = 128\left(\frac{1}{2}\right)^x$, where x is the number of rounds played in the tournament.
    a. Determine whether the function represents exponential growth or decay. Explain.
    b. What does 128 represent in the function?
    c. What percent of the teams are eliminated after each round? Explain how you know.
    d. Graph the function. What is a reasonable domain and range for the function? Explain.

27. **Construct Arguments** The function shown in the graph represents the number of lions in a region after x years, where the rate of decay is 20%. The number of zebras in that same region after x years can be modeled by the function $f(x) = 300(0.95)^x$. A representative for a conservationist group claims there will be fewer lions than zebras within 2 years. Is the representative correct? Justify your answer.

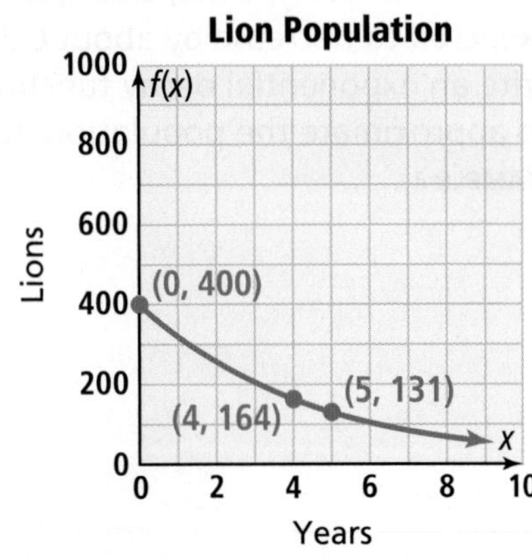

ASSESSMENT PRACTICE

28. The exponential function $g(x) = 3^{x-1} + 6$ is a transformation of the function $f(x) = 3^x$. Does each statement accurately describe how the graph of $g(x)$ compares to the graph of $f(x)$? Select yes or no.

	Yes	No
a. $g(x)$ is translated 6 units up.	❑	❑
b. $g(x)$ is translated 6 units down.	❑	❑
c. $g(x)$ is translated 6 units to the right.	❑	❑
d. $g(x)$ is translated 1 unit to the right.	❑	❑
e. $g(x)$ is translated 1 unit to the left.	❑	❑
f. The horizontal asymptote shifts 1 unit down.	❑	❑

29. **SAT/ACT** Which of the functions defined below could be the one shown in this graph?

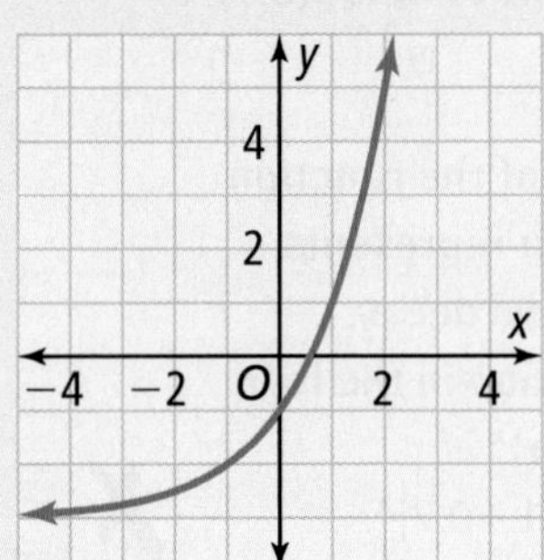

Ⓐ $f(x) = 4(2)^{x-1} + 3$

Ⓑ $f(x) = 4(2)^{x+1} + 3$

Ⓒ $f(x) = 4(2)^{x-1} - 3$

Ⓓ $f(x) = 4(2)^{x+1} - 3$

30. **Performance Task** A radioactive isotope of the element osmium Os-182 has a half-life of 21.5 hours. This means that if there are 100 grams of Os-182 in a sample, after 21.5 hours there will only be 50 grams of that isotope remaining.

Part A Write an exponential decay function to model the amount of Os-182 in a sample over time. Use A_0 for the initial amount and A for the amount after time t in hours.

Part B Use your model to predict how long it would take a sample containing 500 g of Os-182 to decay to the point where it contained only 5 g of Os-182.

5-2 Exponential Models

PearsonRealize.com

I CAN... write exponential models in different ways to solve problems.

VOCABULARY

- compound interest formula
- continuously compounded interest formula
- natural base e

EXPLORE & REASON

Juan is studying exponential growth of bacteria cultures. Each is carefully controlled to maintain a specific growth rate. Copy and complete the table to find the number of bacteria cells in each culture.

Culture	Initial Number of Bacteria	Growth Rate per Day	Time (days)	Final Number of Bacteria
A	10,000	8%	1	
B	10,000	4%	2	
C	10,000	2%	4	
D	10,000	1%	8	

A. What is the relationship between the daily growth rate and the time in days for each culture?

B. Look for Relationships Would you expect a culture with a growth rate of $\frac{1}{2}$% and a time of 16 days to have more or fewer cells than the others in the table? Explain.

ESSENTIAL QUESTION

How can you develop exponential models to represent and interpret situations?

EXAMPLE 1 Rewrite an Exponential Function to Identify a Rate

In 2015, the population of a small town was 8,000. The population is increasing at a rate of 2.5% per year. Rewrite an exponential growth function to find the monthly growth rate.

Write an exponential growth function using the annual rate to model the town's population y, in t years after 2015.

$$y = 8{,}000(1 + 0.025)^t$$

$$y = 8{,}000(1.025)^t$$

initial population: 8,000; annual growth rate: 0.025; years after 2015: t

To identify the monthly growth rate, you need the exponent to be the number of months in t years, or $12t$.

$$y = 8{,}000(1.025)^{\frac{12t}{12}}$$

Multiply the exponent by $\frac{12}{12}$ so that $12t$ represents the number of months.

$$y = 8{,}000\left(1.025^{\frac{1}{12}}\right)^{12t}$$

$$y \approx 8{,}000(1.00206)^{12t}$$

Applying the Power of a Power rule helps to reveal the monthly growth rate by producing an expression with the exponent $12t$.

The monthly growth rate is about $1.00206 - 1 = 0.00206$. The population is increasing about 0.206% per month.

COMMON ERROR
Dividing the annual growth rate by 12 does not give the exact monthly growth rate. This Example shows how to find an expression for the exact monthly rate: $1.025^{\frac{1}{12}} - 1$.

Try It! 1. The population in a small town is increasing annually by 1.8%. What is the quarterly rate of population increase?

CONCEPT Compound Interest

When interest is paid monthly, the interest earned after the first month becomes part of the new principal for the second month, and so on. Interest is earned on interest already earned. This is compound interest.

The **compound interest formula** is an exponential model that is used to calculate the value of an investment when interest is compounded.

$$A = P\left(1 + \frac{r}{n}\right)^{nt}$$

P = the initial principal invested

r = annual interest rate, written as a decimal

n = number of compounding periods per year

A = the value of the account after t years

EXAMPLE 2 Understand Compound Interest

Tamira invests $5,000 in an account that pays 4% annual interest. How much will there be in the account after 3 years if the interest is compounded annually, semi-annually, quarterly, or monthly?

Use the Compound Interest formula to find the amount in Tamira's account after 3 years.

	Compound Interest Formula	Amount After 3 Years ($)
Annually	$A = 5000\left(1+\frac{0.04}{1}\right)^{3(1)}$	5,624.32
Semi-Annually	$A = 5000\left(1+\frac{0.04}{2}\right)^{3(2)}$	5,630.81
Quarterly	$A = 5000\left(1+\frac{0.04}{4}\right)^{3(4)}$	5,634.13
Monthly	$A = 5000\left(1+\frac{0.04}{12}\right)^{3(12)}$	5,636.36

REASON
The more frequently interest is added to the account, the earlier that interest generates more interest. This reasoning supports the trend shown in the table.

As the number of compounding periods increases, the amount in the account also increases.

Try It! 2. $3,000 is invested in an account that earns 3% annual interest, compounded monthly.

a. What is the value of the account after 10 years?

b. What is the value of the account after 100 years?

CONCEPTUAL UNDERSTANDING

EXAMPLE 3 Understanding Continuously Compounded Interest

Consider an investment of $1 in an account that pays a 100% annual interest rate for one year. The equation $A = 1\left(1 + \frac{1}{n}\right)^{n(1)} = \left(1 + \frac{1}{n}\right)^{n}$ gives the amount in the account after one year for the number of compounding periods n. Find the value of the account for the number of periods given in the table.

Number of Periods, n	Value of $\left(1 + \frac{1}{n}\right)^{n}$
1	$\left(1 + \frac{1}{1}\right)^{1} = 2$
10	$\left(1 + \frac{1}{10}\right)^{10} = 2.59374246$
100	$\left(1 + \frac{1}{100}\right)^{100} = 2.704813829$
1000	$\left(1 + \frac{1}{1{,}000}\right)^{1{,}000} = 2.716923932$
10000	$\left(1 + \frac{1}{10{,}000}\right)^{10{,}000} = 2.718145927$
100000	$\left(1 + \frac{1}{100{,}000}\right)^{100{,}000} = 2.718268237$

Notice that as n continues to increase, the value of the account remains very close to 2.718. This special number is called the *natural base.*

The **natural base e** is defined as the value that the expression $\left(1 + \frac{1}{x}\right)^{x}$ approaches as $x \to +\infty$. The number e is an irrational number.

$$e = 2.718281828459\ldots$$

The number e is the base in the **continuously compounded interest formula**.

$A = Pe^{rt}$
- P = the initial principal invested
- e = the natural base
- r = annual interest rate, written as a decimal
- A = the value of the account after t years

Try It! 3. If you continued the table for $n = 1{,}000{,}000$, would the value in the account increase or decrease? How do you know?

EXAMPLE 4 Find Continuously Compounded Interest

Regina invests \$12,600 in an account that earns 3.2% annual interest, compounded continuously. What is the value of the account after 12 years? Round your answer to the nearest dollar.

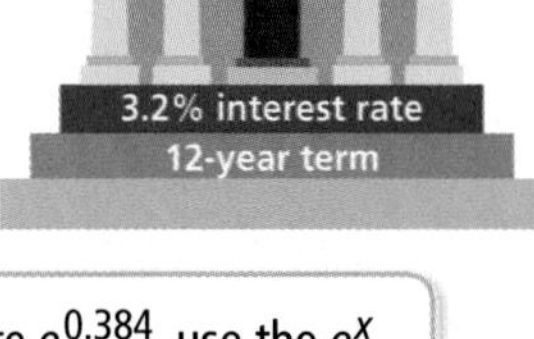

Use the continuously compounded interest formula with $P = 12{,}600$, $r = 0.032$, and $t = 12$.

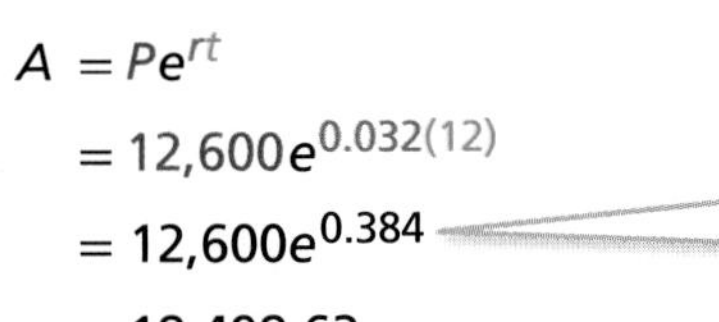

$$\begin{aligned} A &= Pe^{rt} \\ &= 12{,}600e^{0.032(12)} \\ &= 12{,}600e^{0.384} \\ &\approx 18{,}498.63 \end{aligned}$$

To evaluate $e^{0.384}$, use the e^x key on your calculator.

To the nearest dollar, the value of the account after 12 years is \$18,499.

COMMON ERROR
Be sure that when you evaluate $e^{0.032(12)}$ you either simplify 0.032(12) as 0.384 first, or use parentheses to ensure that e is raised to the entire product, rather than just the first factor.

CONTINUED ON THE NEXT PAGE

 **Try It!** 4. You invest $125,000 in an account that earns 4.75% annual interest, compounded continuously.

a. What is the value of the account after 15 years?

b. What is the value of the account after 30 years?

APPLICATION

EXAMPLE 5 Use Two Points to Find an Exponential Model

Tia knew that the number of e-mails she sent was growing exponentially. She generated a record of the number of e-mails she sent each year since 2009. What is an exponential model that describes the data?

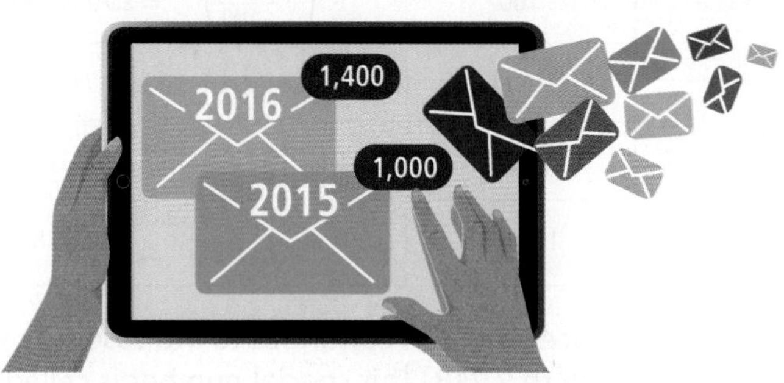

Write an exponential model in the form $y = a \bullet b^x$, with y equal to the number of e-mails in hundreds and x equal to the number of years since 2009. Use the data to find the values of the constants a and b.

COMMON ERROR
Remember that the growth factor $(1 + r)$ is different from the growth rate (r). In this example, the growth factor is 1.4 while the growth rate is 0.4, or 40%.

The growth factor for Tia's e-mails in the two consecutive years was $\frac{14}{10}$, or 1.4.

When data points have consecutive x-values, the growth factor, b, is the ratio of their y-values.

Use the value of b and one of the data points to find the initial value, a.

$y = a \bullet b^x$ .... Write an exponential growth equation.

$14 = a(1.4)^7$ .... Substitute 1.4 for b, 7 for x, and 14 for y.

$\frac{14}{(1.4)^7} = a$ .... Division Property of Equality

$1.33 \approx a$ .... Simplify.

So, the function $y = 1.33(1.4)^x$ models the number of e-mails (in hundreds) Tia sends x years after 2009.

 **Try It!** 5. A surveyor determined the value of an area of land over a period of several years since 1950. The land was worth $31,000 in 1954 and $35,000 in 1955. Use the data to determine an exponential model that describes the value of the land.

APPLICATION

EXAMPLE 6 Use Regression to Find an Exponential Model

Randy is making soup. The soup reaches the boiling point and then, as shown by the data, begins to cool off. Randy wants to serve the soup when it is about 80°F, or about 10 degrees above room temperature (68°F).

x, time (min)	y, Temperature °F
00:00	212°F
02:00	185°F
03:30	170°F
05:00	162°F
07:30	145°F
10:00	138°F
15:00	125°F
20:00	117°F

A. Explain why the temperature might follow an exponential decay curve as it approaches room temperature.

A scatter plot of the data shows the soup cooling toward room temperature. The graph is not a line.

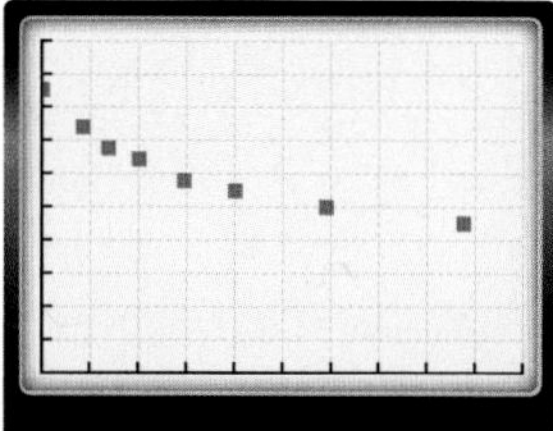

The rate of cooling appears to slow as the graph approaches room temperature, around 68° F. This indicates exponential decay toward an asymptote of $y = 68$.

B. Find an exponential model for the data. Use your model to determine when Randy should serve the soup.

Step 1 Enter the data as lists in a graphing calculator. Because the temperature values approach 68°F, subtract 68 from each temperature value.

Most graphing calculators will only calculate exponential regressions for data values that approach 0. You can subtract 68 so your data will approach 0. Then you can undo the adjustment in **Step 3** below.

L1	L2	L3 2
2	117	
3.5	102	
5	94	
7.5	77	
10	70	
15	57	
20	49	

L2(8)=49

STUDY TIP
The procedure for determining an exponential regression model for data may be slightly different on your graphing calculator, but the steps should be very similar.

Step 2 Use the calculator to find an exponential regression equation. The exponential model that best fits the data is $y = 126.35(0.9492)^x$.

Step 3 Translate this function up vertically by 68 units.

The translated model is $y = 126.35(0.9492)^x + 68$.

Use the translated model to find when the soup has a temperature of about 80°F.

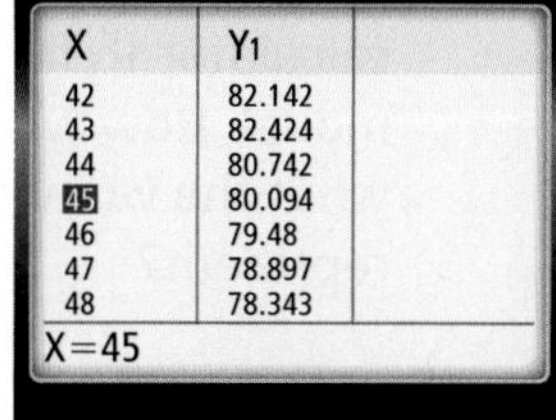

X	Y1
42	82.142
43	82.424
44	80.742
45	80.094
46	79.48
47	78.897
48	78.343

X=45

The soup has a temperature of about 80°F after 45 minutes.

So, Randy should serve the soup about 45 minutes after it begins to cool.

Try It! **6.** According to the model in Example 6, what was the approximate temperature 35 minutes after cooling started?

CONCEPT SUMMARY Writing Exponential Models

	General Exponential Model	Compound Interest	Continuously Compounded Interest
ALGEBRA	$y = a \cdot b^x$	$A = P\left(1 + \frac{r}{n}\right)^{nt}$	$A = Pe^{rt}$
NUMBERS	A necklace costs \$250 and increases in value by 2% per year. $a =$ initial amount \$250 $b =$ growth factor 1.02 $x =$ number of years $y = 250(1.02)^x$	A principal of \$3,000 is invested at 5% annual interest, compounded monthly, for 4 years. $P = 3{,}000$ $r = 5\%$ $n = 12$ compounding periods per year $t = 4$ years $A = 3000\left(1 + \frac{0.05}{12}\right)^{(12)(4)}$	A principal of \$3,000 is invested at 5% continuously compounded interest for 4 years. $P = 3{,}000$ $r = 5\%$ $t = 4$ years $A = 3000e^{(0.05)(4)}$

Do You UNDERSTAND?

1. ESSENTIAL QUESTION Why do you develop exponential models to represent and interpret situations?

2. **Error Analysis** The exponential model $y = 5{,}000(1.05)^t$ represents the amount Yori earns in an account after t years when \$5,000 is invested. Yori said the monthly interest rate of the exponential model is 5%. Explain Yori's error.

3. **Vocabulary** Explain the similarities and differences between compound interest and continuously compounded interest.

4. **Communicate Precisely** Kylee is using a calculator to find an exponential regression model. How would you explain to Kylee what the variables in the model $y = a \cdot b^x$ represent?

Do You KNOW HOW?

The exponential function models the annual rate of increase. Find the monthly and quarterly rates.

5. $f(t) = 2{,}000(1.03)^t$

6. $f(t) = 500(1.055)^t$

Find the total amount of money in an account at the end of the given time period.

7. compounded monthly, $P = \$2{,}000$, $r = 3\%$, $t = 5$ years

8. continuously compounded, $P = \$1{,}500$, $r = 1.5\%$, $t = 6$ years

Write an exponential model given two points.

9. (3, 55) and (4, 70)

10. (7, 12) and (8, 25)

11. Paul invests \$6,450 in an account that earns continuously compounded interest at an annual rate of 2.8%. What is the value of the account after 8 years?

PRACTICE & PROBLEM SOLVING

Scan for Multimedia

Practice Tutorial

Additional Exercises Available Online

UNDERSTAND

12. **Error Analysis** Suppose \$6,500 is invested in an account that earns interest at a rate of 2% compounded quarterly for 10 years. Describe and correct the error a student made when finding the value of the account.

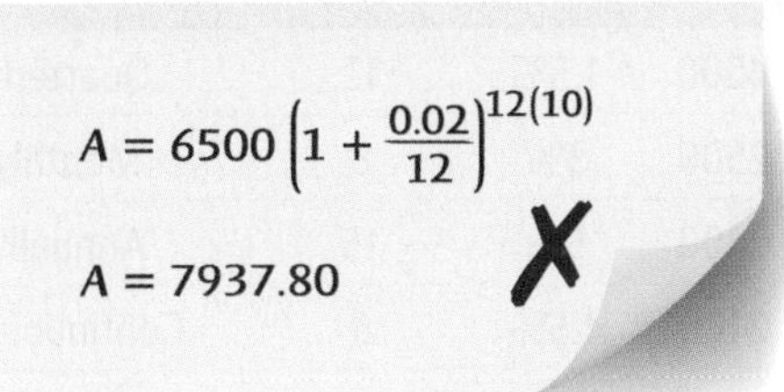

$$A = 6500\left(1 + \frac{0.02}{12}\right)^{12(10)}$$

$$A = 7937.80$$

13. **Communicate Precisely** The points (2, 54.61) and (4, 403.48) are points on the graph of an exponential model in the form $y = a \cdot e^x$.

    a. Explain how to write the exponential model, and then write the model.

    b. How can you use the exponential model to find the value of y when $x = 8$?

14. **Model with Mathematics** Use the points listed in the table for years 7 and 8 to find an exponential model. Then use a calculator to find an exponential model for the data. Explain how to find each model. Predict the amount in the account after 15 years.

Time (yr)	Amount (\$)
1	3,225
2	3,500
3	3,754
4	4,042
5	4,368
6	4,702
7	5,063
8	5,456

15. **Higher Order Thinking** A power model is a type of function in the form $y = a \cdot x^b$. Use the points (1, 4), (2, 8), (3, 16) and (4, 64) and a calculator to find an exponential model and a power model for the data. Then use each model to predict the value of y when $x = 6$. Graph the points and models in the same window. What do you notice?

PRACTICE

Find the amount in the account for the given principal, interest rate, time, and compounding period. SEE EXAMPLES 2 AND 4

16. $P = 800$, $r = 6\%$, $t = 9$ years; compounded quarterly

17. $P = 3{,}750$, $r = 3.5\%$, $t = 20$ years; compounded monthly

18. $P = 2{,}400$, $r = 5.25\%$, $t = 12$ years; compounded semi-annually

19. $P = 1{,}500$, $r = 4.5\%$, $t = 3$ years; compounded daily

20. $P = \$1{,}000$, $r = 2.8\%$, $t = 5$ years; compounded continuously

21. $P = \$16{,}000$, $r = 4\%$, $t = 25$ years; compounded continuously

Write an exponential model given two points.
SEE EXAMPLE 5

22. (9, 140) and (10, 250)

23. (6, 85) and (7, 92)

24. (10, 43) and (11, 67)

25. In 2012, the population of a small town was 3,560. The population is decreasing at a rate of 1.7% per year. How can you rewrite an exponential growth function to find the quarterly decay rate? SEE EXAMPLE 1

26. Selena took a pizza out of the oven and it started to cool to room temperature (68°F). She will serve the pizza when it reaches 150°F. She took the pizza out of the oven at 5:00 P.M. When can she serve it? SEE EXAMPLE 6

Time (min)	Temperature (°F)
5	310
8	264
10	238
15	202
20	186
25	175

Practice Tutorial

Mixed Review Available Online

PRACTICE & PROBLEM SOLVING

APPLY

27. Reason Adam invests \$8,000 in an account that earns 1.25% interest, compounded quarterly for 20 years. On the same date, Jacinta invests \$8,000 in an account that earns continuous compounded interest at a rate of 1.25% for 20 years. Who do you predict will have more money in their account after 20 years? Explain your reasoning.

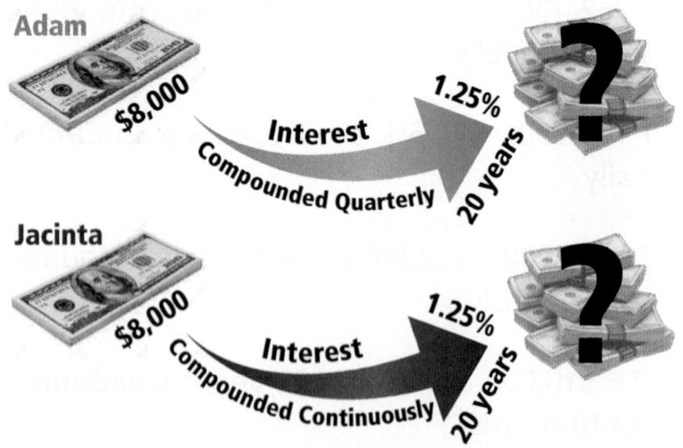

28. Make Sense and Persevere A blogger found that the number of visits to her Web site increases 5.6% annually. The Web site had 80,000 visits this year. Write an exponential model to represent this situation. By what percent does the number of visits increase daily? Explain how you found the daily rate.

29. Use Structure Jae invested \$3,500 at a rate of 2.25% compounded continuously in 2010. How much will be in the account in 2025? How much interest will the account have earned by 2025?

30. Model with Mathematics A scientist is conducting an experiment with a pesticide. Use a calculator to find an exponential model for the data in the table. Use the model to determine how much pesticide remains after 180 days.

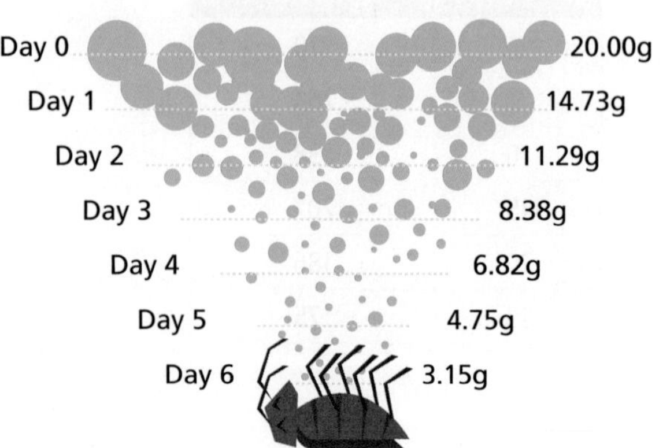

ASSESSMENT PRACTICE

31. The table shows the account information of five investors. Which of the following are true, assuming no withdrawals are made? Select all that apply.

Employee	P	r	t(years)	Compound
Anna	4000	1.5%	12	Quarterly
Nick	2500	3%	8	Monthly
Lori	7200	5%	15	Annually
Tara	2100	4.5%	6	Continuously
Steve	3800	3.5%	20	Semi-annually

Ⓐ After 12 years, Anna will have about \$4,788.33 in her account.

Ⓑ After 8 years, Nick will have about \$3,177.17 in his account.

Ⓒ After 15 years, Lori will have about \$15,218.67 in her account.

Ⓓ After 6 years, Tara will have about \$2,750.93 in her account.

Ⓔ After 20 years, Steve will have about \$7,629.00 in his account.

32. SAT/ACT Rick invested money in a continuous compound account with an interest rate of 3%. How long will it take Rick's account to double?

Ⓐ about 2 years

Ⓑ about 10 years

Ⓒ about 23 years

Ⓓ about 46 years

Ⓔ about 67 years

33. Performance Task Cassie is financing a \$2,400 treadmill. She is going to use her credit card for the purchase. Her card charges 17.5% interest compounded monthly. She is not required to make minimum monthly payments.

Part A How much will Cassie pay in interest if she waits a full year before paying the full balance?

Part B How much additional interest will Cassie pay if she waits two full years before paying the full balance?

Part C If both answers represent a single year of interest, why is the answer in B greater than the answer in A?

EXTENSION

5-2a Analyzing Residuals

I CAN... analyze residuals to determine the goodness of fit of a function model.

VOCABULARY

- residual

ESSENTIAL QUESTION How can you use residuals to determine the goodness of fit of a function model?

EXAMPLE 1 Analyze Residuals

The population of a town since 2010 is shown. A city planner used the exponential function $y = 7{,}520.06 \cdot 1.02589^x$, where x is the number of years since 2010, to model the population growth. How well does the model fit the data?

Evaluate the equation for each x-value to find predicted y-values.

Year	Years since 2010	Actual Population	Predicted Population	Residual
2010	0	7,516	7,520	–4
2011	1	7,724	7,715	9
2012	2	7,908	7,914	–6
2013	3	8,120	8,119	1
2014	4	8,323	8,330	–7
2015	5	8,552	8,545	7
2016	6	8,778	8,766	12
2017	7	8,983	8,993	–10

Calculate the **residuals** by subtracting the predicted y-value from the actual y-value for each x-value.

STUDY TIP
Recall that a **residual** is the difference between the actual y-value and the predicted y-value. Residual = actual y-value – predicted y-value, so for $x = 0$, the residual is 7,516 – 7,520 = –4

Create a scatter plot and a residual plot.

The scatter plot with the curve of best fit suggests that the model is a good fit for the data.

The residual plot is randomly distributed both above and below the x-axis. The values are all clustered near the x-axis, so the model is a good fit for the data.

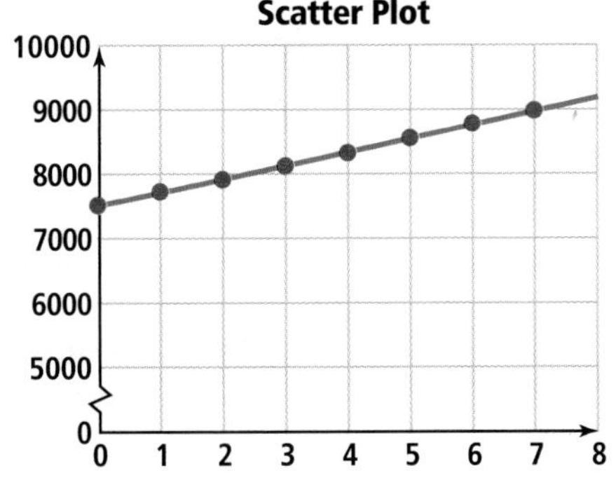

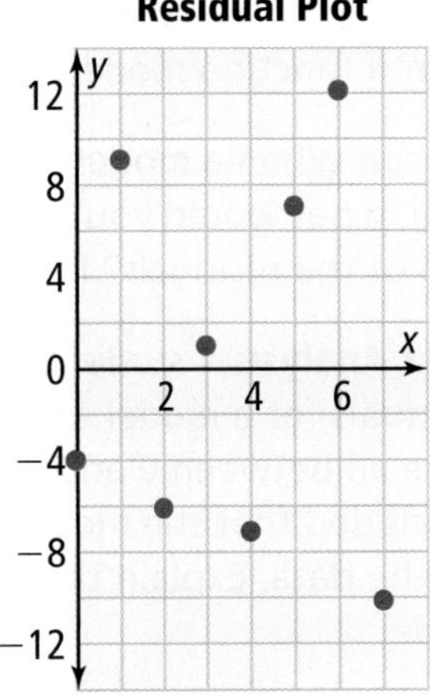

CONTINUED ON THE NEXT PAGE

  Activity  Concept Summary  Assess

EXAMPLE 1 CONTINUED

Try It! 1. A biologist is tracking the population of raccoons in a forest since 2010 as shown in the table. She creates the exponential model $y = 638 \cdot 0.99^x$, where x is the number of years since 2010, to model the population. Use a residual plot to analyze how well the model fits the data.

Year (x)	0	1	2	3	4	5	6	7
Population (y)	635	622	618	615	612	601	597	593

CONCEPT SUMMARY Residuals

A **residual** is the difference between the actual y-value of a data point and the predicted y-value of a model.

residual = actual y-value − predicted y-value

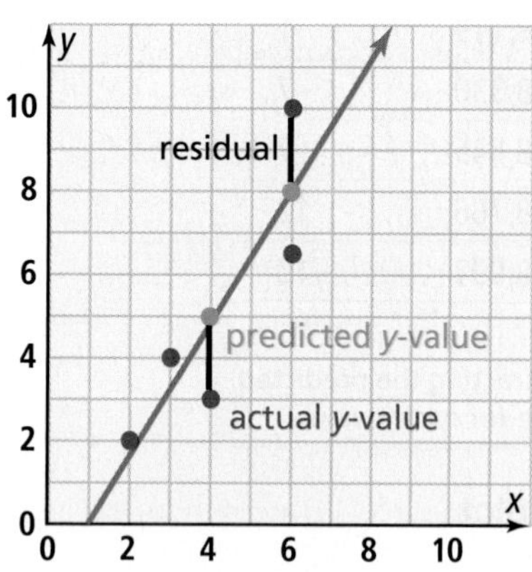

The residual plot of a model shows how well the model fits the data set. If the residuals are randomly distributed on either side of the x-axis and clustered close to the x-axis, then the model is likely a good fit.

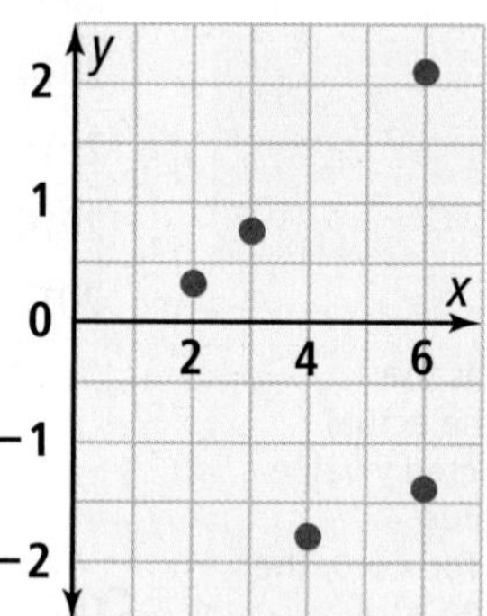

Do You UNDERSTAND?

1. ESSENTIAL QUESTION How can you use residuals to determine the goodness of fit of a function model?

2. **Reason** When a model is a good fit for the data, what would you expect to see in the sum of the residuals? Explain.

3. **Error Analysis** A student calculated the residuals for a model and found that they were all between 0 and 3, so the student concluded that the model was a good fit for the data. Explain the error the student made.

Do You KNOW HOW?

Use the table for Exercises 4–6.

x	0	1	2	3	4	5	6
y	118	129	145	156	178	185	210

4. Use technology to perform an exponential regression on the data.

5. Make a residual plot for the exponential model and the data in the table. How well does the model fit the data? Explain.

6. Use the model to predict the y-value when $x = 12$.

PRACTICE & PROBLEM SOLVING

Practice

UNDERSTAND

7. **Reason** Explain whether the residual plot shown suggests that the model is good fit for the data.

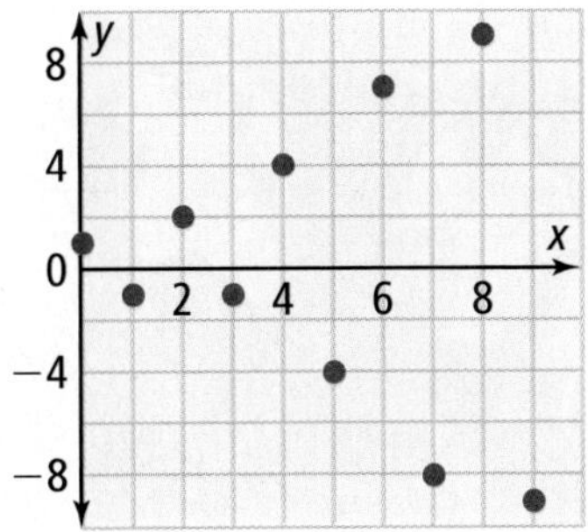

8. **Construct Arguments** Clara and Yvonne performed regressions on a data set. Based on the residual plots, Clara states that her model is a better fit for the data than Yvonne's. Make a mathematical argument to support or refute Clara's claim.

Clara's Plot

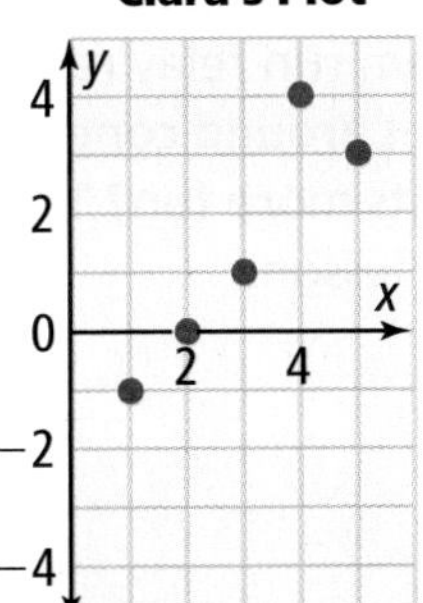

Yvonne's Plot

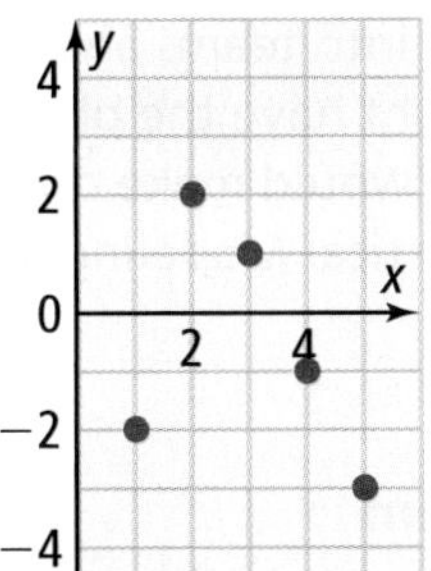

PRACTICE

For each model and data set:

a. Find the residuals to the nearest integer,

b. Create a residual plot for each model, and

c. Explain whether the model is a good fit for the data.

9. Model: $y = 200 \cdot 0.95^x$
Data:

x	0	1	2	3	4	5
y	198	191	180	171	167	153

10. Model: $y = 562 \cdot 1.03^x$
Data:

x	1	2	3	4	5	6
y	585	598	616	641	659	680

APPLY

11. **Model with Mathematics** The number of followers each week of Sara's video site is shown in the table.

Week	Followers
1	90
2	97
3	102
4	109
5	117

a. Find an exponential regression for the data.

b. Create a residual plot for the model.

c. How well does the model represent the data?

d. Use the model to predict the number of followers Sara wil have in week 10.

12. **Make Sense and Persevere** Since the city implemented curbside recycling, the amount of solid waste generated has declined as shown in the table.

Year	Waste (tons)
0	145,251
1	147,510
2	126,096
3	112,840
4	100,885
5	91,355

a. Create an exponential model for the data.

b. Use residuals to explain how well the model fits the data.

c. By approximately what percent is the amount of waste decreasing each year?

d. In what year would you expect the amount of solid waste to be less than 50,000 tons?

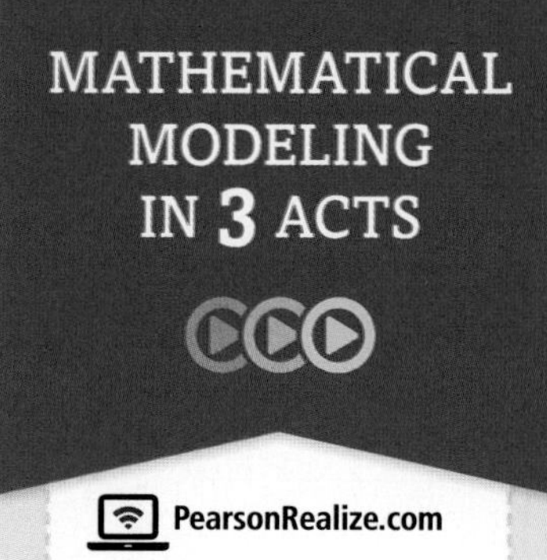

Video

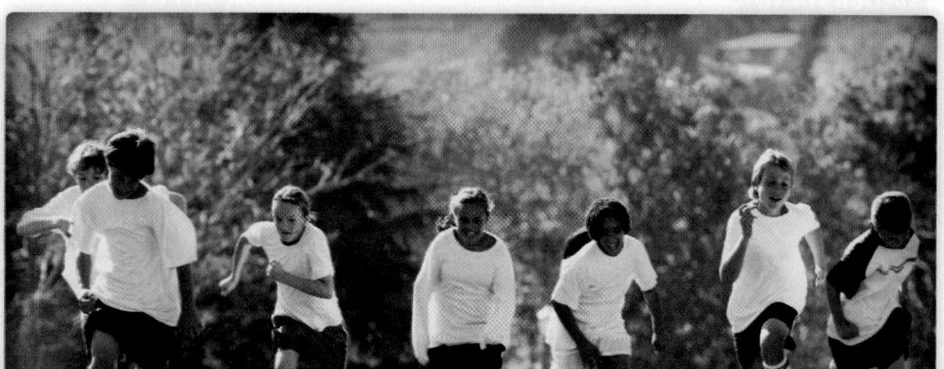

The Crazy Conditioning

Like all sports, soccer requires its players to be well-trained. That is why players often have to run sprints in practice.

To make sprint drills more interesting, many coaches set up competitions. Coaches might split the players into teams and have them run relay races against each other. Or they might have the players sprint around cones and over barriers. What other ways would make doing sprints more fun? Think about this during this Mathematical Modeling in 3 Acts lesson.

ACT 1 Identify the Problem

1. Write down the Main Question you will answer.
2. Make an initial conjecture that answers this Main Question.
3. Explain how you arrived at your conjecture.
4. Write a number that you know is too small.
5. Write a number that you know is too high.
6. What information do you need to know to answer the main question? How can you get it? How will you use that information?

ACT 2 Develop a Model

1. Use the math that you have learned in this Topic to refine your conjecture.
2. Is your refined conjecture between the high and low estimates you came up with earlier?

ACT 3 Interpret the Results

1. Did your refined conjecture match the actual answer exactly? If not, what might explain the difference?

Activity Assess

5-3 Linear, Exponential, and Quadratic Models

PearsonRealize.com

I CAN… determine whether a linear, exponential, or quadratic function best models a data set.

MODEL & DISCUSS

Jacy and Emma use different functions to model the value of a bike x years after it is purchased. Each function models the data in the table.

Jacy's function: $f(x) = -14.20x + 500$

Emma's function: $f(x) = 500(0.85)^x$

Time (yr)	Value ($)
0	500.00
1	485.20
2	472.13
3	461.00
4	452.10

A. Make Sense and Persevere Why did Jacy and Emma not choose a quadratic function to model the data?

B. Whose function do you think is a better model? Explain.

C. Do you agree with this statement? Explain why or why not.

To ensure that you are finding the best model for a table of data, you need to find the values of the functions for the same values of x.

ESSENTIAL QUESTION

How can you determine whether a linear, exponential, or quadratic function best models data?

CONCEPTUAL UNDERSTANDING

EXAMPLE 1 Determine Which Function Type Represents Data

A. How can you determine whether the data in the table can be modeled by a linear function?

First, confirm that the differences in the x-values are constant. Then analyze the *first differences*.

GENERALIZE
Look at the data in the table. What do you notice about the differences between consecutive y-values?

x	y	1st Differences
−2	−1	
−1	1	$1 - (-1) = 2$
0	3	$3 - 1 = 2$
1	5	$5 - 3 = 2$
2	7	$7 - 5 = 2$

(+1 between each consecutive x-value)

The differences between consecutive y-values are the first differences.

A linear function best models the data when the first differences are constant.

CONTINUED ON THE NEXT PAGE

Activity Assess

EXAMPLE 1 CONTINUED

B. How can you determine whether the data in the table can be modeled by a quadratic function?

Analyze the *second differences*.

COMMON ERROR

You may forget to confirm that the differences between the x-values are constant. If differences between the x-values are not constant, then the differences or ratios between the y-values will not be accurate indicators of whether a linear, quadratic, or exponential function best represents the data.

x	y	1st Differences	2nd Differences
0	3		
1	9	$9 - 3 = 6$	
2	19	$19 - 9 = 10$	$10 - 6 = 4$
3	33	$33 - 19 = 14$	$14 - 10 = 4$
4	51	$51 - 33 = 18$	$18 - 14 = 4$

First differences are not constant. Check the second differences.

The differences between consecutive first differences are called the *second differences*.

A quadratic function best models the data when the second differences are constant.

C. How can you determine whether the data in the table can be modeled by an exponential function?

The first differences and second differences are not constant. Find and analyze the ratios of consecutive y-values.

x	y	1st Differences	2nd Differences	Ratios of y-Values
0	1			
1	2	$2 - 1 = 1$		$\frac{2}{1} = 2$
2	4	$4 - 2 = 2$	$2 - 1 = 1$	$\frac{4}{2} = 2$
3	8	$8 - 4 = 4$	$4 - 2 = 2$	$\frac{8}{4} = 2$
4	16	$16 - 8 = 8$	$8 - 4 = 4$	$\frac{16}{8} = 2$

The first differences and second differences are not constant, so the data do not represent a linear or quadratic function.

The ratios of consecutive y-values are the same.

An exponential function best models the data when the ratios of consecutive y-values are the same.

Try It! 1. Does a linear, quadratic, or exponential function best model the data? Explain.

a.

x	0	1	2	3	4
y	−2	−5	−14	−29	−50

b.

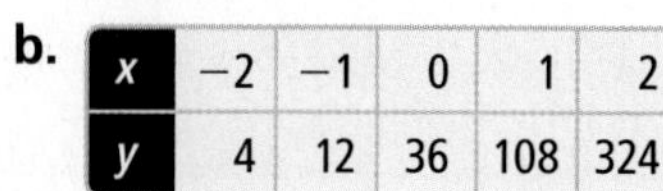

x	−2	−1	0	1	2
y	4	12	36	108	324

APPLICATION

EXAMPLE 2 Choose a Function Type for Real-World Data

The owner of a framing store tracks the cost of bubble wrap for packing pictures like the one shown. How can you use the data to estimate the cost of the bubble wrap for a picture with a length of 75 in.?

75 in.

Length (in.)	Bubble Wrap Cost ($)
6	0.10
12	0.31
18	0.62
24	1.04
30	1.57

Step 1 Determine whether a linear, exponential, or quadratic function model best represents the data.

Analyze at the differences or ratios to determine which model best fits the data.

Length (in.) x	Bubble Wrap Cost ($) y	1st Differences	2nd Differences
6	0.10		
12	0.31	$0.31 - 0.10 = 0.21$	
18	0.62	$0.62 - 0.31 = 0.31$	$0.31 - 0.21 = 0.10$
24	1.04	$1.04 - 0.62 = 0.42$	$0.42 - 0.31 = 0.11$
30	1.57	$1.57 - 1.04 = 0.53$	$0.53 - 0.42 = 0.11$

The first differences are not constant.

The second differences are roughly constant.

A quadratic model best represents the data.

Step 2 Write a quadratic function that represents the data.

Use a graphing calculator to find a quadratic regression. Enter the data as lists, and use the quadratic regression feature.

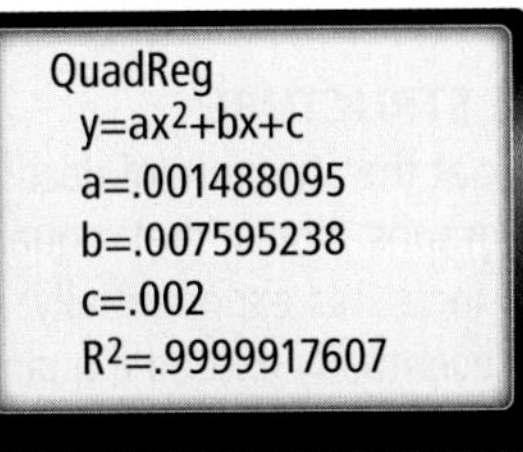

STUDY TIP

You can find a quadratic regression for any set of data whether it is quadratic or not. Because the R^2 value is so close to 1, the quadratic equation generated by the calculator is a good model for the data.

Step 3 Substitute $x = 75$ into the equation.

Enter function $y = 0.0015x^2 + 0.0076x + 0.002$ and evaluate for $x = 75$.

The cost of bubble wrap for a 75-in. picture is about \$9.01.

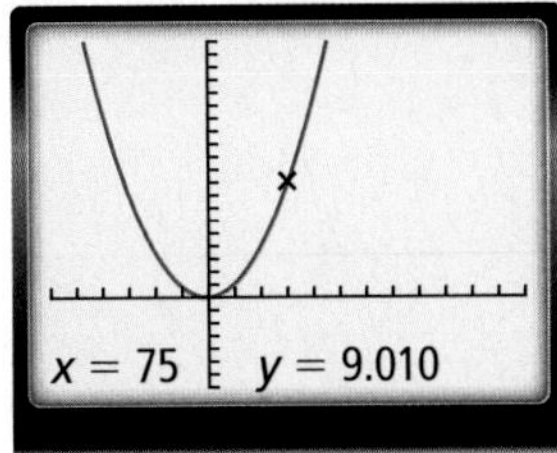

CONTINUED ON THE NEXT PAGE

Try It! 2. Determine whether a linear, quadratic, or exponential function best models the data. Then, use regression to find the function that models the data.

x	0	1	2	3	4
y	100	89.5	78.9	68.4	57.8

EXAMPLE 3 Compare Linear, Exponential, and Quadratic Growth

The graph shows population models for three cities, based on data over a five-year period. If the populations continue to increase in the same ways, when will the population of City C exceed the populations of the other two cities?

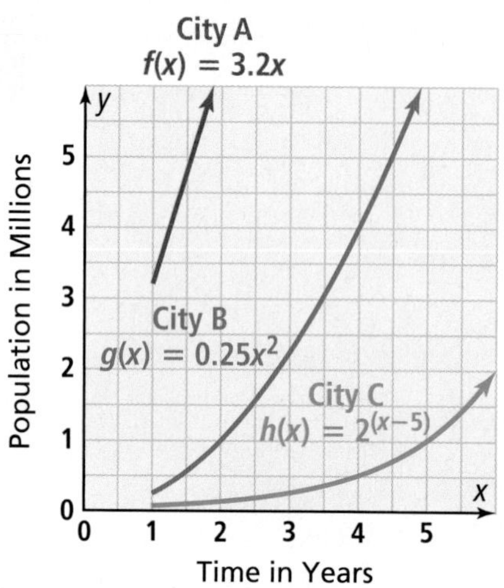

Method 1 Use the table of values.

x	$f(x)$	$g(x)$	$h(x)$
4	12.8	4.0	0.5
5	16.0	6.25	1
6	19.2	9.0	2
7	22.4	12.25	4
8	25.6	16.0	8
9	28.8	20.25	16
10	32.0	25.0	32
11	35.2	30.25	64

The population of City C is greater than those of City A and City B.

Method 2 Use a graphing calculator to determine the points of intersection.

x scale: 10 y scale: 32

Use your calculator to find the point where function h exceeds functions f and g.

USE STRUCTURE
Look at the structure of each of the graphs. Notice that a quantity that increases exponentially will eventually exceed a quantity that increases linearly or quadratically.

After 10 years, the population of City C will exceed the populations of City A and City B. It will continue to outgrow the other cities because it is growing exponentially.

Try It! 3. Compare the functions $f(x) = 3x + 2$, $g(x) = 2x^2 + 3$, and $h(x) = 2^x$. Show that as x increases, $h(x)$ will eventually exceed $f(x)$ and $g(x)$.

CONCEPT SUMMARY Linear, Quadratic, and Exponential Functions

Linear

WORDS The 1st differences are constant.

TABLES

$f(x) = 2x + 3$

x	y	1st Differences
0	3	
1	5	2
2	7	2
3	9	2

GRAPHS

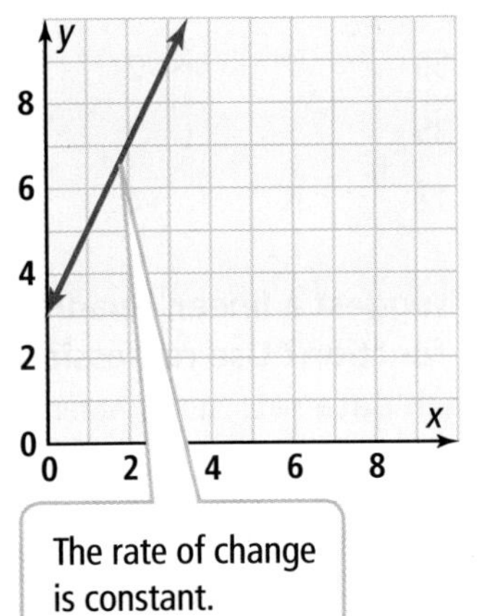

The rate of change is constant.

Quadratic

WORDS The 2nd differences are constant.

TABLES

$f(x) = 0.25x^2 + 0.5x + 0.25$

x	y	Differences 1st	Differences 2nd
0	0.25		
1	1.00	0.75	
2	2.25	1.25	0.5
3	4.00	1.75	0.5

GRAPHS

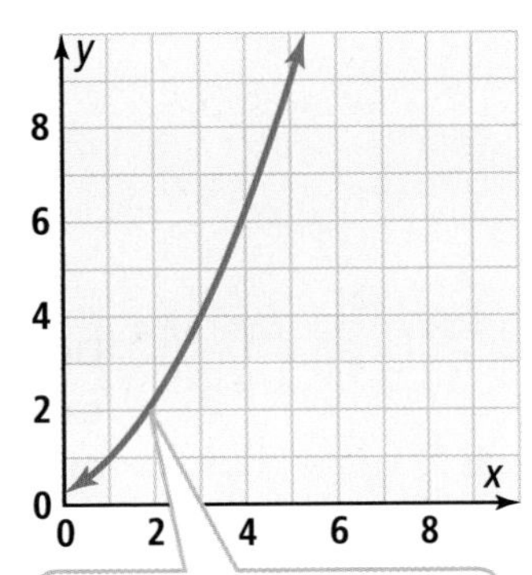

The rate of change in this function increases as the value of *x* increases.

Exponential

WORDS The ratios of consecutive *y*-values are constant.

TABLES

$f(x) = 2^{x-3}$

x	y	Ratios
0	0.125	
1	0.25	$\frac{0.25}{0.125} = 2$
2	0.5	$\frac{0.5}{0.25} = 2$
3	1.00	$\frac{1}{0.5} = 2$

GRAPHS

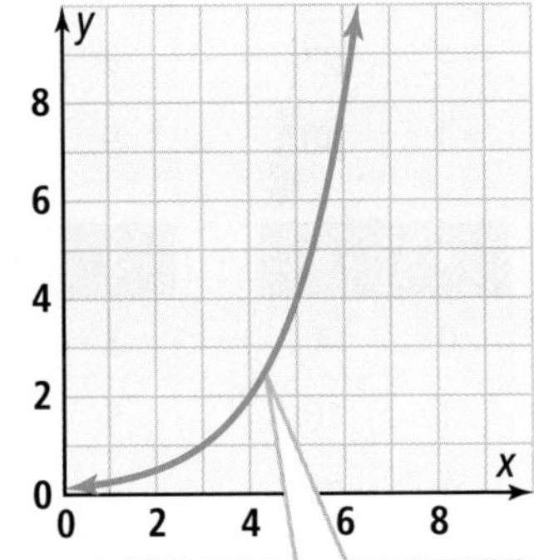

The rate of change in this function increases by equal factors as the value of *x* increases.

Do You UNDERSTAND?

1. **ESSENTIAL QUESTION** How can you determine whether a linear, exponential, or quadratic function best models data?

2. **Reason** The average rate of change of a function is less from $x = 1$ to $x = 4$ than from $x = 5$ to $x = 8$. What type of function could it be? Explain.

3. **Error Analysis** Kiyo used a quadratic function to model data with constant first differences. Explain the error Kiyo made.

Do You KNOW HOW?

Determine whether the data are best modeled by a linear, quadratic, or exponential function.

4.

x	0	1	2	3	4
y	−2	1	10	25	46

5.

x	−2	−1	0	1	2
y	2	7	12	17	22

6. A company's profit from a certain product is represented by $P(x) = -5x^2 + 1{,}125x - 5{,}000$, where *x* is the price of the product. Compare the growth in profits from $x = 120$ to $x = 140$ and from $x = 140$ to $x = 160$. What do you notice?

PRACTICE & PROBLEM SOLVING

Scan for Multimedia

Practice Tutorial

Additional Exercises Available Online

UNDERSTAND

7. **Communicate Precisely** Create a flow chart to show the process to determine whether a given data set represents a function that is linear, quadratic, exponential, or none of these.

8. **Generalize** Calculate the 2nd differences for data in each table. Use a graphing calculator to find the quadratic regression for each data set. Make a conjecture about the relationship between the a values in the quadratic models and the 2nd differences of the data.

x	y
0	0
1	3
2	12
3	27
4	48

x	y
1	0.5
2	2
3	4.5
4	8
5	12.5

x	y
0	4
1	16
2	36
3	64
4	100

x	y
3	58.5
5	162.5
7	318.5
9	526.5
11	786.5

9. **Error Analysis** What is the error in the student's reasoning below? Describe how to correct the statement.

The data can be modeled with a linear function because the first differences are constant.

x	y
-3	-8
-1	-2
0	4
1	10
3	16

10. **Higher Order Thinking** A savings account has a balance of \$1. Savings Plan A will add \$1,000 to an account each month, and Plan B will double the amount each month.

a. Which plan is better in the short run? For how long? Explain.

b. Which plan is better in the long run? Explain.

PRACTICE

Determine whether a linear, quadratic, or exponential function is the best model for the data in each table. SEE EXAMPLE 1

11.

x	y
0	1
1	3
2	9
3	27
4	81

12.

x	y
0	1
1	2
2	7
3	16
4	29

13.

x	y
0	56
1	57
2	50
3	35
4	12

14.

x	y
0	−6
1	−3
2	0
3	3
4	6

Do the data suggest a linear, quadratic, or an exponential function? Use regression to find a model for each data set. SEE EXAMPLE 2

15.

x	0	1	2	3	4
y	−20	−17.5	−15.1	−12.5	−10

16.

x	6	7	8	9	10
y	−19	−12	−7	−4	−3

17. **Use the functions shown.** SEE EXAMPLE 3

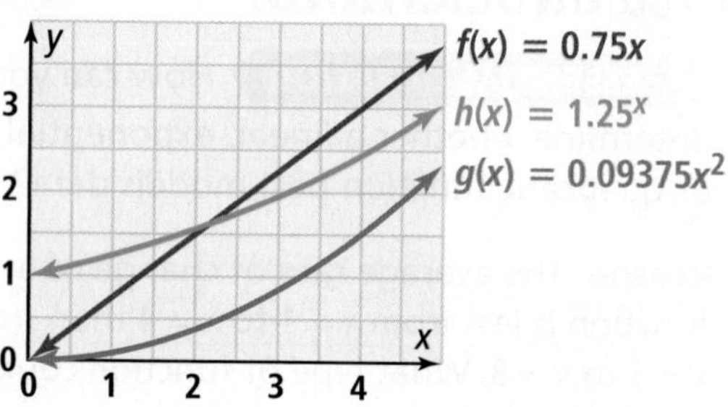

a. Evaluate each function for $x = 6$, $x = 8$ and $x = 12$.

b. When will function h exceed function f and function g?

Mixed Review Available Online

PRACTICE & PROBLEM SOLVING

APPLY

18. Model With Mathematics The data in the table show the population of a city for the past five years. A new water plant will be built when the population exceeds 1 million. Will the city need a new water plant in the next ten years? Use a function model to justify your answer.

Year	2016	2017	2018	2019	2020
Population	794,000	803,000	814,000	822,000	830,000

19. Construct Arguments The graphic shows costs for rectangular lots of different widths. Each lot is twice as long as it is wide.

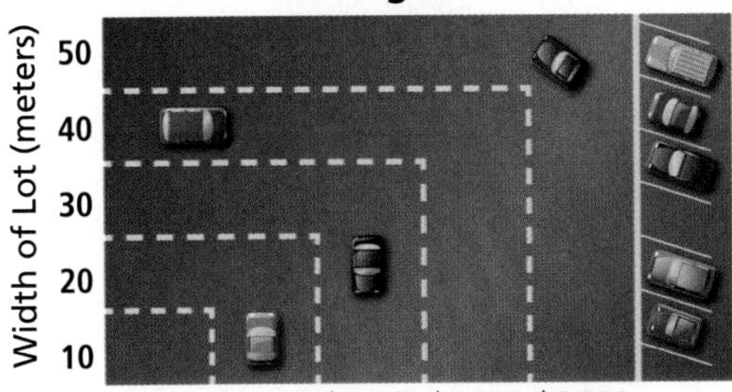

To coat a parking lot 300 m long and 150 m wide, a developer budgeted $20,220, or three times the cost of a lot 50 m wide. Will the budget be sufficient? Justify your answers using a function model.

20. Construct Arguments Carmen is considering two plans to pay off a $10,000 loan. The tables show the amount remaining on the loan after x years.

Plan A	
Year	Amount Remaining
0	10,000
1	9,000
2	8,100
3	7,290
4	6,561

Plan B	
Year	Amount Remaining
0	10,000
1	9,500
2	9,000
3	8,500
4	8,000

Which plan should Carmen use to pay off the loan as soon as possible? Justify your answer using a function model.

ASSESSMENT PRACTICE

21. Function f has constant second differences. Which of the following are true? Select all that apply.

Ⓐ The graph of f is a parabola.

Ⓑ The graph of f is a straight line.

Ⓒ The ratios of the y-values increase as x increases.

Ⓓ The function f is an exponential function.

Ⓔ The function f has constant first differences.

22. SAT/ACT At what point will $f(x) = 3^x$ exceed $g(x) = 2x + 5$ and $h(x) = x^2 + 4$?

Ⓐ (1, 7)

Ⓑ (1.8, 7.3)

Ⓒ (2, 9)

Ⓓ (2.4, 9.8)

23. Performance Task Ella wrote three different computer apps to analyze some data. The tables show the time in milliseconds y for each app to analyze data as a function of the number of data items x.

App A	
x	y
4	81
5	243
6	729
7	2,187
8	6,561

App B	
x	y
4	4,042
5	5,040
6	6,038
7	7,036
8	8,034

App C	
x	y
4	4,400
5	5,375
6	6,550
7	7,925
8	9,500

Part A Use regression on a graphing calculator to find a function that models each data set. Explain your choice of model.

Part B Make a conjecture about which app will require the most time as the number of data items gets very large. How could you support your conjecture?

5-4 Logarithms

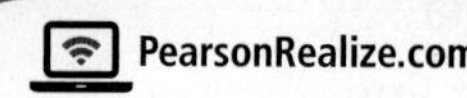

I CAN… evaluate and simplify logarithms.

VOCABULARY

- common logarithm
- logarithm
- logarithmic function
- natural logarithm

Activity Assess

CRITIQUE & EXPLAIN

Earthquakes make seismic waves through the ground. The equation $y = 10^x$ relates the height, or amplitude, in microns, of a seismic wave, y, and the power, or magnitude, x, of the ground-shaking it can cause.

Magnitude, x	Amplitude, y
2	100
3	1,000
?	5,500
4	10,000

Taylor and Chen used different methods to find the magnitude of the earthquake with amplitude 5,500.

Taylor

5,500 is halfway between 1,000 and 10,000.

3.5 is halfway between 3 and 4.

The magnitude is about 3.5.

Chen

$y = 10^x$

$10^3 = 1{,}000$
$10^4 = 10{,}000$
$10^{3.5} \approx 3{,}162$
$10^{3.7} \approx 5{,}012$
$10^{3.8} \approx 6{,}310$
$10^{3.74} \approx 5{,}500$

The magnitude is about 3.74.

A. What is the magnitude of an earthquake with amplitude 100,000? How do you know?

B. Construct Arguments Critique Taylor's and Chen's work. Is each method valid? Could either method be improved?

C. Describe how to express the exact value of the desired magnitude.

ESSENTIAL QUESTION

What are logarithms and how are they evaluated?

CONCEPTUAL UNDERSTANDING

EXAMPLE 1 Understand Logarithms

Solve the equations $2x = 8$ and $2^x = 8$.

You can use inverse operations to solve the first equation.

$$\frac{2x}{2} = \frac{8}{2}$$
$$x = 4$$

Division is the inverse of multiplication, so you can divide both sides by 2 to solve the equation.

The operation in $2^x = 8$ is exponentiation. To solve this equation, you need an inverse for exponentiation that answers the question, "To what exponent would you raise the base 2 to get 8?"

The inverse of exponentiation is called a *logarithm*. To solve the equation $2^x = 8$, you can write $\log_2 8 = x$. Solving this gives $\log_2 8 = 3$ because $2^3 = 8$.

This is read "logarithm base 2 of 8" or "log base 2 of 8."

USE STRUCTURE
Creating the notation $\log_2 x$ to represent the exponent to which you raise 2 to get x is similar to creating the radical notation $\sqrt{x}$ to represent one number you can square to get x.

CONTINUED ON THE NEXT PAGE

EXAMPLE 1 CONTINUED

The **logarithm** base b of x is defined as follows.

$$\log_b x = y \text{ if and only if } b^y = x, \text{ for } b > 0, b \neq 1, \text{ and } x > 0.$$

The **logarithmic function** $y = \log_b x$ is the inverse of the exponential function $y = b^x$.

 **Try It!** **1.** Write the logarithmic form of $y = 8^x$.

CONCEPT Exponential and Logarithmic Forms

Exponential form shows that a base raised to an exponent equals the result.

$$a^b = c$$

Logarithmic form shows that the log of the result with the given base equals the exponent.

$$\log_a c = b$$

When written in logarithmic form, the number that was the result of the exponential equation is often called the argument.

EXAMPLE 2 Convert Between Exponential and Logarithmic Forms

STUDY TIP
Do you remember writing *fact families* for related operations like addition and subtraction? Think of exponential and logarithmic forms as a *fact family* for the three numbers given.

A. What is the logarithmic form of $3^4 = 81$?

The base is 3, the exponent is 4, and the result is 81.

So, in logarithmic form,

$3^4 = 81 \rightarrow \log_3 81 = 4.$

The logarithmic form of $3^4 = 81$ is $\log_3 81 = 4$.

B. What is the exponential form of $\log_{10} 1{,}000 = 3$?

The base is 10, the exponent is 3, and the result (or argument) is 1,000.

So, in exponential form,

$\log_{10} 1{,}000 = 3 \rightarrow 10^3 = 1{,}000.$

The exponential form of $\log_{10} 1{,}000 = 3$ is $10^3 = 1{,}000$.

 **Try It!** **2. a.** What is the logarithmic form of $7^3 = 343$?

b. What is the exponential form of $\log_4 16 = 2$?

EXAMPLE 3 Evaluate Logarithms

What is the value of each logarithmic expression?

GENERALIZE
The output of any exponential function of the form $y = b^x$, with $b > 0$, is always a positive number. Therefore, the input of a logarithmic function must also be a positive number.

A. $\log_5 125$	**B.** $\log_{\frac{1}{4}} 16$
THINK: $5^? = 125$ Since $5^3 = 125$, $\log_5 125 = 3$.	THINK: $\left(\frac{1}{4}\right)^? = 16$ Since $\left(\frac{1}{4}\right)^{-2} = 16$, $\log_{\frac{1}{4}} 16 = -2$.
C. $\log_3 0$ THINK: $3^? = 0$ There is no such power, so $\log_3 0$ is undefined.	**D.** $\log_2 2^8$ THINK: $2^? = 2^8$ Since $2^8 = 2^8$, $\log_2 2^8 = 8$.

Try It! **3.** What is the value of each logarithmic expression?

a. $\log_3\left(\frac{1}{81}\right)$ b. $\log_7(-7)$ c. $\log_5 5^9$

CONCEPT Common Logarithms and Natural Logarithms

The base 10 logarithm is called the **common logarithm** and is written as $\log x$ with the base of 10 implied.

The base e logarithm is called the **natural logarithm** and is written as $\ln x$.

The expressions $\log_{10} x$ and $\log x$ mean the same thing, as do $\ln_e x$ and $\ln x$.

EXAMPLE 4 Evaluate Common and Natural Logarithms

What is the value of each logarithmic expression to the nearest ten-thousandth?

STUDY TIP
Most calculators have keys for the common logarithm (LOG) and the natural logarithm (LN).

A. log 900

$\log 900 \approx 2.9542$ $10^{2.9542} \approx 900$

Check by writing the expression in exponential form and evaluating.

B. ln *e*

$\ln e = 1$ $e^1 = e$

C. ln(−1.87)

$\ln(-1.87)$ $e^? = -1.87$

log(900)
2.954242509
ln(e)
1
ln(−1.87)
Error

There is no exponent to which e can be raised in order to get a negative number, so $\ln(-1.87)$ is undefined.

Try It! **4.** What is the value of each logarithmic expression to the nearest ten-thousandth?

a. log 321 b. ln 1,215 c. log 0.17

EXAMPLE 5 Solve Equations With Logarithms

COMMON ERROR
Remember that 10 is not a coefficient, but a base. You cannot divide both sides by 10 and then add 1 to solve for x.

What is the solution to each equation? Round to the nearest thousandth.

A. $25 = 10^{x-1}$

$25 = 10^{x-1}$

$\log 25 = x - 1$ ········ Convert to logarithmic form.

$1 + \log 25 = x$ ········ Addition Property

$2.398 \approx x$ ········ Use calculator to evaluate.

B. $\ln(2x + 3) = 4$

$\ln(2x + 3) = 4$

$2x + 3 = e^4$ ········ Convert to exponential form.

$2x + 3 \approx 54.598$ ········ Use calculator to evaluate.

$2x \approx 51.598$ ········ Addition Property

$x \approx 25.799$ ········ Multiplication Property

Try It! **5.** Solve each equation. Round to the nearest thousandth.

a. $\log(3x - 2) = 2$ **b.** $e^{x+2} = 8$

APPLICATION

EXAMPLE 6 Use Logarithms to Solve Problems

The seismic energy, x, in joules can be estimated based on the magnitude, m, of an earthquake by the formula $x = 10^{1.5m+12}$. What is the magnitude of an earthquake with a seismic energy of 4.2×10^{20} joules?

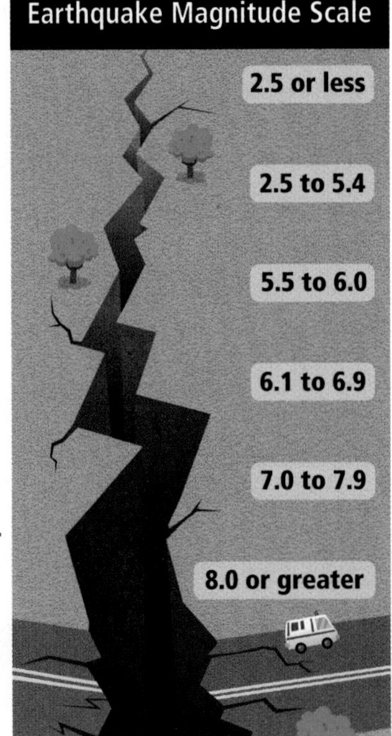

Formulate Substitute 4.2×10^{20} for x in the formula.

$4.2 \times 10^{20} = 10^{1.5m+12}$

Compute Solve the equation for m.

$4.2 \times 10^{20} = 10^{1.5m+12}$ ········ Write the original equation.

$\log(4.2 \times 10^{20}) = 1.5m + 12$ ········ Write the equation in logarithmic form.

$20.6 \approx 1.5m + 12$ ········ Evaluate the logarithm.

$5.75 \approx m$ ········ Solve for m.

Interpret The magnitude of the earthquake is about 5.75.
Verify the answer: $10^{1.5(5.75)+12} \approx 4.2 \times 10^{20}$

Try It! **6.** What is the magnitude of an earthquake with a seismic energy of 1.8×10^{23} joules?

CONCEPT SUMMARY Logarithms

	Exponential Form		Logarithmic Form
ALGEBRA	$b^x = y$	$\leftrightarrow$	$\log_b y = x$
WORDS	The base raised to the exponent is equal to a result.		The logarithm with a base b of the result (or argument) is equal to the exponent.
NUMBERS	$3^4 = 81$	$\leftrightarrow$	$\log_3 81 = 4$

Do You UNDERSTAND?

1. ESSENTIAL QUESTION What are logarithms and how are they evaluated?

2. **Error Analysis** Amir said the expression $\log_5(-25)$ simplifies to -2. Explain Amir's possible error.

3. **Vocabulary** Explain the difference between the common logarithm and the natural logarithm.

4. **Make Sense and Persevere** How can logarithms help to solve an equation such as $10^t = 656$?

Do You KNOW HOW?

Write each equation in logarithmic form.

5. $2^{-6} = \frac{1}{64}$

6. $e^4 \approx 54.6$

Write each equation in exponential form.

7. $\log 200 \approx 2.301$

8. $\ln 25 \approx 3.22$

Evaluate the expression.

9. $\log_4 64$

10. $\log \frac{1}{100}$

11. $\ln e^5$

12. Solve for x. $4e^x = 7$.

PRACTICE & PROBLEM SOLVING

Scan for Multimedia

Additional Exercises Available Online

UNDERSTAND

13. **Make Sense and Persevere** If the LN button on your calculator were broken, how could you still use your calculator to find the value of the expression ln 65?

14. **Error Analysis** Describe and correct the error a student made in solving an exponential equation.

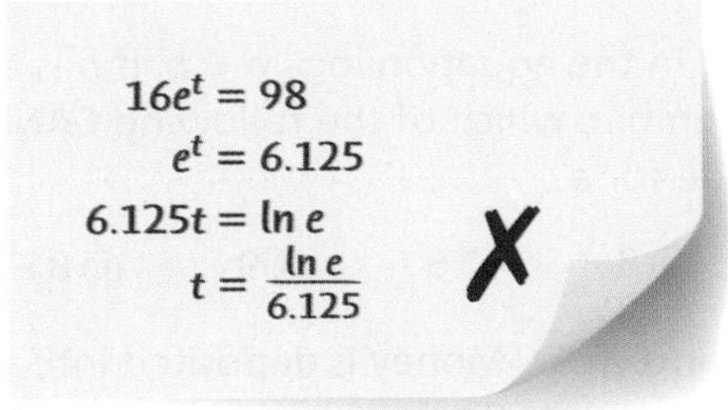

15. **Higher Order Thinking** Use the graph of $y = 3^x$ to estimate the value of $\log_3 50$. Explain your reasoning.

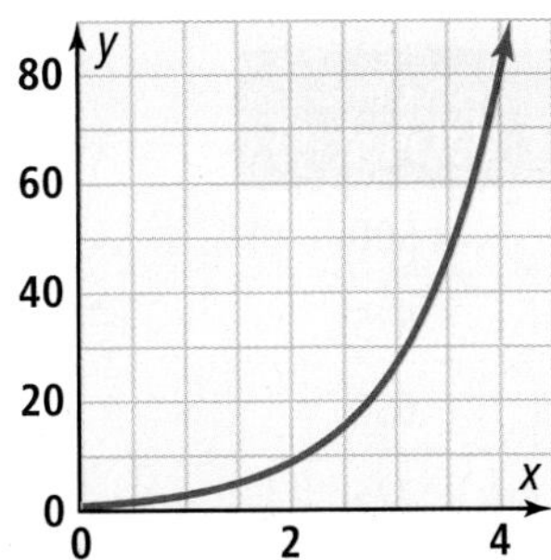

16. **Generalize** For what values of x is the expression $\log_4 x < 0$ true?

17. **Use Structure** A student says that $\log_3(\frac{1}{27})$ simplifies to −3. Is the student correct? Explain.

18. **Use Structure** Explain why the expression ln 1,000 is not equal to 3.

PRACTICE

Write the inverse of each exponential function.
SEE EXAMPLE 1

19. $y = 4^x$
20. $y = 10^x$
21. $y = 7^x$
22. $y = a^x$

Write each equation in logarithmic form.
SEE EXAMPLE 2

23. $3^8 = 6{,}561$
24. $e^{-3} \approx 0.0498$
25. $5^0 = 1$
26. $7^3 = 343$

Write each equation in exponential form.
SEE EXAMPLE 2

27. $\log \frac{1}{100} = -2$
28. $\log_8 64 = 2$
29. $\ln 148.41 \approx 5$
30. $\log_2 \frac{1}{32} = -5$

Evaluate each logarithmic expression. SEE EXAMPLE 3

31. $\log_5 \frac{1}{125}$
32. $\log_6(-216)$
33. $\log_3 3^4$
34. $\log_2 32$
35. $\log_9 729$
36. $\log_8 \frac{1}{64}$
37. $\log_7 0$
38. $\log_7 7^a$

Use a calculator to evaluate each expression. Round to the nearest ten-thousandth. SEE EXAMPLE 4

39. $\log 78.5$
40. $\log 0.24$
41. $\ln(-37)$
42. $\ln 41.5$
43. $\log 12$
44. $\ln 3$

Solve each equation. Round answers to the nearest ten-thousandth. SEE EXAMPLES 5 AND 6

45. $\log(7x + 6) = 3$
46. $2.75e^t = 38.6$
47. $\ln(3x - 1) = 2$
48. $10^{t+1} = 50$
49. $1.5e^t = 27$
50. $\log(x - 3) = -1$

51. How long does it take for \$250 to grow to \$600 at 4% annual percentage rate compounded continuously? Round to the nearest year.

PRACTICE & PROBLEM SOLVING

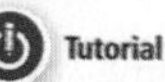

Mixed Review Available Online

APPLY

52. **Model with Mathematics** Michael invests \$1,000 in an account that earns a 4.75% annual percentage rate compounded continuously. Peter invests \$1,200 in an account that earns a 4.25% annual percentage rate compounded continuously. Which person's account will grow to \$1,800 first?

53. **Reason** The Richter magnitude of an earthquake is $R = 0.67\log(0.37E) + 1.46$, where E is the energy (in kilowatt-hours) released by the earthquake.

    a. What is the magnitude of an earthquake that releases 11,800,000,000 kilowatt-hours of energy? Round to the nearest tenth.

    b. How many kilowatt-hours of energy would an earthquake have to release in order to be an 8.2 on the Richter scale? Round to the nearest whole number.

    c. What number of kilowatt-hours of energy would an earthquake have to release in order for walls to crack? Round to the nearest whole number.

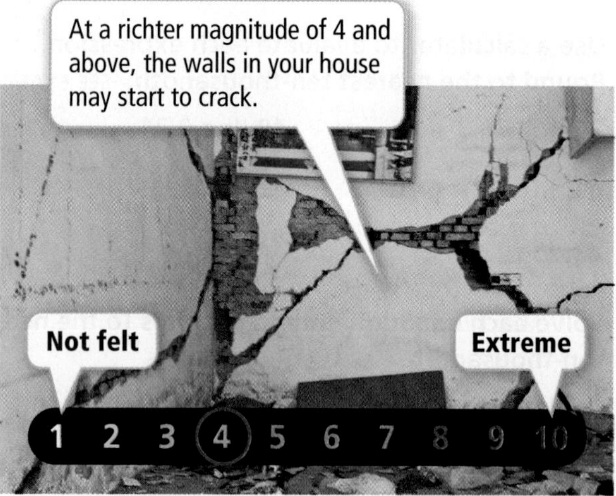

54. **Reason** The function $c(t) = 108e^{-0.08t} + 75$ calculates the temperature, in degrees Fahrenheit, of a cup of coffee that was handed out a drive-thru window t minutes ago.

    a. What is the temperature of the coffee in the instant that it is handed out the window?

    b. After how many minutes is the coffee in the cup 98 degrees Fahrenheit? Round to the nearest whole minute.

ASSESSMENT PRACTICE

55. Given that $\log_b x < 0$, which of the following are true? Select all that apply.

    Ⓐ $b < 0$
    Ⓑ $x < 0$
    Ⓒ $b > 0$
    Ⓓ $x > 0$
    Ⓔ $x < 1$

56. **SAT/ACT** In the equation $\log_3 a = b$, if b is a whole number, which of the following CANNOT be a value for a?

    Ⓐ 1 Ⓑ 3 Ⓒ 6 Ⓓ 9 Ⓔ 81

57. **Performance Task** Money is deposited into two separate accounts. The money in one account is compounded continuously. The money in the other account is not compounded continuously. Neither account has any money withdrawn in the first 6 years.

Year	Account 1 Balance (\$)	Account 2 Balance (\$)
0	400	500
1	433.31	575
2	469.40	650
3	508.50	725
4	550.85	800
5	596.72	875

Part A Write a function to calculate the amount of money in each account given t, the number of years since the account was opened. Describe the growth in each account.

Part B Will the amount of money in Account 1 ever exceed the amount of money in Account 2? Explain. If so, when will that occur?

  Activity  Assess

5-5 Logarithmic Functions

PearsonRealize.com

I CAN... graph logarithmic functions and find equations of the inverses of exponential and logarithmic functions.

EXPLORE & REASON

Compare the graphs.

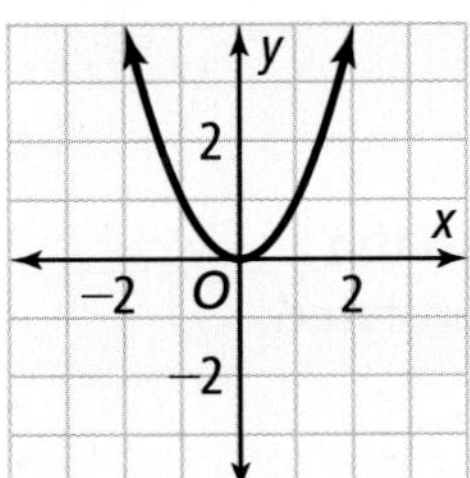

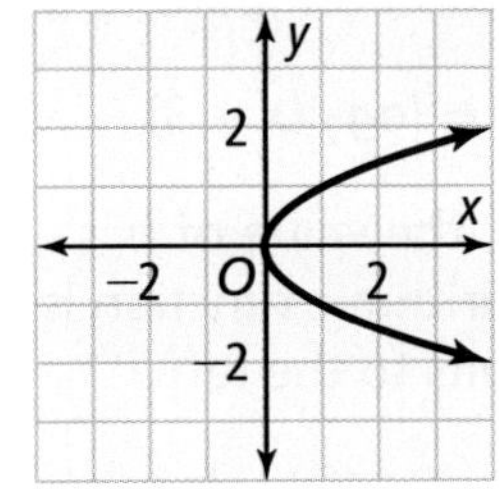

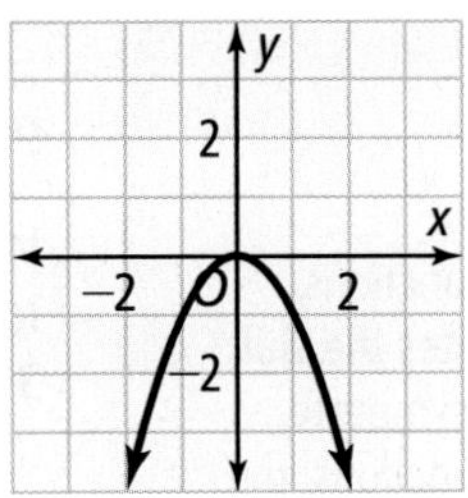

A. Which two graphs represent the inverse of each other? Explain.

B. Look for Relationships What is the relationship between the domain and the range of the two inverse relations?

ESSENTIAL QUESTION

How is the relationship between logarithmic and exponential functions revealed in the key features of their graphs?

EXAMPLE 1 Identify Key Features of Logarithmic Functions

Graph $y = \log_2 x$. What are the domain, range, x-intercept, and asymptote? What is the end behavior of the graph?

Create a table of values for $y = 2^x$.

x	−2	−1	0	1	2
y	0.25	0.5	1	2	4

$y = \log_2 x$ and $y = 2^x$ are inverse functions, so start by making a table of values for $y = 2^x$.

Interchange the corresponding x- and y-values. These ordered pairs represent $y = \log_2 x$.

x	0.25	0.5	1	2	4
y	−2	−1	0	1	2

Graph the ordered pairs.

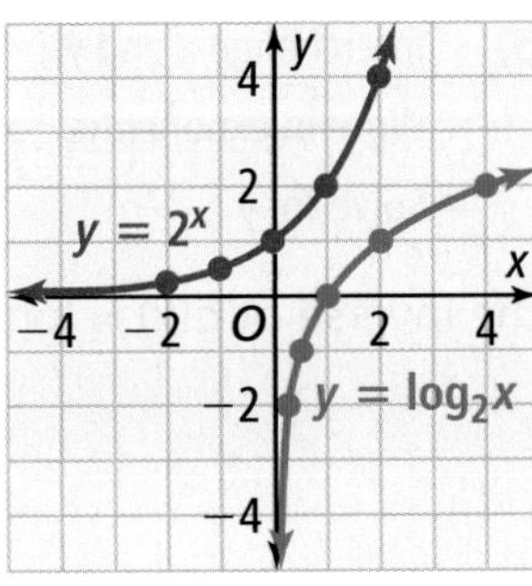

domain: $\{x \mid x > 0\}$

The logarithmic function accepts only positive input values.

range: all real numbers

x-intercept: 1

asymptote: y-axis

The graph of the logarithmic function approaches $x = 0$ but does not touch it.

end behavior: As $x \to 0$, $y \to -\infty$.
As $x \to \infty$, $y \to \infty$.

USE STRUCTURE
The functions $y = \log_2 x$ and $y = 2^x$ are inverse functions. The graphs are reflections of each other across the line $y = x$.

 **Try It!** 1. Graph each function and identify the domain and range. List any intercepts or asymptotes. Describe the end behavior.

a. $y = \ln x$ **b.** $y = \log_{\frac{1}{2}} x$

EXAMPLE 2 Graph Transformations of Logarithmic Functions

Graph the function. How do the asymptote and *x*-intercept of the given function compare to those of the parent function?

$g(x) = \log_2 (x + 3)$

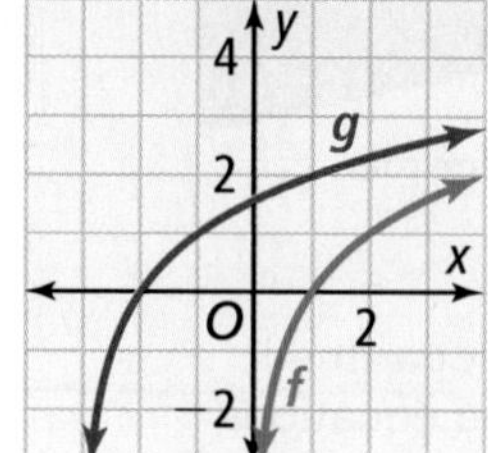

In g, the value of h is −3, so the logarithmic function is translated 3 units to the left.

$$f(x) = \log_2 x$$
$$g(x) = \log_2 (x + 3) = f(x - (-3))$$

The vertical asymptote and the *x*-intercept each shift 3 units to the left.

COMMON ERROR
With exponential functions, the value of k dictates the shift of the horizontal asymptote. With logarithmic functions, the asymptote is vertical. So the value of h determines the shift of the asymptote.

Try It! 2. Describe how each graph compares to the graph of $f(x) = \ln x$.

a. $g(x) = \ln x + 4$

b. $h(x) = 5 \ln x$

CONCEPTUAL UNDERSTANDING

EXAMPLE 3 Inverses of Exponential and Logarithmic Functions

What is the equation of the inverse of the functions?

A. $f(x) = 10^{x+1}$

Write the function in $y = f(x)$ form and then interchange x and y.

$y = 10^{x+1}$ .... Write the function in $y = f(x)$ form.

$x = 10^{y+1}$ .... Interchange x and y.

$y + 1 = \log x$ .... Write in log form.

$y = \log x - 1$ .... Solve for y.

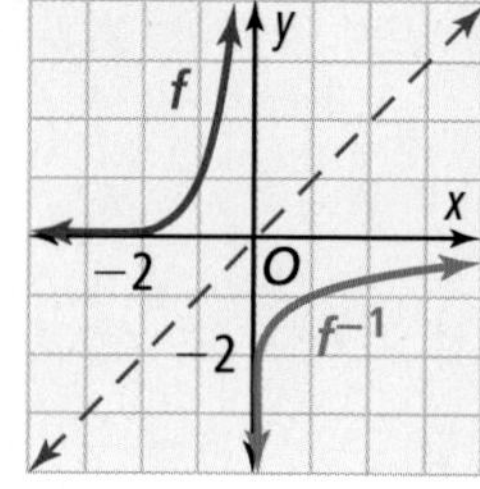

The equation of the inverse of $f(x) = 10^{x+1}$ is $f^{-1}(x) = \log x - 1$.

LOOK FOR RELATIONSHIPS
$f(x)$ is a translation of the parent function $y = 10^x$ one unit left. $f^{-1}(x)$ is a translation of the parent function $y = \log x$ one unit down. Graphical translations of a function and its inverse are directly related, with horizontal and vertical effects switching places.

B. $g(x) = \log_7 (x + 5)$

Write the function in $y = g(x)$ form and then interchange x and y.

$y = \log_7 (x + 5)$ .... Write the function in $y = g(x)$ form.

$x = \log_7 (y + 5)$ .... Interchange x and y.

$y + 5 = 7^x$ .... Write in exponential form.

$y = 7^x - 5$ .... Solve for y.

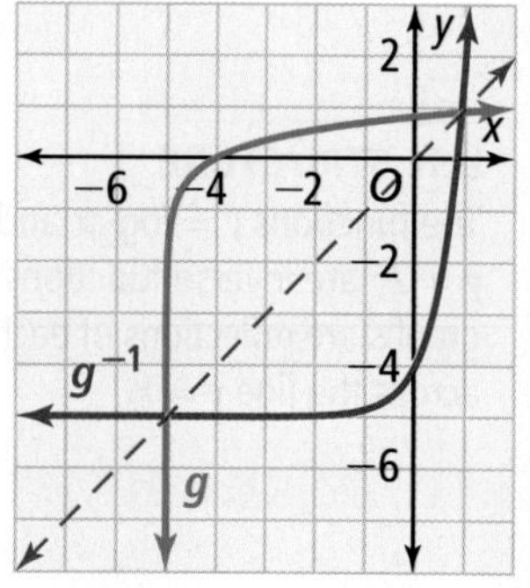

The equation of the inverse of $g(x) = \log_7 (x + 5)$ is $g^{-1}(x) = 7^x - 5$.

Try It! 3. Find the inverse of each function.

a. $f(x) = 3^{x+2}$

b. $g(x) = \log_7 x - 2$

EXAMPLE 4 Interpret the Inverse of a Formula Involving Logarithms

A company uses this function to relate sales revenue R and advertising costs, a:

$$R = 12 \log(a + 1) + 25$$

R is revenue in thousands of dollars. a is advertising costs in thousands of dollars.

STUDY TIP
To find the inverse formula do not interchange the variables. Instead, solve for a in terms of R. The variables a and R have a particular meaning in this context and are not interchangeable.

What is the equation of the inverse of the formula? Which equation would be easier to use to find a value of a for a particular value of R?

$R = 12 \log(a + 1) + 25$ ········ Write the equation in $R = f(a)$ form.

$R - 25 = 12 \log(a + 1)$ ········ Subtract 25 from each side.

$\frac{R - 25}{12} = \log(a + 1)$ ········ Divide each side by 12.

$a + 1 = 10^{\frac{R-25}{12}}$ ········ Rewrite in exponential form.

$a = 10^{\frac{R-25}{12}} - 1$ ········ Subtract 1 from each side.

The inverse of the formula is $a = 10^{\frac{R-25}{12}} - 1$. It would be easier to use the inverse to find a when R is known.

Try It! 4. Describe what happens to the amount of monthly revenue as the cost of advertising increases. How might you determine the optimal advertising budget? Explain.

EXAMPLE 5 Compare Two Logarithmic Functions

Logarithmic functions can approximate the altitude of a plane over time. Which plane's altitude shows the greater rate of change over the interval $10 \leq t \leq 15$?

Plane A

Altitude is approximated by following the function:

$A = 9{,}200 \ln t + 10{,}000$

t is time in minutes after takeoff.

A is altitude in feet.

Plane B

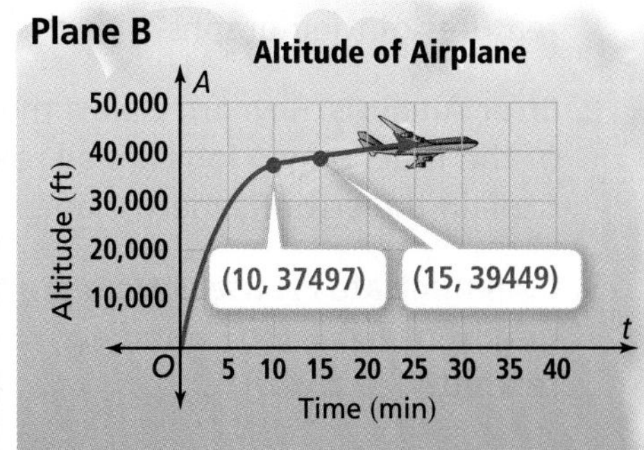

STUDY TIP
The average rate of change is a ratio of the change in altitude to the change in time over the interval.

Step 1 Determine the average rate of change for Plane A.

$$\frac{34{,}914 - 31{,}184}{15 - 10} = \frac{3{,}730}{5} = 746 \text{ ft per min}$$

Find $A(15)$ and $A(10)$ using the function given for Plane A.

Step 2 Determine the average rate of change for Plane B.

$$\frac{39{,}449 - 37{,}497}{15 - 10} = \frac{1{,}952}{5} = 390 \text{ ft per min}$$

Use the points given in the graph for Plane B.

Between 10 and 15 min after takeoff, the average rate of change of the altitude of Plane A is greater than the average rate of change for Plane B.

Try It! 5. For which plane do you think the altitude will change more quickly over the interval $15 \leq t \leq 20$? Explain your reasoning.

  Concept Summary 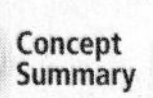  Assess

CONCEPT SUMMARY Logarithmic Functions

GRAPH

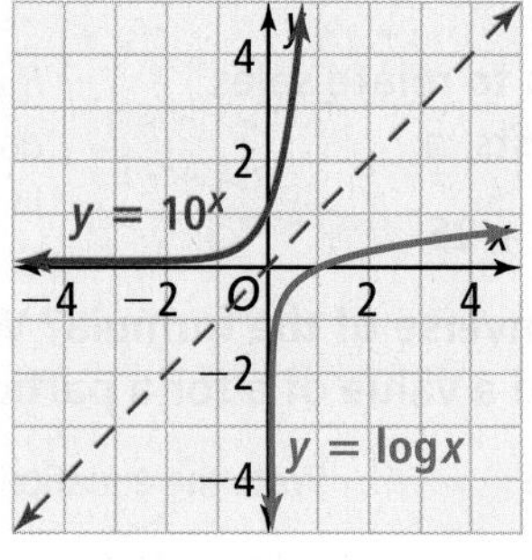

The functions are inverses so their graphs are reflections of each other across the line with equation $y = x$.

EQUATIONS	$y = \log x$	$y = 10^x$
KEY FEATURES	Domain: $\{x \mid x > 0\}$ Range: all real numbers x-intercept: 1 Asymptote: y-axis	Domain: all real numbers Range: $\{y \mid y > 0\}$ y-intercept: 1 Asymptote: x-axis
END BEHAVIOR	As $x \to 0$, $y \to -\infty$ As $x \to \infty$, $y \to \infty$	As $x \to -\infty$, $y \to 0$ As $x \to \infty$, $y \to \infty$

Do You UNDERSTAND?

1. **ESSENTIAL QUESTION** How is the relationship between logarithmic and exponential functions revealed in the key features of their graphs?

2. **Error Analysis** Raynard claims the domain of the function $y = \log_3 x$ is all real numbers. Explain the error Raynard made.

3. **Communicate Precisely** How are the graphs of $f(x) = \log_5 x$ and $g(x) = -\log_5 x$ related?

Do You KNOW HOW?

4. Graph the function $y = \log_4 x$ and identify the domain and range. List any intercepts or asymptotes. Describe the end behavior.

5. Write the equation for the function $g(x)$, which can be described as a vertical shift $1\frac{1}{2}$ units up from the function $f(x) = \ln x - 1$.

6. The function $y = 5 \ln(x + 1)$ gives y, the number of downloads, in hundreds, x minutes after the release of a song. Find the equation of the inverse and interpret its meaning.

y downloads

PRACTICE & PROBLEM SOLVING

Scan for Multimedia  Practice Tutorial

Additional Exercises Available Online

UNDERSTAND

7. **Look for Relationships** Are the logarithmic and exponential functions shown inverses of each other? Explain.

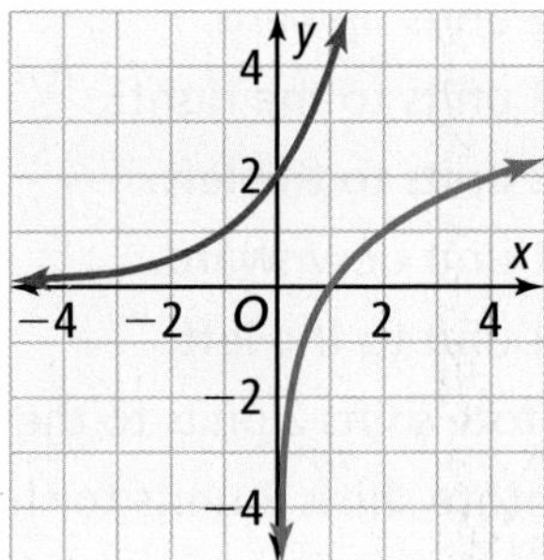

8. **Communicate Precisely** How is the graph of the logarithmic function $g(x) = \log_2 (x - 7)$ related to the graph of the function $f(x) = \log_2 x$? Explain your reasoning.

9. **Error Analysis** Describe and correct the error a student made in finding the inverse of the exponential function $f(x) = 5^{x-6} + 2$.

$y = 5^{x-6} + 2$	Write in $y = f(x)$ form.
$x = 5^{y-6} + 2$	Interchange x and y.
$x - 2 = 5^{y-6}$	Subtract 2 from each side.
$y - 6 = \log_5 x - 2$	Rewrite in logarithmic form.
$y = \log_5 x - 2 + 6$	Add 6 to each side.
$y = \log_5 x + 4$	Simplify.
$f'(x) = \log_5 x + 4$	

10. **Make Sense and Persevere** The number of members m who joined a new workout center w weeks after opening is modeled by the equation $m = 1.6^{w+2}$, where $0 \leq w \leq 10$. Find the inverse of the function and explain what the inverse tells you.

11. **Use Structure** The graph shows a transformation of the parent graph $f(x) = \log_3 x$. Write an equation for the graph.

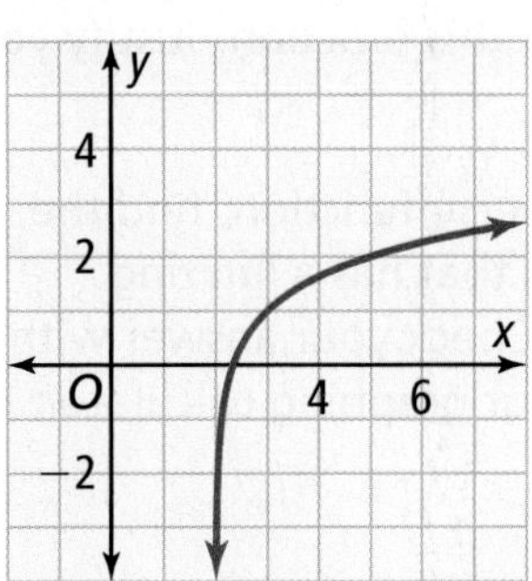

PRACTICE

Graph each function and identify the domain and range. List any intercepts or asymptotes. Describe the end behavior. SEE EXAMPLE 1

12. $y = \log_5 x$

13. $y = \log_8 x$

14. $y = \log_{\frac{3}{10}} x$

15. $y = \log_{0.1} x$

Describe the graph in terms of transformations of the parent function $f(x) = \log_6 x$. Compare the asymptote and x-intercept of the given function to the parent function. SEE EXAMPLE 2

16. $g(x) = \frac{1}{2} \log_6 x$

17. $g(x) = \log_6 (-x)$

18. Describe how the graph of $g(x) = -\ln(x + 0.5)$ is related to the graph of $f(x) = \ln x$. SEE EXAMPLE 2

Find the equation of the inverse of each function. SEE EXAMPLE 3

19. $f(x) = 5^{x-3}$

20. $f(x) = \left(\frac{1}{2}\right)^{x-1}$

21. $f(x) = 6^{x+7}$

22. $f(x) = \log_2 (8x)$

23. $f(x) = \ln (x + 3) - 1$

24. $f(x) = 4 \log_2 (x - 3) + 2$

25. The altitude y, in feet, of a plane t minutes after takeoff is approximated by the function $y = 5{,}000 \ln(.05t) + 8{,}000$. Solve for t in terms of y. What is a situation in which it would be easier to use your new equation rather than the original? SEE EXAMPLE 4

26. Find the average rate of change of the function graphed below over the interval $10 \leq x \leq 50$. Compare it to the average rate of change of $y = 3 \log x + 12$ over the same interval. SEE EXAMPLE 5

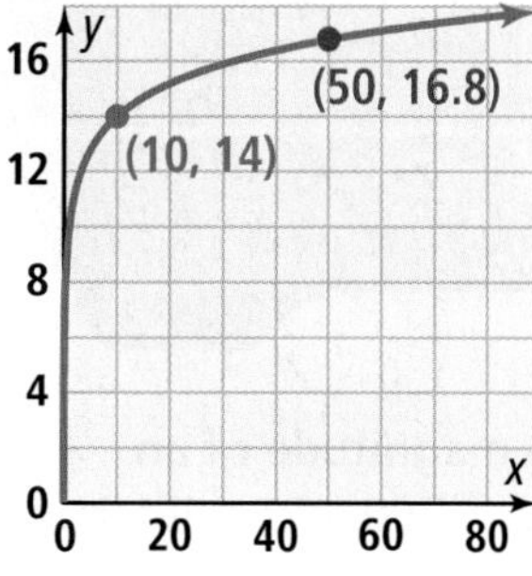

PRACTICE & PROBLEM SOLVING

APPLY

27. Model with Mathematics The equation $r = 90 - 25 \log(t + 1)$ is to model a student's retention r after taking a physics course where r represents a student's test score (as a percent), and t represents the number of months since taking the course.

a. Make a table of values for ordered pairs that represent $r = 90 - 25 \log(t + 1)$, rounding to the nearest tenth. Then sketch the graph of the function on a coordinate plane through those ordered pairs. (You may use a graphing calculator to check.)

b. Find the equation of the inverse. Interpret the meaning of this function.

28. Higher Order Thinking As shown by the diagram, an earthquake occurs below Earth's surface at point F (the focus). Point E, on the surface above the focus, is called the *epicenter*. A seismograph station at point S records the waves of energy generated by the earthquake. The surface wave magnitude M of the earthquake is given by this formula:

$$M = \log\left(\frac{A}{T}\right) + 1.66(\log D) + 3.3$$

In the formula, A is the amplitude of the ground motion in micrometers, T is the period in seconds, and D is the measure of ES in degrees.

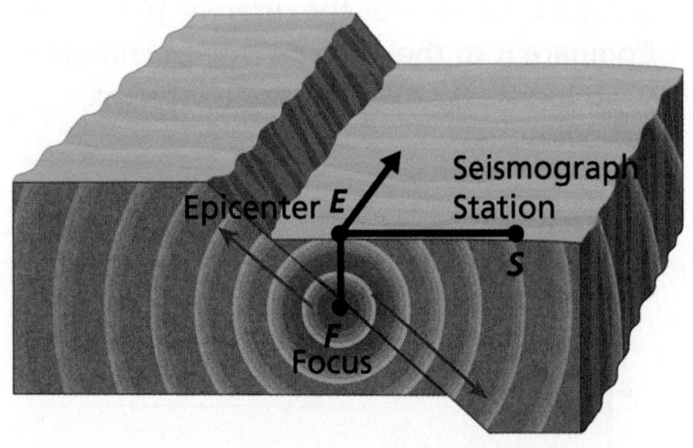

a. Find surface wave magnitude of an earthquake with $A = 700$ micrometers, $T = 2$ and $D = 100°$.

b. In the formula, $20° < D \leq 160°$. By how much can the size of arc ES affect the surface wave magnitude? Explain.

ASSESSMENT PRACTICE

29. The logarithmic function $g(x) = \ln x$ is transformed to $h(x) = \ln(x + 2) - 1$. Which of the following are true? Select **all** that apply.

Ⓐ $g(x)$ is translated 2 units upward.

Ⓑ $g(x)$ is translated 2 units to the right.

Ⓒ $g(x)$ is translated 2 units to the left.

Ⓓ $g(x)$ is translated 1 unit downward.

Ⓔ $g(x)$ is translated 1 unit to the left.

Ⓕ The vertical asymptote shifts 2 units to the left.

Ⓖ The vertical asymptote shifts 2 units to the right.

30. SAT/ACT The graph shows the exponential function $f(x) = 5^{x+1}$. Which of the following functions represents its inverse, $f^{-1}(x)$?

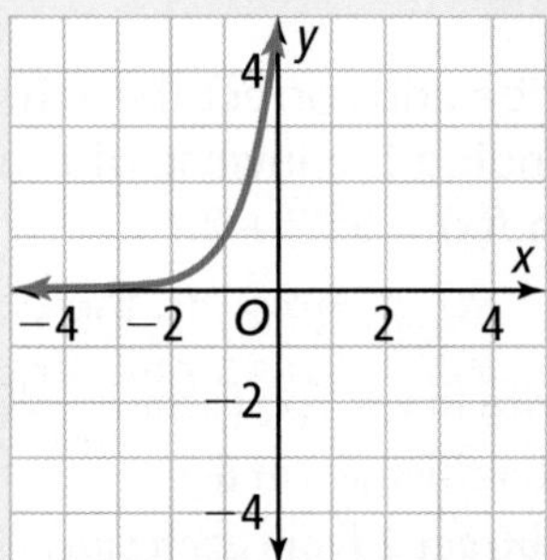

Ⓐ $f^{-1}(x) = 1 + \log_5 x$

Ⓑ $f^{-1}(x) = \log_5 x - 1$

Ⓒ $f^{-1}(x) = \log_5 (x - 1)$

Ⓓ $f^{-1}(x) = \log_5 (x + 1)$

31. Performance Task The logarithmic function $M(d) = 5 \log d + 2$ is used to find the limiting magnitude of a telescope, where d represents the diameter of the lens of the telescope (mm) that is being used for the observation.

Part A Find the limiting magnitude of a telescope having a lens diameter of 40 mm.

Part B Find the equation of the inverse of this function.

Part C Interpret why astronomers may wish to use the inverse of this function. Justify your reasoning.

Part D Using the inverse function, find the diameter of the lens that has a limiting magnitude of 13.5. Check your answer with the table function of your graphing calculator.

5-6 Properties of Logarithms

PearsonRealize.com

I CAN...
use properties of logarithms to rewrite expressions.

VOCABULARY

- Change of Base Formula

Activity

Assess

EXPLORE & REASON

Look at the graph of $y = \log x$ and the ordered pairs shown.

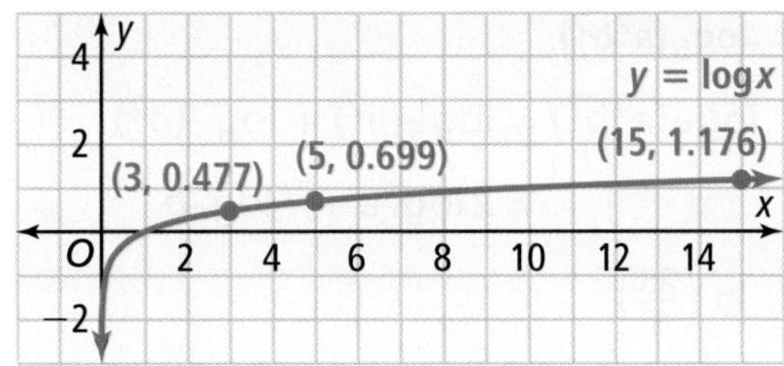

A. Complete the table shown.

x	3	5	15
$\log x$			

B. Look for Relationships What is the relationship between the numbers 3, 5, and 15? What is the relationship between the logarithms of 3, 5, and 15?

C. What is your prediction for the value of log 45? log 75? Explain.

ESSENTIAL QUESTION

How are the properties of logarithms used to simplify expressions and solve logarithmic equations?

CONCEPT Properties of Logarithms

For positive numbers b, m, and n with $b \neq 1$, the following properties hold.

$\log_b mn = \log_b m + \log_b n$ .... Product Property of Logarithms

$\log_b \frac{m}{n} = \log_b m - \log_b n$ .... Quotient Property of Logarithms

$\log_b m^n = n \log_b m$ .... Power Property of Logarithms

EXAMPLE 1 Prove a Property of Logarithms

How can you prove the Product Property of Logarithms?

Let $x = \log_b m$ and $y = \log_b n$. Then $b^x = m$ and $b^y = n$.

$b^x \cdot b^y = m \cdot n$ .... Multiply the expressions b^x and b^y.

$b^{x+y} = mn$ .... Product Property of Exponents

$x + y = \log_b mn$ .... Rewrite the equation in logarithmic form.

$\log_b m + \log_b n = \log_b mn$ .... Substitute.

Try It! **1.** Prove the Quotient Property of Logarithms.

 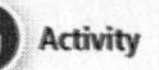

EXAMPLE 2 Expand Logarithmic Expressions

MAKE SENSE AND PERSEVERE
Expanding logarithmic expressions requires the use of a variety of properties. Look at the whole expression first to determine the sequence of properties that will be used.

How can you use the properties of logarithms to expand each expression?

A. $\log_5(a^2b^7)$

$\log_5(a^2b^7) = \log_5(a^2) + \log_5(b^7)$ ······ Product Property of Logarithms

$= 2\log_5 a + 7\log_5 b$ ······ Power Property of Logarithms

B. $\ln\left(\frac{25}{3}\right)$

$\ln\left(\frac{25}{3}\right) = \ln\left(\frac{5^2}{3}\right)$ ······ Rewrite the numerator as a power.

$= \ln(5^2) - \ln 3$ ······ Quotient Property of Logarithms

$= 2\ln 5 - \ln 3$ ······ Power Property of Logarithms

 **Try It!** **2.** Use the properties of logarithms to expand each expression.

a. $\log_7\left(\frac{r^3t^4}{v}\right)$ **b.** $\ln\left(\frac{7}{225}\right)$

EXAMPLE 3 Write Expressions as Single Logarithms

STUDY TIP
Recall that the Properties of Logarithms are each associated with a different operation. Addition signals the Product Property, subtraction signals the Quotient Property, and multiplication by a constant signals the Power Property.

What is each expression written as a single logarithm?

A. $4\log_4 m + 3\log_4 n - \log_4 p$

$4\log_4 m + 3\log_4 n - \log_4 p$

$= \log_4(m^4) + \log_4(n^3) - \log_4 p$ ······ Power Property of Logarithms

$= \log_4(m^4n^3) - \log_4 p$ ······ Product Property of Logarithms

$= \log_4\left(\frac{m^4n^3}{p}\right)$ ······ Quotient Property of Logarithms

B. $3\ln 2 - 2\ln 5$

$3\ln 2 - 2\ln 5 = \ln(2^3) - \ln(5^2)$ ······ Power Property of Logarithms

$= \ln\left(\frac{2^3}{5^2}\right)$ ······ Quotient Property of Logarithms

$= \ln\left(\frac{8}{25}\right)$ ······ Simplify exponents

 **Try It!** **3.** Write each expression as a single logarithm.

a. $5\log_2 c - 7\log_2 n$ **b.** $2\ln 7 + \ln 2$

 Activity  Assess

APPLICATION

EXAMPLE 4 Apply Properties of Logarithms

The pH of a solution is a measure of its concentration of hydrogen ions. This concentration (measured in moles per liter) is written $[H^+]$ and is given by the formula

$$\text{pH} = \log\frac{1}{[H^+]}.$$

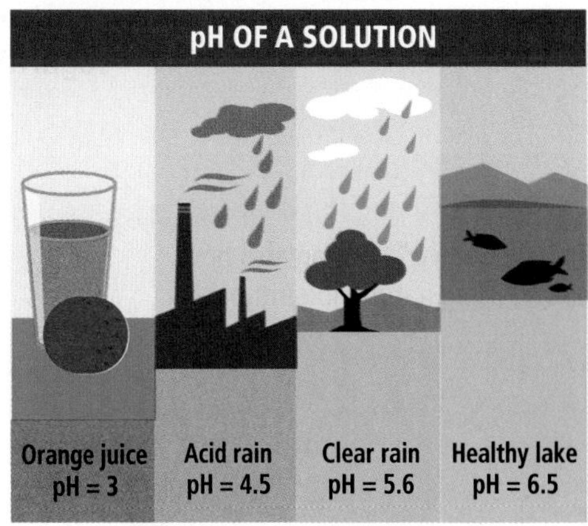

What is the concentration of hydrogen ions in the acid rainfall?

$4.5 = \log\frac{1}{[H^+]}$ ········ Substitute 4.5 for pH.

$4.5 = \log 1 - \log[H^+]$ ········ Quotient Property

$-4.5 = \log[H^+]$ ········ Solve for $\log[H^+]$

$10^{-4.5} = H^+$ ········ Write in exponential form.

The concentration of hydrogen ions in the acid rainfall is $10^{-4.5} \approx 0.0000316$ moles per liter.

COMMON ERROR
The expression $\log\frac{1}{[H^+]}$ is equal to $\log 1 - \log[H^+]$, not $\log[1 - H^+]$.

 **Try It!** 4. What is the concentration of hydrogen ions in a liter of orange juice?

CONCEPTUAL UNDERSTANDING

EXAMPLE 5 Evaluate Logarithmic Expressions by Changing the Base

How can you use base 10 logarithms to evaluate base 2 logarithms?

To evaluate $\log_2 3$ with a calculator, you need to express $\log_2 3$ in terms of base 10 logarithms.

$\log_2 3 = \frac{\log_2 3 \cdot \log 2}{\log 2}$ ········ Multiply $\log_2 3$ by 1 in the form of $\frac{\log 2}{\log 2}$.

$= \frac{\log 2^{\log_2 3}}{\log 2}$ ········ Power Property of Logarithms.

$= \frac{\log 3}{\log 2}$ ········ Since $2^{\log_2 3} = 3$, the numerator simplifies to log 3.

Remember that exponents and logarithms are inverse operations, so they undo one another.

$= \frac{0.477}{0.301} \approx 1.585$ ········ Use a calculator to evaluate.

This illustrates the **Change of Base Formula**:

For positive numbers m, b, and a, with $b \neq 1$ and $a \neq 1$, $\log_b m = \frac{\log_a m}{\log_a b}$.

STUDY TIP
To divide logs with a calculator using one expression, be sure to include parentheses in the correct places. To evaluate $\log_2 3$, press [LOG] [3] [÷] [(] [LOG] [2] [)] [ENTER.]

 **Try It!** 5. Estimate the value of each logarithm. Then use a calculator to find the value of each logarithm to the nearest thousandth.

a. $\log_2 7$

b. $\log_5 3$

EXAMPLE 6 Use the Change of Base Formula

What is the solution of the equation $2^x = 7$? Express the solution as a logarithm and then evaluate. Round to the nearest thousandth.

$2^x = 7$ .... Write the equation.

$x = \log_2 7$ .... Rewrite in logarithmic form.

$x = \frac{\log 7}{\log 2}$ .... Use the Change of Base Formula.

$x \approx 2.807$ .... Use a calculator.

Check $2^{2.807} \approx 7$

STUDY TIP
The equation $2^x = 7$ can also be solved using natural logarithms.

 **Try It!** 6. What is the solution to the equation $3^x = 15$? Express the solution as a logarithm, make an estimate, and then evaluate. Round to the nearest thousandth.

CONCEPT SUMMARY Properties of Logarithms

	Product Property	Quotient Property	Power Property	Change of Base
ALGEBRA	$\log_b(mn) = \log_b m + \log_b n$	$\log_b\left(\frac{m}{n}\right) = \log_b m - \log_b n$	$\log_b(m^n) = n \cdot \log_b m$	$\log_b m = \frac{\log_a m}{\log_a b}$
WORDS	The log of a product is the sum of the logs.	The log of a quotient is the difference of the logs.	The log of a number raised to a power is the power multiplied by the log of the number.	The log base b of a number is equal to the log base a of the number divided by the log base a of b.
NUMBERS	$\log_2(20) = \log_2(4) + \log_2(5)$	$\log_{10}\left(\frac{2}{3}\right) = \log_{10}2 - \log_{10}3$	$\log_3(16) = 4 \cdot \log_3 2$	$\log_5 7 = \frac{\log 7}{\log 5}$

Do You UNDERSTAND?

1. **ESSENTIAL QUESTION** How are the properties of logarithms used to simplify expressions and solve logarithmic equations?

2. **Vocabulary** While it is not necessary to change to base 10 when applying the Change of Base Formula, why is it common to do so?

3. **Error Analysis** Amanda claimed the expanded form of the expression $\log_4(c^2d^5)$ is $5\log_4 c + 5\log_4 d$. Explain the error Amanda made.

Do You KNOW HOW?

4. Use the properties of logarithms to expand the expression $\log_6\left(\frac{49}{5}\right)$.

5. Use the properties of logarithms to write the expression $5\ln s + 6\ln t$ as a single logarithm.

6. Use the formula $\text{pH} = \log\frac{1}{[H^+]}$ to write an expression for the concentration of hydrogen ions, $[H^+]$, in a container of baking soda with a pH of 8.9.

PRACTICE & PROBLEM SOLVING

Scan for Multimedia

Practice Tutorial

Additional Exercises Available Online

UNDERSTAND

7. **Use Structure** Without applying the Change of Base Formula, explain how to use $\log_3 2 \approx 0.631$ and $\log_3 5 \approx 1.465$ to approximate $\log_3\left(\frac{2}{5}\right)$.

8. **Communicate Precisely** Explain what is meant by *expanding a logarithmic expression*. How are the processes of *expanding logarithmic expressions* and *writing logarithmic expressions as a single logarithm* related?

9. **Higher Order Thinking** The graph of $y = \log\left(\frac{1}{x}\right)$ and $y = -\log x$ are shown. Notice the graph is the same for both equations. Use properties of logarithms to explain why the graphs are the same.

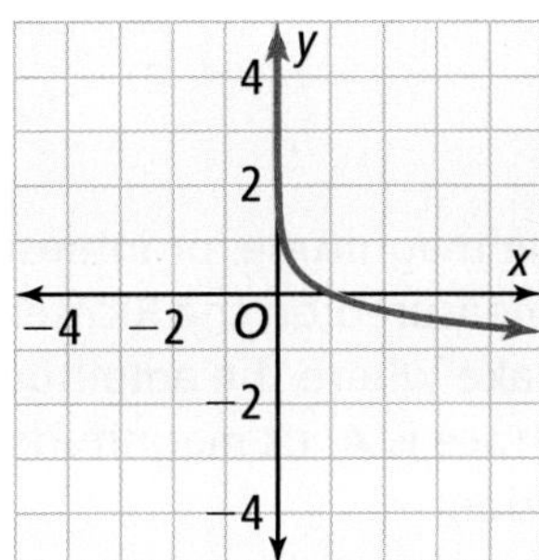

10. **Communicate Precisely** Emma used the Change of Base Formula to solve the equation $6^x = 72$ and found that $x = 2.387$. How can Emma check her solution?

11. **Error Analysis** Describe and correct the error a student made in writing the logarithmic expression in terms of a single logarithm.

$$\log_3 2 + \frac{1}{2}\log_3 y = \log_3 2y^2$$ ✗

12. **Error Analysis** A student wants to approximate $\log_2 9$ with her calculator. She enters the equivalent expression $\frac{\ln 2}{\ln 9}$, but the decimal value is not close to her estimate of 3. What happened?

$$\log_2 9 = \frac{\ln 2}{\ln 9}$$

PRACTICE

13. Use the properties of exponents to prove the Power Property of Logarithms. SEE EXAMPLE 1

Use the properties of logarithms to expand each expression. SEE EXAMPLE 2

14. $\log_5\left(\frac{2}{3}\right)$
15. $\log_6(2m^5n^3)$
16. $\ln 2x^5$
17. $\log_2\left(\frac{x}{5y}\right)$

Use the properties of logarithms to write each expression as a single logarithm. SEE EXAMPLE 3

18. $9\ln x - 6\ln y$
19. $\log_5 6 + \frac{1}{2}\log_5 y$
20. $2\log 10 + 4\log(3x)$
21. $\frac{1}{3}\ln 27 - 3\ln(2y)$
22. $8\log_3 2 + 5\log_3 c + 7\log_3 d$

23. Use properties of logarithms to show that $\text{pH} = \log\frac{1}{[H^+]}$ can be written as $\text{pH} = -\log\,[H^+]$. SEE EXAMPLE 4

Use the Change of Base Formula to evaluate each logarithm. Round to the nearest thousandth. SEE EXAMPLE 5

24. $\log_4 9$
25. $\log_6 5$
26. $\ln 3$
27. $\log_2 7$
28. $\log_9 12$
29. $\ln 23$

Use the Change of Base Formula to solve each equation for *x*. Give an exact solution as a logarithm and an approximate solution rounded to the nearest thousandth. SEE EXAMPLE 6

30. $3^x = 4$
31. $5^x = 11$
32. $8^x = 10$
33. $2^x = 30$
34. $7^x = 100$
35. $4^x = 55$

PRACTICE & PROBLEM SOLVING

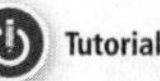

Mixed Review Available Online

APPLY

36. Make Sense and Persevere The loudness of sound is measured in decibels. For a sound with intensity I (in watts per square meter), its loudness $L(I)$ (in decibels) is modeled by the function $L(I) = 10\log\frac{I}{I_0}$, where I_0 represents the intensity of a barely audible sound (approximately 10^{-12} watts per square meter).

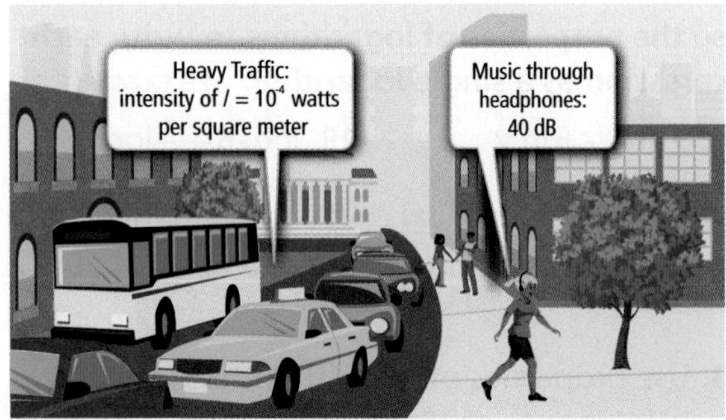

a. Find the decibel level of the sound made by the heavy traffic.

b. Find the intensity of the sound that is made by music playing at 40 decibels.

c. How many times as great is the intensity of the traffic than the intensity of the music?

37. Model with Mathematics Miguel collected data on the attendance at an amusement park and the daily high temperature. He found that the model $A = 2\log t + \log 5$ approximated the attendance A, in thousands of people, at the amusement park, when the daily high temperature is t degrees Fahrenheit.

a. Use properties of logarithms to simplify Miguel's formula.

b. The daily high temperatures for the week are below.

What is the expected attendance on Wednesday? Round to the nearest person.

ASSESSMENT PRACTICE

38. Match each expression with an equivalent expression.

I. $\log_4 20$	Ⓐ $\log_2 20 - \log_2 4$
II. $2\log_2 5$	Ⓑ $\log_4 2 + \log_4 10$
III. $\log_2 5$	Ⓒ $\frac{\log 25}{\log 2}$
VI. $4\log_4 2$	Ⓓ $\log_2 4$

39. SAT/ACT Use the properties of logarithms to write the following expression in terms of a single logarithm.

$$2(\log_3 20 - \log_3 4) + 0.5\log_3 4$$

Ⓐ $\log_3 4$
Ⓑ $\log_3 5$
Ⓒ $\log_3 25$
Ⓓ $\log_3 50$

40. Performance Task The magnitude, or intensity, of an earthquake is measured on the Richter scale. For an earthquake where the amplitude of its seismographic trace is A, its magnitude is modeled by the function:

$$R(A) = \log\frac{A}{A_0},$$

where A_0 represents the amplitude of the smallest detectable earthquake.

Part A An earthquake occurs with an amplitude 200 times greater than the amplitude of the smallest detectable earthquake, A_0. What is the magnitude of this earthquake on the Richter scale?

Part B Approximately how many times as great is the amplitude of an earthquake measuring 6.8 on the Richter scale than the amplitude of an earthquake measuring 5.9 on the Richter scale?

Part C Suppose the intensity of one earthquake is 150 times as great as that of another. How much greater is the magnitude of the more intense earthquake than the less intense earthquake?

Activity Assess

5-7 Exponential and Logarithmic Equations

PearsonRealize.com

I CAN… solve exponential and logarithmic equations.

VOCABULARY
- exponential equation
- logarithmic equation

MODEL & DISCUSS

A store introduces two new models of fitness trackers to its product line. A glance at the data is enough to see that sales of both types of fitness trackers are increasing. Unfortunately, the store has limited space for the merchandise. The manager decides that the store will sell both models until sales of TrackSmart exceed those of FitTracker.

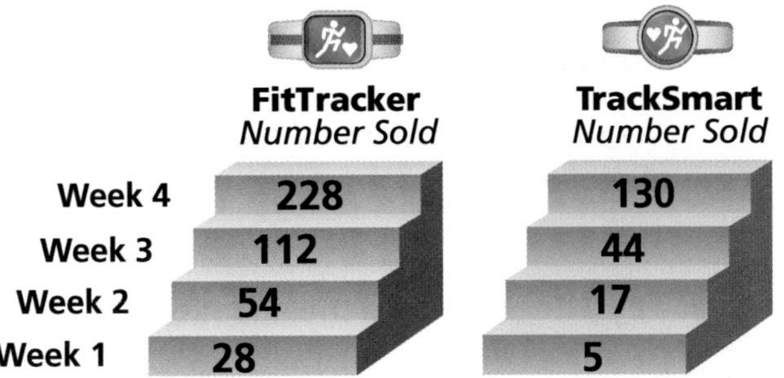

A. **Model With Mathematics** Find an equation of an exponential function that models the sales for each fitness tracker. Describe your method.

B. Based on the equations that you wrote, determine when the store will stop selling FitTracker.

ESSENTIAL QUESTION

How do properties of exponents and logarithms help you solve equations?

VOCABULARY
An **exponential equation** is an equation that contains variables in the exponents.

CONCEPT Property of Equality for Exponential Equations

Symbols Suppose $b > 0$ and $b \neq 1$, then $b^x = b^y$ if and only if $x = y$.

Words If two powers of the same base are equal, then their exponents are equal; if two exponents are equal, then the powers with the same base are equal.

EXAMPLE 1 Solve Exponential Equations Using a Common Base

What is the solution to $\left(\frac{1}{2}\right)^{x+7} = 4^{3x}$?

$\left(\frac{1}{2}\right)^{x+7} = 4^{3x}$ .... Write the original equation.

$(2^{-1})^{x+7} = (2^2)^{3x}$ .... Rewrite each side with a common base.

$2^{-x-7} = 2^{6x}$ .... Power of a Power Property

$-x - 7 = 6x$ .... Property of Equality for Exponential Equations

$-7 = 7x$ .... Add x to each side.

$-1 = x$ .... Divide each side by 7.

Try It! 1. Solve each equation using a common base.

a. $25^{3x} = 125^{x+2}$

b. $0.001 = 10^{6x}$

CONCEPTUAL UNDERSTANDING

EXAMPLE 2 Rewrite Exponential Equations Using Logarithms

How can you rewrite the equation $17 = 4^x$ using logarithms?

There is no common base for 17 and 4. Write each number as a power of 10.

$17 = 4^x$	Write the original equation.
$10^{\log 17} = 10^{\log 4^x}$	Write the equation using the powers of 10.
$\log 17 = \log 4^x$	Property of Equality for Exponential Equations

Rewriting expressions using logarithms can help you solve many types of problems.

Try It! 2. Rewrite the equation $5^x = 12$ using logarithms.

CONCEPT Property of Equality for Logarithmic Equations

Symbols If $x > 0$, then $\log_b x = \log_b y$ if and only if $x = y$.

Words If two logarithms (exponents) of the same base are equal, then the quantities are equal; if two quantities are equal, and the bases are the same, then the logarithms (exponents) are equal.

EXAMPLE 3 Solve Exponential Equations Using Logarithms

What is the solution to $3^{x+1} = 5^x$?

$3^{x+1} = 5^x$	Write the original equation.
$\log(3^{x+1}) = \log(5^x)$	Property of Equality for Logarithmic Equations
$(x + 1) \log 3 = x \log 5$	Power Property of Logarithms
$x \log 3 + \log 3 = x \log 5$	Use the Distributive Property.
$x(\log 3 - \log 5) = -\log 3$	Move terms and factor out x.
$x = \frac{-\log 3}{\log 3 - \log 5}$	Divide.
$x \approx 2.15$	Evaluate.

COMMON ERROR

The entire quantity of $x + 1$ is the exponent, so it must be written as a quantity to be multiplied by the logarithmic expression.

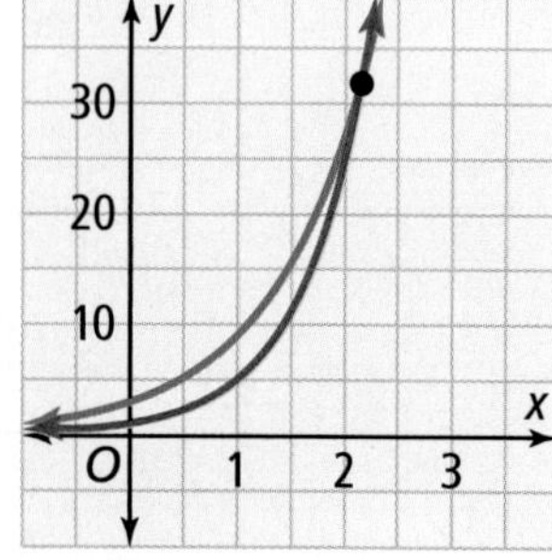

Check

Substitute 2.15 into the equation:

$3^{x+1} = 3^{2.15+1} \approx 31.8$

$5^x = 5^{2.15} \approx 31.8$

The point of intersection of the graphs is about (2.15, 31.8).

Try It! 3. What is the solution to $2^{3x} = 7^{x+1}$?

APPLICATION

EXAMPLE 4 Use an Exponential Model

The diagram shows how a forest fire grows over time. The fire department can contain a 160-acre fire without needing additional resources. About how many minutes does it take for a fire to become too big for the fire department to contain without additional resources? Round to the nearest minute.

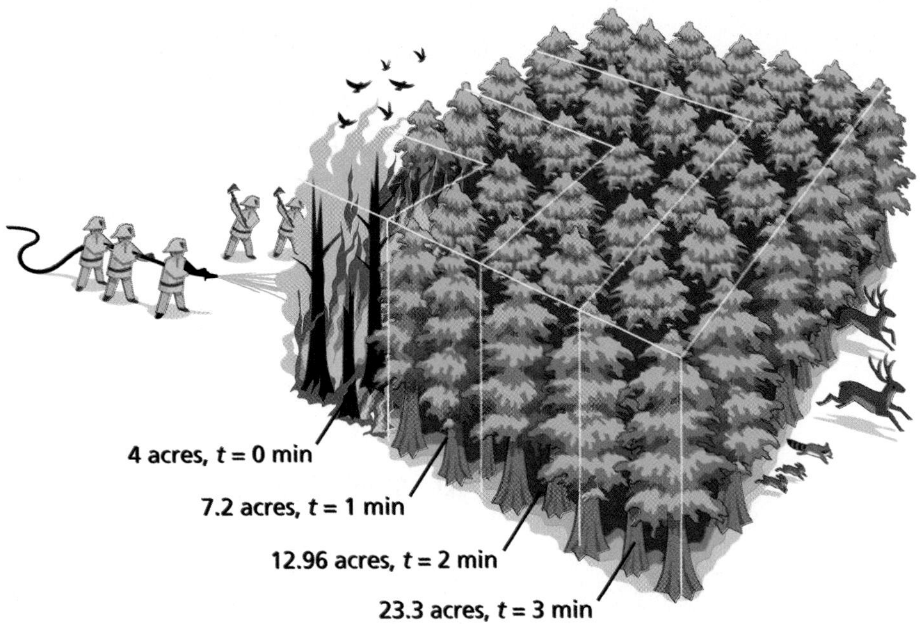

Formulate Because the ratios of the number of acres from the diagram are all 1.8, the exponential growth model uses $b = 1.8$. The model is $160 = 4(1.8)^t$.

Use the model $y = ab^t$ where y represents the number of acres, a is the initial number of acres, b is the growth rate of the fire, and t is the number of minutes the fire has raged.

Compute Solve the equation for t.

$160 = 4(1.8)^t$ .... Write the original equation.

$40 = (1.8)^t$ .... Divide each side by 4.

$\log 40 = \log(1.8)^t$ .... Property of Equality for Logarithmic Equations

$\log 40 = t \log 1.8$ .... Power Property of Logarithms

$\frac{\log 40}{\log 1.8} = t$ .... Isolate the variable t.

$6.276 \approx t$ .... Evaluate.

Interpret Verify the answer by evaluating the expression $4(1.8)^{6.276}$.

$4(1.8)^{6.276} \approx 160.01$

The fire department has a little more than 6 minutes to contain the fire before they will require additional resources.

 **Try It!** **4.** About how many minutes does it take the fire to spread to cover 100 acres?

VOCABULARY
A **logarithmic equation** contains one or more logarithms of variable expressions.

EXAMPLE 5 Solve Logarithmic Equations

What is the solution to $\ln (x^2 - 16) = \ln (6x)$?

$\ln (x^2 - 16) = \ln (6x)$	Write the original equation.
$x^2 - 16 = 6x$	Property of Equality for Logarithmic Equations
$x^2 - 6x - 16 = 0$	Set quadratic equation equal to 0.
$(x - 8)(x + 2) = 0$	Factor.
$x = 8$ or -2	Apply the Zero Product Property.

Check Substitute each value into the original equation.

$x = 8$	$x = -2$
$\ln (8^2 - 16) = \ln (6 \cdot 8)$	$\ln ((-2)^2 - 16) = \ln (6 \cdot (-2))$
$\ln (48) = \ln (48)$ ✔	$\ln (-12) = \ln (-12)$ ✘

Because logarithms are not defined for negative values, only $x = 8$ is a solution. The value $x = -2$ is an extraneous solution.

Try It! 5. Solve each equation.

a. $\log_5 (x^2 - 45) = \log_5 (4x)$ b. $\ln (-4x - 1) = \ln (4x^2)$

EXAMPLE 6 Solve Logarithmic and Exponential Equations by Graphing

USE APPROPRIATE TOOLS
When typing this equation into a calculator, it is helpful to write the equation using the Power Property of Logarithms rather than risking incorrect input of the exponent.

What is the solution to $\log (2x + 1)^5 = x - 2$?

Let $y_1 = 5 \log (2x + 1)$ and $y_2 = x - 2$.

Graph both equations.

Use the INTERSECT feature to find the point(s) of intersection.

The points of intersection, to the nearest thousandth, are (−0.329, −2.329) and (8.204, 6.204).

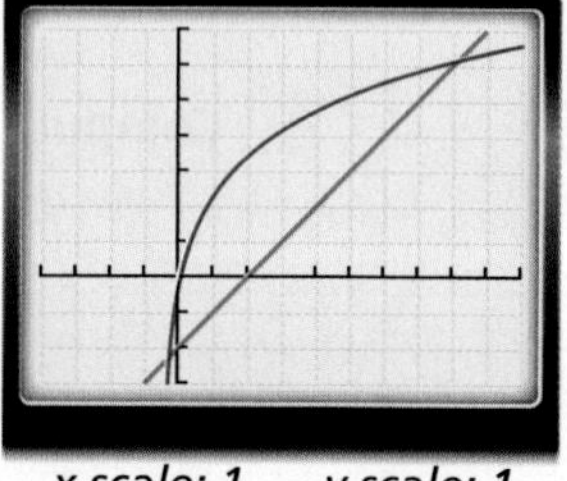
x scale: 1 *y scale: 1*

Check

$\log (2(-0.329) + 1)^5 = -0.329 - 2$	$\log (2(8.204) + 1)^5 = 8.204 - 2$
$\log (0.342)^5 = -2.329$	$\log (17.408)^5 = 6.204$
$-2.329 = -2.329$ ✔	$6.204 = 6.204$ ✔

The solutions are $x \approx -0.329$ and $x \approx 8.204$.

Try It! 6. Solve each equation by graphing. Round to the nearest thousandth.

a. $3(2)^{x+2} - 1 = 3 - x$ b. $\ln (3x - 1) = x - 5$

CONCEPT SUMMARY Exponential and Logarithmic Equations

	Property of Equality for Exponential Equations		Property of Equality for Logarithmic Equations	
ALGEBRA	If b is a positive number other than 1, $b^x = b^y$ if and only if $x = y$.		If b is a positive number other than 1, $\log_b x = \log_b y$ if and only if $x = y$.	
WORDS	If two powers of the same base are equal, then their exponents are equal.	If two exponents are equal, then the powers with the same base are equal.	If two logarithms of the same base are equal, then the arguments are equal.	If two arguments are equal and the bases are the same, then the logarithms are equal.
NUMBERS	If $2^x = 2^4$, then $x = 4$.	If $x = 4$, then $2^x = 2^4$.	If $\log_3 x = \log_3 8$, then $x = 8$.	If $x = 8$, then $\log_3 x = \log_3 8$.

Do You UNDERSTAND?

1. ESSENTIAL QUESTION How do properties of exponents and logarithms help you solve equations?

2. **Vocabulary** Jordan claims that $x^2 + 3 = 12$ is an exponential equation. Is Jordan correct? Explain your thinking.

3. **Communicate Precisely** How can properties of logarithms help to solve an equation such as $\log_6 (8x - 2)^3 = 12$?

Do You KNOW HOW?

Solve. Round to the nearest hundredth, if necessary. List any extraneous solutions.

4. $16^{3x} = 256^{x+1}$

5. $6^{x+2} = 4^x$

6. $\log_5 (x^2 - 44) = \log_5 (7x)$

7. $\log_2 (3x - 2) = 4$

8. $4^{2x} = 9^{x-1}$

9. A rabbit farm had 200 rabbits in 2015. The number of rabbits increases by 30% every year. How many rabbits are on the farm in 2031?

PRACTICE & PROBLEM SOLVING

Scan for Multimedia

Practice Tutorial

Additional Exercises Available Online

UNDERSTAND

10. **Use Structure** Would you use the natural log or the common log when solving the equation $10^{x+2} = 78$? Is it possible to use either the natural log or common log? Explain.

11. **Make Sense and Persevere** Explain why logarithms are necessary to solve the equation $3^{x+2} = 8$, but are not necessary to solve the equation $3^{x+2} = 27^{4x}$.

12. **Reason** Tristen solved the equation $\log_3 (x + 1) - \log_3 (x - 6) = \log_3 (2x + 2)$. Justify each step of solving the equation in Tristen's work. Are both numbers solutions to the equation? Explain.

$$\log_3(x + 1) - \log_3(x - 6) = \log_3(2x + 2)$$
$$\log_3(x + 1) = \log_3(2x + 2) + \log_3(x - 6)$$
$$\log_3(x + 1) = \log_3(2x + 2)(x - 6)$$
$$(x + 1) = (2x + 2)(x - 6)$$
$$x + 1 = 2x^2 - 10x - 12$$
$$0 = 2x^2 - 11x - 13$$
$$x = 6.5 \text{ or } x = -1$$

13. **Error Analysis** The number of milligrams of medicine in a person's system after t hours is given by the function $A = 20e^{-0.40t}$. Thomas sets $A = 0$ to find the number of hours it takes for all of the medicine to be removed from a person's system. What mistake did Thomas make? Explain.

14. **Mathematical Connections** Explain the importance of the Power Property of Logarithms when solving exponential equations.

15. **Error Analysis** Find the student error in the solution of the logarithmic equation.

$$\log (x + 3) + \log x = 1$$
$$\log x (x + 3) = 1$$
$$x(x + 3) = 10^1$$
$$x^2 + 3x - 10 = 0$$
$$(x - 2)(x + 5) = 0$$
$$x = 2, -5$$

X

PRACTICE

Find all solutions of the equation. Round answers to the nearest ten-thousandth. SEE EXAMPLE 1

16. $3^{2-3x} = 3^{5x-6}$

17. $7^{3x} = 54$

18. $25^{x^2}=125^{x+3}$

19. $4^{3x-1} = \left(\frac{1}{2}\right)^{x+5}$

20. $4^{2x+1} = 4^{3x-5}$

21. $6^{x-2} = 216$

Find all solutions of the equation. Round answers to the nearest ten-thousandth. SEE EXAMPLES 2 AND 3

22. $2^{3x-2} = 5$

23. $4 + 5^{6-x} = 15$

24. $6^{3x+1} = 9^x$

25. $-3 = \left(\frac{1}{2}\right)^x - 12$

26. $3^{2x-3} = 4^x$

27. $4^{x+2} = 8^{x-1}$

28. Dale has \$1,000 to invest. He has a goal to have \$2,500 in this investment in 10 years. At what annual rate compounded continuously will Dale reach his goal? Round to the nearest hundredth. SEE EXAMPLE 4

Find all solutions of the equation. Round answers to the nearest thousandth. SEE EXAMPLE 5

29. $\log_2 (4x + 5) = \log_2 x^2$

30. $2\ln (3x - 2) = \ln (5x + 6)$

31. $\log_4 (x^2 - 2x) = \log_4 (3x + 8)$

32. $\ln (5x - 2) = \ln (x - 1)$

33. $\ln (2x^2 + 5x) = \ln (2x + 7)$

34. $2\log (x + 1) = \log (x + 1)$

35. $\log_2 x + \log_2 (x - 3) = 2$

36. $\log_2 (3x - 2) = \log_2 (x - 1) + 4$

37. $\log_6 (x^2 - 2x) = \log_6 (2x - 3) + \log_6 (x + 1)$

Solve by graphing. Round answers to the nearest thousandth. SEE EXAMPLE 6

38. $\log(5x - 3)^2 = x - 4$

39. $\ln(2x) = 3x - 5$

40. $\log(4x) = x + \log x$

PRACTICE & PROBLEM SOLVING

Practice Tutorial

Mixed Review Available Online

APPLY

41. Model With Mathematics The population of a city is modeled by the function $P = 250{,}000e^{0.013t}$, where t is the number of years since 2000. In what year, to the nearest year, will the population reach 450,000?

42. Use Structure Felix invested \$10,000 into a retirement account in 2010. He then projected the amount of money that would be in the account for several years assuming that interest would compound continuously at an annual rate. Later, when he looked back the data, he could not recall the annual rate that he used for the projections. Use the data below to determine the annual rate.

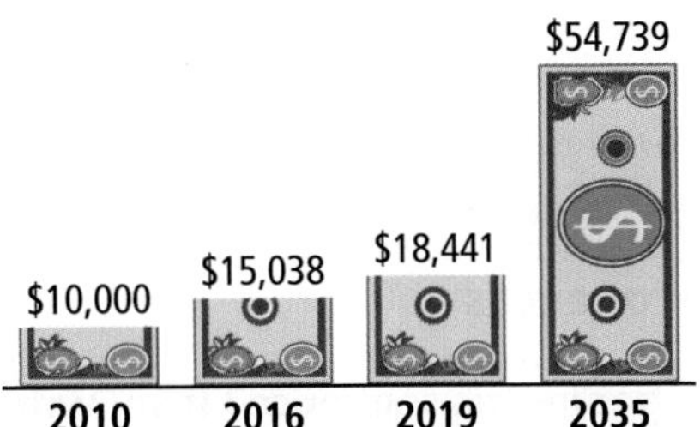

43. Higher Order Thinking A biologist is using the logarithmic model $n = k\log(A)$ to determine the number of a species n, that can live on a land mass of area A. The constant k varies according to the species.

a. Use the graph to determine the constant k for the species that the scientist is studying.

b. Determine the land mass in acres that is needed to support 3,000 of the species.

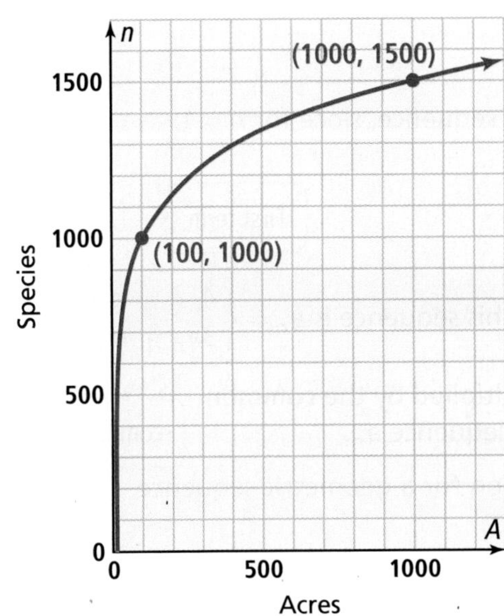

ASSESSMENT PRACTICE

44. Which of the following have the same solution? Select all that apply.

Ⓐ $\log_8(x^2 - 15) = \log_8(2x)$

Ⓑ $\ln(12x + 2) = \ln(2x - 3)$

Ⓒ $\log_2 x + \log_2(x + 4) = 5$

Ⓓ $\log_3(15x + 6)^2 = 8$

Ⓔ $\log_4(3x - 5) = 2$

45. SAT/ACT The graph shows the function $y = 4^x$. Determine when the function shown in the graph is greater than the function $y = 2^{3x-1}$.

Ⓐ $x > 1$

Ⓑ $x < 1$

Ⓒ $x > -1$

Ⓓ $x < -1$

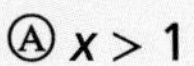

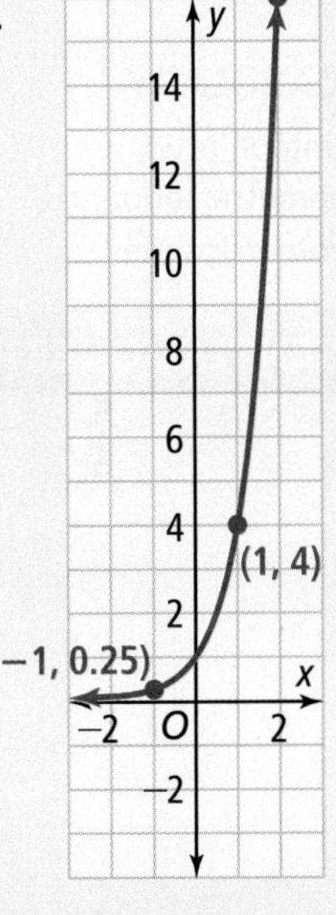

46. Performance Task A professor conducted an experiment to find the relationship between time and memory. The professor determined the model $f(t) = t_0 - 15\log(t + 1.1)$ gives the memory score after t months when a student had an initial memory score of t_0.

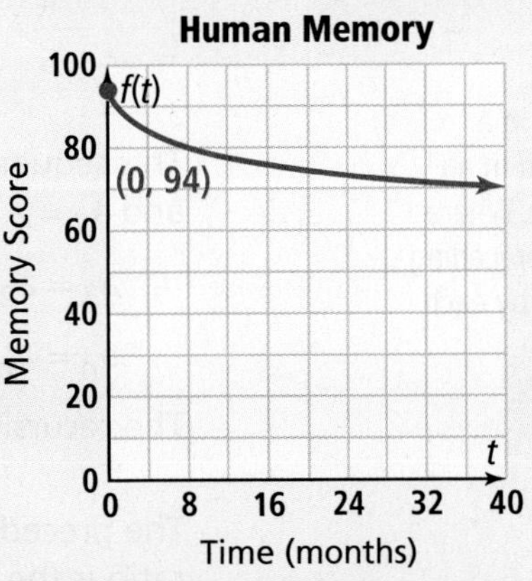

Part A Write a model for a student with the given initial memory score.

Part B After about how many years will the student have a memory score of 65?

Activity Assess

5-8 Geometric Sequences and Series

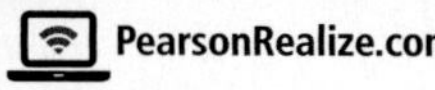
PearsonRealize.com

I CAN… identify, write, and use geometric sequences and series.

VOCABULARY
- common ratio
- geometric sequence
- geometric series

EXPLORE & REASON

A store offered customers two plans for getting bonus points:

A. What expression represents the number of points received each day for Plan A?

B. What expression represents the number of points received each day for Plan B?

C. Reason On the 7th day, which plan would offer the most bonus points? Explain.

ESSENTIAL QUESTION How can you represent and use geometric sequences and series?

EXAMPLE 1 Identify Geometric Sequences

A. Is the sequence shown in the table a geometric sequence? If so, write a recursive definition for the sequence.

A **geometric sequence** is a sequence with a constant ratio between consecutive terms. This ratio is called the **common ratio**, *r*.

Notice the relationship between the terms in this sequence:

Term Number (n)	Term (a_n)
1	4
2	12
3	36
4	108
5	324

x3 x3

Each term is 3 times the preceding term.

STUDY TIP
Notice that *r* serves in a similiar capacity as *d* in an arithmetic sequence. Where *d* is added to each preceding term, *r* is multiplied by each preceding term.

This sequence is a geometric sequence, since for $n = 1$, $a_1 = 4$, $r = 3$, and $a_2 = a_1 \bullet 3$

$a_3 = a_2 \bullet 3$

$a_n = a_{n-1} \bullet 3$

The recursive definition for this sequence is $a_n = \begin{cases} 4, & n = 1 \\ 3a_{n-1}, & n > 1. \end{cases}$

First term — Term number — common ratio

The preceding term a_{n-1} multiplied by the common ratio is the next term in the sequence a_n.

The general recursive defintion for a geometric sequence is $a_n = \begin{cases} a_1, & n = 1 \\ a_{n-1} \bullet r, & n > 1 \end{cases}$

CONTINUED ON THE NEXT PAGE

EXAMPLE 1 CONTINUED

B. Is the sequence 12, 9.6, 7.68, 6.144, ... a geometric sequence? If so, write the recursive definition for the sequence.

Find the ratio between consecutive terms.

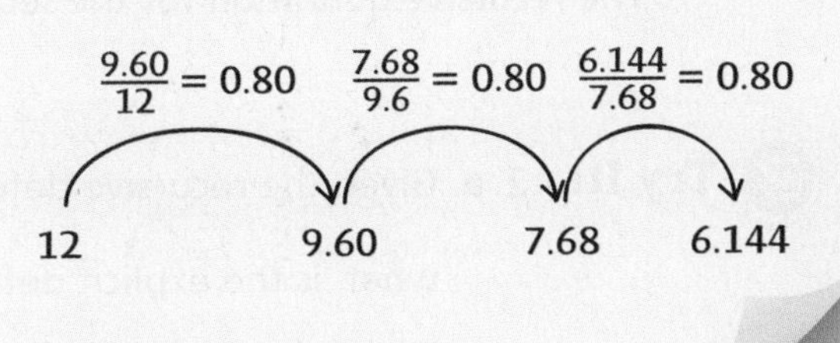

The ratio between the consecutive terms is constant. This is a geometric sequence with $a_1 = 12$ and $r = 0.8$.

The recursive definition for the sequence is $a_n = \begin{cases} 12, & n = 1 \\ 0.8\, a_{n-1}, & n > 1 \end{cases}$

Try It! 1. Is the sequence a geometric sequence? If so, write a recursive definition for the sequence.

a. 1.22, 1.45, 1.68, 1.91, ...

b. −1.5, 0.75, −0.375, 0.1875, ...

EXAMPLE 2 Translate Between Recursive and Explicit Definitions

A. Given the recursive definition $a_n = \begin{cases} 5, & n = 1 \\ \frac{1}{2} a_{n-1}, & n > 1 \end{cases}$ what is the explicit definition for the geometric sequence?

The first term is 5, and the common ratio is $\frac{1}{2}$.

The recursive definition is $a_n = \frac{1}{2}a_{n-1}$. Use this definition to find a pattern:

$a_1 = 5$ .... Identify the first term.

$a_2 = 5\left(\frac{1}{2}\right)$ .... 1 common ratio multiplied to the first term

$a_3 = a_2 \cdot \left(\frac{1}{2}\right) = (5)\left(\frac{1}{2}\right)\left(\frac{1}{2}\right) = (5)\left(\frac{1}{2}\right)^2$ .... 2 common ratios multiplied to the first term

$a_4 = a_3 \cdot \left(\frac{1}{2}\right) = (5)\left(\frac{1}{2}\right)^2\left(\frac{1}{2}\right) = (5)\left(\frac{1}{2}\right)^3$ .... 3 common ratios multiplied to the first term

The pattern reveals the explicit definition for the sequence: $a_n = (5)\left(\frac{1}{2}\right)^{n-1}$.

The general explicit definition for any geometric sequence is: $a_n = a_1 r^{n-1}$.

VOCABULARY
Recall that an explicit definition allows you to find any term in the sequence without knowing the previous term.

CONTINUED ON THE NEXT PAGE

EXAMPLE 2 CONTINUED

B. Given the explicit definition $a_n = 3(2)^{n-1}$, what is the recursive definition for the geometric sequence?

From the explicit definition, $a_1 = 3$ and $r = 2$.

The recursive definition for the sequence is $a_n = \begin{cases} 3, & n = 1 \\ 2a_{n-1}, & n > 1 \end{cases}$.

Try It! **2. a.** Given the recursive definition $a_n = \begin{cases} 12, & n = 1 \\ \frac{1}{3}a_{n-1}, & n > 1 \end{cases}$ what is the explicit definition for the sequence?

b. Given the explicit definition $a_n = 6(1.2)^{n-1}$, what is the recursive definition?

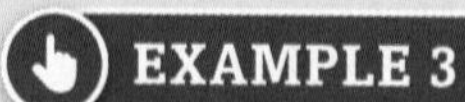

EXAMPLE 3 Solve Problems With Geometric Sequences

A phone tree is when one person calls a certain number of people, then those people each call the same number of people, and so on. In the fifth round of calls, 243 people were called.

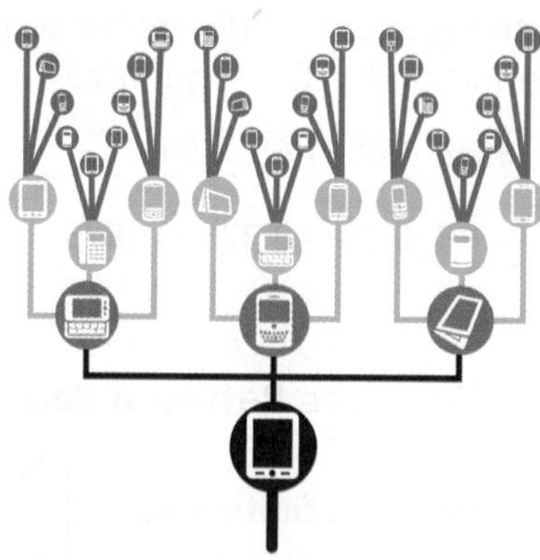

A. Write an explicit definition to find the number of people called in each round.

So $a_1 = 3$ and $a_5 = 243$. Use the explicit definition to find r.

$a_n = a_1 r^{n-1}$ .... Write the general explicit formula.

$243 = 3r^{5-1}$ .... Substitute 243 for a_5, 3 for a_1, and 5 for n.

$81 = r^4$ .... Isolate the power.

$3 = r$ .... Solve. Disregard the negative solution.

The explicit definition is $a_n = 3(3)^{n-1}$.

LOOK FOR RELATIONSHIPS
Notice that the equation for an explicit definition is in the same form as the equation for an exponential function.

CONTINUED ON THE NEXT PAGE

Activity Assess

EXAMPLE 3 CONTINUED

B. How many people were called in the eighth round of the phone tree?

Use the explicit definition and solve for $n = 8$.

$a_r = a_1 r^{n-1}$

$a_8 = 3(3)^{8-1}$ Substitute 8 for n and simplify.

$a_8 = 3(3)^7$

$a_8 = 6{,}561$

On the eighth round, 6,561 people were called.

Try It! 3. A geometric sequence can be used to describe the growth of bacteria in an experiment. On the first day of the experiment there were 9 bacteria in a Petri dish. On the 10th day, there are 3^{20} bacteria in the dish. How many bacteria were in the dish on the 7th day of the experiment?

CONCEPTUAL UNDERSTANDING

EXAMPLE 4 Formula for the Sum of a Finite Geometric Series

A. How can you find the sum of a finite geometric series?

A **geometric series** is the sum of the terms of a geometric sequence. S_n represents the sum of a geometric sequence with n terms.

$S_n = a_1 + a_1 r + a_1 r^2 + a_1 r^3 + \ldots + a_1 r^{n-1}$ Write the equation for a geometric series.

$rS_n = a_1 r + a_1 r^2 + a_1 r^3 + \ldots + a_1 r^{n-1} + a_1 r^n$ Multiply each side by r.

$S_n - rS_n = a_1 - a_1 r^n$ Subtract the second equation from the first equation.

$S_n(1 - r) = a_1(1 - r^n)$ Factor.

$S_n = \dfrac{a_1(1 - r^n)}{(1 - r)}$ for $r \neq 1$ Solve for S_n.

MAKE SENSE AND PERSEVERE
Notice that multiplying each side by r gives you a second equation with many of the same terms as the original equation. How does this help you eliminate terms to find an expression for the sum of a finite geometric series?

B. Write the expanded form of the series $\sum_{n=1}^{7} 3\left(\frac{2}{3}\right)^{n-1}$. What is the sum?

Recall how to use sigma ($\sum$) notation to represent a series.

$$\sum_{m=1}^{n} a_1 r^{m-1} = a_1 + a_1 r + a_1 r^2 + a_1 r^3 + \ldots + a_1 r^{n-1} = \frac{a_1(1 - r^n)}{(1 - r)}.$$

The series is $3 + 2 + \frac{4}{3} + \frac{8}{9} + \frac{16}{27} + \frac{32}{81} + \frac{64}{243}$. To find the sum, use the sum of a finite geometric series formula with $a_1 = 3$, $r = \frac{2}{3}$, and $n = 7$.

$$S_7 = \frac{3\left(1 - \left(\frac{2}{3}\right)^7\right)}{1 - \frac{2}{3}} = \frac{2{,}059}{243}$$

The sum is $\frac{2{,}059}{243}$.

You can check by finding the sum of the terms directly:

$$3 + 2 + \frac{4}{3} + \frac{8}{9} + \frac{16}{27} + \frac{32}{81} + \frac{64}{243} = \frac{2{,}059}{243}.$$

CONTINUED ON THE NEXT PAGE

EXAMPLE 4 CONTINUED

Try It! **4. a.** Write the expanded form of the series $\sum_{n=1}^{5} \frac{1}{2}(3)^{n-1}$. What is the sum?

b. Write the series $-2 + \left(\frac{-2}{3}\right) + \ldots \left(\frac{-2}{243}\right)$ using sigma notation. What is the sum?

EXAMPLE 5 Number of Terms in a Finite Geometric Series

COMMON ERROR
Be careful to calculate the common ratio as a term divided by the previous term, not the next term.

A. How many terms are in the geometric series $200 + 300 + 450 + \ldots + 7{,}688.7$?

Since the series is geometric, you can find that $r = 1.5$. Use the explicit definition to find n, the number of terms.

$$7{,}688.7 = 200(1.5)^{n-1}$$

$$38.4435 = (1.5)^{n-1}$$

Substitute the last term in the series into the explicit definition to determine n.

$$\log 38.4435 = \log (1.5)^{n-1}$$

$$\log 38.4435 = (n-1)\log (1.5)$$

$$\frac{\log 38.4435}{\log 1.5} = n - 1$$

$$n = \frac{\log 38.4435}{\log 1.5} + 1$$

$$n \approx 10$$

There are 10 terms in the geometric series.

B. The sum of a geometric series is 11,718. The first term of the series is 3, and its common ratio is 5. How many terms are in the series?

$$S_n = \frac{a_1(1 - r^n)}{(1 - r)}$$

Substitute for S_n, a_1, and r in the formula for the sum of a geometric series to find n.

$$11{,}718 = \frac{3(1 - 5^n)}{(1 - 5)}$$

$$-46{,}872 = 3(1 - 5^n)$$

$$-15{,}624 = 1 - 5^n$$

$$5^n = 1 + 15{,}624$$

$$\log (5^n) = \log 15{,}625$$

Once you have isolated the term with the exponent, take the logarithm of both sides.

$$n\log 5 = \log 15{,}625$$

$$n = \frac{\log 15{,}625}{\log 5}$$

$$n = 6$$

There are 6 terms in the series.

Try It! **5a.** How many terms are in the geometric series $3 + 6 + 12 + \ldots + 768$?

b. The sum of a geometric series is 155. The first term of the series is 5, and its common ratio is 2. How many terms are in the series?

Activity Assess

APPLICATION

EXAMPLE 6 Use a Finite Geometric Series

Isabel wants to borrow \$24,000 for 6 years with an annual interest rate of 4.5% to purchase a share in a food truck business. What will be her monthly payment?

The formula to calculate a monthly payment is $A = \frac{P}{\sum_{k=1}^{n}\left(\frac{1}{1+i}\right)^{k}}$, where A is the monthly amount, P is the principal, or amount of the loan, n is the number of months, and i is the monthly interest rate.

For Isabel's loan, $P = 24{,}000$, $n = 72$, and $i = 0.00375$. Substitute the values into the formula.

The annual interest rate is 4.5%, so you must divide that by 12 to get the monthly interest rate.

USE APPROPRIATE TOOLS
You can use your calculator's memory feature to use more precise values rather than the estimates used here.

$$A = \frac{24{,}000}{\sum_{k=1}^{72}\left(\frac{1}{1+0.00375}\right)^{k}}$$

The denominator is a finite geometric series with $a_1 \approx 0.996$ and $r \approx 0.996$.

Find the sum.

$$\sum_{k=1}^{72}\left(\frac{1}{1+0.00375}\right)^{k} \approx \frac{0.996(1-0.996^{72})}{(1-0.996)} \approx 62.417$$

Now calculate the amount of the monthly payment:

$$A \approx \frac{24{,}000}{62.417} \approx 384.51$$

Isabel's monthly payment for the loan would be about \$384.51.

Try It! 6. What is the monthly payment for a \$40,000 loan for 4 years with an annual interest rate of 4.8%?

  Concept Summary 

CONCEPT SUMMARY Geometric Sequences and Series

In a geometric sequence, the ratio defined by a term divided by the previous term is a constant, r. Alternately, any term in a geometric sequence multiplied by r gives the next term.

The sequence 1, 5, 25, 125, 625, ... is a geometric sequence, since $r = 5$.

WORDS	ALGEBRA	EXAMPLE
Each term in the sequence is r times the previous term.	The recursive definition for a geometric sequence is $a_n = \begin{cases} a_1, & n = 1 \\ a_{n-1} \cdot r, & n > 1 \end{cases}$	$a_n = \begin{cases} 1 & n = 1 \\ 5a_{n-1}, & n > 1 \end{cases}$
The fourth term in a sequence is the first term multiplied by three common ratios.	The explicit definition is $a_n = a_1 r^{n-1}$	$a_n = 1(5)^{n-1}$
You can find the sum of a certain number of terms in a geometric series.	For a finite geometric series with $r \neq 1$ $\sum_{m=1}^{n} a_1 r^{m-1} = \frac{a_1(1 - r^n)}{(1 - r)}$.	The sum of the first five terms is $\frac{1(1 - 5^5)}{1 - 5} = \frac{-3{,}124}{-4} = 781$

Do You UNDERSTAND?

1. ESSENTIAL QUESTION How can you represent and use geometric sequences and series?

2. **Error Analysis** Denzel claims the sequence 0, 7, 49, 343, ... is a geometric sequence and the next number is 2,401. What error did he make?

3. **Vocabulary** Describe the similarities and differences between a common difference and a common ratio.

4. **Use Structure** What happens to the terms of a sequence if a_1 is positive and $r > 1$? What happens if $0 < r < 1$? Explain.

Do You KNOW HOW?

Find the common ratio and the next three terms of each geometric sequence.

5. 2, −4, 8, −16, ...

6. −64, −16, −4, −1, ...

7. 0.8, 2.4, 7.2, 21.6, ...

8. 2, −10, 50, −250, ...

9. 100, 50, 25, 12.5, ...

10. In a video game, players earn 10 points for finishing the first level and twice as many points for each additional level. How many points does a player earn for finishing the fifth level? How many points will the player have earned in the game up to that point?

PRACTICE & PROBLEM SOLVING

Scan for Multimedia

Practice Tutorial

Additional Exercises Available Online

UNDERSTAND

11. **Reason** True or False: If the first two terms of a geometric sequence are positive, then the third term is positive. Explain your reasoning.

12. **Error Analysis** The first term of a geometric sequence is 4 and grows exponentially by a factor of 3. Murphy writes out the terms and says that the sum of the 4th and 5th terms is 1,296. Explain Murphy's error and correct it.

13. **Construct Arguments** Write a geometric sequence with at least four terms and describe it using both an explicit and recursive definitions. How can you confirm that your sequence is geometric?

14. **Higher Order Thinking** Adam drops a ball from a height of 12 feet. Each bounce is 50% as high as the previous bounce. What is the total vertical distance the ball has traveled when it hits the ground for the 4th time?

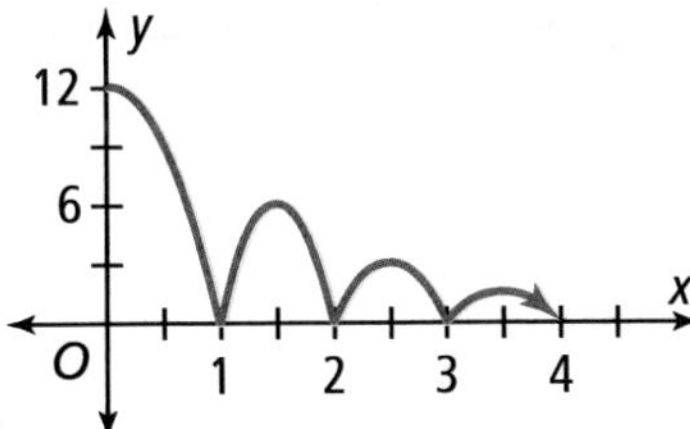

15. **Model with Mathematics** The Sierpinski Triangle is a fractal made by cutting an equilateral triangle into four congruent pieces and removing the center piece, leaving three smaller triangles. The process is repeated on each triangle, creating more triangles that are even smaller. Continuing this pattern, how many triangles would there be after the tenth step in the process?

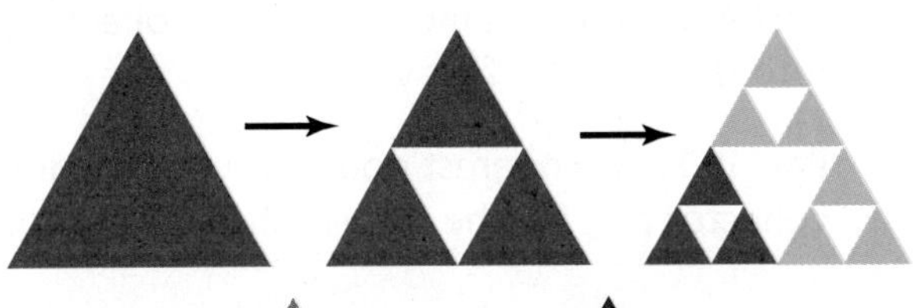

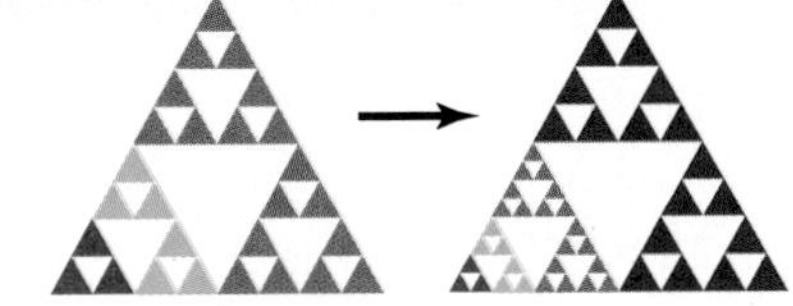

PRACTICE

Is the sequence geometric? If so, write a recursive definition for the sequence. SEE EXAMPLE 1

16. 1, −3, 9, −27, ...
17. 3, −15, 75, −375, ...
18. 4, 5, 6, 7, ...
19. 24, 8, $\frac{8}{3}$, $\frac{8}{9}$, ...
20. 2, 4, 6, 8, ...
21. 10, 40, 160, 640, ...

Translate between the recursive and explicit definitions for each sequence. SEE EXAMPLE 2

22. $a_n = 1{,}024\left(\frac{1}{2}\right)^{n-1}$

23. $a_n = \begin{cases} 2, & n = 1 \\ -2a^{n-1}, & n > 1 \end{cases}$

24. $a_n = 35(2)^{n-1}$

25. $a_n = -6(-3)^{n-1}$

26. $a_n = \begin{cases} 1, & n = 1 \\ \frac{2}{3}a_{n-1}, & n > 1 \end{cases}$

27. In an experiment, the number of bacteria present each day form a geometric sequence. On the first day, there were 100 bacteria. On the eighth day, there were 12,800 bacteria. How many bacteria were there on the fourth day? SEE EXAMPLE 3

Write the expansion of each series. What is the sum? SEE EXAMPLE 4

28. $\sum_{n=1}^{6} 4(2)^{n-1}$
29. $\sum_{n=1}^{20} 6(2)^{n-1}$
30. $\sum_{n=1}^{7} -4(3)^{n-1}$
31. $\sum_{n=1}^{12} (-4)^{n-1}$

Write each series using sigma notation. Find the sum. SEE EXAMPLE 4

32. 8 + 16 + 32 + ... + 1,024

33. −7 − 42 − 252 − ... − 54,432

34. $\frac{1}{5} + \frac{1}{10} + \frac{1}{20} + \ldots + \frac{1}{80}$

35. 4 − 12 + 36 − ... + 2,916

36. The sum of a geometric series is 31.75. The first term of the series is 16, and its common ratio is 0.5. How many terms are in the series? SEE EXAMPLE 5

37. What is the monthly payment for a $12,000 loan for 7 years with an annual interest rate of 2.7%? SEE EXAMPLE 6

Practice Tutorial

Mixed Review Available Online

PRACTICE & PROBLEM SOLVING

APPLY

38. Model With Mathematics Kelley opens a bank account to save for a down payment on a car. Her initial deposit is $250, and she plans to deposit 10% more each month. Kelley's goal is to have $2,000 in the account after six months. Will she meet her goal?

39. Make Sense and Persevere Henry just started his own cleaning business. He is using word-of-mouth from his current clients to promote his business. He currently has seven clients.

a. Five of his clients really like Henry's work and each told two friends the following month. This group each told two friends the following month, and so on for a total of five months. Assuming no one heard twice, how many people have had or heard of a positive experience with Henry's cleaning business?

b. The two unhappy clients each told five people the following month. This group each told five people, and so on, for five months. Assuming no one heard twice, how many people have had or heard of a negative experience with Henry's cleaning business?

40. Model with Mathematics Ricardo bought a motorcycle for $15,000. The value depreciates 15% at the start of every year. What is the value of the motorcycle after three years?

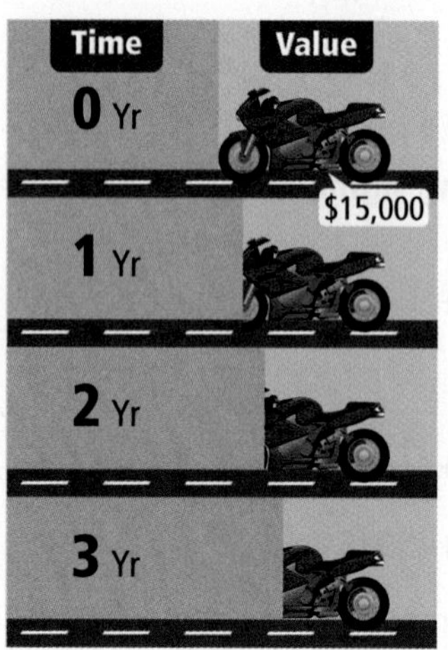

ASSESSMENT PRACTICE

41. The first term of a geometric series is −1, and the common ratio is −2. Fill in the number to complete the sentence.

If the sum of the series is −43, there are ___?___ terms in the series.

42. SAT/ACT What is the value of the 11th term in the following geometric sequence?

$$\frac{1}{27}, \frac{1}{9}, \frac{1}{3}, \ldots$$

Ⓐ 3^4
Ⓑ 3^5
Ⓒ 3^6
Ⓓ 3^7
Ⓔ 3^8

43. Performance Task An avid collector wants to purchase a signed basketball from a particular playoff game. He plans to put away 4% more money each year, in a safe at his home, to save up for the basketball. In the sixth year, he puts $580 in the safe and realizes that he has exactly enough money to purchase the basketball.

Price = Year 5 savings + $580.00

Part A How much money did the collector put into the safe the first year?

Part B To the nearest dollar, how much did the collector pay for the signed playoff basketball?

TOPIC 5

Topic Review

TOPIC ESSENTIAL QUESTION

1. How do you use exponential and logarithmic functions to model situations and solve problems?

Vocabulary Review

Choose the correct term to complete each sentence.

2. A(n) __________ has base e.
3. A(n) __________ has the form $f(x) = a \cdot b^x$.
4. In an exponential function, when $0 < b < 1$, b is a(n) __________.
5. The __________ allows logarithms with a base other than 10 or e to be evaluated.
6. A(n) __________ has base 10.
7. The inverse of an exponential function is a(n) __________.

- decay factor
- exponential function
- logarithmic function
- growth factor
- common logarithm
- natural logarithm
- Change of Base Formula

Concepts & Skills Review

LESSON 5-1 Key Features of Exponential Functions

Quick Review

An **exponential function** has the form $f(x) = a \cdot b^x$. When $a > 0$ and $b > 1$, the function is an **exponential growth function**. When $a > 0$ and $0 < b < 1$, the function is an **exponential decay function**.

Example

Paul invests $4,000 in an account that pays 2.5% interest annually. How much money will be in the account after 5 years?

Write and use the exponential growth function model.

$A(t) = a(1 + r)^n$

$A(5) = 4,000(1 + 0.025)^5$

$A(5) = 4,000(1.025)^5$

$A(5) = 4,525.63$

There will be about $4,525.63 in Paul's account after 5 years.

Practice & Problem Solving

Identify the domain, range, intercept, and asymptote of each exponential function. Then describe the end behavior.

8. $f(x) = 400 \cdot \left(\frac{1}{2}\right)^x$
9. $f(x) = 2 \cdot (3)^x$
10. **Reason** Seth invests $1,400 at 1.8% annual interest for 6 years. How much will Seth have at the end of the sixth year?
11. **Model With Mathematics** Bailey buys a car for $25,000. The car depreciates in value 18% per year. How much will the car be worth after 3 years?
12. Identify the domain, range, intercept, and asymptote.

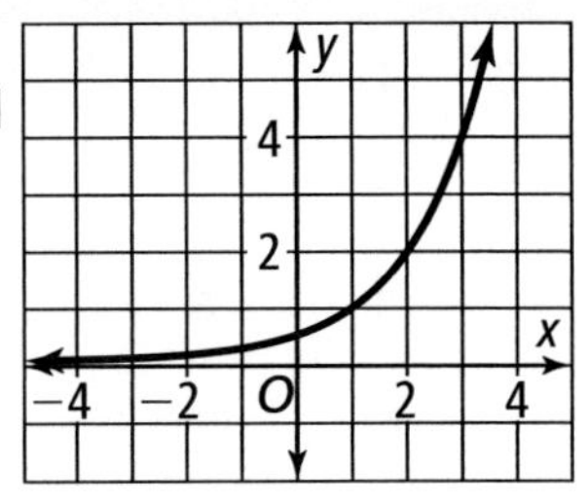

TOPIC 5 REVIEW

LESSON 5-2 Exponential Models

Quick Review

Interest may be compounded over different time periods, such as quarterly, monthly, or daily. The formula $A = P\left(1 + \frac{r}{n}\right)^{nt}$ is used to calculate the amount of money available after it has been invested for an amount of time. The formula $A = Pe^{rt}$ is used to calculate the amount of money available in an account that is compounded continuously. The calculator can be used to find an exponential model for a set of data.

Example

Jenny invests $2,500 in an account that pays 2.4% interest annually. The interest is compounded quarterly. How much will Jenny have in the account after 6 years?

Use the formula $\boldsymbol{A = P\left(1 + \frac{r}{n}\right)^{nt}}$.

$A = 2{,}500\left(1 + \frac{0.024}{4}\right)^{4(6)}$ Substitute for *A*, *P*, *n*, and *r*.

$A = 2{,}500(1.006)^{24}$ Simplify.

$A = 2{,}885.97$ Use a calculator.

Jenny will have about $2,885.97.

Practice & Problem Solving

Find the total amount of money in the account after the given amount of time.

13. Compounded monthly, $P = \$5{,}000$, $r = 2.4\%$, $t = 8$ years

14. Continuously compounded, $P = \$7{,}500$, $r = 1.6\%$, $t = 10$ years

Write an exponential model given two points.

15. (12, 256) and (13, 302)

16. (3, 54) and (4, 74)

17. **Model With Mathematics** Jason's parents invested some money for Jason's education when Jason was born. The table shows how the account has grown.

Number of Years	Amount ($)
1	2,250
7	4,400
13	9,250

Predict how much will be in the account after 18 years.

LESSON 5-3 Linear, Exponential, and Quadratic Models

Quick Review

To determine which function best models a data set, analyze the differences and ratios between consecutive *y*-values when the differences in consecutive *x*-values are constant.

Example

Determine whether the function below is linear, quadratic, or exponential.

x	y	1st Diff.	2nd Diff.	Ratios
0	1			
1	3	2		3
2	9	6	4	3
3	27	18	12	3

Since the ratio between the *y*-values is constant, the function is exponential.

Practice and Problem Solving

18. **Make Sense and Persevere** What is the first step in determining whether a table shows a linear, quadratic, or exponential function?

Determine whether the data in the tables represent a linear, quadratic, or exponential function.

19.

x	0	1	2	3	4
y	3	7	19	39	67

20.

x	−2	0	2	4	6
y	−20	−6	8	22	36

LESSON 5-4 Logarithms

Quick Review

A logarithm is an exponent. Common logarithms have base 10 and natural logarithms have base e. Exponential expressions can be rewritten in logarithmic form, and logarithmic expressions can be converted to exponential form.

$5^3 = 125$ can be rewritten as $\log_5 125 = 3$.

$\log 100 = 2$ can be rewritten as $10^2 = 100$.

Example

Evaluate $\log_2 \frac{1}{8}$.

$\log_2 \frac{1}{8} = x$ ······ Write an equation.

$2^x = \frac{1}{8}$ ······ Rewrite the equation in exponential form.

$2^x = 2^{-3}$ ······ Rewrite the equation with a common base.

$x = -3$ ······ Since the two expressions have a common base, the exponents are equal.

Practice & Problem Solving

Use Structure If an equation is given in exponential form, write the logarithmic form. If an equation is given in logarithmic form, write the exponential form.

21. $4^3 = 64$

22. $10^2 = 100$

23. $\log_6 216 = 3$

24. $\ln 20 = x$

Evaluate each logarithmic expression.

25. $\log_8 \frac{1}{64}$

26. $\log_3 81$

Use Appropriate Tools Evaluate each logarithmic expression using a calculator. Round answers to the nearest thousandth.

27. $\log 628$

28. $\ln 0.55$

Evaluate each logarithmic expression.

29. $\log_5 5^9$

30. $7^{\log_7 49}$

LESSON 5-5 Logarithmic Functions

Quick Review

A logarithmic function is the inverse of an exponential function.

Example

Find the inverse of $f(x) = 10^{x-2}$. Identify any intercepts or asymptotes.

$y = 10^{x-2}$ ······ Write in $y = f(x)$ form.

$x = 10^{y-2}$ ······ Interchange x and y.

$y - 2 = \log x$ ······ Write in log form.

$y = \log x + 2$ ······ Solve for y.

The equation of the inverse is $f^{-1}(x) = \log x + 2$. It has an x-intercept at $x = \frac{1}{100}$ and a vertical asymptote at the y-axis.

Practice & Problem Solving

Look for Relationships Graph each function and identify the domain and range. List any intercepts or asymptotes. Describe the end behavior.

31. $f(x) = \log_4 x$

32. $f(x) = \ln(x - 2)$

Use Structure Find the equation of the inverse of each function.

33. $f(x) = 8^{x-2}$

34. $f(x) = \frac{5^{x-2}}{8}$

LESSON 5-6 Properties of Logarithms

Quick Review

Properties of logarithms can be used to either expand a single logarithmic expression into individual logarithms or condense several logarithmic expressions into a single logarithm.

The Change of Base Formula can be used to find logarithms of numbers with bases other than 10 or *e*.

Example

Use the properties of logarithms to expand the expression $\log_6 \frac{x^3 y^5}{z}$.

$\log_6 \frac{x^3 y^5}{z}$

$= \log_6 x^3 y^5 - \log_6 z$ ...... Quotient Property of Logarithms

$= \log_6 x^3 + \log_6 y^5 - \log_6 z$ ...... Product Property of Logarithms

$= 3\log_6 x + 5\log_6 y - \log_6 z$ ...... Power Property of Logarithms

Practice & Problem Solving

Use Structure Use the properties of logarithms to write each as a single logarithm.

35. $3\log r - 2\log s + \log t$

36. $2\ln 3 + 4\ln 2 - \ln 36$

Evaluate each logarithm.

37. $\log_4 12$

38. $\log_7 70$

Make Sense and Persevere Solve each equation for *x*. Give an exact solution written as a logarithm and use the Change of Base Formula to provide an approximated solution rounded to the nearest thousandth.

39. $5^x = 200$

40. $7^x = 486$

LESSON 5-7 Exponential and Logarithmic Equations

Quick Review

You can solve exponential equations by taking the logarithm of both sides. You can solve a logarithmic equation by combining the logarithmic terms into one logarithm and then converting to exponential form.

Example

Solve $7^{2x} = 10^{x+1}$.

$7^{2x} = 10^{x+1}$

$\log 7^{2x} = \log 10^{x+1}$ ...... Take the common log of each side.

$2x \log 7 = (x + 1) \log 10$ ...... Power Property of Logarithms

$2x \log 7 = x + 1$ ...... Since $\log 10 = 1$

$2x \log 7 - x = 1$ ...... Subtract *x* from each side.

$x(2 \log 7 - 1) = 1$ ...... Factor out *x*.

$x = \frac{1}{2 \log 7 - 1}$ ...... Divide each side by $2 \log 7 - 1$.

$x \approx 1.449$ ...... Use a calculator.

Practice & Problem Solving

Find all solutions of the equation. Round answers to the nearest ten-thousandth.

41. $2^{5x+1} = 8^{x-1}$

42. $9^{2x+3} = 27^{x+2}$

43. $3^{x-2} = 5^{x-1}$

44. $7^{x+1} = 12^{x-1}$

Find all solutions of the equation.

45. $\log_5 (3x - 2)^4 = 8$

46. $\ln(x^2 - 32) = \ln(4x)$

47. $\log_6 (2x - 1) = 2 - \log_6 x$

48. Model With Mathematics Geri has $1,500 to invest. He has a goal to have $3,000 in this investment in 10 years. At what annual rate, compounded continuously, will Geri reach his goal? Round the answer to the nearest tenth.

LESSON 5-8 Geometric Sequences and Series

Quick Review

A geometric sequence is defined by a common ratio between consecutive terms. It can be defined explicitly or recursively. A geometric series is the sum of the terms of a geometric sequence.

Example

A geometric sequence is defined by $a_n = \begin{cases} \frac{1}{9}, & n = 1 \\ 3a_{n-1}, & n > 1 \end{cases}$. What is the sum of the first 10 terms of this sequence?

$a_n = \frac{1}{9}(3)^{n-1}$ Write the explicit definition.

$a_{10} = \frac{1}{9}(3)^9 = 2187$ Find the 10th term.

$S_{10} = \frac{\frac{1}{9}(1 - 3^{10})}{(1 - 3)} = 3280\frac{4}{9}$ Calculate the sum.

Practice & Problem Solving

Determine whether or not each sequence is geometric.

49. 2, 4, 6, 8, 10, 12, ...

50. 2, 4, 8, 16, 32, 64, ...

Convert between recursive and explicit forms.

51. $a_n = \begin{cases} \frac{1}{8}, & n = 1 \\ \frac{3}{2}a_{n-1}, & n > 1 \end{cases}$

52. $a_n = -2(5)^{n-1}$

Find the sum for each geometric series.

53. $\sum_{n=1}^{8} 6(2)^{n-1}$

54. $\sum_{n=1}^{9} 81\left(\frac{1}{3}\right)^{n-1}$

55. Look for Relationships Find the difference $\sum_{n=1}^{10} 10(2)^{n-1} - \sum_{k=2}^{11} 10(2)^{k-1}$. Explain how you found your answer.

56. Make Sense and Persevere The half-life of carbon-14 is 5,730 years. This is the amount of time it takes for half of a sample to decay. From a sample of 24 grams of carbon 14, how long will it take until only 3 grams of the sample remains?

TOPIC 5 REVIEW

TOPIC 6

Trigonometric Functions

? TOPIC ESSENTIAL QUESTION

How are trigonometric functions used to solve real-world problems?

Topic Overview

enVision® STEM Project:
Space Goggles

6-1 Trigonometric Functions and Acute Angles

6-2 Angles and the Unit Circle

6-3 Trigonometric Functions and Real Numbers

6-4 Graphing Sine and Cosine Functions

Mathematical Modeling in 3 Acts:
What Note Was That?

6-5 Graphing Other Trigonometric Functions

6-6 Translating Trigonometric Functions

Topic Vocabulary

- amplitude
- cofunction
- cofunction identities
- cosecant
- cosine
- cotangent
- coterminal angles
- frequency
- initial side
- midline
- period
- periodic function
- phase shift
- radian
- radian measure
- reciprocal trigonometric functions
- reference angle
- reference triangle
- secant
- sine
- standard position
- tangent
- terminal side
- unit circle

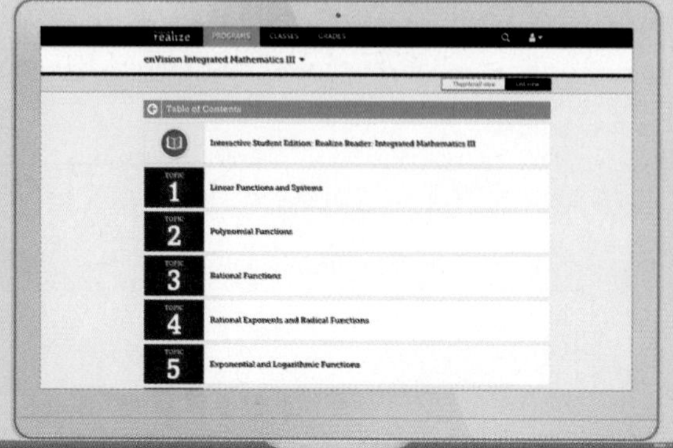

Go online | **PearsonRealize.com**

Digital Experience

INTERACTIVE STUDENT EDITION Access online or offline.

ACTIVITIES Complete ***Explore & Reason, Model & Discuss***, and ***Critique & Explain*** activities. Interact with Examples and Try Its.

ANIMATION View and interact with real-world applications.

PRACTICE Practice what you've learned.

What Note Was That?

Sounds are created by vibrations. As the vibrations travel through the air, they create sound waves. The frequency of a sound is the measurement of the number of cycles of that wave per second, in a unit called hertz (Hz). Music notes can be identified by their frequency.

What information do you need to determine the frequency of a note? How accurate does your data need to be? Think about this during the Mathematical Modeling in 3 Acts lesson.

TOPIC 6

VIDEOS Watch clips to support ***Mathematical Modeling in 3 Acts Lessons*** and **enVision®** ***STEM Projects.***

CONCEPT SUMMARY Review key lesson content through multiple representations.

ASSESSMENT Show what you've learned.

GLOSSARY Read and listen to English and Spanish definitions.

TUTORIALS Get help from ***Virtual Nerd***, right when you need it.

MATH TOOLS Explore math with digital tools and manipulatives.

Video

Did You Know?

In space, all electromagnetic waves move at the same speed: the speed of light, which is 299,792,458 meters per second. The length of 1 meter is defined to be the distance light travels in space in 1/299,792,458 of a second.

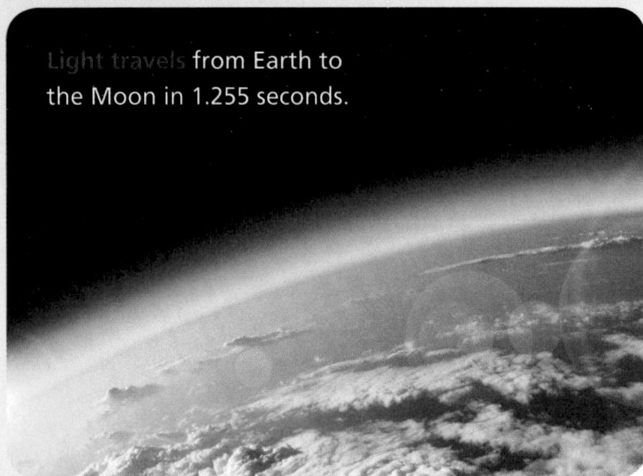
Light travels from Earth to the Moon in 1.255 seconds.

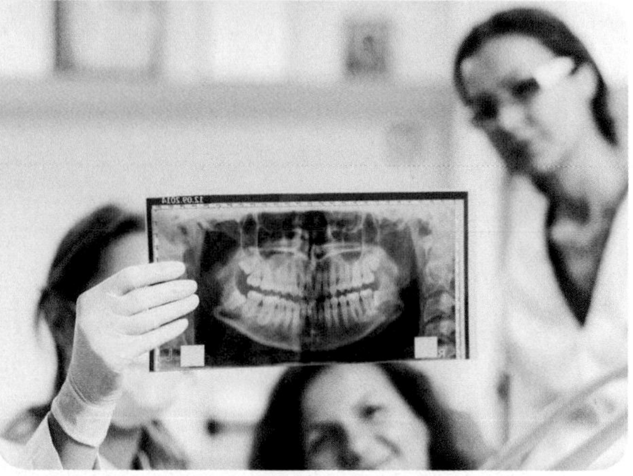
The frequency of an electromagnetic wave is proportional to its energy. X-ray machines range in strength from the low-frequency machines used to examine teeth and bones to the high-frequency machines used to kill cancer cells.

The spectrum of visible light is a very small portion of the electromagnetic spectrum, which includes gamma rays, x-rays, ultraviolet light, infrared radiation, microwaves, and radio waves.

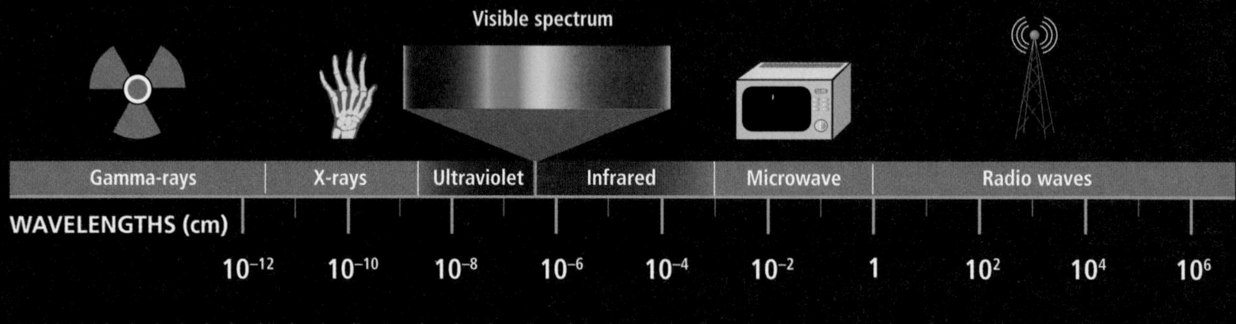

Your Task: Design Space Goggles

You and your classmates will investigate different electromagnetic waves, including the relative energy and dangers of each. Then you will designs space goggles to protect a space traveler's vision.

Go Online | PearsonRealize.com

6-1

Trigonometric Functions and Acute Angles

PearsonRealize.com

I CAN… use trigonometric functions.

VOCABULARY

- cofunction
- cofunction identities
- cosecant
- cosine
- cotangent
- reciprocal trigonometric functions
- secant
- sine
- tangent

 Activity
 Assess

EXPLORE & REASON

In the figure below, $\triangle ABC \sim \triangle DEF$.

A. Write as many ratios as you can using two side lengths from $\triangle ABC$.

B. Write as many ratios as you can using two side lengths from $\triangle DEF$.

C. Look for Relationships What do the results from parts (a) and (b) suggest about the ratios of side lengths in similar right triangles?

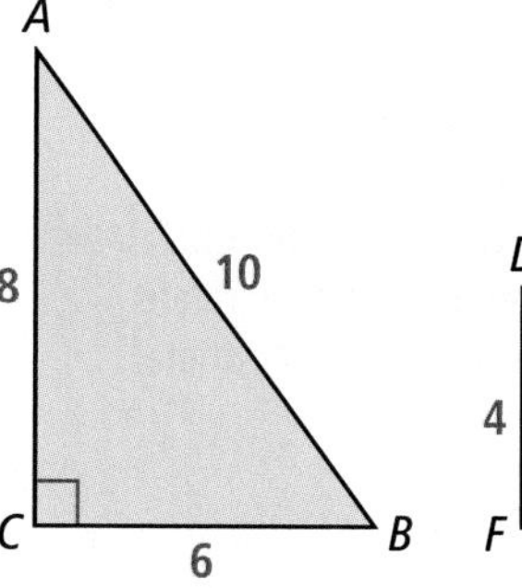

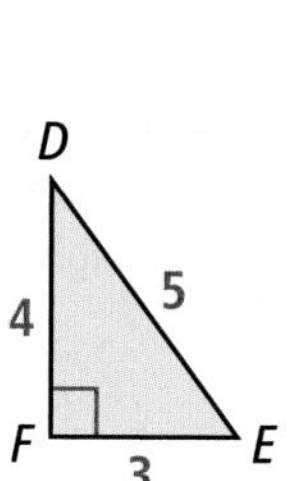

ESSENTIAL QUESTION **How can ratios of lengths of sides within right triangles help determine other lengths and angle measures in the triangles?**

CONCEPT Trigonometric Ratios

The three sides of a right triangle are referred to as the hypotenuse and two legs.

The Greek letter θ, read "theta", is often used to represent an acute angle in a right triangle. Angle θ is an abbreviation for "angle with measure θ".

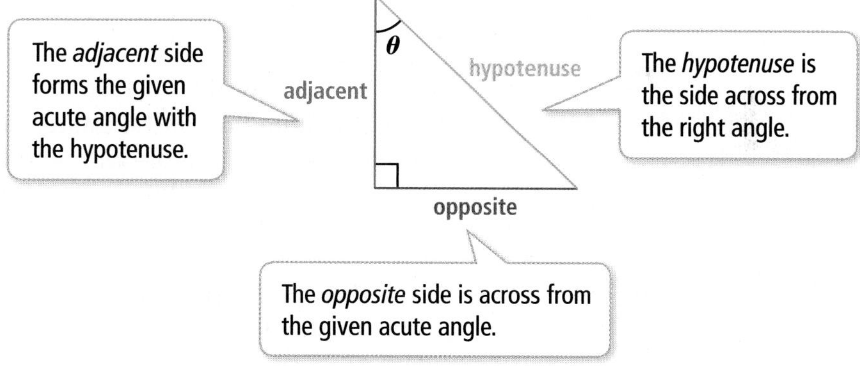

These are the six basic trigonometric functions of the angle θ.

Sine	Cosine	Tangent
$\sin\theta = \dfrac{\text{opposite}}{\text{hypotenuse}}$	$\cos\theta = \dfrac{\text{adjacent}}{\text{hypotenuse}}$	$\tan\theta = \dfrac{\text{opposite}}{\text{adjacent}}$

The **reciprocal trigonometric functions** of the angle θ are formed by exchanging the terms in each ratio.

Cosecant	Secant	Cotangent
$\csc\theta = \dfrac{\text{hypotenuse}}{\text{opposite}}$	$\sec\theta = \dfrac{\text{hypotenuse}}{\text{adjacent}}$	$\cot\theta = \dfrac{\text{adjacent}}{\text{opposite}}$

Activity Assess

EXAMPLE 1 Write Trigonometric Ratios

Given the right triangle below, write the six trigonometric ratios for the given angle with measure θ.

STUDY TIP
Before finding the ratios, it is helpful to label the sides of the triangle "opposite," "adjacent," and "hypotenuse" as they relate to the angle with measure theta.

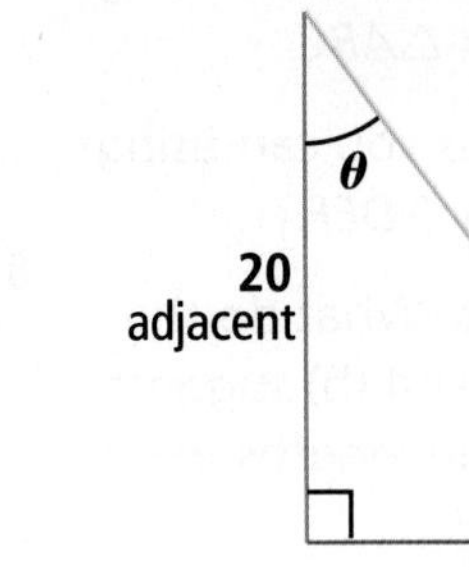

$\sin\theta = \frac{21}{29}$ $\csc\theta = \frac{29}{21}$

$\cos\theta = \frac{20}{29}$ $\sec\theta = \frac{29}{20}$

$\tan\theta = \frac{21}{20}$ $\cot\theta = \frac{20}{21}$

Try It! 1. Write the six trigonometric ratios for the given angle with measure θ.

a.

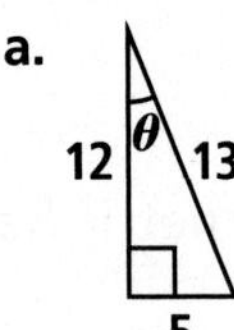

b.

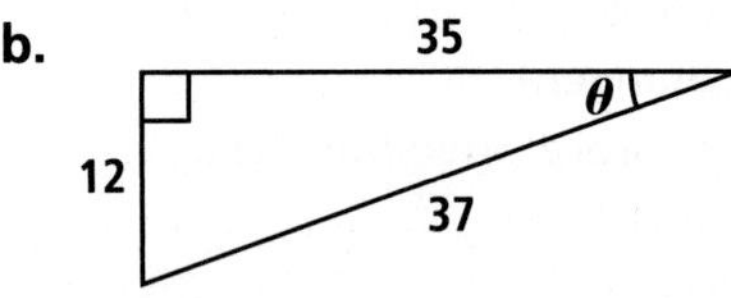

EXAMPLE 2 Use One Trigonometric Ratio to Find Another

Knowing that $\tan\theta = \frac{15}{8}$, what are the other trigonometric ratios for θ?

You can use one trigonometric ratio to find the other five trigonometric ratios.

Step 1 Use the definition of the tangent ratio to draw a right triangle with angle θ.

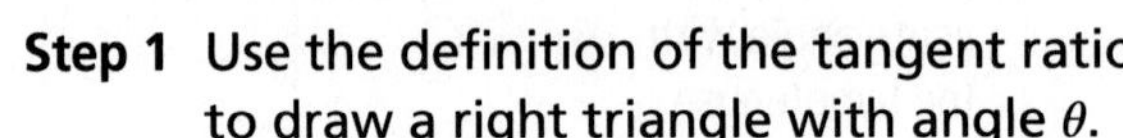

$$\tan\theta = \frac{15}{8} = \frac{\text{opposite}}{\text{adjacent}}$$

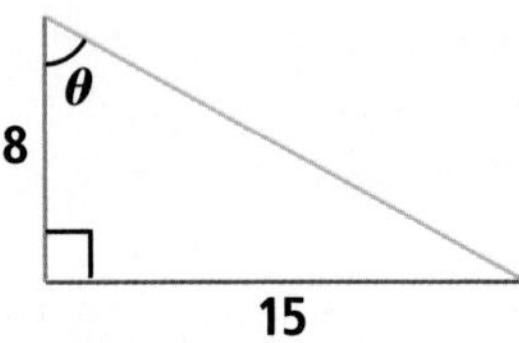

Step 2 Use the Pythagorean Theorem to find the hypotenuse.

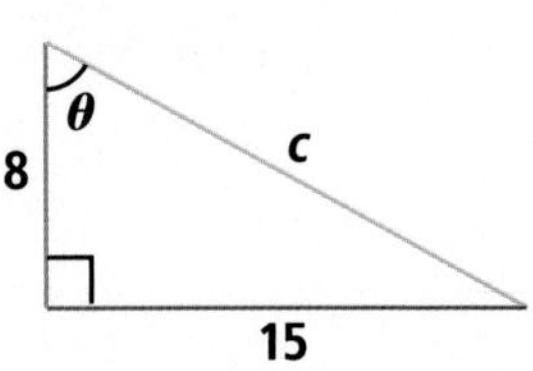

$$a^2 + b^2 = c^2$$

$$(8)^2 + (15)^2 = c^2$$

$$17 = c$$

USE STRUCTURE
Would any right triangle you draw with an angle of measure θ and the given tangent ratio have all six trigonetric ratios in common?

Step 3 Use the side lengths to write the other trigonometric ratios.

Substitute the side lengths into the formulas. For example, since $\sin\theta = \frac{\text{opposite}}{\text{hypotenuse}}$, $\sin\theta = \frac{15}{17}$. Now write the rest of the trigonometric ratios.

$$\sin\theta = \frac{15}{17},\ \cos\theta = \frac{8}{17},\ \csc\theta = \frac{17}{15},\ \sec\theta = \frac{17}{8},\ \cot\theta = \frac{8}{15}$$

Try It! 2. What are the trigonometric ratios of an angle with measure θ in a right triangle in which $\sin\theta = \frac{24}{25}$?

APPLICATION

EXAMPLE 3 Find a Missing Side Length

A fire truck has an 84 ft ladder extended against a building forming a 55° angle with the top of the truck. The truck is 8 ft tall. The firefighters are trying to reach a window that is 75 ft above the ground. Will they be able to reach the window using the ladder set at this angle?

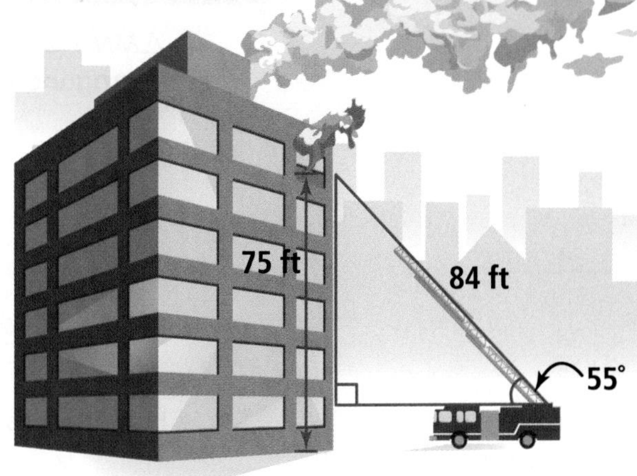

Step 1 Sketch a diagram to represent the situation. Label the sides and angles of your diagram with all of the known information.

Step 2 Decide which trigonometric function to use. You are given the hypotenuse, and you are trying to find the length opposite the angle with a measure of 55°. The ratio that relates the opposite side of an angle to the hypotenuse of the right triangle is the sine ratio.

wall
ladder
84 ft
55°
8 ft
ground

Step 3 Let x represent the length of the side opposite the 55° angle and write an equation.

$$\sin 55^\circ = \frac{x}{84}$$

COMMON ERROR
Make sure that your calculator is set to degrees when you calculate the value of sine.

Step 4 Solve for x.

$$x = 84 \sin 55$$
$$\approx 68.8 \text{ ft}$$

Step 5 Find the height on the building that the ladder will reach.

$$68.8 + 8 = 76.8 \text{ ft}$$

The height the ladder will reach is the side length of the triangle plus 8 ft for the height of the truck.

The ladder will extend to a height of about 76.8, which is longer than 75. The firefighters will be able to reach the window 75 ft above the ground.

Try It! **3.** The sun shines at a 60° angle to the ground. How long is the shadow cast by a 20 ft tall flagpole?

EXAMPLE 4 Evaluate Trigonometric Ratios in Special Triangles

A. $\triangle MNO$ is a 45°-45°-90° triangle with side length $OM = 2$. What are the six trigonometric ratios for angle N with measure θ?

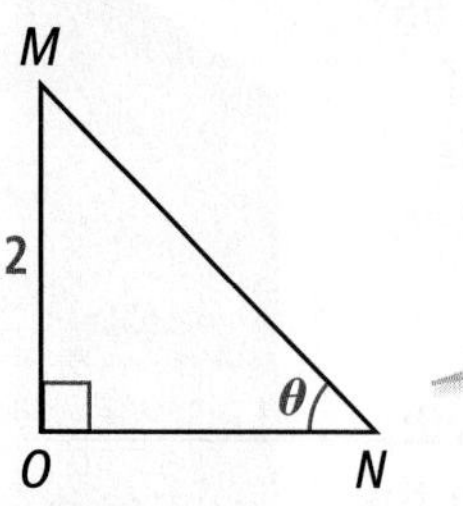

This is an isosceles right triangle so the legs are congruent.

STUDY TIP
Recall that in every 45°-45°-90° triangle, the sides lengths can be expressed as x, x, and $x\sqrt{2}$.

Find the hypotenuse using the Pythagorean Theorem:

$$a^2 + b^2 = c^2$$
$$(2)^2 + (2)^2 = c^2$$
$$c = \sqrt{8} = 2\sqrt{2}$$

The side lengths are $MO = 2$, $NM = 2\sqrt{2}$, and $ON = 2$.

The trigonometric ratios for θ in $\triangle MNO$ are:

GENERALIZE
Recall that in a 45°-45°-90° right triangle, since the two legs are equal, $\sin\theta = \cos\theta$, $\csc\theta = \sec\theta$, and $\tan\theta = \cot\theta = 1$.

$\sin\theta = \frac{2}{2\sqrt{2}} = \frac{\sqrt{2}}{2}$ $\qquad \cos\theta = \frac{2}{2\sqrt{2}} = \frac{\sqrt{2}}{2}$ $\qquad \tan\theta = \frac{2}{2} = 1$

$\csc\theta = \frac{2\sqrt{2}}{2} = \sqrt{2}$ $\qquad \sec\theta = \frac{2\sqrt{2}}{2} = \sqrt{2}$ $\qquad \cot\theta = \frac{2}{2} = 1$

Check your calculations. Use a calculator to evaluate both sin 45° and $\frac{\sqrt{2}}{2}$. They should both be approximately equal to 0.7071.

B. $\triangle JKL$ is a 30°-60°-90° right triangle with side length $LK = 4$ and $m\angle J = 30°$. What are the six trigonometric ratios for angle J with measure θ?

This triangle is half of an equilateral triangle, so the length of the hypotenuse is twice the length of the shortest leg.

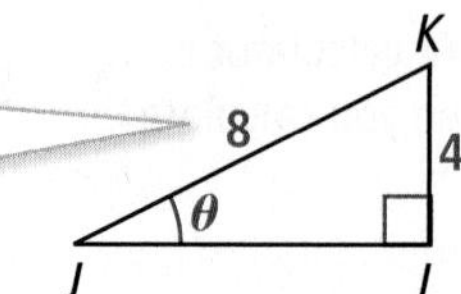

STUDY TIP
Recall that in every 30°-60°-90° triangle, the sides lengths can be expressed as x, $2x$, and $x\sqrt{3}$.

Use the Pythagorean Theorem to find the length of the third side:

$$a^2 + b^2 = c^2$$
$$(4)^2 + b^2 = (8)^2$$
$$b^2 = 48$$
$$b = 4\sqrt{3}$$

The side lengths are $JL = 4\sqrt{3}$, $KJ = 8$, and $LK = 4$.

The trigonometric ratios for θ in $\triangle JKL$ are:

$\sin\theta = \frac{4}{8} = \frac{1}{2}$ $\qquad \cos\theta = \frac{4\sqrt{3}}{8} = \frac{\sqrt{3}}{2}$ $\qquad \tan\theta = \frac{4}{4\sqrt{3}} = \frac{\sqrt{3}}{3}$

$\csc\theta = \frac{8}{4} = 2$ $\qquad \sec\theta = \frac{2}{\sqrt{3}} = \frac{2\sqrt{3}}{3}$ $\qquad \cot\theta = \sqrt{3}$

 **Try It!** 4. The length of the hypotenuse in a 45°-45°-90° triangle is $5\sqrt{2}$. What are the sine and secant ratios for a 45° angle?

CONCEPTUAL UNDERSTANDING

EXAMPLE 5 Explain Trigonometric Identities

A. Which trigonometric ratios are reciprocals of each other?

An **identity** is an equation that is true for all values of the variable for which all expressions in the equation are defined. You have seen that some trigonometric functions include ratios that are reciprocals. One example:

$$\sin\theta = \frac{\text{opposite}}{\text{hypotenuse}} \qquad \csc\theta = \frac{\text{hypotenuse}}{\text{opposite}}$$

Show that the following reciprocal identity is true for all values of θ that measure an acute angle: $\sin\theta = \frac{1}{\csc\theta}$.

Confirm that the equation is true algebraically by using substitution:

$$\sin\theta = \frac{1}{\csc\theta} = \frac{1}{\left(\frac{\text{hypotenuse}}{\text{opposite}}\right)} = \frac{\text{opposite}}{\text{hypotenuse}}$$

STUDY TIP

In a right triangle, the sum of the measures of the two acute angles is 90°, so these angles are complementary.

B. How are the trigonometric ratios of the two non-right angles in a right triangle related to each other?

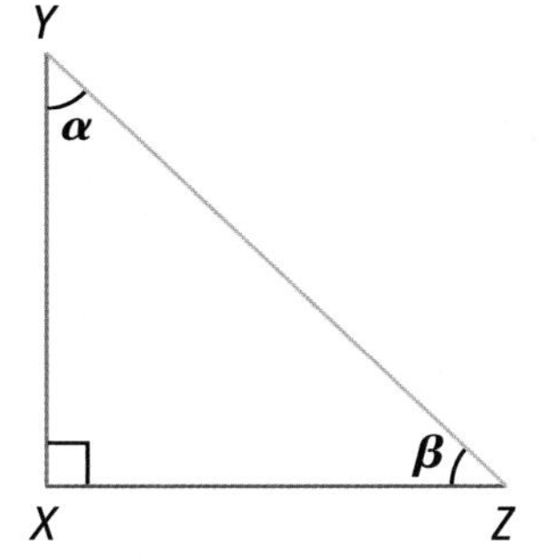

α and β are complementary angles.

$\alpha + \beta = 90°$, so

$\alpha = 90° - \beta$

$\beta = 90° - \alpha$

The Greek letters α (alpha) and β (beta) are often used to represent angles in trigonometry.

Compare sine and cosine for α and β:

$\sin\alpha = \frac{ZX}{YZ}$ $\qquad \sin\beta = \frac{XY}{YZ}$

$\cos\alpha = \frac{XY}{YZ}$ $\qquad \cos\beta = \frac{ZX}{YZ}$

If $\beta = 90° - \alpha$, then $\sin\alpha = \cos\beta$ and $\cos\alpha = \sin\beta$. The trigonometric function for the complement of an angle is called a **cofunction**, so these are the **cofunction identities** for sine and cosine.

C. Triangle *DEF* has right angle, *F*. The $m\angle D = \alpha$ and $m\angle E = \beta$. If $\sin\alpha = \frac{8}{17}$ and $\cos\alpha = \frac{15}{17}$, find $\sin\beta$ and $\cos\beta$.

In a right triangle, where α and β are complementary angles, $\sin\alpha = \cos\beta$ and $\cos\alpha = \sin\beta$.

You are given $\sin\alpha = \frac{8}{17}$ and $\cos\alpha = \frac{15}{17}$.

Use this information to determine that $\sin\beta = \frac{15}{17}$ and $\cos\beta = \frac{8}{17}$.

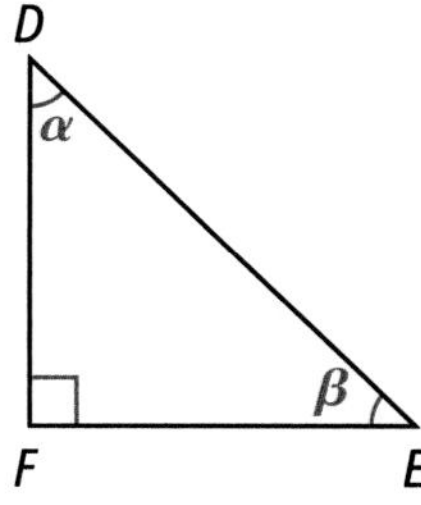

You may confirm your findings by sketching one possible triangle that represents the situation.

In this example, the hypotenuse is 17, the side opposite α is 8, and the side adjacent α is 15.

From this information, you can confirm that $\sin\beta = \frac{15}{17}$ and $\cos\beta = \frac{8}{17}$.

 **Try It!** **5.** What are the cofunction identities for tangent and cotangent?

CONCEPT SUMMARY Trigonometric Functions and Acute Angles

WORDS The ratios of the sides of any right triangle are always the same for a given angle θ. These ratios define the six basic trigonometric functions.

DEFINITIONS

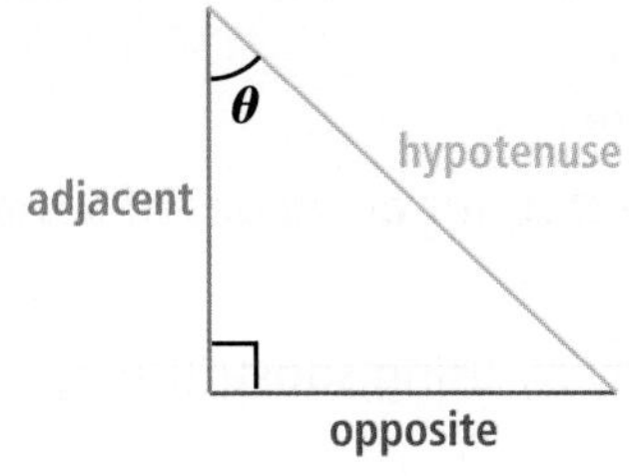

Sine	**Cosine**	**Tangent**
$\sin\theta = \frac{\text{opposite}}{\text{hypotenuse}}$	$\cos\theta = \frac{\text{adjacent}}{\text{hypotenuse}}$	$\tan\theta = \frac{\text{opposite}}{\text{adjacent}}$
Cosecant	**Secant**	**Cotangent**
$\csc\theta = \frac{\text{hypotenuse}}{\text{opposite}}$	$\sec\theta = \frac{\text{hypotenuse}}{\text{adjacent}}$	$\cot\theta = \frac{\text{adjacent}}{\text{opposite}}$

Do You UNDERSTAND?

1. **ESSENTIAL QUESTION** How can ratios of lengths of sides within right triangles help determine other lengths and angle measures in the triangles?

2. **Error Analysis** Terrell said that $\cos\theta$ is the reciprocal of $\sin\theta$. Explain and correct Terrell's error.

3. **Vocabulary** Explain what it means to say that $\tan\theta = \frac{1}{\cot\theta}$ is an identity.

4. **Construct Arguments** Why are the cofunction identities true for all right triangles?

5. **Generalize** How does knowing one trigonometric ratio allow you to find the other five trigonometric ratios?

6. **Look for Relationships** Why do secant and cosecant always have to be greater than 1 or less than −1?

Do You KNOW HOW?

Find $\sin\theta$ using the given trigonometric ratio.

7. $\csc\theta = \frac{7}{3}$

8. $\tan\theta = \frac{5}{12}$

Use the trigonometric ratio given to write the other five trigonometric ratios for θ.

9. $\cos\theta = \frac{5}{13}$

10. $\tan\theta = \frac{3}{4}$

Write the reciprocal identity of the given trigonometric ratio.

11. $\cos\theta$

12. $\sec\theta$

Write the cofunction identity of the given trigonometric ratio.

13. $\csc\theta$

14. $\sec\theta$

15. A right triangle has a side of 16 m adjacent to an angle of 37°. What is the length of the hypotenuse rounded to the nearest whole meter?

16. A flagpole is 24 ft tall. A support wire runs from the top of the flagpole to an anchor in the ground. The wire makes a 73° angle with the ground. To the nearest tenth of a foot, how far from the base of the flagpole is the anchor?

PRACTICE & PROBLEM SOLVING

Scan for Multimedia

Additional Exercises Available Online

UNDERSTAND

17. **Construct Arguments** Yama said you can find any side length or angle measure of a right triangle if you know at least 1 side length and 1 non-right angle measure, or 2 side lengths. Is Yama correct? Explain your reasoning.

18. **Look for Relationships** The sine of an acute angle must be greater than 0 and less than 1. Explain why.

19. **Error Analysis** Describe and correct the error a student made in solving for the length of the hypotenuse in the triangle shown.

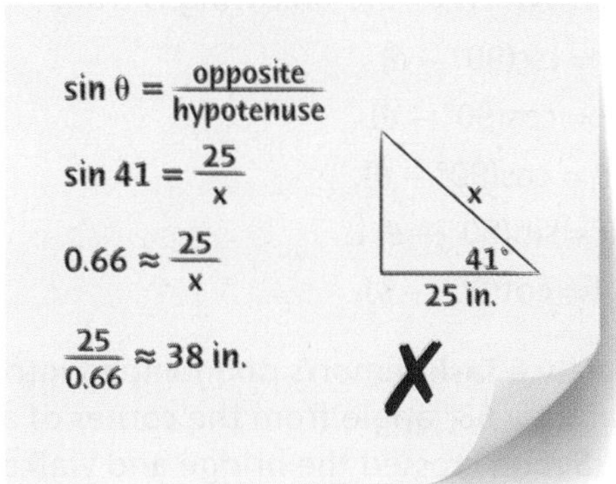

20. **Construct Arguments** Show that the reciprocal identity $\sec \theta = \frac{1}{\cos \theta}$ is true.

21. **Generalize** Knowing all three angle measures of a right triangle does not determine the exact side lengths. However, knowing all three side lengths of a right triangle does determine the exact angle measures. Explain why.

22. **Reason** The sun shines at a 75° angle to the ground. How long is the shadow cast by a 15 ft tall cactus? Round to the nearest foot.

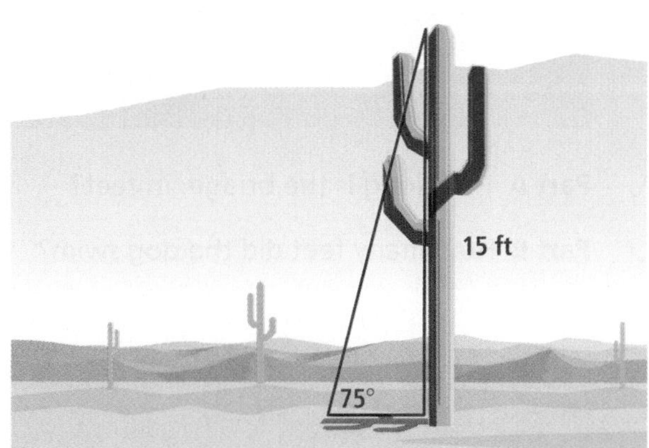

PRACTICE

Write the six trigonometric ratios for θ.
SEE EXAMPLE 1

23.

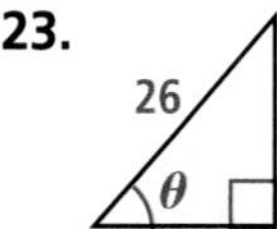

24.

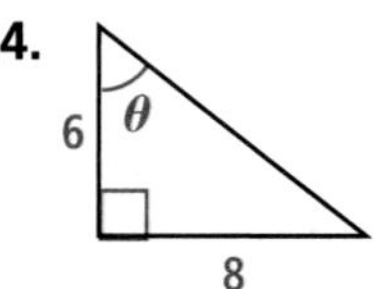

What are the trigonometric ratios of θ in a right triangle with the given value?
SEE EXAMPLE 2

25. $\cos \theta = \frac{4}{5}$

26. $\cot \theta = \frac{12}{16}$

27. $\csc \theta = \frac{17}{15}$

28. $\sec \theta = \frac{52}{20}$

29. A closed umbrella casts a shadow when the sun shines at a 16.3° angle to the ground. How tall is the top of the umbrella to the nearest foot? SEE EXAMPLE 3

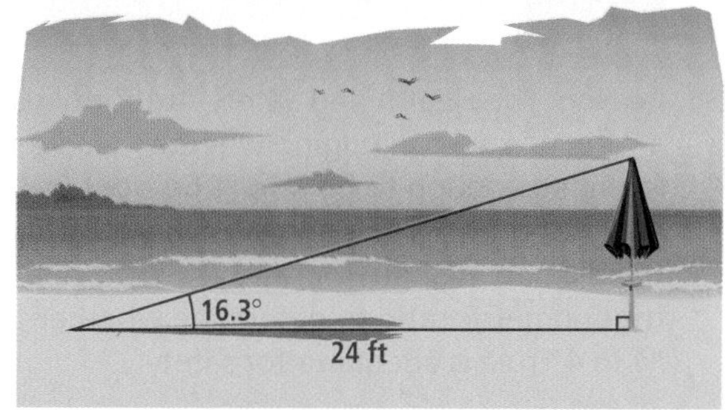

What are the sine and cosine ratios for the special triangles described? SEE EXAMPLE 4

30. A 45°-45°-90° triangle with a leg of 9

31. A 30°-60°-90° triangle with a hypotenuse of 14, when $\theta = 30°$

What is the cofunction identity for the given trigonometric ratio? SEE EXAMPLE 5

32. secant

33. cosine

Practice | Tutorial

Mixed Review Available Online

PRACTICE & PROBLEM SOLVING

APPLY

34. Make Sense and Persevere Roshaun sees two rock formations on the other side of a canyon from where he is hiking. One is directly across the canyon, and the other is across at an angle of 27°. How far apart are the two rock formations? Round your answer to the nearest tenth.

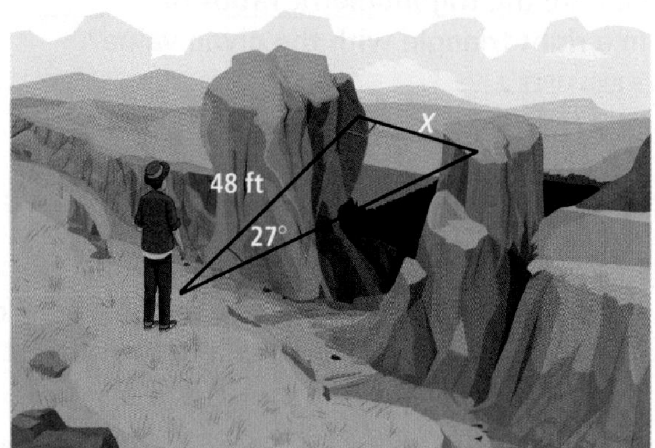

35. Reason The Health and Safety Authority uses a "1 in 4" rule for judging whether a ladder is angled enough to be safe (1 unit out for every 4 units up). The angle measure that is the maximum angle for safety is 75°. Use a trigonometric ratio to determine whether the "1 in 4" rule is adequate for safety.

36. Model With Mathematics An inflatable figure is a decoration on Gabriella's lawn. A rope 42 in. long secures the top of the figure to the ground at an angle of 80°. About how tall is the figure?

37. Make Sense and Persevere A zip line starts 28 feet in the air and ends 11 feet in the air. The zip line drops at an angle of 85°. How long is the zip line cable when completely taut (no rider)? Round your answer to the nearest whole number.

ASSESSMENT PRACTICE

38. Match each trigonometric ratio in the left column with its reciprocal expression in the right column.

I. $\sin\theta$	A. $\frac{1}{\cos\theta}$
II. $\sec\theta$	B. $\frac{1}{\sin\theta}$
III. $\tan\theta$	C. $\frac{1}{\cot\theta}$
IV. $\cos\theta$	D. $\frac{1}{\sec\theta}$
V. $\csc\theta$	E. $\frac{1}{\tan\theta}$
VI. $\cot\theta$	F. $\frac{1}{\csc\theta}$

39. SAT/ACT Which of the following is true?

Ⓐ $\sin\theta = \csc(90° - \theta)$

Ⓑ $\sec\theta = \cos(90° - \theta)$

Ⓒ $\tan\theta = \cos(90° - \theta)$

Ⓓ $\sec\theta = \sin(90° - \theta)$

Ⓔ $\tan\theta = \cot(90° - \theta)$

40. Performance Task Simon's dog jumped into a stream at a 68° angle from the corner of a bridge. Simon crossed the bridge and walked downstream to meet the dog.

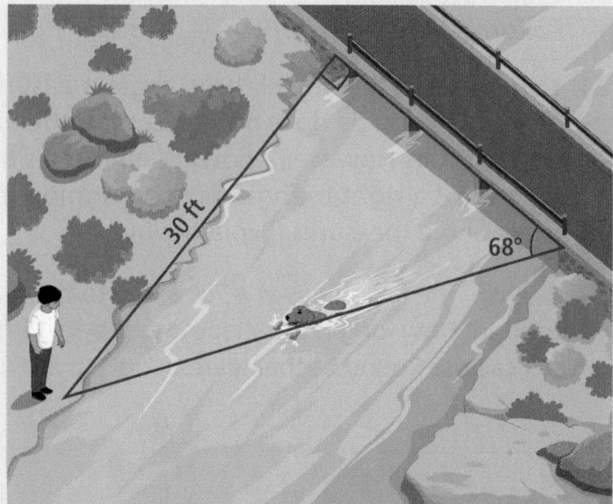

Part A How long is the bridge, in feet?

Part B How many feet did the dog swim?

Activity

Assess

6-2 Angles and the Unit Circle

PearsonRealize.com

I CAN… understand angles in standard position.

VOCABULARY

- coterminal angles
- initial side
- radian
- radian measure
- reference angle
- reference triangle
- standard position
- terminal side
- unit circle

EXPLORE & REASON

A bug is placed at the point (1, 0) of the coordinate plane shown. It starts walking counterclockwise along a circle with radius 1.

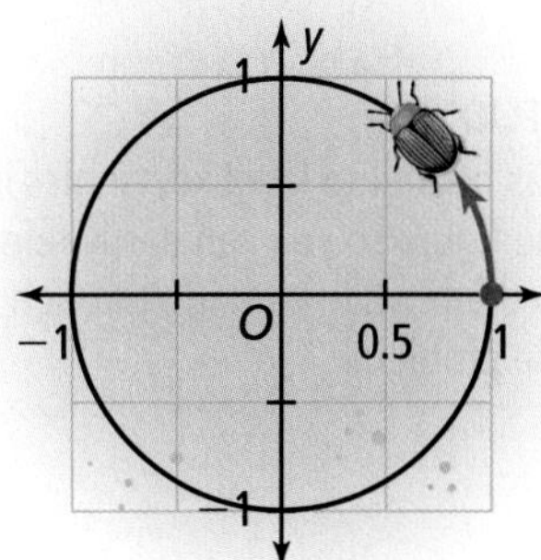

A. Model With Mathematics How can you calculate the distance along the circle the bug has traveled? How can you determine the measure of the central angle?

B. When the bug has traveled $\frac{1}{8}$ of the way along the circle, how far has it traveled? What central angle does its path travel through?

C. What are the distances shown traveled and the central angles when the bug has traveled $\frac{1}{6}$ of the way around the circle and $\frac{4}{5}$ of the way around the circle?

ESSENTIAL QUESTION

How can we extend the trigonometric ratios to angles greater than 90°?

EXAMPLE 1 Find the Measure of an Angle in Standard Position

What is the measure of the angle shown?

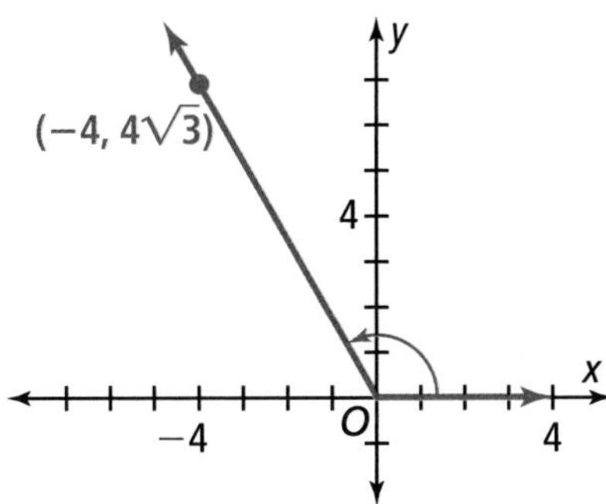

The angle represented by θ is in **standard position**. The vertex is at the origin, and the **initial side** of the angle is the positive x-axis. The **terminal side** is the other ray that forms the angle.

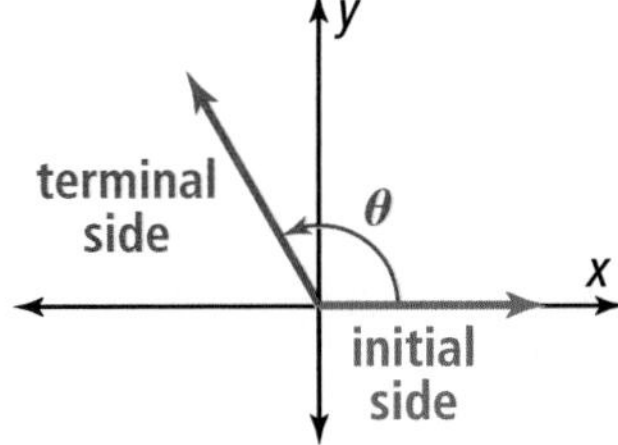

CONTINUED ON THE NEXT PAGE

EXAMPLE 1 CONTINUED

To find the measure of an angle in standard position, create a right triangle and use right triangle trigonometry. Draw a vertical line from the given point to the x-axis to form a right triangle.

STUDY TIP
It is helpful to label key angles in the figure so you can easily refer to them while working through the problem.

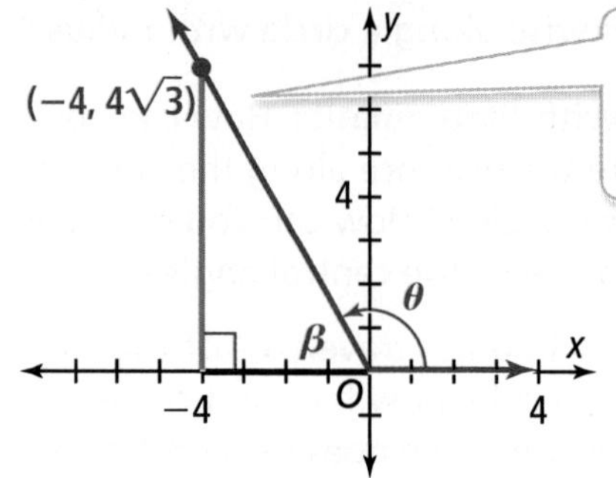

The lengths of the legs are 4 and $4\sqrt{3}$ units. Use the Pythagorean Theorem to find that the hypotenuse is 8.

LOOK FOR RELATIONSHIPS
Recall that in a 30°-60°-90° right triangle, if the length of the shorter leg is x, then the length of the hypotenuse is $2x$, and the length of the longer leg is $x\sqrt{3}$.

Examine the lengths of the sides of the right triangle. The dimensions fit the pattern of a 30°-60°-90° triangle, so $\beta = 60°$. Since β is supplementary to θ, we can can solve for $\theta = 180° - 60°$. Therefore $\theta = 120°$.

An angle in standard position can have its measure described in different ways.

As a positive angle measure	As a negative angle measure	As a positive angle measure greater than 360°
(−4, 4√3); 120°	(−4, 4√3); −240°	(−4, 4√3); 480°
$0 \leq \theta < 360$	$-360 \leq \theta < 0$	$\theta + 360k$, where k is a natural number representing the number of rotations

Because all three of the angles in this exercise are in standard position and share a terminal side, they are **coterminal angles**.

In standard position, the measure of the angle could be 120°, −240°, or $120 + 360k°$, where k is an integer.

CONTINUED ON THE NEXT PAGE

 **Try It!** **1.** Given the initial and terminal sides, find a positive angle measure, a negative angle measure, and an angle measure greater than 360° for each angle below.

a.

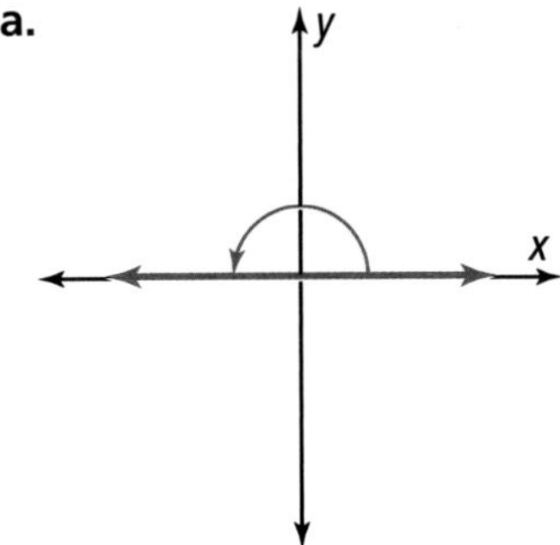

b.

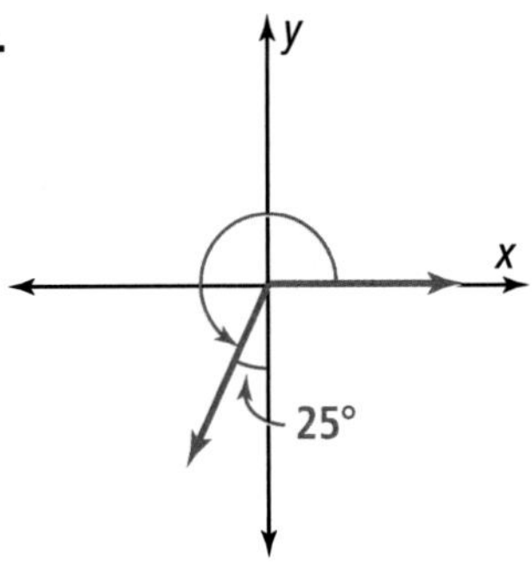

 **EXAMPLE 2** Find Reference Angles

A. What is the reference angle for a 130° angle?

When an angle is in standard position, the **reference angle** is the acute angle formed between the terminal side of the angle and the x-axis.

To find the reference angle for any angle, first sketch the angle by considering the quadrant in which the terminal side lies.

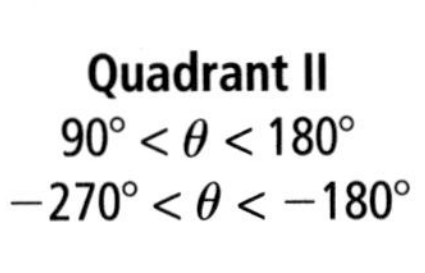

Quadrant II	Quadrant I
$90° < \theta < 180°$	$0° < \theta < 90°$
$-270° < \theta < -180°$	$-360° < \theta < -270°$
Quadrant III	**Quadrant IV**
$180° < \theta < 270°$	$270° < \theta < 360°$
$-180° < \theta < -90°$	$-90° < \theta < 0°$

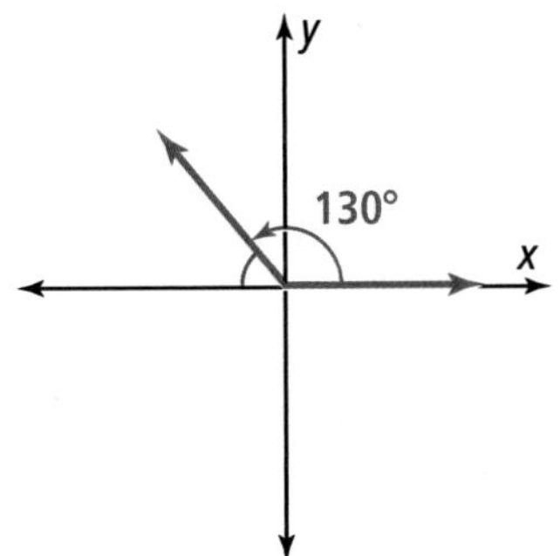

A 130° angle in standard position has its terminal side in Quardrant II. The reference angle is: 180° – 130° = 50°. When the given angle is greater than 90° and less than 180°, it is supplementary to its reference angle.

COMMON ERROR
Make sure you are always using the x-axis to locate the reference angle, not the y-axis.

CONTINUED ON THE NEXT PAGE

EXAMPLE 2 CONTINUED

B. What is the reference angle for a 210° angle?

Sketch the angle to determine in which Quadrant the terminal side lies.

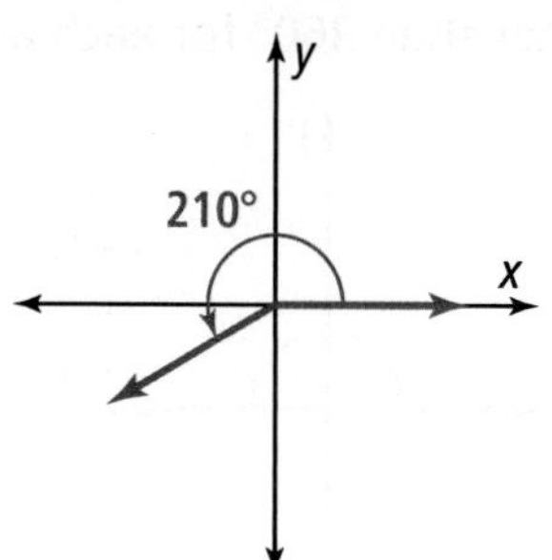

A 210° angle in standard position has its terminal side in Quadrant III. The measure of the reference angle is 180° less than the measure of the given angle: $210° - 180° = 30°$.

C. A reference angle is 45°, and its terminal side lies in Quadrant IV. What are a possible positive measure and negative measure for the angle?

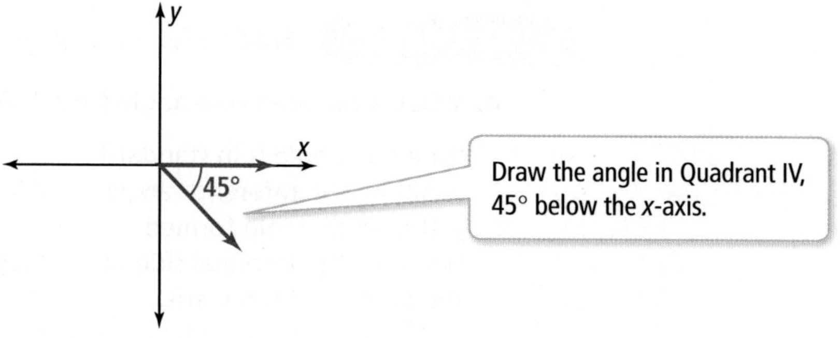

A positive angle measure is $360° - 45° = 315°$.
A negative angle measure is $-45°$.

STUDY TIP
Notice that the sum of the positive angle of measure and the absolute value of the negative angle measure is 360°. This is because, taken together, the two rotations combine to make one full rotation around the circle.

Try It! 2. Give a possible positive angle measure and a possible negative angle measure for each reference angle.

a. 10° in Quadrant III

b. 15° in Quadrant I

CONCEPT The Unit Circle

The unit circle is a circle that has its center at the origin and has a radius of 1.

In any right triangle formed with the radius as the hypotenuse, the length of the hypotenuse is 1.

Based on right triangle trigonometry

$\sin \theta = \frac{y}{1}$, or y $\cos \theta = \frac{x}{1}$, or x

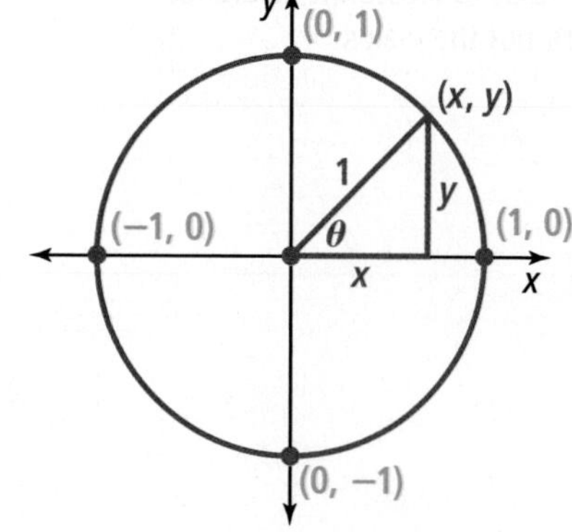

  Activity  Assess

EXAMPLE 3 Find the Coordinates of a Point on the Unit Circle

An angle, θ, has a measure of 60° and a terminal side that intercepts the unit circle at (x, y). What are the values of x and y?

Sketch a figure to represent the problem.

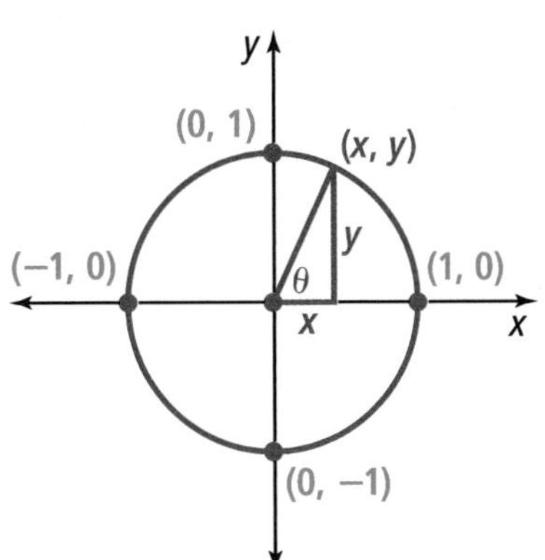

This figure represents the unit circle, so the radius is 1. Draw a **reference triangle**, formed by drawing a perpendicular line from the terminal point of an angle θ in standard position to the x-axis. The length of the hypotenuse of this triangle is 1.

$\sin\theta = \frac{y}{1} = y \quad \cos\theta = \frac{x}{1} = x$

The reference triangle formed is a 30°-60°-90° triangle, so you can use the relationship between the sides to find the value of x and y. The side across from the 30° angle is half of the hypotenuse, or $\frac{1}{2}$. The side across from the 60° angle is $\sqrt{3}$ times the shorter side, or $\frac{\sqrt{3}}{2}$. So, $\sin 60° = \frac{\sqrt{3}}{2}$ and $\cos 60° = \frac{1}{2}$, and the coordinate (x, y) is $\left(\frac{1}{2}, \frac{\sqrt{3}}{2}\right)$.

STUDY TIP
You may also use technology to find $\sin\theta$ and $\cos\theta$.

Try It! 3. An angle, θ, has a measure of 45° and a terminal side that intercepts the unit circle at (x, y). What are the values of x and y?

EXAMPLE 4 Understand Radian Measure on the Unit Circle

A. What is the radian measure of an angle?

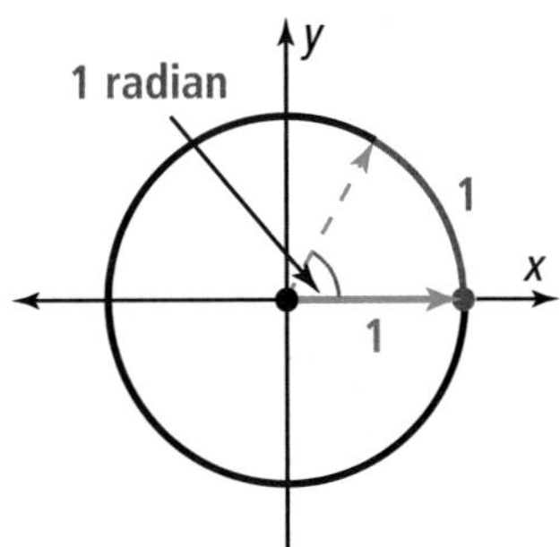

The **radian measure** of a central angle is equal to the length of the arc on the unit circle subtended by that angle.

An angle measure of 1 **radian** subtends an arc on the unit circle with length 1.

The radius of the **unit circle** is 1, so the circumference of the unit circle is $C = 2\pi r = 2\pi(1) = 2\pi$. This implies that a 360° angle, or one complete rotation of the circle, measures 2π radians.

The x- and y-axis divide the unit circle into four congruent arcs, each representing $\frac{\pi}{2}$ radians.

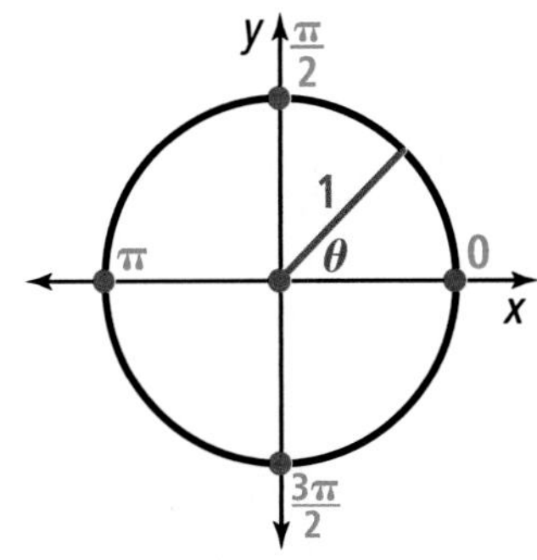

CONTINUED ON THE NEXT PAGE

EXAMPLE 4 CONTINUED

In general, the radian measure, θ, of an angle is the length of the intercepted arc measured in radius units.

$$\theta = \frac{\text{length of intercepted arc}}{\text{radius}}.$$

Since the radius of the unit circle is 1, the radian measure of, θ, of an angle is equal to the length of its intercepted arc on the unit circle.

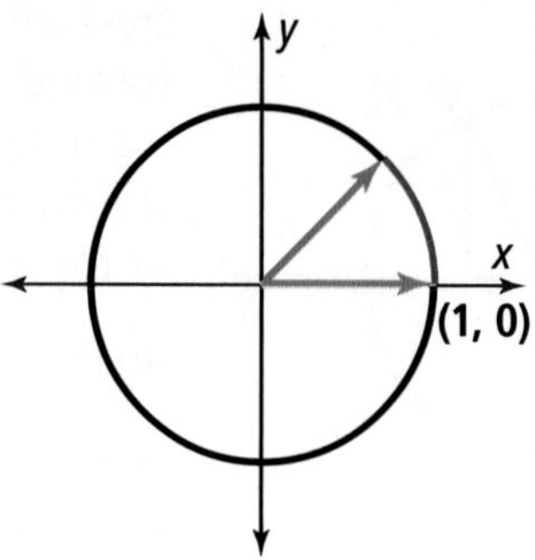

STUDY TIP
The circumference of the unit circle is 2π, and $\frac{2\pi}{8} = \frac{\pi}{4}$, so $\frac{\pi}{4}$ is $\frac{1}{8}$ of the circumference.

For example, if an angle measures $\frac{\pi}{4}$ radians, its intercepted arc is also $\frac{\pi}{4}$ radians. The angle lies in Quadrant I, with a terminal side halfway between 0 and $\frac{\pi}{2}$.

B. How can you use radian measure to sketch an angle?

Suppose an angle measures $\frac{4\pi}{3}$ radians. Its intercepted arc on the unit circle is also $\frac{4\pi}{3}$ radians.

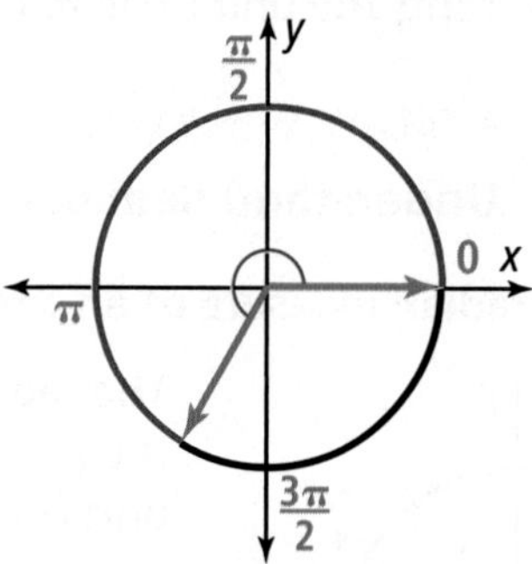

The top half of the circle represents π radians. $\frac{4\pi}{3}$ radians is greater than π radians but less than $\frac{3\pi}{2}$ radians. Therefore an angle with a measure of $\frac{4\pi}{3}$ radians lies in Quadrant III and has a reference angle of $\frac{\pi}{3}$.

Try It! 4. Sketch the graph of an angle that measures $-\frac{5\pi}{6}$ in standard position.

 Activity
 Assess

EXAMPLE 5 Convert Between Degrees and Radians

A. How do you convert between degrees and radians?

One full rotation, or 360°, is the same as 2π radians. Half a rotation, or 180°, is the same as π radians.

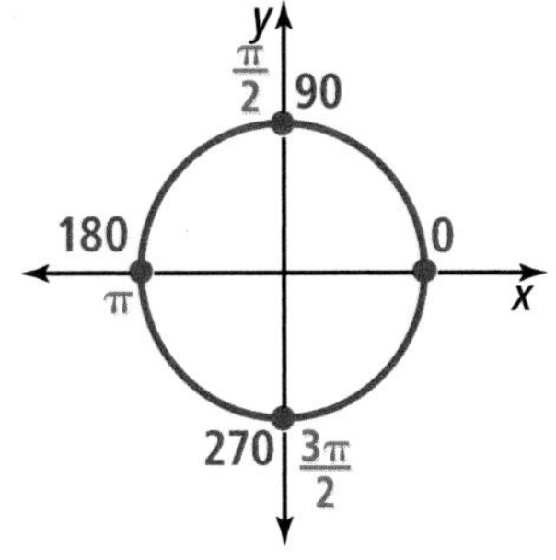

Radian	0	$\frac{\pi}{2}$	π	$\frac{3\pi}{2}$	2π
Degrees	0	90	180	270	360

2π radians $= 360°$

π radians $= 180°$

1 radian $= \frac{180°}{\pi}$

To find the value of 1 radian in terms of degrees, divide both sides by π.

For example, if an angle measures $\frac{\pi}{2}$ radians, what is its measure in degrees?

$\frac{\pi}{2} \bullet \frac{180°}{\pi} = 90°$

To convert any number of radians to degrees, multiply the number of radians by $\frac{180°}{\pi}$.

π radians $= 180°$

1 degree $= \frac{\pi}{180°}$ radians

To find the value of 1 degree in terms of radians, divide both sides by 180°.

For example, if an angle measures 120°, what is its measure in radians?

$120° \bullet \frac{\pi}{180°}$ radians $= \frac{2\pi}{3}$ radians

To convert any number of degrees to radians, multiply the number of degrees by $\frac{\pi}{180°}$.

B. How can you convert each angle measure from radians to degrees or degrees to radians?

$\frac{\pi}{7}$ radians

$\frac{\pi}{7} \bullet \frac{180°}{\pi} \approx 25.7°$

75°

$75° \bullet \frac{\pi}{180°} = \frac{5\pi}{12}$ radians

USE APPROPRIATE TOOLS
Your calculator is able to work with both radians and degrees. Be sure that it is set properly for your calculations.

 **Try It!** 5. Convert the angle measures.

a. 112° to radians

b. $\frac{\pi}{6}$ radians to degrees

APPLICATION

EXAMPLE 6 Use Radians to Find Arc Length

NASA is tracking a satellite traveling in a circular orbit above Earth. It can only be tracked while it orbits through a $\frac{\pi}{6}$ angle. The radius of Earth is 6,400 km. What is the distance the satellite travels while it is being tracked?

The satellite travels through an arc surrounding Earth.

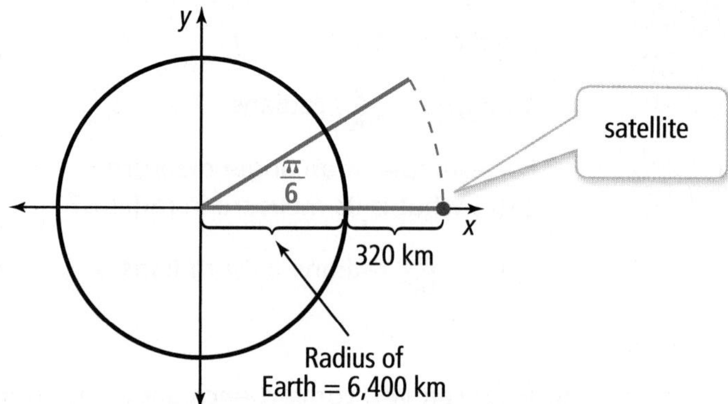

The total distance from the center of Earth to the satellite is 6,400 km + 320 km, or 6,720 km.

Use the formula for the radian measure of an arc to find the distance through which the satellite can be tracked.

$$\text{Radian Measure} = \frac{\text{length of intercepted arc}}{\text{Radius}}$$

$$\text{Length of Intercepted Arc} = \text{Radian Measure} \times \text{Radius}$$

$$\text{Length of Intercepted Arc} = \left(\frac{\pi}{6}\right)(6{,}720 \text{ km})$$

$$\approx 3{,}519 \text{ km}$$

The satellite can be tracked for about 3,519 km.

STUDY TIP
Make sure that the units are the same for the radius and the arc length.

 **Try It!** 6. If the satellite could be tracked for 5,000 km, what angle in radians would it pass through?

CONCEPT SUMMARY Angles and the Unit Circle

STANDARD POSITION

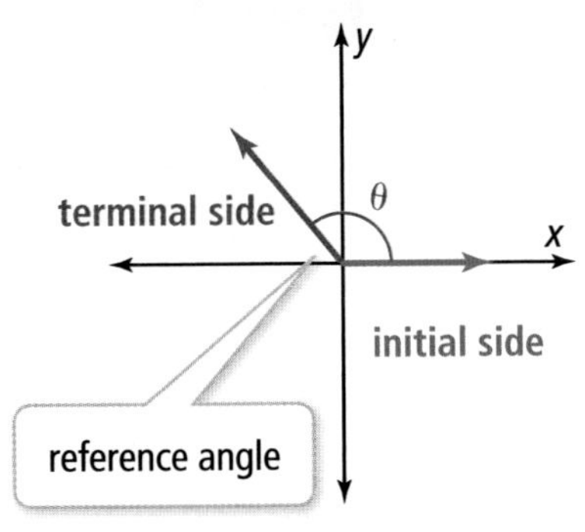

An angle is in standard position when its initial side is the positive x-axis and its vertex is at the origin.

The reference angle is the acute angle formed by the terminal side and the x-axis.

DEGREES AND RADIANS

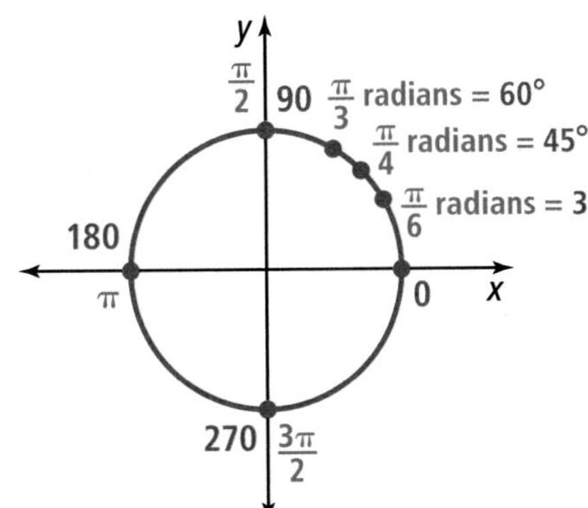

$$\text{radians} = \frac{\pi}{180} \bullet \text{degrees}$$

$$\text{degrees} = \frac{180}{\pi} \bullet \text{radians}$$

Do You UNDERSTAND?

1. ESSENTIAL QUESTION How can we extend the trigonometric ratios to angles greater than 90°?

2. **Error Analysis** Camilla said that θ and its reference angle are always supplementary angles. Explain and correct Camilla's error.

3. **Vocabulary** What two features distinguish a circle as the unit circle?

4. **Reason** If given an angle measure in radians, how can you determine in which quadrant its terminal side will be, without converting to degrees?

5. **Make Sense And Persevere** If you are using a calculator to find the measure of an angle in degrees, what type of measure might make you question whether your calculator is actually in radian mode? Explain.

Do You KNOW HOW?

The angles given are in standard position. What is the reference angle for each given angle?

6. 65°

7. 145°

In what quadrant does the angle, given in radians, lie?

8. $\frac{\pi}{6}$

9. $\frac{5\pi}{3}$

What is the negative angle of rotation for the angle with given positive angle of rotation?

10. 270°

11. 110°

Convert each radian measure to a degree measure.

12. $\frac{\pi}{3}$

13. $\frac{7\pi}{4}$

Convert each degree measure to a radian measure.

14. $-30°$

15. 480°

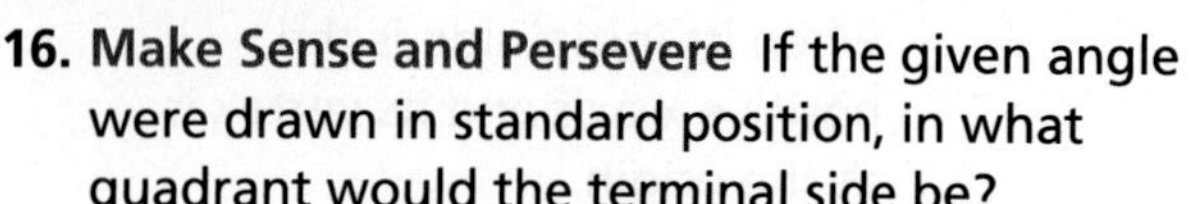

PRACTICE & PROBLEM SOLVING

Scan for Multimedia

Practice | Tutorial

Additional Exercises Available Online

UNDERSTAND

16. Make Sense and Persevere If the given angle were drawn in standard position, in what quadrant would the terminal side be?

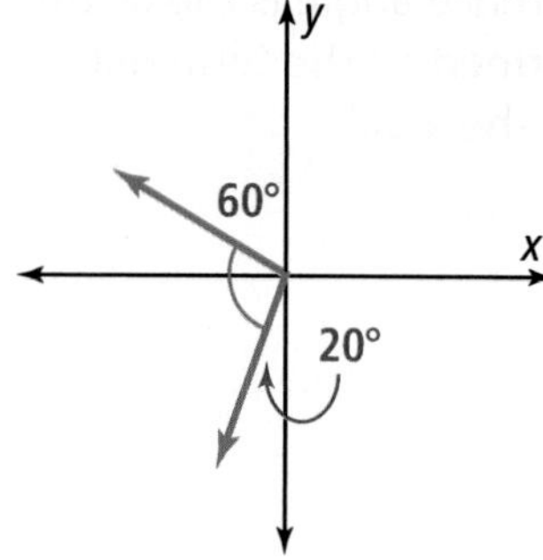

17. Look for Relationships Explain why the length of an intercepted arc on the unit circle always equals the corresponding central angle measure in radians.

18. Error Analysis Describe and correct the error a student made in converting $\frac{\pi}{2}$ radians to degrees.

$$\frac{\pi}{2} \text{ radians} = x^\circ$$
$$\frac{\pi}{2} \times \frac{\pi}{180} = x^\circ$$
$$\frac{\pi^2}{360} = x^\circ$$
$$\frac{25}{0.66} \approx 0.03^\circ$$

✗

19. Generalize What is the relationship between a positive angle and a negative angle that share a common terminal side? Write a formula that relates the two measures.

20. Higher Order Thinking At what coordinates does the terminal side of a 60° angle intersect the unit circle?

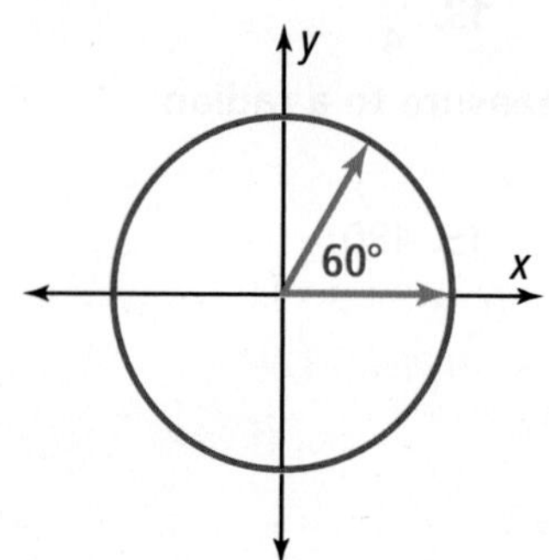

PRACTICE

Find the measure of each angle as a positive angle measure, a negative angle measure, and an angle measure that is greater than 360°. SEE EXAMPLE 1

21. **22.**

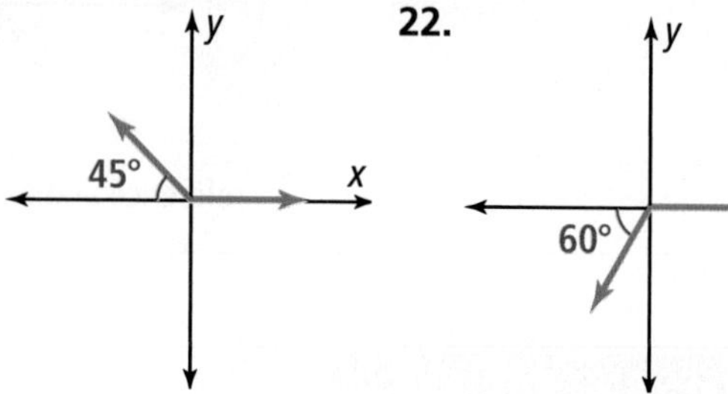

Find the measure of an angle in standard position for each reference angle. SEE EXAMPLE 2

23. 15° in Quadrant II

24. 75° in Quadrant IV

25. 8° in Quadrant III

26. 56° in Quadrant I

Sketch each angle in standard position.
SEE EXAMPLE 3

27. 30°

28. −45°

29. −210°

30. 130°

Sketch each angle in standard position.
SEE EXAMPLE 4

31. $\frac{3\pi}{4}$

32. $\frac{\pi}{3}$

33. $\frac{-2\pi}{3}$

34. $\frac{3\pi}{2}$

Convert each angle measure to radians. Round to the nearest hundredth. SEE EXAMPLE 5

35. 148°

36. 20°

Convert each angle measure to degrees.
SEE EXAMPLE 5

37. $\frac{2\pi}{3}$

38. $\frac{5\pi}{6}$

Solve using the formula given. SEE EXAMPLE 6

39. Earth's radius is 6,400 km. If a satellite is orbiting at 200 km above Earth's surface and can be tracked while it orbits through a $\frac{\pi}{3}$ radian angle, what is the distance the satellite travels while being tracked? Round your answer to the nearest tenth.

PRACTICE & PROBLEM SOLVING

APPLY

40. Make Sense and Persevere Physicists use the Large Hadron Collider in France and Switzerland to observe particle collisions. A circular chamber with beam pipes to track the particles circular path has a radius of 4.3 km. One beam pipe tracks a particle's movement over an angle of $\frac{\pi}{4}$ radians. What is the distance traveled by the particle being tracked by the one beam pipe?

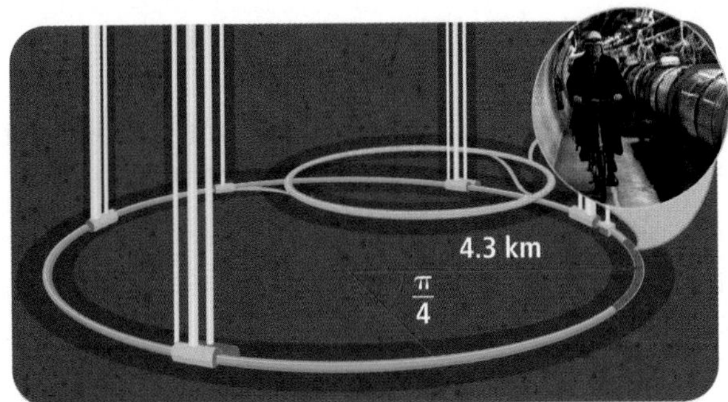

41. Reason The steps into a hot tub need to span a 60° section of the tub. How can you modify the formula for finding the intercepted arc length from an angle in radians to use degrees instead?

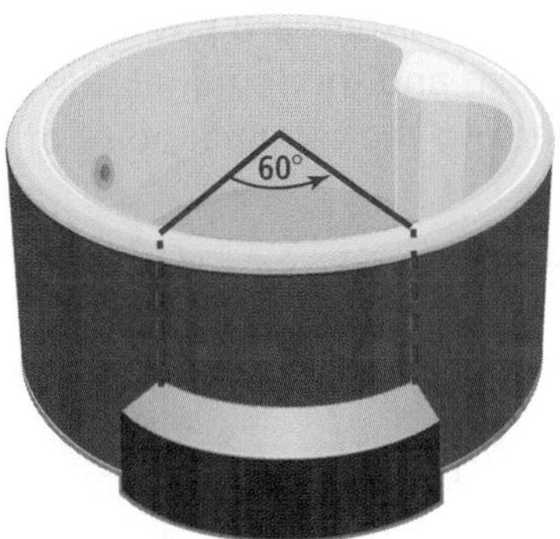

42. Make Sense and Persevere Riders on a Ferris wheel get on a seat, then the Ferris wheel turns and stops to load the next seat. The radius of the Ferris wheel is 18 m. The riders travel 5.5 m in a circular path before stopping. What angle is the Ferris wheel turning between stops?

ASSESSMENT PRACTICE

43. Match each angle measure in degrees in the left column with its corresponding measure in radians in the right column.

I. 60°	A. $\frac{\pi}{8}$
II. −15°	B. $-\frac{\pi}{12}$
III. −200°	C. $\frac{4\pi}{3}$
IV. −108°	D. $-\frac{10\pi}{9}$
V. 22.5°	E. $-\frac{3\pi}{5}$
VI. 240°	F. $\frac{\pi}{3}$

44. SAT/ACT What is another way to represent an angle in standard position that has a measure of 530°?

Ⓐ 370°

Ⓑ 170°

Ⓒ 10°

Ⓓ −10°

Ⓔ −170°

45. Performance Task A center-pivot circular irrigator has sprayers that follow concentric circular paths as the irrigator rotates. The radius of the innermost path is 20 m and to the outermost path is 420 m more.

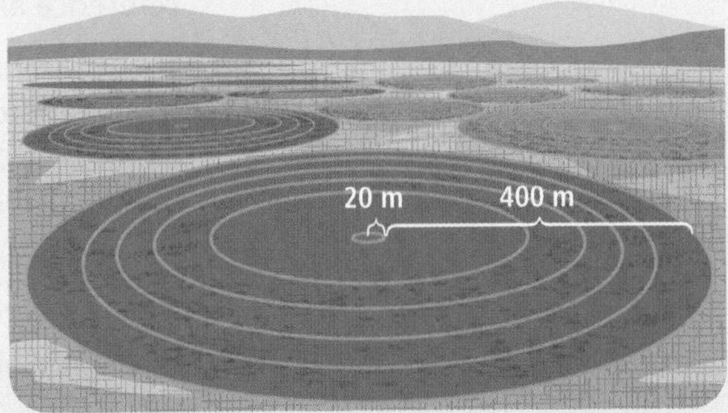

Part A What is the length of the path covered by the innermost sprayer when the irrigator rotates through an angle of $\frac{3\pi}{2}$ radians?

Part B What angle must the irrigator rotate through for the outermost sprayer to cover a path of the same length?

6-3 Trigonometric Functions and Real Numbers

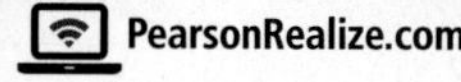

PearsonRealize.com

I CAN… use the unit circle to evaluate the trigonometric functions of any angle.

Activity Assess

EXPLORE & REASON

The graph shows the terminal sides of an angle with measure θ and its supplement, $180 - \theta$, on the unit circle.

A. How are the coordinates of the intersection of the terminal side of an angle with measure θ and the unit circle related to the sine and cosine of the angle?

B. What do you notice about θ and the measure of the acute angle formed by the terminal side of $180 - \theta$ and the x-axis?

C. Draw the terminal sides of angles in Quadrants III and IV that form the same acute angle with the x-axis as the angles in Quadrants I and II. How are these angles related to θ?

D. Communicate Precisely How are all four terminal sides related geometrically on the coordinate plane?

ESSENTIAL QUESTION

How is the unit circle related to trigonometric functions?

CONCEPTUAL UNDERSTANDING

EXAMPLE 1 Use Reference Triangles to Evaluate Sine and Cosine

A. What are the sine and cosine of the angle $\frac{2\pi}{3}$?

Recall that a reference triangle for an angle θ in standard position includes the acute angle formed by the x-axis and the terminal side of θ, and a right angle that is formed by connecting the terminal point of θ to the x-axis.

The reference triangle for $\frac{2\pi}{3}$ includes the reference angle $\frac{\pi}{3}$, (which is $\pi - \frac{2\pi}{3}$). The coordinates of the terminal point of the reference angle $\frac{\pi}{3}$ are $\left(\cos\frac{\pi}{3}, \sin\frac{\pi}{3}\right)$, or $\left(\frac{1}{2}, \frac{\sqrt{3}}{2}\right)$.

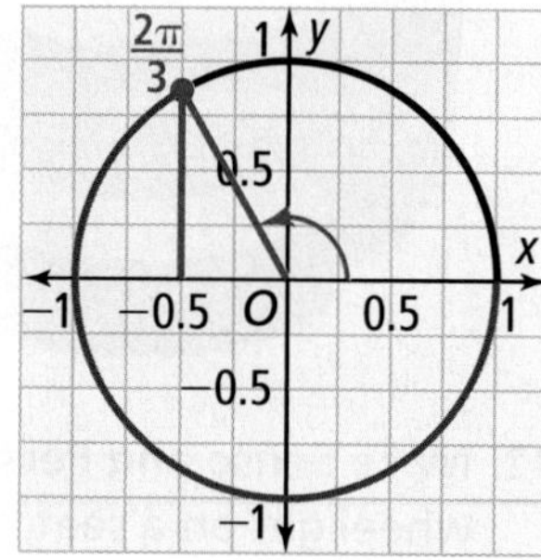

The reference triangle and the triangle with the reference angle in standard position are congruent. So once the values of sine and cosine of the reference angle are found, only the signs of the values are left to be determined.

Since the terminal point of $\frac{2\pi}{3}$ lies in Quadrant II, the coordinates of the terminal point are $\left(-\frac{1}{2}, \frac{\sqrt{3}}{2}\right)$.

Therefore, $\cos\frac{2\pi}{3} = -\frac{1}{2}$ and $\sin\frac{2\pi}{3} = \frac{\sqrt{3}}{2}$.

CONTINUED ON THE NEXT PAGE

REASON
When working on the unit circle, how do you know if the sine and cosine of an angle are positive or negative?

EXAMPLE 1 CONTINUED

B. What are the sine and cosine of a –45° angle?

A –45° angle has a reference triangle that includes a 45° reference angle. The coordinates of the terminal point of 45° are $\left(\frac{\sqrt{2}}{2}, \frac{\sqrt{2}}{2}\right)$. This reference triangle is congruent to the triangle in standard position with the reference angle 45°. Since the –45° angle lies in Quadrant IV, the point on the unit circle is $\left(\frac{\sqrt{2}}{2}, -\frac{\sqrt{2}}{2}\right)$.

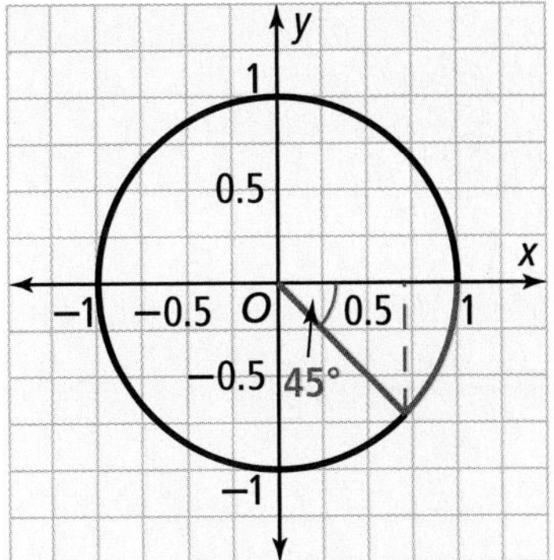

Therefore, $\cos -45° = \frac{\sqrt{2}}{2}$ and $\sin -45° = -\frac{\sqrt{2}}{2}$.

Try It! **1. What are the sine and cosine of each angle?**

a. $\frac{4\pi}{3}$ b. $\frac{3\pi}{4}$

EXAMPLE 2 Use the Pythagorean Identity $\sin^2\theta + \cos^2\theta = 1$

What is $\sin\theta$ if $\cos\theta = -\frac{3}{5}$ and the angle with measure θ is in Quadrant III?

Sketch the angle with measure θ and its reference triangle on the unit circle, as shown.

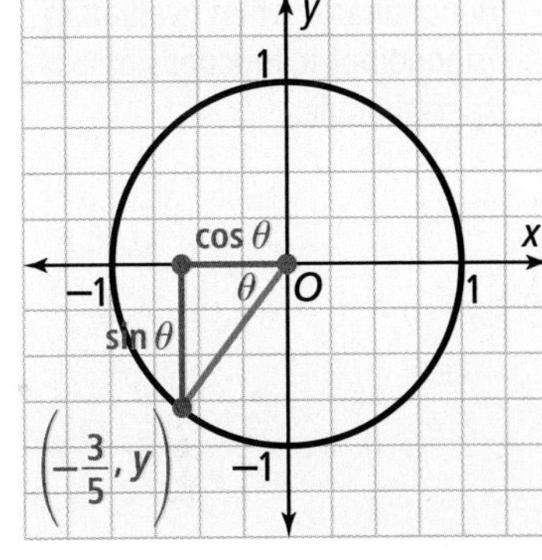

STUDY TIP
Note the absolute value signs: the *coordinates* $\sin\theta$ and $\cos\theta$ might be positive or negative, but the *lengths* of the sides of the triangle are always positive.

The coordinates of the point where the terminal side of the angle intersects the unit circle are $(\cos\theta, \sin\theta)$. The reference triangle has sides of length $|\cos\theta|$ and $|\sin\theta|$.

The hypotenuse of the reference triangle has length 1. The length of the side of the triangle opposite θ is $\sin\theta$. The length of the side of the triangle adjacent to θ is $\cos\theta$, or in this case, $\left|\frac{-3}{5}\right|$, or $\frac{3}{5}$.

Relate these values to those used in the Pythagorean Theorem to find the third side of the triangle. This will give you the *y*-coordinate of the terminal point, or $\sin\theta$.

COMMON ERROR
Be careful not to interpret the notation $\sin^2\theta$ as $\sin(\theta^2)$ or $\sin(\theta \bullet \theta)$. The notation $\sin^2\theta$ means $(\sin\theta)(\sin\theta)$.

$\sin^2\theta + \cos^2\theta = 1$ — This equation is called The Pythagorean Identity.

Given $\cos\theta = -\frac{3}{5}$, you can solve for $\sin\theta$:

$\sin^2\theta + \cos^2\theta = 1$ ········ Write the Pythagorean Identity.

$\sin^2\theta + \left(-\frac{3}{5}\right)^2 = 1$ ········ Substitute $-\frac{3}{5}$ for $\cos\theta$.

$\sin^2\theta + \frac{9}{25} = 1$ ········ Evaluate $\left(-\frac{3}{5}\right)^2$.

$\sin^2\theta = \frac{16}{25}$ ········ Subtract $\frac{9}{25}$ from both sides.

$\sin\theta = \pm\frac{4}{5}$ ········ Take the square root of both sides.

Since the angle is in Quadrant III, the *y*-coordinate $\sin\theta$ must be negative. Therefore, $\sin\theta = -\frac{4}{5}$.

CONTINUED ON THE NEXT PAGE

Activity Assess

EXAMPLE 2 CONTINUED

Try It! 2. a. What is $\sin\theta$ if $\cos\theta = \frac{\sqrt{2}}{2}$ and $0 < \theta < \frac{\pi}{2}$?

b. What is $\cos\theta$ if $\sin\theta = -0.8$ and θ is in Quadrant IV?

EXAMPLE 3 Use the Unit Circle to Evaluate Tangents

A. What is $\tan\left(-\frac{5\pi}{6}\right)$?

To find $\tan\left(-\frac{5\pi}{6}\right)$, start by finding $\sin\left(-\frac{5\pi}{6}\right)$ and $\cos\left(-\frac{5\pi}{6}\right)$, then use the identity $\tan\theta = \frac{\sin\theta}{\cos\theta}$ to find $\tan\left(-\frac{5\pi}{6}\right)$.

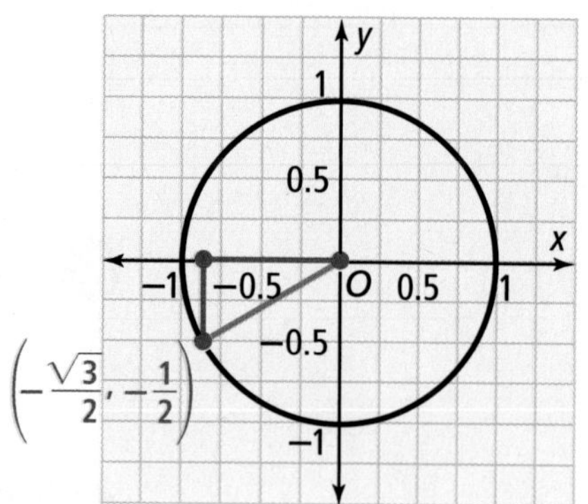

The angle with measure $-\frac{5\pi}{6}$ is in Quadrant III. Its reference angle is $\frac{\pi}{6}$, or 30°.

The reference triangle is a 30°-60°-90° triangle.

The length of the hypotenuse is 1, the length of the shorter leg is $\frac{1}{2}$, and the length of the longer leg is $\frac{\sqrt{3}}{2}$.

STUDY TIP
Consider rationalizing the denominator when evaluating trigonometric functions of special angles.

By considering the signs of a point in Quadrant III, you can determine that the coordinate of the point where the terminal side of the angle meets the unit circle is $\left(-\frac{\sqrt{3}}{2}, -\frac{1}{2}\right)$.

Use the reciprocal identity for tangent:

$$\tan\left(-\frac{5\pi}{6}\right) = \frac{\sin\left(-\frac{5\pi}{6}\right)}{\cos\left(-\frac{5\pi}{6}\right)}$$

$$= \frac{-\frac{1}{2}}{-\frac{\sqrt{3}}{2}}$$

$$= \frac{\sqrt{3}}{3}$$

So the tangent of $-\frac{5\pi}{6}$ is $\frac{\sqrt{3}}{3}$.

B. What is $\tan(3\pi)$?

$3\pi = 2\pi + \pi$, so 3π is coterminal with π. The terminal point of π has coordinates (−1, 0).

Since $\tan\theta = \frac{\sin\theta}{\cos\theta}$, $\tan\theta = \frac{y}{x}$.

From this you can conclude that $\tan(3\pi) = \frac{0}{-1} = 0$.

Try It! 3. What is the tangent of each angle?

a. $-\frac{3\pi}{2}$

b. 675°

EXAMPLE 4 Evaluate the Reciprocal Functions

Evaluate the secant, cosecant, and cotangent of a 135° angle.

The coordinates of the terminal point on the unit circle are $\left(-\frac{\sqrt{2}}{2}, \frac{\sqrt{2}}{2}\right)$.

$\sec\theta = \frac{1}{\cos\theta}$ $\quad \sec 135° = \frac{1}{-\frac{\sqrt{2}}{2}} = -\frac{2}{\sqrt{2}} = -\sqrt{2}$

$\csc\theta = \frac{1}{\sin\theta}$ $\quad \csc 135° = \frac{1}{\frac{\sqrt{2}}{2}} = \sqrt{2}$

$\cot\theta = \frac{1}{\tan\theta}$ $\quad \cot 135° = \frac{1}{-1} = -1$

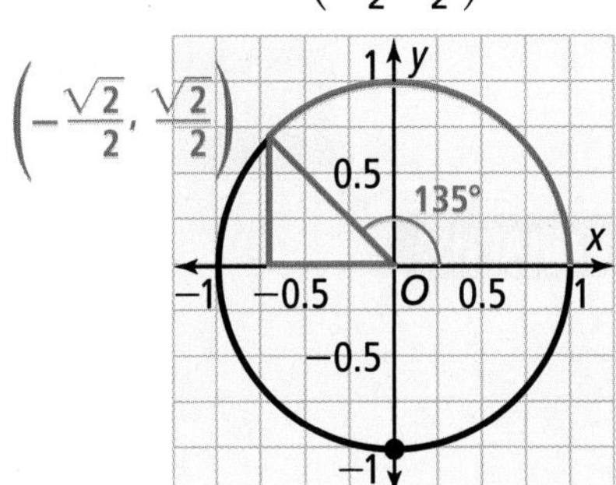

Try It! 4. What are the secant, cosecant, and cotangent for each angle?

a. 210°

b. $-\frac{10\pi}{4}$

APPLICATION

EXAMPLE 5 Use Any Circle Centered at the Origin

A rescue team is searching a circular area in a 4-mi radius around their camp. The team travels on a path 30° east of south from the camp. What is their final position relative to their camp?

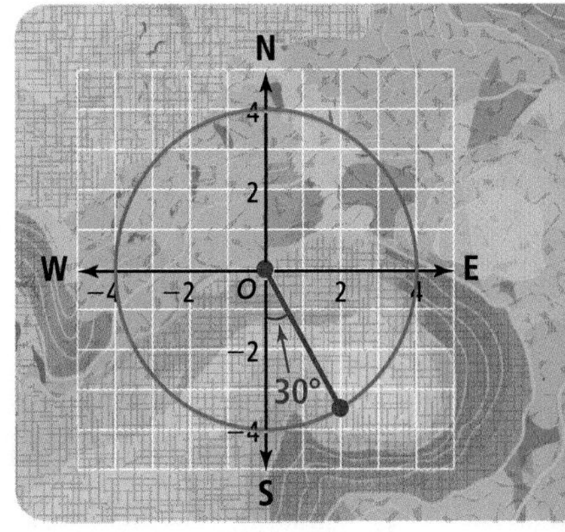

Formulate Draw a circle with radius 4 to represent the search perimeter with the camp as the origin. Show the path of the team by drawing a radius at 30° east of south. This corresponds to an angle of 300°.

Compute Draw a perpendicular line from the team's final position to the *x*-axis, creating a right triangle with hypotenuse 4.

This triangle is similar to a triangle on the unit circle. The scale factor between the triangles is 4, since your triangle has hypotenuse 4 and the unit circle triangle has hypotenuse 1.

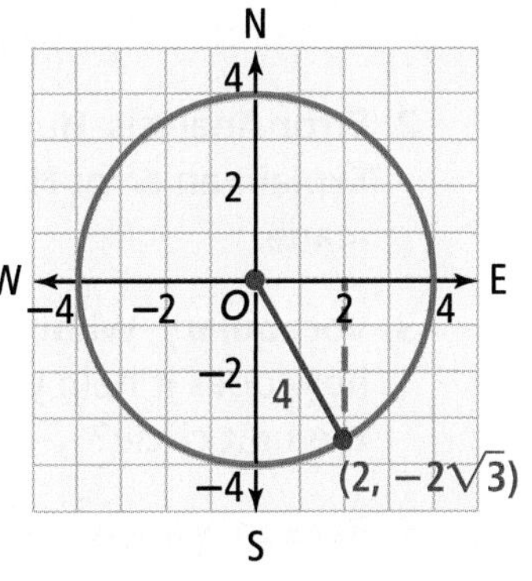

The team's final position will have coordinates 4 times those of the terminal point of 300° on the unit circle. On the unit circle, the terminal point of 300° is $\left(\frac{1}{2}, -\frac{\sqrt{3}}{2}\right)$. So the team's final position on the search perimeter circle will be at $4\left(\frac{1}{2}, -\frac{\sqrt{3}}{2}\right)$, or $(2, -2\sqrt{3})$.

Interpret The point $(2, -2\sqrt{3})$ represents a position that is 2 mi east and about 3.5 mi south of the camp.

Try It! 5. What is the final position of a search team relative to the camp if they walk 30° north of due west for 5 mi from their base camp?

CONCEPT SUMMARY Trigonometric Functions and the Unit Circle

A reference triangle is formed using the terminal side of an angle and a perpendicular segment from the terminal point to the *x*-axis. This can help you find the coordinates of the terminal point on the unit circle.

	Trigonometric Functions on the Unit Circle	Trigonometric Functions on Any Circle
GRAPHS	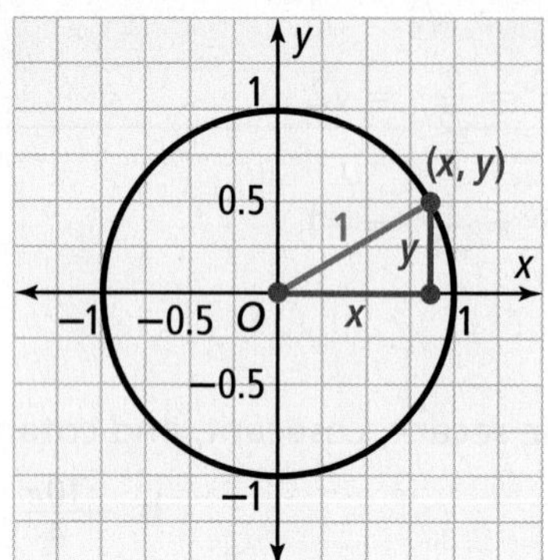	
WORDS	For an angle with measure θ in standard position with terminal point (x, y) on the unit circle:	For an angle with measure θ in standard position with terminal point (x, y) on any circle:
	$\sin\theta = y$ $\csc\theta = \frac{1}{y}$	$\sin\theta = \frac{y}{r}$ $\csc\theta = r \cdot \frac{1}{y}$
	$\cos\theta = x$ $\sec\theta = \frac{1}{x}$	$\cos\theta = \frac{x}{r}$ $\sec\theta = r \cdot \frac{1}{x}$
	$\tan\theta = \frac{y}{x}$ $\cot\theta = \frac{x}{y}$	$\tan\theta = \frac{y}{x}$ $\cot\theta = \frac{x}{y}$

Do You UNDERSTAND?

1. ESSENTIAL QUESTION How is the unit circle related to trigonometric functions?

2. **Error Analysis** Hugo said $\sin \frac{5\pi}{2} = -1$. Explain an error Hugo could have made.

3. **Vocabulary** What is a reference triangle and how does it help you work with angles on the unit circle?

4. **Reason** Why is $\cos 30° = \cos(-30°)$?

Do You KNOW HOW?

Find the sine and cosine of each angle.

5. $\frac{5\pi}{4}$

6. $120°$

7. What is $\sin\theta$ if $\cos\theta = \frac{4}{5}$ and θ is in Quadrant II?

8. What is $\cos\theta$ if $\sin\theta = -\frac{1}{2}$ and θ is in Quadrant III?

Find the tangent of each angle.

9. $\frac{\pi}{6}$

10. $-45°$

11. Evaluate the secant, cosecant, and tangent of a $135°$ angle.

PRACTICE & PROBLEM SOLVING

Scan for Multimedia

Additional Exercises Available Online

UNDERSTAND

12. **Reason** Nadeem said the tangent of 270° is 0. Is he correct? Explain your reasoning.

13. **Make Sense and Persevere** In your own words explain how you can convert an angle measured in radians to an angle measured in degrees.

14. **Error Analysis** Describe and correct the error a student made in evaluating the secant of a 135° angle.

The coordinates of the terminal point on the unit circle are

$\left(-\frac{\sqrt{2}}{2}, \frac{\sqrt{2}}{2}\right)$.

$\sec 135° = \frac{-\frac{\sqrt{2}}{2}}{1} = -\frac{\sqrt{2}}{2}$ ✗

15. **Generalize** In which quadrant(s) are all six trigonometric functions positive? Explain.

16. **Construct Arguments** Can a reference angle have a negative measure? Justify your reasoning.

17. **Communicate Precisely** How many coterminal angles does a given angle have? Explain.

18. **Model With Mathematics** Through how many radians does the minute hand of an analog clock rotate in 50 min?

19. **Error Analysis** If the coordinates of the terminal point of an angle θ on the unit circle are (−3, 4), describe and correct the error a student made in finding tan θ.

$\tan \theta = \frac{x}{y} = -\frac{3}{4}$ ✗

PRACTICE

Find the sine and cosine of each angle.
SEE EXAMPLE 1

20. $\frac{5\pi}{6}$

21. 225°

22. 270°

23. $\frac{29\pi}{4}$

24. What is $\sin\theta$ if $\cos\theta = \frac{8}{17}$ and θ is in Quadrant I? SEE EXAMPLE 2

25. What is $\cos\theta$ if $\sin\theta = -\frac{24}{25}$ and θ is in Quadrant IV? SEE EXAMPLE 2

Find the tangent of each angle. SEE EXAMPLE 3

26. $\frac{7\pi}{3}$

27. 405°

Find the secant, cosecant, and cotangent for each angle. SEE EXAMPLE 4

28. −315°

29. $\frac{13\pi}{4}$

30. 750°

31. $-\frac{2\pi}{3}$

32. Scientists are making an aerial study of a volcano. Their helicopter is circling at an 8 km radius around the volcano's crater, and one of the scientists notices a new vent that is 45° east of due north from the crater. What is the position of the new vent relative to the crater? SEE EXAMPLE 5

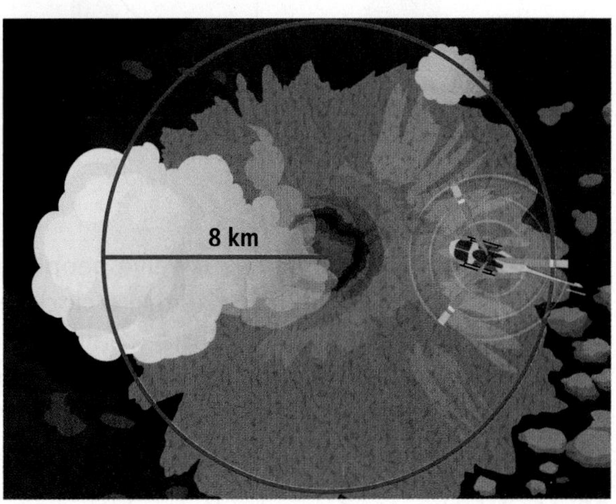

PRACTICE & PROBLEM SOLVING

Practice Tutorial

Mixed Review Available Online

APPLY

33. Model With Mathematics The horizontal distance d (in feet) traveled by a projectile launched at an angle θ and with an initial speed v (in feet per second) is given by the formula: $d = \frac{v^2}{32} \sin 2\theta$. Suppose you kick a soccer ball with an initial speed of 35 ft/sec projected at an angle of 45°. How many feet will the soccer ball travel horizontally before hitting the ground? Round to the nearest foot.

34. Make Sense and Persevere A circular carnival ride has a diameter of 120 ft. Suppose you board a gondola at the bottom of the circular ride, which is 6 ft above the ground, and rotate 240° counterclockwise before the ride temporarily stops. How many feet above ground are you when the ride stops?

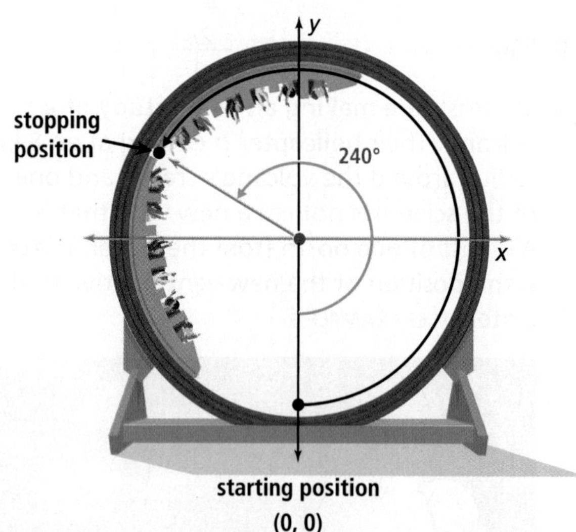

35. Make Sense and Persevere Twelve people sit at a round table. Alani, in the five o'clock seat, passes a piece of paper to Carla, at nine o'clock. What are the degree and radian measures of the angle through which the piece of paper passes?

36. Model With Mathematics Kelsey boards one of the outer horses of a carousel that has a 32 ft diameter. She represents her starting position at the point (16, 0) on a coordinate plane. The carousel rotates 300° and stops.

a. Find the coordinates (x, y) of Kelsey's horse when the ride stopped.

b. How far from her starting position was she when the ride stopped?

ASSESSMENT PRACTICE

37. What is $\sin\theta$ if $\cos\theta = -\frac{5}{13}$ and θ is in Quadrant II?

Ⓐ $-\frac{12}{13}$

Ⓑ $-\frac{8}{13}$

Ⓒ $\frac{8}{13}$

Ⓓ $\frac{12}{13}$

38. SAT/ACT Which of the following is $\tan\left(\frac{4\pi}{6}\right)$?

Ⓐ $-\sqrt{3}$

Ⓑ $-\frac{\sqrt{3}}{2}$

Ⓒ $-\frac{\sqrt{3}}{3}$

Ⓓ $-\frac{1}{2}$

39. Performance Task In navigation, the term *bearing* is used to describe the location of an object, or the clockwise-directed measure of the angle from due north. Suppose a ship's bearing is 30° from a lighthouse, as shown.

Part A Sketch the diagram on a coordinate plane, placing the lighthouse at the origin.

Part B What is the measure of the angle in standard position that describes the ship's location?

Part C If the distance from the lighthouse to the ship is 20 mi, find the coordinates of the point that represent its position on the coordinate plane.

6-4 Graphing Sine and Cosine Functions

I CAN... create and use graphs of sine and cosine functions.

VOCABULARY

- amplitude
- frequency
- midline
- period
- periodic function

Activity Assess

EXPLORE & REASON

The graph shows a rider's height above the platform when riding a Ferris wheel *t* minutes after entering the Ferris wheel car.

Height (m)
Time (min)

A. Sketch a graph of a rider's height if the Ferris wheel is twice as high. How does the graph represent the change in height?

B. Sketch a graph of a rider's height if the Ferris wheel is the same height as the first but goes twice as fast. How does the graph represent the change in speed?

C. Communicate Precisely How are the three graphs similar? How are they different?

ESSENTIAL QUESTION

How can you identify key features of sine and cosine functions?

CONCEPTUAL UNDERSTANDING

EXAMPLE 1 Understand the Graph of a Periodic Function

A. What is the period of the graph of $f(x) = \sin x$?

A **periodic function** is a function for which the outputs repeat at regular intervals. When a function is periodic, $f(x) = f(x + p)$, for some real number p. The smallest such value of p is called the **period**.

LOOK FOR RELATIONSHIPS
Notice that the function values that repeat occur at coterminal angles in the circle.

To understand the period of the function, you could use a table of values with radian measures on the unit circle to graph $f(x) = \sin x$.

x	0	$\frac{\pi}{6}$	$\frac{\pi}{4}$	$\frac{\pi}{3}$	$\frac{\pi}{2}$	$\frac{2\pi}{3}$	π	$\frac{5\pi}{4}$	$\frac{3\pi}{2}$	$\frac{11\pi}{6}$	2π	$\frac{13\pi}{6}$	$\frac{9\pi}{4}$
$f(x)$	0	$\frac{1}{2}$	$\frac{\sqrt{2}}{2}$	$\frac{\sqrt{3}}{2}$	1	$\frac{\sqrt{3}}{2}$	0	$-\frac{\sqrt{2}}{2}$	-1	$-\frac{1}{2}$	0	$\frac{1}{2}$	$\frac{\sqrt{2}}{2}$

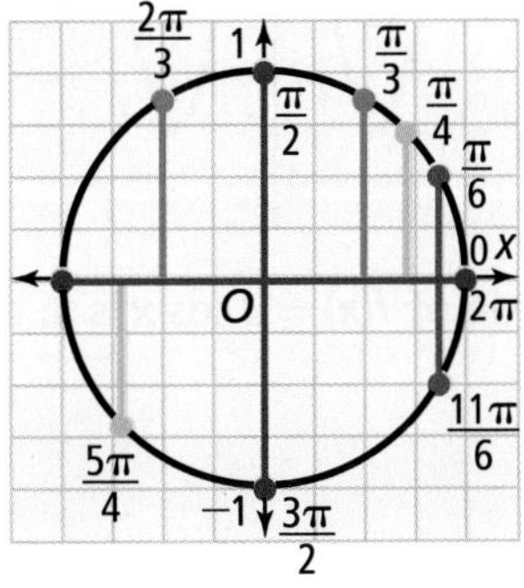

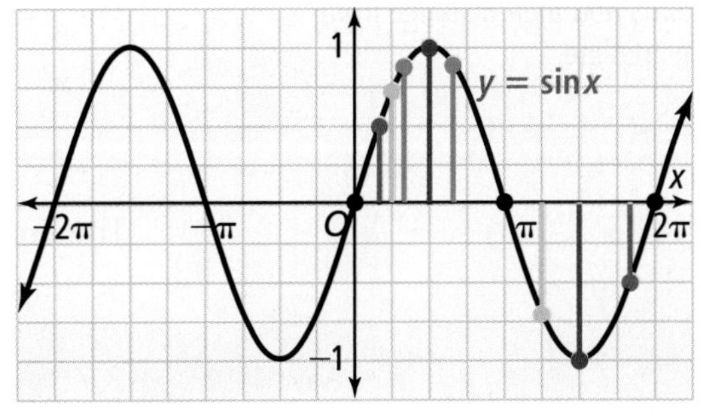

Notice that the y-values begin to repeat themselves after $x = 2\pi$. For this periodic function, $\sin(x + 2\pi) = \sin x$, for all x

The period of the function $f(x) = \sin x$ is 2π.

CONTINUED ON THE NEXT PAGE

EXAMPLE 1 CONTINUED

B. What are the other key features of the graph of $f(x) = \sin x$?

The **midline** is the horizontal line halfway between the maximum and minimum points of the graph. The **amplitude** is the distance from the midline to the minimum or maximum value of the graph.

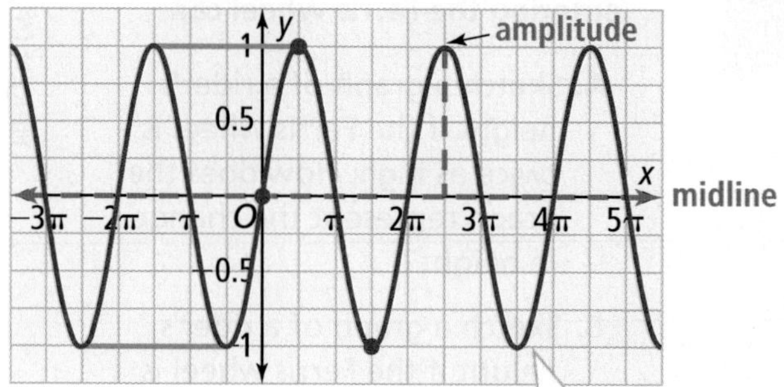

The minimum and maximum values of −1 and 1 occur at $\frac{3\pi}{2} + 2\pi k$ and $\frac{\pi}{2} + 2\pi k$, respectively, for all integers k.

The domain is $(-\infty, \infty)$ and there are infinitely many zeros, occurring at every integer multiple of π. The range is $[-1, 1]$.

The graph of $f(x) = \sin x$ has a midline at $y = 0$ and amplitude of 1.

Try It! **1. a.** What is the period of the function $f(x) = \cos x$?

b. What are the other key features of the function?

EXAMPLE 2 Identify Amplitude and Period

A. What are the amplitude and period of $f(x) = 3\cos x$?

Graph both $f(x) = 3\cos x$ and the parent function $f(x) = \cos x$.

STUDY TIP
When looking for the amplitude of a sine or cosine function, find the minimum and maximum points and their distance from the midline.

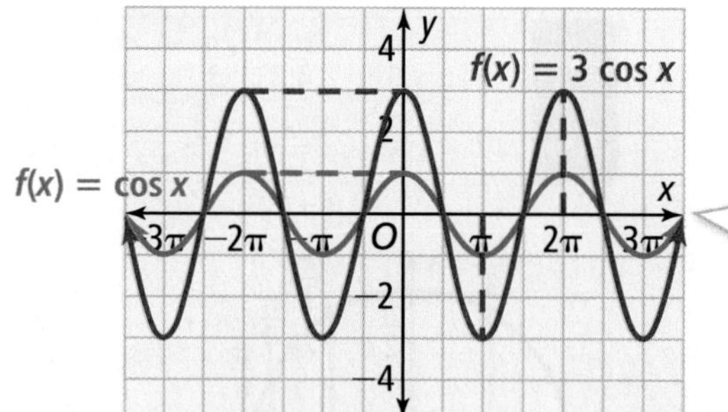

The midline is $y = 0$ and there are minimum values at −3 and maximum values at 3, which are 3 times those of $f(x) = \cos x$.

The amplitude of $f(x) = 3\cos x$ is 3, and the period is 2π.

CONTINUED ON THE NEXT PAGE

EXAMPLE 2 CONTINUED

B. What are the amplitude and period of $y = -\sin 2x$?

$$y = -\sin 2x$$

As with other functions, the graph of $y = -f(x)$ is a reflection of the graph of the parent function over the x-axis.

As with other functions, the graph of $y = f(2x)$ is a horizontal compression of the graph of the parent function by a factor of $\frac{1}{2}$.

Neither of these transformations changes the amplitude, so the amplitude of $y = -\sin 2x$ is 1.

The period is compressed by a factor of $\frac{1}{2}$. Since $\frac{1}{2}(2\pi) = \pi$, the period of $y = -\sin 2x$ is π.

Check with a graph:

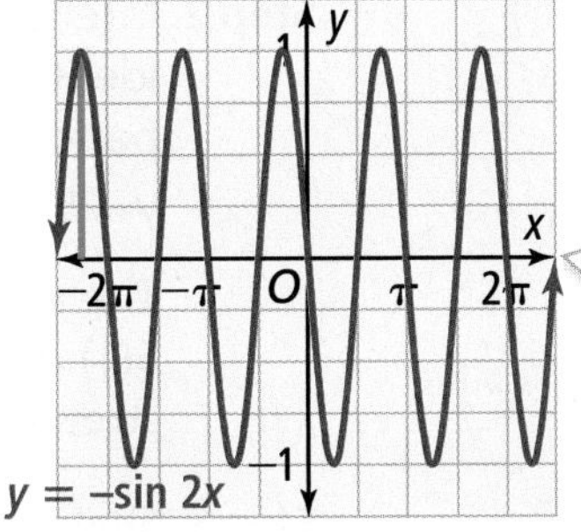

The function has an amplitude of 1, and the values of the function repeat at multiples of π.

STUDY TIP

Since the period of the graph of $y = \sin x$ is 2π, multiplying the x by 2 will make the graph repeat itself twice as often, so the period of the graph of $y = \sin 2x$ is half the period of the graph of $y = \sin x$.

Try It! 2. What are the amplitude and period of each function?

a. $y = \frac{1}{3} \cos \frac{1}{2}x$

b. $y = 2 \sin \pi x$

CONCEPT: Frequency

Frequency is the reciprocal of the period.

$y = \sin x$ and $y = \cos x$ each have a period of 2π and a frequency of $\frac{1}{2\pi}$. The function repeats itself one time from 0 to 2π.

$y = -\sin 2x$ has a period of π, and a frequency of $\frac{1}{\pi}$. The function repeats itself one time from 0 to π.

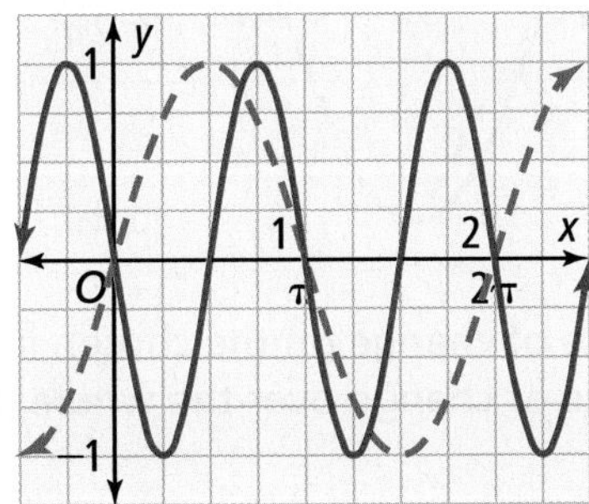

EXAMPLE 3 Graph $y = a\sin bx$ and $y = a\cos bx$

A. What is the frequency of the graph of $y = 5\sin\frac{1}{2}x$?

Step 1 Identify transformations to the parent function $y = \sin x$.

$$y = 5\sin\frac{1}{2}x$$

In an equation of the form $y = a\sin bx$ the parameter a indicates a vertical stretch or compression.

The parameter b indicates a horizontal stretch or compression.

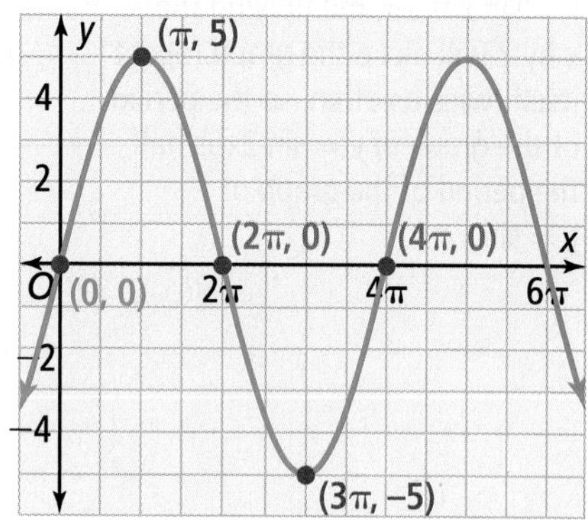

Step 2 Interpret the parameters to identify the amplitude and period of the graph of $y = 5\sin\frac{1}{2}x$.

The amplitude is stretched to $5(1) = 5$. The period is stretched to $2(2\pi) = 4\pi$.

COMMON ERROR
Use key points to determine if a graph's appearance is different because of a change in the viewing window or a change in the period of a function.

Step 3 Sketch the graph. Divide one period into fourths. Plot in order, a zero, a maximum, a zero, a minimum, and a zero.

The frequency of the graph is $\frac{1}{4\pi}$. The graph goes through one period every 4π units.

B. How does the average rate of change differ within one period of the function $y = 5\sin\frac{1}{2}x$?

Choose different intervals in $[0, 4\pi]$, and determine each average rate of change:

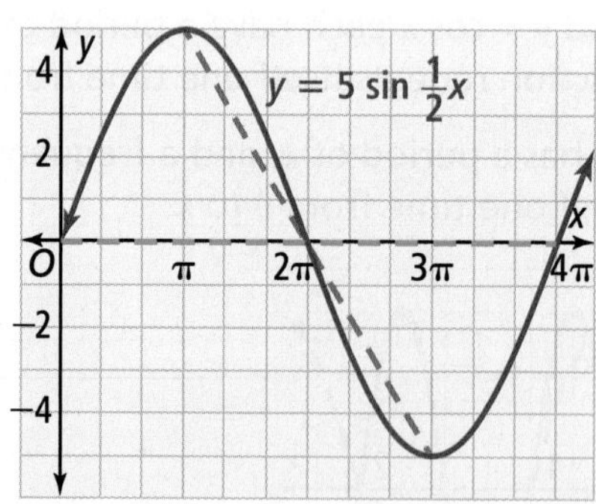

Interval	Endpoints	Average Rate of Change
$[0, \pi]$	$(0, 0)$ to $(\pi, 5)$	$\frac{5-0}{\pi-0} = \frac{5}{\pi}$
$[\pi, 2\pi]$	$(\pi, 5)$ to $(2\pi, 0)$	$\frac{0-5}{2\pi-\pi} = \frac{-5}{\pi}$
$[0, 2\pi]$	$(0, 0)$ to $(2\pi, 0)$	$\frac{0-0}{2\pi-0} = 0$
$[2\pi, 3\pi]$	$(2\pi, 0)$ to $(3\pi, -5)$	$\frac{-5-0}{3\pi-2\pi} = \frac{-5}{\pi}$
$[0, 4\pi]$	$(0, 0)$ to $(4\pi, 0)$	$\frac{0-0}{4\pi-0} = 0$

The average rate of change on the chosen intervals varies between $\frac{-5}{\pi}$ and $\frac{5}{\pi}$. The average rate of change over the whole period $[0, 4\pi]$ is 0.

Try It! **3. a.** Graph $y = \frac{3}{2}\cos 3\pi x$. What is the frequency?

b. What is the average rate of change over the interval $[0, 1]$?

APPLICATION

EXAMPLE 4 Develop a Graph and an Equation From a Description

A math teacher has a clock centered at the origin of a coordinate system. The hour hand of the clock is 5 in. long. Graph the relationship between *x*, in hours, and *y*, in inches between the horizontal axis and the tip of the hour hand. Let midnight represent 0 h, and graph the relationship for the time between midnight and 11:59 P.M. Write the equation describing the relationship you graphed.

Formulate Construct a diagram to represent the clock:

Think of the horizontal axis as the midline.

The tip of the hour hand starts 5 in. above the horizontal axis at midnight.

3 h later it reaches the horizontal axis.

At 6:00 A.M. it is 5 in. below the horizontal axis.

At 9:00 A.M. it is back to the horizontal axis.

At noon, after 12 h, the cycle starts over again.

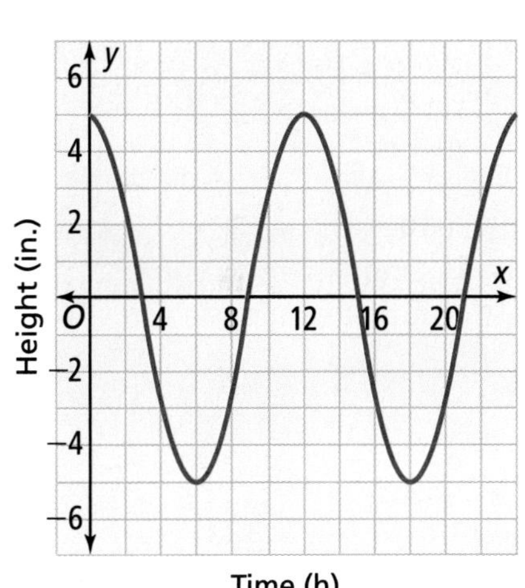

Compute The function starts at (0, 5) for midnight, then crosses (3, 0) at 3 A.M. and (6, −5) at 6 A.M. The hour hand travels back up to (9, 0) and then at noon is at (12, 5) before repeating the cycle again to end at (24, 5) at midnight the next day.

Interpret The graph has a *y*-intercept at the maximum value, so the equation is $y = a \cos bx$.

The minimum and maximum values occur at −5 and 5 respectively, so the midline is $y = 0$ and the amplitude is $a = 5$.

The minimum value repeats after 12 h, so the period is 12.

$$12 = \frac{2\pi}{b}, \text{ so } b = \frac{\pi}{6}.$$

The equation describing the relationship is $y = 5 \cos \frac{\pi}{6}x$.

Try It! 4. Construct a graph over 3 h for the tip of the minute hand *t* minutes after noon if the minute hand is 8 in. long. What is the period?

EXAMPLE 5 Compare Key Features of Two Periodic Functions

The equation for *f* and the graph of *g* are given below. How do the period and amplitude of the functions compare?

STUDY TIP

The period of a trigonometric graph can be determined using any two points, usually the two minimum points or maximum points closest to each other.

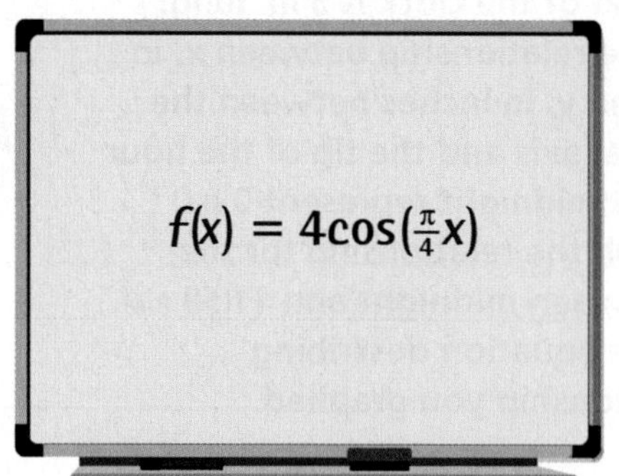

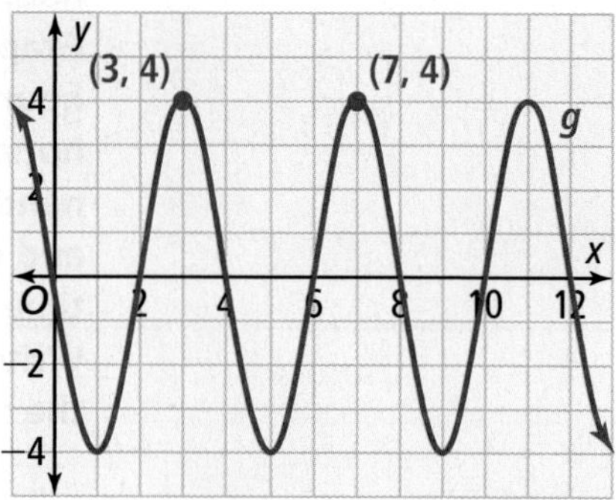

Find the period of *f* by dividing the period of the parent function by the parameter $\frac{\pi}{4}$.

The period of *f* is $\frac{2\pi}{\frac{\pi}{4}}$, or 8.

Find the amplitude of *f* by multiplying the amplitude of the parent function by the parameter 4.

The amplitude of *f* is 1(4), or 4.

Find the period of *g* by measuring the distance from one maximum to the next.

The period of *g* is 4.

Find the amplitude of *g* by measuring the distance from the midline to a maximum or minimum.

The midline of *g* is the line with equation $y = 0$, so the distance to a maximum is 4.

The amplitude of *g* is 4.

The two functions have the same amplitude, but the period of *f* is twice as long as the period of *g*.

Try It! **5. a.** How do the frequencies of *f* and *g* compare?

b. What else is different about the two functions? Explain.

 Concept Summary  Assess

CONCEPT SUMMARY Key Features of Sine and Cosine Graphs

WORDS

The general equation for a sine function is $y = a \sin bx$, just as the general equation for a cosine function is $y = a \cos bx$. In both cases, the amplitude is $|a|$ and the frequency is $\frac{b}{2\pi}$.

The equation for the graph below is $y = \frac{1}{2} \sin 4x$.

GRAPH

The amplitude is the distance between a minimum or maximum point and the midline, or $\frac{1}{2}$.

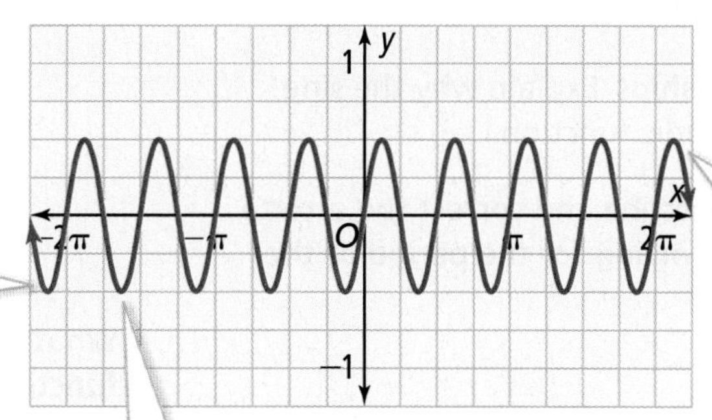

The x-axis, or $y = 0$, is the midline, which is halfway between the maximum points and minimum points.

The period is $\frac{\pi}{2}$, or the length of one cycle. The frequency is $\frac{2}{\pi}$, because the function repeats 2 times from 0 to π.

Do You UNDERSTAND?

1. ESSENTIAL QUESTION How can you identify key features of sine and cosine functions?

2. **Error Analysis** Christy said that the function $y = 3 \cos 4x$ has an amplitude of 3 and a period of $\frac{\pi}{4}$. Explain and correct Christy's error.

3. **Vocabulary** Explain the difference between the period and the amplitude of a periodic function.

4. **Reason** What is the range of the cosine function? How does the range compare to the amplitude of the function?

Do You KNOW HOW?

Find the period and amplitude of each function.

5. 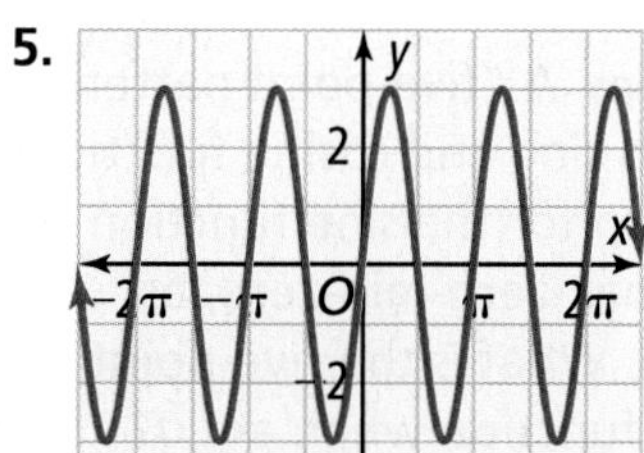

6. 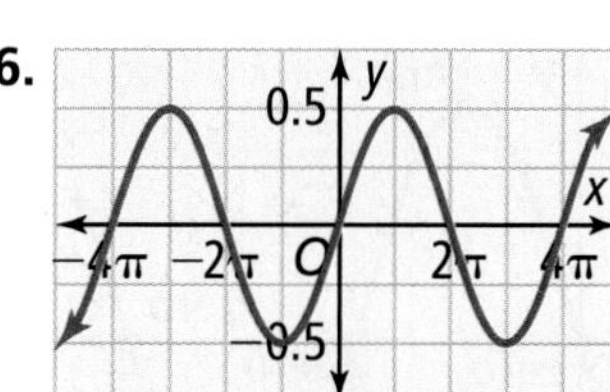

7. Use the graph from Exercise 6. How many cycles does the function have in the interval from 0 to 2π?

UNDERSTAND

8. **Use Structure** Write the equations of three cosine functions that have an amplitude of $\frac{1}{2}$ and that have periods of $\frac{1}{2}$, 2, and 4. Then graph and label all three equations on the same coordinate plane.

9. **Look for Relationships** Explain why the sine function is a periodic function.

10. **Error Analysis** Describe and correct the error a student made in solving for the period of the given function.

$y = \frac{1}{4} \sin \frac{2}{3}x$

period $= \frac{2\pi}{\frac{1}{4}}$

period $= \frac{2\pi}{1} \times \frac{4}{1}$

period $= 8\pi$ ✗

11. **Look for Relationships** A "five-point pattern" can be used to graph sine and cosine functions. The five-point pattern for the sine function when $a > 0$ is zero-max-zero-min-zero, as shown on the graph. What is the five-point pattern for the sine function when $a < 0$?

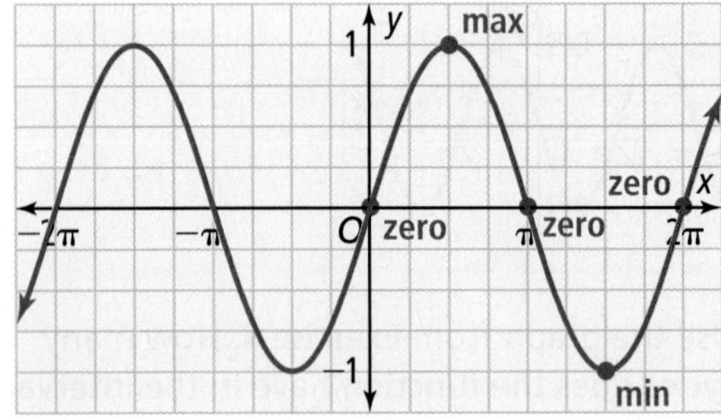

12. **Higher Order Thinking** Use a graphing calculator to graph $y = \sin x$ and $y = \csc x$. What do you notice about the graph of $y = \csc x$ where $y = 0$ on the graph of $y = \sin x$? (*Hint*: $y = \csc x$ is equivalent to $y = \frac{1}{\sin x}$.)

PRACTICE

13. Identify the domain, range, and period of the function $y = \cos x$. SEE EXAMPLE 1

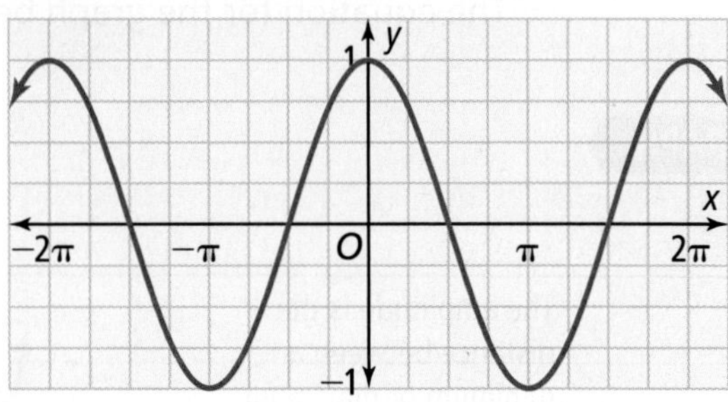

What are the amplitude and period of each function? SEE EXAMPLE 2

14. $y = \frac{1}{2} \cos \frac{1}{8}x$

15. $y = 5 \sin \frac{1}{4}x$

16. Use technology to graph $y = \frac{3}{4} \sin 2x$. What is the frequency? What is the average rate of change on the interval $[0, \pi]$? SEE EXAMPLE 3

17. A particle in the ocean moves with a wave. The motion of the particle can be modeled by the cosine function. If a 14 in. wave occurs every 6 s, write a function that models the height of the particle in inches y as it moves in seconds x. What is the period of the function? SEE EXAMPLE 4

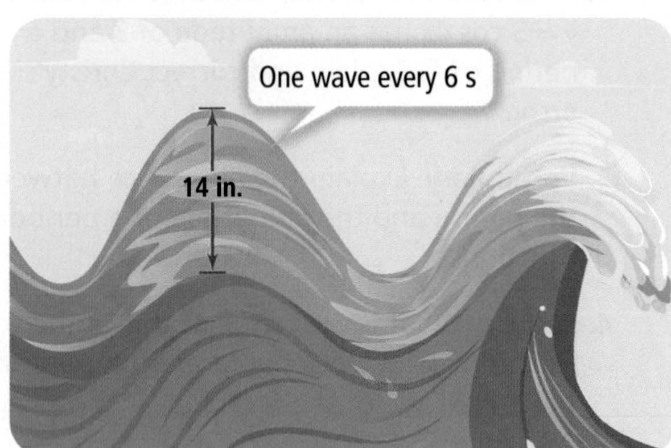

18. How do the periods of the two functions compare? SEE EXAMPLE 5

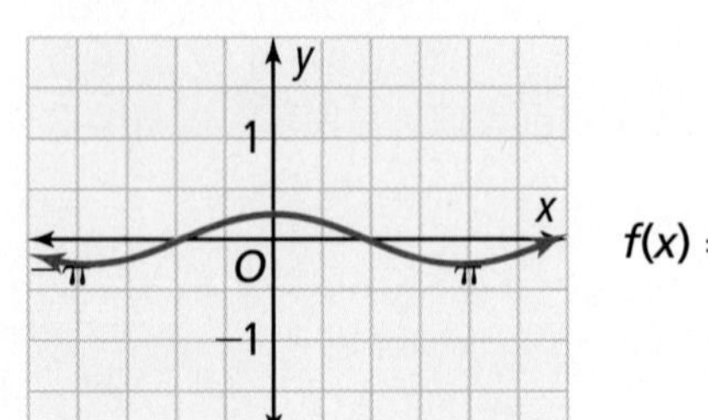

$f(x) = \frac{1}{4} \cos \frac{\pi}{3}x$

PRACTICE & PROBLEM SOLVING

Mixed Review Available Online

APPLY

19. Make Sense and Persevere The relationship between the height of a point on a unicyle wheel, in feet, and time, in seconds, can be modeled by the sine function. A unicycle wheel has a diameter of 2 ft. A marker was placed on the wheel at time $t = 0$ s with a height of $h = 0$ ft. When Esteban is riding the unicycle, it takes $\frac{\pi}{2}$ s for the unicycle wheel to make one complete revolution.

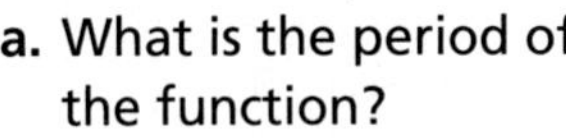

a. What is the period of the function?

b. What is the amplitude of the function?

c. Write an equation to represent this situation.

d. Graph the function.

e. How many revolutions will the unicycle wheel make in 4π s when Esteban is riding the unicycle?

20. Model With Mathematics A solar day is 24 h and a lunar day is 24 h 50 min. A lunar day is 50 min longer than a solar day because the moon revolves around Earth, and Earth rotates around its axis in the same direction. This means it takes Earth 50 min longer to catch up with the moon. Each lunar day, two high tides and two low tides occur. High tides occur 12 h 25 min apart. Yesterday, high tide was measured at 8 ft above sea level and low tide was measured at 2 ft above sea level. A cosine function models the depth of the water in feet, D, at time t in hours.

a. What is the period of the function?

b. The amplitude is the difference between the depth of the water at high tide and the average depth of the water. What is the amplitude?

c. Write an equation to represent D as a function of t.

ASSESSMENT PRACTICE

21. Find the key features of the function $y = 8\cos\left(\frac{\pi}{6}x\right)$. Write the correct value from the box next to each key feature.

amplitude =

period =

frequency =

midline =

3	8	12
$\frac{1}{8}$	$\frac{1}{12}$	$\frac{\pi}{3}$
$x = 0$		$y = 0$

22. SAT/ACT What is the equation of the graph?

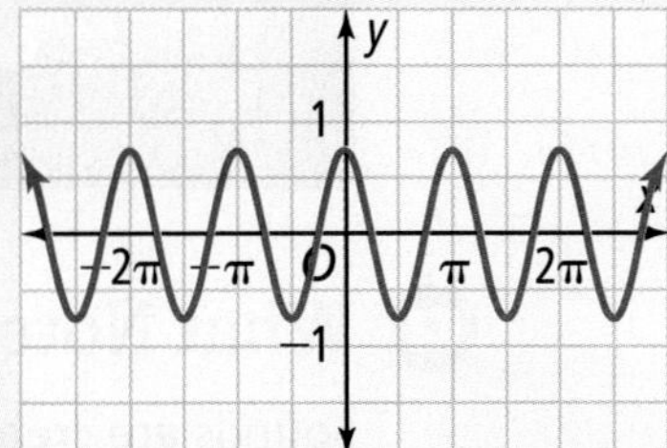

Ⓐ $y = \frac{3}{4}\cos(2x)$

Ⓑ $y = \frac{3}{2}\cos x$

Ⓒ $y = \frac{3}{4}\sin(2x)$

Ⓓ $y = \frac{3}{2}\sin x$

23. Performance Task Danielle is investigating how the signs of the parameters a and b create transformations of the sine function.

Part A Graph $y = (\sin 2x)$ and $y = -\sin(2x)$ on the same coordinate plane.

Part B How are the graphs of $y = \sin(2x)$ and $y = -\sin(2x)$ related?

Part C Graph $y = \sin(2x)$ and $y = \sin(-2x)$ on the same coordinate plane.

Part D How are the graphs of $y = \sin 2x$ and $y = \sin(-2x)$ related?

Part E How is the graph of $y = a\sin(bx)$ affected when a or b is replaced with its opposite? Explain.

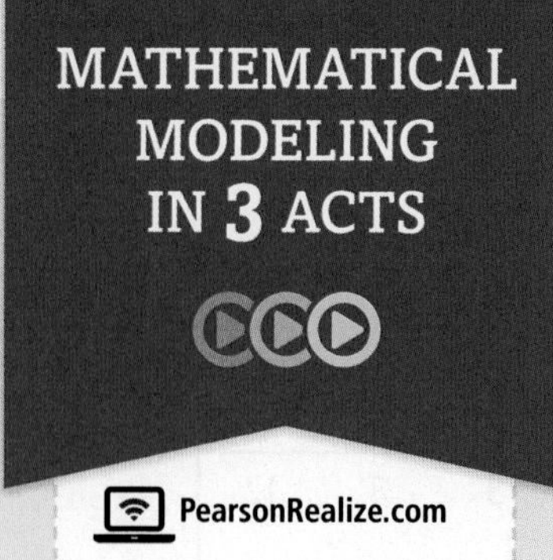

PearsonRealize.com

What Note Was That?

Sounds are created by vibrations. As the vibrations travel through the air, they create sound waves. The frequency of a sound is the measurement of the number of cycles of that wave per second, in a unit called hertz (Hz). Music notes can be identified by their frequency.

What information do you need to determine the frequency of a note? How accurate does your data need to be? Think about this during the Mathematical Modeling in 3 Acts lesson.

Scan for Multimedia 

ACT 1 Identify the Problem

1. What is the first question that comes to mind after watching the video?
2. Write down the main question you will answer about what you saw in the video.
3. Make an initial conjecture that answers this main question.
4. Explain how you arrived at your conjecture.
5. What information will be useful to know to answer the main question? How can you get it? How will you use that information?

ACT 2 Develop a Model

6. Use the math that you have learned in this Topic to refine your conjecture.

ACT 3 Interpret the Results

7. Did your refined conjecture match the actual answer exactly? If not, what might explain the difference?

6-5

Graphing Other Trigonometric Functions

I CAN... sketch the graphs of the ratio and reciprocal trigonometric functions.

EXPLORE & REASON

Use the graphs of $f(x) = x + 3$ and $g(x) = \frac{1}{x+3}$ to compare these reciprocal functions.

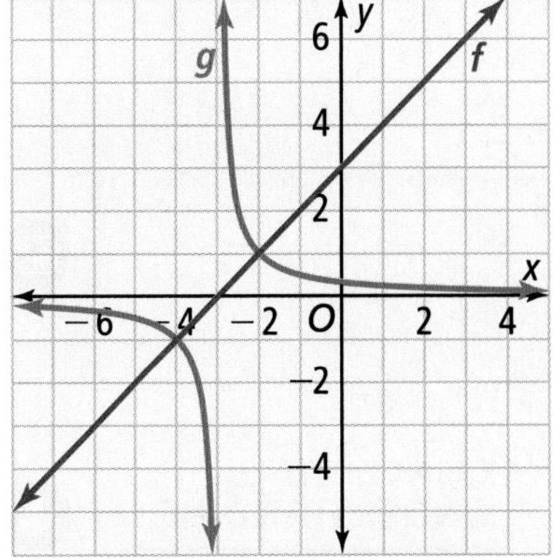

A. Identify the zeros of each function.

B. Identify the asymptotes of $y = g(x)$. Describe how the rule for g can be used to predict the horizontal and vertical asymptotes of its graph.

C. Look for Relationships How can you use the graph of f to predict a vertical asymptote in the graph of g?

ESSENTIAL QUESTION

How do key features of one trigonometric function relate to key features of other trigonometric functions?

EXAMPLE 1 Graph $y = \tan x$

How can the unit circle help you sketch the graph of $y = \tan x$?

Use what you know about the unit circle to create a table of values.

LOOK FOR RELATIONSHIPS
How does the unit circle relate to the graph of the function $y = \tan x$? A semicircle on the unit circle corresponds to one period of the function's graph.

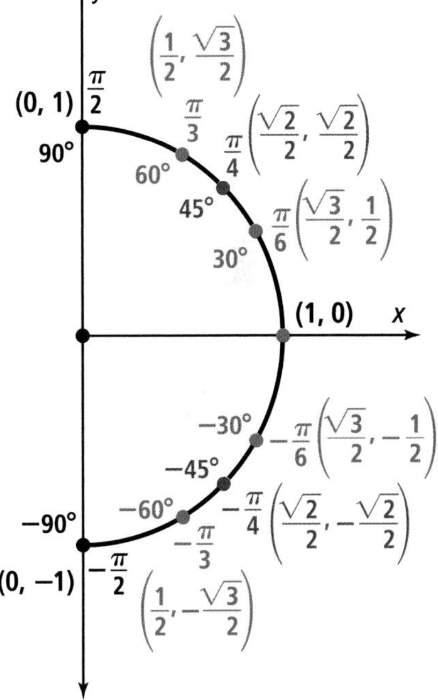

x	$-\frac{\pi}{2}$	$-\frac{\pi}{3}$	$-\frac{\pi}{4}$	$-\frac{\pi}{6}$	0	$\frac{\pi}{6}$	$\frac{\pi}{4}$	$\frac{\pi}{3}$	$\frac{\pi}{2}$
$\tan x$	undefined	$-\sqrt{3}$	-1	$-\frac{\sqrt{3}}{3}$	0	$\frac{\sqrt{3}}{3}$	1	$\sqrt{3}$	undefined

The graph of $y = \tan x$ goes through one complete cycle from $-\frac{\pi}{2} < x < \frac{\pi}{2}$. Over this interval the range is all real numbers.

CONTINUED ON THE NEXT PAGE

EXAMPLE 1 CONTINUED

Notice that at the boundaries of this interval, $y = \tan x$ is undefined: these are the values where $\cos x = 0$. Since $\tan x = \frac{\sin x}{\cos x}$, the graph of $y = \tan x$ will have vertical asymptotes at these values.

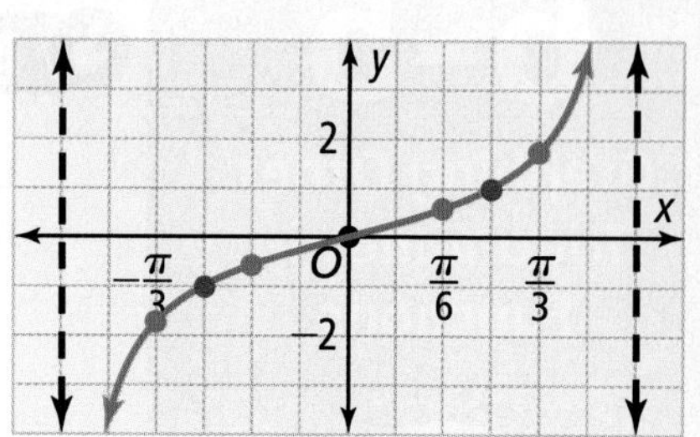

Try It! **1.** Create a table of values, and use the unit circle to help you sketch the graph of $y = \cot x$. Plot the function's zeros and asymptotes in your sketch.

CONCEPTUAL UNDERSTANDING

EXAMPLE 2 Describe Key Features of Tangent Functions

What are the key features (domain, range, period, zeros, and asymptotes) of the graph of $y = \tan x$?

Refer back to the table of values and sketch you made in Example 1.

GENERALIZE
What do you notice about the key features of the graph? Points and characteristics repeat every π units. If you understand the graph for $-\frac{\pi}{2} < x < \frac{\pi}{2}$, then you understand the graph everywhere.

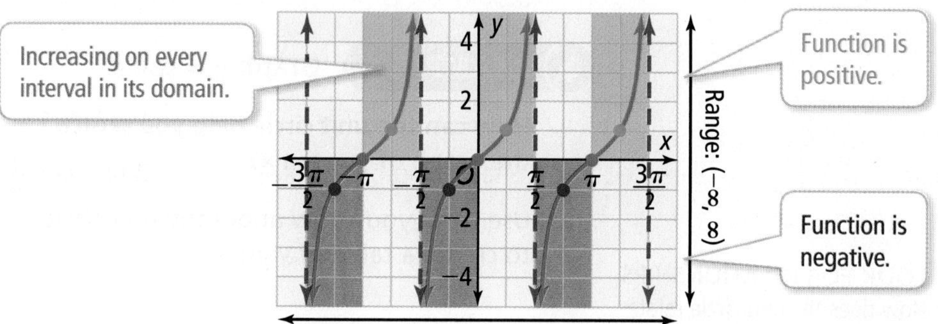

Domain: $\left\{x: x \neq \frac{\pi}{2} + n\pi, \text{ where } x \text{ is a real number and } n \text{ is an integer}\right\}$;

Range: $(-\infty, \infty)$

Period: π

$y = \tan x = \frac{\sin x}{\cos x}$

Function has zeros whenever $\sin x = 0$.

Function has vertical asymptotes whenever $\cos x = 0$.

The function is increasing everywhere.

The function is positive for every interval $\left(0 + n\pi, \frac{\pi}{2} + n\pi\right)$ where n is an integer: these correspond to the green shaded regions on the graph.

The function is negative for every interval $\left(-\frac{\pi}{2} + n\pi, n\pi\right)$ where n is an integer. These correspond to the purple shaded regions on the graph.

Try It! **2.** Describe the key features of the graph of the function $y = \cot x$. Refer to your graph from Example 1, Try It!

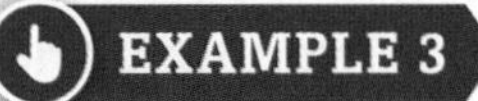

EXAMPLE 3 Graph $y = a \tan bx$

How can you use transformations to sketch the graph of the function $y = a \tan bx$?

To sketch a graph using transformations, first consider how the parameters a and b change the graph of the parent function.

$$y = 2 \tan 4x$$

$a = 2$; the coefficient of the tangent function stretches the graph of the function vertically.

$b = 4$; a larger coefficient of x corresponds to a smaller period, so the graph appears to be the parent graph compressed horizontally.

The vertical stretch makes the graph of $y = 2 \tan 4x$ rise more steeply than the graph of $y = \tan x$.

The horizontal compression changes the period of the function:

The period of the graph of $y = \tan x$ is π.

The period of the graph of $y = 2 \tan 4x$ is $\frac{\pi}{4}$.

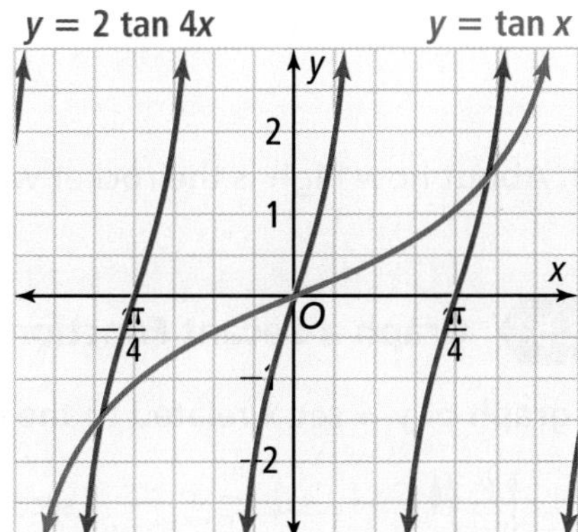

COMMON ERROR

Since the function $y = 2 \cos x$ has an amplitude of 2, you may think that the function $y = 2 \tan 4x$ has an amplitude of 2. The tangent function, however, has no maximum or minimum values, so it has no amplitude.

Try It! **3.** Sketch the graph of the function $y = \frac{1}{2} \cot 3x$.

APPLICATION

EXAMPLE 4 Model With a Trigonometric Function

MODEL WITH MATHEMATICS
Why does the function involve the tangent? Could you use a sine or cosine function to model this problem instead?

Seth is observing today's rocket launch at Cape Canaveral from the viewing area about 3 mi away. Write a function to model the height *h* of the rocket as a function of the angle of inclination *θ*, from Seth's position in the viewing area to the rocket. Identify an appropriate domain, and use the function to describe the motion of the rocket.

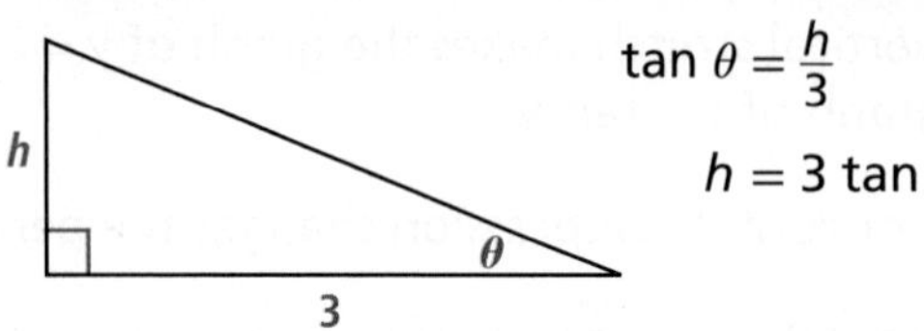

$$\tan \theta = \frac{h}{3}$$

$$h = 3 \tan \theta$$

The rocket will never be directly overhead, because there is always a horizontal distance of 3 mi.

In this context, the domain of the function is $\left\{\theta \mid 0 < \theta < \frac{\pi}{2}\right\}$ because the rocket will never be directly overhead. The range is $\{h \mid h > 0\}$, because the height of the rocket is always positive.

Try It! 4. About how high is the rocket when the angle of inclination is $\frac{\pi}{3}$?

EXAMPLE 5 Graph a Secant Function

STUDY TIP
Use the unit circle to help you learn the values of sine and cosine for key angle measures. You can then use this knowledge to find values and sketch the graphs of the remaining trigonometric functions.

How is the graph of $y = \sec x$ related to the graph of $y = \cos x$?

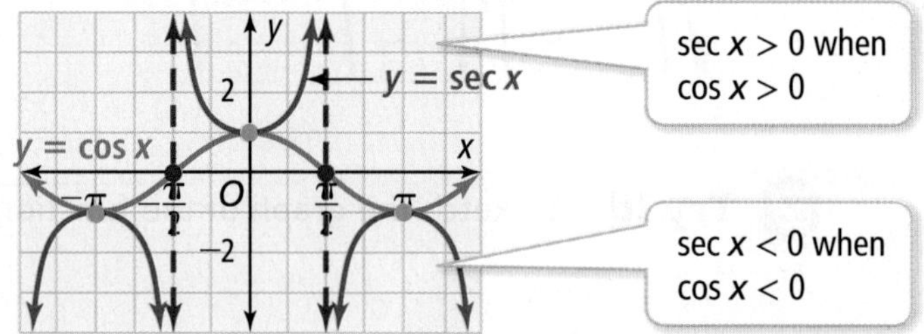

sec $x > 0$ when cos $x > 0$

sec $x < 0$ when cos $x < 0$

The domain of $y = \sec x$ is $\left\{x: x \neq \frac{\pi}{2} + n\pi, \text{ integer } n\right\}$. The graph of $y = \sec x$ has a vertical asymptote wherever $x = \frac{\pi}{2} + n\pi$ for any integer n. This makes sense, since $\sec x = \frac{1}{\cos x}$ and $\cos x$ is 0 for any $\frac{\pi}{2} + n\pi$. Since the graph of $y = \cos x$ changes sign at those values, the graph of $y = \sec x$ approaches $+\infty$ on one side of the asymptote and $-\infty$ on the other.

Try It! 5. How is the graph of $y = \csc x$ related to the graph of $y = \sin x$?

  Concept Summary  Assess

CONCEPT SUMMARY Graph Ratios and Reciprocals of Sine and Cosine

	Tangent and Cotangent		Secant and Cosecant	
ALGEBRA	$y = \tan x = \frac{\sin x}{\cos x}$	$y = \cot x = \frac{\cos x}{\sin x}$	$y = \sec x = \frac{1}{\cos x}$	$y = \csc x = \frac{1}{\sin x}$
GRAPHS	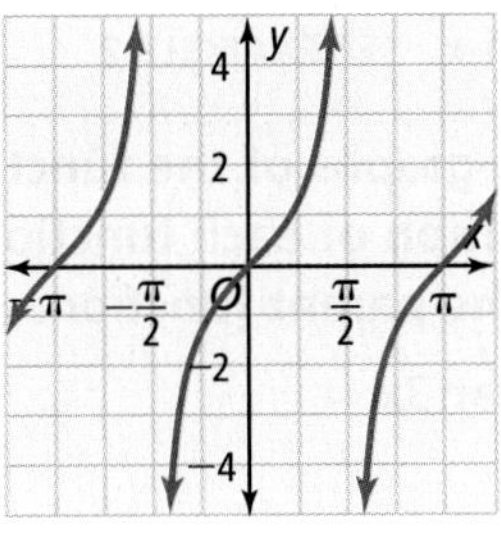	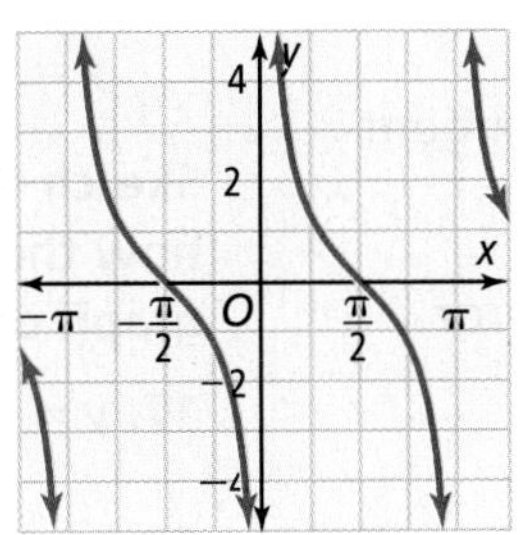	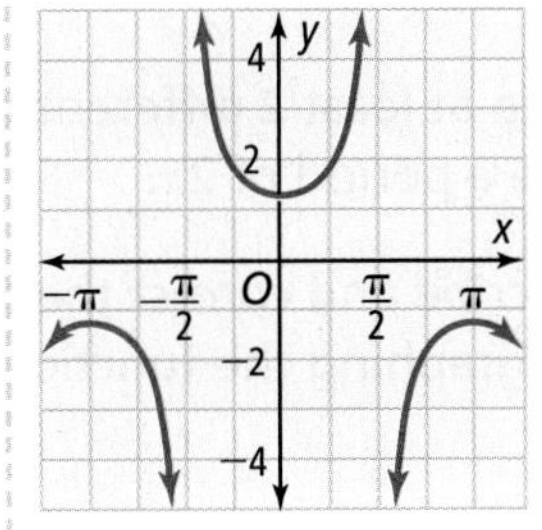	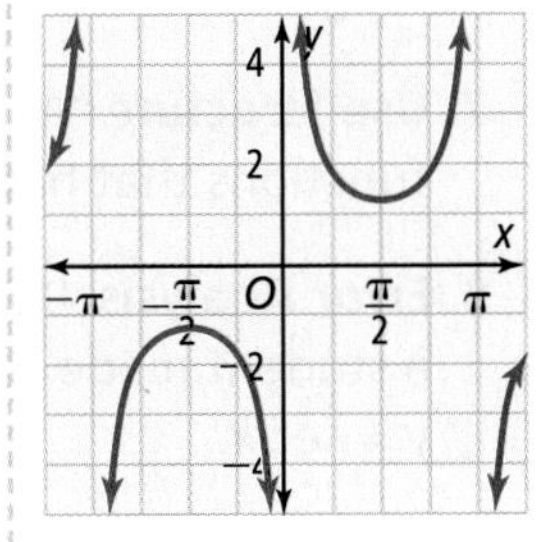
KEY FEATURES	• Zeros in denominators ⇔ vertical asymptotes • tan x increasing; cot x decreasing • Period = π		• Zeros in denominators ⇔ vertical asymptotes • Sign of reciprocal matches sign of denominator • Period = 2π	

Do You UNDERSTAND?

1. **ESSENTIAL QUESTION** How do key features of one trigonometric function relate to key features of other trigonometric functions?

2. **Error Analysis** Mia said the period of the tangent function is 2π. Explain an error that Mia could have made.

3. **Reason** Explain why the graph of $y = \tan x$ does not have an amplitude.

Do You KNOW HOW?

4. Sketch the graph of the function $y = \frac{1}{2} \tan x$ over the interval $-\frac{\pi}{2} < x < \frac{\pi}{2}$. How does this graph differ from the graph of $y = \tan x$?

5. Find the period of the function $y = \tan 3x$.

UNDERSTAND

6. **Look for Relationships** Describe the relationship between the ranges of the sine and cosine graphs and the ranges of the secant and cosecant graphs. What values do all their ranges share?

7. **Use Structure** Write at least 2 different tangent functions that have a period of 2π.

8. **Error Analysis** Describe and correct the error a student made in graphing the function $y = \sec x$.

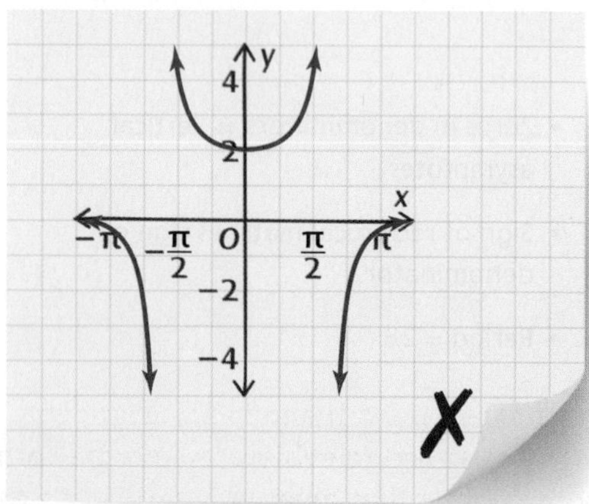

9. **Construct Arguments** Explain why the cosecant function is undefined at multiples of π radians or 180°.

10. **Generalize** For what values of x is the function $y = \tan x$ undefined? Explain.

11. **Look for Relationships** Explain how the periods of the tangent and cotangent functions differ from the periods of the other four trigonometric functions.

12. **Generalize** Identify all the asymptotes of the graph of $y = \sec x$.

13. **Use Structure** Write a tangent function that has a period of $\frac{\pi}{3}$. Graph the function.

14. **Higher Order Thinking** A function f is considered even if $f(-x) = f(x)$ for all x in the domain of f; a function is odd if $f(-x) = -f(x)$ for all x in the domain of f. Which of the six trigonometric functions are even, and which are odd?

PRACTICE

15. Sketch the graph of $y = \tan x$ over the domain $-\pi$ to π. SEE EXAMPLE 1

16. Describe the domain, range, period, zeros, and asymptotes of the function $y = \tan x$. SEE EXAMPLE 2

Sketch the graphs of the functions. Then describe how the graph of each function compares to the graph of the parent function. SEE EXAMPLE 3

17. $y = \frac{1}{2}\tan 3x$

18. $y = 2\cot \frac{1}{2}x$

19. Stacy is observing a glass elevator from a bench 20 ft away from the elevator's entrance. SEE EXAMPLE 4

   a. Write a function to model the height h of the elevator as a function of the angle of inclination θ from Stacy's position to the elevator.

   b. Identify an appropriate domain, and use the function to graph and describe the motion of the elevator.

   c. About how high is the elevator when the angle of inclination is $\frac{\pi}{4}$?

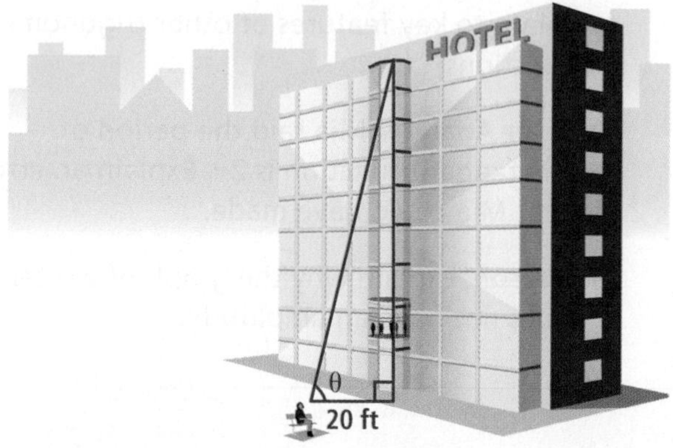

20. Graph the function $y = \csc x$. Describe how the graph of $y = \csc x$ is related to the graph of $y = \sin x$. SEE EXAMPLE 5

PRACTICE & PROBLEM SOLVING

APPLY

21. Make Sense and Persevere An architect is designing a sloped rooftop that is triangular from the side view.

a. Write a function that models the height of the triangle where θ is the angle indicated.

b. Graph the function over the domain $\left[0, \frac{\pi}{4}\right]$.

c. What is the height of the triangle if θ is $\frac{\pi}{10}$? Round to the nearest tenth of a foot.

22. Make Sense and Persevere A carpenter is constructing a hexagonal floor for a treehouse. The floor will be made of six isosceles triangles placed together as shown.

a. Write a function that models the height of one of the triangles where θ is the measure of one of the base angles and the base of the triangle is 16 ft in length.

b. Graph the function over the domain (0, 60°).

ASSESSMENT PRACTICE

23. Fill in the blanks to complete each statement regarding the properties of the tangent function.

a. The domain is the set of all real numbers, except odd multiples of ____.

b. The range is the set of ________.

c. The x-intercepts are $\{\ldots, -2\pi,$ ____, $0, \pi, 2\pi,$ ____ $\ldots\}$; the y-intercept is 0.

d. Vertical asymptotes occur at $x = \ldots,$ ____, $-\frac{\pi}{2},$ ____ $\frac{3\pi}{2}, \ldots$.

24. SAT/ACT Which equation is represented by the graph?

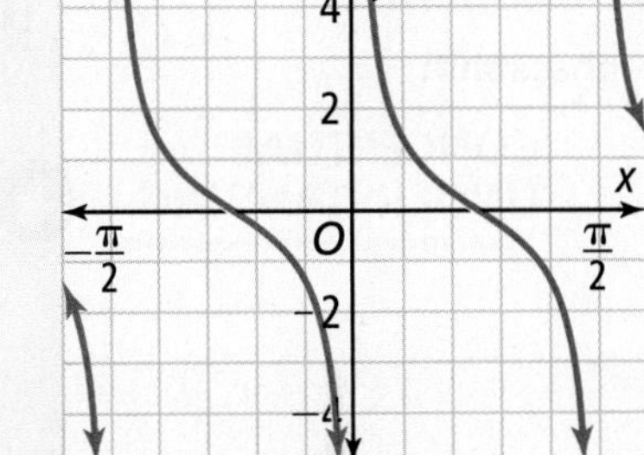

Ⓐ $y = 2 \cot x$

Ⓑ $y = \cot 2x$

Ⓒ $y = 2 \tan x$

Ⓓ $y = \tan 2x$

25. Performance Task A homeowner wants to move a flat screen television around the corner of two hallways that meet at a right angle as shown. One hallway is 6 ft wide, and the other hallway is only 4 ft wide. The length L of the diagonal through which the television must pass, as a function of θ, is $L(\theta) = \frac{4}{\sin \theta} + \frac{6}{\cos \theta}$.

Part A Write the function in terms of $\csc \theta$ and $\sec \theta$.

Part B Use your graphing calculator to graph the function for $0 < \theta < 90°$ in order to determine the greatest length the television could have to the nearest foot.

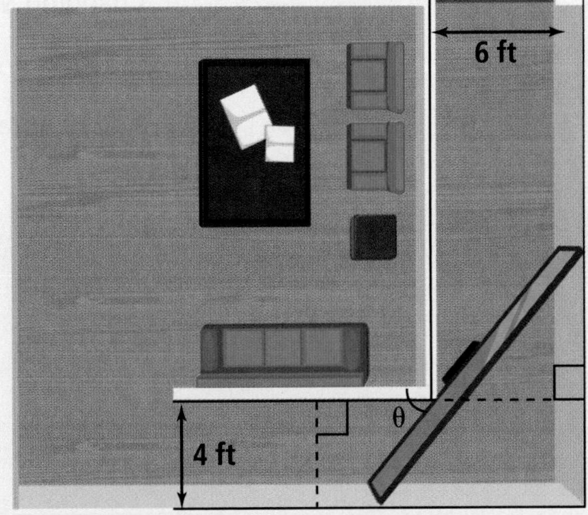

6-6 Translating Trigonometric Functions

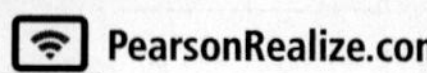
PearsonRealize.com

I CAN… use transformations to analyze and sketch graphs of trigonometric functions.

VOCABULARY

- phase shift

Activity

Assess

CRITIQUE & EXPLAIN

Sadie and Zhang use translations to relate the graphs of sine and cosine. Sadie claims that $\sin x = \cos\left(x - \frac{\pi}{2}\right)$. Zhang insists that $\cos x = \sin\left(x + \frac{\pi}{2}\right)$.

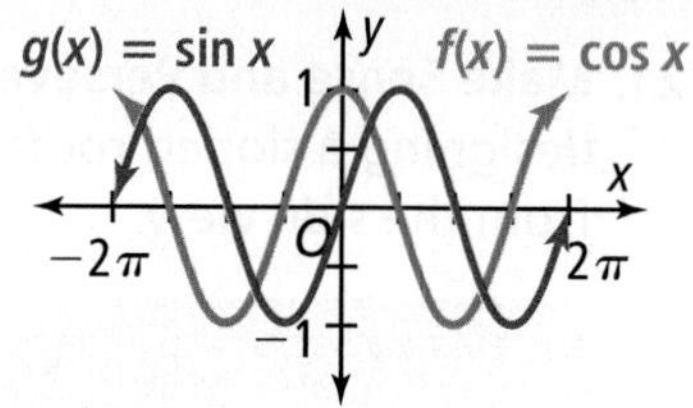

A. Who is correct? How do you know?

B. **Communicate Precisely** Victor claims that knowing $\sin 0 = \cos\frac{\pi}{2}$ can be used to determine who is correct. Is Victor's suggestion helpful? If so, explain why. If not, explain why not.

ESSENTIAL QUESTION

How can you find and use translations of graphs of trigonometric functions?

CONCEPTUAL UNDERSTANDING

EXAMPLE 1 Understand Phase Shift as a Horizontal Translation

How can you identify a horizontal translation from the rule of a trigonometric function?

A. How does changing the value of h affect the graph of $y = 2\sin(x - h)$?

Sketch the graphs:

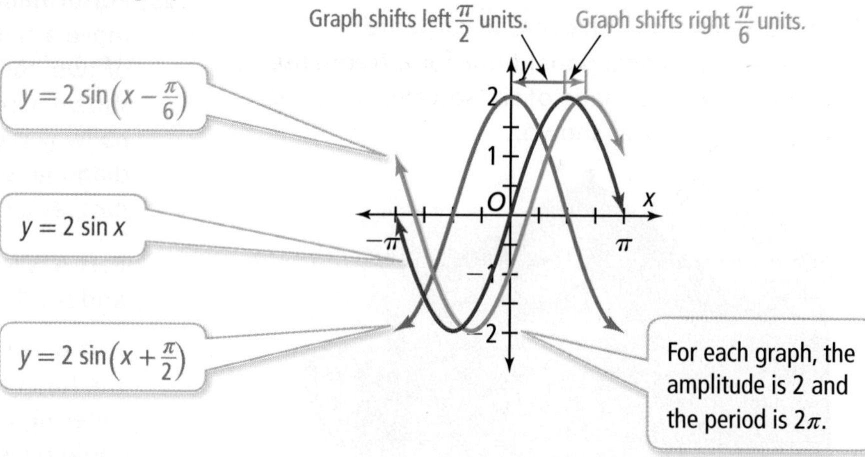

LOOK FOR RELATIONSHIPS
Just as with other functions you have studied, adding or subtracting a constant value from x shifts the graph of the function *horizontally*. Adding or subtracting a constant value from y shifts the graph of the function *vertically*.

Changing h translates the graph left or right.

It does not change the amplitude or period.

A horizontal translation of a periodic function is called a **phase shift**.

CONTINUED ON THE NEXT PAGE

  Activity  Assess

COMMON ERROR
You may think that the period of $y = \sin 2x$ is twice the period of $y = \sin x$, or 4π. In fact, the period of $y = \sin 2x$ is half the period of $y = \sin x$, or π.

EXAMPLE 1 CONTINUED

B. How does changing the value of h affect the graph of $y = \sin 2(x - h)$?

Sketch the graphs:

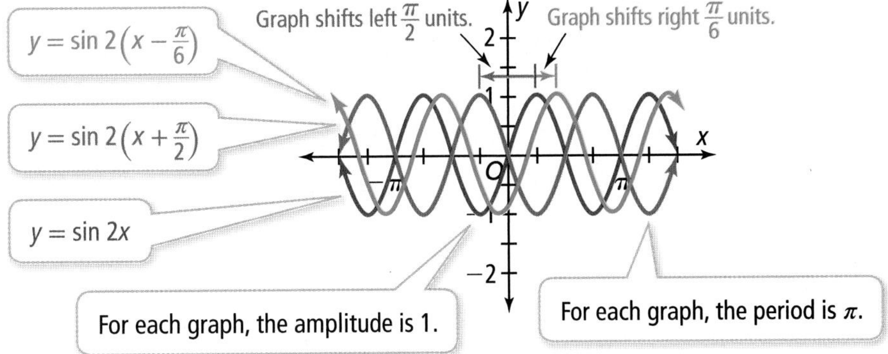

Changing h shifts the graph left or right as before.

The amplitude and period are the same for all three graphs.

Try It! 1. Sketch the graph.

a. $y = 3\cos\left(x + \frac{\pi}{4}\right)$ **b.** $y = \cos\left(3x + \frac{3\pi}{4}\right)$.

EXAMPLE 2 Graph a Sine or Cosine Function

How can knowledge of transformations help you sketch the graph of $y = 2\sin\frac{x}{2} + 3$?

USE STRUCTURE
Make sure you understand which parameter influences each feature of the function $y = a \sin b(x - c) + d$.
$|a|$: amplitude
b: period
c: phase shift
d: vertical shift

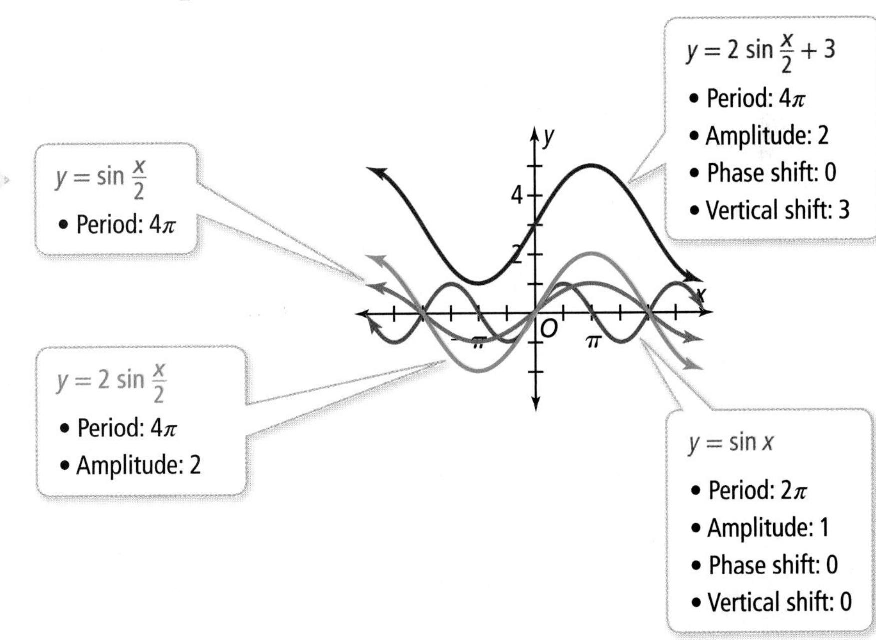

Try It! 2. Sketch the graph of the function $y = \frac{2}{3}\cos\left(x - \frac{\pi}{2}\right) + 1$.

Activity Assess

EXAMPLE 3 Analyze a Sine or Cosine Function

A. What are the key features of the graph of the function $y = 4\cos(3x) + 1$?

$y = 4\cos 3x + 1$

Amplitude $= |4| = 4$ — The amplitude is the absolute value of the coefficient of cosine.

Period $= \frac{2\pi}{3}$ — To calculate the period, divide 2π by the coefficient of x.

Vertical shift $= 1$ — The graph of $y = 4\cos 3x$ has been shifted up 1 unit.

There is no phase shift. The graph has not been shifted horizontally from that of $y = \cos x$. In terms of the general form, $y = a\cos[b(x - c)] + d$, $c = 0$.

Sketching the graph can help make sense of these parameters.

The amplitude of $y = \cos x$ is 1. Notice that, for this function, the maximum value is $4 + 1$, or 5, and the minimum value is $-4 + 1$, or -3.

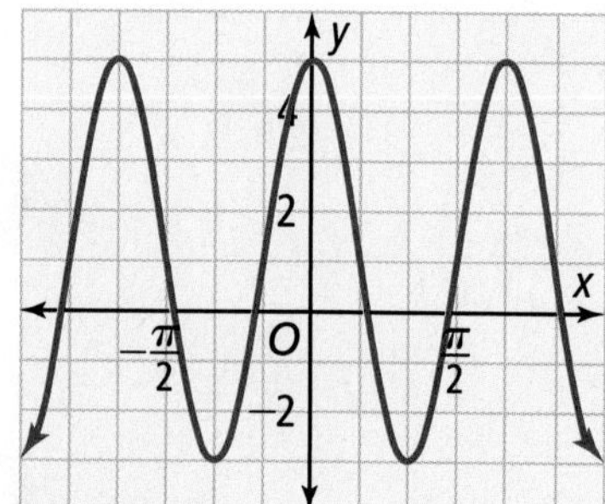

USE APPROPRIATE TOOLS
Why is it important to identify the key features of a function, even if you intend to graph it on a calculator?

B. What are the key features of the graph of the function $y = -3\sin\left(x + \frac{\pi}{2}\right) - 2$?

$y = -3\sin\left(x + \frac{\pi}{2}\right) - 2$ — Since the coefficient of the sine function is negative, this graph is a reflection over the x-axis of the parent function.

Amplitude $= |-3| = 3$

Period $= 2\pi$

Vertical shift $= 2$ units down

Phase shift $= \frac{\pi}{2}$ units left

Sketch the graph to check.

Notice that the combined effects of the reflection and the phase shift produce a graph that could be interpreted as a sine graph without a reflection and with a phase shift $\frac{\pi}{2}$ units right.

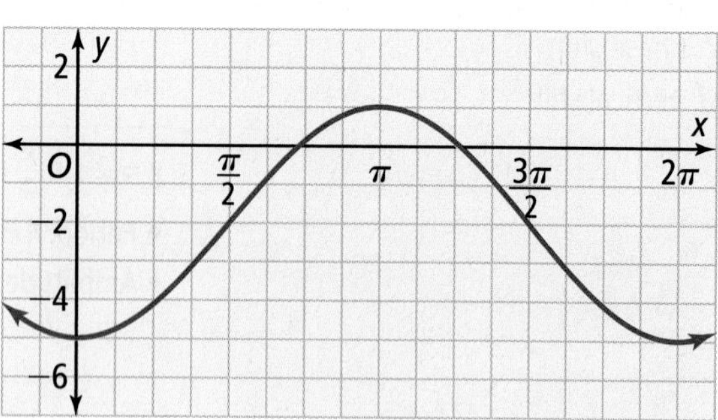

Try It! 3. Identify the amplitude, period, phase shift, vertical shift, and the maximum and minimum values of each function.

a. $y = \frac{1}{2}\sin\left(x - \frac{\pi}{3}\right) - 4$

b. $y = 2\cos\left(2x + \frac{\pi}{4}\right) + 2$

APPLICATION

EXAMPLE 4 Write the Equation of a Translation

An assembly-line machine stamps a company's logo on each product coming down the line. The graph models the stamp's height from the machine's axle, *y*, at time *x* seconds since the machine turns on. What is an equation that models this motion? Interpret the graph's *y*-intercept in terms of the context.

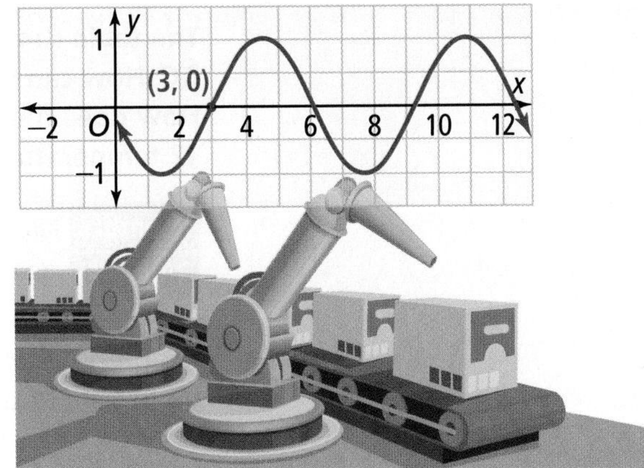

STUDY TIP

Because sine and cosine are simply phase shifts of each other, you can build the equation using either function.

The sine function has a general form

$$y = a \sin b(x - c) + d.$$

The amplitude here is 1, so $a = 1$.

The period is 2π, so $b = 1$ also.

There is no vertical shift—the midline is the *y*-axis, just like the midline of $y = \sin x$. So $d = 0$.

This graph contains the point (3, 0), where the corresponding point on $y = \sin(x)$ would be (0, 0).

There is a horizontal shift of 3, so $c = 3$.

So an equation for the graph is $y = \sin(x - 3)$.

At $x = 0$, when the equipment is turned on, the equipment is near the midline of its cycle, moving down.

Try It! 4. Write an equation that models the function represented by the graph.

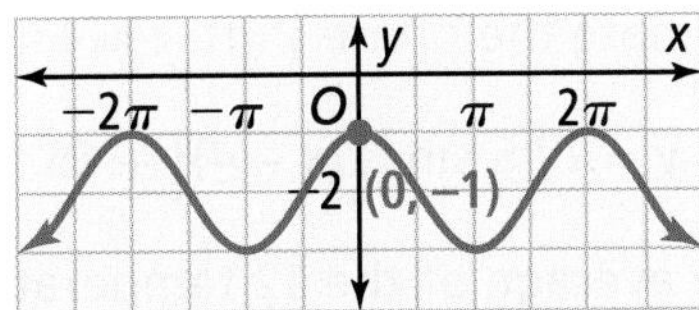

Activity Assess

APPLICATION

EXAMPLE 5 Find a Trigonometric Model

The table shows the average high temperature by month for Washington, DC. How can these temperatures be modeled with a trigonometric graph? How does the midline function value compare with the average of the 12 temperatures?

Month	Jan.	Feb.	Mar.	April	May	June	July	Aug.	Sept.	Oct.	Nov.	Dec.
High (°F)	43	47	56	67	75	84	88	87	80	68	58	47

Formulate Assign numbers to represent the months of the year, and create a scatter plot to show the pattern of temperatures in the table repeating over a span of two years.

Washington D.C. Average High Temperature (°F)

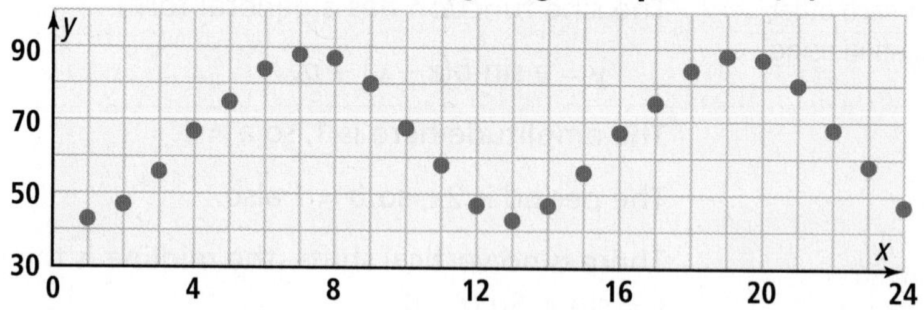

The temperatures can be modeled by a function in the form $y = a \sin b(x - c) + d$.

Compute Average the maximum and minimum temperatures to find the midline (vertical shift). $\frac{88 + 43}{2} = 65.5$, so the vertical shift is $d = 65.5$.

Find the amplitude.

$$\text{amplitude} = \frac{\max - \min}{2} = \frac{88 - 43}{2} = 22.5$$

so the amplitude $a = 22.5$

The period is 12 months, so $b = \frac{2\pi}{12} = \frac{\pi}{6}$.

Estimate the phase shift: $c \approx 4$

> Determine the phase shift by looking for the point where the graph crosses the midline. In the parent function, there is a zero exactly at the origin.

$$y = 22.5 \sin\left[\frac{\pi}{6}(x - 4)\right] + 65.5$$

Interpret The average of the 12 temperatures, 66.7°F, is close to the midline value, 65.5°F.

Try It! 5. Write a trigonometric function to model the average high temperatures for Philadelphia, Pennsylvania. How does the midline value compare with the average of the 12 temperatures?

Month	Jan.	Feb.	Mar.	Apr.	May	June	July	Aug.	Sept.	Oct.	Nov.	Dec.
High (°F)	40	44	53	64	74	83	87	85	78	67	56	45

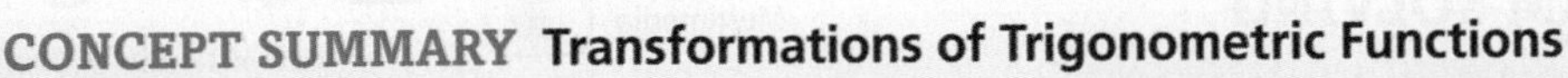

CONCEPT SUMMARY Transformations of Trigonometric Functions

GRAPH

$y = 2\sin\left[\frac{1}{2}\left(x - \frac{\pi}{2}\right)\right] + 1$

$y = \sin x$

WORDS AND SYMBOLS

$y = a \sin b\,(x - c) + d$

$y = 2\sin\left[\frac{1}{2}\left(x - \frac{\pi}{2}\right)\right] + 1$

Amplitude $= |a| = |2| = 2$

Stretches the graph by a factor of 2

Period $= \frac{2\pi}{b} = \frac{2\pi}{\frac{1}{2}} = 4\pi$

Cycle repeats every 4π units.

Phase Shift $= c = \frac{\pi}{2}$

Graph is shifted $\frac{\pi}{2}$ units to the right.

Vertical Shift $= d = 1$

Graph is shifted up one unit.

Do You UNDERSTAND?

1. **ESSENTIAL QUESTION** How can you find and use translations of graphs of trigonometric functions?

2. **Vocabulary** What is a *phase shift*?

3. **Error Analysis** Felipe said the function $y = \frac{1}{2}\cos\left[3\left(x + \frac{\pi}{4}\right)\right] - 3$ has a phase shift $\frac{\pi}{4}$ units to the right and a vertical shift 3 units down. Describe and correct the error Felipe made.

4. **Use Structure** Write a sine function that has an amplitude of $\frac{1}{6}$, a period of $\frac{8\pi}{3}$, a phase shift of 2π units to the right, and a vertical shift of 5 units up.

Do You KNOW HOW?

Identify the amplitude, period, phase shift, and vertical shift of the function.

5. $y = 4\sin\left(x - \frac{\pi}{6}\right) + 2$

6. $y = \frac{1}{3}\cos\left[2\left(x + \frac{\pi}{2}\right)\right] - 1$

7. Write an equation for the function represented by the graph using the cosine function.

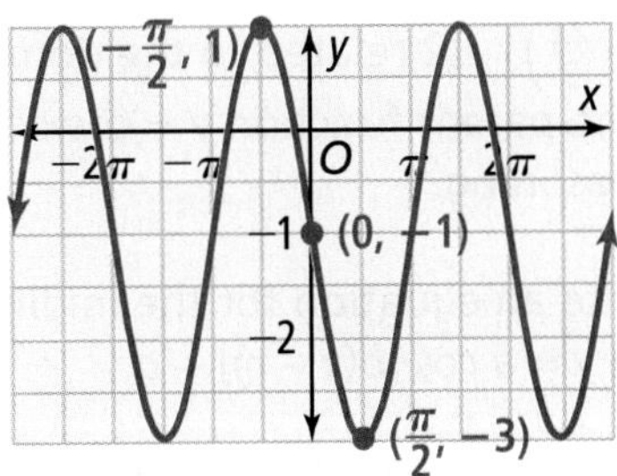

8. Sketch a graph of the function $y = \sin\left[2\left(x + \frac{\pi}{2}\right)\right] + 1$.

PRACTICE & PROBLEM SOLVING

Scan for Multimedia

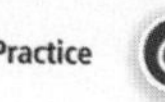

Practice Tutorial

Additional Exercises Available Online

UNDERSTAND

9. **Use Structure** Write a sine function and a cosine function for the graph.

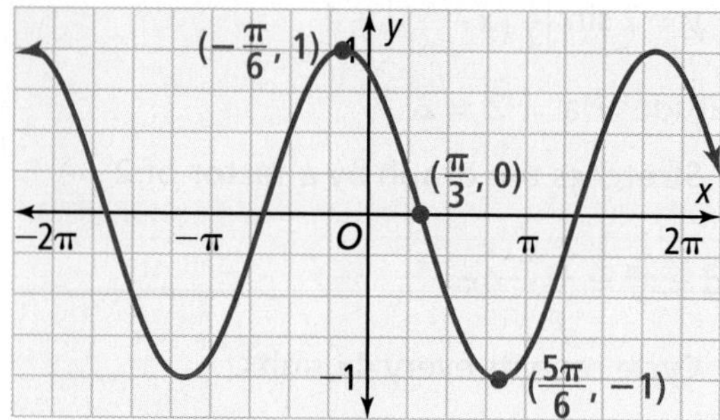

10. **Error Analysis** Describe and correct the error a student made in finding the phase shift of the given function.

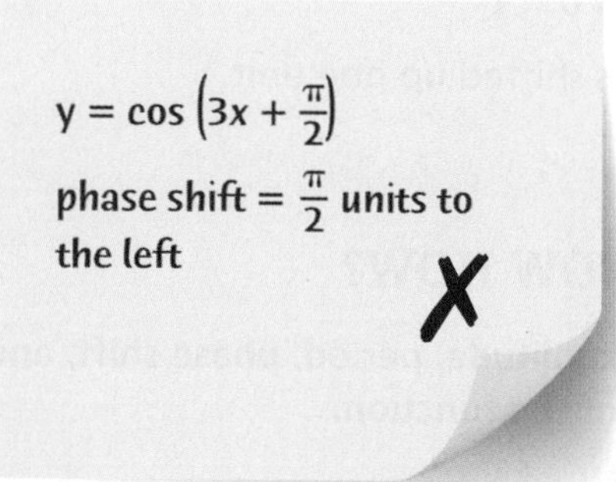

11. **Generalize** Describe the phase shift and vertical shift of a function in the form $y = a \sin [b(x - c)] + d$.

12. **Higher Order Thinking** How are the domain and range of the function $y = \frac{1}{4}\cos\left[3\left(x - \frac{2\pi}{3}\right)\right] + 2$ related to the domain and range of the parent function $y = \cos x$? Explain your reasoning.

13. **Generalize** Write an equation for the midline of the function $y = a \cos [b(x - c)] + d$.

14. **Reason** How are the zeros of the function $y = \sin\left(x + \frac{\pi}{3}\right)$ related to the zeros of the parent function $y = \sin x$?

15. **Mathematical Connections** In the equation $y = a \sin [b(x - c)] + d$, which of the parameters a, b, c, and d can have an effect on the y-intercept of the graph? Explain.

PRACTICE

Sketch the graph of the function. SEE EXAMPLE 1

16. $y = \cos\left(x - \frac{\pi}{4}\right)$

17. $y = 2 \sin\left(x + \frac{3\pi}{4}\right)$

Sketch the graph of the function. SEE EXAMPLE 2

18. $y = \frac{1}{3}\cos\left(x + \frac{\pi}{2}\right) - 2$

19. $y = 3 \sin\left(x - \frac{\pi}{6}\right) + 1$

Identify the amplitude, period, phase shift, vertical shift, and the maximum and minimum values of the function. SEE EXAMPLE 3

20. $y = \frac{2}{3}\sin\left(x + \frac{\pi}{3}\right) + 3$

21. $y = \frac{1}{2}\cos\left[2\left(x - \frac{\pi}{4}\right)\right] - 1$

22. Write an equation for the function represented by the graph using the sine function. SEE EXAMPLE 4

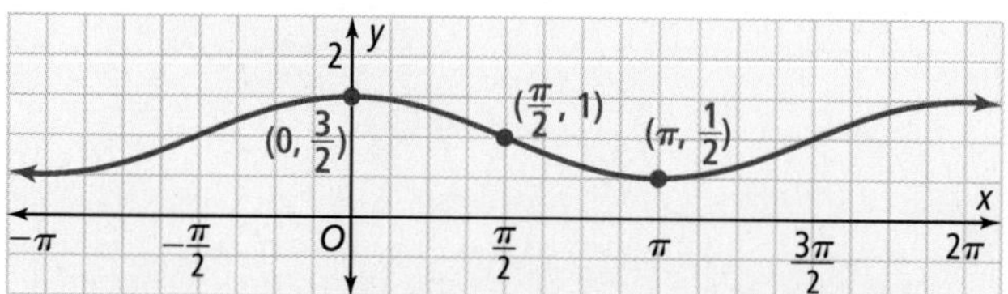

23. The table shows the brightness of the moon at the end of eight consecutive weeks. How can you model this with a trigonometric function? How does the midline of the function compare with the average of the 8 visibility levels? SEE EXAMPLE 5

Week	Percent Visible	
1	50%	
2	0%	
3	48%	
4	100%	
5	67%	
6	5%	
7	34%	
8	95%	

APPLY

24. Model With Mathematics Alternating current is the flow of charge that periodically changes direction. Alternating current is used to deliver power. The function $V(t) = E\cos\left(wt + \frac{\pi}{2}\right)$ gives the voltage in amps for t seconds.

a. Edgar wants to find the voltage when $E = 40$ volts and $w = 188$ radians per second. Write a function to represent this situation.

b. Rewrite the function so that the coefficient of t is 1.

c. What is the amplitude of the function?

d. What is the period of the function?

e. What is the phase shift of the function?

f. Graph the function.

25. Make Sense and Persevere The table shows the average amount of rainfall in inches by month for Junction City, California.

Month	Rainfall (in.)
January	6.46
February	5.83
March	4.84
April	2.52
May	1.81
June	0.79
July	0.29
August	0.16
September	0.59
October	2.28
November	5.39
December	7.87

a. How can these rainfall amounts be modeled with a trigonometric graph?

b. How does the midline function value compare with the average of the 12 rainfall amounts?

c. Graph the function.

ASSESSMENT PRACTICE

26. Determine if each statement about the function $y = \frac{3}{4}\cos\left[3\left(x + \frac{\pi}{6}\right)\right] - 5$ is true. Write *yes* or *no*.

A. The amplitude is $\frac{3}{4}$.

B. The period is 3.

C. The phase shift is $\frac{\pi}{6}$ units to the right.

D. The vertical shift is 5 units down.

27. SAT/ACT Kathryn graphed the function $y = 2\sin\left(x + \frac{\pi}{2}\right) - 1$ but forgot to label the x-axis. What is the value of d on the x-axis?

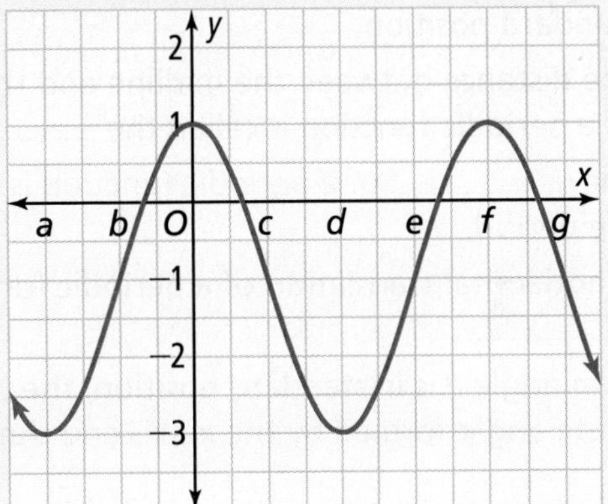

Ⓐ $\frac{\pi}{2}$ Ⓑ π Ⓒ $\frac{3\pi}{2}$ Ⓓ 2π

28. Performance Task Micah is investigating phase shifts of the parent sine function, $y = \sin x$. He wants to map the sine function onto itself.

Part A Write an equation of a function that has an identical graph but includes a phase shift.

Part B Write an equation that will map the parent sine function onto itself by shifting the parent function to the right.

Part C What do the equations in part (a) and part (b) tell you about the period of the sine function?

Part D How many equations can you write to map the parent sine function onto itself? Explain.

TOPIC 6

Topic Review

TOPIC ESSENTIAL QUESTION

1. How are trigonometric functions used to solve real-world problems?

Vocabulary Review

Choose the correct term to complete each sentence.

2. The __________ of an angle in standard position is along the positive x-axis.
3. The __________ of an angle is the other side of an angle in standard position.
4. The distance between the midline and the minimum or maximum of a periodic function is called the __________.
5. The __________ of a periodic function is the reciprocal of the period.
6. A horizontal translation of a periodic function is often called a __________.
7. If an angle θ is in standard position, the __________ for θ is the acute angle formed by the x-axis and the terminal side of θ.

- amplitude
- frequency
- initial side
- phase shift
- reference angle
- terminal side

Concepts & Skills Review

LESSON 6-1 Trigonometric Functions and Acute Angles

Quick Review

$\sin\theta = \dfrac{\text{opposite}}{\text{hypotenuse}}$ $\csc\theta = \dfrac{\text{hypotenuse}}{\text{opposite}}$

$\cos\theta = \dfrac{\text{adjacent}}{\text{hypotenuse}}$ $\sec\theta = \dfrac{\text{hypotenuse}}{\text{adjacent}}$

$\tan\theta = \dfrac{\text{opposite}}{\text{adjacent}}$ $\cot\theta = \dfrac{\text{adjacent}}{\text{opposite}}$

Example

Write the six trigonometric ratios for the angle θ in the given triangle.

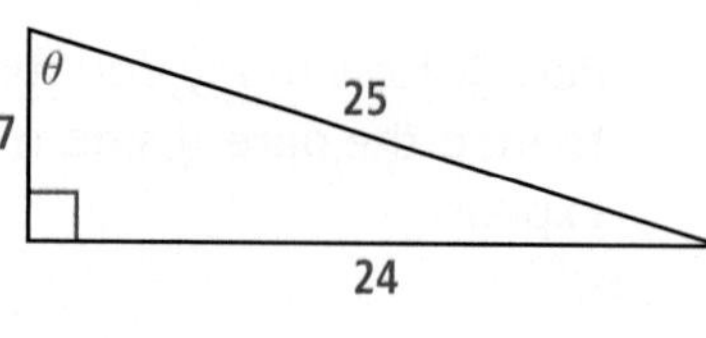

$\sin\theta = \frac{24}{25}$ $\csc\theta = \frac{25}{24}$

$\cos\theta = \frac{7}{25}$ $\sec\theta = \frac{25}{7}$

$\tan\theta = \frac{24}{7}$ $\cot\theta = \frac{7}{24}$

Practice & Problem Solving

Write the six trigonometric ratios for the angle θ in each given triangle.

8. 

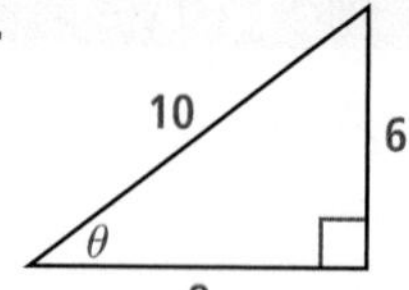

9. 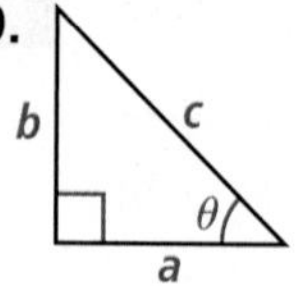

What are the trigonometric ratios of θ in a right triangle with the given value?

10. $\sin\theta = \frac{5}{13}$

11. $\cot\theta = \frac{56}{33}$

12. **Look for Relationships** What trigonometric ratio is given by the cofunction identity $\sec(90^\circ - \theta)$?

13. **Make Sense and Persevere** A 15-foot ladder is leaning against the side of a house at a 65° angle. What is the distance from the house to the base of the ladder? Round to the nearest hundredth.

LESSON 6-2 Angles and the Unit Circle

Quick Review

An angle is in **standard position** when its vertex is at the origin and the initial side lies on the *x*-axis. Angles in standard position may be named with positive values or negative values.

The **unit circle** is a circle that has its center at the origin and has a radius of 1. An angle of full circle rotation, or 360°, has a measure of 2π radians.

Example

What is the measure of this angle as a positive number of degrees and in radians? As a negative number of degrees and in radians?

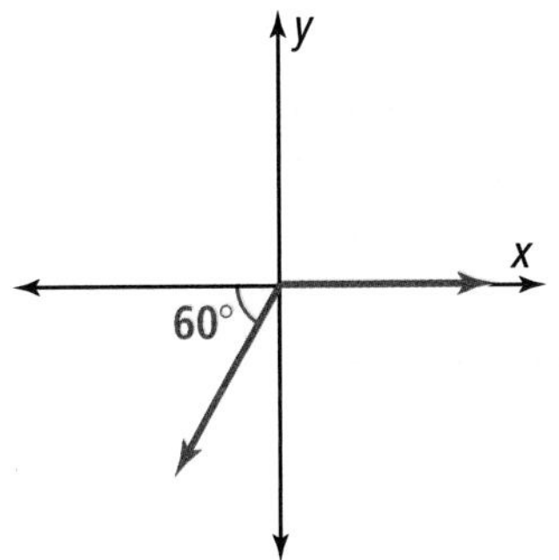

$m\angle\theta = 180° + 60° = 240°$

$m\angle\theta = 240°\left(\frac{\pi}{180°}\right) = \frac{4\pi}{3}$

$m\angle\theta = 240° - 360° = -120°$

$m\angle\theta = -120°\left(\frac{\pi}{180°}\right) = -\frac{2\pi}{3}$

Practice & Problem Solving

Find a positive angle measure for each reference angle.

14. 67° in Quadrant I

15. 63° in Quadrant IV

16. 25° in Quadrant II

17. 14° in Quadrant III

Convert the angle measures.

18. 136° to radians

19. $\frac{2\pi}{3}$ radians to degrees

20. 80° to radians

21. $-\frac{\pi}{3}$ radians to degrees

For each angle give the reference angle and Quadrant.

22. $-\frac{3\pi}{4}$ radians

23. 330°

24. **Communicate Precisely** Why is it convenient to express an angle in radians when you want to compute arc length?

25. **Model With Mathematics** The radius of a pond is about 840 feet. After walking around the pond through an angle of $\frac{2\pi}{3}$, you pick up a plastic bottle. You carry it to a recycle bin at a point where you have walked through an angle of $\frac{5\pi}{4}$. How far did you carry the bottle?

LESSON 6-3 Trigonometric Functions and Real Numbers

Quick Review

The domains of the sine and cosine functions are extended to all real numbers using the unit circle. The coordinates of the point where the terminal side of an angle in standard position intersects the unit circle are ($\cos\theta$, $\sin\theta$). The values of the other trigonometric functions can be calculated from this result.

Example

Use the unit circle to evaluate $\tan\frac{\pi}{6}$.

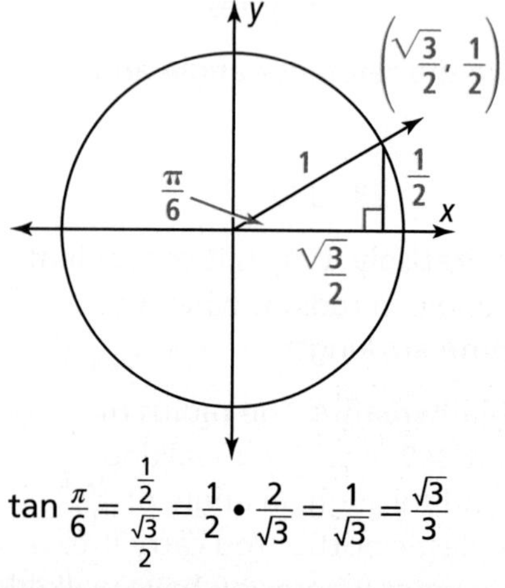

$$\tan\frac{\pi}{6} = \frac{\frac{1}{2}}{\frac{\sqrt{3}}{2}} = \frac{1}{2} \bullet \frac{2}{\sqrt{3}} = \frac{1}{\sqrt{3}} = \frac{\sqrt{3}}{3}$$

Practice & Problem Solving

Find the sine and cosine for each angle.

26. $\frac{4\pi}{3}$

27. 135°

28. $\frac{5\pi}{6}$

29. 420°

Find the tangent for each angle.

30. 120°

31. $-\frac{\pi}{4}$

Find the secant, cosecant, and cotangent for each angle.

32. −135°

33. $\frac{8\pi}{3}$

34. **Use Structure** What is $\sin\theta$ if $\cos\theta = \frac{3}{5}$ and θ is in Quadrant IV?

35. **Reason** A scout team is searching a circular region in a 6-mile radius around a camp. Two of the scouts travel on a route that is 45° east of south from the camp. What is their final position, relative to the camp?

LESSON 6-4 Graphing Sine and Cosine Functions

Quick Review

The distance between the midline and the minimum or maximum point is the **amplitude**. The **period** is the interval of the domain for which the function does not repeat. **Frequency** is the reciprocal of the period.

Example

What are the amplitude, period, and frequency of $y = 2\sin x$?

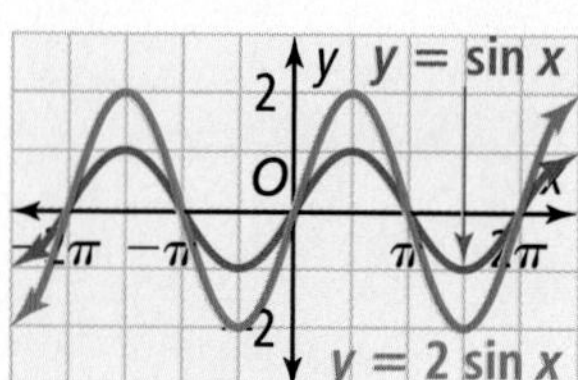

The distance between the midline and maximum point is 2, so the amplitude is 2. The period is 2π. The frequency is $\frac{1}{2\pi}$.

Practice & Problem Solving

What are the amplitude, period, and frequency of each function?

36. $y = \frac{1}{4}\cos(4x)$

37. $y = 3\sin\left(\frac{1}{2}\right)x$

38. $y = 4\sin 2x$

39. $y = -2\cos 6x$

40. **Use Structure** What equation represents the graph?

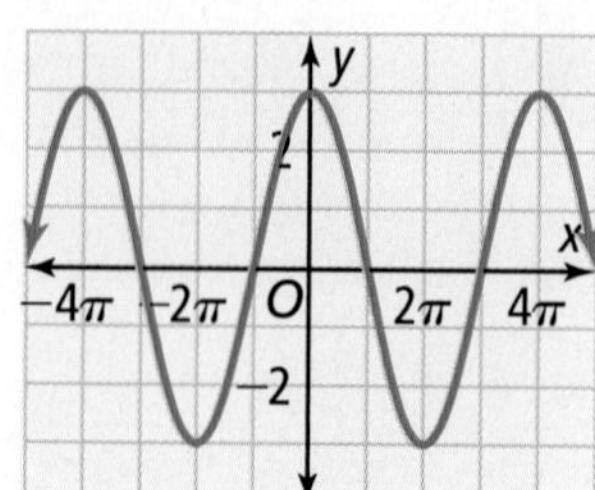

LESSON 6-5 Graphing Other Trigonometric Functions

Quick Review

When graphing $y = a \tan bx$, a stretches the graph of the parent function vertically and b compresses the graph of the parent function horizontally. The period of the tangent function can be found using period $= \frac{\pi}{|b|}$.

Example

How can you use transformations of the parent function to sketch the graph of the function $y = 2 \tan \frac{1}{4} x$?

$a = 2$, so stretch the graph vertically by a factor of 2.

$b = \frac{1}{4}$, so stretch the graph horizontally by a factor of 4.

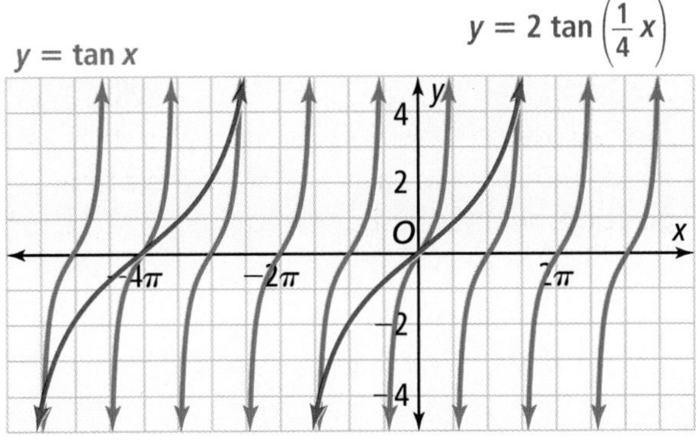

Practice & Problem Solving

Sketch the graph of the function. Then describe how the parent graph of the function was affected by the transformations.

41. $y = \frac{1}{4} \tan 4x$

42. $y = \frac{1}{2} \cot 6x$

43. **Use Structure** Describe the domain, range, period, zeros, and asymptotes of the function $y = \cot x$.

44. **Reason** Write a function that represents the height, h, of the triangle where θ is the angle indicated. Graph the function over the domain $[0, \frac{\pi}{2}]$.

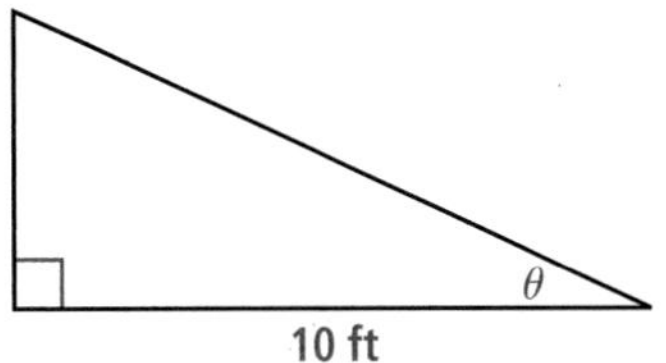

45. **Make Sense and Persevere** The function $y = 3 \sec \theta$ models the length of a pole leaning against a wall as a function of the measure of the angle θ formed by the pole and the horizontal when the bottom of the pole is 3 ft from the wall. Graph the function and find the length the pole when $\theta = 62°$. Round to the nearest hundredth.

LESSON 6-6 Translating Trigonometric Functions

Quick Review

A horizontal translation of a periodic function is the **phase shift**. When graphing $y = a \sin b(x - c) + d$ or $y = a \cos b(x - c) + d$, $|a|$ is the amplitude, $\frac{|b|}{2\pi}$ is the frequency, c is the phase shift, and d is the vertical shift.

Example

What are the key features of the function $y = 5 \cos 2(x - 1) + 6$.

$a = 5$, so the amplitude is 5.

$b = 2$, so the frequency is 2, which means the period is $\frac{2\pi}{2} = \pi$.

$c = 1$, so the phase shift is 1 unit to the right.

$d = 6$, so the vertical shift is 6 units up.

Practice & Problem Solving

Identify the amplitude, period, phase shift, and vertical shift of the function.

46. $y = -4 \sin (x + 4\pi) - 8$

47. $y = \frac{1}{4} \cos\left[6\left(x + \frac{\pi}{2}\right)\right] + 2$

48. **Use Structure** Write an equation that models the function represented by the graph using the cosine function.

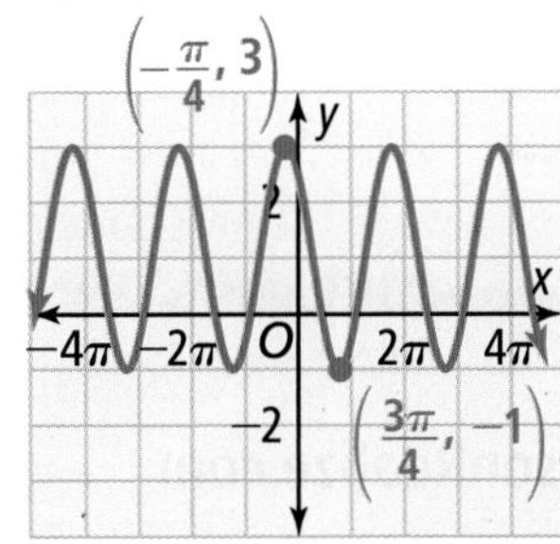

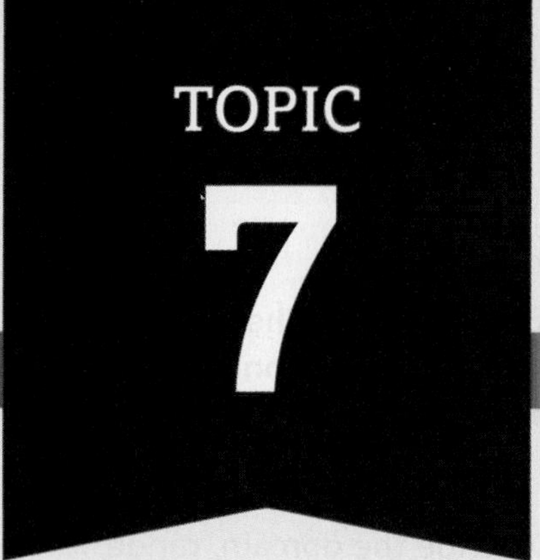

Trigonometric Equations and Identities

TOPIC ESSENTIAL QUESTION

How do trigonometric identities and equations help you solve problems involving real or complex numbers?

Topic Overview

Topic Vocabulary

- angle of depression
- angle of elevation
- Law of Cosines
- Law of Sines
- trigonometric identity

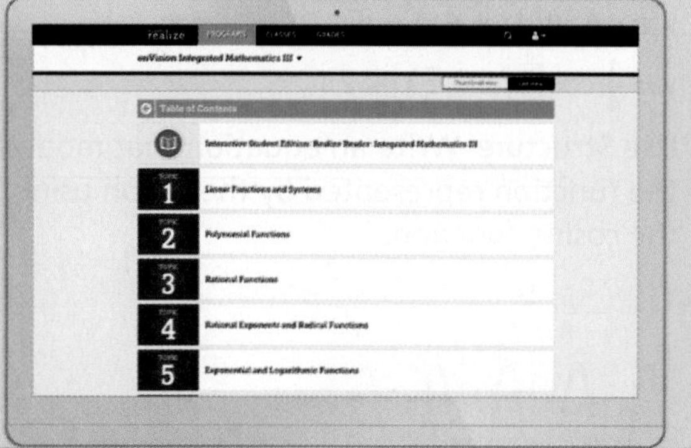

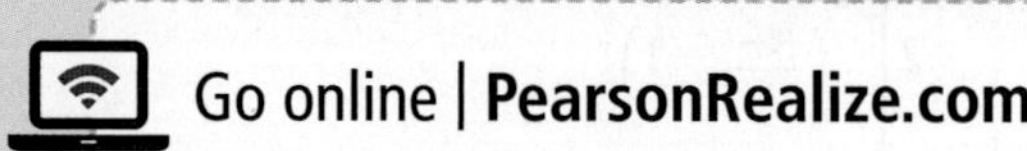
Go online | **PearsonRealize.com**

Digital Experience

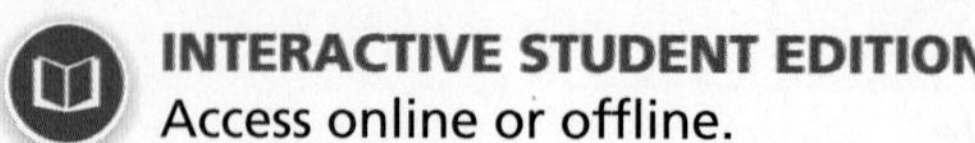

INTERACTIVE STUDENT EDITION Access online or offline.

ACTIVITIES Complete ***Explore & Reason, Model & Discuss***, and ***Critique & Explain*** activities. Interact with Examples and Try Its.

ANIMATION View and interact with real-world applications.

PRACTICE Practice what you've learned.

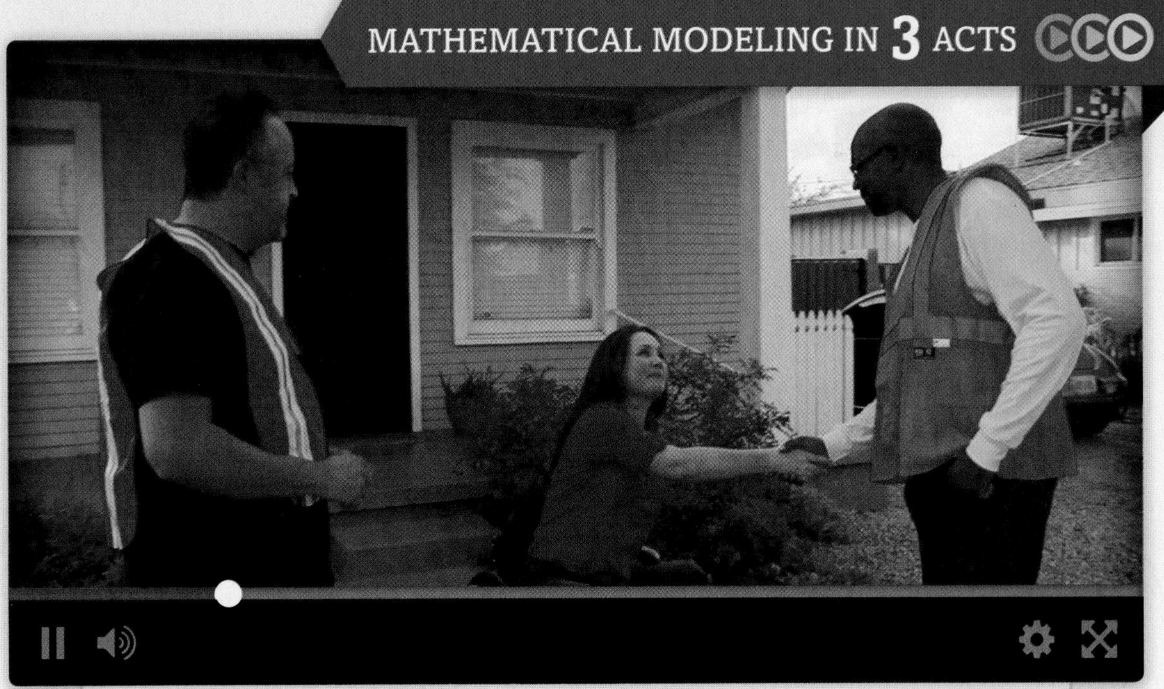

Ramp Up Your Design

Wheelchair users and others with mobility challenges require ramps or elevators to access buildings and other public spaces. Most public buildings are required to have accessible ramps through the Americans with Disabilities Act. However, most homes do not have such ramps. Wheelchair users who move into a home with steps will have to have a new ramp installed.

The construction of accessibility ramps must follow strict guidelines. If ramps are not accurately built to follow these guidelines, they can be dangerous to use. Think about this during the Mathematical Modeling in 3 Acts lesson.

VIDEOS Watch clips to support ***Mathematical Modeling in 3 Acts Lessons*** and **enVision® *STEM Projects.***

CONCEPT SUMMARY Review key lesson content through multiple representations.

ASSESSMENT Show what you've learned.

GLOSSARY Read and listen to English and Spanish definitions.

TUTORIALS Get help from ***Virtual Nerd***, right when you need it.

MATH TOOLS Explore math with digital tools and manipulatives.

Video

Did You Know?

A roller coaster has no engine. The first car in the train is pulled to the top of the first hill, after which gravity and momentum take over.

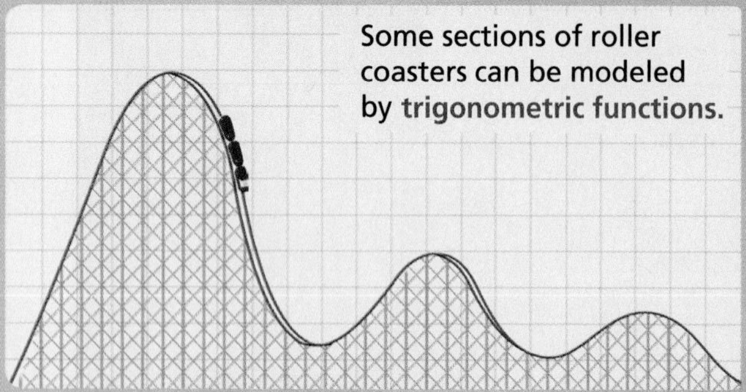

Some sections of roller coasters can be modeled by trigonometric functions.

Materials used to build Big One steel roller coaster =

1,270 pilings

+

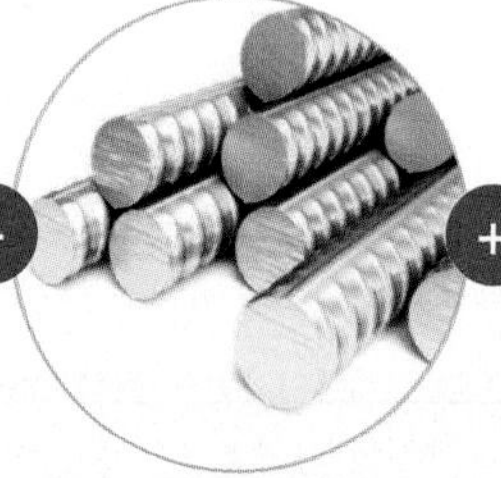

2,212 tons of steel

+

60,000 bolts

+

42,000 square feet of paint

Your Task: Design a Roller Coaster

You and your classmates will design a roller coaster following a track modeled on trigonometric functions.

Activity Assess 

7-1 Solving Trigonometric Equations Using Inverses

I CAN… use inverse trigonometric functions.

CRITIQUE & EXPLAIN

Marisol and Nadia are both asked to find θ given $\sin \theta = \frac{\sqrt{3}}{2}$.

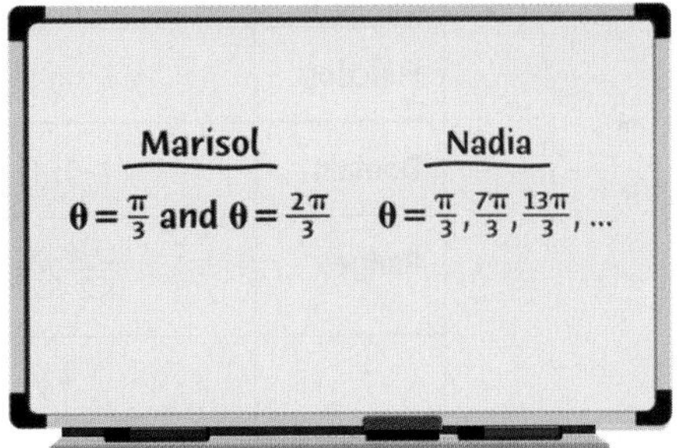

A. Is either student correct? Explain.

B. Make Sense and Persevere What are all of the correct solutions for θ?

ESSENTIAL QUESTION

How can you use an inverse function to find all the solutions of a trigonometric equation?

CONCEPTUAL UNDERSTANDING

EXAMPLE 1 Define Inverse Trigonometric Functions

How can we derive inverse trigonometric functions? Why use an inverse function?

For a relation to be a function, each value in the domain can have only one output. For an inverse relation to be a function, it must map each value in the range of the original function to only one value in the domain of the original function.

By definition, the sine function is periodic so the values of the range repeat throughout the domain. To create a valid inverse function, restrict the domain of $y = \sin x$.

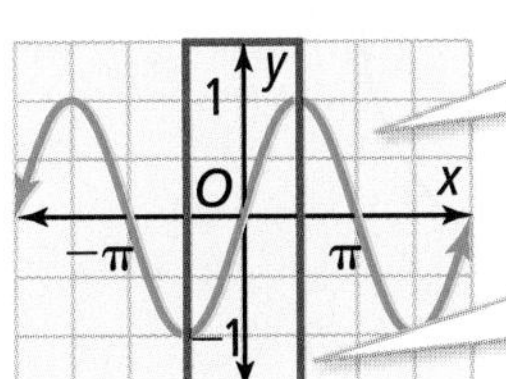

Choose a portion of the graph where the function is always increasing (or decreasing) and includes 0.

Every value in the range from −1 to 1 is represented exactly once, and none are missing.

The inverse function can be defined as $y = \sin^{-1} x$ where $x = \sin y$ for $-\frac{\pi}{2} \leq y \leq \frac{\pi}{2}$.

Given an angle, the sine function outputs the y-coordinate where the terminal side of the angle, in standard position, intersects the unit circle. The inverse sine function allows you to input the value of the output of the original function from a limited range of the sine function and obtain the measure of the angle.

How do the domain and range of the sine function relate to those of its inverse function?

 **Try It!** **1.** How should the domain of $y = \cos x$ be restricted to define the inverse cosine function?

CONCEPT Inverse Trigonometric Functions

	Inverse sine	Inverse cosine	Inverse tangent
Function	$y = \sin^{-1} x$	$y = \cos^{-1} x$	$y = \tan^{-1} x$
Domain	$[-1, 1]$	$[-1, 1]$	$(-\infty, \infty)$
Range	$\left[\frac{-\pi}{2}, \frac{\pi}{2}\right]$	$[0, \pi]$	$\left(\frac{-\pi}{2}, \frac{\pi}{2}\right)$
Graph			

EXAMPLE 2 Evaluate Inverse Trigonometric Functions

COMMUNICATE PRECISELY
The expression $\sin^{-1} x$ asks for the angle measure that has x for its sine.

What is $\sin^{-1}\left(\frac{1}{2}\right)$?

Recall that the range of the inverse sine function is $\frac{-\pi}{2} \leq x \leq \frac{\pi}{2}$, or $-90°$ to $90°$. The expression $\sin^{-1}\left(\frac{1}{2}\right)$ represents the angle in the given range that has a sine value of $\frac{1}{2}$. Consider the unit circle. The sine function of an angle is positive in Quadrant I and Quadrant II, but the range of the inverse sine function does not include Quadrant II.

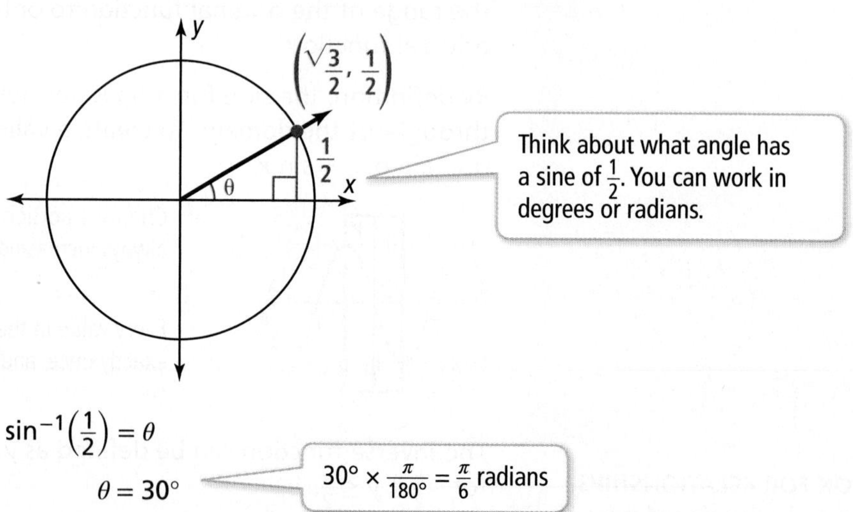

$\sin^{-1}\left(\frac{1}{2}\right) = \theta$

$\theta = 30°$

$30° \times \frac{\pi}{180°} = \frac{\pi}{6}$ radians

Try It! 2. a. What is $\cos^{-1}\left(\frac{\sqrt{2}}{2}\right)$?

b. What is $\tan^{-1}(-\sqrt{3})$?

  Activity  Assess

EXAMPLE 3 Find All Angles With a Given Trigonometric Value

COMMON ERROR
When using technology to solve trigonometric functions, make sure you have the correct *system of angle measure* selected.

A. What are all of the angles that have a cosine value of 0.57?

Step 1 Write the inverse cosine function $\cos^{-1}(0.57) = \theta$.

Step 2 Use the inverse cosine function on your calculator to find the value for θ, $\cos^{-1}(0.57) = 55.25°$, or 0.96 radians.

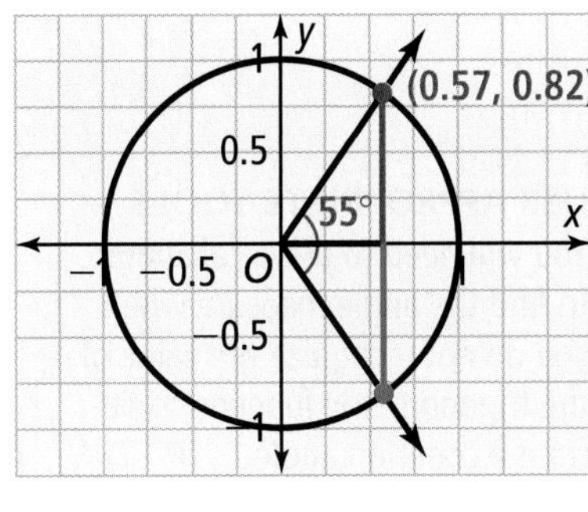

Step 3 Draw the angle on a unit circle. Look for all angles that have an x-coordinate equal to 0.57.

The x-coordinate is positive in Quadrants I and IV, so −55.25°, or −0.96 radians, also has a cosine of 0.57.

Step 4 Identify all coterminal angles.

55.25° is coterminal with $55.25° + (360°)k$, or $0.96 + (2\pi)k$, where k is an integer.

−55.25° is coterminal with $-55.25° + (360°)k$, or $-0.96 + (2\pi)k$, where k is an integer.

So the angle measures that have a cosine value of 0.57 are $55.25° + (360°)k$ and $-55.25° + (360°)k$, where k is an integer.

STUDY TIP
When asked to solve an equation involving an inverse trig function, use the domain and range of the function. When asked about all possible angles, provide a complete list, such as $55.25° + (360°)k$ or $-55.25° + (360°)k$.

B. What are all of the angles that have a tangent value of −0.35?

Step 1 Write the inverse tangent function $\tan^{-1}(-0.35) = \theta$.

Step 2 Use the inverse tangent function on your calculator to find the value for θ: $\tan^{-1}(-0.35) = -19.29°$, or −0.34 radians.

Step 3 Draw the angle on a unit circle. An angle of −19.29° is in Quadrant IV. The tangent function is also negative in Quadrant II. The angle in Quadrant II with the same value of tangent is $180° - 19.29° = 160.71°$, or 2.80 radians.

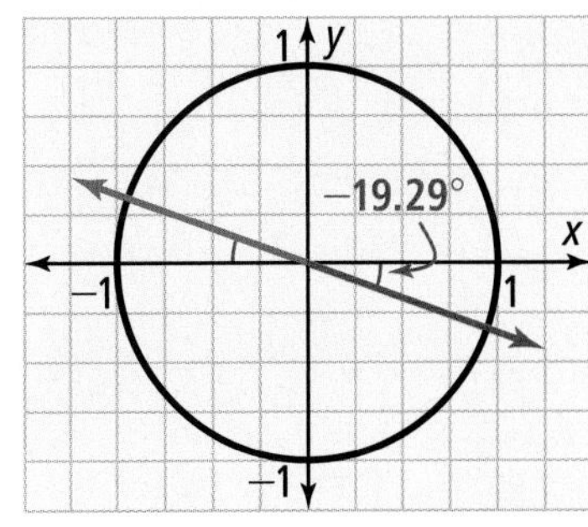

Step 4 Identify all coterminal angles. Since the two angles are on the same line, each angle coterminal with −19.29° is 180° from angles coterminal with 160.71°. So all of the angles are given by $-19.29° + (180°)k$, where k is an integer, or $-0.34 + \pi k$, where k is an integer.

So the angles that have a tangent value of −0.35 are $-19.29° + (180°)k$, where k is an integer.

 **Try It!** 3. a. What are all of the angles that have a sine value of 0.95?

b. What are all of the angles that have a cosine value of 0.54?

EXAMPLE 4 Solve a Trigonometric Equation

How can you solve the trigonometric equation $6 \sin \theta = 3 \sin \theta + 2$ for values between 0 and 2π?

$6 \sin \theta = 3 \sin \theta + 2$ .... Write the original equation.

$3 \sin \theta = 2$ .... Subtract $3 \sin \theta$ from both sides of the equation.

$\sin \theta = \frac{2}{3}$ .... Isolate the sine function.

$\theta = \sin^{-1}\left(\frac{2}{3}\right)$ .... Apply inverse sine function.

$\theta \approx 0.73$ radians or $41.81°$ .... Use technology to find θ.

USE APPROPRIATE TOOLS
You will need to use a calculator to find the angle measure when you do not recognize the value of the trigonometric function to be from a common angle.

If you reflect the terminal side of an angle with measure 0.73 radians across the *y*-axis, that angle will also have a sine of $\frac{2}{3}$. That angle is $\pi - 0.73 \approx 2.41$ radians, or $138.19°$.

Try It! 4. a. What is the value for θ when $0.25 \cos \theta + 1 = 1.5 \cos \theta$ for values between 0 and 2π?

b. What is the value for θ when $3 \tan \theta - 4 = \tan \theta$ for values between 0 and π?

APPLICATION

EXAMPLE 5 Use a Trigonometric Model

The average monthly temperature in New Zealand is modeled by the function $T = 4 \cos\left(\frac{\pi x}{6}\right) + 14$, where T is the temperature in °C, and x is the month, with the beginning of January being 1. In what months will the average temperature be less than 15°C?

CONTINUED ON THE NEXT PAGE

EXAMPLE 5 CONTINUED

To determine the months during which the temperature is less than 15°C, find the values of x that make the value of the function less than 15. Start by considering the period of the function.

Recall that you can find the period of the function $f(x) = \cos(bx)$ by dividing 2π by b. In this example, $b = \frac{\pi}{6}$.

$$\text{Period} = 2\pi \div \frac{\pi}{6}, \text{ or } 12$$

Since we are looking at the temperature over one year, a period of 12 (or 12 months) makes sense.

Now, solve for x to find the points over the period when the temperature is equal to 15°C.

$T = 4\cos\left(\frac{\pi x}{6}\right) + 14$ ...... Write the original equation.

$15 = 4\cos\left(\frac{\pi x}{6}\right) + 14$ ...... Substitute 15 for T.

$1 = 4\cos\left(\frac{\pi x}{6}\right)$ ...... Subtract 14 from both sides.

$\frac{1}{4} = \cos\left(\frac{\pi x}{6}\right)$ ...... Isolate the cosine function.

$\cos^{-1}\left(\frac{1}{4}\right) = \frac{\pi x}{6}$ ...... Rewrite as an inverse cosine function.

$\frac{6\cos^{-1}\left(\frac{1}{4}\right)}{\pi} = x$ ...... Multiply both sides by $\frac{6}{\pi}$ to isolate x.

$x \approx 2.5$ ...... Use technology to find x.

STUDY TIP

Just as when you are solving a linear equation, your goal here is to isolate the variable using inverse operations.

One solution for x is about 2.5. However, the cosine function is periodic so the value of the function will equal 15 at another point over the 12-month period. Graph the function to find the second point and then determine over which interval the value of the function is less than 15.

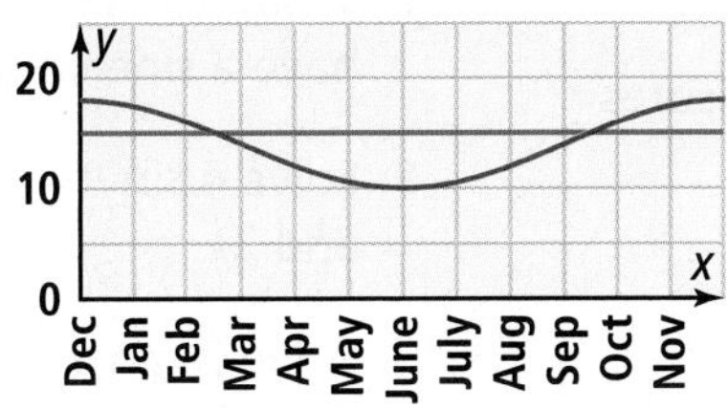

Using technology, you can see that, in addition to $x = 2.5$ (or mid February), the temperature function has a value of 15 at $x = 9.5$ (or mid September).

The graph of $y = 4\cos\frac{\pi x}{6} + 14$ is less than the graph of $y = 15$ between 2.5 and 9.5. This interval represent the months from mid-February to mid-September.

So, the average monthly temperature is below 15°C from mid-February to mid-September.

Try It! 5. The average monthly high temperature in a city is modeled by the function $T = 30\sin\left(\frac{\pi}{6}x - 1.8\right) + 61$, where T is the temperature in °F, x is the month, and $x = 1$ corresponds to January. Use this function to determine the months that have a monthly high temperature of 54°.

CONCEPT SUMMARY Inverse Trigonometric Functions

	Inverse sine	Inverse cosine	Inverse tangent
FUNCTION	$y = \sin^{-1} x$	$y = \cos^{-1} x$	$y = \tan^{-1} x$
DOMAIN	$[-1, 1]$	$[-1, 1]$	$(-\infty, \infty)$
RANGE	$\left[\frac{-\pi}{2}, \frac{\pi}{2}\right]$	$[0, \pi]$	$\left(\frac{-\pi}{2}, \frac{\pi}{2}\right)$
GRAPHS	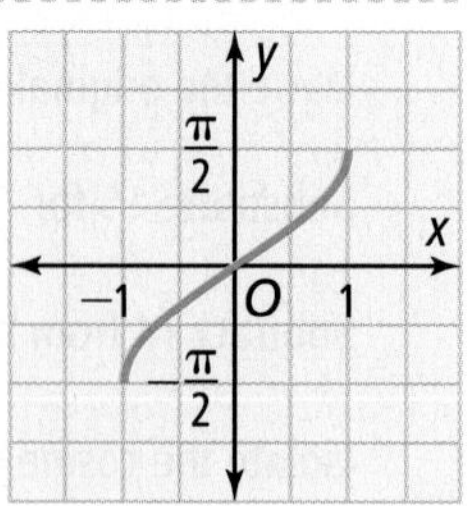	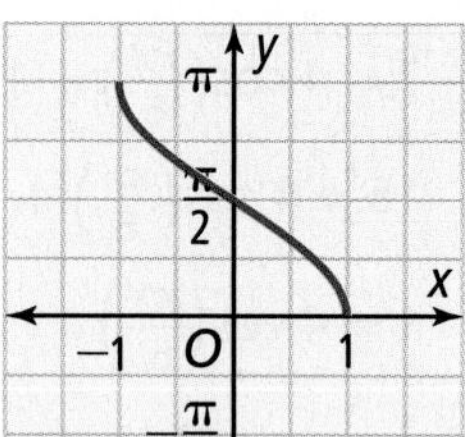	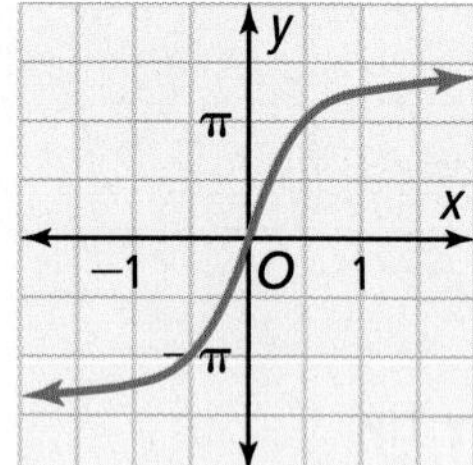

Do You UNDERSTAND?

1. ESSENTIAL QUESTION How can you use an inverse function to find all the solutions of a trigonometric equation?

2. **Error Analysis** Luis said that the inverse of $y = \cos x$ is a function. Explain and correct Luis's error.

3. **Use Structure** What are the radian measures of the angles whose sine is 1?

4. **Error Analysis** Describe and correct the error a student made when asked to find the radian measures of the angles whose sine is 1.

$\sin(0 + \pi x) = 1$

✗

Do You KNOW HOW?

5. What is $\sin^{-1}\left(\frac{\sqrt{2}}{2}\right)$?

6. What is $\tan^{-1}(\sqrt{3})$?

7. What are all of the angles (in degrees) that have a cosine value of 0.74?

8. What are all of the angles (in degrees) that have a sine value of 0.83?

9. Solve $4 \sin \theta - 1 = 0$ for values between 0 and 2π.

10. Solve $2 \tan \theta + 3 = 0$ for values from 0° to 360°. Round angle measures to the nearest degree.

PRACTICE & PROBLEM SOLVING

Scan for Multimedia

Practice Tutorial

Additional Exercises Available Online

UNDERSTAND

11. Use Structure Find the radian measures of the angles θ whose cosine is -1.5. Explain your reasoning.

12. Communicate Precisely In order to define the inverse sine, inverse cosine, and inverse tangent functions, the domains of the sine, cosine, and tangent functions must be restricted. Explain why.

13. Error Analysis Describe and correct the error a student made in solving the following trigonometric equation for θ.

$$2\sin\theta + 3 = 4$$
$$2\sin\theta = 1$$
$$\sin\theta = \frac{1}{2}$$
$$\theta = \sin^{-1}\left(\frac{1}{2}\right)$$
$$\theta = \frac{\pi}{3} + 2\pi n \text{ or } \frac{5\pi}{3} + 2\pi n$$

✗

14. Construct Arguments Explain why there is no solution for $\theta = \cos^{-1} 3.75$.

15. Generalize Find $\sec^{-1}\left(\frac{1}{2}\right)$. Justify your answer.

16. Higher Order Thinking Evaluate or simplify.

a. $\cos^{-1}\left(\cos\left(\frac{\pi}{8}\right)\right)$

b. $\tan(\tan^{-1}(-3.6))$

c. $\sin^{-1}\left(\tan\left(-\frac{\pi}{4}\right)\right)$

17. Generalize Find the value(s) of $\sin\theta$, if $\sin^2\theta = 1$.

18. Mathematical Connections Write a trigonometric equation with solutions of 240° and 300° in the domain [0, 360°].

PRACTICE

19. How would you restrict the domain of the cotangent function to define the inverse cotangent function? SEE EXAMPLE 1

Evaluate the inverse trigonometric functions at the given value. Keep the angle values within the range of each inverse function. Give answers in both radian and degree measures. SEE EXAMPLE 2

20. $\tan^{-1}\left(\frac{\sqrt{3}}{3}\right)$

21. $\sin^{-1}\left(\frac{\sqrt{3}}{2}\right)$

22. $\tan^{-1}(-1)$

23. $\cos^{-1}\left(-\frac{1}{2}\right)$

Find all the angle values of the trigonometric functions that have the given values. Give answers in degree measures rounded to the nearest tenth. SEE EXAMPLE 3

24. $\sin x = 0.64$

25. $\cos x = -0.6293$

26. $\sin x = -0.39$

27. $\tan x = -0.6293$

Solve each trigonometric equation for values between 0 and 2π. SEE EXAMPLE 4

28. $\sqrt{3}\tan x + 1 = 0$

29. $2\sin x + \sqrt{3} = 0$

30. $2\cos^2\theta - 1 = 0$

31. $2\sin^2\theta + \sin\theta - 1 = 0$ (*Hint*: Factor the trinomial).

32. A sprint car with a loud engine is racing around a track. The engine's volume V, in dB, is defined as $V = -12\sin\left(\frac{2\pi}{15}t\right) + 70$, where t is the time in minutes since the sprint car has passed your position. When will the sound of the sprint car first be below 65 dB?

PRACTICE & PROBLEM SOLVING

Practice | Tutorial

Mixed Review Available Online

APPLY

33. Make Sense and Persevere A pendulum is pulled away from its resting position and released. The equation $h = 2\cos(\pi t) + 6$ models the height h in inches as a function of time at t seconds.

a. Solve the equation for t.

b. Find the first time at which the pendulum is at a height of 5 in. Round to the nearest hundredth second.

34. Model With Mathematics Air traffic controllers at LaGuardia Airport have asked an aircraft to maintain a holding pattern near the airport. The function $d(x) = 70\sin(0.60x) + 120$ represents the horizontal distance d, in miles, of the aircraft from the airport at time x, in minutes.

a. When the aircraft enters the holding pattern, $x = 0$, how far is it from LaGuardia Airport?

b. During the first 15 min after the aircraft enters the holding pattern, at what time, x, is the aircraft exactly 187 mi from the airport?

35. Make Sense and Persevere A photographer stands 60 ft from the White House, which is, 60 ft, 4 in. tall, and photographs a bird sitting on the roof. Provided the line of sight of the photographer is 6 ft above the ground, find the angle of elevation of the line of sight of the photographer to the roof of the White House. Round the angle measure to the nearest degree.

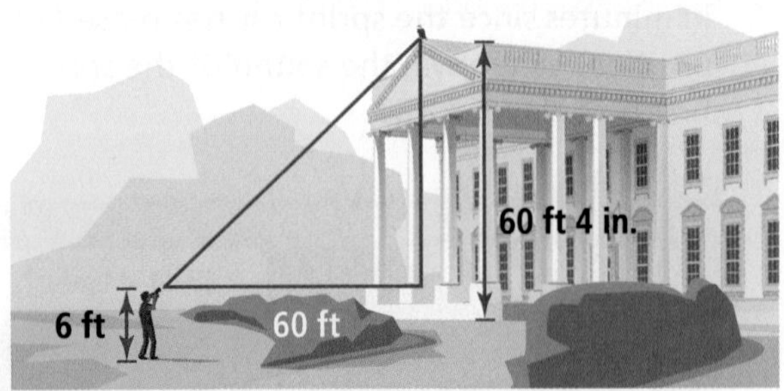

36. Model With Mathematics The tides at a particular North Carolina beach could be modeled by $h = 4.5\cos\frac{3\pi}{17}t$, where h is the height of the tide in feet above the mean water level and t is the number of hours past midnight. At what time will the tide be about $2\frac{1}{2}$ ft above the mean water level?

ASSESSMENT PRACTICE

37. Solve the equation $4\sin^2\theta - 3 = 0$ for θ measured in radians. Determine if each of the following are part of the solution set. Select *Yes* or *No*.

	Yes	No
a. $\frac{\pi}{6} + 2k\pi$, where k is an integer	❑	❑
b. $\frac{\pi}{3} + k\pi$, where k is an integer	❑	❑
c. $\frac{\pi}{3} + 2k\pi$, where k is an integer	❑	❑
d. $\frac{2\pi}{3} + 2k\pi$, where k is an integer	❑	❑
e. $\frac{2\pi}{3} + k\pi$, where k is an integer	❑	❑
f. $\frac{5\pi}{6} + k\pi$, where k is an integer	❑	❑

38. SAT/ACT What is the approximate measure of the angle θ in the triangle shown?

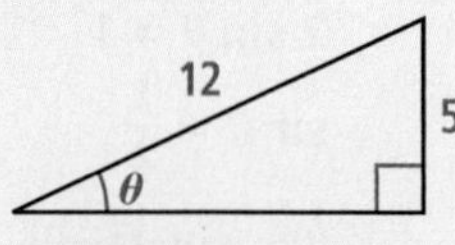

Not drawn to scale

Ⓐ $\theta = 22.6°$

Ⓑ $\theta = 24.6°$

Ⓒ $\theta = 65.4°$

Ⓓ $\theta = 67.4°$

39. Performance Task The Washington Monument is 555 ft tall. The angle of elevation from the end of the monument's shadow to the top of the monument has a cosecant of 1.10.

Part A What is the measure of the angle θ?

Part B What is the distance d from the end of the monument's shadow to the top of the monument? Round to the nearest tenth of a foot.

Part C What is the length l of the monument's shadow? Round to the nearest tenth of a foot.

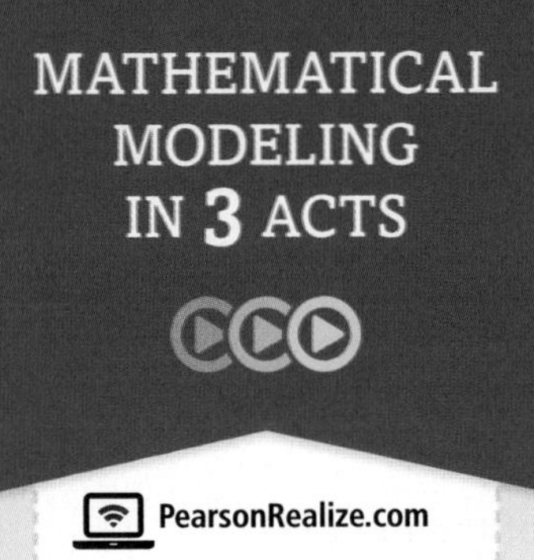

PearsonRealize.com

Ramp Up Your Design

Wheelchair users and others with mobility challenges require ramps or elevators to access buildings and other public spaces. Most public buildings are required to have accessible ramps through the Americans with Disabilities Act. However, most homes do not have such ramps. Wheelchair users who move into a home with steps will have to have a new ramp installed.

The construction of accessibility ramps must follow strict guidelines. If ramps are not accurately built to follow these guidelines, they can be dangerous to use. Think about this during the Mathematical Modeling in 3 Acts lesson.

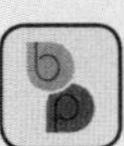

ACT 1 Identify the Problem

1. What is the first question that comes to mind after watching the video?
2. Write down the main question you will answer about what you saw in the video.
3. Make an initial conjecture that answers this main question.
4. Explain how you arrived at your conjecture.
5. What information will be useful to know to answer the main question? How can you get it? How will you use that information?

ACT 2 Develop a Model

6. Use the math that you have learned in this Topic to refine your conjecture.

ACT 3 Interpret the Results

7. Did your refined conjecture match the actual answer exactly? If not, what might explain the difference?

Activity Assess

7-2 Law of Sines and Law of Cosines

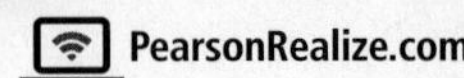

PearsonRealize.com

I CAN… use the Law of Sines and the Law of Cosines to solve for unknown angles and sides of a triangle.

VOCABULARY

- Law of Cosines
- Law of Sines

MODEL & DISCUSS

A biologist measures the slant height of a conical termite mound to be about 32 ft. The angle from the ground to the top of the mound is 51°. The base of the mound has a diameter of about 40 ft.

A. Draw a model to help the biologist.

B. Make Sense and Persevere What is the height of the mound?

ESSENTIAL QUESTION

How can you use the sine and cosine functions with non-right triangles?

CONCEPT Law of Sines and Law of Cosines

The Law of Sines and the Law of Cosines allow you to apply trigonometric functions to non-right triangles. Given $\triangle ABC$, with angles A, B, and C and opposite-side lengths a, b, and c:

Law of Sines: $\frac{\sin A}{a} = \frac{\sin B}{b} = \frac{\sin C}{c}$

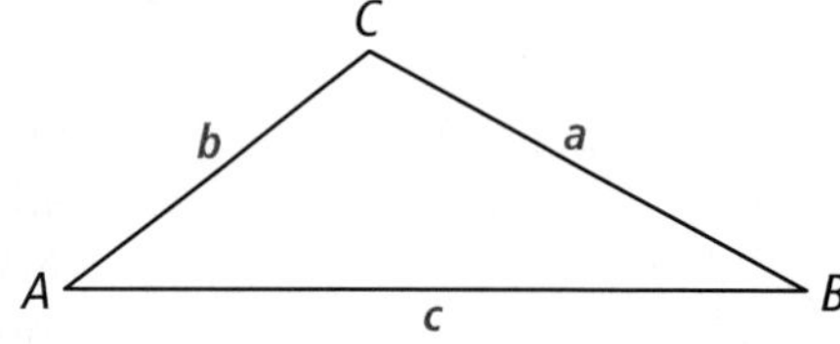

Law of Cosines:

$a^2 = b^2 + c^2 - 2bc(\cos A)$

$b^2 = a^2 + c^2 - 2ac(\cos B)$

$c^2 = a^2 + b^2 - 2ab(\cos C)$

EXAMPLE 1 Prove the Law of Sines

How can you derive the Law of Sines?

STUDY TIP
Drawing an altitude allows you to create two right triangles and apply trigonometric functions.

Step 1 Draw $\triangle ABC$ with an altitude from C to side c with length x.

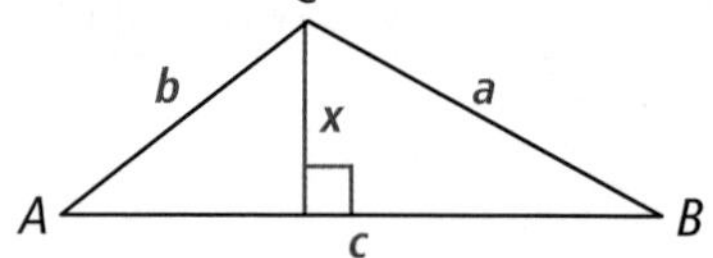

Step 2 Write the sine function for angles A and B.

$\sin A = \frac{x}{b}$ or $x = b \sin A$

$\sin B = \frac{x}{a}$ or $x = a \sin B$

Step 3 Since you have two statements that are both equal to x, you can set them equal to each other.

$b \sin A = a \sin B$

Step 4 Divide both sides of the equation by ab.

$\frac{\sin A}{a} = \frac{\sin B}{b}$

The ratio of the sine of an angle to its opposite side is the same for all angles in the same triangle.

Try It! 1. How can you derive the Law of Sines for angles B and C?

Activity Assess

APPLICATION

EXAMPLE 2 Use the Law of Sines

A. Nicholas is walking along an obstacle course that begins at point *X*. He starts going straight on the path. It then takes a wide right turn onto a second path (at point *Y*) and continues for 1,000 feet before turning on to the final path (at point *Z*). What is the angle between the second path and the final path (point *Z*)? Round to the nearest tenth of a degree.

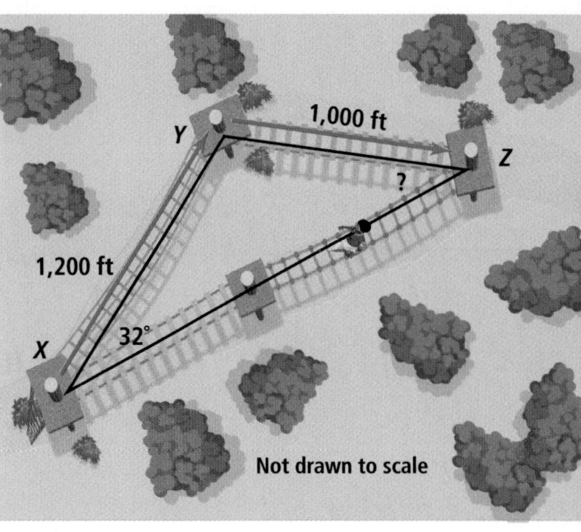

USE STRUCTURE
In order to apply the Law of Sines, you must know the measure of one angle and the length of the side opposite the angle.

$\frac{\sin A}{a} = \frac{\sin B}{b}$ ······ Use Law of Sines, since an angle and its opposite side length are given.

$\frac{\sin 32°}{1{,}000} = \frac{\sin Z}{1{,}200}$ ······ Substitute.

$\frac{6 \sin 32°}{5} = \sin Z$ ······ Isolate the sine function.

$\sin^{-1}\left(\frac{6 \sin 32°}{5}\right) = m\angle Z$ ······ Use the inverse sine function.

$m\angle Z \approx 39.5°$ ······ Solve.

Since the turn at $\angle Y$ is described as wide, $\angle Y$ must be an obtuse angle, and $\angle Z$ must be acute. This means you do not need to check for other angles with the same sine value.

The angle between the second path and the trail is about 39.5°.

REASON
Could you have used $\angle L$ to solve the problem instead?

B. Amaya is flying her zeppelin balloon. The string is 90 ft long, and the angle of elevation to the balloon from the ground is 60°. Across the park, Rochelle is watching the balloon which is between Rochelle and Amaya. The angle of elevation from Rochelle's feet to the balloon is 75°. How far apart are Amaya and Rochelle standing? Round to the nearest tenth of a foot.

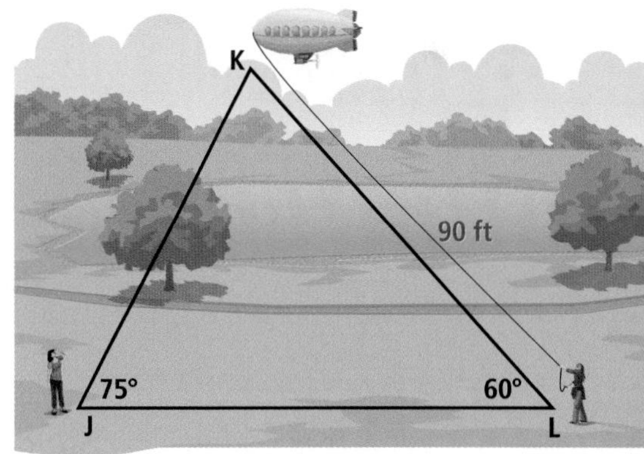

To use the Law of Sines to find *JL*, you need to know the measure of the angle opposite *JL*.

Find $m\angle K$ using the measures of the other two angles in the triangle.

$m\angle K = 180° - 75° - 60° = 45°$.

CONTINUED ON THE NEXT PAGE

EXAMPLE 2 CONTINUED

$\frac{\sin A}{a} = \frac{\sin B}{b}$ .... Use the Law of Sines.

$\frac{\sin 45^\circ}{k} = \frac{\sin 75^\circ}{90}$ .... Substitute.

$\frac{90 \sin 45^\circ}{\sin 75^\circ} = k$ .... Isolate the variable.

$k \approx 65.9$ ft .... Solve.

Amaya and Rochelle are standing about 65.9 ft apart.

 **Try It!** 2. In $\triangle NPQ$, $m\angle N = 105^\circ$, $n = 12$, and $p = 10$.

a. To the nearest degree, what is $m\angle Q$?

b. What is the length of side q? Round to the nearest tenth of a unit.

CONCEPTUAL UNDERSTANDING

EXAMPLE 3 Understand the Ambiguous Case

In $\triangle CDE$, $CD = 8$, $DE = 6$, and $m\angle C = 30^\circ$. What is $m\angle E$ in $\triangle CDE$? Round to the nearest degree.

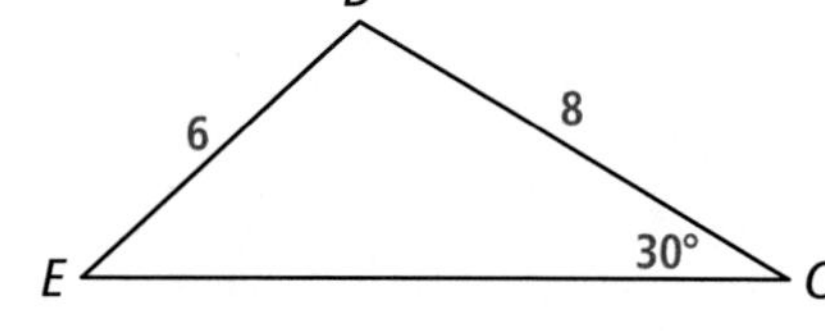

Start by drawing a sketch of the given information. It is not necessary to try to make your sketch to scale as you will not be relying on measurements of the sketch to find the missing information.

Because you know one side and the angle opposite that side, you can use the Law of Sines to find a second angle.

$\frac{\sin A}{a} = \frac{\sin B}{b}$ .... Use the Law of Sines.

$\frac{\sin 30^\circ}{6} = \frac{\sin E}{8}$ .... Substitute.

$\frac{8 \sin 30^\circ}{6} = \sin E$ .... Isolate the variable.

$\sin^{-1}\left(\frac{4 \sin 30^\circ}{3}\right) = m\angle E$ .... Use the inverse sine function.

$m\angle E \approx 42^\circ$ .... Solve.

So you could conclude that the angles in the triangle measure 30°, 42°, and 108°. However, there is another angle which has the same sine value as the 42° angle.

Using the unit circle, you can see that an angle with measure 138° has the same sine value.

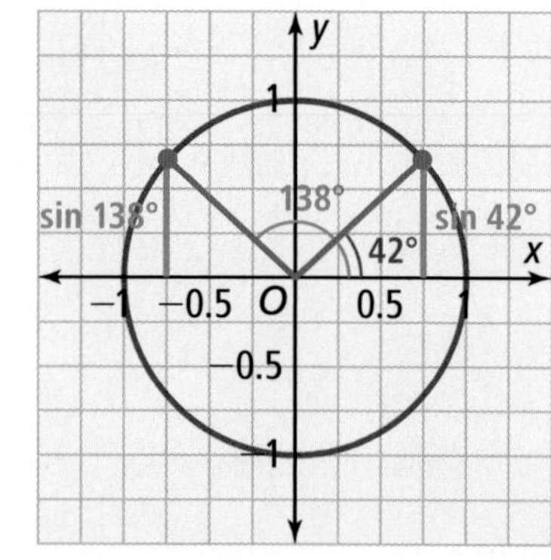

LOOK FOR RELATIONSHIPS
If a triangle has one obtuse angle given, there is only one possible triangle. If one acute angle is given, then *two* triangles may be possible.

CONTINUED ON THE NEXT PAGE

STUDY TIP
Regardless of what information a problem is asking for or how it is being solved, do not rely on the appearance of an angle to guide your answers. Always work measurements out mathematically.

EXAMPLE 3 CONTINUED

So the angles in the triangle could also measure 30°, 138°, and 12°. The triangle would look quite different than the original sketch, but it does match all of the information given in the problem.

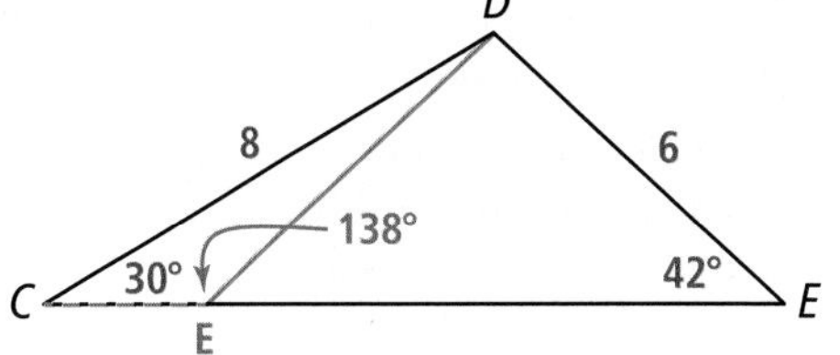

There are two possible triangles that could have the given information, one where $m\angle E = 42°$ and one where $m\angle E = 138°$.

Try It! 3. In $\triangle ABC$, $m\angle A = 30°$, $a = 5$, and $b = 8$. Find $m\angle B$. How many possible triangles are there?

EXAMPLE 4 Prove the Law of Cosines

Prove the Law of Cosines $a^2 = b^2 + c^2 - 2bc(\cos A)$ for an acute angle A.

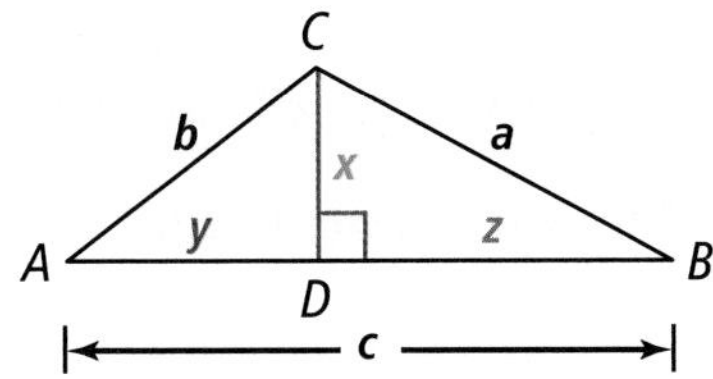

Step 1 The Law of Cosines resembles the Pythagorean Theorem. To prove the Law of Cosines, start by thinking of a right triangle in which a is the hypotenuse.

The drawing shows $\triangle ABC$ with an altitude of length x that divides length c into y and z at point D, so that two right triangles are formed.

Step 2 Since z is in the right triangle with hypotenuse a, find an expression for z using b, c, and $\angle A$, the variables on the right side of the Law of Cosines equation.

$$\cos A = \frac{y}{b} \text{ or } y = b \cos A$$

$$c = y + z \text{ or } z = c - y$$

$$z = c - b \cos A$$

Substitute $b \cos A$ for y.

Step 3 Now you need an expression for x in terms of b, c, and $\angle A$. You can get one by finding $\sin A$.

$$\sin A = \frac{x}{b} \text{ or } x = b \sin A$$

CONTINUED ON THE NEXT PAGE

EXAMPLE 4 CONTINUED

COMMON ERROR
Be careful to square both quantities correctly. The first quantity is a monomial while the second is a binomial.

Step 4 Use the Pythagorean Theorem for $\triangle BCD$, and substitute to obtain an equation relating a, b, c, and $\angle A$. Simplify.

$$a^2 = x^2 + z^2$$
$$a^2 = (b \sin A)^2 + (c - y)^2$$
$$a^2 = (b \sin A)^2 + c^2 - 2cy + y^2$$
$$a^2 = b^2 \sin^2 A + c^2 - 2bc(\cos A) + b^2 \cos^2 A$$
$$a^2 = b^2(\sin^2 A + \cos^2 A) + c^2 - 2bc(\cos A)$$
$$a^2 = b^2 + c^2 - 2bc(\cos A)$$

$y = b \cos A$

This result is the Law of Cosines for $\angle A$.

Try It! **4. a.** How can you derive the Law of Cosines for an obtuse angle C?

b. How does the equation compare to the equation for an acute angle?

EXAMPLE 5 Use the Law of Cosines

What is t? Round to the nearest tenth.

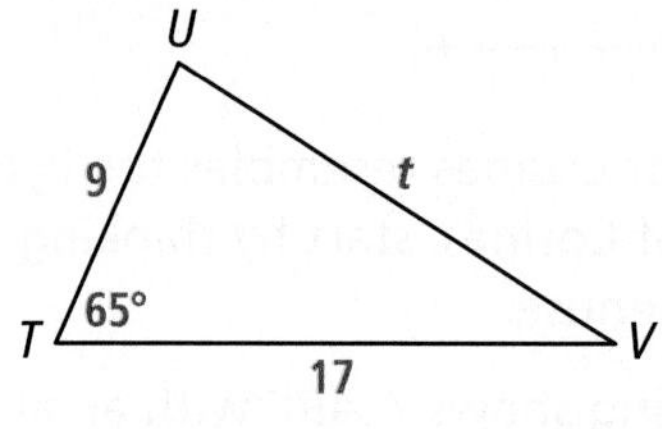

COMMON ERROR
Make sure to assign the correct values for a, b, and c based on their relationship to the given angle.

$a^2 = b^2 + c^2 - 2bc(\cos A)$	Write the original equation.
$t^2 = 9^2 + 17^2 - 2(9)(17) \cos 65^\circ$	Substitute.
$t^2 = 81 + 289 - 306 \cos 65^\circ$	Simplify.
$t^2 \approx 240.68$	Compute using technology.
$t \approx \sqrt{240.68}$	Take the square root of both sides.
$t \approx 15.5$	Solve.

To the nearest tenth, $t \approx 15.5$.

Try It! **5. a.** In $\triangle JKL$, $j = 15$, $k = 13$, and $l = 12$. What is $m\angle J$?

b. In $\triangle ABC$, $a = 11$, $b = 17$, and $m\angle C = 42^\circ$. What is c?

Activity Assess

APPLICATION

EXAMPLE 6 Use the Law of Cosines and the Law of Sines

STUDY TIP
It is necessary to use the Law of Cosines and Law of Sines, because the flagpole is not perpendicular to the ground; if it were, you could use trigonometric ratios.

A wire 5.3 m long is attached to the top of a flagpole that leans to the left in a strong wind. The wire is anchored to the ground 1.2 m to the right of the pole. The wire forms a 68° angle with the ground. What angle does the wire form with the top of the flagpole? Round to the nearest degree.

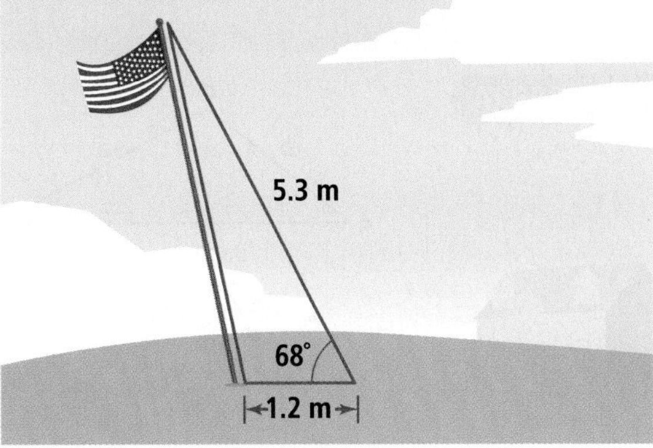

Since the lengths of two sides and the measure of the included angle are given, use the Law of Cosines to find the length h of the flagpole.

$a^2 = b^2 + c^2 - 2bc(\cos A)$ .... Write the original equation.

$h^2 = 1.2^2 + 5.3^2 - 2(1.2)(5.3)\cos 68°$ .... Substitute.

$h^2 = 1.44 + 28.09 - 12.72\cos 68°$ .... Simplify.

$h^2 \approx 24.77$ .... Compute using technology.

$h \approx \pm\sqrt{24.77}$ .... Take the square root of both sides.

$h \approx 4.98$ m .... Solve.

Now that an angle and its opposite length are known, use the Law of Sines to find the angle θ that the wire forms with the flagpole.

$\frac{\sin A}{a} = \frac{\sin B}{b}$ .... Use the Law of Sines.

$\frac{\sin 68°}{4.98} = \frac{\sin \theta}{1.2}$ .... Substitute.

$\frac{1.2 \sin 68°}{4.98} = \sin \theta$ .... Isolate the sine function.

$\sin^{-1}\left(\frac{1.2 \sin 68°}{4.98}\right) = \theta$ .... Take the inverse sine.

$12.9° \approx \theta$ .... Solve.

The angle formed by the wire and the flagpole is about 13°.

Try It! 6. A bike race follows a triangular path, represented by triangle ABC. If A is the starting point and the measure of the angle at point B is 70°, what is the measure of the angle formed by path BC and path CA?

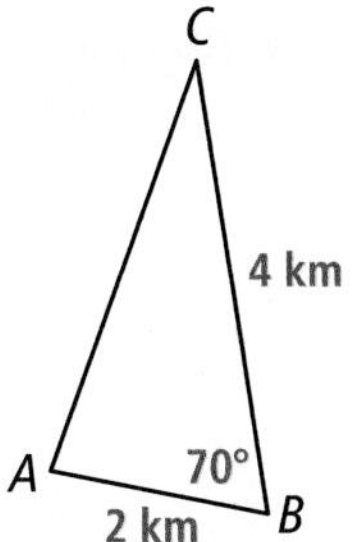

CONCEPT SUMMARY Law of Sines and Law of Cosines

	Law of Sines	Law of Cosines
ALGEBRA	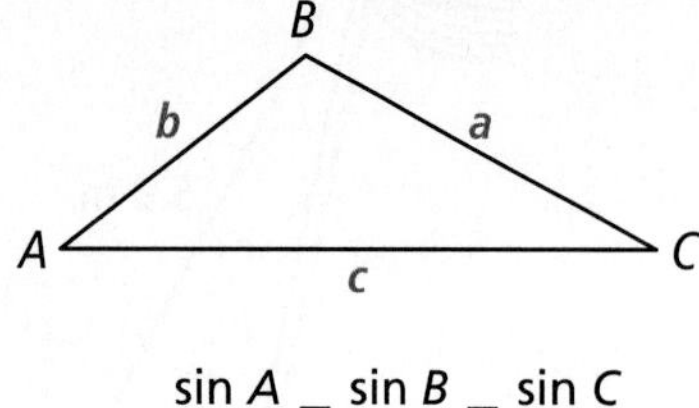 $\frac{\sin A}{a} = \frac{\sin B}{b} = \frac{\sin C}{c}$	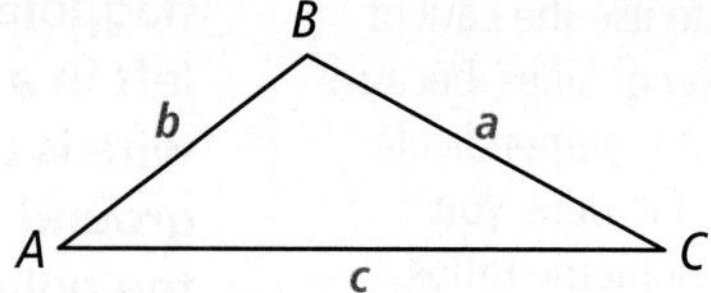 $a^2 = b^2 + c^2 - 2bc(\cos A)$ $b^2 = a^2 + c^2 - 2ac(\cos B)$ $c^2 = a^2 + b^2 - 2ab(\cos C)$
NUMBERS	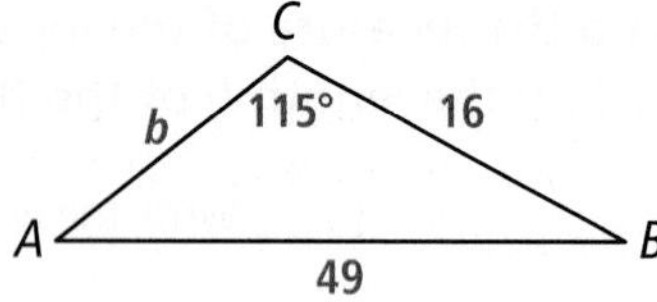 **Find the measure of $\angle A$.** $\frac{\sin A}{a} = \frac{\sin C}{c}$ so $\frac{\sin A}{16} = \frac{\sin 115^\circ}{49}$ $\frac{\sin A}{16} = \frac{\sin 115^\circ}{49}$ $\sin A \approx 0.2959$ $A \approx \sin^{-1} 0.2959$; $m\angle A \approx 17.2^\circ$	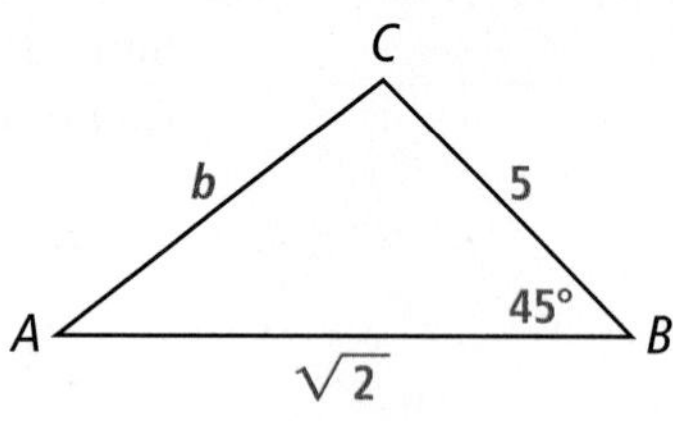 **Find b.** $b^2 = a^2 + c^2 - 2ac(\cos B)$ $b^2 = 5^2 + (\sqrt{2})^2 - 2(5)(\sqrt{2})(\cos 45^\circ)$ $b^2 = 25 + 2 - 10(\sqrt{2})\left(\frac{\sqrt{2}}{2}\right)$ $b^2 = 17$; $b \approx 4.1$

Do You UNDERSTAND?

1. ESSENTIAL QUESTION How can you use the sine and cosine functions with non-right triangles?

2. **Error Analysis** Alejandro said the Law of Sines always gives one answer. Explain and correct Alejandro's error.

3. **Construct Arguments** Consider the Law of Cosines as $a^2 = b^2 + c^2 - 2bc(\cos A)$. Explain why the negative square root of a is not a valid solution.

4. **Reason** In what situations do you use the Law of Sines? Law of Cosines?

Do You KNOW HOW?

Use the Law of Sines or the Law of Cosines to find the indicated measure in $\triangle ABC$.

5. $m\angle A = 50^\circ$, $a = 4.5$, $b = 3.8$; find $m\angle B$.

6. $m\angle A = 72^\circ$, $a = 61$, $c = 58$; find $m\angle C$.

7. $m\angle A = 18^\circ$, $m\angle C = 75^\circ$, $c = 101$; find a.

8. $m\angle B = 112^\circ$, $m\angle C = 20^\circ$, $c = 1.6$; find b.

9. $m\angle C = 45^\circ$, $a = 15$, $b = 8$; find c.

10. $m\angle A = 82^\circ$, $b = 2.5$, $c = 6.8$; find a.

11. $a = 14$, $b = 12$, $c = 5.8$; find $m\angle A$.

Scan for Multimedia

Practice Tutorial

Additional Exercises Available Online

UNDERSTAND

12. **Construct Arguments** Lourdes said that you can use the Law of Sines if you have any two angles and any side, or any two sides and any angle. Is Lourdes correct? Explain your reasoning.

13. **Generalize** Knowing a particular combination of the sides and/or angles in a triangle leads to the ambiguous case. What is that combination?

14. **Error Analysis** Describe and correct the error a student made in using the Law of Cosines to find a.

$a^2 = 14^2 + 9^2 - 2(14)(9)(\cos 140)$
$a^2 = 196 + 81 - 252(-.766)$
$a^2 = 277 - 193.03$
$a^2 = 83.97$
$a \approx 9.16$ ✗

15. **Communicate Precisely** Two students are solving for d in the triangle shown, using the Law of Cosines. One says the answer is 20 in., and the other says the answer is 20.3 in. Is either student incorrect? Explain your reasoning.

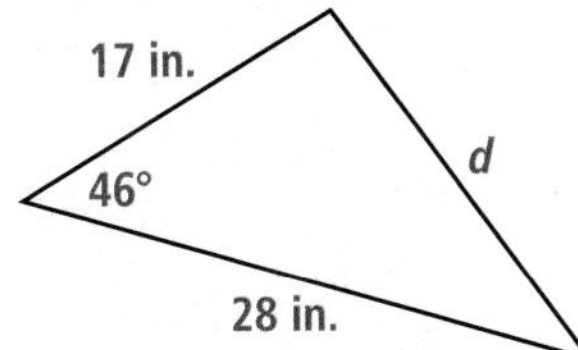

16. **Look for Relationships** Show that the Law of Cosines is equivalent to the Pythagorean Theorem when the given angle is 90°.

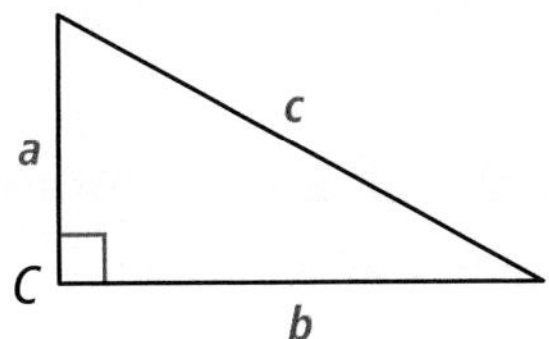

17. **Higher Order Thinking** The ambiguous case only causes a problem when the given angle is acute, not when an obtuse angle is given. Explain why.

PRACTICE

How can you derive the Law of Sines for the given angles? SEE EXAMPLE 1

18. E and F

19. F and G

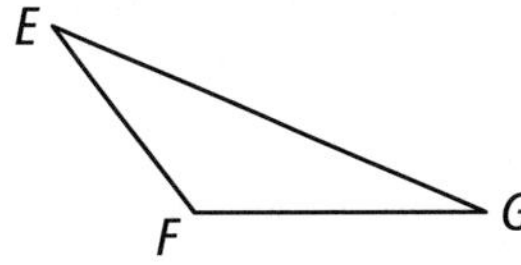

Use the Law of Sines to solve. SEE EXAMPLE 2

20. In $\triangle HJK$, $m\angle J = 122°$, $j = 17$, and $k = 8$. What is $m\angle K$?

21. In $\triangle RST$, $m\angle R = 45°$, $m\angle S = 19°$, and $r = 15$. What is s?

Find the number of possible triangles for each set of measures. Then find the angle measure(s). SEE EXAMPLE 3

22. In $\triangle WXY$, $m\angle X = 104°$, $x = 7$, and $y = 2$. Find $m\angle Y$.

23. In $\triangle DEF$, $m\angle D = 28°$, $d = 8$, and $e = 15$. Find $m\angle E$.

24. In $\triangle RST$, $m\angle R = 30°$, $r = 14$, and $t = 32$. Find $m\angle T$.

How can you derive the Law of Cosines for obtuse angle K? SEE EXAMPLE 4

25.

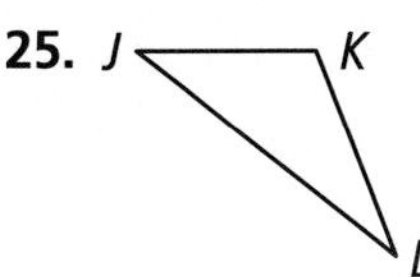

In $\triangle PQR$, find $m\angle P$. SEE EXAMPLE 5

26. $p = 5$, $q = 8$, $r = 9$

27. $p = 14$, $q = 6$, $r = 12$

What is the measure of angle Z? SEE EXAMPLE 6

28.

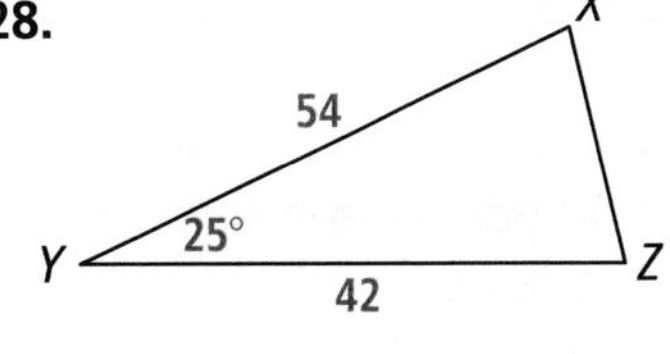

29.

PRACTICE & PROBLEM SOLVING

Practice Tutorial

Mixed Review Available Online

APPLY

30. Model with Mathematics The head sail for Melissa's sailboat is a triangle with the three sides having lengths of 24 ft, 23 ft, and 12 ft. What is the measure of the sail's greatest angle?

31. Use Structure An art sculpture is made of rotated scalene triangles, as shown. The triangles are all congruent. What is the length of the longest side of each triangle?

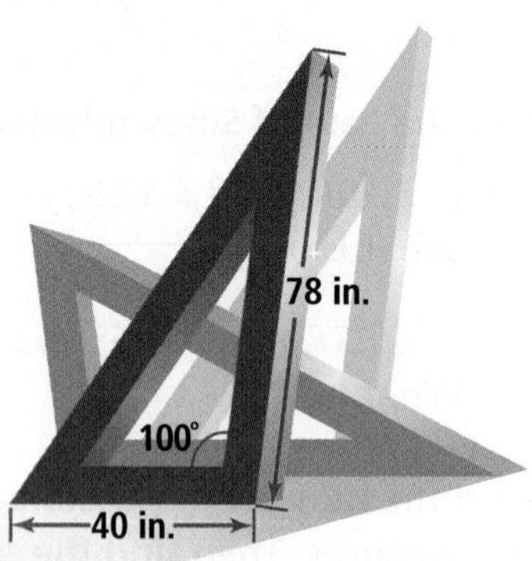

32. Make Sense and Persevere The course for a race follows three roads as shown. How far do the runners travel along Jappa Road?

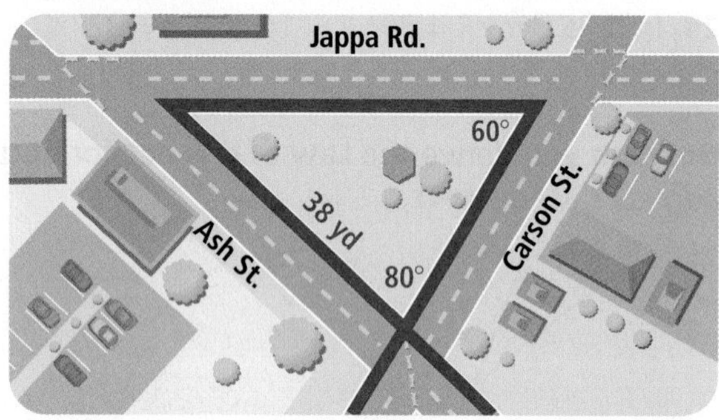

33. Model With Mathematics Noemi throws a ball to Parker, who is 6 m away. When Parker catches the ball, he turns 50°, and then throws the ball 7 m to Shandra. What angle does Shandra turn to throw back to Noemi?

34. Make Sense and Persevere Tamika parked her car and walked 300 yd down a path. She then made a 135° turn onto a new path. She walked another 40 yd along a river to her fishing spot. If Tamika turns to face the direction of her car, what angle does she need to turn?

ASSESSMENT PRACTICE

35. In $\triangle EFG$, $m\angle E = 35°$, $e = 5.8$, and $f = 10$. Choose *Yes* or *No* to tell whether each is a possible value for $m\angle F$.

	Yes	No
There are no possible values.	❑	❑
6.2°	❑	❑
60.3°	❑	❑
81.5°	❑	❑
98.5°	❑	❑
119.7°	❑	❑

36. SAT/ACT In $\triangle ABC$, $a = 29.7$, $b = 48.5$, and $B = 92°$. What is $m\angle A$?

Ⓐ There is no possible value.
Ⓑ 37.7°
Ⓒ 56.3°
Ⓓ 123.7°
Ⓔ 142.3°

37. Performance Task Teo is standing 80 yd from the base of a Mayan pyramid. The side of the pyramid is 100 ft from base to peak.

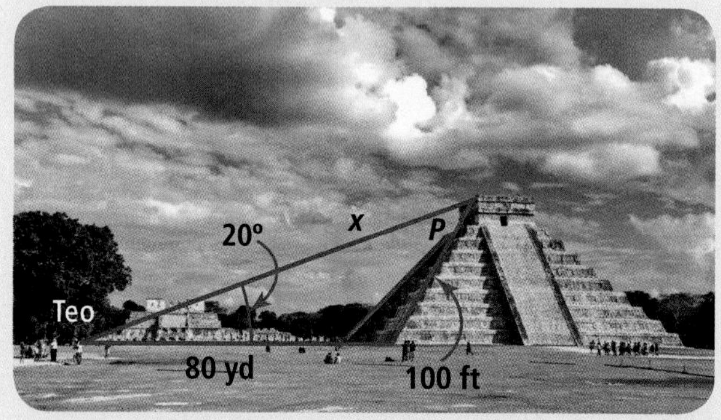

Part A How many feet from the base of the pyramid is Teo?

Part B What is the measure of angle P formed by the side of the pyramid and Teo's line of sight?

Part C What is the distance in a straight line from Teo to the peak x?

Activity Assess

7-3 Problem Solving With Trigonometry

PearsonRealize.com

I CAN… use trigonometry to solve problems.

VOCABULARY

- angle of depression
- angle of elevation

MODEL & DISCUSS

A search-and-rescue team is having a nighttime practice drill. Two members of the team are in a helicopter that is hovering at 2,000 feet above ground level.

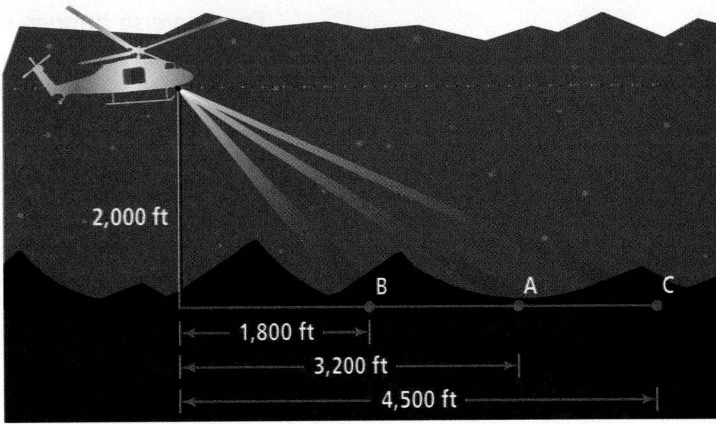

A. The team first tries to locate object A. At what angle from the horizontal line even with the helicopter should they position the spotlight so that it shines on object A?

B. Next, they shine the spotlight on object B. How does the angle of the spotlight from the horizontal line change?

C. Use Structure In general, how does the angle of the spotlight from the horizontal change as the light moves from object A to object B? From object A to object C?

ESSENTIAL QUESTION

How can trigonometry be used to solve real-world and mathematical problems?

EXAMPLE 1 Identify Angles of Elevation and Depression

Identify ∠2 as an angle of elevation or an angle of depression. Do the same for ∠3. Explain your reasoning.

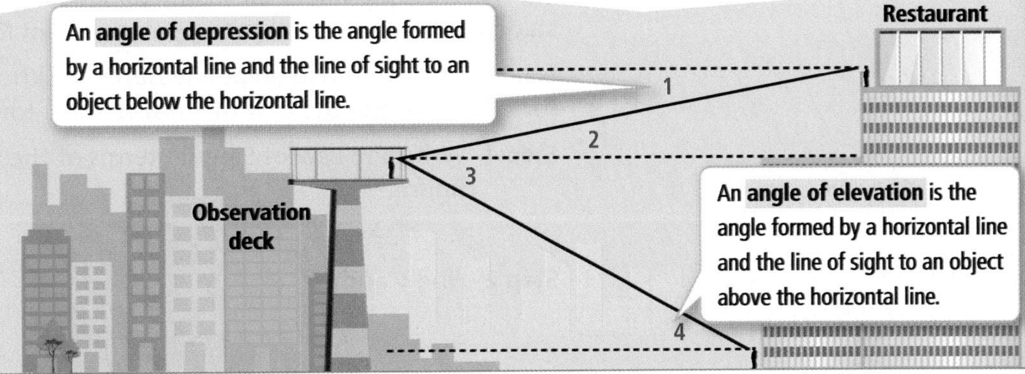

STUDY TIP
When solving problems involving angle of elevation or angle of depression, use a diagram and look for right triangles.

To see the person above, the person on the observation deck is looking up from the horizontal, so ∠2 is an angle of elevation.

To see the person below, the person on the observation deck is looking down from the horizontal, so ∠3 is an angle of depression.

Try It! **1.** In Example 1, how does the angle of depression, ∠1, compare with the angle of elevation, ∠2? Explain your reasoning.

APPLICATION

EXAMPLE 2 Use Angles of Elevation and Depression

For a reverse bungee ride, Reagan stands halfway between two vertical posts. Two bungee cords extend from the top of the posts to Reagan's waist at a height 1 m above the ground. How tall are the vertical posts?

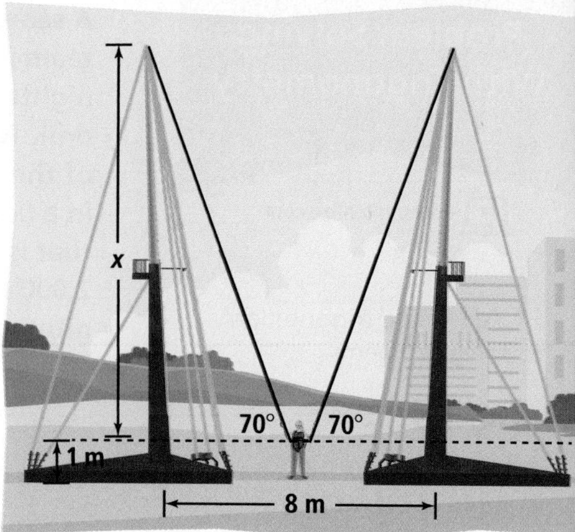

Write an equation to determine x m, the vertical distance from the top of a post to a point 1 meter above the ground.

$$\tan 70° = \frac{x}{4}$$

$$x = 4 \tan 70°$$

$$x \approx 10.9899$$

The unknown length and the 4-m length are opposite and adjacent to a 70° angle. So use the tangent function.

COMMON ERROR
Be careful not to forget the distance between Reagan's waist and the ground.

Find the height of the vertical posts.

$$11 + 1 = 12$$

The vertical posts are about 12 meters tall.

Try It! 2. Nadeem sees the tour bus from the top of the tower. To the nearest foot, how far is the bus from the base of the tower?

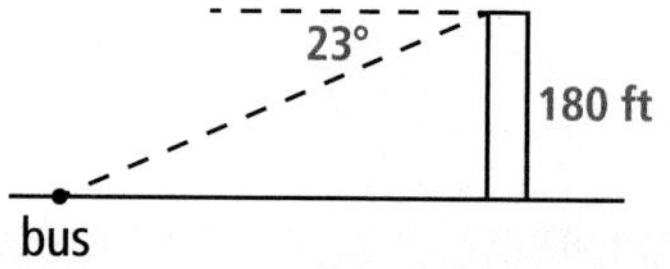

APPLICATION

EXAMPLE 3 Use Trigonometry to Solve Problems

An instructor holds a safety rope at point C for a student to rappel from the anchor point T. The rope between them currently measures 61 ft. How much more rope should the instructor let out so the student can make it to a resting point at point R?

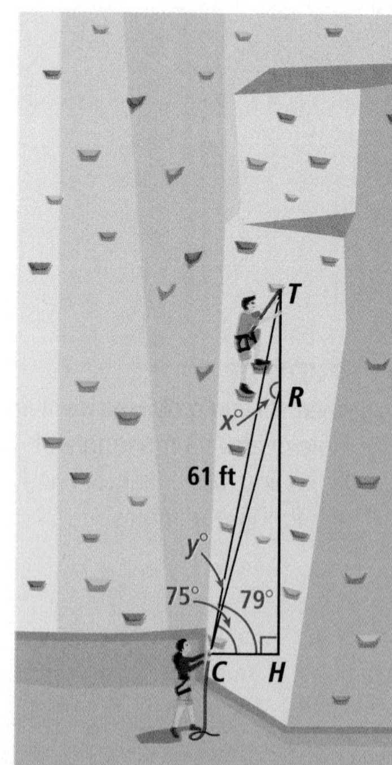

A side length and two angle measures are known for $\triangle TRC$. So, use the Law of Sines to solve for TR.

Step 1 Write the Law of Sines in terms of the figure.

$$\frac{\sin x°}{CT} = \frac{\sin y°}{TR}$$

Step 2 Find y and x.

$$y = 79 - 75 = 4$$

$$m\angle CRH = 90 - 75 = 15$$

$$x = 180 - 15 = 165$$

COMMUNICATE PRECISELY
Think about how you could check the reasonableness of your answer. What theorems or definitions could you use?

Step 3 Use the proportion to solve for TR.

$$\frac{\sin 165°}{61} = \frac{\sin 4°}{TR}$$

$$TR = \frac{61(\sin 4°)}{\sin 165°} \approx 16$$

The instructor should let out about 16 ft of rope.

CONTINUED ON THE NEXT PAGE

EXAMPLE 3 CONTINUED

Try It! 3. In Example 3, how far is the student from the instructor at the resting point?

CONCEPTUAL UNDERSTANDING

EXAMPLE 4 Use Trigonometry to Find Triangle Area

A. How can you use trigonometry to find the area of $\triangle ABC$?

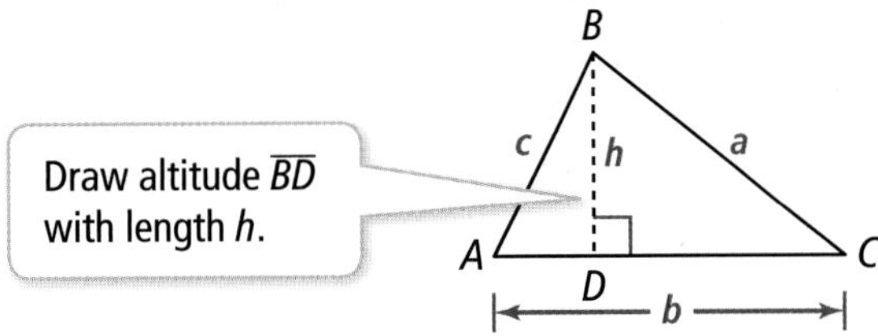

To write a formula with side lengths b and c and included $\angle A$, apply the area formula for a triangle.

$$\text{area} = \frac{1}{2}bh$$
$$= \frac{1}{2}b(c \sin A)$$
$$= \frac{1}{2}bc \sin A$$

In $\triangle ABD$, $\sin A = \frac{h}{c}$, so $h = c \sin A$.

You can apply the same reasoning to $\angle B$ and $\angle C$ to write the following area formulas.

$$\text{area} = \frac{1}{2}ac \sin B \qquad \text{area} = \frac{1}{2}ab \sin C$$

B. What is the area of $\triangle FEG$?

In the triangle, the lengths of sides g and f are 3 cm and 4 cm, respectively, and the measure of the included angle is 116°.

$$\text{area} = \frac{1}{2}gf \sin E$$
$$= \frac{1}{2}(3)(4) \sin 116°$$
$$= 6 \sin 116°$$
$$\approx 5.4$$

F, g, 116°, E, f, G

The area of the triangle is about 5.4 cm^2.

STUDY TIP

In order to use the formula area $= \frac{1}{2}bc \sin A$, you must know two side lengths and the measure of the included angle.

Try It! 4. a. What is the area of $\triangle JKL$?

b. What is the area of $\triangle PQR$? *Hint:* First apply the Law of Cosines to find the measure of the angle included between $\overline{PQ}$ and $\overline{PR}$. Then apply the area formula with the sine of the angle measure.

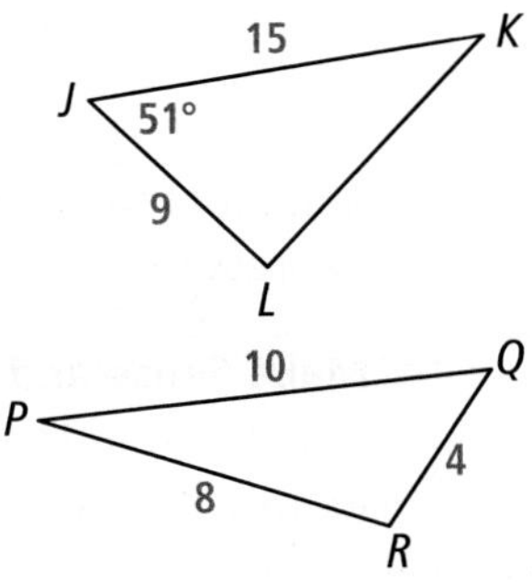

CONCEPT SUMMARY Using Trigonometry to Solve Problems

	Angles of Elevation or Depression	Area Formulas
DIAGRAMS	angle of elevation; object; h; 37°; 42°; 60 ft; 25 ft; d; angle of depression; object	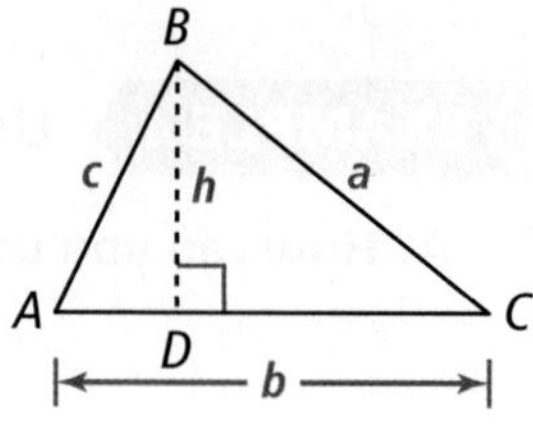
SYMBOLS	$\tan 37° = \frac{h}{60}$ $\sin 42° = \frac{25}{d}$	area $= \frac{1}{2}bc \sin A$ area $= \frac{1}{2}ac \sin B$ area $= \frac{1}{2}ab \sin C$

Do You UNDERSTAND?

1. **ESSENTIAL QUESTION** How can trigonometry be used to solve real-world and mathematical problems?

2. **Error Analysis** What error does Jamie make in finding the area?

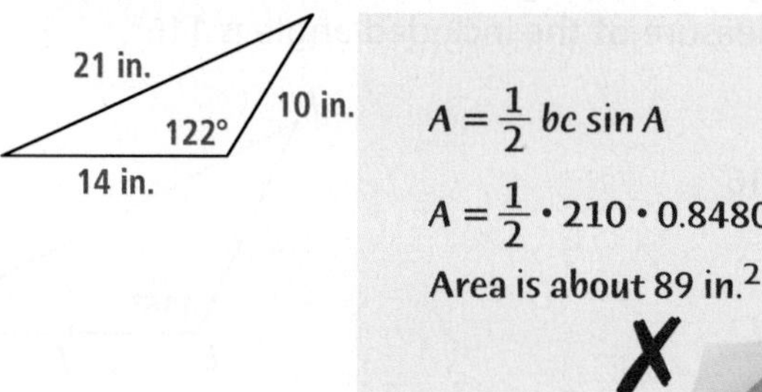

3. **Vocabulary** A person on a balcony and a person on a street look at each other. Draw a diagram to represent the situation and label the angles of elevation and depression.

4. **Make Sense and Persevere** How do you find the area of a triangle when given only the lengths of three sides?

Do You KNOW HOW?

5. A person rides a glass elevator in a hotel lobby. As the elevator goes up, how does the angle of depression to a fixed point on the lobby floor change?

6. A person observes the top of a radio antenna at an angle of elevation of 5°. After getting 1 mile closer to the antenna, the angle of elevation is 10°. How tall is the antenna to the nearest tenth of a foot?

5°
10°
5,280 ft

7. Triangle ABC has $AB = 13$, $AC = 15$, and $m\angle A = 59$. What is the area of the triangle to the nearest tenth?

8. Triangle DEF has $DE = 13$, $DF = 15$, and $EF = 14$. What is the area of the triangle to the nearest tenth?

9. A temporary pen for cattle is built using 10-foot sections of fence arranged in a triangle. One side of the pen has 4 sections, one has 5 sections, and the last has 6 sections. What is the area enclosed by the pen?

PRACTICE & PROBLEM SOLVING

Scan for Multimedia

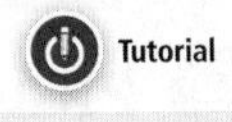

Additional Exercises Available Online

UNDERSTAND

10. **Construct Arguments** How is the area of a triangle determined if the lengths of two sides and the measure of the included angle are given?

11. **Error Analysis** Leah is asked to find AC. What is her error?

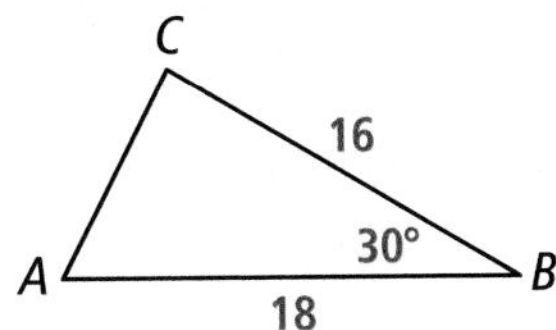

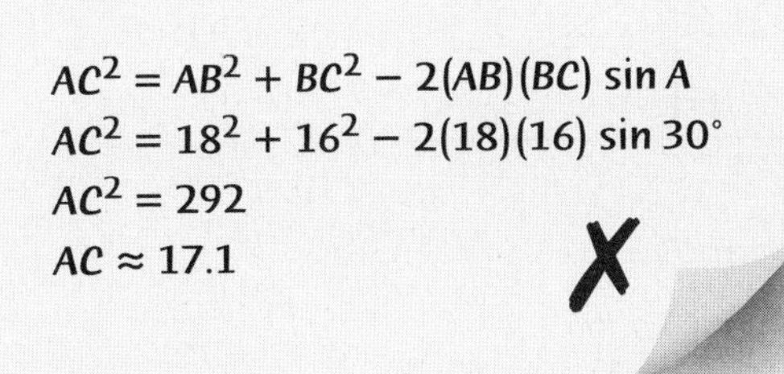

$AC^2 = AB^2 + BC^2 - 2(AB)(BC)\sin A$

$AC^2 = 18^2 + 16^2 - 2(18)(16)\sin 30°$

$AC^2 = 292$

$AC \approx 17.1$

12. **Mathematical Connections** Find the length of the diagonal of the isosceles trapezoid. Then find the length of the fourth side.

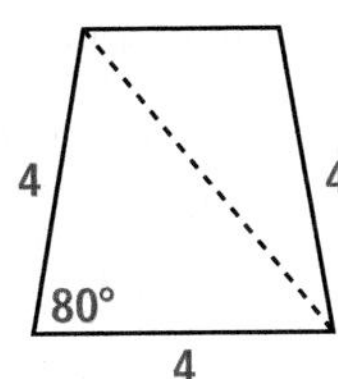

13. **Use Appropriate Tools** For each triangle, write an equation for x using a trigonometric function.

a.

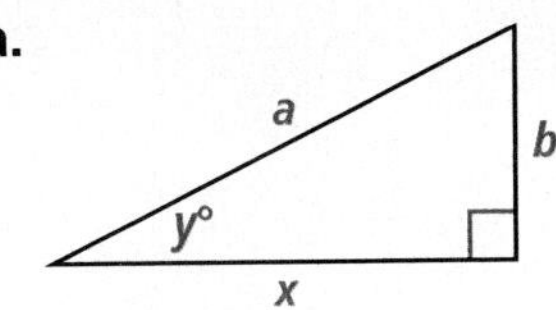

b.

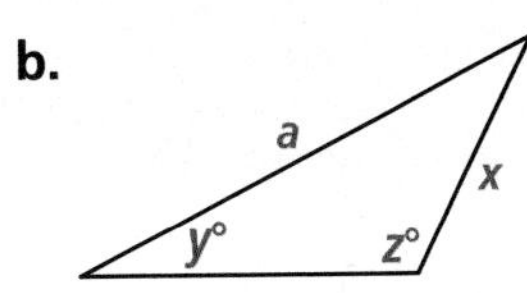

14. **Higher Order Thinking** What is a formula for the area of the parallelogram in the figure? Explain.

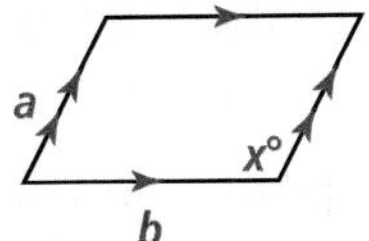

PRACTICE

15. What is the angle of elevation to a building 1,000 m away that is 300 m high? SEE EXAMPLE 1

16. To what angle of depression should the security camera be adjusted in order to have the lens aimed at point P on the ground? SEE EXAMPLE 2

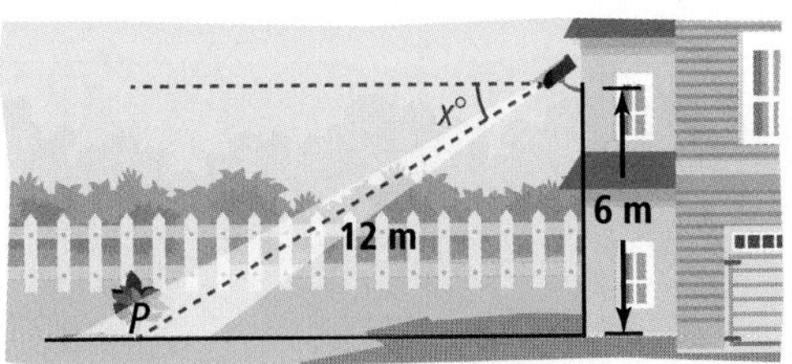

17. The angle of elevation to the sun is 21.5°. What is the length of the shadow cast by a person 5 ft 6 in. tall? SEE EXAMPLE 2

18. Libby's eyes are 5 ft above the ground, and the angle of elevation of her line of sight to the top of the monument is 74°. How far is she from the monument? SEE EXAMPLE 3

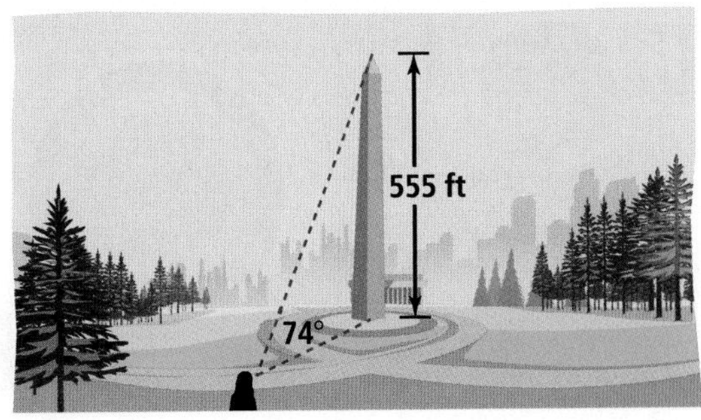

19. Triangle GHJ has $GH = 13$, $GJ = 15$, and $m\angle G = 74$. What is the area of the triangle? SEE EXAMPLE 4

20. What is the area of the triangle? SEE EXAMPLE 4

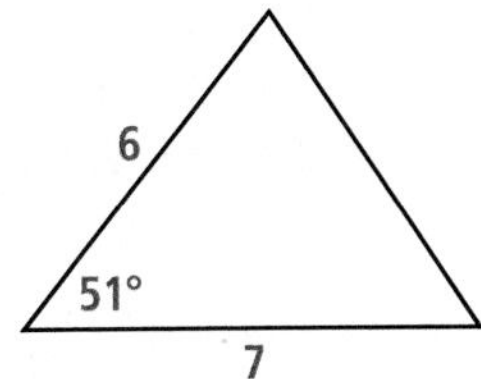

21. Triangle KLM has $KL = 22$, $KM = 27$, and $LM = 29$. What is the area of the triangle? SEE EXAMPLE 4

22. What is the area of the triangle? SEE EXAMPLE 4

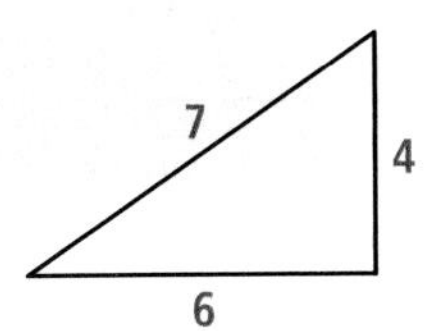

PRACTICE & PROBLEM SOLVING

APPLY

23. Model With Mathematics A research submarine dives at a speed of 100 ft/min directly toward the research lab. How long will it take the submarine to reach the lab from the surface of the ocean to the nearest tenth of a minute?

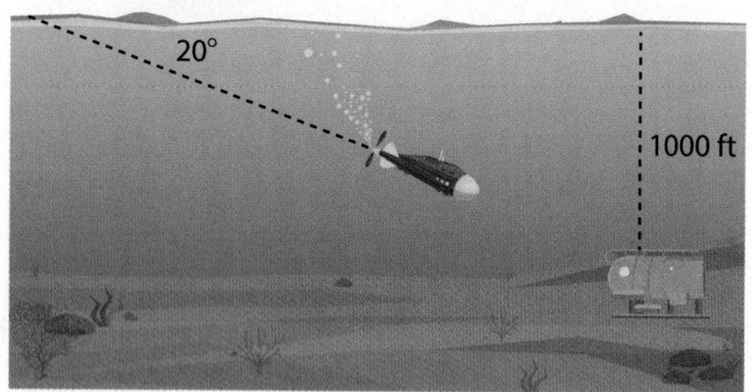

24. Make Sense and Persevere Benito aims for the center of the target from a distance of 70 meters. If Benito shoots an arrow at a 0.055° angle of depression below the center, will he hit the yellow circle? Explain.

25. Reason Ramona is climbing a hill with a 10° incline and wants to know the height of the rock formation. She walks 100 ft up the hill and uses a clinometer to measure the angle of elevation to the top of the formation. She then walks another 229.4 ft to the top of the hill. What is the height h of the rock formation?

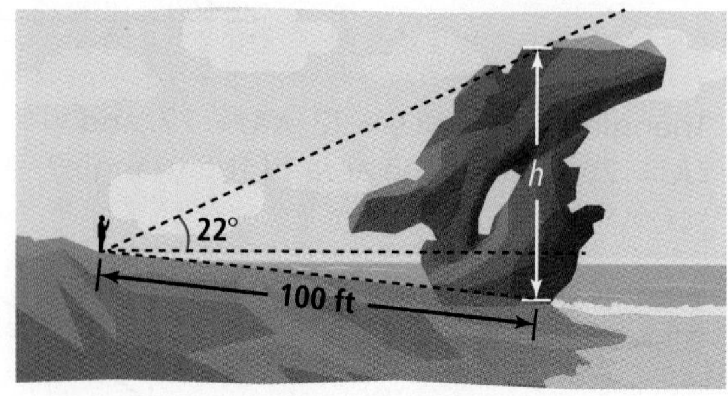

ASSESSMENT PRACTICE

26. What is the area of the triangle? Round to the nearest one hundredth of a square unit.

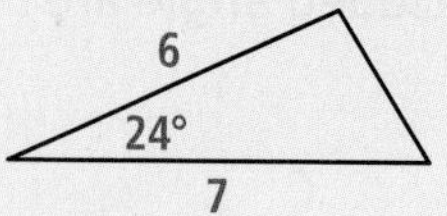

27. SAT/ACT Which of the following equations is true?

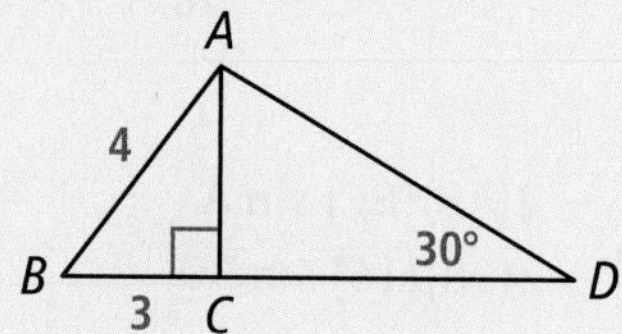

I. $\tan B = \frac{4}{3}$

II. $AD = 2\sqrt{7}$

III. $AB^2 = BD^2 + AD^2 - 2 \bullet (BD) \bullet (AD)\cos 30°$

Ⓐ I only
Ⓑ II only
Ⓒ III only
Ⓓ II and III only

28. Performance Task An amateur astronomer sets up his telescope in the center of a circular field. The field is surrounded by trees 20 m tall. The tripod holding the telescope pivots 1 m above the ground.

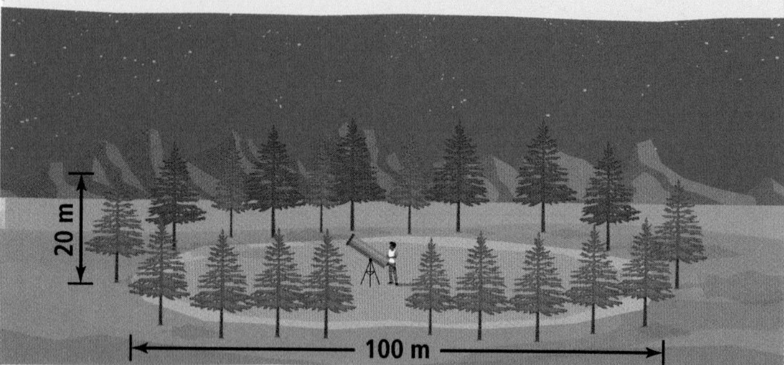

Part A What is the lowest angle of elevation at which the astronomer can observe a star?

Part B If the astronomer wants to observe a star 15° above the horizon to the east, how far west must the astronomer move the telescope to see the star?

Part C If the astronomer sets up the telescope in the center of the field on the bed of a truck 1.5 meters above the ground, what is the lowest angle at which he can observe?

  Activity  Assess

APPLICATION

EXAMPLE 5 Model With Sum and Difference Formulas

Noise-reducing headphones create a sound wave that effectively cancels out other noises around you. Does a noise with a sound wave modeled by $y = \sin(1{,}100\pi x)$ get cancelled out by another noise with a sound wave modeled by $y = \sin\left[1{,}100\pi\left(x - \frac{1}{220}\right)\right]$?

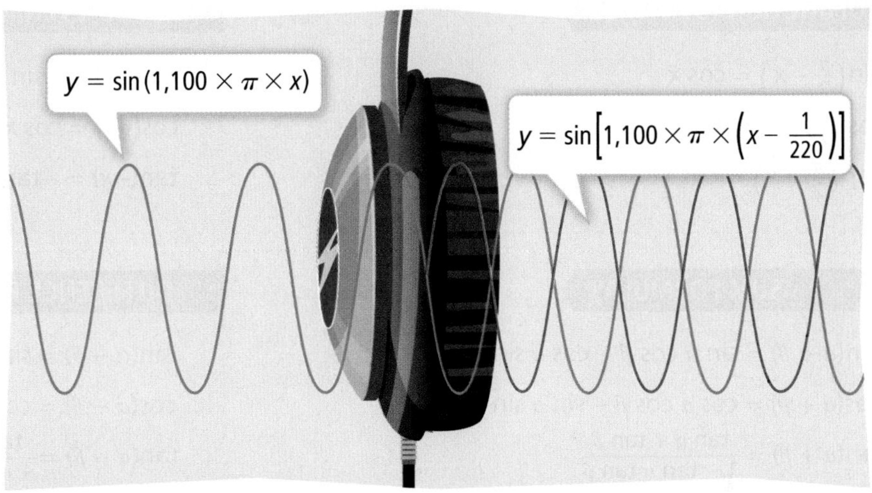

Formulate ◀ Add the sound waves together to combine the noises. If the two waves do, in fact, cancel each other out, their sum will be 0.

Compute ◀

$$\sin(1{,}100\pi x) + \sin\left[1{,}100\pi\left(x - \frac{1}{220}\right)\right]$$

$$= \sin(1{,}100\pi x) + \sin[1{,}100\pi x - 5\pi]$$

$$= \sin(1{,}100\pi x) + \sin(1{,}100\pi x)[\cos(5\pi)] - \cos(1{,}100\pi x)[\sin(5\pi)]$$

$$= \sin(1{,}100\pi x) + \sin(1{,}100\pi x)(-1) - \cos(1{,}100\pi x)(0)$$

$$= 0$$

Interpret ◀ Since the sum of the sound waves is 0 for all values of x, the noises cancel each other out.

 **Try It!** **5.** The sound wave for a musical note of A is modeled by $y = \sin(880\pi x)$. The sound wave for a different A note is modeled by $y = \sin\left[880\pi\left(x + \frac{1}{440}\right)\right]$. What is the simplified form of an equation that models the sound wave if the two notes are played at the same time?

CONCEPT SUMMARY Trigonometric Identities

QUOTIENT IDENTITY

$\tan x = \frac{\sin x}{\cos x}$

PYTHAGOREAN IDENTITY

$\sin^2 x + \cos^2 x = 1$

COFUNCTION IDENTITIES

$\sin\left(\frac{\pi}{2} - x\right) = \cos x$

$\cos\left(\frac{\pi}{2} - x\right) = \sin x$

$\tan\left(\frac{\pi}{2} - x\right) = \cot x$

ODD-EVEN IDENTITIES

$\sin(-x) = -\sin x$

$\cos(-x) = \cos x$

$\tan(-x) = -\tan x$

SUM FORMULAS

$\sin(\alpha + \beta) = \sin \alpha \cos \beta + \cos \alpha \sin \beta$

$\cos(\alpha + \beta) = \cos \alpha \cos \beta - \sin \alpha \sin \beta$

$\tan(\alpha + \beta) = \frac{\tan \alpha + \tan \beta}{1 - \tan \alpha \tan \beta}$

DIFFERENCE FORMULAS

$\sin(\alpha - \beta) = \sin \alpha \cos \beta - \cos \alpha \sin \beta$

$\cos(\alpha - \beta) = \cos \alpha \cos \beta + \sin \alpha \sin \beta$

$\tan(\alpha - \beta) = \frac{\tan \alpha - \tan \beta}{1 + \tan \alpha \tan \beta}$

Do You UNDERSTAND?

1. **ESSENTIAL QUESTION** How can you verify and apply relationships between trigonometric functions?

2. **Error Analysis** Sarah said that because of the odd-even identities, both the sine and cosine functions are odd functions. Explain and correct Sarah's error.

3. **Vocabulary** Explain what it means to say that $\cos(-x) = \cos x$ is a trigonometric identity.

4. **Reason** Why do the cofunction identities apply to an angle θ of any size?

5. **Make Sense and Persevere** How can the quotient identity help you to identify angles for which the tangent is undefined?

Do You KNOW HOW?

Verify each identity.

6. $\sin \theta \sec \theta \cot \theta = 1$

7. $\sec \theta \cot \theta = \csc \theta$

Find a simplified form of each expression.

8. $\frac{\tan \theta}{\sin \theta}$

9. $\frac{\sec \theta}{\sin \theta}(1 - \cos^2 \theta)$

Use a sum or difference formula to find the exact value of each of the following.

10. $\sin 15°$

11. $\cos 105°$

PRACTICE & PROBLEM SOLVING

Scan for Multimedia

Practice Tutorial

Additional Exercises Available Online

UNDERSTAND

12. **Generalize** Explain the process that is used to verify that a trigonometric equation is an identity.

13. **Construct Arguments** Benjamin said that he had worked out a trigonometric identity: $\cos 2\theta = \cos^2 \theta - \sin^2 \theta$. Is Benjamin correct? Explain.

14. **Mathematical Connections** Show that $f(x) = \tan x$ is an odd function by verifying that $\tan(-x) = -\tan x$.

15. **Error Analysis** Describe and correct the error a student made in applying the cosine difference formula to find the exact value of cos 15°.

$$\cos 15° = \cos(45° - 30°)$$
$$= \cos 45° \cos 30° - \sin 45° \sin 30°$$
$$= \frac{\sqrt{2}}{2} \cdot \frac{\sqrt{3}}{2} - \frac{\sqrt{2}}{2} \cdot \frac{1}{2}$$
$$= \frac{\sqrt{6}}{4} - \frac{\sqrt{2}}{4}$$
$$= \frac{\sqrt{6} - \sqrt{2}}{4}$$

✗

16. **Construct Arguments** Show that the quotient identity $\cot \theta = \frac{\cos \theta}{\sin \theta}$ is true algebraically.

17. **Higher Order Thinking** Use the Pythagorean Identity $\sin^2 x + \cos^2 x = 1$ to algebraically derive each of the following identities.

    a. $1 + \tan^2 x = \sec^2 x$

    b. $1 + \cot^2 x = \csc^2 x$

18. **Look for Relationships** Using the Pythagorean Identity, express $\sin \theta$ in terms of $\cos \theta$.

19. **Use Structure** Restate the Cofunction Identities using degrees instead of radians. What can you conclude about sin 15°? cos 60°?

PRACTICE

20. Does the relationship between $\csc(-\theta)$ and $-\csc \theta$ indicate whether $\csc \theta$ is odd or even? SEE EXAMPLE 1

21. Does the relationship between $\sec(-\theta)$ and $-\sec \theta$ indicate whether $\sec \theta$ is odd or even? SEE EXAMPLE 1

22. Does the relationship between $\cot(-\theta)$ and $-\cot \theta$ indicate whether $\cot \theta$ is odd or even? SEE EXAMPLE 1

Find a simplified form of each expression. SEE EXAMPLE 2

23. $\frac{\cos \theta}{\sin \theta \cot \theta}$

24. $[\cot(-x)](\sin x)$

Prove each of the following sum and difference formulas. SEE EXAMPLE 3

25. $\tan(\alpha + \beta) = \frac{\tan \alpha + \tan \beta}{1 - \tan \alpha \tan \beta}$

26. $\tan(\alpha - \beta) = \frac{\tan \alpha - \tan \beta}{1 + \tan \alpha \tan \beta}$

Find the exact value of each expression. Then evaluate the function on your calculator, comparing the calculator value to the approximation for your exact value. SEE EXAMPLE 4

27. tan 105°

28. $\sin\left(\frac{3\pi}{4} + \frac{5\pi}{6}\right)$

29. cos 225°

30. sin 75°

31. Does a noise with a sound wave modeled by $y = \sin(660\pi x)$ get cancelled out by another noise with a sound wave modeled by $y = \sin\left[660\pi\left(x - \frac{1}{220}\right)\right]$? Explain. SEE EXAMPLE 5

32. The sound wave for a musical note is modeled by $y = \sin(1{,}320\pi x)$. The sound wave for a different note is modeled by $y = \sin\left[1{,}320\pi\left(x + \frac{1}{220}\right)\right]$. What is the simplified form of an equation that models the sound wave if the two notes are played simultaneously? SEE EXAMPLE 5

PRACTICE & PROBLEM SOLVING

Practice Tutorial

Mixed Review Available Online

APPLY

33. **Make Sense and Persevere** The diagram shows a gear with a radius of 5 in. Point Q represents a 30° counterclockwise rotation of point $P(5, 0)$. Point R represents a further θ-degree rotation. The coordinates of R are $(5\cos(\theta + 30°), 5\sin(\theta + 30°))$. Express these coordinates in terms of $\cos\theta$ and $\sin\theta$.

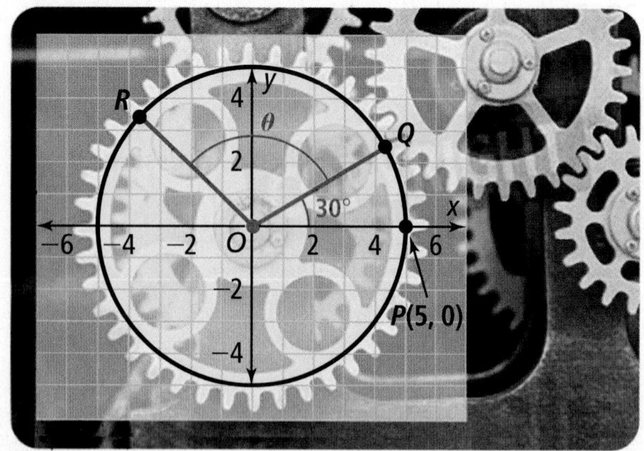

34. **Look for Relationships** The force required to push an object at a certain angle from its resting position can be modeled by $F = Mg\tan\theta$, where F is the force, M is the mass of the object, g is the acceleration due to gravity, and θ is the angle at which the object is being pushed. Write an equivalent equation for this formula in terms of $\sin\theta$ and $\sec\theta$.

35. **Reason** The length s of a shadow cast by a vertical *gnomon* (the column or shaft on a sundial that projects a shadow) of height h when the angle of the sun above the horizon is θ can be modeled by the equation $s = \frac{h\sin(90° - \theta)}{\sin\theta}$. Show that this equation is equivalent to $s = h\cot\theta$. (*Hint*: Convert degrees to radians and use a cofunction identity).

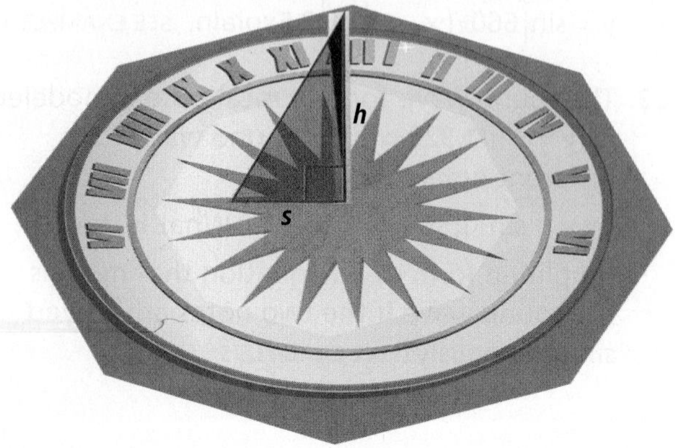

ASSESSMENT PRACTICE

36. Fill in each blank to complete an expression equivalent to $\frac{\csc x(\sin^2 x + \cos^2 x\tan x)}{\sin x + \cos x}$.

    a. $\sin^2 x +$ ______

    b. ________ $- \cos^2 x$

37. **SAT/ACT** Find the exact value of tan 75°.

    Ⓐ $2 + \sqrt{3}$

    Ⓑ $2 - \sqrt{3}$

    Ⓒ $-2 + \sqrt{3}$

    Ⓓ $-2 - \sqrt{3}$

38. **Performance Task** In order for motor vehicles to negotiate a curve in the road without skidding or running off of it, the angle of incline of the road must be determined. The angle of incline, or *angle of inclination,* is the nonnegative acute angle that the vehicle makes with the horizontal, and it is represented by the equation $\tan\theta = \frac{v^2}{gR}$, where R is the radius of the circular path, v is the speed that the vehicle is traveling in meters per second, and g is the acceleration due to gravity, 9.8 m/s^2.

Part A Find the angle of inclination of a curve with a 120-m radius, when a vehicle is traveling at 60 km/h (16.7 m/s) around the curve. Round to the nearest tenth of a degree.

Part B Write an equivalent equation in terms of $\sin\theta$, rather than $\tan\theta$.

TOPIC 7

Topic Review

TOPIC ESSENTIAL QUESTION

1. How do trigonometric identities and equations help you solve problems involving real or complex numbers?

Vocabulary Review

Choose the correct term to complete each sentence.

2. A(n) __________ is a trigonometric equation that is true for all values of the variable for which both sides of the equation are defined.
3. The angle formed by a horizontal line and a line of sight to an object above the line is a(n) __________ .
4. The __________ gives a relationship between the sine of each angle in a triangle and the length of the side opposite the angle.

- angle of depression
- angle of elevation
- Law of Sines
- Law of Cosines
- trigonometric identity

Concepts & Skills Review

LESSON 7-1 Solving Trigonometric Equations Using Inverses

Quick Review

An inverse trigonometric function allows you to input the values in a limited range of a trigonometric function and find the corresponding measure of an angle in the domain of the trigonometric function.

Example

Solve the trigonometric equation $5 \sin \theta = 3 \sin \theta + 1$ for values between 0 and 2π.

$5 \sin \theta = 3 \sin \theta + 1$ ········ Write the original equation.

$2 \sin \theta = 1$ ········ Subtract $3 \sin \theta$.

$\sin \theta = \frac{1}{2}$ ········ Divide by 2.

$\theta = \sin^{-1}\left(\frac{1}{2}\right)$ ········ Find the sine inverse.

$\theta = \frac{\pi}{6}$ ········ Solve.

Reflect the angle $\frac{\pi}{6}$ across the y-axis; that angle will also have a sine of $\frac{1}{2}$. That angle is $\pi - \frac{\pi}{6} = \frac{5\pi}{6}$.

Practice & Problem Solving

Evaluate each function. Angle values must be within the range of each inverse function. Give answers in radians and in degrees.

5. $\tan^{-1}(\sqrt{3})$
6. $\sin^{-1}\left(\frac{\sqrt{2}}{2}\right)$
7. $\tan^{-1}(-1)$
8. $\cos^{-1}\left(-\frac{1}{2}\right)$

Solve each trigonometric equation for values between 0 and 2π.

9. $3 \tan x - \sqrt{3} = 0$
10. $2 \cos x + \sqrt{2} = 0$
11. **Reason** Why is the domain of the inverse sine function restricted to the interval $[-1, 1]$?
12. **Make Sense and Persevere** A bird flies 78 ft from the top of a 4 ft tall bird feeder to the top of a 65 ft tree. To the nearest degree, find the angle of elevation of the line of sight from the top of the bird feeder to the top of the tree.

TOPIC 7 REVIEW

LESSON 7-2 Law of Sines and Law of Cosines

Quick Review

The Law of Sines and the Law of Cosines allow you to apply trigonometric functions to non-right triangles.

Law of Sines: $\frac{\sin A}{a} = \frac{\sin B}{b} = \frac{\sin C}{c}$

Law of Cosines: $a^2 = b^2 + c^2 - 2bc(\cos A)$

Example

In $\triangle ABC$, $m\angle A = 93°$, $a = 15$, and $b = 11$. To the nearest degree, what is $m\angle B$?

$\frac{\sin A}{a} = \frac{\sin B}{b}$ ······ Use the Law of Sines.

$\frac{\sin 93}{15} = \frac{\sin B}{11}$ ······ Substitute.

$\frac{11 \sin 93}{15} = \sin B$ ······ Isolate the sine function.

$\sin^{-1}\left(\frac{11 \sin 93}{15}\right) = B$ ······ Use the inverse sine function.

$m\angle B \approx 47°$ ······ Solve.

Practice & Problem Solving

Use the Law of Sines to solve.

13. In $\triangle MNP$, $m\angle N = 112°$, $n = 14$, and $p = 6$. What is $m\angle P$?

14. In $\triangle XYZ$, $m\angle X = 40°$, $m\angle Y = 25°$, and $x = 13$. What is y?

In $\triangle QRS$, find $m\angle Q$.

15. $q = 7$, $r = 6$, $s = 10$

16. $q = 8$, $r = 5$, $s = 6$

17. Look for Relationships How do you know whether to use the Law of Sines or the Law of Cosines to solve a problem?

18. Make Sense and Persevere Mark went to the beach, parked his car, and walked 500 yd down a path toward the beach. Mark then turned onto a boardwalk at a 125° angle to his path and walked another 140 yd along the boardwalk to a pier. If Mark turns to face his car, what angle does he turn?

LESSON 7-3 Problem Solving With Trigonometry

Quick Review

Many problems, such as those with angles of elevation or depression, can be modeled with triangles.

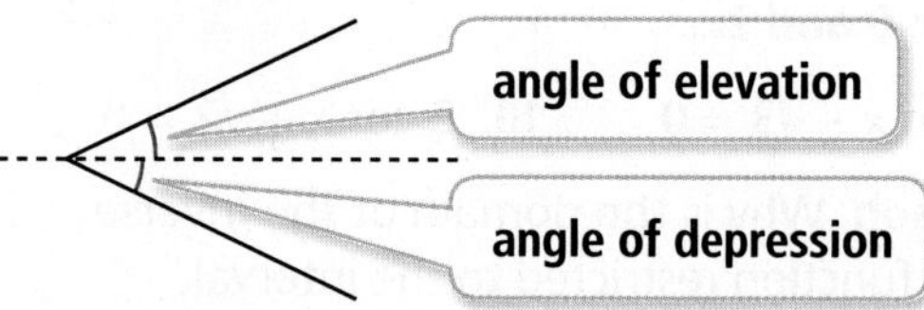

You can use trigonometric ratios, the Law of Sines, or the Law of Cosines to solve those problems.

Example

The angle of depression from the top to the bottom of a well is 62°. If the well is 4.5 feet in diameter, how deep is it?

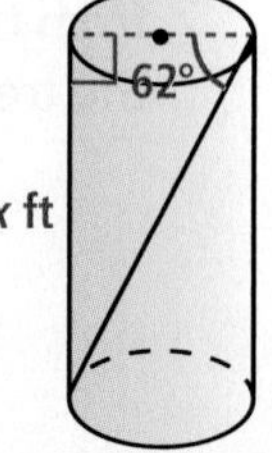

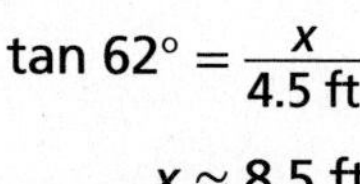

$\tan 62° = \frac{x}{4.5 \text{ ft}}$

$x \approx 8.5$ ft

Practice & Problem Solving

Find the area of each triangle.

19. **20.**

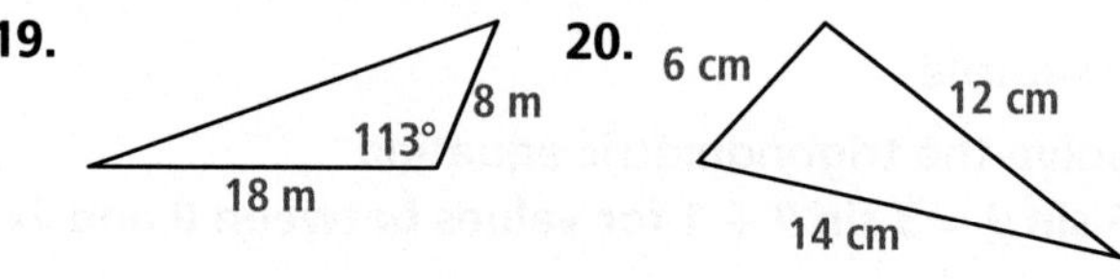

21. **22.**

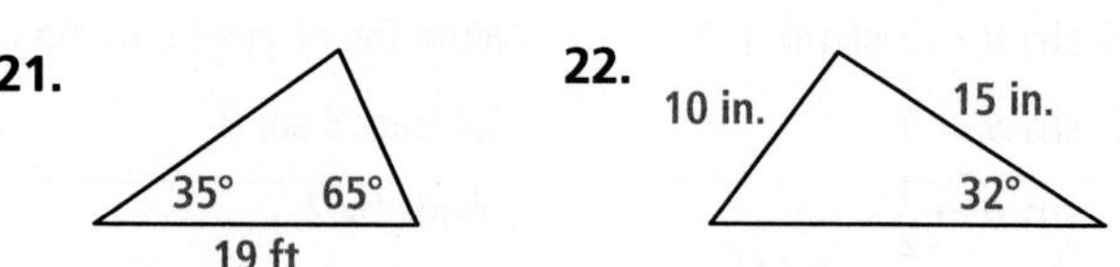

23. Communicate Precisely A hiker whose eyes are $5\frac{1}{2}$ feet above ground looks down at a kayaker on the far side of the river below. How could you find the approximate width of the river?

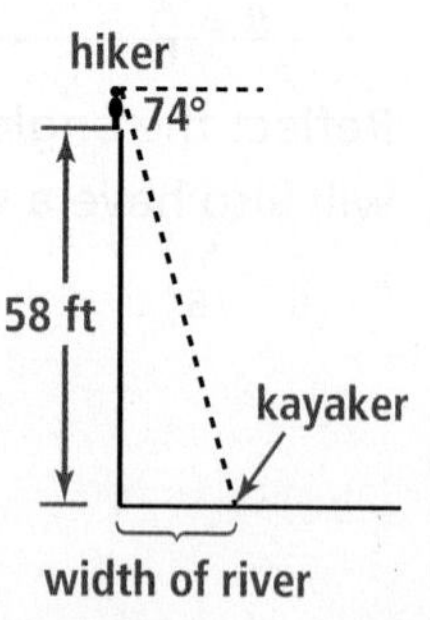

LESSON 7-4 Trigonometric Identities

Quick Review

Quotient Identity: $\tan x = \frac{\sin x}{\cos x}$

Pythagorean Identity: $\sin^2 x + \cos^2 x = 1$

Cofunction Identities: $\sin\left(\frac{\pi}{2} - x\right) = \cos x$

$\cos\left(\frac{\pi}{2} - x\right) = \sin x$

Odd-Even Identities: $\sin(-x) = -\sin x$

$\cos(-x) = \cos x$

Sum and Difference Formulas:

$\sin(\alpha \pm \beta) = \sin\alpha\cos\beta \pm \cos\alpha\sin\beta$

$\cos(\alpha \pm \beta) = \cos\alpha\cos\beta \mp \sin\alpha\sin\beta$

$\tan(\alpha \pm \beta) = \frac{\tan\alpha \pm \tan\beta}{1 \mp \tan\alpha\tan\beta}$

Example

What is the simplified form of $\frac{\csc^2 x - 1}{\csc^2 x}$?

$\frac{\csc^2 x - 1}{\csc^2 x} = \frac{\csc^2 x}{\csc^2 x} - \frac{1}{\csc^2 x}$ Rewrite the fraction.

$= 1 - \sin^2 x$ Use the definition of sine.

$= \cos^2 x$ Apply the Pythagorean Identity.

Practice & Problem Solving

Use a trigonometric identity to write a different form of each expression.

24. $\tan^2 x + 1$

25. $\tan x + \cot x$

26. $\frac{1 + \tan^2 x}{1 - \tan^2 x}$

27. $\frac{\sec x - 1}{\sec x + 1}$

Find the exact value of each expression. Then evaluate the function on your calculator. Compare the calculator value to your exact value.

28. $\sin 15°$

29. $\cos 105°$

30. $\tan\left(\frac{\pi}{4} + \frac{\pi}{3}\right)$

31. $\cos\left(\frac{\pi}{4} - \frac{\pi}{6}\right)$

32. Use Structure Find expressions for $\sin 2\theta$ and $\cos 2\theta$.

33. Model With Mathematics Is a noise with a sound wave modeled by $y = \sin(1{,}500\pi x)$ cancelled out by another noise with a sound wave modeled by $y = \sin\left[1{,}500\pi\left(x - \frac{1}{250}\right)\right]$? Explain.

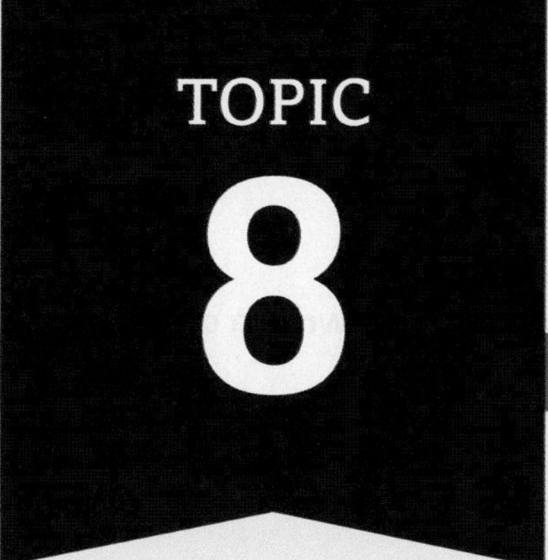

Data Analysis and Statistics

TOPIC ESSENTIAL QUESTION

What questions can you answer by using statistics and normal distributions?

Topic Overview

Topic Vocabulary

- alternative hypothesis
- bias
- control group
- experiment
- experimental group
- margin of error
- normal distribution
- null hypothesis
- observational study
- parameter
- random sample
- sample survey
- sampling distribution
- standard deviation
- statistic
- *z*-score

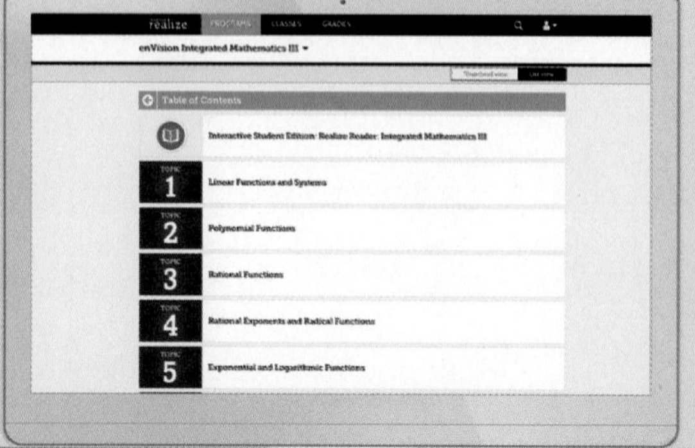

Go online | **PearsonRealize.com**

Digital Experience

INTERACTIVE STUDENT EDITION Access online or offline.

ACTIVITIES Complete ***Explore & Reason, Model & Discuss***, and ***Critique & Explain*** activities. Interact with Examples and Try Its.

ANIMATION View and interact with real-world applications.

PRACTICE Practice what you've learned.

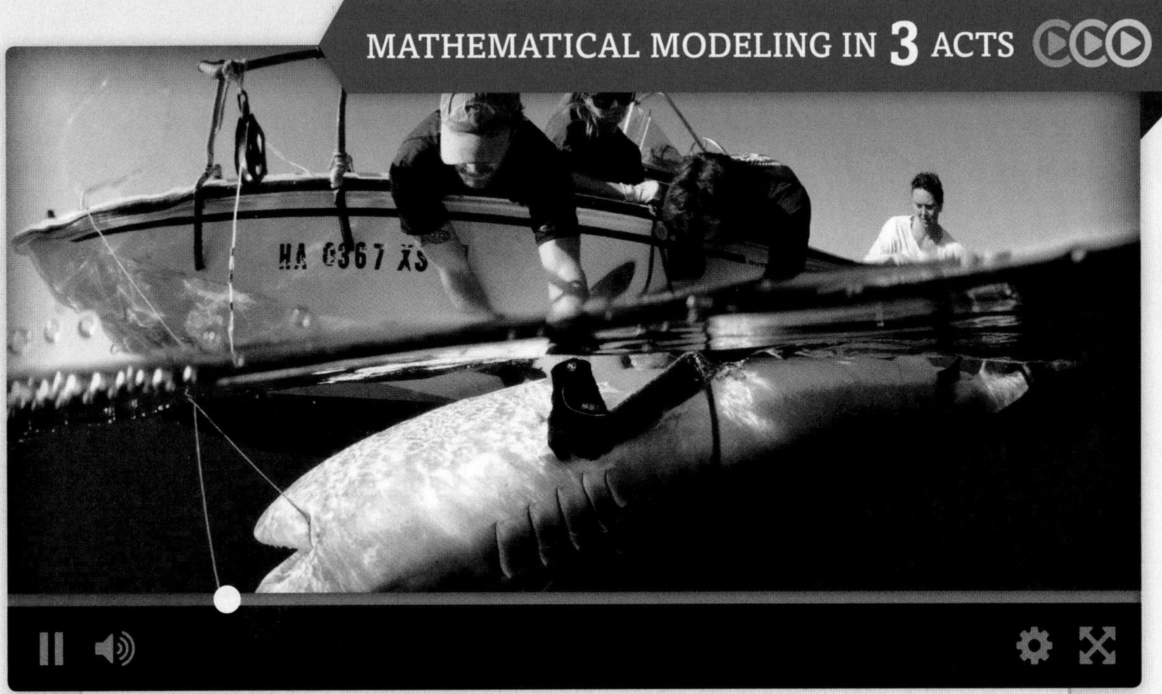

Mark and Recapture

It wouldn't take very long for you to count the number of people who live in your home or the number of socks in your drawer. How about the number of deer in Yellowstone National Park or the number of sharks in the waters around Hawaii?

The mark and recapture method is a popular way researchers can estimate an animal population. You will see an example of this method in the Mathematical Modeling in 3 Acts lesson.

TOPIC 8

VIDEOS Watch clips to support ***Mathematical Modeling in 3 Acts Lessons*** and **enVision®** ***STEM Projects.***

CONCEPT SUMMARY Review key lesson content through multiple representations.

ASSESSMENT Show what you've learned.

GLOSSARY Read and listen to English and Spanish definitions.

TUTORIALS Get help from ***Virtual Nerd***, right when you need it.

MATH TOOLS Explore math with digital tools and manipulatives.

Video

Did You Know?

Community officials and planners use **surveys and statistics** to decide how best to use public spaces.

How Would You Use Your Park?

Camping

Cycling

Picnicking

Hiking

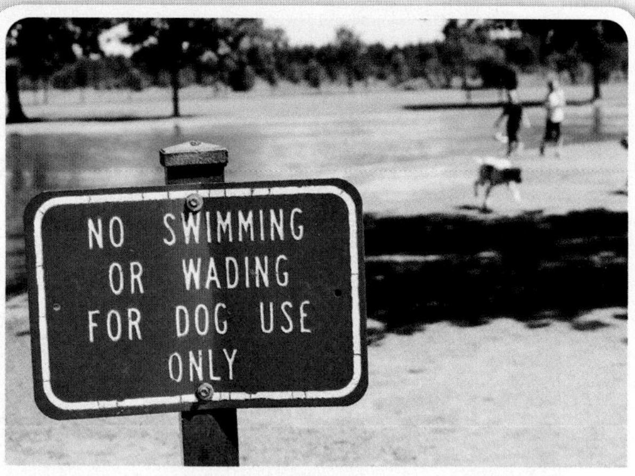

Dog parks are the fastest-growing type of urban park in the United States. Off-leash dog parks encourage **physical activity** and **social interaction**.

Public spaces come in different shapes and sizes. The many uses of public spaces include **ice-skating, bicycling, and skateboarding.**

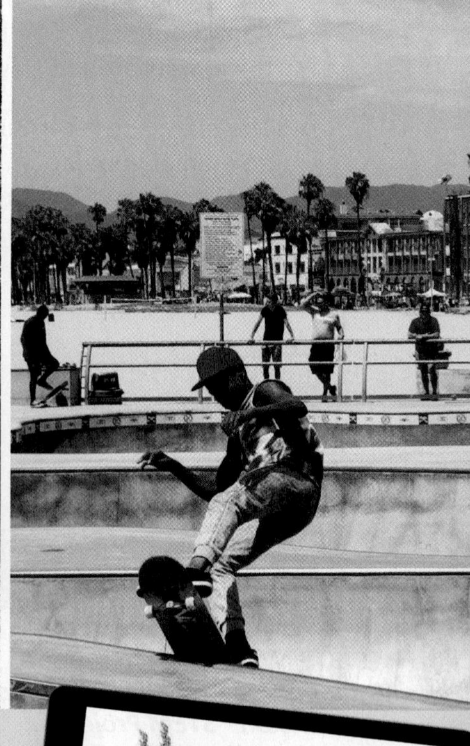

Your Task: Plan a Public Space

You and your classmates will draft a survey about preferred uses of a public space and poll your community. You will analyze and present the data along with your conclusions.

8-1 Statistical Questions and Variables

I CAN… use vocabulary related to statistical questions and variables.

VOCABULARY

- categorical variable
- parameter
- population
- quantitative variable
- sample
- statistic
- statistical question
- statistical variable

EXPLORE & REASON

A state questioned some of its high schools about the price they were charging for prom tickets. The results are summarized in the histogram.

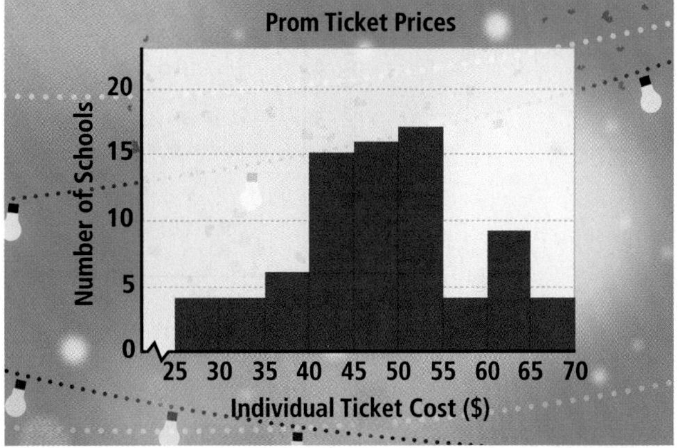

A. What questions can be answered using the data in this histogram?

B. Who might be interested in the answers to these questions? Explain.

C. Construct Arguments Anastasia is surprised that the median cost of a prom ticket is not higher, given that her school is charging $60 per ticket. What are some possible reasons for the data not conforming to her expectations?

ESSENTIAL QUESTION

What kinds of questions about quantities and relationships among quantities can be answered with statistics?

APPLICATION

EXAMPLE 1 Understand Statistical Questions

A. Consider the following questions.

I. "*In what month is your birthday?*"

II. "*What month has the most birthdays of students at your school?*"

What is the difference between the two questions?

Question I can be answered using one piece of information.

Question II can be answered by collecting many pieces of information and summarizing them.

Question I could be asked as *part* of an investigation into Question II. But a specific interview question is different from the general statistical question the investigation is trying to answer.

Question II is a **statistical question** because it can be answered by collecting many pieces of information, or data, and summarizing the data.

STUDY TIP
The answers to statistical questions can be summarized in different types of displays such as bar graphs, line graphs, scatter plots, and frequency charts.

CONTINUED ON THE NEXT PAGE

EXAMPLE 1 CONTINUED

B. Does each graph represent the answer to a statistical question?

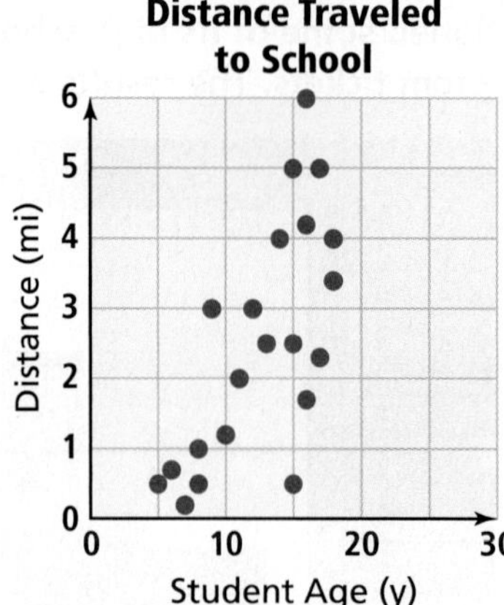

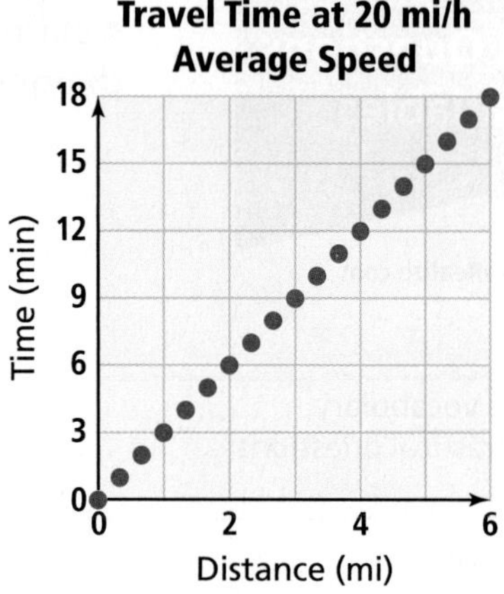

COMMON ERROR
The word *"data"* is a plural noun, so use it with plural verbs like *"these data are"* or *"the data indicate."* However, *"set"* and *"value"* are singular, so use singular verbs for them, like *"this data set is"* or *"the data value is."*

The graph of distance traveled to school is a scatter plot and represents some students' answers to the question *"How far do you travel to get to school?"* This is a statistical question because it is answered by gathering and summarizing varying data about many students.

The graph of travel time is a function model and represents answers to the question *"How long does it take to travel x miles at 20 mi/h?"* This is a question that has a predetermined answer. The answer varies predictably with x, so it is not a statistical question.

 **Try It!** 1. Is the given question a statistical question?

a. "Which is the most popular visual art form: photography, painting, sculpting, or drawing?"

b. "How many lithographs were created by the artist M.C. Escher?"

CONCEPTUAL UNDERSTANDING

EXAMPLE 2 Understand Statistical Variables

COMMUNICATE PRECISELY
Variables in mathematics can be used to represent an unknown number, such as the price of a shirt at a store. Statistical variables represent a quantity that varies between observations, such as the price of the shirt at every store in the country.

A. What type of statistical variable is represented by the following question and corresponding chart?

"What is your favorite Summer Olympic sport?"

A **statistical variable** is a quantity or quality that can be measured or counted, and for which data are expected to differ from one observation to another. Two main types are categorical and quantitative.

Answers to the question above will be different Olympic sports, as shown by the chart summarizing the various responses. Data that fall into categories, or that indicate a qualitative rather than quantitative attribute, represent a **categorical variable.** "Favorite Olympic sport"

CONTINUED ON THE NEXT PAGE

EXAMPLE 2 CONTINUED

is a categorical variable because the values belong to a limited set of possible categories.

B. What type of statistical variable is represented by the following question and corresponding graph?

"What is the typical number of apps a teenager has on a smartphone?"

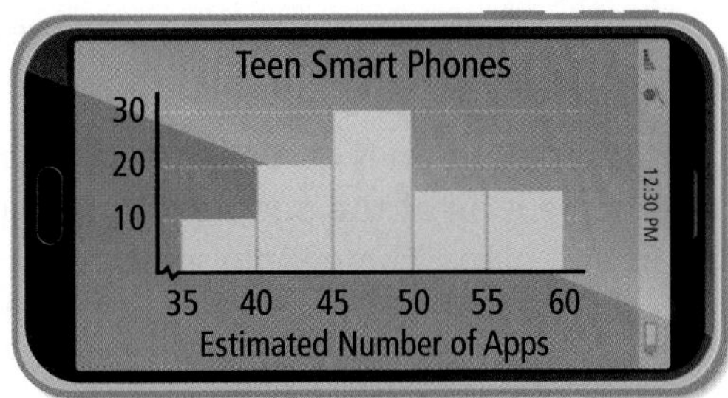

STUDY TIP
Some variables, such as month or semester grade, can be categorical or quantitative depending on the context.

Responses to this question are *quantities* representing the number of apps on a phone. Numerical data like these, that in the context of the data can be compared, added, subtracted or otherwise operated on, represent a second type of statistical variable, a **quantitative variable.** "Number of apps on a phone" is a quantitative variable because the values are numbers that you could meaningfully count, add, subtract and so on.

Try It! 2. What is the statistical variable represented by each of the following questions, and is it categorical or quantitative?

a. *"What breed of dog is most likely to be adopted from an animal shelter?"*

b. *"What is the average number of students per activity participating in after-school activities at Jefferson High School?"*

APPLICATION

EXAMPLE 3 Distinguish Between Populations and Samples

A. A school newspaper randomly selects 30 students from each grade level to participate in a survey to determine the opinions of students at the school. What is the relationship between the sophomores surveyed, all the students surveyed, and all the students at the school?

In statistics, the set of all members of a group that you want to know something about is called a **population**. The group of all the students at the school is the population that the school newspaper is studying in their survey.

COMMON ERROR
In statistics, a "population" does not have to be made up of people. The population is whatever whole group that is under statistical study—it could be a group of corporations, a group of bodies of water, or a group of cars of different models.

CONTINUED ON THE NEXT PAGE

EXAMPLE 3 CONTINUED

A **sample** is a subset of the population that is being studied to answer a statistical question about the population. The group of all the students who were surveyed is a sample of all the students at the school, as is the group of sophomores who were surveyed.

B. A polling organization randomly chose eligible voters in the state of Illinois to ask who they would vote for in an upcoming election for governor, to determine who will win the election. What are the sample and the population in this scenario?

The population is all the voters in Illinois who are eligible to vote. The sample is all of the people the polling organization asked about their voting plans. The people selected by the polling organization are a subset of the voting population of Illinois.

 **Try It!** **3.** A city worker collects five vials of water from each of ten randomly selected locations all over the city to test the levels of bacteria in the city water supply.

a. What is the sample in this experiment?

b. What is the population?

APPLICATION

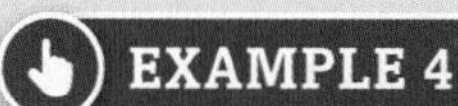

EXAMPLE 4 Distinguish Between Parameters and Statistics

Is each quantity a statistic or a parameter?

A. A high school has three lunch periods. In a randomly selected lunch period, 24% of students brought lunch from home.

A **parameter** is a measure that describes a population. A **statistic** is a measure that describes a sample of the population. In this situation, the population is the set of all students in the school. The figure 24% describes a sample of that population, the students who were in the selected lunch period. Therefore, it is a statistic.

GENERALIZE
Categorical data are often summarized using proportions while quantitative data are often summarized using a median or a mean.

B. At the end of its first year of business, a movie theater collected data on how well its concession stand operated that year. The theater used its total yearly concessions sales and number of tickets sold to calculate that the mean amount spent at concessions by a moviegoer was $8.14. Is this a statistic or a parameter?

The value $8.14 describes the concession purchases of all of the moviegoers who attended the theater that year. This value is a parameter since the theater included all moviegoers to determine how well the concession stand is doing.

Try It! **4.** Is the given data summary a parameter or statistic?

a. 53.2% of a district's eligible voters voted for the sitting U.S. House Representative.

b. The median age of a car in 20 randomly selected spaces in the school parking lot is 7 years.

CONCEPT SUMMARY Statistics and Statistical Variables

A statistical question is a question that can be answered by collecting many pieces of information, or data.

"What is the average number of pets owned by students at your school?"

"What is the most popular type of pet owned by students at your school?"

Number of Pets	Types of Pets		
	Dog	Cat	Other
3	X	X	
0			
1			X
⋮	⋮	⋮	⋮

The value of a statistical variable will vary from one observation to another.

A quantitative variable has numerical values that can be meaningfully compared, added, subtracted, or otherwise operated upon.

A categorical variable has a limited number of possible responses that are not quantitative.

A parameter is a piece of information about a variable that is based on the entire population, or group of people or things that is being studied.

A statistic is a piece of information about a variable that is based on a sample or subgroup chosen from the population.

Do You UNDERSTAND?

1. ESSENTIAL QUESTION What kinds of questions about quantities and relationships among quantities can be answered with statistics?

2. **Error Analysis** Dyani says she identified a quantitative variable and conducted a survey when she asked her fellow classmates in her homeroom about their favorite style of sweatshirt from the categories: hoodie, pullover, or zip-up. Explain her error.

3. **Vocabulary** Explain the difference between a categorical variable and a quantitative variable.

4. **Communicate Precisely** Suppose Hana wants to find out the most commonly driven type of vehicle among the students at her high school. Since 1,560 students attend her high school, she asks every tenth student who enters the building one morning what kind of vehicle he or she drives. What is the population in this scenario?

Do You KNOW HOW?

5. Is the following question a statistical question?

   "During which month did your family take a vacation?"

6. What is the statistical variable represented by the following question, and is it categorical or quantitative?

   "How many TV sets are owned by families?"

7. Forty randomly-selected members of a high school music program were asked to report the number of hours they spend practicing each week. If you were to compute the mean number of hours, would your answer be a parameter or a statistic? Explain.

Scan for Multimedia

Additional Exercises Available Online

UNDERSTAND

8. Communicate Precisely Does the scatterplot below relate to a statistical question? Explain.

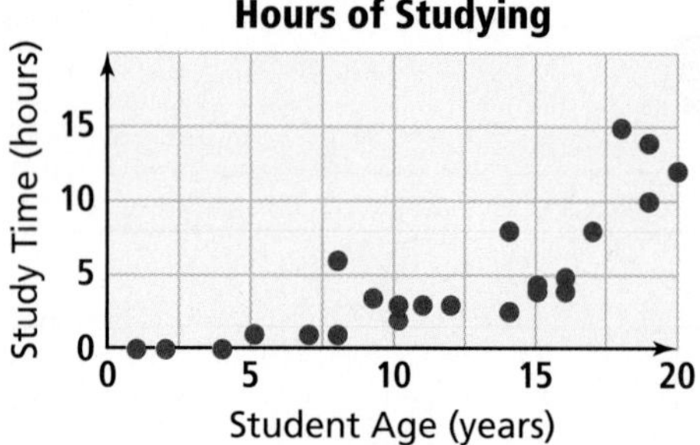

9. Make Sense and Persevere At the end of the month, a restaurant manager used the total food sales for the month and the total number of customers for the month to calculate that the mean amount spent per customer during that month was $12.59. Is this value a statistic or a parameter? Explain.

10. Error Analysis Describe and correct the error a student made in responding to the question regarding the following scenario.

A Detroit, Michigan, radio station polled its listeners about whether they supported a citywide tax increase to renovate the city's professional football stadium to determine whether city residents support the increase. What are the sample and the population in this scenario?

> The sample is the listeners of the radio station.
> The population is all the registered voters in the state of Michigan. ✗

11. Higher Order Thinking Write a response to the following items regarding statistical variables.

a. Write a statistical question that uses a categorical variable.

b. Write a statistical question that uses a quantitative variable.

PRACTICE

12. Is the given question a statistical question? Explain. SEE EXAMPLE 1

a. *"What is the tallest building in Chicago, Illinois?"*

b. *"What is the most popular store in the Turtlecreek Mall among teenagers?"*

13. What type of statistical variable is represented by the graph shown? SEE EXAMPLE 2

Most Popular H.S. Sport to Watch

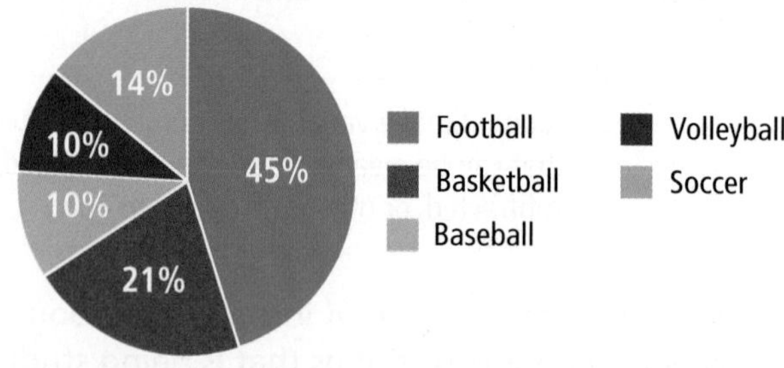

14. A biology teacher wants to know which dissection his students liked best this semester, so he randomly selects eight students from each of his five classes to participate in a survey.

a. What is the sample in this situation?

b. What is the population? SEE EXAMPLE 3

15. The data below were collected from all race participants to answer the question, "What is the average age of runners in the Fall Harvest 5K?" Does this histogram represent data related to a parameter or statistic? Explain your response. SEE EXAMPLE 4

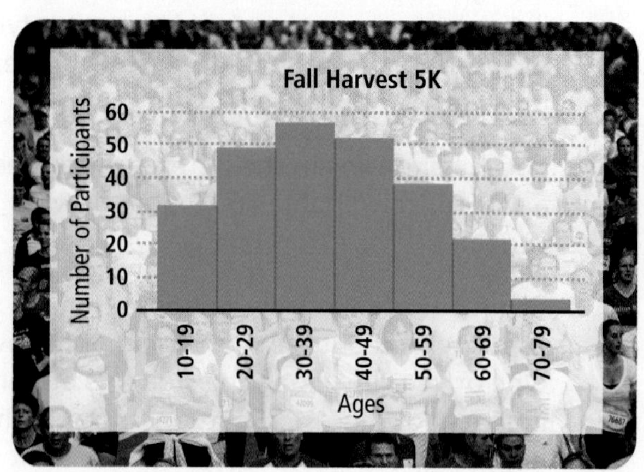

PRACTICE & PROBLEM SOLVING

Practice Tutorial

Mixed Review Available Online

APPLY

16. Is the given question a statistical question? Explain.

a. *"Which is the most popular category of children's literature: biography, science fiction, fantasy, or mystery?"*

b. *"For which category of children's literature is J.K. Rowling best known?"*

17. Make Sense and Persevere Can the graph below be helpful in answering a statistical question? Explain.

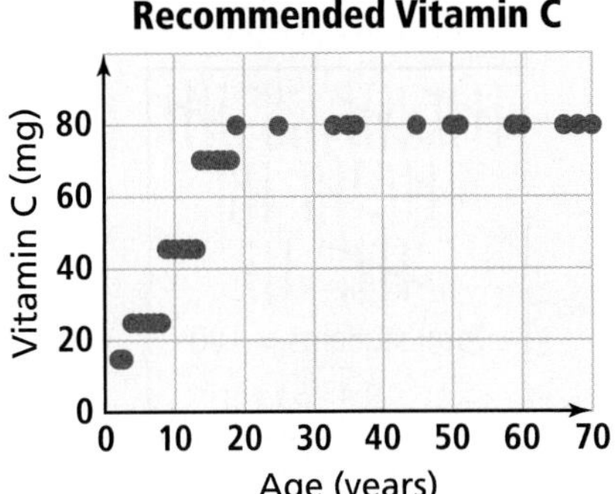

18. Use Structure What type of statistical variable is represented by the following question and corresponding graph?

"How many pets does your family own?"

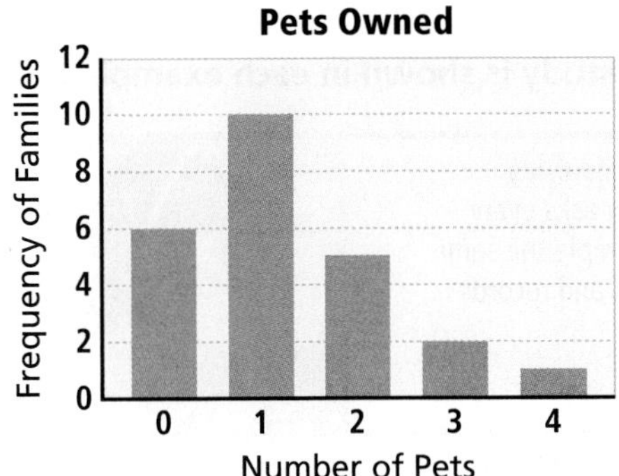

19. Look For Relationships Ms. Lee wants to know what kinds of things her students do to prepare for her tests. Ms. Lee placed the names of her students into a box. To determine who she would ask about their study habits she asked a student to draw names from the box.

a. What is the sample in this situation?

b. What is the population?

ASSESSMENT PRACTICE

20. The average length of all the trout in a river is 60 cm. This data summary represents a ____________. (parameter/statistic)

21. SAT/ACT If the Hamilton High School freshmen class is the sample in a statistical study, then which is **not** a possible population for the study?

Ⓐ the student body of Hamilton High School

Ⓑ the students in Hamilton High School's district

Ⓒ the students in Ms. Anderson's science class

Ⓓ all freshmen students in the state

22. Performance Task A state randomly questioned some of its high schools about the average percentages of their students who attend home football games. The results are summarized in the histogram below.

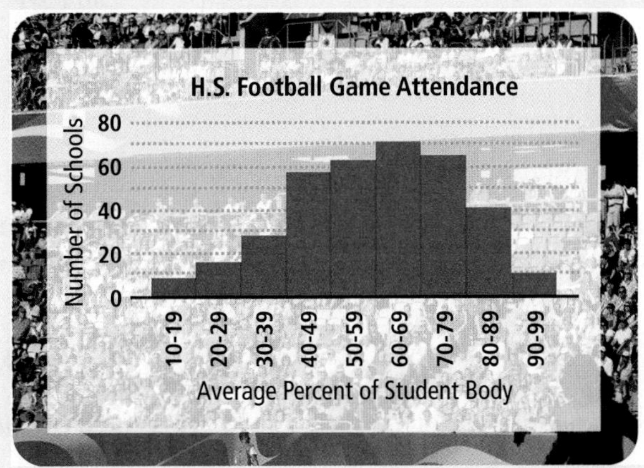

Part A Describe the population and the sample for these data. Are these data quantitative or categorical? Explain.

Part B What is an example of a statistical question that could be answered with these data?

Part C Joshua was surprised that the median of the data was not a much lower number. What is a possible reason that Joshua could be surprised by these results?

8-2 Statistical Studies and Sampling Methods

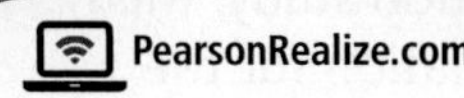
PearsonRealize.com

I CAN… design a statistical study.

VOCABULARY
- bias
- control group
- experiment
- experimental group
- observational study
- sample survey
- simple random sample

Activity Assess

CRITIQUE & EXPLAIN

Jacinta and Felix were each asked to design a study to answer the question: "What proportion of students at this school listen to music while studying?"

A. What group did Jacinta select from to conduct her study? What group did Felix select from?

B. How did Jacinta choose which members of her group to question? How did Felix choose which members from his group to observe?

C. Look for Relationships Who designed a better study, Jacinta or Felix? Explain.

Jacinta

Friends in Gym Class	yes	no
Cameron	X	
Dana	X	
Emma		X
Henry		X
Jung	X	
Keisha		X
Marisol		X

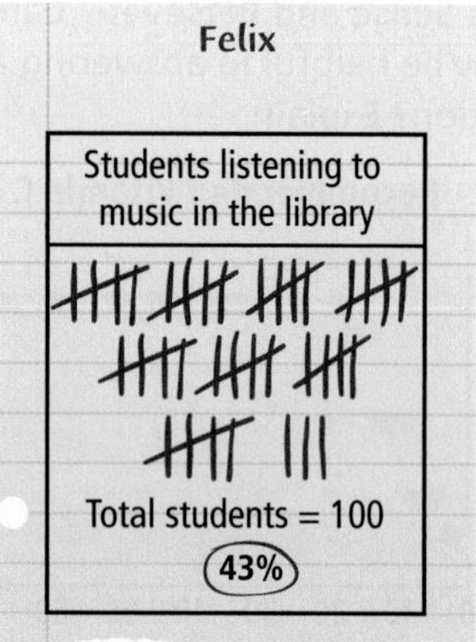

ESSENTIAL QUESTION

How can you choose the best type of study to answer a given statistical question and choose a reasonable sample?

EXAMPLE 1 Choose a Type of Study

A. Which of the three main types of study is shown in each example below?

A newspaper polls randomly selected residents in a town about which mayoral candidate they prefer.

This is a **sample survey**. A sample survey asks every member of a sample the same set of questions and records the answers.

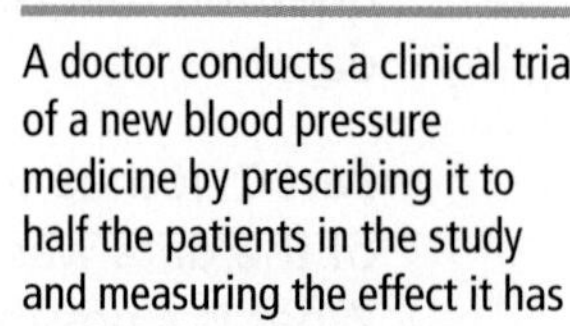
A doctor conducts a clinical trial of a new blood pressure medicine by prescribing it to half the patients in the study and measuring the effect it has on their blood pressure.

This is an **experiment**. An experiment involves applying a treatment to some group or groups and measuring the affects of the treatments.

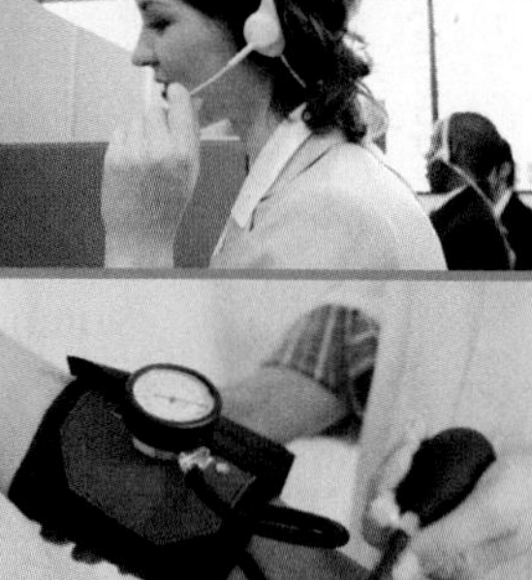

A grocery store wonders how many customers bring reusable grocery bags to the store. They have an employee stand at the checkout and count the number of people using reusable bags.

This is an **observational study**. In an observational study, you measure or observe members of a sample in such a way that they are not affected by the study.

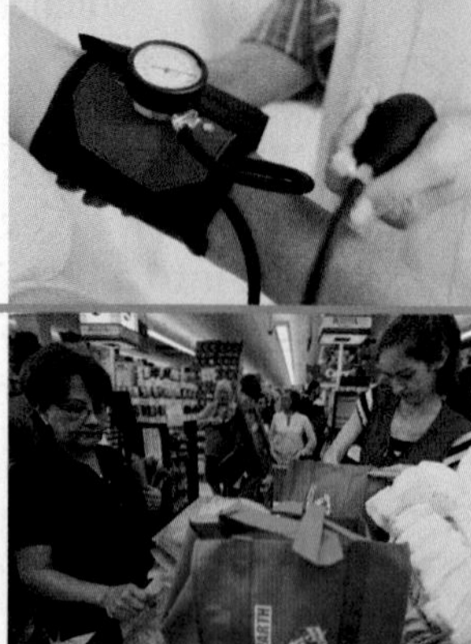

LOOK FOR RELATIONSHIPS
In which type of study might a person be unaware that he or she is a participant?

CONTINUED ON THE NEXT PAGE

EXAMPLE 1 CONTINUED

B. What type of study could you use to answer the following questions?

Question	Study
Does urban pollution have an effect on rates of asthma?	Observational study: observe residents of urban and non-urban areas, and compare the rates of asthma over a long period of time.
How many students in a school would like the cafeteria to serve breakfast?	Sample survey: ask randomly chosen students in the school their opinion and record the results.
A group of plants is not growing well compared to the rest. What should you change to improve their growth?	Experiment: split the plants into groups randomly, and give each group different conditions such as more light, more water, or different fertilizer. Leave one group under the current conditions to see if the new treatments show improvement.

COMMON ERROR

Conducting an experiment might be the most efficient way to answer a question, but it may be unethical to do so. For example, you would not intentionally expose people to pollution to test its affect on asthma rates. In these cases, an observational study is more appropriate.

Try It! 1. What type of study is described?

a. A gym asks its customers if they would prefer the gym to open earlier in the morning.

b. A gym tries out a new weightlifting method to see if it will build muscle for their customers faster than their current method.

c. A gym counts the customers who come before 8 A.M.

CONCEPTUAL UNDERSTANDING

Determine Sources of Bias

In the following situations, are the differences between groups potentially due to bias?

A. A psychologist is conducting surveys to study the happiness levels of people who live in a neighborhood. She asks the same questions to the two samples below chosen from the population of the neighborhood.

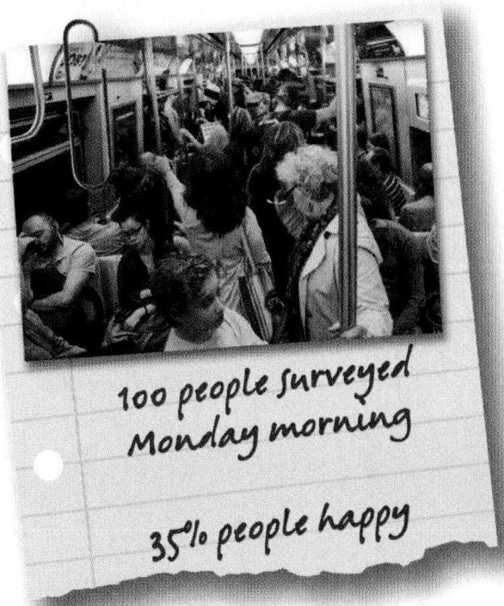

The difference between the results of these surveys is due to bias, because the circumstances when the two samples were surveyed may influence their responses. A study has **bias** if it systematically produces results that misrepresent a population.

STUDY TIP

Personal bias, or a personal inclination for or against something, and statistical bias are different. While personal bias can lead to statistical bias, statistical bias has many other possible causes.

CONTINUED ON THE NEXT PAGE

Activity

Assess

EXAMPLE 2 CONTINUED

Bias might also arise if a sample is more likely to include a certain category of the population than another. For example, a poll on a website is more likely to select frequent Internet users than those who do not go online often.

Bias can be introduced in other ways. For example, a survey might have questions that influence the answers in some way.

B. A school wants to know the average height of its students. The school randomly chooses some students and measures their height. Some students are under 5 feet tall and some are over 6 feet, 5 inches tall.

MAKE SENSE AND PERSEVERE
Why should you determine whether any differences in the collected data are due to a biased study or from natural variability in a population?

The fact that some of the data collected are either very high or very low is not necessarily the result of bias. A population like students in a high school will naturally have people with a wide variety of heights. A true random sample may have members from both extremes.

Try It! 2. A soft drink company calls 500 people at random and asks, "Is our product or our rival's product the best soft drink on the market?" Why is this question a potential source of bias?

CONCEPT Sampling Methods

In order to select a sample that is likely to be representative of the population, you need to choose members of the sample using randomness. The simplest way to use randomness is with a **simple random sample**. In a simple random sample, each member of the population is equally likely to chosen, and each possible sample of the size you want is equally likely to be chosen.

Some sampling methods can involve randomness in other ways to select a sample. Some sampling methods do not use enough randomness to give reliable results.

Care must be taken to avoid bias.			High Risk of Bias	
Stratified sampling is when a population is divided into groups with similar characteristics and a sample is randomly chosen from each group.	Cluster sampling is when a population is divided into convenient clusters, and entire clusters are chosen at random as the sample.	Systematic sampling is when you start with one member chosen at random then use a rule, such as "every 3rd member of the population," to select members of the sample.	Convenience sampling is only choosing subjects that are in close proximity or easy to get to.	Self-selected sampling is using a sample made up of volunteers.

EXAMPLE 3 Identify a Sampling Method

What sampling method is used in the following examples? Is the method likely to be biased?

Study	Sampling Method
A. Starting with a randomly chosen ID number, every fifth student ID number was chosen and that student was asked to fill out a survey.	This is systematic sampling. The rule is that every fifth number was chosen. This method unlikely to be biased.
B. A retailer put feedback cards at the front of its store. They got responses from 22% of their customers.	This is a self-selected sample, which only includes people who decided to respond to the survey. This method is not random and likely biased.
C. A city wants to know what percent of people in the city own a dog or a cat. A city worker goes door to door in the neighborhood around city hall to ask people about their pets.	This is convenience sampling because only the neighborhood around city hall was sampled. The process is likely to be biased because pets may be more or less common in other parts of the city.

CONSTRUCT ARGUMENTS
How could you redesign the biased studies here so that the samples are not biased?

Try It! **3.** What sampling method is used in the following examples? Is the method likely to be biased or not?

a. The population is grouped according to age and a random sample is chosen from each group.

b. A number of hospitals around the country were randomly chosen. Within each hospital, all of the nurses were chosen.

APPLICATION

EXAMPLE 4 Randomize Experiments

Describe a design for a controlled experiment to test a new drug for treating the flu on mice. How does randomization apply to your design?

In a simple controlled experiment, randomly assign mice to one of two groups. One group, the **experimental group**, receives the treatment. The other group, the **control group**, does not. Then use statistics to compare the effect of the treatment to the effect of no treatment.

Mice are assigned randomly to either group, and all mice are infected with the flu. The control group does not receive the drug. The experimental group receives the new drug. The results are analyzed to see whether the new drug affects the progression of flu in a way that is significantly different from receiving no treatment. The random assignment to experimental and control groups should ensure that the difference between the two groups is due to the drug rather than some other cause.

STUDY TIP
Some experiments can have more than two groups, especially if you are testing multiple variables. Some experiments do not have a control group and just compare different treatments.

Try It! **4.** Design an experiment to test whether drinking coffee improves memory. How will you choose the experimental and control groups?

  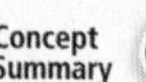 

CONCEPT SUMMARY Statistical Studies and Sampling Methods

TYPES OF STUDIES

- An **experiment** involves randomly dividing a population into two groups, applying a different treatment to each group, and measuring the difference between the treatments.
- A **sample survey** asks every member of a randomly selected sample the same set of questions and records the answers to try to draw a conclusion about the population.
- In an **observational study,** you do not assign treatments to the subjects being studied. The subjects are already affected by the treatments under investigation.

TYPES OF SAMPLING

Care must be taken to avoid bias.			High Risk of Bias	
Stratified sampling is when a population is divided into groups with similar characteristics and a sample is randomly chosen from each group.	Cluster sampling is when a population is divided into convenient clusters, and entire clusters are chosen at random as the sample.	Systematic sampling is when you start with one member chosen at random then use a rule, such as "every 3rd member of the population," to select members of the sample.	Convenience sampling is only choosing subjects that are in close proximity or easy to get to.	Self-selected sampling is using a sample made up of volunteers.

Do You UNDERSTAND?

1. ESSENTIAL QUESTION How can you choose the best type of study to answer given statistical question and choose a reasonable sample?

2. **Vocabulary** A city is weighing whether to increase fares for public transit, or to provide more funding to public transit through the city's general fund, which is primarily funded by local property taxes. A survey of public transit riders was conducted to determine popular opinion. What is this sampling method an example of?

3. **Error Analysis** When Lila conducted an experiment on citywide pond water, all of her samples came from the pond in her uncle's backyard. Explain her error.

Do You KNOW HOW?

4. An ice cream shop asks its customers if they would like the shop to offer containers of ice cream to take home. What type of study does this describe?

5. A television news program asks its viewers to call in to give their opinions on an upcoming ballot question. What type of sampling method does this represent?

6. A doctor assigns people to treatment groups based on data from their medical records. Is this method of selecting treatment groups biased or unbiased? Explain.

PRACTICE & PROBLEM SOLVING

UNDERSTAND

7. **Reason** Suppose a civic engineer wants to conduct a survey to find out if residents of a city would be in favor of widening one of the city's roadways for increased traffic flow.

   a. Would a sample consisting of residents who utilize that roadway to travel to work each morning be representative? Explain.

   b. Would a sample consisting of residents who live along that roadway be representative? Explain.

   c. Would a random sample of homeowners in the city be representative? Explain.

8. **Make Sense and Persevere** A pharmaceutical company is developing a new oral medication for the treatment of psoriasis, a skin disease marked by red, itchy, scaly patches. Describe how you could design a controlled experiment to test the effect of the medication. How could you keep participants from knowing whether or not they were in the treatment group?

9. **Error Analysis** Describe and correct the error a student made when responding to the following question.

   A website wants to post a blog about the most popular type of pet in the Seattle area. Would a sample consisting of every tenth ticket holder to the local dog show be representative? Explain.

   Yes; since the sample is a systematic random sample, it would be representative of the population.

10. **Higher Order Thinking** Suppose a grocery store manager wishes to survey the store's employees in order to determine whether they prefer expanding the existing break room or building an outdoor patio for the employees.

    a. How could the manager conduct an unbiased stratified sampling?

    b. How could the manager conduct an unbiased systematic sampling?

PRACTICE

11. **What type of study is described?** SEE EXAMPLE 1

    a. Managers of a forest preserve want to know what percent of the visitors with dogs keep their dogs on a leash. The park assigns an employee to count the numbers of visitors that do and do not use a leash.

    b. A local newspaper polls citizens of a city about whether they support a local tax levy.

12. A researcher wants to know the average growth of a certain plant one week after germination. The greenhouse where he grows the plants has 12 trays with 36 plants on each tray. He picks one tray from the greenhouse and measures the heights of each plant. The results are shown in the dot plot.

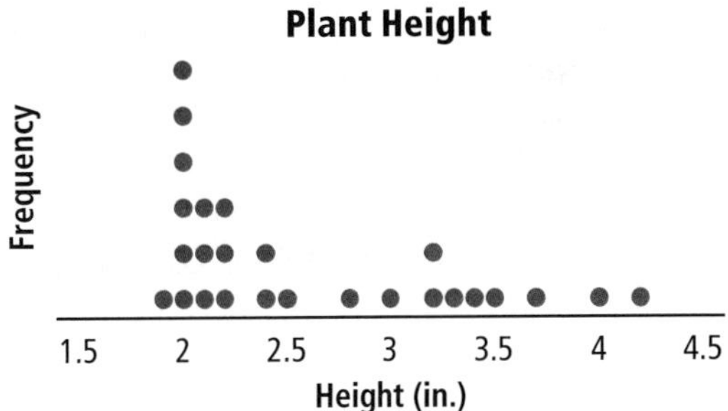

When analyzing the data, he sees that the heights of the plants are clustered around 2 in. Could this be the result of bias in his sampling method? Explain. SEE EXAMPLE 2

13. **What sampling method is used in the following examples? Is the method biased or not?** SEE EXAMPLE 3

    a. A clothing manufacturing company divided its employees up by units, and then they randomly selected three employees from each unit to represent the company at a convention in Las Vegas.

    b. Mr.Yotsey put names of all students at his school on identical slips of paper in a box and distributed surveys to the students whose names he pulled.

14. Researchers want to find out if warm water therapy increases muscle strength in people 65 years of age and older. Describe a design for a controlled study of this question. What are some potential sources of bias in your study? SEE EXAMPLE 4

PRACTICE & PROBLEM SOLVING

Practice

Tutorial

Mixed Review Available Online

APPLY

15. Make Sense and Persevere Suppose a major oil company hired a survey organization to conduct a study of citizens living within 5 mi of the coast.

The survey question is, *"Do you want to save money at the gas pump? Well then you would be in favor of off shore drilling, right?"*

Explain the bias that exists in this scenario.

16. Communicate Precisely A group of farmers wants to test a new fertilizer being produced for soybean crops. Explain how the farmers could set up the control group and the experimental group for this study.

17. Make Sense and Persevere At Miami University in Oxford, OH, there is a university seal located in the heart of campus. There is a long-standing tradition that claims if you step on the seal you will fail your next exam.

Natalie spends several hours over several different days, at varying times, counting the number of students who pass along the walkway and the number of students who step on the seal. Which of the three main types of study does Natalie use in her project?

18. Model With Mathematics A commercial developer hires a market research company to determine the mean household income of those who live within a 10 mi radius of the site of a proposed upscale shopping center.

a. Explain why the commercial developer would do this.

b. How might the market research company get the information?

19. A newspaper hires a polling company to determine the level of support in the county for raising property taxes in order to increase funding for local schools. The polling company calls phone numbers chosen at random from a phone number registry between the hours of 5:00 P.M. and 7:00 P.M. What are some potential sources of bias in this sampling method?

ASSESSMENT PRACTICE

20. Choose Yes or No to tell whether each of the following describes a convenience sampling method.

	Yes	No
A manager surveys every fourth customer about their level of satisfaction with their shopping experience.	❑	❑
When a school district wishes to get feedback on the district's new webpage, they survey the entire population of randomly selected schools.	❑	❑
When Sheila wanted to find out what type of music was most popular among the students in her history class, she asked the two students who sat on either side of her.	❑	❑
The quality control officer of a ladder manufacturer walked into the shop, pulled the five closest ladders, and gave them several stress tests checking for potential defects.	❑	❑

21. SAT/ACT A researcher studies differences in career goals between boys and girls in middle school. All of the students in the seventh grade schools in a particular county answer a list of questions. What type of study is this?

Ⓐ experiment
Ⓑ sample survey
Ⓒ observational study
Ⓓ random trial

22. Performance Task A grocery store surveys every fifth customer to determine whether it should consider expanding its organic foods department. The results of the 500 customers surveyed are shown in the table.

In favor of expanded organic dept.?	
Yes	378
No	97
Indifferent	25

Part A What type of sampling method was used? Does it seem valid?

Part B Based upon the results of this survey, about what percent of the store's customers would favor the expansion?

Part C What is the statistical variable in this study? Is this a quantitative or categorical variable?

8-3 Data Distributions

PearsonRealize.com

I CAN… evaluate data distributions

VOCABULARY

- normal distribution
- skewed distribution
- standard deviation
- symmetrical distribution

CRITIQUE & EXPLAIN

Chen and Dakota were asked to estimate the mean and median of the following data set. Chen said, "The middle value is 11. Both the mean and median are approximately 11." Dakota said, "Most of the data are the left. I think the mean and median will be about 9, with the mean slightly larger."

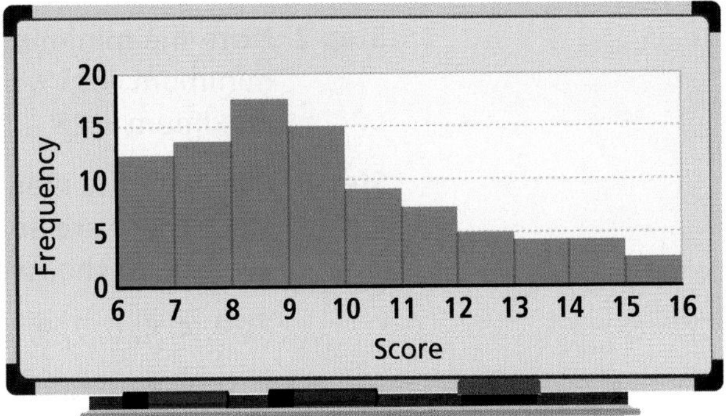

A. Is either Chen or Dakota correct? Explain.

B. What strategies could you use to approximate the exact mean and median?

C. **Reason** Which measure of center is more representative in this case, the mean or the median? Explain.

ESSENTIAL QUESTION **How can you interpret the distribution of data in a data set?**

EXAMPLE 1 Find Measures of Center and Spread

A. What are the mean and standard deviation of the following data set?

4, 12, 15, 9, 14, 16, 13, 6, 7, 6, 25, 3, 13, 17, 22, 4

The mean, or average, of a data set is the sum of the values in the data set divided by the number of values in the data set. The **standard deviation** is a measure of how much the values in a data set vary, or deviate, from the mean. It is a measure of the variability or spread of the data.

The mean and the standard deviation are used together to measure the center and spread of the data.

STUDY TIP
Most technology has the ability to calculate mean and standard deviation.

You can use a spreadsheet to calculate the mean and standard deviation.

	A	B	C	D	E	F	G	H	I	J	K	L	M	N	O	P	Q	R
1																		
2	4	12	15	9	14	16	13	6	7	6	25	3	13	17	22	4	Mean	11.625
3																	SD	6.313
4																		

The mean is $\overline{x} \approx 11.6$, and the standard deviation is $\sigma \approx 6.3$.

CONTINUED ON THE NEXT PAGE

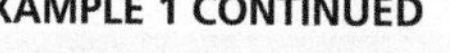

Activity Assess

EXAMPLE 1 CONTINUED

B. What is the five-number summary of the data set?

The five-number summary includes the minimum value, first quartile, median, third quartile, and maximum value.

Step 1 Rearrange the data in ascending numerical order.

3, 4, 4, 6, 6, 7, 9, 12, 13, 13, 14, 15, 16, 17, 22, 25

Step 2 Note the minimum and maximum values:

minimum = 3

maximum = 25

Step 3 Calculate the median, the number in the middle of the data set. Since there are an even number of values, the median is the average of the two middle values, or 12.5.

{3, 4, 4, 6, 6, 7, 9, 12,} {13, 13, 14, 15, 16, 17, 22, 25}

1st quartile median 3rd quartile

Step 4 Calculate the first and third quartiles. The quartiles show how the data are distributed. The first quartile is the median of the lower half of the data, 6. The third quartile is the median of the upper half of the data, 15.5.

COMMON ERROR

Remember that for a data set that has an odd number of values, the median IS the middle value. Do not consider this value when finding the quartiles.

These data can be represented in a box-and-whisker plot. Notice that the one quartile is closer to the median than the other.

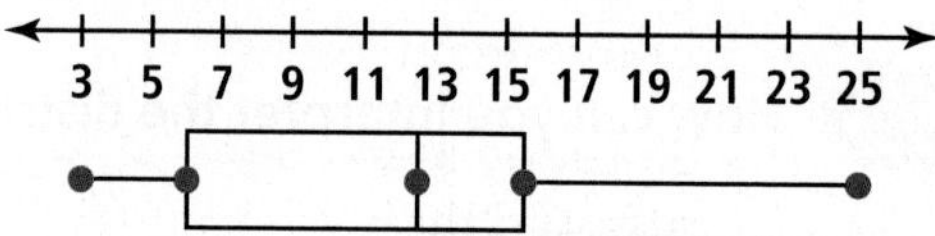

The five-number summary of this data set is: minimum = 3, 1st quartile = 6, median = 12.5, 3rd quartile = 15.5, maximum = 25

Try It! 1. List the mean, standard deviation, and five-number summary of the following data set.

3 4 9 12 12 14 15 19 25 30 32 33 34 34 35

EXAMPLE 2 Use Appropriate Statistics to Compare Data Sets

A. How can you describe different types of distributions?

To compare the different types of distributions, look at the shape, the center, and the spread of the distributions.

The standard deviation, range, and the interquartile range are three measures of spread. The range of a data set is the difference between the maximum and minimum values. The interquartile range is the difference between the third quartile and the first quartile.

When measuring center and spread, median and interquartile range are used together, and mean and standard deviation are used together.

A **skewed distribution** is one with a shape that is stretched out in either the positive or negative direction. A **symmetrical distribution** has a shape that, when reflected across the mean, the display is roughly the same.

CONTINUED ON THE NEXT PAGE

EXAMPLE 2 CONTINUED

The shape of a distribution can affect the measures of center and spread and determine which measures of center and spread best describe the data.

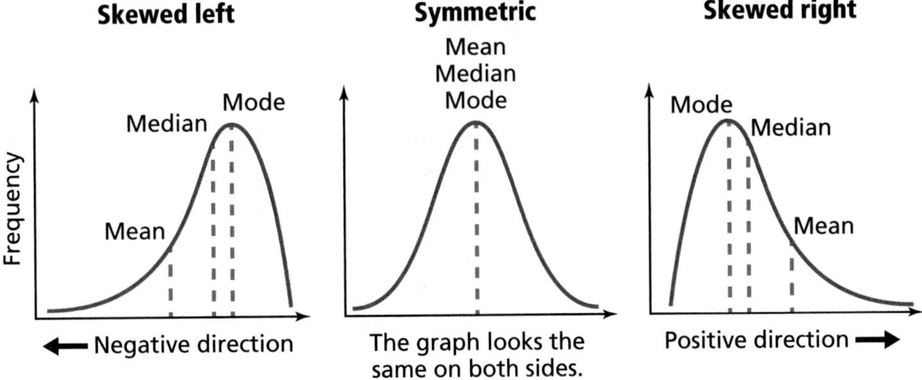

The mean, median, and mode are all about the same in a symmetric distribution. You can use the mean and the standard deviation to describe the center and spread.

B. What measures of center and spread would you use for the following data set?

10 13 16 21 22 26 29 29 30 32 33 33 33 35 37

You can use a histogram to determine the shape.

Frequency (0, 2, 4, 6); Data Values (0, 5, 10, 15, 20, 25, 30, 35, 40)

Since the mean is more affected than the median by a data distribution that is skewed, it is better to use the median and interquartile range as the measures of center and spread. Also, the quartiles show how the data are distributed differently on either side of the center.

The data are already in numerical order.

{10 13 16 21 22 26 29} 29 {30 32 33 33 33 35 37}

1st quartile   median   3rd quartile

The range is $37 - 10 = 27$, and the interquartile range is $33 - 21 = 12$.

USE APPROPRIATE TOOLS
What are some other ways you can determine the shape of the distribution of these data?

Try It! **2.** What are the better measures of center and spread of the following data sets?

a. 55 55 57 57 57 58 58 59 59 59 61 61

b. 110 110 110 120 120 130 140 150 160 170 180 190

CONCEPTUAL UNDERSTANDING

EXAMPLE 3 Recognize a Normal Distribution

Are the following variables likely to have a normal distribution?

A. The heights of all the people in a large group

A **normal distribution** can be modeled by a particular bell-shaped curve that is symmetric about the mean. This is called a normal curve.

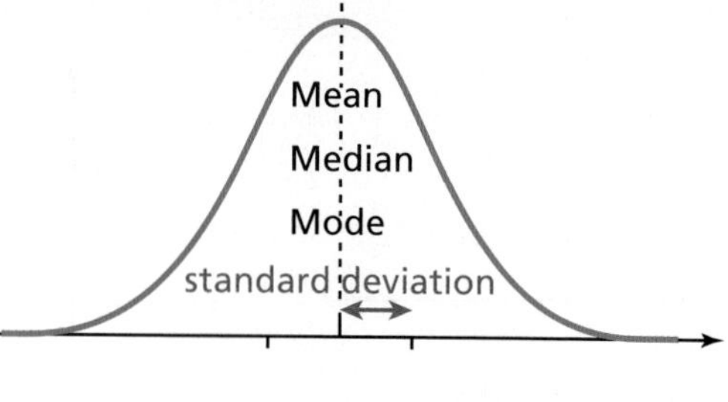

Approximately normal distributions can be found in many real-world situations where the data are symmetric and mostly clustered near the mean.

The heights of people in a large group are likely to be normally distributed.

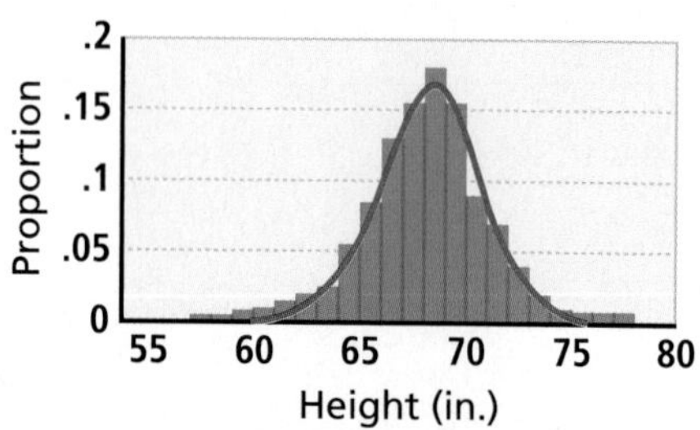

STUDY TIP

Notice that for real-world examples, the data in a normal distribution might not be perfectly normally distributed but can be modeled by a normal curve.

B. The probability of landing on each of 8 equal parts of a spinner

This data set is not normally distributed because each outcome has the same probability of occurring as any other.

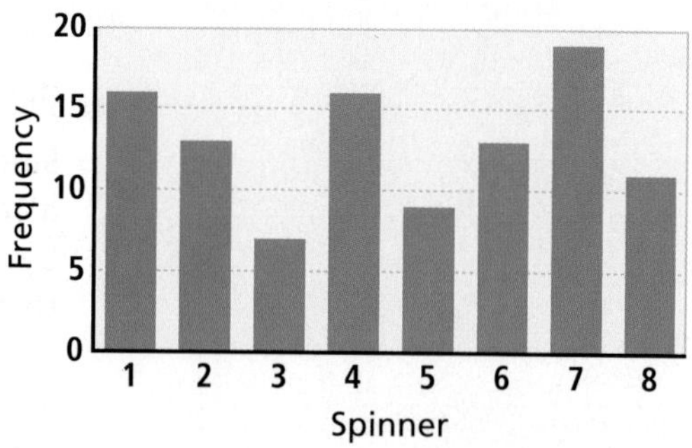

C. The scores on an easy test

The scores on an easy test are often skewed left and not normally distributed, because more students will receive higher scores.

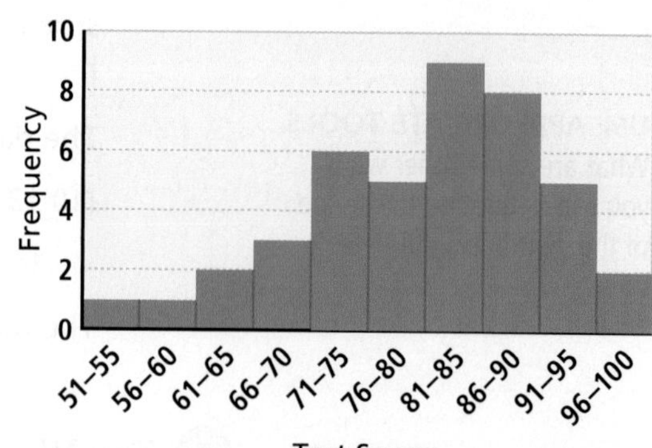

CONTINUED ON THE NEXT PAGE

EXAMPLE 3 CONTINUED

D. The number of children in a family

The number of children in a family is not normally distributed. The distribution is skewed right because many families have 0, 1, 2, or 3 children, but very few families have 10 or more children.

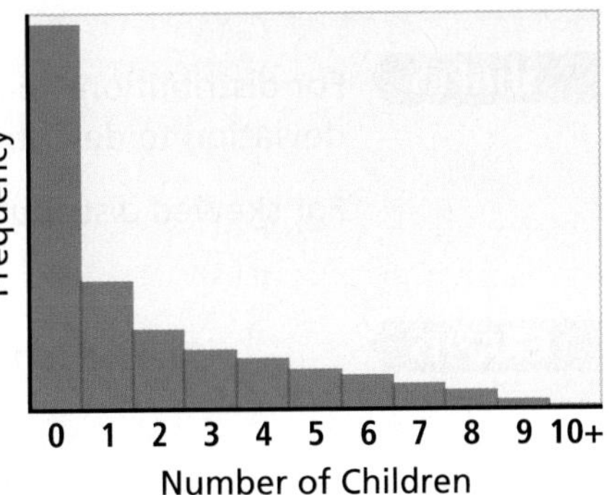

Try It! 3. Is each situation likely to be normally distributed? Explain.

a. weight of individuals in a population

b. the scores on a difficult test

EXAMPLE 4 Classify a Data Distribution

How would you classify the following data set? Describe the shape of the distribution and the center and spread of the data.

106, 96, 86, 120, 98, 76, 112, 64, 99, 72, 119, 115, 76, 120, 97

STUDY TIP

If the median and the mean are equal or very close, then the data are likely to be symmetric.

Step 1 Make a histogram of the data.

Step 2 Analyze the shape of the histogram.

Since the data are bunched to the right and have a long tail to the left, the data are skewed left.

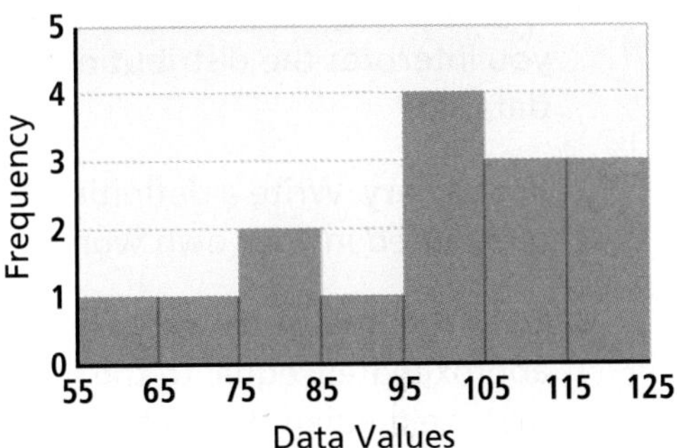

Step 3 Determine the center and spread of the data. Use the median and interquartile range.

64 72 76 76 86 96 97 98 99 106 112 115 119 120 120

1st quartile = 76, median = 98, 3rd quartile = 115

The interquartile range is 115 – 76 = 39. Notice that the 3rd quartile is closer to the median than the 1st quartile is. This is characteristic of a distribution that is skewed left.

The distribution is skewed left with median 98 and interquartile range 39.

Try It! 4. What is the type of distribution and the center and spread of the data? 20, 17, 17, 12, 18, 21, 19, 18, 13, 14, 17, 23, 25

CONCEPT SUMMARY Data Distributions

SHAPES For distributions that are approximately normal, use mean and standard deviation to describe the data.

For skewed distributions, use median and quartiles to describe the data.

GRAPHS

Skewed left

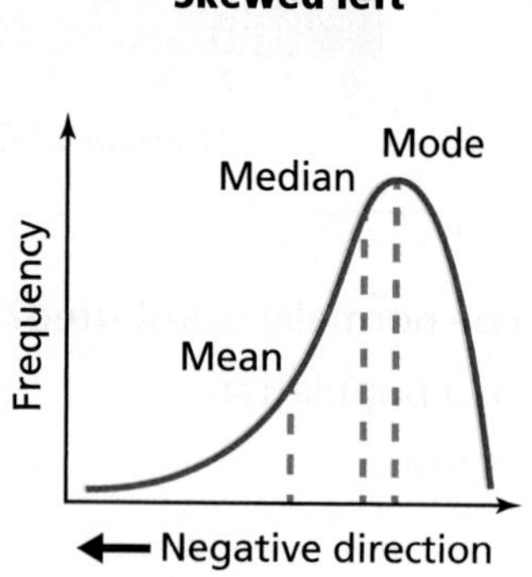

← Negative direction

Normal (no skew)

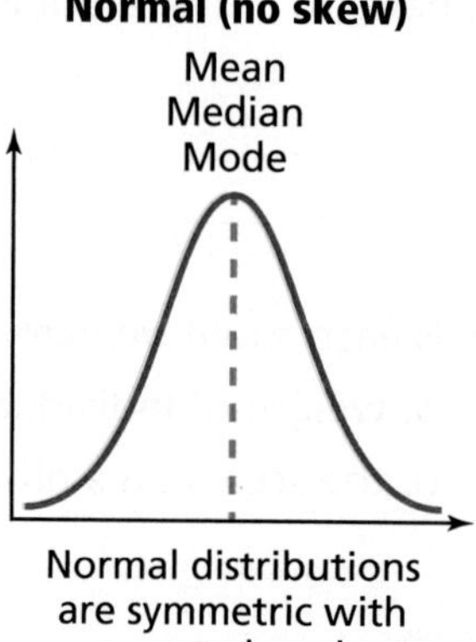

Normal distributions are symmetric with a central peak.

Skewed right

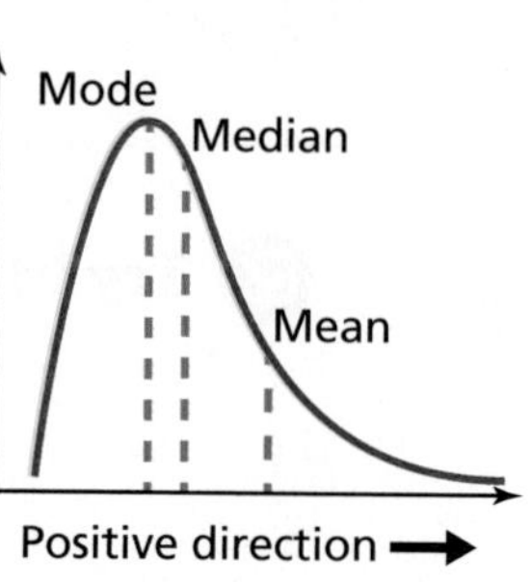

Positive direction →

Do You UNDERSTAND?

1. ESSENTIAL QUESTION How can you interpret the distribution of data in a data set?

2. **Vocabulary** Write a definition for *normally distributed* in your own words.

3. **Error Analysis** A data set has a mean that is approximately equal to the median. Ralph says the median should be used to describe the measure of center, and the quartiles should be used to describe the measure of spread. Explain his error.

4. **Communicate Precisely** Explain how to determine if the data distribution shown is skewed left, right, or is symmetric.

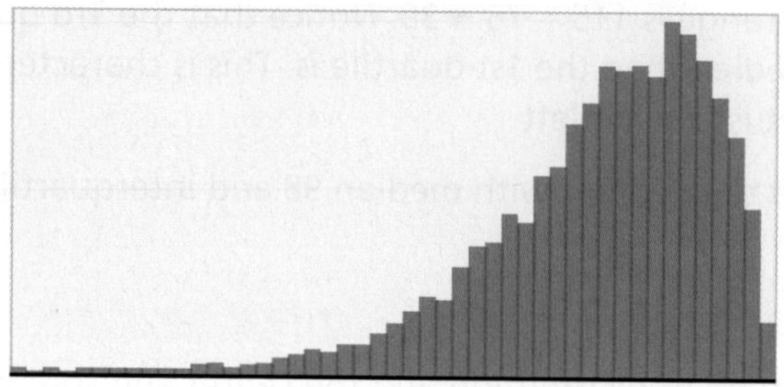

Do You KNOW HOW?

Determine the mean, standard deviation, and five-number summary of each data set. Round to the nearest hundredth, if necessary.

5. 5, 8, 5, 9, 6, 14, 9, 3, 8, 7, 10, 12

6. 10.5, 2.25, 7.75, 8.8, 3.4, 9.2, 6.5, 4.3, 3.9, 6.4

Describe the shape of the data summarized in the histograms.

7.

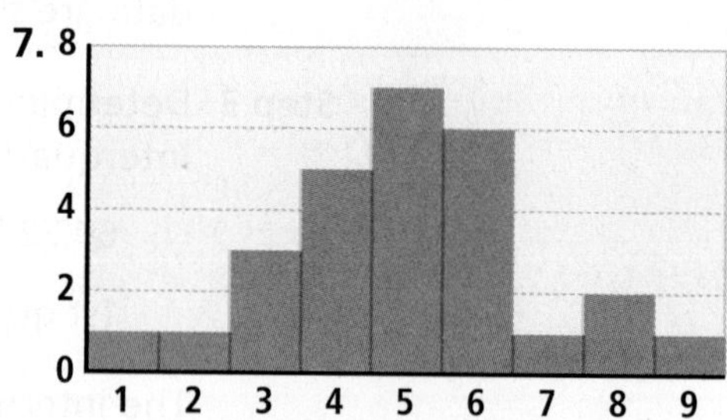

8.

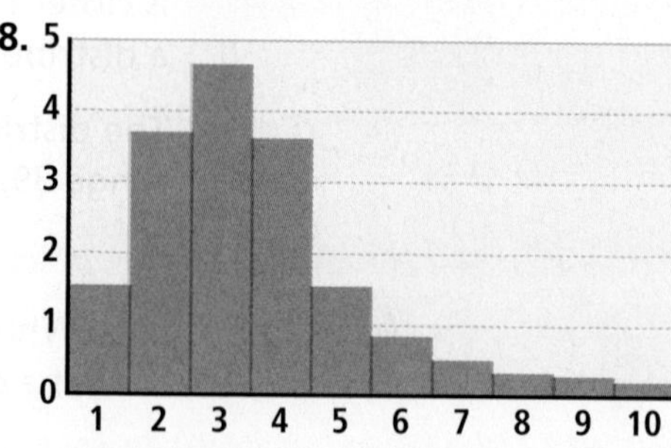

PRACTICE & PROBLEM SOLVING

Scan for Multimedia

Additional Exercises Available Online

UNDERSTAND

9. Communicate Precisely Describe a situation that is likely to produce the following data distribution.

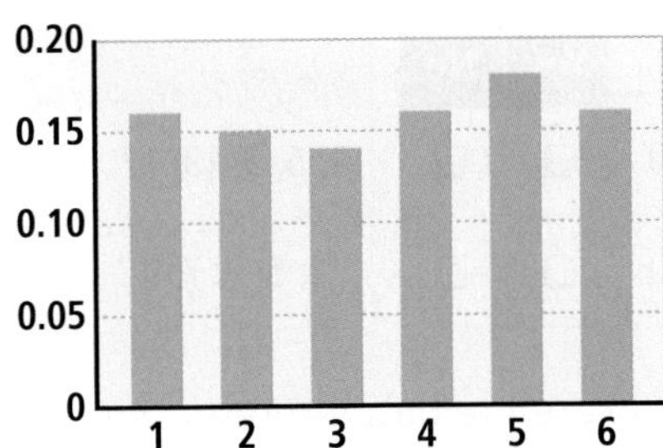

10. Error Analysis Maurice's teacher asked him to compare the mean and median of the data distribution. Explain and correct Maurice's error in comparing the mean and median.

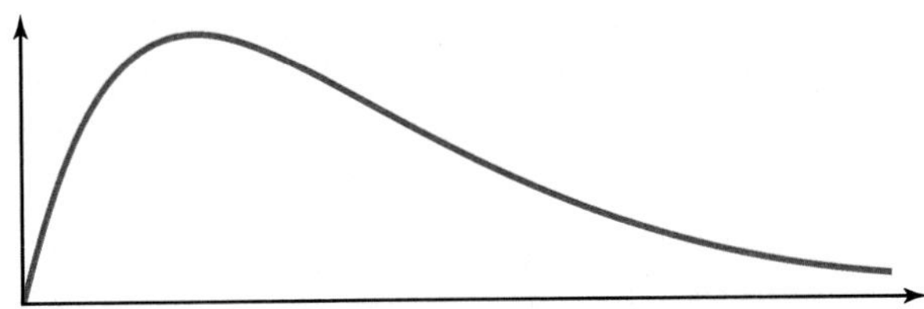

The distribution is skewed right.
This implies the mean is less than the median. ✗

11. Higher Order Thinking Dale drew the following box plot to represent a data set.

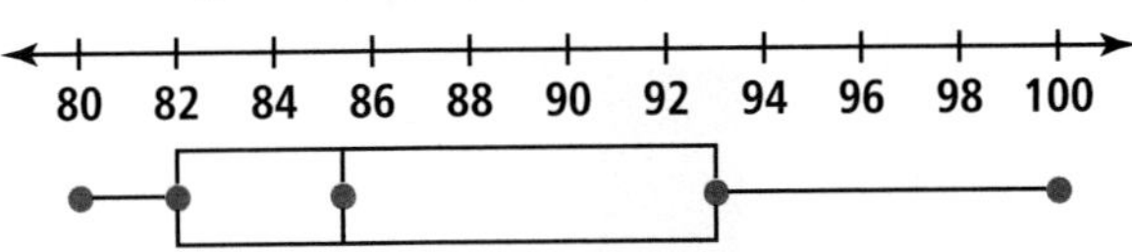

a. Identify the five-number summary of the data.

b. Explain how to use the five-number summary to write a data set with 14 data values to match the box plot. Then write such a data set.

PRACTICE

Find the mean, standard deviation, and five-number summary of each data set. Round to the nearest tenth, if necessary. SEE EXAMPLE 1

12. 9, 15, 17, 21, 23, 31, 33, 39, 46, 50

13. 35, 12, 25, 33, 27, 48, 30, 34, 35, 41, 14

14. 9, 24, 10, 11, 5, 16, 18, 30, 19, 22, 12, 28, 9, 33

For each set of data, describe the shape of the distribution and determine which measures of center and spread best represent the data. SEE EXAMPLE 2

15. 28, 13, 23, 34, 55, 38, 44, 65, 49, 33, 50, 59, 67, 45

16. 3.1, 2.3, 8.8, 2.8, 3.2, 3.5, 3.9, 4.3, 4.5, 2.9, 3.9, 5.5

17. 12, 2, 14, 4, 1, 6, 11, 7, 8, 5, 9, 10, 8, 15

Determine if each situation is likely to be uniformly distributed, normally distributed, skewed left, or skewed right. SEE EXAMPLE 3

18. The age at which people die in the United States

19. number of pets owned by students at your school

20. Selling price of cars in 2018

21. The height of all adult females in Connecticut

Determine the type of distribution and the best measure of center and spread of each data set. Round to the nearest hundredth, if necessary. SEE EXAMPLE 4

22. 3, 6, 12, 14, 17, 17, 18, 21, 21, 22, 23, 28

23. 17, 9, 27, 13, 15, 19, 19, 21, 11, 23, 17, 25

24. 7.8, 4.9, 5.7, 24.2, 3.3, 6.2, 9.1, 10.6, 11.9, 3.9, 12.3, 17.2, 18

25. 53, 24, 65, 26, 60, 32, 41, 7, 44, 49, 50, 52, 55, 46

PRACTICE & PROBLEM SOLVING

Mixed Review Available Online

APPLY

26. **Make Sense and Persevere** The test scores from a history test are 88, 95, 92, 60, 86, 78, 95, 98, 92, 96, 70, 80, 89, and 96.

    a. Find the mean and standard deviation of the test scores.

    b. Find the five-number summary of the test scores.

    c. Describe the type of distribution. Explain.

    d. Do you think the test was an easy test or a hard test for these students? Explain.

27. **Reason** The salaries of some employees at a company are shown.

Employee Salary

$40,000

$50,000

$75,000

$175,000

$55,000

$90,000

$100,000

$60,000

    a. Describe the type of distribution.

    b. Find an appropriate measure of center and measure of spread. Explain your choice.

28. A real estate agent wants to convince a client to raise the asking price on his home so she can earn a higher commission. Based on the data shown, should she tell her client the mean or median home price? Explain.

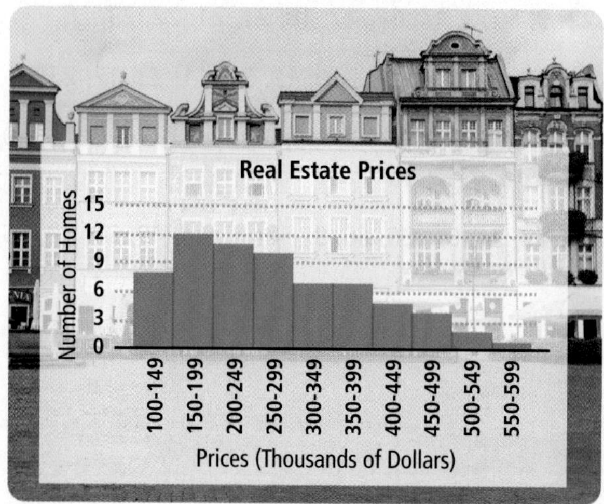

ASSESSMENT PRACTICE

29. Does each five-number summary represent a data distribution that is normally distributed? Check *Yes* or *No*.

	Yes	No
2; 7; 8; 9; 10	❑	❑
2; 4; 6; 8; 10	❑	❑

	Yes	No
1; 5; 9; 13; 17	❑	❑
1; 5; 6; 7; 9	❑	❑

30. **SAT/ACT** How are the data representing the age of people who purchased movie tickets at a senior citizen discount likely to be distributed?

    Ⓐ uniformly distributed
    Ⓑ skewed right
    Ⓒ normally distributed
    Ⓓ skewed left

31. **Performance Task** A voice coach looks up the ages of all the contestants on a popular singing competition and creates two graphs by grouping the data differently.

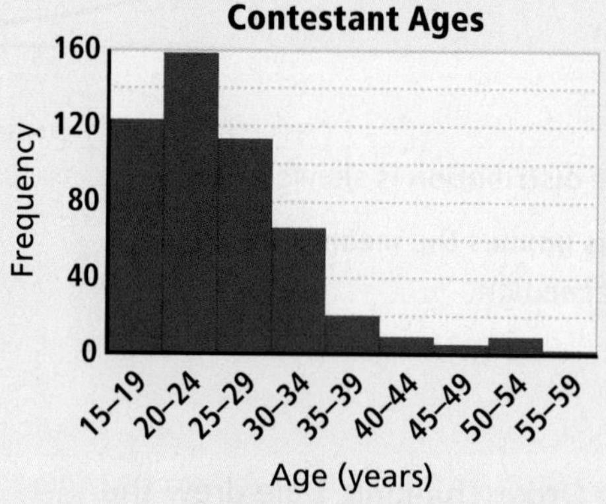

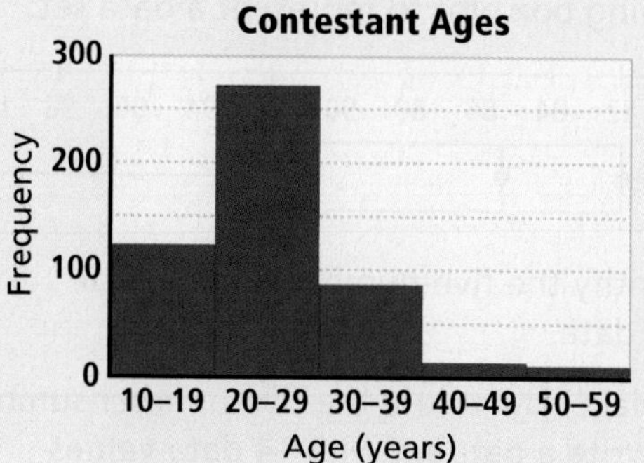

Part A Describe the shape of the data. How would you expect the mean and median to compare?

Part B Which graph would be better to convince students that they should continue singing lessons into 20s? Which graph would be better to convince students to continue lessons into their 30s?

8-4 Normal Distributions

PearsonRealize.com

I CAN... understand where a data value falls in relation to other values in a normal distribution.

VOCABULARY

- percentile
- standard normal distribution
- *z*-score

Activity Assess

EXPLORE & REASON

The owner of an apple orchard and the owner of an orange grove create histograms to display fruit production data.

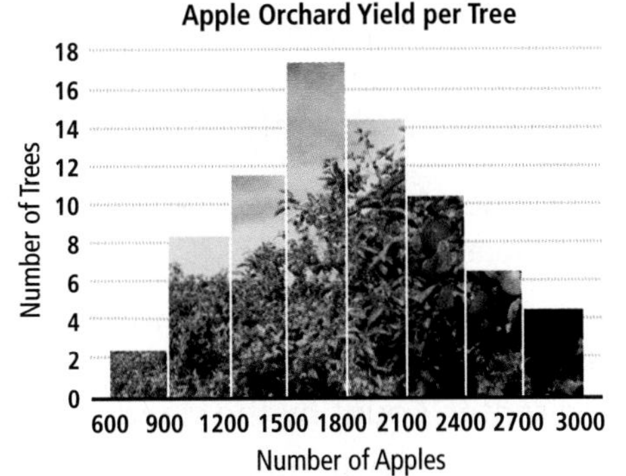

mean = 1,750
standard deviation = 296

mean = 210
standard deviation = 47

A. Describe the shape of each distribution. Discuss how the distributions are alike and how they are different.

B. Use Structure Explain how you could estimate the mean from the graphs. The standard deviation measures spread from the mean. Which data values are within a standard deviation of the mean on each graph?

ESSENTIAL QUESTION

How can you use the normal distribution to explain where data values fall within a population?

CONCEPT The Empirical Rule

The normal distribution has a special property called The Empirical Rule. The approximate percentage of data values falling in any interval of the range of the data can be determined using just the mean and the standard deviation.

For a population, the mean is denoted by μ and the standard deviation by σ.

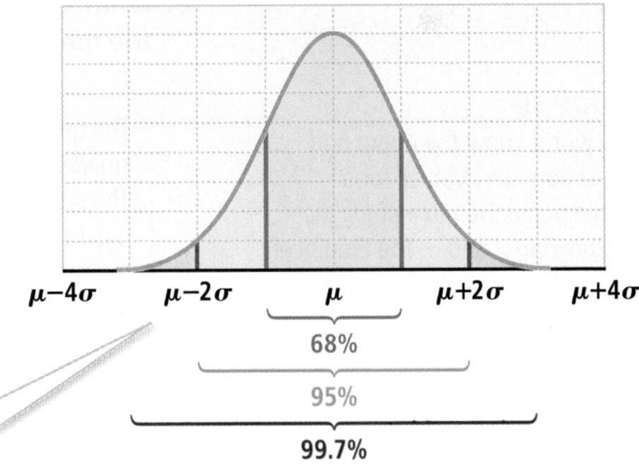

How far from the mean does a value in a normal distribution fall?

- About 68% of all values fall within 1 standard deviation.
- About 95% of all values fall within 2 standard deviations.
- About 99.7% of all values fall within 3 standard deviations.

The rule applies *only* to normal distributions.

EXAMPLE 1 Find Population Intervals

An example of an early application of statistics was in the year 1817. A study of chest circumference among a group of Scottish men exhibited an approximately normal distribution. Their chest circumferences ranged from 33 to 48 in., with a mean chest measurement of 40 in. and a standard deviation of 2 in. Use the Empirical Rule to help you understand the distribution of chest circumferences in the study.

A. What range of chest measurements contains the 68% which fall closest to the mean?

To draw the graph, first draw the horizontal axis. Draw the "bell curve" of the normal distribution and add the labels to the axis with the mean at the center. Count by the standard deviation to each end of the curve.

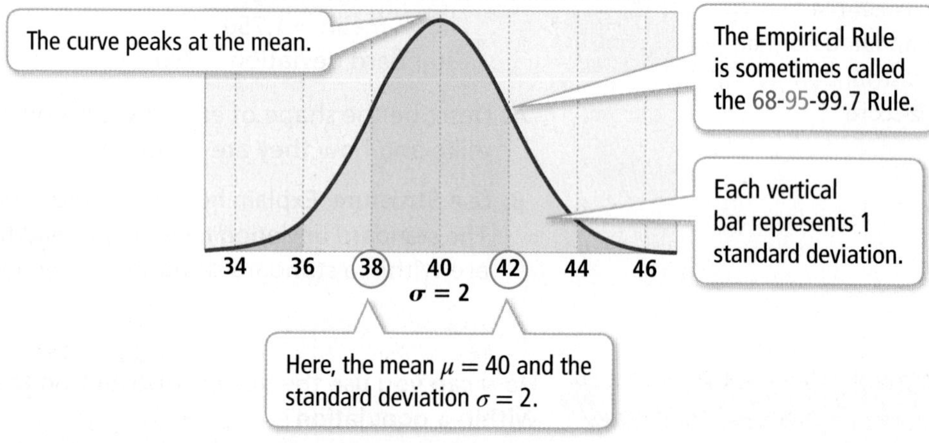

LOOK FOR RELATIONSHIPS
One standard deviation from the mean is where the curve changes from opening upward to downward (left of mean), and from opening downward to upward (right of mean).

You would expect approximately 68% of the men in the population had chest measurements between 38 and 42 in.

B. What would you expect the chest measurements to be for the 2.5% of the men with the smallest chest measurements in the population?

STUDY TIP
You won't know the upper and lower boundary values for a whole population in a study just by knowing μ and σ. The Empirical Rule only covers 99.7% of the values, not the farthest 0.3% from the mean.

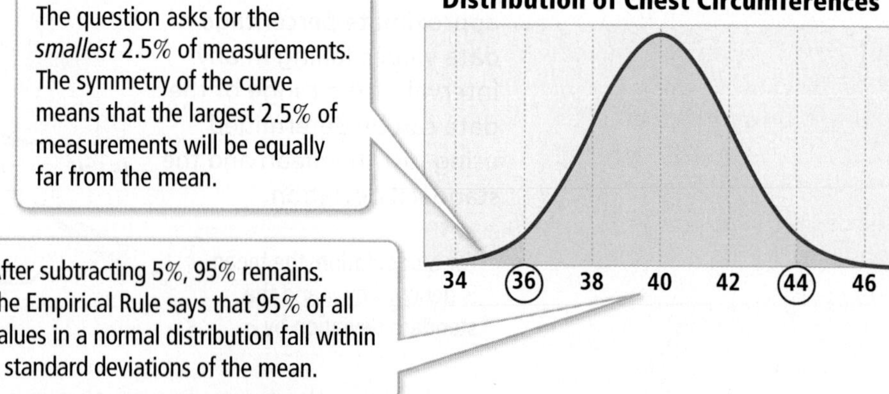

You would expect 2.5% of the men in the population to have chests measuring less than 36 in.

CONTINUED ON THE NEXT PAGE

 **Try It!** **1. a.** What would you expect to be the smallest and largest chest measurements of the "middle" 95% of the men?

b. What would you expect to be the measurements of the 16% of the men with the largest chests in the population?

EXAMPLE 2 Use The Empirical Rule

Recent SAT scores for college-bound seniors are normally distributed with mean score 508 and standard deviation 121. How does the Empirical Rule help you understand the performances of individual students?

A. What proportion of students received scores between 387 and 629?

Sketch the graph to see where the numbers 387 and 629 fall in terms of the distribution.

Distribution of SAT Math Scores

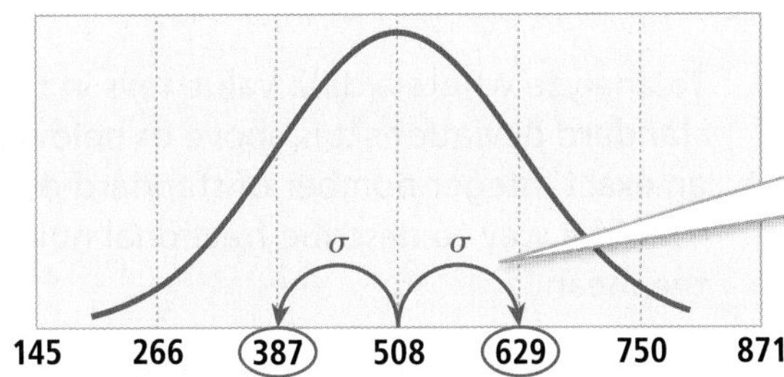

When you compute the numbers for the horizontal scale, 387 and 629 are each 1 standard deviation from the mean.

According to the Empirical Rule, 68% of scores are within 1 standard deviation of the mean. That means that approximately 68% of students received SAT Math scores between 387 and 629.

B. What proportion of students received scores greater than 387?

Distribution of SAT Math Scores

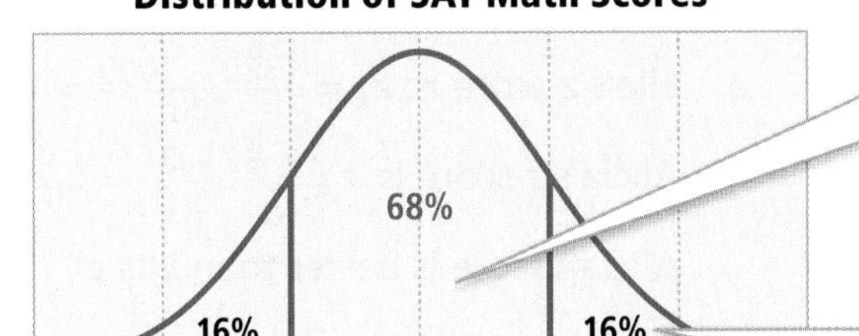

100% − 68% = 32% of students earned scores either greater than 629 or less than 387.

The symmetry of the curve means half, or 16%, of the remaining 32% of scores are greater than 629, and half are less than 387.

So 68% + 16% = 84% of students received scores greater than 387.

USE APPROPRIATE TOOLS
Consulting an accurate sketch of the distribution under consideration will help tell you determine whether the Empirical Rule applies.

 **Try It!** **2.** Find the proportion of students who earned SAT Math scores in the following ranges.

a. between 266 and 750

b. between 266 and 629

CONCEPTUAL UNDERSTANDING

EXAMPLE 3 Compare Values Using z-Scores

Ella and Alicia are comparing scores on their college entrance exams. Ella's SAT score is 1380. Alicia's ACT score is 32. The mean SAT score is 1000 with a standard deviation of 200. The mean ACT score is 21 with a standard deviation of 5. Who has the better score?

You cannot compare their scores directly, but you can compare their relative position within each distribution.

Distribution of SAT Scores

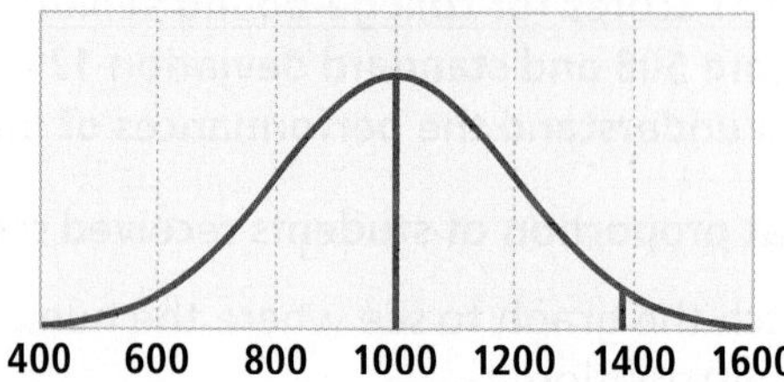

Ella's score is *less than* 2 standard deviations greater than the mean.

Distribution of ACT Scores

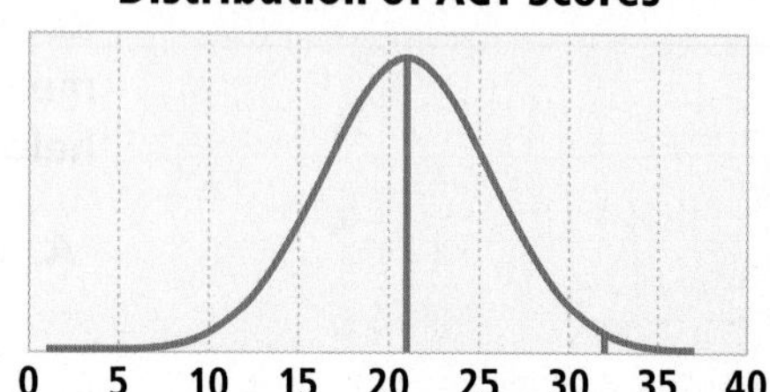

Alicia's score is *more than* 2 standard deviations greater than the mean.

To analyze where a data value falls in the distribution, find how many standard deviations it is above or below the mean. Most data values are not an exact integer number of standard deviations from the mean, so we need to find a way to describe fractional numbers of standard deviations from the mean.

The **z-score** counts how many standard deviations a data value is above or below the mean, because it divides the difference from the mean by the distance of a standard deviation. These distributions are normal, but you can use z-scores with any distribution.

> **COMMON ERROR**
> You may think that a positive *z*-score is always better than a negative one. Be careful to consider the context, though.
> - Test scores: higher is better
> - Golf scores: lower is better
> - Height: no "better" score

$$z = \frac{\text{data value} - \text{mean}}{\text{standard deviation}}$$

Ella's *z*-score is: $z_E = \frac{1380 - 1000}{200} = 1.9$

Ella's score: 1380
Mean SAT score: 1000
Standard deviation of scores: 200

Alicia's *z*-score is: $z_A = \frac{32 - 21}{5} = 2.2$

Alicia's score: 32
Mean ACT score: 21
Standard deviation of scores: 5

Alicia's score is better than Ella's.

 **Try It!** **3.** How does an SAT score of 1120 compare to an ACT score of 23?

APPLICATION

EXAMPLE 4 Use a z-Score to Compute Percentage

The weight of captive adult female lowland gorillas is normally distributed with a mean of $\mu = 82.30$ kg and standard deviation of $\sigma = 15.33$ kg. Calculate a z-score for Sasha. How can you use this score to find the percentage of captive adult female lowland gorillas whose weights are less than or equal to Sasha's?

LOOK FOR RELATIONSHIPS

$z = \frac{x - \mu}{\sigma}$

The formula for the z-score can be used to determine part of the transformation of the standard normal distribution into the normal distribution with mean μ and standard deviation σ. For example, there is a horizontal translation of μ units.

Sasha's weight of 61.8 kg gives her a z-score of $\frac{61.8 - 82.3}{15.33} \approx -1.34$.

When you calculate the z-score for a data value, you are finding its corresponding value on the *standard normal distribution*. The **standard normal distribution** is the normal distribution with mean $\mu = 0$ and standard deviation $\sigma = 1$.

The total area under the curve of the standard normal distribution is equal to 1, and represents 100% of the data values.

Standard Normal Distribution

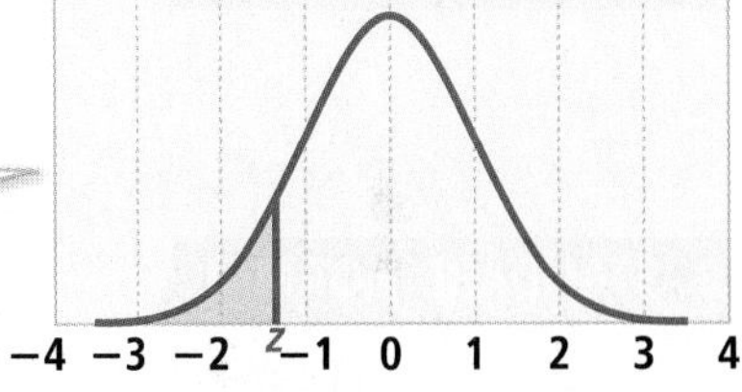

The percentage of values less than or equal to a particular data value is equal to the percentage of the total area under the distribution curve for that population to the left of that data value. This percentage is called the **percentile** of the data value. The percentage of area to the left of a data value is equal to the area to the left of the value's z-score under the standard normal distribution.

To calculate the area under the curve of the standard normal distribution to the left of $z = -1.34$, use a spreadsheet program or a calculator.

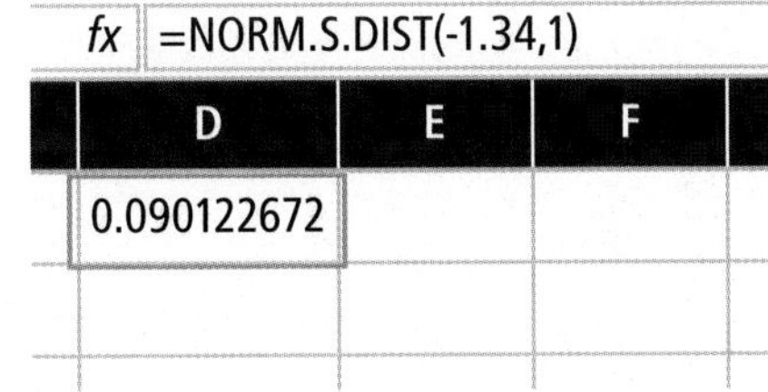

The percentile of Sasha's weight or of a z-score of −1.34 is approximately 9%. This means that about 9% of all captive adult female lowland gorillas have a weight less than or equal to Sasha's weight.

 **Try It!** **4.** Find the percentage of all values in a normal distribution with $z \leq 1.85$.

CONCEPT SUMMARY Using Normal Distributions in the Real World

EMPIRICAL RULE

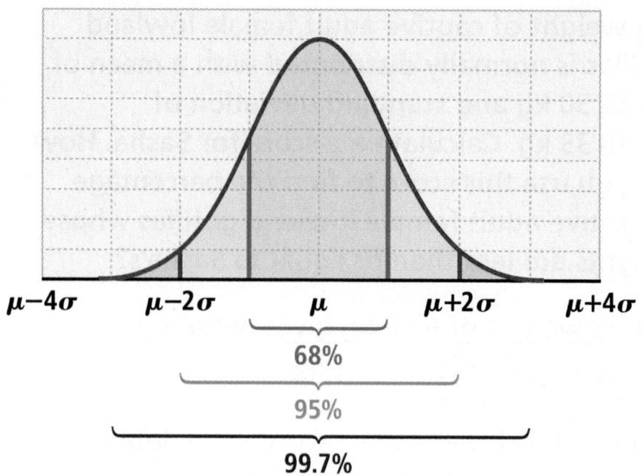

Approximately 68% of data values in a normal distribution fall within 1 standard deviation of the mean.

Approximately 95% of data values in a normal distribution fall within 2 standard deviations of the mean.

Approximately 99.7% of data values in a normal distribution fall within 3 standard deviations of the mean.

***z*-SCORES**

$$z = \frac{\text{data value} - \text{mean}}{\text{standard deviation}}$$

z tells how many standard deviations a data value is above or below the mean.

STANDARD NORMAL DISTRIBUTION

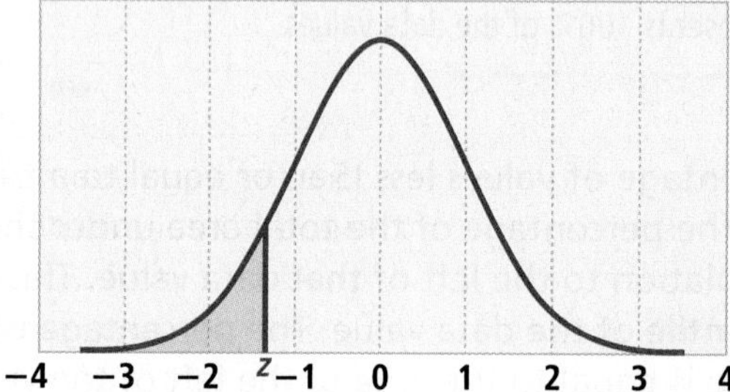

Mean: 0
Standard Deviation: 1

Along with *z*-scores, the standard normal distribution allows you to compare values across different population distributions.

Normal distributions are predictable, allowing you to calculate percentiles using tables, calculators, or spreadsheets.

Do You UNDERSTAND?

1. ESSENTIAL QUESTION How can you use the normal distribution to explain where data values fall within a population?

2. **Vocabulary** Write a definition for *z-score* using your own words.

3. **Look for Relationships** Why is it useful to compare a normal distribution to the standard normal distribution?

Do You KNOW HOW?

A data set with a mean of 75 and a standard deviation of 3.8 is normally distributed.

4. What value is three standard deviations above the mean?

5. What percent of the data is from 67.4 to 82.6?

6. What is the *z*-score for a data value of 69.3?

PRACTICE & PROBLEM SOLVING

Scan for Multimedia

Practice Tutorial

Additional Exercises Available Online

UNDERSTAND

7. **Communicate Precisely** Explain how to use the Empirical Rule to find the percentage of the population that falls in a given interval of values.

8. **Mathematical Connections** How could you use the standard normal curve to verify the Empirical Rule? Show your computations.

9. **Error Analysis** The cost of movie tickets at several movie theaters is normally distributed with a mean ticket price of \$10 and a standard deviation of \$0.50. Kenji bought a movie ticket for \$9.25. Explain and correct the error in finding the z-score.

$$z = \frac{\text{mean - data value}}{\text{standard deviation}}$$

$$z = \frac{\$10 - \$9.25}{\$0.5} = 1.5$$

✗

10. **Higher Order Thinking** Skyler took an English test and a French test. The mean score for both tests was 84. Skyler got an 88 on the English test and a 92 on the French test. What condition would have to exist so that Skyler's score on the English test was more impressive relative to her classmates' scores than on the French test?

11. **Use Structure** The graph of normally distributed data is shown. What are the mean and standard deviation of the data? Explain how you know.

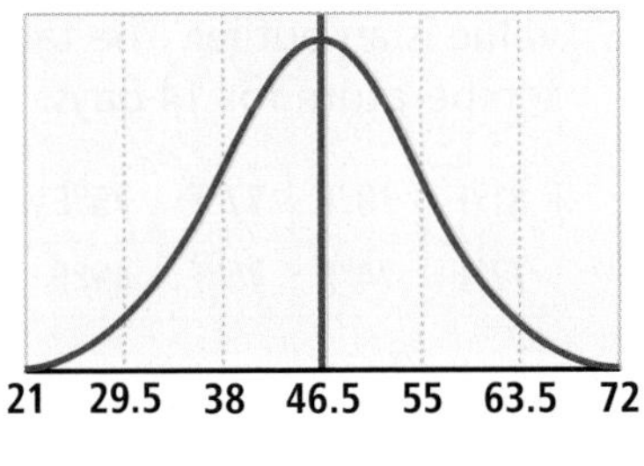

12. **Reason** The monthly cost of joining a gym is normally distributed with a mean of \$50 and a standard deviation of \$5. The cost of the gym Tyler joined was exactly two standard deviations away from the mean.

    a. What are possible z-scores of Tyler's cost?

    b. Suppose the cost of Tyler's gym stays the same, but other gyms change their prices. How would your answer to part (a) be affected?

PRACTICE

The lifespan of a certain brand of car tires is approximately normally distributed. The car tires have a mean lifespan of 50,000 miles and a standard deviation of 7,500 miles. SEE EXAMPLE 1

13. What range of car tire lifespan contains the 95% closest to the mean?

14. What would the lifespan be for the 2.5% of the tires with the greatest lifespan in the population?

The price of a certain brand of printers is normally distributed with mean cost of \$215 and standard deviation \$35. SEE EXAMPLE 2

15. What proportion of printers cost between \$110 and \$320?

16. What proportion of printers cost less than \$145?

17. What proportion of printers cost more than \$250?

18. In their last basketball game, Holly scored 25 points and Juanita scored 16 points. The mean number of points Holly scores is 20 with a standard deviation of 2. The mean number of points Juanita scores is 12 with a standard deviation of 1.25. Whose score is better relative to her average number of points per game? SEE EXAMPLE 3

Find the percentage of all values in a normal distribution for each z-score.
SEE EXAMPLE 4

19. $z \leq 2.15$

20. $z \leq 1.25$

21. $z \geq 0.62$

22. $z \leq 0.48$

23. $z \geq -1.39$

24. $z \leq -2.26$

Given the mean μ and standard deviation σ, find the z-score for each data point x.

25. $\mu = 0;\ \sigma = 2;\ x = 3$

26. $\mu = 1;\ \sigma = 0.15;\ x = 0.70$

27. $\mu = 100;\ \sigma = 15;\ x = 70$

28. $\mu = 2.7;\ \sigma = 0.5;\ x = 3.0$

PRACTICE & PROBLEM SOLVING

Practice Tutorial

Mixed Review Available Online

APPLY

29. Make Sense and Persevere Mrs. Burleson surveyed the students in her class to find the number of minutes they spent doing homework each night. She found that the data was normally distributed with $\mu = 30$ min and $\sigma = 10$ min.

a. What range of time spent doing homework contains the 68% closest to the mean?

b. How much time spent on homework would you expect from the 2.5% of the students with the least time spent on homework?

c. Jeffrey studied 25 min last night. What percent of the students studied fewer minutes than Jeffrey? Round to the nearest hundredth.

30. Reason A random sample of attendance numbers for last year's soccer matches for a local team are shown.

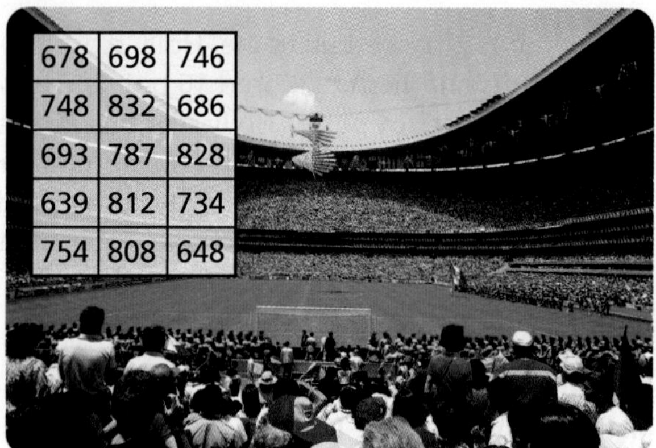

678	698	746
748	832	686
693	787	828
639	812	734
754	808	648

a. Find the mean and standard deviation of the attendance numbers to the nearest tenth.

b. Use the data given in the problem to find what percent of last year's games had at least 808 people in attendance. Round to the nearest tenth of a percent.

c. Given that the data is normally distributed, estimate the percent of games that will have at least 808 people in attendance.

31. Anna scored an 89 on an exam with $\mu = 68$ points and $\sigma = 10$ points. Damian scored a 95 on an exam with $\mu = 76$ points and $\sigma = 12$ points. If both exams had normally distributed scores, what was the z-score for each student? Who did better on their exam? Explain.

ASSESSMENT PRACTICE

32. A normally distributed data set has a mean of 35 and a standard deviation of 5.23. Complete the table to find the probability that a randomly selected value is in the given interval. Round to the nearest hundredth percent, if necessary.

Interval	Probability (%)
at most 43	
at least 48	
between 32 and 38	
at least 41.6	
between 30.2 and 42.6	
at most 36.25	

33. SAT/ACT In a set of data that is normally distributed, the value that is 1 standard deviation above the mean is 93. The value that is 2 standard deviations below the mean is 39. What is the mean of the set of data?

Ⓐ 3 Ⓑ 18 Ⓒ 57 Ⓓ 75

34. Performance Task Outliers can be identified using the interquartile method. Multiply the interquartile range by 1.5. If a data value has a distance below the first quartile or above the third quartile greater than this product, it is an outlier. Another way is to use the *z*-score method. If a data value falls more than 3 standard deviations from the mean, the data value is an outlier. The table shows the high temperature for 14 days.

81°F	78°F	77°F	75°F	80°F	81°F	80°F
77°F	74°F	75°F	49°F	71°F	72°F	80°F

Part A Identify the mean, standard deviation, first quartile, third quartile, and interquartile range of the data.

Part B Which data values, if any, are outliers using the interquartile method? Explain your reasoning.

Part C Which data values, if any, are outliers using the *z*-score method? Explain your reasoning.

8-5 Margin of Error

I CAN… use margin of error to estimate a population parameter accurately.

VOCABULARY
- margin of error
- sampling distribution

MODEL & DISCUSS

With a partner or a group, toss a number cube 30 times and record the number showing on each toss.

A. Compute the means of the numbers in the first five tosses, the first ten tosses, and all thirty tosses.

B. **Use Appropriate Tools** Compile the results for your entire class in three sets of data: the means of the first five tosses, the means of the first ten tosses, and the means of all thirty tosses. Create a histogram for each data set.

C. Compare the histograms. Describe how the distribution of the mean changes as the number of tosses increases.

ESSENTIAL QUESTION

How can you determine how far a statistic is likely to be from a parameter?

APPLICATION

EXAMPLE 1 Estimate a Population Parameter

Seth selects a random sample of students from a local college. He asks students their year in college and how far the college is from their home in miles. How can Seth's sample estimate the proportion of freshmen in the population? How accurate is the estimate likely to be?

Seth's Data

Sophomore	5	Senior	60
Junior	50	Senior	20
Freshman	65	Junior	10
Sophomore	200	Sophomore	110
Junior	120	Sophomore	75
Junior	2	Junior	30
Sophomore	180	Senior	15
Freshman	800	Freshman	45
Junior	100	Sophomore	15
Freshman	90	Sophomore	25

You can use sample statistics, such as proportion and mean, to estimate the corresponding population parameters. The proportion of freshmen in a sample can be used to estimate the proportion of freshmen in the population.

COMMUNICATE PRECISELY
Different samples include different individuals with different characteristics. Results should be reported clearly, explaining how measures were obtained.

$$\text{Ratio of freshmen to students in the population} = \frac{\text{number of freshmen in sample}}{\text{number of participants in sample}}$$

$$= \frac{4}{20}$$

$$= \frac{1}{5} \text{ or } 0.20$$

0.20 of the sample, or 20%, are freshmen.

The accuracy of this estimate depends on the number of participants in the sample and how well the sample represents the population.

If by chance the sample clusters away from the true mean, estimates will not be very accurate.

Larger samples usually provide more accurate estimates than smaller samples.

CONTINUED ON THE NEXT PAGE

EXAMPLE 1 CONTINUED

 **Try It!** **1.** Use the sample data to estimate the mean distance from home. Estimate the proportion of seniors to the total population at the college.

APPLICATION

EXAMPLE 2 Make an Inference Using Multiple Samples

Tia is contributing to the same project as Seth and has sampled a different group of students. The proportion of freshmen in her sample is 0.40 or 40%. How can Seth and Tia determine whose result is a better representation of the population?

Tia's Data

Junior	120	Freshman	60
Sophomore	320	Freshman	200
Senior	240	Sophomore	130
Freshman	150	Freshman	120
Freshman	20	Junior	15
Sophomore	25	Freshman	30
Senior	5	Junior	70
Freshman	30	Sophomore	60
Sophomore	20	Freshman	10
Senior	100	Junior	15

Tia and Seth decide to examine more samples. Everyone in their class completed the same survey. They compared the 50 total samples of 20 college students. Seth and Tia create a histogram of the proportion of freshmen in each sample.

GENERALIZE
Most samples provide a reasonable estimate of the parameter. The average value of a set of sample statistics will approximate the population parameter with high precision.

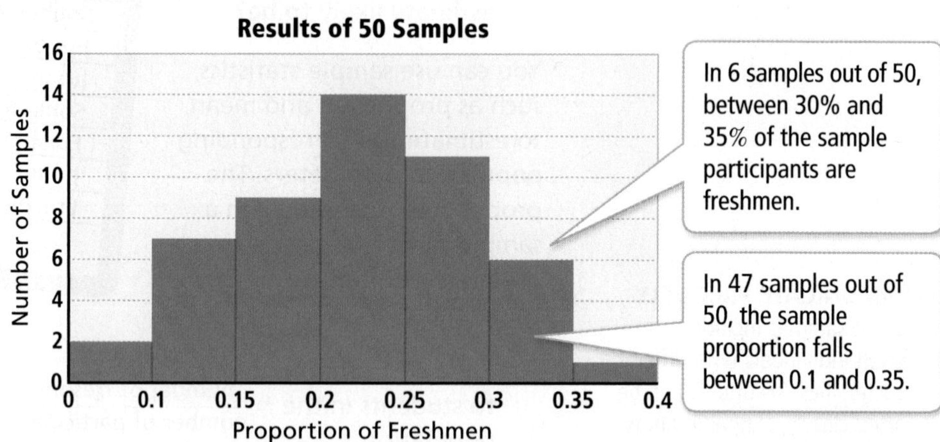

The distribution of sample results is approximately normal. There is natural variability among the samples, but most of the samples return statistics between 0.1 and 0.35. It is reasonable to predict that the actual proportion of freshmen at the college is between 0.1 and 0.35.

Seth's result of 0.20 is in the middle of the range and is likely a good representation of the population proportion. Tia's result of 0.40 falls outside the range of most of the results, so it is more likely that her estimate is further away from the true mean.

CONTINUED ON THE NEXT PAGE

EXAMPLE 2 CONTINUED

Try It! 2. Each classmate calculates the mean distance from home in miles reported by participants. Seth and Tia create this histogram to investigate the sample statistics. How many samples reported an average distance from home between 101 and 125 mi? Use the histogram to suggest a reasonable interval to estimate the population parameter.

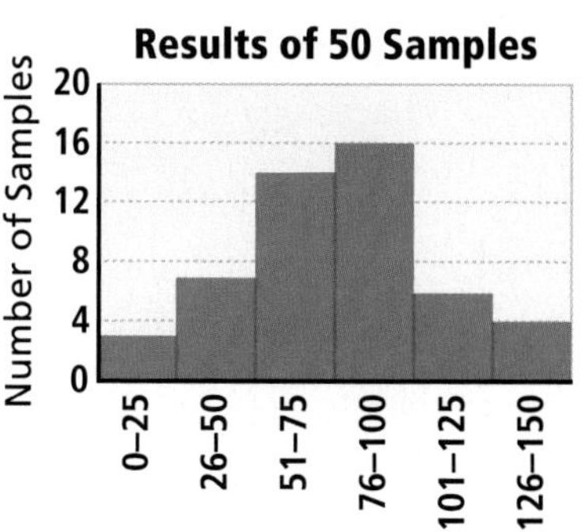

CONCEPTUAL DEVELOPMENT

EXAMPLE 3 Use a Simulation to Evaluate a Claim

Gabriela wants proof of Alex's claim that he is a 75% free-throw shooter. She observes Alex shoot 50 free throws, of which he makes 30. Gabriela notes his 60% success rate, but Alex points out that this is a reasonable result due to the natural variability that happens from sample to sample. Is he correct?

USE APPROPRIATE TOOLS
A random number generator allows you to generate many samples based on a possible population parameter. These samples will provide a collection of statistics with natural variability. You can evaluate a statistic by comparing it to this collection.

A. How can you use random numbers to investigate Alex's claim?

Assume Alex does make 75% of his free throws. Use a random number generator on a calculator or spreadsheeet to simulate the outcome of a random sample of shots.

Create a list of 50 random numbers ranging from 1–100. Numbers 1–75 represent successful free throws, and numbers 76–100 represent missed shots.

fx =RANDBETWEEN(1,100)

D	E	F	G	H	I
50	10	66	61	15	
9	82	50	22	78	
49	13	26	76	48	
19	12	11	35	4	
95	18	15	16	17	
61	55	86	58	22	
74	78	100	40	58	
65	25	89	82	84	
35	22	57	66	22	
1	64	88	65	30	

A formula like this generates a random number between 1 and 100.

In this sample, 39 out of 50 shots, or 0.78, are successful.

While the simulated proportion 0.78 is much higher than 0.60 or 60%, this one simulation does not refute Alex's reasoning about natural variability. Gabriela needs more evidence.

CONTINUED ON THE NEXT PAGE

  Activity  Assess

EXAMPLE 3 CONTINUED

Continue the simulation, analyzing 100 samples of 50 shots each. The distribution of sample statistics, such as means or proportions from different samples of the same population, is called the **sampling distribution.**

This sampling distribution of the number of successes in 50 shots for 100 simulated samples is approximately normal.

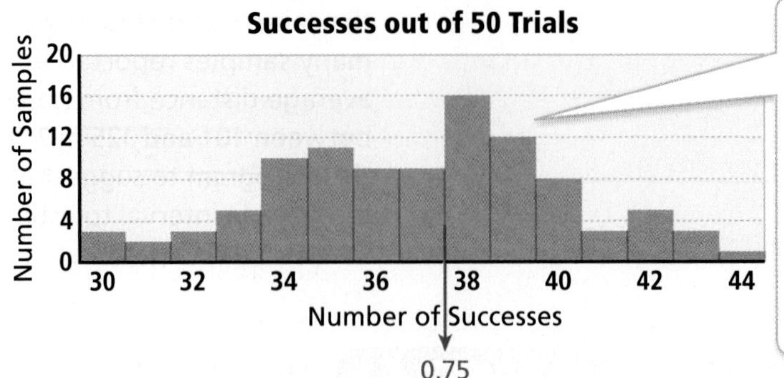

Most sample proportions are clustered near the 75% success rate, but many random samples have different proportions of successes.

As the number of samples increases, the distribution will more accurately reflect the population parameter.

B. How can you interpret the sampling distribution?

This simulated sampling distribution is based on the assumption that Alex makes 75% of his free throws.

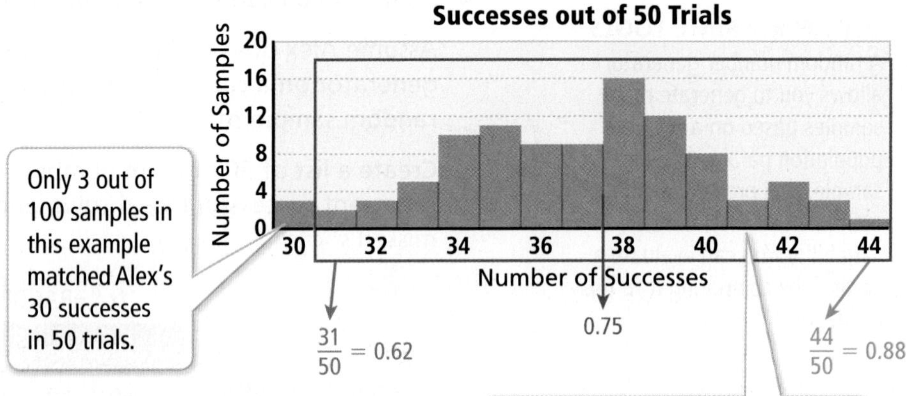

Only 3 out of 100 samples in this example matched Alex's 30 successes in 50 trials.

$\frac{31}{50} = 0.62$ $\frac{44}{50} = 0.88$

Select a range of data that is centered on the mean and includes about 95% of the samples.

Most samples (47 of 50, or 0.94) have a proportion of success between 0.62 and 0.88. This is as much as 0.13 above or below the central value of 0.75.

You can say that 0.13 or 13% represents a reasonable difference from the target that could appear through natural variability.

Based on the simulation, a basketball player who actually shoots free throws with 75% accuracy can reliably be expected to make 62%–88% of free throws in a 50-shot trial.

It would be very unusual for a real 75%-shooter to make only 30 shots out of 50. It is likely that Alex's low performance shows that he does not make 75% of his free throws overall.

COMMON ERROR
Do not assume that Alex's "true" free-throw percentage *must* be less than 75%. It is unlikely, but it is still possible that his lower actual success rate of 60% is due to chance, or other adverse factors.

CONTINUED ON THE NEXT PAGE

 **Try It!** 3. How would your conclusion in Example 3 differ if you did 100 simulations of 10 shots each? How would it differ if you did 100 simulations of 1,000 shots each?

CONCEPT Margin of Error

The sampling distributions of means and proportions tend to be normal. The mean of such a sampling distribution is the population parameter, and the standard deviation decreases as the sample size increases.

According to the Empirical Rule, 95% of values in a normal distribution fall within two standard deviations of the mean.

So, 95% of all sample results fall within two standard deviations of the population parameter being evaluated.

The **margin of error** gives the maximum expected difference between the sample result and the population parameter.

These formulas give the maximum difference between the parameter and the statistic for 95% of samples.

Quantitative Data	Categorical Data
Margin of Error $\approx \frac{2\sigma}{\sqrt{n}}$	Margin of Error $\approx \frac{1}{\sqrt{n}}$
σ = population standard deviation	for samples of size n.
n = sample size.	

EXAMPLE 4 Use a Margin of Error for a Mean

The College Board recently reported that the mean score on the SAT mathematics exam is 508, with standard deviation 121. Washington High believes that its seniors score considerably higher than the national average, so the school randomly sampled scores from 200 seniors, finding a mean score of 550. Is Washington High correct in its belief?

STUDY TIP
Before calculating margin of error, identify the type of data being analyzed. Formulas are different for categorical and quantitative values.

Since the data in this example is quantitative, the margin of error for SAT data is $\frac{2\sigma}{\sqrt{n}} = \frac{2(121)}{\sqrt{200}} \approx 17$.

So, about 95% of random samples with 200 participants will have mean values within 17 points of the population parameter, $\mu = 508$. Find the range of reasonable means.

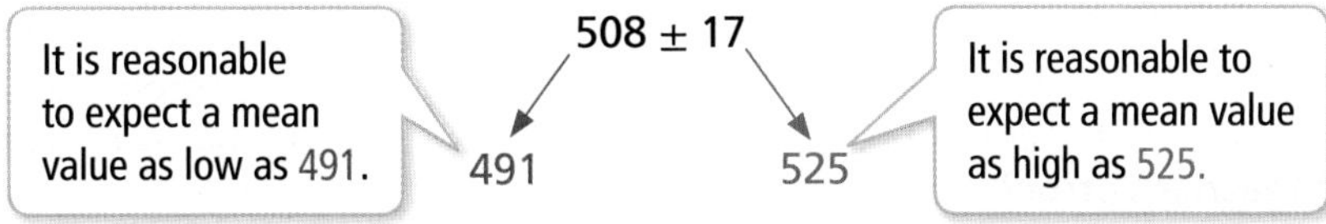

Washington High's sample mean score of 550 is above the range of reasonable means, so they can conclude that their seniors perfom better than the national average.

CONTINUED ON THE NEXT PAGE

 **Try It!** 4. A random sample of 100 Washington High seniors reveals that 40% plan to take the SAT this year. Use the margin of error to predict the actual proportion of seniors planning to take the exam.

CONCEPT SUMMARY Understanding Sampling Distributions

SAMPLING DISTRIBUTION

Sample statistics tend to be normally distributed (for samples of the same size).

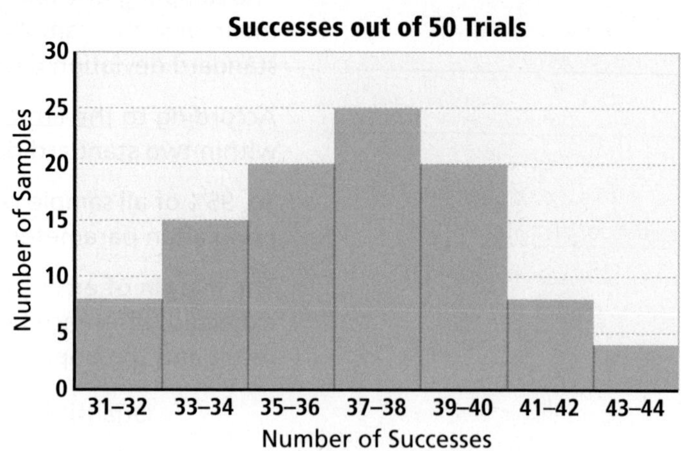

MARGIN OF ERROR

Quantitative Data

Margin of Error $\approx \frac{2\sigma}{\sqrt{n}}$

σ = population standard deviation

n = sample size

Categorical Data

Margin of Error $\approx \frac{1}{\sqrt{n}}$

n = sample size

Do You UNDERSTAND?

1. ESSENTIAL QUESTION How can you determine how far a statistic is likely to be from a parameter?

2. **Error Analysis** In a sample of 16 students from a teacher's physical education classes, students attempted to do as many sit-ups as possible in one minute. The mean was 10 with a standard deviation of 2. The teacher said that the margin of error was $\frac{1}{4}$. What is the teacher's error?

3. **Vocabulary** Explain what a sampling distribution is in your own words.

4. **Communicate Precisely** Suppose you want to find the margin of error for a certain sample. Explain when to use the formula Margin of Error $= \frac{2\sigma}{\sqrt{n}}$ and when to use the formula Margin of Error $= \frac{1}{\sqrt{n}}$.

Do You KNOW HOW?

Suppose an event occurs x times in a sample size of n. Find the sample proportion and the margin of error to the nearest percent.

5. $x = 80$ and $n = 700$

6. $x = 45$ and $n = 1,200$

Suppose a sample has a standard deviation of σ and a sample size of n. Find the margin of error to the nearest tenth.

7. $\sigma = 21.26$ and $n = 500$

8. $\sigma = 122.18$ and $n = 850$

9. **Model With Mathematics** In a sample of 400 adults, 348 have never been to Australia. Find the sample proportion for those who have never been to Australia. Write the answer as a percent.

PRACTICE & PROBLEM SOLVING

Scan for Multimedia

Additional Exercises Available Online

UNDERSTAND

10. Reason Erin found the margin of error of a certain random sample. Suppose she triples the sample size. How is the margin of error affected?

11. Make Sense and Persevere A poll reports that 48% of voters are going to vote for Candidate A. The poll reports a margin of error of ±4%. Estimate the number of voters in the poll. Explain how you found your answer.

12. Error Analysis Describe and correct the error a student made in finding the range of reasonable means.

The nationwide mean height of players on a high school basketball team is 71 in., with standard deviation of 5 in. A random sample of 150 players was used to determine the range of reasonable means.

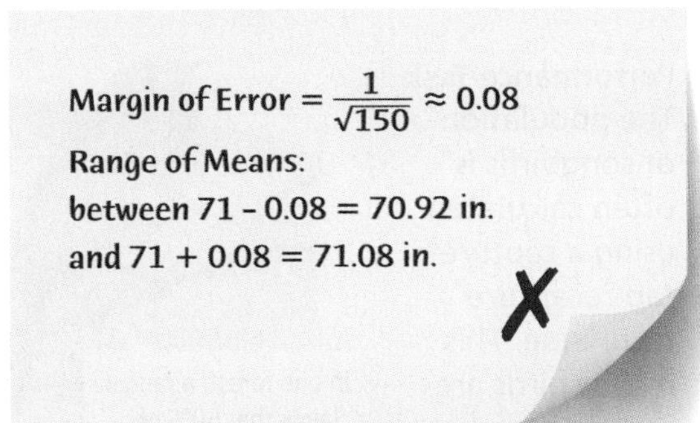

13. Higher Order Thinking The students in Mr. Morrison's science class measured the heights of flowers in the school's playground area. The class took six random samples by measuring a group of flowers. The table shows the standard deviation of each sample. Use the information in the table to determine which was likely the smallest sample. Explain your reasoning.

Sample	Standard Deviation
A	1.45
B	2.03
C	1.12
D	1.35
E	2.78
F	1.84

PRACTICE

14. Ryan selects a random sample of students from a high school. Students were asked how long it takes them to get ready for school. Use the sample data in the table to estimate the mean time to get ready for school. Estimate the proportion of juniors at the school. SEE EXAMPLE 1

Junior	45 min
Sophomore	30 min
Junior	15 min
Senior	25 min
Sophomore	60 min
Freshman	10 min
Sophomore	35 min
Junior	40 min
Senior	10 min
Freshman	30 min

15. Ryan's classmates each calculated the mean time it takes to get ready for school reported by a sample of 100 participants. Ryan created this histogram of the sample means. How many samples reported an average time to get ready between 11 and 20 min? Suggest a reasonable interval to estimate the population parameter. SEE EXAMPLE 2

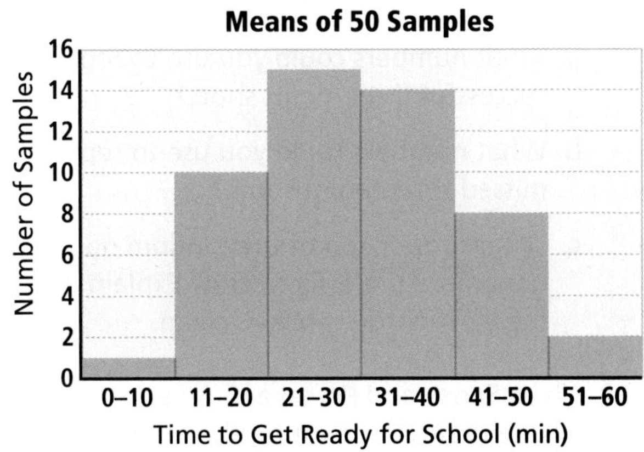

16. Jake makes 80% of the field goals he attempts. Suppose Jake attempts 100 field goals. Use technology to simulate 50 trials with 100 field goals each. Identify the range that contains the middle 95% of results. SEE EXAMPLE 3

17. The mean score on a statewide science test is 72, with standard deviation 12. Hailey believes that the scores in her school are considerably higher than the state average. A random sample of 100 students from Hailey's school showed a mean score of 76. Is Hailey correct in her belief? Explain. SEE EXAMPLE 4

PRACTICE & PROBLEM SOLVING

Mixed Review Available Online

APPLY

18. **Reason** A survey of 2,390 employees found that 7% are left-handed.
    a. Find the margin of error for the sample. Round to the nearest percent.
    b. Use the margin of error to find an interval that will likely include the population proportion of the employees that are left-handed.

19. **Model With Mathematics** Lydia wants proof of Mike's claim that he is a 40% three-point shooter in basketball. She observes him make 17 out of 50 three-point shots. Lydia used a random number generator to simulate the outcome of a random sample of shots.

16	22	53	51	62	81	69	68	59	29
69	71	29	83	79	34	67	82	64	50
30	79	68	94	33	24	6	28	91	59
33	59	42	89	13	56	15	6	75	97
83	6	89	55	39	61	69	17	20	89

    a. What numbers could you use to represent successful three-point shots?
    b. What numbers could you use to represent missed three-point shots?
    c. What proportion of the random numbers generated were successful? Explain what this means regarding Mike's claim.

20. **Make Sense and Persevere** An app estimates phone usage by counting the number of times a phone screen is unlocked during the course of a day. A sample of 25 users is shown.

123	65	119	145	114
125	114	91	113	125
88	141	105	116	121
186	136	65	128	107
97	126	101	90	10

    a. What is the mean and standard deviation?
    b. Assuming the sample standard deviation matches the population standard deviation, what is the margin of error?
    c. When Isabel says, "I check my phone at least 100 times a day," is she exaggerating, or could her claim be reasonable? Explain.

ASSESSMENT PRACTICE

21. In a random survey of 60 customers, 46 prefer Cracker A. Fill in the blank with the correct value.
    a. The sample proportion is about ________.
    b. The margin of error is about ________.
    c. The interval likely to contain the true population proportion is between ________ and ________.

22. **SAT/ACT** A manufacturing company wants to randomly sample customers about their satisfaction rating on products. The company will give a gift certificate worth $25 to every customer who completes the survey. How much will it cost the company to obtain a margin of error of ±5%?

    Ⓐ $400
    Ⓑ $1,000
    Ⓒ $4,000
    Ⓓ $10,000

23. **Performance Task** The population of songbirds is often calculated using a *capture-tag-recapture* technique. This means birds are captured and then tagged. After being tagged, the birds are released. A group of researchers is investigating a ranger's claim about the percentage of songbirds that are tagged. They recapture 10 birds, and only 3 have tags.

Part A Use a calculator or spreadsheet to simulate 25 samples with 10 birds recaptured by selecting 10 random numbers.

Part B After simulating 25 trials, analyze the proportion of successes in each trial and create a histogram to display the sampling distribution.

Part C Identify the range of values that contains the middle 95% of results. Does the ranger's claim seem reasonable?

Activity Assess

8-6 Introduction to Hypothesis Testing

PearsonRealize.com

I CAN… state two hypotheses for a statistics question and decide if the data support one of the hypotheses.

VOCABULARY

- alternative hypothesis
- hypothesis
- null hypothesis

EXPLORE & REASON

The tables below each show the results of flipping a coin 30 times.

Coin 1					
H	H	H	H	H	T
H	T	T	H	H	T
T	T	H	H	T	H
H	H	T	T	T	H
H	T	T	H	T	H

Coin 2					
T	T	H	T	H	H
H	T	T	T	H	T
T	T	H	T	T	T
H	T	T	T	T	T
T	T	T	H	T	T

A. How many heads and how many tails resulted from flipping each coin 30 times?

B. How many heads and how many tails would you expect from flipping a fair coin 30 times? Are either of these coins close to what you would expect?

C. Construct Arguments Can you conclude with certainty that either of the coins is fair? Can you conclude that either of the coins is unfair?

ESSENTIAL QUESTION How do you formulate and test a hypothesis using statistics?

CONCEPTUAL UNDERSTANDING

EXAMPLE 1 Write Hypotheses

A car has been getting 34.6 miles per gallon. With a fuel additive, the car gets 35.3 miles per gallon. What hypotheses would you test to determine whether the increase in mileage is due to the additive?

The first step in determining whether the additive is effective is to formulate *hypotheses* to test using statistical methods.

Step 1 Determine what your question means in terms of a parameter.

The additive works if a car gets a higher mean gas mileage when using the additive than the mean gas mileage when not using the additive.

Step 2 State this information about the parameter mathematically.

Let μ represent the mean gas mileage for the car with the additive. You want to know if $\mu > 34.6$. This is a **hypothesis**, a possible explanation of one or more observed occurrences.

Step 3 State what would happen if this hypothesis is not true.

If the fuel additive does not cause an increase in gas mileage, then $\mu = 34.6$. This is also a hypothesis.

COMMUNICATE PRECISELY
Exactly one of the hypotheses can be true. Data from an experiment will provide evidence to help you argue for which hypothesis is more likely true.

CONTINUED ON THE NEXT PAGE

EXAMPLE 1 CONTINUED

Step 4 Write the *null hypothesis* and *alternative hypothesis*.

The hypothesis that there is no increase with the additive is the **null hypothesis** and is denoted H_0. In this case you would write H_0 as $\mu = 34.6$.

The **alternative hypothesis** is H_a: $\mu > 34.6$ because it includes only the possibility of difference between the quantities of interest.

Stating hypotheses is useful because it gives you two possibilities to test using statistics. The hypotheses used to determine whether the fuel additive causes an increase in gas mileage are:

$$H_0: \mu = 34.6$$

$$H_a: \mu > 34.6.$$

Try It! **1.** A soccer goalie saved 46.4% of her opponents' tiebreaker attempts. After her coach adjusted her position in the goal, she saved 47.3% of the attempts. Write the null hypothesis and alternative hypothesis for a statistical study to evaluate the population parameter *P*, the proportion of tiebreaker goals she saves after working with her coach.

APPLICATION

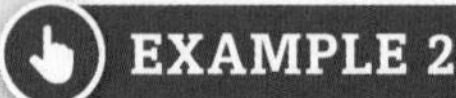

EXAMPLE 2 Examine Data from an Experiment

A car company performed an experiment to determine whether the fuel additive from Example 1 increases a particular type of car's gas mileage.

The company recorded the gas mileage of ten identical cars all driven under the same conditions with and without the use of the fuel additive.

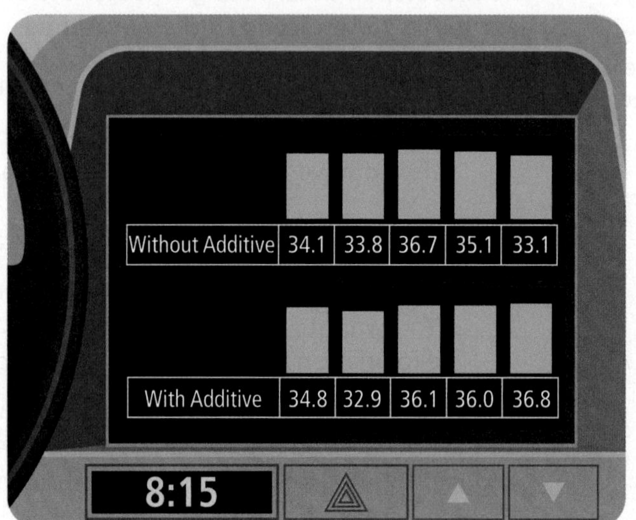

Without Additive	34.1	33.8	36.7	35.1	33.1
With Additive	34.8	32.9	36.1	36.0	36.8

CONTINUED ON THE NEXT PAGE

Activity Assess

EXAMPLE 2 CONTINUED

How can you use the data to compare the effectiveness of the additive?

If there were no difference in the gas mileages with or without the additive, the means of the gas mileages would be equal and their difference would be 0. If the additive increases gas mileage, the difference of the means would be greater than 0.

Let μ_1 be the mean of the gas mileage with the additive and let μ_2 be the mean of the gas mileage without the additive. The null hypothesis and alternative hypothesis for this situation are,

$$H_0: \mu_1 - \mu_2 = 0$$
$$H_A: \mu_1 - \mu_2 > 0$$

The sample means are $\bar{x}_1 = 34.56$ and $\bar{x}_2 = 35.32$.

Recall that the notation $\bar{x}$ represents the sample mean. Note that the hypotheses use the population mean μ.

The difference of the sample means is $35.32 - 34.56 = 0.76$.

The average gas mileage with the additive was *0.76 miles per gallon greater* than the average without it. But is this due to the additive, or to random variation?

USE APPROPRIATE TOOLS
You can use technology or draw slips of paper from a container to sort the data randomly into two new groups.

It is extremely unlikely that all ten cars will have exactly the same gas mileage, even if the additive has no effect. There will always be some amount of variation. It is possible that by chance alone the cars with the higher gas mileage were grouped together and the cars with the lower gas mileage were grouped together.

One way to test the hypotheses is to randomly assign the data to two new groups many times and look at the variability of the differences of the means. The table shows one such assignment.

New Group 1	34.8	33.8	36.7	36.1	33.1
New Group 2	34.1	35.1	36.0	32.9	36.8

Mean of New Group 1 = 34.9

Mean of New Group 2 = 34.98

If there is no difference in mileage between the groups with or without the additive, reassigning the data into two groups repeatedly will likely result in differences closely distributed around zero. If there is a difference in mileage, there is likely to be large variability in the distribution of differences.

In this regrouping of the data, the difference of the sample means is 0.08, which is closer to 0 than the original difference of sample means, 0.76.

While this provides one basis of comparison for testing the null hypothesis, many more resamples and many more comparisons are needed before you can possibly reject the null hypothesis. You will see this in Example 3.

Try It! 2. In one particular randomization one group has these data values: 34.1, 36.7, 35.1, 36.1, 36.8.

a. Identify the data values for the other group.

b. Calculate the difference of the means for the two groups.

EXAMPLE 3 Use Simulation Results to Test Hypotheses

How can continued randomization of the gas mileage data be used to test the hypotheses in Example 2?

In Example 2, you randomly reassigned the data into two new groups to make a comparison. If you randomize the data many times, you can create a distribution that you can use to evaluate the hypotheses. To do this, follow these steps.

- Pool all data values into a single set.
- Create two new groups of data values at random from the pool. Each data value must be used exactly once.
- Calculate the difference of the means for the new groups.
- Repeat. The histogram below shows the result of 200 randomizations.

When data values were assigned to new groups at random, the differences of the means were greater than 0.76 almost a quarter of the time.

COMMON ERROR

The initial experiment relied on a very small sample. It is difficult to establish definitive results with a small sample. Repeat the experiment with a greater number of trials.

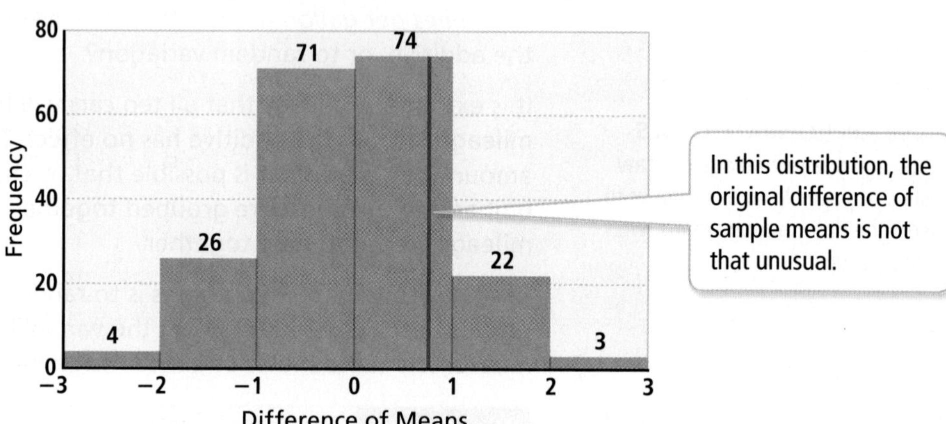

The initial difference of means could reasonably be attributed to the variability inherent in random sampling.

This small experiment *does not* give convincing evidence that the fuel additive improved the car's gas mileage. More testing, possibly with larger samples, is needed. For now, we cannot reject the null hypothesis, that there is no difference in the means of the gas mileage with and without the additive, and that any variation is due to chance alone.

Try It! 3. The fuel additive was tested again, resulting in the data displayed below. Use a simulation to randomly assign the data into two new groups. Find the difference of the means of the original sample and the new groups you just created. How do they differ? Explain what additional information you need to be able to test the hypotheses from Example 2.

Without Additive	34.1	32.8	33.8	30.9	36.7
	33.4	35.1	32.1	30.4	33.1
With Additive	34.8	35.1	32.9	35.3	36.1
	36.9	36.0	37.2	36.3	36.8

 Activity
 Assess

APPLICATION

EXAMPLE 4 Evaluate a Report Based on Data

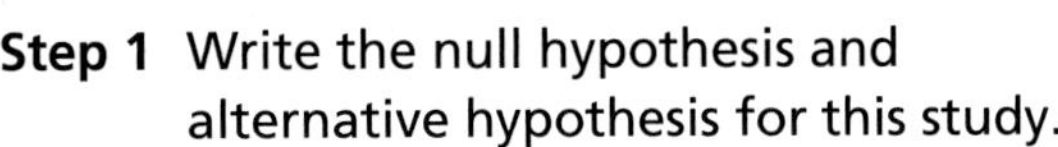

Best Bet Mac & Cheese reports that the average price for a box of their product is \$1.45. A marketing company selects a national sample of 100 retail prices. The standard deviation of prices nationally is \$0.20 and the mean of the prices of the sample is \$1.65. Does this study provide strong evidence that Best Bet's claim is false?

$\bar{x} = \$1.65$
$\sigma = \$0.20$

Best Bet
MAC
&
CHEESE

Step 1 Write the null hypothesis and alternative hypothesis for this study.

H_0: $\mu = 1.45$ The mean price of Best Bet Mac & Cheese is \$1.45.

H_A: $\mu \neq 1.45$ The mean price of Best Bet Mac & Cheese is NOT \$1.45.

STUDY TIP
You can use margin of error to find the range of reasonable means for a study. If the mean in a claim is within that range, then the data do not disprove the claim.

Step 2 Calculate the margin of error for the new sample.

Use the formula $m = \frac{2\sigma}{\sqrt{n}}$, where σ is the population standard deviation of \$0.20, and n is 100, the number of prices sampled.

$$m = \frac{2(0.20)}{\sqrt{100}} = 0.04$$

Step 3 Use the sample statistic and margin of error to predict a range of reasonable values estimating the population parameter.

Sample mean $\pm$ margin of error

$1.65 \pm 0.04 = 1.61$ to 1.69

Based on sampling, we would predict the value of the mean price to fall between \$1.61 and \$1.69.

Step 4 Compare the claim to the predicted interval.

The claim falls outside the range of reasonable values predicted by the statistical study. This evidence suggests you should reject the null hyothesis.

Try It! **4.** Best Bet revises their claim and reports an average retail price of \$1.60. A second marketing study sampled 300 prices for Best Bet Mac & Cheese finding a mean price of \$1.64.

a. What is the margin of error for the new sample?

b. Is Best Bet's revised claim supported by this new study? Explain why or why not.

CONCEPT SUMMARY Using Statistical Data to Test Claims

SET UP Write two statements.

Null hypothesis, H_0: The observed statistic in a treatment group is equal to the corresponding population parameter, and any variation is due to chance.

Alternative hypothesis, H_a: The observed statistic in a treatment group differs from the corresponding population parameter, and the variation is not due to chance alone.

COMPARE Compare two groups by comparing their distributions, means, standard deviations, proportions, or other statistics.

Analyze the data to determine how likely it is that differences between the two groups occurred by chance.

DECIDE Decide whether the differences could be attributed to natural variability.

Likely to have occurred by chance?

Then there is no reason to reject the null hypothesis.

Too different to be coincidence?

Strong evidence that the difference is not due to chance points to the truth of the alternative hypothesis.

Do You UNDERSTAND?

1. ESSENTIAL QUESTION How do you formulate and test a hypothesis using statistics?

2. **Error Analysis** When presented with an experiment about teeth whitening strips claiming to deliver visibly whiter teeth within two weeks, Mercedes said the null hypothesis of the experiment was that the teeth would become significantly whiter after two weeks of using the whitening strips. Explain Mercedes' error.

3. **Vocabulary** Explain the difference between a *null hypothesis* and an *alternative hypothesis*.

4. **Communicate Precisely** If the null hypothesis of an experiment is H_0: $\mu \leq 10.8$, then what is the alternative hypothesis H_a?

Do You KNOW HOW?

5. A baseball player's career batting average was .278. After working with a new coach, the player batted .315. Write the null hypothesis and alternative hypothesis for a study of the effect of the change.

6. A lumber company claims that at least 80% of its plywood is made from recycled materials. It tests 25 pieces of the plywood and finds that the mean of the percentage of recycled material in the sample is 78%. The standard deviation of the population is 3%. Give an interval of reasonable values for the percentage of recycled material in the plywood. Is the company's claim likely true?

7. Terrence grows two varieties of tomatoes, TomTom and Hugemato. Hugemato claims to grow 10% heavier tomatoes. Find the difference of sample means for the samples shown. Resample randomly and find the new difference of sample means. How do they compare?

TomTom	10.1	10.5	9.9	10.4	11.2
Hugemato	13.1	11	12.1	11.4	12.9

PRACTICE & PROBLEM SOLVING

Scan for Multimedia

Practice Tutorial

Additional Exercises Available Online

UNDERSTAND

8. **Communicate Precisely** Becky buys a new hybrid grass seed that is supposed to require only a small amount of water to grow. After Becky plants the new seed, it rains every other day for a two-week period, and the grass grows well. Explain why this particular situation cannot be used to support the claim about the water required to grow the seed.

9. **Error Analysis** Jake's average bowling score was 230. Jake bought a new bowling ball. Since using the new bowling ball Jake's average score has improved to 250. He wrote the null hypothesis and alternative hypothesis for a statistical study to evaluate the effect of the new ball on his bowling sscore. Explain his error.

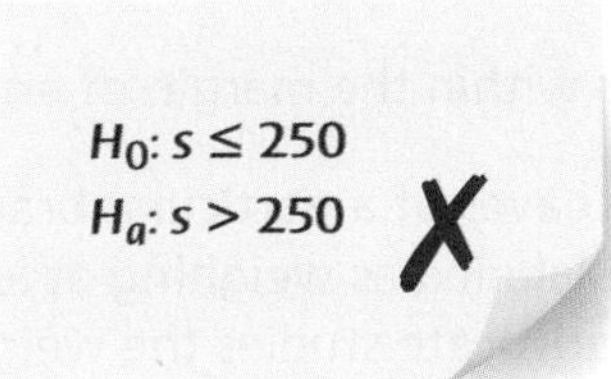

10. **Generalize** Using the formula for margin of error, $m = \frac{2\sigma}{\sqrt{n}}$, explain why the larger a sample size is, the smaller the margin of error should be.

11. **Reason** Answer the following questions about randomizing samples.

    a. Why is the method of randomizing samples used when working with experimental data sets?

    b. If the red vertical line in the histogram shown represents the difference in the means of the original samples, then how does it compare to the differences of the means in the randomly generated samples?

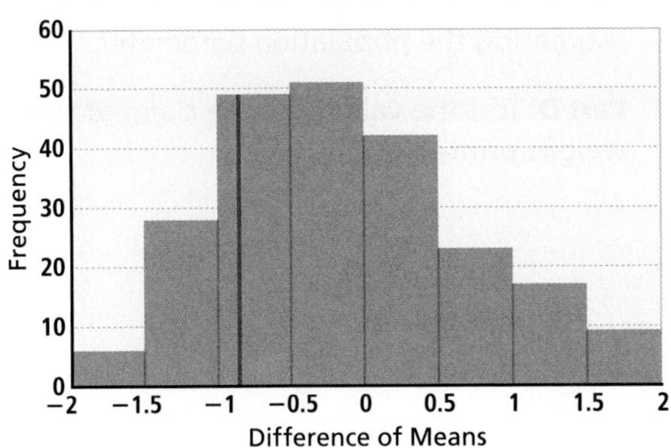

PRACTICE

12. Tavon had an average time for the 100-yd dash of 18 seconds. Since starting a strength-training program, he has been running the 100-yd dash in an average time of 15 seconds. Write the null hypothesis and alternative hypothesis for a statistical study to evaluate the effect of the training on Tavon's time in the 100-yd dash. SEE EXAMPLE 1

13. The coach wants to perform an experiment to determine whether strength training impacts a runner's speed. The coach completed several trials and recorded the speeds of the 100-yd dash (in seconds) of a sample of five track athletes both before and after they tried strength training. SEE EXAMPLE 2

Without Training	18	20	16	15	14
With Training	15	19	17	16	14

    a. Find the sample means and their difference. Resample the data so that one group has these data values: 15, 20, 17, 15, 14.

    b. Identify the data values for the other group.

    c. Calculate the difference of the means for the two resample groups.

14. The training regimen was tested again, resulting in the data displayed below. Use a simulation to randomize the data without replacement, creating 50 new groupings. Create a histogram of the differences between group means to display your results. Use the data to draw a conclusion about the initial hypothesis. SEE EXAMPLE 3

Without Vitamins	14	12	18	19	15
With Vitamins	15	12	16	18	14

15. Grain Goodness reports the average price for a box of their granola is \$3.87. A marketing company selects a national sample of 100 retail prices and states the mean price was \$4.42. The standard deviation was \$0.60. What is the margin of error for this new sample? SEE EXAMPLE 4

Mixed Review Available Online

PRACTICE & PROBLEM SOLVING

APPLY

16. Model with Mathematics A botanist is doing an experimental research study to determine whether a certain fertilizer will increase the yield of soybean plants. The botanist included several soybean farmers in his study. The average yield of soybeans for each farmer (in bushels per acre) of the crops with and without fertilizer are recorded in the table shown.

Without Fertilizer	40	42	45	50	47
With Fertilizer	42	40	46	49	48

Find the means of both samples and their difference. State how the average yield of the soybean crops with the fertilizer compares to the average yield of the soybean crops without fertilizer.

17. Communicate Precisely A randomization of the data from Exercise 16, placed into two new random groups, is shown in the table.

New Group 1	46	50	40	42	47
New Group 2	40	49	42	48	45

a. Find the difference between the sample means of the new groups.

b. Does it provide evidence that the difference in the original two sample means is due to the effects of the fertilizer or just due to chance?

18. Make Sense and Persevere The rules state that a baseball must have a certain circumference. What hypotheses would you test to determine whether the baseballs made on a new machine are within the specifications?

ASSESSMENT PRACTICE

19. What are the different types of hypotheses used in a statistical study? Select all that apply

Ⓐ experimental
Ⓑ supported
Ⓒ alternative
Ⓓ strategic
Ⓔ null

20. SAT/ACT A survey found that 72% of freshmen planned to take at least one spring break trip while in college with a margin of error of ±3.5%. Central U claims that 75% of freshman plan trips. Is their claim reasonable?

Ⓐ No, their claim is not within the margin of error.
Ⓑ No, their claim is within the margin of error.
Ⓒ Yes, their claim is not within the margin of error.
Ⓓ Yes, their claim is within the margin of error.

21. Performance Task Loaves of a particular brand of wheat bread are labeled as weighing at least 16 oz. A consumer advocate studies the weights of 500 loaves of this bread.

Part A Find H_0 and H_a.

Part B Calculate the margin of error.

Part C Predict a range of reasonable values estimating the population parameter.

Part D Test the validity of the claim of the weight printed on the labels.

MATHEMATICAL MODELING IN 3 ACTS

PearsonRealize.com

Video

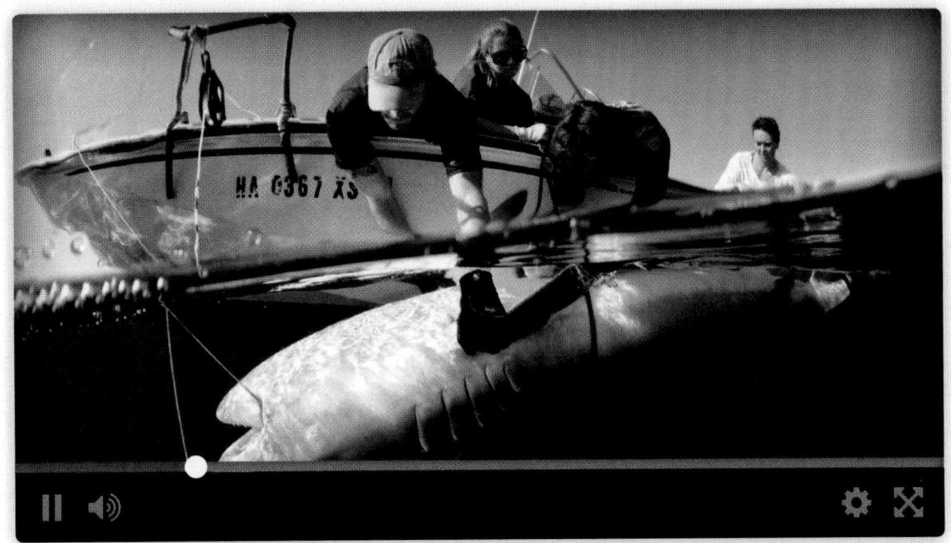

Mark and Recapture

It wouldn't take very long for you to count the number of people who live in your home or the number of socks in your drawer. How about the number of deer in Yellowstone National Park or the number of sharks in the waters around Hawaii?

The mark and recapture method is a popular way researchers can estimate an animal population. You will see an example of this method in the Mathematical Modeling in 3 Acts lesson.

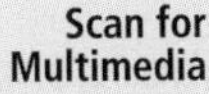
Scan for Multimedia

ACT 1 Identify the Problem

1. What is the first question that comes to mind after watching the video?
2. Write down the main question you will answer about what you saw in the video.
3. Make an initial conjecture that answers this main question.
4. Explain how you arrived at your conjecture.
5. What information will be useful to know to answer the main question? How can you get it? How will you use that information?

ACT 2 Develop a Model

6. Use the math that you have learned in this Topic to refine your conjecture.

ACT 3 Interpret the Results

7. Did your refined conjecture match the actual answer exactly? If not, what might explain the difference?

  Activity  Assess

8-7 Probability and Decision Making

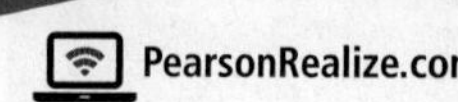
PearsonRealize.com

I CAN… use probability to make decisions.

CRITIQUE & EXPLAIN

Your friend offers to play the following game with you "If the product of the roll of two number cubes is 10 or less, I win. If not, you win!"

A. If you were to play the game many times, what percent of the games would you expect to win?

B. Is the game fair? Should you take the offer? Explain.

C. Make Sense and Persevere Suggest a way to change the game from fair to unfair, or vice versa, while still using the product of the two number cubes. Explain.

ESSENTIAL QUESTION

How can you use probability to make decisions?

APPLICATION

EXAMPLE 1 Use Probability to Make Fair Decisions

Sadie, Tamira, River, Victor, and Jae are candidates to represent their school at an event. How can you use random integers to select 2 students from the 5 candidates, so that each one is equally likely to be selected?

MAKE SENSE AND PERSEVERE Consider how you would assign integers from 1 to 10 among the 5 students. How do you adjust this for a random number generator that gives a number r from the interval $0 \leq r < 1$?

There are 5 students. Assign a number to each student.

1	2	3	4	5
Sadie	Tamira	River	Victor	Jae

To select a student, use a calculator or other random number generator to generate a random integer from 1 to 5. Repeat to select the second student.

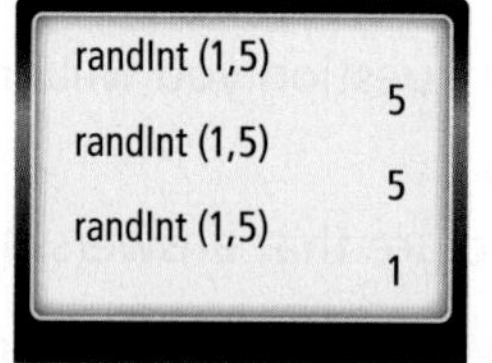

Ignore the duplicate 5. Some calculators may have a function that eliminates duplicates.

Jae (5) and Sadie (1) are selected.

Try It! 1. Your trainer creates training programs for you. How can you use index cards to randomly choose the following: Strength training 1 day per week; Cardio training 2 days per week, with no consecutive days; Swimming 1 day per week.

CONCEPTUAL UNDERSTANDING

EXAMPLE 2 Determine Whether a Decision Is Fair or Unfair

Thato places three cards in a hat and challenges Helena to a game.

A. Thato says, "If you draw a number greater than 2, you earn 2 points. Otherwise, I earn 2 points." Is the game fair, or unfair? If it is unfair, which player has the advantage? Explain.

In each round, Thato either wins 2 points or loses 2 points.

> If Helena draws a "3" and gets 2 points, Thato considers this a loss of 2 points for himself.

Find the probability of each outcome. Then find the expected value.

$P(-2) = \frac{1}{3}$ and $P(+2) = \frac{2}{3}$.

$$E = -2 \cdot \left(\frac{1}{3}\right) + 2 \cdot \left(\frac{2}{3}\right)$$

$$= \frac{2}{3}$$

> A game is considered "fair" if and only if the expected value is 0.

COMMON ERROR
Recall that the expected value is the sum of the products of the outcomes' values by their respective probabilities. Be careful not to use the sum of the probabilities.

The game is unfair and is skewed to Thato's advantage. The probability of his scoring 2 points is twice the probability of Helena scoring 2 points.

B. Helena proposes a change to the scoring of the game. She says, "If I draw a number greater than 2, I get 2 points. Otherwise, you get 1 point." Is the game fair, or unfair? If it is unfair, which player has the advantage? Explain.

In each round, Thato either scores 1 point or he loses 2 points.

Find the probability of each outcome. Then find the expected value.

$P(-2) = \frac{1}{3}$ and $P(+1) = \frac{2}{3}$.

$$E = -2 \cdot \left(\frac{1}{3}\right) + 1 \cdot \left(\frac{2}{3}\right)$$

$$= -\frac{2}{3} + \frac{2}{3} = 0$$

This is a fair game because the expected value is 0. Neither player has an advantage over the other.

Try It! **2.** Justice and Tamika use the same 3 cards but change the game. In each round, a player draws a card and replaces it, and then the other player draws. The differences between the two cards are used to score each round. Order matters, so the difference can be negative. Is each game fair? Explain.

a. If the difference between the first and second cards is 2, Justice gets a point. Otherwise Tamika gets a point.

b. They take turns drawing first. Each round, the first player to draw subtracts the second player's number from her own and the result is added to her total score.

APPLICATION

EXAMPLE 3 Make a Decision Based on Expected Value

The Silicon Valley Company manufactures tablets and computers. Their tablets are covered by a warranty for one year, so that if the tablet fails, the company replaces it. Since the failure rate of their model TAB5000 tablet is high, the head of production has a plan for replacing certain components inside the TAB5000 and calling the new model TAB5001.

If you were the head of production, would you recommend switching to selling the TAB5001?

Formulate ◀ Find the expected profit for each model.

Expected profit = price − cost − (cost to replace)(failure rate)

Compute ◀

$$\begin{aligned}\text{Expected profit of TAB5000} &= \$150 - \$100 - (\$130)(0.05)\\ &= \$50 - \$6.50\\ &= \$43.50\end{aligned}$$

$$\begin{aligned}\text{Expected profit of TAB5001} &= \$150 - \$105 - (\$135)(0.01)\\ &= \$45 - \$1.35\\ &= \$43.65\end{aligned}$$

Interpret ◀ The expected profit of the TAB5001 is more than the expected profit of the TAB5000. It makes sense to sell the TAB5001 instead of the TAB5000. Also, customers who bought a tablet would be more likely to be pleased with their purchase and buy from the same company in the future.

Try It! **3.** Additional data is collected for the TAB5000 and TAB5001. The production and replacement costs for the TAB5001 remain unchanged.

a. The production and replacement costs for the TAB5000 increased by $10. What would the expected profit be for the TAB5000?

b. The failure rate for the TAB5001 increased by 1%. What would the expected profit be for the TAB5001?

c. As a consultant for the company, what would you recommend they do to maximize their profit?

EXAMPLE 4 Use a Binomial Distribution to Make Decisions

An airport shuttle company takes 8 reservations for each trip because 25% of their reservations do not show up. Is this a reasonable policy?

Find the probability that more passengers show up than the van can carry.

For 8 reservations, the graph shows the number of possible combinations of passengers showing up.

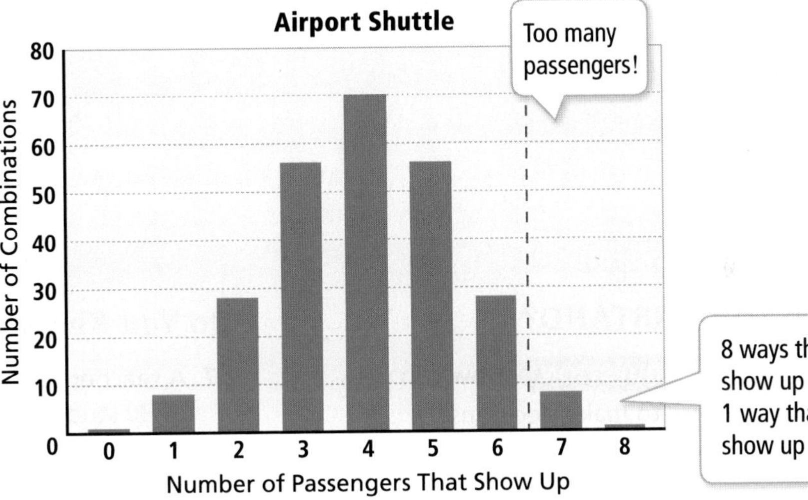

USE APPROPRIATE TOOLS
How does the graph of the number of combinations help you think about the situation?

To find the probability that too many reservations show up, compute the probability that either 7 or 8 passengers show up. Each reservation has a 75% chance of showing up and a 25% chance of not showing up. Use $P(r) = {}_nC_r\, p^r(1 - p)^{n-r}$.

Find the probability that 7 reservations show up.

$$P(7) = {}_8C_7(0.75)^7(0.25)^1 \approx 8(0.1335)(0.25) \approx 0.267$$

Find the probability that 8 reservations show up.

$$P(8) = {}_8C_8(0.75)^8(0.25)^0 \approx 1(0.1001)(1) \approx 0.100$$

The probability that more reservations will show up than the van can carry is $P(7) + P(8)$, or about $0.267 + 0.100 = 0.367$.

Over one third of the trips will have passengers who can not get a seat in the van. This will result in dissatisfied customers, so this is not a reasonable policy.

Try It! 4. A play calls for a crowd of 12 extras with non-speaking parts. Because 10% of the extras have not shown up in the past, the director selects 15 students as extras. Find the probabilities that 12 extras show up to the performance, 15 extras show up to the performance, and more than 12 extras show up to the performance.

  Concept Summary  Assess

CONCEPT SUMMARY Using Probability to Make Decisions

METHOD	DESCRIPTION	APPLICATIONS
Simple Probability	Find the probability of random events.	• Select the most favorable among random events.
Expected Value	Multiply the probability of each outcome by its value. Add to find the expected value.	• Compare expected values to choose the best of several options. • Compare expected values to decide if a game is fair.
Probability Distribution	Find the probability distribution of all possible outcomes.	• Compare probabilities of outcomes in a binomial experiment. • Create a graph of a probability distribution to present the distribution visually.

Do You UNDERSTAND?

1. ESSENTIAL QUESTION How can you use probability to make decisions?

2. **Reason** How can you use random numbers to simulate rolling a standard number cube?

3. **Error Analysis** Explain the error in Diego's reasoning.

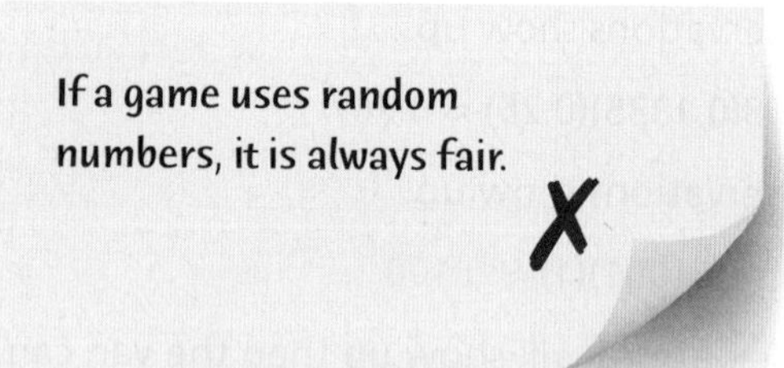

4. **Use Structure** Describe what conditions are needed for a fair game.

5. **Use Appropriate Tools** Explain how you can visualize probability distributions to help you make decisions.

6. **Reason** Why must the expected value of a fair game of chance equal zero?

Do You KNOW HOW?

7. A teacher assigns each of 30 students a unique number from 1 to 30. The teacher uses the random numbers shown to select students for presentations. Which student was selected first? second?

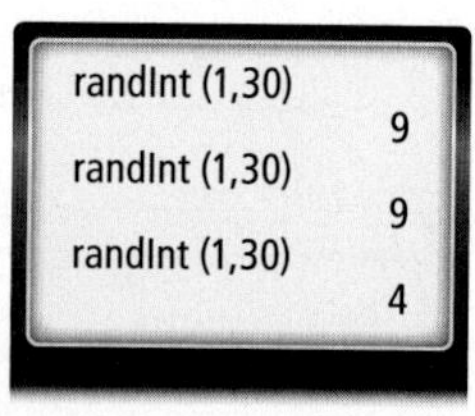

8. Three friends are at a restaurant and they all want the last slice of pizza. Identify three methods involving probability that they can use to determine who gets the last slice. Explain mathematically why each method will guarantee a fair decision.

9. Edgar rolls one number cube and Micah rolls two. If Edgar rolls a 6, he wins a prize. If Micah rolls a sum of 7, she gets a prize. Is this game fair? Explain.

10. The 10 parking spaces in the first row of the parking lot are reserved for the 12 members of the Student Council. Usually an average of ten percent of the Student Council does not drive to school dances. What is the probability that more members of the Student Council will drive to a dance than there are reserved parking spaces?

PRACTICE & PROBLEM SOLVING

Scan for Multimedia

Practice Tutorial

Additional Exercises Available Online

UNDERSTAND

11. **Reason** Suppose Chris has pair of 4-sided dice, each numbered from 1 to 4, and Carolina has a pair of 10-sided dice, each numbered from 1 to 10. They decide to play a series of games against each other, using their own dice.

    a. Describe a game that would be fair. Explain.

    b. Describe an unfair game. Explain.

12. **Construct Arguments** Mr. and Ms. Mitchell have 3 children, Luke, Charlie, and Aubrey. All 3 children want to sit in the front seat. Charlie suggests that they flip a coin two times to decide who will sit in the front seat. The number of heads determines who sits in the front seat. Is this a fair method? Explain.

Number of Heads	Front Seat Passenger
0	Luke
1	Charlie
2	Aubrey

13. **Error Analysis** Mercedes is planning a party for 10 people. She knows from experience that about 20% of those invited will not show up. If she invites 12 people, how can she calculate the probability that more than 10 people will show up. What error did she make? What is the correct probability?

Use the binomial distribution for 12 trials, with a 20% probability, and more than 10 show up.
$(12)(0.80)^1(0.20)^{11} +$
$(1)(0.80)^0(0.20)^{12}$ ✗

PRACTICE

14. How can you use random integers to select 3 students from a group of 8 to serve as student body representatives, so that each student is equally likely to be selected? SEE EXAMPLE 1

Explain whether each game is fair or unfair. SEE EXAMPLE 2

15. When it is your turn, roll a standard number cube. If the number is even, you get a point. If it is odd, you lose a point.

16. When it is your turn, roll two standard number cubes. If the product of the numbers is even, you get a point. If the product is odd, you lose a point.

Fatima is a contestant on a game show. So far, she has won \$34,000. She can keep the \$34,000 or spin the spinner shown below and add or subtract the amount shown from \$34,000. SEE EXAMPLE 3

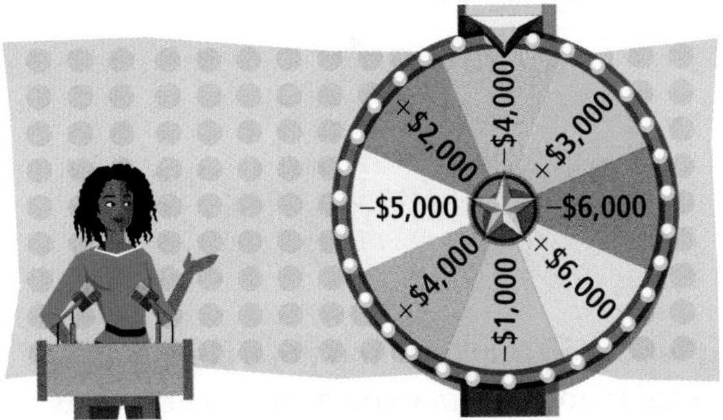

17. If Fatima spins the spinner, what are her expected total winnings?

18. Would you advise Fatima to keep the \$34,000 or to spin the spinner? Explain your reasoning.

19. Suppose 0.5% of people who file federal tax returns with an adjusted gross income (AGI) between \$50,000 and \$75,000 are audited. Of 5 people in that tax bracket for whom ABC Tax Guys prepared their taxes, 2 were audited. SEE EXAMPLE 4

    a. If 5 people with an AGI between \$50,000 and \$75,000 are selected at random from all the people who filed federal tax returns, what is the probability that at least 2 people are audited?

    b. Would you recommend that a friend with an AGI between \$50,000 and \$75,000 use ABC Tax Guys to prepare her tax returns? Explain.

PRACTICE & PROBLEM SOLVING

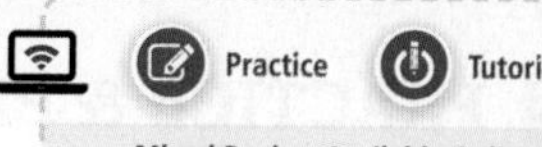

APPLY

20. Model With Mathematics For $5.49 per month, Ms. Corchado can buy insurance to cover the cost of repairing a leak in the natural gas lines within her house. She estimates that there is a 3% chance that she will need to have such repairs made next year.

a. What is the expected cost of a gas leak, if Ms. Corchado does not buy insurance? Use the cost shown in the middle of the graph.

b. With more recent information, Ms. Corchado learns that repair costs could be as much as $1,200 dollars with an 8% probability of a leak. What is the expected cost of a gas leak with these assumptions?

c. Would you advise Ms. Corchado to buy the insurance? Explain.

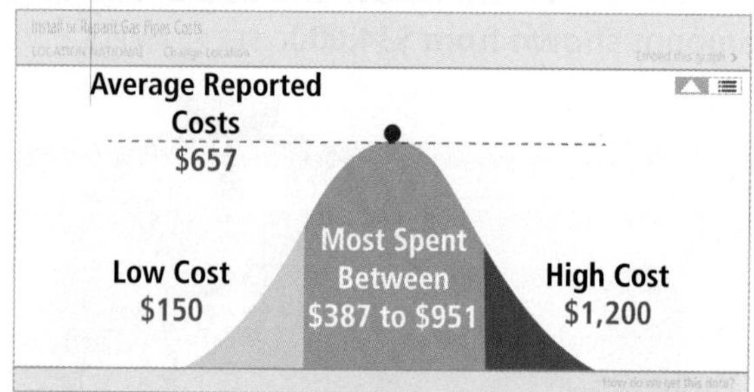

21. Higher Order Thinking You are a consultant to a company that manufactures components for cell phones. One of the components the company manufactures has a 4% failure rate. Design changes have improved the quality of the component. A test of 50 of the new components found that only one of the new components is defective.

a. Before the design improvements what was the probability that among 50 of the items, at most one of the items was defective?

b. Is it reasonable to conclude that the new components have a lower failure rate than 4%?

c. Would you recommend further testing to determine whether the new parts have a lower failure rate than 4%? Explain.

ASSESSMENT PRACTICE

22. Paula, Sasha, and Yumiko live together. They want a system to determine who will wash the dinner dishes on any given night. Select all of the methods that are fair.

Ⓐ Roll a standard number cube. If the result is 1 or 2, Paula does the dishes; if 3 or 4, Sasha; if 5 or 6, Yumiko.

Ⓑ Roll a standard number cube. If the result is 1, Paula does the dishes; if 2, Sasha; if 4, Yumiko. If the result is 3, 5, or 6, roll again.

Ⓒ Roll two standard number cubes. If the sum of the numbers that come up is less than 6, Paula washes the dishes; if the sum is 8, 9, or 12, Sasha; if the sum is 6 or 7, Yumiko. If the sum is 10 or 11, roll again.

Ⓓ Write the name of each girl on a slip of paper, place the slips in a box, mix them up, and select one at random. The person whose name is selected does the dishes.

23. SAT/ACT A fair choice among a group of students may be made by flipping three coins in sequence, and noting the sequences of heads and tails. If each student is assigned one of these sequences, how many students can be selected fairly by this method?

Ⓐ 4 Ⓑ 5 Ⓒ 6 Ⓓ 7 Ⓔ 8

24. Performance Task Acme Tire Company makes two models of steel belted radial tires, Model 1001 and Model 1002.

Model	1001
Blowouts per 200,000 tires	2
Profits before any lawsuits	$60

Model	1002
Blowouts per 200,000 tires	1
Profits before any lawsuits	$56

If one of these tires fails and the company is sued, the average settlement is $1,200,000.

Part A Find the expected profit for both models of tires after any potential lawsuits. Explain.

Part B Would you recommend that the company continue selling both models? Explain.

TOPIC 8

Topic Review

TOPIC ESSENTIAL QUESTION

1. What questions can you answer by using statistics and normal distributions?

Vocabulary Review

Choose the correct term to complete each sentence.

2. __________ is used to find a range of reasonable values used to estimate the population parameter based on a sample statistic.
3. A(n) __________ involves applying a treatment to some group or groups and measuring the effects of the treatment.
4. The __________ is a statement that expresses that there is no difference between the parameter and the benchmark.
5. A(n) __________ can be answered by collecting many pieces of information, or data, and summarizing the data.
6. The __________ counts how many standard deviations a data value is from the mean.

- experiment
- margin of error
- null hypothesis
- statistical question
- *z*-score

Concepts & Skills Review

LESSON 8-1 Statistical Questions and Variables

Quick Review

A **statistical variable** is a quantity or quality for which data are expected to differ. A **categorical variable** has values that belong to a limited set of possible qualitative responses. A **quantitative variable** has values that are numbers that you could meaningfully compare, add, subtract, and so on.

A **population** represents all the members of a group studied by a statistical question. A **sample** is a subset of the population—one that is being studied to answer a statistical question about the population.

Example

A political volunteer asked passersby about who they would vote for in an upcoming election for city council to try to determine who would win. What are the sample and the population in this scenario?

The population is all the voters in the city who plan to vote in the election. The sample is all of the passersby who responded.

Practice & Problem Solving

Is the given question a statistical question?

7. How many days are in September?
8. Do football coaches generally get paid more than swimming coaches?
9. **Communicate Precisely** Explain how to determine if a quantity is a statistic or a parameter.
10. **Make Sense and Persevere** What type of statistical variable is represented by the graph?

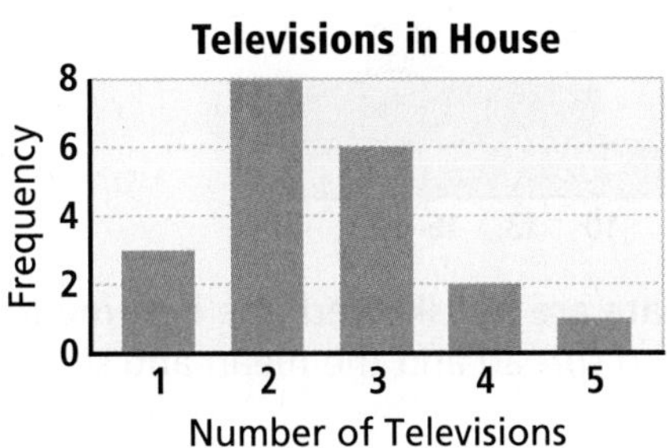

TOPIC 8 REVIEW

LESSON 8-2 Statistical Studies and Sampling Methods

Quick Review

An **experiment** is a statistical study where a researcher applies treatment(s) to the sample. In an **observational study** researchers observe the sample without intentionally affecting it. Researchers use **sample surveys** to ask sample members the same set of questions.

Example

What sampling method is used in the following example? Is the method biased?

The first ten students who enter the school are sampled.

This is convenience sampling because only the first ten students were sampled. The method is biased.

Practice & Problem Solving

In Exercises 11–12, describe what king of study you would conduct to answer each statistical question.

11. Is the lifespan of giraffes affected by the number of offspring they produce?

12. Do employees at a company want vending machines with healthy snacks?

13. Communicate Precisely Explain the difference between an experimental group and a control group.

14. Look for Relationships What sampling method is used below? Is the method biased?

Every 10th person in line was chosen to fill out a survey.

LESSON 8-3 Data Distributions

Quick Review

The **standard deviation** is a measure of how much the values in a data set vary, or deviate, from the mean.

For **skewed distributions,** use the median and interquartile range to describe the data. For distributions that are symmetric, use the mean and standard deviation to describe the data.

Example

Which measures of center and spread are best for describing this set of data?

9 2 17 12 3 20 5 22 7 11 6 14 3 15 10 19

Draw a histogram of the data.

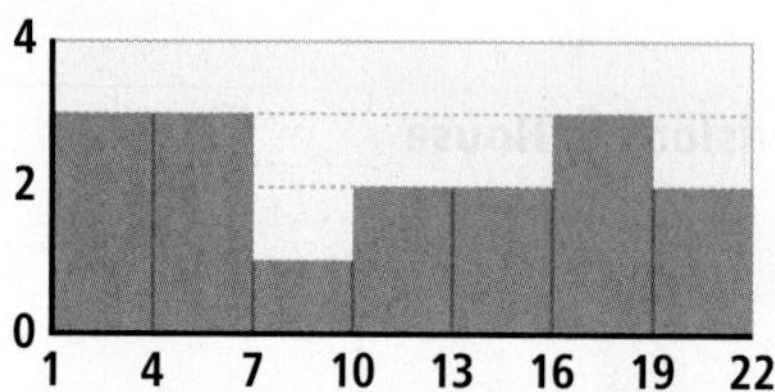

Since the data are not skewed, the best measures of center and spread and the mean and standard deviation.

Practice & Problem Solving

Find the mean, standard deviation, and five-number summary of the data set. Round to the nearest tenth, if necessary.

15. 23 35 19 27 33 24 18 26 38 29

16. 82 77 88 65 68 73 81 74 68 83 80

Which measures of center and spread describe each data set best?

17. 13 28 14 30 18 22 29 24 26 12 20 16

18. 45 56 38 48 41 35 59 46 52 79 62

19. Communicate Precisely Describe a situation that could produce a data distribution similar to this one.

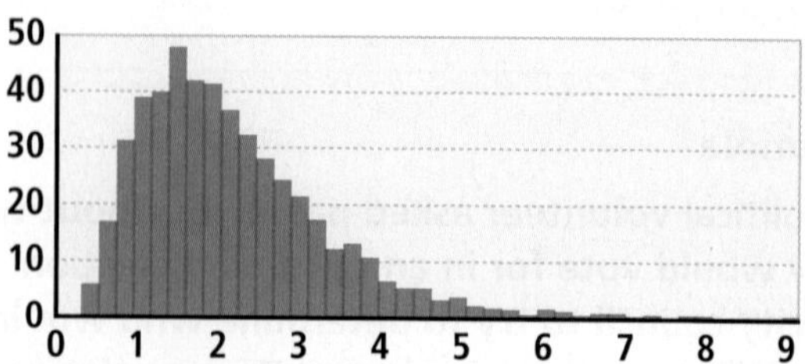

20. Use Structure A data set has a mean that is equal to the median. What is the likely shape of the distribution of the data? Explain.

LESSON 8-4 Normal Distributions

Quick Review

The Empirical Rule gives the percentage of data values falling near the mean.

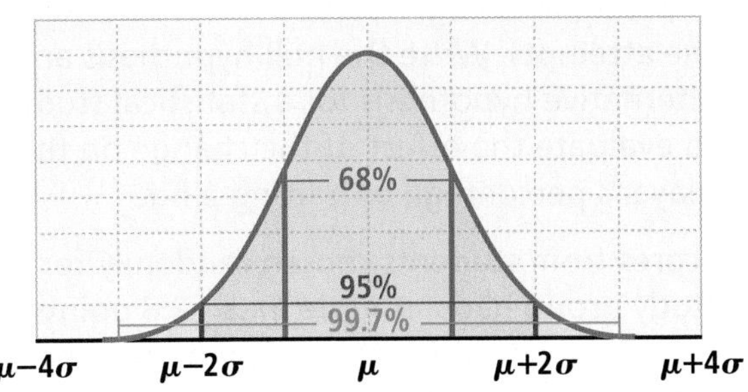

Example

Suppose test scores are normally distributed with mean score 78 and standard deviation 3. What portion of the students scored between 72 and 84?

The interval between 72 and 84 includes all the scores within two standard deviations of the mean.

According to the Empirical Rule, 95% of students scored between 72 and 84.

Practice & Problem Solving

Find the percentage of all values in a normal distribution for each *z*-score.

21. $z \leq 0.29$
22. $z \leq 1.45$
23. $z \leq 0.89$
24. $z \geq 2.11$
25. $z \geq -0.67$
26. $z \leq -1.55$

27. The heart rate of a random sample of people is approximately normally distributed. The mean heart rate is 73 beats per minutes and the standard deviation is 6 beats per minute. What range of heart rates contains the 95% closest to the mean?

28. **Error Analysis** Hana said the percentage of all values in a normal distribution with $z \geq 1.05$ is 85.31%. Describe and correct Hana's error.

29. **Reason** Suppose travel times of employees at a company are normally distributed with mean travel time of 18 min and standard deviation of 3.25 min. What portion of the employees have a travel time between 14.75 and 22.5 min?

TOPIC 8 REVIEW

LESSON 8-5 Margin of Error

Quick Review

Margin of Error (ME)	
Quantitative Data $ME \approx \frac{2\sigma}{\sqrt{n}}$ σ = standard deviation n = sample size	Categorical Data $ME \approx \frac{1}{\sqrt{n}}$ n = sample size

Example

A random sample of 100 Jefferson High seniors reveals that 80% plan to go to college next year. Use the margin of error to predict the actual proportion of seniors planning to go to college.

The data is categorical, so the margin of error is $\frac{1}{\sqrt{100}} = 0.1 = 10\%$.

Range: $80\% - 10\% = 70\%$ and $80\% + 10\% = 90\%$

The proportion of seniors planning to go to college next year is between 70% and 90%.

Practice & Problem Solving

30. Find the sample proportion and margin of error to the nearest percent for an event that occurs 67 times in a sample size of 400.

31. Suppose a population has standard deviation 32.5 and the sample size is 350. Find the margin of error to the nearest tenth.

32. **Communicate Precisely** What happens to the margin of error when the sample size increases? Explain.

33. **Reason** Kimberly makes 20% of the goals she attempts in lacrosse. Use technology to simulate 50 trials with 100 goals each. Identify the range that contains the middle 95% of results.

Quick Review

The **null hypothesis** H_0 is a statement that expresses that there is no difference between the quantities of interest. The **alternative hypothesis** H_a is the statement that expresses that there is a difference between the quantities.

Example

Keen Beenz reports that the average price for a can of their beans is $0.85. A sample of 100 retail prices of their beans has a mean price of $1.15. The standard deviation of prices nationally is $0.25. Does this study provide strong evidence that Keen Beenz' claim is true or false?

Write the hypotheses: H_0: $\mu = 0.85$; H_a: $\mu \neq 0.85$

Calculate the margin of error: $\frac{2\sigma}{\sqrt{n}} = \frac{2(0.25)}{\sqrt{100}} = 0.05$

Predict a range of reasonable values:

sample mean $\pm$ margin of error $= 1.15 \pm 0.05$

The range of values is 1.10 to 1.20.

The claim falls outside the range of reasonable values predicted by the statistical study. This evidence suggests that the claim is false.

Practice & Problem Solving

34. A baseball player got a hit in 30.5% of his attempts. After his coach attempted to improve his swing, he got a hit in 32.8% of the attempts. Write the null hypothesis and alternative hypothesis for a statistical study to evaluate the effect of the change on the player's percentage of getting a hit.

35. Scores from students chosen randomly for a study group had a sample mean 2.8 points higher than that for students who studied alone. The data were randomized 50 times, producing this histogram. Can you conclude that the study group improved scores? Explain.

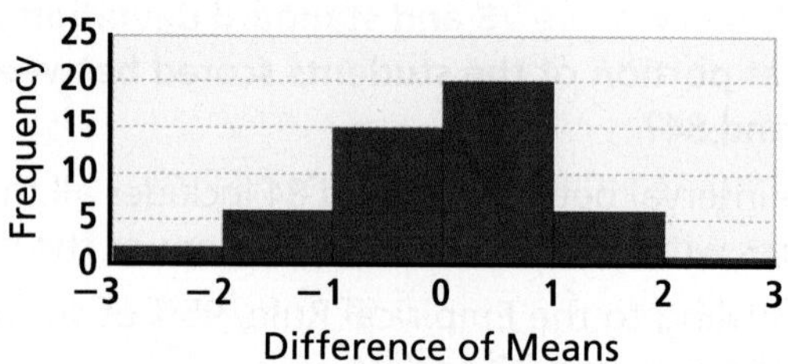

36. Make Sense and Persevere SportORiffic reports that they sell a daily average of 25 athletic tops per day. A national sample of 100 SportORiffic stores is selected, and mean number of athletic tops sold was 23 per day. The standard deviation is 12 per day. Does this study provide strong evidence that SportORiffic's claim is true or false? Explain.

LESSON 8-7 Probability and Decision Making

Quick Review

Combined with probability, expected value can be used to help make decisions.

Example

Frederica is playing a game tossing 20 beanbags from a choice of three lines. Frederica has a 90% chance of success from the 5-point line, a 65% chance of success from the 10-point line, and a 20% chance from the 20-point line. Frederica wants to toss every beanbag from the same line, and thinks she should toss from the 5-point line since it has the highest probability of success. Is Frederica correct?

Find the expected points per toss, or expected value.

5-point line:
5 points • 0.90 = 4.5 points per toss

10-point line:
10 points • 0.65 = 6.5 points per toss

20-point line:
20 points • 0.20 = 4 points per toss

Frederica should toss the beanbag from the 10-point line.

Practice & Problem Solving

Both situations have the same expected value. Find the missing information.

37. Situation 1: Paul hits a dart target worth 15 points 45% of the time.

Situation 2: He hits a dart target worth 10 points x% of the time.

38. Situation 1: Lenora has a success rate of 25% when selling bracelets at $15 each.

Situation 2: She has a success rate of 20% when selling bracelets at $$x$ each.

39. **Make Sense of Problems** Use the information from the Example. Frederica practices her shots and increases her chances from the 20-point line to 30%. Should she now toss the beanbag from the 20-point line? Explain your reasoning.

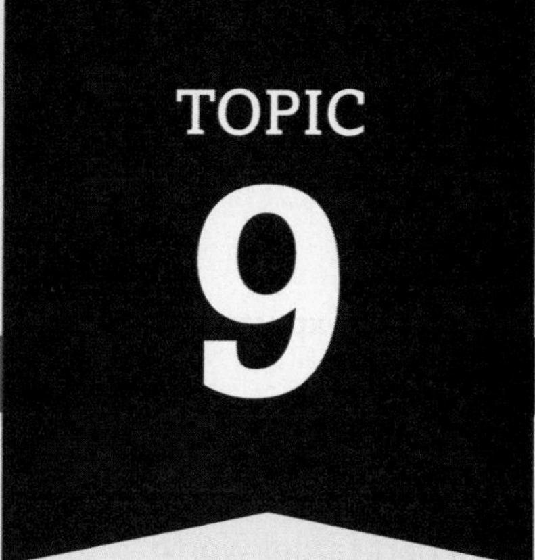

Coordinate Geometry

TOPIC ESSENTIAL QUESTION

How can geometric relationships be proven by applying algebraic properties to geometric figures represented in the coordinate plane?

Topic Overview

enVision® STEM Project:
Design a Solar Collector

9-1 Basic Constructions

Extension 9-1a: Constructions in Triangles

9-2 Slopes of Parallel and Perpendicular Lines

9-3 Polygons in the Coordinate Plane

Mathematical Modeling in 3 Acts:
You Be the Judge

9-4 Proofs Using Coordinate Geometry

Extension 9-4a: Partitioning a Line Segment

9-5 Circles in the Coordinate Plane

9-6 Parabolas in the Coordinate Plane

Topic Vocabulary

- angle bisector
- construction
- directrix
- focus
- parabola
- perpendicular bisector

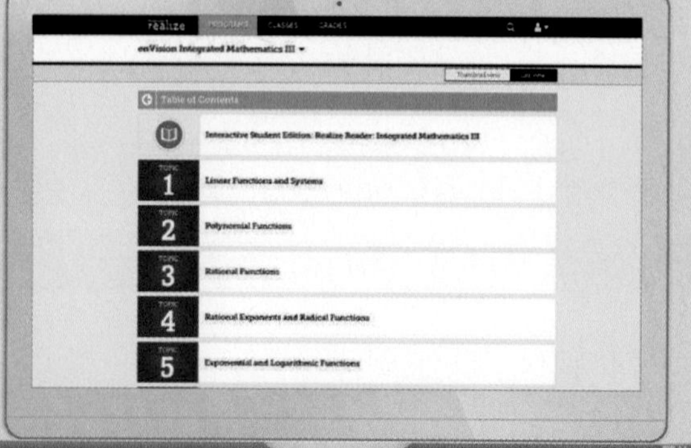

Go online | **PearsonRealize.com**

Digital Experience

INTERACTIVE STUDENT EDITION Access online or offline.

ACTIVITIES Complete ***Explore & Reason, Model & Discuss***, and ***Critique & Explain*** activities. Interact with Examples and Try Its.

ANIMATION View and interact with real-world applications.

PRACTICE Practice what you've learned.

MATHEMATICAL MODELING IN 3 ACTS

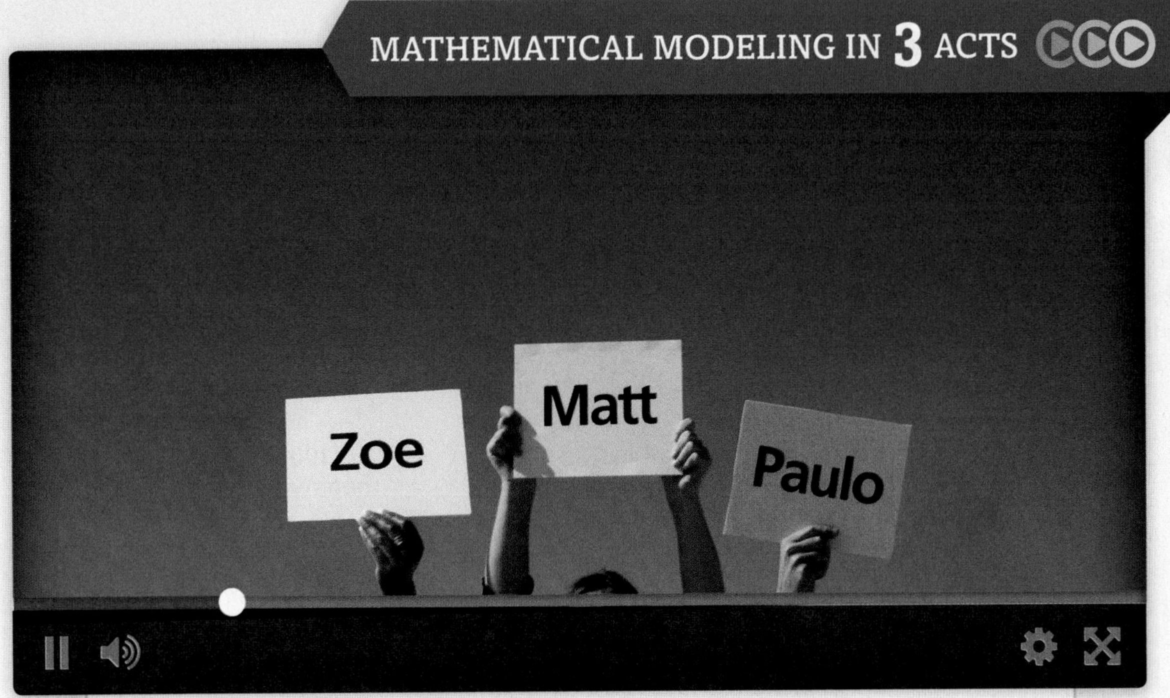

You Be the Judge

Have you ever been a judge in a contest or competition? What criteria did you use to decide the winner? If you were one of many judges, did you all agree on who should win?

Often there is a set of criteria that judges use to help them score the performances of the contestants. Having criteria helps all of the judges be consistent regardless of the person they are rating. Think of this during the Mathematical Modeling in 3 Acts lesson.

TOPIC 9

VIDEOS Watch clips to support ***Mathematical Modeling in 3 Acts Lessons*** and **enVision® *STEM Projects.***

CONCEPT SUMMARY Review key lesson content through multiple representations.

ASSESSMENT Show what you've learned.

GLOSSARY Read and listen to English and Spanish definitions.

TUTORIALS Get help from ***Virtual Nerd***, right when you need it.

MATH TOOLS Explore math with digital tools and manipulatives.

Video

Did You Know?

Solar reflectors are made of mirrors or pieces of glass in many shapes and sizes. Parabolic reflectors collect the sun's rays from a wide area and focus them on a small area, concentrating the energy.

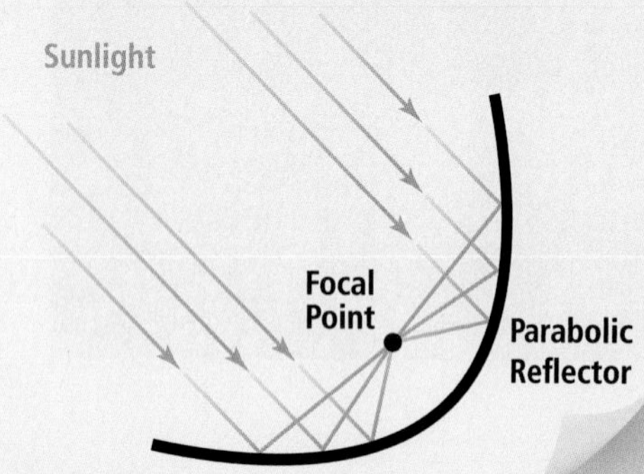

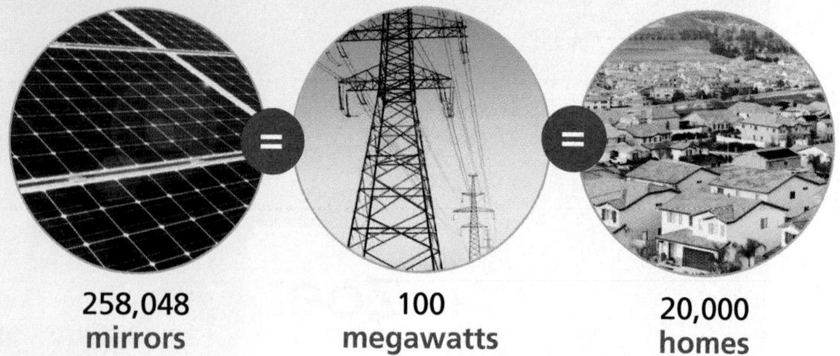

The world's largest power station, the SHAMS 1 in the United Arab Emirates, uses 258,048 mirrors. That's enough to generate 100 megawatts of electricity per day and power 20,000 homes.

In 2016, the United States produced more than 40 billion kilowatt-hours of solar energy, 40 times more than it did a decade earlier.

Your Task: Design a Solar Collector

Giant solar power plants are not the only place to see parabolic trough collectors—you might find a water purifier made from a single 6 ft-x-4 ft mirror in a neighbor's back yard! You and your classmates will analyze parabolas and design a solar collector for use in your school or community.

Go Online | PearsonRealize.com

9-1 Basic Constructions

PearsonRealize.com

Activity Assess

EXPLORE & REASON

Using a compass, make a design using only circles like the one shown.

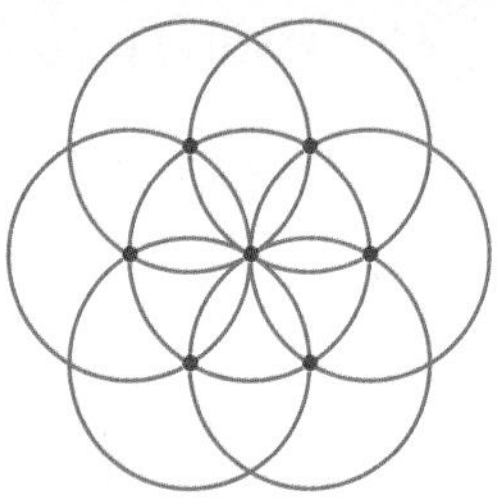

A. What instructions can you give to another student so they can make a copy of your design?

B. Make Sense and Persevere Use a ruler to draw straight line segments to connect points where the circles intersect. Are any of the segments that you drew the same length? If so, why do you think they are?

I CAN… use a straightedge and compass to construct basic figures.

VOCABULARY

- angle bisector
- construction
- perpendicular bisector

ESSENTIAL QUESTION How are a straightedge and compass used to make basic constructions?

CONCEPTUAL UNDERSTANDING

EXAMPLE 1 Copy a Segment

How can you copy a segment using only a straightedge and compass?

A straightedge is a tool for drawing straight lines. A compass is a tool for drawing arcs and circles of different sizes and can be used to copy lengths.

Step 1 To copy $\overline{AB}$, first use a straightedge to draw line ℓ. Mark point M on line ℓ.

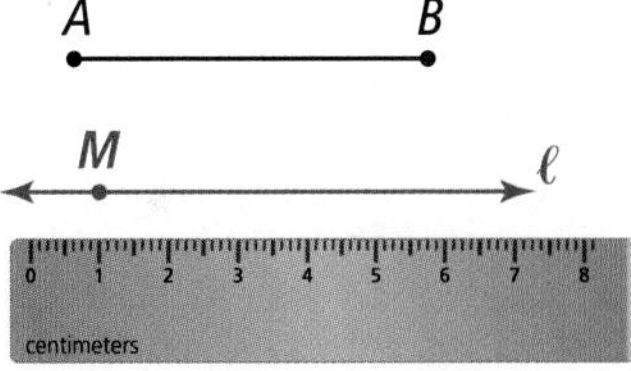

STUDY TIP
Remember, with constructions, only use a ruler as a straightedge, not as a measuring tool.

Step 2 Place the compass point at A, and open the compass to length AB.

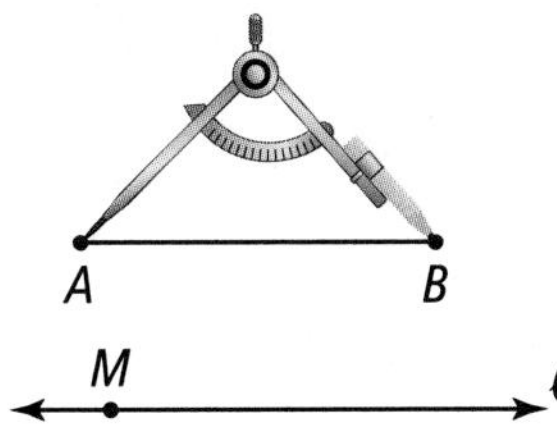

Step 3 Using the same setting, place the compass point at M, and draw an arc through line ℓ. Mark point N at the intersection.

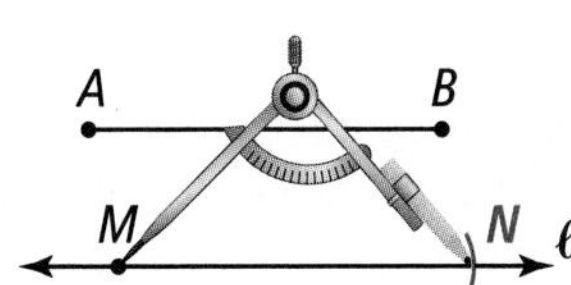

The constructed segment MN is a copy of $\overline{AB}$. A copy of a line segment is a type of *construction*. A **construction** is a geometric figure made with only a straightedge and compass.

Try It! 1. How can you construct a copy of $\overline{XY}$?

X ———————— Y

EXAMPLE 2 Copy an Angle

How can you construct a copy of ∠A?

Step 1 Mark a point X. Use a straightedge to draw a ray with endpoint X.

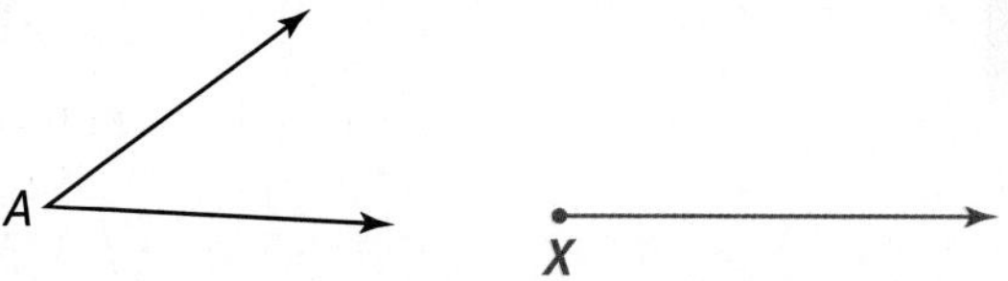

Step 2 Place the compass point at A. Draw an arc that intersects both rays of ∠A. Label the points of intersection B and C.

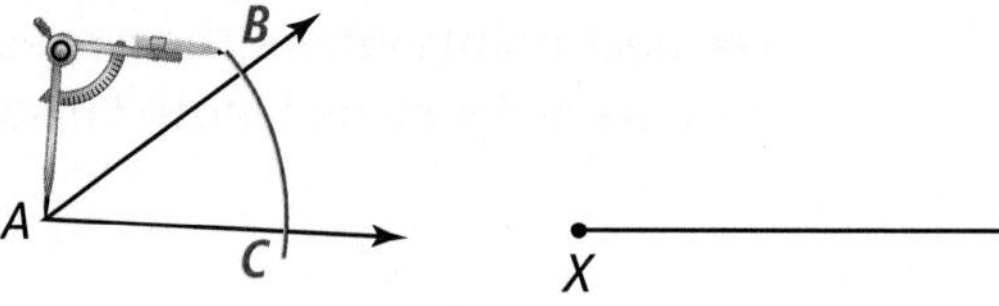

Step 3 Without changing the setting, place the compass point at X and draw an arc intersecting the ray. Mark the point Y at the intersection.

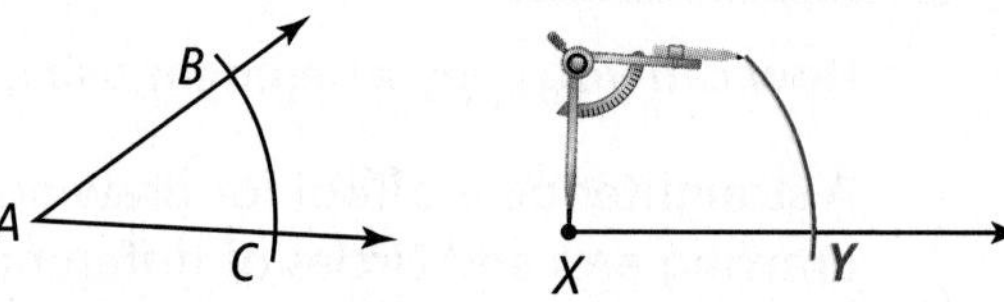

Step 4 Place the compass point at C, and open the compass to the distance between B and C.

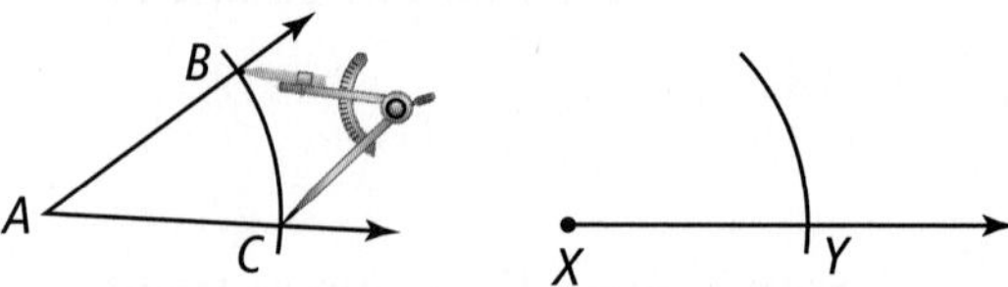

Step 5 Without changing the setting, place the compass point at Y and draw an arc. Label the point Z where the two arcs intersect. Use a straightedge to draw $\overrightarrow{XZ}$.

STUDY TIP
You can use a protractor to confirm that the two angles are congruent.

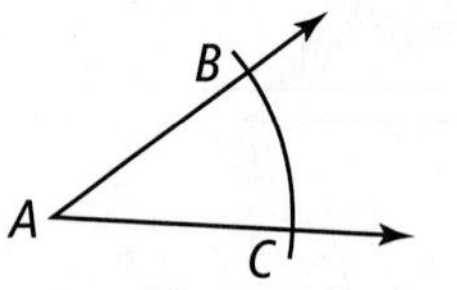

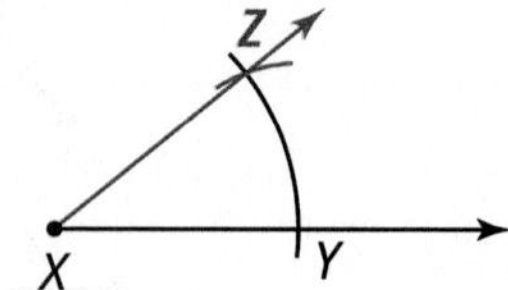

The constructed angle, ∠YXZ, is a copy of ∠A.

Try It! 2. How can you construct a copy of ∠B?

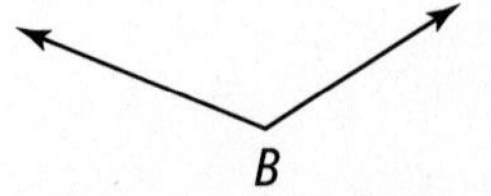

EXAMPLE 3 Construct a Perpendicular Bisector

How can you construct the perpendicular bisector of $\overline{AB}$?

A **perpendicular bisector** of a segment is a line, segment, or ray that is perpendicular to the segment and divides the segment into two congruent segments.

You can use a straightedge and compass to construct the perpendicular bisector of a segment.

Step 1 With a setting greater than $\frac{1}{2}AB$, place the compass point at A. Draw arcs above and below $\overline{AB}$.

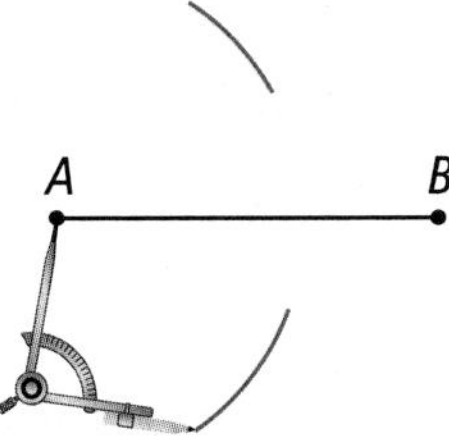

Step 2 With the same setting, place the compass point at B. Draw arcs above and below $\overline{AB}$.

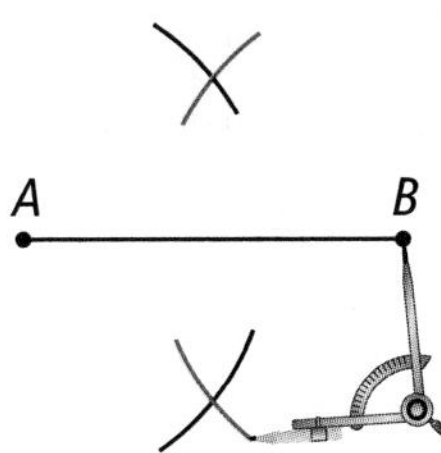

Step 3 Label the points of intersection of the arcs E and F. Use a straightedge to draw $\overleftrightarrow{EF}$.

USE APPROPRIATE TOOLS
Consider the tools you can use to verify that a segment bisects another segment. What tool can you use?

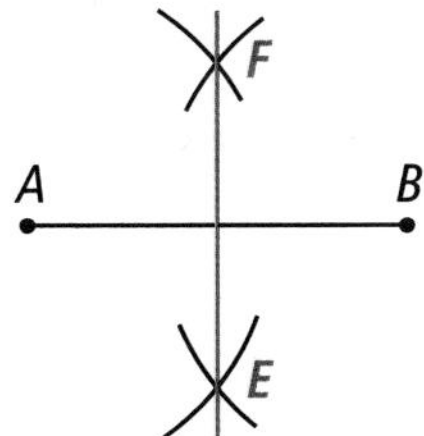

The constructed line, $\overleftrightarrow{EF}$, is the perpendicular bisector of $\overline{AB}$.

Try It! **3.** How can you construct the perpendicular bisector of $\overline{JK}$?

J ———— K

EXAMPLE 4 Construct an Angle Bisector

How can you construct the *angle bisector* of $\angle A$?

An **angle bisector** is a ray that divides an angle into two congruent angles. You can use a straightedge and compass to construct an angle bisector.

Step 1 Place the compass point at A. Draw an arc intersecting both rays of $\angle A$. Label the points of intersection B and C.

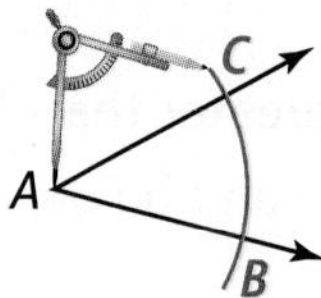

Step 2 Place the compass point at B. Draw an arc in the interior of $\angle A$. With the same setting, place the compass point at C and draw an arc intersecting the arc drawn from B.

COMMON ERROR
Be sure to set the compass greater than $\frac{1}{2}$ the distance from A to C.

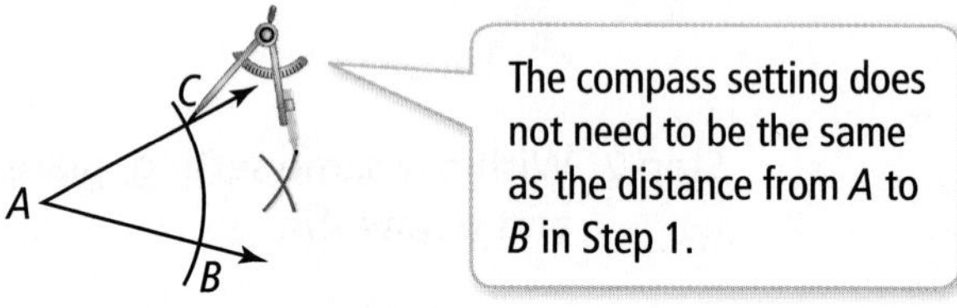

Step 3 Label the point of intersection of the two arcs D. Use a straightedge to draw $\overrightarrow{AD}$.

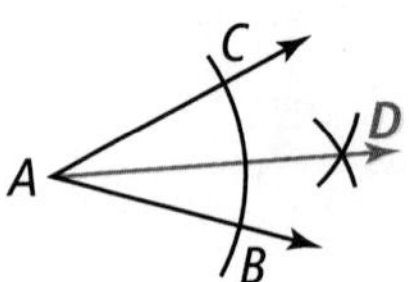

The constructed ray, $\overrightarrow{AD}$, is the bisector of $\angle A$.

 **Try It!** 4. How can you construct the angle bisector of $\angle G$?

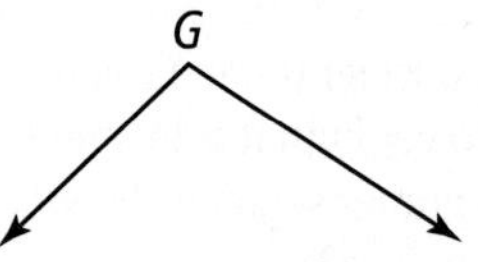

APPLICATION

EXAMPLE 5 Use Constructions

An artist wants to center-align a new sculpture with the bay window in the museum lobby. He also wants to center-align it with the entrance. Where should the sculpture be placed?

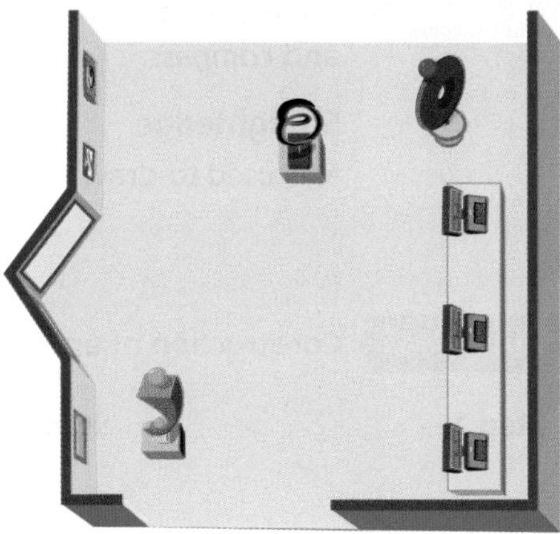

Formulate If the sculpture is center-aligned with the bay window, it lies on the angle bisector of the bay window. If it is center-aligned with the entrance, it lies on the perpendicular bisector of the entrance.

Compute Construct the angle bisector of the bay window and the perpendicular bisector of the entrance.

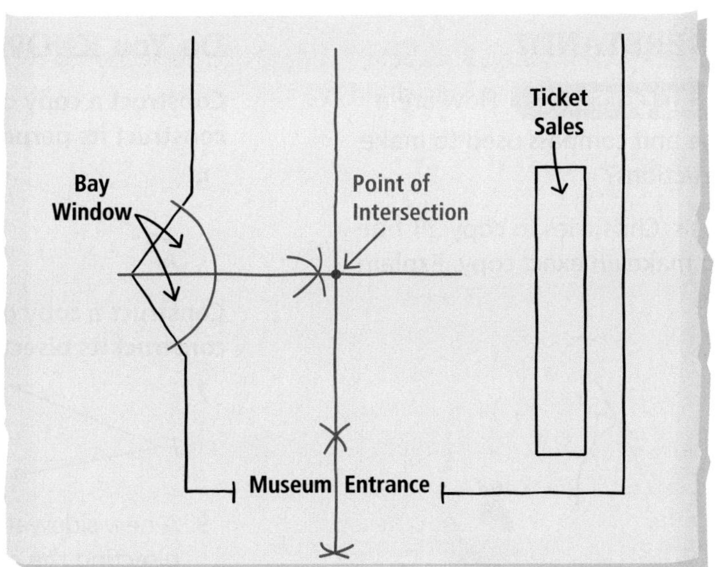

Interpret The center of the sculpture should be placed at the point of intersection of the angle bisector of the bay window and the perpendicular bisector of the museum entrance.

Try It! 5. Where should the sculpture be placed if it is to be center-aligned with the museum entrance and the center of the ticket sales desk?

CONCEPT SUMMARY Constructions

WORDS A **construction** is a geometric figure that can be made using only a straightedge and compass.

Straightedge
- is used to draw segments, lines and rays.

Compass
- is used to draw circles and arcs.
- is used to measure and copy length.

DIAGRAMS Construction of an Angle Bisector

Step 1

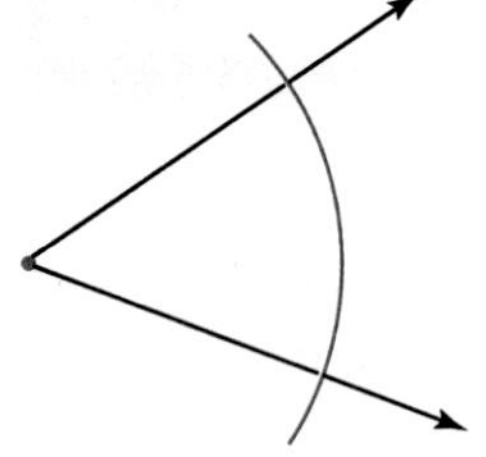

Step 2

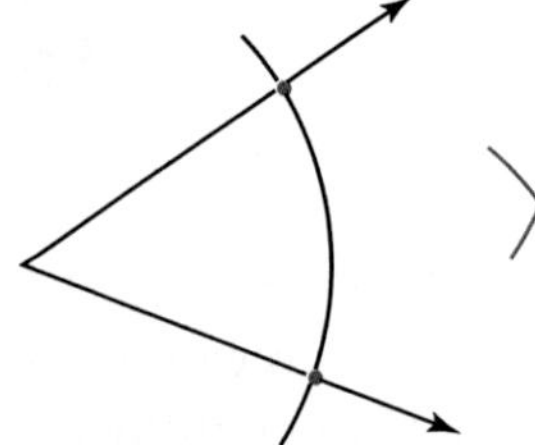

Use a compass to make arcs.

Step 3

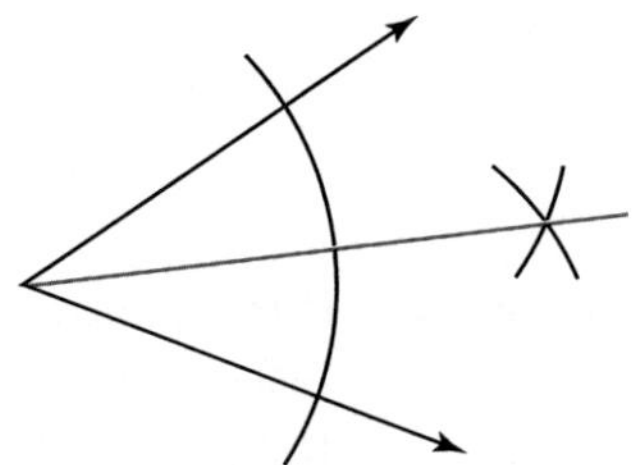

Use a straightedge to draw the bisector.

Do You UNDERSTAND?

1. ESSENTIAL QUESTION How are a straightedge and compass used to make basic constructions?

2. **Error Analysis** Chris tries to copy $\angle T$ but is unable to make an exact copy. Explain Chris's error.

3. **Vocabulary** What is the difference between a line that is perpendicular to a segment and the perpendicular bisector of a segment?

4. **Look for Relationships** Darren is copying $\triangle ABC$. First, he constructs $\overline{DE}$ as a copy of $\overline{AB}$. Next, he constructs $\angle D$ as a copy of $\angle A$, using $\overline{DE}$ as one of the sides. Explain what he needs to do to complete the copy of the triangle.

A, B, C

Do You KNOW HOW?

Construct a copy of each segment, and then construct its perpendicular bisector.

5.

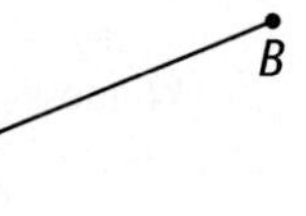

6.

Construct a copy of each angle, and then construct its bisector.

7.

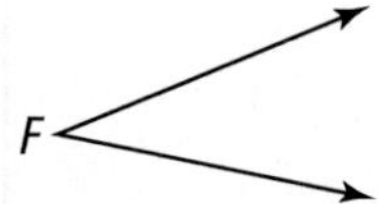

8.

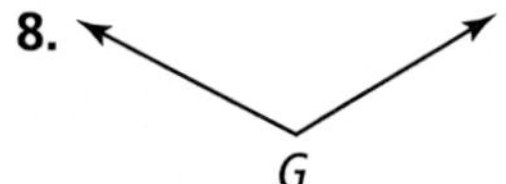

9. A new sidewalk is perpendicular to and bisecting the existing sidewalk. At the point where new sidewalk meets the fence around the farmer's market, a gate is needed. At about what point should the gate be placed?

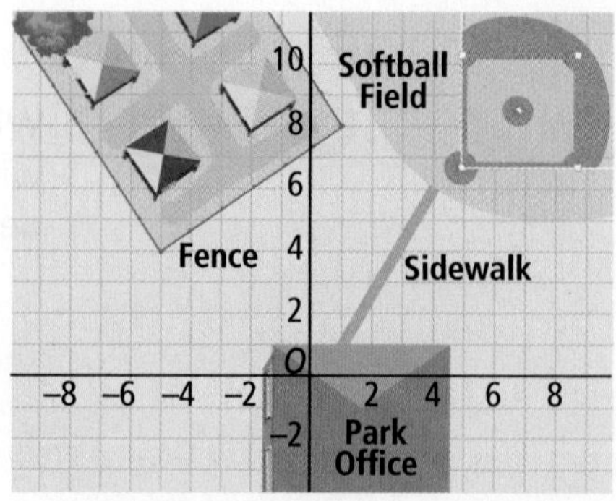

PRACTICE & PROBLEM SOLVING

Scan for Multimedia

Practice Tutorial

Additional Exercises Available Online

UNDERSTAND

10. Use Appropriate Tools How could you use a compass to determine if two segments are the same length?

11. Higher Order Thinking You can divide a segment into *n* congruent segments by bisecting segments repeatedly. What are some of the possible values of *n*? Give a rule for *n*.

12. Make Sense and Persevere In the figure shown, suppose $m\angle ABC = n$ and $m\angle ABD = 2(m\angle DBC)$. The angle bisector of $\angle DBC$ is $\overrightarrow{BE}$. What is $m\angle EBC$?

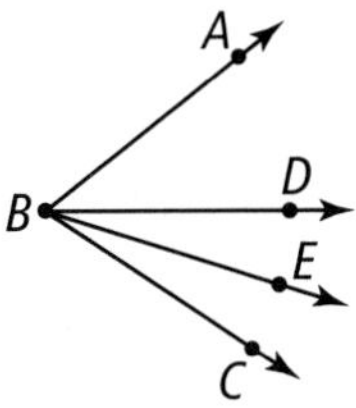

13. Make Sense and Persevere There are other methods for making constructions, such as paper folding. Follow the steps to use paper folding to construct the perpendicular bisector of a segment.

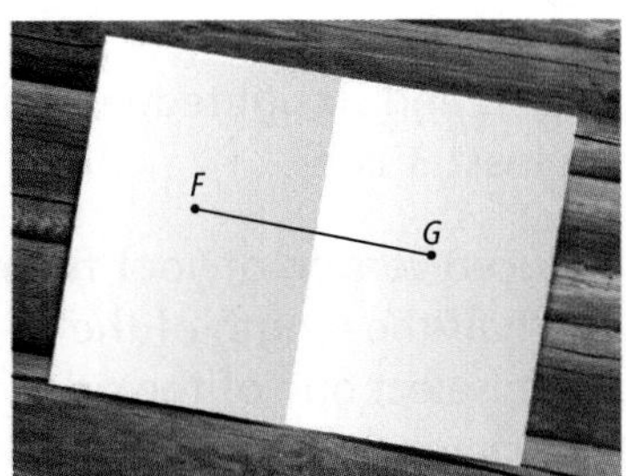

- On a sheet of paper, draw $\overline{FG}$.
- Fold the paper so that *F* is on top of *G*.
- Crease the paper along the fold.
- Unfold the paper. The crease line represents the perpendicular bisector.

Why must *F* and *G* be aligned when you fold the paper?

14. Error Analysis Adam is asked to construct the bisector of $\angle R$. Explain the error in Adam's work.

PRACTICE

Copy the segments. SEE EXAMPLE 1

15. **16.**

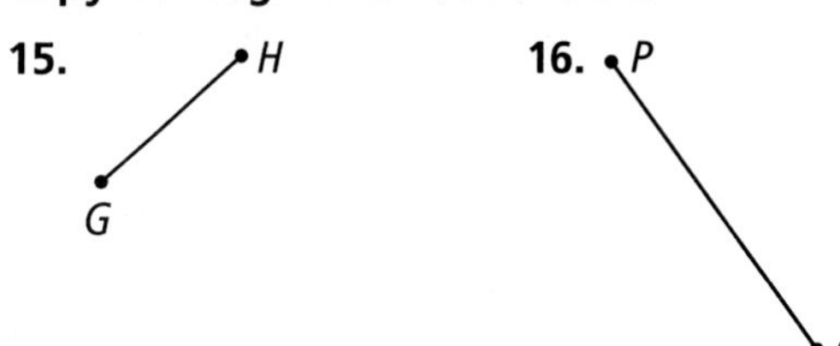

Copy the angles. SEE EXAMPLE 2

17. **18.**

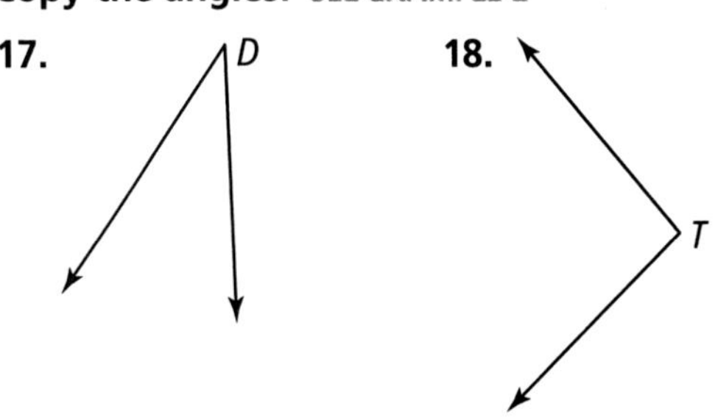

Copy and bisect the segments. SEE EXAMPLE 3

19. **20.**

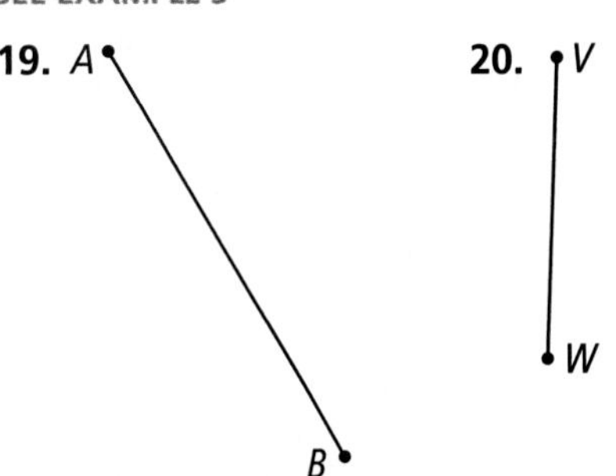

Copy and bisect the angles. SEE EXAMPLE 4

21. **22.**

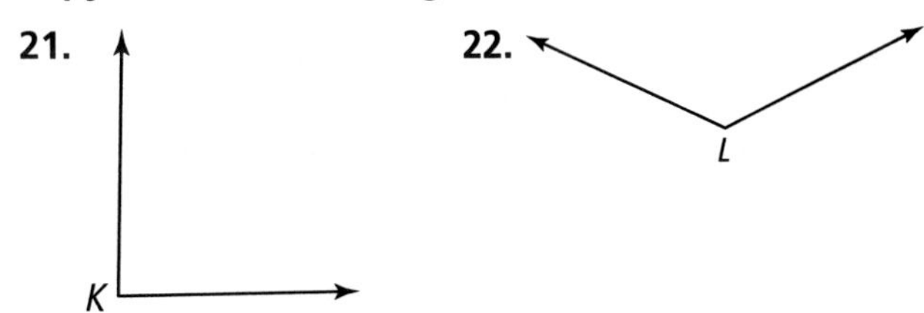

23. Where is the intersection of the perpendicular bisector of $\overline{GF}$ and the angle bisector of $\angle E$? SEE EXAMPLE 5

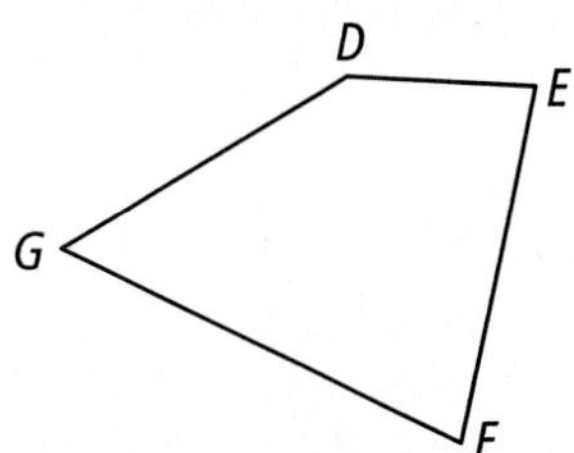

PRACTICE & PROBLEM SOLVING

Practice Tutorial

Mixed Review Available Online

APPLY

24. Communicate Precisely The quilt block is designed from a square using only perpendicular bisectors and angle bisectors. Write instructions for constructing the pattern in square *ABCD*. You may find it helpful to name some additional points.

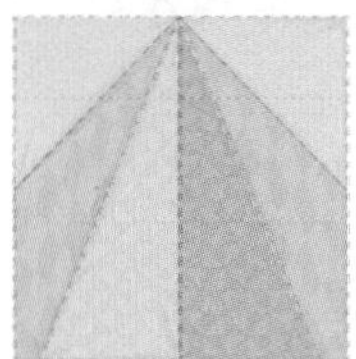

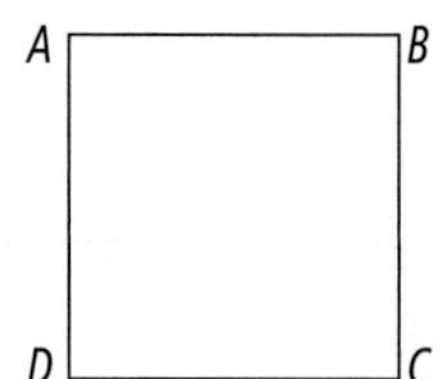

25. Mathematical Connections A school gym is divided for a fair by bisecting its width and its length. Each half of the length is then bisected, forming 8 sections in all. What are the dimensions and area of each section?

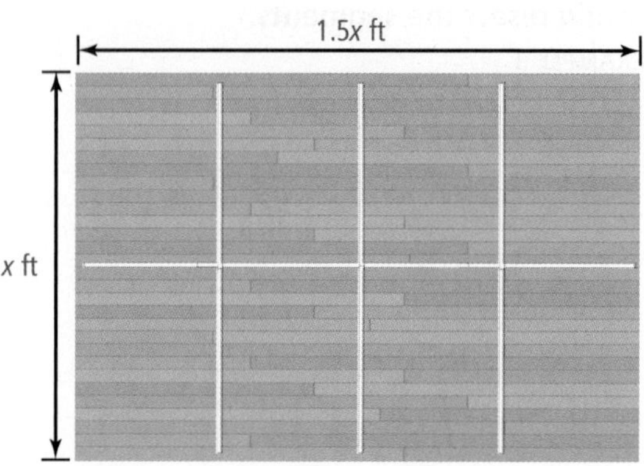

26. Model With Mathematics A sixth wind turbine will be placed near the intersections of the bisector of $\angle BCD$ and the perpendicular bisectors of $\overline{AE}$ and $\overline{ED}$. What is a possible location for the sixth turbine?

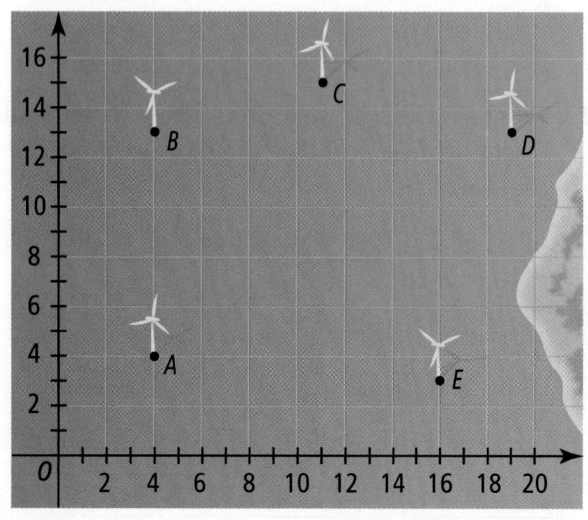

ASSESSMENT PRACTICE

27. The angle bisector of $\angle NPM$ is $\overrightarrow{PQ}$. Write an equation to describe the relationship between $m\angle NPM$ and $m\angle QPM$

28. SAT/ACT A perpendicular bisector of $\overline{DC}$ is $\overleftrightarrow{AB}$, and a perpendicular bisector of $\overline{AB}$ is $\overline{DC}$. The intersection of $\overline{AB}$ and $\overline{DC}$ is at *E*. Which equation is true?

Ⓐ $AB = CD$

Ⓑ $CE = CD$

Ⓒ $DE = CE$

Ⓓ $AE = DE$

Ⓔ $EB = CD$

29. Performance Task Reducing or enlarging images can be useful when you need a smaller or larger version of a picture or graph for a report or poster.

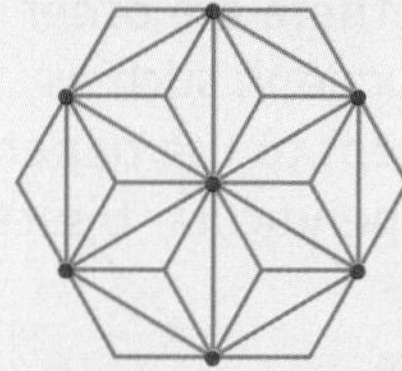

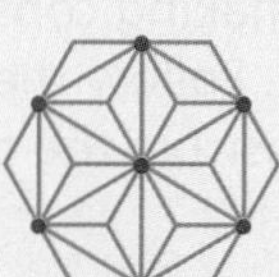

Part A Use a compass and straightedge to draw a polygon with at least 3 sides.

Part B Make a reduced version of your figure with sides that are half the length of the original figure. First, select one of the sides, bisect it, and then copy one of the halves. Next, copy one of the angles that is adjacent. Repeat until you have a reduced version of your figure.

Part C Think about how you can double the length of the line segment. Make an enlarged version of your figure with sides that are twice the length of the original figure. Describe how you made the enlarged figure.

EXTENSION

9-1a Constructions in Triangles

I CAN… construct the circumscribed and inscribed circles of a triangle.

ESSENTIAL QUESTION How can you construct the circumscribed and inscribed circles of a triangle?

EXAMPLE 1 Construct the Circumscribed Circle of a Triangle

How can you construct the circumscribed circle of a triangle?

Recall that a circle circumscribes a triangle if the circle contains the triangle and the vertices of the triangle are on the circle.

All points on a circle are equidistant from the center of the circle.

The vertices of the triangle must be equidistant from the center of the circle.

How do you know that a circle centered on the circumcenter passing through any vertex of the triangle will also pass through the other two vertices?

Step 1 Construct the perpendicular bisectors of two sides of the triangle to find the point equidistant from the vertices.

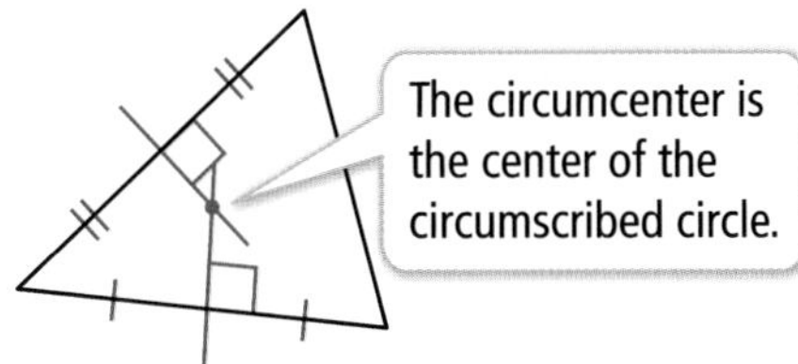

Step 2 Construct the circle centered on the circumcenter passing through any vertex of the triangle.

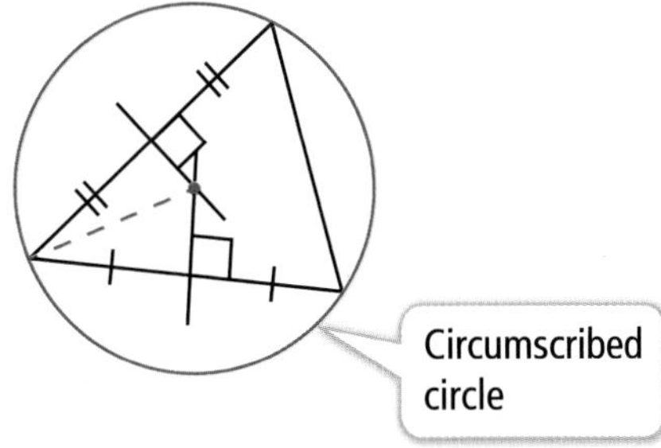

Circumscribed circle

Try It! 1. Draw an obtuse triangle. Construct the circumscribed circle of the triangle.

EXAMPLE 2 Construct the Inscribed Circle of a Triangle

How can you construct the inscribed circle of a triangle?

The circle that intersect each side of a triangle at exactly one point and has no points outside the triangle is the inscribed circle of the triangle.

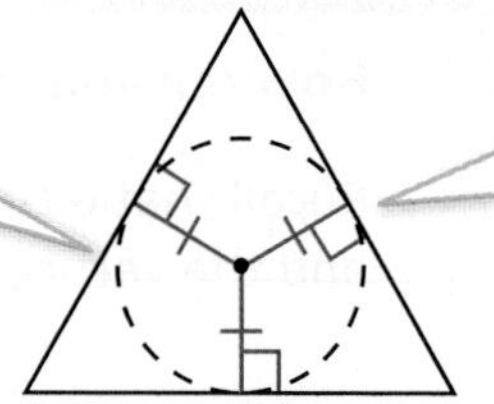

STUDY TIP
The parts of the word *incenter* can help you remember what it means. It is the *center* of the circle that is *inside* the triangle.

Step 1 Construct two angle bisectors to find the point that is equidistant from the sides of the triangle.

Step 2 Construct a perpendicular segment from the incenter to any side.

Step 3 Construct the circle centered on the incenter passing through the point of intersection of the perpendicular segment and side.

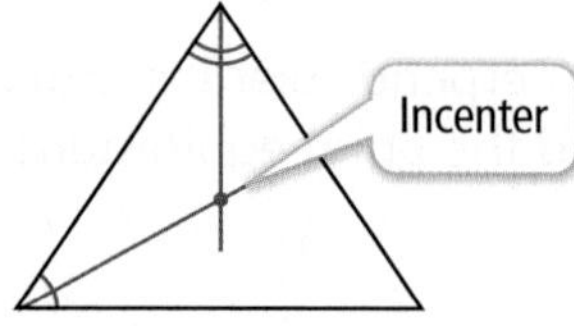

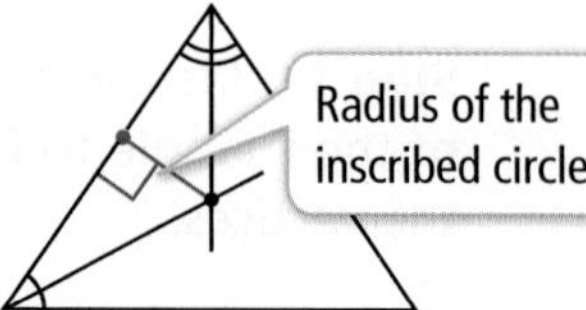

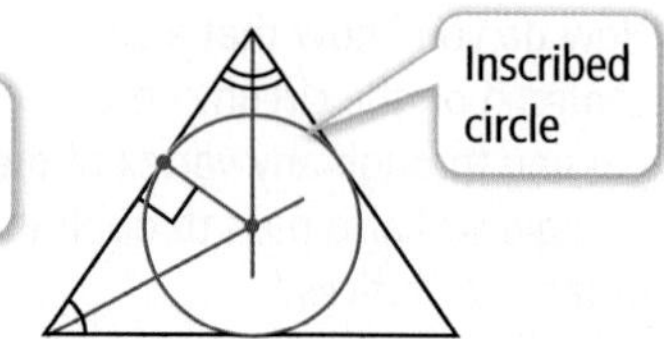

 **Try It!** 2. Draw an obtuse triangle. Construct the inscribed circle of the triangle.

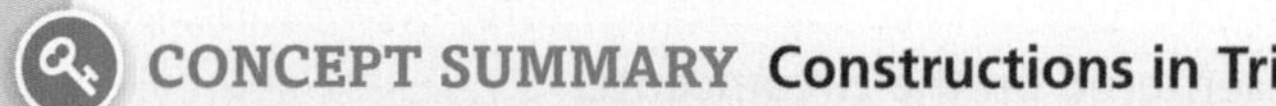

CONCEPT SUMMARY Constructions in Triangles

Construct the circumcenter of a triangle to locate the center of the circumscribed circle of the triangle.

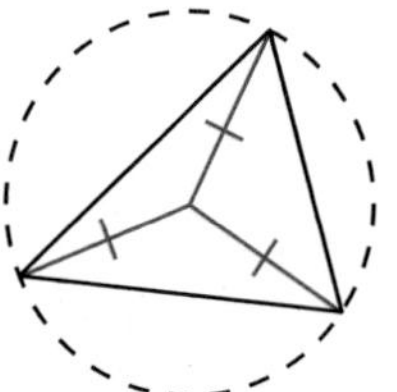

Construct the incenter of a triangle to locate center of the inscribed circle of the triangle.

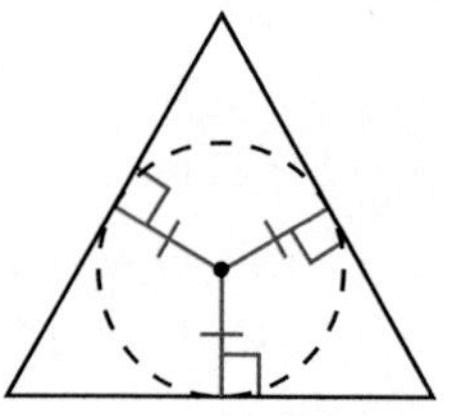

Do You UNDERSTAND?

1. ESSENTIAL QUESTION How can you construct the circumscribed and inscribed circles of a triangle?

2. **Vocabulary** What parts of the triangle is the *circumcenter* equidistant from? What parts of the triangle is the *incenter* equidistant from?

Do You KNOW HOW?

3. Draw an acute triangle and label it $\triangle GHJ$. Construct the circumscribed circle of $\triangle GHJ$.

4. Draw an obtuse triangle and label it $\triangle RST$. Construct the inscribed circle of $\triangle RST$.

PRACTICE & PROBLEM SOLVING

Practice

UNDERSTAND

5. **Error Analysis** Terrence constructed the circumscribed circle for $\triangle XYZ$. Explain Terrence's error.

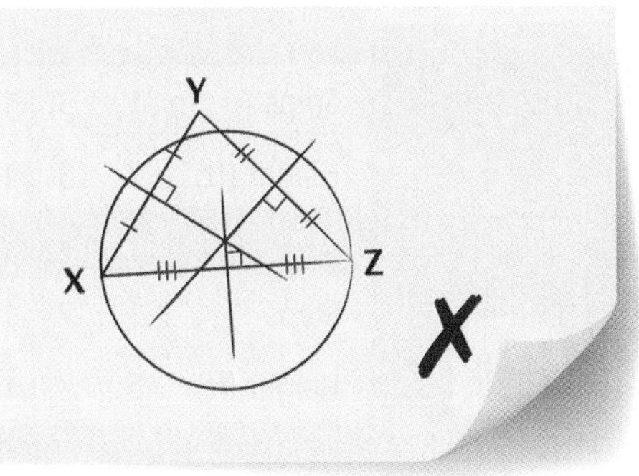

6. **Reason** Is it possible for the circumscribed circle and the inscribed circle of a triangle to be the same? Explain your reasoning.

7. What conjecture can you make about the location of the circumcenter for acute, right, and obtuse triangles?

8. Do you think that the incenter of a triangle can ever be located on a side of the triangle? Explain.

9. **Construct Arguments** A right triangle has vertices $X(0, 0)$, $Y(0, 2a)$, $Z(2b, 0)$. What are the coordinates of the circumcenter of the triangle? Make a conjecture about the diameter of a circle that is circumscribed about a right triangle.

PRACTICE

Use the diagram below for Exercises 10 and 11. Points *D*, *E*, and *F* are midpoints of the sides of $\triangle ABC$.

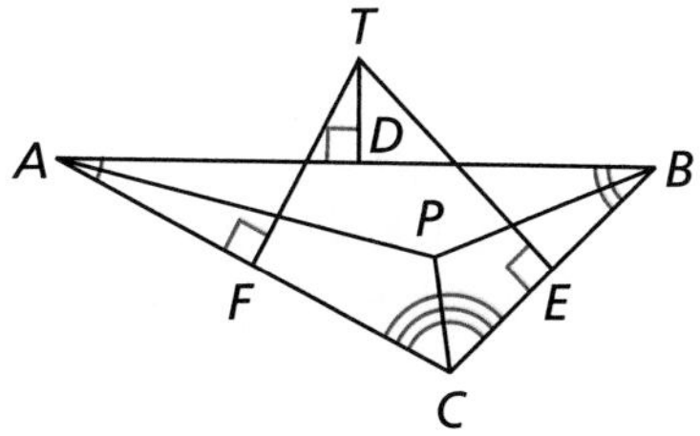

10. Which point is the center of a circle that contains *A*, *B*, and *C*?

11. Which point is the center of a circle that intersects each side of $\triangle ABC$ at exactly one point?

12. The perpendicular bisectors of $\triangle DEF$ are $\overline{TM}$, $\overline{UM}$, and $\overline{VM}$. What is the circumcenter of $\triangle DEF$? Explain your reasoning.

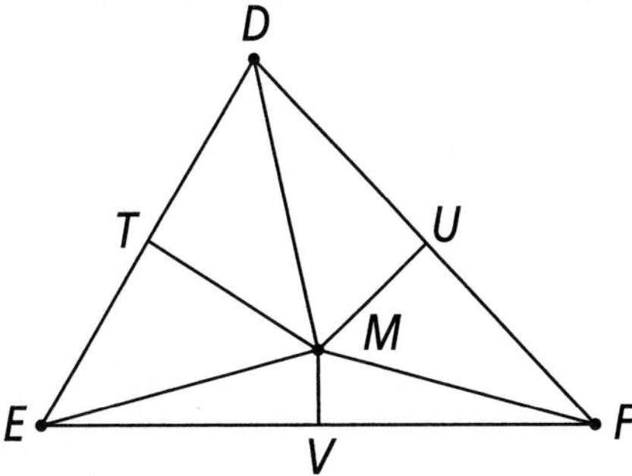

APPLY

13. **Model With Mathematics** A maintenance crew wants to build a shed at a location that is the same distance from each path. Where should the shed be located? Justify your answer with a diagram.

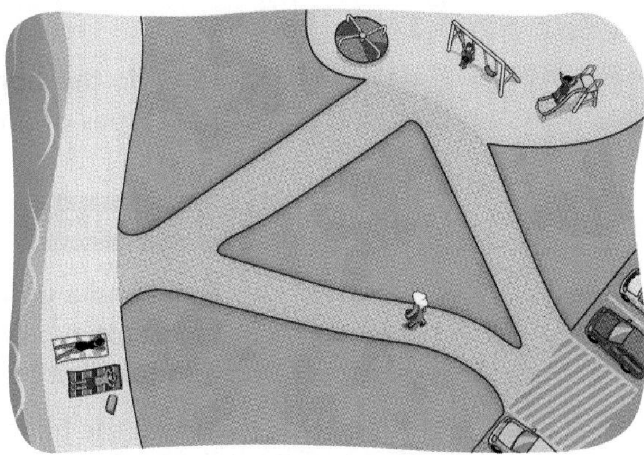

14. Edison High School is designing a new triangular pennant. The school mascot will be inside a circle, and the circle must touch each side of the pennant.

Using a straightedge and compass, construct four different types of triangles for the pennant. Construct an inscribed circle in each triangle.

Activity Assess

9-2 Slopes of Parallel and Perpendicular Lines

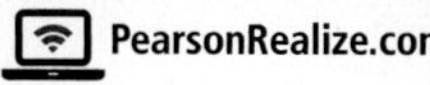

I CAN… use slope to solve problems about parallel and perpendicular lines.

MODEL & DISCUSS

Pilar and Jake begin climbing to the top of a 100-ft monument at the same time along two different sets of steps at the same rate. The tables show their distances above ground level after a number of steps.

Pilar				
Steps	1	3	17	25
Height (ft)	2	3	10	14

Jake				
Steps	1	7	15	29
Height (ft)	5	8	12	19

A. How many feet does each student climb after 10 steps? Explain.

B. Will Pilar and Jake be at the same height after the same number of steps? Explain.

C. Reason What would you expect the graphs of each to look like given your answers to parts A and B? Explain.

ESSENTIAL QUESTION How do the slopes of lines that are parallel to each other compare? How do the slopes of lines that are perpendicular to each other compare?

CONCEPTUAL UNDERSTANDING

EXAMPLE 1 Slopes of Parallel Lines

A hill and a gondola line 20 ft above the ground that goes up the hill both have slope $\frac{1}{2}$. What is the geometric relationship between the hill and the gondola line?

Model the hill and gondola line on a coordinate plane where x represents the horizontal distance from the base of the hill and y represents the vertical distance from the base of the hill.

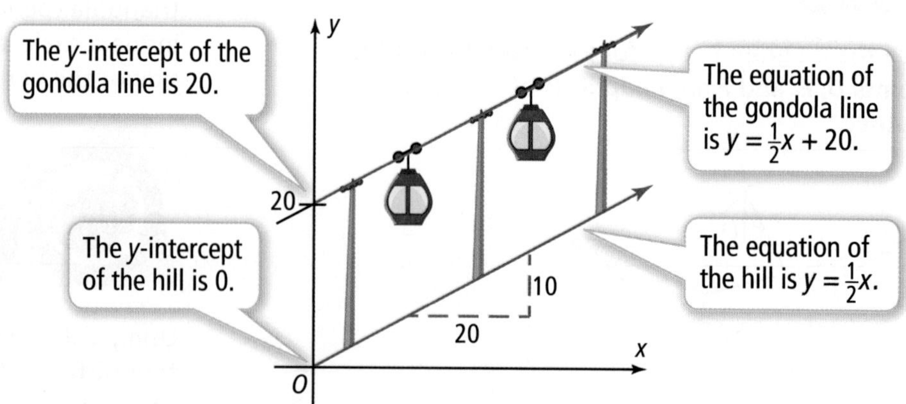

MODEL WITH MATHEMATICS
Would you describe a different relationship between the slopes of parallel lines if the y-intercept for the hill were not at (0, 0)?

Because the slope of the hill is $\frac{1}{2}$, the hill gains one foot of height for every two feet of horizontal distance. The same is true for the gondola. It never gets any closer or farther away from the hill.

Conjecture: If two linear equations have the same slope, then the graphs of the equations are parallel.

CONTINUED ON THE NEXT PAGE

EXAMPLE 1 CONTINUED

 **Try It!** **1.** Suppose another line for a chair lift is placed at a constant distance c below the gondola line. What is an equation of the new line? Is the new line also parallel to the hill? Explain.

THEOREM 9-1

Two non-vertical lines are parallel if and only if their slopes are equal.

Any two vertical lines are parallel.

PROOF: SEE LESSON 7-5.

If... p and q are both not vertical

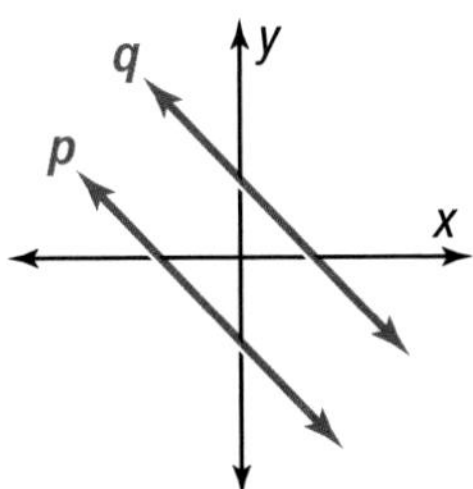

Then... $p \parallel q$ if and only if the slope of line p = slope of line q

If... p and q are both vertical

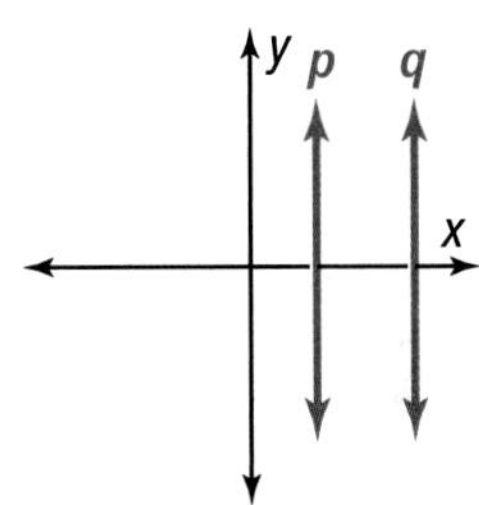

Then... $p \parallel q$

EXAMPLE 2 Check Parallelism

Are lines k and n parallel?

COMMON ERROR
Be sure that the first numbers in both subtraction expressions are the coordinates of the same point.

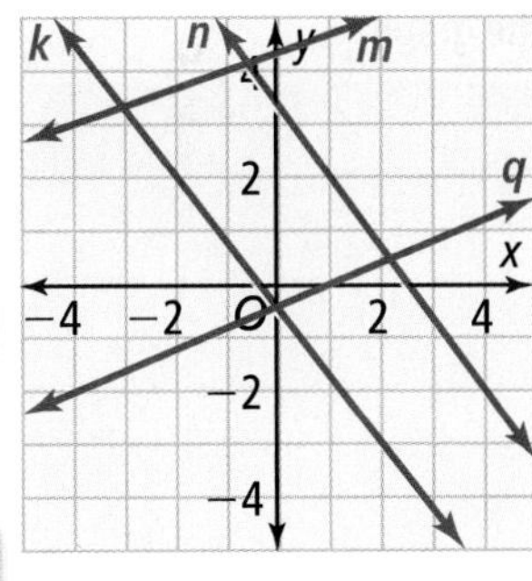

Step 1 Find the slope of line k.

$$m = \frac{-3 - 2}{2 - (-2)} = -\frac{5}{4}$$

Line k passes through (−2, 2) and (2, −3).

Step 2 Find the slope of line n.

$$m = \frac{-2 - 2}{4 - 1} = -\frac{4}{3}$$

Line n passes through (1, 2) and (4, −2).

Step 3 Compare the slopes.

Parallel lines have equal slope, but $-\frac{5}{4} \neq -\frac{4}{3}$. Thus, lines k and n are not parallel.

 **Try It!** **2.** Are lines m and q parallel?

THEOREM 9-2

Two non-vertical lines are perpendicular if and only if the product of their slopes is -1.

A vertical line and a horizontal line are perpendicular to each other.

PROOF: SEE LESSON 7-4.

If... p and q are both not vertical

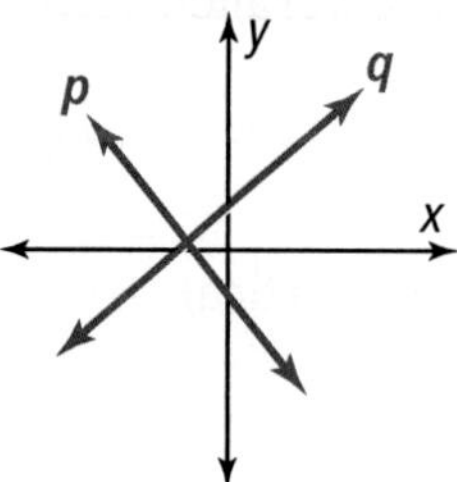

Then... $p \perp q$ if and only if the product of their slopes is -1

If... one of p and q is vertical and the other is horizontal

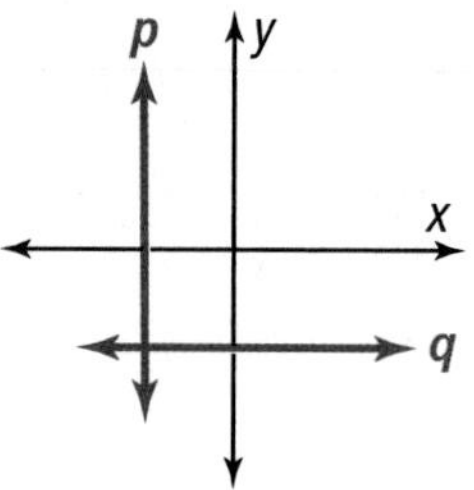

Then... $p \perp q$

EXAMPLE 3 Check Perpendicularity

Are lines j and k perpendicular?

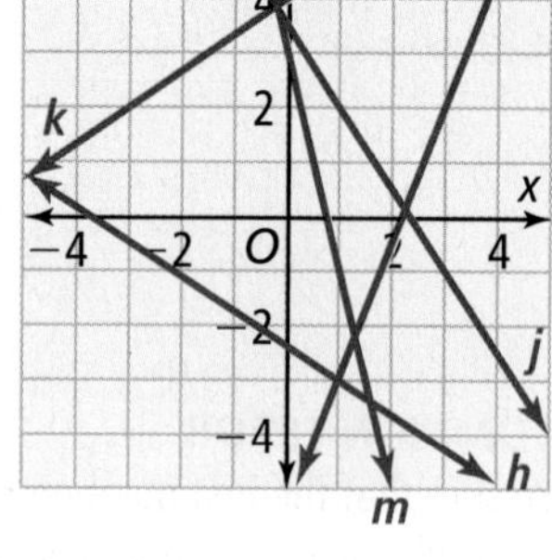

STUDY TIP
Look for two points on each line where you can easily read the coordinates of the points from the graph.

Step 1 Find the slope of line j.

$$m = \frac{2 - 5}{1 - (-1)} = -\frac{3}{2}$$

Line j passes through $(-1, 5)$ and $(1, 2)$.

Step 2 Find the slope of line k.

$$m = \frac{4 - 2}{0 - (-3)} = \frac{2}{3}$$

Line k passes through $(-3, 2)$ and $(0, 4)$.

Step 3 Compare the slopes.

Perpendicular lines have slopes with a product of -1, and $-\frac{3}{2} \cdot \frac{2}{3} = -1$. Thus, lines j and k are perpendicular.

Try It! **3. a.** Are lines h and ℓ perpendicular?

b. Are lines k and m perpendicular?

EXAMPLE 4 Write Equations of Parallel and Perpendicular Lines

A. What is an equation of the line through P that is parallel to ℓ?

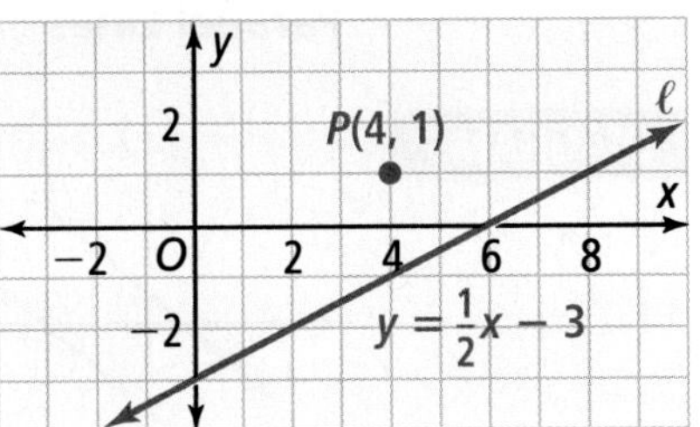

Step 1 Identify the slope of the parallel line.

The slope of ℓ is $\frac{1}{2}$. Parallel lines have equal slope, so the slope of the parallel line is $\frac{1}{2}$.

Step 2 Solve for the y-intercept of the parallel line.

$y = mx + b$

$1 = \frac{1}{2}(4) + b$ — Use the point (4, 1).

$b = -1$

Step 3 Write an equation of the line.

$y = \frac{1}{2}x - 1$

The line parallel to ℓ passing through P is $y = \frac{1}{2}x - 1$.

GENERALIZE
If the slope of a line is $\frac{a}{b}$, what is the slope of any line perpendicular to it? How do you know?

B. What is the equation of the line through P that is perpendicular to ℓ?

Step 1 Identify the slope of the perpendicular line.

The slope of ℓ is $\frac{1}{2}$. Perpendicular lines have slopes with a product of -1, so the slope of the perpendicular line is -2.

Step 2 Solve for the y-intercept of the perpendicular line.

$y = mx + b$

$1 = -2(4) + b$ — Use the point (4, 1).

$b = 9$

Step 3 Write the equation of the line.

$y = -2x + 9$

The line perpendicular to ℓ passing through P is $y = -2x + 9$.

Try It! 4. What are equations of lines parallel and perpendicular to the given line k passing through point T?

a. $y = -3x + 2$; $T(3, 1)$

b. $y = \frac{3}{4}x - 5$; $T(12, -2)$

CONCEPT SUMMARY Slopes of Parallel and Perpendicular Lines

	Parallel Lines	Perpendicular Lines
DIAGRAMS	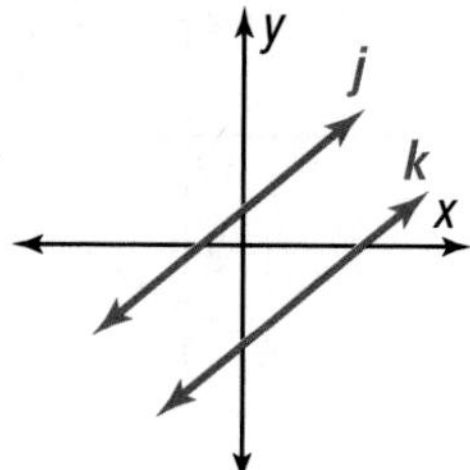	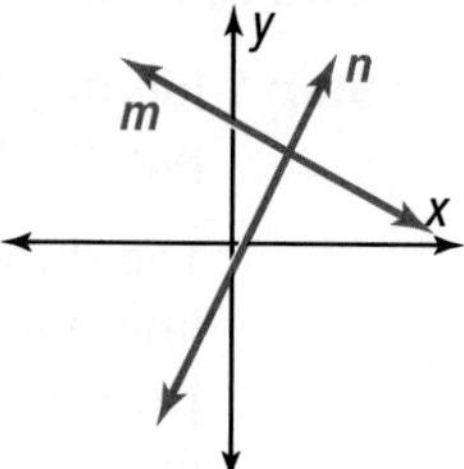
SYMBOLS	$j \parallel k$ if and only if the slopes are the same.	$m \perp n$ if and only if the product of the two slopes is -1.

Do You UNDERSTAND?

1. ESSENTIAL QUESTION How do the slopes of lines that are parallel to each other compare? How do the slopes of lines that are perpendicular to each other compare?

2. **Error Analysis** Katrina said that the lines $y = -\frac{2}{3}x + 5$ and $y = -\frac{3}{2}x + 2$ are perpendicular. Explain Katrina's error.

3. **Reason** Give an equation for a line perpendicular to the line $y = 0$. Is there more than one such line? Explain.

4. **Communicate Precisely** What are two different if-then statements implied by Theorem 9-1?

5. **Error Analysis** Devin said that $\overleftrightarrow{AB}$ and $\overleftrightarrow{CD}$ for $A(-2, 0)$, $B(2, 3)$, $C(1, -1)$, and $D(5, -4)$ are parallel. Explain and correct Devin's error.

slope of $\overleftrightarrow{AB}$: $\frac{3-0}{2-(-2)} = \frac{3}{4}$

slope of $\overleftrightarrow{CD}$: $\frac{-1-(-4)}{5-1} = \frac{3}{4}$

slopes are equal, so $\overleftrightarrow{AB} \parallel \overleftrightarrow{CD}$ 

Do You KNOW HOW?

Use the diagram for Exercises 6–9.

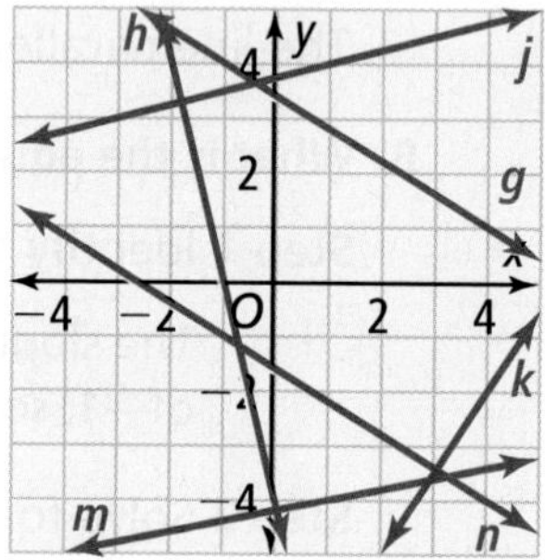

6. Are lines g and n parallel?

7. Are lines j and m parallel?

8. Are lines n and k perpendicular?

9. Are lines h and j perpendicular?

10. What is an equation for the line parallel to $y = -x + 7$ that passes through $(7, -2)$?

11. What is an equation for the line perpendicular to $y = 3x - 1$ that passes through $(-9, -2)$?

12. The graph of a roller coaster track goes in a straight line through coordinates (10, 54) and (42, 48), with coordinates in feet. A support beam runs parallel 12 feet below the track. What equation describes the support beam?

PRACTICE & PROBLEM SOLVING

Scan for Multimedia

Practice Tutorial

Additional Exercises Available Online

UNDERSTAND

13. Look for Relationships What are the equations of lines m and q?

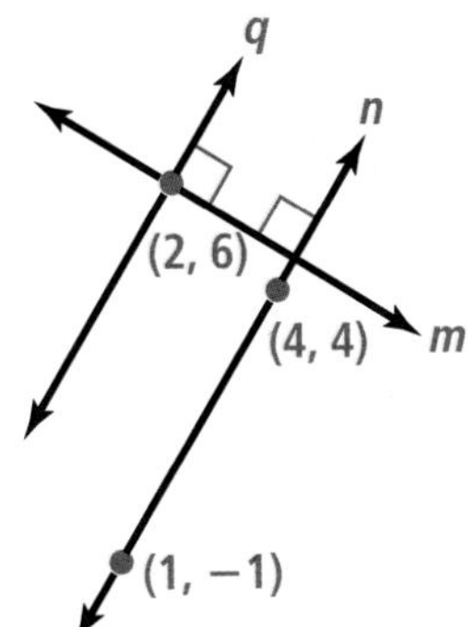

14. Reason Why can you not say that two vertical lines have equal slope? Why can you not say that the product of the slopes of a vertical and horizontal line is −1?

15. Higher Order Thinking Lines k and n intersect on the y-axis.

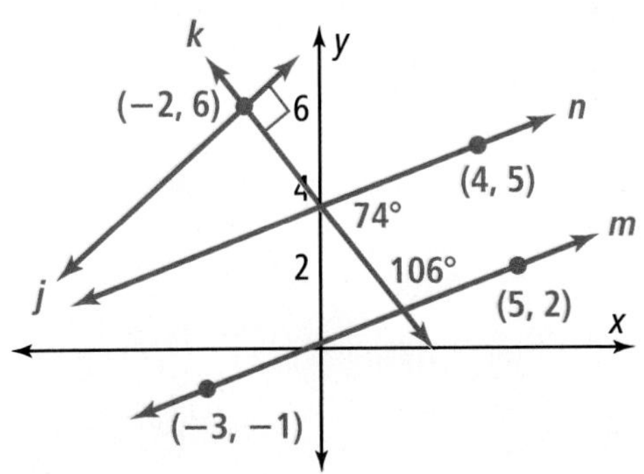

a. What is the equation of line k in slope-intercept form?

b. What is the equation of line j in slope-intercept form?

16. Construct Arguments Line m passes through points X and Y. Line n passes through points X and Z. If m and n have equal slope, what can you conclude about points X, Y, and Z? Explain.

17. Error Analysis Shannon says that the lines $y = -3x - 4$, $y = -\frac{1}{3}x + 6$, $y = -4x - 5$, and $y = \frac{1}{4}x - 5$ could represent the sides of a rectangle. Explain Shannon's error.

PRACTICE

Compare the slopes of the lines for $y = f(x)$ and $y = g(x)$ to determine if each pair of lines is parallel.
SEE EXAMPLE 1

18.

x	$f(x)$	$g(x)$
0	20	22
1	35	37
2	50	52
3	65	67

19.

x	$f(x)$	$g(x)$
0	5	10
1	7	15
2	9	20
3	11	25

Determine if each pair of lines is parallel.
SEE EXAMPLE 2

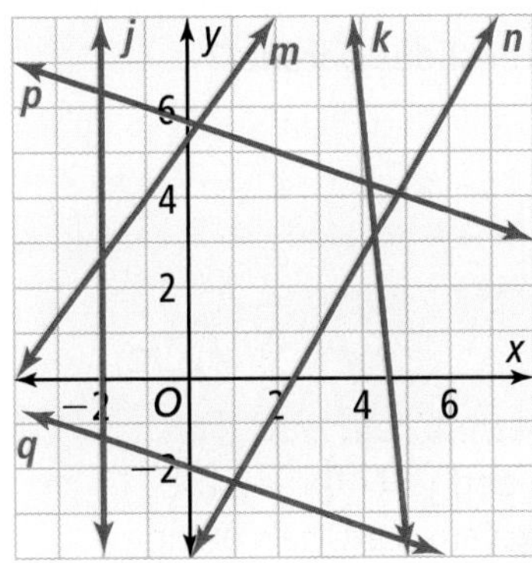

20. j and k **21.** m and n **22.** p and q

Determine if each pair of lines is perpendicular.
SEE EXAMPLE 3

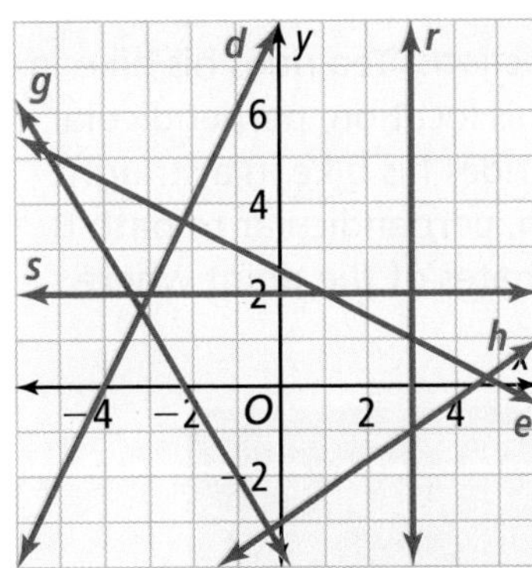

23. d and e **24.** g and h **25.** r and s

Write the equations for the lines parallel and perpendicular to the given line j that passes through Q. SEE EXAMPLE 4

26. $y = -4x + 1$; $Q(6, -1)$

27. $y = \frac{3}{2}x + 4$; $Q(-1, 1)$

PRACTICE & PROBLEM SOLVING

APPLY

28. Model With Mathematics The table shows locations of several sites at a high school campus. A landscaper wants to connect two sites with a path perpendicular to the path connecting the cafeteria and the library. Which two sites should he connect?

Locations	
Cafeteria (5, 5)	Library (11, 14)
Office (4, 12)	Gym (15, 8)
Woodshop (11, 6)	Art Studio (3, 16)

29. Make Sense and Persevere Are the steepest parts of the two water slides parallel? Explain.

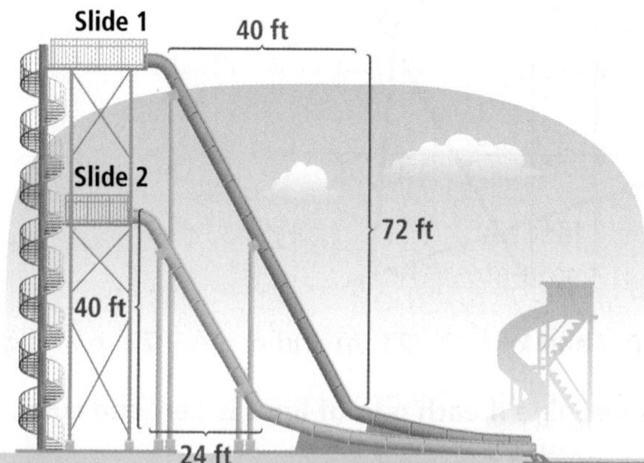

30. Mathematical Connections Teo rides his bike in a straight line from his location, perpendicular to path A, and Luke rides his bike in a straight line from his location, perpendicular to path B. What are the coordinates of the point where they meet?

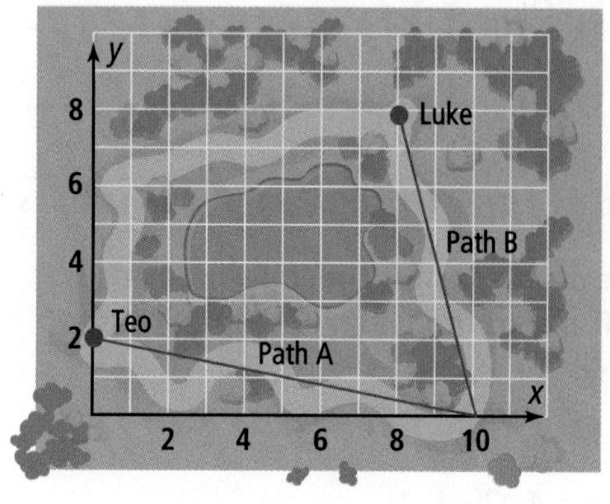

ASSESSMENT PRACTICE

31. $\overleftrightarrow{AB} \perp \overleftrightarrow{BC}$ for $A(-3, 2)$ and $C(2, 7)$. Which of the following could be the coordinates of B? Select all that apply.

Ⓐ (8, 0)
Ⓑ (−2, 2)
Ⓒ (−4, 5)
Ⓓ (1, 3)
Ⓔ (−1, −1)
Ⓕ (−3, 7)

32. SAT/ACT Line k passes through (2, −3) and (8, 1). Which equation represents a line that is parallel to k?

Ⓐ $y = -\frac{2}{3}x - \frac{5}{3}$
Ⓑ $y = \frac{2}{3}x - \frac{13}{3}$
Ⓒ $y = \frac{3}{2}x - 6$
Ⓓ $y = -\frac{3}{2}x$

33. Performance Task A knight travels in a straight line from the starting point to Token 1. The knight can only make right-angle turns to get to Tokens 2 and 3.

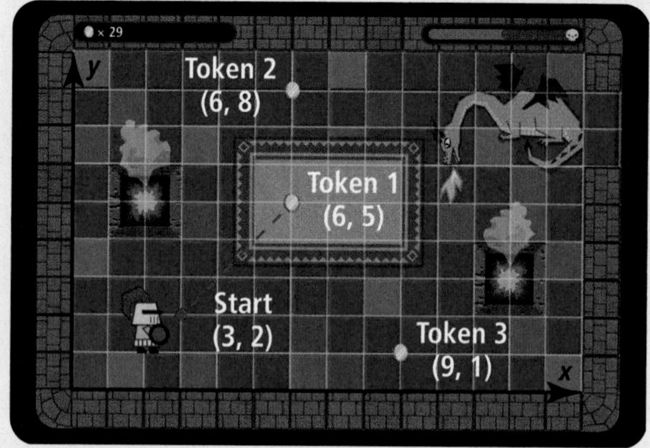

Part A Since the knight can only make right-angle turns, what are the slopes of the straight line paths the knight can travel?

Part B What equations describe a path that the knight can follow from the starting point to reach the tokens for the arrangement shown?

Part C What is the fewest number of turns that the knight can take in order to get all three tokens?

9-3 Polygons in the Coordinate Plane

PearsonRealize.com

I CAN… use the coordinate plane to analyze geometric figures.

Activity Assess

EXPLORE & REASON

Players place game pieces on the board shown and earn points from the attributes of the piece placed on the board.

- 1 point for a right angle
- 2 points for a pair of parallel sides
- 3 points for the shortest perimeter

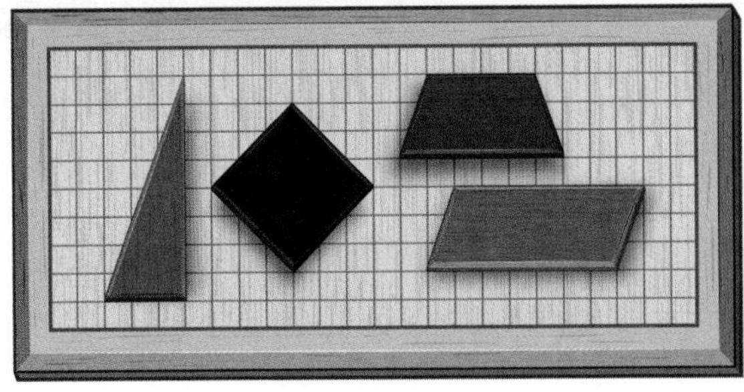

A. Which game piece is worth the greatest total points? Explain.

B. Make Sense and Persevere Describe a way to determine the perimeters that is different from the way you chose. Which method do you consider better? Explain.

ESSENTIAL QUESTION How are properties of geometric figures represented in the coordinate plane?

CONCEPTUAL UNDERSTANDING

EXAMPLE 1 Connect Algebra and Geometry Through Coordinates

What formulas can you use to identify properties of figures on the coordinate plane?

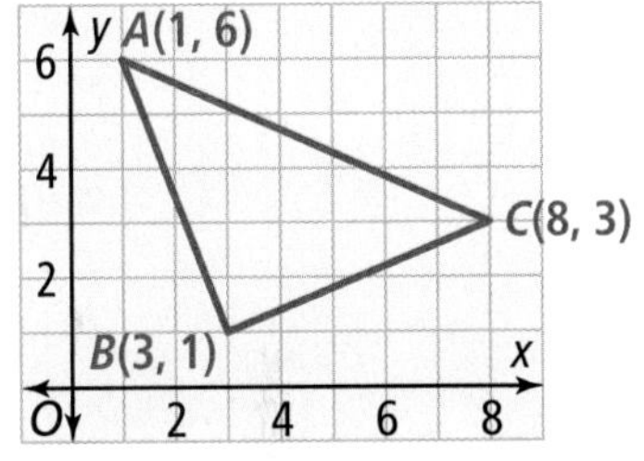

A. Which formula can you use to find *AB*?

Use the Distance Formula to find segment length.

$$AB = \sqrt{(3-1)^2 + (1-6)^2} = \sqrt{29}$$

B. What point bisects $\overline{AB}$?

Use the Midpoint Formula to find a segment bisector.

$$\text{midpoint of } \overline{AB} = \left(\frac{1+3}{2}, \frac{6+1}{2}\right) = \left(2, \frac{7}{2}\right)$$

C. Why do slopes of $\overline{AB}$ and $\overline{BC}$ show that $m\angle ABC = 90°$?

Use the slopes of the two segments to show that they are perpendicular.

$$\text{slope of } \overline{AB} = \frac{1-6}{3-1} = -\frac{5}{2}$$

$$\text{slope of } \overline{BC} = \frac{3-1}{8-3} = \frac{2}{5}$$

The product of the slopes is −1. So $\overline{AB} \perp \overline{BC}$, and $m\angle ABC = 90°$.

COMMON ERROR

Recall that the slope of a line is the ratio of the difference in the *y*-coordinates to the difference in the *x*-coordinates. Be careful not to reverse the ratio.

Try It! 1. Given $\triangle ABC$ in Example 1, what is the length of the line segment connecting the midpoints of $\overline{AC}$ and $\overline{BC}$?

EXAMPLE 2 Classify a Triangle on the Coordinate Plane

A. Is $\triangle XYZ$ equilateral, isosceles, or scalene?

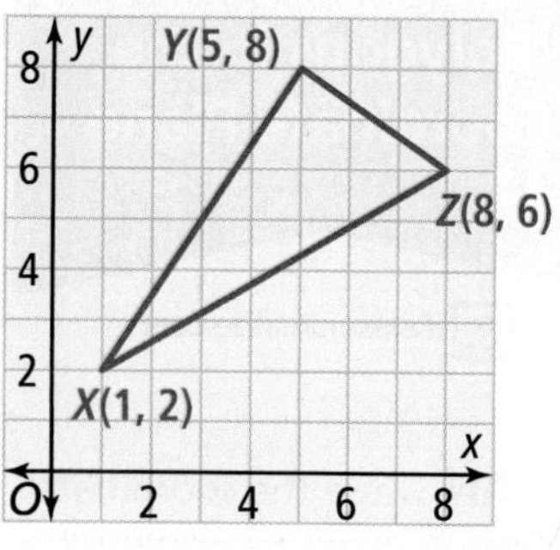

Find the length of each side.

$$XY = \sqrt{(5-1)^2 + (8-2)^2} = \sqrt{52}$$

$$YZ = \sqrt{(8-5)^2 + (6-8)^2} = \sqrt{13}$$

$$XZ = \sqrt{(8-1)^2 + (6-2)^2} = \sqrt{65}$$

No two sides are congruent. The triangle is scalene.

B. Is $\triangle XYZ$ a right triangle?

If $\triangle XYZ$ is a right triangle, then $\overline{XZ}$ is the hypotenuse because it is the longest side, and XY, YZ, and XZ satisfy the Pythagorean Theorem.

$$(\sqrt{52})^2 + (\sqrt{13})^2 \stackrel{?}{=} (\sqrt{65})^2$$

$$65 = 65 \checkmark$$

Triangle XYZ is a right triangle.

Try It! 2. The vertices of $\triangle PQR$ are $P(4, 1)$, $Q(2, 7)$, and $R(8, 5)$.

a. Is $\triangle PQR$ equilateral, isosceles, or scalene? Explain.

b. Is $\triangle PQR$ a right triangle? Explain.

EXAMPLE 3 Classify a Parallelogram on the Coordinate Plane

What type of parallelogram is $RSTU$?

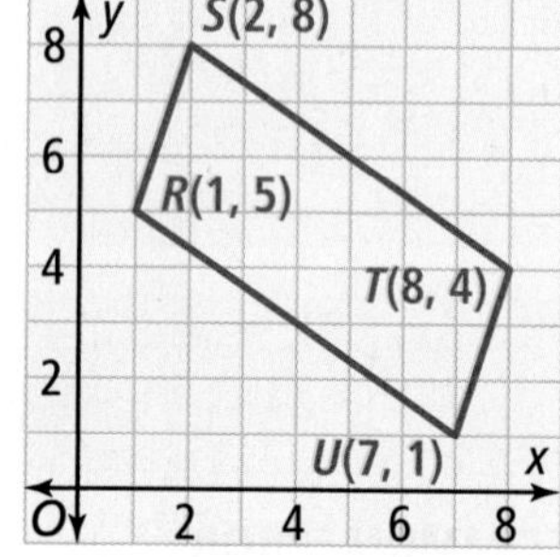

Determine whether $RSTU$ is a rhombus, a rectangle, or a square. First calculate ST and SR:

$$ST = \sqrt{(2-8)^2 + (8-4)^2} = \sqrt{52}$$

$$RS = \sqrt{(2-1)^2 + (8-5)^2} = \sqrt{10}$$

Since not all side lengths are equal, $RSTU$ is not a rhombus or a square.

Check for right angles by finding the slopes.

$$\text{slope of } \overline{ST} = \frac{4-8}{8-2} = -\frac{2}{3}$$

$$\text{slope of } \overline{RS} = \frac{8-5}{2-1} = 3$$

The product of the slopes is not -1, so $\overline{ST}$ and $\overline{RS}$ are not perpendicular. At least one angle is not a right angle, and $RSTU$ is not a rectangle. Therefore, quadrilateral $RSTU$ is a parallelogram that is neither a square, nor a rhombus, nor a rectangle.

MAKE SENSE AND PERSEVERE

Consider other formulas you use on the coordinate plane. What are some ways to show that a quadrilateral is not a rectangle or a rhombus?

Try It! 3. The vertices of a parallelogram are $A(-2, 2)$, $B(4, 6)$, $C(6, 3)$, and $D(0, -1)$.

a. Is $ABCD$ a rhombus? Explain.

b. Is $ABCD$ a rectangle? Explain.

EXAMPLE 4 Classify Quadrilaterals as Trapezoids and Kites on the Coordinate Plane

A. Is *ABCD* a trapezoid?

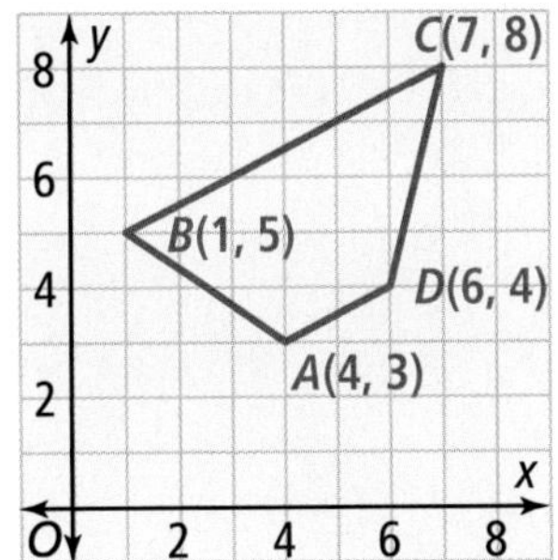

A trapezoid has exactly one pair of parallel sides. Use the slope formula to determine if only one pair of opposite sides is parallel.

COMMUNICATE PRECISELY
Think about the properties of a trapezoid. Why do you need to find the slopes for all four sides?

slope of $\overline{AB} = \frac{5-3}{1-4} = -\frac{2}{3}$

slope of $\overline{BC} = \frac{8-5}{7-1} = \frac{1}{2}$

slope of $\overline{CD} = \frac{4-8}{6-7} = \frac{4}{1}$

slope of $\overline{AD} = \frac{4-3}{6-4} = \frac{1}{2}$

Since only the slopes of $\overline{BC}$ and $\overline{AD}$ are equal, $\overline{BC} \parallel \overline{AD}$, and only one pair of opposite sides is parallel. Therefore, quadrilateral *ABCD* is a trapezoid.

B. Is *JKLM* a kite?

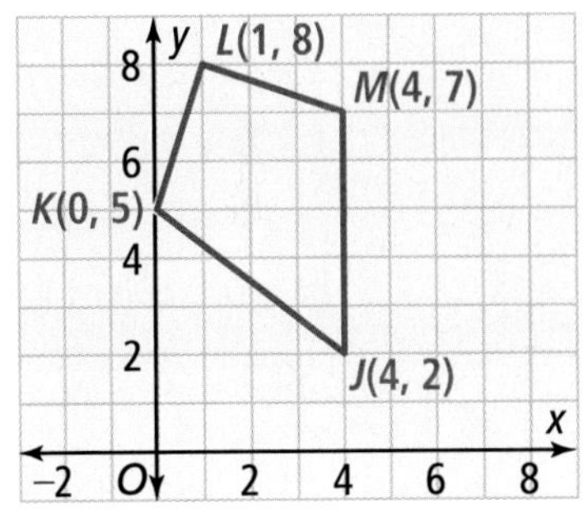

A kite has two pairs of consecutive congruent sides and no opposite sides congruent. Use the Distance Formula to find the lengths of the sides.

$JK = \sqrt{(0-4)^2 + (5-2)^2} = 5$

$KL = \sqrt{(1-0)^2 + (8-5)^2} = \sqrt{10}$

$LM = \sqrt{(4-1)^2 + (7-8)^2} = \sqrt{10}$

$MJ = \sqrt{(4-4)^2 + (2-7)^2} = 5$

Consecutive pair $\overline{KL}$ and $\overline{LM}$ and consecutive pair $\overline{JK}$ and $\overline{MJ}$ are congruent. No opposite pair is congruent, so *JKLM* is a kite.

Try It! **4.** Is each quadrilateral a kite, trapezoid, or neither?

a. Q(2, 5), R(7, 6), S(6, 1), P(2, 1)

b.

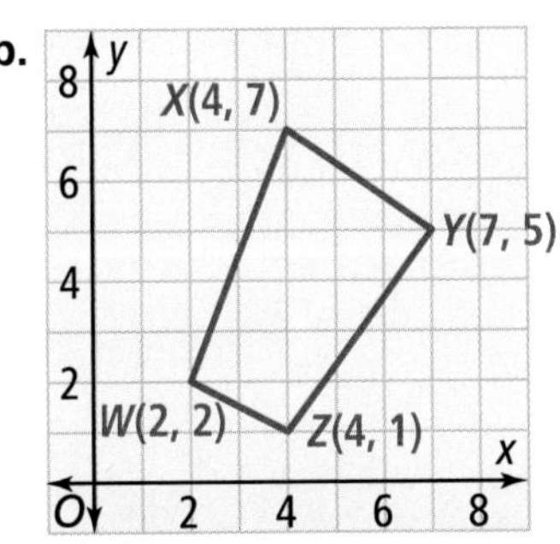

APPLICATION

EXAMPLE 5 Find Perimeter and Area

Dylan draws up a plan to fence in a yard for his chickens. The distance between grid lines is 1 foot.

A. Is 30 feet of fencing enough to enclose the yard?

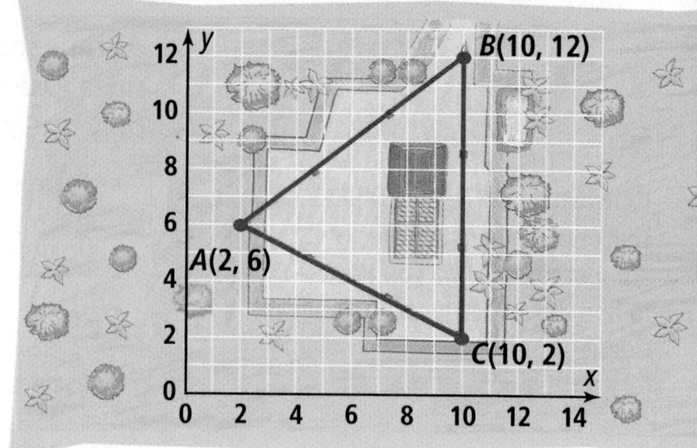

Find the lengths of the sides.

$AB = \sqrt{(2-10)^2 + (6-12)^2} = 10$ ft

$BC = \sqrt{(10-10)^2 + (12-2)^2} = 10$ ft

$AC = \sqrt{(2-10)^2 + (6-2)^2} = \sqrt{80}$ ft

Find the perimeter of the yard.

$P = 10 + 10 + \sqrt{80}$

≈ 28.9 ft

The perimeter is about 28.9 feet, which is less than 30 feet. Dylan has enough fencing material.

B. For a healthy flock, each chicken needs at least 8 square feet of space. What is the maximum number of chickens Dylan can put in the yard?

CONSTRUCT ARGUMENTS
Consider the properties of an isosceles triangle. What property of an isosceles triangle justifies that $\overline{BX}$ is a height of the triangle?

The yard is an isosceles triangle. To find the area, you need the height of the triangle. The height of $\triangle ABC$ is BX, where X is the midpoint of $\overline{AC}$.

Find the midpoint of $\overline{AC}$.

$X = \left(\frac{2+10}{2}, \frac{6+2}{2}\right) = (6, 4)$

Find the height of $\triangle ABC$.

$BX = \sqrt{(10-6)^2 + (12-4)^2} = \sqrt{80}$ ft

Then find the area of the yard.

area of $\triangle ABC = \frac{1}{2}(\sqrt{80})(\sqrt{80}) = 40$ ft^2

Divide 40 by 8 to find the number of chickens.

$40 \div 8 = 5$

Dylan can keep as many as 5 chickens in the yard.

Try It! 5. The vertices of $WXYZ$ are $W(5, 4)$, $X(2, 9)$, $Y(9, 9)$, and $Z(8, 4)$.

a. What is the perimeter of $WXYZ$?

b. What is the area of $WXYZ$?

CONCEPT SUMMARY Connecting Algebra and Geometry

You can use algebra to determine properties of and to classify geometric figures on the coordinate plane.

WORDS

Use the Distance Formula to find the lengths of segments to classify figures.

Use the Slope Formula to determine whether two lines or segments are parallel or perpendicular.

Use the Midpoint Formula to determine if a point bisects a segment.

GRAPH

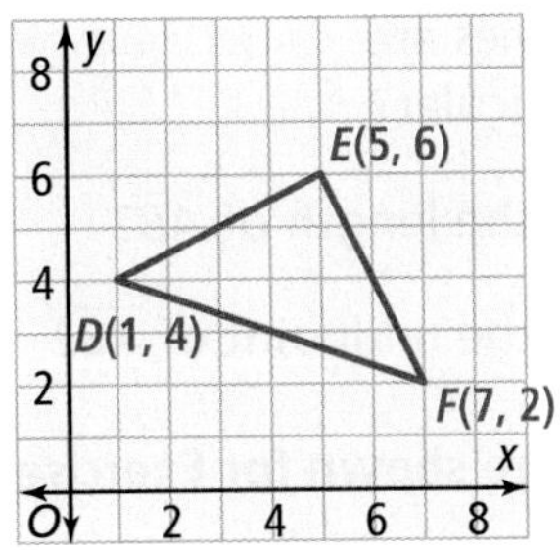

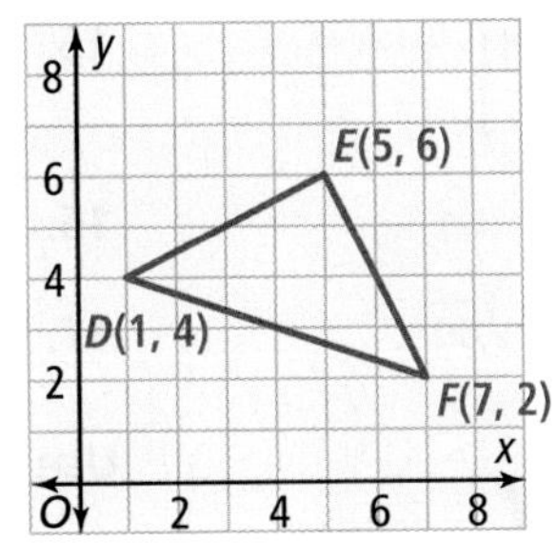

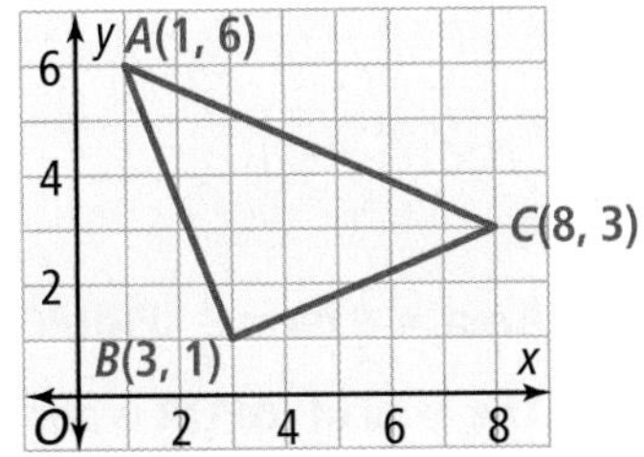

NUMBERS

$DE = \sqrt{(5 - 1)^2 + (6 - 4)^2}$
$= \sqrt{20}$

slope of $\overline{DE} = \frac{6 - 4}{5 - 1}$
$= \frac{1}{2}$

midpoint of $\overline{DF}$
$= \left(\frac{1 + 7}{2}, \frac{4 + 2}{2}\right) = (4, 3)$

Do You UNDERSTAND?

1. **ESSENTIAL QUESTION** How are properties of geometric figures represented in the coordinate plane?

2. **Error Analysis** Chen is asked to describe two methods to find *BC*. Why is Chen incorrect?

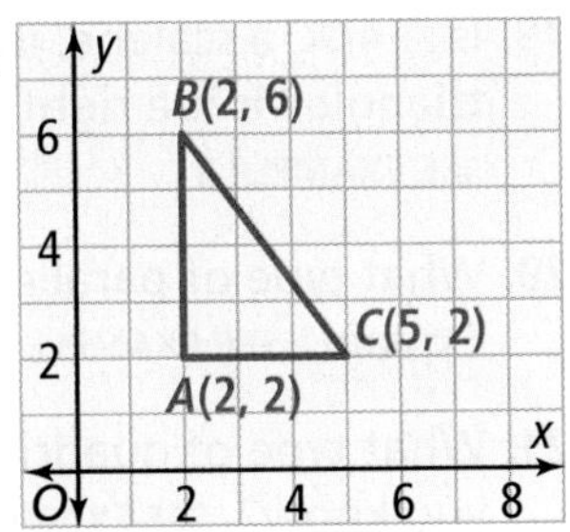

The only possible method is to use the Distance Formula because you only know the endpoints of $\overline{BC}$.

3. **Communicate Precisely** Describe three ways you can determine whether a quadrilateral is a parallelogram given the coordinates of the vertices.

Do You KNOW HOW?

Use *JKLM* for Exercises 4–6.

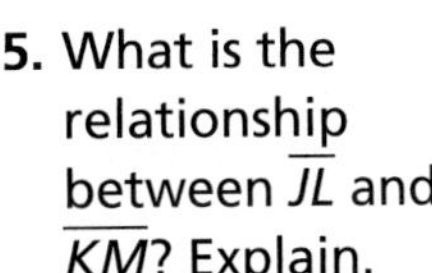

4. What is the perimeter of *JKLM*?

5. What is the relationship between $\overline{JL}$ and $\overline{KM}$? Explain.

6. What type of quadrilateral is *JKLM*? Explain.

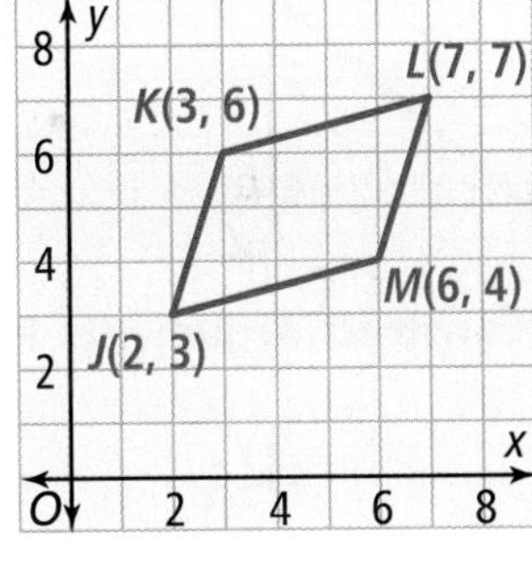

Use △*PQR* for Exercises 7 and 8.

7. What kind of triangle is *PQR*? Explain.

8. What is the area of *PQR*?

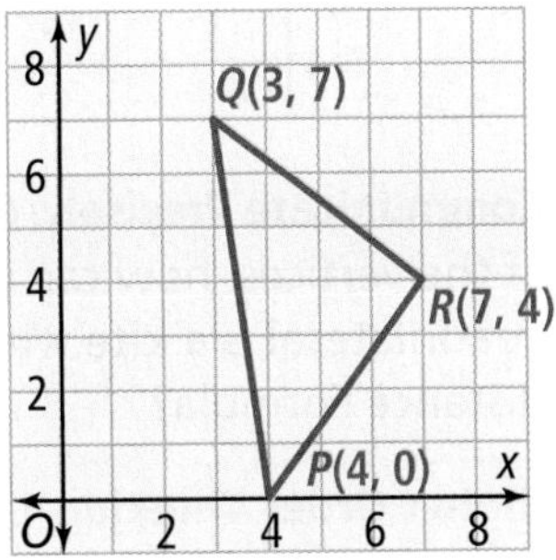

PRACTICE & PROBLEM SOLVING

Scan for Multimedia 

Additional Exercises Available Online

UNDERSTAND

9. **Error Analysis** What error did Kelley make in finding the area of $\triangle PQR$?

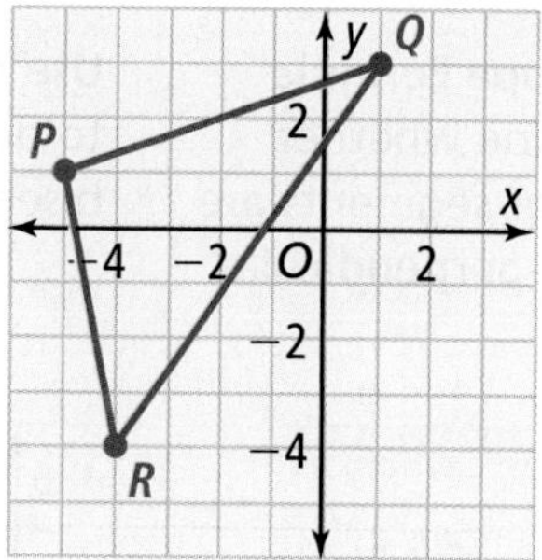

Area $= \frac{1}{2}bh = \frac{1}{2}(PR)(PQ) = \frac{1}{2}\sqrt{26}\sqrt{40}$

The area of ΔPQR is about 16.12 square units. ✗

10. **Mathematical Connections** Find the equation of the line that passes through point R and is perpendicular to line m.

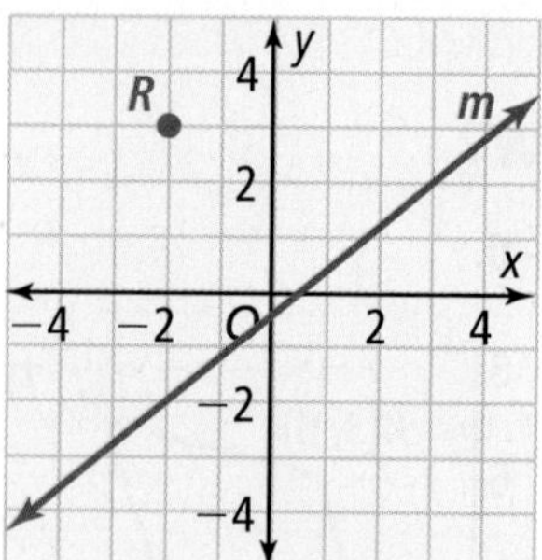

11. **Construct Arguments** Prove $\triangle ABC \cong \triangle DEF$.

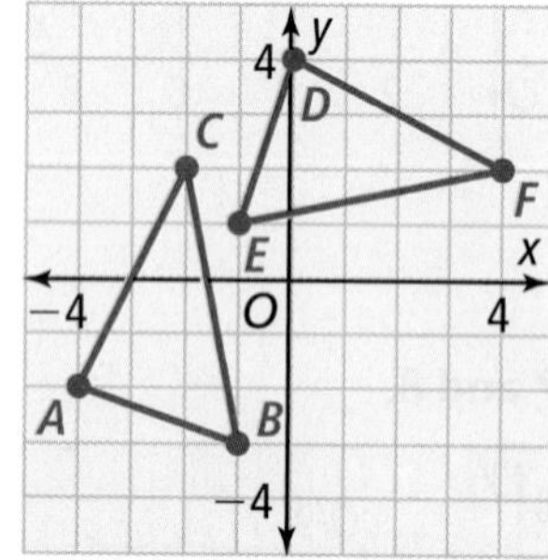

12. **Communicate Precisely** Given the coordinates of the vertices, how can you show that a quadrilateral is a kite without using the Distance Formula?

13. **Higher Order Thinking** Let line p be the perpendicular bisector of $\overline{AB}$ that has endpoints and $A(x_1, y_1)$ and $B(x_2, y_2)$. Describe the process for writing a general equation in slope-intercept form for line p.

PRACTICE

Use the figure shown for Exercises 14–17.
SEE EXAMPLE 1

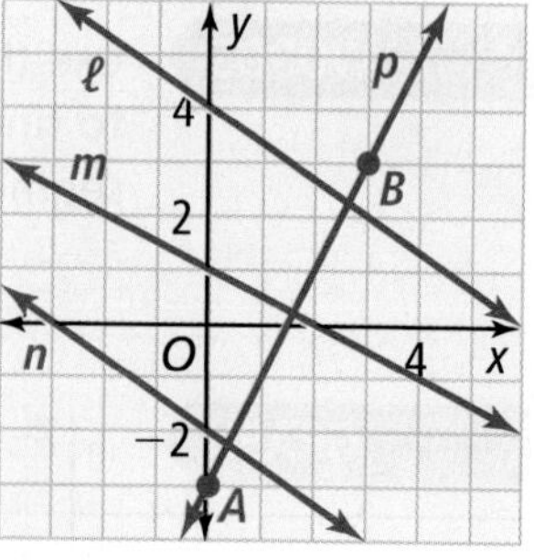

14. Which lines are parallel?

15. Which lines are perpendicular?

16. What is the length of $\overline{AB}$?

17. What is the midpoint of $\overline{AB}$?

Use the figure shown for Exercises 18–23.

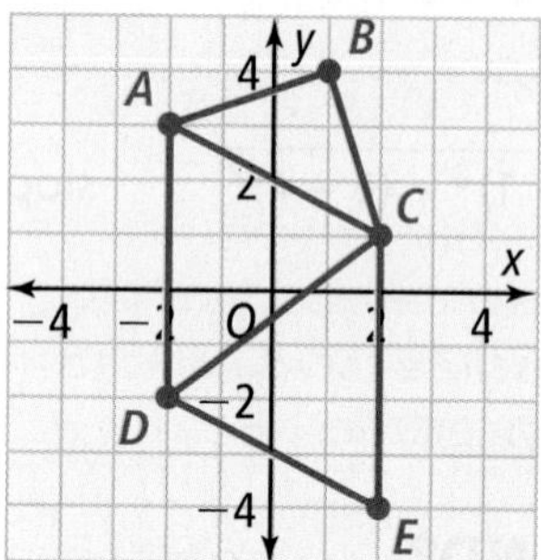

18. Is $\triangle ABC$ a scalene, isosceles, or equilateral triangle? Is it a right triangle? Explain.
SEE EXAMPLE 2

19. Is $\triangle ADC$ a scalene, isosceles, or equilateral triangle? Is it a right triangle? Explain.
SEE EXAMPLE 2

20. What type of parallelogram is $ACED$? Explain. SEE EXAMPLE 3

21. What type of quadrilateral is $ABCD$? How do you know? SEE EXAMPLE 4

22. Find the area and perimeter of $\triangle ABC$.
SEE EXAMPLE 5

23. Find the area and perimeter of $ABCD$.
SEE EXAMPLE 6

Three vertices of a quadrilateral are $P(-2, 3)$, $Q(2, 4)$, and $R(1, 0)$. SEE EXAMPLE 3

24. Suppose $PQRS$ is a parallelogram. What are the coordinates of vertex S? What type of parallelogram is $PQRS$?

25. Suppose $PQSR$ is a parallelogram. What are the coordinates of vertex S? What type of parallelogram is $PQSR$?

PRACTICE & PROBLEM SOLVING

Practice Tutorial

Mixed Review Available Online

APPLY

26. Use Appropriate Tools An architect overlays a coordinate grid on her plans for attaching a greenhouse to the side of a house. She wants to locate point D so that $ABCD$ is a trapezoid and $\overline{CD}$ is perpendicular to the house. What are the coordinates for point D?

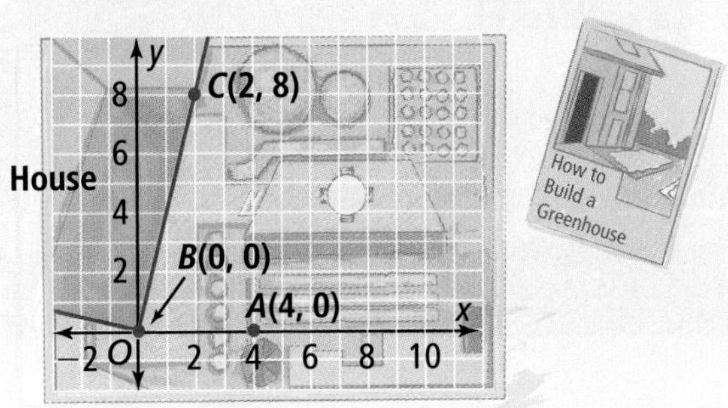

27. Model With Mathematics Yuson thinks the design she made is symmetric across the dashed line she drew. How can she use coordinates to show that her design is symmetric?

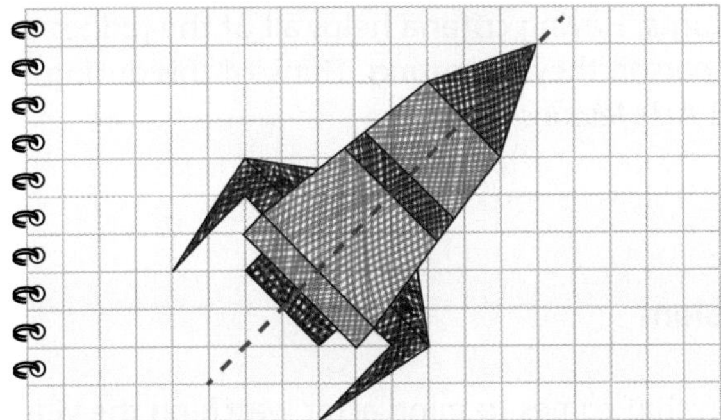

28. Construct Arguments The map shows the regions that Anna and Richard have explored. Each claims to have explored the greater area. Who is correct? Explain.

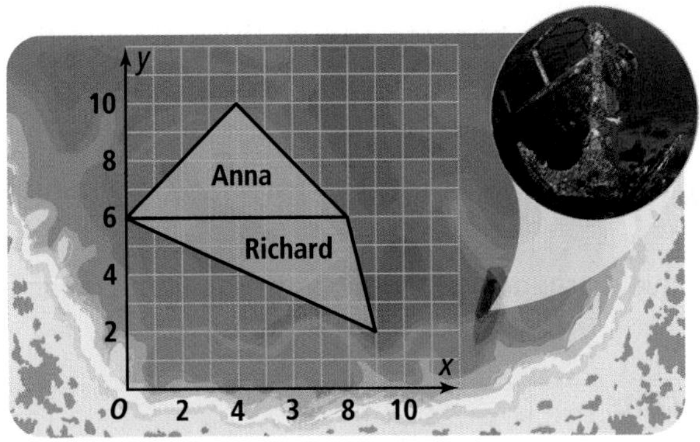

ASSESSMENT PRACTICE

29. Triangle ABC has vertices $A(2, 5)$, $B(6, 8)$, and $C(5, 1)$. Determine whether each statement about $\triangle ABC$ is true. Select *Yes* or *No*.

	Yes	No
$\overline{AB} \cong \overline{AC}$	❑	❑
$BC = AB\sqrt{2}$	❑	❑
The midpoint of BC is (5.5, 4).	❑	❑
The perimeter is 12.5 units.	❑	❑

30. SAT/ACT Quadrilateral $JKLM$ has vertices $J(1, -2)$, $K(7, 1)$, $L(8, -1)$, and $M(2, -4)$. Which is the most precise classification of $JKLM$?

Ⓐ rectangle

Ⓑ rhombus

Ⓒ trapezoid

Ⓓ kite

31. Performance Task Dana draws the side view of a TV stand that has slanted legs. Each unit in his plan equals half of a foot.

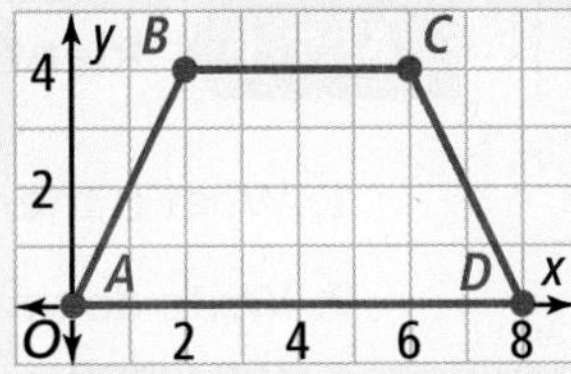

Part A Dana thinks his TV stand is in the shape of isosceles trapezoid. Is he correct? Explain.

Part B Dana adds an additional support by connecting the midpoints of the legs. How long is the support?

Part C Dana decides he wants to make the TV stand a half foot higher by placing B at (2, 5) and C at (6, 5). How much longer will the legs and support connecting the midpoints be?

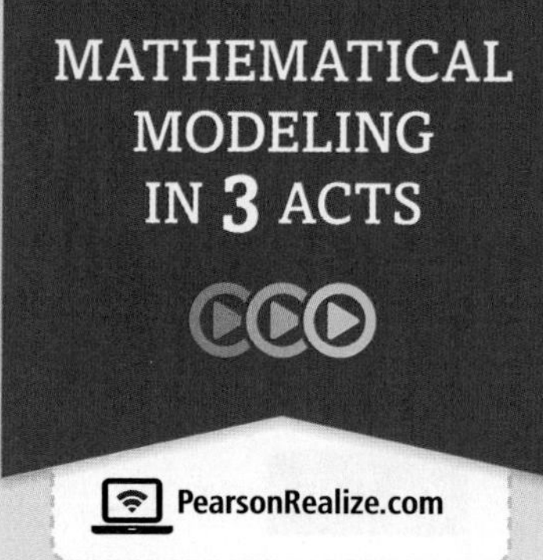

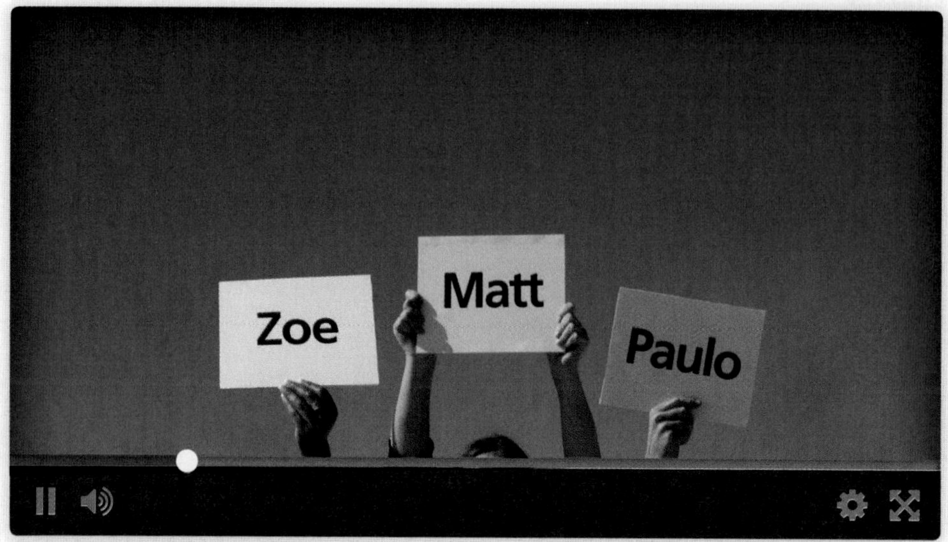

You Be the Judge

Have you ever been a judge in a contest or competition? What criteria did you use to decide the winner? If you were one of many judges, did you all agree on who should win?

Often there is a set of criteria that judges use to help them score the performances of the contestants. Having criteria helps all of the judges be consistent regardless of the person they are rating. Think of this during the Mathematical Modeling in 3 Acts lesson.

ACT 1 Identify the Problem

1. What is the first question that comes to mind after watching the video?
2. Write down the main question you will answer about what you saw in the video.
3. Make an initial conjecture that answers this main question.
4. Explain how you arrived at your conjecture.
5. What information will be useful to know to answer the main question? How can you get it? How will you use that information?

ACT 2 Develop a Model

6. Use the math that you have learned in this Topic to refine your conjecture.

ACT 3 Interpret the Results

7. Did your refined conjecture match the actual answer exactly? If not, what might explain the difference?

9-4 Proofs Using Coordinate Geometry

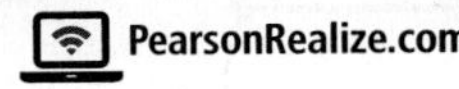

I CAN… prove geometric theorems using algebra and the coordinate plane.

CRITIQUE & EXPLAIN

Dakota and Jung are trying to show that $\triangle ABC$ is a right triangle. Each student uses a different method.

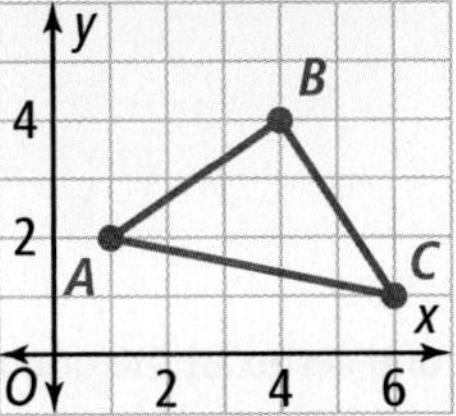

Dakota

slope of $\overline{AB} = \frac{2}{3}$, slope of $\overline{BC} = -\frac{3}{2}$

slope of $\overline{AB} \cdot$ slope of $\overline{BC} = -1$

Triangle ABC is a right triangle.

Jung

$AB = BC = \sqrt{13}$, $AC = \sqrt{26}$

$(\sqrt{13})^2 + (\sqrt{13})^2 = (\sqrt{26})^2$

Triangle ABC is a right triangle.

A. Did Dakota and Jung both show $\triangle ABC$ is a right triangle? Explain.

B. Reason If the coordinates of $\triangle ABC$ were changed to (2, 3), (5, 5), and (7, 2), how would each student's method change? Explain.

ESSENTIAL QUESTION

How can geometric relationships be proven algebraically in the coordinate plane?

CONCEPTUAL UNDERSTANDING

EXAMPLE 1 Plan a Coordinate Proof

How can you use coordinates to prove geometric relationships algebraically? Plan a proof for the Trapezoid Midsegment Theorem.

Draw and label a diagram that names all points to be used in the proof.

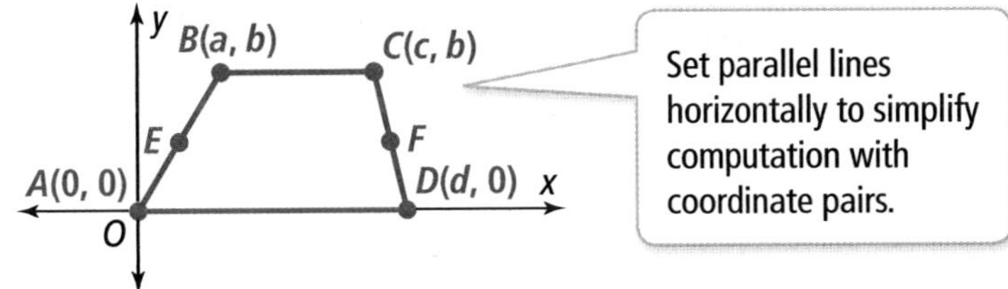

Restate the Trapezoid Midsegment Theorem so the statement can be proved using algebra on the coordinate plane.

Theorem: The midsegment of a trapezoid is parallel to each base and its length is one half the sum of the lengths of the bases.

Restatement: If $\overline{EF}$ is the midsegment of trapezoid $ABCD$, then slope $\overline{EF}$ = slope $\overline{AD}$ = slope $\overline{BC}$ and $EF = \frac{AD + BC}{2}$.

Plan: To show that the midsegment is parallel to the bases, show that their slopes are equal. Then show that the mean of the base lengths is the length of the midsegment.

USE STRUCTURE
Variables are used according to the properties of trapezoids. Why is the proof valid for all trapezoids?

Try It! **1.** Plan a proof to show that the diagonals of a square are congruent and perpendicular.

PROOF

EXAMPLE 2 Write a Coordinate Proof

Write a coordinate proof of the Trapezoid Midsegment Theorem. Use the conditional statement from Example 1 to decide what is given and what is to be proved.

STUDY TIP
Placing one vertex at the origin makes calculations of slopes and distances easier. If a figure is symmetrical, align the line of symmetry along one of the axes to simplify calculations.

Given: Trapezoid $ABCD$, with midpoints E and F

Prove: $\overline{EF} \parallel \overline{AD} \parallel \overline{BC}$ and $EF = \frac{AD + BC}{2}$

Plan: Apply the plan and diagram from Example 1. Use the coordinates in the diagram to show that slope $\overline{EF}$ = slope $\overline{AD}$ = slope $\overline{BC}$, and $EF = \frac{AD + BC}{2}$.

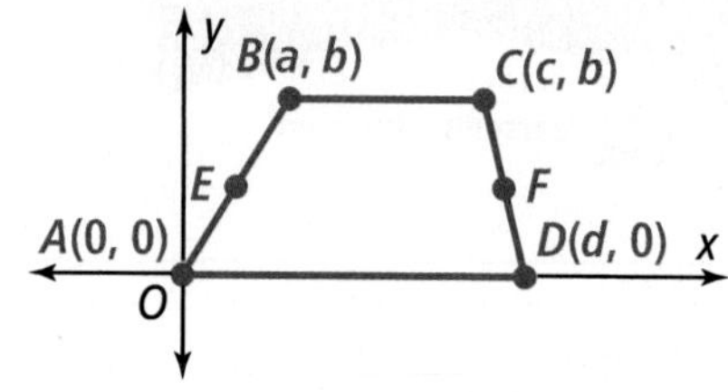

Proof:

Step 1 Use the Midpoint Formula to find the coordinates of points E and F.

$$E = \left(\frac{0 + a}{2}, \frac{0 + b}{2}\right) = \left(\frac{a}{2}, \frac{b}{2}\right) \qquad F = \left(\frac{c + d}{2}, \frac{b + 0}{2}\right) = \left(\frac{c + d}{2}, \frac{b}{2}\right)$$

Step 2 The slopes of $\overline{AD}$, $\overline{BC}$, and $\overline{EF}$ all equal zero, because the segments are horizontal.

Therefore, $\overline{EF} \parallel \overline{AD} \parallel \overline{BC}$.

Step 3 Determine AD, BC, and EF.

Since the segments are horizontal lines, the lengths are differences of the x-coordinates.

$$AD = d - 0 = d \qquad BC = c - a \qquad EF = \frac{c + d}{2} - \frac{a}{2} = \frac{c + d - a}{2}$$

Step 4 Use algebra to show that $\frac{AD + BC}{2} = EF$.

$$\frac{AD + BC}{2} = \frac{d + (c - a)}{2} = \frac{c + d - a}{2} = EF$$

The bases and the midsegment are parallel, and the length of the midsegment is equal to the mean of the base lengths.

Therefore, $\overline{EF} \parallel \overline{AD} \parallel \overline{BC}$ and $EF = \frac{AD + BC}{2}$.

 **Try It!** 2. Use coordinate geometry to prove that the diagonals of a rectangle are congruent.

PROOF

EXAMPLE 3 Plan and Write a Coordinate Proof

Write a coordinate proof of the Concurrency of Medians Theorem.

Given: $\triangle ABC$ with medians $\overline{AD}$, $\overline{BE}$, and $\overline{CF}$

Prove: The medians are concurrent at point P such that

$$AP = \frac{2}{3}AD,\ BP = \frac{2}{3}BE, \text{ and } CP = \frac{2}{3}CF.$$

Plan: Draw and label a triangle in the coordinate plane. Then use the Midpoint Formula to locate the midpoints. Draw two medians and locate the point of intersection P. Use algebra to determine that the medians are concurrent at P. Finally, find the distance from P to each vertex.

Proof: Draw the triangle with the coordinates shown.

Find the coordinates of D, E, and F using the Midpoint Formula.

$D = (a + c, b)$ $\quad E = (c, 0)$ $\quad F = (a, b)$

Then find the slopes of the lines containing the medians $\overline{AD}$ and $\overline{CF}$.

slope of $\overline{AD} = \frac{b - 0}{a + c - 0} = \frac{b}{a + c}$

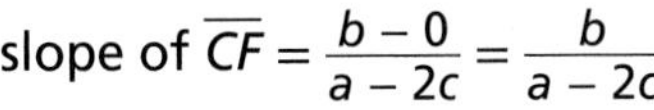

slope of $\overline{CF} = \frac{b - 0}{a - 2c} = \frac{b}{a - 2c}$

Write equations for $\overleftrightarrow{AD}$ and $\overleftrightarrow{CF}$ using point-slope form.

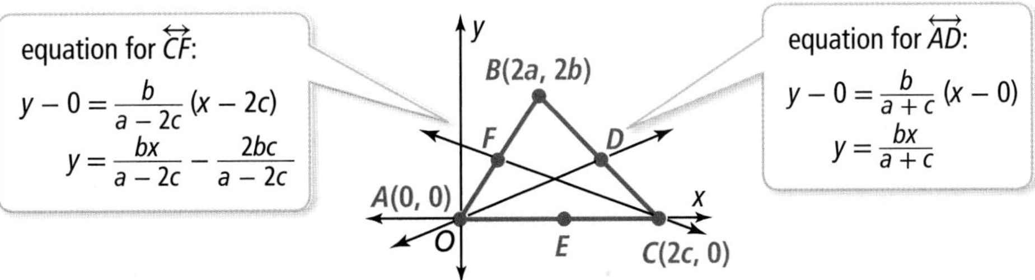

Set the expressions for y equal to each other. Solve for x to get $x = \frac{2(a + c)}{3}$.
Then substitute the expression for x into $y = \frac{bx}{a + c}$ to get $y = \frac{2b}{3}$.
Let point P be $\left(\frac{2(a + c)}{3}, \frac{2b}{3}\right)$.

To show that point P is on $\overline{BE}$, find an equation for the line containing $\overline{BE}$. Start by finding the slope of $\overline{BE}$.

slope of $\overline{BE} = \frac{0 - 2b}{c - 2a} = -\frac{2b}{c - 2a}$

Then, using point-slope form, an equation for $\overleftrightarrow{BE}$ is $y = -\frac{2bx}{c - 2a} + \frac{2bc}{c - 2a}$.

Substituting $\frac{2(a + c)}{3}$ for x into the equation results in $y = \frac{2b}{3}$, so point P is on $\overline{BE}$. The three medians are concurrent at P.

To complete the proof in the Try It, use the Distance Formula to show that $AP = \frac{2}{3}AD$, $BP = \frac{2}{3}BE$, and $CP = \frac{2}{3}CF$.

CONTINUED ON THE NEXT PAGE

COMMON ERROR
Do not confuse the Midpoint and Distance Formulas. The x-coordinate of a midpoint is the average of the x-coordinates of the endpoints and the y-coordinate is the average of the y-coordinates.

  Activity  Assess

 **Try It!** 3. To complete the proof in Example 3, use the coordinates to show that $AP = \frac{2}{3}AD$, $BP = \frac{2}{3}BE$, and $CP = \frac{2}{3}CF$.

APPLICATION

EXAMPLE 4 Use Coordinate Proofs to Solve Problems

An interior designer wants the center of a circular fountain to be equidistant from the corners of a triangular lobby. Where should he place the center of the fountain?

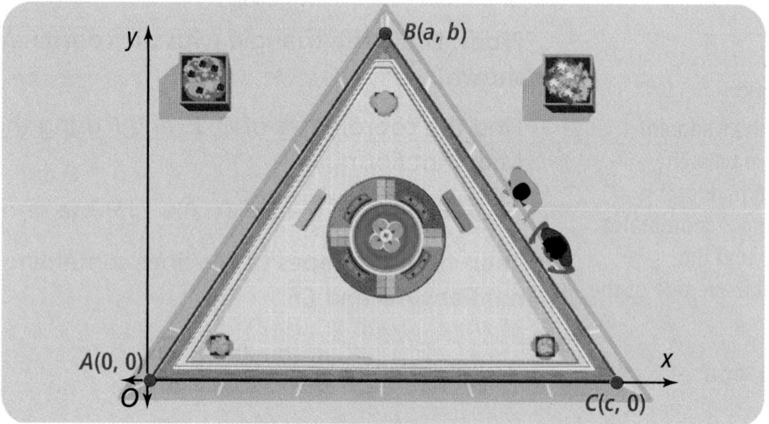

Formulate The center of the fountain must be at the circumcenter of the triangle. Find the point of intersection of the perpendicular bisectors of two sides of the triangle.

Compute Determine the intersection of the perpendicular bisectors of $\overline{AC}$ and $\overline{AB}$.

An equation of the perpendicular bisector of $\overline{AC}$ is $x = \frac{c}{2}$.

The perpendicular bisector of $\overline{AB}$ contains the point $\left(\frac{a}{2}, \frac{b}{2}\right)$ and has slope $-\frac{a}{b}$. Its point-slope equation is $y - \frac{b}{2} = -\frac{a}{b}\left(x - \frac{a}{2}\right)$, which simplifies to $y = -\frac{a}{b}x + \frac{a^2 + b^2}{2b}$.

Calculate the intersection of the two lines.

$$y = -\frac{a}{b}x + \frac{a^2 + b^2}{2b}$$

$$y = -\frac{a}{b} \cdot \frac{c}{2} + \frac{a^2 + b^2}{2b}$$

Substitute $\frac{c}{2}$ for x, and then solve for y.

$$y = \frac{a^2 - ac + b^2}{2b}$$

Interpret The center of the fountain should be at the point $\left(\frac{c}{2}, \frac{a^2 - ac + b^2}{2b}\right)$.

Try It! 4. A table has a top that is a right triangle and a single support leg. Where should the center of the leg be placed so it corresponds with the center of gravity of the table top? Plan a coordinate geometry proof to find its location.

CONCEPT SUMMARY Writing a Coordinate Proof

WORDS

- Determine which numerical relationships you must calculate to show the statement is true.
- Draw and label a figure on a coordinate plane. Choose coordinates that simplify computations.
- Calculate the numerical values needed to prove a statement or solve a problem.

DIAGRAMS

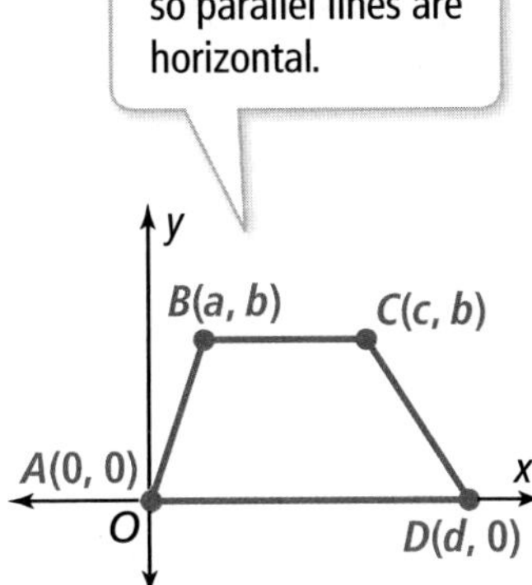

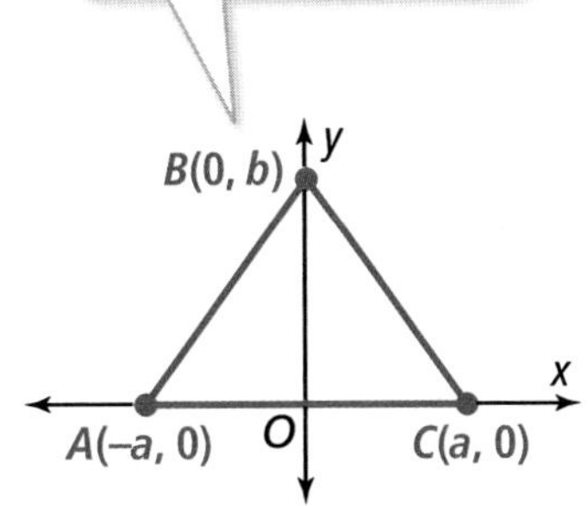

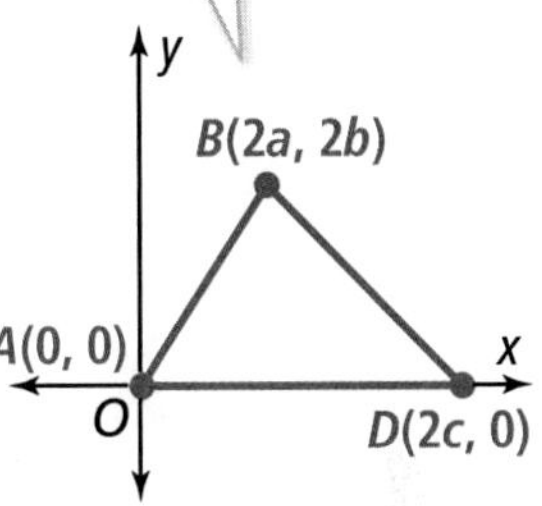

Do You UNDERSTAND?

1. **ESSENTIAL QUESTION** How can geometric relationships be proven algebraically in the coordinate plane?

2. **Error Analysis** Venetta tried to find the slope of $\overline{AB}$. What is her error?

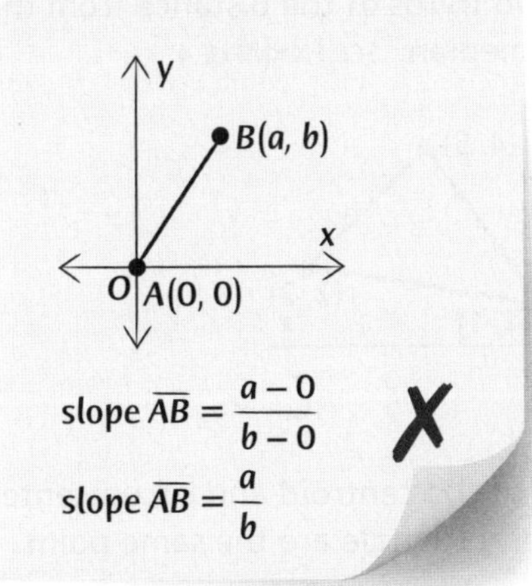

$$\text{slope } \overline{AB} = \frac{a-0}{b-0}$$

$$\text{slope } \overline{AB} = \frac{a}{b}$$

3. **Communicate Precisely** What is a coordinate geometry proof?

4. **Reason** Describe why it is important to plan a coordinate proof.

5. **Use Structure** What coordinates would you use to describe an isosceles triangle on a coordinate plane? Explain.

Do You KNOW HOW?

For Exercises 6–8, write a plan for a coordinate proof.

6. The diagonals of a rhombus are perpendicular.

7. The area of a triangle with vertices $A(0, 0)$, $B(0, a)$ and $C(b, c)$ is $\frac{ab}{2}$.

8. The lines that contain the altitudes of a triangle are concurrent.

For Exercises 9–12, plan and write a coordinate proof.

9. A point on the perpendicular bisector of a segment is equidistant from the endpoints.

10. The diagonals of a kite are perpendicular.

11. All squares are similar.

12. The area of a rhombus is half the product of the lengths of its diagonals.

PRACTICE & PROBLEM SOLVING

UNDERSTAND

13. **Communicate Precisely** What coordinates would you use to describe an equilateral triangle in the coordinate plane? Explain.

14. **Error Analysis** Tonya drew a diagram to prove the Perpendicular Bisector Theorem using coordinate geometry. What coordinates should she use for point C?

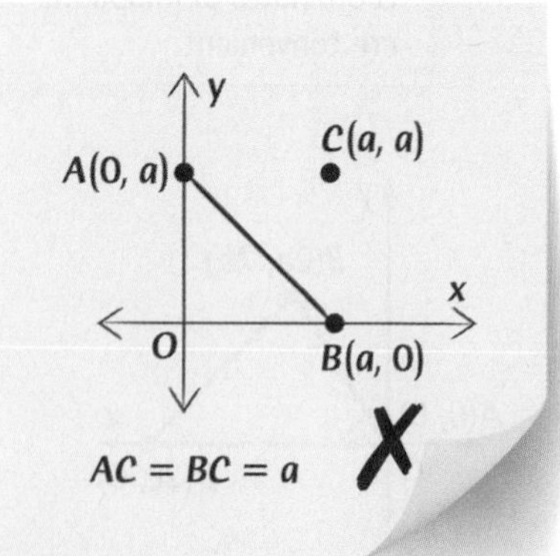

For Exercises 15 and 16, use the graph.

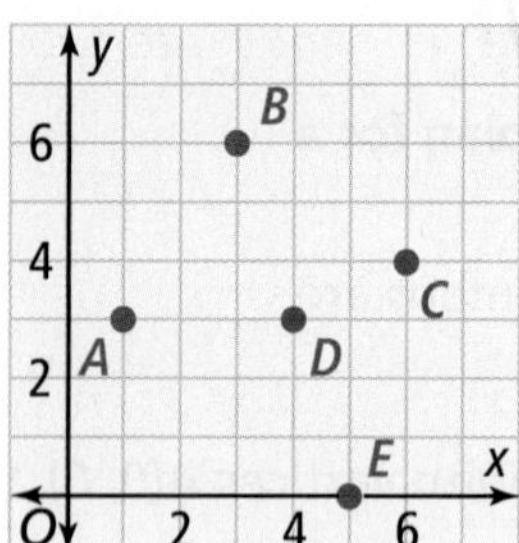

15. **Make Sense and Persevere** How would you plan a proof to show that $\triangle ABC$ is a right triangle?

16. **Make Sense and Persevere** Describe how you would prove points B, D, and E are collinear.

17. **Mathematical Connections** What is the equation of the line containing the perpendicular bisector of $\overline{AB}$?

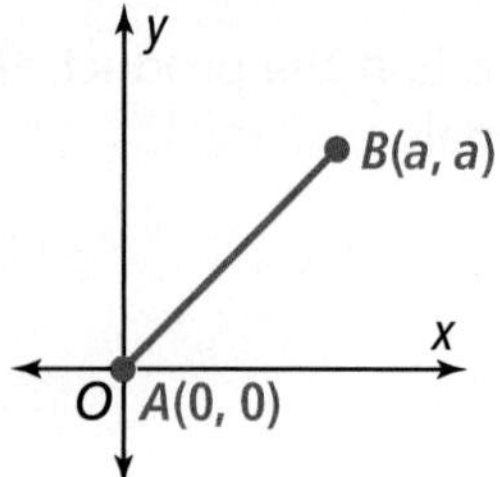

PRACTICE

For Exercises 18–21, write a plan for a coordinate proof. SEE EXAMPLE 1

18. The diagonals of a parallelogram that is not a rectangle are not congruent.

19. The length of a diameter of a circle is twice that of its radius.

20. The diagonals of a parallelogram bisect each other.

21. The area of $\triangle XYZ$ is twice the area of $\triangle XWZ$, where W is the midpoint of $\overline{YZ}$.

For Exercises 22–25, plan and write a coordinate proof. SEE EXAMPLES 2 AND 3

22. The length of a diagonal of a rectangle is the square root of the sum of the squares of the lengths of two adjacent sides.

23. All right triangles with one acute angle measuring 30° are similar.

24. One and only one diagonal of a kite bisects the other.

25. The length of the median to the hypotenuse of a right triangle is half the length of the hypotenuse.

26. Find the centroid of the triangle by finding the point two thirds of the distance from the vertex on one median. SEE EXAMPLE 4

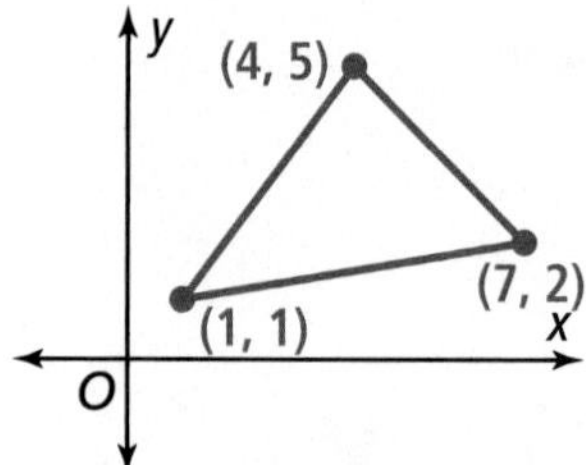

27. Show that the centroid and circumcenter of an equilateral triangle are the same point.

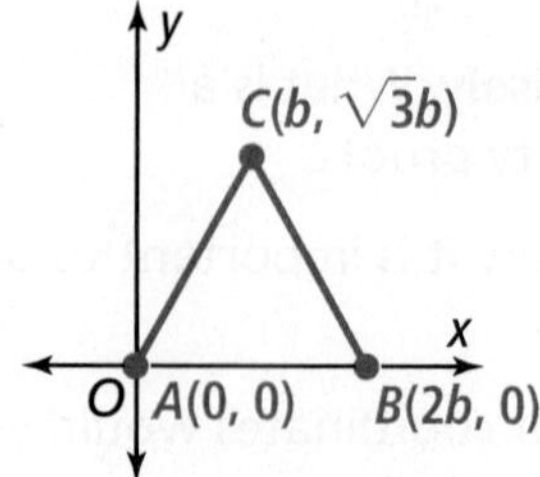

PRACTICE & PROBLEM SOLVING

Mixed Review Available Online

APPLY

28. **Model With Mathematics** Each student in a woodworking class inlays brass wire along the lines connecting the midpoints of adjacent sides of a trivet. A trivet is six square inches. If the wire costs \$0.54 per inch, what is the cost of the wire for making 12 trivets?

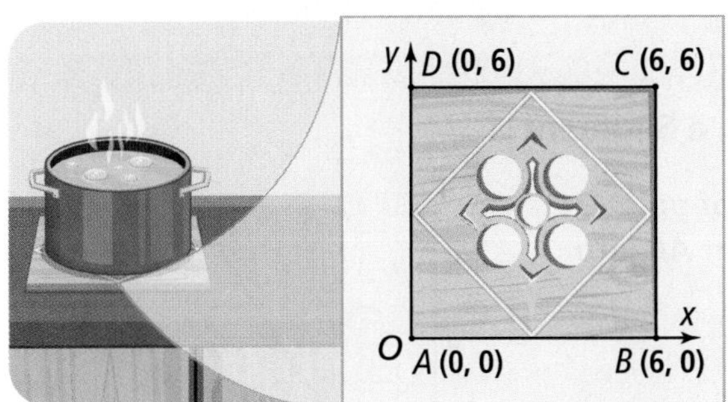

29. **Make Sense and Persevere** The owner of an animal park wants a quadrilateral trail that connects the four sides of the iscosceles-trapezoid-shaped park, with all sides of the trail the same length. Deon says that if the trail connects the midpoint of each side to the midpoints of the adjacent sides, the trail will be a rhombus. Write a coordinate proof to show that Deon is correct.

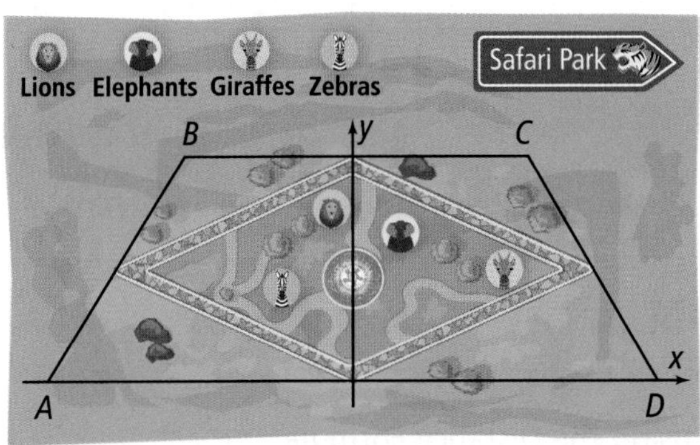

30. **Higher Order Thinking** The front of a sculpture is symmetric about the y-axis. Point A is located at $(-3, 0)$, and $\overline{AC}$ is the longest side of $\triangle ABC$. The perimeter of $\triangle ABC$ is 16. What is the value of a?

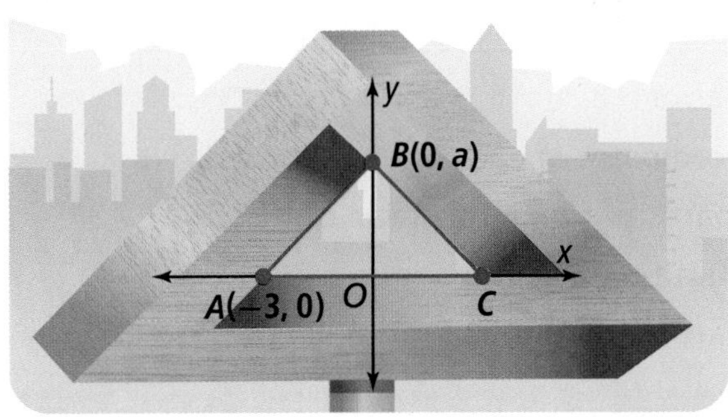

ASSESSMENT PRACTICE

31. A coordinate proof requires a __?__ and then uses __?__ on the __?__ of the points in the diagram to complete the proof.

32. **SAT/ACT** Which statements are true?

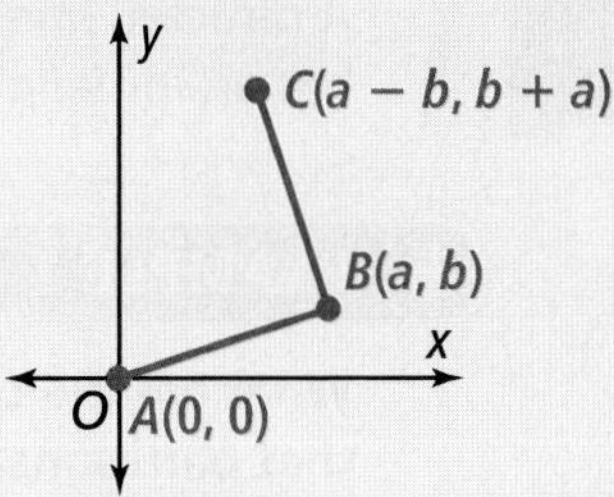

I. $AB = BC$

II. $\overline{AB} \perp \overline{BC}$

III. $AC = 2a^2 + 2b^2$

Ⓐ I only

Ⓑ II only

Ⓒ I and II only

Ⓓ I, II, and III

33. **Performance Task** Consider $\triangle ABC$ on the coordinate plane. Points D, E, and F are the midpoints of the sides.

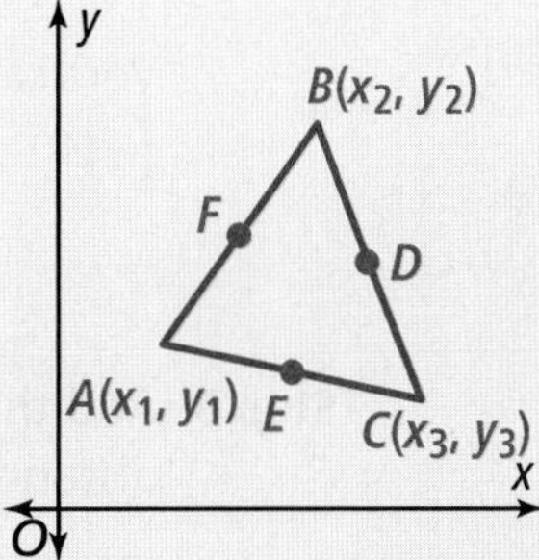

Part A What are the coordinates of D, E, and F?

Part B Prove that the coordinates of the point of concurrency of the medians is the average of the x and y coordinates of the vertices.

$\left(\frac{x_1 + x_2 + x_3}{3}, \frac{y_1 + y_2 + y_3}{3}\right)$

Hint: Apply the Concurrency of Medians Theorem and find the point $\frac{2}{3}$ of the way from A to D.

Part C Explain why it does not make sense to place one of the coordinates at the origin for this proof.

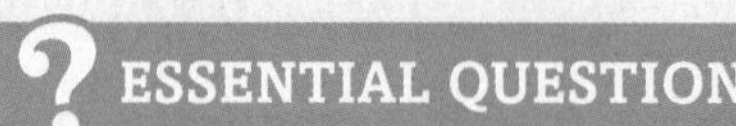

EXTENSION

9-4a Partitioning a Line Segment

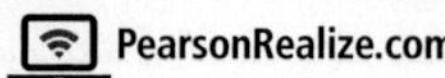

I CAN… find a point on a directed line segment between two given points to partition the segment in a given ratio.

VOCABULARY

- directed line segment

LOOK FOR RELATIONSHIPS
Think about how number lines are related to the x- and y-axes. How can you relate partitioning on a number line to partitioning on a coordinate plane?

ESSENTIAL QUESTION How can you find a point on a directed line segment between two given points that partitions the segment in a given ratio?

CONCEPT Directed Line Segment

A **directed line segment** has distance and direction. Directed line segment $\overline{AB}$ has an *initial point* at point *A* and an *end point* at point *B*.

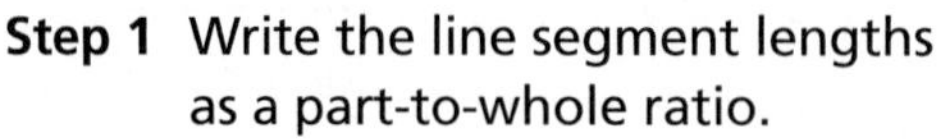

EXAMPLE 1 Partition a Segment

What are the coordinates of point *P* that partitions line segment $\overline{AB}$ into a ratio of 3 : 2?

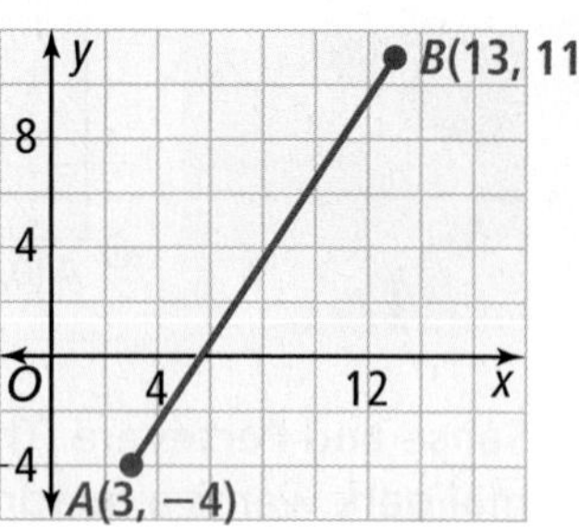

Step 1 Write the line segment lengths as a part-to-whole ratio.

$\frac{\overline{AP}}{\overline{AB}} = \frac{3}{5}$

Step 2 Find $\frac{3}{5}$ of the horizontal and vertical distances from *A* to *B*.

Horizontal distance:
$\frac{3}{5}|13 - 3| = \frac{3}{5}(10) = 6$

Vertical distance:
$\frac{3}{5}|11 - (-4)| = \frac{3}{5}(15) = 9$

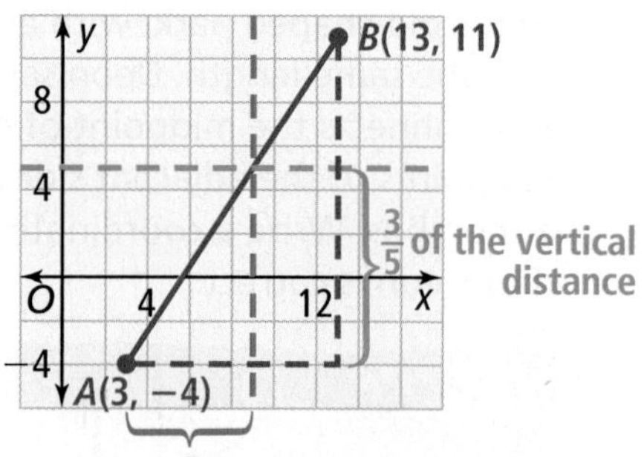

Step 3 Add the horizontal distance to the *x*-coordinate and the vertical distance to the *y*-coordinate of point *A*(3, −4).

$(3 + 6, -4 + 9) = (9, 5)$

Point *P*(9, 5) partitions $\overline{AB}$ into a ratio of 3 : 2.

Step 4 Check your answer using the Distance Formula.

$$\overline{AP} = \sqrt{|9 - 3|^2 + |5 - (-4)|^2} = \sqrt{36 + 81} = \sqrt{117}$$

$$\overline{PB} = \sqrt{|13 - 9|^2 + |11 - 5|^2} = \sqrt{16 + 36} = \sqrt{52}$$

The ratio $\frac{\overline{AP}}{\overline{PB}} = \frac{\sqrt{117}}{\sqrt{52}} = \sqrt{\frac{9}{4}} = \frac{3}{2}$.

Try It!

1. Find the coordinates of each point described.
   a. Point *Q* partitions $\overline{AB}$ into a ratio of 7 : 3.
   b. Point *R* partitions $\overline{AB}$ into a ratio of 4 : 1.
   c. Point *T* partitions $\overline{BA}$ into a ratio of 4 : 1.

CONCEPTUAL UNDERSTANDING

EXAMPLE 2 Use Similar Triangles

How can you use similar triangles to find the coordinates of *P* that partition the line segment between *A*(−5, −3) and *B*(7, 6) into a ratio of 2 : 1?

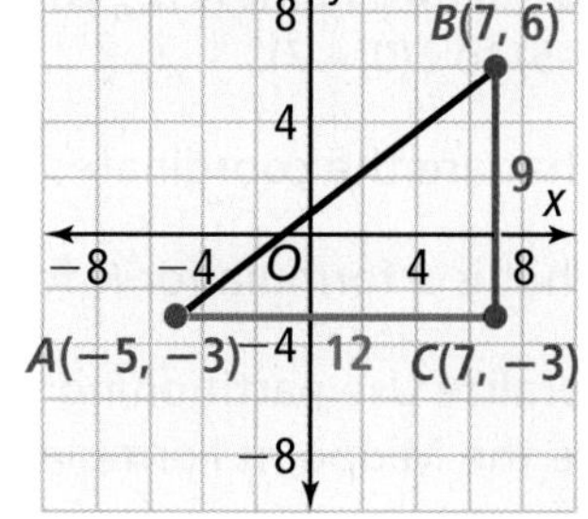

CONSTRUCT ARGUMENTS
Explain why this strategy still works if you choose *C*(−5, 6).

Find point *C* such that $\overline{AC} \perp \overline{BC}$.

Consider $\triangle ABC$ with point *P* such that $\frac{AP}{PB} = \frac{2}{1}$.

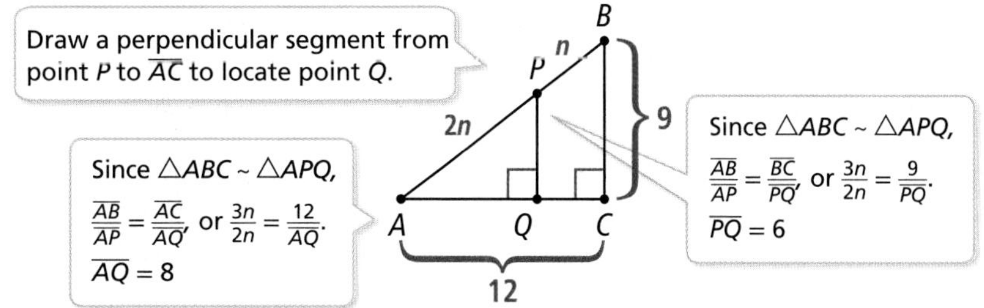

Point *P* is 8 units to the right and 6 units above *A*, at (3, 3).

Try It!

2. Use similar triangles to find the coordinates of *P* that partition the line segment between *A*(–5, 6) and *B*(5, –18) into a ratio of 2 : 3.

Do You UNDERSTAND?

1. **ESSENTIAL QUESTION** How can you find a point on a directed line segment between two given points that partitions the segment in a given ratio?

2. **Vocabulary** Compare and contrast directed line segment $\overline{AB}$ with directed line segment $\overline{BA}$.

3. **Error Analysis** Corey found the coordinates of *P* that divides the line segment between (1, 1) and (7, 13) into a ratio of 1 : 2. What is Corey's error?

Horizontal: $\frac{1}{2}(7 - 1) = 3$

Vertical: $\frac{1}{2}(13 - 1) = 6$

$P = (1 + 3, 1 + 6) = (4, 7)$

✗

Do You KNOW HOW?

$\overline{PQ}$ has endpoints at *P*(−5, 4) and *Q*(7, −5).

4. What are the coordinates of the point that partitions $\overline{PQ}$ in a ratio 2 : 1?

5. Use similar triangles to find the point that partitions $\overline{PQ}$ in a ratio 2 : 3?

6. A chair lift at a ski resort travels along the cable as shown.

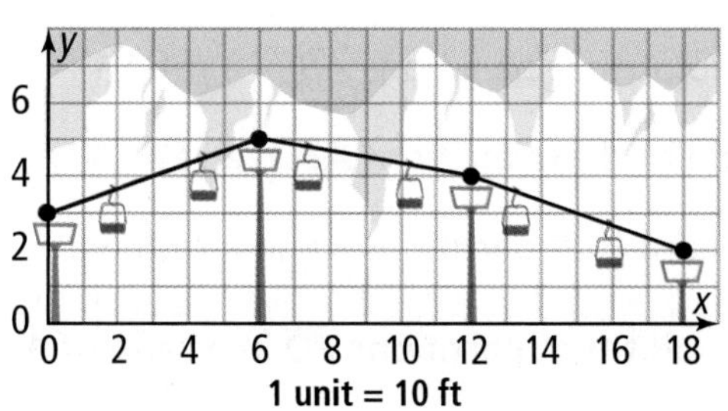

Additional supports will be added along each section of cable so that the ratio of the lower length of cable to the higher length of cable is 3 : 2.

a. Where will each support be placed?

b. How tall will each support need to be?

PRACTICE & PROBLEM SOLVING

UNDERSTAND

7. **Use Structure** Point K is $\frac{1}{n}$ of the way from $J(4, -5)$ to $L(0, -7)$.

   a. What are the coordinates of K if $n = 4$?

   b. What is a formula for K for any positive n?

8. **Generalize** Use partitioning of segments to prove the Midpoint Formula.

$$M = \left(\frac{x_1 + x_2}{2}, \frac{y_1 + y_2}{2}\right)$$

9. **Mathematical Connections** Point M partitions $\overline{FG}$ into segments with a ratio of 1 : 3. Can you determine the value of a? Explain.

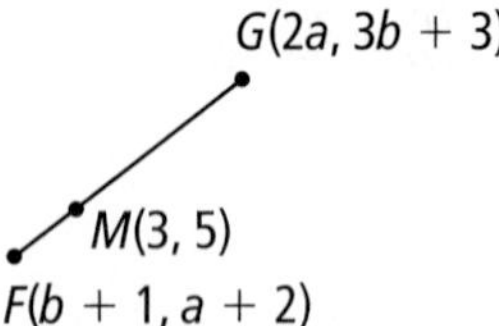

10. **Reason** Suppose $\overline{PQ}$ has endpoint P at (0, 0). How would you find Q if (2, 5) is $\frac{1}{4}$ of the way from P to Q?

PRACTICE

Find the coordinates of each given point on $\overline{AB}$.

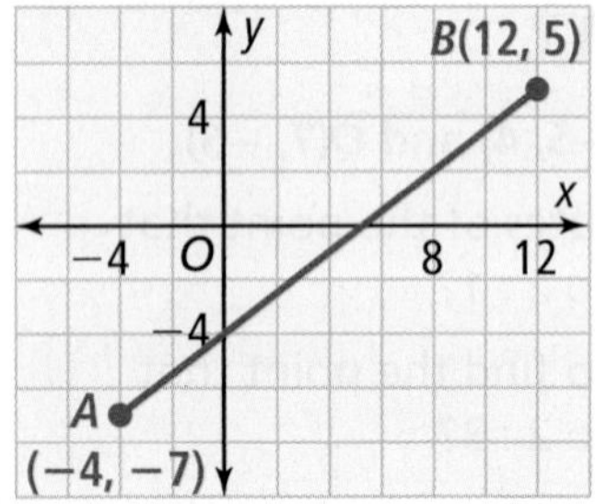

11. The point that partitions $\overline{AB}$ in a ratio 3 : 7.

12. The point that partitions $\overline{AB}$ in a ratio 1 : 3.

13. The point that partitions $\overline{AB}$ in a ratio 3 : 2.

14. The point that partitions $\overline{AB}$ in a ratio 9 : 1.

Find the point that partitions $\overline{PQ}$ in a ratio of 1 : 2.

15. $P(3, 5)$, $Q(-2, 13)$

16. $P(-2, 2.5)$, $Q(1.6, 4)$

17. $P\left(4\frac{1}{3}, 3\frac{1}{6}\right)$, $Q\left(-2\frac{1}{5}, 3\frac{2}{3}\right)$

Find the point that partitions each segment in a ratio of 3 : 2.

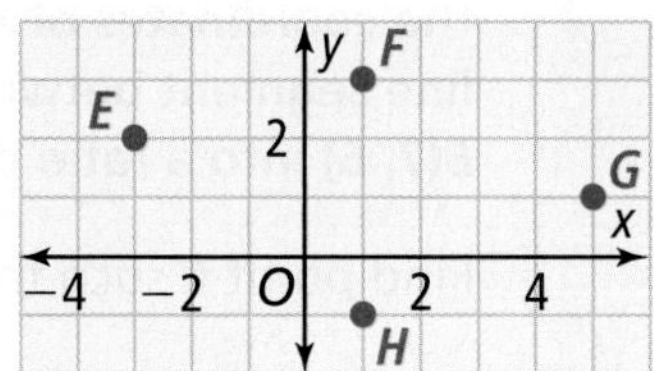

18. $\overline{EF}$

19. $\overline{FG}$

20. $\overline{GH}$

21. $\overline{EH}$

APPLY

22. **Model With Mathematics** A university is building a new student center that is two-thirds the distance from the arts center to the residential housing. What are the coordinates of the new student center?

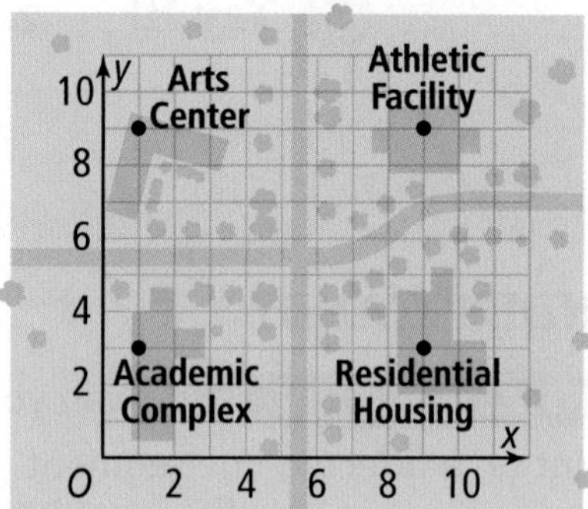

23. **Mathematical Connections** Three reflective buoys will be placed equidistantly on a line between the pier and the lighthouse.

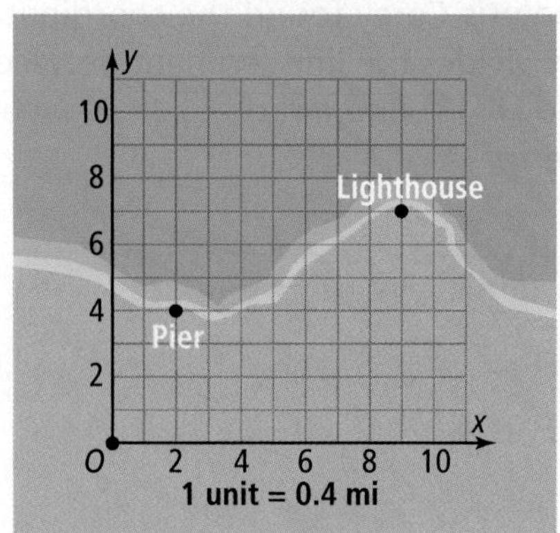

   a. What are the coordinates of each buoy?

   b. What are the vertical and horizontal distances between each buoy?

9-5 Circles in the Coordinate Plane

PearsonRealize.com

I CAN… use the equations and graphs of circles to solve problems.

Activity Assess

MODEL & DISCUSS

Damian uses an app to find all pizza restaurants within a certain distance of his current location.

A. What is the shape of the region that the app uses to search for pizza restaurants? Explain how you know.

B. What information do you think the app needs to determine the area to search?

C. **Construct Arguments** If Damian's friend is using the same app from a different location, could the app find the same pizza restaurant for both boys? Explain.

? ESSENTIAL QUESTION

How is the equation of a circle determined in the coordinate plane?

CONCEPTUAL UNDERSTANDING

EXAMPLE 1 Derive the Equation of a Circle

What equation defines a circle in the coordinate plane?

Draw a circle with point (h, k) as the center of the circle. Then select any point (x, y) on the circle.

Use the Distance Formula to find the distance r between the two points.

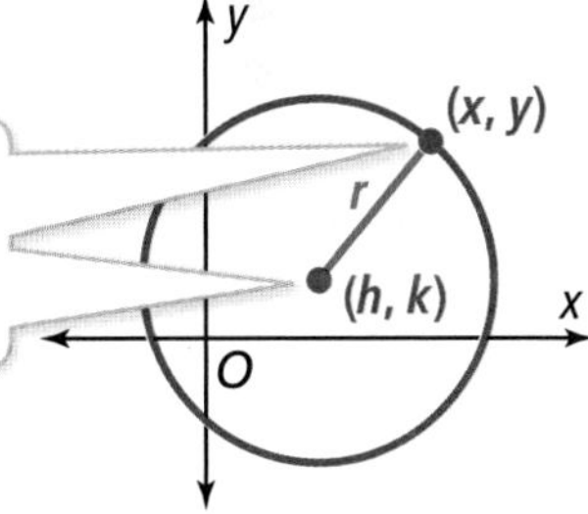

Use variables that can apply to any circle on the coordinate plane.

$$d = \sqrt{(x_2 - x_1)^2 + (y_2 - y_1)^2}$$
$$(x - h)^2 + (y - k)^2 = r^2$$

Because the radius is the same from the center to any point (x, y) on the circle, this equation satisfies all points of the circle.

GENERALIZE
What other formula or formulas compares the sum of two squares to a third square? How do these formulas relate?

Try It! 1. What are the radius and center of the circle with the equation $(x - 2)^2 + (y - 3)^2 = 25$?

THEOREM 9-3 Equation of a Circle

An equation of a circle with center (h, k) and radius r is $(x - h)^2 + (y - k)^2 = r^2$.

If...

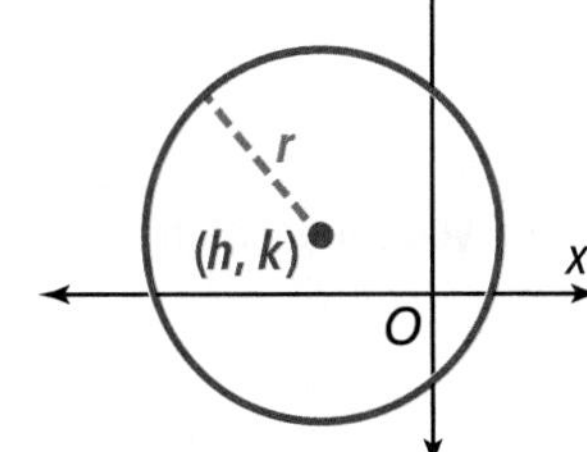

Then... $(x - h)^2 + (y - k)^2 = r^2$

PROOF: SEE EXERCISE 13.

EXAMPLE 2 Write the Equation of a Circle

What is the equation for $\odot A$?

The notation $\odot A$ means a circle with center at point A.

Step 1 Find the radius r.

The radius is the distance from P to A.

$$r = \sqrt{(-1-1)^2 + (2-5)^2} = \sqrt{13}$$

The radius of the circle is $\sqrt{13}$.

Step 2 Use the radius and center to write the equation.

$$(x-h)^2 + (y-k)^2 = r^2$$ Use the equation of a circle.

$$(x-(-1))^2 + (y-2)^2 = (\sqrt{13})^2$$ Substitute values for h, k, and r.

$$(x+1)^2 + (y-2)^2 = 13$$

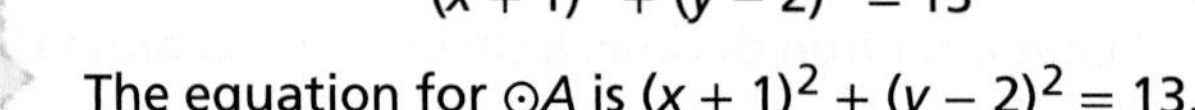

The equation for $\odot A$ is $(x+1)^2 + (y-2)^2 = 13$.

COMMON ERROR
Be careful with the signs of coordinates. Coordinates of the center are subtracted, so if a coordinate is negative, the expression will convert to addition.

Try It! 2. What is the equation for each circle?

a.

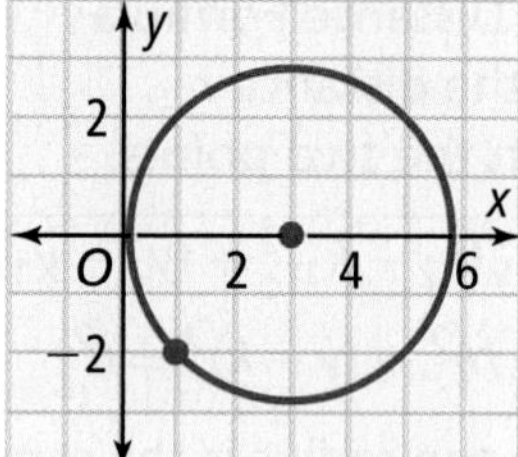

b.

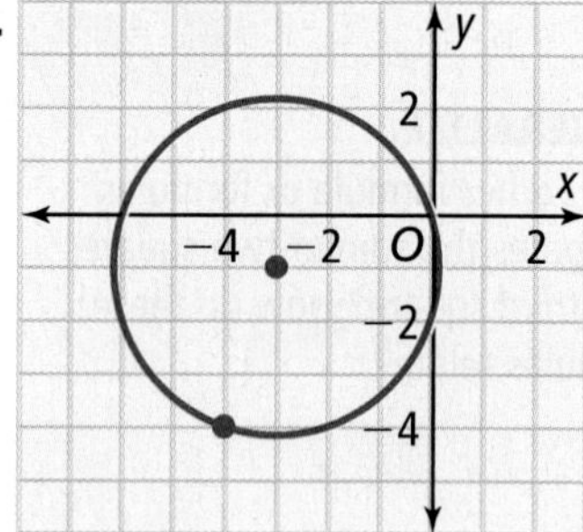

EXAMPLE 3 Determine Whether a Point Lies on a Circle

Circle Q has radius 7 and is centered at the origin. Does the point $(-3\sqrt{2}, 5)$ lie on $\odot Q$?

Step 1 Write the equation for $\odot Q$.

$$(x-h)^2 + (y-k)^2 = r^2$$
$$(x-0)^2 + (y-0)^2 = 7^2$$
$$x^2 + y^2 = 49$$

Step 2 Test the point $(-3\sqrt{2}, 5)$ in the equation.

$$(-3\sqrt{2})^2 + 5^2 \stackrel{?}{=} 49$$
$$18 + 25 \stackrel{?}{=} 49$$
$$43 \neq 49$$

The point $(-3\sqrt{2}, 5)$ does not lie on $\odot Q$.

STUDY TIP
Remember that to square an expression $a\sqrt{b}$, you square both factors: $(a\sqrt{b})^2 = a^2(\sqrt{b})^2$.

Try It! 3. Determine whether each point lies on the given circle.

a. $(-3, \sqrt{11})$; circle with center at the origin and radius $2\sqrt{5}$

b. $(6, 3)$; circle with center at $(2, 4)$ and radius $3\sqrt{3}$

EXAMPLE 4 Graph a Circle from Its Equation

What is the graph of $(x-3)^2+(y+4)^2=9$?

Write the equation in the form $(x-h)^2+(y-k)^2=r^2$ to identify the center and radius.

$(x-3)^2+(y-(-4))^2=3^2$

center $(h, k) = (3, -4)$

radius $r = 3$

Plot the point (3, −4).

Plot points 3 units above, below, left, and right of the center. Use the points as a guide to draw the circle.

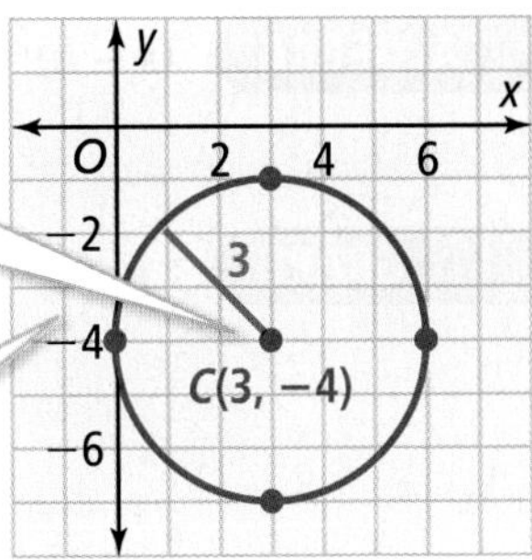

 **Try It!** 4. What is the graph of each circle?

a. $(x+2)^2+y^2=25$ b. $(x+1)^2+(y-2)^2=1$

APPLICATION

EXAMPLE 5 Use the Graph and Equation of a Circle to Solve Problems

Doppler radar detects precipitation within a 90-mile radius. Doppler radar gear in Grafton and Meyersville does not extend to Clear Lake or Davis.

Where can a third Doppler station be placed so all towns are covered?

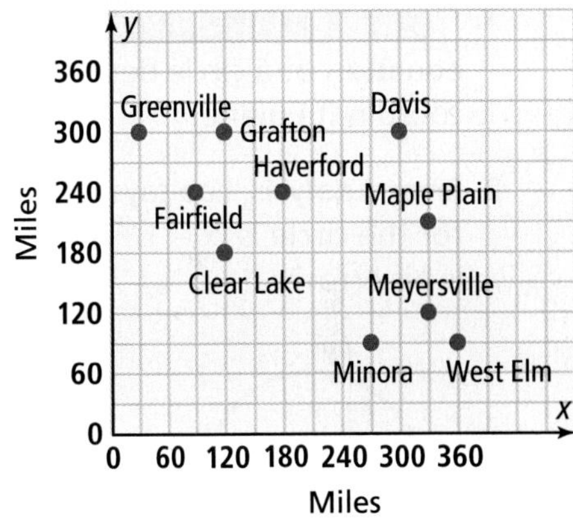

Draw circles with a 90-mile radius with centers at Grafton and Meyersville.

A circle with a 90-mile radius has a diameter of 180 miles, so 180 miles is the farthest distance between two locations covered by the same radar.

REASON
Think about the parts of the equation for a circle. How could you write an inequality to determine whether a point is within a circle?

Use the Distance Formula to find the distance between Clear Lake and Davis.

$$\sqrt{(300-180)^2+(300-120)^2} \approx 216$$

The towns are more than 180 miles apart. Adding one more Doppler radar will not cover all the towns.

 **Try It!** 5. If one or both of the existing radar stations could be moved to another town, would three radar stations be sufficient to cover all the towns? Explain.

Concept Summary Assess

CONCEPT SUMMARY Equations and Graphs of Circles

WORDS A circle is the set of points equidistant from a fixed point. The fixed point is the center.

ALGEBRA $(x - h)^2 + (y - k)^2 = r^2$ where (h, k) is the center and r is the radius.

GRAPH

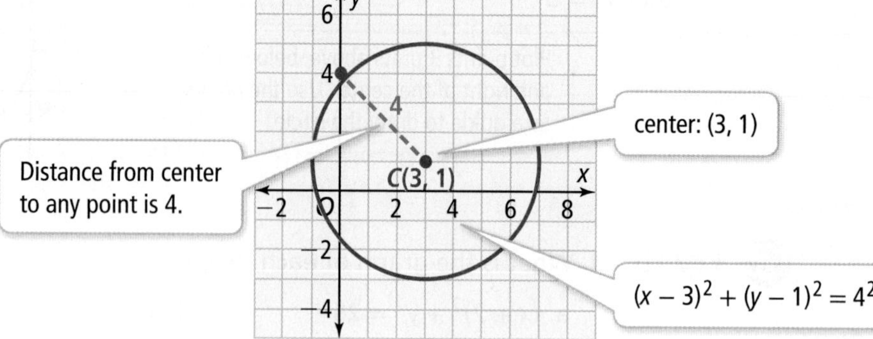

Do You UNDERSTAND?

1. **ESSENTIAL QUESTION** How is the equation of a circle determined in the coordinate plane?

2. **Error Analysis** Leo says that the equation for the circle is $(x - 1)^2 + (y - 2)^2 = 3$. What is his error?

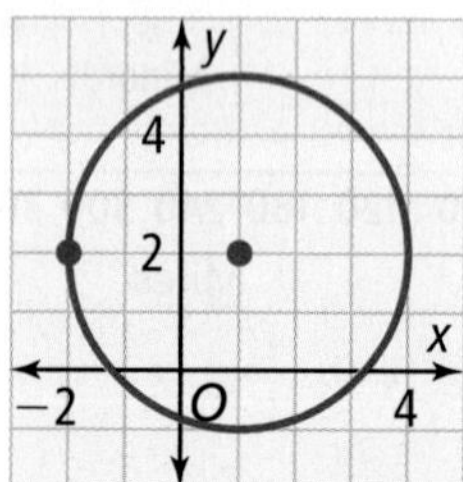

3. **Construct Arguments** If you are given the coordinates of the center and one point on a circle, can you determine the equation of the circle? Explain.

4. **Make Sense and Persevere** How could you write the equation of a circle given only the coordinates of the endpoints of its diameter?

Do You KNOW HOW?

5. What are the center and radius of the circle with equation $(x - 4)^2 + (y - 9)^2 = 1$?

6. What is the equation for the circle with center (6, 2) and radius 8?

7. What are the center and radius of the circle with equation $(x + 7)^2 + (y - 1)^2 = 9$?

8. What is the equation for the circle with center (–9, 5) and radius 4?

For Exercises 9 and 10, write an equation for each circle shown.

9.

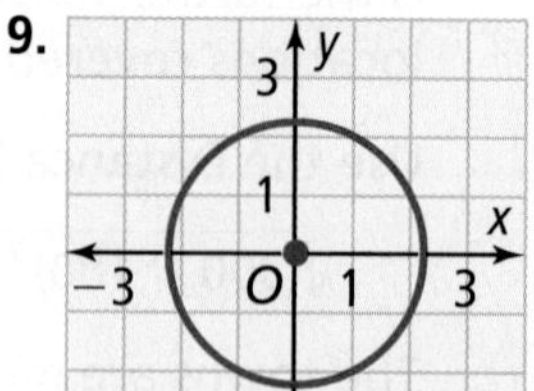

10.

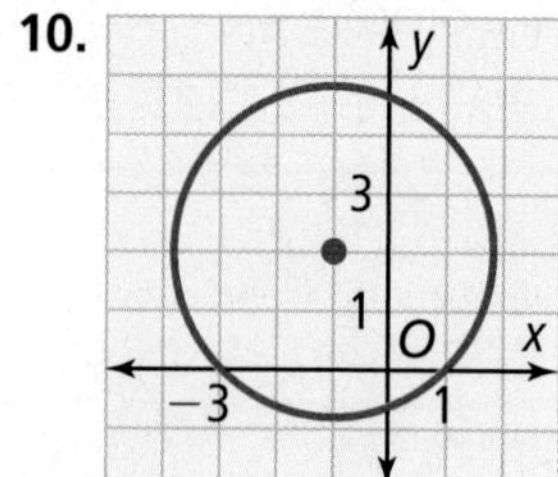

11. Is point (5, –2) on the circle with radius 5 and center (8, 2)?

12. What is the equation for the circle with center (5, 11) that passes through (9, –2)?

Scan for Multimedia

Practice Tutorial

Additional Exercises Available Online

UNDERSTAND

13. **Construct Arguments** Write a proof of Theorem 9-3.

14. **Mathematical Connections** What are the point(s) of intersection of $x^2 + y^2 = 25$ and $y = 2x - 5$? Graph both equations to check your answer.

15. **Error Analysis** LaTanya was asked to determine if $(3\sqrt{5}, 4)$ lies on the circle with radius 7 centered at (0, –2). What is her error?

$x^2 + (y-2)^2 = 49$
$(3\sqrt{5})^2 + (4-2)^2 \stackrel{?}{=} 49$
$45 + 4 = 49$

The point $(3\sqrt{5}, 4)$ lies on the circle with radius 7 and center (0, –2). ✗

16. **Communicate Precisely** Describe the graph of $(x - a)^2 + (y - b)^2 = 0$.

17. **Reason** If the area of square *ABCD* is 50, what is the equation for ⊙*R*?

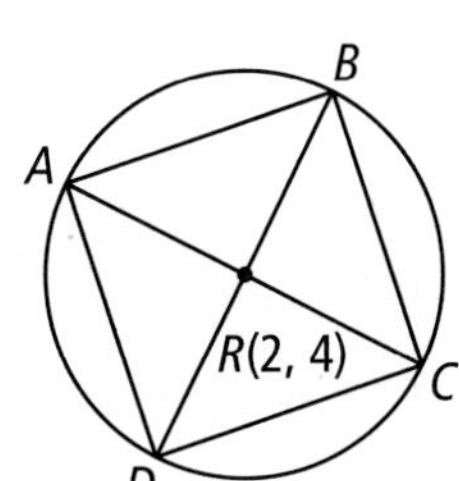

18. **Construct Arguments** The points (*a*, *b*) and (*c*, *d*) are the endpoints of a diameter of a circle. What are the center and radius of the circle?

19. **Higher Order Thinking** Isabel says the graph shows the circle with center (–2, 2) and radius 3. Nicky says the graph shows all possible centers for a circle that passes through (–2, 2) with radius 3. Which student is correct? Explain.

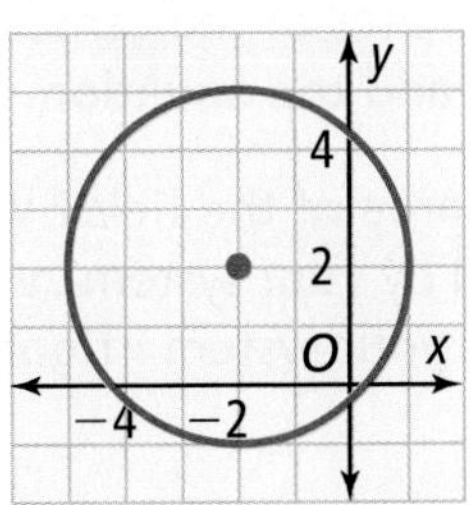

PRACTICE

For Exercises 20–23, find the center and radius for each equation of a circle. SEE EXAMPLE 1

20. $(x - 4)^2 + (y + 3)^2 = 64$

21. $(x + 2)^2 + y^2 = 13$

22. $(x + 5)^2 + (y + 11)^2 = 32$

23. $(x - 8)^2 + (y - 12)^2 = 96$

For Exercises 24 and 25, write the equation for the circle shown in each graph. SEE EXAMPLE 2

24.

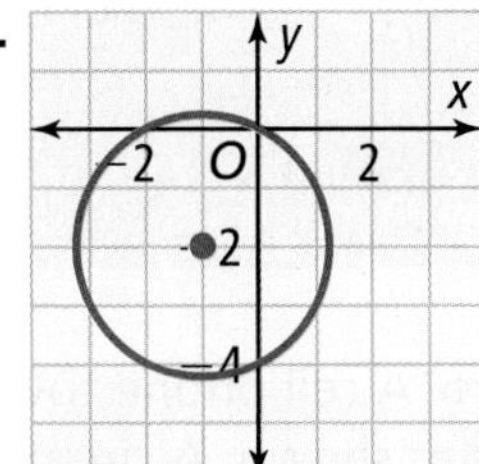

25.

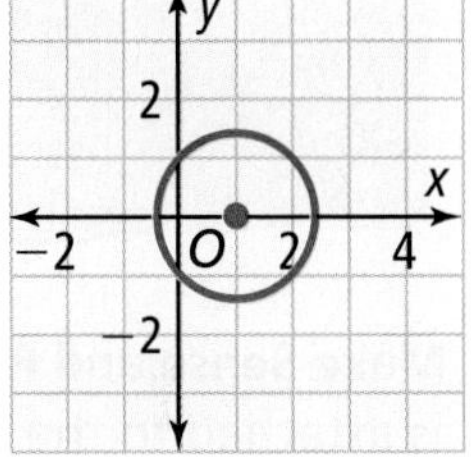

For Exercises 26–29, write the equation for each circle with the given radius and center. SEE EXAMPLE 2

26. radius: 4, center: (5, 1)

27. radius: 9, center: (–3, 8)

28. radius: $5\sqrt{5}$, center: (2, –4)

29. radius: $\sqrt{13}$, center: (–5, –9)

For Exercises 30–32, determine whether each given point lies on the circle with the given radius and center. SEE EXAMPLE 3

30. (2, 4); radius: 4, center: (–1, 1)

31. $(\sqrt{17}, 8)$; radius: 9, center: (0, 0)

32. (2, 0); radius: $\sqrt{10}$, center: (3, –9)

For Exercises 33–35, graph each equation. SEE EXAMPLES 4 AND 5

33. $(x - 5)^2 + (y + 1)^2 = 4$

34. $x^2 + (y - 1)^2 = 16$

35. $(x + 3)^2 + (y + 4)^2 = 9$

36. The point (2, *b*) lies on the circle with radius 5 and center (–1, –1). What are the possible values of *b*?

37. Is (7, 2) inside, outside, or on the circle $(x - 4)^2 + y^2 = 25$? Explain.

PRACTICE & PROBLEM SOLVING

Practice Tutorial
Mixed Review Available Online

APPLY

38. **Model With Mathematics** After an earthquake, a circle-shaped tsunami travels outward from the epicenter at an average speed of 420 miles per hour. If the earthquake with the epicenter shown occurred at 5:48 A.M., at what time will the tsunami reach Port Charles? Justify your answer.

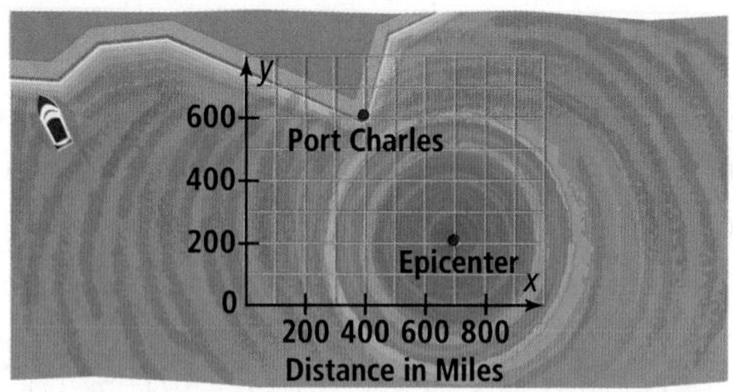

39. **Make Sense and Persevere** A cell phone tower is attached to the ground as shown. A circular security fence must be placed around the tower 10 feet from where the guy wires are attached to the ground. Can a cell phone tower be placed in the region enclosed by the red border? If so, what are possible coordinates of the tower?

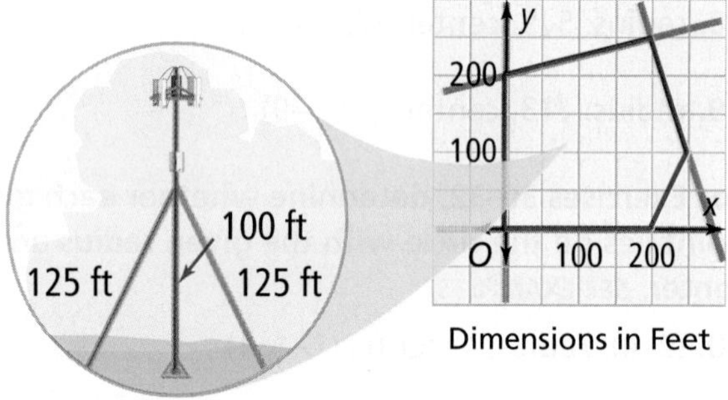

40. **Reason** Semitrailer trucks can be up to 14 feet tall. Should they be allowed in the outer lanes of the semicircular tunnel? Explain.

ASSESSMENT PRACTICE

41. A circle has center (0, 0) and passes through the point (−5, 2). Which other points lie on the circle? Select all that apply.

Ⓐ (0, 6)
Ⓑ $(\sqrt{11}, 3\sqrt{2})$
Ⓒ (2, 5)
Ⓓ (−5, −2)
Ⓔ $(4, -\sqrt{13})$
Ⓕ $(-\sqrt{29}, 0)$

42. **SAT/ACT** Which equation represents the circle with center (−3, 7) and radius 9?

Ⓐ $(x + 3)^2 + (y - 7)^2 = 3^2$
Ⓑ $(x - 3)^2 + (y + 7)^2 = 9^2$
Ⓒ $(x - 7)^2 + (y + 3)^2 = 9^2$
Ⓓ $(x + 3)^2 + (y - 7)^2 = 9^2$
Ⓔ $(x + 7)^2 + (y - 3)^2 = 3^2$

43. **Performance Task** A farmer can use up to four rotating sprinklers for the field shown. He has ten 50-meter sections that can be combined to form rotating arms with lengths from 50 m to 500 m. The irrigation circles cannot overlap and must not extend beyond the edges of the field. The distance between grid lines is 50 m.

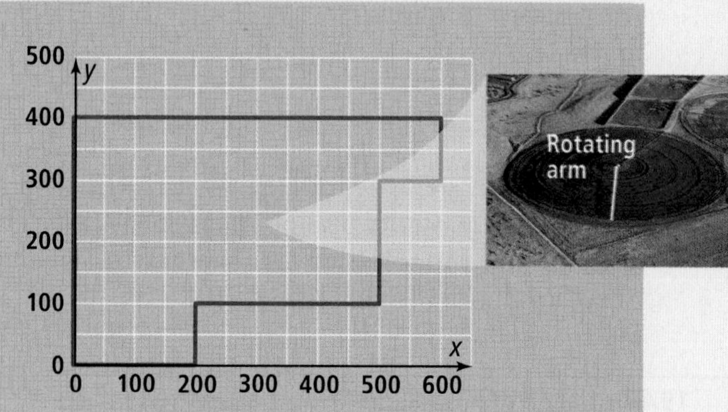

Part A Design an irrigation system for the field that irrigates as much of the field as possible. Draw a sketch of your system. For each sprinkler, give the coordinates of the center of the sprinkler, the radius, and the equation.

Part B What is the total area of the field? What is the total area irrigated by your system? What percent of the field does your system irrigate?

9-6 Parabolas in the Coordinate Plane

PearsonRealize.com

I CAN… use the equations and graphs of parabolas to solve problems.

VOCABULARY
- directrix
- focus
- parabola

EXPLORE & REASON

Consider two points and two intersecting lines.

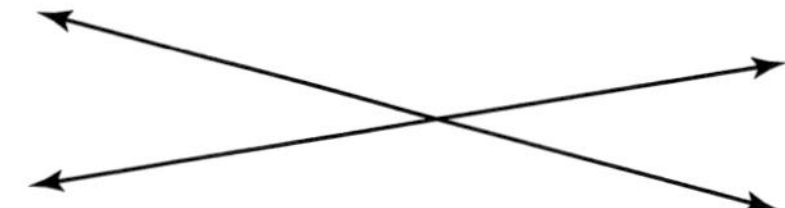

A. Describe the set of points that is equidistant from two points. Draw a diagram to support your answer.

B. Describe the set of points that is equidistant from each of two intersecting lines. Draw a diagram to support your answer.

C. Look for Relationships What do you think a set of points that is equidistant from a line and a point would look like? Draw a diagram to support your answer.

ESSENTIAL QUESTION **How does the geometric description of a parabola relate to its equation?**

CONCEPTUAL UNDERSTANDING

EXAMPLE 1 Explore the Graph of a Parabola

What is the set of points that are equidistant from the graph of the equation $y = -2$ and the point (0, 2)?

Graph the line and the point.

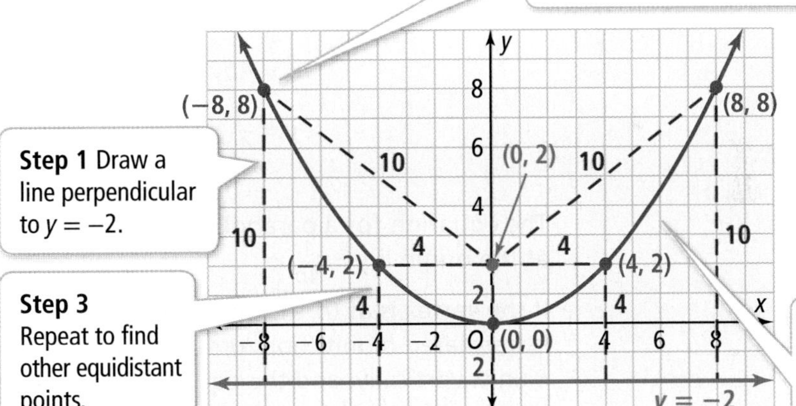

The set of points equidistant from (0, 2) and $y = -2$ is a curve called a *parabola*.

MAKE SENSE AND PERSEVERE Think about the relationship between the point and line. How would the shape of the parabola change if the line and point were closer together or farther apart?

Try It! **1.** The set of points equidistant from (3, 5) and the line $y = 9$ is also a parabola.

a. What is the vertex of the parabola?

b. Describe the graph of the parabola.

EXAMPLE 2 Derive the Equation of a Parabola

What is the equation of a parabola?

A **parabola** is the set of all points in a plane that are the same distance from a fixed point F, the **focus**, as they are from a line d, the **directrix**.

STUDY TIP
The focus is p units above the vertex, so the directrix must be p units below the vertex.

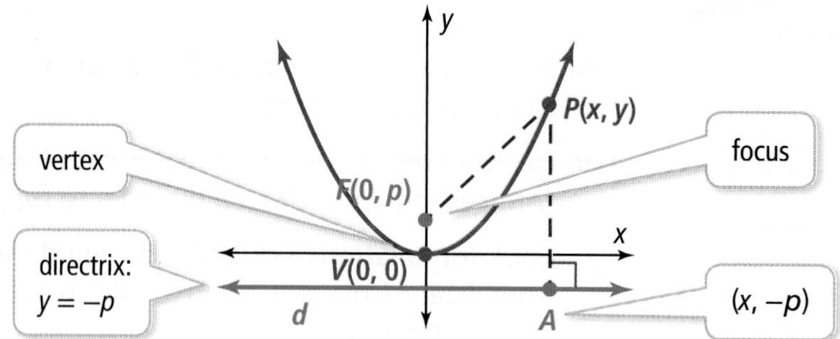

Every point on the parabola is equidistant from F and line d.

$$PF = PA$$

$$\sqrt{(x-0)^2 + (y-p)^2} = \sqrt{(x-x)^2 + (y-(-p))^2} \quad \text{Distance Formula}$$

$$\sqrt{x^2 + (y-p)^2} = \sqrt{(y+p)^2} \quad \text{Simplify.}$$

$$x^2 + (y-p)^2 = (y+p)^2 \quad \text{Square each side.}$$

$$x^2 + y^2 - 2py + p^2 = y^2 + 2py + p^2 \quad \text{Simplify.}$$

$$x^2 - 2py = 2py$$

$$x^2 = 4py$$

$$y = \frac{1}{4p}x^2 \quad \text{Solve for } y.$$

The equation for a parabola with vertex at the origin is $y = \frac{1}{4p}x^2$.

If the vertex is at (h, k), then the parabola is translated h units horizontally and k units vertically, and the equation is $y - k = \frac{1}{4p}(x - h)^2$.

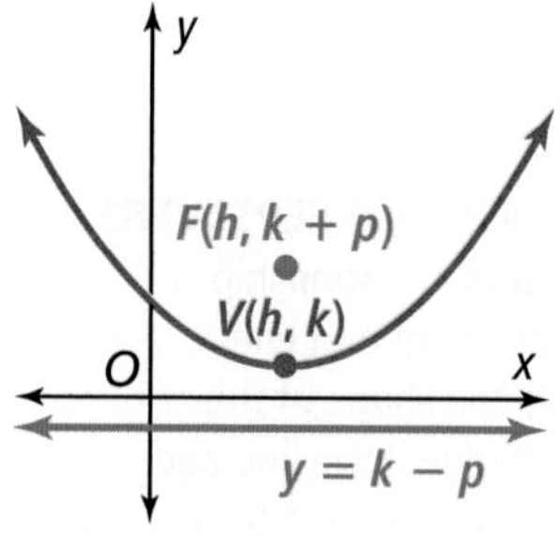

 **Try It!** 2. What expression represents the distance between the focus and the directrix?

CONCEPT Equation of a Parabola

Vertex at origin:

$$y = \frac{1}{4p}x^2$$

Vertex at (h, k):

$$y - k = \frac{1}{4p}(x - h)^2$$

The variable p represents the distance between the focus and the vertex.

EXAMPLE 3 Write the Equation of a Parabola

A. What equation represents the parabola with focus (5, 5) and directrix $y = 1$?

Graph the focus and directrix to determine the vertex and p.

The vertex is the midpoint of the segment connecting the focus and the directrix.

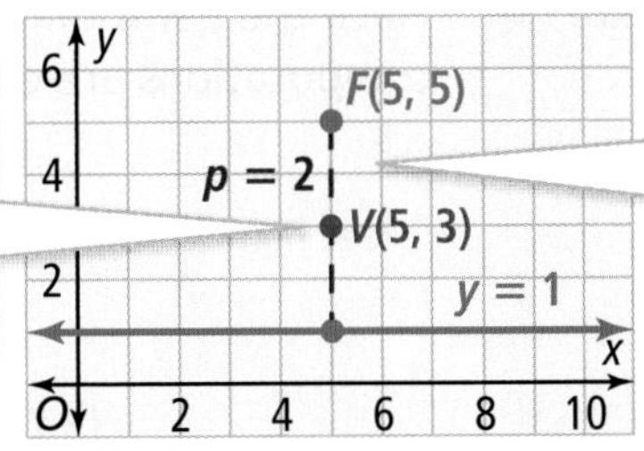

The value of p is the distance between the focus and the vertex.

Write the equation for the parabola with vertex (5, 3) and $p = 2$.

$$y - k = \frac{1}{4p}(x - h)^2$$

Write the formula for a parabola with vertex (h, k).

$$y - 3 = \frac{1}{4(2)}(x - 5)^2$$

$$y = \frac{1}{8}(x - 5)^2 + 3$$

COMMON ERROR
When substituting values into the equation of a parabola, be sure to use the coordinates of the vertex, not the coordinates of the focus.

B. Graph the parabola from part A.

Use the equation to make a table of values to help you sketch the graph.

x	y	(x, y)
1	$\frac{1}{8}(1 - 5)^2 + 3$	$(1, 5)$
3	$\frac{1}{8}(3 - 5)^2 + 3$	$\left(3, 3\frac{1}{2}\right)$
8	$\frac{1}{8}(8 - 5)^2 + 3$	$\left(8, 4\frac{1}{8}\right)$

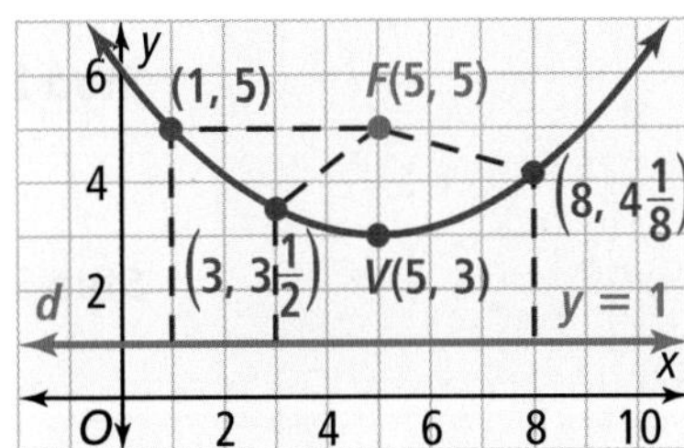

Try It! **3. a.** What equation represents the parabola with focus (−1, 4) and directrix $y = -2$?

b. What equation represents the parabola with focus (3, 5) and vertex (3, −1)?

APPLICATION

EXAMPLE 4 Apply the Equation of a Parabola

The cross section of a satellite dish is a parabola, with the feed horn at the focus. How long do the braces holding the feed horn need to be?

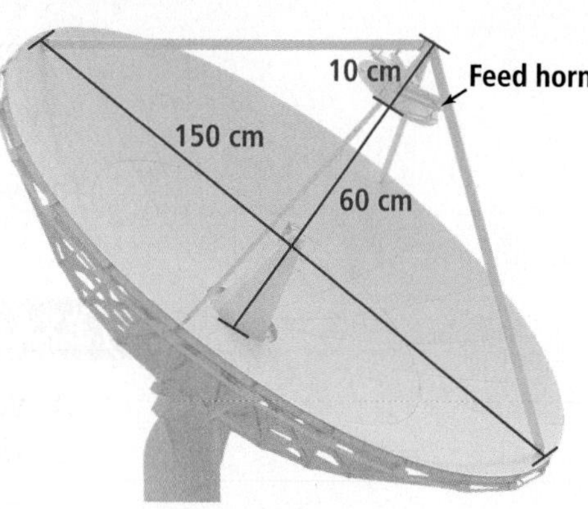

Formulate ◀ Place the parabola on a coordinate plane. Parabolas are symmetric, so computations are easier for a parabola with its vertex at the origin.

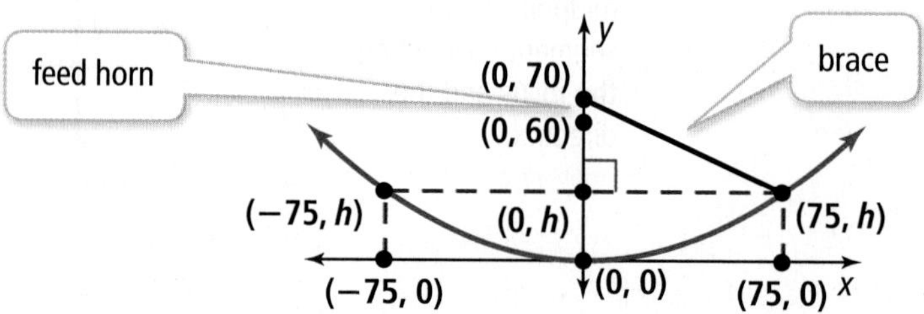

Write an equation for the parabola, and then use the equation to find the height h of the dish. Finally, use the Pythagorean Theorem to find the length of the brace.

Compute ◀ **Step 1** Write the equation.

$$y = \frac{1}{4p}x^2$$

Write the equation for a parabola with vertex at the origin, where p is the distance between the focus and the vertex.

$$y = \frac{1}{4(60)}x^2$$

Substitute 60 for p.

$$y = \frac{1}{240}x^2$$

Step 2 Evaluate for $x = 75$ to find the height h of the dish.

$$h = \frac{1}{240}(75)^2 \approx 23.4 \text{ cm}$$

Step 3 Use the Pythagorean Theorem to find the length of the brace.

$$(70 - 23.4)^2 + 75^2 = b^2$$

$$7{,}796.56 = b^2$$

$$b \approx 88.3$$

(0, 70)

(0, 23.4)

(75, 23.4)

Interpret ◀ The braces need to be 88.3 cm long.

Try It! 4. On a different satellite dish, the feed horn is 38 inches above the vertex. If the height of the dish is 22 inches, what is its width?

CONCEPT SUMMARY Parabolas

WORDS A parabola is the set of points equidistant from a focus and a directrix.

ALGEBRA $y - k = \frac{1}{4p}(x - h)^2$

where (h, k) is the vertex and p is the distance from the vertex to the focus

GRAPH

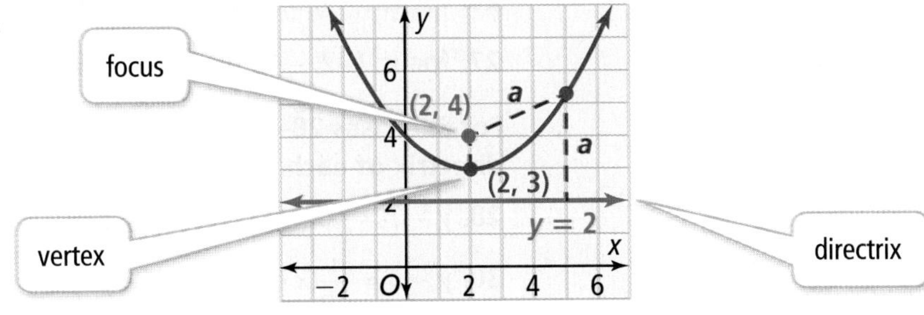

Do You UNDERSTAND?

1. ESSENTIAL QUESTION How does the geometric description of a parabola relate to its equation?

2. **Error Analysis** Arthur says that an equation of the parabola with directrix $y = 0$ and focus $= (0, 6)$ is $y - 3 = \frac{1}{24}x^2$. What is his error?

3. **Vocabulary** How could the word *direction* help you remember that the directrix is a line?

4. **Reason** What are the coordinates of point P? Show your work.

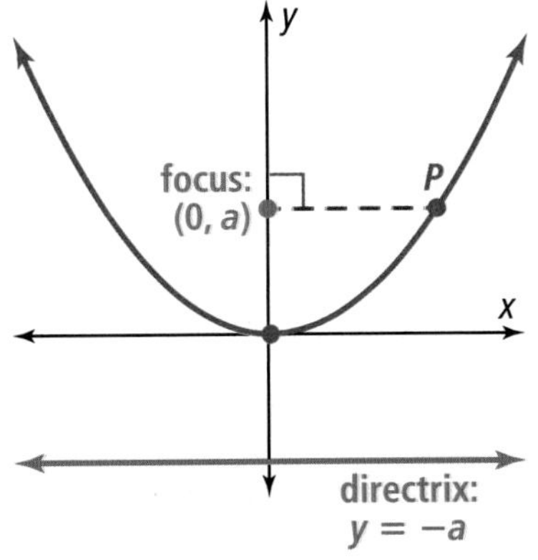

5. **Communicate Precisely** Given vertex (a, b) and focus (a, c), describe how you would write an equation for the parabola.

Do You KNOW HOW?

For Exercises 6–9, write an equation of each parabola with the given focus and directrix.

6. focus: (0, 4); directrix: $y = -4$

7. focus: (5, 1); directrix: $y = -5$

8. focus: (4, 0); directrix: $y = -4$

9. focus: (2, −1); directrix: $y = -4$

For Exercises 10–13, give the vertex, focus, and directrix of each parabola.

10. $y = \frac{1}{8}x^2$

11. $y - 2 = \frac{1}{6}x^2$

12. $y - 6 = \frac{1}{4}(x - 1)^2$

13. $y + 3 = \frac{1}{20}(x - 9)^2$

For Exercises 14–17, write an equation of each parabola with the given focus and vertex.

14. focus: (6, 2); vertex: (6, −4)

15. focus: (−1, 8); vertex: (−1, 7)

16. focus: (4, 0); vertex: (4, −2)

17. focus: (−3, −1); vertex: (−3, −4)

18. Consider the parabola $y = \frac{1}{36}x^2$.

    a. What are the focus and directrix?

    b. The parabola passes through (12, 4). Show that this point is equidistant from the focus and the directrix.

PRACTICE & PROBLEM SOLVING

Scan for Multimedia

Practice Tutorial

Additional Exercises Available Online

UNDERSTAND

19. Communicate Precisely Use the graph to answer the questions. Line m is the directrix of the parabola.

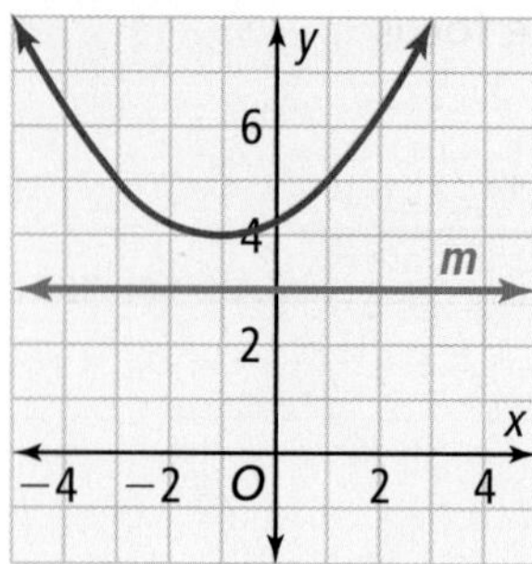

a. How would you find the vertex of the parabola? Explain.

b. How would you find the focus of the parabola? Explain.

c. How would you find an equation of the parabola? Explain.

20. Communicate Precisely Define a parabola as a set of points. What is the relationship of the points to the lines and points associated with the parabola?

21. Mathematical Connections The general form of the equation of a parabola is $y = x^2 - 6x + 9$. What are the focus, vertex, and directrix of the parabola?

22. Reason How does changing the distance from the focus to the directrix change the shape of a parabola in the coordinate plane? Explain.

23. Construct Arguments The parabola has its focus at $\left(0, \frac{1}{4}\right)$ and vertex at (0, 0). How would you find the equation of the parabola?

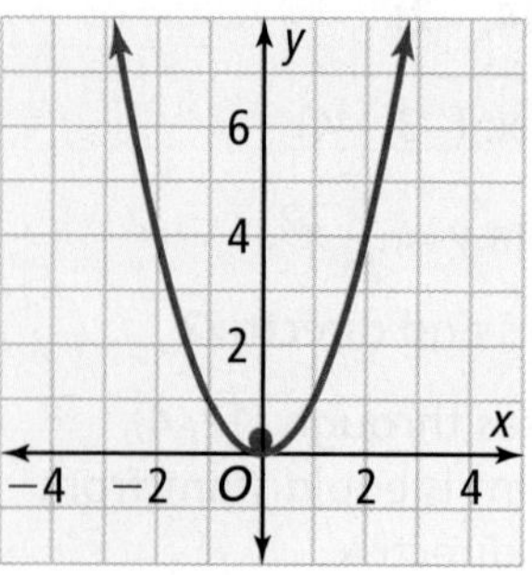

PRACTICE

For Exercises 24–27, find the vertex of each parabola. SEE EXAMPLE 1

24. focus: (3, 7); directrix: $y = -1$

25. focus: (6, 2); directrix: $y = -4$

26. focus: (−4, 3); directrix: $y = 0$

27. focus: (−2, −1); directrix: $y = -6$

For Exercises 28–31, find the vertex, focus and directrix of each parabola. SEE EXAMPLE 2

28. $y - 7 = \frac{1}{8}(x - 3)$

29. $y + 4 = \frac{1}{36}(x - 1)$

30. $y - 3 = \frac{1}{16}(x + 6)$

31. $y + 5 = \frac{1}{2}(x - 10)$

For Exercises 32–34, write an equation of each parabola with the given focus and directrix. SEE EXAMPLE 3

32. focus: (0, 4); directrix: $y = 0$

33. focus: (5, 1); directrix: $y = -9$

34. focus: (−4, 5); directrix: $y = 2$

For Exercises 35–37, write an equation of each parabola with the given focus and vertex. SEE EXAMPLE 3

35. focus: (4, 5); vertex: (4, −1)

36. focus: (−4, 9); vertex: (−4, 5)

37. focus: (2, 4); vertex: (2, 0)

For Exercises 38–40, use the graph of the parabola shown to answer each question. SEE EXAMPLE 4

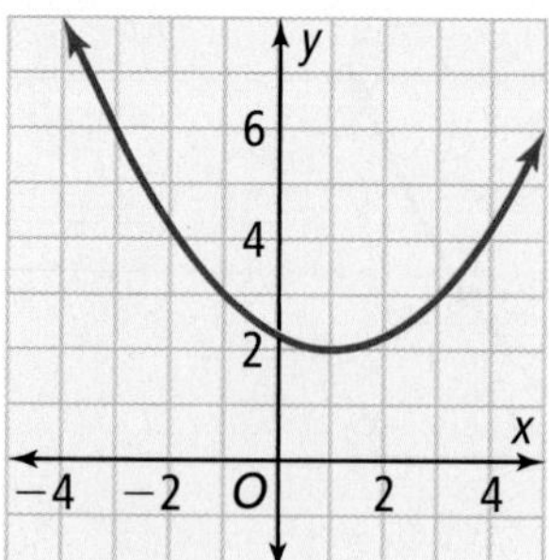

38. What is the vertex of the parabola?

39. Using a point on the parabola and the equation $y - k = \frac{1}{4p}(x - h)^2$, what is p?

40. What is the focus of the parabola?

Practice Tutorial
Mixed Review Available Online

PRACTICE & PROBLEM SOLVING

APPLY

41. Reason Henry is building a model of the Clifton Suspension Bridge using a scale factor of 100 ft : 1 in. The cables between the towers are in the shape of a parabola. He writes an equation of the parabola to describe the model he is building and uses the equation to determine the distances from the cable to the deck of the bridge. Suppose the deck is the x-axis and the vertex lies on the y-axis. What is the equation that Henry writes?

42. Model With Mathematics Devin builds a solar hot dog cooker for the science fair. Suppose the base of the cooker is the x-axis and the hot dog is on the y-axis at the focus. What is the equation of the parabola that models the cooker?

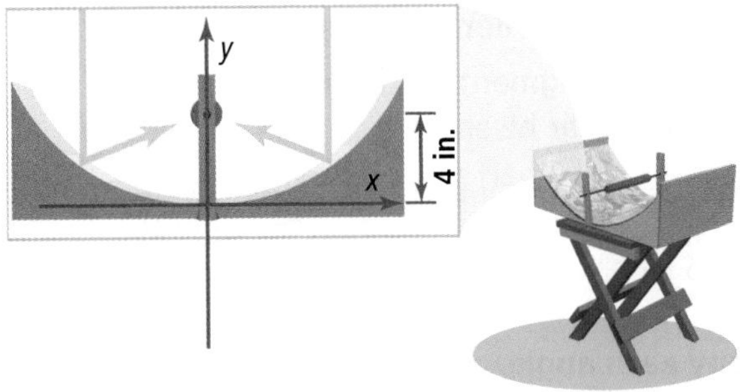

43. Higher Order Thinking An engineer is making an impact analysis on a car bumper. He graphs the kinetic energy of a 2-kg steel ball as a function of the velocity of the ball. Kinetic energy is measured in joules (J) and velocity is measured in meters per second.

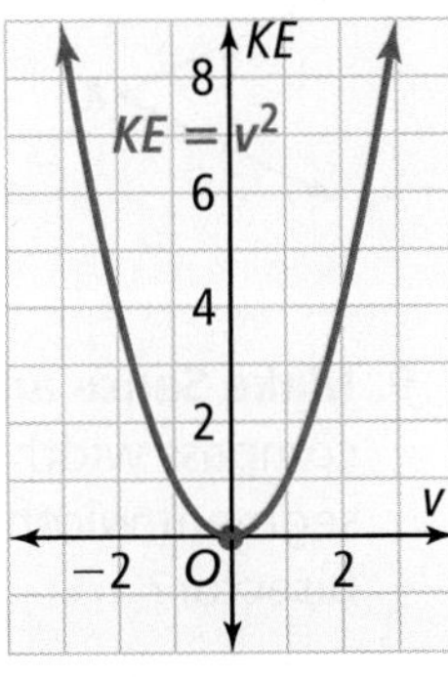

a. What are the vertex, focus, and directrix of the parabola?

b. The car bumper has to withstand an impact of 25 J from the 2-kg steel ball without any damage. How fast is the ball moving when it strikes the bumper with that amount of energy?

ASSESSMENT PRACTICE

44. An equation of a parabola is $y - 5 = \frac{1}{8}(x - 4)$. Select all that apply.

Ⓐ The vertex of the parabola is (5, 4).

Ⓑ $p = 2$

Ⓒ The focus of the parabola is (4, 7).

Ⓓ The directrix of the parabola is $y = 3$.

45. SAT/ACT Which is the vertex of the parabola represented by the equation $y + 5 = 6(x - 6)^2$?

Ⓐ (6, 5)

Ⓑ (−6, −5)

Ⓒ (6, −5)

Ⓓ (−6, 25)

46. Performance Task Some flashlights are designed so that a parabolic mirror reflects light forward from a light source.

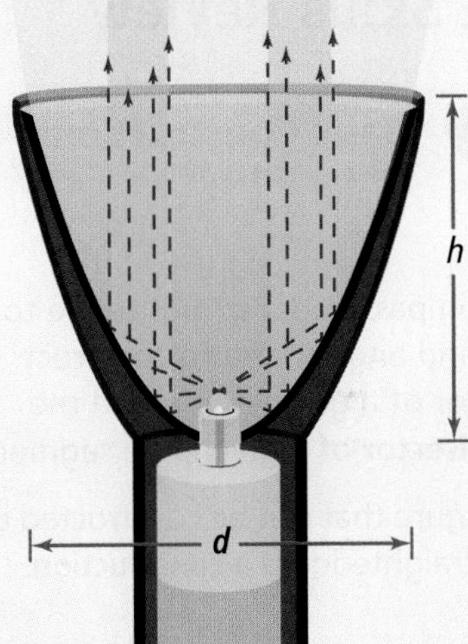

For the flashlight to work best, the light source is placed at the focus of the parabola. Deon designs a flashlight so $d = 4$ in. and $h = 3$ in.

Part A How could Deon model the mirror on the coordinate plane? What is an equation for the mirror?

Part B At what point above the vertex would Deon place the light source?

Part C Suppose Deon wants to place the light source $\frac{1}{2}$ in. farther from the vertex with the same $h = 3$ in. Will the mirror be narrower or wider? Explain.

TOPIC 9

Topic Review

TOPIC ESSENTIAL QUESTION

1. How can geometric relationships be proven by applying algebraic properties to geometric figures represented in the coordinate plane?

Vocabulary Review

Choose the correct term to complete each sentence.

2. All the points on a parabola are the same distance from a fixed point, the ________ as they are from a line, the ________.
3. A ________ is a set of points equidistant from a point.
4. A ________ is the highest or lowest point on the graph of a function.

- circle
- directrix
- focus
- parabola
- radius
- vertex

Concepts & Skills Review

LESSON 9-1 Basic Constructions

Quick Review

You can use a compass and a straightedge to copy segments and angles, and to construct the **angle bisector** of a given angle and the **perpendicular bisector** of a given line segment.

Any geometric figure that can be constructed using a compass and straightedge is a **construction**.

Example

Construct the angle bisector of $\angle A$.

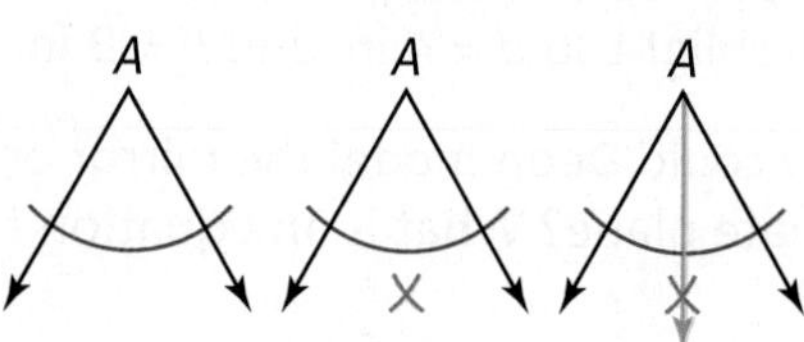

From the vertex, draw an arc that intersects both sides of the angle.

Next, using the same compass setting at each intersection, draw intersecting arcs within the angle.

Finally, draw the angle bisector from the vertex through the intersecting arcs.

Practice & Problem Solving

Copy each segment, and construct the perpendicular bisector.

5. S T

6. U V

Copy each angle, and construct its bisector.

7. K

8. L

9. **Make Sense and Persevere** Why must the compass width be larger than half the segment width to draw a perpendicular bisector?

10. **Model With Mathematics** The sides of a roof meet at a 120° angle. A strip of wood extends down from the vertex so that it bisects the angle. Draw a diagram of the roof with the bisecting strip of wood.

LESSON 9-2 Slopes of Parallel and Perpendicular Lines

Quick Review

Two non-vertical lines are parallel if they have the same slope. Two vertical lines are parallel to each other.

Two non-vertical lines are perpendicular if the product of the slopes is -1. A vertical line is perpendicular to a horizontal line.

Example

What is the equation of a line that is parallel to the line $y = 3x - 9$ and passes through (6, 12)?

The slope of the line is 3.
Solve for the y-intercept of the parallel line:

$$y = mx + b$$
$$12 = (3)(6) + b$$
$$b = -6$$

The equation of the parallel line is $y = 3x - 6$.

Practice & Problem Solving

Use the figure for Exercises 11–12. Show the calculations you use to answer each question.

11. Are lines p and q parallel?

12. Are lines w and t perpendicular?

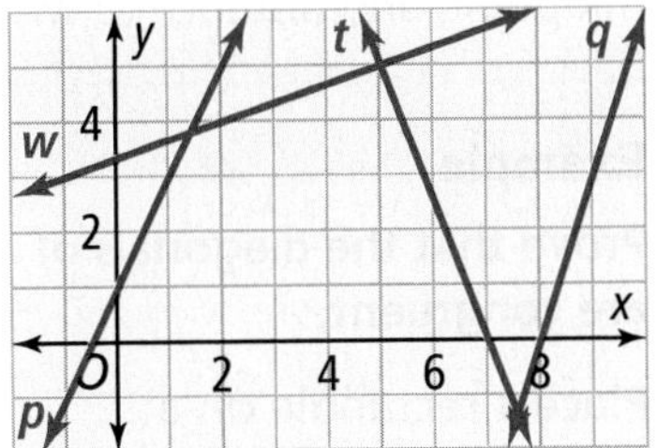

13. **Reason** Theorem 9-3 states that two non-vertical lines are perpendicular if and only if the product of their slopes is -1. Why are vertical lines excluded?

14. **Use Structure** Write an equation for each line that passes through (2, 7) and is parallel or perpendicular to the line $y = -3x - 6$.

TOPIC 9 REVIEW

LESSON 9-3 Polygons in the Coordinate Plane

Quick Review

When a geometric figure is represented in a coordinate plane, you can use slope, distance, and midpoints to analyze properties of the figure.

Example

Is $\triangle ABC$ an isosceles triangle? Explain.

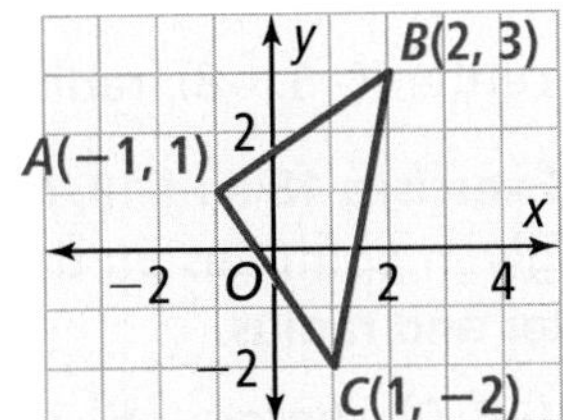

A triangle is isosceles if two sides are congruent. Use the Distance Formula to find the side lengths.

$$AB = \sqrt{(2 - (-1))^2 + (3 - 1)^2} = \sqrt{13}$$
$$BC = \sqrt{(1 - 2)^2 + (-2 - 3)^2} = \sqrt{26}$$
$$CA = \sqrt{(1 - (-1))^2 + (-2 - 1)^2} = \sqrt{13}$$

Since $AB = CA$, $\triangle ABC$ is isosceles.

Practice & Problem Solving

For Exercises 15–18, determine whether each figure is the given type of figure.

15. $F(-2, 4)$, $G(0, 0)$, $H(3, 1)$; right triangle

16. $A(7, 2)$, $B(3, -1)$, $C(3, 4)$; equilateral triangle

17. $J(-4, -4)$, $K(-7, 0)$, $L(-4, 4)$, $M(-1, 0)$; rhombus

18. What are the area and perimeter of $PQRS$?

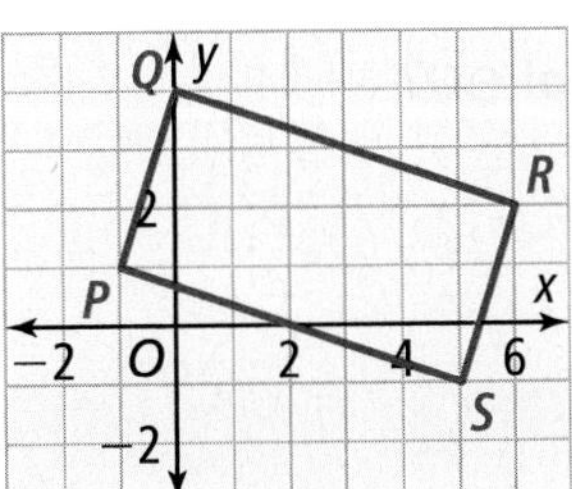

19. **Make Sense and Persevere** Parallelogram $WXYZ$ has coordinates $W(a, b)$, $X(c, d)$, $Y(f, g)$, and $Z(h, j)$. What equation can you use to determine whether $WXYZ$ is a rhombus? Explain.

LESSON 9-4 Proofs Using Coordinate Geometry

Quick Review

To prove theorems using coordinate geometry, place the figure on the coordinate plane. Use slope, midpoint, and distance to write an algebraic proof.

Example

Prove that the diagonals of a rectangle are congruent.

Place a rectangle on a coordinate plane with one vertex at the origin and two sides along the axes.

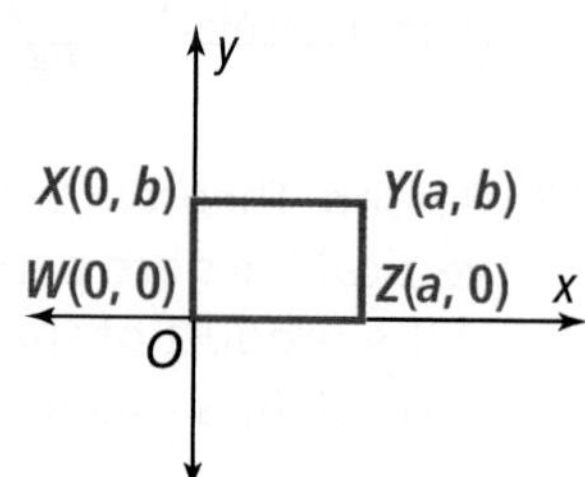

$$WY = \sqrt{(a-0)^2 + (b-0)^2} = \sqrt{a^2 + b^2}$$

$$XZ = \sqrt{(a-0)^2 + (0-b)^2} = \sqrt{a^2 + b^2}$$

Since $WY = XZ$, the diagonals of a rectangle are congruent.

Practice & Problem Solving

For Exercises 20–22, give the coordinates of each missing vertex.

20. $ABCD$ is a parallelogram; $A(0, 0)$, $B(p, q)$, $D(t, 0)$

21. $JKLM$ is a kite; $J(0, 0)$, $K(a, b)$, $L(0, c)$

22. $WXYZ$ is a rhombus; $W(0, 0)$, $Y(0, h)$, $Z(j, k)$

23. **Communicate Precisely** If you are given the coordinates of a quadrilateral, how can you prove that the quadrilateral is an isosceles trapezoid?

24. The diagram shows a fenced garden area, where $PX = PY$. The gardener is dividing the garden with a fence from P to the midpoint of $\overline{XY}$. Will the new fence be perpendicular to $\overline{XY}$? Use coordinate geometry to explain.

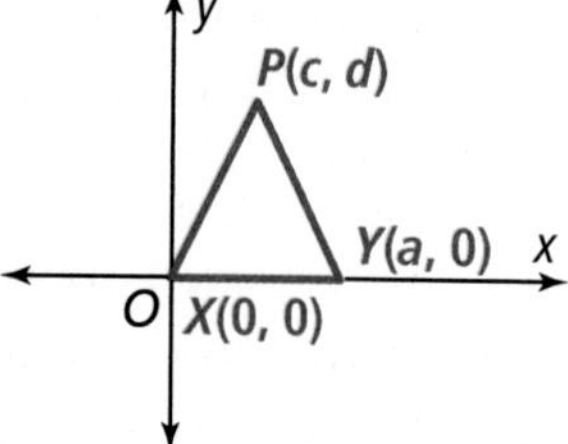

LESSON 9-5 Circles in the Coordinate Plane

Quick Review

The equation of a circle in the coordinate plane is

$$(x-h)^2 + (y-k)^2 = r^2$$

where (h, k) is the center of the circle and r is the radius.

Example

What is the equation of $\odot Q$?

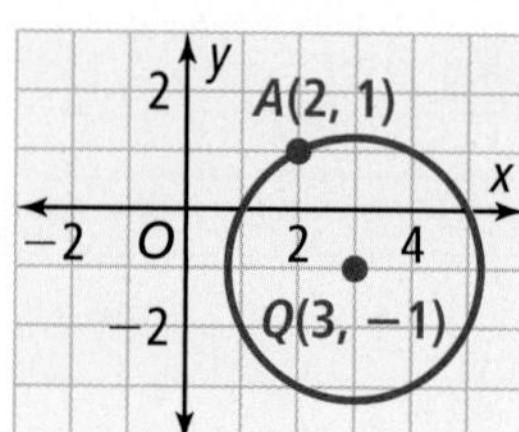

The center of the circle is $(3, -1)$, and the radius is QA.

$$QA = \sqrt{(2-3)^2 + (1-(-1))^2} = \sqrt{5}$$

So, the equation of $\odot Q$ is $(x-3)^2 + (y+1)^2 = 5$.

Practice & Problem Solving

For Exercises 25–27, write the equation for the circle with the given center and radius.

25. center: $(0, 0)$, radius: 9

26. center: $(-2, 3)$, radius: 5

27. center: $(-5, -8)$, radius: $\sqrt{13}$

For Exercises 18 and 19, determine whether the given point lies on the circle with the given center and radius.

28. $(-3, 0)$; center: $(-5, 2)$, radius: $2\sqrt{2}$

29. $(11, -1)$; center: $(4, 4)$, radius: $6\sqrt{2}$

30. Suppose that $\overline{AB}$, with $A(1, 15)$ and $B(13, -1)$, and $\overline{CD}$, with $C(15, 13)$ and $D(-1, 1)$, are diameters of $\odot T$. What is the equation of $\odot T$?

31. **Construct Arguments** Is it possible to write the equation of a circle given only two points on the circle? Explain.

LESSON 9-6 Parabolas in the Coordinate Plane

Quick Review

A **parabola** is the set of points that are equidistant from a fixed point, the **focus**, and a line, the **directrix**. The equation for a parabola in the coordinate plane is

$$y - k = \frac{1}{4p}(x - h)^2$$

where (h, k) is the vertex and p is the distance between the vertex and focus.

Example

What is the equation of the parabola with focus (4, 2) and directrix $y = 0$?

The vertex is the midpoint of the segment connecting the focus and the directrix, so the vertex is (4, 1). Since p is the distance between the focus and the vertex, $p = 1$. So, the equation of the parabola is

$$y - 1 = \frac{1}{4}(x - 4)^2.$$

Practice & Problem Solving

For Exercises 32 and 33, write the equation for the parabola with the given focus and directrix.

32. focus: (0, 0), directrix: $y = -6$

33. focus: (−1, −3), directrix: $y = -4$

34. **Reason** Point F is the focus and $y = -p$ is the directrix of the parabola shown. What is AB? Explain how you found your answer.

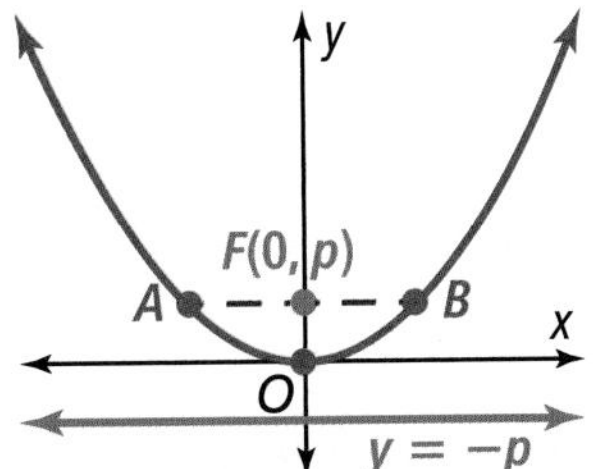

35. The cables for a suspension bridge are parabolic. The support towers are 40 m tall and 100 m apart. At its lowest point, the cable is 15 m above the bridge deck. If the bridge deck represents the x-axis and the vertex is on the y-axis, what equation represents the bridge cables?

TOPIC 9 REVIEW

TOPIC 10

Circles

TOPIC ESSENTIAL QUESTION

When a line or lines intersect a circle how are the figures formed related to the radius, circumference, and area of the circle?

Topic Overview

Topic Vocabulary

- arc length
- central angle
- chord
- inscribed angle
- intercepted arc
- major arc
- minor arc
- point of tangency
- radian
- secant
- sector of a circle
- segment of a circle
- tangent to a circle

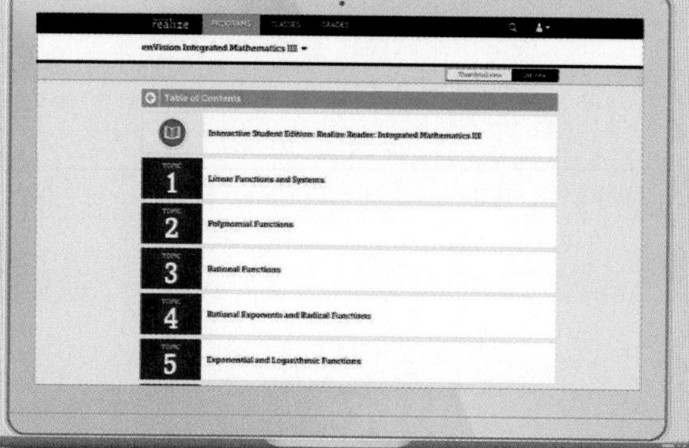

Go online | **PearsonRealize.com**

Digital Experience

INTERACTIVE STUDENT EDITION Access online or offline.

ACTIVITIES Complete ***Explore & Reason, Model & Discuss***, and ***Critique & Explain*** activities. Interact with Examples and Try Its.

ANIMATION View and interact with real-world applications.

PRACTICE Practice what you've learned.

MATHEMATICAL MODELING IN 3 ACTS

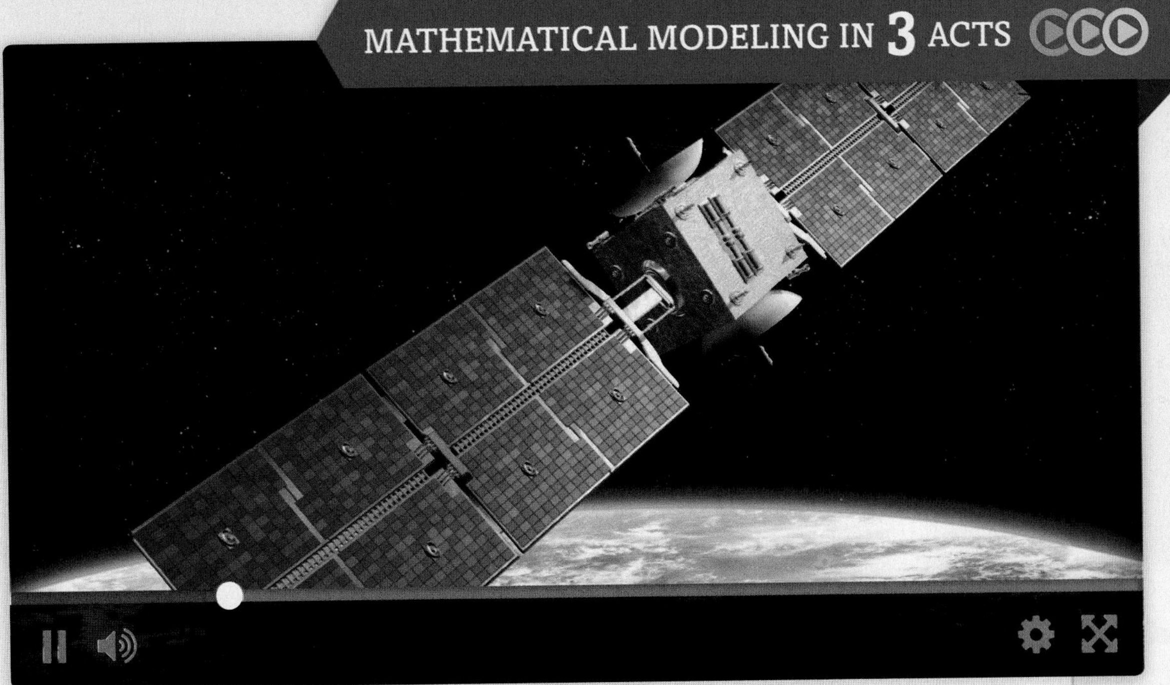

Earth Watch

Scientists estimate that there are currently about 3,000 operational man-made satellites orbiting Earth. These satellites serve different purposes, from communication to navigation and global positioning. Some are weather satellites that collect environmental information.

The International Space Station is the largest man-made satellite that orbits Earth. It serves as a space environment research facility, and it also offers amazing views of Earth. Think about this during the Mathematical Modeling in 3 Acts lesson.

VIDEOS Watch clips to support ***Mathematical Modeling in 3 Acts Lessons*** and **enVision®** ***STEM Projects.***

CONCEPT SUMMARY Review key lesson content through multiple representations.

ASSESSMENT Show what you've learned.

GLOSSARY Read and listen to English and Spanish definitions.

TUTORIALS Get help from ***Virtual Nerd***, right when you need it.

MATH TOOLS Explore math with digital tools and manipulatives.

Video

Did You Know?

Astronauts, six at a time, have lived and worked in the International Space Station (ISS) since 2000. Residents of 17 countries have visited the ISS.

The size of a football field, ISS circles the Earth every 90 minutes at an **altitude of 248 miles** and a speed of about **17,500 miles per hour.**

At its closest, the planet Mars is **150 times as far from Earth** as the Moon is. Despite the distance, the United States and Russia have been landing spacecraft and scientific instruments on Mars for several decades.

Your Task: Design Space Cities

Suppose it's 500 years in the future. Space stations the size of small cities are journeying through space. Use trigonometry and the geometry of circles to calculate the measurements of two of these stations, then design, measure, and describe a group of three "space cities."

10-1 Arcs and Sectors

PearsonRealize.com

I CAN… find arc length and sector area of a circle and use them to solve problems.

VOCABULARY

- arc length
- central angle
- intercepted arc
- major arc
- minor arc
- radian
- sector of a circle
- segment of a circle

Activity

Assess

EXPLORE & REASON

Darren bends a piece of wire using a circular disc to make the shape as shown.

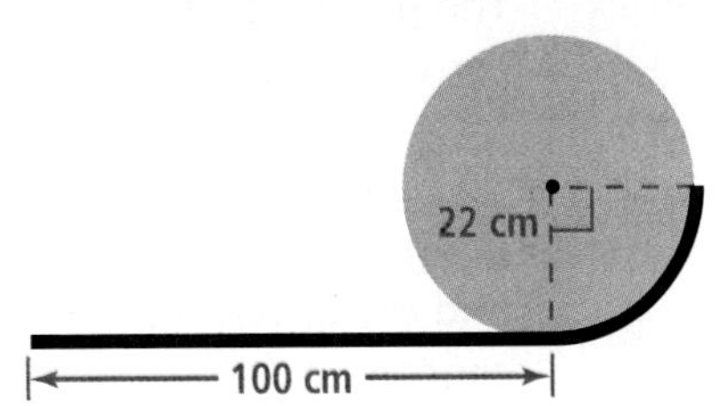

A. How long does the piece of wire need to be to make the shape? Explain.

B. Construct Arguments What information do you think is needed to find part of the circumference of a circle? Justify your answer.

ESSENTIAL QUESTION

How are arc length and sector area related to circumference and area of a circle?

EXAMPLE 1 Relate Central Angles and Arc Measures

What are $m\overset{\frown}{AB}$ and $m\overset{\frown}{ACB}$?

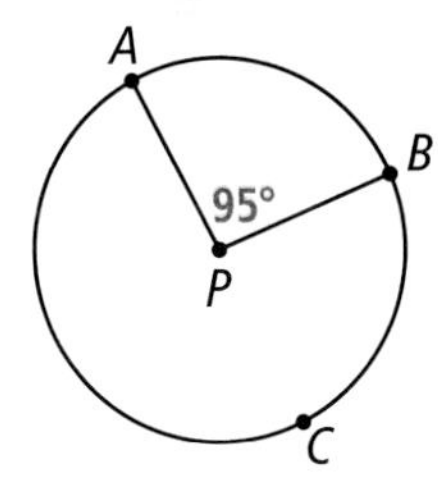

A **central angle** of a circle is an angle formed by two radii with the vertex at the center of the circle. Angle APB is a central angle.

A central angle creates two intercepted arcs. An **intercepted arc** is the part of a circle that lies between two segments, rays, or lines that intersect the circle.

A central angle and its intercepted minor arc have equal measure.

STUDY TIP
A minor arc may be written with just two letters, as in $\overset{\frown}{AB}$. Use the third point between the endpoints of an arc to name a major arc, as in $\overset{\frown}{ACB}$.

$\angle APB$ is a central angle, and $\overset{\frown}{AB}$ is its corresponding intercepted arc.

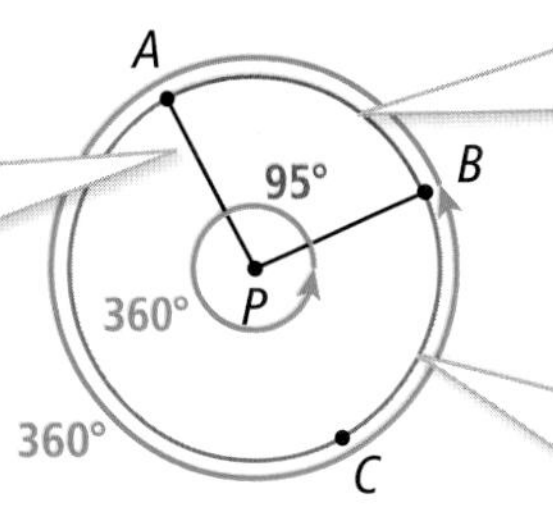

A **minor arc** of a circle is an arc that is smaller than a semicircle. $\overset{\frown}{AB}$ is a minor arc.

A **major arc** of a circle is an arc that is larger than a semicircle. $\overset{\frown}{ACB}$ is a major arc.

Find $m\overset{\frown}{AB}$.

$$m\overset{\frown}{AB} = m\angle APB = 95$$

The degree measure of $\overset{\frown}{AB}$ is equal to the measure of its corresponding central angle $\angle APB$.

Find $m\overset{\frown}{ACB}$.

$$m\overset{\frown}{ACB} = 360 - 95 = 265$$

Try It! 1. Use $\odot W$.

a. What is $m\overset{\frown}{XZ}$?

b. What is $m\overset{\frown}{XYZ}$?

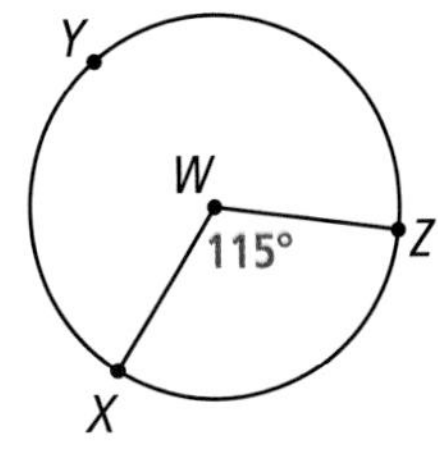

CONCEPT Arc Measure

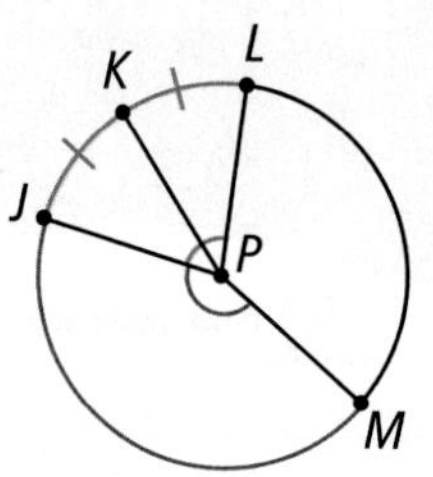

The measure of an arc is equal to the measure of its corresponding central angle.

$m\widehat{JM} = m\angle JPM$

Congruent central angles intercept congruent arcs, and congruent arcs are intercepted by congruent central angles.

$\angle JPK \cong \angle KPL$ $\widehat{JK} \cong \widehat{KL}$

CONCEPTUAL UNDERSTANDING

EXAMPLE 2 Relate Arc Length to Circumference

A. How do you find the length *s* of an arc measured in degrees?

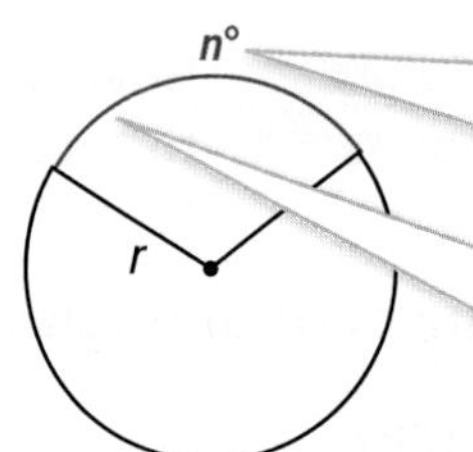

The *measure* of an arc is a fraction of 360°

The **arc length** is a fraction of the circumference.

$$\frac{\text{arc length}}{\text{circumference}} = \frac{\text{arc measure}}{360}$$

$$\frac{s}{2\pi r} = \frac{n}{360}$$

$$s = \frac{n}{360} \cdot 2\pi r$$

Use a proportion to represent the relationship between arc length *s*, radius *r*, and arc measure *n*.

The formula to find the length of an arc is $s = \frac{n}{360} \cdot 2\pi r$.

B. How do you find the length *s* of an arc measured in radians?

Besides degrees, angle measures can be expressed in *radians*.

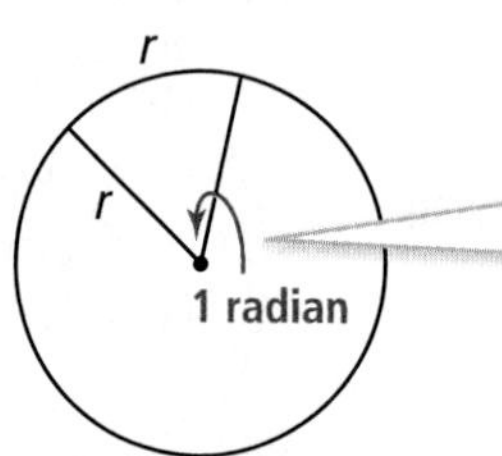

A **radian** is equal to the measure of a central angle that intercepts an arc with length equal to the radius of the circle.

Circumference is $2\pi r$, which is 2π arcs of length *r*. Since each arc of length *r* corresponds to 1 radian, there are 2π radians in a circle. So, 2π radians is equivalent to 360°.

To find the arc length, use the following proportion.

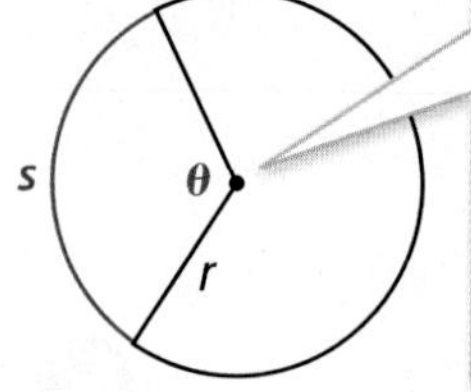

The variable theta (θ) is often used for angles measured in radians.

$$\frac{\text{arc length}}{\text{circumference}} = \frac{\text{arc measure (radians)}}{2\pi}$$

$$\frac{s}{2\pi r} = \frac{\theta}{2\pi}$$

$$s = \frac{\theta}{2\pi} \cdot 2\pi r = \theta r$$

Arc length is proportional to radius, with θ as the constant of proportionality.

To find the length of an arc measured in radians, use the formula $s = \theta r$.

STUDY TIP
Remember that the circumference measures the distance around all of the circle and the arc length is the distance around part of the circle.

CONTINUED ON THE NEXT PAGE

EXAMPLE 2 CONTINUED

Try It! **2. a.** In a circle with radius 4, what is the length of an arc that has a measure of 80? Round to the nearest tenth.

b. In a circle with radius 6, what is the length of an arc that has a measure of π radians? Round to the nearest tenth.

CONCEPT Arc Length

The length s of an arc of a circle is the product of the ratio relating the measure of the central angle in degrees to 360 and the circumference of the circle. The length of the arc is also the product of the radius and the central angle measure in radians.

Central angle in degrees:

$$s = \frac{n}{360} \cdot 2\pi r$$

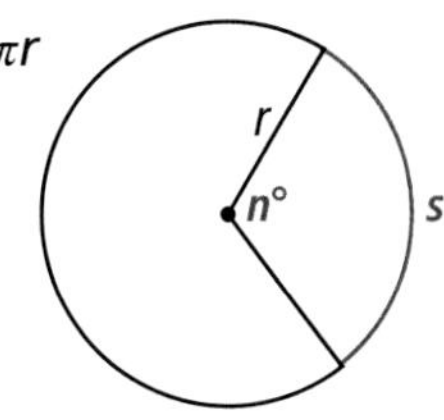

Central angle in radians:

$$s = \theta r$$

EXAMPLE 3 Apply Arc Length

What is the length of $\widehat{AD}$? Express the answer in terms of π.

Step 1 Find the arc measure.

$$m\widehat{AD} = 360 - m\widehat{AB} - m\widehat{BC} - m\widehat{CD}$$
$$= 360 - 73 - 43 - 104$$
$$= 140$$

Each arc measure is equal to the measure of the corresponding central angle.

Step 2 Find the arc length.

$$s = \frac{n}{360} \cdot 2\pi r$$
$$= \frac{140}{360} \cdot 2\pi(4) = \frac{28}{9}\pi$$

Use the formula for arc length for angles given in degrees.

The length of $\widehat{AD}$ is $\frac{28}{9}\pi$.

MAKE SENSE AND PERSEVERE
Think about when you should express arc lengths in terms of π and when you should give approximate answers. How would you decide?

Try It! **3.** Use $\odot Q$. Express answers in terms of π.

a. What is the length of $\widehat{JK}$?

b. What is the length of $\widehat{HK}$?

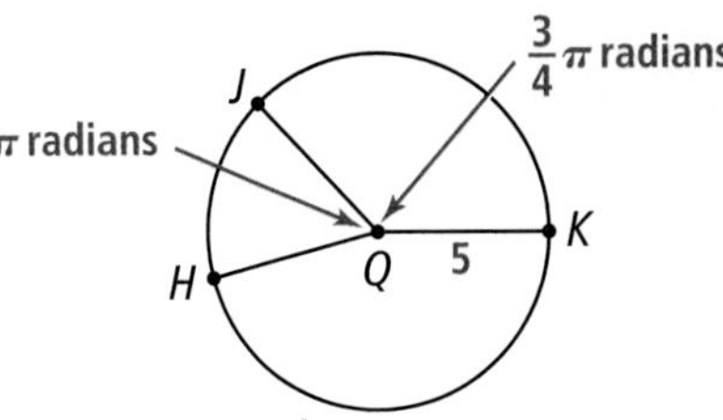

EXAMPLE 4 Relate the Area of a Circle to the Area of a Sector

A sector of a circle is the region bounded by two radii and the intercepted arc. What is the area of sector MQN?

To find the area of the sector, find $\frac{78}{360}$ of the area of the circle.

$$A = \frac{78}{360} \bullet \pi r^2$$

$$= \frac{78}{360} \bullet \pi(10)^2 = \frac{65}{3}\pi$$

The area of sector MQN is $\frac{65}{3}\pi$ cm^2.

In general, the area of a sector is $A = \frac{n}{360} \bullet \pi r^2$, where $n°$ is the measure of the intercepted arc and r is the radius of the circle.

GENERALIZE
Compare the formulas for arc length and sector area. What relationships do you see between the arc length and sector area for any given arc?

Try It! 4. What is the area of each sector?

a. (circle with center F, points A and B, radius 3, central angle 165°)

b.

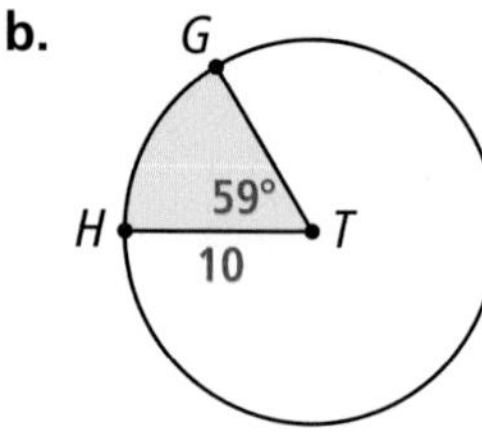

EXAMPLE 5 Find the Area of a Segment of a Circle

A segment of a circle is the part of a circle bounded by an arc and the segment joining its endpoints. What is the area of the shaded region?

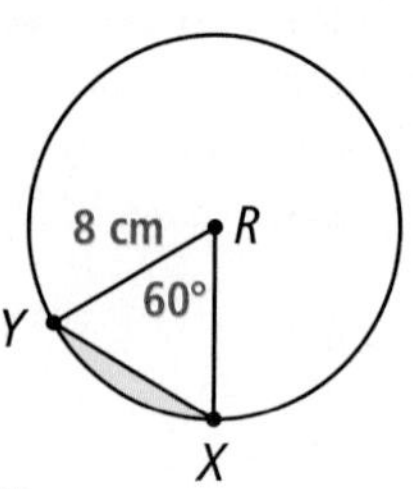

To find the area of the segment, subtract the area of the triangle from the area of the sector.

Step 1 Find the area of the sector.

$$A = \frac{n}{360} \bullet \pi r^2 = \frac{32}{3}\pi$$

Use the formula for area of a sector.

Step 2 Find the area of the triangle.

Since $\overline{RX}$ and $\overline{RY}$ are both radii and the angle between them is 60°, $\triangle RYX$ is equilateral.

STUDY TIP
To find areas of triangles in circles, you may need to apply trigonometric ratios to find the base and height.

Use the Pythagorean Theorem to find h.

$$4^2 + h^2 = 8^2$$

$$h^2 = 8^2 - 4^2$$

$$h = \sqrt{48} = 4\sqrt{3}$$

Find the area of the triangle.

$$A = \frac{1}{2}bh$$

$$= \frac{1}{2}(8)(4\sqrt{3}) = 16\sqrt{3}$$

Step 3 Find the area of the segment.

area of segment = area of sector − area of triangle

$$= \frac{32}{3}\pi - 16\sqrt{3} \approx 5.8$$

The area of the shaded region is about 5.8 cm^2.

CONTINUED ON THE NEXT PAGE

Try It! **5.** What is the area of each segment?

a.

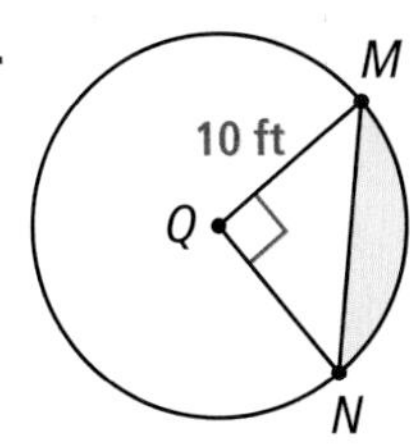

b.

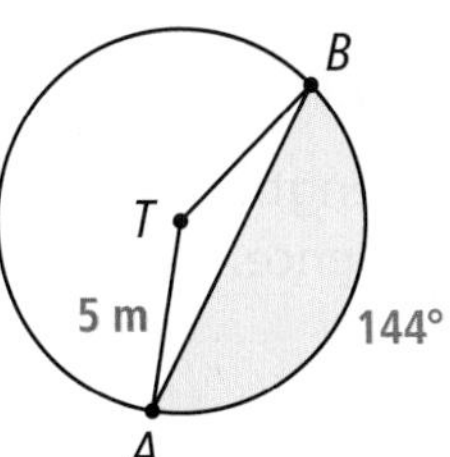

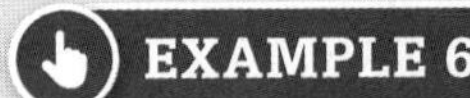

APPLICATION

EXAMPLE 6 Solve Problems Involving Circles

Chen uses circular corkboards to make 18 watermelon coasters to sell at a craft fair.

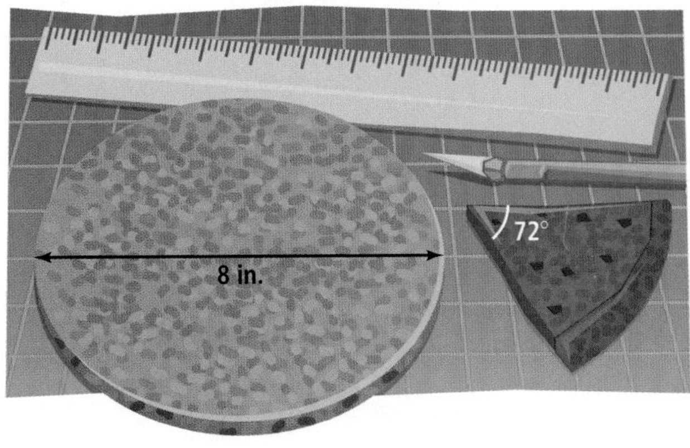

A. He paints one side of each coaster with special paint. Each jar of paint covers 200 in.^{2}. Will one jar of paint be enough to paint all the coasters?

Find the area of one watermelon coaster. Use 3.14 for π.

$$A = \frac{n}{360} \cdot \pi r^2$$

Use the formula for area of a sector.

$$= \frac{72}{360} \cdot \pi(4)^2$$

$$\approx 10.0$$

The area of one watermelon coaster is about 10 in.^{2}.

Chen can paint $200 \div 10 = 20$ coasters with one jar of paint, so he has enough paint for 18 coasters.

COMMON ERROR

Be careful not to confuse the formula for the area of a sector with the formula for arc length. Remember that the area of a sector is proportional to the area of the circle, and the arc length is proportional to the circumference.

B. He puts decorative tape around the edge of each coaster. How much tape does he need for each coaster?

The perimeter of the coaster consists of two radii and an arc.

$$P = r + r + \frac{n}{360} \cdot 2\pi r$$

$$= 4 + 4 + \frac{72}{360} \cdot 2\pi(4)$$

$$\approx 13.0$$

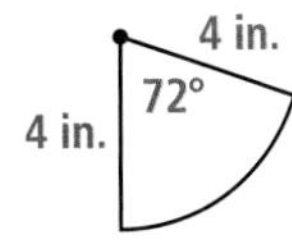

Chen needs about 13 inches of tape for each coaster.

Try It! **6.** What is the area and perimeter of sector QNR? Round to the nearest tenth.

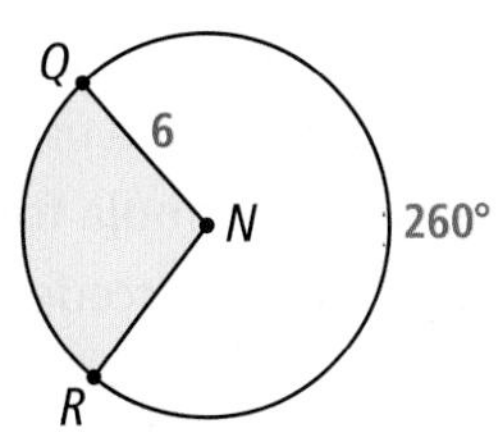

CONCEPT SUMMARY Arc Length and Sector Area

WORDS	DIAGRAMS
Arc Length The arc length is a fraction of the circumference.	**Degrees** 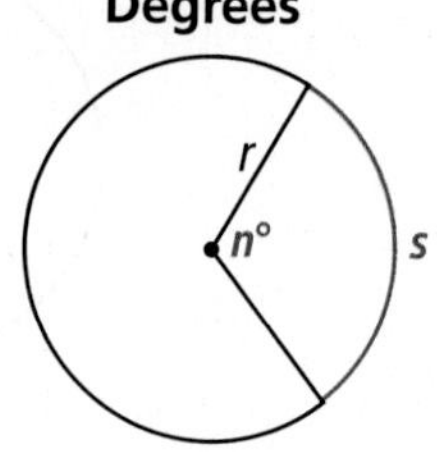 $s = \frac{n}{360} \cdot 2\pi r$ **Radians** $s = \theta r$
Sector A sector of a circle is the region bounded by two radii and the intercepted arc.	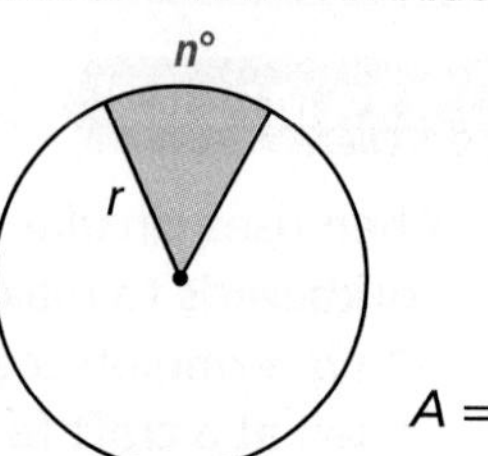 $A = \frac{n}{360} \cdot \pi r^2$
Segment A segment of a circle is the part of a circle bounded by an arc and the segment joining its endpoints.	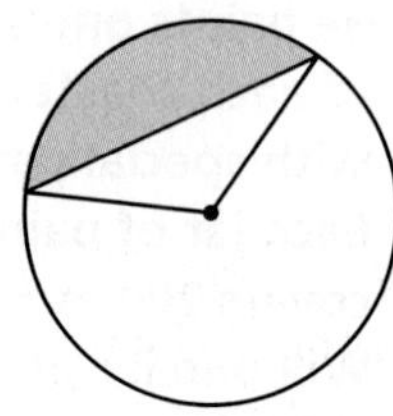 segment area = sector area − triangle area

Do You UNDERSTAND?

1. **ESSENTIAL QUESTION** How are arc length and sector area related to circumference and area of a circle?

2. **Error Analysis** Luke was asked to compute the length of $\overset{\frown}{AB}$. What is Luke's error?

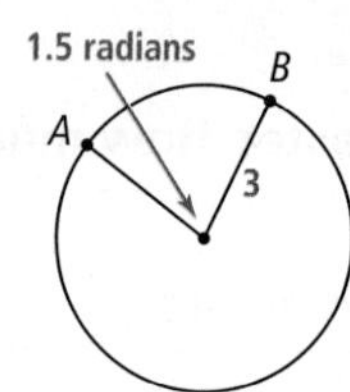

$S = \frac{n}{360} \cdot 2\pi r$

$= \frac{1.5}{360} \cdot 2\pi(3)$

$= 0.0785$ ✗

3. **Vocabulary** How can the word *segment* help you remember what a *segment of a circle* is?

4. **Reason** Mercedes says that she can find the area of a quarter of a circle using the formula $A = \frac{1}{4}\pi r^2$. Using the formula for the area of a sector, explain why Mercedes is correct.

Do You KNOW HOW?

For Exercises 5 and 6, find the measures and lengths of each arc. Express the answers in terms of π.

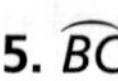

5. $\overset{\frown}{BC}$

6. $\overset{\frown}{ABC}$

7. Circle P has radius 8. Points Q and R lie on circle P, and the length of $\overset{\frown}{QR}$ is 4π. What is $m\angle QPR$ in radians?

8. What is the area of sector EFG? Express the answer in terms of π.

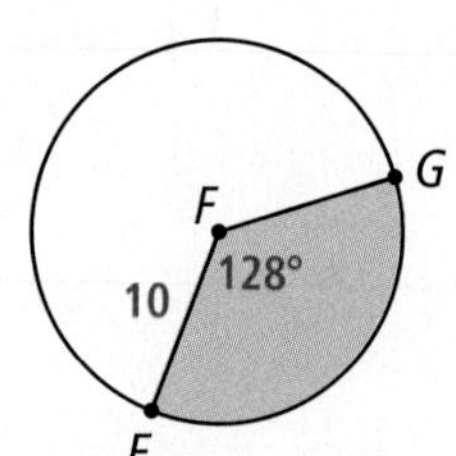

9. What is the area of the segment? Express the answer in terms of π.

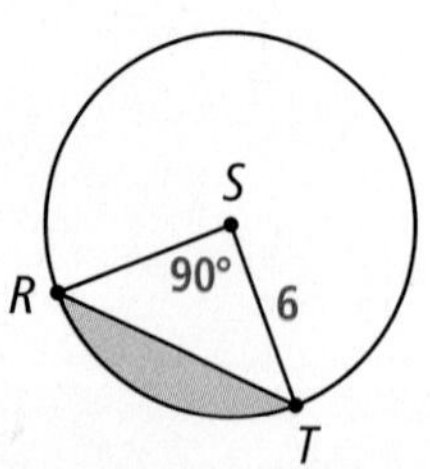

PRACTICE & PROBLEM SOLVING

Scan for Multimedia

Practice Tutorial

Additional Exercises Available Online

UNDERSTAND

10. **Generalize** Is it always true that two arcs with the same length have the same measure? Explain.

11. **Error Analysis** Steve is asked to compute the area of the shaded region. What is his error?

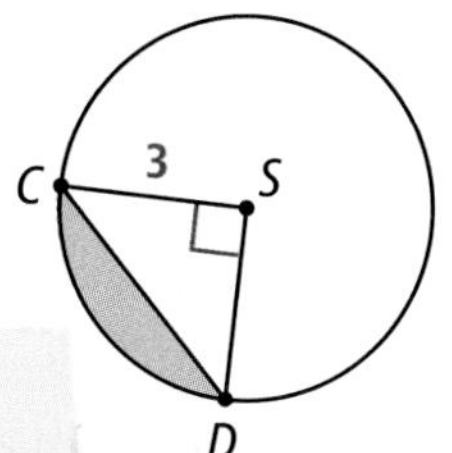

Segment area = sector area − triangle area

$= \frac{90}{360} \cdot 2\pi(3) - \frac{1}{2}(3)(3)$

≈ 0.21

12. Mathematical Connections The equation $(x-2)^2 + (y-3)^2 = 25$ represents ⊙T. Points $X(-2, 6)$ and $Y(-1, -1)$ lie on ⊙T. What is $m\widehat{XY}$? Explain how you know.

13. **Reason** Figure $GHJKL$ is a regular pentagon. Rounded to the nearest tenth, what percent of the area of ⊙T is not part of the area of $GHJKL$? Explain.

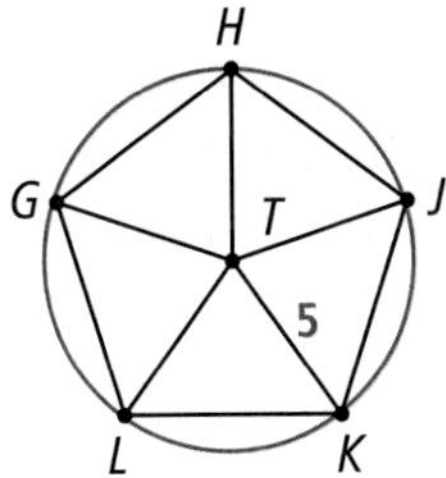

14. **Use Structure** Explain why the length of an arc with arc measure $a°$ is proportional to the radius of the circle.

15. Higher Order Thinking The areas of sectors ACB and DEF are equal. What expression gives the value of x? Show your work.

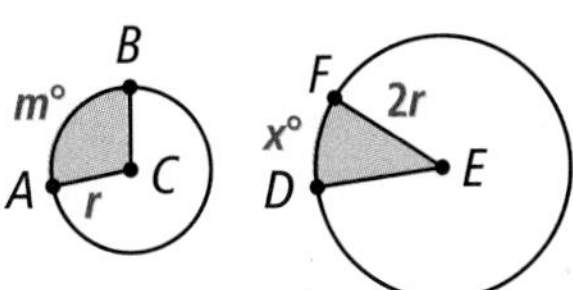

PRACTICE

For Exercises 16–19, find each arc measure.
SEE EXAMPLE 1

16. $m\widehat{FE}$

17. $m\widehat{BC}$

18. $m\widehat{CE}$

19. $m\widehat{CFE}$

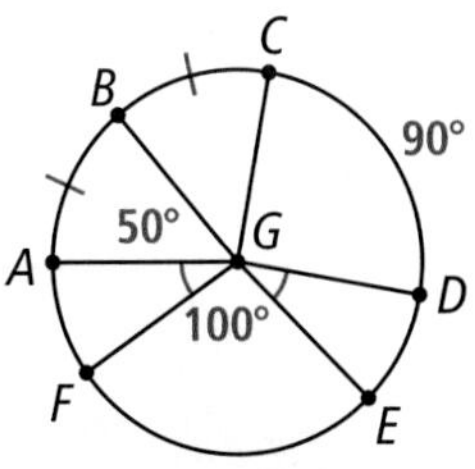

For Exercises 20 and 21, find each arc length in terms of π. SEE EXAMPLES 2 AND 3

20. length of $\widehat{JK}$

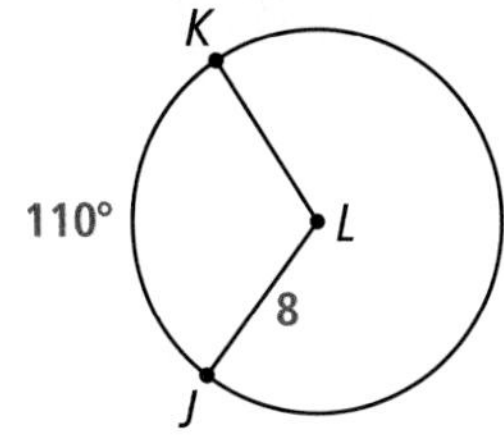

21. length of $\widehat{XYZ}$

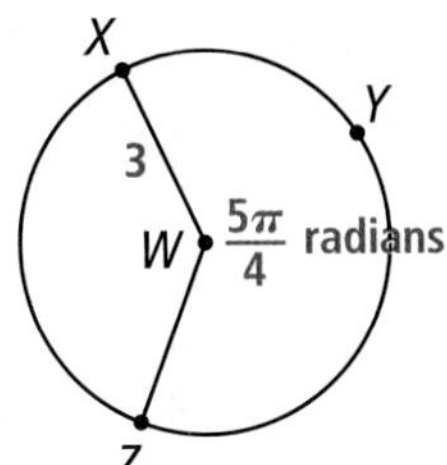

For Exercises 22 and 23, find the area of each sector. Round to the nearest tenth. SEE EXAMPLES 4 AND 6

22. sector DEF

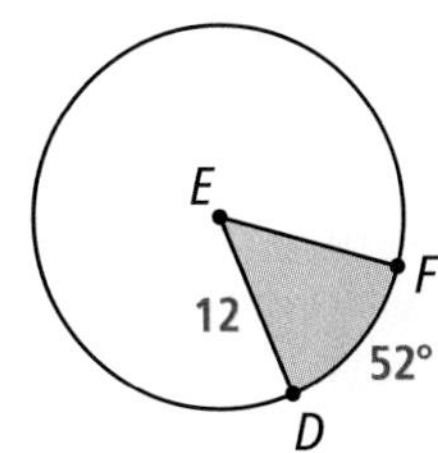

23. sector GHJ

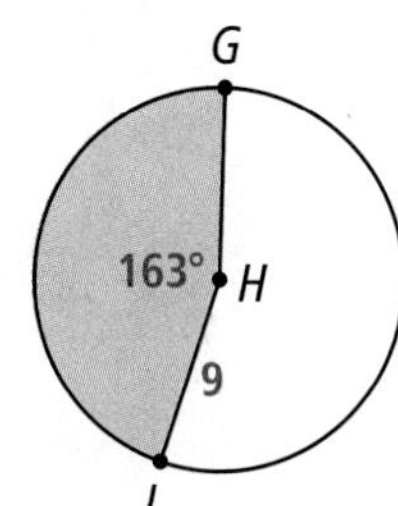

For Exercises 24 and 25, find the area of each segment. Round to the nearest tenth. SEE EXAMPLE 5

24.

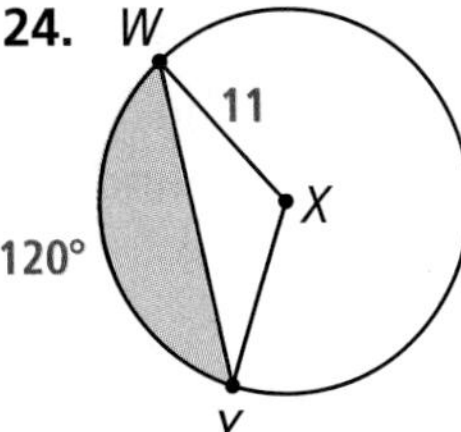

25.

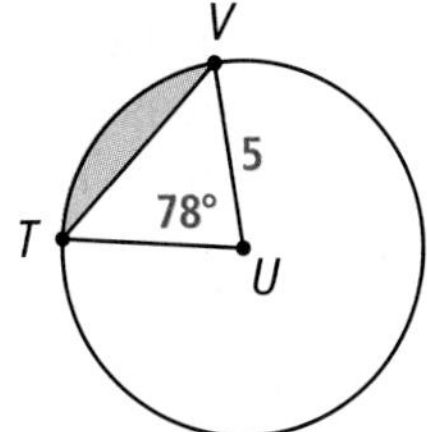

26. The length of $\widehat{ABC}$ is 110 ft. What is the radius of ⊙D? Round to the nearest tenth.

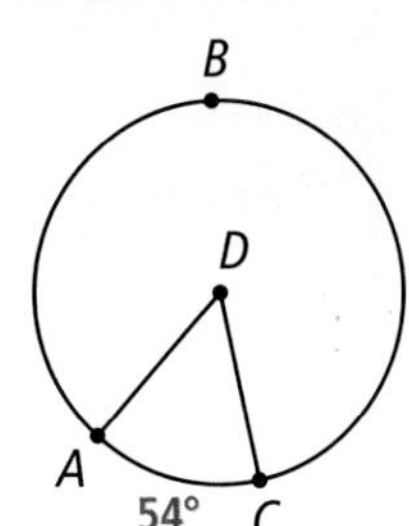

Practice Tutorial
Mixed Review Available Online

PRACTICE & PROBLEM SOLVING

APPLY

27. Make Sense and Persevere Aubrey and Fatima will each run 150 m on the two inside lanes of the track, so the end markers need to be placed correctly. To the nearest hundredth, what are x and y?

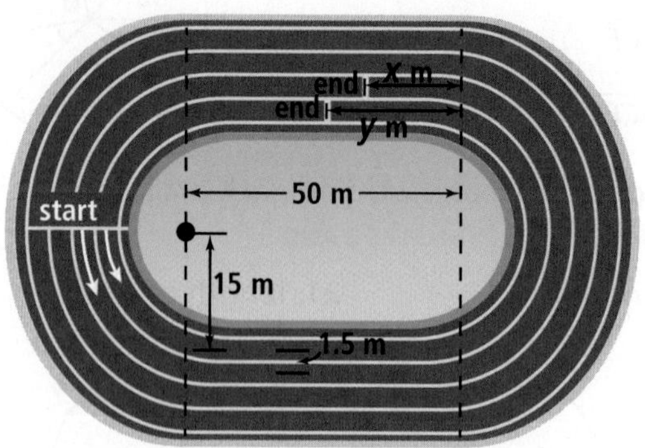

28. Reason Charlie is designing a dart board and wants the red sections to be 25% of the total area. What should be the radius of the inner circle? Round to the nearest tenth.

29. Look for Relationships Enrique is selling the drop-leaf table and wants to include the area of the table when the leaves are down in his ad. What is the area of the center section when the leaves are down? Round to the nearest square inch. Explain how you found your answer.

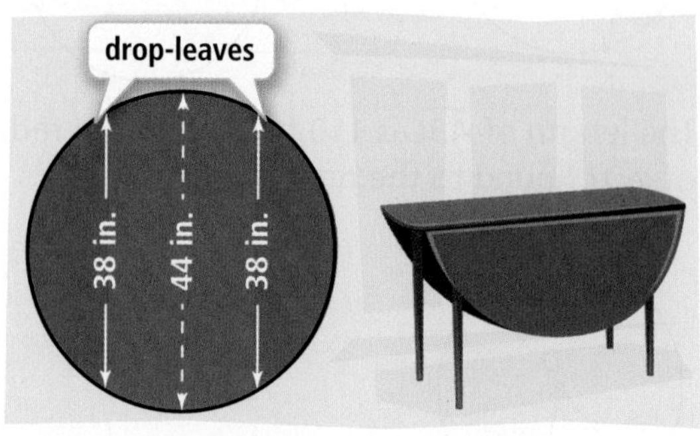

ASSESSMENT PRACTICE

30. What is the diameter of $\odot T$?

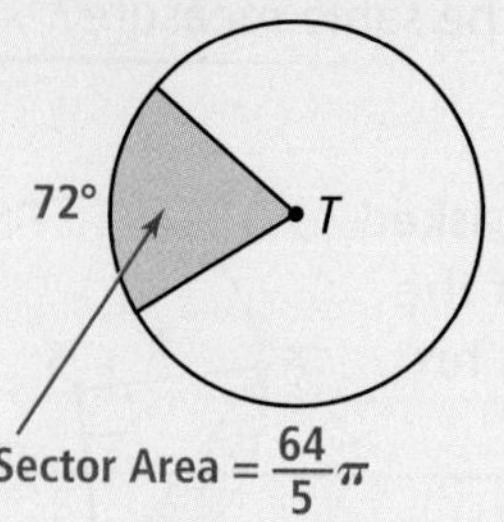

31. SAT/ACT An arc has a central angle of $\frac{2}{5}\pi$ radians and a length of 6π. What is the circumference of the circle?

Ⓐ 12π Ⓑ 15π Ⓒ 30π Ⓓ 36π

32. Performance Task A carpenter is constructing the stage for a concert.

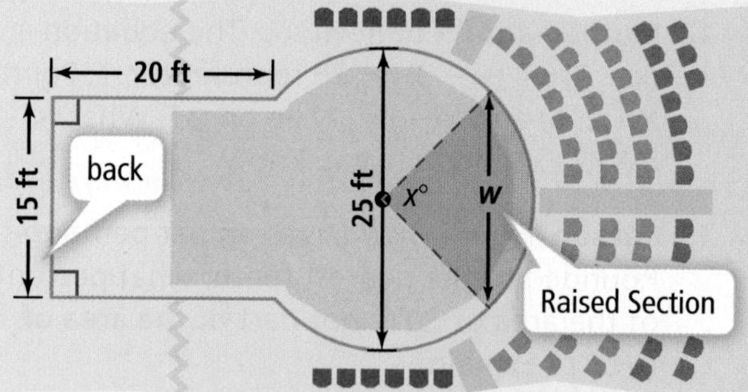

Part A What is the total amount of flooring needed to cover the stage? Round to the nearest square foot. Explain how you found your answer.

Part B A string of lights will be strung along the sides and front of the stage. What is the total length of light string needed? Show your work.

Part C One portion of the stage can be raised during the concert. The lift mechanism can lift a maximum area of 180 ft^2, but the band needs the width w of the raised area to be at least 20 ft. What could be the value of x? Justify your answer.

Activity Assess

10-2 Lines Tangent to a Circle

I CAN... use properties of tangent lines to solve problems.

VOCABULARY

- point of tangency
- tangent to a circle

CRITIQUE & EXPLAIN

Alicia and Renaldo made conjectures about the lines that intersect a circle only once.

Alicia

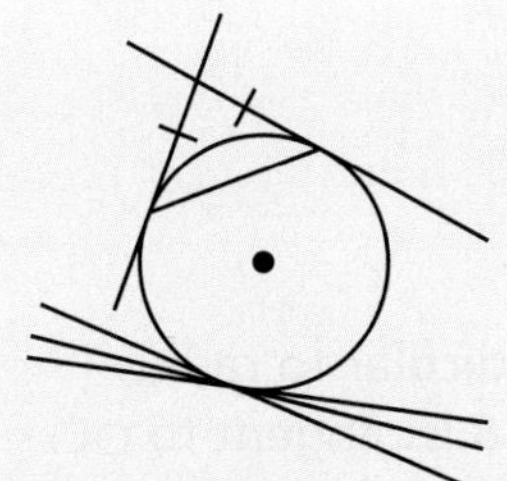

- Many lines intersect the circle once at the same point.
- Two lines that intersect the circle once and the segment connecting the points form an isosceles triangle.

Renaldo

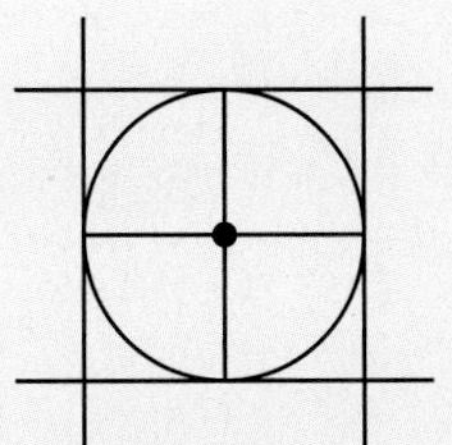

- Parallel lines intersect the circle at opposite ends of the same diameter.
- The lines intersecting the circle at one point are perpendicular to a diameter of the circle.

A. Use Appropriate Tools Which of the four conjectures do you agree with? Which do you disagree with? Draw sketches to support your answers.

B. What other conjectures can you make about lines that intersect a circle at one point?

ESSENTIAL QUESTION **How is a tangent line related to the radius of a circle at the point of tangency?**

CONCEPTUAL UNDERSTANDING

EXAMPLE 1 Understand Tangents to a Circle

What is the relationship between a circle and a tangent to the circle?

A **tangent to a circle** is a line in the plane of the circle that intersects the circle in exactly one point. That point is the **point of tangency**.

Circle C has tangent line m with point of tangency X. Point Y is any other point on m.

GENERALIZE
Point Y represents any point other than the point of tangency. Would the result be true no matter where point Y is located on m?

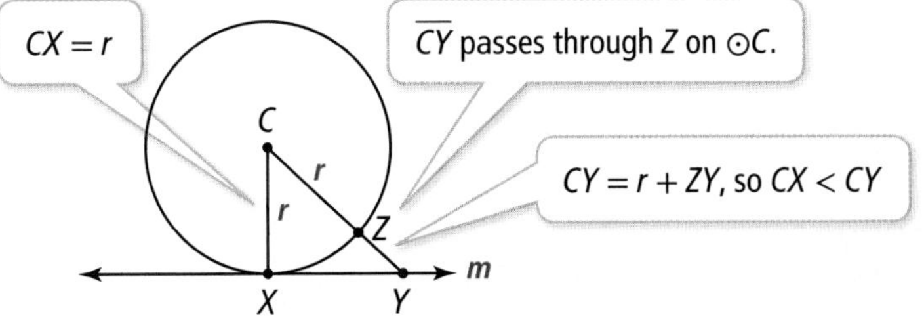

So, $\overline{CX}$ is the shortest segment from C to line m. Since the shortest segment from a point to a line is perpendicular to the line, $\overline{CX} \perp m$.

Try It! 1. Does Example 1 support Renaldo's conjecture that parallel lines intersect the circle at opposite ends of the same diameter? Explain.

THEOREM 10-1 AND THE CONVERSE

Theorem

If $\overleftrightarrow{AB}$ is tangent to $\odot C$ at P, then $\overleftrightarrow{AB}$ is perpendicular to $\overline{CP}$.

If...

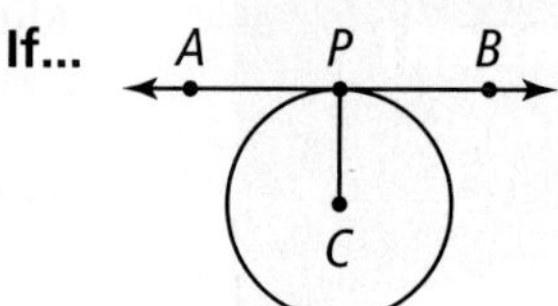

Then... $\overleftrightarrow{AB} \perp \overline{CP}$

Converse

If $\overleftrightarrow{AB}$ is perpendicular to radius $\overline{CP}$ at P, then $\overleftrightarrow{AB}$ is tangent to $\odot C$.

If... A P B C

Then... $\overleftrightarrow{AB}$ is tangent to $\odot C$.

PROOF: SEE EXERCISES 12 AND 13.

EXAMPLE 2 Use Tangents to Solve Problems

A. Is $\overline{KJ}$ tangent to $\odot P$ at J?

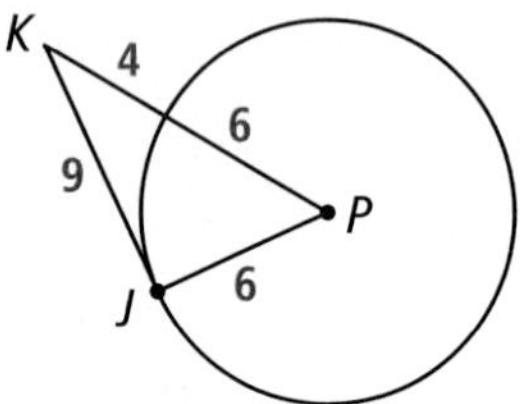

A segment or ray that intersects a circle in one point is tangent to the circle if it is part of a tangent line.

If $\overline{KJ}$ is part of a line that is tangent to $\odot P$ at J, then $\overline{PJ} \perp \overline{JK}$ and $\triangle PJK$ is a right triangle.

$$9^2 + 6^2 \stackrel{?}{=} (4 + 6)^2$$

$$117 \neq 100$$

Use the Converse of the Pythagorean Theorem to determine whether $\triangle PJK$ is a right triangle.

So, $\overline{PJ}$ is not perpendicular to $\overline{KJ}$.

Therefore, $\overline{KJ}$ is not tangent to $\odot P$ at J.

B. Segment ST is tangent to $\odot R$. What is the radius of $\odot R$?

Since $\overline{ST}$ is tangent to $\odot R$, $\triangle RST$ is a right triangle.

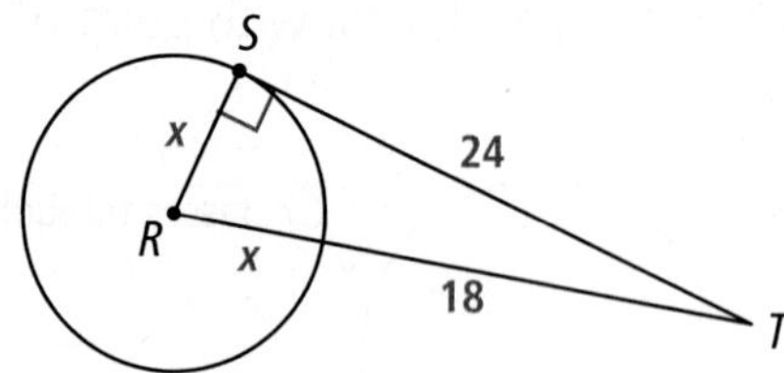

$$x^2 + 24^2 = (x + 18)^2$$

$$x^2 + 576 = x^2 + 36x + 324$$

$$252 = 36x$$

$$7 = x$$

Use the Pythagorean Theorem with length of the hypotenuse $x + 18$.

The radius of $\odot R$ is 7.

COMMON ERROR

You may incorrectly square just the terms x and 18. Recall how to square a binomial. It may be helpful to first write $(x + 18)^2$ as $(x + 18)(x + 18)$ and multiply.

CONTINUED ON THE NEXT PAGE

EXAMPLE 2 CONTINUED

C. Line *m* is tangent to ⊙*T* at *B*, and line *n* is tangent to ⊙*T* at *C*. What is the value of *x*?

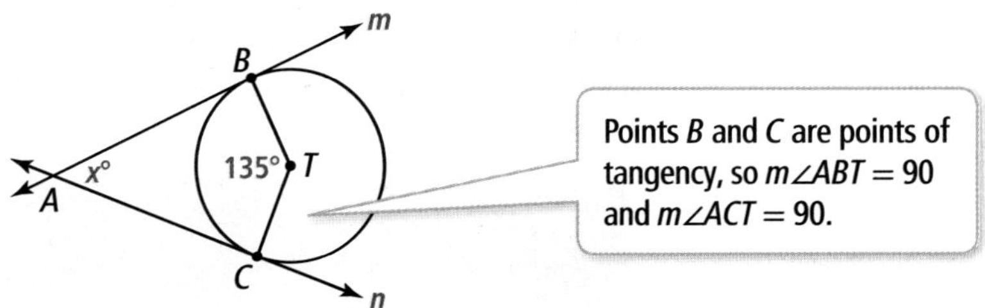

STUDY TIP
Remember that for any convex polygon, the sum of the interior angles is $(n - 2)180°$, where n is the number of sides.

Use the Polygon Angle-Sum Theorem to find *x*.

$$m\angle BAC + m\angle ACT + m\angle CTB + m\angle TBA = 360$$
$$x + 90 + 135 + 90 = 360$$
$$x = 45$$

Try It! 2. Use ⊙*N*.

a. Is $\overleftrightarrow{MP}$ tangent to ⊙*N*? Explain.

b. If $\overline{LK}$ is tangent to ⊙*N* at *L*, what is *KN*?

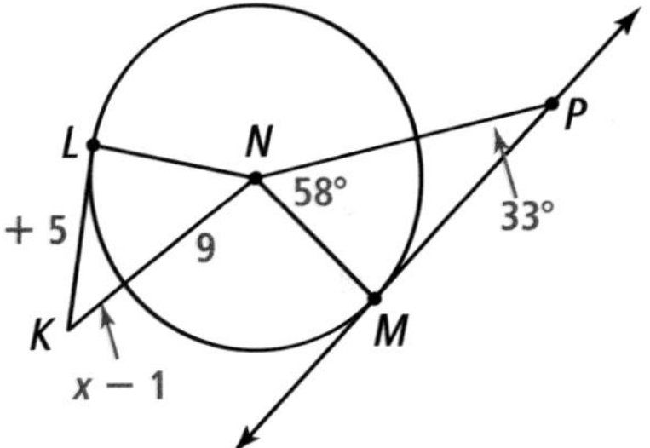

EXAMPLE 3 Find Lengths of Segments Tangent to a Circle

What is the relationship between $\overline{YZ}$ and $\overline{XZ}$?

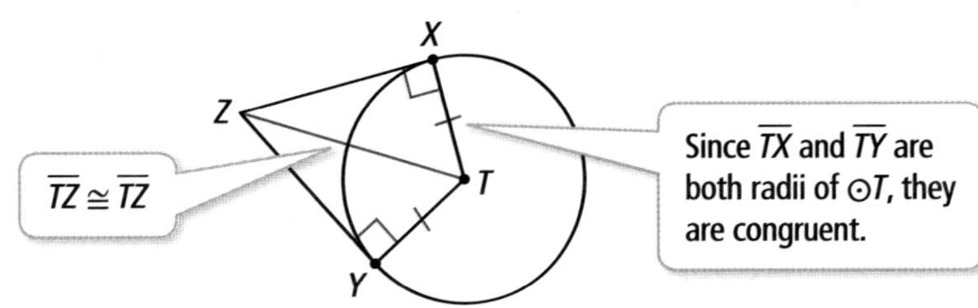

By HL, $\triangle TXZ \cong \triangle TYZ$, so $\overline{YZ} \cong \overline{XZ}$ by CPCTC.

Try It! 3. If $TX = 12$ and $TZ = 20$, what are XZ and YZ?

THEOREM 10-2 Segments Tangent to a Circle Theorem

If two segments with a common endpoint exterior to a circle are tangent to the circle, then the segments are congruent.

If...

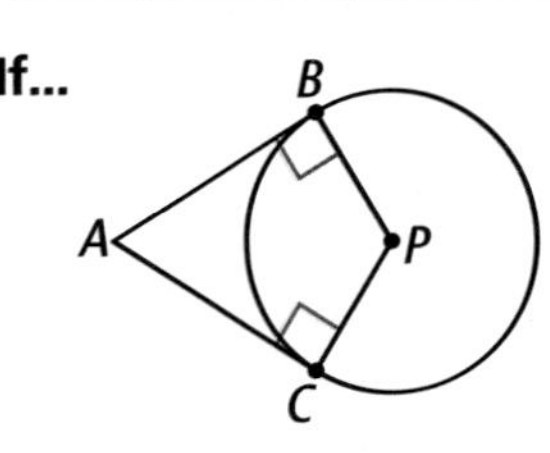

PROOF: SEE EXERCISE 14.

Then... $\overline{AB} \cong \overline{AC}$

APPLICATION

EXAMPLE 4 Find Measures Involving Tangent Lines

A satellite requires a line of sight for communication. Between the ground stations farthest from the satellite, what is the amount of time needed for a signal to go from one station up to the satellite, and then down to the other station?

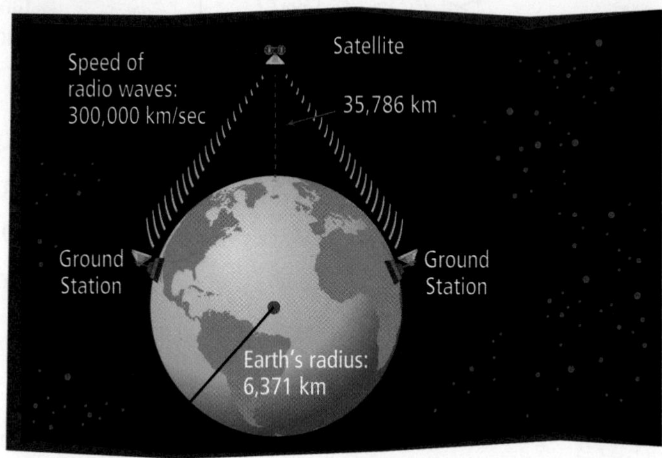

Formulate ◀ The lines from the satellite to the farthest ground stations are tangent to Earth's surface.

Use the Pythagorean Theorem to compute the distance to the ground stations. Then compute the time for radio waves to travel twice this distance.

Compute ◀ **Step 1** Find the distance from the farthest ground stations to the satellite.

$$x^2 + 6{,}371^2 = (6{,}371 + 35{,}786)^2$$

$$x^2 + 40{,}589{,}641 = 1{,}777{,}212{,}649$$

$$x^2 = 1{,}736{,}623{,}008$$

$$x \approx 41{,}673$$

Satellite
35,786 km
x
Ground Station
6,371 km
Center of Earth
6,371 km

Step 2 Find the time for radio waves to travel this distance twice.

$$(41{,}673 \times 2)\text{ km} \div 300{,}000\text{ km/sec} \approx 0.28\text{ sec}$$

Interpret ◀ The amount of time for a signal to travel from one of the farthest ground stations to the satellite and back to the other ground station is about 0.28 second.

 **Try It!** **4.** What is the perimeter of *ABCD*?

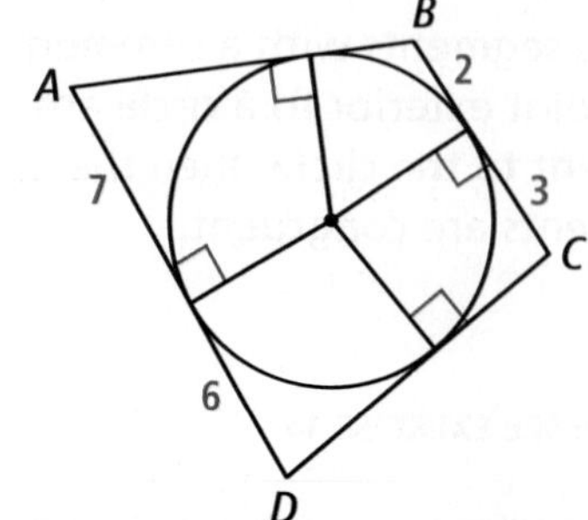

EXAMPLE 5 Construct Tangent Lines

How do you construct a tangent to ⊙*P* passing through point *T*?

COMMON ERROR
You may think that *A* is the midpoint of $\overline{PT}$. However, the construction of a perpendicular line here is different from constructing the perpendicular bisector of $\overline{PT}$.

Step 1 Use a straightedge to draw $\overline{PT}$. Label point *A* where $\overline{PT}$ intersects the circle.

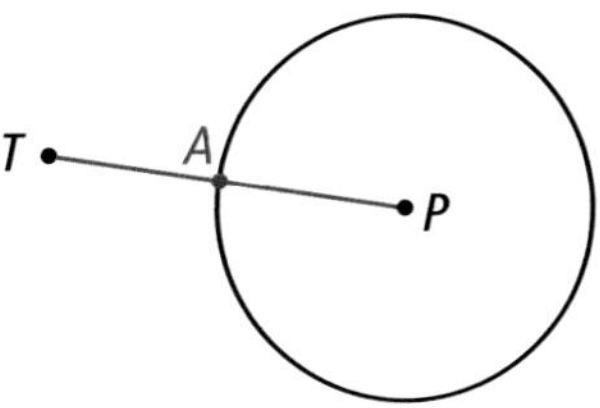

Step 2 Use a compass to construct a circle with center *P* and passing through *T*. Construct a perpendicular to $\overline{PT}$ at *A*. Label point *B* where the perpendicular intersects the outer circle.

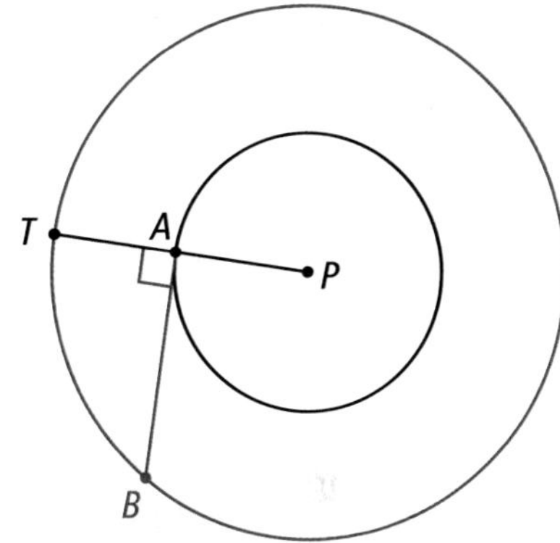

Step 3 Use a straightedge to construct $\overline{BP}$. Label point *C* where $\overline{BP}$ intersects the inner circle.

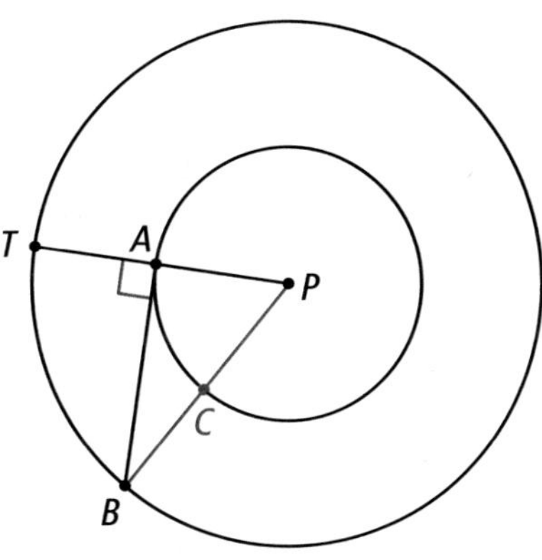

Step 4 Use a straightedge to construct $\overline{TC}$.

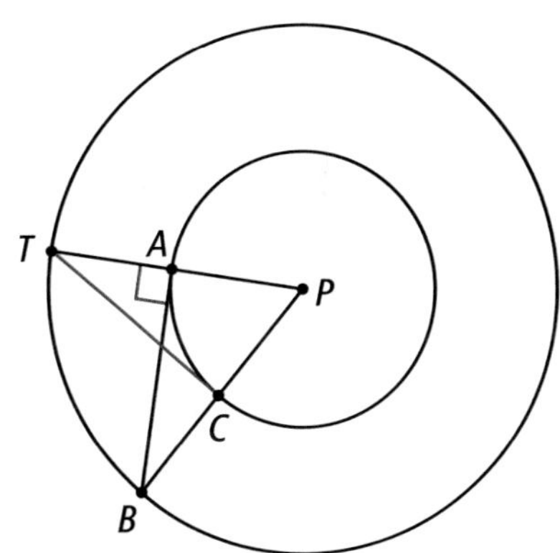

The tangent to ⊙*P* passing through *T* is $\overline{TC}$.

Try It! **5.** Prove that $\overline{TC}$ is tangent to ⊙*P*.

Given: Two circles share center *P*, points *A* and *C* on the smaller circle, points *T* and *B* on the larger circle, $\overline{AB} \perp \overline{PT}$

Prove: $\overline{TC}$ is tangent to ⊙*P* at *C*.

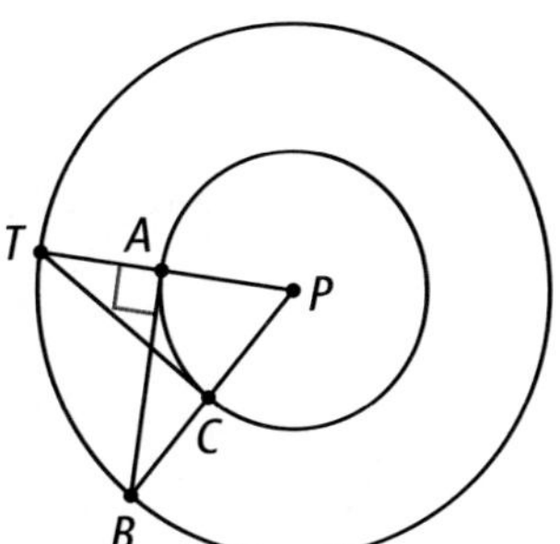

CONCEPT SUMMARY Tangents to a Circle

WORDS A tangent to a circle intersects the circle at exactly one point. The radius that contains the point of tangency is perpendicular to the tangent.

DIAGRAM

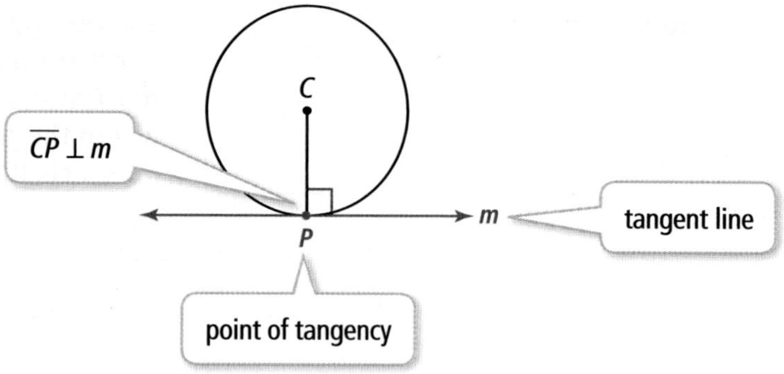

C

$\overline{CP} \perp m$

m tangent line

P

point of tangency

Do You UNDERSTAND?

1. **ESSENTIAL QUESTION** How is a tangent line related to the radius of a circle at the point of tangency?

2. **Error Analysis** Kona looked at the figure shown and said that $\overline{AB}$ is tangent to $\odot G$ at A because it intersects $\odot G$ only at A. What was Kona's error?

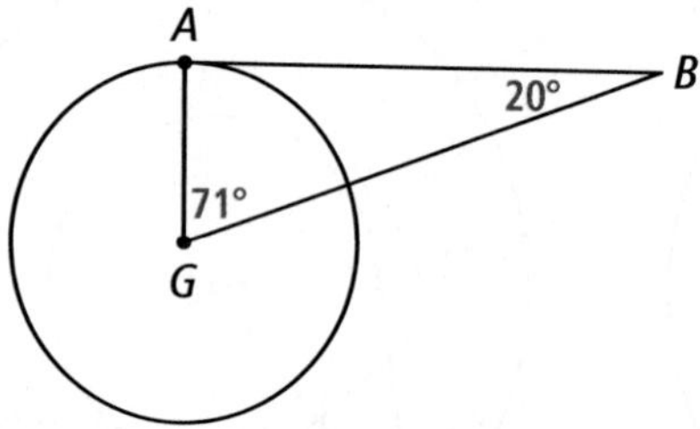

3. **Vocabulary** Can any point on a circle be a *point of tangency*? Explain.

4. **Reason** Lines m and n are tangent to circles A and B. What are the relationships between $\angle PAS$, $\angle PQS$, $\angle RQS$, and $\angle RBS$? Explain.

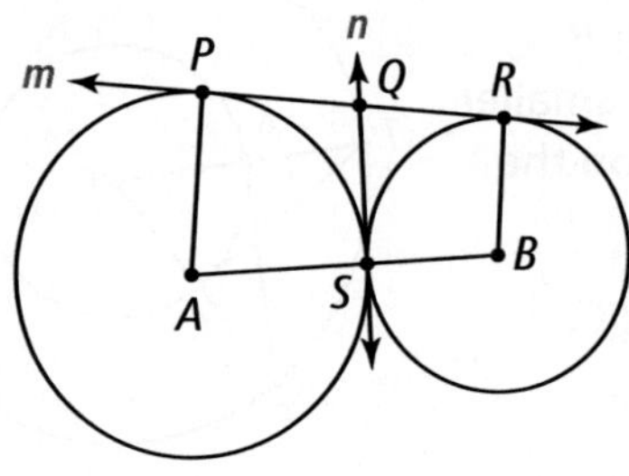

Do You KNOW HOW?

Tell whether each line or segment is a tangent to $\odot B$.

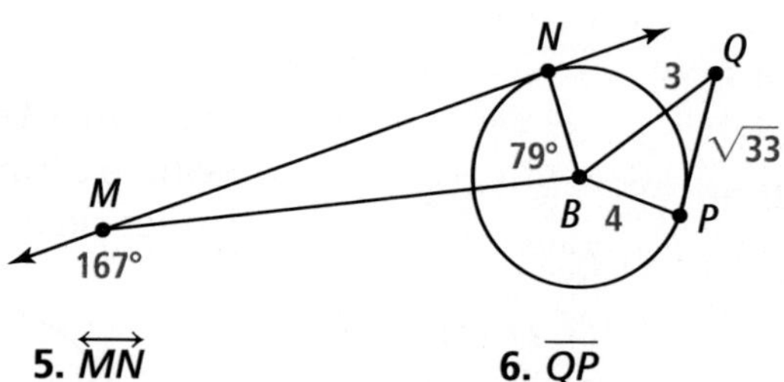

5. $\overleftrightarrow{MN}$

6. $\overline{QP}$

Segment AC is tangent to $\odot D$ at B. Find each value.

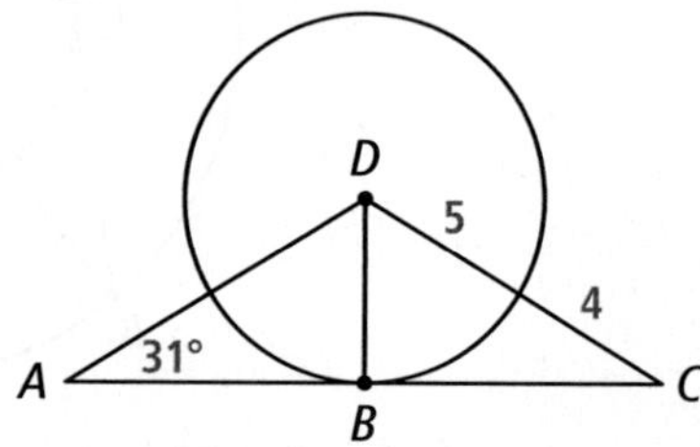

7. $m\angle ADB$

8. BC

Segment FG is tangent to $\odot K$ at F and $\overline{HG}$ is tangent to $\odot K$ at H. Find each value.

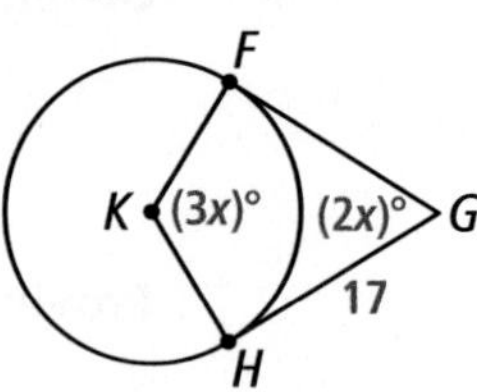

9. FG

10. $m\angle FGH$

PRACTICE & PROBLEM SOLVING

Scan for Multimedia

Additional Exercises Available Online

UNDERSTAND

11. Error Analysis Segments $\overline{DF}$, $\overline{DH}$, and $\overline{GF}$ are tangent to the circle. Andrew was asked to find *DF*. Explain Andrew's error.

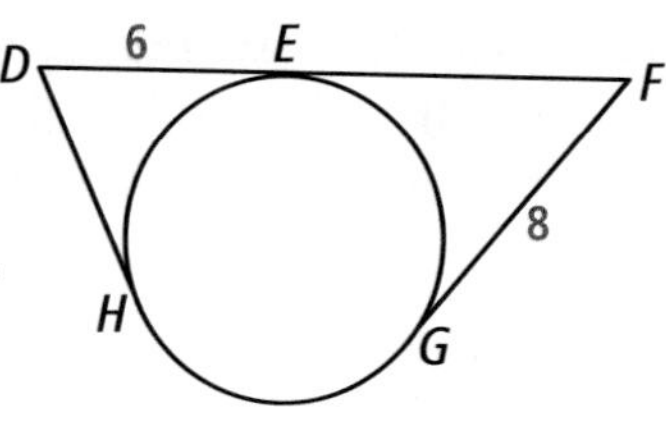

$DF = DE + EF$

By Theorem 10-2, $DE = EF$.

So, $DF = 6 + 6 = 12$. ✗

12. Construct Arguments Use the following outline to write an indirect proof of Theorem 10-1.

Given: Line *m* is tangent to ⊙*T* at *G*.

Prove: $\overline{GT} \perp m$

- Assume that $\overline{GT}$ is not perpendicular to *m*.
- Draw $\overline{HT}$ such that $\overline{HT} \perp m$.
- Use triangles to show that $GT > HT$.
- Show that this is a contradiction, since *H* is in the exterior of ⊙*T*.

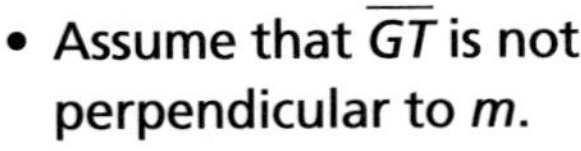

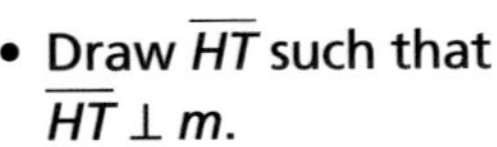

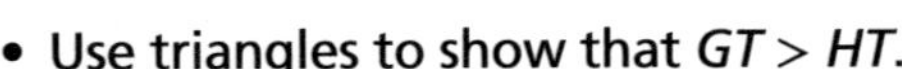

13. Construct Arguments Prove the Converse of Theorem 10-1.

Given: $\overline{QR} \perp n$

Prove: *n* is tangent to ⊙*Q* at *R*

Hint: Select any other point *S* on line *n*. Show that $\overline{QS}$ is the hypotenuse of △*QRS*, so $QS > QR$ and therefore *S* lies outside ⊙*Q*.

14. Construct Arguments Prove Theorem 10-2.

Given: $\overline{DE}$ and $\overline{DF}$ are tangent to ⊙*T*.

Prove: $\overline{DE} \cong \overline{DF}$

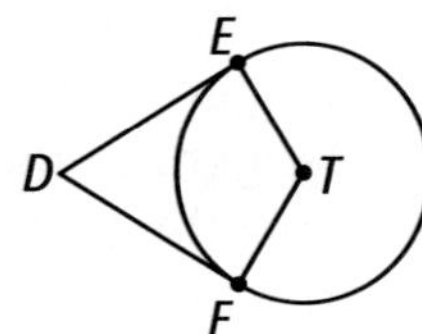

15. Higher Order Thinking If $AC = x$, what is the perimeter of △*BCE*? Explain.

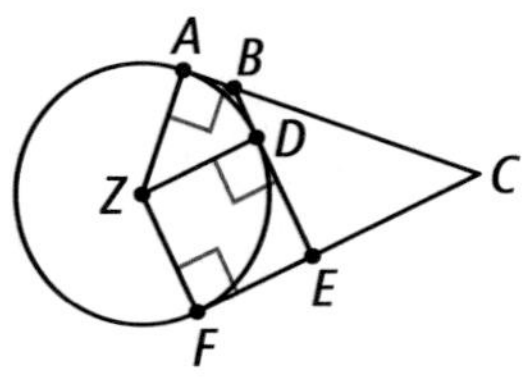

PRACTICE

The segments $\overline{AB}$ and $\overline{CD}$ are tangent to ⊙*T*. Find each value. SEE EXAMPLES 1 AND 2

16. *AB*

17. *m*∠*TDC*

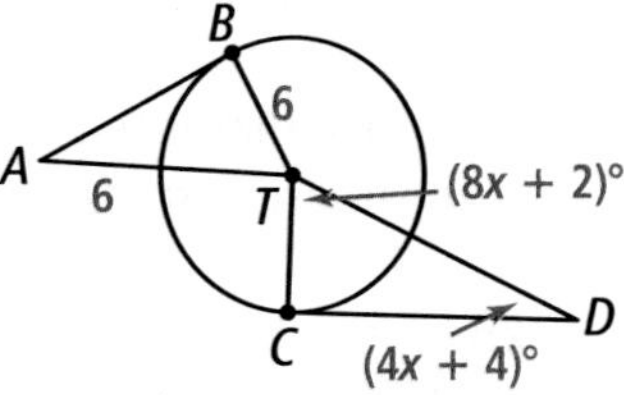

For Exercises 18–20, the segments are tangent to the circle. Find each value. SEE EXAMPLES 3 AND 4

18. *DG*

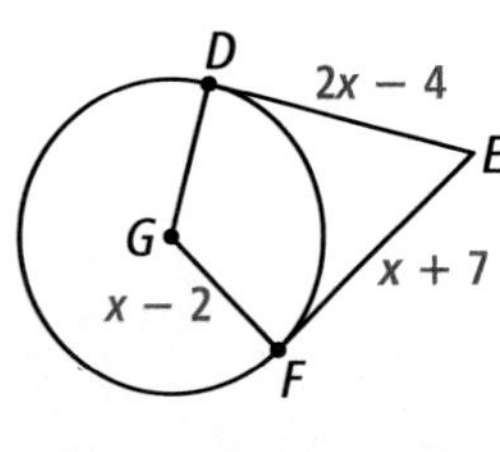

19. Perimeter of *JLNQ*

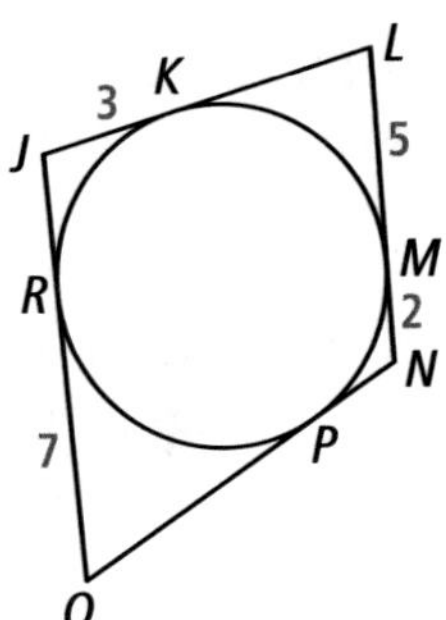

20. *AC*

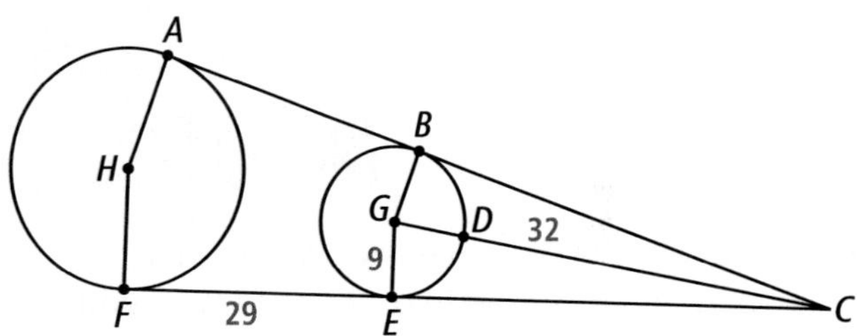

21. Trace ⊙*P* and point *A*. Construct a tangent to ⊙*P* that passes through *A*. SEE EXAMPLE 5

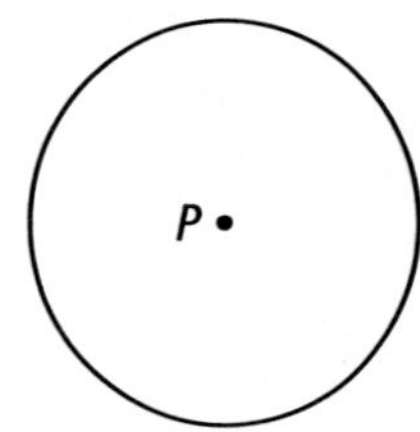

22. The diameter of ⊙*F* is 8; $AB = 10$; and $\overline{AB}$, $\overline{BC}$, and $\overline{AC}$ are tangent to ⊙*F*. What is the perimeter of △*ABC*?

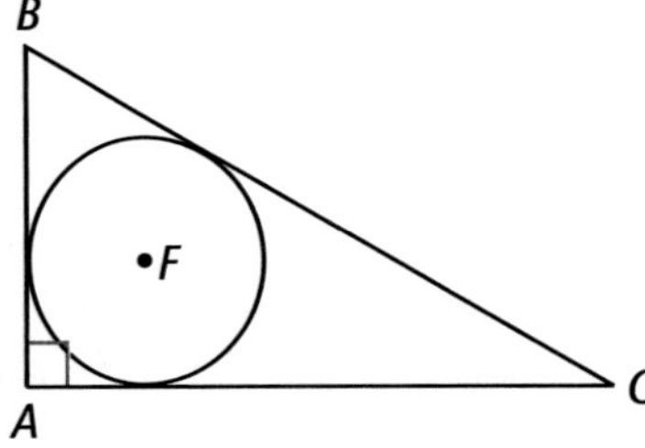

Mixed Review Available Online

PRACTICE & PROBLEM SOLVING

APPLY

23. Make Sense and Persevere Yumiko is shopping for a stand for a decorative glass ball with an 8-inch diameter. She is considering the stand shown and wants to know the height h of the portion of the ball that will be visible if the sides of the stand are tangent to the sphere. What is the value of h?

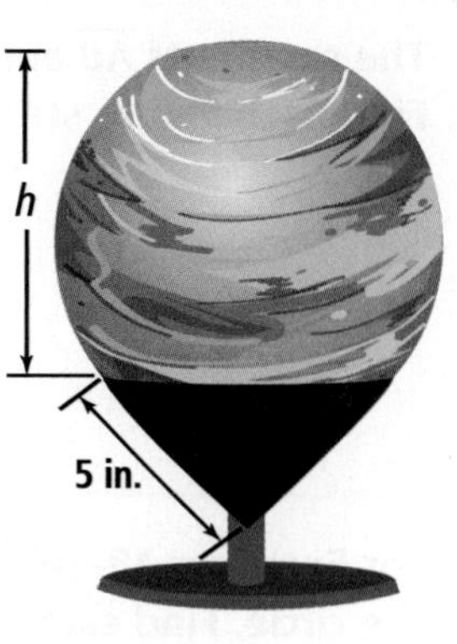

24. Use Structure Samantha is looking out from the 103rd floor of the Willis Tower on a clear day. How far away is the horizon? Earth's radius is about 6,400 km.

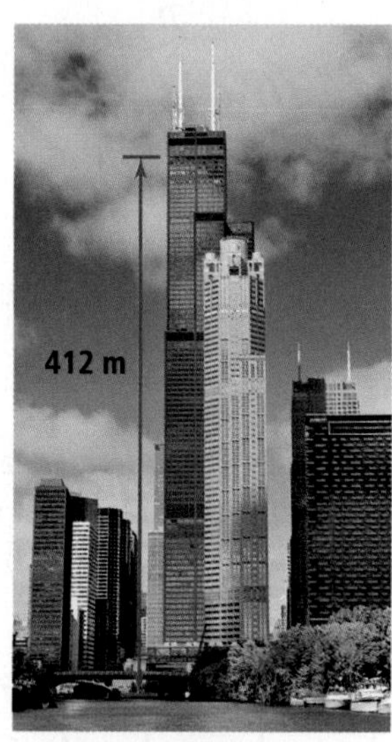

25. Mathematical Connections Rail planners want to connect the two straight tracks with a curved track as shown. Any curves must have a radius of at least 450 m.

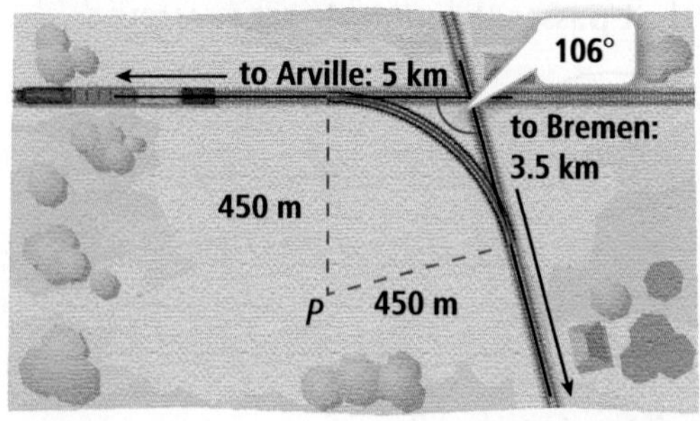

a. Explain how engineers can locate point P, the center of the curved section of track.

b. Once the curved track is constructed, what distance will trains travel between Arvillle and Bremen? Justify your answer.

ASSESSMENT PRACTICE

26. Circle P is described by the equation $(x + 3)^2 + (y - 2)^2 = 25$. Which of the following lines are tangent to $\odot P$? Select all that apply.

Ⓐ $y = x + 3$
Ⓑ $y = 5$
Ⓒ $y = x$
Ⓓ $x = 2$
Ⓔ $y = -3$
Ⓕ $y = x - 3$

27. SAT/ACT Line m is tangent to $\odot A$ at B. What is the area of $\triangle ABC$?

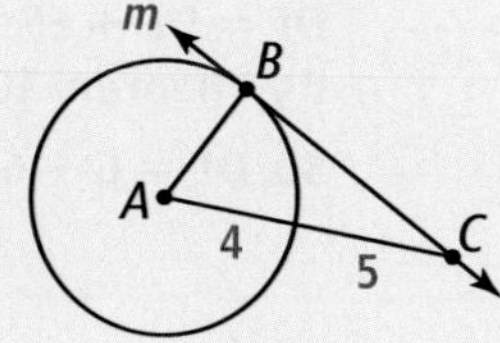

Ⓐ 10
Ⓑ 18
Ⓒ $2\sqrt{65}$
Ⓓ $\frac{5\sqrt{65}}{2}$

28. Performance Task The African art design below is based on circles that are tangent to each other.

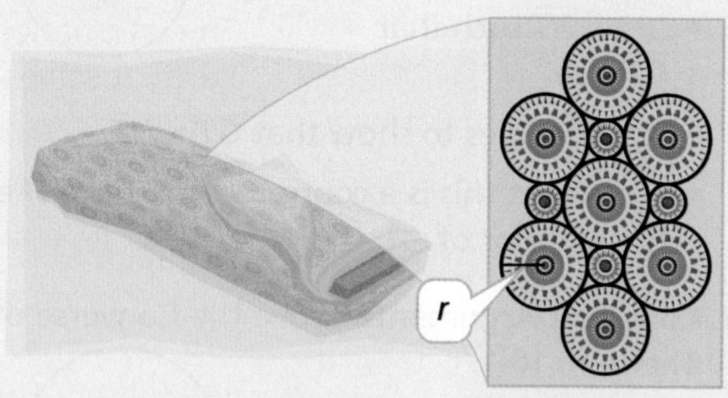

Part A If the radius of the larger circles is r, what is the radius of the smaller circles?

Part B Choose a value for the larger radius and draw the pattern. Measure the radii of the small and large circles. Are the values related in the way you described in Part A?

Part C In your diagram for Part B, mark the points where the small and large circles are tangent to each other. Add lines that are tangent to the circles at these points. Describe how the tangent lines you drew illustrate Theorems 10-1 and 10-2.

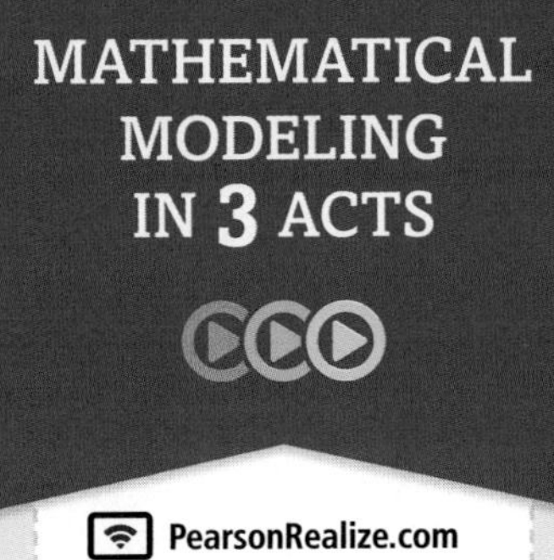

PearsonRealize.com

Earth Watch

Scientists estimate that there are currently about 3,000 operational man-made satellites orbiting Earth. These satellites serve different purposes, from communication to navigation and global positioning. Some are weather satellites that collect environmental information.

The International Space Station is the largest man-made satellite that orbits Earth. It serves as a space environment research facility, and it also offers amazing views of Earth. Think about this during the Mathematical Modeling in 3 Acts lesson.

ACT 1 Identify the Problem

1. What is the first question that comes to mind after watching the video?
2. Write down the main question you will answer about what you saw in the video.
3. Make an initial conjecture that answers this main question.
4. Explain how you arrived at your conjecture.
5. What information will be useful to know to answer the main question? How can you get it? How will you use that information?

ACT 2 Develop a Model

6. Use the math that you have learned in this Topic to refine your conjecture.

ACT 3 Interpret the Results

7. Did your refined conjecture match the actual answer exactly? If not, what might explain the difference?

10-3 Chords

PearsonRealize.com

I CAN… relate the length of a chord to its central angle and the arc it intercepts.

VOCABULARY

- chord

Activity | Assess

EXPLORE & REASON

Use the diagram to answer the questions.

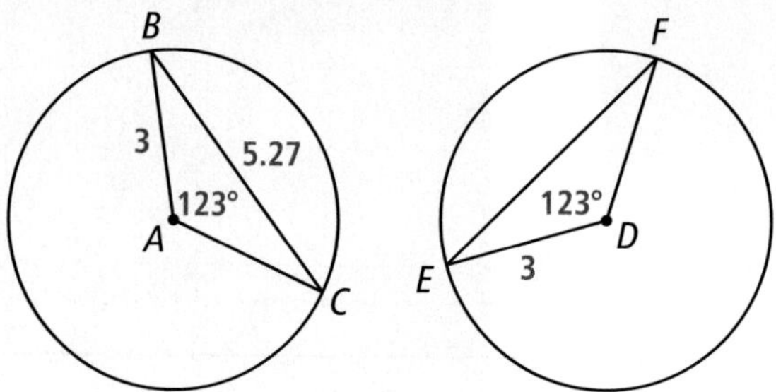

A. What figures in the diagram are congruent? Explain.

B. Look for Relationships How can you find EF?

ESSENTIAL QUESTION

How are chords related to their central angles and intercepted arcs?

CONCEPTUAL UNDERSTANDING

EXAMPLE 1 Relate Central Angles and Chords

A chord is a segment whose endpoints are on a circle. Why is $\overline{RS} \cong \overline{UT}$?

$\angle RQS \cong \angle UQT$ because they are vertical angles.

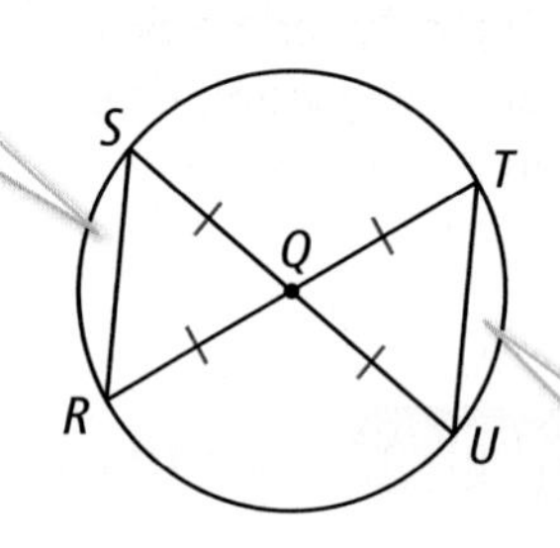

$\overline{SQ} \cong \overline{TQ} \cong \overline{UQ} \cong \overline{RQ}$ because all radii of a circle are $\cong$.

STUDY TIP

Refer to the diagram as you read the proof. Note which parts of the triangles are congruent.

By the SAS Congruence Theorem, $\triangle QRS \cong \triangle QUT$. Therefore $\overline{RS} \cong \overline{UT}$ because they are corresponding parts of congruent triangles.

Try It! **1.** Why is $\angle BAC \cong \angle DAE$?

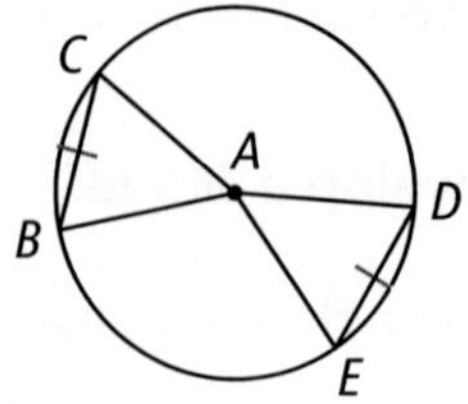

THEOREM 10-3 AND THE CONVERSE

Theorem

If two chords in a circle or in congruent circles are congruent, then their central angles are congruent.

Converse

If two central angles in a circle or in congruent circles are congruent, then their chords are congruent.

PROOF: SEE EXERCISES 12 AND 13.

If... $\overline{MN} \cong \overline{PQ}$
Then... $\angle MTN \cong \angle PTQ$

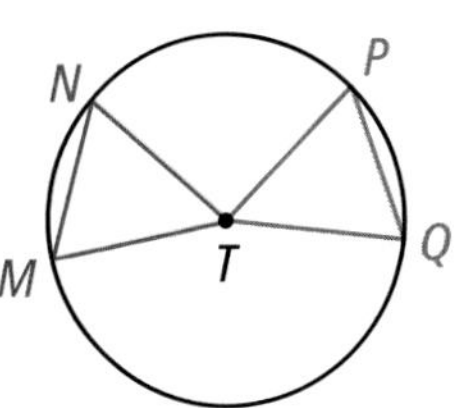

If... $\angle MTN \cong \angle PTQ$
Then... $\overline{MN} \cong \overline{PQ}$

THEOREM 10-4 AND THE CONVERSE

Theorem

If two arcs in a circle or in congruent circles are congruent, then their chords are congruent.

Converse

If two chords in a circle or in congruent circles are congruent, then their arcs are congruent.

PROOF: SEE EXAMPLE 2 AND EXAMPLE 2 TRY IT.

If... $\widehat{MN} \cong \widehat{PQ}$
Then... $\overline{MN} \cong \overline{PQ}$

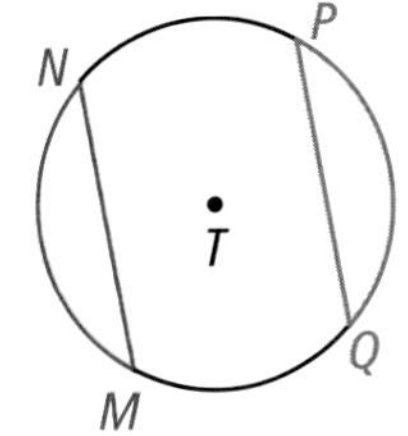

If... $\overline{MN} \cong \overline{PQ}$
Then... $\widehat{MN} \cong \widehat{PQ}$

PROOF

EXAMPLE 2 Relate Arcs and Chords

Write a proof of Theorem 10-4.

Given: $\widehat{AB} \cong \widehat{CD}$

Prove: $\overline{AB} \cong \overline{CD}$

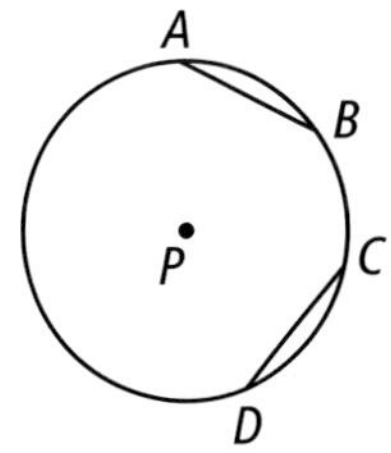

MAKE SENSE AND PERSEVERE Think about other strategies you can use. How could you use congruent triangles to prove the relationship?

Plan: Use the relationship between central angles and arcs by drawing the radii $\overline{PA}$, $\overline{PB}$, $\overline{PC}$, and $\overline{PD}$.

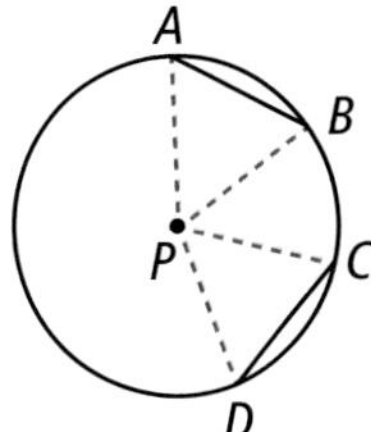

Proof: Since $\widehat{AB} \cong \widehat{CD}$, you know that $m\widehat{AB} = m\widehat{CD}$. And since the measure of a central angle is equal to the measure of its arc, $m\angle APB = m\widehat{AB}$ and $m\angle CPD = m\widehat{CD}$. By substitution, $m\angle APB = m\angle CPD$ and $\angle APB \cong \angle CPD$. So, by the Converse of Theorem 10-3, $\overline{AB} \cong \overline{CD}$.

 **Try It!** **2.** Write a flow proof of the Converse of Theorem 10-4.

THEOREM 10-5 AND THE CONVERSE

Theorem

If chords are equidistant from the center of a circle or the centers of congruent circles, then they are congruent.

Converse

If chords in a circle or in congruent circles are congruent, then they are equidistant from the center or centers.

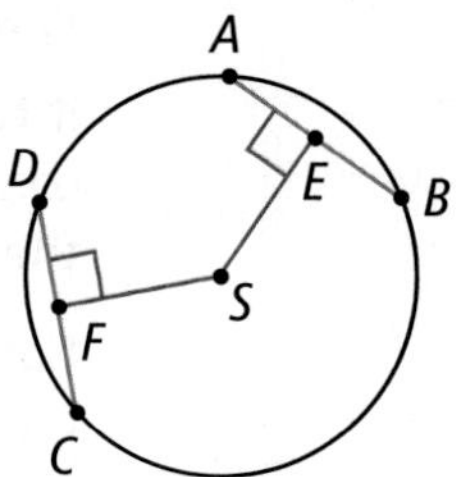

If... $\overline{SE} \cong \overline{SF}$, **Then...** $\overline{AB} \cong \overline{CD}$

If... $\overline{AB} \cong \overline{CD}$, **Then...** $\overline{SE} \cong \overline{SF}$

PROOF: SEE EXAMPLE 3 AND EXAMPLE 3 TRY IT.

PROOF

EXAMPLE 3 Relate Chords Equidistant from the Center

COMMON ERROR
Be sure to construct the triangles with corresponding parts that yield the desired conclusion.

Write a proof of Theorem 10-5.

Given: $\odot P$ with $\overline{AB} \perp \overline{PE}$, $\overline{CD} \perp \overline{PF}$, $\overline{PE} \cong \overline{PF}$

Prove: $\overline{AB} \cong \overline{CD}$

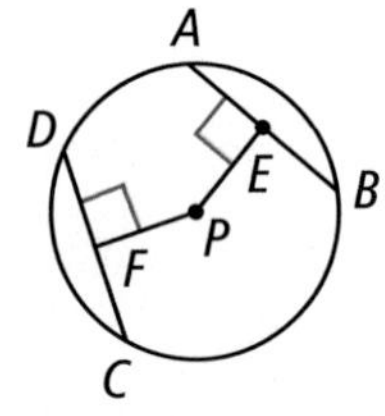

Plan: Construct triangles by drawing the radii $\overline{PA}$, $\overline{PB}$, $\overline{PC}$, and $\overline{PD}$. Then show that the triangles are congruent in order to apply CPCTC.

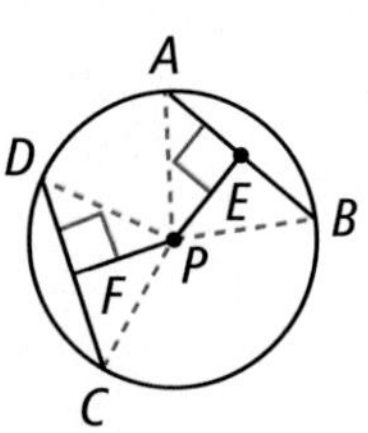

Proof:

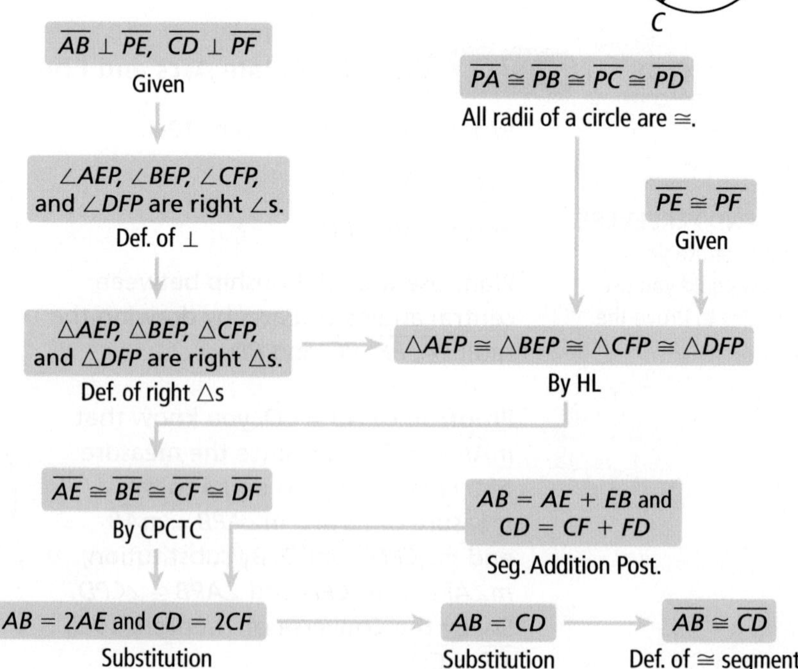

Try It! **3.** Write a flow proof of the Converse of Theorem 10-5.

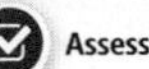

EXAMPLE 4 Construct a Regular Hexagon Inscribed in a Circle

STUDY TIP
Remember, a regular polygon is both equilateral and equiangular.

How do you draw a regular hexagon inscribed in ⊙*P*?

Step 1 Mark point *Q* on the circle.

Step 2 Set the compass the radius of the circle. Place the compass point at *Q* and draw an arc through the circle.

Step 3 Keep the compass setting. Move the compass point to the intersection of the arc and the circle. Draw another arc through the circle. Each point of intersection is a vertex of the hexagon. Continue this way until you have five arcs.

Step 4 Draw chords connecting consecutive points on the circle.

The side lengths of the resulting figure are all congruent because they have the same length as the radius of the circle.

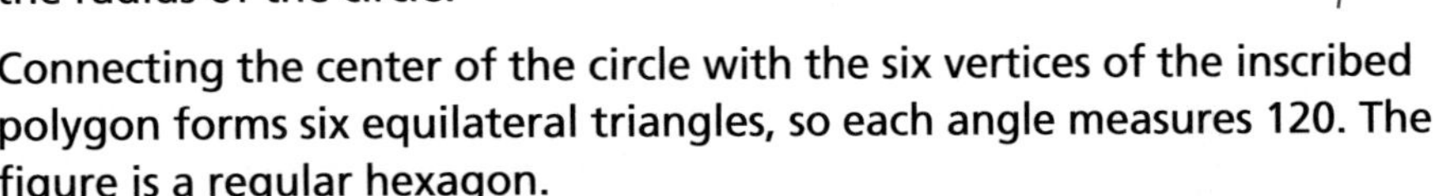

Connecting the center of the circle with the six vertices of the inscribed polygon forms six equilateral triangles, so each angle measures 120. The figure is a regular hexagon.

Try It! **4.** Construct an equilateral triangle inscribed in a circle.

THEOREM 10-6 AND THE CONVERSE

Theorem

If a diameter is perpendicular to a chord, then it bisects the chord.

Converse

If a diameter bisects a chord (that is not a diameter), then it is perpendicular to the chord.

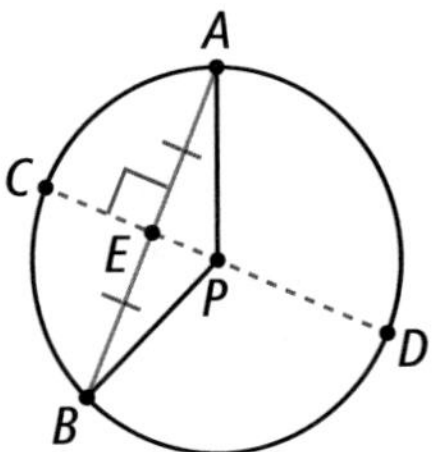

If... $\overline{CD}$ is a diameter, $\overline{AB} \perp \overline{CD}$
Then... $\overline{AE} \cong \overline{BE}$

If... $\overline{CD}$ is a diameter, $\overline{AE} \cong \overline{BE}$
Then... $\overline{AB} \perp \overline{CD}$

PROOF: SEE EXERCISES 15 AND 16.

THEOREM 10-7

The perpendicular bisector of a chord contains the center of the circle.

If...

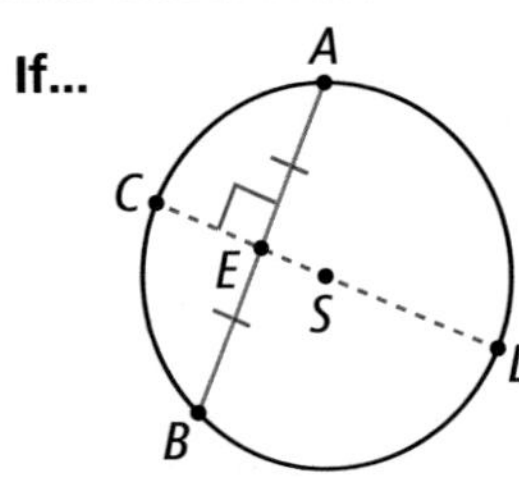

Then... *S* is on $\overline{CD}$

PROOF: SEE EXERCISE 28.

APPLICATION

EXAMPLE 5 Solve Problems Involving Chords of Circles

An engineer is designing a service tunnel to accommodate two trucks simultaneously. If the tunnel can accommodate a width of 18 ft, what is the greatest truck height that the tunnel can accommodate? Subtract 0.5 ft to account for fluctuations in pavement.

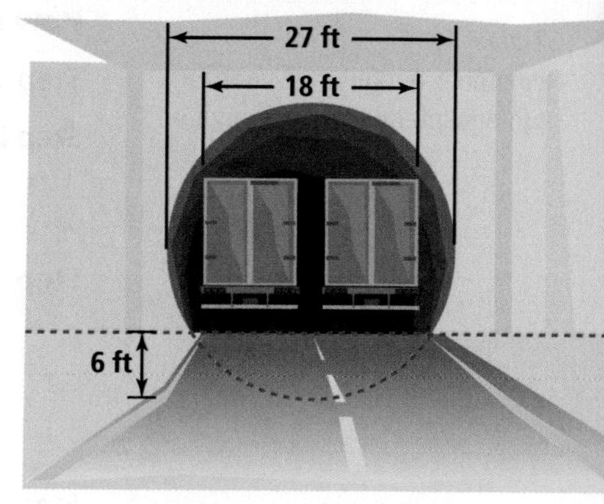

Formulate Draw and label a sketch to help solve the problem.

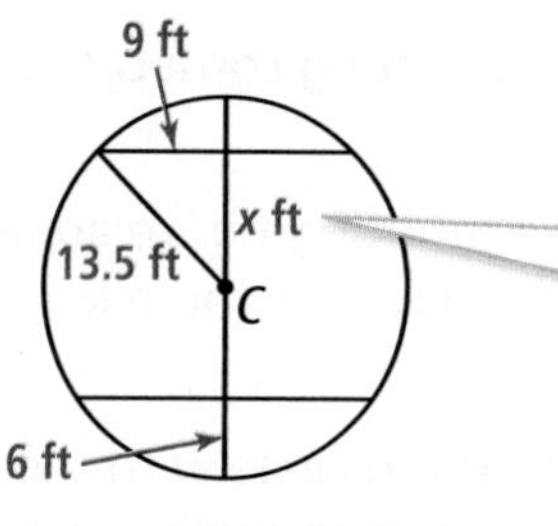

Let x be the distance from the center to the greatest height. The radius is 13.5 ft.

Compute Write and solve an equation for x.

$$9^2 + x^2 = 13.5^2$$

Use the Pythagorean Theorem.

$$x^2 = 13.5^2 - 9^2$$

$$x = \sqrt{13.5^2 - 9^2}$$

$$x \approx 10.06$$

Add the distance from the ground to the center $13.5 - 6 = 7.5$ to x and subtract 0.5 ft to account for fluctuations in pavement.

$$7.5 + 10.06 - 0.5 = 17.06$$

Interpret The greatest height that the tunnel can accommodate is about 17.06 ft.

Try It! 5. Fresh cut flowers need to be in at least 4 inches of water. A spherical vase is filled until the surface of the water is a circle 5 inches in diameter. Is the water deep enough for the flowers? Explain.

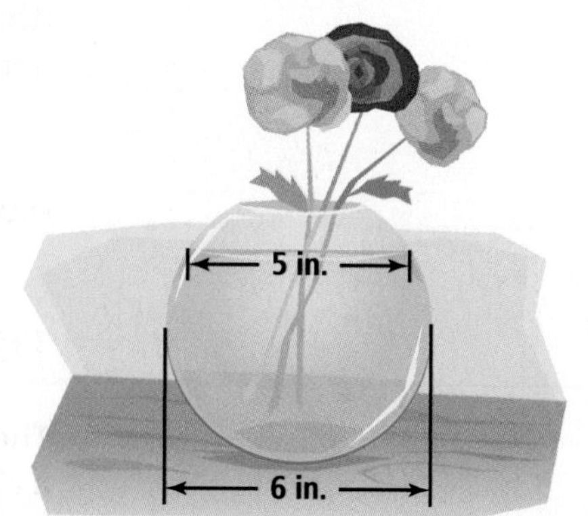

CONCEPT SUMMARY Chords

	Chords and Central Angles	Chords and Arcs
WORDS	Two chords in a circle or in congruent circles are congruent if and only if the central angles of the chords are congruent.	Two chords in a circle or in congruent circles are congruent if and only if the chords intercept congruent arcs.
DIAGRAMS	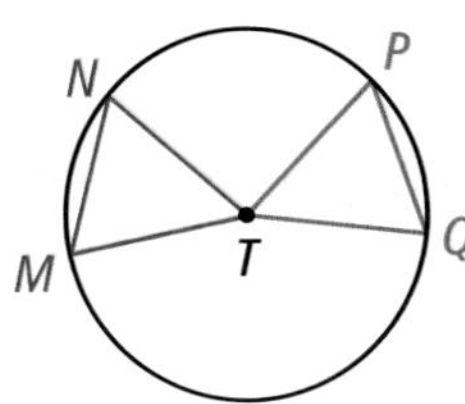 $\angle MTN \cong \angle PTQ$ if and only if $\overline{MN} \cong \overline{PQ}$.	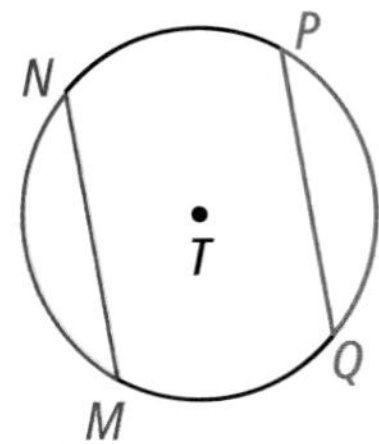 $\overset{\frown}{MN} \cong \overset{\frown}{PQ}$ if and only if $\overline{MN} \cong \overline{PQ}$.

Do You UNDERSTAND?

1. ESSENTIAL QUESTION How are chords related to their central angles and intercepted arcs?

2. **Error Analysis** Sasha writes a proof to show that two chords are congruent. What is her error?

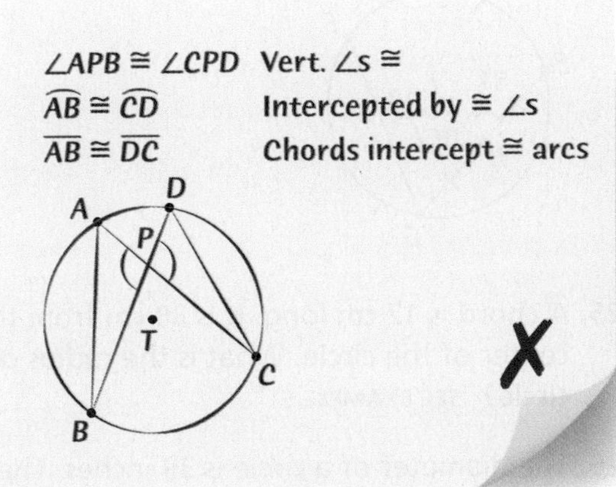

$\angle APB \cong \angle CPD$	Vert. $\angle$s $\cong$
$\overset{\frown}{AB} \cong \overset{\frown}{CD}$	Intercepted by $\cong$ $\angle$s
$\overline{AB} \cong \overline{DC}$	Chords intercept $\cong$ arcs

3. **Vocabulary** Explain why all diameters of circles are also chords of the circles.

4. **Reason** Given $\overset{\frown}{RS} \cong \overset{\frown}{UT}$, how can you find UT?

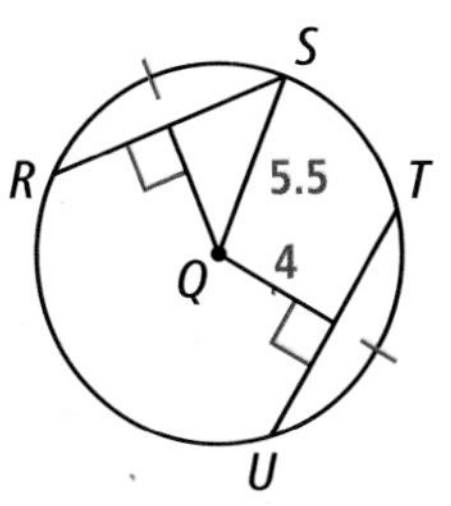

Do You KNOW HOW?

For Exercises 5–10, in $\odot P$, $m\overset{\frown}{AB} = 43°$, and $AC = DF$. Find each measure.

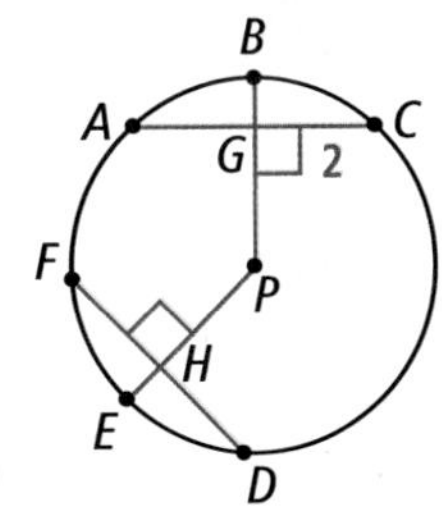

5. DF
6. $m\overset{\frown}{ABC}$
7. FH
8. $m\overset{\frown}{DE}$
9. AC
10. $m\overset{\frown}{DF}$

11. For the corporate headquarters, an executive wants to place a company logo that is six feet in diameter with the sides of the H five feet tall on the front wall. What is the width x of the crossbar for the H?

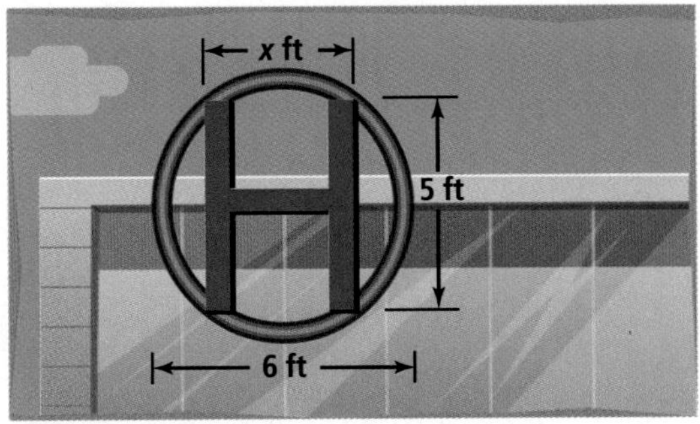

PRACTICE & PROBLEM SOLVING

Scan for Multimedia

Additional Exercises Available Online

UNDERSTAND

12. Construct Arguments Write a paragraph proof of Theorem 10-3.

Given: $\overline{AB} \cong \overline{CD}$

Prove: $\angle AEB \cong \angle CED$

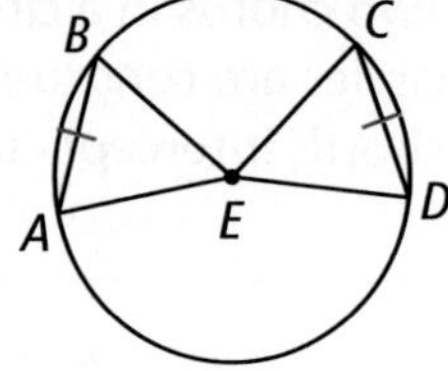

13. Construct Arguments Write a two-column proof of the Converse of Theorem 10-3.

Given: $\angle AEB \cong \angle CED$

Prove: $\overline{AB} \cong \overline{CD}$

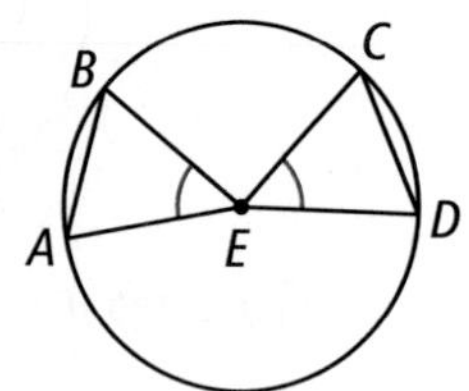

14. Error Analysis What is Ashton's error?

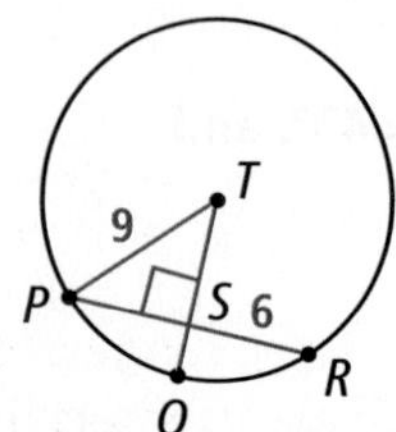

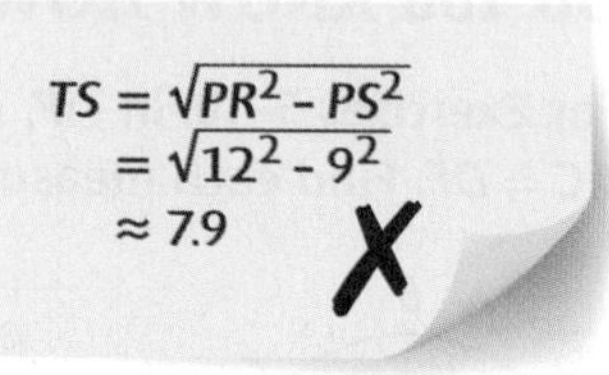

15. Construct Arguments Write a proof of Theorem 10-6.

Given: $\overline{LN}$ is a diameter of $\odot Q$; $\overline{LN} \perp \overline{KM}$

Prove: $\overline{KP} \cong \overline{MP}$

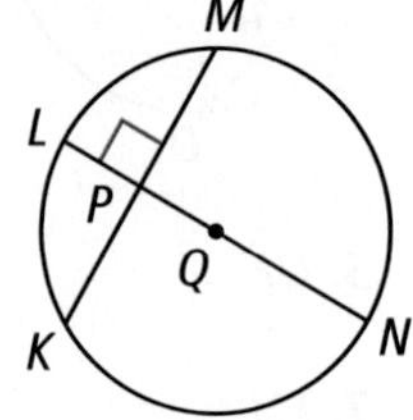

16. Construct Arguments Write a proof of the Converse of Theorem 10-6.

Given: $\overline{LN}$ is a diameter of $\odot Q$; $\overline{KP} \cong \overline{MP}$

Prove: $\overline{LN} \perp \overline{KM}$

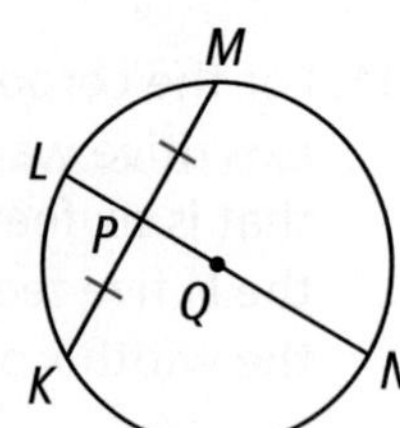

17. Higher Order Thinking $\triangle ABP \sim \triangle CDE$. How do you show that $\widehat{AB} \cong \widehat{CD}$?

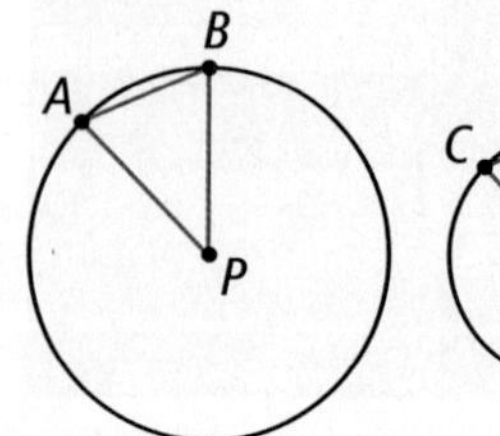

PRACTICE

For Exercises 18–21, in $\odot B$, $m\angle VBT = m\widehat{PR} = 90$, and $QR = TU$. SEE EXAMPLES 1 AND 2

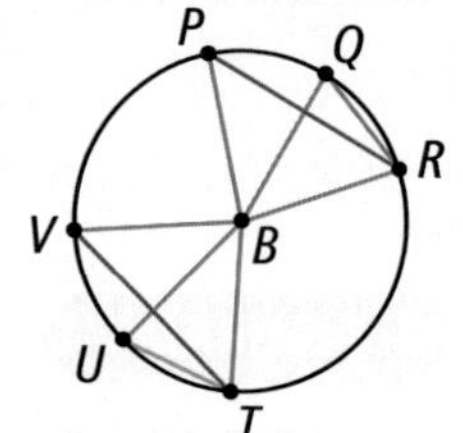

18. Find $m\angle PBR$.

19. Find $m\widehat{TV}$.

20. Which angle is congruent to $\angle QBR$?

21. Which segment is congruent to $\overline{TV}$?

22. Construct a square inscribed in a circle. How is drawing an inscribed square different from drawing an inscribed hexagon or triangle? SEE EXAMPLE 4

23. Find CD. SEE EXAMPLE 3

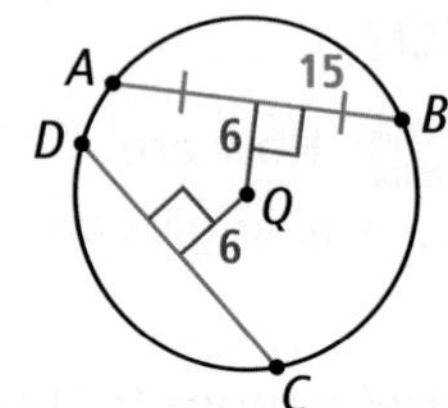

24. Find FG. SEE EXAMPLE 3

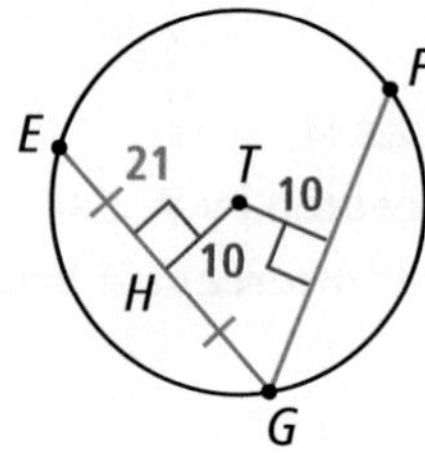

25. A chord is 12 cm long. It is 30 cm from the center of the circle. What is the radius of the circle? SEE EXAMPLE 5

26. The diameter of a circle is 39 inches. The circle has two chords of length 8 inches. What is the distance from each chord to the center of the circle?

27. A chord is 4 units from the center of a circle. The radius of the circle is 5 units. What is the length of the chord?

28. Write a proof of Theorem 10-7.

Given: $\overline{QR}$ is a chord in $\odot P$; $\overline{AB}$ is the perpendicular bisector of $\overline{QR}$.

Prove: $\overline{AB}$ contains P.

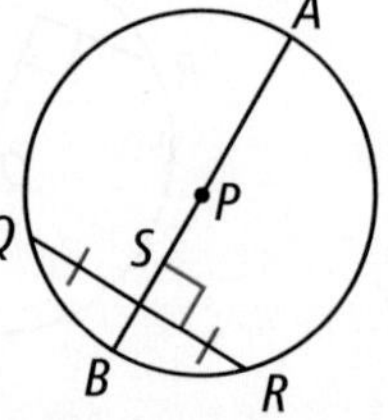

PRACTICE & PROBLEM SOLVING

APPLY

29. Mathematical Connections Nadia designs a water ride and wants to use a half-cylindrical pipe in the construction. If she wants the waterway to be 8 ft wide when the water is 2 ft deep, what is the diameter of the pipe?

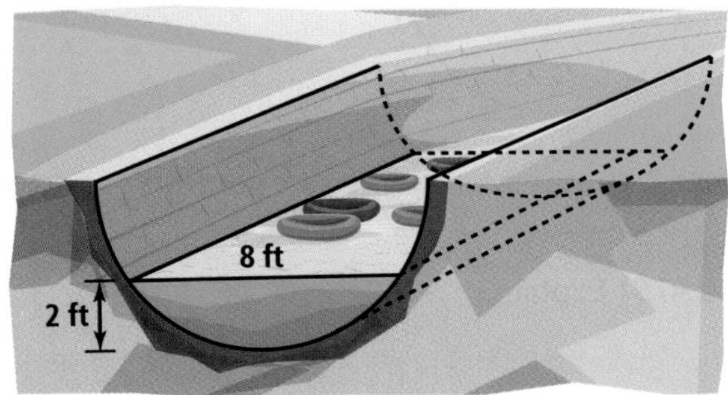

30. Model With Mathematics A bike trail has holes up to 20 in. wide and 5 in. deep. If the diameter of the wheels of Anna's bike is 26 in., can she ride her bike without the wheels hitting the bottom of the holes? Explain.

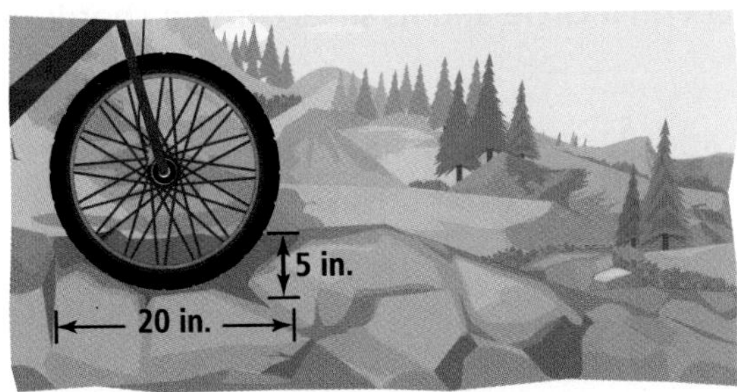

31. Make Sense and Persevere The bottom of a hemispherical cake has diameter 8 in.

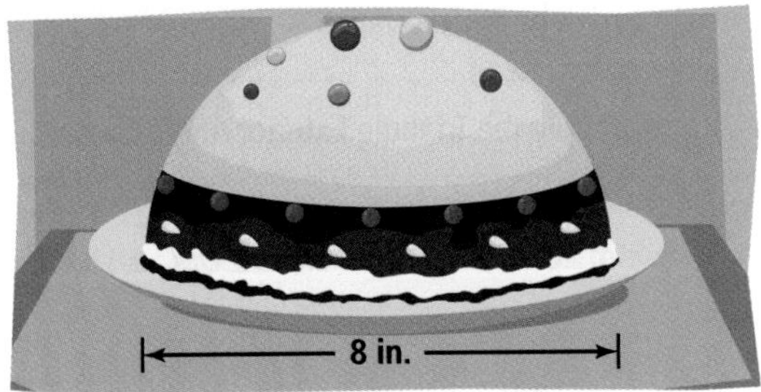

a. If the cake is sliced horizontally in half so each piece has the same height, would the top half fit on a plate with diameter 6 in.? Explain.

b. If the cake is sliced horizontally in thirds so each piece has the same height, would the top third fit on a plate with diameter 5 in.? Explain.

ASSESSMENT PRACTICE

32. Which must be true? Select all that apply.

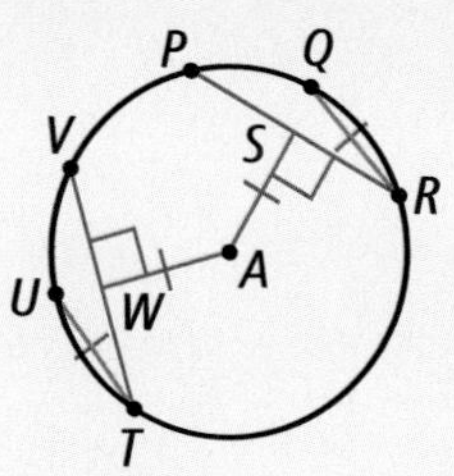

Ⓐ $\overset{\frown}{QR} \cong \overset{\frown}{TU}$

Ⓑ $PR = TV$

Ⓒ $VW = AS$

Ⓓ $PS = SR$

33. SAT/ACT The radius of the semicircle is r, and $CD = \frac{3}{4} \cdot AB$. What is the distance from the chord to the diameter?

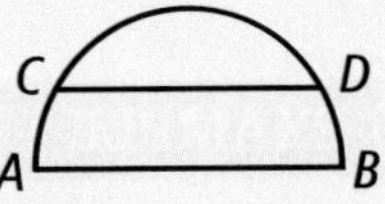

Ⓐ $\frac{5}{4}r$ Ⓑ $\frac{\sqrt{7}}{4}r$ Ⓒ $\frac{\sqrt{7}}{4}\pi r$ Ⓓ $\frac{5}{4}\pi r$

34. Performance Task The radius of the range of a radar is 50 miles. At 1:00 P.M., a plane enters the radar screen flying due north. At 1:04 P.M. the aircraft is due east of the radar. At 1:08 P.M., the aircraft leaves the screen. The plane is moving at 8 miles per minute.

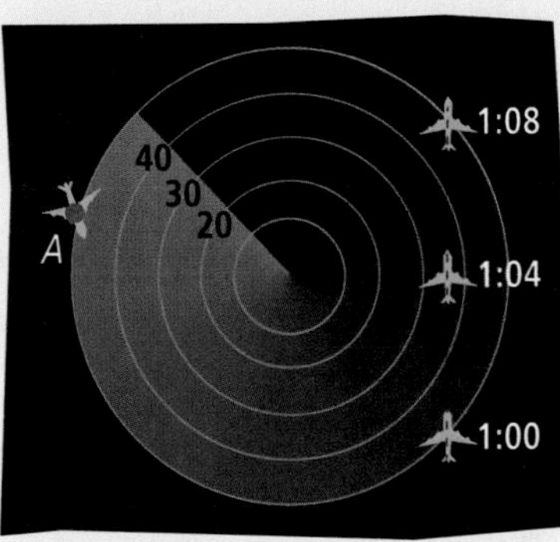

Part A What distance does the plane fly on the controller's screen?

Part B What is the distance of the plane from the radar at 1:04 P.M.?

Part C Another plane enters the screen at point A at 1:12 P.M. and flies in a straight line at 9 miles per minute. If it gets no closer than 40 miles from the radar, at what time does it leave the screen? Explain.

Activity Assess

10-4 Inscribed Angles

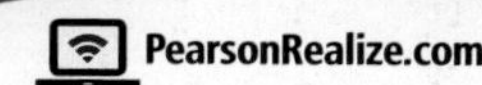
PearsonRealize.com

I CAN... use the relationships between angles and arcs in circles to find their measures.

VOCABULARY

- inscribed angle

EXPLORE & REASON

Consider $\odot T$.

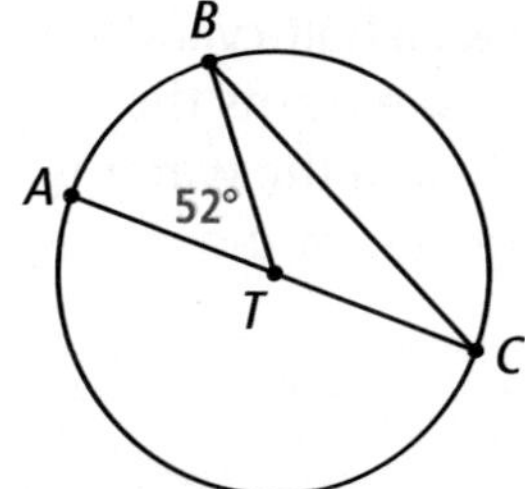

A. Make Sense and Persevere List at least seven things you can conclude about the figure.

B. How is $\angle ACB$ related to $\angle ATB$? Explain.

ESSENTIAL QUESTION How is the measure of an inscribed angle related to its intercepted arc?

CONCEPTUAL UNDERSTANDING

EXAMPLE 1 Relate Inscribed Angles to Intercepted Arcs

What is the relationship between $\overset{\frown}{AB}$ and $\angle ACB$?

An **inscribed angle** has its vertex on a circle and its sides contain chords of the circle.

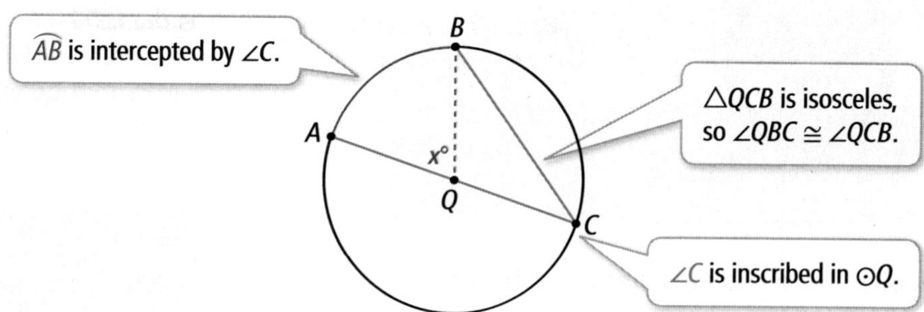

Draw radius $\overline{QB}$ to form $\triangle QCB$ and central angle $\angle AQB$.

$$m\angle QBC + m\angle QCB = x$$

Apply the Triangle Exterior Angle Theorem.

$$2(m\angle QCB) = x$$

$m\angle QBC = m\angle QCB$ since $\angle QBC \cong \angle QCB$.

$$m\angle QCB = \frac{1}{2}x$$

$$m\angle ACB = \frac{1}{2}m\overset{\frown}{AB}$$

$m\angle QCB = m\angle ACB$ and $x = m\overset{\frown}{AB}$.

STUDY TIP

There are an infinite number of inscribed angles that intercept the arc. These inscribed angles all have the same angle measure.

The measure of an inscribed angle $\angle ACB$ is half the measure of the intercepted arc $\overset{\frown}{AB}$.

Try It! **1.** Given $\odot P$ with inscribed angle $\angle S$, if $m\overset{\frown}{RT} = 47$, what is $m\angle S$?

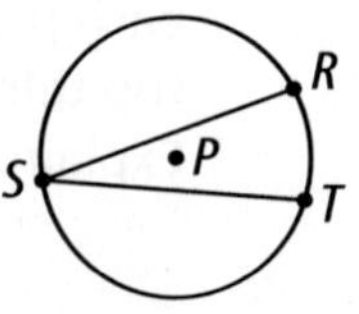

THEOREM 10-8 Inscribed Angles Theorem

The measure of an inscribed angle is half the measure of its intercepted arc.

Case 1

The center is on one side of the angle.

If...

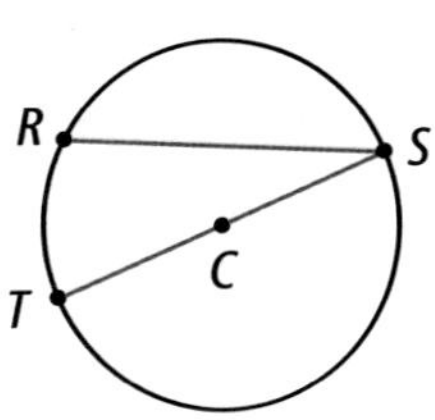

Then... $m\angle S = \frac{1}{2}m\widehat{RT}$

Case 2

The center is inside the angle.

If...

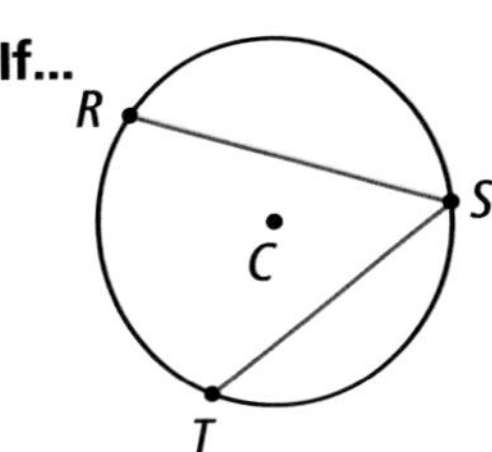

Then... $m\angle S = \frac{1}{2}m\widehat{RT}$

Case 3

The center is outside the angle.

If...

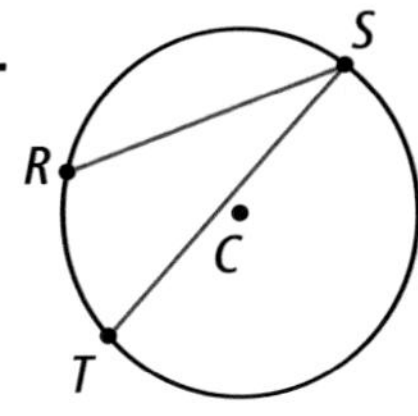

Then... $m\angle S = \frac{1}{2}m\widehat{RT}$

PROOF: SEE EXERCISES 19, 32, AND 33.

EXAMPLE 2 Use the Inscribed Angles Theorem

A. If $m\widehat{DG} = 45.6$, what are $m\angle E$ and $m\angle F$?

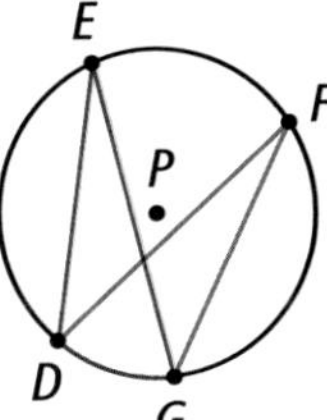

$m\angle E = \frac{1}{2}m\widehat{DG}$

$= \frac{1}{2}(45.6) = 22.8$

$m\angle F = \frac{1}{2}m\widehat{DG}$

$= \frac{1}{2}(45.6) = 22.8$

B. If $\widehat{RT}$ is a semicircle, what is $m\angle RST$?

$m\angle S = \frac{1}{2}m\widehat{RT}$

$= \frac{1}{2}(180) = 90$

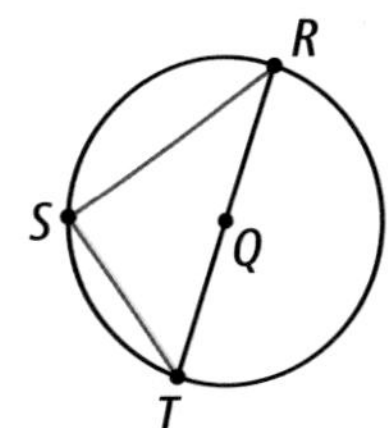

LOOK FOR RELATIONSHIPS
The diameter of a circle is a straight angle. What is the measure of the arc intercepted by a diameter?

C. If $m\widehat{ABC} = 184$ and $m\widehat{BCD} = 242$, what are the measures of the angles of quadrilateral $ABCD$?

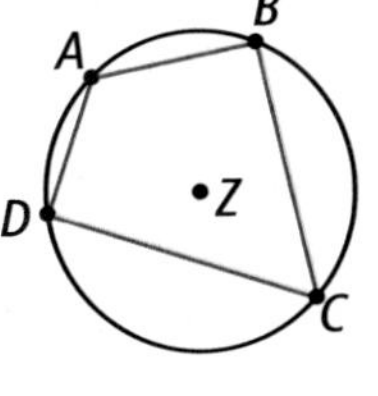

$m\angle A = \frac{1}{2}m\widehat{BCD}$

$= \frac{1}{2}(242) = 121$

$m\angle B = \frac{1}{2}m\widehat{ADC}$

$= \frac{1}{2}(360 - 184) = 88$

$m\angle D = \frac{1}{2}m\widehat{ABC}$

$= \frac{1}{2}(184) = 92$

$m\angle C = 360 - (121 + 88 + 92)$

$= 59$

Try It! **2. a.** If $m\widehat{RST} = 164$, what is $m\angle RVT$?

b. If $m\angle SPU = 79$, what is $m\widehat{STU}$?

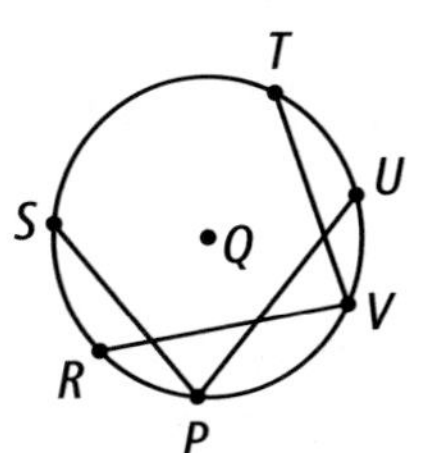

COROLLARIES TO THE INSCRIBED ANGLES THEOREM

Corollary 1

Two inscribed angles that intercept the same arc are congruent.

If...

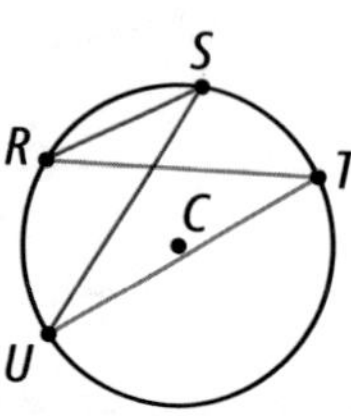

Then... $\angle S \cong \angle T$

Corollary 2

An angle inscribed in a semicircle is a right angle.

If... $m\widehat{RS} = 180$

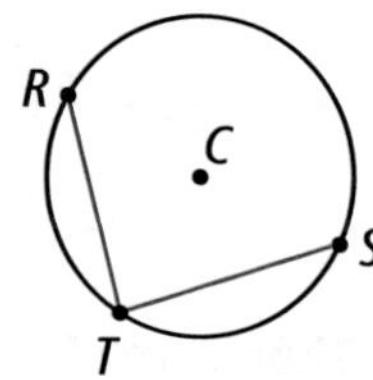

Then... $m\angle T = 90$

Corollary 3

The opposite angles of an inscribed quadrilateral are supplementary.

If...

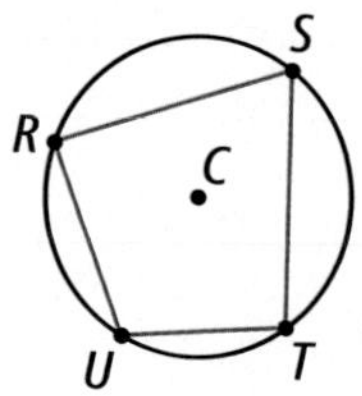

Then...

$m\angle R + m\angle T = 180$

$m\angle S + m\angle U = 180$

EXAMPLE 3 Explore Angles Formed by a Tangent and a Chord

Given chord $\overline{FH}$ and $\overleftrightarrow{HJ}$ tangent to $\odot E$ at point H, what is the relationship between $\angle FHJ$ and $\widehat{FGH}$?

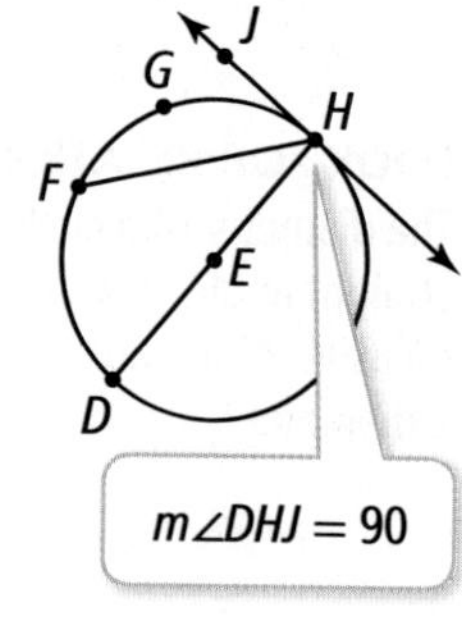

Consider the angles and arcs formed by the chord, tangent line, and diameter.

Let $m\angle FHJ = x$, so $m\angle FHD = 90 - x$.

$$m\angle FHD = \frac{1}{2}m\widehat{DF}$$

Use the Inscribed Angles Theorem.

$$90 - x = \frac{1}{2}m\widehat{DF}$$

$$m\widehat{DF} = 180 - 2x$$

Since $\overline{DH}$ is a diameter, $m\widehat{DFH} = 180$.

$$m\widehat{DF} + m\widehat{FGH} = m\widehat{DFH}$$

$$180 - 2x + m\widehat{FGH} = 180$$

$$m\widehat{FGH} = 2x$$

$$m\widehat{FGH} = 2m\angle FHJ$$

$$m\angle FHJ = \frac{1}{2}m\widehat{FGH}$$

COMMON ERROR

Be careful not to assume arc measure relationships such as assuming $m\widehat{DF} = m\widehat{FH}$. Think about concepts and theorems you can apply when writing mathematical statements.

Try It! **3. a.** Given $\overleftrightarrow{BD}$ tangent to $\odot P$ at point C, if $m\widehat{AC} = 88$, what is $m\angle ACB$?

b. Given $\overleftrightarrow{EG}$ tangent to $\odot P$ at point F, if $m\angle GFC = 115$, what is $m\widehat{FAC}$?

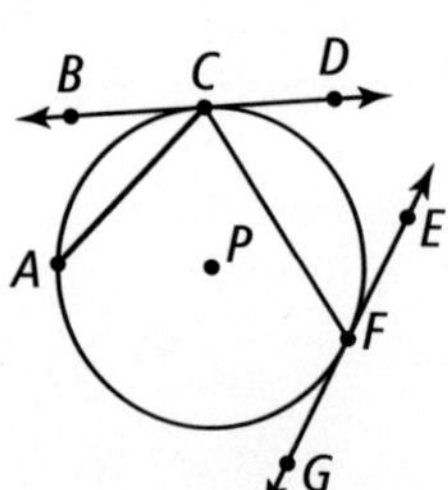

THEOREM 10-9

The measure of an angle formed by a tangent and a chord is half the measure of its intercepted arc.

If...

PROOF: SEE EXERCISE 34.

Then... $m\angle AED = \frac{1}{2}m\widehat{ABE}$

APPLICATION

EXAMPLE 4 Use Arc Measure to Solve a Problem

A director wants to position two cameras to capture an entire circular backdrop behind two newscasters. Where should he position the cameras?

Formulate ◀ Represent the set as a chord $\overline{AB}$ of a circle that intercepts an arc measuring 90°.

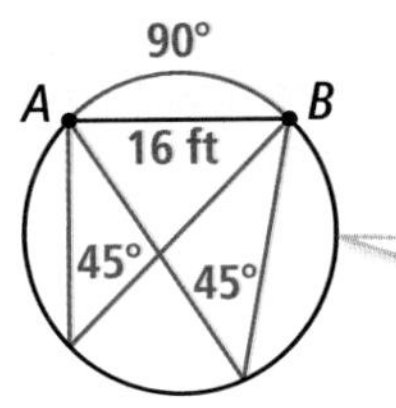

Any point on the major arc $\widehat{AB}$ is the vertex of a 45° angle that intercepts arc $\widehat{AB}$.

To find the size of the circle, find the radius of the circle.

Compute ◀ Let P be the center of the circle.

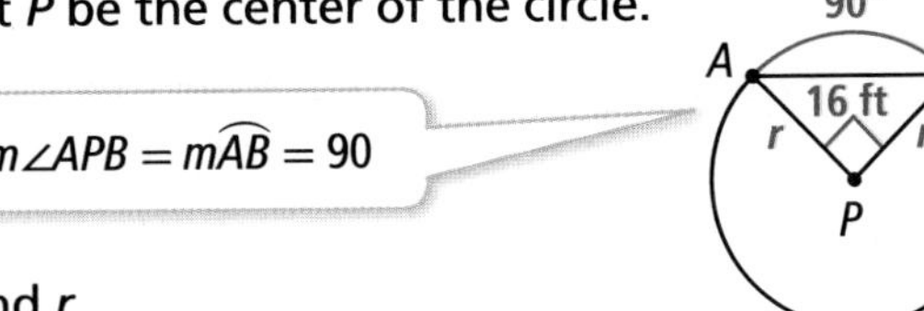

$m\angle APB = m\widehat{AB} = 90$

Find r.

$$\sqrt{2} \cdot r = 16$$
$$r = \frac{16}{\sqrt{2}}$$
$$r = 8\sqrt{2}$$

$\triangle APB$ is a 45°-45°-90° triangle, and the length of the hypotenuse is 16.

Center P is on the perpendicular bisector of $\overline{AB}$, so P is 8 ft from the midpoint of $\overline{AB}$.

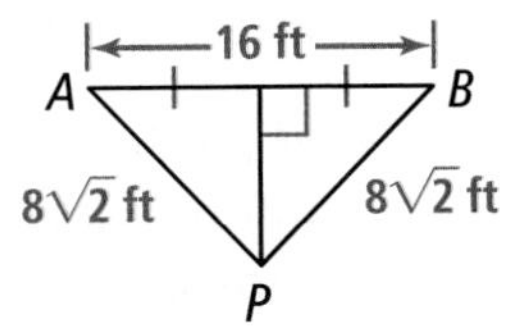

Interpret ◀ Position a camera on any point of circle with radius $8\sqrt{2}$ ft and center 8 ft from the midpoint of the set.

Try It! **4. a.** Given $\overleftrightarrow{WY}$ tangent to $\odot C$ at point X, what is $m\widehat{XZ}$?

b. What is $m\angle VXW$?

CONCEPT SUMMARY Inscribed Angles and Intercepted Arcs

	Inscribed Angles	Angles Formed by a Tangent and a Chord
WORDS	The measure of an inscribed angle is one-half the measure of its intercepted arc.	The measure of an angle formed by a tangent and a chord is one-half the measure of its intercepted arc.
DIAGRAMS	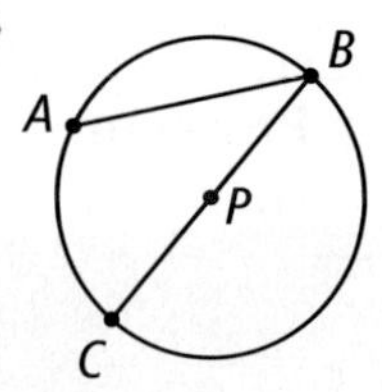 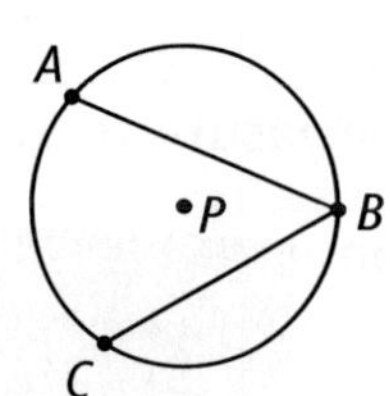 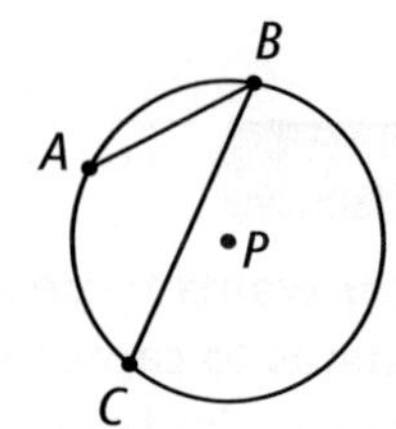	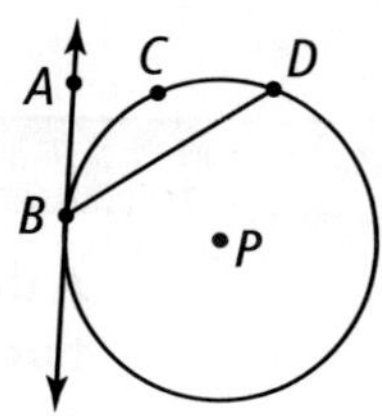
SYMBOLS	$m\angle ABC = \frac{1}{2}m\widehat{AC}$	$m\angle ABD = \frac{1}{2}m\widehat{BCD}$

Do You UNDERSTAND?

1. ESSENTIAL QUESTION How is the measure of an inscribed angle related to its intercepted arc?

2. **Error Analysis** Darren is asked to find $m\widehat{XZ}$. What is his error?

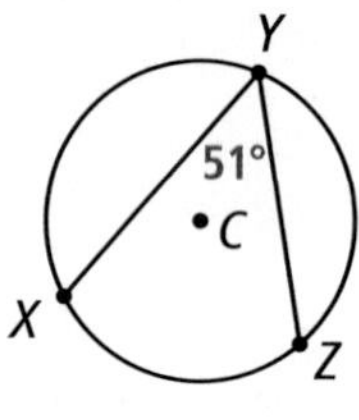

$m\widehat{XZ} = \frac{1}{2}\ m\angle XYZ$

$= \frac{1}{2}(51)$ ✗

$= 25.5$

3. **Reason** Can the measure of an inscribed angle be greater than the measure of the intercepted arc? Explain.

4. **Make Sense and Persevere** Is there enough information in the diagram to find $m\widehat{RST}$? Explain.

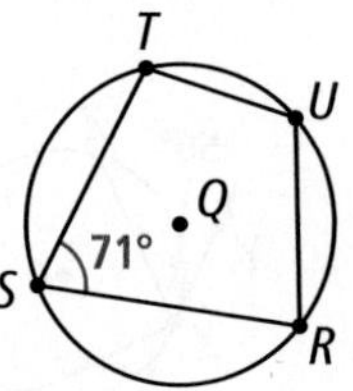

Do You KNOW HOW?

For Exercises 5–8, find each measure in ⊙*Q*.

5. $m\widehat{JKL}$

6. $m\widehat{MJ}$

7. $m\angle KJM$

8. $m\angle KLM$

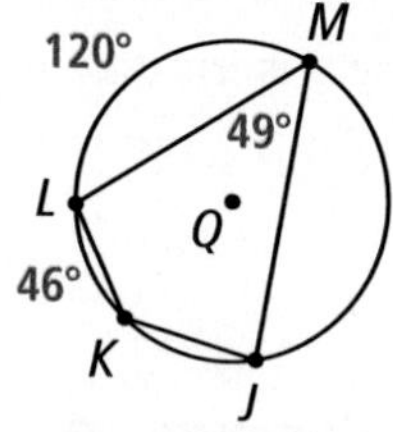

For Exercises 9–12, $\overleftrightarrow{DF}$ is tangent to ⊙*Q* at point *E*. Find each measure.

9. $m\widehat{EGH}$

10. $m\widehat{EKJ}$

11. $m\angle HEJ$

12. $m\angle DEJ$

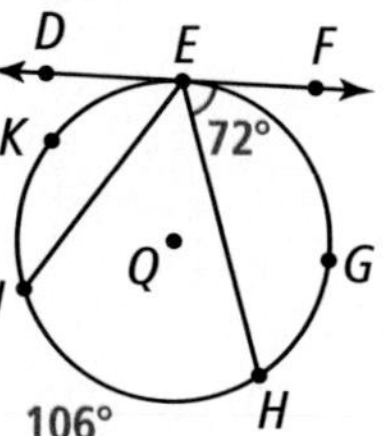

For Exercises 13–16, find each measure in ⊙*M*.

13. $m\angle PRQ$

14. $m\angle PTR$

15. $m\angle RST$

16. $m\angle SRT$

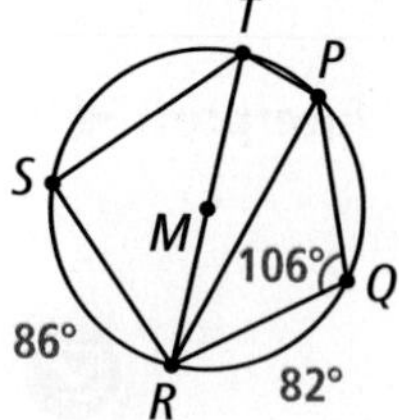

PRACTICE & PROBLEM SOLVING

Scan for Multimedia   

Additional Exercises Available Online

UNDERSTAND

17. Mathematical Connections Given $m\widehat{ABC} = x$, what is an expression for $m\widehat{DAB}$ in terms of x? Explain.

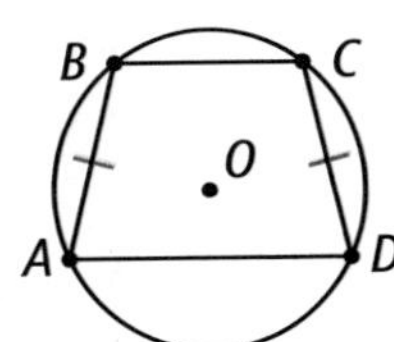

18. Error Analysis Casey is asked to find $m\widehat{WVZ}$. What is Casey's error?

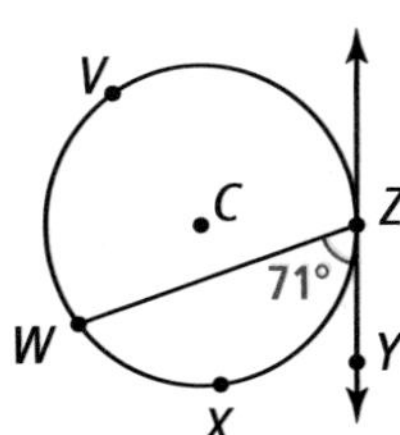

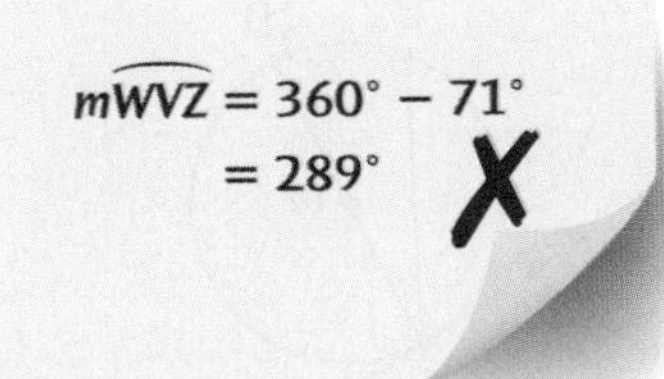

19. Higher Order Thinking Write a proof of the Inscribed Angles Theorem, Case 2.

Given: Center C is inside $\angle RST$.

Prove: $m\angle RST = \frac{1}{2}m\widehat{RT}$

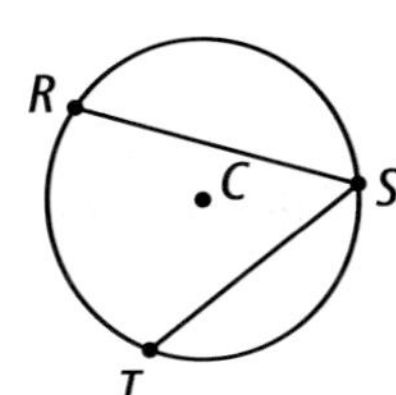

20. Construct Arguments Margaret measures $\angle HGK$ with a protractor and says that it is 98°. Is Margaret's answer reasonable? Explain.

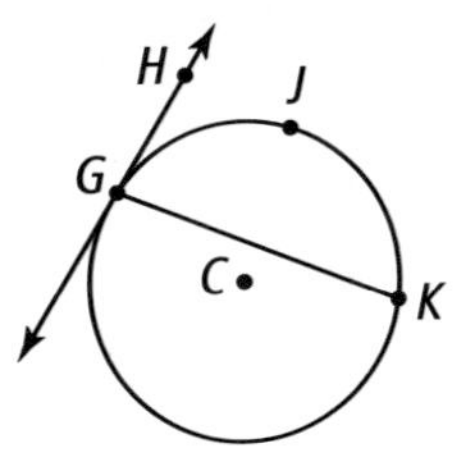

21. Use Structure Given $\odot Q$ with diameter $\overline{AC}$, if point B is located on $\odot Q$, can $\angle ABC$ ever be less than 90°? Can it ever be greater than 90°? Explain.

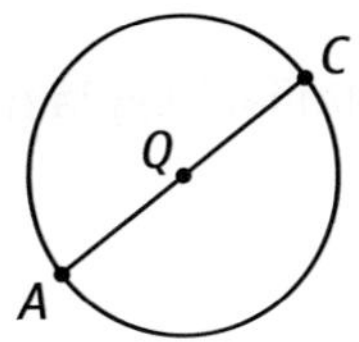

PRACTICE

For Exercises 22–25, find each measure in $\odot P$.
SEE EXAMPLES 1 AND 2

22. $m\widehat{AD}$

23. $m\widehat{BDC}$

24. $m\angle ADC$

25. $m\angle BAD$

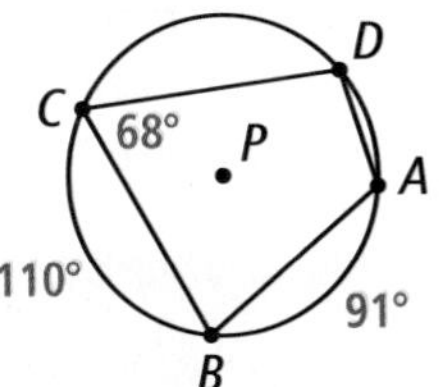

For Exercises 26–28, $\overleftrightarrow{SU}$ is tangent to $\odot P$ at point T. Find each measure. SEE EXAMPLES 2 AND 3

26. $m\widehat{TVW}$

27. $m\angle TWX$

28. $m\angle TWV$

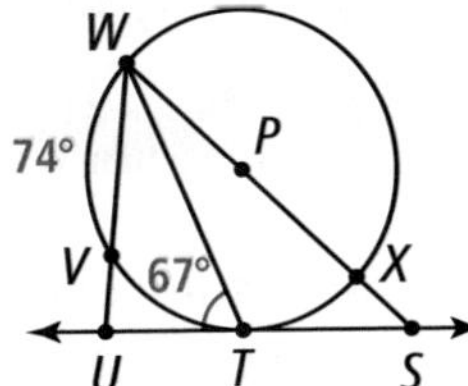

For Exercises 29–31, $\overleftrightarrow{HK}$ is tangent to $\odot C$ at point J. Find each measure. SEE EXAMPLES 3 AND 4

29. $m\angle KJM$

30. $m\angle MJN$

31. $m\angle HJN$

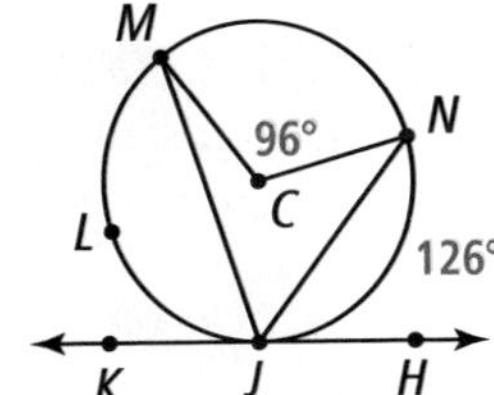

32. Write a proof of the Inscribed Angles Theorem, Case 1.

Given: Center C is on $\overline{ST}$.

Prove: $m\angle RST = \frac{1}{2}m\widehat{RT}$

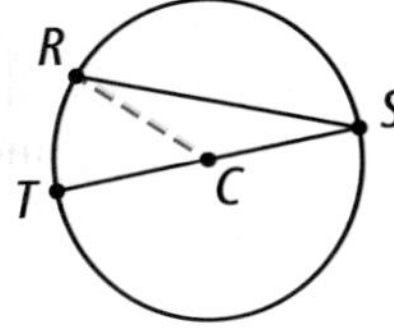

33. Write a proof of the Inscribed Angles Theorem, Case 3.

Given: Center C is outside $\angle RST$.

Prove: $m\angle RST = \frac{1}{2}m\widehat{RT}$

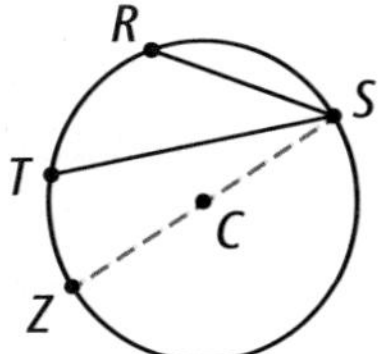

34. Write a two-column proof of Theorem 10-9.

Given: $\overleftrightarrow{AB}$ tangent to $\odot P$ at point B.

Prove: $m\angle ABD = \frac{1}{2}m\widehat{BCD}$

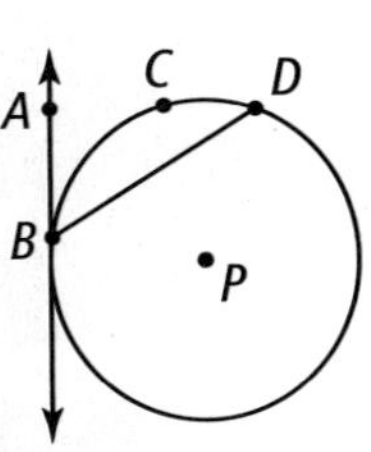

PRACTICE & PROBLEM SOLVING

Practice | Tutorial

Mixed Review Available Online

APPLY

35. Construct Arguments Deondra needs to know the angle measure for each notch in the 16-notch socket wrench she is designing. The notches will be the same size. What is the angle measure?

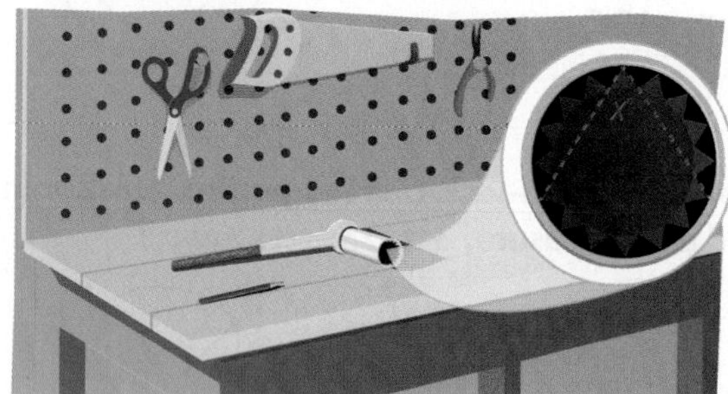

36. Use Structure Cheyenne wants to make a replica of an antique sundial using the fragment of the sundial she acquired. Is there enough information for her to determine the diameter of the sundial? Explain.

37. Use Appropriate Tools Malcom sets up chairs for a home theater showing on his television. His optimal viewing angle is 50°. Besides at chair A, where else could he sit with the same viewing angle? Draw a diagram and explain.

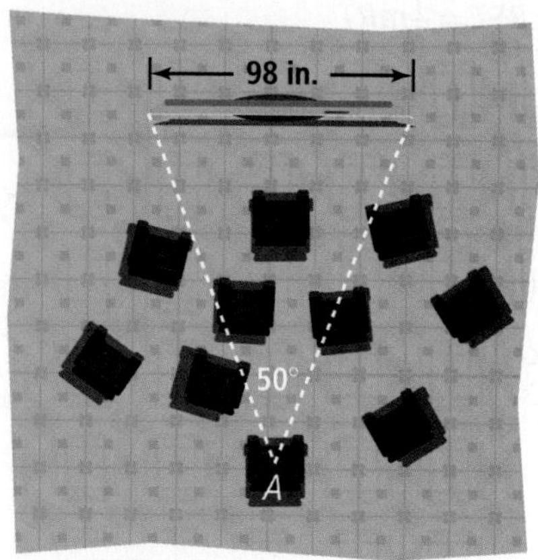

ASSESSMENT PRACTICE

38. Write an expression that represents $m\angle DGF$.

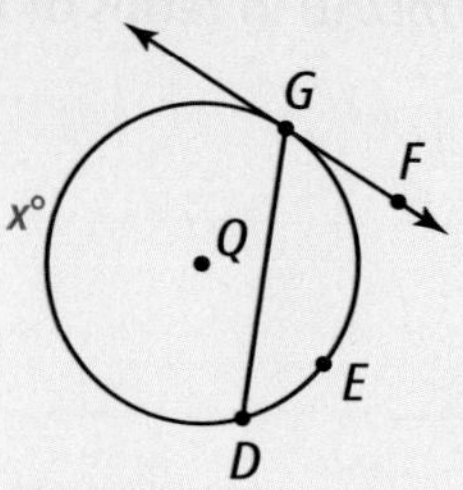

39. SAT/ACT Segment AB is tangent to $\odot M$ at Point A. What is $m\angle DAC$?

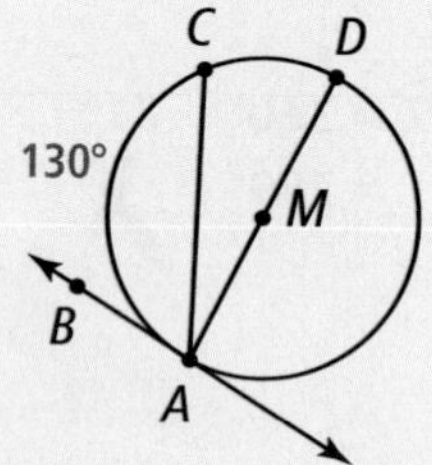

Ⓐ 25

Ⓑ 65

Ⓒ 50

Ⓓ 90

Ⓔ 100

40. Performance Task Triangle DEF is inscribed in $\odot G$, and $\overline{AB}$, $\overline{BC}$, and $\overline{AC}$ are tangent to $\odot G$.

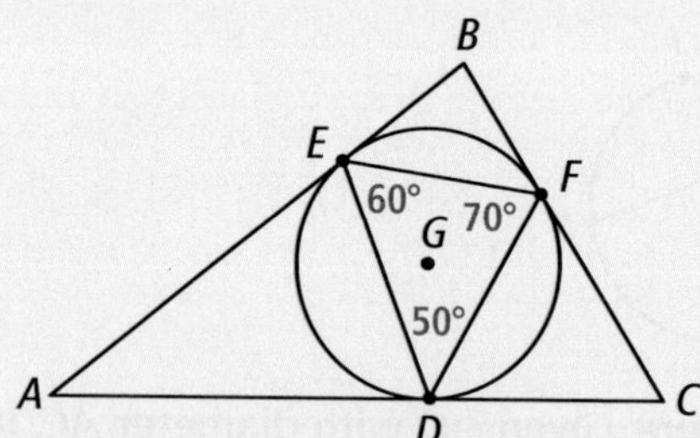

Part A Are there any isosceles triangles in the diagram? If so, explain why the triangles are isosceles. If not, explain why not.

Part B Are $\triangle ABC$ and $\triangle DEF$ similar? Explain.

  Activity 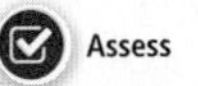 Assess

10-5 Secant Lines and Segments

PearsonRealize.com

I CAN… use angle measures and segment lengths formed by intersecting lines and circles to solve problems.

VOCABULARY

- secant

EXPLORE & REASON

Skyler made the design shown. Points *A*, *B*, *C*, and *D* are spaced evenly around the circle.

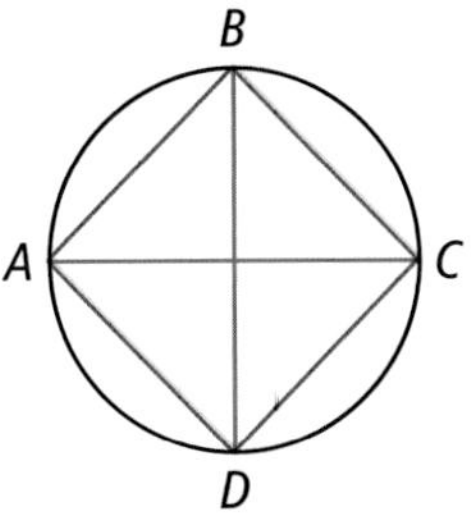

A. Using points *A*, *B*, *C*, and *D* as vertices, what congruent angles can you find? How can you justify that they are congruent?

B. Make Sense and Persevere What strategy did you use to make sure you found all congruent angles?

ESSENTIAL QUESTION

How are the measures of angles, arcs, and segments formed by intersecting secant lines related?

CONCEPTUAL UNDERSTANDING

EXAMPLE 1 Relate Secants and Angle Measures

A secant is a line, ray, or segment that intersects a circle at two points. Secants $\overleftrightarrow{AC}$ and $\overleftrightarrow{BD}$ intersect to form ∠1. How can you use arc measures to find $m\angle 1$?

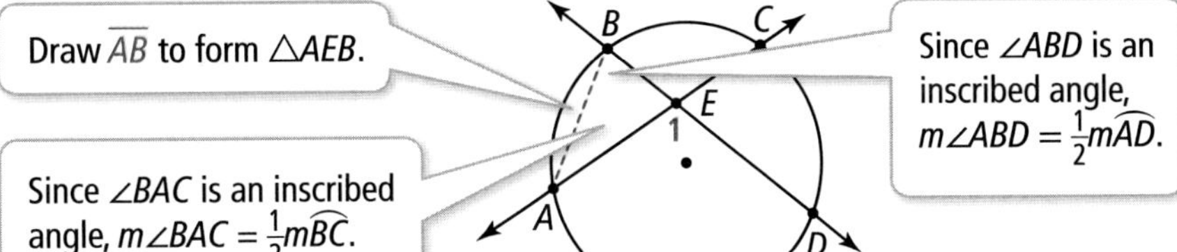

MAKE SENSE AND PERSEVERE Consider other relationships in the diagram. What is an alternate plan you could use to solve the problem?

Apply the Triangle Exterior Angle Theorem.

$$m\angle 1 = m\angle ABD + m\angle BAC$$
$$= \frac{1}{2}m\widehat{AD} + \frac{1}{2}m\widehat{BC}$$

So the measure of the angle is half the sum of the measures of the two intercepted arcs.

Try It! **1.** If $m\widehat{AD} = 155$ and $m\widehat{BC} = 61$, what is $m\angle 1$?

THEOREM 10-10

The measure of an angle formed by two secant lines that intersect inside a circle is half the sum of the measures of the intercepted arcs.

If...

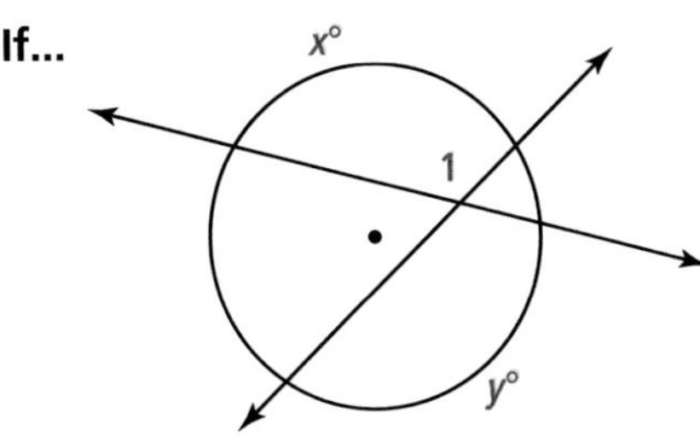

Then... $m\angle 1 = \frac{1}{2}(x + y)$

PROOF: SEE EXERCISE 18.

THEOREM 10-11

The measure of an angle formed by two lines that intersect outside a circle is half the difference of the measures of the intercepted arcs.

Case 1	Case 2	Case 3
If... 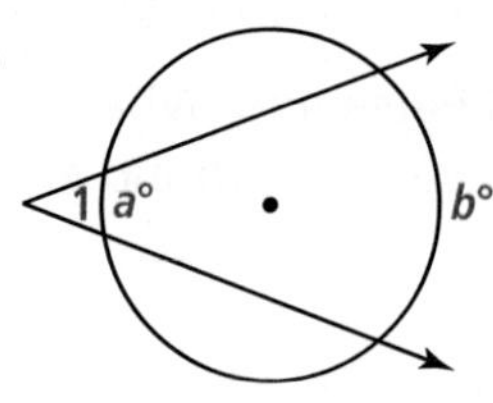	**If...** 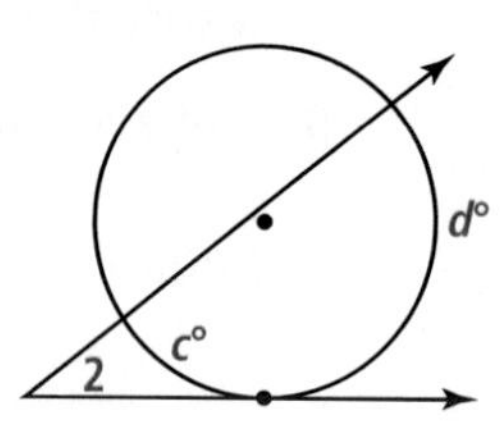	**If...** 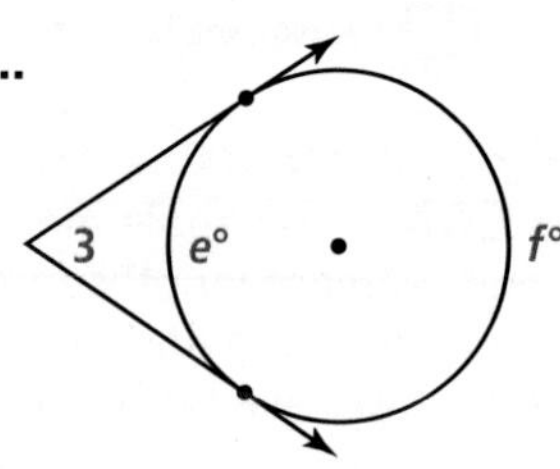
Then... $m\angle 1 = \frac{1}{2}(b - a)$	**Then...** $m\angle 2 = \frac{1}{2}(d - c)$	**Then...** $m\angle 3 = \frac{1}{2}(f - e)$

PROOF: SEE EXAMPLE 2, TRY IT 2, AND EXERCISE 19.

EXAMPLE 2 Prove Theorem 10-11, Case 1

Write a proof for Theorem 10-11, Case 1.

Given: Secants $\overrightarrow{PS}$ and $\overrightarrow{PT}$

Prove: $m\angle P = \frac{1}{2}(m\widehat{ST} - m\widehat{QR})$

Proof:

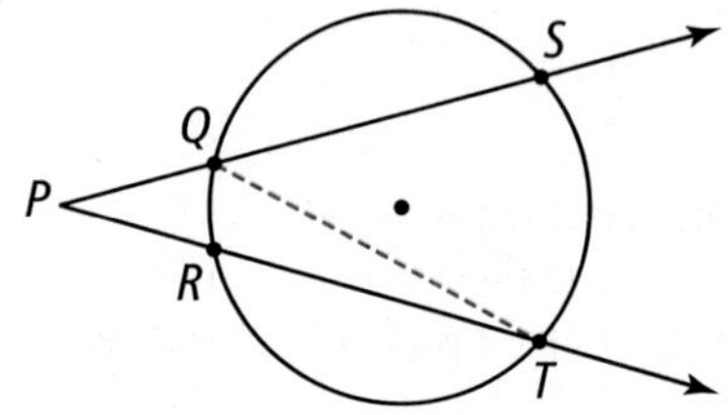

Statement	Reason
1) $\overrightarrow{PS}$ and $\overrightarrow{PT}$ are secants.	**1)** Given
2) Draw $\overline{QT}$.	**2)** Two points determine a segment.
3) $m\angle QTP = \frac{1}{2}m\widehat{QR}$	**3)** Inscribed Angles Theorem
4) $m\angle SQT = \frac{1}{2}m\widehat{ST}$	**4)** Inscribed Angles Theorem
5) $m\angle SQT = m\angle P + m\angle QTP$	**5)** Triangle Exterior Angle Theorem
6) $m\angle P = m\angle SQT - m\angle QTP$	**6)** Subtraction Property of Equality
7) $m\angle P = \frac{1}{2}m\widehat{ST} - \frac{1}{2}m\widehat{QR}$	**7)** Substitution
8) $m\angle P = \frac{1}{2}(m\widehat{ST} - m\widehat{QR})$	**8)** Distributive Property

STUDY TIP
Remember to look for helpful relationships that you can draw on the given figure when completing a proof. Drawing $\overline{QT}$ forms inscribed angles, which are needed for this proof.

Try It! **2.** Prove Theorem 10-11, Case 2.

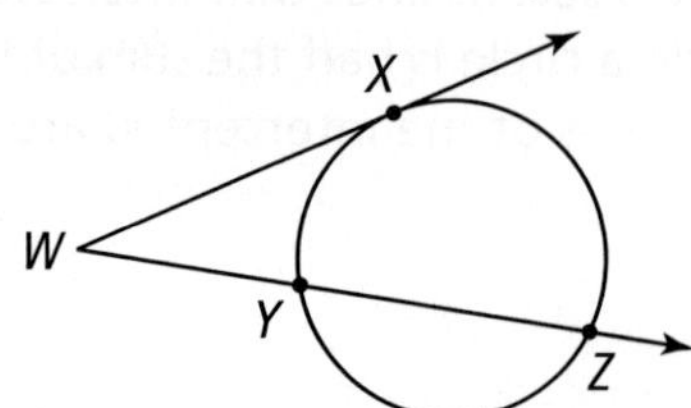

EXAMPLE 3 Use Secants and Tangents to Solve Problems

A. What is $m\angle ABD$?

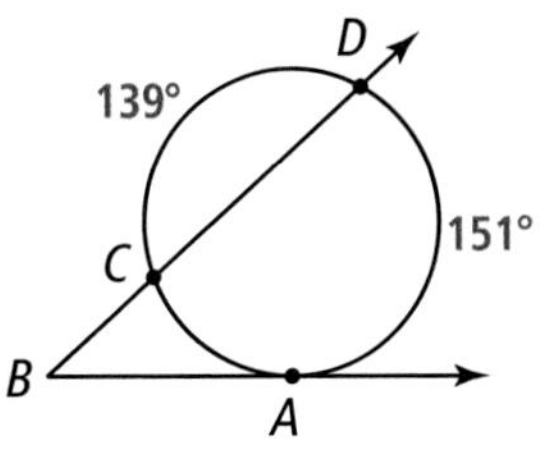

Step 1 Find $m\widehat{AC}$.

$$m\widehat{AC} = 360 - m\widehat{AD} - m\widehat{CD}$$
$$= 360 - 151 - 139$$
$$= 70$$

Step 2 Find $m\angle ABD$.

$$m\angle ABD = \frac{1}{2}(m\widehat{AD} - m\widehat{AC})$$
$$= \frac{1}{2}(151 - 70)$$
$$= 40.5$$

Since the angle is formed outside the circle by a secant and a tangent, apply Theorem 10-11, Case 2.

B. What is $m\widehat{LM}$?

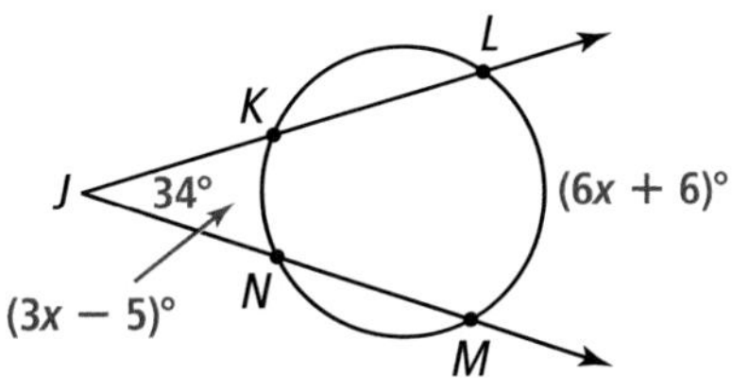

Step 1 Find x.

$$m\angle LJM = \frac{1}{2}(m\widehat{LM} - m\widehat{KN})$$
$$34 = \frac{1}{2}((6x + 6) - (3x - 5))$$
$$34 = \frac{1}{2}(3x + 11)$$
$$68 = 3x + 11$$
$$19 = x$$

Since the angle is formed outside the circle by two secants, apply Theorem 10-11, Case 1.

COMMON ERROR
Remember to add the arc measures when the vertex is inside the circle and to subtract them when it is outside the circle.

Step 2 Find $m\widehat{LM}$.

$$m\widehat{LM} = 6x + 6$$
$$= 6(19) + 6$$
$$= 120$$

Substitute the value of x found in Step 1.

Try It! **3. a.** What is $m\widehat{WX}$?

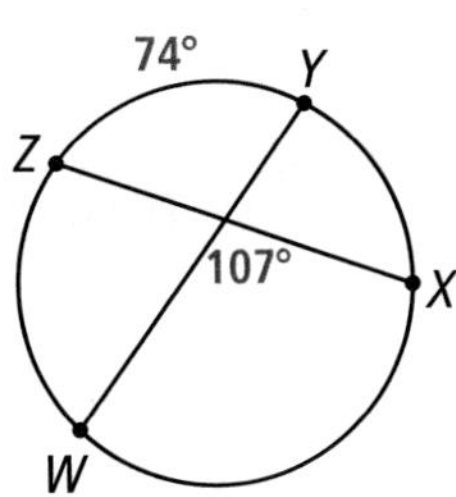

b. What is $m\angle PSQ$?

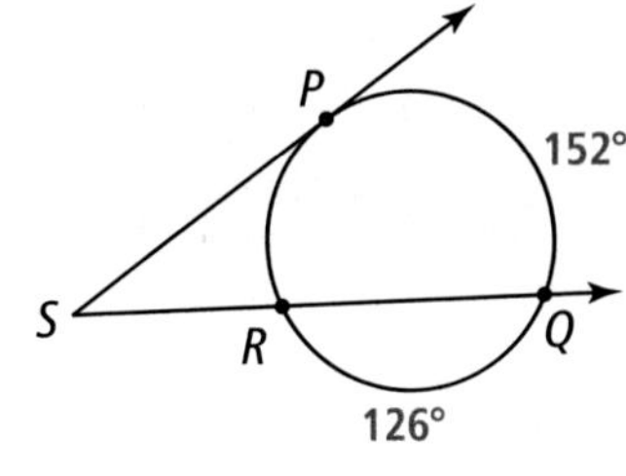

EXAMPLE 4 Develop Chord Length Relationships

What is the value of x?

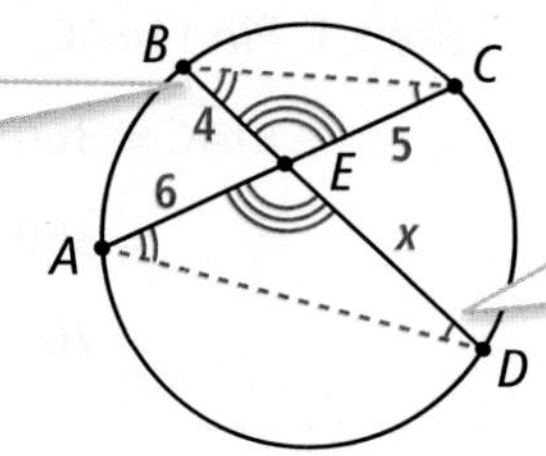

By the Angle-Angle Similarity Theorem, $\triangle AED \sim \triangle BEC$.

$$\frac{ED}{EC} = \frac{EA}{EB}$$

$$\frac{x}{5} = \frac{6}{4}$$

$$4 \cdot x = 6 \cdot 5$$

$$x = 7.5$$

The ratios of corresponding sides of similar triangles are equal.

The value of x is 7.5.

COMMON ERROR
Be careful to correctly identify corresponding sides in similar triangles. The sides opposite congruent angles are the corresponding sides.

Try It! **4.** What is the value of y?

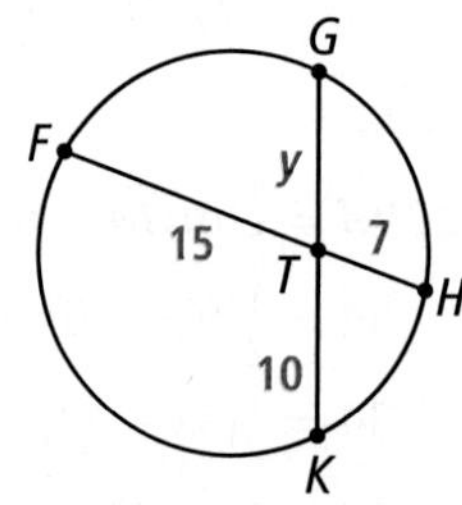

THEOREM 10-12

For a given point and circle, the product of the lengths of the two segments from the point to the circle is constant along any line through the point and circle.

Case 1	Case 2	Case 3
If... 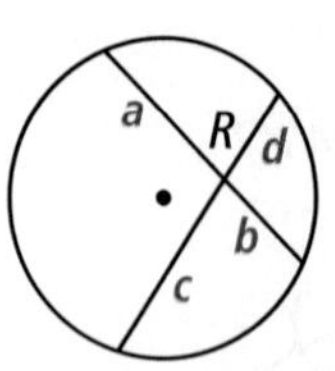	**If...** 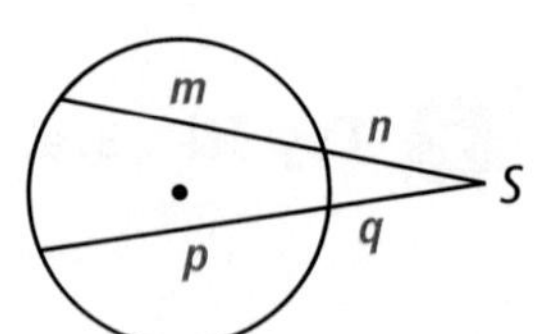	**If...** 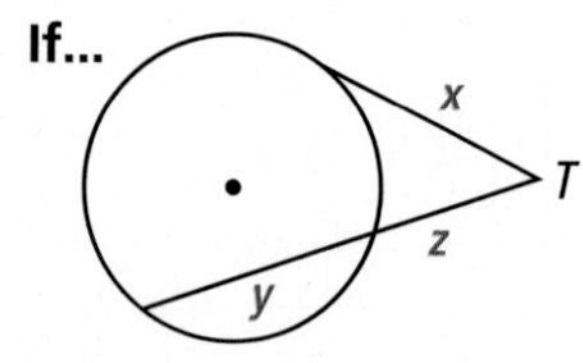
Then... $ab = cd$	**Then...** $(n + m)n = (q + p)q$	**Then...** $x^2 = (z + y)z$

PROOF: SEE EXERCISES 11, 23, and 24.

Activity

Assess

APPLICATION

EXAMPLE 5 Use Segment Relationships to Find Lengths

Archaeologists found part of the circular wall that surrounds an ancient city. They measure the distances shown. The 272-m segment lies on a line through the center of the circular wall. What was the diameter of the circular wall?

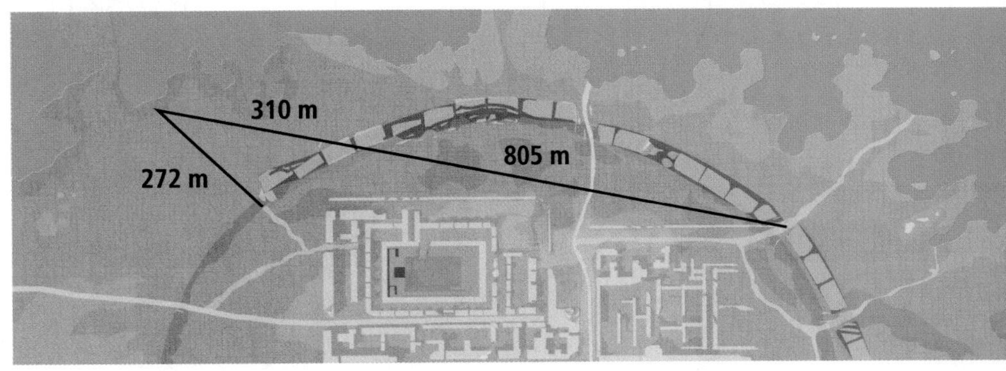

Draw a diagram to represent the situation.

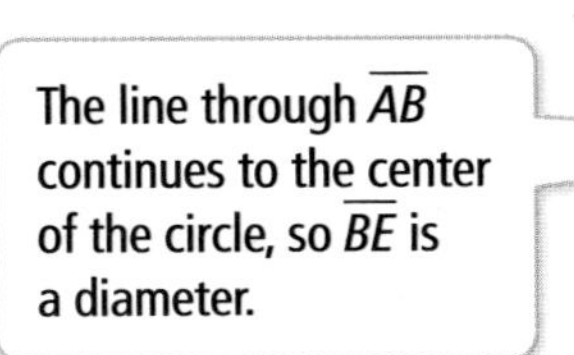

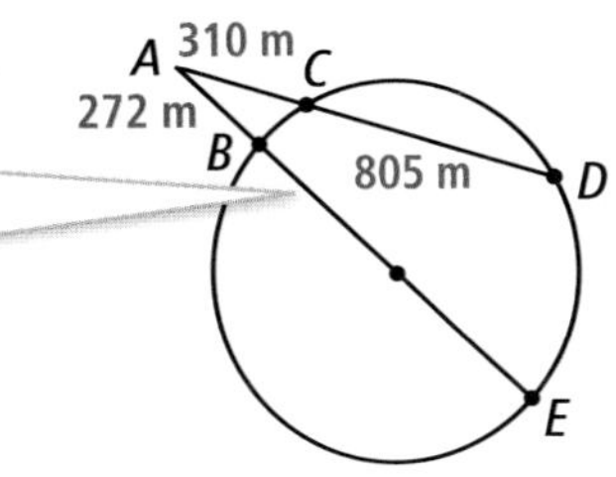

MAKE SENSE AND PERSEVERE Are there other measurements that archaeologists could have taken to help find the diameter using another method?

Write an equation to relate the segment lengths.

$$(AB + BE)AB = (AC + CD)AC$$

$$(272 + BE)(272) = (310 + 805)(310)$$

Apply Theorem 10-12 and substitute known segment lengths.

$$73{,}984 + 272 \cdot BE = 345{,}650$$

$$272 \cdot BE = 271{,}666$$

$$BE \approx 998.8$$

The diameter of the circular wall was about 998.8 meters.

Try It! **5. a.** What is the value of a?

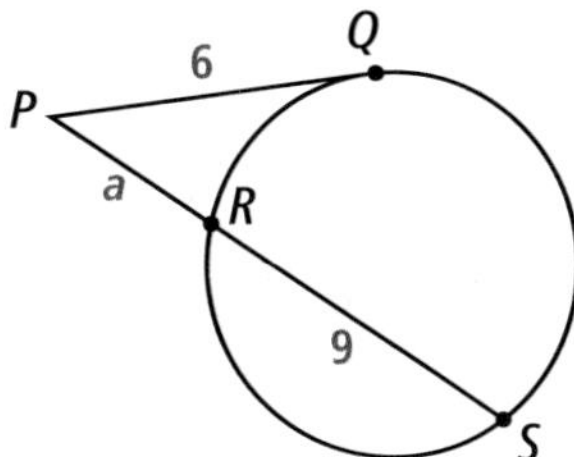

b. What is EC?

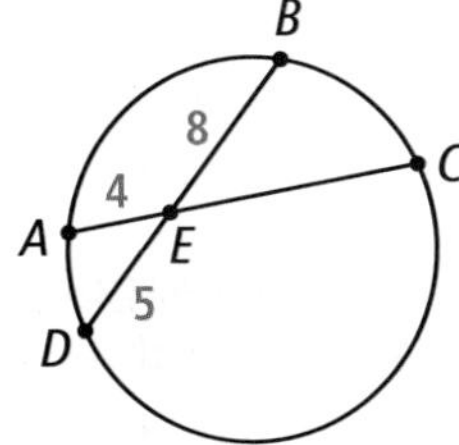

  Concept Summary  Assess

CONCEPT SUMMARY Angle and Segment Relationships in a Circle

	Vertex Inside the Circle	Vertex Outside the Circle
ANGLES	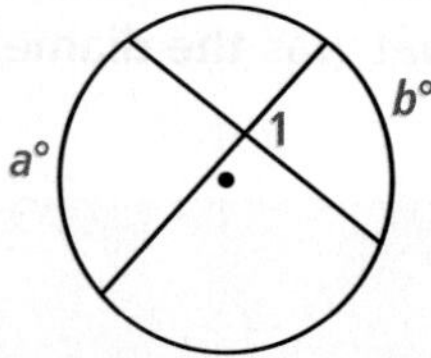 $m\angle 1 = \frac{1}{2}(a + b)$	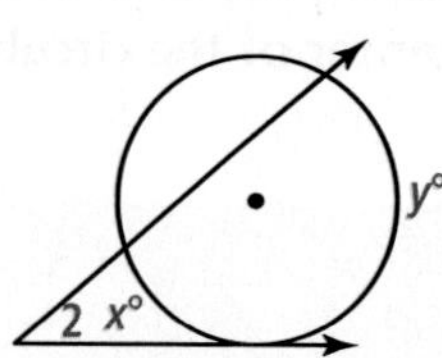 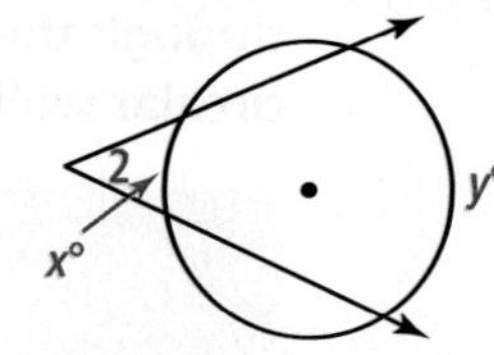 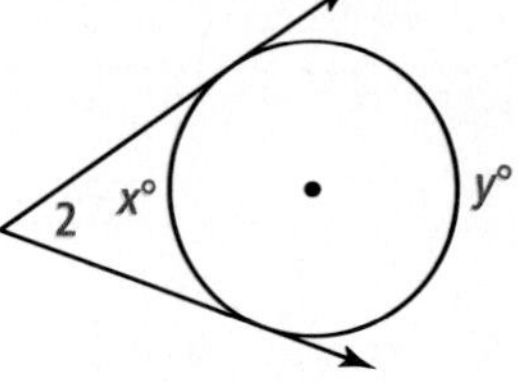 $m\angle 2 = \frac{1}{2}(y - x)$
SEGMENTS	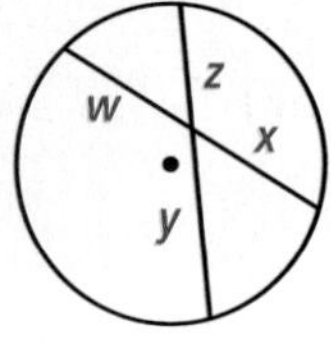 $wx = yz$	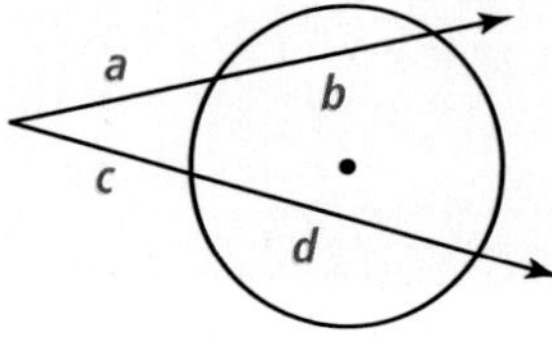 $(a + b)a = (c + d)c$ 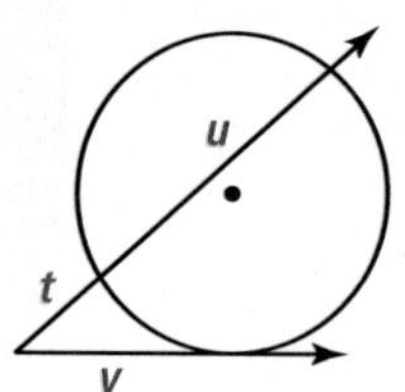 $(t + u)t = v^2$

Do You UNDERSTAND?

1. ESSENTIAL QUESTION How are the measures of angles, arcs, and segments formed by intersecting secant lines related?

2. **Error Analysis** Derek is asked to find the value of x. What is his error?

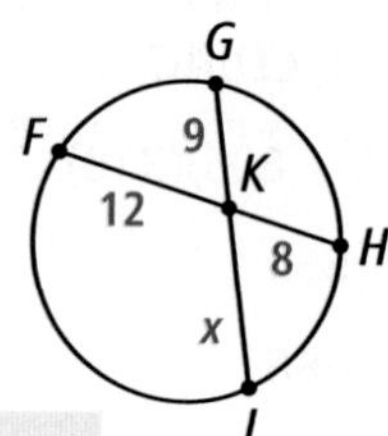

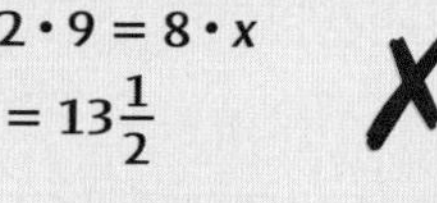

$GK \cdot FK = HK \cdot JK$
$12 \cdot 9 = 8 \cdot x$
$x = 13\frac{1}{2}$

3. **Vocabulary** How are *secants* and *tangents* to a circle alike and different?

4. **Construct Arguments** The rays shown are tangent to the circle. Show that $m\angle 1 = (x - 180)$.

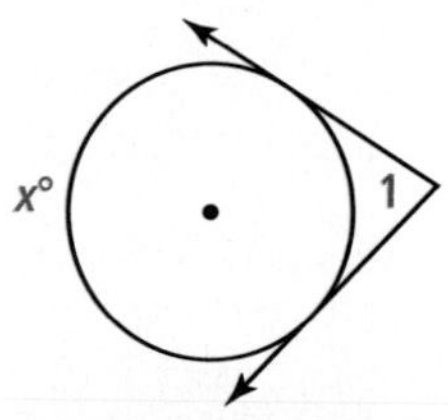

Do You KNOW HOW?

For Exercises 5 and 6, find each angle measure. Rays *QP* and *QR* are tangent to the circle in Exercise 6.

5. $m\angle BEC$

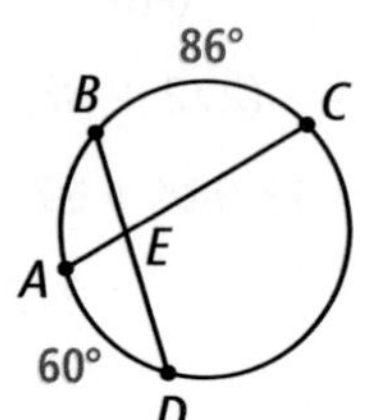

6. $m\angle PQR$

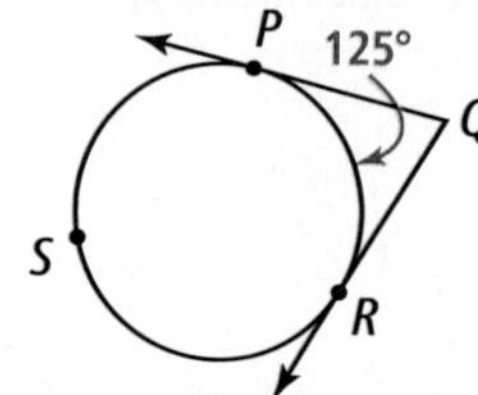

For Exercises 7 and 8, find each length. Ray *HJ* is tangent to the circle in Exercise 7.

7. *GF*

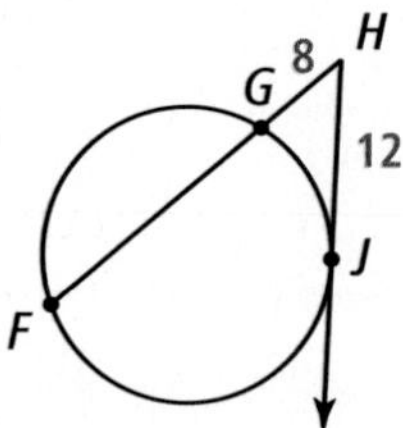

8. *LM*

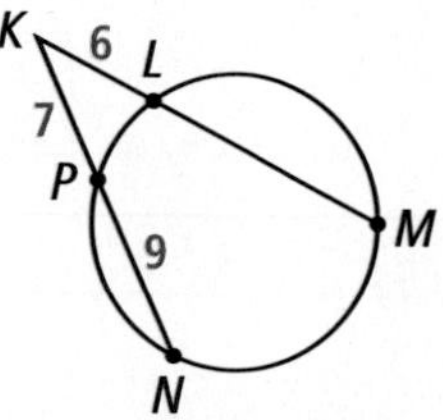

For Exercises 9 and 10, $\overline{AE}$ is tangent to ⊙*P*. Find each length.

9. *BC*

10. *EF*

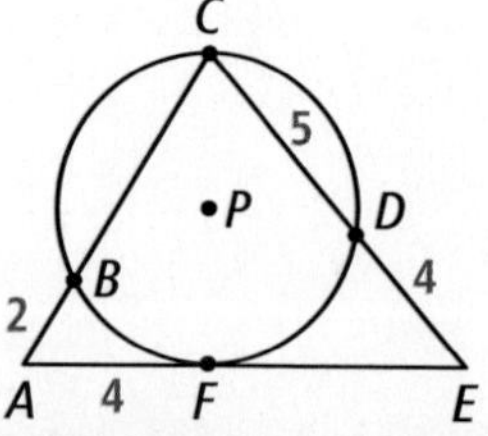

PRACTICE & PROBLEM SOLVING

UNDERSTAND

11. Construct Arguments Given ⊙*X*, write a two-column proof of Theorem 10-12, Case 2.

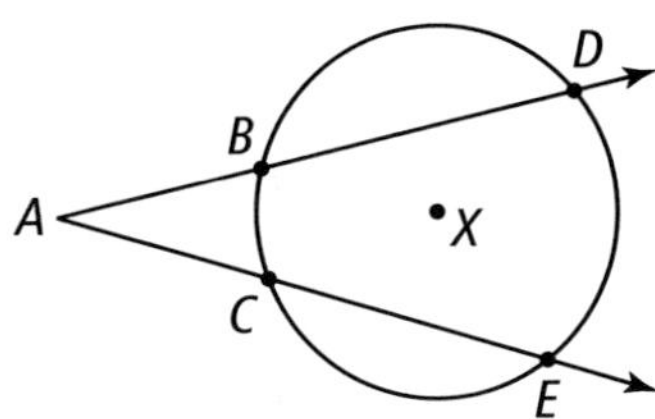

12. Error Analysis Cindy is asked to find $m\angle VXZ$. What is her error?

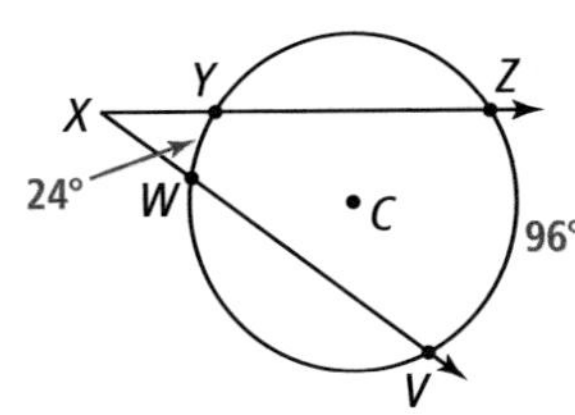

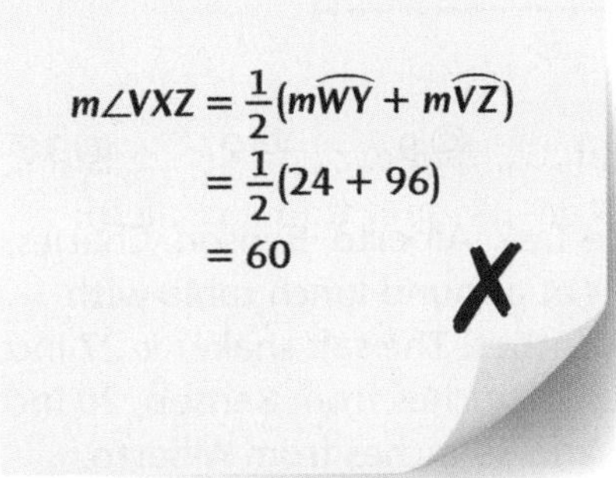

$$m\angle VXZ = \frac{1}{2}(m\widehat{WY} + m\widehat{VZ})$$
$$= \frac{1}{2}(24 + 96)$$
$$= 60$$

13. Mathematical Connections Given ⊙*P*, secant $\overrightarrow{CA}$, and tangent $\overrightarrow{CD}$, what is the area of ⊙*P*?

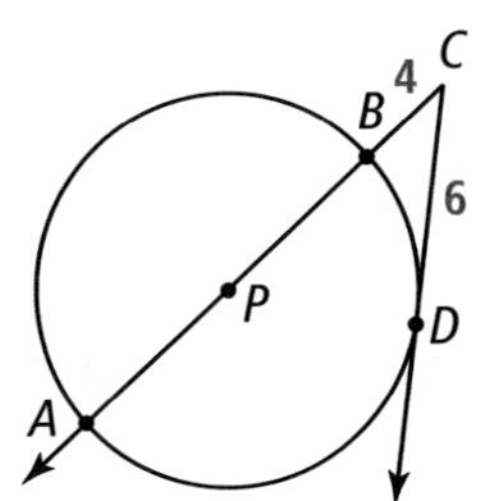

14. Higher Order Thinking Given ⊙*T*, and tangents $\overline{AD}$ and $\overline{CD}$, what is the measure of $\angle ADC$?

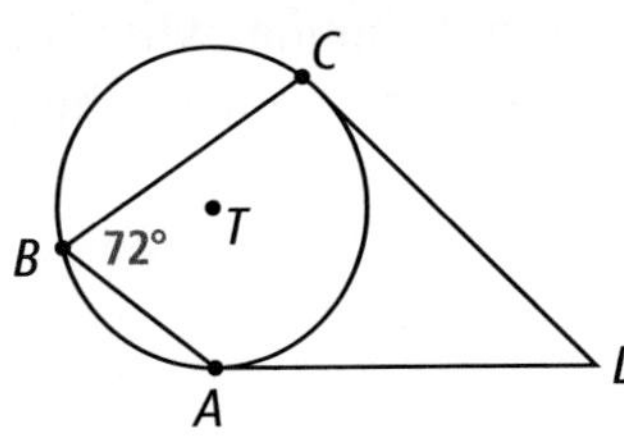

15. Communicate Precisely How would you describe each case of Theorem 10-11?

PRACTICE

For Exercises 16 and 17, find each measure.

SEE EXERCISE 1

16. $m\angle 1$

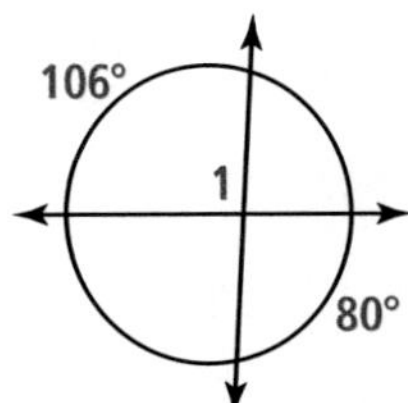

17. x

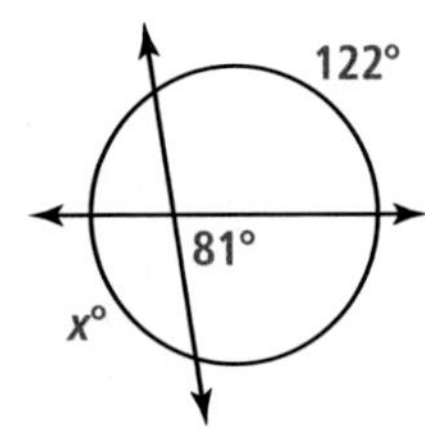

18. Given ⊙*A* and secants $\overline{PR}$ and $\overline{QS}$, write a paragraph proof of Theorem 10-10. SEE EXAMPLE 1

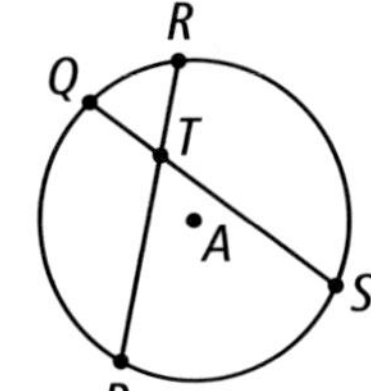

19. Given ⊙*Q* and tangents $\overrightarrow{AB}$ and $\overrightarrow{AC}$, write a two-column proof of Theorem 10-11, Case 3.
SEE EXAMPLE 2

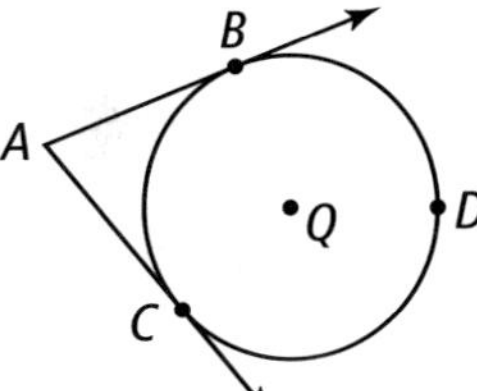

20. Given ⊙*C*, inscribed angle $\angle RWV$, and secants $\overrightarrow{TR}$ and $\overrightarrow{TV}$, what is the measure of $\angle RTV$?
SEE EXAMPLE 3

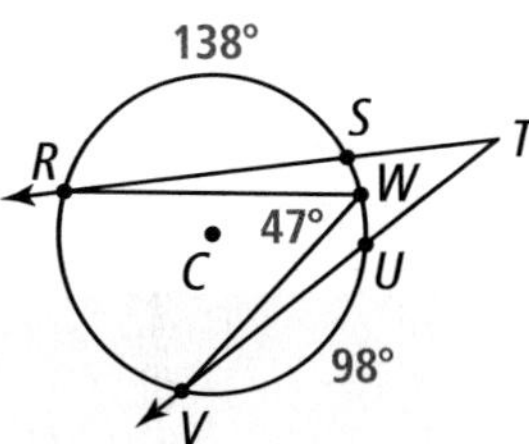

For Exercises 21 and 22, find each length.

SEE EXERCISE 4

21. a

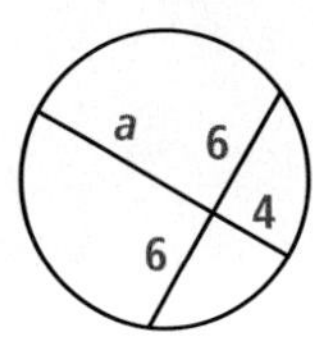

22. b

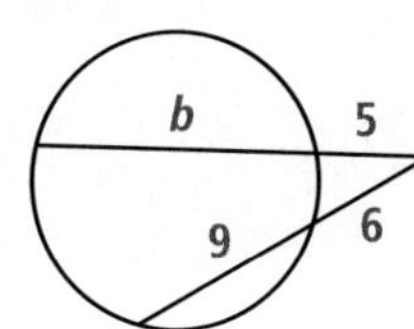

23. Given ⊙*T* and secants $\overline{JK}$ and $\overline{LM}$ intersecting at point *N*, write a paragraph proof of Theorem 10-12, Case 1.
SEE EXAMPLE 4

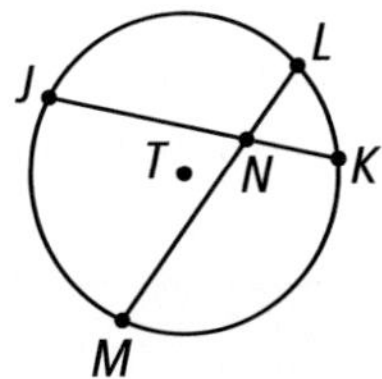

24. Given ⊙*C*, secant $\overrightarrow{QS}$ and tangent $\overline{PQ}$, write a two-column proof of Theorem 10–12, Case 3.
SEE EXAMPLE 5

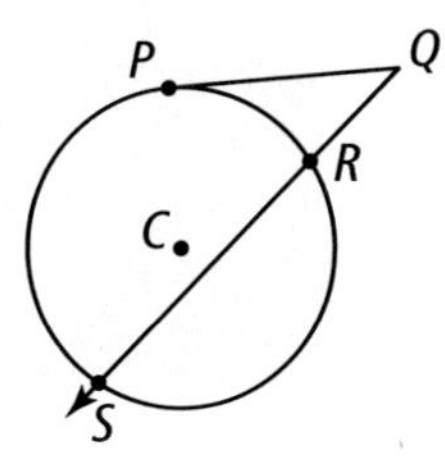

PRACTICE & PROBLEM SOLVING

Practice Tutorial

Mixed Review Available Online

APPLY

25. Use Structure Chris stands in the position shown to take a picture of a sculpture with a circular base.

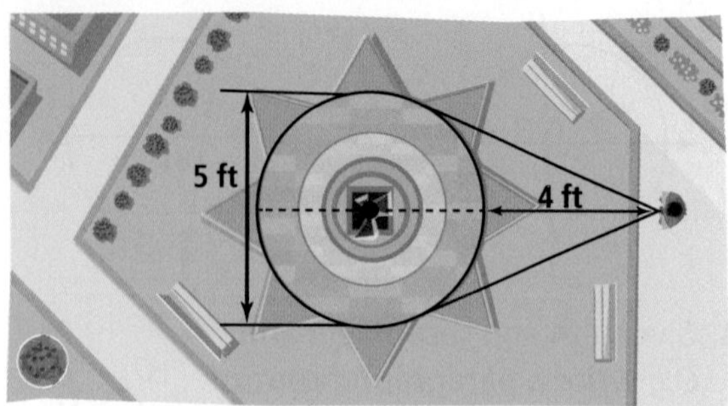

a. Chris is deciding on which lens to use. What is the minimum view angle from where he stands so he can get as much of the base as possible in his picture?

b. If Chris uses a lens with a view angle of 40°, what is the shortest distance he could stand from the sculpture?

26. Reason A satellite orbits above the equator of Mars as shown and transmits images back to a scientist in the control room. What percent of the equator is the scientist able to see? Explain.

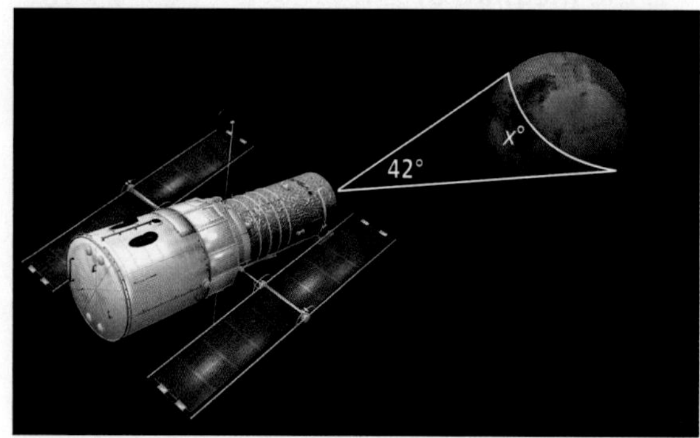

27. Use Structure Carolina wants to etch the design shown onto a circular piece of glass. At what measure should she cut ∠1? Explain.

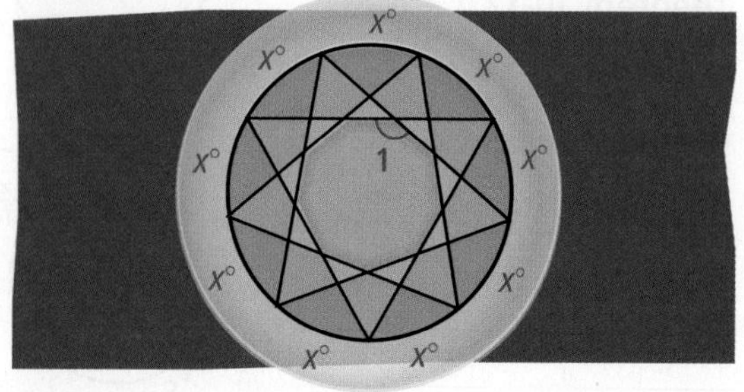

ASSESSMENT PRACTICE

28. For what measure of $\overset{\frown}{UW}$ does $m\angle TVX = 34$?

$m\overset{\frown}{UW} =$ ______

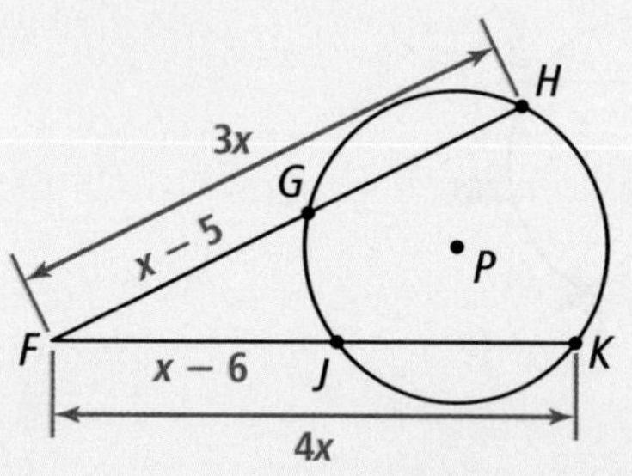

29. SAT/ACT Given ⊙P and secants $\overline{FH}$ and $\overline{FK}$, what is FG?

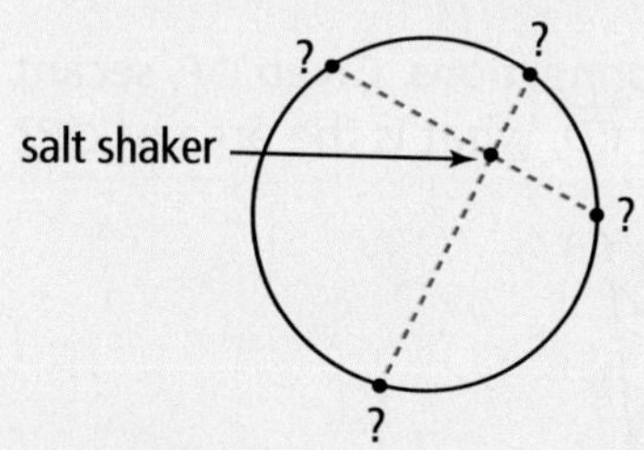

Ⓐ 3 Ⓑ 4 Ⓒ 9 Ⓓ 27 Ⓔ 36

30. Performance Task Alberto, Benson, Charles, and Deon sit at a round lunch table with diameter 54 inches. The salt shaker is 27 inches from Charles, 18 inches from Benson, 20 inches from Deon, and 30 inches from Alberto.

salt shaker ?

Part A In what order around the table are they seated? Explain.

Part B Alberto, Benson, Charles, and Deon change the positions of their seats and sit evenly spaced around the table. If the location of the salt shaker does not change, what is the closest that one of them could be from the salt shaker? What is the farthest?

TOPIC 10

Topic Review

TOPIC ESSENTIAL QUESTION

1. When a line or lines intersect a circle how are the figures formed related to the radius, circumference, and area of the circle?

Vocabulary Review

Choose the correct term to complete each sentence.

2. A(n) __________ is a region of a circle with two radii and an arc of the circle as borders.
3. A(n) __________ is an angle with its vertex on the circle.
4. A(n) __________ and the corresponding circle have exactly one point in common.
5. When both rays of an angle intersect a circle, the __________ is the portion of the circle between the rays.

- central angle
- chord
- inscribed angle
- intercepted arc
- secant
- sector of a circle
- segment of a circle
- tangent to a circle

Concepts & Skills Review

TOPIC 10 REVIEW

LESSON 10-1 Arcs and Sectors

Quick Review

Arc length and the area of a **sector of a circle** are proportional to the corresponding central angle.

The length of an arc is $\frac{n}{360}$ of the circumference, where n is the measure of the central angle in degrees, and the area of a sector is $\frac{n}{360}$ of the area of the circle.

Example

Circle J has a radius of 6 cm. What is the area of a sector with a central angle of 80°?

Write the formula for the area of a sector:

$$A = \frac{n}{360} \cdot \pi r^2$$

$$= \frac{80}{360} \cdot \pi(6)^2$$

$$\approx 25.1$$

The area of the sector is about 25.1 cm^2.

Practice & Problem Solving

Find each arc length in terms of π.

6. $\widehat{JK}$

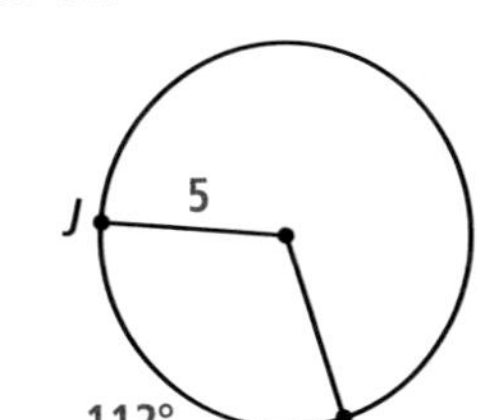

7. $\widehat{ABC}$

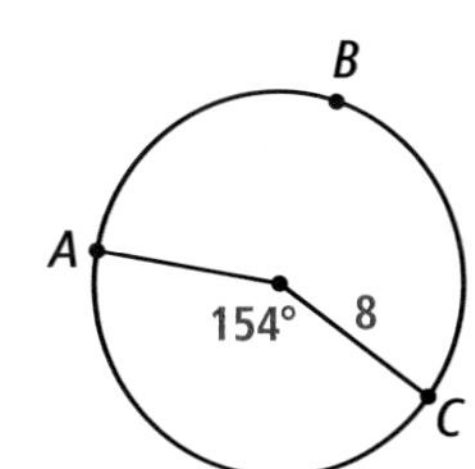

Find the area of each sector in terms of π.

8. sector NRM

N
10
63°
R
M

9. sector DSE

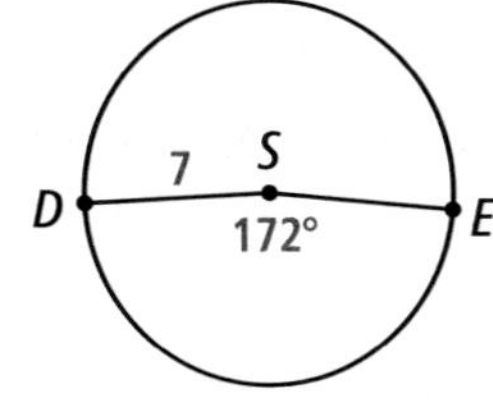

10. **Reason** If you know the circumference of a circle and the area of a sector of the circle, how could you determine the central angle of the sector? Explain.

LESSON 10-2 Lines Tangent to a Circle

Quick Review

A **tangent to a circle** is perpendicular to the radius of the circle at the **point of tangency**. You can use properties of right triangles to solve problems involving tangents.

Example

Lines m and n are tangent to $\odot T$. What is $m\angle ATB$?

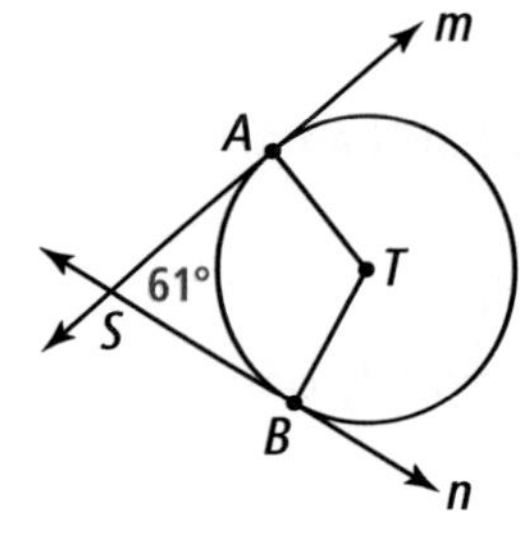

Since lines m and n are tangent lines, $m\angle SAT = m\angle SBT = 90$. Points A, T, B, and S form a quadrilateral, so use the angle sum of a quadrilateral to solve the problem.

$$m\angle SAT + m\angle ASB + m\angle SBT + m\angle ATB = 360$$
$$90 + 61 + 90 + m\angle ATB = 360$$
$$m\angle ATB = 119$$

So, $m\angle ATB = 119$.

Practice & Problem Solving

For Exercises 11–12, $\overline{QR}$ and $\overline{AB}$ are tangent to the circle. Find each value.

11. QR

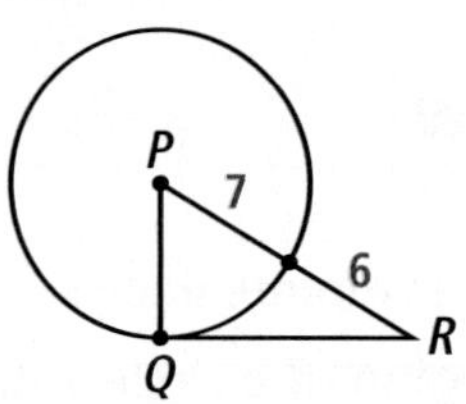

12. $m\angle CAB$

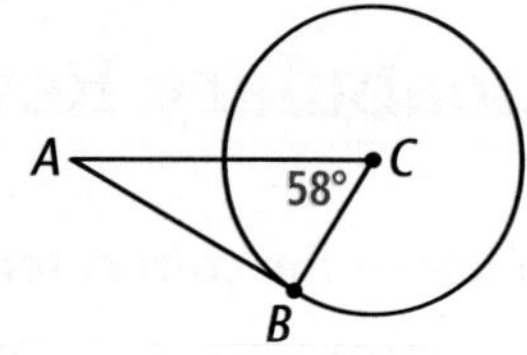

13. **Construct Arguments** If $\overline{GH}$ is a diameter of $\odot T$, is it possible to draw tangents to G and H from the same point external to $\odot T$? Explain.

14. Segment MN is tangent to $\odot L$. What is the radius of the circle? Explain.

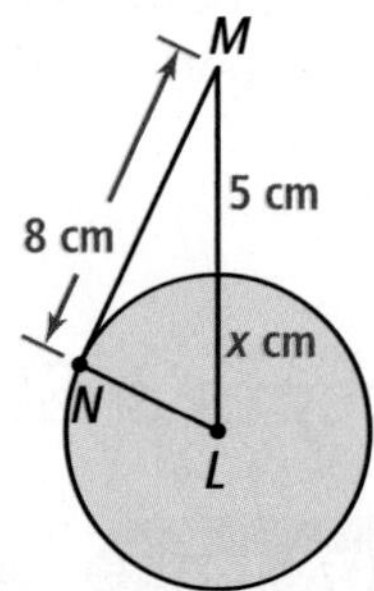

LESSON 10-3 Chords

Quick Review

Chords in a circle have the following properties:

- Two chords in the same circle with the same length have congruent central angles, have congruent arcs, and are equidistant from the center of the circle.
- Chords are bisected by the diameter of the circle that is perpendicular to the chord.

Example

What is the radius of $\odot T$?

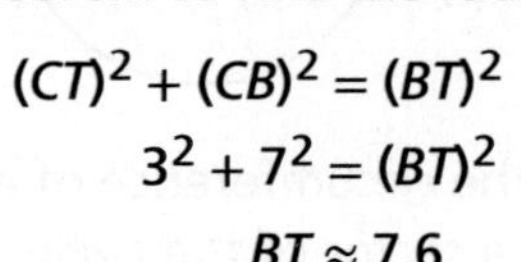

Since $\overline{CT} \perp \overline{AB}$, $\overline{CT}$ bisects $\overline{AB}$. So, $CB = 7$. Use the Pythagorean Theorem to find the radius.

$$(CT)^2 + (CB)^2 = (BT)^2$$
$$3^2 + 7^2 = (BT)^2$$
$$BT \approx 7.6$$

The radius of $\odot T$ is about 7.6.

Practice & Problem Solving

For Exercises 15–17, the radius of $\odot T$ is 7. Find each value. Round to the nearest tenth.

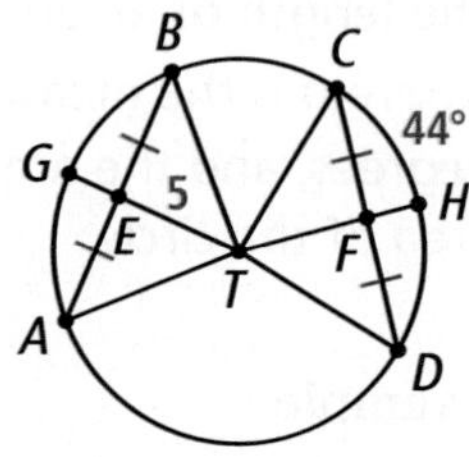

15. FH

16. CD

17. $m\angle BTA$

18. **Look for Relationships** Circles T and S intersect at points A and B. What is the relationship between $\overline{AB}$ and  $\overleftrightarrow{TS}$? Explain.

19. A contractor cuts off part of a circular countertop so that it fits against a wall. What should be the length x of the cut? Round to the nearest tenth.

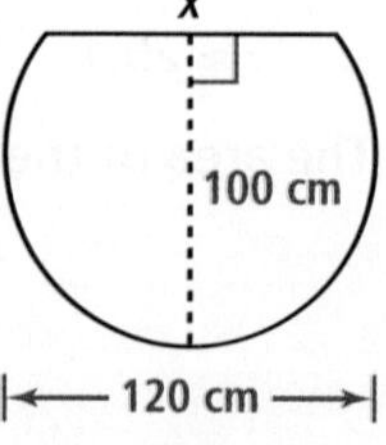

LESSON 10-4 Inscribed Angles

Quick Review

The measure of an **inscribed angle** is half the measure of its intercepted arc. As a result:

- Opposite angles of an inscribed quadrilateral are supplementary.
- The measure of an angle formed by a tangent and chord is half the measure of the intercepted arc.

Example

What are the angle measures of $\triangle ABC$?

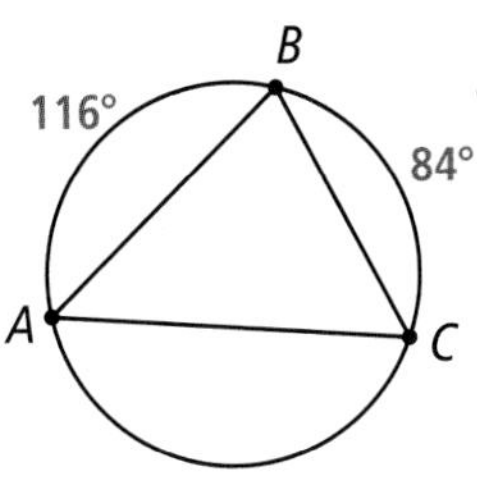

Use inscribed angles:

$m\angle BAC = \frac{1}{2}(84) = 42$

$m\angle BCA = \frac{1}{2}(116) = 58$

$m\angle ABC = 180 - 42 - 58 = 80$

Practice & Problem Solving

Find each value.

20. $m\widehat{EF}$

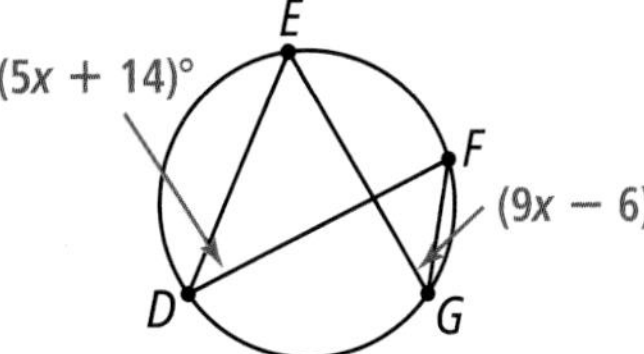

21. $m\angle MNP$

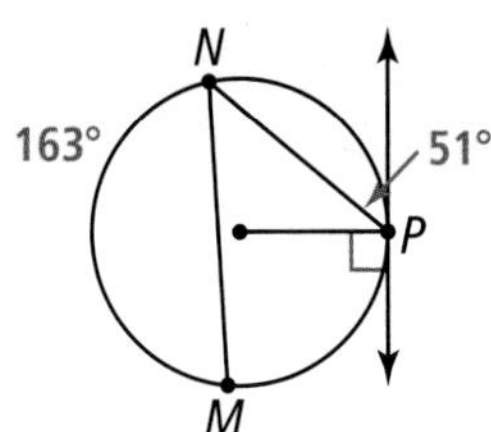

22. $m\angle WZY$

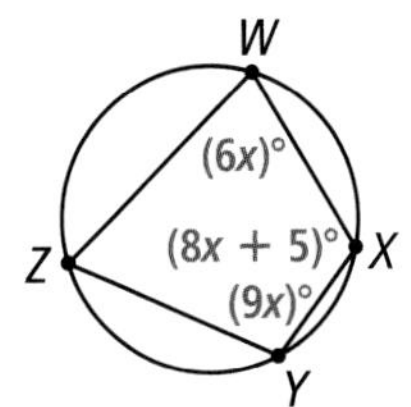

23. $m\angle QPR$

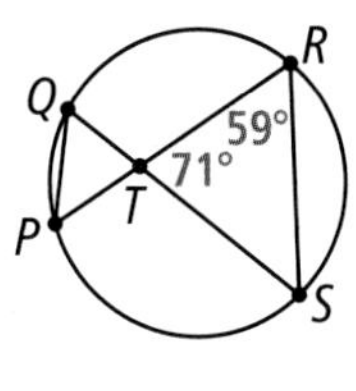

24. Generalize If a rectangle is inscribed in a circle, what must be true about the diagonals of the rectangle? Explain.

LESSON 10-5 Secant Lines and Segments

Quick Review

Secant lines form angles with special relationships:

- The measure of an angle formed by secants intersecting inside a circle is half the sum of the measures of the intercepted arcs.
- The measure of an angle formed by secants intersecting outside a circle is half the difference of the measures of the intercepted arcs.

Example

What is the value of *x*?

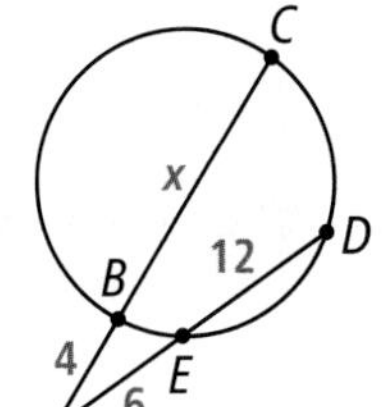

Use secant segment relationships.

$$(AE)(AE + ED) = (AB)(AB + BC)$$
$$6(6 + 12) = 4(4 + x)$$
$$108 = 16 + 4x$$
$$92 = 4x$$
$$23 = x$$

The value of x is 23.

Practice & Problem Solving

For Exercises 25 and 26, find each value in the figure shown.

25. QR

26. $m\angle NRP$

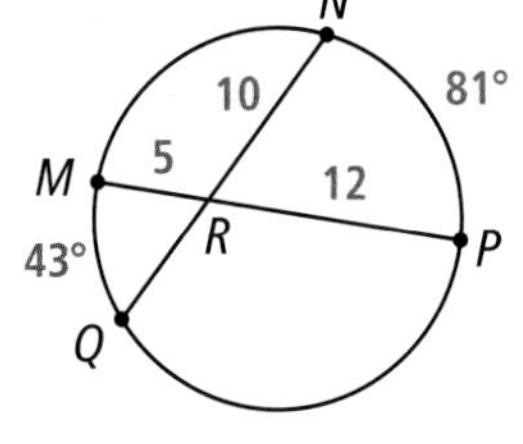

For Exercises 27 and 28, find each value in the figure shown. The segment $\overline{WZ}$ is tangent to the circle.

27. WZ

28. $m\widehat{XZ}$

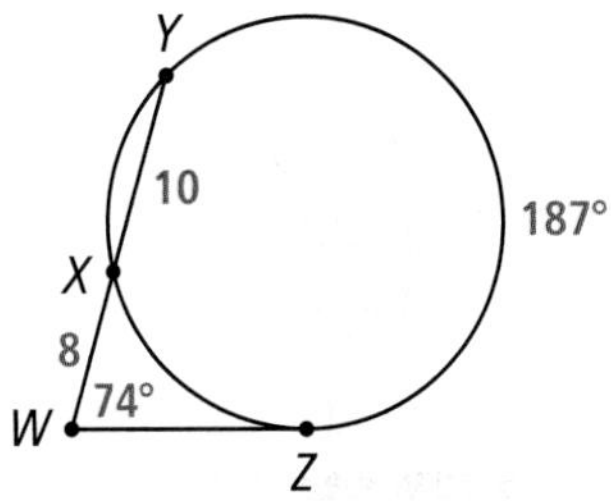

29. Construct Arguments A student said that if $\angle A$ is formed by two secants intersecting outside of a circle, then $m\angle A < 90$. Do you agree? Explain.

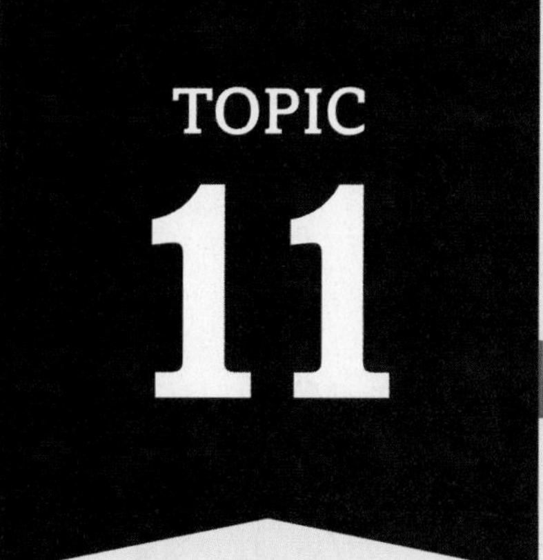

Two- and Three-Dimensional Models

TOPIC ESSENTIAL QUESTION

How is Cavalieri's Principle helpful in understanding the volume formulas for solids?

Topic Overview

enVision® STEM Project:
Design a Rigid Package

11-1 Three-Dimensional Figures and Cross Sections

11-2 Volumes of Prisms and Cylinders

Mathematical Modeling in 3 Acts:
Box 'Em Up

11-3 Pyramids and Cones

11-4 Spheres

Topic Vocabulary

- Cavalieri's Principle
- hemisphere
- oblique cylinder
- oblique prism

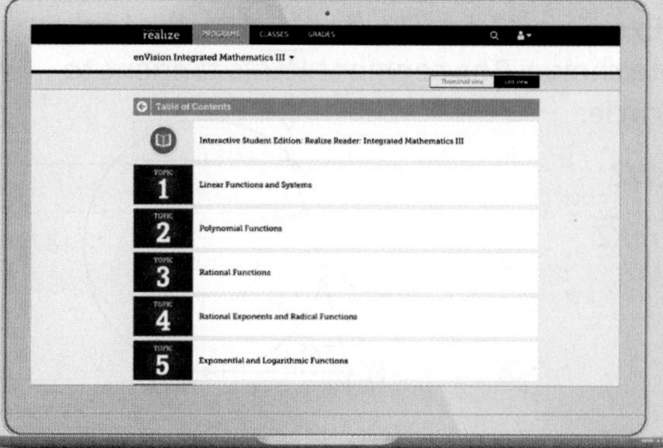

Digital Experience

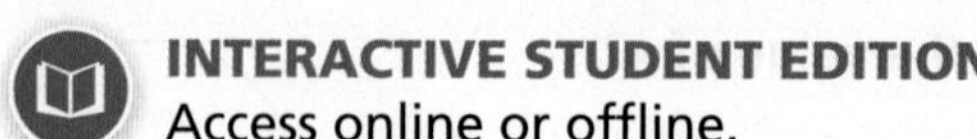

INTERACTIVE STUDENT EDITION Access online or offline.

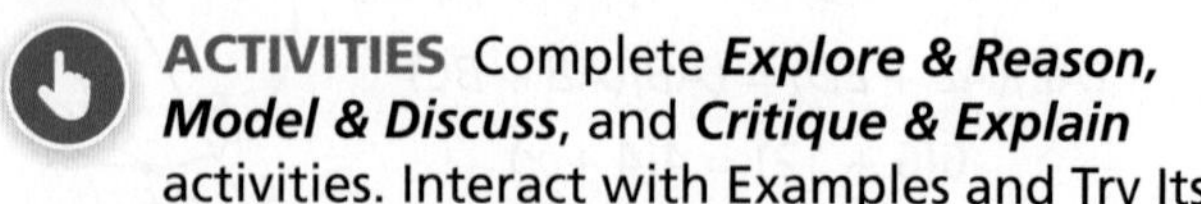

ACTIVITIES Complete ***Explore & Reason, Model & Discuss***, and ***Critique & Explain*** activities. Interact with Examples and Try Its.

ANIMATION View and interact with real-world applications.

PRACTICE Practice what you've learned.

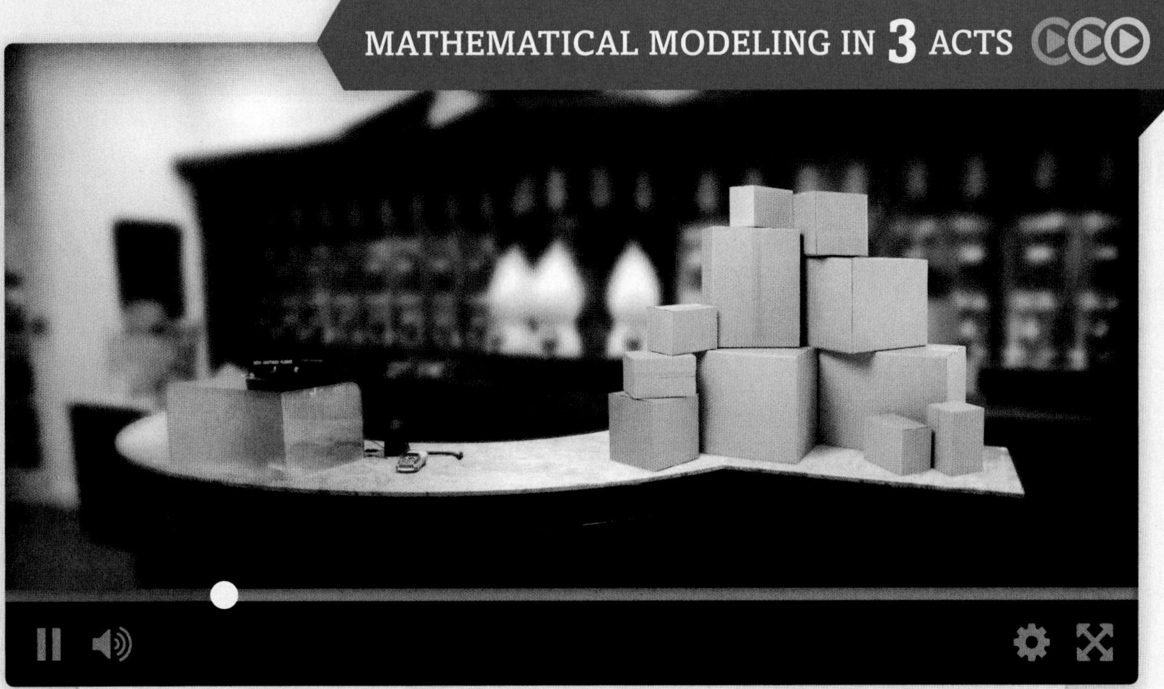

Box 'Em Up

With so many people and businesses shopping online, retailers, and especially e-retailers, ship more and more packages every day. Some of the products people order have unusual sizes and shapes and need custom packaging. Imagine how you might package a surfboard, or a snow blower, or even live crawfish to ship to someone's house!

Think about this during the Mathematical Modeling in 3 Acts lesson.

TOPIC 11

VIDEOS Watch clips to support ***Mathematical Modeling in 3 Acts Lessons*** and **enVision® *STEM Projects.***

CONCEPT SUMMARY Review key lesson content through multiple representations.

ASSESSMENT Show what you've learned.

GLOSSARY Read and listen to English and Spanish definitions.

TUTORIALS Get help from *Virtual Nerd*, right when you need it.

MATH TOOLS Explore math with digital tools and manipulatives.

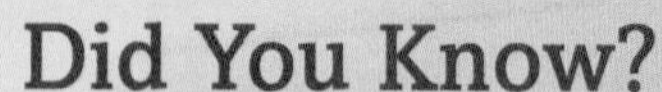

Did You Know?

Cardboard boxes look simple, but the machines that make them are not. This **cartoning machine** is capable of making **15,000 boxes per day**.

Packages come in many shapes. The familiar milk carton shape is called a **gable-top carton** because of its resemblance to a house gable. **Cylindrical** packaging is often used for sugar, tea and grains that don't have rigid shapes.

Manufacturers consider many factors when designing a package.

- ☑ Marketing appeal
- ☑ Cost of materials
- ☑ Simplicity
- ☑ Safety
- ☑ Recyclability

Your Task: Design a Rigid Package

You will design a rigid package for a product of your choice. Your design will address factors such as attractiveness, protection for the product, and cost. You will then draw two- and three-dimensional representations of your package and build a prototype.

11-1 Three-Dimensional Figures and Cross Sections

I CAN… identify three-dimensional figures and their relationships with polygons to solve problems.

EXPLORE & REASON

Consider a cube of cheese. If you slice straight down through the midpoints of four parallel edges of the cube, the outline of the newly exposed surface is a square.

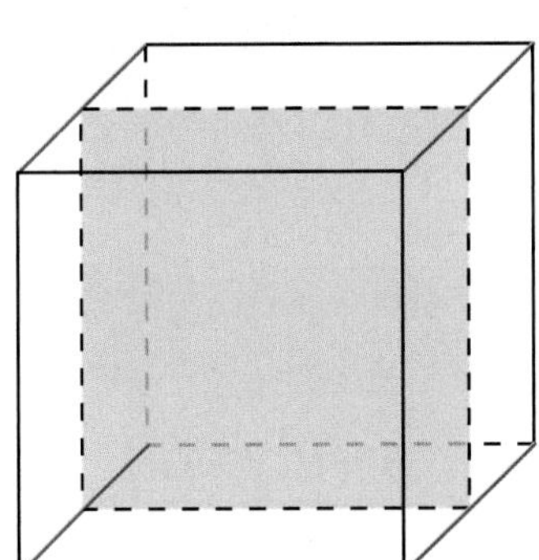

A. How would you slice the cube to expose a triangular surface?

B. **Communicate Precisely** How would you slice the cube to expose a triangular surface with the greatest possible area?

ESSENTIAL QUESTION

How are three-dimensional figures and polygons related?

CONCEPTUAL UNDERSTANDING

EXAMPLE 1 Develop Euler's Formula

How many faces, vertices, and edges does each prism contain? Do you notice any patterns in these quantities?

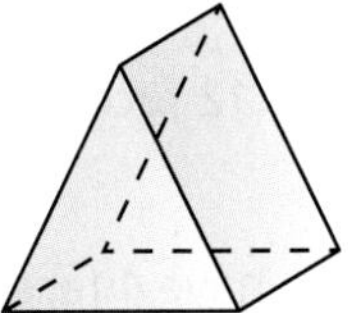
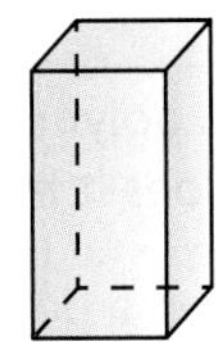
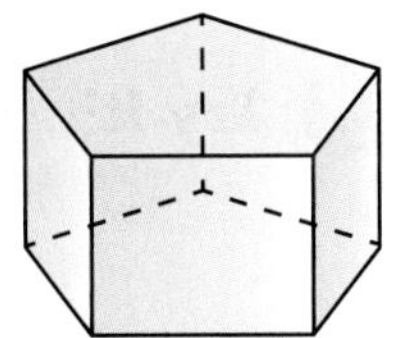
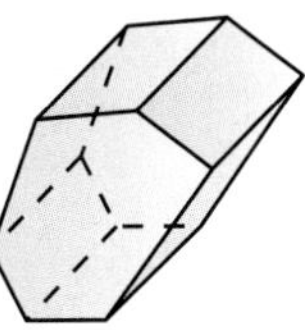

Make a table of the number of vertices, edges, and faces for each prism. Look for patterns and relationships.

Type of Prism	Faces (F)	Vertices (V)	Edges (E)
triangular	5	6	9
rectangular	6	8	12
pentagonal	7	10	15
hexagonal	8	12	18

For each additional face on the prism, the prism gains 2 vertices and 3 edges.

Look at the sums of the faces and vertices. Compare it to the number of edges.

$5 + 6 = 9 + 2$
$6 + 8 = 12 + 2$
$7 + 10 = 15 + 2$
$8 + 12 = 18 + 2$

The sum of the faces and vertices is always 2 more than the number of edges.

MODEL WITH MATHEMATICS
Look at the relationships between the number of vertices, faces, and edges. How might you represent these relationships in an equation?

Try It! 1. How many faces, vertices, and edges do the pyramids have? Name at least three patterns you notice.

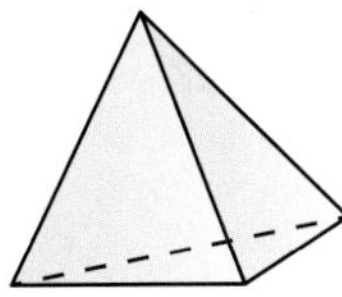
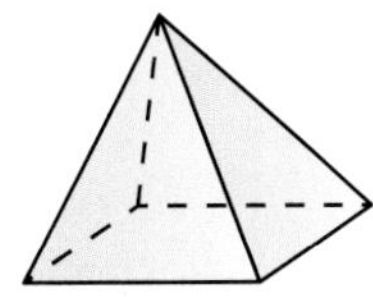
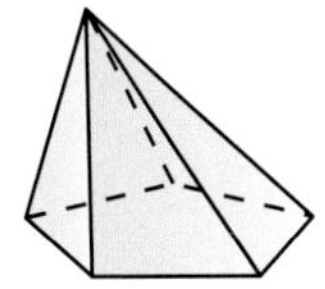
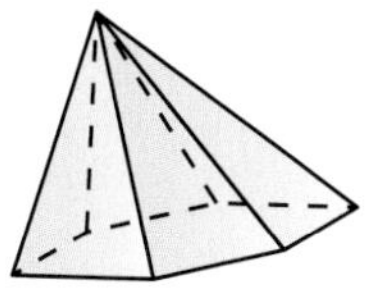

CONCEPT Euler's Formula

The sum of the number of faces (F) and vertices (V) of a polyhedron is 2 more than the number of its edges (E).

$F + V = E + 2$

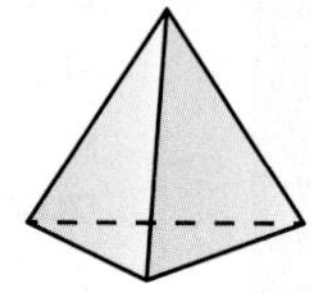

$$F + V = E + 2$$
$$4 + 4 = E + 2$$
$$E = 6$$

APPLICATION

EXAMPLE 2 Apply Euler's Formula

To make polyhedron-shaped game pieces using a 3D printer, Juanita enters the number of faces, edges, and vertices into a program. If she wants a game piece with 20 faces and 30 edges, how many vertices does the piece have?

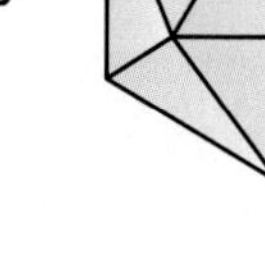

COMMON ERROR
Remember to add the number of faces and vertices on one side of the equation and to add the number of edges plus 2 on the other side of the equation.

$$F + V = E + 2$$
$$20 + V = 30 + 2$$
$$V = 12$$

Apply Euler's Formula.

The game piece has 12 vertices.

Try It! **2. a.** A polyhedron has 12 faces and 30 edges. How many vertices does it have?

b. Can a polyhedron have 4 faces, 5 vertices, and 8 edges? Explain.

EXAMPLE 3 Describe a Cross Section

Plane M and plane N intersect the regular octahedron as shown. What is the shape of each cross section?

STUDY TIP
Recall that a *cross section* is the intersection of a solid and a plane.

Plane M slices the octahedron in half through the top and bottom vertices. The cross section is a rhombus.

Plane N slices horizontally between the bases of two square pyramids. The cross section is a square.

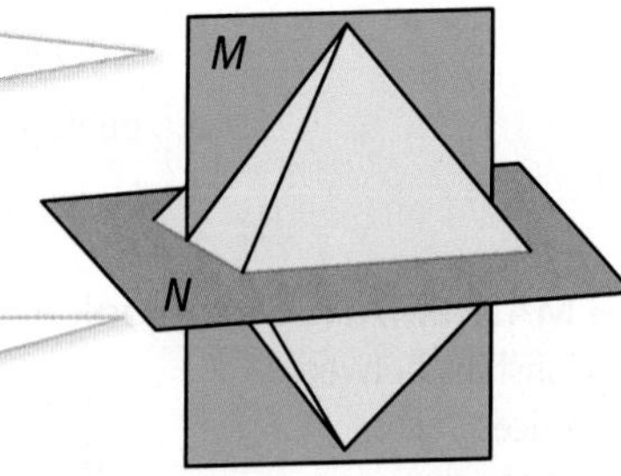

Try It! **3. a.** What shape is the cross section shown?

b. What shape is the cross section if the plane is perpendicular to the base and passes through the vertex of the pyramid?

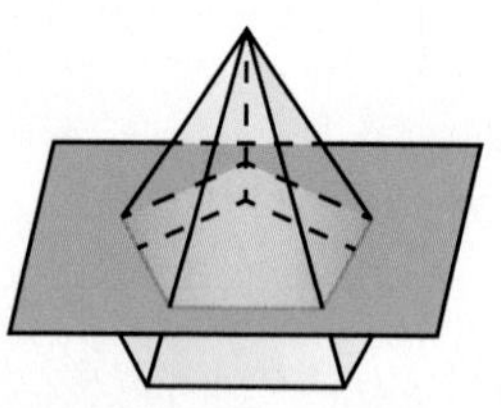

Activity Assess

EXAMPLE 4 Draw a Cross Section

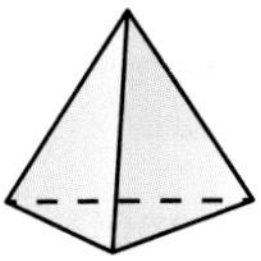

A plane intersects a tetrahedron parallel to the base. How do you draw the cross section?

Step 1 Visualize the plane intersecting the tetrahedron.

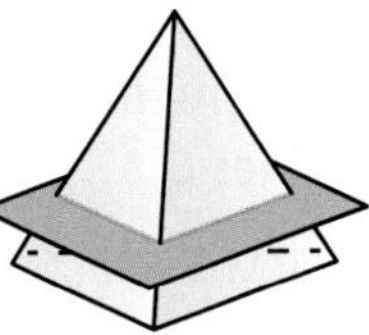

Step 2 Draw lines where the plane cuts the surface of the polyhedron.

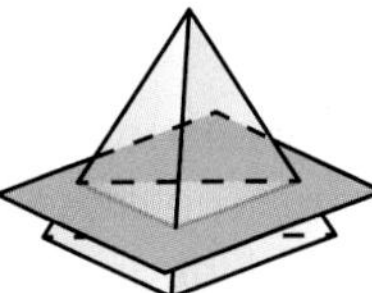

Step 3 Shade the cross section.

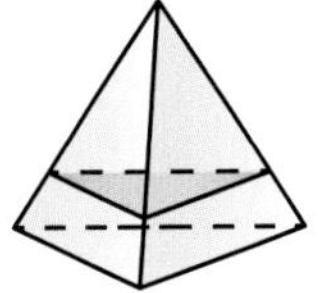

STUDY TIP
It is not possible for a polyhedron with n faces to have a cross section with more than n sides.

Try It! **4. a.** Draw the cross section of a plane intersecting the tetrahedron through the top vertex and perpendicular to the base.

b. Draw the cross section of a plane intersecting a hexagonal prism perpendicular to the base.

EXAMPLE 5 Rotate a Polygon to Form a Three-Dimensional Figure

If you rotate an isosceles triangle about the altitude, what three-dimensional figure does the triangle form?

As the triangle rotates, each point on the sides traces out a circle about the axis of rotation.

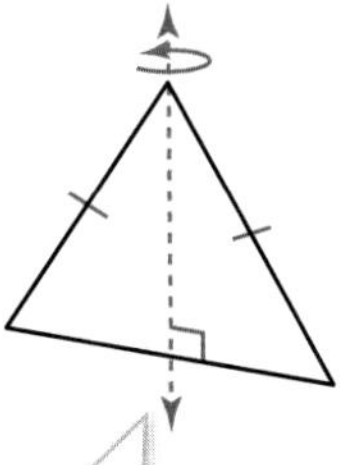

The line containing the altitude is the axis of rotation.

The rotation forms a stack of circles.

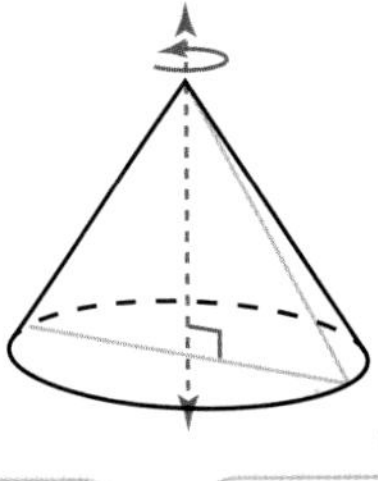

The three-dimensional figure is a cone.

Try It! **5. a.** What three-dimensional figure is formed by rotating equilateral triangle $\triangle ABC$ about $\overline{BD}$?

b. What three-dimensional figure is formed by rotating $\triangle ABC$ about $\overline{BC}$?

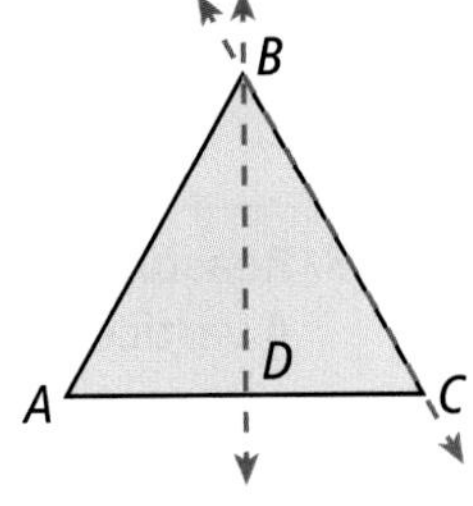

CONCEPT SUMMARY Polyhedrons, Cross Sections, and Rotating a Polygon

WORDS | **DIAGRAMS**

Euler's Formula The faces of a polyhedron are polygons. The sum of the number of faces F and vertices V of a polyhedron is 2 more than the number of its edges E.

$$F + V = E + 2$$

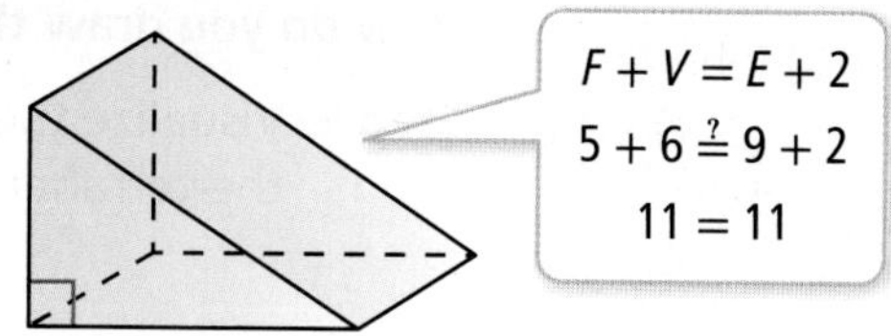

Cross Sections A cross section is the intersection of a plane and a solid. The cross section of a plane and a convex polyhedron is a polygon.

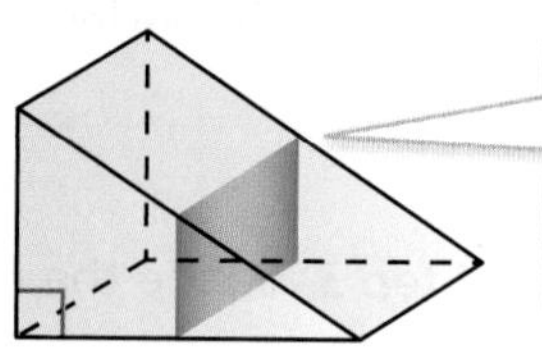

A cross section perpendicular to the base of the triangular prism is a rectangle.

Rotation of Polygons Rotating a polygon about an axis forms a three-dimensional figure with at least one circular cross section.

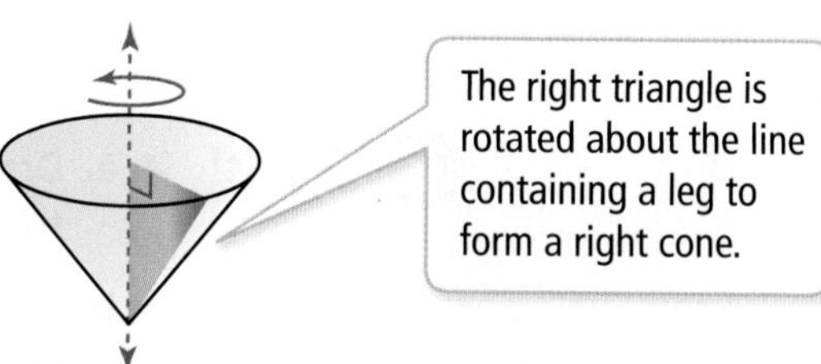

Do You UNDERSTAND?

1. **ESSENTIAL QUESTION** How are three-dimensional figures and polygons related?

2. **Error Analysis** Nicholas drew a figure to find a cross section of an icosahedron, a polyhedron with 20 faces. What is Nicholas's error?

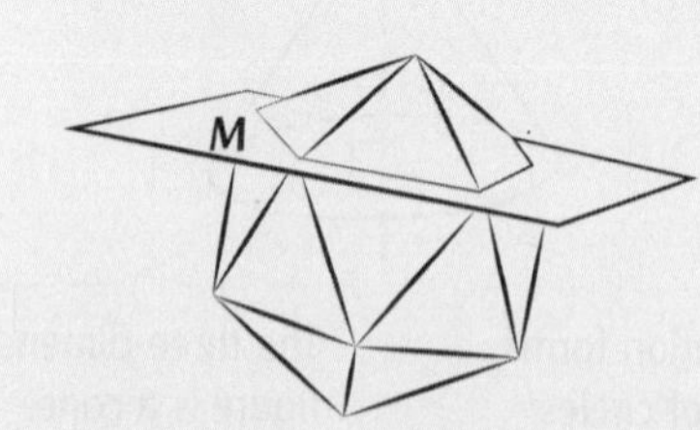

3. **Reason** Can a polyhedron have 3 faces, 4 vertices, and 5 edges? Explain.

Do You KNOW HOW?

For Exercises 4–7, copy and complete the table.

	Faces	Vertices	Edges
4.	5	6	
5.	8		18
6.		12	20
7.	22	44	

8. What polygon is formed by the intersection of plane N and the octagonal prism shown?

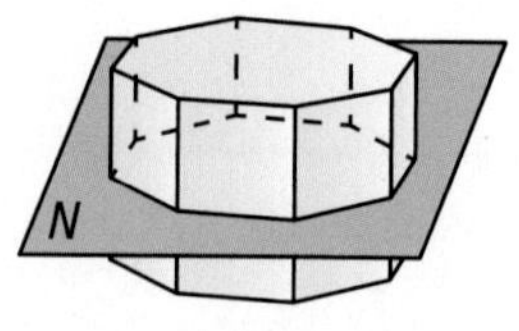

9. Describe the three-dimensional figure that is formed from rotating the isosceles right triangle about the hypotenuse.

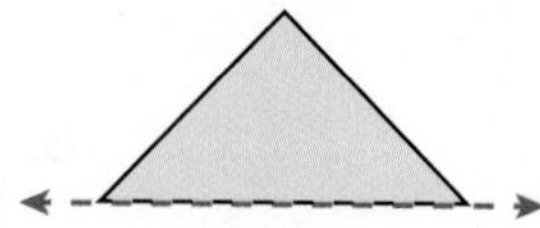

PRACTICE & PROBLEM SOLVING

Scan for Multimedia

Practice | Tutorial

Additional Exercises Available Online

UNDERSTAND

10. Mathematical Connections If you rotate rectangle $ABCD$ about $\overleftrightarrow{CD}$, what is the volume of the resulting three-dimensional figure?

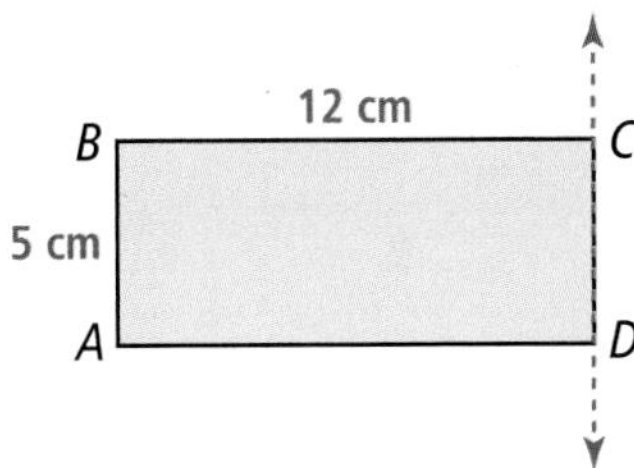

11. Error Analysis Philip was asked to find the number of vertices of a polyhedron with 32 faces and 60 edges. What is his error?

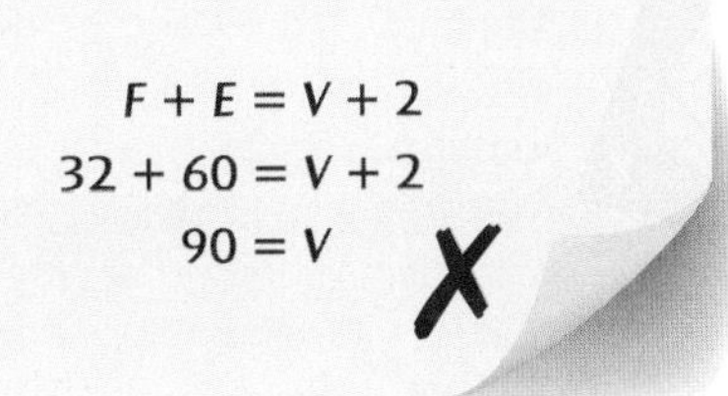

$$F + E = V + 2$$
$$32 + 60 = V + 2$$
$$90 = V$$

X

12. Make Sense and Persevere A tetrahedron is a polyhedron with four triangular faces. Can a plane intersect the tetrahedron shown to form a cross section with four sides? Explain.

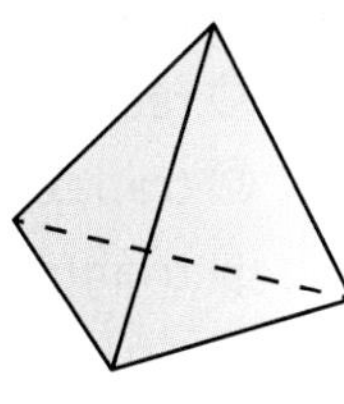

13. Use Appropriate Tools Can the intersection of a plane and a triangular prism produce a rectangular cross section? Draw a diagram to explain.

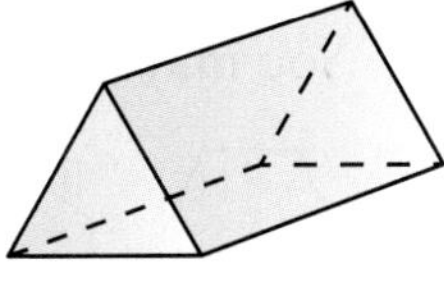

14. Higher Order Thinking Is it possible to rotate a polygon to form a cube? Explain.

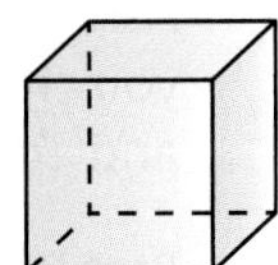

15. Make Sense and Persevere Use the polyhedron shown.

a. Does the figure have a cross section with five sides? Copy the figure and draw the cross section or explain why not.

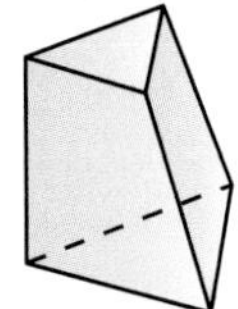

b. What is the maximum number of sides that a cross section of this figure can have?

PRACTICE

For Exercises 16–20, find the missing number for each polyhedron. SEE EXAMPLES 1 AND 2

16. A polyhedron has 24 edges and 12 vertices. How many faces does it have?

17. A polyhedron has 20 faces and 12 vertices. How many edges does it have?

18. A polyhedron has 8 faces and 15 edges. How many vertices does it have?

19. A polyhedron has 16 edges and 10 vertices. How many faces does it have?

20. Draw the cross section formed by the intersection of plane A and the polyhedron shown. What type of polygon is the cross section? SEE EXAMPLE 3

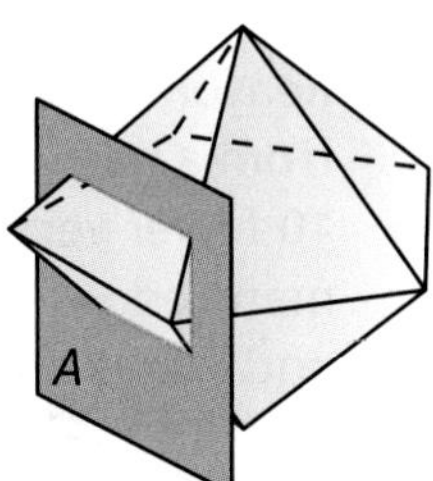

For Exercises 20 and 21, use the square pyramid shown. SEE EXAMPLE 4

21. Visualize a plane intersecting the square pyramid parallel to the base. Describe the cross section.

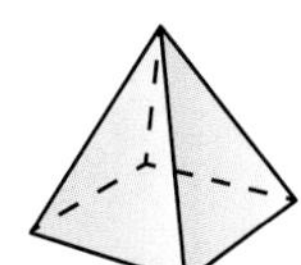

22. Visualize a plane intersecting the square pyramid through the vertex and perpendicular to opposite edges of the base. Describe the cross section.

23. Describe the three-dimensional figure that is formed from by rotating the rectangle about the side. SEE EXAMPLE 5

24. Describe the three-dimensional figure that is formed by rotating the pentagon about the line shown. SEE EXAMPLE 5

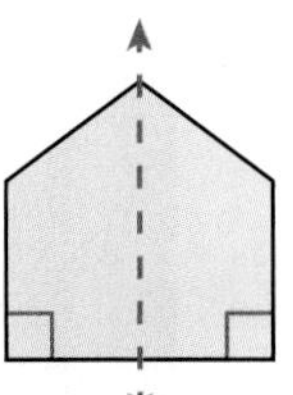

25. Describe the three-dimensional figure that is formed by rotating the circle about a diameter.

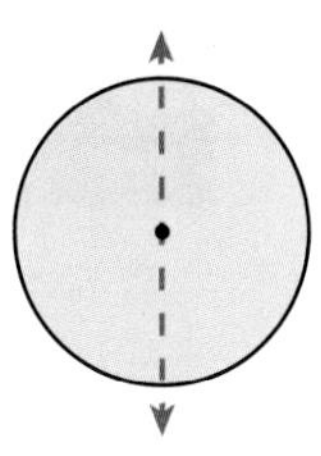

APPLY

26. Model With Mathematics Parker cuts 12 pentagons and 20 hexagons out of fabric to make the pillow shown. The pillow has 60 vertices. If it takes 20 inches of thread per seam to connect the edges of the polygons, how many inches of thread does Parker need to make the pillow?

27. Reason A gem cutter cuts a polyhedral crystal from a garnet gemstone. The crystal has 10 fewer vertices than edges and twice as many edges as faces. How many faces, vertices, and edges does the crystal have?

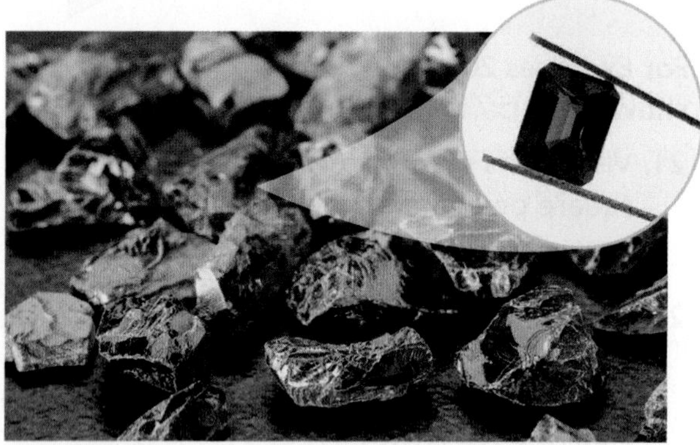

28. Communicate Precisely Rebecca wants to install a safety mat under the path of a revolving door. What shape should she make the mat? Explain.

ASSESSMENT PRACTICE

29. Complete the table for each polyhedron.

Polyhedron	Faces (F)	Vertices (V)	Edges (E)
regular dodecahedron	12		30
heptagonal pyramid	8	9	
octahedron	8		12
rhombohedron		8	12

30. SAT/ACT Which best describes the cross section of plane X and the polyhedron shown?

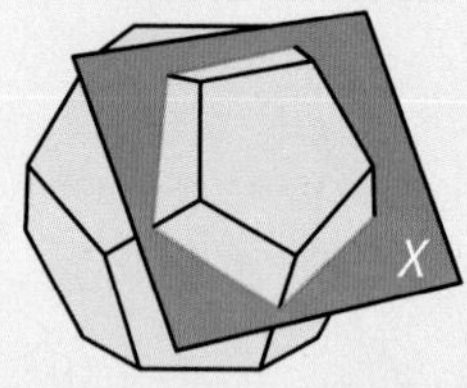

Ⓐ hexagon
Ⓑ pentagon
Ⓒ rectangle
Ⓓ trapezoid
Ⓔ triangle

31. Performance Task Draw a polyhedron with the fewest possible faces, vertices, and edges. Choose the faces from the polygons shown. You may use a polygon more than once.

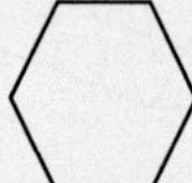 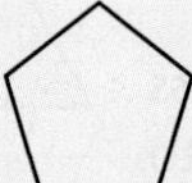 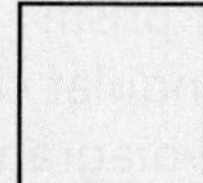 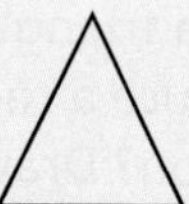

Part A Explain why the polygon or polygons you chose minimize the number of vertices and edges.

Part B How do you know that there is no polyhedron with fewer faces, vertices, or edges than the one you drew?

11-2 Volumes of Prisms and Cylinders

Activity Assess

I CAN… use the properties of prisms and cylinders to calculate their volumes.

VOCABULARY

- Cavalieri's Principle
- oblique cylinder
- oblique prism

MODEL & DISCUSS

The Environmental Club has a piece of wire mesh that they want to form into an open-bottom and open-top compost bin.

A. Using one side as the height, describe how you can form a compost bin in the shape of a rectangular prism using all of the mesh with no overlap.

B. **Construct Arguments** Which height would result in the largest volume? Explain.

C. Suppose you formed a cylinder using the same height as a rectangular prism. How would the volumes compare?

? ESSENTIAL QUESTION **How does the volume of a prism or cylinder relate to a cross section parallel to its base?**

CONCEPTUAL UNDERSTANDING

EXAMPLE 1 Develop Cavalieri's Principle

How are the volumes of the two different stacks of index cards related?

The first stack forms a right prism. The second stack forms an *oblique prism*. An **oblique prism** is a prism such that some or all of the lateral faces are nonrectangular.

VOCABULARY
Remember that in a right prism, the sides are perpendicular to the bases. In an *oblique prism*, one or more sides are not perpendicular to the bases.

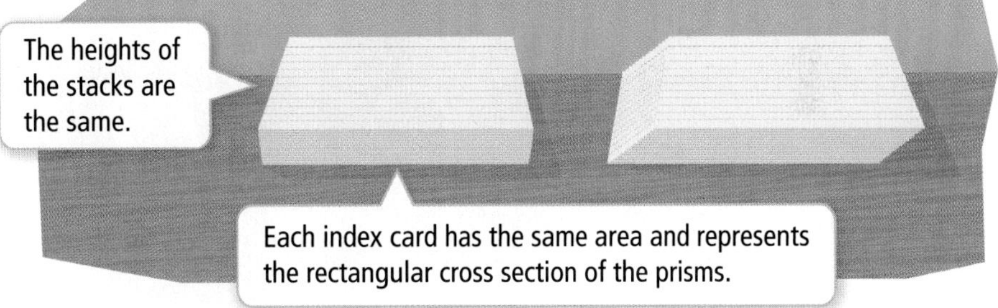

The volumes of the two stacks are the same because the sums of the areas of the cards are the same.

Try It! **1.** Do you think that right and oblique cylinders that have the same height and cross-sectional area also have equal volume? Explain.

CONCEPT Cavalieri's Principle

Cavalieri's Principle states that if two three-dimensional figures have the same height and the same cross-sectional area at every level, then they have the same volume.

If…

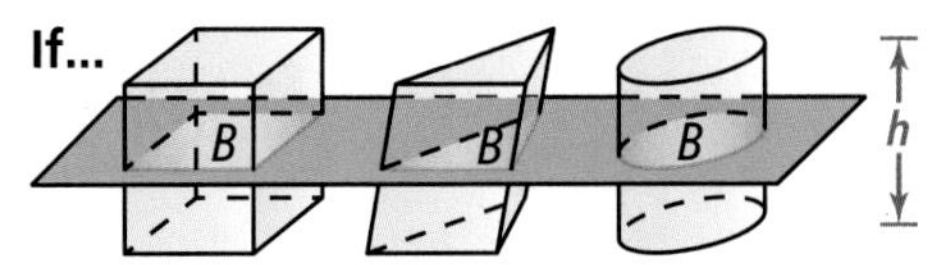

Then… the volumes are equal.

CONCEPT Volumes of Prisms and Cylinders

The volume of a prism is the product of the area of the base and the height of the prism.

$V = Bh$

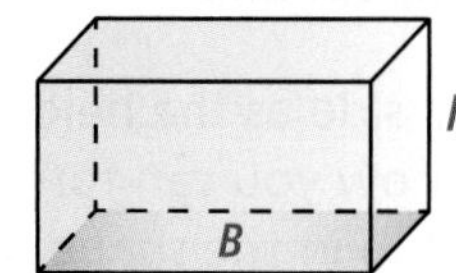

The volume of a cylinder is the product of the area of the base and the height of the cylinder.

$V = Bh$

$V = \pi r^2 h$

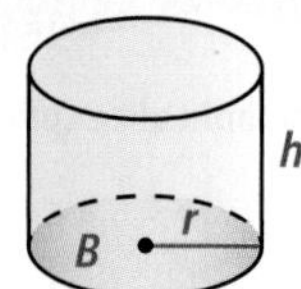

EXAMPLE 2 Find the Volumes of Prisms and Cylinders

A. Lonzell needs to store 20 ft^3 of firewood. Could he use the storage rack shown?

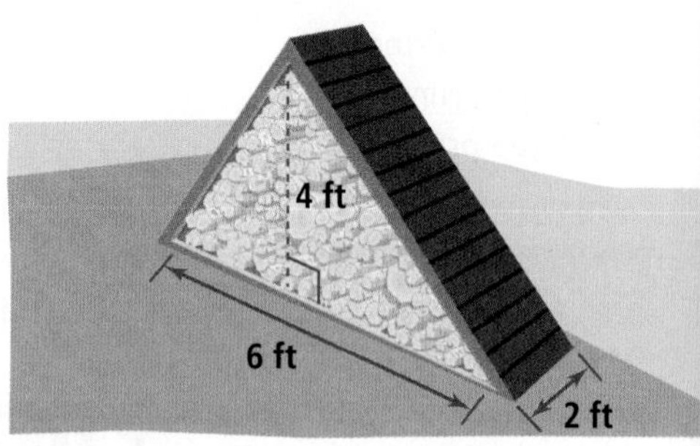

The rack is a triangular prism.

$$V = Bh$$
$$= \left[\frac{1}{2}(4)(6)\right](2) = 24$$

The volume of the storage rack is 24 ft^3, so Lonzell can store his firewood in the rack.

B. Keisha is deciding between the two canisters shown. Which canister holds more? What is the volume of the larger canister?

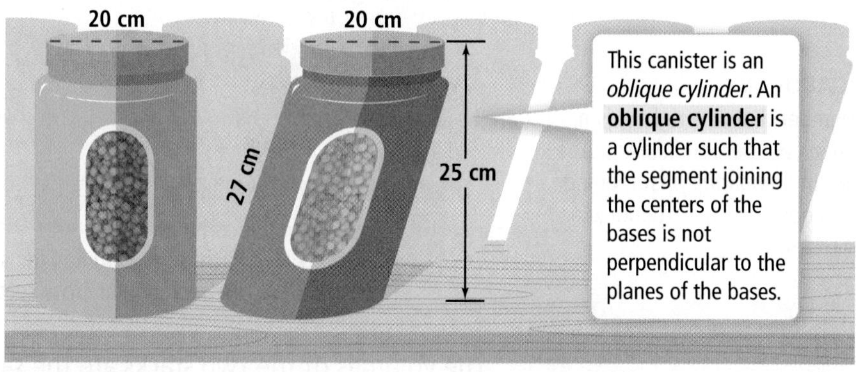

The canisters have the same cross-sectional area at every height. So, by Cavalieri's Principle, the canisters have the same volume.

Use the volume formula to find the volume of the canister on the left.

$$V = \pi r^2 h$$
$$= \pi(10)^2(25) \approx 7{,}854$$

The diameter is 20 cm, so the radius is 10 cm.

The volume of both canisters is about 7,854 cm^3.

COMMON ERROR
The height of an oblique cylinder or prism is the length perpendicular to the bases, not the length of the sides of the figure.

 **Try It!** 2. a. How would the volume of the storage shed change if the length of the triangular base is reduced by half?

b. How would the volume of the canisters change if the diameter is doubled?

APPLICATION

EXAMPLE 3 Apply the Volumes of Prisms to Solve Problems

Marta is repurposing a sandbox as a garden and is buying the soil from her school's fundraiser. Estimate the number of bags she should buy.

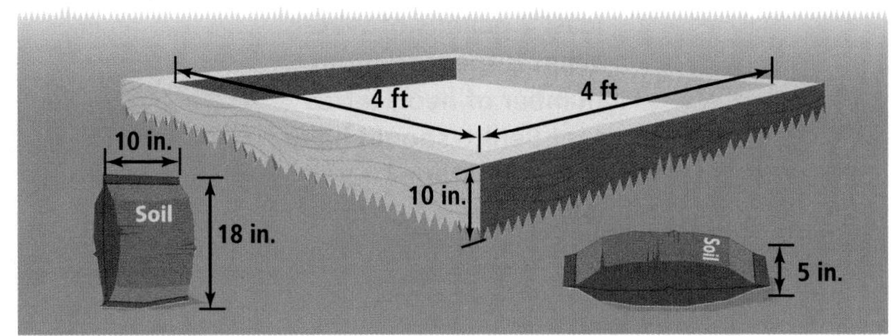

Step 1 Determine the volume of soil needed.

Compute the volume of the sandbox in cubic inches.

$$V = Bh$$
$$= (48 \cdot 48)(10)$$
$$= 23{,}040$$

Use 4 ft = 48 in.

Marta needs 23,040 in.^{3} of soil.

Step 2 Estimate the volume of soil in each bag by modeling the bag of soil as a rectangular prism.

The height of the bag is tapered on the ends, but thicker in the middle, so we still use 5 inches to estimate the height.

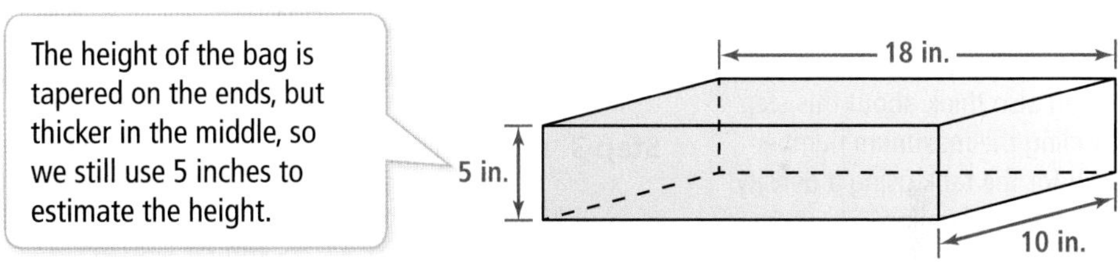

$$V = Bh$$
$$= (10 \cdot 18)(5) = 900$$

The volume of one bag of soil is about 900 in.^{3}.

MODEL WITH MATHEMATICS Think about other ways to model the bag. Is a rectangular prism with the values used a reasonable model?

Step 3 Estimate the number of bags needed.

$$23{,}040 \div 900 \approx 26$$

Marta should buy 26 bags of soil to fill the sandbox.

 **Try It!** 3. Kathryn is using cans of juice to fill a cylindrical pitcher that is 11 in. tall and has a radius of 4 in. Each can of juice is 6 in. tall with a radius of 2 in. How many cans of juice will Kathryn need?

EXAMPLE 4 Apply Volume of Cylinders to Solve Problems

Benito has 15 neon tetras in his aquarium. Each neon tetra requires at least 2 gallons of water. What is the maximum number of neon tetras that Benito should have in his aquarium? (*Hint:* 1 gal = 231 in.^{3})

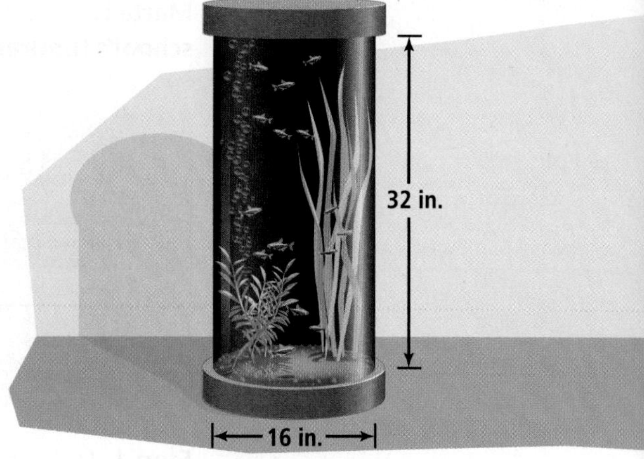

Step 1 Compute the volume of water in cubic inches.

$$V = \pi r^2 h$$
$$= \pi(8)^2(32)$$
$$\approx 6{,}434$$

The radius is half the diameter.

The volume of the water in the aquarium is about 6,434 in.^{3}.

Step 2 Find the volume of water in gallons.

$$6{,}434 \text{ in.}^3 \cdot \frac{1 \text{ gal}}{231 \text{ in.}^3} \approx 27.85 \text{ gal}$$

The volume of the water in the aquarium is about 27.85 gal.

STUDY TIP
You can also think about this step as finding the maximum number of fish for the tank using a density of 0.5 tetra per gallon.

Step 3 Compute the number of neon tetras that Benito's tank should hold.

Use a proportion to find the maximum number x of neon tetras that should be in 27.85 gal of water.

$$\frac{x \text{ fish}}{27.85 \text{ gal}} = \frac{1 \text{ fish}}{2 \text{ gal}}$$
$$\frac{x}{27.85} = \frac{1}{2}$$
$$2x = 27.85$$
$$x = 13.925$$

Benito should have no more than 13 neon tetras in his aquarium.

Try It! **4.** Benito is considering the aquarium shown. What is the maximum number of neon tetras that this aquarium can hold?

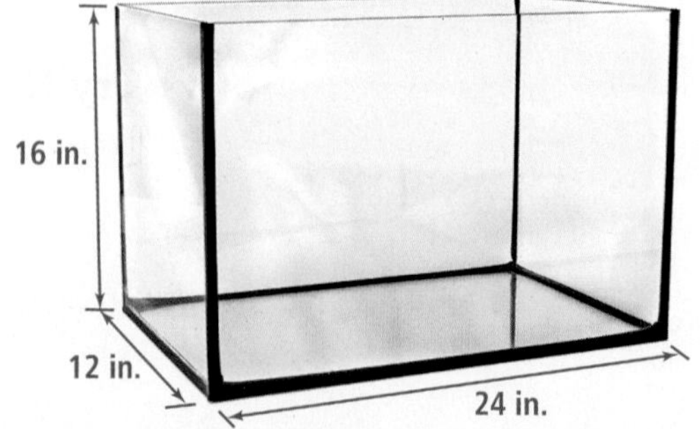

APPLICATION

EXAMPLE 5 Determine Whether Volume or Surface Area Best Describes Size

A forester surveys giant sequoias by gathering data about the heights and circumference of the trees.

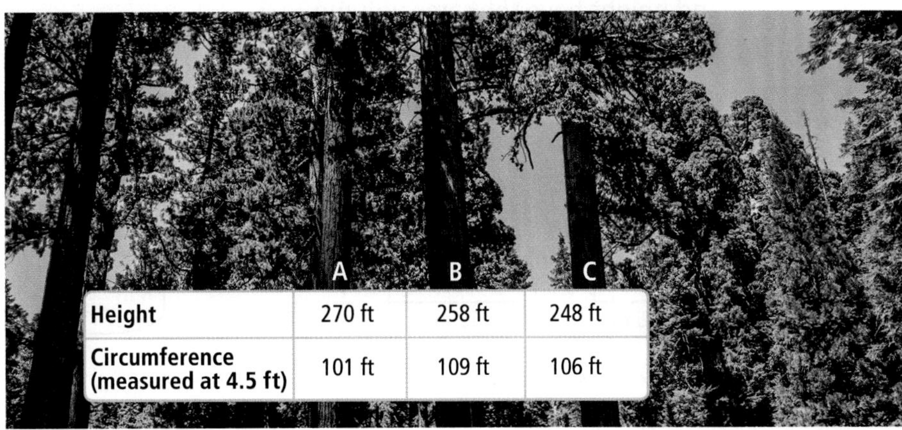

	A	B	C
Height	270 ft	258 ft	248 ft
Circumference (measured at 4.5 ft)	101 ft	109 ft	106 ft

A. Should the forester use surface area or volume to describe the sizes of the sequoias? Explain.

The amount of wood in a tree is represented by its volume, so she should use volume to determine the size of a giant sequoia.

MODEL WITH MATHEMATICS
Think about other shapes you could use to represent the tree. What is another mathematical model you could use for this problem?

B. What are the sizes of the sequoias shown? Rank them in order by size from largest to smallest.

Although the sequoias have branches and the trunk tapers gradually toward the top of the tree, each tree can be modeled as a cylinder. Find the volume of each cylinder to estimate the volume of each tree.

	Radius (ft)	Volume of Trunk (ft^3)
Tree A 270 ft	$r = \frac{101}{2\pi} \approx 16.1$	$V = \pi r^2 h$ $= \pi(16.1)^2(270)$ $\approx 219{,}870$
Tree B 258 ft	$r = \frac{109}{2\pi} \approx 17.3$	$V = \pi r^2 h$ $= \pi(17.3)^2(258)$ $\approx 242{,}584$
Tree C 248 ft	$r = \frac{106}{2\pi} \approx 16.9$	$V = \pi r^2 h$ $= \pi(16.9)^2(248)$ $\approx 222{,}523$

In order from largest to smallest, the three trees are: Tree B, Tree C, Tree A.

Try It! **5.** Describe a situation when surface area might be a better measure of size than volume.

CONCEPT SUMMARY Volumes of Prisms and Cylinders

WORDS

Cavalieri's Principle Figures with the same height and same cross-sectional area at every level have the same volume.

As a result, right and oblique prisms and cylinders with the same base area and height have the same volume.

DIAGRAMS

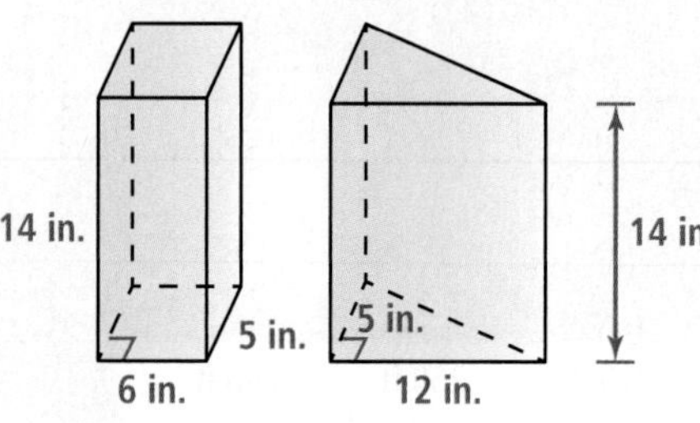

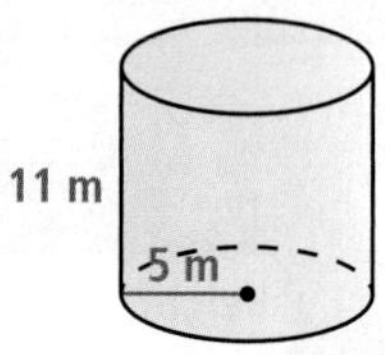

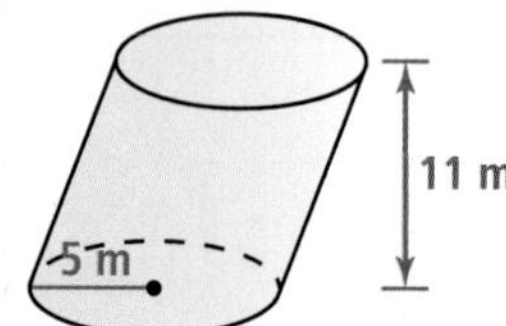

$V = Bh$

$V = 30 \cdot 14$

$V = 420$ cubic inches

$V = Bh$

$V = \pi r^2 h$

$= \pi \cdot 5^2 \cdot 11$

$= 863.9$ cubic meters

Do You UNDERSTAND?

1. **ESSENTIAL QUESTION** How does the volume of a prism or cylinder relate to a cross section parallel to its base?

2. **Error Analysis** Sawyer says that Cavalieri's Principle proves that the two prisms shown have the same volume. Explain Sawyer's error.

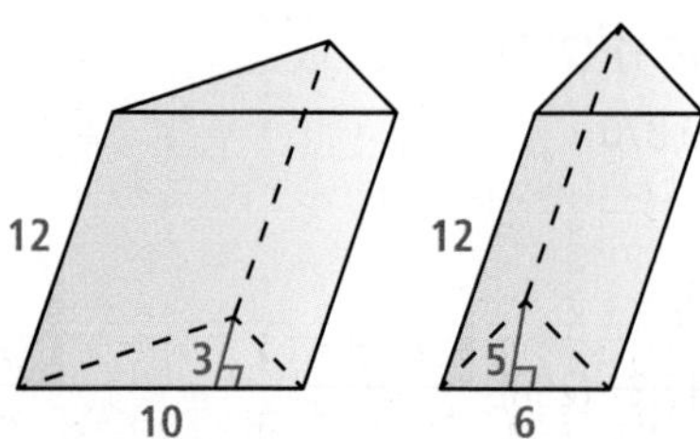

3. **Vocabulary** How are an oblique prism and an oblique cylinder alike and different?

4. **Reason** The circumference of the base of a cylinder is x, and the height of the cylinder is x. What expression gives the volume of the cylinder?

5. **Construct Arguments** Denzel kicks a large dent into a trash can and says that the volume does not change because of Cavalieri's Principle. Do you agree with Denzel? Explain.

Do You KNOW HOW?

For Exercises 6–11, find the volume of each figure. Round to the nearest tenth.

6.

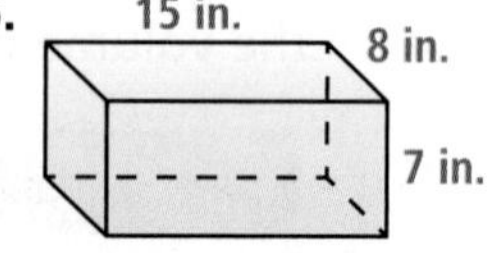

7.

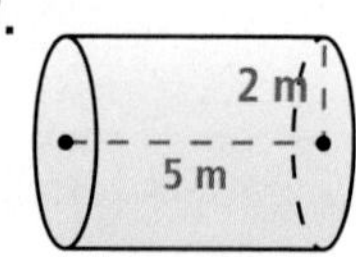

8.

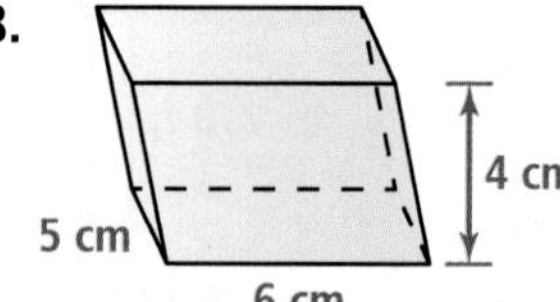

9.

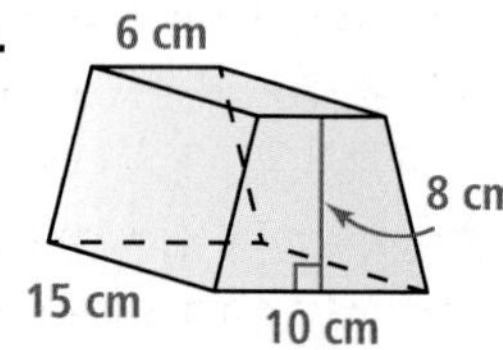

10.

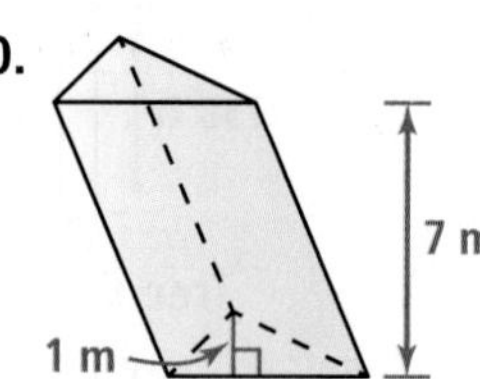

11.

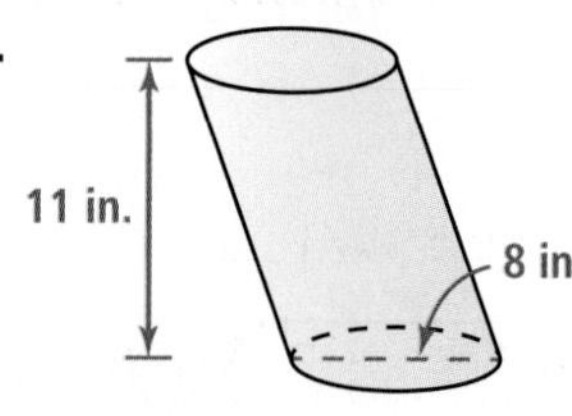

12. Which figures have the same volume? Explain.

A — 4 ft, 2 ft

B — 4 ft, π ft, 1 ft

C — 4 ft, 2 ft

Scan for Multimedia

Practice Tutorial

Additional Exercises Available Online

UNDERSTAND

13. **Error Analysis** Dylan compares the volumes of two bottles. What is Dylan's error?

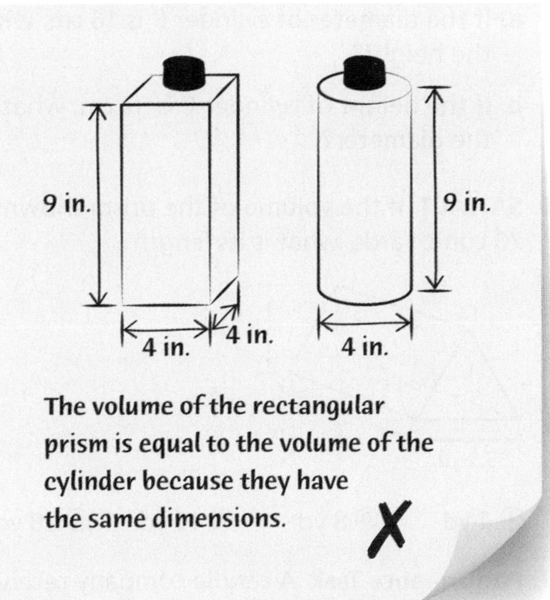

14. **Higher Order Thinking** Does Cavalieri's Principle apply to the volumes of the cones shown? Explain.

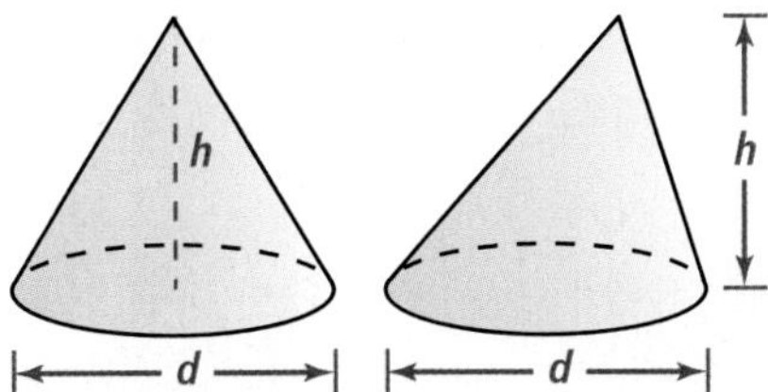

15. **Mathematical Connections** Does rotating the rectangle about line *m* result in a cylinder with the same volume as rotating the rectangle about line *n*? Explain.

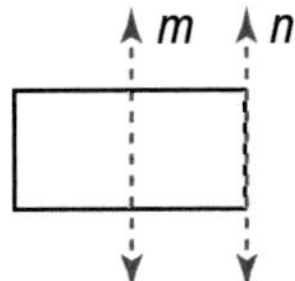

16. **Use Appropriate Tools** Do the prisms shown have equivalent volumes? Explain.

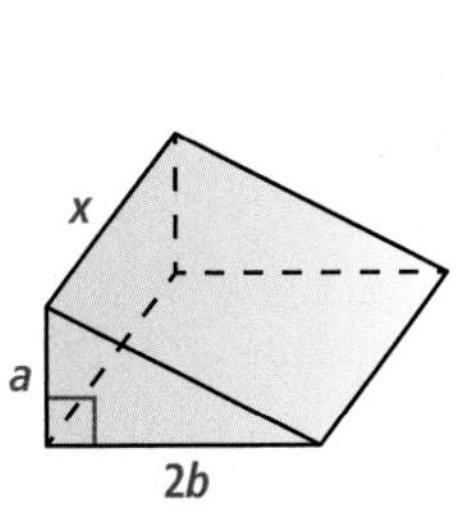

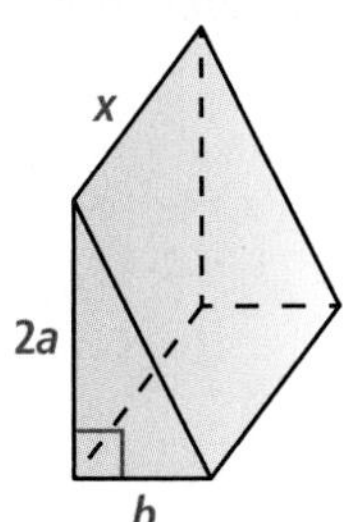

PRACTICE

17. Katrina buys the two vases shown. How do the volumes of the vases compare? Explain. SEE EXAMPLE 1

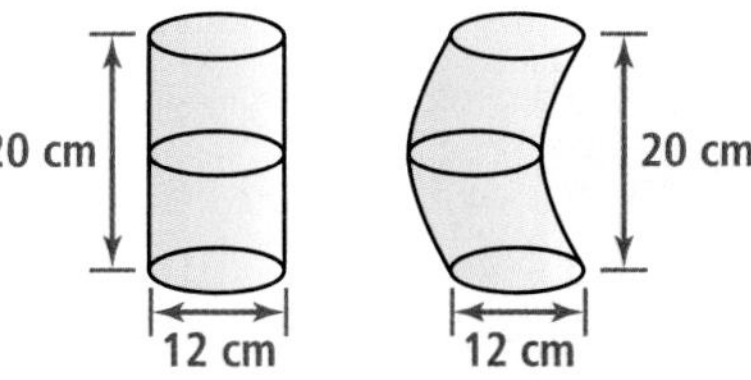

18. Talisa plans a 6-foot deep pond. While digging, she hits rock 5 feet down. How can Talisa modify the radius to maintain the original volume of the pond? SEE EXAMPLE 2

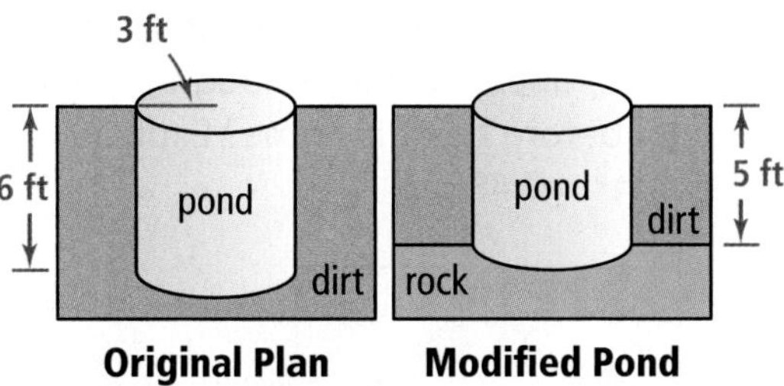

19. The instructions for plant food say to use 0.25 gram per cubic inch of soil. How many grams of plant food should Jordan use if the planter box shown is full of soil? SEE EXAMPLE 3

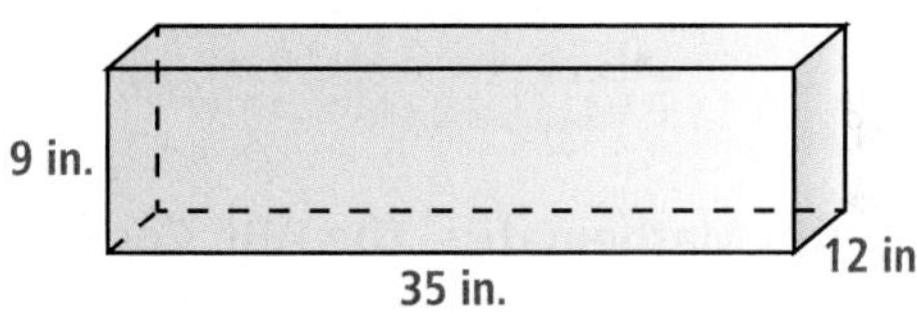

20. If a stack of 40 nickels fits snugly in the coin wrapper shown, how thick is 1 nickel? Round to the nearest hundredth. SEE EXAMPLE 4

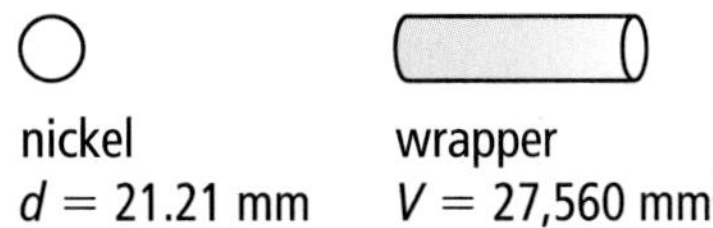

21. Sections of two flood-control ditches are shown. Which one holds the greater volume of water per foot? Explain. SEE EXAMPLE 5

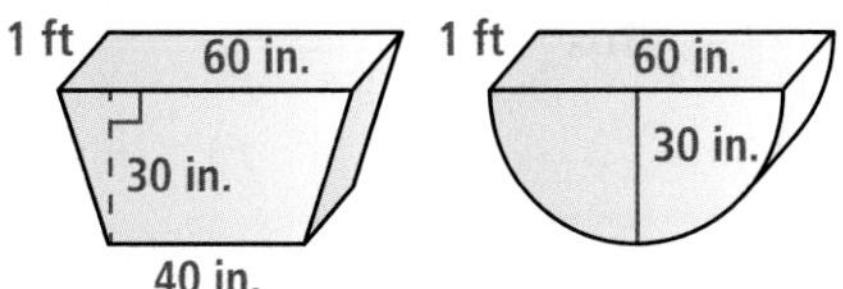

PRACTICE & PROBLEM SOLVING

Practice Tutorial

Mixed Review Available Online

APPLY

22. Use Appropriate Tools How many 3-inch-thick bags of mulch should Noemi buy to cover 100 square feet at a depth of 4 inches?

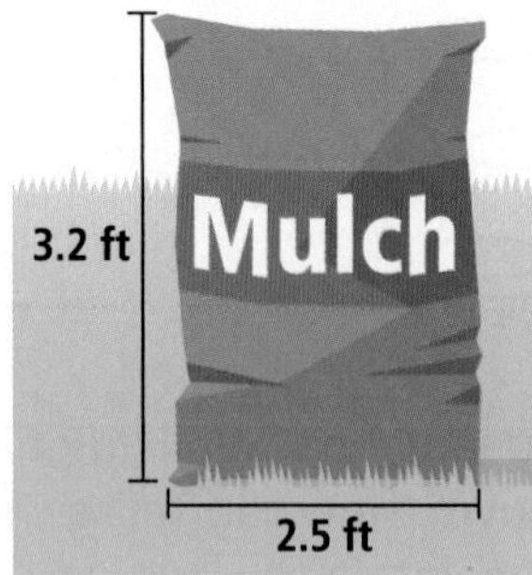

23. Reason Ines's younger brother will be home in a half hour. If her garden hose flows at a rate 24 gal/min, does she have enough time to fill the pool before he gets home? Explain. (*Hint:* 1 ft^3 = 7.48 gal)

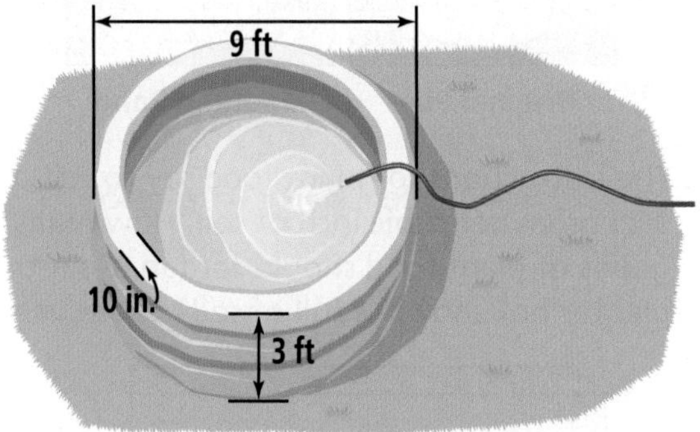

24. Model With Mathematics The ABC Cookie Company wants to promise an average of "12 chocolate chips per cookie." Assuming that the cookies fill about 80% of the box by volume, will 600 chocolate chips for each box of cookies be sufficient to make the claim? Explain.

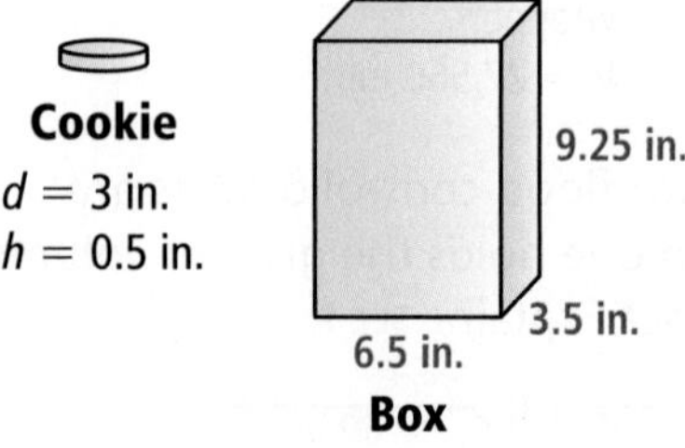

ASSESSMENT PRACTICE

25. Cylinders A, B, and C have the same volume. Cylinder A has diameter 12 cm and height 8 cm.

a. If the diameter of cylinder B is 16 cm, what is the height?

b. If the height of cylinder C is 32 cm, what is the diameter?

26. SAT/ACT If the volume of the prism shown is 70 cubic yards, what is its length?

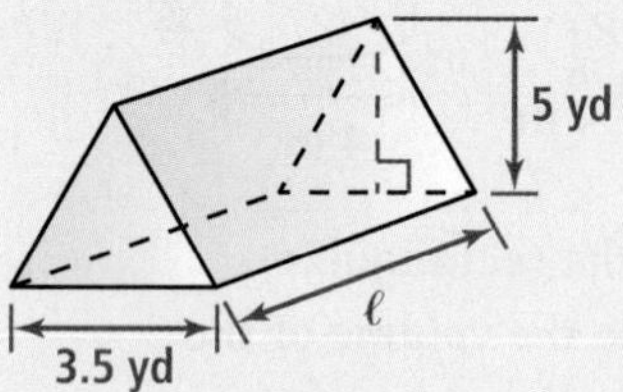

Ⓐ 4 yd Ⓑ 8 yd Ⓒ 16 yd Ⓓ 28 yd

27. Performance Task A candle company receives an order for an overnight delivery of 8 short candles and 6 tall candles. The overnight service has a weight limit of 23 kg.

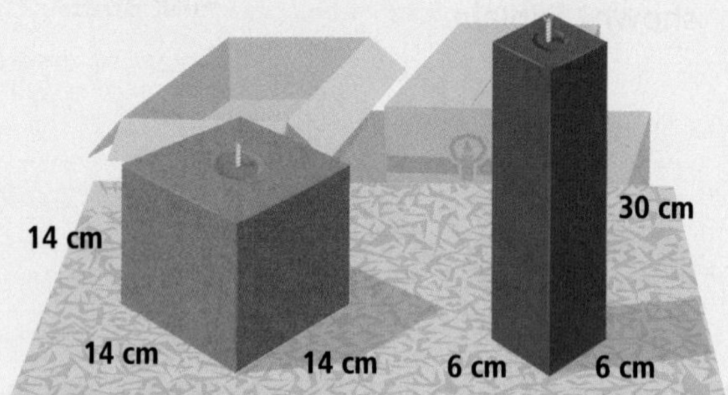

Part A The density of the wax used to make each candle is 0.0009 kg/cm^3. What is the weight of the order? Can the order be filled and shipped for delivery?

Part B If no tall candles are included in the order, what is the greatest number of short candles that can be delivered?

Part C What combination of tall and short candles can be delivered if the total number of candles delivered is 10?

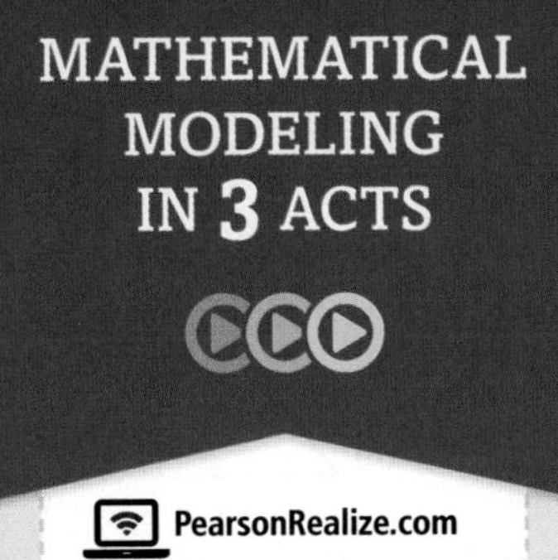

PearsonRealize.com

Video

Box ‘Em Up

With so many people and businesses shopping online, retailers, and especially e-retailers, ship more and more packages every day. Some of the products people order have unusual sizes and shapes and need custom packaging. Imagine how you might package a surfboard, or a snow blower, or even live crawfish to ship to someone's house!

Think about this during the Mathematical Modeling in 3 Acts lesson.

ACT 1 Identify the Problem

1. What is the first question that comes to mind after watching the video?
2. Write down the main question you will answer about what you saw in the video.
3. Make an initial conjecture that answers this main question.
4. Explain how you arrived at your conjecture.
5. What information will be useful to know to answer the main question? How can you get it? How will you use that information?

ACT 2 Develop a Model

6. Use the math that you have learned in this Topic to refine your conjecture.

ACT 3 Interpret the Results

7. Did your refined conjecture match the actual answer exactly? If not, what might explain the difference?

11-3 Pyramids and Cones

PearsonRealize.com

I CAN… use the volumes of right and oblique pyramids and cones to solve problems.

Activity | Assess

EXPLORE & REASON

Consider the cube and pyramid.

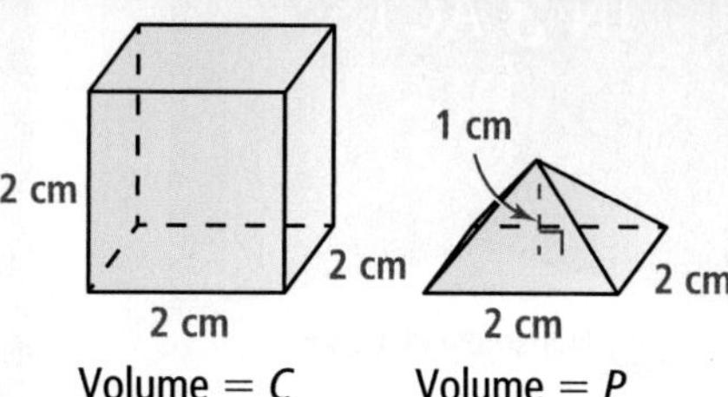

A. How many pyramids could you fit inside the cube? Explain.

B. Write an equation that shows the relationship between C and P.

C. **Look for Relationships** Make a conjecture about the volume of any pyramid. Explain your reasoning.

ESSENTIAL QUESTION

How are the formulas for volume of a pyramid and volume of a cone alike?

CONCEPTUAL UNDERSTANDING

EXAMPLE 1 Apply Cavalieri's Principle to Pyramids and Cones

How are the volumes of pyramids and cones with the same base area and height related?

Imagine a set of cardboard discs, each with a slightly smaller radius than the previous disc. You can stack the discs in different ways.

GENERALIZE
Think about the shape formed by the stacks. What would happen if the number of discs increases while the difference in the radii and the thickness of each disc decreases?

The heights of the stacks are the same, and the area at each level is the same. The total volume of cardboard in each stack is the same.

The stacks approximate cones. You can apply Cavalieri's Principle to cones and pyramids.

If two figures have the same height and equal area at every cross section, they have equal volumes.

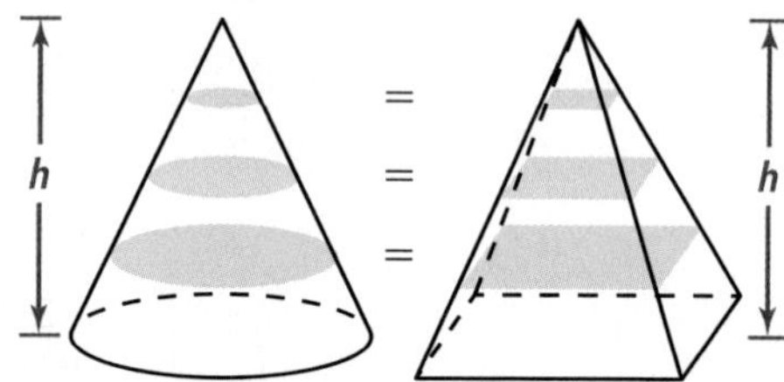

Try It! 1. Is it possible to use only Cavalieri's Principle to show that a cone and a cylinder have equal volumes? Explain.

CONCEPT Volumes of Pyramids and Cones

The volume of a pyramid is one-third the product of the area of the base and the height of the pyramid.

$V = \frac{1}{3}Bh$

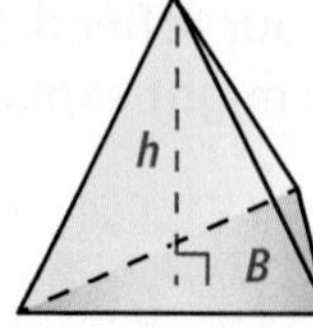

The volume of a cone is one-third the product of the area of the base and the height of the cone.

$V = \frac{1}{3}Bh$

$V = \frac{1}{3}\pi r^2 h$

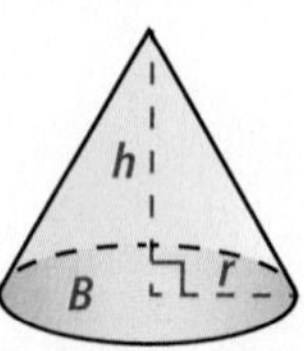

  Activity  Assess

EXAMPLE 2 Find the Volumes of Pyramids and Cones

A. Kyle's truck can haul 1.75 tons of corn per load. One cubic meter of corn weighs 0.8 ton. How many loads will Kyle haul to move this pile of corn?

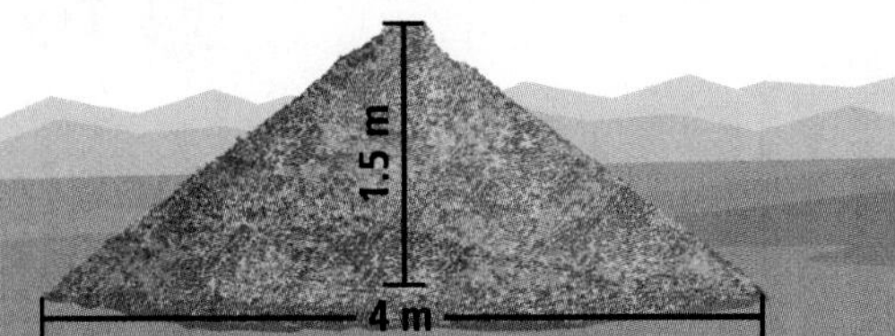

$V = \frac{1}{3}\pi r^2 h$

$= \frac{1}{3}\pi(2)^2(1.5) \approx 6.3 \text{ m}^3$

The pile is shaped like a cone, so use the volume formula for cones.

Since $6.3 \text{ m}^3 \cdot 0.8 \text{ ton/m}^3 = 5.04$ tons, Kyle will need to haul $5.04 \div 1.75 = 2.88$ or 3 loads.

B. Jason is using the mold to make 12 candles. How many cubic inches of wax does he need?

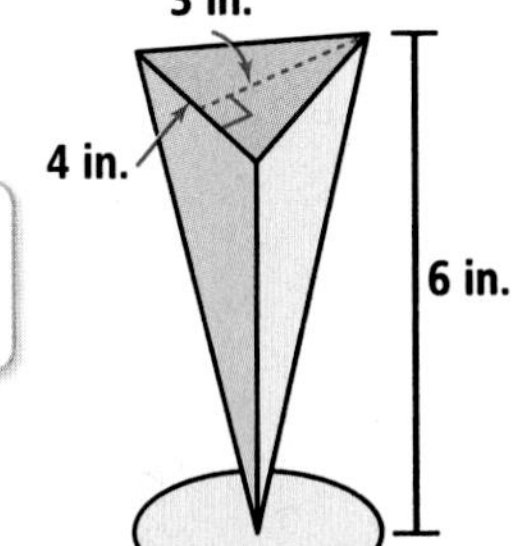

$V = \frac{1}{3}Bh$

$= \frac{1}{3}\left[\frac{1}{2}(4)(3)\right](6) = 12 \text{ in.}^3$

Use the volume formula for a pyramid.

Use the area formula for a triangle to find the base.

STUDY TIP
The base of a pyramid can be any polygon, so the formula you use to determine the area of the base B depends on the shape of the base.

For 12 candles, Jason needs $12 \text{ in.}^3 \cdot 12$, or 144 in.^3 of wax.

Try It! 2. a. What is the volume of a cone with base diameter 14 and height 16?

b. What is the volume of a pyramid with base area 10 and height 7?

EXAMPLE 3 Apply the Volumes of Pyramids to Solve Problems

Dyani is 1.8 m tall and wants to be able to stand inside her new tent. Should she buy this tent?

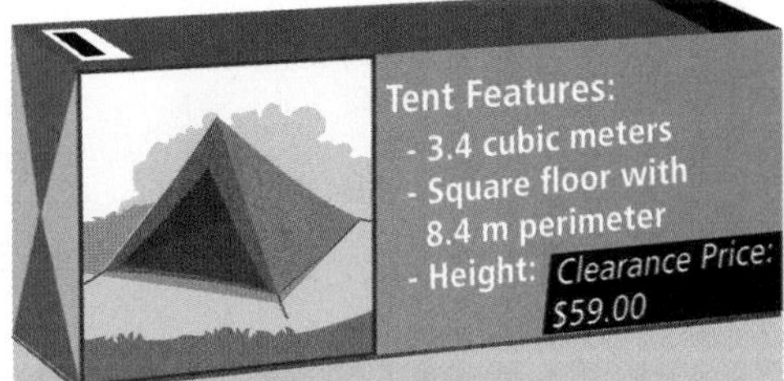

Step 1 Draw and label a square pyramid to represent the tent.

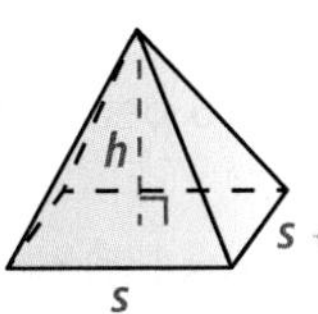

Since the perimeter of the square floor is 8.4 m, $s = 2.1$ m.

Step 2 Find the height of the pyramid.

$V = \frac{1}{3}Bh$

$3.4 = \frac{1}{3}(2.1)^2 h$

$h \approx 2.3$

The height of the pyramid is approximately 2.3 m.

Dyani will be able to stand in the tent, so she should buy this tent.

CONTINUED ON THE NEXT PAGE

EXAMPLE 3 CONTINUED

Try It! 3. A rectangular pyramid has a base that is three times as long as it is wide. The volume of the pyramid is 75 ft^3 and the height is 3 ft. What is the perimeter of the base?

APPLICATION

EXAMPLE 4 Apply the Volumes of Cones to Solve Problems

A restaurant sells smoothies in two sizes. Which size is a better deal?

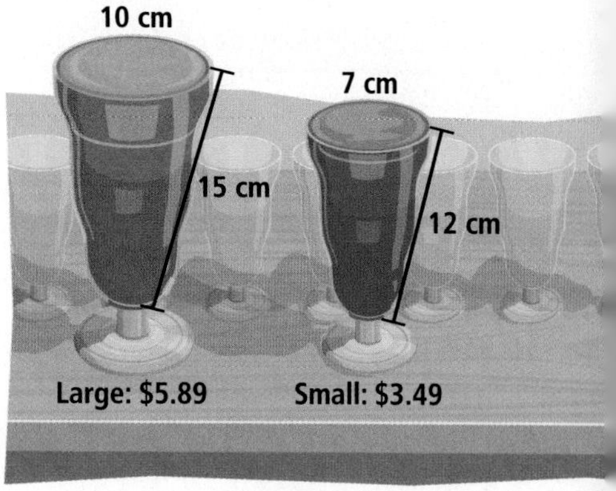

Formulate Compare the prices by determining the cost per cubic centimeter for each size.

The volume of fruit smoothie in each glass can be approximated as the volume of a cone.

Compute **Step 1** Calculate the height of each cone using the Pythagorean Theorem.

Large

$$5^2 + h^2 = 15^2$$
$$h^2 = 200$$
$$h \approx 14.1$$

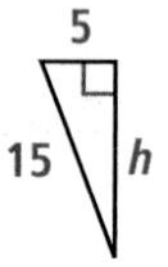

The height of the large cone is approximately 14.1 cm.

Small

$$3.5^2 + h^2 = 12^2$$
$$h^2 = 131.75$$
$$h \approx 11.5$$

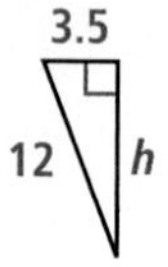

The height of the small cone is approximately 11.5 cm.

Step 2 Calculate the volume of each cone.

Large

$$V = \frac{1}{3}\pi r^2 h$$
$$= \frac{1}{3}\pi(5)^2(14.1)$$
$$\approx 369.1$$

The volume of the large cone is approximately 369.1 cm^3.

Small

$$V = \frac{1}{3}\pi r^2 h$$
$$= \frac{1}{3}\pi(3.5)^2(11.5)$$
$$\approx 147.5$$

The volume of the small cone is approximately 147.5 cm^3.

Step 3 Calculate the cost per cubic centimeter for each size.

Large

$$\frac{\$5.89}{369.1 \text{ cm}^3} \approx \$0.016 \text{ per cm}^3$$

Small

$$\frac{\$3.49}{147.5 \text{ cm}^3} \approx \$0.024 \text{ per cm}^3$$

Interpret The large size smoothie costs less per cubic centimeter, so the large size smoothie is a better deal.

CONTINUED ON THE NEXT PAGE

EXAMPLE 4 CONTINUED

 **Try It!** **4.** A cone has a volume of 144π and a height of 12.

a. What is the radius of the base?

b. If the radius of the cone is tripled, what is the new volume? What is the relationship between the volumes of the two cones?

APPLICATION

EXAMPLE 5 Measure a Composite Figure

Kaitlyn is making a concrete animal sculpture. Each bag of concrete mix makes 0.6 ft^3 of concrete. How many bags of concrete mix does Kaitlyn need?

Calculate the volume of each part.

Step 1 Calculate the volume of one of the legs.

$$V = \pi r^2 h$$
$$= \pi(2)^2(16)$$
$$\approx 201 \text{ in.}^3$$

The legs are oblique cylinders.

Step 2 Calculate the volume of the body.

$$V = Bh$$
$$= (22 \cdot 18)(15)$$
$$= 5{,}940 \text{ in.}^3$$

The body is a rectangular prism.

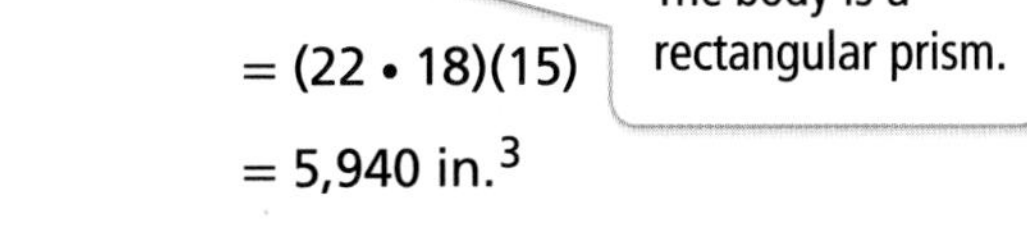

Step 3 Calculate the volume of the head.

$$V = \frac{1}{3}Bh$$
$$= \frac{1}{3}(16 \cdot 16)(20)$$
$$\approx 1{,}707 \text{ in.}^3$$

The head is a square pyramid.

Step 4 Calculate the total volume.

$$V = 4(201) + 5{,}940 + 1{,}707$$
$$= 8{,}451$$

Add the volumes of the parts of the sculpture.

The total volume is 8,451 in.^{3}. Convert to cubic feet to determine the amount of concrete needed.

$$8{,}451 \cdot \frac{1}{1{,}728} = 4.9$$

$1 \text{ ft}^3 = (12 \text{ in.})^3 = 1{,}728 \text{ in.}^3$

To make the sculpture, 4.9 ft^3 of concrete is needed. Kaitlyn needs $4.9 \div 0.6 \approx 8.2$ or 9 bags of concrete mix.

COMMON ERROR
When multiple parts of a composite figure have the same volume, make sure you account for each part in your total.

 **Try It!** **5.** A cone-shaped hole is drilled in a prism. The height of the triangular base is 12 cm. What is the volume of the remaining figure? Round to the nearest tenth.

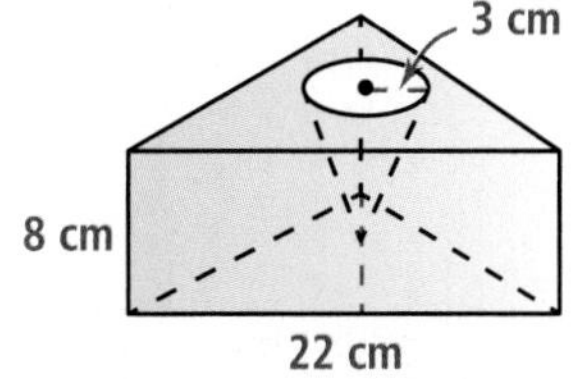

CONCEPT SUMMARY Pyramids and Cones

WORDS

The volume of a pyramid is one-third the volume of a prism with the same base area and height.

The volume of a cone is one-third the volume of a cylinder with the same base area and height.

DIAGRAMS

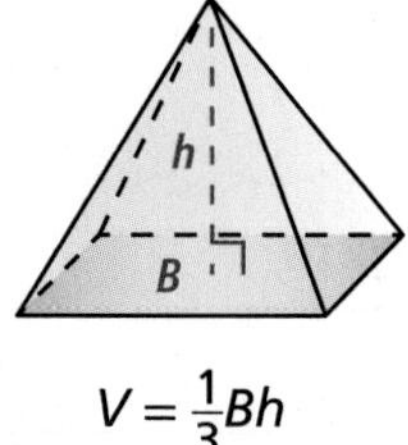

$V = \frac{1}{3}Bh$

h
B
r

$V = \frac{1}{3}Bh$ or $V = \frac{1}{3}\pi r^2 h$

Do You UNDERSTAND?

1. **ESSENTIAL QUESTION** How are the formulas for volume of a pyramid and volume of a cone alike?

2. **Error Analysis** Zhang is finding the height of a square pyramid with a base side length of 9 and a volume of 162. What is his error?

$V = Bh$
$162 = 9^2(h)$
$h = 2$
✗

3. **Reason** A cone and cylinder have the same radius and volume. If the height of the cone is h, what is the height of the cylinder?

4. **Construct Arguments** Do you have enough information to compute the volume of the cone? Explain.

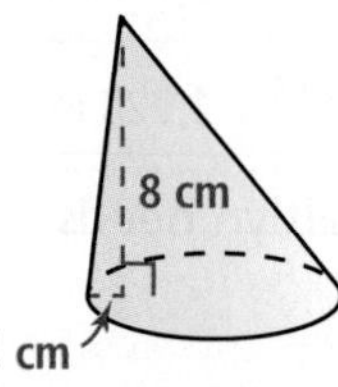

Do You KNOW HOW?

For Exercises 5–10, find the volume of each figure. Round to the nearest tenth. Assume that all angles in each polygonal base are congruent.

5.
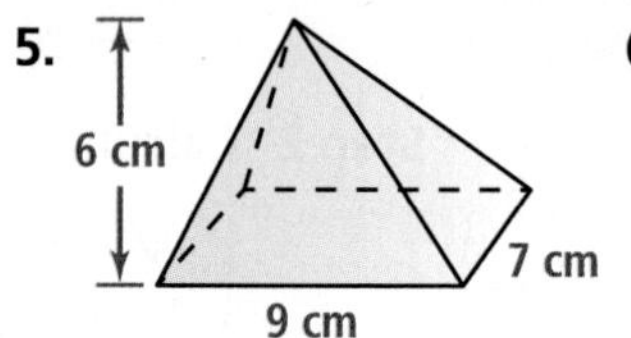

6.
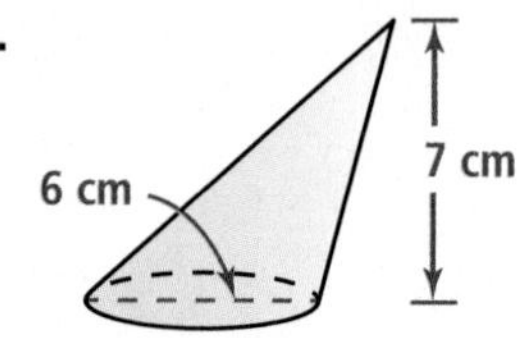

7.
8 in.
3 in.

8.
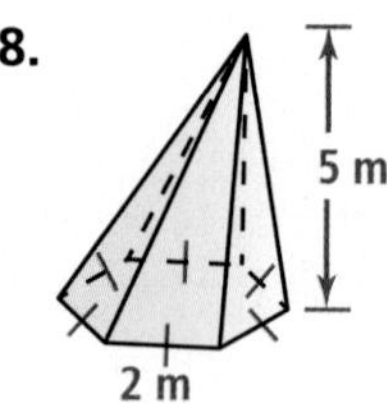

9.
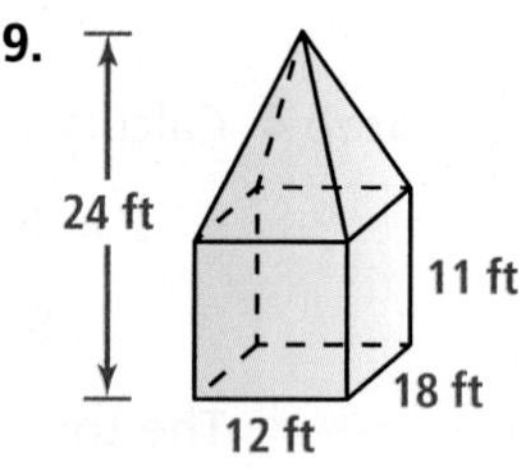

10.
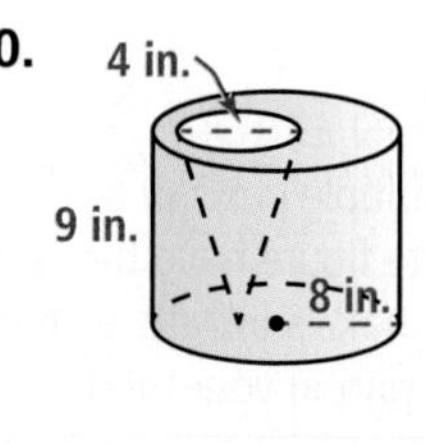

11. A solid metal square pyramid with a base side length of 6 in. and height of 9 in. is melted down and recast as a square pyramid with a height of 4 in. What is the base side length of the new pyramid?

PRACTICE & PROBLEM SOLVING

Scan for Multimedia

 Practice  Tutorial

Additional Exercises Available Online

UNDERSTAND

12. Construct Arguments A stack of 39 pennies is exactly as tall as a stack of 31 nickels. Do the two stacks have the same volume? Explain.

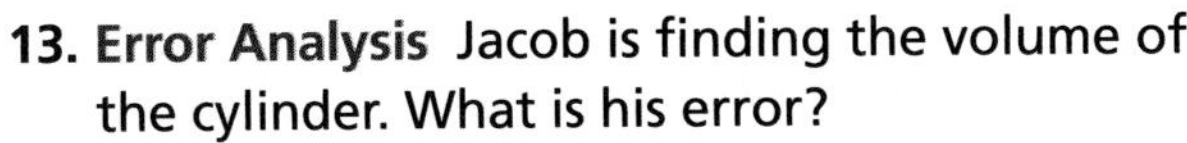

13. Error Analysis Jacob is finding the volume of the cylinder. What is his error?

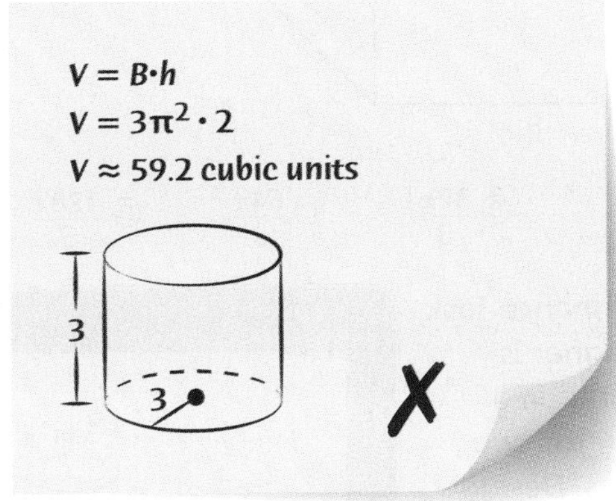

14. Communicate Precisely How would you find the volume of a right square pyramid with a base side length of 10 cm, and the altitude of a triangular side is 13 cm? Explain.

15. Mathematical Connections In terms of the radius *r*, what is the volume of a cone whose height is equal to its radius?

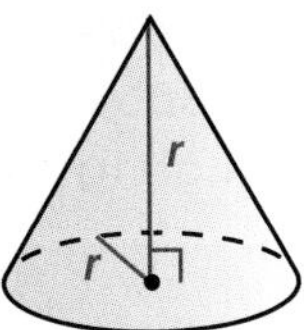

16. Higher Order Thinking A plane slices a cone parallel to the base at one-half of the height of the cone. What is the volume of the part of the cone lying below the plane?

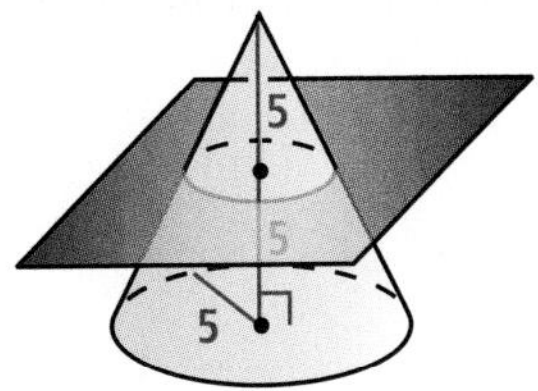

PRACTICE

17. The plane intersects sections of equal area in the two solids. Are the volumes equal? SEE EXAMPLE 1

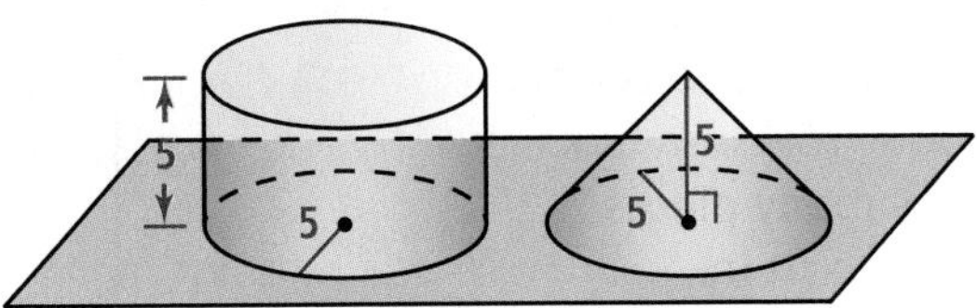

For Exercises 18–21, find the volume of each solid. Assume that all angles in each polygonal base are congruent. SEE EXAMPLE 2

18.

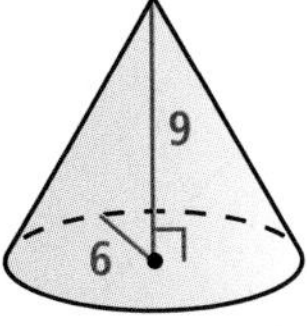

19.

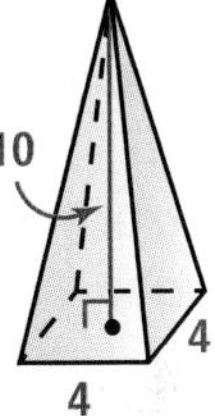

20.

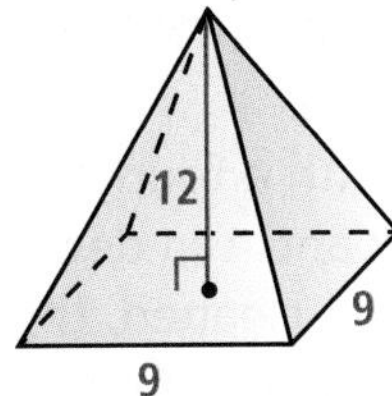

21.

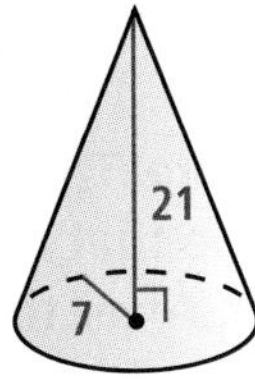

22. A cone is inscribed in a right square pyramid. What is the remaining volume if the cone is removed? SEE EXAMPLES 3 AND 4

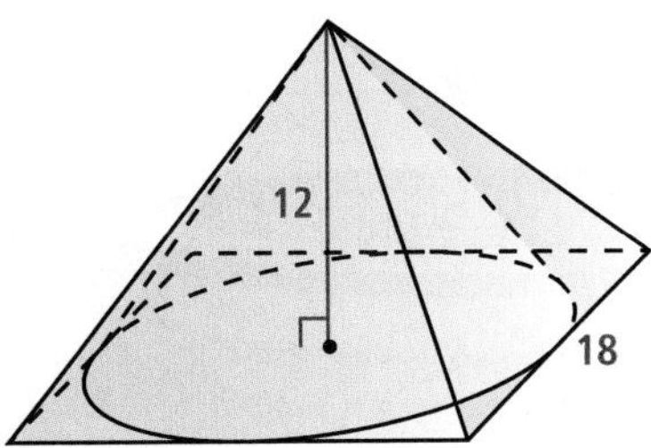

For Exercises 23 and 24, find the volume of each composite figure. SEE EXAMPLE 5

23.

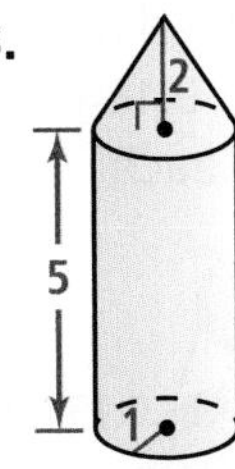

24.

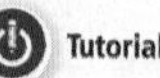

Mixed Review Available Online

PRACTICE & PROBLEM SOLVING

APPLY

25. Make Sense and Persevere Chiang makes gift boxes in the shape of a right square pyramid. She fills each box with chocolate cubes with $\frac{7}{8}$-in. sides. She can fill about 75% of a box. How many pieces can she fit in each box?

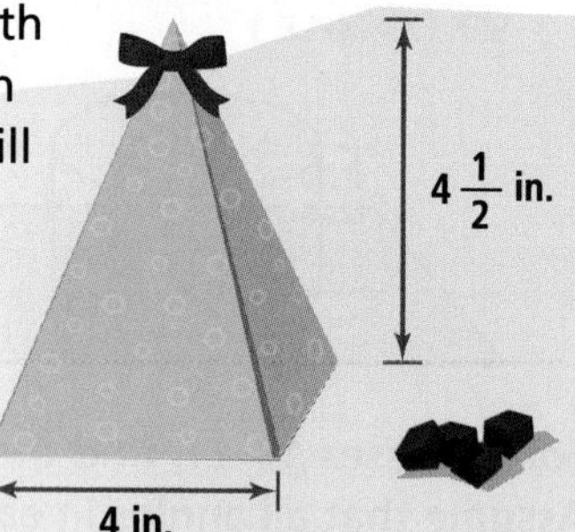

26. Reason A pile of snow is plowed into the shape of a right cone. How many trucks with a capacity of 10 yd^3 per truck will be needed to move the pile?

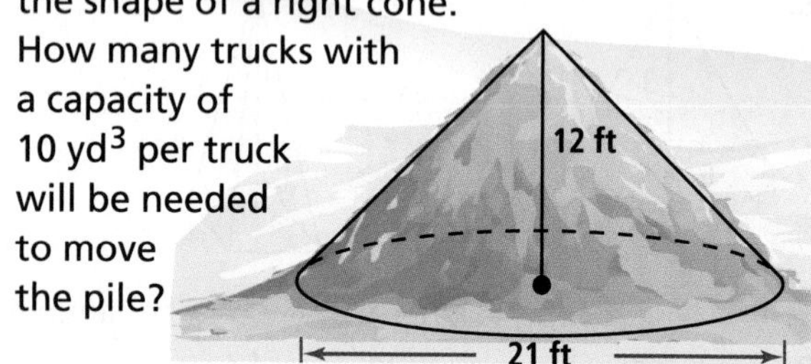

27. Use Structure The basin beneath a fountain is a right cone that is 7 m across and 1 m deep at the center. After the fountain is cleaned, the pool is refilled at a rate of 300 L/min. One cubic meter is 1,000 L. How long does it take to refill the pool?

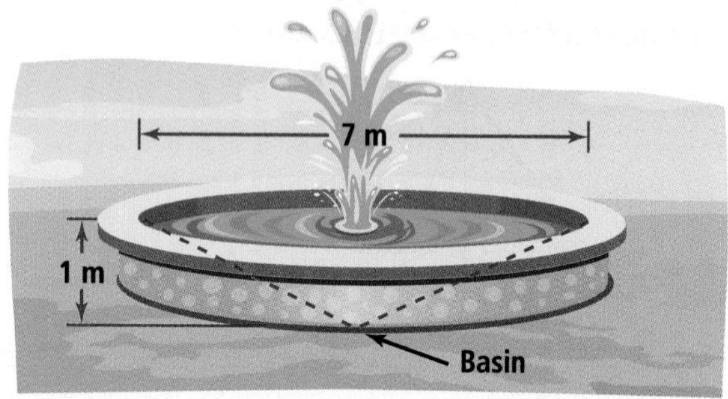

28. Model With Mathematics A physicist wants to know what percentage of gas is empty space. A molecule of methane can be modeled by a regular tetrahedron with side length 0.154 nm ($1 \text{ nm} = 1 \times 10^{-9}$ m). The altitude of each triangular side is 0.133 nm. If 6.022×10^{23} molecules make up 0.0224 m^3 of gas, how does the volume of the molecules compare to the volume of the gas?

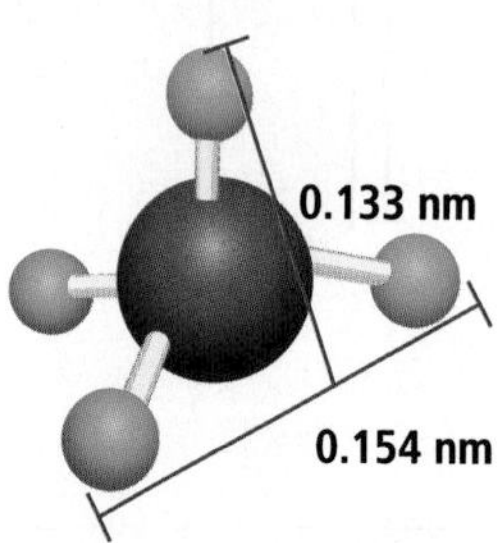

ASSESSMENT PRACTICE

29. Cavalieri's Principle states that if two solids have the same __?__ and the same __?__ at every cross section, then the two solids have the same __?__.

30. SAT/ACT Which is the volume of the largest cone that will fit entirely within the right square prism?

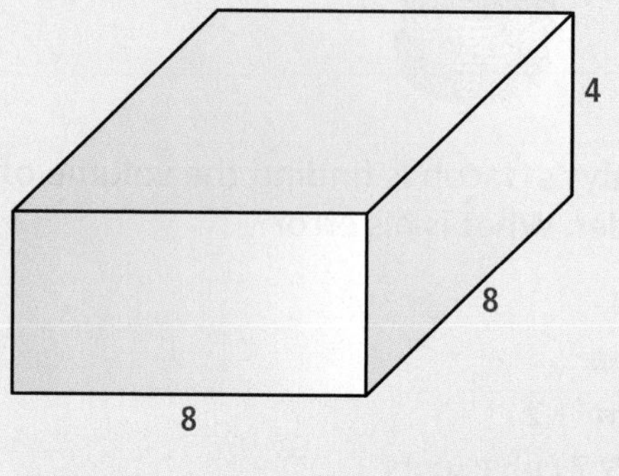

Ⓐ $\frac{16\pi}{3}$ Ⓑ $\frac{32\pi}{3}$ Ⓒ $\frac{64\pi}{3}$ Ⓓ $\frac{128\pi}{3}$

31. Performance Task A designer is working on a design for two goblets. Design A is based on a cylinder and design B is based on a cone. The client wants both goblets to be the same height and width.

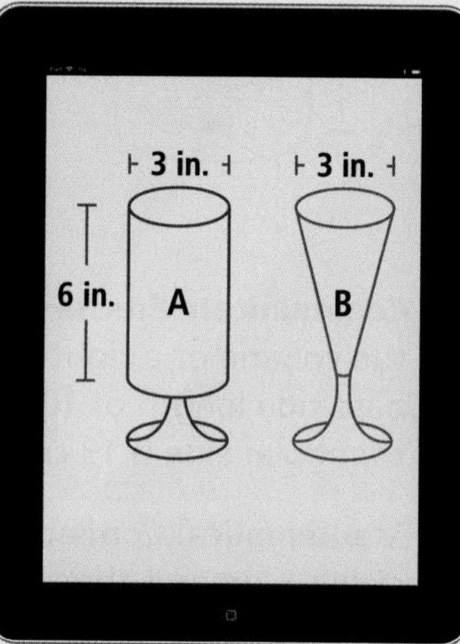

Part A The client wants the smaller goblet to hold at least 10 fl oz. One fluid ounce is 1.8 $in.^3$. Will design B be large enough to meet the client's requirements? Explain.

Part B The client wants the larger goblet to hold 20 fl oz. Does design A meet the client's requirement? Explain.

Part C How could design B be changed if the client wants the smaller goblet to hold at least 12 fl oz?

Activity Assess

11-4 Spheres

I CAN... calculate the volume of a sphere and solve problems involving the volumes of spheres.

VOCABULARY

- hemisphere

CRITIQUE & EXPLAIN

Ricardo estimates the volume of a sphere with radius 2 by placing the sphere inside a cylinder and placing two cones inside the sphere. He says that the volume of the sphere is less than 16π and greater than $\frac{16}{3}\pi$.

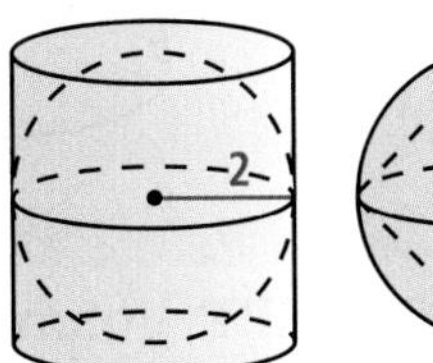

A. Do you agree with Ricardo? Explain.

B. Reason How might you estimate the volume of the sphere?

ESSENTIAL QUESTION

How does the volume of a sphere relate to the volumes of other solids?

CONCEPTUAL UNDERSTANDING

EXAMPLE 1 Explore the Volume of a Sphere

What is the volume of a sphere? Why does the volume formula for a sphere make sense?

A plane, parallel to the bases, intersects half of a sphere with radius r and a cylinder with radius r and height r. The cylinder has a cone with radius r and height r removed from its center.

USE APPROPRIATE TOOLS
Think about how you can draw the section of the cylinder with the cone removed. What does the cross section look like?

By the Pythagorean Theorem, the cross section is a circle with radius $\sqrt{r^2 - h^2}$.

The cross section of the cylinder has radius r. The cross section of the cone has radius h.

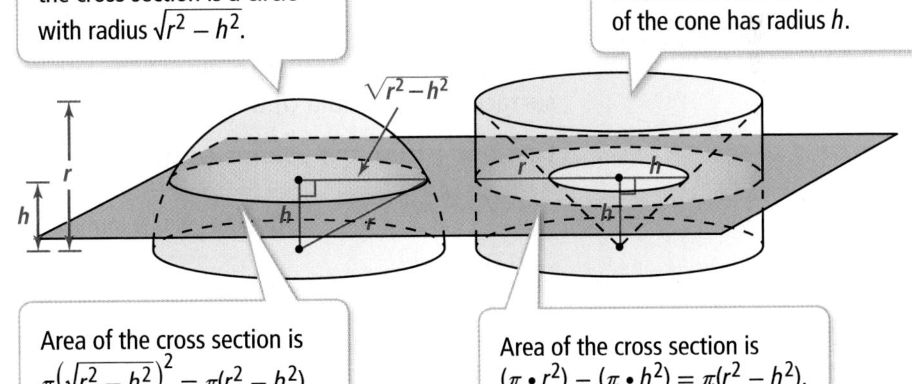

Area of the cross section is $\pi\left(\sqrt{r^2 - h^2}\right)^2 = \pi(r^2 - h^2)$.

Area of the cross section is $(\pi \cdot r^2) - (\pi \cdot h^2) = \pi(r^2 - h^2)$.

Once the cone is removed, the areas of the cross sections of the solids are equal at any height. Therefore, by Cavalieri's Principle, the two solids have the same volume.

$$\text{volume of half a sphere} = \text{volume of cylinder} - \text{volume of cone}$$
$$= \pi r^2 \cdot r - \frac{1}{3}\pi r^2 \cdot r$$
$$= \frac{2}{3}\pi r^3$$

The volume of a sphere is twice the volume of half of the sphere, so the volume of a sphere with radius r is $\frac{4}{3}\pi r^3$.

CONTINUED ON THE NEXT PAGE

EXAMPLE 1 CONTINUED

 **Try It!** 1. Find the volumes of the three solids. What do you notice?

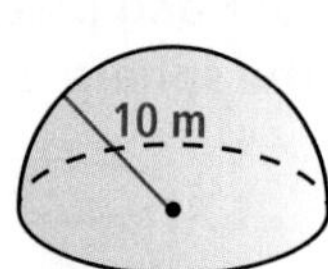

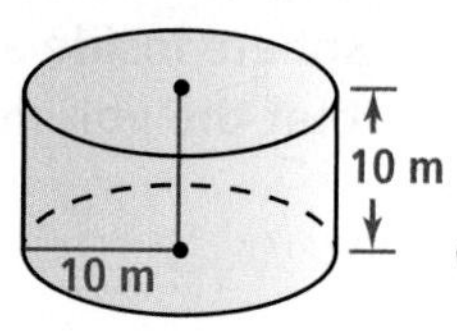

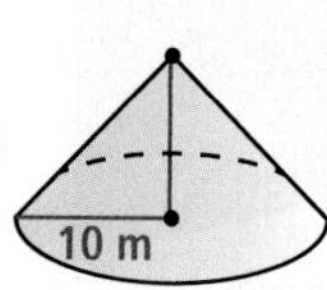

CONCEPT Volume of a Sphere

The volume of a sphere is four-thirds of the product of π and the cube of the radius of the sphere.

$$V = \frac{4}{3}\pi r^3$$

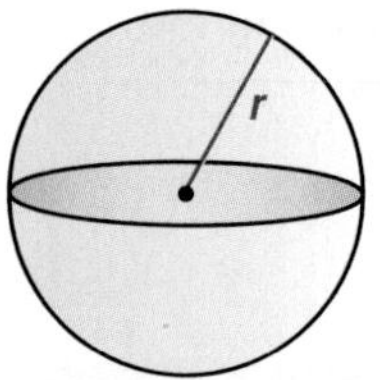

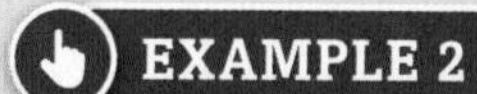

EXAMPLE 2 Use the Volumes of Spheres to Solve Problems

The drama club makes a big ball from foam to hang above the stage for a play. They plan to cover the surface of the ball with metallic fabric. What is the minimum number of square meters of fabric that the club needs?

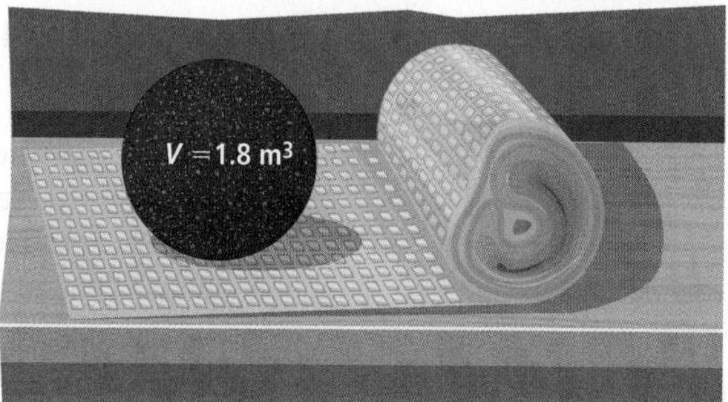

Use the volume formula to determine the radius of the ball. Then use the surface area formula of a sphere.

First find r from the volume of the ball.

$$V = \frac{4}{3}\pi r^3$$ Use the volume formula.

$$1.8 = \frac{4}{3}\pi r^3$$

$$r^3 = \frac{1.35}{\pi}$$ Use a calculator to find the cube root.

$$r \approx 0.75$$

STUDY TIP
Remember that the surface area of a sphere is four times the area of a circle with the same radius.

The radius of the ball is about 0.75 m. Next, calculate the surface area.

The surface area of a sphere with radius r is S.A. $= 4\pi r^2$.

$$\text{S.A.} = 4\pi r^2$$

$$\text{S.A.} = 4\pi(0.75)^2$$ Substitute the radius into the surface area formula.

$$\text{S.A.} \approx 7.1$$

The club needs at least 7.1 m^2 of fabric.

 **Try It!** 2. What is the largest volume a sphere can have if it is covered by 6 m^2 of fabric?

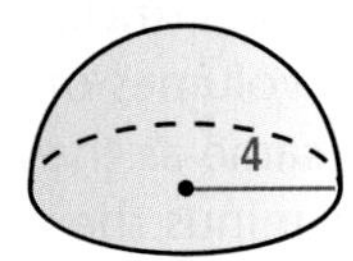

EXAMPLE 3 Find the Volumes of Hemispheres

What is the volume of the hemisphere?

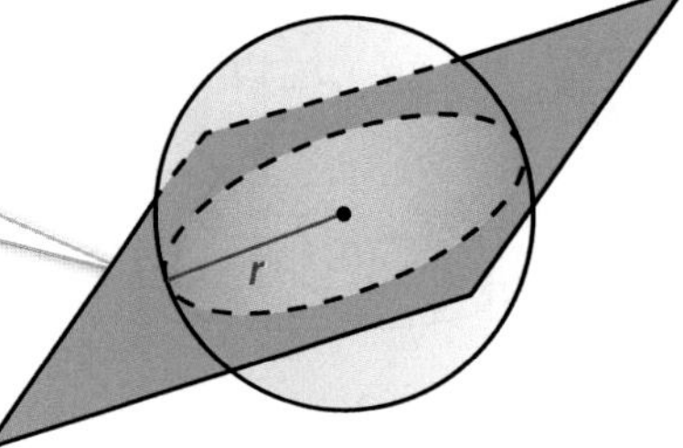

A *great circle* is the intersection of a sphere and a plane containing the center of the sphere.

VOCABULARY
The prefix *hemi* is from the Greek and means *half*. Thus, hemisphere means half-sphere.

A great circle divides a sphere into two **hemispheres**.

The volume of a hemisphere is one-half the volume of a sphere with the same radius.

$V = \frac{2}{3}\pi r^3$

$V = \frac{2}{3}\pi \cdot 4^3 \approx 134.04$

Try It! **3. a.** What is the volume of a hemisphere with radius 3 ft?

b. What is the volume of a hemisphere with diameter 13 cm?

EXAMPLE 4 Find the Volumes of Composite Figures

A solid is composed of a right cylinder and a hemisphere as shown. If the density of the solid is 100 kg/m^3, what is the mass of the solid?

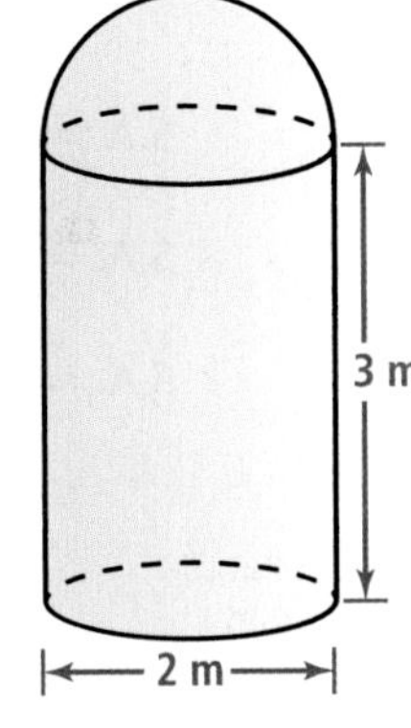

Find the volume of the solid.

volume of solid = volume of cylinder + volume of hemisphere

$= \pi r^2 h + \frac{2}{3}\pi r^3$

$= \pi(1)^2(3) + \frac{2}{3}\pi(1)^3$

≈ 11.5

COMMON ERROR
As you break a composite figure into figures or parts of figures you are familiar with, be careful not to mix up the measurements of each figure.

The volume of the solid is about 11.5 m^3. Next, find the mass of the solid.

$11.5 \cdot 100 = 1{,}150$

The mass of the solid is about 1,150 kg.

Try It! **4.** What is the volume of the space between the sphere and the cylinder?

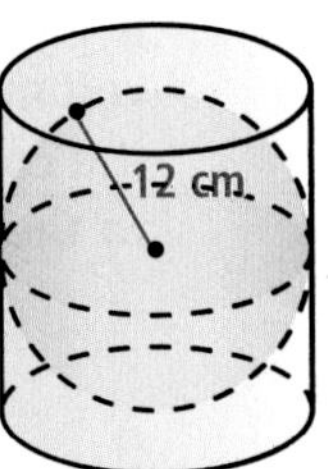

CONCEPT SUMMARY Volume of Spheres

WORDS Cavalieri's Principle can be used to show how the volume of the sphere is related to the volumes of a cylinder and cone. The area of a cross section of a hemisphere is the same as the area of a cross section of a cylinder with height equal to the radius minus the cross section of a cone with height equal to the radius.

DIAGRAMS

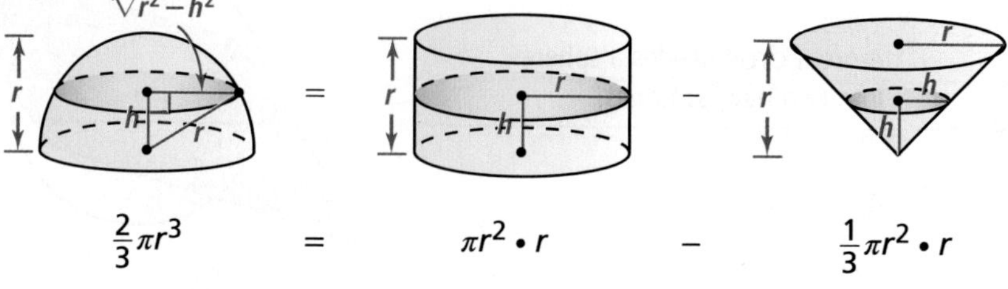

$$\frac{2}{3}\pi r^3 \quad = \quad \pi r^2 \cdot r \quad - \quad \frac{1}{3}\pi r^2 \cdot r$$

Do You UNDERSTAND?

1. **ESSENTIAL QUESTION** How does the volume of a sphere relate to the volumes of other solids?

2. **Error Analysis** Reagan is finding the volume of the sphere. What is her error?

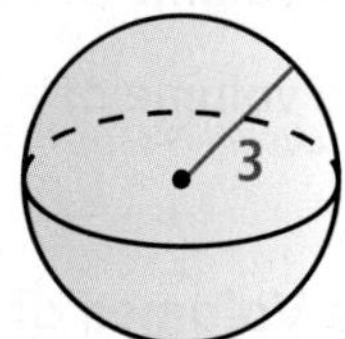

$$S.A. = \frac{4}{3}\pi r^3$$

$$S.A. = \frac{4}{3} \cdot \pi \cdot 3^3$$

S.A. ≈ 113.1 square units

3. **Vocabulary** How does a great circle define a hemisphere?

4. **Reason** The radius of a sphere, the base radius of a cylinder, and the base radius of a cone are r. What is the height of the cylinder if the volume of the cylinder is equal to the volume of the sphere? What is the height of the cone if the volume of the cone is equal to the volume of the sphere?

Do You KNOW HOW?

For Exercises 5 and 6, find the surface area of each solid.

5. 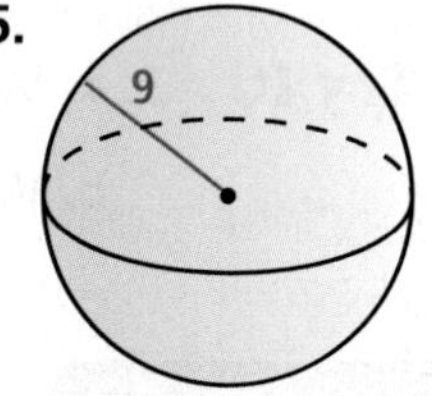

6. 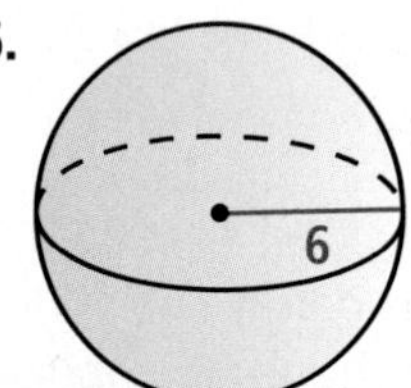

For Exercises 7 and 8, find the volume of each solid.

7. 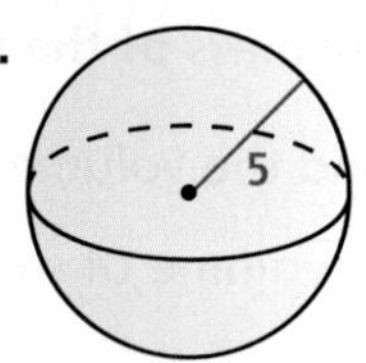

8. 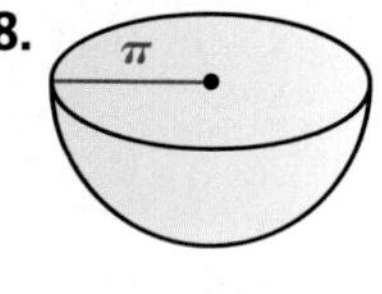

9. Find the volume of the largest sphere that can fit entirely in the rectangular prism.

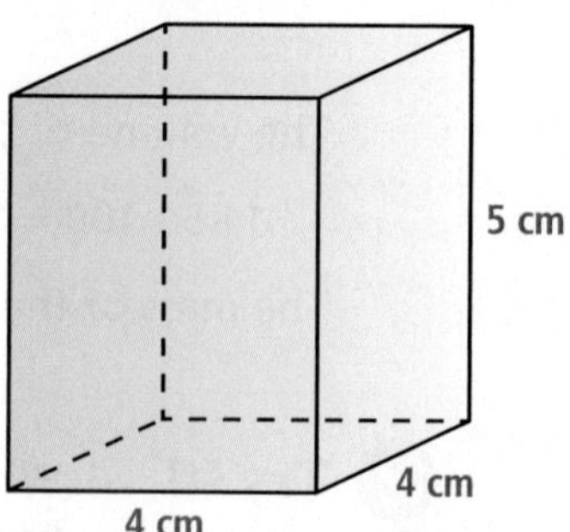

10. Find the volume and surface area of a sphere with radius 1.

PRACTICE & PROBLEM SOLVING

Scan for Multimedia

Practice Tutorial

Additional Exercises Available Online

UNDERSTAND

11. Construct Arguments How does Cavalieri's Principle apply to finding the volume of a hemisphere? Explain.

12. Error Analysis Kayden is finding the surface area of the sphere. What is her error?

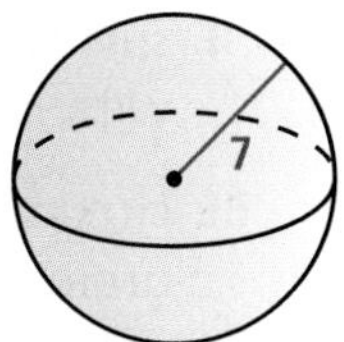

S.A. $= 4\pi r^2$

S.A. $= 4 \cdot \pi \cdot 14^2$

S.A. $\approx$ 2,463.0 square units ✗

13. Mathematical Connections Given the surface area of a sphere, write a formula for the volume of a sphere in terms of the surface area.

14. Construct Arguments Fifteen cylinders and 15 rectangular prisms are stacked. Each cylinder has the same top surface area and height as each rectangular prism. What can you determine about the volumes of the two stacks of 15 solids? Explain.

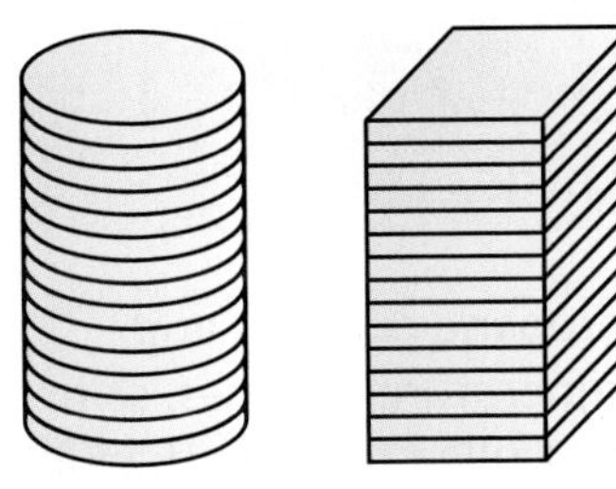

15. Reason A sphere is divided by two great circles that are perpendicular to each other. How would you find the surface area and volume of each part of the sphere between the two planes containing the great circles? Explain.

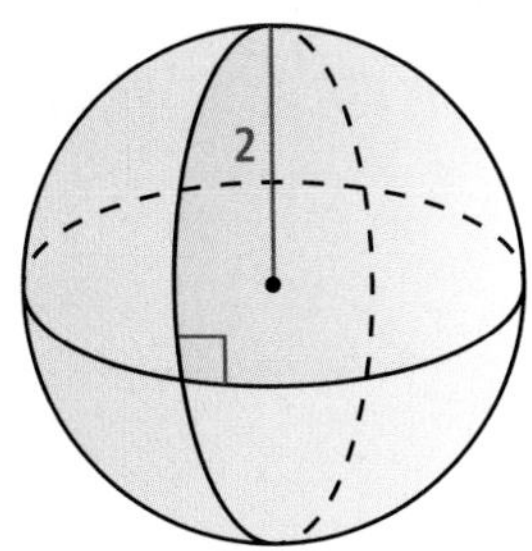

PRACTICE

For Exercises 16–18, find the area of each cross section. SEE EXAMPLE 1

16.

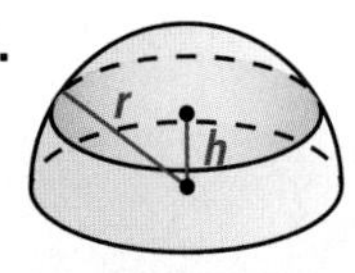

17.

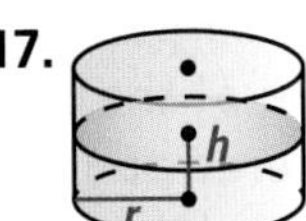

18.

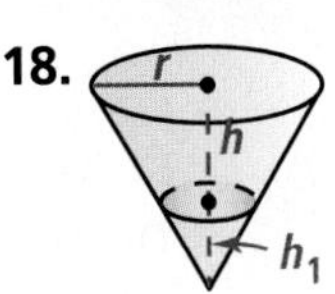

For Exercises 19–22, find the surface area of each solid to the nearest tenth. SEE EXAMPLE 2

19.

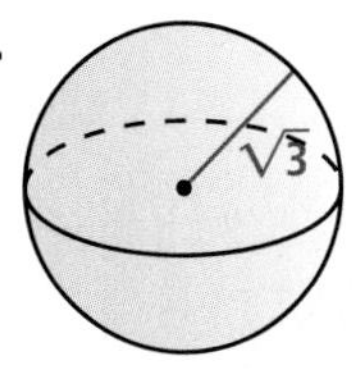

20.

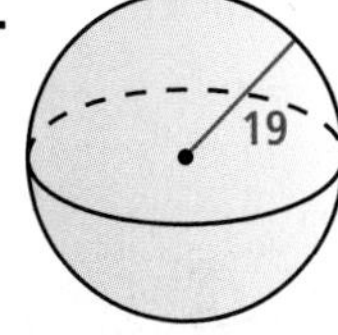

21. sphere with volume 35 cm^3

22. sphere with volume 100 in.^3

For Exercises 23–26, find the volume of each solid to the nearest tenth. SEE EXAMPLES 2 AND 3

23.

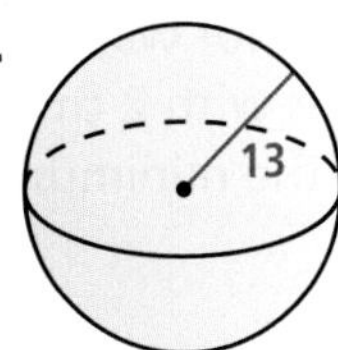

24.

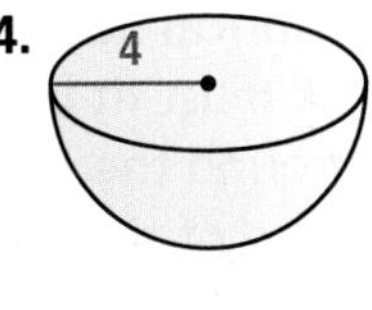

25. hemisphere with radius 12 ft

26. sphere with radius 25 m

For Exercises 27 and 28, find the volume of each composite figure to the nearest tenth.
SEE EXAMPLE 4

27.

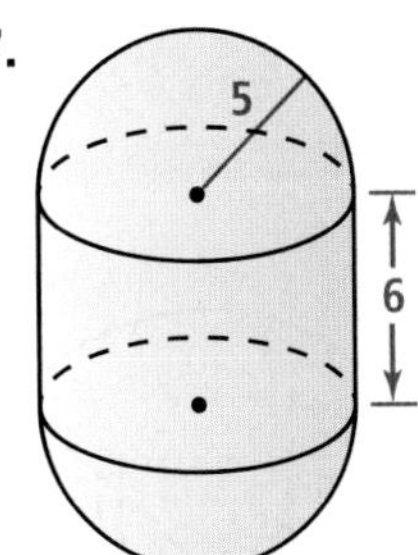

28.

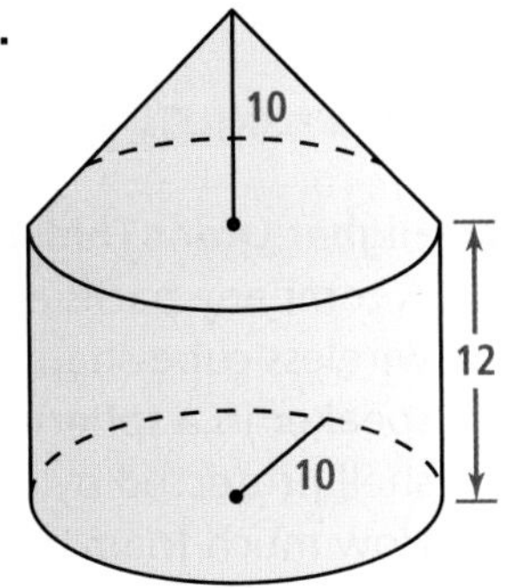

PRACTICE & PROBLEM SOLVING

Practice Tutorial

Mixed Review Available Online

APPLY

29. Make Sense and Persevere To reach the regulation pressure for a game ball, the amount of air pumped into a ball is 1.54 times the volume of the ball. A referee adds 15 in.^{3} of air for each pump of air. How many pumps of air will it take the referee to fill an empty ball?

30. Reason Jeffery uses a block of clay to make round beads. How many beads can he make from the block?

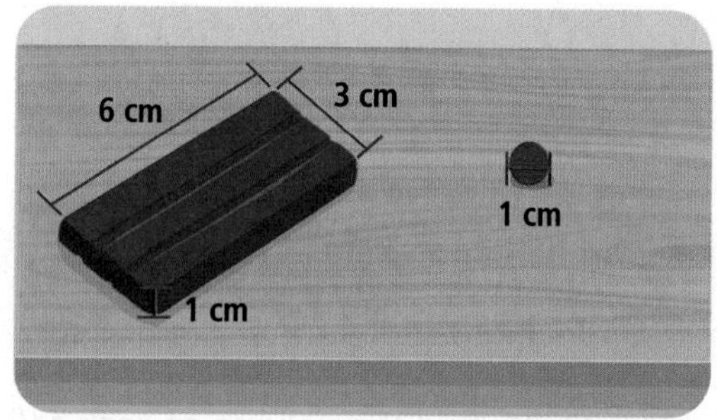

31. Felipe places a spherical round-bottom flask in a cylindrical beaker containing hot water. The flask must fit into the beaker with 2 cm of space around the flask. What is the minimum diameter *d* of the beaker?

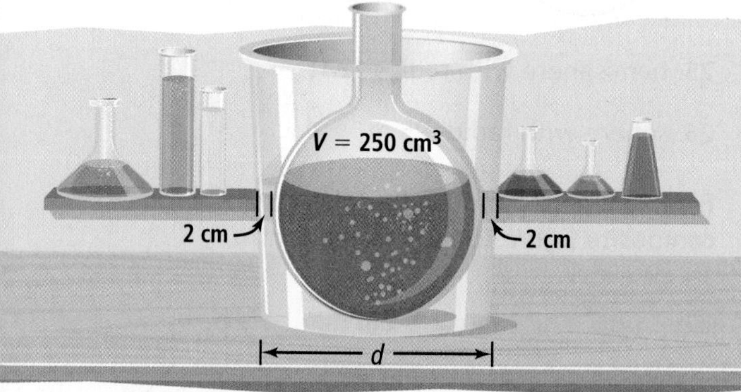

32. Higher Order Thinking A company packs each wireless cube-shaped speaker in a spherical shell protected by foam. How much foam does the company use for each speaker?

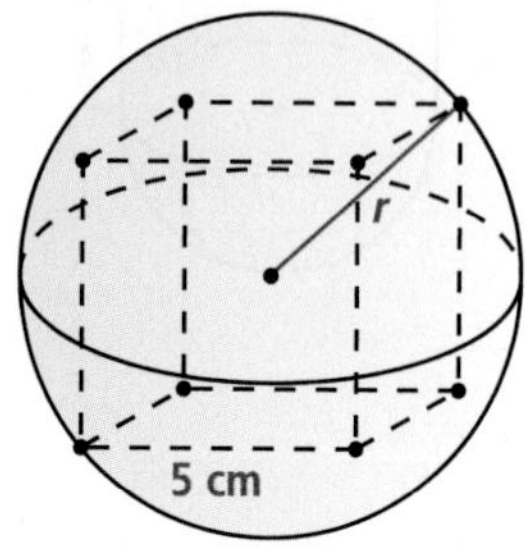

ASSESSMENT PRACTICE

33. Match each description with its expression.

I. volume of a sphere with radius 1	**A.** $\frac{4}{3}\pi$
II. surface area of a sphere with radius 2	**B.** $\frac{16}{3}\pi$
III. circumference of a great circle for a sphere with radius 3	**C.** 6π
IV. volume of a hemisphere with radius 2	**D.** 16π

34. SAT/ACT The surface area of a sphere is 64π ft^2. What is the radius of the sphere?

Ⓐ 64 ft

Ⓑ 16 ft

Ⓒ 8 ft

Ⓓ 4 ft

35. Performance Task Jayesh is to fill the tank shown with liquid propane.

Part A The liquid propane expands and contracts as the temperature changes, so a propane tank is never filled to more than 80% capacity with liquid propane. How much liquid propane should Jayesh put in the tank?

Part B If Jayesh has 20 m^3 of liquid propane to fill another tank, what are the dimensions of the tank if the length of the cylindrical part is three times the diameter?

TOPIC 11

Topic Review

? TOPIC ESSENTIAL QUESTION

1. How is Cavalieri's Principle helpful in understanding the volume formulas for solids?

Vocabulary Review

Choose the correct term to complete each sentence.

2. A prism is ________ if one or more faces are not perpendicular to the bases.
3. ________ describes the relationship between the volumes of three-dimensional figures that have the same height and the same cross sectional area at every level.
4. A great circle divides a sphere into two ________.

- Cavalieri's Principle
- cones
- cylinders
- hemispheres
- oblique
- right
- spheres

Concepts & Skills Review

LESSON 11-1 Three-Dimensional Figures and Cross Sections

Quick Review

The faces of a polyhedron are polygons. Euler's Formula states that the relationship between the number of faces F, number of vertices V, and number of edges E is

$$F + V = E + 2$$

The cross section of a plane and a convex polyhedron is a polygon.

Rotating a polygon about an axis forms a three-dimensional figure.

Example

A triangular prism has 5 faces and 9 edges. How many vertices does it have?

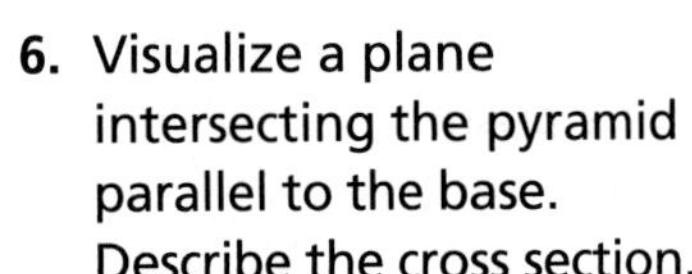

$$F + V = E + 2$$

$$5 + V = 9 + 2$$

$$V = 6$$

The prism has 6 vertices.

Practice & Problem Solving

For Exercises 5 and 6, use the pyramid shown.

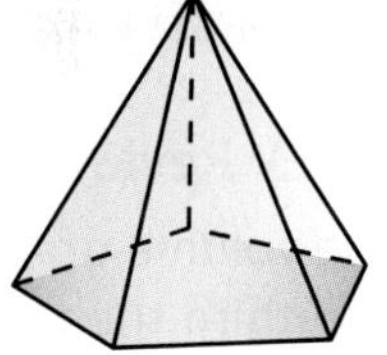

5. The pyramid has 6 vertices and 10 edges. How many faces does it have?
6. Visualize a plane intersecting the pyramid parallel to the base. Describe the cross section.
7. Describe the three-dimensional figure that is formed by rotating the rectangle about the line shown.

8. **Reason** Can a polyhedron have the same number of faces, edges, and vertices? Explain.

TOPIC 11 REVIEW

LESSON 11-2 Volumes of Prisms and Cylinders

Quick Review

Cavalieri's Principle states that figures with the same height and same area at every horizontal cross section have the same volume.

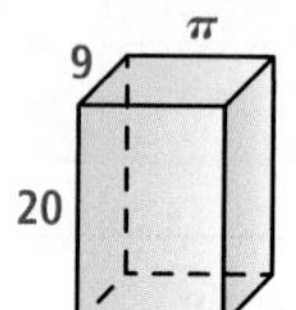

$V = Bh$
$V = (\ell \cdot w)h$
$V = (9\pi)(20)$
$V = 180\pi$

6
20

$V = Bh$
$V = (\pi r^2)h$
$V = (9\pi)(20)$
$V = 180\pi$

Example

Do the cylinders have the same volume? Explain.

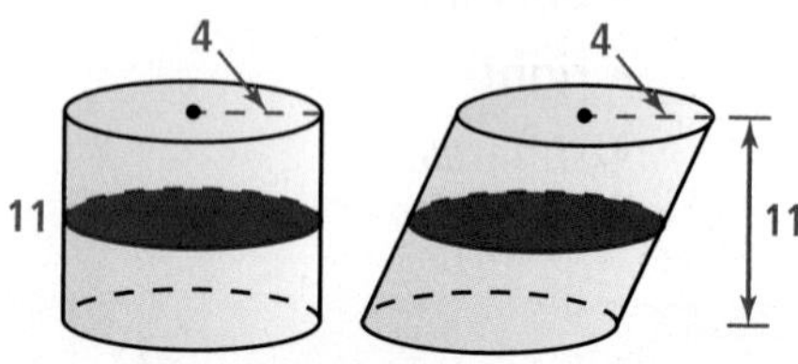

Yes, cylinders with the same base area and height have the same volume. The height of each cylinder is 11. The area of the base of each cylinder is $\pi(4)^2$, or 16π.

Practice & Problem Solving

For Exercises 9 and 10, find the volume of each figure. Round to the nearest tenth.

9.

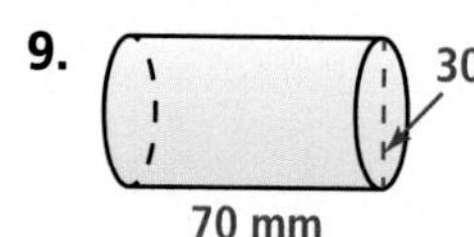

10.

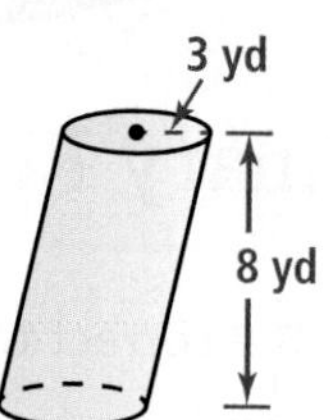

11. Reason What does the expression $\frac{3}{4}xyz$ represent for the prism shown?

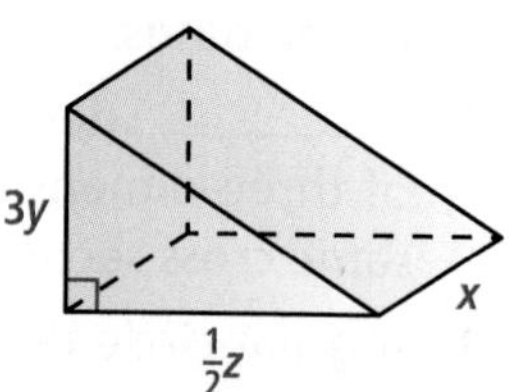

12. Malia pours wax in molds to make candles. Compare the amount of wax each mold holds.

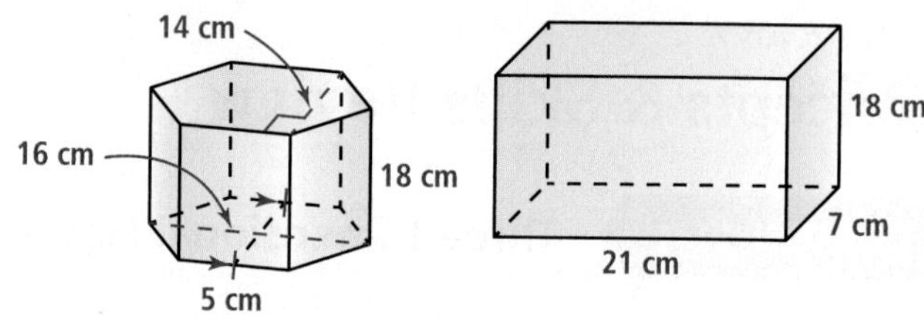

LESSON 11-3 Pyramids and Cones

Quick Review

The volume of a pyramid is one-third the volume of a prism with the same base area and height. $V = \frac{1}{3}Bh$

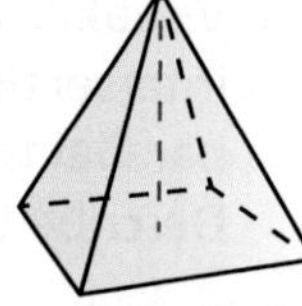

The volume of a cone is one-third the volume of a cylinder with the same base area and height. $V = \frac{1}{3}Bh$

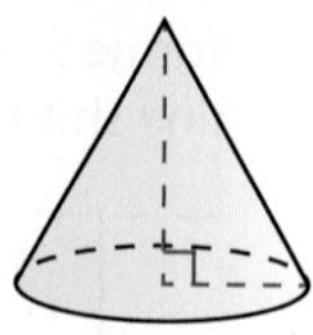

Example

What is the volume?

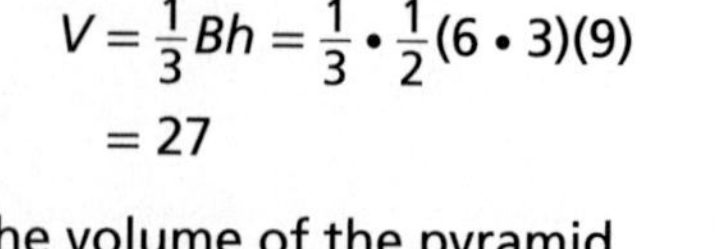

$V = \frac{1}{3}Bh = \frac{1}{3} \cdot \frac{1}{2}(6 \cdot 3)(9)$

$= 27$

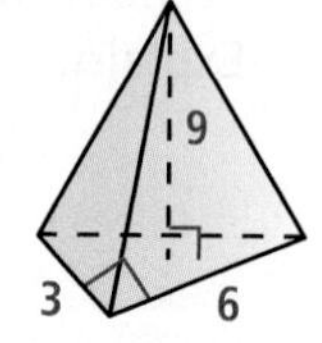

The volume of the pyramid is 27 cubic units.

Practice & Problem Solving

For Exercises 13 and 14, find the volume of each figure. Round to the nearest tenth.

13.

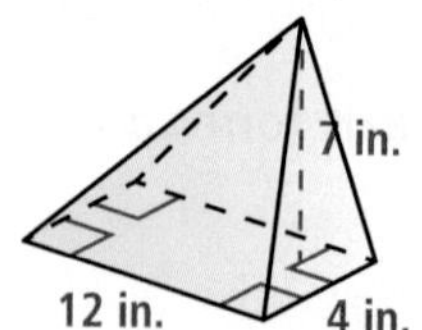

14.

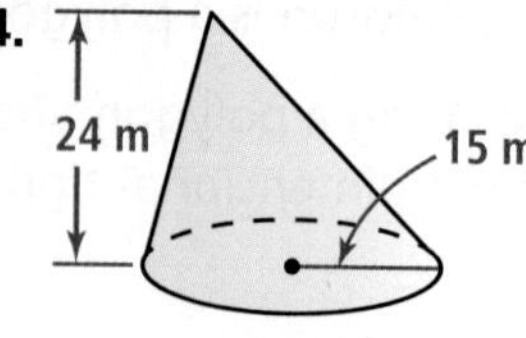

15. A sculptor cuts a pyramid from a marble cube with volume t^3 ft^3. The pyramid is t ft tall. The area of the base is t^2 ft^2. Write an expression for the volume of marble removed.

16. A company cuts 2 in. from the tops of the solid plastic cones. How much less plastic is used in the new design?

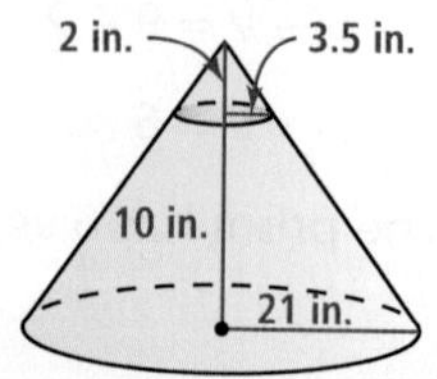

LESSON 11-4 Spheres

Quick Review

The volume of a sphere is $V = \frac{4}{3}\pi r^3$.

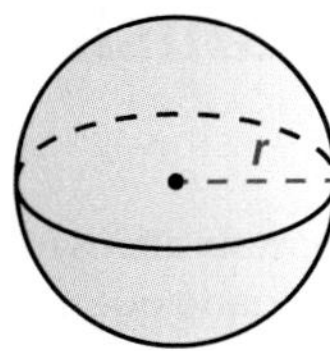

The volume of a hemisphere is one-half the volume of a sphere with the same radius, $V = \frac{2}{3}\pi r^3$.

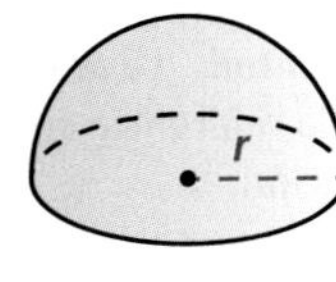

Example

What is the volume of the sphere shown?

$$V = \frac{4}{3}\pi r^3$$
$$= \frac{4}{3}\pi(3)^3 = 36\pi$$

The volume of the sphere is 36π m^3.

Practice & Problem Solving

For Exercises 17 and 18, find the volume of each figure. Round to the nearest tenth.

17. 2.4 in.

18.

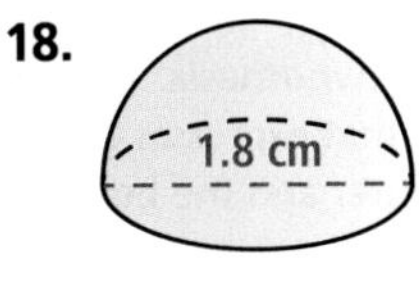

19. **Use Structure** A golf ball has a radius of r centimeters. What is the least possible volume of a rectangular box that can hold 2 golf balls?

20. A capsule of liquid cold medicine is shown. If 1 dose is about 23 ml, how many capsules make up 1 dose? (*Hint:* 1 ml = 1 cm^3)

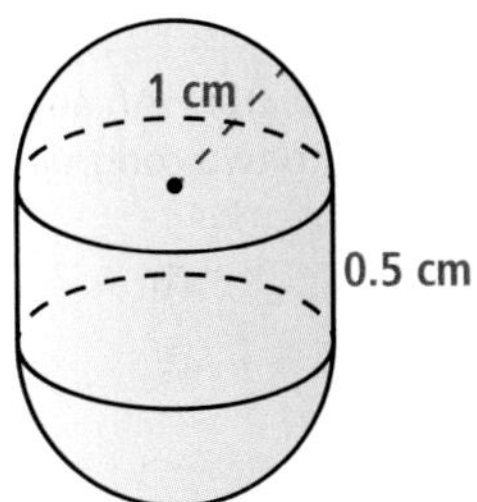

Visual Glossary

English

Spanish

A

Alternative hypothesis An alternative hypothesis is a statement that expresses that there is a difference between the parameter and the benchmark.

Hipótesis alternativa Una hipótesis alternativa es un enunciado que expresa que hay una diferencia entre el parámetro y el punto de referencia.

Amplitude The amplitude of a periodic function is half the difference between the maximum and minimum values of the function.

Amplitud La amplitud de una función periódica es la mitad de la diferencia entre los valores máximo y mínimo de la función.

Example The maximum and minimum values of $y = 4 \sin x$ are 4 and −4, respectively.
amplitude $= \frac{4 - (-4)}{2} = 4$

Angle bisector An angle bisector is a ray that divides an angle into two congruent angles.

Bisectriz de un ángulo La bisectriz de un ángulo es una semirrecta que divide al ángulo en dos ángulos congruentes.

Example

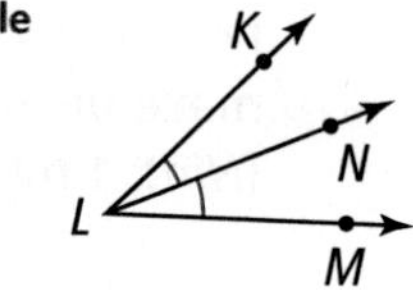

$\overrightarrow{LN}$ bisects $\angle KLM$.
$\angle KLN \cong \angle NLM$.

Angle of elevation or depression An angle of elevation (depression) is the angle formed by a horizontal line and the line of sight to an object above (below) the horizontal line.

Ángulo de elevación o depresión Un ángulo de elevación (depresión) es el ángulo formado por una línea horizontal y la recta que va de esa línea a un objeto situado arriba (debajo) de ella.

Example

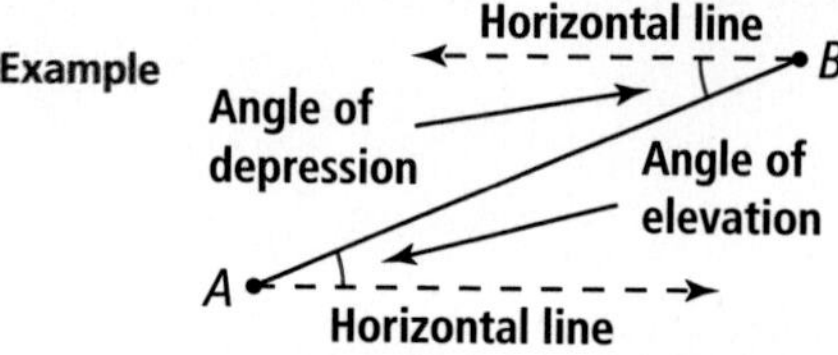

Arc length The length of an arc of a circle is the product of the circumference of the circle and the ratio of the corresponding central angle measure in degrees and 360. The length of the arc is also the product of the radius and central angle measure in radians.

Longitud de un arco La longitud del arco de un círculo es el producto de la circunferencia del círculo y la razón de la medida del ángulo central correspondiente en grados y 360. La longitud del arco es también el producto del radio y de la medida del ángulo central en radianes.

Example

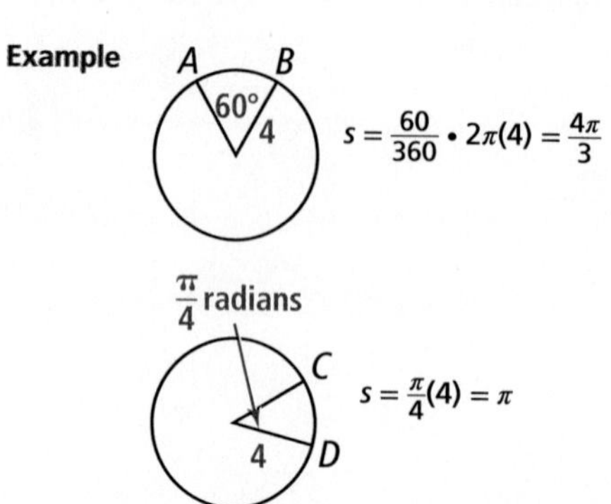

$s = \frac{60}{360} \cdot 2\pi(4) = \frac{4\pi}{3}$

$s = \frac{\pi}{4}(4) = \pi$

English	Spanish
Arithmetic sequence An arithmetic sequence is a number sequence formed by adding a fixed number to each previous term to find the next term. The fixed number is called the common difference.	**Secuencia aritmética** Una secuencia aritmética es una secuencia de números que se forma al sumar un número fijo a cada término para hallar el término que le sigue. El número fijo se denomina diferencia común.

Example The arithmetic sequence 1, 5, 9, 13, . . . has a common difference of 4.

Arithmetic series An arithmetic series is the sum of the terms in an arithmetic sequence.

Serie aritmética Una serie aritmética es la suma de los términos de una progresión aritmética.

Example $1 + 5 + 9 + 13 + 17 + 21$ is an arithmetic series with six terms.

Average rate of change The average rate of change is the slope of the line segment between the points $(a, f(a))$ and $(b, f(b))$.

Tasa de cambio promedio La tasa de cambio promedio es la pendiente del segmento de recta entre los puntos $(a, f(a))$ y $(b, f(b))$.

Example For the parabola $y = x^2$, the average rate of change through the points (2, 4) and (4, 16) is $\frac{16-4}{4-2} = \frac{12}{2} = 6$.

B

Bias A bias is a systematic error that results in a sample that misrepresents a population.

Sesgo El sesgo es un error sistemático que produce una muestra que no representa con precisión a una población.

C

Categorical variable A categorical variable is a variable for which the possible values belong to a limited set of qualitative responses.

Variable categórica Una variable categórica es una variable cuyos valores posibles pertenecen a un conjunto limitado de respuestas cualitativas.

Cavalieri's Principle If two space figures have the same height and the same cross-sectional area at every level, then they have the same volume.

Principio de Cavalieri Si dos figuras sólidas tienen la misma altura y la misma área transversal en todos los niveles, entonces también tienen el mismo volumen.

Example

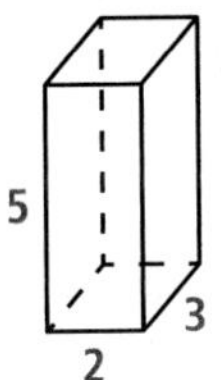

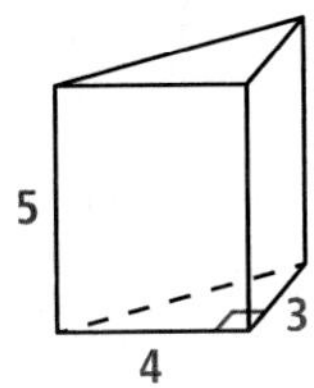

Both figures are prisms with height 5 units and horizontal cross-sectional area 6 square units.

$V = B \cdot h = (6)(5) = 30$ cubic units

Center of rotation A center of rotation is the fixed point of a rotation.

Centro de rotación Un centro de rotación es el punto fijo de una rotación.

Example

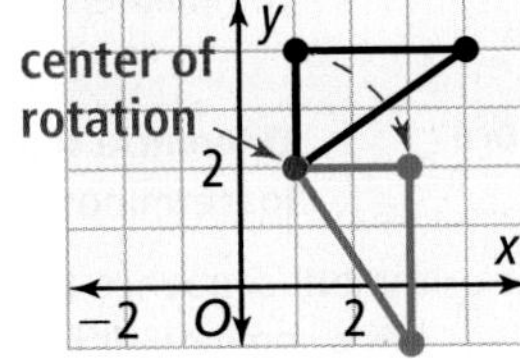

English | Spanish

Central angle A central angle of a circle is an angle whose vertex is at the center of a circle.

Ángulo central El ángulo central de un círculo es un ángulo cuyo vértice está situado en el centro del círculo.

Example

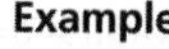

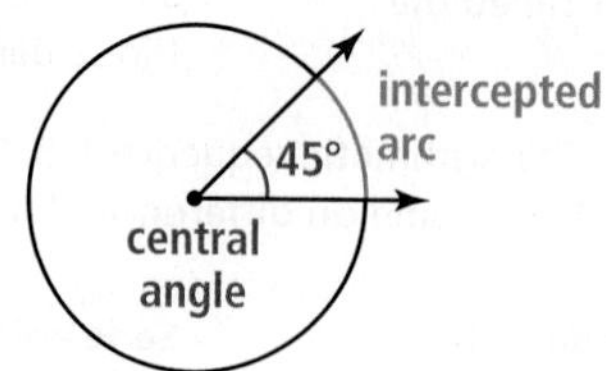

Change of Base Formula This formula allows logarithms with a base other than 10 and *e* to be evaluated. $\log_b m = \frac{\log_a m}{\log_a b}$, where *m*, *b*, and *a* are positive numbers, and $b \neq 1$ and $a \neq 1$.

Fórmula de cambio de base Esta fórmula permite evaluar logaritmos con base distinta de 10 y *e*. $\log_b m = \frac{\log_a m}{\log_a b}$, donde *m*, *b*, y *a* son números positivos y $b \neq 1$ y $a \neq 1$.

Example $\log_3 8 = \frac{\log 8}{\log 3} \approx 1.8928$

Chord A chord of a circle is a segment whose endpoints are on the circle.

Cuerda Una cuerda de un círculo es un segmento cuyos extremos son dos puntos del círculo.

Example

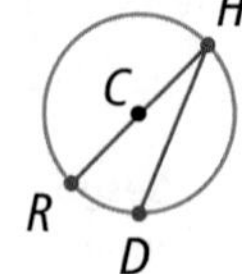

$\overline{HD}$ and $\overline{HR}$ are chords of $\odot C$.

Circle A circle is the set of all points in a plane that are a given distance, the radius, from a given point, the center. The standard form for an equation of a circle with center (*h*, *k*) and radius *r* is $(x - h)^2 + (y - k)^2 = r^2$.

Círculo Un círculo es el conjunto de todos los puntos de un plano situados a una distancia dada, el radio, de un punto dado, el centro. La fórmula normal de la ecuación de un círculo con centro (*h*, *k*) y radio *r* es $(x - h)^2 + (y - k)^2 = r^2$.

Example

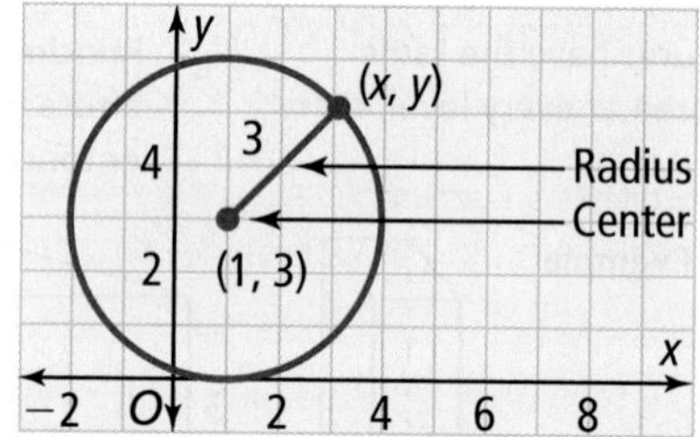

The equation of the circle whose center is (1, 3) and whose radius is 3 is $(x - 1)^2 + (y - 3)^2 = 9$.

Cofunction A cofunction is the trigonometric function for the complement of an angle.

Cofunción Una cofunción es la función trigonométrica para el complemento de un ángulo.

Cofunction identities A cofunction identity is an equation that represents a trigonometric function with an equivalent trigonometric function related to its complement.

Identidades de cofunción Una identidad de cofunción es una ecuación que representa una función trigonométrica con una función trigonométrica equivalente relacionada con su complemento.

Common difference A common difference is the difference between consecutive terms of an arithmetic sequence.

Diferencia común La diferencia común es la diferencia entre los términos consecutivos de una progresión aritmética.

Example The arithmetic sequence 1, 5, 9, 13, . . . has a common difference of 4.

English | Spanish

Common logarithm A common logarithm is a logarithm that uses base 10. You can write the common logarithm $\log_{10} y$ as $\log y$.

Logaritmo común El logaritmo común es un logaritmo de base 10. El logaritmo común $\log_{10} y$ se expresa como $\log y$.

Example $\log 1 = 0$
$\log 10 = 1$
$\log 50 = 1.698970004\ldots$

Common ratio A common ratio is the ratio of consecutive terms of a geometric sequence.

Razón común Una razón común es la razón de términos consecutivos en una secuencia geométrica.

Example The geometric sequence 2.5, 5, 10, 20, . . . has a common ratio of 2.

Compass A compass is a tool for drawing arcs and circles of different sizes and can be used to copy lengths.

Compás El compás es un instrumento que se usa para dibujar arcos y círculos de diferentes tamaños, y que se puede usar para copiar longitudes.

Composite space figures A composite space figure is the combination of two or more figures into one object.

Figuras geométricas compuestas Una figura geométrica compuesta es la combinación de dos o más figuras en un mismo objeto.

Example

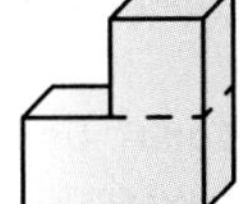

Composition of functions A composition of functions is the operation that forms composite functions.

Composición de funciones Una composición de funciones es la operación que forma funciones compuestas.

Example $f \circ g(x) = f(g(x))$
$g \circ f(x) = g(f(x))$

Compound fraction A compound fraction is a fraction that has one or more fractions in the numerator and/or the denominator.

Fracción compuesta Una fracción compuesta está en forma de fracción y tiene una o más fracciones en el numerador o el denominador.

Example $\dfrac{\frac{x}{4} + \frac{x+2}{2}}{\frac{x-1}{3}}$

Compound inequality A combination of two or more inequalities is a compound inequality.

Desigualdad compuesta Una combinación de dos o más desigualdades es una desigualdad compuesta.

Example $-1 < x$ and $x \leq 3$
$x < -1$ or $x \geq 3$

VISUAL GLOSSARY

English | Spanish

Compression A compression is a transformation that decreases the distance between the points of a graph and a given line by the same factor.

Compresión La compresión es una transformación que reduce por el mismo factor la distancia entre los puntos de una gráfica y una recta dada.

Example

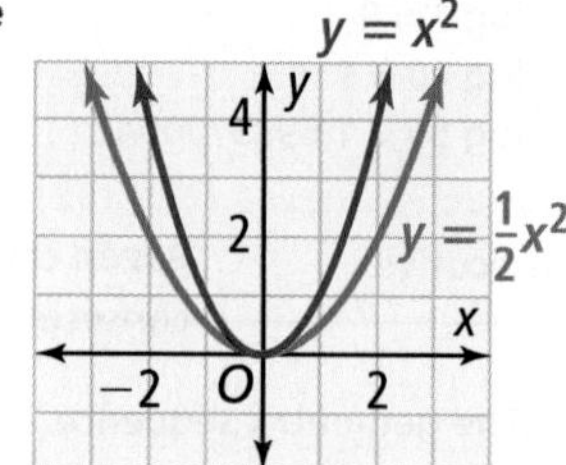

The graph of $y = \frac{1}{2}x^2$ is a compression of the graph of $y = x^2$.

Concentric circles Concentric circles lie in the same plane and have the same center.

Círculos concéntricos Los círculos concéntricos están en el mismo plano y tienen el mismo centro.

Example

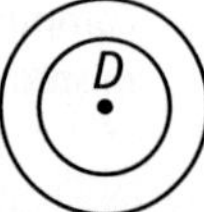

The two circles both have center D and are therefore concentric.

Cone A cone is a three-dimensional figure that has a circular *base*, a *vertex* not in the plane of the circle, and a curved lateral surface, as shown in the diagram. The *altitude* of a cone is the perpendicular segment from the vertex to the plane of the base. The *height* is the length of the altitude. In a *right* cone, the altitude contains the center of the base. The *slant height* of a right cone is the distance from the vertex to the edge of the base.

Cono Un cono es una figura tridimensional que tiene una *base* circular, un *vértice* que no está en el plano del círculo y una superficie lateral curvada (indicada en el diagrama). La *altura* de un cono es el segmento perpendicular desde el vértice hasta el plano de la base. La *altura*, por extensión, es la longitude de la altura. Un *cono recto* es un cono cuya altura contiene el centro de la base. La *longitude de la generatriz* de un cono recto es la distancia desde el vértice hasta el borde de la base.

Example

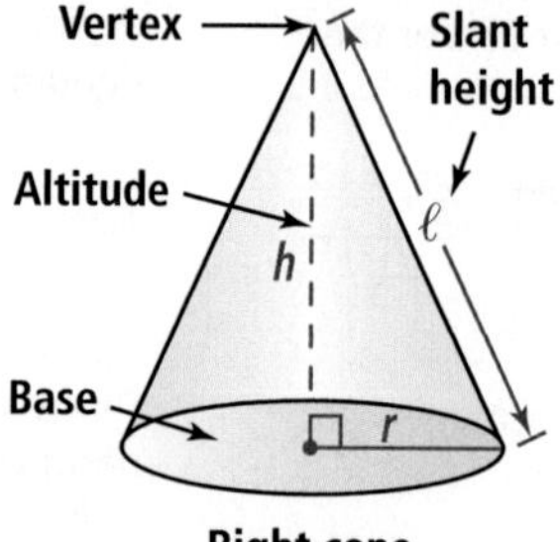

Congruent arcs Congruent arcs are arcs that have the same measure and are in the same circle or congruent circles.

Arcos congruentes Arcos congruentes son arcos que tienen la misma medida y están en el mismo círculo o en círculos congruentes.

Example

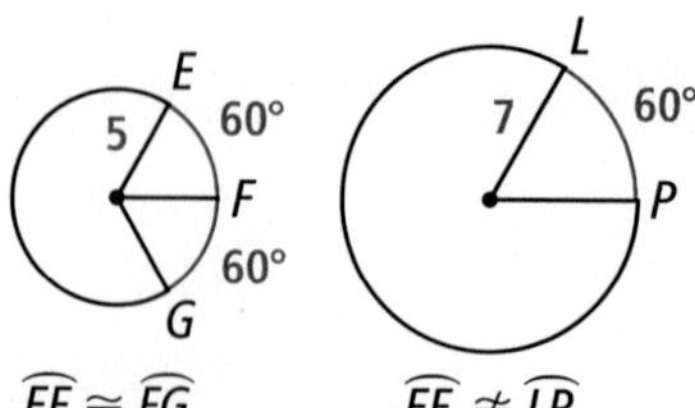

English	Spanish

Congruent circles Congruent circles are circles whose radii are congruent.

Círculos congruentes Los círculos congruentes son círculos cuyos radios son congruentes.

Example

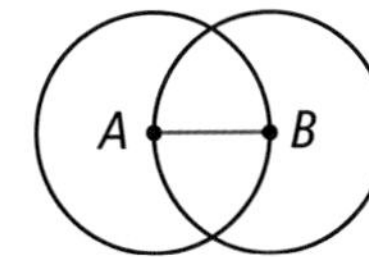

$\odot A$ and $\odot B$ have the same radius, so $\odot A \cong \odot B$.

Constant of variation The constant of variation is the ratio of the two variables in a direct variation and the product of the two variables in an inverse variation.

Constante de variación La constante de variación es la razón de dos variables en una variación directa y el producto de las dos variables en una variación inversa.

Example In $y = 3.5x$, the constant of variation k is 3.5. In $xy = 5$, the constant of variation k is 5.

Construction A construction is a geometric figure made with only a straightedge and compass.

Construcción Una construcción es una figura geométrica trazada solamente con una regla sin graduación y un compás.

Example

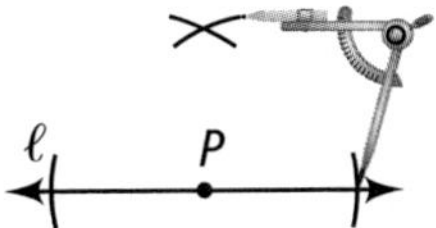

The diagram shows the construction (in progress) of a line perpendicular to a line ℓ through a point P on ℓ.

Continuously compounded interest formula This formula is a model for interest that has an infinitely small compounding period. The number e is the base in the formula $A = Pe^{rt}$.

Fórmula de interés compuesto continuo Esta fórmula es un modelo para calcular el interés que tiene un período de capitalización muy reducido. El número e es la base de la fórmula $A = Pe^{rt}$.

Example Suppose that $P = \$1200$, $r = 0.05$, and $t = 3$. Then

$$A = 1200e^{0.05 \cdot 3}$$
$$= 1200(2.718 \ldots)^{0.15}$$
$$\approx 1394.20$$

Control group In an experiment, the group chosen to not receive the treatment is the control group.

Grupo controlado En un experimento, el grupo no manipulado es el grupo controlado.

Cosecant function The cosecant (csc) function is the reciprocal of the sine function. For all real numbers θ except those that make $\sin\theta = 0$, $\csc\theta = \frac{1}{\sin\theta}$.

Función cosecante La función cosecante (csc) se define como el recíproco de la función seno. Para todos los números reales θ, excepto aquéllos para los que $\sin\theta = 0$, $\csc\theta = \frac{1}{\sin\theta}$.

Example If $\sin\theta = \frac{5}{13}$, then $\csc\theta = \frac{13}{5}$

Cosine In a right triangle, the cosine of an acute angle is the ratio of the length of the side adjacent to the angle to the length of the hypotenuse.

Coseno En un triángulo rectángulo, el coseno de un ángulo agudo es la razón de la longitud del cateto adyacente al ángulo a la longitud de la hipotenusa.

Example

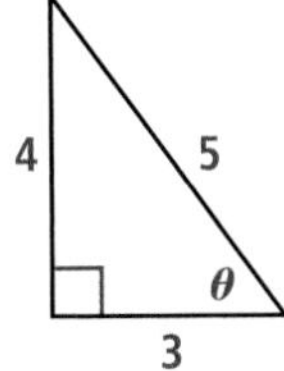

In the triangle, $\cos\theta = \frac{3}{5}$.

VISUAL GLOSSARY

English	Spanish

Cotangent function The cotangent (cot) function is the reciprocal of the tangent function. For all real numbers θ except those that make $\tan \theta = 0$, $\cot \theta = \frac{1}{\tan \theta}$.

Función cotangente La función cotangente (cot) es el recíproco de la función tangente. Para todos los números reales θ, excepto aquéllos para los que $\tan \theta = 0$, $\cot \theta = \frac{1}{\tan \theta}$.

Example If $\tan \theta = \frac{5}{12}$, then $\cot \theta = \frac{12}{5}$.

Coterminal angles Two angles in standard position are coterminal if they have the same terminal side.

Ángulo coterminal Dos ángulos que están en posición normal son coterminales si tienen el mismo lado terminal.

Example

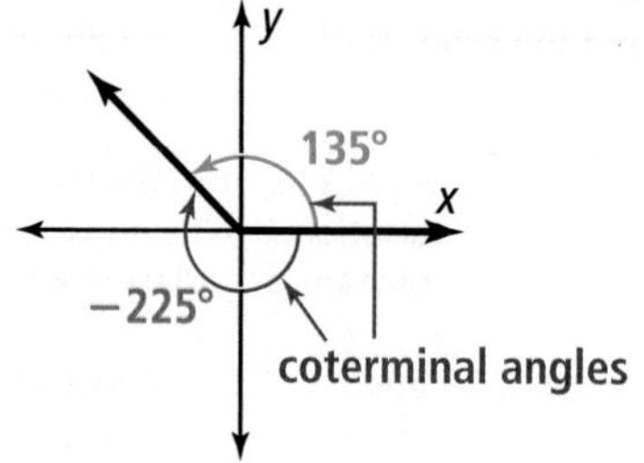

Angles that have measures 135° and –225° are coterminal.

Cross section A cross section is the intersection of a solid and a plane.

Sección de corte Una sección de corte es la intersección de un plano y un cuerpo geométrico.

Example

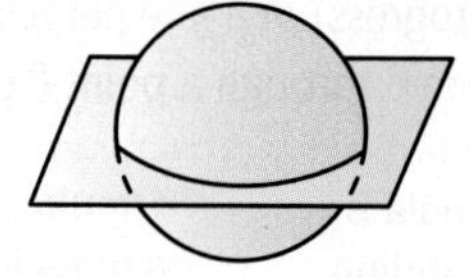

The cross section is a circle.

Cylinder A cylinder is a three-dimensional figure with two congruent circular bases that lie in parallel planes. An *altitude* of a cylinder is a perpendicular segment that joins the planes of the bases. Its length is the *height* of the cylinder. In a *right cylinder*, the segment joining the centers of the bases is an altitude. In an *oblique cylinder*, the segment joining the centers of the bases is not perpendicular to the planes containing the bases.

Cilindro Un cilindro es una figura tridimensional con dos bases congruentes circulares en planos paralelos. Una *altura* de un cilindro es un segmento perpendicular que une los planos de las bases. Su longitud es, por extensión, la *altura* del cilindro. En un *cilindro* recto, el segmento que une los centros de las bases es una altura. En un *cilindro oblicuo*, el segmento que une los centros de las bases no es perpendicular a los planos que contienen las bases.

Example

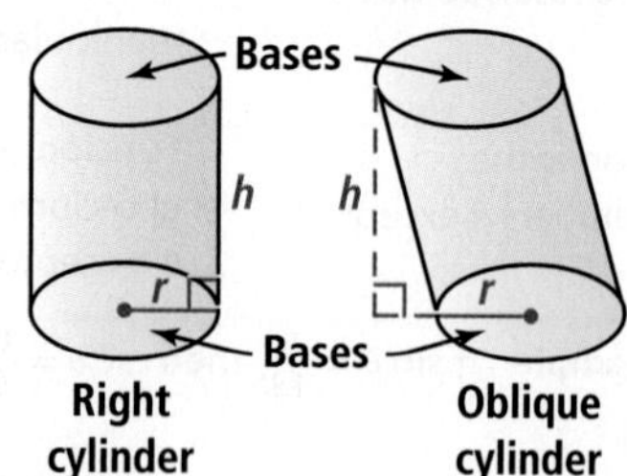

English | Spanish

Decay factor In an exponential function of the form $y = ab^x$, b is the decay factor if $0 < b < 1$.

Factor de decaimiento En la función exponencial de la forma $y = ab^x$, b es el factor de decaimiento si $0 < b < 1$.

Example In the equation $y = 0.3^x$, 0.3 is the decay factor.

Degree of a polynomial The degree of a polynomial is the greatest degree among its monomial terms.

Grado de un polinomio El grado de un polinomio es el grado mayor entre los términos de monomios.

Example $P(x) = x^6 + 2x^3 - 3$ has degree 6

Diameter of a sphere The diameter of a sphere is a segment passing through the center, with endpoints on the sphere.

Diámetro de una esfera El diámetro de una esfera es un segmento que contiene el centro de la esfera y cuyos extremos están en la esfera.

Example

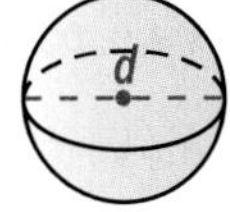

Domain The domain of a relation is the set of all inputs.

Dominio El dominio de una relación es el conjunto de todos los valores de entrada.

Examples In the relation {(0, 1), (0, 2), (0, 3), (0, 4), (1, 3), (1, 4), (2, 1)}, the domain is {0, 1, 2}. In the function $f(x) = x^2 - 10$, the domain is all real numbers.

End behavior End behavior of the graph of a function describes the directions of the graph as you move to the left and to the right, away from the origin.

Comportamiento extremo El comportamiento extremo de la gráfica de una función describe las direcciones de la gráfica al moverse a la izquierda y a la derecha, apartándose del origen.

Even function A function that is symmetric about the y-axis is an even function; $f(x) = f(-x)$ for all x-values.

Función par Una función que es simétrica respecto del eje y es una función par; $f(x) = f(-x)$ para todos los valores de x.

Example $f(x) = x^2$ is an even function since $f(-x) = (-x)^2 = x^2$.

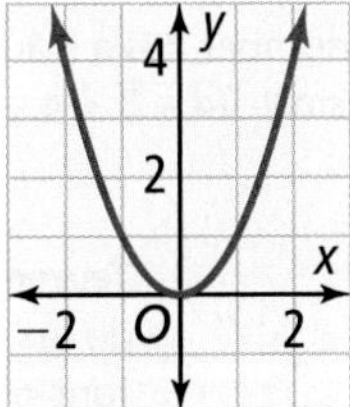

Explicit definition An explicit definition allows any term in a sequence to be found without knowing the previous term.

Definición explícita Una definición explícita permite hallar cualquier término de una progresión aunque no se conozca el término anterior.

Example The explicit definition $a_n = 3 + 4(n - 1)$ allows the 7th term to be calculated directly: $a_7 = 3 + 4(7 - 1) = 27$.

VISUAL GLOSSARY

English	Spanish

Exponential decay function Exponential decay is modeled by a function of the form $y = ab^x$ with $a > 0$ and $0 < b < 1$.

Función de decaimiento El decaimiento exponencial se expresa con una función $y = ab^x$ donde $a > 0$ y $0 < b < 1$.

Exponential equation An exponential equation contains the form b^{cx}, with the exponent including a variable.

Ecuación exponencial Una ecuación exponencial tiene la forma b^{cx}, y su exponente incluye una variable.

Example

$$\begin{aligned} 5^{2x} &= 270 \\ \log 5^{2x} &= \log 270 \\ 2x \log 5 &= \log 270 \\ 2x &= \frac{\log 270}{\log 5} \\ 2x &\approx 3.4785 \\ x &\approx 1.7392 \end{aligned}$$

Exponential function An exponential function is any function of the form $f(x) = ab^x$ where a and b are constants with $a \neq 0$, $b > 0$, and $b \neq 1$.

Función exponencial Una función exponencial es cualquier función de la forma $f(x) = ab^x$ donde a y b son constantes con $a \neq 0$, $b > 0$ y $b \neq 1$.

Example

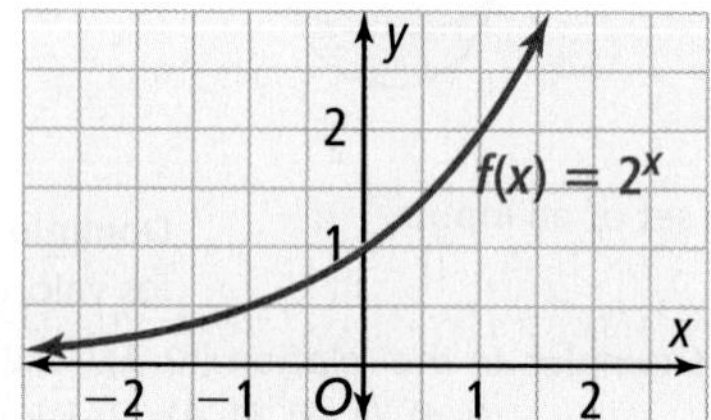

Exponential growth function Exponential growth is modeled by a function of the form $y = ab^x$ with $a > 0$ and $b > 1$.

Función de crecimiento exponencial El crecimiento exponencial se expresa con una función de la forma $y = ab^x$ donde $a > 0$ y $b > 1$.

Extraneous solution An extraneous solution is a solution of an equation derived from an original equation, but it is not a solution of the original equation.

Solución extraña Una solución extraña es una solución de una ecuación derivada de una ecuación dada, pero que no satisface la ecuación dada.

Example

$$\begin{aligned} \sqrt{x-3} &= x - 5 \\ x - 3 &= x^2 - 10x + 25 \\ 0 &= x^2 - 11x + 28 \\ 0 &= (x-4)(x-7) \\ x &= 4 \text{ or } 7 \end{aligned}$$

The number 7 is a solution, but 4 is not, since $\sqrt{4-3} \neq 4 - 5$.

F

Factor Theorem The expression $x - a$ is a linear factor of a polynomial if and only if the value of a is a root of the related polynomial function.

Teorema de factores La expresión $x - a$ es un factor lineal de un polinomio si y sólo si el valor de a es una raíz de la función polinomial con la que se relaciona.

Example The value 2 makes the polynomial $x^2 + 2x - 8$ equal to zero. So, $x - 2$ is a factor of $x^2 + 2x - 8$.

Frequency For a periodic function, the frequency is the reciprocal of the period.

Frecuencia En una función periódica, la frecuencia es el recíproco del período.

Example The period of $y = \sin x$ is 2π so the frequency is $\frac{1}{2\pi}$.

English	Spanish

Frequency table A table that groups a set of data values into intervals and shows the frequency for each interval.

Tabla de frecuencias Tabla que agrupa un conjunto de datos en intervalos y muestra la frecuencia de cada intervalo.

Example

Interval	Frequency
0–9	5
10–19	8
20–29	4

Function A function is a relation in which each element of the domain corresponds with exactly one element in the range.

Función Una función es una relación en la que cada elemento del dominio corresponde exactamente con un elemento del rango.

Example The relation $y = 3x^3 - 2x + 3$ is a function. $f(x) = 3x^3 - 2x + 3$ is the same relation written in function notation.

G

Geometric sequence A geometric sequence is a sequence with a constant ratio between consecutive terms.

Secuencia geométrica Una secuencia geométrica es una secuencia con una razón constante entre términos consecutivos.

Example The geometric sequence 2.5, 5, 10, 20, 40 . . . , has a common ratio of 2.

Geometric series A geometric series is the sum of the terms in a geometric sequence.

Serie geométrica Una serie geométrica es la suma de términos en una progresión geométrica.

Example One geometric series with five terms is $2.5 + 5 + 10 + 20 + 40$.

Great circle A great circle is the intersection of a sphere and a plane containing the center of the sphere. A great circle divides a sphere into two *hemispheres*.

Círculo máximo Un círculo máximo es la intersección de una esfera y un plano que contiene el centro de la esfera. Un círculo máximo divide una esfera en dos *hemisferios*.

Example

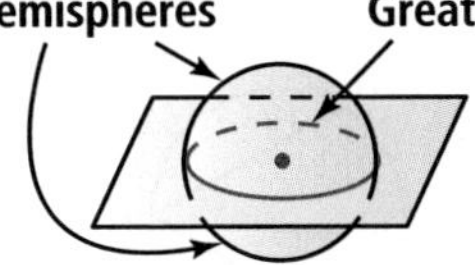

Greatest common factor The greatest common factor (GCF) of an expression is the common factor of each term of the expression that has the greatest coefficient and the greatest exponent.

Máximo factor común El máximo factor común de una expresión es el factor común de cada término de la expresión que tiene el mayor coeficiente y el mayor exponente.

Example The GCF of $4x^2 + 20x - 12$ is 4.

Growth factor In an exponential function of the form $y = ab^x$, b is the growth factor if $b > 1$.

Factor de incremento En una función exponencial de la forma $y = ab^x$, b es el factor de incremento si $b > 1$.

Example In the exponential equation $y = 2^x$, 2 is the growth factor.

English	Spanish

I

Inconsistent system A system of equations that has no solution is an inconsistent system.

Sistema incompatible Un sistema incompatible es un sistema de ecuaciones para el cual no hay solución.

Example $\begin{cases} y = 2x + 3 \\ -2x + y = 1 \end{cases}$ is a system of parallel lines, so it has no solution. It is an inconsistent system.

Index With a radical sign, the index indicates the degree of the root.

Índice Con un signo de radical, el índice indica el grado de la raíz.

Example index 2 index 3 index 4
$\sqrt{16}$ $\sqrt[3]{16}$ $\sqrt[4]{16}$

Initial side When an angle is in standard position, the initial side of the angle is given to be on the positive x-axis. The other ray is the terminal side of the angle.

Lado inicial Cuando un ángulo está en posición normal, el lado inicial del ángulo se ubica en el eje positivo de las x. El otro rayo, o semirrecta, forma el lado terminal del ángulo.

Example

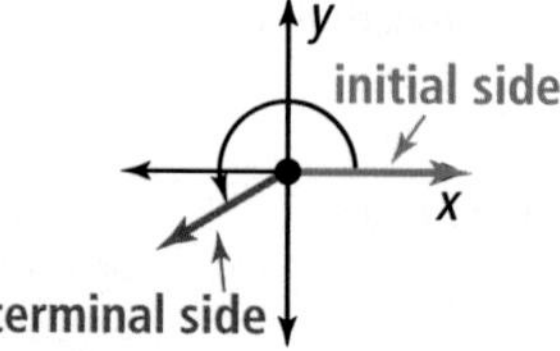

Inscribed angle An angle is inscribed in a circle if the vertex of the angle is on the circle and the sides of the angle are chords of the circle.

Ángulo inscrito Un ángulo está inscrito en un círculo si el vértice del ángulo está en el círculo y los lados del ángulo son cuerdas del círculo.

Example

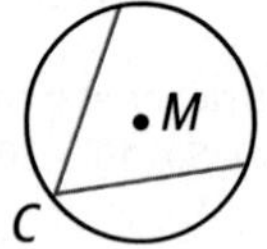

$\angle C$ is inscribed in $\odot M$.

Intercepted arc An intercepted arc is the part of a circle that lies between two segments that intersect the circle.

Arco interceptor Un arco interceptor es la parte de un círculo que yace entre dos segmentos de recta que intersecan al círculo.

Example

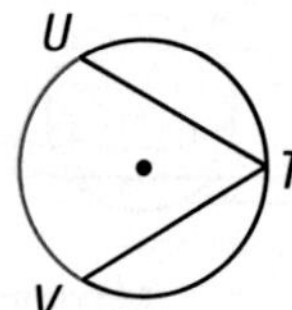

$\overset{\frown}{UV}$ is the intercepted arc of inscribed $\angle T$.

Interquartile range The interquartile range of a set of data is the difference between the third and first quartiles.

Intervalo intercuartil El rango intercuartil de un conjunto de datos es la diferencia entre el tercero y el primer cuartiles.

Example The first and third quartiles of the data set {2, 3, 4, 5, 5, 6, 7, 7} are 3.5 and 6.5. The interquartile range is $6.5 - 3.5 = 3$.

Interval notation Interval notation represents a set of real numbers with a pair of values that are its left (minimum) and right (maximum) boundaries.

Notación de intervalo La notación de intervalo representa un conjunto de números reales con un par de valores que son sus límites a la izquierda (mínimo) y a la derecha (máximo).

Example The interval (2, 7] represents the inequality $2 < x \leq 7$.

English	Spanish

Inverse function If function f pairs a value b with a, then its inverse, denoted f^{-1}, pairs the value a with b. If f^{-1} is also a function, then f and f^{-1} are inverse functions.

Funcion inversa Si la función f empareja un valor b con a, entonces su inversa, cuya notación es f^{-1}, empareja el valor a con b. Si f^{-1} también es una función, entonces f y f^{-1} son funciones inversas.

Example If $f(x) = x + 3$, then $f^{-1}(x) = x - 3$.

Inverse relation An inverse relation is formed when the roles of the independent and dependent variables are reversed.

Relación inversa Una relación inversa se forma cuando se invierten los roles de las variables independientes y dependientes.

Inverse variation An inverse variation is a relation represented by an equation of the form $xy = k$, $y = \frac{k}{x}$, or $x = \frac{k}{y}$, where $k \neq 0$.

Variación inversa Una variación inversa es una relación representada por la ecuación $xy = k$, $y = \frac{k}{x}$, ó $x = \frac{k}{y}$, donde $k \neq 0$.

Example

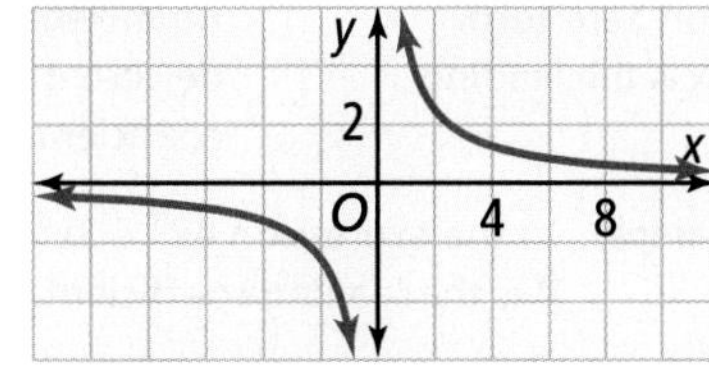

$xy = 5$, or $y = \frac{5}{x}$

L

Lateral area The lateral area of a prism or pyramid is the sum of the areas of the lateral faces. The lateral area of a cylinder or cone is the area of the curved surface.

Área lateral El área lateral de un prisma o pirámide es la suma de las áreas de sus caras laterales. El área lateral de un cilindro o de un cono es el área de la superficie curvada.

Example

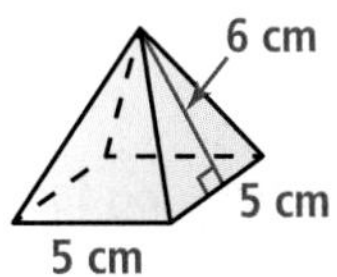

$$\text{L.A. of pyramid} = \frac{1}{2}p\ell = \frac{1}{2}(20)(6) = 60 \text{ cm}^2$$

Law of Cosines In $\triangle ABC$, let a, b, and c represent the lengths of the sides opposite $\angle A$, $\angle B$, and $\angle C$, respectively. Then
$a^2 = b^2 + c^2 - 2bc \cos A$,
$b^2 = a^2 + c^2 - 2ac \cos B$, and
$c^2 = a^2 + b^2 - 2ab \cos C$

Ley de cosenos En $\triangle ABC$, sean a, b y c las longitudes de los lados opuestos a $\angle A$, $\angle B$ y $\angle C$, respectivamente. Entonces
$a^2 = b^2 + c^2 - 2bc \cos A$,
$b^2 = a^2 + c^2 - 2ac \cos B$ y
$c^2 = a^2 + b^2 - 2ab \cos C$

Example

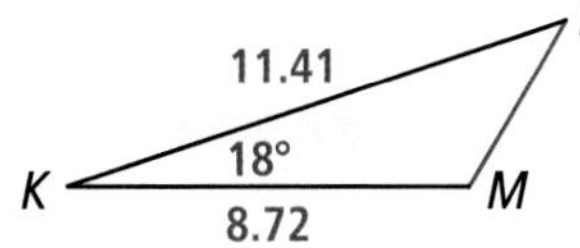

$LM^2 = 11.41^2 + 8.72^2 - 2(11.41)(8.72) \cos 18°$
$LM^2 \approx 16.9754$
$LM \approx 4.12$

VISUAL GLOSSARY

English | Spanish

Law of Sines In $\triangle ABC$, let a, b, and c represent the lengths of the sides opposite $\angle A$, $\angle B$, and $\angle C$, respectively. Then $\frac{\sin A}{a} = \frac{\sin B}{b} = \frac{\sin C}{c}$.

Ley de senos En $\triangle ABC$, sean a, b y c las longitudes de los lados opuestos a $\angle A$, $\angle B$ y $\angle C$, respectivamente. Entonces $\frac{\text{sen } A}{a} = \frac{\text{sen } B}{b} = \frac{\text{sen } C}{c}$.

Example

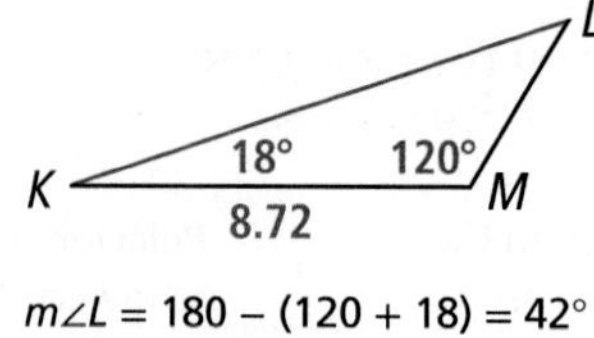

$$m\angle L = 180 - (120 + 18) = 42°$$
$$\frac{KL}{\sin 120°} = \frac{8.72}{\sin 42°}$$
$$KL = \frac{8.72 \sin 120°}{\sin 42°}$$
$$KL \approx 11.29$$

Leading coefficient In a polynomial, the non-zero term that is multiplied by the greatest power of x is the leading coefficient.

Coeficiente principal En un polinomio, el término distinto de cero que se multiplica por la potencia de x mayor es el coeficiente principal.

Example In the expression $4x^5 + 3x^2 - x - 6$, 4 is the leading coefficient.

Like radicals Like radicals are radical expressions that have the same index and the same radicand.

Radicales semejantes Los radicales semejantes son expresiones radicales que tienen el mismo índice y el mismo radicando.

Example $4\sqrt[3]{7}$ and $\sqrt[3]{7}$ are like radicals.

Logarithm For $b > 0$, $b \neq 1$, and $x > 0$, the logarithm base b of a positive number x is defined as follows: $\log_b x = y$, if and only if $x = b^y$.

Logaritmo Para $b > 0$, $b \neq 1$ y $x > 0$, la base del logaritmo b de un número positivo x se define como $\log_b x = y$, si y sólo si $x = b^y$.

Example $\log_2 8 = 3$
$\log_{10} 100 = \log 100 = 2$
$\log_5 5^7 = 7$

Logarithmic equation A logarithmic equation is an equation that includes a logarithm involving a variable.

Ecuación logarítmica Una ecuación logarítmica es una ecuación que incluye un logaritmo con una variable.

Example $\log_3 x = 4$

Logarithmic function A logarithmic function is the inverse of an exponential function.

Función logarítmica Una función logarítmica es la inversa de una función exponencial.

Example

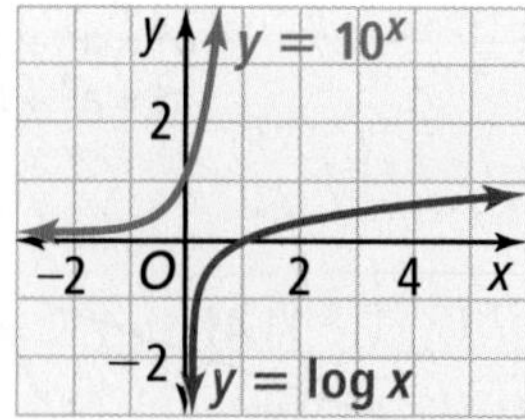

Major arc A major arc of a circle is an arc that is larger than a semicircle.

Arco mayor Un arco mayor de un círculo es cualquier arco más grande que un semicírculo.

Example

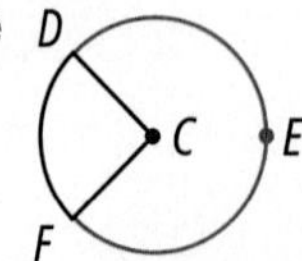

$\overparen{DEF}$ is a major arc of $\odot C$.

English / Spanish

Margin of error The margin of error of a sample statistic is the maximum expected difference between the sample statistic and the population parameter.

Margen de error El margen de error de una estadística de muestreo aleatorio es la diferencia máxima que se espera entre la estadística de muestreo y el parámetro de la población.

Example The standard deviation of a sample is 5.0 and the number of trials is 30. The margin of error at a 95% confidence level is $ME \approx \frac{2 \cdot 5.0}{\sqrt{30}} \approx 1.8$.

Maximum The maximum of a function is the greatest value that the function attains in its domain. It is the *y*-coordinate of the highest point on the graph of the function.

Máximo El valor máximo de una función es el mayor valor que la función alcanza en su dominio. Es la coordenada *y* del punto más alto de la gráfica de la función.

Example

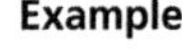

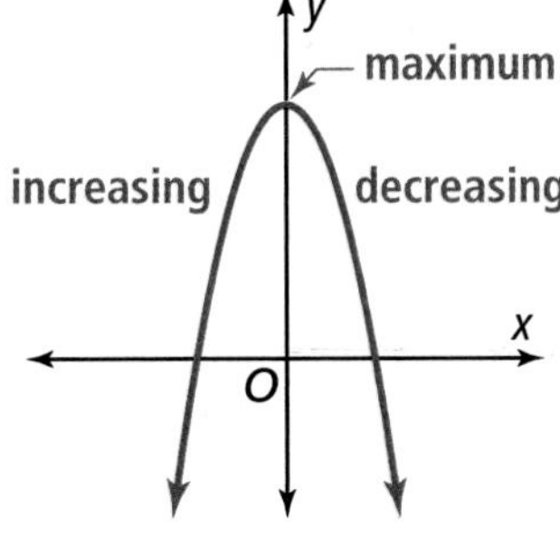

Mean The mean of a data set is the sum of the data values divided by the number of data values.

Media La media de un conjunto de datos es la suma de los valores de datos dividida por el número de valores de los datos.

Example {1, 2, 3, 3, 6, 6}

$$\text{mean} = \frac{1 + 2 + 3 + 3 + 6 + 6}{6} = \frac{21}{6} = 3.5$$

Measure of an arc The measure of a minor arc is the measure of its central angle. The measure of a major arc is 360° minus the measure of its related minor arc.

Medida de un arco La medida de un arco menor es la medida de su ángulo central. La medida de un arco mayor es 360° menos la medida en grados de su arco menor correspondiente.

Example

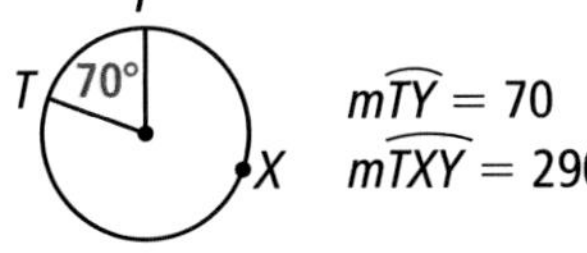

$m\overparen{TY} = 70$

$m\overparen{TXY} = 290$

Median The median is the middle value in a data set. If the data set contains an even number of values, the median is the mean of the two middle values.

Mediana La mediana es el valor situado en el medio en un conjunto de datos. Si el conjunto de datos contiene un número par de valores, la mediana es la media de los dos valores del medio.

Example {1, 2, 3, 3, 4, 5, 6, 6}

$$\text{median} = \frac{3 + 4}{2} = \frac{7}{2} = 3.5$$

VISUAL GLOSSARY

English

Spanish

Midline The horizontal line through the average of the maximum and minimum values.

Línea media Recta horizontal que pasa a través de la media de los valores máximos y mínimos.

Example

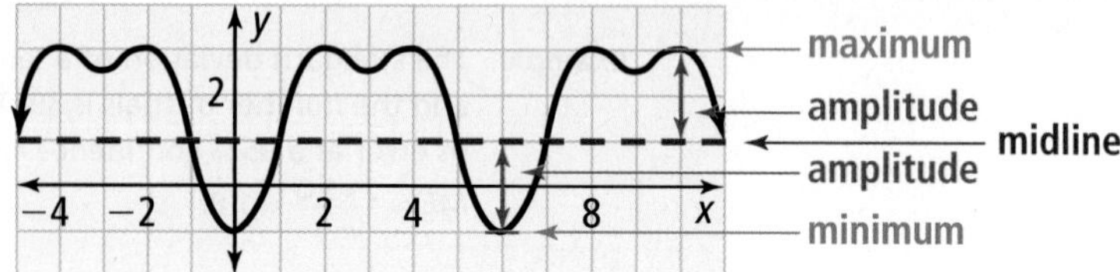

Minimum The minimum of a function is the least value that the function attains in its domain. It is the *y*-coordinate of the lowest point on the graph of the function.

Mínimo El valor mínimo de una función es el menor valor que la función alcanza en su dominio. Es la coordenada y del punto más bajo de la gráfica de la función.

Example

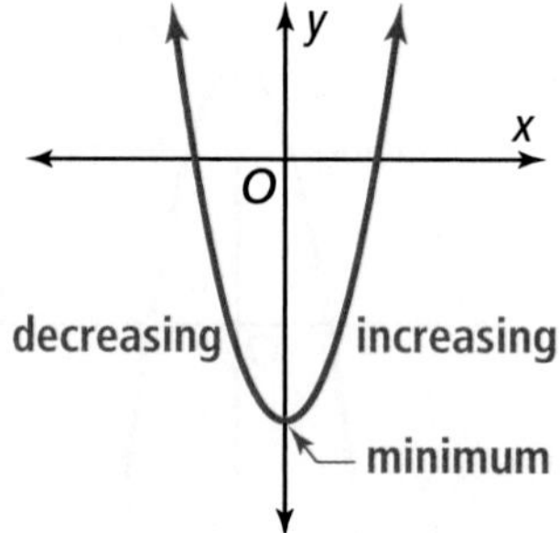

Minor arc A minor arc is an arc that is smaller than a semicircle.

Arco menor Un arco menor de un círculo es un arco más corto que un semicírculo.

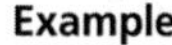
Example

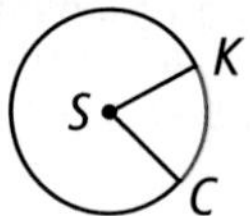

$\overset{\frown}{KC}$ is a minor arc of $\odot S$.

Monomial A monomial is either a real number, a variable, or a product of real numbers and variables with whole number exponents.

Monomio Un monomio es un número real, una variable o un producto de números reales y variables cuyos exponentes son números enteros.

Example $1, x, 2z, 4ab^2$

Multiplicity The multiplicity of a zero of a polynomial function is the number of times the related linear factor is repeated in the factored form of the polynomial.

Multiplicidad La multiplicidad de un cero de una función polinomial es el número de veces que el factor lineal relacionado se repite en la forma factorizada del polinomio.

Example The zeros of the function $P(x) = 2x(x - 3)^2(x + 1)$ are 0, 3, and −1. Since $(x - 3)$ occurs twice as a factor, the zero 3 has multiplicity 2.

N

***n*th root** For any real numbers *a* and *b*, and any positive integer *n*, if $a^n = b$, then a is an *n*th root of *b*.

raíz *n*-ésima Para todos los números reales *a* y *b*, y todo número entero positivo *n*, si $a^n = b$, entonces *a* es la *n*-ésima raíz de *b*.

Example $\sqrt[5]{32} = 2$ because $2^5 = 32$.
$\sqrt[4]{81} = 3$ because $3^4 = 81$.

Natural base e The value that the expression $(1 + \frac{1}{x})^x$ approaches as $x \to \infty$. The value is approximately 2.7818282 . . .

Base natural e El valor al que se acerca la expresión $(1 + \frac{1}{x})^x$ a medida que $x \to \infty$. El valor es aproximadamente igual a 2.7818282 . . .

English	Spanish

Natural logarithmic function A natural logarithmic function is a logarithmic function with base e. The natural logarithmic function $y = \ln x$ is $y = \log_e x$. It is the inverse of $y = e^x$.

Función logarítmica natural Una función logarítmica natural es una función logarítmica con base e. La función logarítmica natural $y = \ln x$ es $y = \log_e x$. Ésta es la función inversa de $y = e^x$.

Example

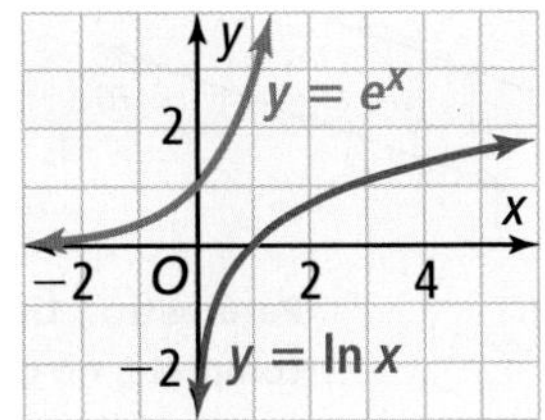

$\ln e^3 = 3$
$\ln 10 \approx 2.3026$
$\ln 36 \approx 3.5835$

Normal distribution A normal distribution shows data that vary randomly from the mean in the pattern of a bell-shaped curve.

Distribución normal Una distribución normal muestra, con una curva en forma de campana, datos que varían alcatoriamento respecto de la media.

Example

Distribution of Test Scores

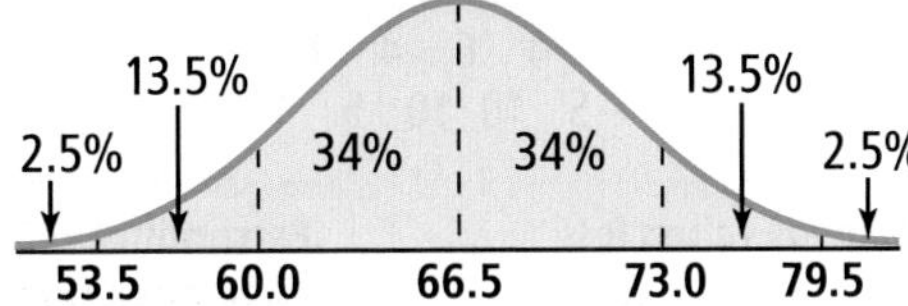

In a class of 200 students, the scores on a test were normally distributed. The mean score was 66.5 and the standard deviation was 6.5. The number of students who scored greater than 73 percent was about 13.5% + 2.5% of those who took the test.
16% of 200 = 32
About 32 students scored 73 or higher on the test.

Null hypothesis A null hypothesis is a statement that expresses that there is no difference between the parameter and the benchmark.

Hipótesis nula Una hipótesis nula es un enunciado que expresa que no hay diferencia entre el parámetro y el punto de referencia.

Observational study In an observational study, you measure or observe members of a sample in such a way that they are not affected by the study.

Estudio de observación En un estudio de observación, se miden u observan a los miembros de una muestra de tal manera que no les afecte el estudio.

Odd function An odd function is a function that is symmetric about the origin; $f(-x) = -f(x)$ for all x-values.

Función impar Una función impar es una función que es simétrica respecto del origen; $f(-x) = -f(x)$ para todos los valores de x.

Example $f(x) = x^3$ is an odd function since $f(-x) = (-x)^3 = -x^3$.

English / Spanish

Parallel lines Two lines are parallel if they lie in the same plane and do not intersect. The symbol || means "is parallel to."

Rectas paralelas Dos rectas son paralelas si están en el mismo plano y no se cortan. El símbolo || significa "es paralelo a".

Example $\ell \parallel m$

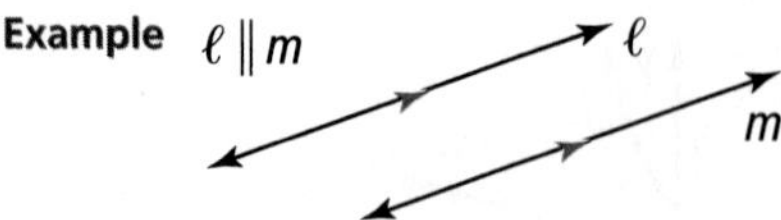

The red symbols indicate parallel lines.

Parameter A parameter is a piece of data from a whole population, not from a sample.

Parámetro Un parámetro es un dato de una población completa, no de una muestra.

Pascal's Triangle Pascal's Triangle is a triangular array of numbers in which the first and last number in each row is 1. Each of the other numbers in the row is the sum of the two numbers above it.

Triángulo de Pascal El Triángulo de Pascal es una distribución triangular de números en la cual el primer número y el último número son 1. Cada uno de los otros números en la fila es la suma de los dos números de encima.

Example **Pascal's Triangle**

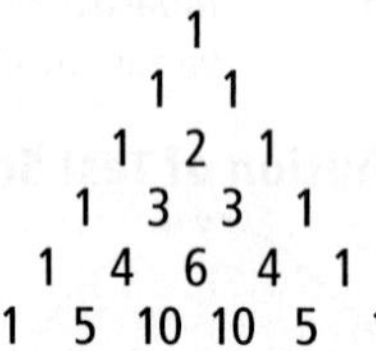

Percentile A percentile is the percentage of values less than or equal to a particular data value. It is equal to the percentage of the total area under the distribution curve for the population to the left of that value.

Percentil Un percentil es el porcentaje de valores que es menor que o igual a un valor de datos en particular. Es igual al porcentaje del área total bajo la curva de distribución para la población a la izquierda de ese valor.

Period The period of a periodic function is the horizontal length of one cycle.

Período El período de una función periódica es el intervalo horizontal de un ciclo.

Example

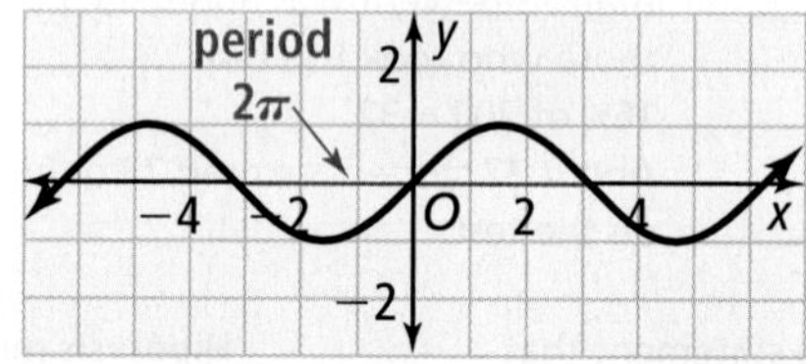

The periodic function $y = \sin x$ has period 2π.

Periodic function A periodic function repeats a pattern of y-values at regular intervals.

Función periódica Una función periódica repite un patrón de valores y a intervalos regulares.

Example

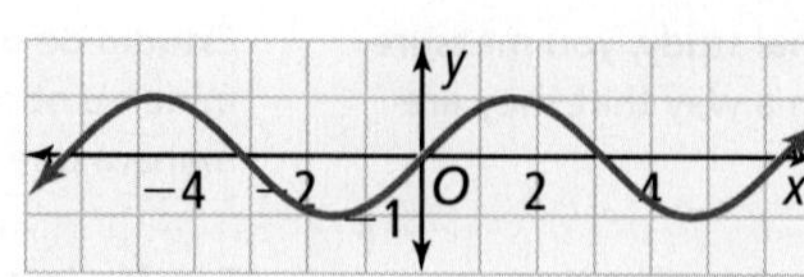

$y = \sin x$

English | Spanish

Perpendicular bisector The perpendicular bisector of a segment is a line, segment, or ray that is perpendicular to the segment and divides the segment into two congruent segments.

Mediatriz La mediatriz de un segmento es una recta, segmento o semirrecta que es perpendicular al segmento y que divide al segmento en dos segmentos congruentes.

Example

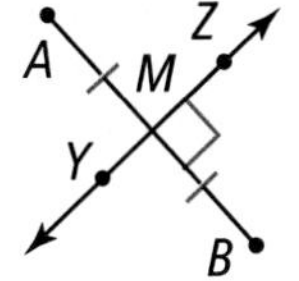

$\overleftrightarrow{YZ}$ is the perpendicular bisector of $\overline{AB}$. It is perpendicular to $\overline{AB}$ and intersects $\overline{AB}$ at midpoint M.

Perpendicular lines Perpendicular lines are lines that intersect and form right angles. The symbol ⊥ means "is perpendicular to."

Rectas perpendiculares Las rectas perpendiculares son rectas que se cortan y forman ángulos rectos. El símbolo ⊥ significa "es perpendicular a".

Example

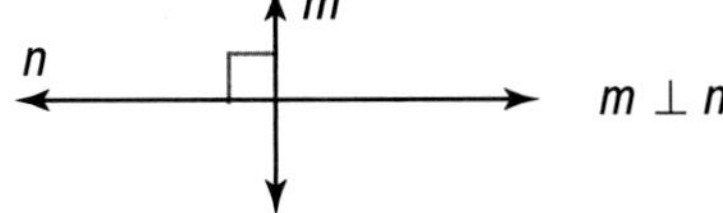

Phase shift A horizontal translation of a periodic function is a phase shift.

Cambio de fase Una traslación horizontal de una función periódica es un cambio de fase.

Example

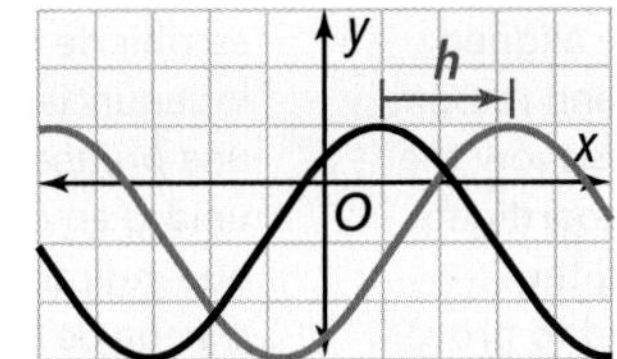

$g(x)$: horizontal translation of $f(x)$

$g(x) = f(x - h)$

Piecewise-defined function A piecewise-defined function has different rules for different parts of its domain.

Función definida por partes Una función de fragmentos tiene reglas diferentes para diferentes partes de su dominio.

Polyhedron A polyhedron is a three-dimensional figure whose surfaces, or *faces*, are polygons. The vertices of the polygons are the *vertices* of the polyhedron. The intersections of the faces are the *edges* of the polyhedron.

Poliedro Un poliedro es una figura tridimensional cuyas superficies, o *caras*, son polígonos. Los vértices de los polígonos son los *vértices* del poliedro. Las intersecciones de las caras son las *aristas* del poliedro.

Example

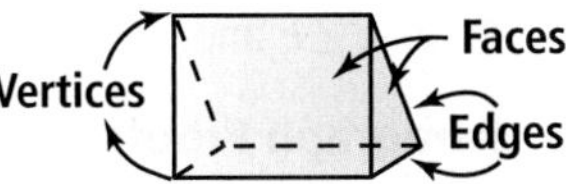

Polynomial A polynomial is a monomial or the sum or difference of two or more monomials.

Polinomio Un polinomio es un monomio o la suma o la diferencia de dos o más monomios.

Example $3x^3 + 4x^2 - 2x + 5$

$8x$

$x^2 + 4x + 2$

Polynomial function A polynomial function is a function whose rule is a polynomial.

Función polinomial Una función polinomial es una función cuya regla es un polinomio.

Example $P(x) = a_n x^n + a_{n-1}x^{n-1} + \ldots + a_1x + a_0$ is a polynomial function, where n is a nonnegative integer and the coefficients $a_n, \ldots, a_0$ are real numbers.

English

Spanish

Population A population is all the members of a set.

Población Una población está compuesta por los miembros de un conjunto.

Prism A prism is a polyhedron with two congruent and parallel faces, which are called the *bases*. The other faces, which are parallelograms, are called the *lateral faces*. An *altitude* of a prism is a perpendicular segment that joins the planes of the bases. Its length is the *height* of the prism. A *right prism* is one whose lateral faces are rectangular regions and a lateral edge is an altitude. In an *oblique prism*, some or all of the lateral faces are nonrectangular.

Prisma Un prisma es un poliedro con dos caras congruentes paralelas llamadas *bases*. Las otras caras son paralelogramos llamados *caras laterales*. La *altura* de un prisma es un segmento perpendicular que une los planos de las bases. Su longitud es también la *altura* del prisma. En un *prisma rectangular*, las caras laterales son rectangulares y una de las aristas laterales es la altura. En un *prisma oblicuo*, algunas o todas las caras laterales no son rectangulares.

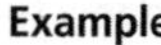

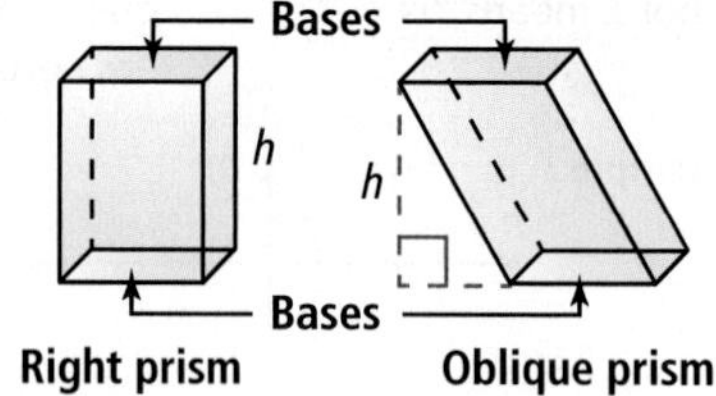

Proof A proof is a convincing argument that uses deductive reasoning. A proof can be written in many forms. In a two-column proof, the statements and reasons are aligned in columns. In a paragraph proof, the statements and reasons are connected in sentences. In a flow proof, arrows show the logical connections between the statements. In a coordinate proof, a figure is drawn on a coordinate plane and the formulas for slope, midpoint, and distance are used to prove properties of the figure. An indirect proof involves the use of indirect reasoning.

Prueba Una prueba es un argumento convincente en el cual se usa el razonamiento deductivo. Una prueba se puede escribir de varias maneras. En una *prueba de dos columnas*, los enunciados y las razones se alinean en columnas. En una *prueba de párrafo*, los enunciados y razones están unidos en oraciones. En una *prueba de flujo*, hay flechas que indican las conexiones lógicas entre enunciados. En una *prueba de coordenadas*, se dibuja una figura en un plano de coordenadas y se usan las fórmulas de la pendiente, punto medio y distancia para probar las propiedades de la figura. Una *prueba indirecta* incluye el uso de razonamiento indirecto.

Example

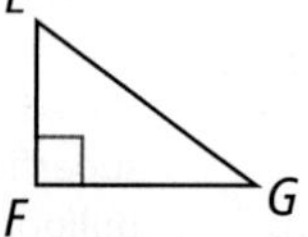

Given: $\triangle EFG$, with right angle $\angle F$
Prove: $\angle E$ and $\angle G$ are complementary.

Paragraph Proof: Because $\angle F$ is a right angle, $m\angle F = 90$. By the Triangle Angle-Sum Theorem, $m\angle E + m\angle F + m\angle G = 180$. By substitution, $m\angle E + 90 + m\angle G = 180$. Subtracting 90 from each side yields $m\angle E + m\angle G = 90$. $\angle E$ and $\angle G$ are complementary by definition.

English	Spanish
Pyramid A pyramid is a polyhedron in which one face, the *base*, is a polygon and the other faces, the *lateral faces*, are triangles with a common vertex, called the *vertex* of the pyramid. An *altitude* of a pyramid is the perpendicular segment from the vertex to the plane of the base. Its length is the *height* of the pyramid. The *slant height* of a regular pyramid is the length of an altitude of a lateral face.	**Pirámide** Una pirámide es un poliedro en donde una cara, la *base*, es un polígono y las otras caras, las *caras laterales*, son triángulos con un vértice común, llamado el *vértice* de la pirámide. Una *altura* de una pirámide es el segmento perpendicular que va del vértice hasta el plano de la base. Su longitude es, por extensión, la *altura* de la pirámide. La *apotema* de una pirámide regular es la longitude de la altura de la cara lateral.

Example

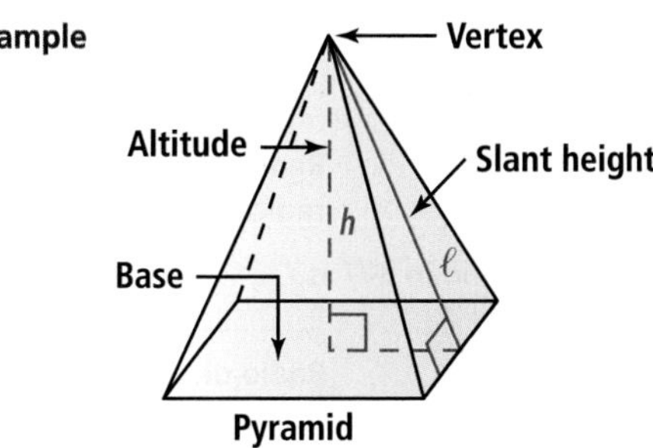

Quantitative variable A quantitative variable is a variable for which the possible values are numbers that can be meaningfully counted, added, subtracted, and so on.	**Variable cuantitativa** Una variable cuantitativa es una variable para la cual los valores posibles son números que se pueden contar, sumar, restar, y así, de manera significativa.

Example "Number of apps on a phone" is a quantitative variable.

Quartile Quartiles are values that separate a finite data set into four equal parts. The second quartile (Q_2) is the median of the data. The first and third quartiles (Q_1 and Q_3) are the medians of the lower half and upper half of the data, respectively.	**Cuartil** Los cuartiles son valores que separan un conjunto finito de datos en cuatro partes iguales. El segundo cuartil (Q_2) es la mediana de los datos. Los cuartiles primero y tercero (Q_1 y Q_3) son las medianas de la mitad superior e inferior de los datos, respectivamente.

Example {2, 3, 4, 5, 5, 6, 7, 7}
$Q_1 = 3.5$
Q_2 (median) $= 5$
$Q_3 = 6.5$

R

Radian A radian is the measure of a central angle that intercepts an arc with length equal to the radius of the circle.	**Radián** Un radián es la medida de un ángulo central que interseca a un arco que tiene una longitud igual al radio del círculo.

Example

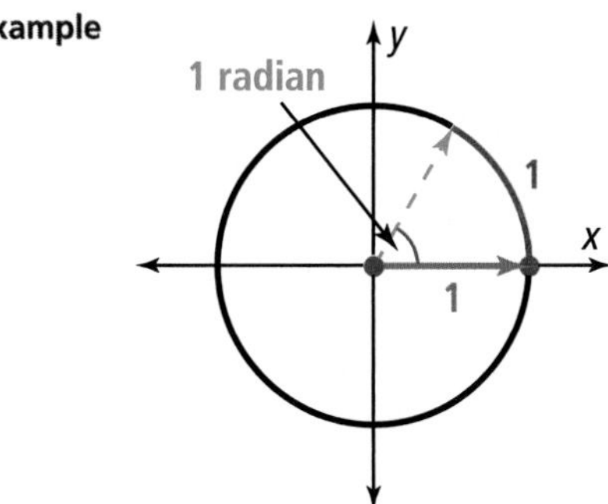

Radian measure Radian measure is the ratio of the length of an intercepted arc and the radius.	**Medida en radianes** La medida del radián es la razón de la longitud de un arco interceptado y el radio.

VISUAL GLOSSARY

English	Spanish

Radical function A radical function is a function that can be written in the form $f(x) = a\sqrt[n]{x - h} + k$, where $a \neq 0$. For even values of n, the domain of a radical function is the real numbers $x \geq h$.

Función radical Una función radical es una función quepuede expresarse como $f(x) = a\sqrt[n]{x - h} + k$, donde $a \neq 0$. Para n par, el dominio de la función radical son los números reales tales que $x \geq h$.

Example $f(x) = \sqrt{x - 2}$

Radical symbol The symbol denoting a root is a radical symbol.

Símbolo de radical El símbolo que expresa una raíz es un símbolo de radical.

Example $\sqrt{}$

Radicand The number under a radical sign is the radicand.

Radicando La expresión que aparece debajo del signo radical es el radicando.

Example The radicand in $3\sqrt[4]{7}$ is 7.

Radius of a sphere The radius of a sphere is a segment that has one endpoint at the center and the other endpoint on the sphere.

Radio de una esfera El radio de una esfera es un segmento con un extremo en el centro y otro en la esfera.

Example

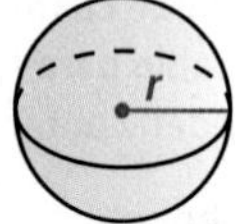

Range The range of a relation is the set of all values of the output, or dependent, variable of a relation or function.

Rango El rango de una relación es el conjunto de todos los valores de la salida, o variable dependiente, de una relación o una función.

Example In the relation {(0, 1), (0, 2), (0, 3), (0, 4), (1, 3), (1, 4), (2, 1)}, the range is {1, 2, 3, 4}. In the function $f(x) = |x - 3|$, the range is the set of real numbers greater than or equal to 0.

Range of a set of data The range of a set of data is the difference between the greatest and least values.

Rango de un conjunto de datos El rango de un conjunto de datos es la diferencia entre el valor máximo y el valor mínimo de los datos.

Example The range of the set {3.2, 4.1, 2.2, 3.4, 3.8, 4.0, 4.2, 2.8} is $4.2 - 2.2 = 2$.

Rational equation A rational equation is an equation that contains a rational expression.

Ecuación racional Una ecuación racional es una ecuación que contiene una expresión racional.

Rational expression A rational expression is the quotient of two polynomials.

Expresión racional Una expresión racional es el cociente de dos polinomios.

English	Spanish
Rational function A rational function $f(x)$ can be written as $f(x) = \frac{P(x)}{Q(x)}$, where $P(x)$ and $Q(x)$ are polynomial functions. The domain of a rational function is all real numbers except those for which $Q(x) = 0$.	**Función racional** Una función racional $f(x)$ se puede expresar como $f(x) = \frac{P(x)}{Q(x)}$, donde $P(x)$ y $Q(x)$ son funciones de polinomios. El dominio de una función racional son todos los números reales excepto aquéllos para los cuales $Q(x) = 0$.

Example

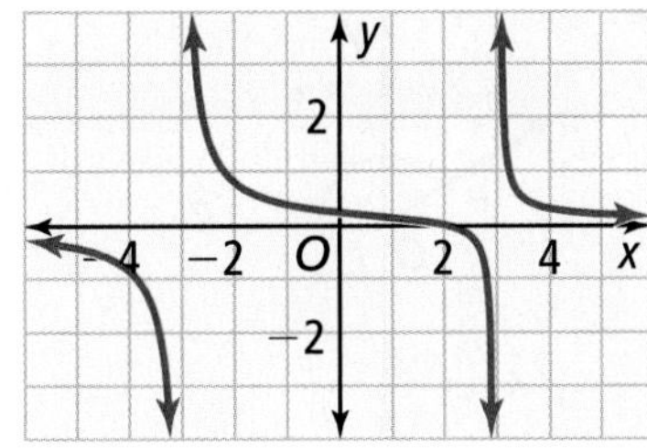

The function $y = \frac{x-2}{x^2-9}$ is a rational function with three branches separated by asymptotes $x = -3$ and $x = 3$.

Reciprocal function The reciprocal function maps every non-zero real number to its reciprocal.	**Función recíproca** La función recíproca establece una correspondencia entre cada número real distinto de cero y su recíproco.

Example The function $f(x) = \frac{1}{x}$ is the reciprocal function.

Reciprocal trigonometric functions Trigonometric functions formed by inverting the ratio of a given trigonometric function are reciprocal trigonometric functions.	**Funcións trigonométrica recíproca** Las funciones trigonométricas que se forman al invertir la razón de una función trigonométrica dada son funciones trigonométricas recíprocas.

Example Cosecant, secant, and cotangent are the reciprocal trigonometric functions.

Recursive definition A recursive definition of a sequence is a rule in which each term is defined by operations on the previous term.	**Definición recursiva** Una definición recursiva de una sucesión es una regla en la cual cada término se define por operaciones efectuadas en el término anterior.

Example Let $a_n = 2.5a_{n-1} + 3a_{n-2}$.
If $a_5 = 3$ and $a_4 = 7.5$, then
$a_6 = 2.5(3) + 3(7.5) = 30$.

Reduced radical form Reduced radical form is the form of an expression for which all nth roots of perfect nth powers in the radicand have been simplified and no radicals remain in the denominator.	**Forma radical reducida** La forma radical reducida es la forma de una expresión en la cual todas las raíces enésimas de potencias enésimas perfectas en el radicando se han simplificado y no quedan radicales en el denominador.

Example The reduced radical form of $\sqrt{50x^7} = 5x^3\sqrt{2x}$.

Reference angle For an angle in standard position, the reference angle is the acute angle formed between the terminal side of the angle and the x-axis.	**Ángulo de referencia** Para un ángulo en posición estándar, el ángulo de referencia es el ángulo agudo que se forma entre el lado terminal del ángulo y el eje x.

Example

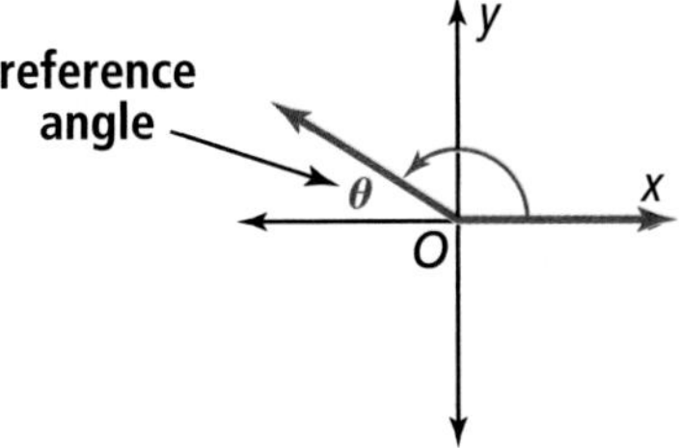

VISUAL GLOSSARY

English

Spanish

Reference triangle A reference triangle is the triangle formed by drawing a perpendicular line from the terminal point on the unit circle of an angle in standard position to the *x*-axis.

Triángulo de referencia Un triángulo de referencia es el triángulo que se forma al trazar una recta perpendicular desde el punto terminal en el círculo unitario de un ángulo en posición estándar hasta el eje *x*.

Example

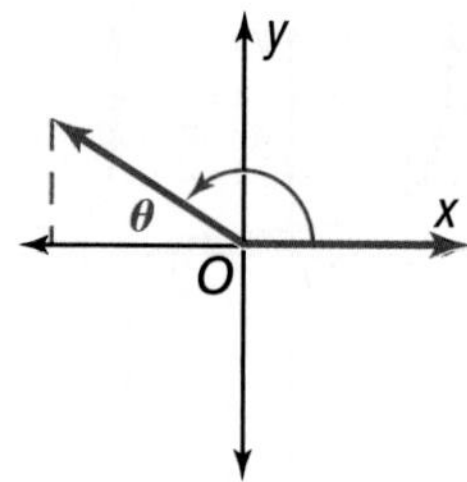

Reflection A reflection flips the graph of a function across a line, such as the *x*- or *y*-axis. Each point on the graph of the reflected function is the same distance from the line of reflection as is the corresponding point on the graph of the original function.

Reflexión Una reflexión voltea la gráfica de una función sobre una línea, como el eje de las *x* o el eje de las *y*. Cada punto de la gráfica de la función reflejada está a la misma distancia del eje de reflexión que el punto correspondiente en la gráfica de la función original.

Example

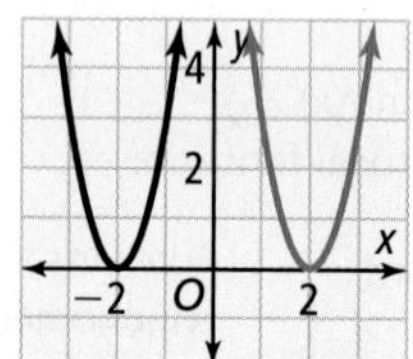

reflection across *y*-axis

Relative maximum (minimum) A relative maximum (minimum) is the value of the function at an up-to-down (down-to-up) turning point.

Máximo (minimo) relativo El máximo (mínimo) relativo es el valor de la función en un punto de giro de arriba hacia abajo (de abajo hacia arriba).

Example

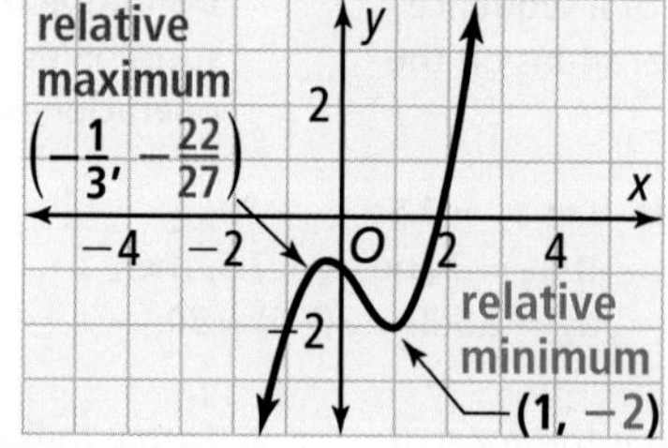

Remainder Theorem If you divide a polynomial $P(x)$ of degree $n > 1$ by $x - a$, then the remainder is $P(a)$.

Teorema del residuo Si divides un polinomio $P(x)$ con un grado $n > 1$ por $x - a$, el residuo es $P(a)$.

Example If $P(x) = x^3 - 4x^2 + x + 6$ is divided by $x - 3$, then the remainder is $P(3) = 3^3 - 4(3)^2 + 3 + 6 = 0$ (which means that $x - 3$ is a factor of $P(x)$).

English / Spanish

Sample A sample from a population is some of the population.

Muestra Una muestra de una población es una parte de la población.

Example Let the set of all males between the ages of 19 and 34 be the population. A random selection of 900 males between those ages would be a sample of the population.

Sample survey A sample survey is a survey in which every member of a sample is asked the same set of questions.

Encuesta muestral Una encuesta muestral es una encuesta en la cual a cada miembro de una muestra se le hace el mismo conjunto de preguntas.

Sampling distribution A sampling distribution is the distribution of sample statistics from different samples of the same population.

Distribución muestral La distribución muestral es la distribución de las estadísticas muestrales de diferentes muestras de la misma población.

Secant A secant is a line, ray, or segment that intersects a circle at two points.

Secante Una secante es una recta, semirrecta o segmento que corta un círculo en dos puntos.

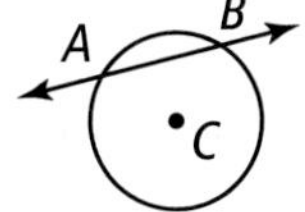

$\overleftrightarrow{AB}$ is a secant of $\odot C$.

Secant function The secant (sec) function is the reciprocal of the cosine function. For all real numbers θ except those that make $\cos\theta = 0$, $\sec\theta = \frac{1}{\cos\theta}$.

Función secante La función secante (sec) es el recíproco de la función coseno. Para todos los números reales θ, excepto aquéllos para los que $\cos\theta = 0$, $\sec\theta = \frac{1}{\cos\theta}$.

Example If $\cos\theta = \frac{5}{13}$, then $\sec\theta = \frac{13}{5}$.

Sector of a circle A sector of a circle is the region bounded by two radii and the intercepted arc.

Sector de un círculo Un sector de un círculo es la región limitada por dos radios y el arco abarcado por ellos.

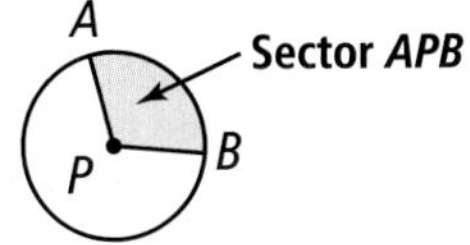

Segment of a circle A segment of a circle is the part of a circle bounded by an arc and the segment joining its endpoints.

Segmento de un círculo Un segmento de un círculo es la parte de un círculo bordeada por un arco y el segmento que une sus extremos.

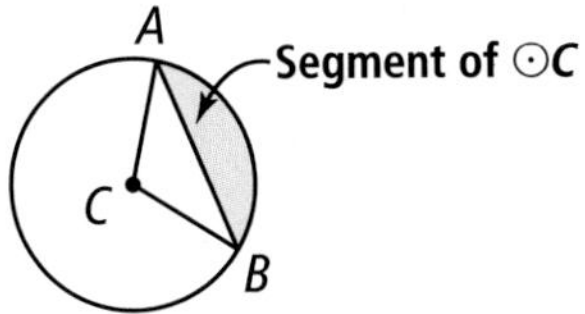

Self-selected sampling In self-selected sampling you select only members of the population who volunteered for the sample.

Muestra de voluntarios En una muestra de voluntarios se seleccionan sólo a los miembros de la población que se ofrecen voluntariamente para ser parte de la muestra.

Sequence A sequence is an ordered list of numbers that often forms a pattern.

Progresión Una progresión es una sucesión de números que suelen formar un patrón.

Example 1, 4, 7, 10, . . .

VISUAL GLOSSARY

English	Spanish

Series A series is the sum of the terms of a sequence.

Serie Una serie es la suma de los términos de una secuencia.

Example The series $3 + 6 + 9 + 12 + 15$ corresponds to the sequence 3, 6, 9, 12, 15. The sum is 45.

Set-builder notation Set-builder notation uses a verbal description or an inequality to describe the numbers in a set.

Notación conjuntista La notación conjuntista usa una descripción verbal o una desigualdad para describir los números.

Example $\{x \mid x \text{ is a real number}\}$
$\{x \mid x > 3\}$

Sigma notation Sigma notation denotes a sum of terms. The terms to be added are formed by evaluating an expression for a specified range of values.

Notación sigma La notación sigma indica una suma de sumandos. Los sumandos que se deben sumar se identifican al evaluar una expresión para un rango determinado de valores.

Example $\sum_{n=1}^{5} 2n - 1 = 1 + 3 + 5 + 7 + 9 = 25$

Simple Random Sample A simple random sample is a sample where each member of the population is equally likely to be chosen, and for all n, each sample of size n is equally likely to be chosen.

Muestra aleatoria simple Una muestra aleatoria simple es una muestra donde la probabilidad de ser seleccionado es igual para todos los miembros de la población, y para todos los valores de n, la probabilidad de ser seleccionado es igual para cada muestra de tamaño n.

Simplest form of a radical expression A radical expression with index n is in simplest form if there are no radicals in any denominator, no denominators in any radical, and any radicand has no nth power factors.

Mínima expresión de una expresión radical Una expresión radical con índice n está en su mínima expresión si no tiene radicales en ningún denominador ni denominadores en ningún radical y los radicandos no tienen factores de potencia.

Simplified form of a rational expression A rational expression is in simplified form if its numerator and denominator are polynomials that have no common divisor other than 1.

Forma simplificada de una expresión racional Una expresión racional se encuentra en su mínima expresión si su numerador y su denominador son polinomios que no tienen otro divisor aparte de 1.

Example $\frac{x^2 - 7x + 12}{x^2 - 9} = \frac{(x-4)(x-3)}{(x+3)(x-3)} = \frac{x-4}{x+3}$, where $x \neq -3$

Sine In a right triangle, the sine of an acute angle is the ratio of the length of the side opposite the angle to the length of the hypotenuse.

Seno En un triángulo rectángulo, el seno de un ángulo agudo es la razón de la longitud del cateto opuesto al ángulo a la longitud de la hipotenusa.

Example

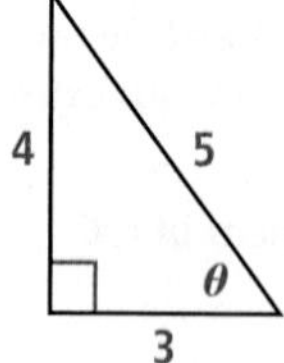

In this triangle, $\sin \theta = \frac{4}{5}$.

English	Spanish

Skewed distribution A skewed distribution is a distribution whose shape is stretched out in either the positive or negative direction.

Distribución asimétrica Una distribución asimétrica es una distribución cuya forma se extiende en dirección positiva o en dirección negativa.

Example

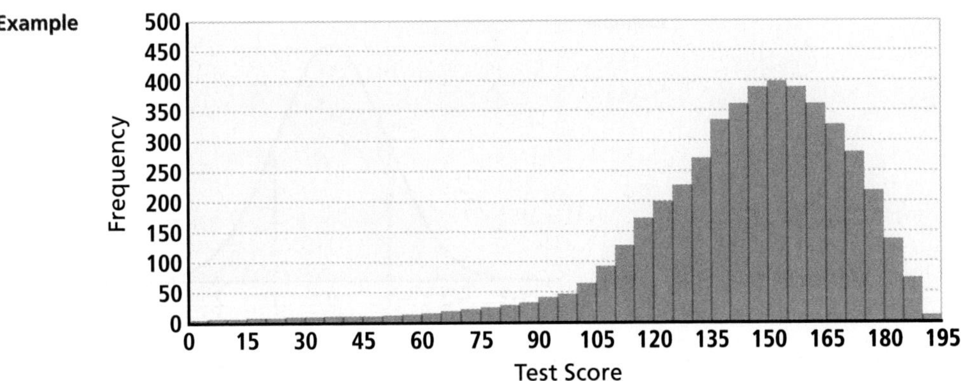

This distribution is skewed left.

Solution of a system of linear equations A solution of a system of linear equations is a set of values for the variables that makes all the equations true.

Solución de un sistema de ecuaciones lineales Una solución de un sistema de ecuaciones lineales es un conjunto de valores para las variables que hace que todas las ecuaciones sean verdaderas.

Sphere A sphere is the set of all points in space that are a given distance *r*, the *radius*, from a given point *C*, the *center*. A *great circle* is the intersection of a sphere with a plane containing the center of the sphere. The *circumference* of a sphere is the circumference of any great circle of the sphere.

Esfera Una esfera es el conjunto de los puntos del espacio que están a una distancia dada *r*, el *radio*, de un punto dado *C*, el *centro*. Un *círculo máximo* es la intersección de una esfera y un plano que contiene el centro de la esfera. La *circunferencia* de una esfera es la circunferencia de cualquier círculo máximo de la esfera.

Example

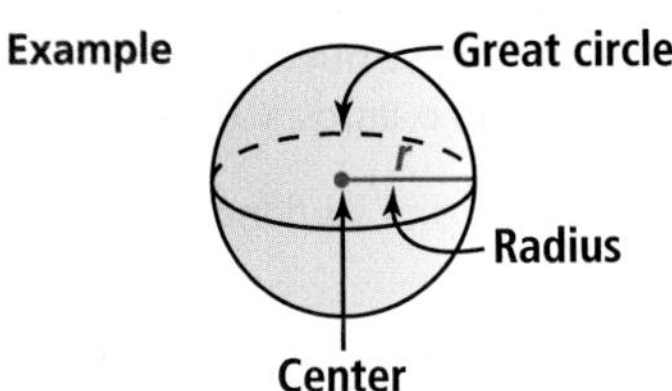

Standard deviation Standard deviation is a measure of how much the values in a data set vary, or deviate, from the mean, $\bar{x}$.

Desviación típica La desviación típica denota cuánto los valores de un conjunto de datos varían, o se desvían, de la media, $\bar{x}$.

Example {0, 2, 3, 4, 6, 7, 8, 9, 10, 11}
$\bar{x} = 6$
standard deviation $= \sqrt{12} \approx 3.46$

Standard form of a polynomial function The standard form of a polynomial function arranges the terms by degree in descending numerical order. A polynomial function, $P(x)$, in standard form is $P(x) = a_nx^n + a_{n-1}x^{n-1} + \cdots + a_1x + a_0$, where n is a nonnegative integer and $a_n, \ldots, a_0$ are real numbers.

Forma normal de una función polinomial La forma normal de una función polinomial organiza los términos por grado en orden numérico descendiente. Una función polinomial, $P(x)$, en forma normal es $P(x) = a_nx^n + a_{n-1}x^{n-1} + \cdots + a_1x + a_0$, donde n es un número entero no negativo y $a_n, \ldots, a_0$ son números reales.

Example $2x^3 - 5x^2 - 2x + 5$

VISUAL GLOSSARY

English	Spanish
Standard normal distribution The standard normal distribution is a normal distribution with mean 0 and standard deviation 1.	**Distribución normal estándar** La distribución normal estándar es una distribución normal con una media de 0 y una desviación típica de 1.

Example

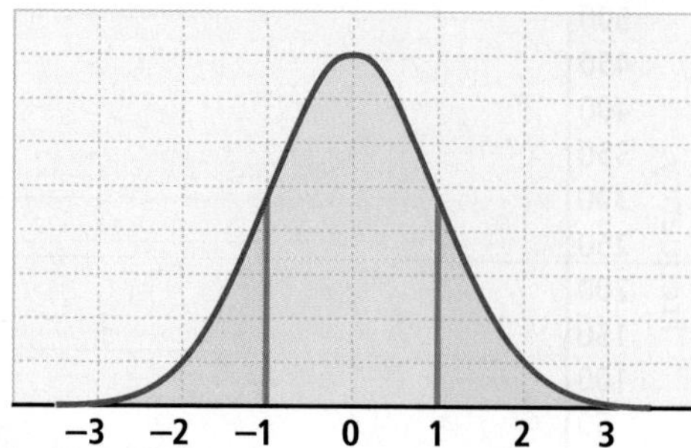

English	Spanish
Standard position An angle in the coordinate plane is in standard position when the vertex is at the origin and one ray is on the positive *x*-axis.	**Posición estándar** Un ángulo en el plano de coordenadas se encuentra en posición estándar si el vértice se encuentra en el origen y una semirrecta se encuentra en el eje *x* positivo.

Example

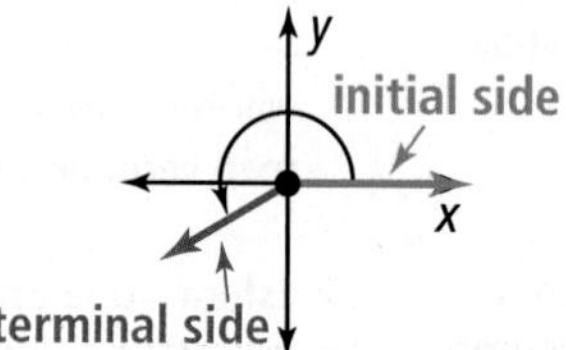

English	Spanish
Statistic A statistic is a piece of data from a sample, not a whole population.	**Estadística** Una estadística es un dato tomado de una muestra, no de una población completa.
Statistical question A statistical question is a question that can be answered by collecting many pieces of information, or data, and summarizing the data.	**Pregunta estadística** Una pregunta estadística es una pregunta que se puede responder reuniendo mucha información, o datos, y resumiéndola.

Example "What month has the most birthdays of students at your school?"

English	Spanish
Statistical variable A statistical variable is a quantity or quality for which data are expected to differ.	**Variable estadística** Una variable estadística es una cantidad o cualidad para la cual se anticipan variaciones en los datos.
Step function A step function pairs every number in an interval with a single value. The graph of a step function can look like the steps of a staircase.	**Función escalón** Una función escalón empareja cada número de un intervalo con un solo valor. La gráfica de una función escalón se puede parecer a los peldaños de una escalera.

Go Online | PearsonRealize.com

English / Spanish

Straightedge A straightedge is a tool for drawing straight lines.

Regla sin graduación Una regla sin graduación es un instrumento para dibujar líneas rectas.

Stretch A stretch is a transformation that increases the distance between the points of a graph and a given line by the same factor.

Estiramiento Un estiramiento es una transformación que aumenta por el mismo factor la distancia entre los puntos de una gráfica y una recta dada.

Example

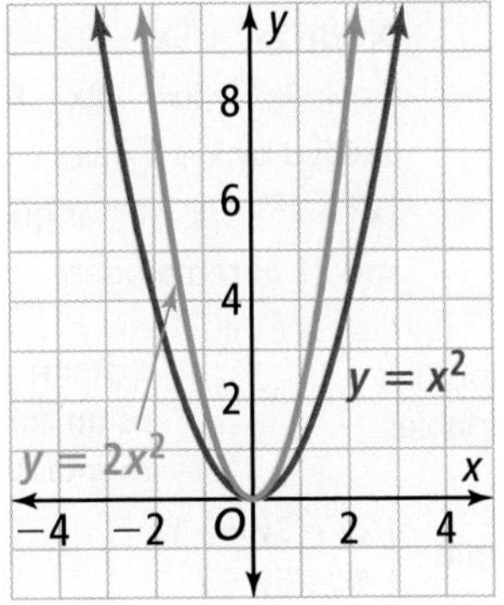

Surface area The surface area of a prism, cylinder, pyramid, or cone is the sum of the lateral area and the areas of the bases. The surface area of a sphere is four times the area of a great circle.

Área El área de un prisma, pirámide, cilindro o cono es la suma del área lateral y las áreas de las bases. El área de una esfera es igual a cuatro veces el área de un círculo máximo.

Example

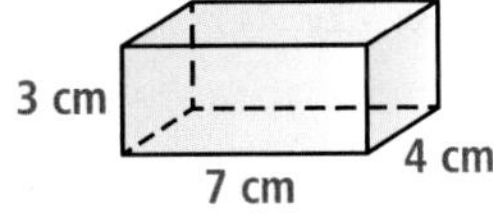

$$\begin{aligned}\text{S.A. of prism} &= \text{L.A.} + 2B \\ &= 66 + 2(28) \\ &= 122\text{ cm}^2\end{aligned}$$

Symmetric distribution A symmetric distribution is a distribution whose shape is evenly distributed around the mean.

Distribución simétrica Una distribución simétrica es una distribución cuya forma está distribuida en forma pareja alrededor de la media.

Example

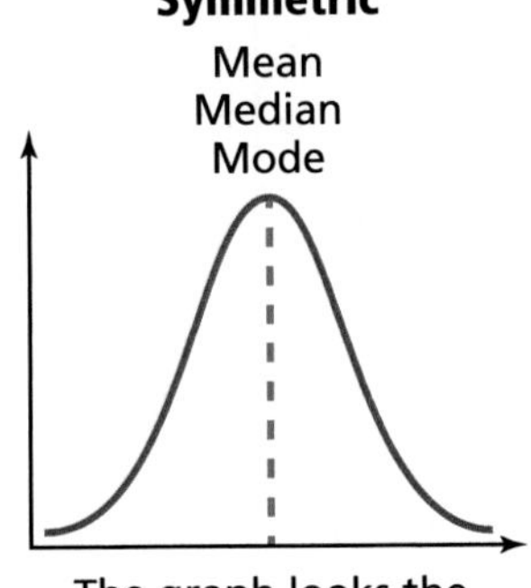

The graph looks the same on both sides.

English	Spanish

Synthetic division Synthetic division is a process for dividing a polynomial by a linear expression $x - a$.

División sintética La división sintética es un proceso para dividir un polinomio por una expresión lineal $x - a$.

Example

$$\begin{array}{r|rrrrr} -3 & 2 & 5 & 0 & -2 & -8 \\ & & -6 & 3 & -9 & 33 \\ \hline & 2 & -1 & 3 & -11 & 25 \end{array}$$

Divide $2x^4 + 5x^3 - 2x - 8$ by $x + 3$. $2x^4 + 5x^3 - 2x - 8$ divided by $x + 3$ gives $2x^3 - x^2 + 3x - 11$ as quotient and 25 as remainder.

System of linear equations A system of equations is a set of two or more equations using the same variables.

Sistema de ecuaciones lineales Un sistema de ecuaciones es un conjunto de dos o más ecuaciones que contienen las mismas variables.

Example $\begin{cases} 2x - 3y = -13 \\ 4x + 5y = 7 \end{cases}$

System of linear inequalities A system of linear inequalities is a set of two or more linear inequalities using the same variables.

Sistema de desigualdades lineales Un sistema de desigualdades lineales es un conjunto de dos o más desigualdades lineales que contienen las mismas variables.

Example $x + 2y < 5$
$3x - 2y > -1$

Tangent In a right triangle, tangent of an acute angle is the ratio of the length of the side opposite the angle to the length of the side adjacent to the angle. It is also equal to the ratio of the sine of the angle to the cosine of the angle.

Tangente En un triángulo rectángulo, la tangente de un ángulo agudo es la razón de la longitud del cateto opuesto al ángulo a la longitud del cateto adyacente a dicho ángulo. También es igual a la razón del seno del ángulo al coseno de dicho ángulo.

Tangent to a circle A tangent to a circle is a line in the plane of the circle that intersects the circle in exactly one point. That point is the *point of tangency*.

Tangente de un círculo Una tangente de un círculo es una recta en el plano del círculo que corta el círculo en exactamente un punto. Ese punto es el *punto de tangencia*.

Example

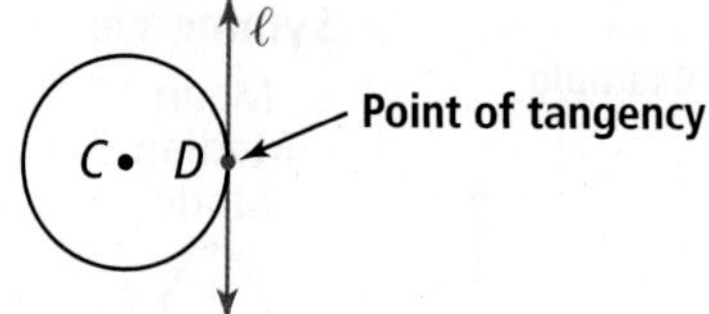

Line ℓ is tangent to $\odot C$. Point D is the point of tangency.

Term of an expression A term is a number, a variable, or the product of a number and one or more variables.

Término de una expresión Un término es un número, una variable o el producto de un número y una o más variables.

Example The expression $4x^2 - 3y + 7.3$ has 3 terms.

Terminal side *See* **Initial side.**

Lado terminal *Ver* **Initial side.**

English	Spanish

Transformation A transformation of a function maps each point of its graph to a new location.

Transformación Una transformación de una función desplaza cada punto de su gráfica a una ubicación nueva.

Example $g(x) = 2(x - 3)$ is a transformation of $f(x) = x$.

Translation A translation shifts the graph of the parent function horizontally, vertically, or both.

Traslación Una traslación desplaza la gráfica de la función madre horizontalmente, verticalmente o en ambas direcciones.

Example

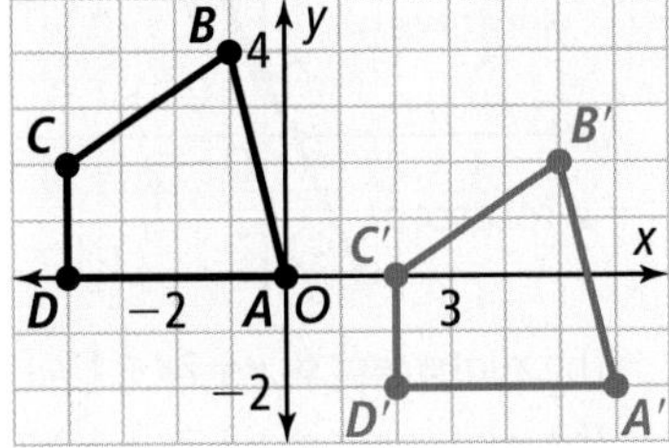

Trigonometric identity A trigonometric identity in one variable is a trigonometric equation that is true for all values of the variable for which both sides of the equation are defined.

Identidad trigonométrica Una identidad trigonométrica en una variable es una ecuación trigonométrica que es verdadera para todos los valores de la variable para los cuales se definen los dos lados de la ecuación.

Example $\tan \theta = \dfrac{\sin \theta}{\cos \theta}$

Turning point A turning point of the graph of a function is a point where the graph changes direction from upward to downward or from downward to upward.

Punto de giro Un punto de giro de la gráfica de una función es un punto donde la gráfica cambia de dirección de arriba hacia abajo o vice versa.

Two-way frequency table A two-way frequency table is a table that displays frequencies in two different categories.

Tabla de frecuencias de doble entrada Una tabla de frecuencias de doble entrada es una tabla de frecuencias que contiene dos categorías de datos.

Example

	Male	Female	Totals
Juniors	3	4	7
Seniors	3	2	5
Totals	6	6	12

The last column shows a total of 7 juniors and 5 seniors.
The last row shows a total of 6 males and 6 females.

U

Unit circle The unit circle has a radius of 1 unit and its center is at the origin of the coordinate plane.

Círculo unitario El círculo unitario tiene un radio de 1 unidad y el centro está situado en el origen del plano de coordenadas.

Example

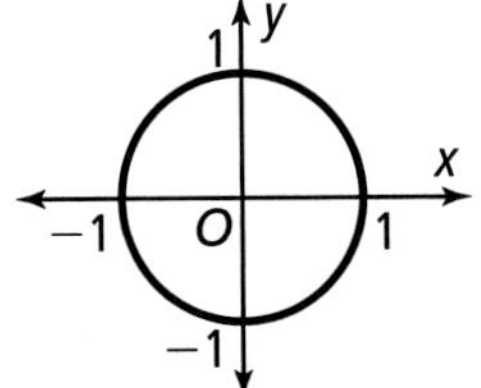

English / Spanish

Volume Volume is a measure of the space a figure occupies.

Volumen El volumen es una medida del espacio que ocupa una figura.

x-intercept, y-intercept The point at which a line crosses the x-axis (or the x-coordinate of that point) is an x-intercept. The point at which a line crosses the y-axis (or the y-coordinate of that point) is a y-intercept.

Intercepto en x, intercepto en y El punto donde una recta corta el eje x (o la coordenada x de ese punto) es el intercepto en x. El punto donde una recta cruza el eje y (o la coordenada y de ese punto) es el intercepto en y.

Example

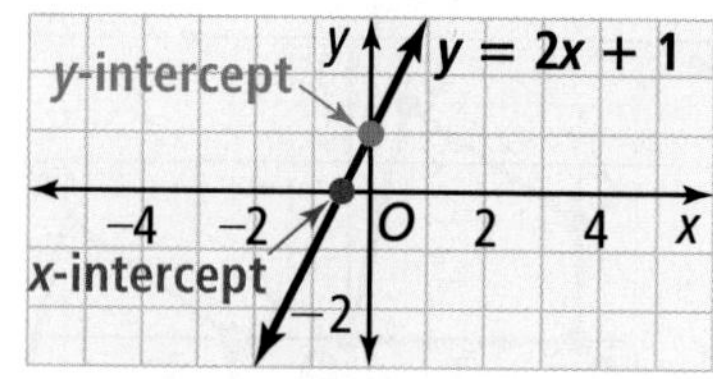

The x-intercept of $y = 2x + 1$ is $\left(-\frac{1}{2}, 0\right)$ or $-\frac{1}{2}$

The y-intercept of $y = 2x + 1$ is $(0, 1)$ or 1.

Z

Zero of a function A zero of a function is an x-intercept of the graph of a function.

Cero de una función Un cero de una función es un intercepto en x de la gráfica de una función.

Example

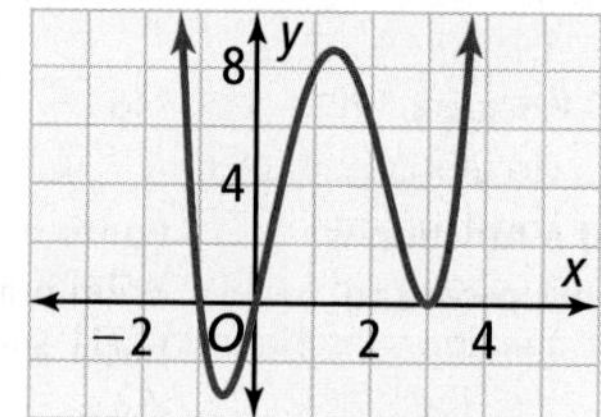

Zero-Product Property If the product of two or more factors is zero, then at least one of the factors must be zero.

Propiedad del cero del producto Si el producto de dos o más factores es cero, entonces al menos uno de los factores debe ser cero.

Example $(x - 3)(2x - 5) = 0$

$x - 3 = 0$ or $2x - 5 = 0$

z-score The z-score of a value is the number of standard deviations that the value is from the mean.

Puntaje z El puntaje z de un valor es el número de desviaciones normales que tiene ese valor de la media.

Example $\{0, 2, 3, 4, 6, 7, 8, 9, 10, 11\}$

$\bar{x} = 6$

standard deviation $= \sqrt{12} \approx 3.46$

For 8, z-score $= \frac{8 - 6}{\sqrt{12}} \approx 0.58$.

Index

D

E

F

G

H

I

K

L

R

S

Acknowledgments

Photographs

Cover:
Excellent backgrounds/Shutterstock

Topic 01:
3 Dibas99/Fotolia; **4** (TL) EV_Korobov/Fotolia, (TC) National Motor Museum/Motoring Picture Library/Alamy Stock Photo, (TR) Drive Images/Alamy Stock Photo, (CL) Kolopach/Shutterstock, (CR) Denebola_h/Fotolia, (CL) Jaochainoi/Shutterstock, (BC) PhoelixDE/Shutterstock, (CR) Gorbovoi81/Fotolia, (B) 3DDock/Shutterstock; **6** The lefty/Fotolia; **7** Steve Lovegrove/Fotolia; **19** Jan Gorzynik/123RF; **46** Artazum/Shutterstock; **53** Dibas99/Fotolia

Topic 02:
59 Danmorgan12/Fotolia; **60** (TL) Peter Tsai Photography/Alamy Stock Photo, (TR) Fotokostic/Shutterstock, (C) Mark Herreid/Alamy Stock Photo, (B) Andrejco/Fotolia; **100** Danmorgan12/Fotolia; **108** (T) Roger costa morera/123RF, (B) Mkos83/Fotolia; **116** (L) Stratos Giannikos/Fotolia, (R) Georgiy Pashin/Fotolia

Topic 03:
121 Aerogondo/iStock/Getty Images; **122** (T) Monty Rakusen/Cultura Creative/Alamy Stock Photo, (C) Roger Bacon/Reuters/Alamy Stock Photo, (B) Minerva Studio/Fotolia; **125** Alex Master/Shutterstock; **135** Urbanhearts/Fotolia; **162** Aerogondo/iStock/Getty Images

Topic 04:
167 Christian Fallini/Fotolia; **168** (TL) Furtseff/Fotolia, (TC) 32 pixels/Fotolia, (TR) Chris Stock / Lebrecht Music & Arts/Lebrecht Music and Arts Photo Library/Alamy Stock Photo, (CL) PrinceOfLove/Shutterstock, (CR) Fosin/Shutterstock, (B) Scanrail1/Shutterstock; **171** Willoughby Owen/Moment/Getty Images; **175** Paul A. Hebert/Invision/AP Images; **191** Netfalls/Fotolia; **194** Kris Wiktor/Shutterstock; 202 Christian Fallini/Fotolia

Topic 05:
225 Fuse/Corbis/Getty Images; **226** (TL) RedlineVector/Shutterstock, (TC) Nobelus/Shutterstock, (TR) Blan-k/Shutterstock, (CL) Denis Rozhnovsky/Shutterstock, (C) ImageFlow/Shutterstock, (CR) Castaldostudio/Shutterstock, (B) Africa Studio/Shutterstock; 246 Fuse/Corbis/Getty Images; **260** John Henshall/Alamy Stock Photo;

Topic 06:
296 (TL) Studio023/Fotolia, (TR) ShutterDivision/Shutterstock, (C) Designua/Fotolia, (B) Andrey Armyagov/Shutterstock; **315** epa european pressphoto agency b.v./Alamy Stock Photo

Topic 07:
354 (T) David Kleyn/Alamy Stock Photo, (L) littleny/Fotolia, (CL) 3desc/Fotolia, (CR) Angelo.Gi/Fotolia, (R) Stevecuk/Fotolia, (B) Megastocker/Fotolia; **358** Kovgabor/Shutterstock; **362** Hisham Ibrahim/The Image Bank/Getty Images; **372** Premium Collection/Fotolia; **386** Zhao Jiankang/123RF

Acknowledgments

Topic 08:
391 Animal Stock/Alamy Stock Photo; **392** (T) Heather Drake/Alamy Stock Photo, (CL) Greg Gard/Alamy Stock Photo, (C) Kumar Sriskandan/Alamy Stock Photo, (CR) Michael Ventura/Alamy Stock Photo, (B) MaxAlex/Fotolia; **395** (TL) Blue Jean Images/Alamy Stock Photo, (TR) David Schaffer/Caia Image/Alamy Stock Photo, (BL) H.Mark Weidman Photography/Alamy Stock Photo, (BR) Phil Boorman/Cultura Creative (RF)/Alamy Stock Photo; **400** (T) Koji Niino/MIXA/Alamy Stock Photo, (C) Hybrid Images/Cultura Creative (RF)/Alamy Stock Photo, (B) Richard Levine/Alamy Stock Photo; **401** (T) Andy Dean Photography/Shutterstock/Asset Library, (B) David Grossman/Alamy Stock Photo; **414** Neirfy/Fotolia; **415** (T) Budimir Jevtic/Fotolia, (B) Olaf Speier/Fotolia; **419** Eric Gevaert/123RF; **422** Aflo Co., Ltd./Alamy Stock Photo; **439** Animal Stock/Alamy Stock Photo; **445** Blackregis/123RF

Topic 09:
454 (TL) Hayate/Fotolia, (TC) Aleksandr Lesik/Fotolia, (TR) Andy Dean/Fotolia, (C) Jdoms/Fotolia, (B) Mike Flippo/Shutterstock; **461** Sabelskaya/Fotolia; **479** Karen Doody/Stocktrek Images,Inc./Alamy Stock Photo; **496** Rgb Ventures/SuperStock/Ed Darack/Alamy Stock Photo; 500 Africa Rising/Shutterstock; **503** Stocker1970/Shutterstock

Topic 10:
509 Paul Fleet/Shutterstock; **510** (T) 3Dsculptor/Shutterstock, (CL) Tryfonov/Fotolia, (CR) Olekcii Mach/Alamy Stock Photo, (B) Algol/Shutterstock; **526** Songquan Deng/Shutterstock; **527** Paul Fleet/Shutterstock; **542** Vasilii Gubskii/Shutterstock; **550** Friedrich Saurer/Alamy Stock Photo

Topic 11:
555 Andersphoto/Shutterstock; **556** (T) Heiner Heine/ImageBroker/Alamy Stock Photo, (C) Katyr/Fotolia, (B) AD Hunter/Shutterstock; **562** (T) Perutskyi Petro/Shutterstock, (CL) Imfotograf/Fotolia, (CR) Yellow Cat/Shutterstock, (B) Monkey Business/Fotolia; **566** Cynoclub/Fotolia; **567** Joerg Hackemann/123RF; **571** Andersphoto/Shutterstock; **584** Sorapong Chaipanya/123RF